Contents

KT-130-414

Introduction to
New Zealand

Kiwis – the people, not the emblematic flightless bird – can't believe their luck at being born in what they call "Godzone" (God's own country). Year after year, travellers list New Zealand in the top ten of places they'd like to visit – and you rarely meet anyone who has been and didn't love the place. And what's not to like? With craggy coastlines, sweeping beaches, primeval forests, snowcapped mountains and explosive geysers, the scenery is truly majestic. The forests come inhabited by strange birds that have evolved to fill evolutionary niches normally occupied by mammals, while penguins, whales and seals ring the coast. And in a land that's larger than the UK and two-thirds the size of California, there are only around 4.7 million people. Māori have been here for around eight hundred years and retain distinct and fascinating customs overlaid by colonial European – and increasingly Asian – cultures that together create a vibrant, if understated, urban life.

Given this stunning backdrop it's not surprising that there are boundless diversions, ranging from strolls along moody windswept beaches and multi-day tramps over alpine passes to adrenaline-charged adventure activities such as bungy jumping, skiing, sea-kayaking and whitewater rafting. Some visitors treat the country as a large-scale adventure playground, aiming to tackle as many challenges as possible in the time available.

Much of the scenic drama comes from tectonic or volcanic forces, as the people of Canterbury know only too well following the **Christchurch earthquakes** of 2010 and 2011. The quakes, along with several thousand aftershocks, devastated the city but it is well on the way to recovery.

So many residents have left Christchurch that **Wellington** now outranks it as the country's second largest city, both well behind **Auckland**. Elsewhere, you can travel through stunning countryside without seeing a soul: there are spots so remote that, it's reliably contended, no human has yet visited them.

THE ROUGH GUIDE TO
NEW ZEALAND

ROUGH
GUIDES

This tenth editi
Gerard Hin
Rachel Mill

C800644507

Geologically, New Zealand split away from the super-continent of Gondwana early, developing a unique **ecosystem** in which birds adapted to fill the role of mammals, many becoming flightless because they had no predators. That all changed about eight hundred years ago with the arrival of Polynesian navigators, when the land they called **Aotearoa** – "the land of the long white cloud" – became the last major landmass to be settled by humans. On disembarking from their canoes, these **Māori** proceeded to unbalance the fragile ecosystem, dispatching forever the giant ostrich-sized moa, which formed a major part of their diet. The country once again settled into a fragile balance before the arrival of **Pakeha** – white Europeans, predominantly of British origin – who swarmed off their square-rigged ships full of colonial zeal in the mid-nineteenth century and altered the land forever.

An uneasy coexistence between **Māori** and **European** societies informs the current conflicts over cultural identity, land and resource rights. The 1840 **Treaty of Waitangi**, New Zealand's founding document, effectively ceded New Zealand to the British Crown while guaranteeing Māori hegemony over their land and traditional gathering and fishing rights. As time wore on and increasing numbers of settlers demanded ever larger parcels of land from Māori, antipathy surfaced and escalated into hostility. Once Māori were subdued, a policy of partial integration all but destroyed **Maoritanga** – the Māori way of doing things.

DRIVING CREEK RAILWAY, COROMANDEL

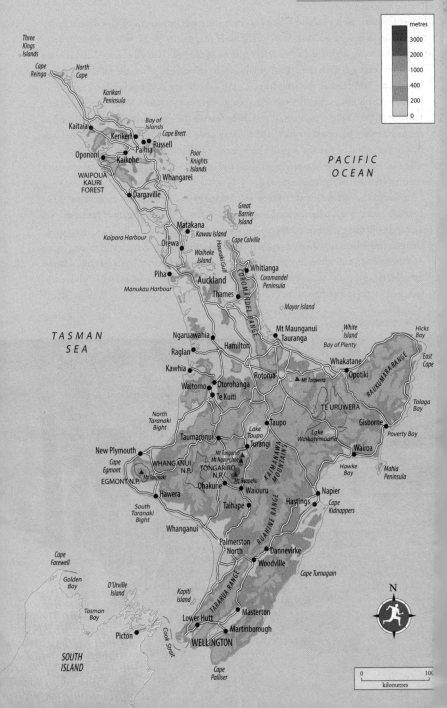

NORTH ISLAND

metres
3000
2000
1000
400
200
0

Three Kings Islands

Cape Reinga

North Cape

Karikari Peninsula

Kaitaia

Bay of Islands

Cape Brett

Kerikeri

Paihia

Russell

Opononi

Kaikohe

Poor Knights Islands

WAIPOUA KAURI FOREST

Whangarei

Dargaville

PACIFIC OCEAN

Matakana

Great Barrier Island

Kaipara Harbour

Kawau Island

Orewa

Cape Colville

Hauraki Gulf

Piha

Waiheke Island

Whitianga

Auckland

Coromandel Peninsula

Manukau Harbour

Thames

COROMANDEL RANGE

Mayor Island

Ngaruawahia

Mt Maunganui

White Island

Hicks Bay

TASMAN SEA

Hamilton

Tauranga

Bay of Plenty

Raglan

Whakatane

East Cape

Kawhia

Rotorua

Opotiki

RAUKUMARA RANGE

Waitomo

Otorohanga

Mt Tarawera

Te Kuiti

TE URUWERA

Tolaga Bay

North Taranaki Bight

Lake Taupo

Taupo

Lake Waikaremoana

Gisborne

Taumarunui

Turangi

Poverty Bay

New Plymouth

Mt Tongariro

Mt Ngauruhoe

Wairoa

Cape Egmont

WHANGANUI N.P.

TONGARIRO N.P.

KAIMANAWA MOUNTAINS

EGMONT N.P.

Mt Taranaki

Mt Ruapehu

Hawke Bay

Mahia Peninsula

Ohakune

Waiouru

Waioru

Napier

Hawera

Taihape

Hastings

Cape Kidnappers

South Taranaki Bight

RUAHINE RANGE

Whanganui

Palmerston North

Dannevirke

Cape Turnagain

Cape Farewell

Golden Bay

Woodville

D'Urville Island

Kapiti Island

TARARUA RANGE

Tasman Bay

Masterton

Lower Hutt

Picton

Cook Strait

Martinborough

WELLINGTON

SOUTH ISLAND

Cape Palliser

N

0   100
kilometres

SOUTH ISLAND

NORTH ISLAND

metres
3000
2000
1000
400
200
0

Cape Farewell
Farewell Spit
Golden Bay
D'Urville Island
Kapiti Island
Marlborough Sounds
WELLINGTON
Collingwood
Takaka
ABEL TASMAN N.P.
Tasman Bay
Picton
Cook Strait
Cape Palliser
KAHURANGI N.P.
Nelson
Blenheim
Karamea Bight
Karamea
St Arnaud
KAIKOURA RANGES
Westport
Murchison
Cape Foulwind
PAPAROA N.P.
NELSON LAKES N.P.
Kaikoura
Reefton
Punakaiki
Hanmer Springs
Lewis Pass
Greymouth
Lake Brunner
TASMAN SEA
Hokitika
Arthur's Pass
ARTHUR'S PASS N.P.
Pegasus Bay
Ross
Arthur's Pass Village
Christchurch
Banks Peninsula
Whataroa
Lyttelton
Franz Josef Glacier
Methven
Akaroa
Fox Glacier
WESTLAND N.P.
Aoraki/Mount Cook
AORAKI/MOUNT COOK N.P.
Ashburton
Aoraki/Mount Cook Village
Lake Tekapo
Canterbury Bight
Haast
Lake Pukaki
Timaru
Twizel
Jackson Bay
Haast Pass
Lake Ohau
MOUNT ASPIRING N.P.
Mount Aspiring
Lake Hawea
Lindis Pass
Lake Wanaka
PACIFIC OCEAN
Milford Sound
Mount Tutoko
Wanaka
Oamaru
Milford Sound
Arrowtown
Moeraki
George Sound
Glenorchy
Cromwell
Ranfurly
Palmerston
Queenstown
Alexandra
Lake Te Anau
Otago Peninsula
Secretary Island
FIORDLAND N.P.
Lake Wakatipu
Dunedin
Doubtful Sound
Te Anau
Lumsden
Manapouri
Lake Manapouri
Ohai
Gore
Balclutha
Resolution Island
Lake Hauroko
Dusky Sound
Tuatapere
Invercargill
Puyseger Point
Riverton
Bluff
Foveaux Strait
Oban (Halfmoon Bay)
RAKIURA N.P.
Stewart Island

SOUTHERN ALPS

N

0   100
kilometres

FACT FILE

- At latitude 41° south, Wellington is the world's **southernmost capital city** and shares the honour of being the most remote with Canberra, over 2000km away.
- At 85 characters, a hill near Porangahau has one of the **longest names** in the world: Taumatawhakatangihangakoauauotama-teaturipukakapikimaungahoronukupokai whenuakitanatahu.
- Kiwis enjoy foreign affirmation: **Flight of the Conchords** was turned down by domestic television and only became a local success after their HBO hit series.
- New Zealand was the first self-governing country in the world in which **all women** had the right to vote in parliamentary elections (in 1893).
- There are **no snakes** in New Zealand, and only a few enomous spiders, rarely seen.
- The numerous **Māori words** that have crept into everyday conversation easily confound visitors: *aroha* is love; *kia kaha* means be strong; *kia ora* can be hi or might signify agreement; and *koha* is a donation or offering.
- New Zealand's **eels** live to 80 years and only breed once, at the end of their lives – and they swim all the way to Tonga to do it.

Māori, however, were left well outside the new European order, where difference was perceived as tantamount to a betrayal of the emergent sense of nationhood. Although elements of this still exist and Presbyterian and Anglican values have proved hard to shake off, the Kiwi psyche has become infused with Māori generosity and hospitality, coupled with a colonial mateyness and the unerring belief that whatever happens, "she'll be right".

Only in the last forty years has New Zealand come of age and developed a true national self-confidence, something partly forced on it by Britain severing the colonial apron strings, and by the resurgence of Māori identity. Māori demands have been nurtured by a willingness on the part of most Pakeha to redress the wrongs perpetrated over the last 175 years, as long as it doesn't impinge on their high standard of living or overall feeling of control. More recently, integration has been replaced with a policy

of **biculturalism** – the somewhat fraught notion of promoting two cultures alongside each other, but with maximum interaction. This policy has been somewhat weakened by relatively recent and extensive **immigration** from China, Korea and South Asia.

Despite having and achieving much to give them confidence, Kiwis (unlike their Australian neighbours) retain an underlying shyness that borders on an inferiority complex: you may well find yourself interrogated about your opinions on the country almost before you've even left the airport. Balancing this is an extraordinary enthusiasm for **sports** and **culture**, which generate a swelling pride in New Zealanders when they witness plucky Kiwis taking on and sometimes beating the world.

Where to go

New Zealand packs a lot into a small space, meaning you can visit many of the main sights in a couple of weeks, but allow at least a month (ideally two) for a proper look around. The scenery is the big draw, and most people only pop into the big cities on arrival and departure (easily done with open-jaw air tickets, allowing you to fly into Auckland and out of Christchurch) or when travelling to Wellington from the South Island across the **Cook Strait**.

Sprawled around the sparkling Waitemata Harbour, **Auckland** looks out over the island-studded Hauraki Gulf. Most people head south from here, missing out on **Northland**, the cradle of both Māori and Pakeha colonization, cloaked in wonderful subtropical forest that harbours New Zealand's largest kauri trees. East of Auckland the coast follows the isolated greenery and long, golden beaches of the

MĀORI CULTURE

Tribal costume is only worn on special occasions, facial tattoos are fairly rare and you'll probably only see a *haka* performed at a rugby match or cultural show. In fact, Māori live very much in the modern world. But peel back the veneer of the song-dance-and-hangi performance and you'll discover a parallel world that non-Māori are only dimly aware of.

Knowledge of **whakapapa** (tribal lineage) is central to Māori identity. **Spirituality** connects Māori to their traditional local mountain or river, while **oratory**, and the ability to produce a song at a moment's notice, are both highly valued. All New Zealanders understand **mana**, a synthesis of prestige, charisma and influence, which is enhanced through brave or compassionate actions.

Nevertheless, inequality and discrimination remain serious issues, with Māori faring significantly worse than non-Māori counterparts on many social and economic indicators.

Hope for redress comes through a **bicultural** approach stressing equality and integration while allowing for parallel identities

For more on what it means to be Māori, and how visitors are likely to tap into it, see page 713.

Coromandel Peninsula, before running down to the beach towns of the **Bay of Plenty**. Immediately south your senses are assailed by the ever-present sulphurous whiff of **Rotorua**, with its spurting geysers and bubbling pools of mud, and the volcanic plateau centred on the trout-filled waters of **Lake Taupo**, overshadowed by three snowcapped volcanoes. Cave fans will want to head west of Taupo for the eerie limestone caverns of **Waitomo**; alternatively it's just a short hop from Taupo to the delights of canoeing the

HOT POOLS, GEYSERS AND BOILING MUD

One of New Zealand's most sensual pleasures is lying back in a **natural hot pool** surrounded by the bush and gazing up at the stars. The country lies on the Pacific Ring of Fire, and earthquakes and volcanic activity are common. Superheated steam escapes as **geysers** (around Rotorua), **boiling mud pools** (Rotorua and Taupo) and **hot springs** – around eighty of them across the northern two-thirds of the North Island and another fifteen along a thin thread down the western side of the Southern Alps.

Many are commercial **resorts** offering tepid swimming pools, near-scalding baths, mineral mud and hydrothermal pampering. The remainder are **natural pools** – in the bush, beside a stream or welling up from below a sandy beach – which require a little sleuthing; locals like to keep the best spots to themselves. Check out ⓦ nzhotpools.co.nz, read the notes on **amoebic meningitis** (see page 63) and sample the following (listed north to south).

Polynesian Spa Commercial resort in Rotorua with something for everyone: mineral pools, family spa, adult-only open-air complex and all manner of body treatments. See page 240
Hot Water Beach Come at low tide, rent a spade and dig a hot pool beside the cool surf. See page 226
Maruia Springs Small resort in the hills 200km north of Christchurch. Particularly magical in winter. See page 534
Welcome Flat Hot Springs Four natural pools sited amid mountain scenery just south of Fox Glacier. It is a six- to seven-hour walk in and you can stay at the adjacent DOC hut. See page 492

Whanganui River, a broad, emerald-green waterway banked by virtually impenetrable bush thrown into relief by the cone of **Mount Taranaki**, whose summit is accessible in a day. East of Taupo lie ranges that form the North Island's backbone, and beyond them the **Hawke's Bay wine country**, centred on the Art Deco city of Napier. Further south, the wine region of Martinborough is just an hour or so from the capital, **Wellington**, its centre squeezed onto reclaimed harbourside, the suburbs slung across steep hills overlooking glistening bays. Politicians and bureaucrats give it a well-scrubbed and urbane sophistication, enlivened by an established café society and after-dark scene.

The **South Island** kicks off with the world-renowned wineries of **Marlborough** and appealing **Nelson**, a pretty and compact spot surrounded by lovely beaches and within easy reach of the hill country around the **Nelson Lakes National Park** and the fabulous sea-kayaking of the **Abel Tasman National Park**. From the top of the South Island you've a choice of nipping behind the 3000m summits of the Southern Alps and following the West Coast to the fabulous, if rapidly shrinking, **glaciers** at Fox and Franz Josef, or sticking to the east, passing the whale-watching territory of **Kaikoura** en route to the South Island's largest centre, **Christchurch**. Its British architectural heritage may have been ravaged by earthquakes – but the city is bouncing back, and remains one of the most exciting urban spaces.

From here you can head across country to the West Coast via Arthur's Pass on the scenic TranzAlpine train trip, or shoot southeast across the patchwork Canterbury Plains to the foothills of the **Southern Alps** and **Aoraki/Mount Cook** with its distinctive drooping-tent summit.

The patchwork-quilt fields of Canterbury run, via the grand architecture of **Oamaru**, to the unmistakably Scottish-influenced city of **Dunedin**, a base for exploring the wildlife of the **Otago Peninsula**, with its albatross, seal, sea lion and penguin colonies. In the middle of the nineteenth century, prospectors arrived here and rushed inland to gold strikes throughout central Otago and around stunningly set **Queenstown**, now a commercialized activity centre where bungy jumping, rafting, jetboating and skiing hold sway. Just up the road is Glenorchy, a tramping heartland, from which the **Routeburn Track** sets out to rain-sodden **Fiordland**; its neighbour, Te Anau, is the launch pad for many of New Zealand's most famous treks, including the **Milford Track**. Further south you'll feel the bite of the Antarctic winds, which reach their peak on New Zealand's third landmass, isolated **Stewart Island**, covered mostly by dense coastal rainforest that offers a great chance of spotting a kiwi in the wild.

When to go

With ocean in every direction it is no surprise that New Zealand has a maritime climate, warm in the summer months, December to March, and never truly cold, even in winter. **Weather** patterns are strongly affected by prevailing westerlies, which suck up moisture from the Tasman Sea and dump it on the western side of both islands. The South Island gets the lion's share, with the West Coast and Fiordland ranking among the world's wettest places. Mountain ranges running the length of both islands cast long rain shadows eastward, making those locations considerably drier. The south is a few degrees cooler than elsewhere, and subtropical Auckland and Northland are appreciably more humid. In the North Island, warm, damp summers fade imperceptibly into cool, wet winters, while the further south you travel the more the weather divides the year into four distinct seasons.

Most people visit New Zealand in the summer, but it is a viable destination at any time provided you pick your target. From December to March you'll find everything open, though often busy with holidaying Kiwis from Christmas to mid-January. In general, you're better off joining the bulk of foreign visitors during the **shoulder seasons** – October, November and April – when sights and attractions are quieter, and accommodation easier to come by. **Winter** (May–Sept) is the wettest, coldest and consequently least popular time, unless you are enamoured of winter sports, in which case it's fabulous. The switch to prevailing southerly winds tends to bring periods of crisp, dry and cloudless weather to the West Coast and heavy snowfalls to the Southern Alps and Central North Island, allowing for some of the most varied and least-populated **skiing and snowboarding** in the world.

PORIRUA

Author picks

Our authors have bussed, walked, rafted and ridden the length and breadth of New Zealand. These are some of their own favourite travel experiences.

Superb natural hot pool Kerosene Creek has no changing rooms, no café, no gift shop – just a naturally heated stream which tumbles over a short waterfall into a bath-like pool. Bliss. See page 253.

The kleptomaniac kea It's hard not to love these trickster alpine parrots, even if one has just shredded your windscreen wipers. See page 51.

DIY caving There's something raw and thrilling about an unaided exploration of Cave Stream, a 600m-long tunnel carved by an alpine stream. See page 536.

Most entertaining stroll For a diverse slice of Kiwi life, take a late evening wander along Auckland's Karangahape Road, a grungy yet vibrant strip of cafés and shops where boozy suits, LGBTQ couples and dining suburbanites all mix to kaleidoscopic effect. See page 79.

Seafood restaurant heaven At *Fleur's Place*, a quirky shed restaurant, you know the fish is fresh as you can see Fleur's fishing boat bobbing in the bay outside. See page 573.

Best coastal drive Savour the Picton–Kaikoura route, with Sauvignon Blanc vineyards heralding a craggy coastal ribbon of crashing azure waves backed by the magnificent Kaikoura Ranges. See page 449.

Southern sky stargazing Join the excellent Earth & Sky stargazing trips to the summit of Mt John near Lake Tekapo, or simply gaze overhead from your tent. See page 548.

Hiking the Hump Ridge Track A dream combination of thick bush, subalpine tops and coastal scenery with a smattering of pioneer logging heritage make this a wonderful hike. Pay a little extra for nightly hot showers and helicopter bag transfer up the stiffest climb. See page 665.

Our author recommendations don't end here. We've flagged up our favourite places – a perfectly sited hotel, an atmospheric café, a special restaurant – throughout the Guide, highlighted with the ★ symbol.

FRESH SEAFOOD

VINEYARDS, MARLBOROUGH

25

things not to miss

It's not possible to see everything that New Zealand has to offer in one trip – so don't try. What follows, in no particular order, is a selective taste of the islands' highlights, including outstanding national parks, natural wonders, adventure activities and exotic wildlife. All highlights have a page reference to take you straight into the Guide, where you can find out more. Coloured numbers refer to chapters in the Guide.

1

1 MILFORD SOUND
See page 654
Experience the grandeur and beauty of Fiordland on the area's most accessible fiord, great in bright sunshine and wonderfully atmospheric in the mist with the waterfalls at their most impressive.

2 FAREWELL SPIT
See page 443
This slender 25km arc of sand dunes and beaches is a nature reserve protecting a host of birds including black swans, wrybills, curlews and dotterels.

3 TAIERI GORGE RAILWAY AND OTAGO CENTRAL RAIL TRAIL
See page 580
Pair a dramatic journey on this stately old train through otherwise inaccessible mountain landscapes with a cycle ride down a rugged 150km bike trail.

4 WHALE WATCHING
See page 452
An impressive range of cetaceans populate the deep canyons off the Kaikoura Peninsula, visited on a cruise or spied from a plane or helicopter.

5 WHITE ISLAND
See page 265
Take an appealing boat trip out to New Zealand's most active volcano, and stroll through the sulphurous lunar landscape to peer into the steaming crater.

6 NINETY MILE BEACH
See page 174
This seemingly endless wave-lashed golden strand is a designated highway, plied by tour buses that regularly stop to let passengers toboggan down the steep dunes.

7 EAST CAPE
See page 326
A varied coastline, tiny, predominantly Māori communities and the slow pace of life make this isolated region a place to linger.

8 THE GLACIERS
See page 486
The steep and dramatic Fox and Franz Josef glaciers can be explored by valley walking, ice climbing or heli-hiking.

9 EXPERIENCE MĀORI CULTURE
See page 713
Gain an insight into Māori history, arts, food and culture – and see the spectacular Pohutu geyser – at the Whakarewarewa Thermal Reserve, outside Rotorua.

10 DIVING AT THE POOR KNIGHTS ISLANDS
See page 149
Two-dive day-trips visit one of the world's best diving destinations. A couple of scuttled navy boats nearby add to the possibilities.

9

10

11 THE CATLINS
See page 682
Seals and dolphins and a
laidback approach to life
make this rugged coast a
great place to unwind for a
few days.

12 MUSEUM OF NEW ZEALAND (TE PAPA)
See page 368
A celebration of the people,
culture and art of New
Zealand that's as appealing
to kids as it is to adults, with
an impressive use of state-
of-the-art technology.

13 HOKIANGA HARBOUR
See page 178
As a low-key antidote to the
commercialization of the Bay
of Islands, the sand dunes,
quiet retreats and crafts
culture of this vast inlet are
hard to beat.

14 CHRISTCHURCH REBUILD
See page 500
Witness the rebirth of a
new city, a creative blend of
coffee shops, art galleries and
contemporary architecture.

15 ABEL TASMAN NATIONAL PARK
See page 450
Visitors flock to this
accessible coastal park to
hike its Coast Track and
kayak its magnificent
coastline.

13

14

15

16 SURFING AT RAGLAN
See page 197
One of the world's longest left-hand breaks, reliable swells and a chilled-out vibe make this New Zealand's prime surfing destination.

17 ZEALANDIA
See page 372
On the edge of Wellington, this beautiful fenced-in nature reserve is stocked with purely native flora and fauna.

18 WAI-O-TAPU
See page 253
The best of Rotorua's geothermal sites offers beautiful, mineral-coloured lakes, a geyser that erupts on cue each morning and pools of plopping mud.

19 WHANGANUI RIVER JOURNEY
See page 312
This relaxing three-day canoe trip along a historic waterway takes you through some of the North Island's loveliest scenery.

20 WINE
See page 44
Spend a day or two sampling fine wines and dining overlooking the vines in Hawke's Bay, Martinborough, Marlborough, Central Otago or any of half-a-dozen other major wine regions.

17

18

19

20

21 THE ROUTEBURN TRACK
See page 608
One of the country's finest walks, showcasing forested valleys, rich birdlife, thundering waterfalls, river flats, lakes and wonderful mountain scenery.

22 MOERAKI BOULDERS
See page 572
Stroll along the beach to visit these large, perfectly round, natural spheres with honeycomb centres, just sitting in the surf.

23 TONGARIRO ALPINE CROSSING
See page 289
A superb one-day hike through the volcanic badlands of the Tongariro National Park, passing the cone of Mount Ngauruhoe.

24 ART DECO NAPIER
See page 347
The world's most homogeneous collection of Art Deco architecture owes its genesis to the 1931 earthquake that flattened this lovely provincial city.

25 THE PENGUIN PLACE
See page 587
Watch yellow-eyed penguins waddle up the beach to their nests each night from hides and viewing platforms all along the South Island's southwestern coast.

Itineraries

The following itineraries pick out New Zealand's best sights, giving everything from a quick overview combining beaches, Māori culture, cool cities and majestic scenery, to more specific recommendations – check out the strange birdlife, soak in hot pools and stargaze, or opt for one of the many adventurous options.

THE GRAND TOUR

New Zealand really packs in the sights, so allow at least three weeks for this comprehensive itinerary.

❶ Auckland New Zealand's biggest city has vibrant and diverse cultural, culinary and nightlife scenes. See page 70

❷ Northland The winterless north features sweeping beaches, vast sand dunes, quaint harbours and the Waitangi Treaty Grounds, perhaps the most symbolic place in the country. See page 134

❸ Rotorua In this geothermal wonderland of geysers and boiling mud pools, *haka*, dance and an earth-steamed *hangi* dinner showcase Māori culture. See page 236

❹ Napier The small-scale Art Deco architecture provides the backdrop to Hawke's Bay's fine food and some of New Zealand's best Bordeaux-style red wines. See page 347

❺ Wellington The capital is New Zealand's most beguiling city, with a walkable heart of museums, cafés and lively bars around a picturesque harbour. See page 362

❻ Nelson and Golden Bay Golden beaches, hippy markets and the coastal pleasures of the Abel Tasman National Park make this the most blissed-out corner of the country. See page 417

❼ The West Coast Native bush and precipitous glaciers plunge steeply to the crashing surf along this wild and fabulously scenic coast. See page 458

❽ Aoraki/Mount Cook New Zealand's highest peak stands as snowy sentinel over the impossibly blue lakes and golden grasses of the Mackenzie Country. See page 551

❾ Queenstown Don't miss the fabulous mountain scenery, incredible concentration of adventure activities and some of the South Island's best restaurants and bars. See page 591

❿ Fiordland Cruise, kayak or even dive the waters of Milford and Doubtful sounds in between multi-day tramps along the Kepler Track or the exalted Milford Track. See page 642

NATURAL NEW ZEALAND

Geysers, fiords, alpine parrots, cute penguins, whales and several species of dolphin supplement clear skies and stunning scenery. Allow at least two and a half weeks for this itinerary.

❶ Kiwi spotting in the kauri forest Move quietly among the kauri forest night as kiwi call plaintively and maybe – just maybe – show themselves. See page 181

❷ Hot Water Beach Dig a hole in the sand and ease into a shallow pool of hot water occasionally cooled by the surf. See page 226

❸ Birds on Kapiti Island Explore this island sanctuary full of intriguing birds – bush parrots, parakeets, fantails, little spotted kiwis and even a few of the 250 takahe left in the world. See page 387

❹ Swimming with seals Give the dolphins a break: seals are often more playful, particularly in the waters off Kaikoura. See page 453

❺ Night sky viewing Tekapo offers wonderful stargazing, helped by the fact it sits within the country's first Dark Sky Reserve. See page 548

❻ Otago Peninsula wildlife Dunedin's doorstep harbours a fabulous concentration of wildlife with two species of penguin, seals and a colony of albatross. See page 586

❼ Stewart Island After being welcomed by flocks of parrots, visit saddlebacks, red-crowned parakeets and bellbirds on Ulva Island, then spot kiwi at Mason Bay. See page 675

ADVENTURE NEW ZEALAND

Nowhere in the world has as many adrenaline-fuelled and low-key adventures as New Zealand. Allow at least three weeks for this itinerary.

❶ Raft the Kaituna Short and sweet, the Kaituna packs in a gorgeous verdant gorge, plunging rapids and a 7m waterfall. See page 244

❷ Lost World caving The ground below Waitomo is riddled with limestone caverns, best explored by a massive abseil followed by squeezes and scrambles. See page 206

❸ Hiking the Tongariro Alpine Crossing Take on New Zealand's finest one-day tramp across the barren volcanic wastes of the Tongariro National Park. See page 289

❹ Kayaking Abel Tasman National Park Opt for an overnight paddle on the sheltered, warm waters then camp beside a golden beach. See page 434

❺ Glacier hike Franz Josef Get choppered up onto the glacier and left for a couple of hours of guided hiking across snowfields and through ice caves. See page 486

❻ Canyon the Niger Stream Jump into deep pools and abseil down waterfalls in Wanaka's beautiful canyons. See page 621

❼ Bungy the Nevis Go for the big one, a 134m monster from a gondola eight freefall seconds above a tiny stream. See page 596

❽ Bike the Wakatipu Basin Easy lakeside jaunts, great cross-country rides, and the country's only cable-car-assisted downhill mountain-bike tracks. See page 562

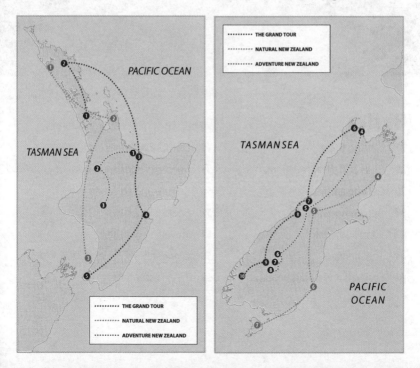

JETBOATING, QUEENSTOWN

Basics

Getting there

The quickest, easiest and cheapest way to get to New Zealand is to fly. It is possible to arrive by sea, but there are no international passenger ferries, so unless you own a boat this means joining a cruise, crewing on a private yacht, or paying for your passage on a cargo ship (a rewarding experience for those who like sea journeys – find out more at ⓦ freightertravel.co.nz).

Air fares depend on the season, with the highest during the New Zealand summer (Dec–Feb); prices drop during the shoulder seasons (Sept–Nov & March–May) and you'll get the cheapest rates during the low (ski) season (June–Aug).

Arriving in New Zealand, your only real choice, unless you're coming from Australia, is between the **international airports at Auckland and Christchurch**. Christchurch receives fewer direct flights but many scheduled airlines have a codeshare shuttle from Auckland at no extra cost. The most desirable option is an **open-jaw ticket** (flying into one and out of the other), which usually costs no more than an ordinary return. **Internal flights** within NZ are best booked online (see page 30).

Tourists and those on short-term working visas (see page 58) are generally required by New Zealand immigration to arrive with an **outward bound ticket**, so one-way tickets are really only viable for Australian and New Zealand residents.

If you've purchased a return ticket and find you want to stay longer or head off on a totally different route, it's possible to **change** the dates and, more rarely, the route, with the airline or travel agent, depending on the conditions of your ticket, though there is often a fee.

Flights from the UK and Ireland

Over a dozen airlines compete to fly you **from Britain** to New Zealand for as little as £645, but prices depend upon the time of year, and can be double that amount at Christmas. Going for the **cheapest flight** typically means sacrificing some comfort (multiple stops, longer layovers), which you may regret, given that even the shortest journey will last at least 24 hours including an obligatory refuelling stop. From Northern Ireland to New Zealand, you'll need to factor in the short hop to Dublin or London (£100 return, cheaper with internet deals) or an additional stop in the Far East or Australia.

Most **scheduled flights** allow multiple **stopovers** either in North America and the Pacific, or Asia and Australia. Most direct scheduled flights depart from London Heathrow, though some services operate from London Gatwick, and regional airports including Manchester and Newcastle.

Flights from the US and Canada

Direct trans-Pacific flights to Auckland operate from Los Angeles, San Francisco (12 hours) and Vancouver (13 hours). Assorted codeshare partners sell tickets to New Zealand, usually offering several connections a day to Wellington and Christchurch.

From the US a direct LA–Auckland or San Francisco–Auckland round-trip fare goes for around US$1000 during the southern winter, rising to around US$1400 or more in peak southern summer season. Flights from all other US cities are usually routed via California. Off-peak you might expect to pay US$1400–1600 from New York or Chicago, but shopping around should save you money.

From Canada, you can fly direct to Auckland. Depending on the season, fares from Vancouver are around CA$1600; from Toronto, around CA$1800; and from Montréal, around CA$1800. Substantial savings can often be made through discount travel companies and websites.

Apart from an **RTW** ticket (see page 28), an alternative approach from North America is to fly **via Asia**, which may work out cheaper. Another option is to stop off at a **Pacific island** or two along the way, which often costs less than US$200 per stopover.

A BETTER KIND OF TRAVEL

At Rough Guides we are passionately committed to travel. We believe it helps us understand the world we live in and the people we share it with – and of course tourism is vital to many developing economies. But the scale of modern tourism has also damaged some places irreparably, and climate change is accelerated by most forms of transport, especially flying. All Rough Guides' flights are carbon-offset, and every year we donate money to a variety of environmental charities.

Flights from Australia and South Africa

Prices for flights between **Australia** and New Zealand vary enormously depending on demand (book well in advance in summer), but the level of competition generally keeps them reasonable – as low as AU$250 return from Australia's east coast (including a basic baggage allowance) if you're prepared to go for non-refundable tickets. Return flights from Perth start at around AU$480.

Flying time from Sydney or Melbourne to New Zealand is around three and a half hours. Auckland, Christchurch, Dunedin, Rotorua, Queenstown and Wellington international airports all have direct flights to/from Australia.

From Australia, there's a huge variety of **package holidays** to New Zealand, including short **city-breaks** (flight and accommodation), winter skiing packages and **fly-drive** deals for little more than the cost of the regular air fare.

Travelling to New Zealand **from South Africa** invariably involves flying via Australia. Expect to pay around ZAR14,000–30,000, depending on the season and airline.

Round-the-world flights

If New Zealand is only one stop on a longer journey, you might consider buying a **Round-the-World (RTW)** ticket. An "off-the-shelf" RTW ticket will have you touching down in about half a dozen cities (Auckland is on many itineraries), or you can assemble one tailored to your needs, though this is liable to be more expensive.

INTERNATIONAL AIRLINES

Air Canada (W aircanada.com)
Air New Zealand (W airnewzealand.com)
American Airlines (W aa.com)
British Airways (W ba.com)
Cathay Pacific (W cathaypacific.com)
China Southern (W csair.com/en)
Emirates (W emirates.com)
Etihad (W etihad.com)
Fiji Airways (W fijiairways.com)
LATAM Airlines (W latam.com)
Malaysia (W malaysiaairlines.com)
Qantas (W qantas.com.au)
South African Airways (W fly.saa.com)
Thai (W thaiairways.com)
Virgin Australia (W virginaustralia.com)

Agents and operators

If time is limited and you have a clear idea of what you want to do, numerous companies offer **organized tours**, from backpacker excursions to no-expense-spared extravaganzas. Full "see-it-all" packages, with most meals and transport included, can be good value, considering what you'd be spending anyway. Some companies offer tours specifically for those aged 18–35, seniors, or the adventurous. You can also find tours to suit your interest (such as hiking or kayaking). There are plenty of New Zealand-based tour operators to choose from (see page 53).

A number of companies operate **flexible bus tours**, which you can hop off whenever you like and rejoin a day or two later when the next bus comes through (see page 31).

Pretty much all the major tour operators can also book you onto **tramping trips**, including some of the guided Great Walks (see page 50); you'll still need to book way in advance, though. For **skiing trips**, the cheapest option is usually to contact ski clubs at the fields directly (contact details at W snow.co.nz).

Even if an all-in package doesn't appeal, it still may be worth investigating potential savings by pre-booking some accommodation, tours or a rental vehicle.

AGENTS AND OPERATORS

Adventures Abroad W adventures-abroad.com. US-based agent with a broad range of New Zealand options.
Backpackers World Travel Australia T 1800 997 325, W backpackersworld.com.
Contiki W contiki.com. 18–35 package tour bracket.
Intrepid W intrepidtravel.com. Adventurous, excellently led small-group tours.
North South Travel UK T 01245 608 291, W northsouthtravel. co.uk. Competitive travel agency, offering discounted fares worldwide. Profits are used to support projects in the developing world, especially the promotion of sustainable tourism.
Road Scholar W roadscholar.org. Not-for-profit educational and adventure tours, mostly small-group, with strong package of New Zealand options.
STA Travel UK T 0333 321 0099, US T 1 800 781 4040, Australia T 134 782, NZ T 0800 474 400, South Africa T 0861 781 781, UK; W statravel.co.uk. Worldwide specialists in independent travel; also student IDs, travel insurance, car rental, rail passes and more. Good discounts for students and under-26s. Experts on NZ travel with branches in major Kiwi cities.
Trailfinders UK T 0207 368 1200, Ireland T 01 677 7888; W trailfinders.com. One of the best-informed and most efficient agents for independent travellers.
Travel Cuts Canada T 1 800 667-2887, W travelcuts.com. Canadian student-travel organization.
USIT Ireland T 01 602 1906, Australia T 1800 092 499; W usit.ie. Ireland's main student and youth travel specialists.

Visas and entry requirements

All visitors to New Zealand need a passport, which must be valid for at least three months beyond the time you intend to stay. When flying to New Zealand you'll probably need to show you have an onward or return booking **before they'll let you board the plane.**

On arrival, British citizens are automatically issued with a permit to stay for up to six months, and a three-month permit is granted to citizens of most other European countries, Southeast Asian nations, Japan, South Africa, the US and Canada, and several other countries. Australian citizens can stay indefinitely.

Other nationalities need to obtain a visitor visa in advance from a New Zealand embassy, costing the local equivalent of NZ$165 and usually valid for three months. Visas are issued by Immigration New Zealand (🌐 immigration.govt.nz). See page 58 for advice on working visas.

Websites and contact details for all NZ embassies and consulates **abroad** can be found at 🌐 nzembassy.com.

Quarantine and customs

In a country all too familiar with the damage that can be caused by introduced plants and animals, **biosecurity** is taken seriously (🌐 mpi.govt.nz/biosecuritynz). On arrival you'll be asked to **declare any food**, plants or parts of plants, animals (dead or alive), equipment used with animals, wooden products (including musical instruments), camping gear, golf clubs, bicycles, biological specimens and hiking boots. Outdoor equipment and walking boots will be inspected and perhaps cleaned then returned shortly thereafter. After a long flight it can seem a bit of a pain, but such precautions are important and there are huge fines for non-compliance. Be sure to dispose of any fresh fruit, vegetables and meat in the bins provided or you're liable for an instant $400 fine (even for that orange you forgot about in the bottom of your bag). Processed foods are usually allowed through, but must be declared.

Visitors aged eighteen and over are entitled to a **duty-free allowance** (🌐 customs.govt.nz) of fifty cigarettes (or fifty grams of cigars or tobacco products), 4.5 litres of wine or beer, three 1125ml bottles of spirits, and up to $700 worth of goods. There are **export restrictions** on wildlife, plants, antiquities and works of art.

Getting around

New Zealand is a relatively small country and getting around is easy, with some form of public transport going to many destinations, though sometimes limited to one service per day. There are still a few places that are hard to access, yet all of these can be reached with will, flexibility and a little ingenuity.

Internal **flights** are reasonably priced if booked well in advance, but you'll appreciate the scenery better by travelling at ground level. The cheapest and easiest, though slowest, way to get around is by **bus** (coaches or shuttle buses). The **rail service**, by contrast, is limited and expensive.

Rental **cars** and campervans, particularly the little ones (see page 33), can be remarkably good value for two or more people, but if you are staying in the country for more than a couple of months, it's more economical to buy a vehicle. New Zealand's green countryside encourages **cyclists**, but even the keenest vary their transport options.

Competition on the **ferries** connecting the North and South islands means passenger fares are good value, though transporting vehicles is pricey. Planes and boats give limited access to offshore islands and the parts of the mainland that remain stubbornly impenetrable by road, though more specialist **tours** make getting into the wilds easier.

The frequency of long-distance bus, train and plane services is listed, where relevant, in each chapter in "Arrival and departure", while local buses and trains, again where relevant, appear in "Getting around".

By plane

Many visitors fly into Auckland at the beginning of their trip and out from Christchurch at the end, so don't touch **domestic flights**, but those with a tight timetable wanting to hit a few key sights in a short time might be tempted by reasonable-value internal fares.

The biggest domestic operator is **Air New Zealand**, serving all the main centres and numerous minor ones (20 destinations). The main competition is from **Jetstar**, which serves Auckland, Wellington, Christchurch, Queenstown, Dunedin, Napier, New Plymouth, Nelson and Palmerston North. Air New Zealand runs single-class planes with **fares** that come in four levels, offering lower fares for decreased flexibility: there are fewer low-cost fares at popular times. Jetstar has a similar system. For example, a one-way

INTERNAL FLIGHTS

If you decide to use **internal flights**, booking tickets online can save you up to fifty percent. Check out Air New Zealand's (ⓦairnewzealand.com) **air passes** if you've used the airline to get to New Zealand. You can buy one-way tickets to create your own multi-stop itinerary. Jetstar (ⓦjetstar.com) offers similar multi-destination tickets at less favourable rates. Air New Zealand also offer last minute (or 1hr 30min before departure, to be precise) Regional Gotta Go fares. Their discount website ⓦgrabaseat.co.nz has cheap seats as well as a weekly reverse seat auction.

standard flight between Auckland and Christchurch is about $200, a seat+bag $139, seat only (no hold baggage) as little as $59 – or only $45 on ⓦgrabaseat.co.nz. Other flights you might take are scenic jaunts from Auckland to Great Barrier Island, the hop over Cook Strait, or the short trip from Invercargill to Stewart Island.

AIRLINES

Air New Zealand ☎ 0800 737 000, ⓦ airnewzealand.co.nz.
Fly My Sky ☎ 0800 222 123, ⓦ flymysky.co.nz. Flights between Auckland and Great Barrier Island.
Great Barrier Airlines ☎ 0800 900 600, ⓦ barrierair.kiwi. Flights between Great Barrier Island, Northland and Auckland.
Jetstar ☎ 0800 800 995, ⓦ jetstar.com.
Soundsair ☎ 0800 505 005, ⓦ soundsair.com. Small planes across Cook Strait.
Stewart Island Flights ☎ 03 218 9129, ⓦ stewartislandflights.com. Scheduled services between Invercargill and Stewart Island.

By bus

You can get most places on long-distance **buses** ("coaches") and smaller **shuttle buses**, which essentially offer the same service but are more likely to drop you off and pick up at hotels, hostels and the like. Services are generally reliable and reasonably comfortable, and competition keeps prices competitive. The larger buses are usually air-conditioned and may have wi-fi. Some have toilets, though all services stop every couple of hours, at wayside tearooms and points of interest along the way. Most of your fellow passengers are likely to be visitors to New Zealand so drivers often give a commentary, the quality of which varies.

InterCity

The biggest operator, **InterCity**, runs high-quality full-size buses all over the country – they also operate Great Sights, Gray Line and Newmans (premium sightseeing and coach companies). All InterCity buses have wi-fi and InterCity GOLD has soft leather reclining chairs and individual charging ports.

Fares vary dramatically, but as an example, a flexi one-way fare on the North Island, Auckland to Rotorua, might be $72 (standard non-refundable tickets start at $22), while on the South Island, Christchurch to Queenstown, it's $81 (nonrefundable $53). Prices drop during off-peak periods.

Book early for the best prices. There's one $1 seat sold on each service, but as they're available a year in advance, you may feel you've better odds of spotting a hobbit. YHA, VIP, ISIC and BBH cardholders get small discounts off Flexible Fares but you'll find cheaper deals by chasing down the various nonrefundable fares.

InterCity also offers numerous **passes**. Fixed-route TravelPasses include Auckland to Paihia (Bay Escape $125); Auckland to Wellington via Matamata (includes Hobbiton tour), Rotorua and Taupo (Big Fish: $219); or Nelson to Queenstown via the west coast ($179). For complete freedom and a pass that's valid for 12 months, choose a Flexipass (see page 32).

Other buses

Other companies compete directly with InterCity on the main routes and fill in the gaps around the country, often linking with the major operators, to take you off the beaten track. Generally they cost less (sometimes appreciably) and can be more obliging when it comes to drop-offs and pick-ups, though seldom as comfortable over distance.

Relative newcomer **ManaBus** is competing on a few North Island routes, offering leather seats, free wi-fi and onboard toilets, with a one-way fare from Auckland to Rotorua of $1 to $3. We've listed a number of other operators below, but there are many more mentioned in the appropriate sections of this guide.

Official (i-SITE) visitor centres carry **timetables** of bus and shuttle companies operating in their area, so you can compare frequencies and prices. **Fare structures** are generally straightforward, with fixed prices and no complicated discounts. Auckland to Rotorua, on the North Island, costs about $20, while on the South Island, Christchurch to Queenstown will be roughly $50.

BACKPACKER BUSES

One of the cheapest ways to cover a lot of ground is on a **backpacker bus**, which combines some of the flexibility of independent travel with the convenience of a tour. You typically purchase a ticket for a fixed route (usually valid for 12 months), and then take it at your own pace. You can either stick with the one bus for the entire journey with nights spent at various towns along the route, or stop off longer in places and hop on a later bus. During peak times some buses may be full, so you'll need to plan onward travel several days in advance. Most companies operate year-round, though services are reduced in winter.

The emphasis is on **experiencing the country** rather than travelling from one town to the next, so you'll be stopping off to bungy jump, hike or some such. Being part of a group of forty rowdy backpackers arriving at some idyllic spot isn't everyone's idea of a good time and, by using assorted public transport, it is often just as cheap to make your own way around New Zealand. But if you want almost everything organized for you, and a ready-made bunch of like-minded fellow travellers, this sort of travel might appeal.

It can be slightly **cheaper** to book before you arrive, as some deals are not available once you step off the plane: check the websites. You might also save a few dollars by being a YHA, VIP, BBH or ISIC cardholder. Tickets don't generally cover accommodation, activities (although these are often discounted), side trips, food or travel between the North and South islands.

Operators are listed below. Those interested in multi-day tours and adventure activities should check out "Outdoor activities" (see page 48), where more intimate and specialized excursions are listed.

Flying Kiwi Wilderness Expeditions (W flyingkiwi.com). Operator specializing in tours that get off the beaten track and eschew city hostels in favour of camping. Converted buses are equipped with bikes, canoes, kitchen, awning, fridge, mattresses, tents and hot shower, and everyone mucks in with domestic chores. Trips operate all year and once on board you stick with the same group. Options range from the Northern Express from Wellington to Auckland via Taupo (2 days; $255) to a full NZ tour (27 days; $4499 including food and camping fees).

Haka Tours (W hakatours.com). Fully guided, small-group tours. You'll travel together, sleep together (all tours include accommodation), and breakfast together. Save money by booking activity packages in advance — useful if you're worried you might squander that money you saved for a dolphin-swim on beer. Tours include the Epic (24 days; $4399 including handful of activities) and the South Island LICK (7 days; $1349 with a trip on the TranzAlpine).

Kiwi Experience (W kiwiexperience.com). With a deserved reputation for attracting high-spirited party animals, Kiwi Experience offers a huge array of passes, from a trip to the Bay of Islands and Cape Reinga starting in Auckland (min 4 days; $219) to the Whole Kit and Caboodle (minimum 30 days; $1649).

Stray (W straytravel.com). Stray see themselves as a bit more intrepid than Kiwi Experience; you're as likely to be necking beers around a campfire as a city bar. Trips include a South Island circuit (minimum 15 days; from $1855) and a North Island circuit (minimum 13 days; from $1295).

By train

Not much is left of New Zealand's passenger train service besides **commuter** services in Wellington and Auckland and a few inter-city trains. The **long-distance services** that exist are scenic runs, primarily used by tourists; trains are so slow that they have ceased to be practical transport for New Zealanders. Minimal investment in infrastructure and rolling stock is beginning to have an effect on standards, but railway travel remains a pleasant experience.

Long-distance trains are all run by **KiwiRail Scenic Trains** (T 0800 872 467, W greatjourneysofnz.co.nz), which operates three passenger routes. Trains have reclining seats, buffet cars with reasonable food, beer, panoramic windows, glass-backed observation cars or open-air viewing decks. Tickets guarantee a seat: passengers check in on the platform before boarding and bags are carried in a luggage van.

The longest is the **Northern Explorer** between Auckland and Wellington, past the volcanic peaks of the Tongariro National Park. Interesting **stops along the way** include Otorohanga (where the train is met by a shuttle bus to Waitomo Caves) and National Park (with access to Mount Ruapehu and the Tongariro Alpine Crossing). The service leaves Auckland on Monday, Wednesday and Saturday, and Wellington on Sunday, Tuesday and Friday at 7.45am and reaches its destination around 6.25pm.

In the South Island, the **Coastal Pacific** makes a pretty five-hour run **between Christchurch and Picton**, sometimes hugging the coast. Since the earthquake in 2016, however, this line has been out of action. It is expected to reopen in 2019.

The finest rail journey in New Zealand is the **TranzAlpine between Christchurch and Greymouth** on the West Coast (see page 519).

TRAVEL PASSES

If you're doing a lot of travelling by bus and train, there are savings to be made with travel passes. The Scenic Rail Pass (🌐 scenicrailpass.com) is a great option if you plan to travel by train, but since the 2016 earthquake, the Coastal Pacific section of the railway has been closed: check the latest online.

InterCity (🌐 intercity.co.nz) offer their own **FlexiPass**, allowing you to buy bus travel by the hour – the more hours you buy the better the savings. You would typically need 45 hours ($355) to cover one of the main islands, and 60 hours upwards ($459) for a full tour. If that's not enough, you can top-up your pass with, say, 15 hours ($132). Travellers with a fixed itinerary who want to move around pretty quickly might be better off with their **TravelPass**; both passes are valid for 12 months, include the Interislander Ferry, and journeys can be booked online.

The backpacker tour buses (see page 31) offer lower prices in return for older buses and – often – a more boisterous time.

Fares are higher than the comparable bus tickets, but with discounts and the use of a **travel pass** (see above), travelling is still reasonably good value. Most people get the standard or **Flexi Fare**, which gives a discount in return for advance booking and a full refund if you cancel or change more than 48 hours before the departure time. As an example, a standard, one-way ticket from Auckland to Wellington or from Christchurch to Greymouth is around $199. Seniors (60-plus) can get discounts on standard fares, though most folk would do better by going for a Scenic Rail Pass, once they are back on sale (see above).

Apart from a couple of short-run steam trains, the only other passenger trains are along the **Taieri Gorge Railway** (see page 580) between Dunedin and Middlemarch, an extremely beautiful route again run almost entirely for the benefit of tourists.

By car

For maximum flexibility, it's hard to beat **driving** around New Zealand: you'll be able to get to places beyond the reach of public transport and to set your own timetable. With the freedom to camp or stay in cheaper places away from town centres this can be a very economical option for two or more people.

Plan routes carefully to allow sufficient time to enjoy your journey: even the highways may be narrower, steeper and more winding than you are used to.

In order to drive in New Zealand you need a valid **licence** from your home country, or an -International Driver's Licence (valid for up to a year in New Zealand). You must always carry the licence when driving.

In New Zealand you **drive on the left** and will find **road rules** similar to those in the UK, Australia and the US. All occupants must wear **seatbelts** and drivers must park in the same direction as the traffic flow. The

Transport Agency (🌐 nzta.govt.nz) publish guides in several languages on *Driving in New Zealand*.

The **speed limit** for the open road is 100kmph, reduced to 70kmph or 50kmph in built-up areas. Speeding fines start at $30 and rapidly increase as the degree of transgression increases. Some drivers flash their headlights at oncoming cars to warn of lurking police patrols, but there are also hidden cameras on the roads. **Drink driving** has traditionally been a problem in New Zealand: as part of a campaign to cut the death toll the alcohol limit is low, random breath tests exist and offenders are dealt with severely.

Road conditions are generally good and traffic is relatively light except around Auckland and Wellington in the rush hour. Most roads are sealed (paved), although a few have a metalled surface, composed of an aggregate of loose chippings. Clearly marked on most maps, these are slower to drive along, prone to washouts and landslides after heavy rain, and demand considerably more care and attention from the driver. Always check conditions locally before setting off on these routes. All rental companies should insure you on gravel (unsealed) roads, though some prohibit the use of their cars on the worst – typically those at Skippers Canyon and around the northern tip of Coromandel Peninsula.

Other **hazards** include one-lane bridges: a sign before the bridge will indicate who has right of way, and on longer examples there'll be a passing place halfway across.

Unleaded and super unleaded **petrol** and diesel are available in New Zealand, and in larger towns petrol stations are open 24hr. In smaller towns, they may close after 8pm, so be sure to fill up for long evening or night journeys.

If you're driving your own vehicle, check if the **New Zealand Automobile Association** (🌐 aa.co.nz) has reciprocal rights with motoring organizations from your own country. Apart from a free 24hr **emergency breakdown** service (📞 0800 500 222) – excluding vehicles bogged on beaches – membership entitles you to free maps, accommodation guides and legal assistance, discounts on some rental cars and accommodation, plus access to insurance and pre-purchase vehicle inspection services.

Car rental

Visitors driving in New Zealand typically pick up a car in Auckland, tour the North Island to Wellington where they leave the first vehicle, cross Cook Strait, pick up a second car in Picton, then drive around the South Island dropping off the car in Christchurch. The whole thing can be done in reverse, and may work out cheaper, or you can stick with the same car across Cook Strait, which doesn't entail a big price hike from domestic companies (though some international agencies forbid it).

You'll see rental deals for under $19 a day, though only for older, small cars rented for over a month in winter (June–Aug). Demand is high over the main summer season and prices rise accordingly.

Most of the major **international companies** are represented and offer good deals for virtually new cars. **Domestic** firms offer cheaper rates partly by minimizing overheads and offering older (but perfectly serviceable) vehicles. You may find even cheaper deals with cut-rate local companies, which are fine for short stints, though for general touring domestic nationwide companies are the best bet. Their infrastructure helps when it comes to crossing between the North and South islands (see page 377) and they typically offer free breakdown assistance.

In peak season it usually pays to have a car **booked in advance**. At quieter times you can often pick up something cheaper once you arrive; and in winter (except in ski areas) you can almost name your price. Provided your rental period is four days or more the deal will be for **unlimited kilometres**. The rates

quoted below are for summer season assuming a two-week rental period, but don't be afraid to haggle at any time.

As a general rule, Ace, Apex, Omega and Pegasus offer reasonably new cars at moderate prices, while the rest of the companies listed below try desperately to undercut each other and offer **low prices**.

Based on a two-week rental in summer, for two people, a **small car** (1.3–1.8 litre) might cost $45–80 a day from the majors and $40–60 from domestic national firms. A **medium-sized car** (2–3 litre) might cost $90–120 from the majors and $60–70 from domestic national companies. Unless you're here in winter and want to get up to the ski-fields without tyre chains you don't really need a **4WD**, which generally cost $70–140 a day; you'll be better off renting one for short trips in specific areas.

If you are renting for several weeks, there is often no **drop-off fee** for leaving the vehicle somewhere other than where you picked it up. For shorter rental periods you may be charged around $200, though if you're travelling south to north, you may be able to sweet-talk your way out of drop-off charges. At different times in the season Wellington, Picton, Christchurch and Queenstown have a glut of cars that are needed elsewhere, and companies will offer **relocation deals**. Look at hostel notice boards or call the firms listed below. Some companies want quick delivery, while others will allow you to spend a few more days en route for a reduced rental rate.

You must have a full, clean **driver's licence** and be over 21; drivers under 25 often pay more for insurance. In most cases insurance is included in the quoted cost but you are liable for any windscreen damage and the first $2000 of any damage. With some of the major international companies, and also cheaper companies, this excess can be as much as $3500 if the accident is your fault. This can usually be reduced to $350 or zero by paying an additional $10–25 a day Collision Damage Waiver. Usually before giving you a car rental companies take a credit-card imprint or a cash bond from you for $2000. If you have an accident, the bond is used to pay for any damage: in some cases you can pay anything up to the value of the bond; in others you pay the entire bond no matter how slight the damage. Read the small print, look around the car for any visible **defects**, so you won't end up being charged for someone else's mistakes, and check whether there are any restrictions on driving along certain roads.

BUS COMPANIES

Atomic Shuttles 📞 03 349 0697, 🌐 atomictravel.co.nz. Major long-distance bus operator in the South Island.
InterCity Auckland call centre 📞 09 583 5780, 🌐 intercity. co.nz. Long-distance buses nationwide.
Manabus 🌐 manabus.com.
NakedBus 📞 0900 62533 (premium rate), 🌐 nakedbus. com. Cheap trips on both islands, including free wi-fi – and beds.

DOMESTIC CAR-RENTAL AGENCIES

Ace Rental Cars ☎ 0800 502 277, ⓦ acerentalcars.co.nz.
Apex ☎ 0800 500 660, ⓦ apexrentals.co.nz.
Bargain Rental Cars ☎ 0800 001 122, ⓦ bargainrentalcars.co.nz.
ezi car rental ☎ 0800 545 000, ⓦ ezi-car-rental.co.nz.
Jucy ☎ 0800 399 736, ⓦ jucy.co.nz.
Omega ☎ 0800 525 210, ⓦ omegarentalcars.com.
Pegasus ☎ 0800 803 580, ⓦ rentalcars.co.nz.

Campervan rental

Throughout the summer, roads are clogged with **campervans**, almost all driven by foreign visitors who rent them for a few weeks and drive around the country staying in campsites and freedom camping (see page 40). A medium campervan is generally suitable for two adults and a couple of kids and comes with a fold-down bed and compact kitchen. Larger models sleep four or more and often have a shower and toilet.

Medium **campervan rentals** (based on a 3-week rental) can be anywhere between $150 and $400 a day during the high season (Dec–Feb), dropping to $70–240 for a couple of months either side and plummeting to $40–150 in winter. The most well-known brands (Kea, Britz, Mighty and Maui) are effectively one company. The smaller firms (listed below) offer cheaper rates, often saving 30 percent or more.

Small vans are often cramped and aimed at backpackers prepared to sacrifice comfort to save money. These typically cost $60–140 a day during summer, $30–90 in the shoulder season and $25–35 in the depths of winter. The trend is for wildly painted bodywork, often with arcane, quirky or downright offensive comments graffitied on them: Escape Rentals and Wicked Campers. Other good bets are the distinctive orange Spaceships that have been imaginatively converted to suit two adults. For an affordable and slightly offbeat experience go for a restored, classic VW campervan (possibly with a pop-top), from Auckland-based Kiwi Kombis, who charge $180–265 a day, depending on dates and van.

For all vans you get unlimited kilometres, a kitchen kit and perhaps airport transfer. If you're renting for less than a week, there may be an additional charge, especially in high summer. Insurance is included but you'll be liable for the first $3000–4000 and you should seriously consider paying extra fees to get this liability reduced. Most companies have a supply of tents, camping kits, outdoor chairs and tables that can be rented for a few dollars.

No special **licence** is required to drive a campervan, but some caution is needed, especially in high winds and when climbing hills and going around tight corners.

CAMPERVAN RENTALS: MEDIUM TO LARGE

Adventure ☎ 0800 123 555, ⓦ nzmotorhomes.co.nz.
Britz ☎ 0800 831 900, ⓦ britz.com.
Eurocampers ☎ 03 347 3285, ⓦ eurocamper.co.nz.
Freedom Campers ☎ 0800 325 939, ⓦ freedomcampers.co.nz.
Jucy ☎ 0800 399 736, ⓦ jucy.co.nz.
Kea Campers ☎ 0800 520 052, ⓦ keacampers.com.
Maui ☎ 0800 651 080, ⓦ maui-rentals.com/nz/en.
Mighty Cars and Campers ☎ 800 422 267, ⓦ mightycampers.com.

SMALL VANS AND CONVERSIONS

Escape ☎ 0800 216 171, ⓦ escaperentals.co.nz.
Jucy ☎ 0800 399 736, ⓦ jucy.co.nz.
Kiwi Kombis ☎ 09 533 9335, ⓦ kiwikombis.com.
Spaceships ☎ 0800 772 237, ⓦ spaceshipsrentals.co.nz.
Wicked Campers ☎ 0800 246 870, ⓦ wickedcampers.co.nz.

Buying a used vehicle

Buying a **used vehicle** can be cost-effective if you are staying in the country for more than a couple of months. Reselling can recoup enough of the price to make it cheaper than using public transport or renting. However, if you buy cheap there's a greater risk of breakdowns and expensive repairs. The majority of people buy cars in Auckland and then try to sell them in Christchurch, so there's something to be said for buying in Christchurch where you'll often have more choice and a better bargaining position.

Some of the best deals are found on backpacker **hostel notice boards** where older cars and vans are typically offered for $500–5000. Realistically you can expect to pay upwards of $3000 for something half-decent. It may not look pretty and with a **private sale** there's no guarantee the vehicle will make yet another trip around the country, but you might get an added bonus like camping gear thrown in with the car (or offered at a snip).

For a little more peace of mind, buy from a **dealership**. There are plenty all over the country, especially in Auckland, Christchurch and Wellington. Prices begin at around $5000 and some yards offer a **buy-back service**, usually paying about fifty percent of the purchase price. If you're confident of your ability to spot a lemon, you can try to pick up a cheap car at an **auction**; they're held weekly in Auckland and Christchurch and are advertised in the local press. Be aware that you'll usually be liable for a **buyer's premium** of around ten percent over your bid.

Before you commit yourself, consult the My Vehicle section of the NZ Transport Agency website (🅦 nzta. govt.nz), which has good advice on buying and the pitfalls. Their **tips for buying a used car** are particularly helpful.

Unless you really know your big end from your steering column you'll want to arrange a **mobile vehicle inspection**, either from the AA (☎ 0800 907 788, 🅦 aa.co.nz; members $149, nonmembers $169) or the Car Inspection Services (from $145; ☎ 0800 500 800 in Auckland and Wellington, 🅦 carinspections. co.nz). The inspection may give you enough ammunition to negotiate a price reduction. Finally, before you close a private sale, call LemonCheck (☎ 0800 536 662, 🅦 lemoncheck.co.nz) – its staff will fill you in on the vehicle history, including possible odometer tampering ($20) and let you know about any debts on the vehicle ($7.50).

All vehicles over three years old must have a **Warrant of Fitness** (WOF), which is a test of its mechanical worthiness and safety. WOFs are carried out and issued by specified garages and testing stations and last for a year if the vehicle was registered this century, or six months if older. Check the expiry date, as any vehicle for sale must have had a WOF carried out no more than one month before sale. The vehicle should also have a current **vehicle licence** ("rego"), which must be renewed before it expires (six months, starting at $26.15; twelve months $52.11 for petrol-driven, private vehicles of 1301–2600cc): post offices and AA offices are the most convenient for this, though you can also do it online at 🅦 nzta.govt.nz.

You **transfer ownership** by completing buyer and seller forms online (buyers can also complete forms at a post office or AA office): the licence plates stay with the vehicle. Next, even though it's not compulsory, you'll want **insurance**: Comprehensive (which covers your vehicle and any other damaged vehicles), or Third Party, Fire & Theft (which covers your own vehicle against fire and theft, but only pays out on damage to other vehicles in case of an accident). Shop around as prices vary widely, but expect to pay a minimum of $150 for six months' Third Party, Fire & Theft cover (depending on age, experience, car value and so on).

By motorcycle

Visitors from most countries can ride in New Zealand with their normal or international licence, though it must specify motorbikes. **Helmets** are compulsory, and you'll need to be prepared to ride on gravel roads from time to time.

Few people bring their own bike but **bike rental** is available from the companies running guided bike tours (see below). It isn't cheap: expect to pay $110–190 a day for a 650cc machine in summer, and up to $350 for a Harley tourer. GoTourNZ Global (see below) has a standard Suzuki 650 from $155 per day. Alternatively, try the same channels as for "Buying a used vehicle" (see page 34).

MOTORBIKE TOURS

Organized tours come in self-guided or guided varieties, usually incorporating top-of-the-range accommodation, restaurants and bikes.

GoTourNZ Global 🅦 gotournz.com. Nelson-based company providing upmarket, small-group guided or self-guided tours around the South Island, with itineraries tweaked to suit and a luxury coach in your wake. Rates start at $9190 for a guided 12-day trip on a relatively modest bike.

New Zealand Motorcycle Rentals & Tours 🅦 nzbike.com. Another specialist top-end company, offering guided all-inclusive tours staying in quality accommodation, semi-guided tours and bike rental. A fully guided 19-day tour round both islands will set you back about $10,245, staying in hotels and riding a modest bike.

Te Waipounamu Motorcycle Hire & Tours 🅦 motorcycle-hire. co.nz. These folk do upscale tours across New Zealand and bike rentals including Beamers at $259/day in the high season.

By bike

If you have time, **cycling** is an excellent way of getting around. Distances aren't enormous, the weather is generally pretty benign, traffic is light, and the countryside is gorgeous. Most everywhere you go you'll find hostels and campsites well set up for campers, but also equipped with rooms and cabins for when the weather really fails.

But there are downsides. New Zealand's road network is skeletal, so in many places you'll find yourself riding on main roads or unsealed minor roads. You'll also experience a fair bit of wind and rain and have to climb quite a lot of hills.

Cycling the **South Island** is an easier proposition than the **North Island**. The South Island's alpine backbone presents virtually the only geographical barrier, while the eastern two-thirds of the island comprise a flat plain. In the North Island you can barely go 10km without encountering significant hills – and you have to contend with a great deal more traffic, including intimidating logging trucks.

New Zealand law requires all cyclists to wear a **helmet**. Some **fitness** is important, but distances don't have to be great and you can take things at

NGA HAERENGA – THE NEW ZEALAND CYCLE TRAIL

With quiet roads, brilliant scenery and superb camping, New Zealand has long been on the cycle touring map and is set to become a major off-road cycle touring destination.

The government has funded a series of **22 Great Rides**, stand-alone, mostly off-road routes that comprise **Nga Haerenga** (Ⓦ nzcycletrail.com). Most of the rides (from a few hours to several days) are now complete and it's hoped that they will emulate the successful Otago Central Rail Trail (see page 634), providing superb riding while boosting the local economy. Eventually these may be linked together in an end-to-end network along the lines of Te Araroa (see page 48).

Rent a bike locally and just tackle rides such as "From the Mountains to the Sea" in the north and "The Old Ghost Road" in the south, or come for a month or so and collect the set.

your own pace. It might be a good idea to go with a **guided group** (see page 53).

For more **information**, and to plan your trip, use the Kennett brothers' Classic New Zealand Cycle Trail (the 2018 edition expanded the Tour Aotearoa section that features the two month ride from Cape Reinga to Bluff). Great online resources include Ⓦ nzcycletrail.com and Ⓦ newzealandcycletouring.blogspot.co.uk.

The bike

Since the vast majority of riding will be on sealed roads with only relatively short sections of gravel, it is perfectly reasonable (and more efficient) to get around New Zealand on a touring bike. But fashion dictates most people use a **mountain bike** fitted with fat but relatively smooth tyres.

On long trips it's cheaper to **bring your own bike**, already set up to your liking. Most inter-national airlines simply count bikes as a piece of luggage and don't incur any extra cost as long as you don't exceed your baggage limit. However, they do require you to use a **bike bag** or box, or at the very least remove pedals and handle-bars and wrap the chain. Some airlines will sell you a cardboard bike box at the airport. Soft bags are probably the most convenient (they're easy to carry on the bike once you arrive), but if you are flying out from the same city you arrive in you can often store hardshell containers (free or for a small fee) at the backpacker hostel where you spend your first and last nights: call around.

Renting bikes for more than the odd day can be an expensive option, costing anything from $30–60 a day, depending on whether you want a bike with little more than pedals and brakes, a tourer or state-of-the-art mountain bike. Specialist cycle shops do more economical monthly rentals for around $200–250 for a tourer and $300 or more for a full-suspension superbike.

For long-distance cycle touring, it's generally cheaper to **buy a bike**. It will cost at least $1500 to get fully kitted out with new equipment, but it's worth checking hostel notice boards for **secondhand bikes** (under $500 is a reasonable deal), often accompanied by essential extras such as wet-weather gear, lights, a helmet and a pump. Some cycle shops offer **buy-back deals**, guaranteeing to refund about fifty percent of the purchase price at the end of your trip – contact Adventure Cycles, 9 Premier Ave, Western Springs, in Auckland (☎ 09 940 2453, Ⓦ adventure-auckland.co.nz/adventurecycles). If you're bringing your own bike, the same folk will let you store the bike box you transported your machine in ($20 a month, free if you buy stuff from their shop), help organize an emergency package of spare parts and extra clothing to be forwarded at your request, and give your bike a once-over before you set off.

Transporting bikes

Lethargy, boredom, breakdowns or simply a need to shift your bike between islands mean you'll use **public transport** at some point. You can usually get your bike onto a bus (generally $10–15) or train ($10/journey), though space is often limited so book well in advance. Crossing Cook Strait, the Interislander and Blue Bridge ferries charge around $15.

Air New Zealand and Jetstar will fly your bike free, if it is packed in a bike bag and is within your baggage allowance.

By ferry

The **ferries** you're most likely to use (see page 377) are vehicle-carrying services plying Cook Strait between Wellington on the North Island and Picton on the South Island.

Passenger ferries link Bluff, in the south of the South Island, to Stewart Island, and vehicle ferries connect Auckland with the Hauraki Gulf islands, principally Waiheke and Great Barrier. Information about these short trips is included in the sections on Invercargill and Auckland and around. Most visitors spend more boat time on cruises – whale watching, dolphin swimming, sightseeing – or **water taxis**.

Accommodation

Accommodation will take up a fair chunk of your money while in New Zealand, but the good news is that standards are uniformly excellent. Almost every town has a motel or hostel of some description, so finding accommodation is seldom a problem – though it's essential to book ahead during the peak summer season from Christmas to the end of March.

Kiwis travel widely at home, most choosing to self-cater at the country's huge number of well-equipped **campsites** (a.k.a. holiday parks) and **motels**, shunning **hotels**, which cater mainly to package holiday-makers and the business community. The range of **backpacker hostels**, **B&Bs**, **homestays**, **farmstays** and **lodges** forms an appealing alternative, covering the whole spectrum from a room in someone's suburban home to pampered luxury in a country mansion.

Wherever you stay, you can expect unstinting hospitality and a truckload of valuable advice on local activities and onward travel. Many places are now accredited using the nationwide **Qualmark** system (Ⓦ qualmark.co.nz), which grades different types of accommodation from one to five stars. Most fall between three stars (very good) and four plus (at the top end of excellent), but there is no way of knowing whether, for example, a four-star backpacker is superior to rooms at a five-star holiday park. Many places choose not to join the system, but may be just as good or better.

ACCOMMODATION GUIDES AND WEBSITES

AA Accommodation Guide Ⓦ aatravel.co.nz. Accommodation providers pay to be in this annual guide for the whole country that concentrates mostly on motels and holiday parks. Also a B&B guide and various regional variants. Available free from most motels and i-SITE offices.

BookABach Ⓦ bookabach.co.nz. Many Kiwis own a holiday home (a.k.a. *bach* or *crib*), which they may rent out when they're not using them. Some are in superb locations next to beaches or lakes. Some have a two- or three-night minimum stay, rising to a week from Christmas to late February when rates rise dramatically and availability is reduced. There are real bargains in winter. Holiday houses (Ⓦ holidayhouses.co.nz) has a similar range of places.

Charming places to stay Ⓦ charmingaccommodation.co.nz. Glossy B&B guide concentrating on mid-range places but also country and farmstays. View online, download as one massive PDF, get the book for the price of postage, or pick up (often free) at B&Bs.

Hotels, motels and pubs

In New Zealand, **hotel** is a term frequently used to describe old-style **pubs**, once legally obliged to provide rooms for drinkers to recuperate. Many no longer provide accommodation, but some have transformed themselves into backpacker hostels, while others are dedicated to preserving the tradition. At their best, such hotels offer comfortable rooms in historic buildings (for $100–140/night), though just as often lodgings are rudimentary. Hotel bars are frequently at the centre of -small-town life and at weekends in particular can be pretty raucous, so you may find a budget room at a hostel a better bet.

In the cities and major resorts, you'll also come across **hotels** in the conventional sense ($150–400), predominantly business- or tour-bus-oriented places. Rack rates are generally high but bargains can definitely be had, particularly at weekends, by checking their websites.

Most Kiwi families on the move prefer the astonishingly well-equipped **motels** ($100–250) which congregate along the roads running into town, making them more convenient for drivers than for those using trains or buses. They usually come with Sky TV, bathroom, some sort of kitchen

---

ACCOMMODATION PRICES

Accommodation rates quoted represent the cheapest available **double or twin room in high season**, though we have generally ignored the short spike in prices around Christmas and New Year. Single rooms usually cost only ten to twenty percent less than doubles or twins. In hostels and campsites where individual dorm beds are available, we have given the full price assuming no discount cards. YHA members get ten percent discount at YHAs and associate YHAs, while BBH members typically save $3 at BBH-affiliated establishments. DOC hut and **camping fees** are also per person, unless otherwise stated.

Our prices always include the fifteen percent Goods and Services Tax (GST).

BOOKING ACCOMMODATION

You should **book accommodation** at major towns and popular tourist locales at least a few days in advance from December to March. Reserving several weeks ahead is a good idea if you're particular about where you stay. Most Kiwis take two to three weeks off from Christmas onwards, so from **December 26 to mid-January** anywhere near a nice beach or lake is likely to be packed, particularly holiday parks (campsites) and motels, which usually rack up their prices considerably during this period. Places that don't attract Kiwi holiday-makers can be relatively peaceful at this time. Towns near **ski resorts** are typically busiest between July and September, particularly on weekends and during school holidays.

and tea and coffee, but are often fairly functional concrete-block places with little to distinguish one from another. Rooms range from all-in-one **studios**, with beds, kettle, toaster and a microwave, through **one-bedroom units**, usually with a full and separate kitchen, to two- and **three-bedroom suites**, sleeping six or eight. Suites generally go for the same basic price as a one-bedroom unit, with each additional adult paying $20–30, making them an economical choice for groups travelling together. Anything calling itself a **motor inn** ($140–240) or similar will be quite luxurious, with a bar, restaurant, swimming pool and sauna but no cooking facilities.

B&Bs, lodges and boutique hotels

While families might prefer the freedom and adaptability of a motel, couples are often better served by a **bed and breakfast** (B&B; $120–250). This might be a simple room with a bathroom down the hall and some toast and cereal included in the price. But the term also encompasses luxurious colonial homes with well-furnished en-suite rooms and sumptuous home-cooked breakfasts. Those at the top end – and sometimes more basic places – fashion themselves as **lodges**, **boutique hotels** and "exclusive retreats" ($300–2000), where standards of service, comfort and prices can reach extraordinary levels.

Rates drop in the low season, when these places can often be good value. If you're travelling alone, want to be chatting to people and don't fancy hostels, B&Bs are a good alternative, usually charging **lone travellers** 60–80 percent of the double room rate, though some only ask fifty percent.

Homestays and farmstays

Homestays ($100–200) usually offer a guest room or two in an ordinary house where you muck in with the owners and join them for breakfast the following morning. Staying in such places can be an excellent way to meet ordinary New Zealanders; you'll be well looked after, sometimes to the point of being overwhelmed by your hosts' generosity. It is courteous to **call in advance**, and bear in mind you'll usually have to **pay in cash**. Rural versions often operate as **farmstays** ($120–200), where you're encouraged to stay a couple of nights and might be able to spend the intervening day trying your hand at farm tasks: rounding up sheep, milking cows, fencing, whatever might need doing. Both homestays and farmstays charge for a double room; some cook breakfast or dinner on request for $15–75 per person, and you may pay a small fee for lunch if you spend the day at the farm or for a packed lunch.

Hostels, backpackers and YHAs

New Zealand has over 350 budget and self-catering places, pretty much interchangeably known as **hostels** or **backpackers** and offering a dorm bed or bunk for around $20–32. They're often in superb locations – bang in the centre of town, beside the beach, close to a ski-field or amid magnificent scenery in a national or forest park – and are great places to meet other travellers and pick up local information. Backpacker hostels range in size from as few as four beds up to huge premises accommodating several hundred. Beds are generally fully made up (sleeping bags were banned years ago to prevent the spread of bed bugs); you should bring your own towel, though you can rent one for a few dollars. Wi-fi is pretty standard, though a few rural places intentionally eschew such mod cons. Depending on the area, there may be a pool, barbecue, bike and/or canoe rental and information on local work opportunities. Many offer cupboards for your gear, though you'll usually need your own padlock. Almost all hostels are affiliated with local and international organizations that offer **accommodation discounts** to members, along with an array of other travel- and activity-related savings.

Some hostels allow you to pitch a tent or park a van in the grounds and use the facilities for around $20 per person, but generally the most basic and cheapest accommodation is in a six- to twelve-bunk **dorm** ($20–28), with three- and four-bed rooms (also known as three-shares and four-shares) usually priced a couple of dollars higher. Most hostels also have **double**, **twin** and **family rooms** ($65–120 for two), the more expensive ones with en-suite bathrooms. Lone travellers who don't fancy a dorm can sometimes get a **single room** ($50–80), and many larger places (especially YHAs and Base backpackers) also offer **women-only dorms**.

YHA

YHA New Zealand (Ⓦyha.co.nz) has more than 35 hostels across the country, made up of YHA managed and independently owned associate hotels. They operate as a not-for-profit, and are committed to sustainability, with the YHA-managed network recently becoming carboNZero certified. Hostel facilities include fully-equipped kitchens, comfortable shared lounge and dining spaces, and a variety of accommodation options. Most hostels have private double or family rooms, en-suite options, and single-sex or mixed dorms. Staff are well-trained, knowledgeable and keen to help.

Nonmembers pay the price we've quoted but you can save 10 percent if you've got a **Hostelling International Card**. You may be better off getting $25 annual YHA membership in New Zealand, which aside from accommodation discounts nets you further discounts on travel and activities like skydiving, whale-watching, white-water rafting and glacier hikes.

You can **book ahead** online, from another hostel through the YHA National Reservations Centre or through Hostelling International offices in your home country.

BBH

YHAs are vastly outnumbered by other **backpacker hostels**, where the atmosphere is more variable; some are friendly and relaxed, others more party-oriented. Many are aligned with the NZ-based **Budget Backpacker Hostels** (Ⓦbbh.co.nz), and are listed (along with current prices) in the *BBH Accommodation Guide*, widely available from hostels and visitor centres. The entries are written by the hostels and don't pretend to be impartial, but each is also given a customer **rating** which is determined by an annual survey and by online voting. These are a fairly reliable quality indicator, though city hostels tend not to

rate as well as similarly appointed places next to nice beaches. Anything above 80 percent will be excellent: those rating below 60 percent should be treated with suspicion.

Savings can be made by buying a **BBH Club Card** ($45), which nets a $3–4 discount on each night's stay. Cards are available from BBH and all participating hostels, as well as major i-SITE visitor centres and online, and you also get a Vodafone SIM card thrown in for free.

Base and Nomads

Two Australasian hostel chains, **Base** (Ⓦstayatbase. com) and **Nomads** (Ⓦnomadsworld.com), each run hostels across the country;Base are in eleven major tourist hangouts whereas Nomads are only in Auckland, Queenstown and Wellington. Both offer discounts if you sign up to a card or accommodation package.

Holiday parks, cabins and camping

New Zealand has some of the world's best **camping** facilities, and even if you've never camped before, you may well find yourself using **holiday parks** (also known as **motor camps**), which come with space to pitch tents, numerous powered sites (or hook-ups) for campervans and usually a broad range of dorms, cabins and motel units. You'll find more down-to-earth camping at wonderfully located **DOC sites**.

Camping is largely a summer activity (Nov–May), especially in the South Island. At worst, New Zealand can be very wet, windy and plagued by voracious winged **insects**, so the first priority for tent campers is good-quality gear with a fly sheet which will repel the worst that the elements can dish out, and an inner tent with bug-proof ventilation for hot mornings.

Busy times at motor camps fall into line with the school holidays, making Easter and the summer period from Christmas to the end of January the most hectic. Make **reservations** as far in advance as possible at this time, and a day or two before you arrive through February and March. DOC sites are not generally bookable, and while this is no

For advice on **backcountry camping** and **trampers' huts**, see the "Outdoor activities" section (see page 50).

problem through most of the year, Christmas can be a mad free-for-all.

Responsible overnight stops outside official areas, otherwise known as freedom camping, is also possible (see below).

Holiday parks

Holiday parks are typically located on the outskirts of towns and are invariably well equipped, with a communal kitchen, TV lounge, games area, laundry and sometimes a swimming pool. You should bring your own pans, plates and cutlery, though some places have limited supplies and full sets can be rented for a few dollars a night. Nonresidents can often get **showers** for around $2–5. **Campers** usually get the quietest and most sylvan corner of the site and are charged around $15–25 per person; camping prices throughout the Guide are per person unless followed or preceded by "per site". There is often no distinction between tent pitches and the **powered sites** set aside for campervans, but the latter usually cost an extra $2–5 per person for the use of power hook-ups and dump stations.

Most holiday parks also have some form of on-site accommodation (see page 40). **Sheets and towels** may not be included at the cheaper end, so bring a sleeping bag or be prepared to pay to rent bed linen (typically $5–15/stay).

Holiday parks are independently run but often align themselves with nationwide organizations that set minimum standards. Look out for **Top 10** sites (Ⓦtop10.co.nz), which maintain a reliably high standard in return for slightly higher prices and a degree of identikit sameness. By purchasing a **membership card** ($49) you save ten percent on each night's stay and get local discounts; the card (valid 2 years) can also be used at some sites in Australia.

HOLIDAY PARK ACCOMMODATION OPTIONS

Tent site ($15–25/person). Usually a patch of grass with a tap nearby.
Powered site ($20–30/person). Patch of grass or concrete with electrical hook-up and a dump station nearby. Fancier places charge a minimum of two people per site.
Lodge or backpackers ($20–30/person). Dorm accommodation, often 8–12 bunks.
Standard cabin ($50–90 for two, plus $10–15 for each extra person). Often little more than a shed with bunks and perhaps a table. They sleep 2–4 and bedding is usually extra.
Kitchen cabin ($70–120 for two, plus $10–20 for each extra person). Like a standard cabin but with some cooking facilities, table and chairs, and pans and plates provided. Often sleeps four and bedding is extra.

Tourist cabin/flat ($80–140 for two, plus $15–25 for each extra person). A kitchen cabin but with your own shower, toilet and maybe TV. Sometimes known as a self-contained unit, it typically sleeps four, and bedding is sometimes included.
Motel unit ($100–200 for two, plus $15–30 for each extra person). Larger than cabins and probably with one or more separate bedrooms and TV/DVD. Bedding and towels included.

DOC campsites

Few holiday parks can match the idyllic locations of the 250 or so **campsites** operated by the **Department of Conservation** (DOC; Ⓦdoc.govt.nz) in national parks, reserves, maritime and forest parks, the majority beautifully set by sweeping beaches or deep in the bush. This is back-to-nature camping, low-cost and with simple **facilities**, though sites almost always have running water and toilets of some sort. Listed in DOC's free North Island and South Island *Conservation Campsites* booklets (available from DOC offices or online), the sites fall into one of five categories: **Basic** (free), usually with nothing but a long-drop toilet and water nearby; **Backcountry** ($6), with perhaps a cooking shelter and/or fireplace; the more common **Standard** ($8), all with vehicular access and many with barbecues, fireplaces, picnic tables and refuse collection; **Scenic** ($13), popular coastal sites with toilets, tap water and possibly cold showers, barbecues and bins; and the rare **Serviced** ($18), which are similar in scope to the regular holiday parks. Children aged 5–17 are usually charged half the adult price. Serviced sites and some Scenic and Standard sites must be **booked in advance** from October to April.

Freedom camping

One of the pleasures of driving a campervan around New Zealand is the ability to sneak the odd free night in wayside rest areas or in car parks beside beaches. This **freedom camping** has never been strictly legal, but when numbers were small nobody worried too much. However, the popularity of the privilege and indiscriminate littering took its toll and a new law now gives councils the power to hand out **instant fines** (minimum $200) to people found camping where they are instructed not to. "No Camping" signs have sprung up in likely spots all over the country, forcing freedom campers to quieter places between towns.

Freedom camping is definitely getting tougher but the approach varies throughout the country. Almost everyone takes a dim view of freedom camping in vehicles without a plumbed-in toilet. **Full self-contained campers** (with a blue warrant, and rear vehicle sticker) have more options. Some councils impose a blanket ban on freedom camping within 10km of town, other places designate specific spots for freedom campers. DOC have responded to the changes by opening up more **campsites**; there's also sites like ⓦcampable. com, a scheme where travellers in campervans can stay free on hosts' property. Guests need to download an app to access member properties spread all over the country.

We've listed many of the best and most convenient camping areas throughout the Guide, but there's lots more information out there. Consult ⓦfreedomcamping.org for guidelines on freedom camping and useful links including the AA maps of dump stations and public toilets. There are also useful **apps**; try the free ones from ⓦcampermate. co.nz showing camping spots, toilets, budget accommodation and wi-fi hotspots all over the country, and **Respect NZ** (ⓦrankers.co.nz/respect), which focuses on the camping but has deeper coverage.

Food and drink

New Zealand's food scene is brilliant all round, from the quality of the ingredients and cooking, to its presentation and the places where it's served.

Kiwi **gastronomy** has its roots in the British culinary tradition – an unfortunate heritage that still informs cooking patterns for older New Zealanders – and it is only comparatively recently that the country's chefs have woken up to the possibilities presented by the fabulous larder of super-fresh, top-quality ingredients available locally. Along with tender lamb, succulent beef and venison, and superb seafood you'll find some of the world's best dairy products and stone and pip fruit which, at harvest time, can be bought for next to nothing from roadside stalls.

All this has been combined into what might be termed **Modern Kiwi cuisine**, drawing on Californian and contemporary Australian cooking, and combining it with flavours drawn from the **Mediterranean**, **Asia** and the **Pacific Rim**: sun-dried tomatoes, lemongrass, basil, ginger, coconut, and many more. Restaurants and cafés throughout the country feel duty-bound to fill their menus with as broad a spectrum as possible, lining up seafood linguini, couscous, sushi, Thai food, venison meatballs and chicken korma alongside the rack of lamb and gourmet pizza. Sometimes this causes gastronomic overload, but often it is simply mouthwatering.

Meat and fish

New Zealanders have a taste for **meat**, the quality of which is superb, with New Zealand lamb often at the head of the menu but matched in flavour by venison and beef.

With the country's extensive coastline, it's no surprise that **fish and seafood** also loom large. The white, flaky flesh of the **snapper** is the most common saltwater fish (though trevally or kingfish is a more sustainable choice), but you'll also come across blue cod, tuna, John Dory, groper (often known by its Māori name of **hapuku**), flounder, gurnard, and the firm, delicately flavoured **tarakihi**. Salmon is common, but not trout, which cannot be bought or sold, though most hotels and restau-

---

THE HANGI

To sample traditional cooking methods go to a **hangi** (pronounced nasally as "hungi"), where meat and vegetables are steamed for hours in an earth oven then served to the assembled masses. The ideal way to experience a *hangi* is as a guest at a private gathering, but most people have to settle for one of the commercial affairs in Rotorua or Christchurch. There you'll be a paying customer rather than a guest but the *hangi* flavours will be authentic, though sometimes the operators may have been creative in the more modern methods they've used to achieve them.

At a traditional *hangi*, the men first light a fire and place river stones in its embers. While these are heating, they dig a suitably large pit and place the hot stones in the bottom, covering them with wet sacking. Meanwhile the women prepare lamb, pork, chicken, fish, shellfish and vegetables (particularly *kumara*), wrapping the morsels in leaves then arranging them in baskets (originally of flax, but now more commonly of steel mesh). The baskets are lowered into the cooking pit and the *hangi* is covered over, sealing in the steam and flavours. A couple of hours later, the baskets are disinterred, revealing fabulously tender steam-smoked meat and vegetables with a faintly earthy flavour. A reverential silence, broken only by munching and appreciative murmurs, usually descends.

rants will cook one if you've caught it. This archaic law was originally intended to protect sportfishing when trout were introduced to New Zealand in the nineteenth century. All these fish are very tasty smoked, but smoked *tarakihi*, *hapuku*, blue cod, marlin and eel are particularly good.

One much-loved delicacy is **whitebait**, a collective name for five species of tiny, silvery, native fish mostly caught on the West Coast and eaten whole in fritters during the August to November season.

Shellfish are a real New Zealand speciality. You'll occasionally come across **tuatua**, dug from Northland beaches, on menus, but you're more likely to find fabulous **Bluff oysters** (see page 674), scallops and sensational **green-lipped mussels**, which have a flavour and texture that's hard to beat and are farmed in the cool, clear waters of the Marlborough Sounds, especially around Havelock. Live green-lipped mussels can be bought from any decent supermarket.

Wonderfully rich and delicate **crayfish** is also available round the coast and should be sought out, particularly when touring Kaikoura and the East Cape.

Māori and International food

In New Zealand restaurants you'll find few examples of Polynesian or **Māori cuisine**, though the cooking style does now have a foothold in forward-looking establishments where you might find a fern frond salad, or steak rubbed with peppery *horopito* leaves. Māori potato (*taewa tutaekuri*) is an unusual deep purple potato that's making a comeback, and foraged herbs are also gaining more popularity in the mainstream. To sample Māori food you'll really need to get along to a *hangi*, most likely in Rotorua.

One Pacific staple you'll certainly come across is **kumara** (sweet potato), which features in *hangi* and is often deep-fried as *kumara* chips.

A major influx of immigrants from south and east Asia has really changed the Kiwi restaurant scene over the last couple of decades; there's barely a town in the land without an **Indian** or **Chinese** restaurant. **Thai** is also common though you'll need to go to larger towns to find **Malaysian**, **Singaporean**, **Japanese** and **Korean** places. In the bigger cities there has recently been a resurgence of **Mexican** restaurants after years out of favour.

Vegetarian and vegan food

In recent years, **vegetarian** and **vegan** food has become far more mainstream in New Zealand. You'll have no problem finding excellent veggie options on the menu, and organic plant-based and raw food outlets are popping up everywhere, particularly in the affluent neighbourhoods of Auckland, Wellington and Christchurch. Outside the major centres dedicated vegetarian restaurants are rare and you will have to rely on the ubiquitous veggie-burger served in most cafés. Ⓦ happycow.net is a great resource for finding nearby veggie- and vegan-friendly places to eat (there are 176 in Auckland alone).

If you are taking a multi-day expedition on which food is provided, give the operator plenty of notice of your dietary needs.

Eating out

The quality of **cafés** and **restaurants** in New Zealand is typically superb, portions are respectable, and many are good value for money. In most restaurants you can expect to pay upwards of $25

THE EDMONDS COOKERY BOOK AND KIWI DESSERTS

Almost every Kiwi household has a battered copy of the **Edmonds Cookery Book**, first published in 1908 and still selling over 20,000 copies a year, parents often giving their kids a copy when they first leave home. The recipes are wide-ranging but the focus is on baking, usually using Edmond's baking powder, which is still prominent on supermarket shelves. The book is the first place people turn to for making the sort of cakes and desserts that fill the shelves of rural tearooms. Fancier modern cafés are now reinventing these retro Kiwi classics.

Afghans The origin of the name is lost, but these chocolate-and-cornflake-dough biscuits topped with cocoa icing are a perennial favourite.

Anzac biscuit Textured cookie made with oats and coconut.

Carrot cake A Kiwi favourite found in cafés and tearooms all over.

Lamington A light sponge slice slathered in pink icing and desiccated coconut.

Pavlova No more than a giant, soft meringue covered in cream and fruit, the "pav" is the apotheosis of Kiwi desserts.

for a main course, perhaps $55 for three courses without wine. There is no expectation of a tip, though a reward for exceptional service (usually around 10 percent) is welcomed. On **public holidays** you may be expected to pay a surcharge (typically 15 percent) to ensure staff get financially compensated for giving up a statutory holiday.

The traditional staple of the Kiwi dining scene is the **tearoom**, a self-service cafeteria-style establishment with old school atmosphere, cheap sandwiches, unsavoury savouries, sticky cakes and very average coffee. You'll still find such places in rural towns: long-distance buses sometimes make their comfort stops at them.

In more urban areas, tearooms are replaced by **cafés** selling everything from often excellent espresso and muffins to full breakfasts and lunch with a range of wines. Many close around 4pm, but others stay open late, transforming into **restaurants**. There is minimal distinction between the two so you may find yourself eating a full meal alongside folk just out for a beer or coffee. At a café you normally order and pay at the front counter and then are brought your food. In restaurants full table service is the norm, although you may be expected to settle the bill at the counter after your meal.

Restaurants, and many cafés, have alcohol licences, but some still maintain the old **BYO** tradition. Corkage fees are typically $5–20 per bottle, though some places charge per person.

Most **bars** serve **pub meals**, often the best-value budget eating around, with straightforward steak and chips, lasagne, pizza or burgers for under $20. The country's ever-burgeoning wine industry has also spawned a number of moderate-to-expensive **vineyard restaurants**, particularly in the growing areas of Hawke's Bay and Marlborough. The food is almost invariably excellent, with many of the dishes matched to that vineyard's wines.

Snacks and takeaways

In the cities you'll come across **food courts**, usually in shopping malls with a dozen or so stalls selling bargain plates of all manner of international dishes. Traditional **burger bars** continue to serve constructions far removed from the limp international-franchise offerings: weighty buns with juicy patties, thick ketchup, a stack of lettuce and tomato and the ever-present Kiwi favourite, slices of beetroot. **Meat pies** are another snack-time stalwart; sold in bakeries and from warming cabinets in pubs everywhere, the traditional steak

TOP 5 FOR FISH & CHIPS
Kai Kart Stewart Island. See page 682
Kaiaua Fisheries Kaiaua. See page 115
The Smokehouse Mapua. See page 429
Tiki's Takeaway Kaikoura. See page 455
The Chippery Wellington. See page 381

and mince varieties now augmented by bacon and egg, venison, steak and cheese, steak and oyster, smoked fish and *kumara* and, increasingly, vegetarian and gluten-free versions.

Fish and chips are also rightly popular – the fish is often shark (euphemistically called lemon fish or flake), though tastier species are always available for a small premium. Look out too for **paua fritters** – battered slabs of minced abalone that are something of an acquired taste.

Self-catering and farmers' markets

If you're **self-catering**, your best bet for cheap supplies is the local supermarket: Pak'n Save is usually the cheapest; New World usually has the widest variety of quality foods. In emergencies you can top up with supplies from the plethora of convenience corner shops (known as "dairies") stocking bog-standard essentials. These, along with shops at campsites and those in isolated areas with a captive market, tend to have inflated prices.

Gourmet foodstuffs are best sought at small independent outlets, offering predominantly local and/or organic supplies. **Farmers' markets** are another good source of local produce; every town of any size now seems to have one, usually on Saturday or Sunday morning – we've mentioned several throughout the Guide.

Drinking

Licensed cafés and restaurants across the land make a point of stocking a wide range of New Zealand wines and beers, but for the lowest prices and a genuine Kiwi atmosphere you can't beat the **pub**. It's a place where folk stop off on their way home from work, its emphasis on consumption and back-slapping camaraderie rather than ambience and decor. In the cities, where competition from cafés is strong, pubs tend to be more comfortable and relaxing, but in the sticks little has changed. Rural pubs can initially be daunting for strangers, but once you get chatting, barriers soon drop. Drinking hours are barely limited; theoretically you can drink in most bars until at least

TOP 5 WINERIES

Poderi Crisci Waiheke Island. See page 124
Mills Reef Near Tauranga. See page 262
Muirlea Rise Martinborough. See page 391
Lawson's Dry Hills Marlborough. See page 415
Amisfield Near Queenstown. See page 616

midnight on weeknights and until 4am or later at weekends though places often close much earlier if there are few customers. The **drinking age** is 18. Smokers are banished to the open air, often in small, purpose-built shelters.

Beer

Beer is drunk widely and often. Nearly all of it is produced by two huge conglomerates – Lion and DB – who market countless variations on the lager and Pilsener theme, as well as insipid, deep-brown fizzy liquid dispensed from taps and in bottles as "draught" – a distant relation of British-style bitter. One popular favourite is Steinlager, also marketed in a "no-additive" version called Pure. There really isn't a lot to choose between the beers except for alcohol content, normally around four percent, though five percent is common for premium beers usually described as "export".

Beer consumption generally is declining, but there has been a boom in microbreweries making **craft beers**. Tap into the craft beer scene at **ⓦ** realbeer. co.nz and **ⓦ** beertourist.co.nz.

Draught beer is usually sold in **pints** (just over half a litre). Keep in mind that a half-pint will always be served as a ten fluid ounce glass and

therefore will be a little over half the price of a pint. In rural areas, traditions die hard and you can buy a one-litre **jug**, which is then decanted into the required number of glasses, usually a **seven** (originally seven fluid ounces, or 200ml), a **ten**, or even an elegantly fluted **twelve**.

Prices vary enormously, but you can expect to pay $7–10 for a pint. It is much cheaper to buy in bulk from a **bottle shop** (off-licence or liquor store) which will stock a fair range of mainstream and boutique beers, usually in a six-pack of 330ml bottles (around $12–15) or multiple thereof.

Wine

Kiwis are justifiably loyal to New Zealand winemakers, who now produce **wines** that are among the best in the world, especially **white wines**. New Zealand is rapidly encroaching on the Loire's standing as the world benchmark for Sauvignon Blanc, while the bold fruitiness of its Chardonnay and apricot and citrus palate of its Rieslings attract many fans. **Red wines** were once of the broad-shouldered Aussie variety, but this has changed as improved canopy management and better site selection have brought Kiwi reds up alongside their Australian cousins. Today there are some superb wines based on Cabernet Sauvignon and Merlot (particularly from Waiheke Island and Hawke's Bay), but the reds garnering the most praise are Pinot Noirs from Central Otago, Marlborough and Martinborough, and Hawke's Bay Syrah – essentially a Shiraz but made in a subtler fashion than the Aussie style.

A liking for **champagne** no longer implies "champagne tastes" in New Zealand: you can still buy the wildly overpriced French stuff, but good Kiwi Méthode Traditionelle (fermented in the bottle in the time-honoured way) starts at around $13 a bottle.

QUALITY FOOD AND DRINK TO LOOK OUT FOR

Ice cream Firm scooped ice cream in a cone is a Kiwi institution and is sold all over. To taste some of the best head for a good supermarket and look for Kapiti or Kohu Road, both available in numerous delicious flavours.

Jams and preserves Artisans sell preserves at various farmers' markets but supermarket brands Anathoth Farm and Te Horo are amazingly flavoursome at modest prices.

Cheese Bland cheddar is the de facto national standard, but New Zealand now makes a wide range of delicious cheeses, with the Kapiti brand widely available. Their super-rich Kikorangi blue is particularly good. Look out, too, for smaller producers such as Whitestone, Meyer and Puhoi Valley.

Beer Shun the mainstream stuff and zero in on small-batch craft brews such as Auckland's Brothers Beer; Croucher from Rotorua; McCashin's, from Stoke outside Nelson; Emerson's from Dunedin; and the deep south's Invercargill Brewery. Most are available in bottle stores and good supermarkets.

MAJOR WINE AREAS

The following wine areas are listed from north to south:

Henderson and Kumeu Most of these wineries, 15km west of Auckland, source their grapes elsewhere, making this a good place to sample wines from around the country, though Chardonnay and Merlot are particular highlights.

Hawke's Bay Premium wine area around Napier and Hastings with over seventy wineries open to the public, some with tours and restaurants. Produces some of the country's best Chardonnay, Cabernet Sauvignon blends and Syrahs.

Martinborough The most accessible cluster of vineyards, many within walking distance of the town, with fine Pinot Noir and Sauvignon Blanc, as well as dessert wines.

Marlborough Seventy percent of New Zealand's grapes are grown around Blenheim and Renwick, with a huge range of fantastic vineyards, several with restaurants. Famous for its Sauvignon Blanc, the region also produces excellent Pinot Noir and other aromatic white wines.

Central Otago Cool-climate wine growing at the limit of practicability, mostly around Bannockburn near Queenstown. Excellent Pinot Noir in particular.

Montana's Lindauer Brut is widely available, and justly popular. Many people round out their restaurant meal with **dessert wines** (or "stickies"), with the sweetest made from grapes withered on the vine by the **botrytis** fungus, the so-called "noble rot".

Most bars and licensed restaurants have a tempting range of wines, many sold by the glass ($8–12; $9 and up for dessert wine), while in shops the racks groan under bottles starting from $12 ($15–25 for good quality).

If you want to try before you buy, visit a few wineries, where you can sample half a dozen different wines; occasionally these are free of charge, but more often you will pay a small fee ($10–15), especially to try the reserve wines. A good starting point for information on the Kiwi wine scene is Ⓦnzwine.com.

Spirits

The big success story for New Zealand spirits is **42 Below vodka** (Ⓦ42below.com). It has won awards and comes infused with fruity flavourings including kiwifruit, passionfruit, and local favourites feijoa and manuka honey. With 42 Below purchased by Bacardi in 2008, the vodka's Kiwi creators have turned their hand to producing delicious South Gin (Ⓦsouthgin.com).

The commercial success of these tipples has spawned domestic pretenders such as Stolen Rum (Ⓦthisisstolen.com), Smoke & Oakum's rum (Ⓦgunpowderrum.com), Broken Shed vodka (Ⓦbrokenshed.com) and others.

A few places, mostly in the south of the South Island, produce single malt **whisky**, the best being Oamaru's New Zealand Malt Whisky Co. (Ⓦthenzwhisky.com). Minor players dabble in fruit **liqueurs**; some are delicious, though few visitors develop an enduring taste for the sickly sweet kiwifruit or feijoa varieties, which are mostly sold through souvenir shops.

Tea and coffee

Tea is usually a down-to-earth Indian blend (sometimes jocularly known as "gumboot"), though you may also have a choice of a dozen or so flavoured, scented and herbal varieties. **Coffee** drinking has been elevated to an art form with a specialized terminology: an Italian-style espresso is known as a **short black**; an espresso diluted with hot water is a **long black** (with the hot water occasionally served on the side); an espresso topped with velvety smooth hot milk becomes a **flat white**. Better places will serve all these decaffeinated, skinny or made with soya milk. Flavoured syrups are widely available. Reusable takeaway cups are encouraged and most places will offer a discount if you bring your own.

The media

For a country of only 4.6 million inhabitants, New Zealand has a vibrant media scene. Auckland claims to have more radio stations per capita than any other city in the world, and magazine racks are crammed with Kiwi-produced weeklies and monthlies. The standard of media coverage sometimes leaves a little to be desired, but for the most part this is a well-informed country with sophisticated tastes. Online, a good starting point is Ⓦpublicaddress.net, the leading Kiwi blog site.

TV

New Zealanders receive five main free-to-air **broadcast channels**, a handful of local channels and Sky TV (which you'll find in most motels).

The biggest broadcaster is the state-owned **TVNZ**, which operates two advertising-heavy channels. TV ONE has slightly older and more information-based programming while TV2 is younger and more entertainment-oriented. Both channels present a diet of local news, current affairs, sport, drama and entertainment, plus a slew of US, British and Australian programmes: you'll find most of your favourites, often three to six months behind. Visitors may already be acquainted with long-running, home-grown Kiwi soap opera, *Shortland Street*, set in the fictional suburb of Ferndale in Auckland.

The main opposition comes from **TV3**, which pitches itself roughly between TV ONE and TV2, and **Prime**, backed by Sky TV, which often has quirkier programming.

Māori TV launched in 2004 with substantial government support (though it also has ads). Broadcasting in Māori and English, it promotes the language and culture but is far from a stuffy educational channel. Along with good movies and engaging Māori language lessons, you might catch Māori cooking shows, lifestyle makeovers, sitcoms and Māori angles on news, current affairs and sport.

Radio

New Zealand has few countrywide radio stations, but syndication means that some commercial stations can be heard in many parts of the country, with local commercials. All websites listed stream the channel over the **internet**.

For news, current affairs and a thoughtful look at the arts and music, tune into the government-funded **Radio New Zealand National** (101.0–101.7 FM; ⓦradionz.co.nz), which is the nearest New Zealand gets to, say, NPR or BBC Radio 4. You'll pick it up most places, though there are blank spots. Its sister station, **Radio New Zealand Concert** (89–100 FM), concentrates on classical music.

Though often amateurish, **student radio stations** provide excellent and varied "alternative" listening in their home cities. In Auckland tune to bFM (95.0; ⓦ95bfm.co.nz); in Wellington to Active (88.6; ⓦradioactive.co.nz); in Christchurch to RDU (98.5; ⓦrdu.org.nz); and in Dunedin to Radio One (91.0; ⓦr1.co.nz).

The rest of the airwaves are clogged by **commercial stations**: keep an ear out for **KiwiFM** (102.1–102.5; ⓦkiwifm.co.nz), predominantly Kiwi music to Auckland, Wellington and Canterbury.

Newspapers and magazines

New Zealand has no national **daily newspaper**, but rather four major regional papers (all published Mon–Sat mornings) as well as a plethora of minor rags of mostly local interest. All are politically fairly neutral. The North Island is shared between the Auckland-based *New Zealand Herald* (ⓦnzherald.co.nz) and Wellington's *Dominion Post*, while *The Press* covers Christchurch and its environs (the *Dominion Post* and *The Press* are both available online at ⓦstuff.co.nz), and the *Otago Daily Times* (ⓦodt.co.nz) serves the far south of the country. All offer a pretty decent selection of national and international news, sport and reviews, often relying heavily on wire services and syndication deals with major British and American newspapers. On **Sunday**, check out the tabloid-style *Sunday News*; the superior broadsheet *Sunday Star-Times*; or Auckland's *Herald on Sunday*.

Kiwi newspaper journalists get little scope for imaginative or investigative journalism, though the broad-ranging and slightly left-leaning **weekly magazine** the *Listener* (ⓦnoted.co.nz) does its best. With coverage of politics, art, music, TV, radio, books, science, travel, architecture and much more, it's perhaps the best overall insight into what makes New Zealand tick.

Topics are covered in greater depth in the nationwide **monthly** *North and South*, though for an insight into the aspirations of Aucklanders you might be better off with the snappier glossy, *Metro* (both also at ⓦnoted.co.nz).

Specialist magazines cover the range: *Wilderness* (ⓦwildernessmag.co.nz) has a good spread of tramping, kayaking, climbing and mountain biking, and *Rip It Up* (ⓦripitupnz.tumblr.com) is the best of the music mags.

Sadly, Māori newspapers and magazines have struggled in recent years. *Mana* (ⓦmanaonline.co.nz), which pitched itself as presenting "the Māori perspective", and gave an insight into what sometimes seems like a parallel world barely acknowledged by the mainstream media paused publication in 2017 – it's unclear if it will continue.

Festivals and public holidays

In the southern hemisphere, Christmas falls near the start of the school summer holidays, which run from mid-December until early February. From Boxing Day through to the middle of January Kiwis hit the beaches en masse and during this time you'll find a lot more people about. Motels and campsites can be difficult to book and often raise their prices, though B&Bs and hostels rarely up their rates.

To help you chart a path through the chaos, i-SITE visitor centres are open longer hours, as are many other tourist attractions. **Other school holidays** last for two weeks in mid- to late April, a fortnight in early to mid-July and the first two weeks of October, though these have a less pronounced effect.

Public holidays are big news in New Zealand and it can feel like the entire country has taken to the roads, so it's worth staying put rather than trying to travel on these days. Each region also takes one day a year to celebrate its **Anniversary Day**, remembering the founding of the original provinces that made up New Zealand, and generally celebrated with an agricultural show, horse-jumping, sheepshearing, cake-baking and best-vegetable contests and novelty events (such as gumboot throwing). We've listed official dates below, but days are usually observed on the nearest Monday (or occasionally Friday) to make a long weekend.

PUBLIC HOLIDAYS AND FESTIVAL CALENDAR

Many of the festivals listed below are covered in more detail in the relevant section of the Guide. **PH** indicates a public holiday.
January 1 New Year's Day (PH) Whaleboat Racing Regatta, Kawhia (Ⓦ kawhiaharbour.co.nz); Highland Games, Waipu (Ⓦ waipugames.co.nz).
January 2 (PH)
First Saturday in January Glenorchy Races (Ⓦ glenorchycommunity.nz).
January 17 Anniversary Day (PH in Southland).
Mid-January in odd-numbered years Wings over Wairarapa (Ⓦ wings.org.nz).
January 22 Anniversary Day (PH in Wellington).
January 29 Anniversary Day (PH in Auckland, Northland, Waikato, Coromandel, Taupo and the Bay of Plenty), celebrated with a massive regatta on Auckland's Waitemata Harbour.
February 1 Anniversary Day (PH in Nelson).
February 6 Waitangi Day (PH); formal events at Waitangi.

First Saturday in February Martinborough Fair, Martinborough Ⓦ martinboroughfair.org.nz.
Second Saturday in February Tuki Festival, Glendhu Bay, Lake Wanaka Ⓦ tukifestival.nz.
Second Saturday in February Wine Marlborough Festival, Blenheim (Ⓦ wine-marlborough-festival.co.nz).
Second weekend in February Coast-to-Coast multisport race, South Island (Ⓦ coasttocoast.co.nz).
Third weekend in February Art Deco Festival, Napier (Ⓦ artdeconapier.com).
Late February to late March NZ International Arts Festival, Wellington (even-numbered years only; Ⓦ festival.co.nz).
Last weekend in February or first weekend in March Golden Shears sheepshearing competition in Masterton (Ⓦ goldenshears.co.nz).
Three weeks in March Wellington Fringe Festival (Ⓦ fringe.org.nz).
First Saturday in March Martinborough Fair, Martinborough (Ⓦ martinboroughfair.org.nz).
Second Saturday in March Pasifika Festival, Auckland (Ⓦ aucklandnz.com/pasifika); Wildfoods Festival, Hokitika (Ⓦ wildfoods.co.nz).
Mid-March WOMAD world music festival, New Plymouth.
Mid-March Round-the-Bays Sunday fun run, Auckland (Ⓦ roundthebays.co.nz).
Third weekend in March Te Houtaewa Challenge, Ahipara (see page 172).
Closest Saturday to March 17 Ngaruawahia Māori Regatta, near Hamilton (see page 194).
March 23 Anniversary Day (PH in Otago).
March 31 Anniversary Day (PH in Taranaki).
Late March to late April Good Friday (PH) and Easter Sunday (PH).
Easter week Royal Easter Show, Auckland (Ⓦ eastershow.co.nz); Warbirds Over Wanaka airshow (even-numbered years only; see page 622); National Jazz Festival, Tauranga (Ⓦ jazz.org.nz).
Early April Festival of Colour, Wanaka (odd-numbered years only; five-days; see page 622).
April 25 ANZAC Day (PH). Dawn services at cenotaphs around the country.
Mid-April to late April Arrowtown Autumn Festival (Ⓦ arrowtownautumnfestival.org.nz).
First Monday in June Queen's Birthday (PH).
Three weeks in June Food and Wine Classic: Winter, Hawke's Bay (Ⓦ fawc.co.nz).
Mid-June Fieldays, the southern hemisphere's largest agricultural show, Hamilton (Ⓦ fieldays.co.nz).
Mid- to late June Matariki, Māori New Year festivities (Ⓦ matarikifestival.org.nz).
Late June to early July Queenstown Winter Festival (Ⓦ winterfestival.co.nz).
Early July to late November New Zealand International Film Festival, held for two weeks each in 14 sites around the country (Ⓦ nzff.co.nz).

Third weekend in June Deco Winter Weekend, Napier (W artdeconapier.com).

End August Taranaki International Festival of the Arts (odd-numbered years only).

Late September to early October Alexandra Blossom Festival (W blossom.co.nz).

Late September to early October World of Wearable Art Awards (WOW), Wellington (W worldofwearableart.com).

Fourth Monday in October Labour Day (PH).

October 31 Halloween.

Late October to early November Taranaki Garden Spectacular, New Plymouth.

November 1 Anniversary Day (PH in Hawke's Bay and Marlborough).

November 5 Guy Fawkes' Night fireworks.

Second week in November New Zealand Cup & Show Week, Canterbury (W nzcupandshow.co.nz).

Third Friday in November Anniversary Day (PH in Canterbury).

Third Sunday in November Toast Martinborough Wine, Food & Music Festival (W toastmartinborough.co.nz).

December 1 Anniversary Day (PH in Westland).

Mid-December to January Festival of Lights, New Plymouth.

December 25 Christmas Day (PH).

December 26 Boxing Day (PH).

Late Dec Rhythm and Vines three-day music festival, culminating on New Year's Eve, Gisborne (W rhythmandvines.co.nz).

Outdoor activities

Life in New Zealand is tied to the great outdoors, and no visit would be complete without spending a fair chunk of your time in intimate contact with nature.

Kiwis have long taken it for granted that within a few minutes' drive of their home they can find a deserted beach or piece of "bush" and wander freely through it, an attitude enshrined in a fabulous collection of national, forest and maritime parks. They are all administered by the **Department of Conservation** (DOC; W doc.govt.nz), which seeks to balance the maintenance of a fragile environment with the demands of tourism. For the most part it manages remarkably well, providing a superb network of signposted paths studded with trampers' huts, and operating visitor centres that present highly informative material about the local history, flora and fauna.

The lofty peaks of the Southern Alps offer challenging **mountaineering** and great **skiing**, while the lower slopes are ideal for multi-day **tramps** which cross low passes between valleys choked with subtropical and temperate rainforests. Along the coasts there are sheltered lagoons and calm harbours for gentle **swimming** and **boating**, but also sweeping strands battered by some top-class **surf**.

The country also promotes itself as the **adventure tourism** capital of the world. All over New Zealand you'll find places to bungy jump, whitewater or cave raft, jetboat, skydive, mountain bike, scuba dive, paddleboard and much more – you name it, someone somewhere organizes it. While thousands of people participate in these activities every day without incident, standards of instructor training vary. It seems to be a point of honour for operators, instructors and guides to put the wind up you as much as possible. Such bravado shouldn't be interpreted as a genuine disregard for safety, but the fact remains that there have been a few well-publicized injuries and deaths – a tragic situation that's addressed by industry-regulated codes of practice, an independent system of accreditation and home-grown organizations that insist upon high levels of professionalism and safety instruction.

Before engaging in any adventure activities, check your insurance cover (see page 63).

Tramping

Tramping, trekking, bushwalking, hiking – call it what you will, it is one of the most compelling reasons to visit New Zealand, and for many the sole objective.

Hikes typically last three to five days, following well-worn trails through relatively untouched wilderness, often in one of the country's national parks. Along the way you'll be either camping out or staying in trampers' huts, and will consequently be lugging a pack over some rugged terrain, so a moderate level of fitness is required. If this sounds daunting, you can

---

TE ARAROA – THE LONG PATHWAY

Since the mid-1970s it has been a Kiwi dream to have a continuous path from one end of the country to the other. **Te Araroa** (W teararoa.org.nz) opened in 2011 under the auspices of the private Te Araroa Trust, which linked a fragmented network of existing tracks into a continuous 3000km route from Cape Reinga to Bluff. Much of the impressively varied route runs through fairly remote country, although it intentionally visits small communities so that trampers can resupply.

Some hardy souls have tramped the whole route but most people tackle short sections.

sign up with one of the guided tramping companies that maintain more salubrious huts or luxury lodges, provide meals and carry much of your gear. Details are given throughout the Guide.

The main tramping season is in summer, from October to May, although the most popular tramps – the Milford, Routeburn and Kepler – are in the cooler southern half of the South Island, where the season is shorter by a few weeks at either end.

The tramps

Rugged terrain and a history of track-bashing by explorers and deer hunters has left New Zealand with a web of tramps following river valleys and linking up over passes, high above the bushline. As far as possible, we've indicated the degree of difficulty of all tramps covered in the Guide, broadly following DOC's classification system: a **path** is level, well graded and often wheelchair-accessible; **walking tracks** and **tramping tracks** (usually way-marked with red and white or orange flashes on trees) are respectively more arduous affairs requiring some fitness and proper walking equipment; and a **route** requires considerable tramping experience to cope with an ill-defined trail, frequently above the bushline. DOC's estimated **walking times** can trip you up: along paths likely to be used by families, for example, you can easily find yourself finishing in under half the time specified, but on serious routes aimed at fit trampers you might struggle to keep pace. We've given estimates for moderately fit individuals and, where possible, included the distance and amount of climbing involved, aiding route planning.

Invaluable information on walking directions, details of access, huts and an adequate map are contained in the excellent DOC tramp **leaflets** (usually a couple of dollars but downloadable free at ⓦ doc.govt.nz) for major walking tracks).

The maps in each DOC leaflet should be sufficient for trampers sticking to the designated route, but experienced walkers planning independent routes and folk after a more detailed vision of the terrain should fork out for specialized **maps** that identify all the features along the way. Most trampers' huts have a copy of the local area map pinned to the wall or laminated into the table. In describing tramps we have used "**true directions**" in relation to rivers and streams, whereby the left bank (the "true left") is the left-hand side of the river looking downstream.

Eight of New Zealand's finest, most popular tramps, plus one river journey, have been classified by DOC as **Great Walks** and are covered in detail in the Guide; a ninth tramp, the Paproa Track and Pike29 Memorial

Track, opens in 2019. Great Walks get the lion's share of DOC track spending, resulting in relatively smooth, broad walkways, with boardwalks over muddy sections and bridges over almost every stream – a sanitized side of New Zealand tramping.

Access to tracks is seldom a problem in the most popular tramping regions, though it does require planning. Most finish some distance from their start, so taking your own vehicle is not much use; besides, cars parked at trailheads are an open invitation to thieves. Great Walks always have transport from the nearest town, but there are often equally stunning and barely used tramps close by which require a little more patience and tenacity to get to – we've included some of the best of the rest in the Guide, listed under "Tramps" in the index.

Backcountry accommodation: huts and camping

New Zealand's backcountry is strung with a network of over 950 **trampers' huts**, sited less than a day's walk apart, frequently in beautiful surroundings. All are simple, communal affairs that fall into four distinct categories as defined by DOC.

Basic Huts (free) are often crude and rarely encountered on the major tramps. Next up is the **Standard Hut** ($5/person/night): basic, weatherproof, usually equipped with individual bunks or sleeping platforms accommodating a dozen or so, an external long-drop toilet and a water supply. There is often a wood-burning stove but there are no cooking facilities. **Serviced Huts** ($15) tend to be larger, sleeping twenty or more on bunks with mattresses. Water is piped indoors to a sink, and flush toilets are occasionally encountered. Again, you'll need to bring your own stove and cooking gear, but heating is provided; if the fire is a wood-burning one, you should replace any firewood you use. More sophisticated still are the **Great Walk Huts** ($22–70), found along the Great Walks. They tend to have separate bunkrooms, gas rings for cooking (but no utensils), stoves for heating, a drying room and occasionally solar-powered lighting and flush toilets. Under-18s pay half the adult fee at Serviced and Standard huts and stay free on Great Walks – though you must still book in advance.

Hut fees are best paid in advance online, at the local DOC office, visitor centre or other outlet close to the start of the track. For Great Walks you need to book (and pay for) specific nights at each hut where you want to stay, then carry the confirmation with you, otherwise the wardens will charge you for each hut again. The booking guarantees you a bed and can

TREMENDOUS TRAMPS

Eight of New Zealand's finest tramps, and one river journey, have been classified as Great Walks, with a ninth opening in 2019; even the most well-trodden of these reveal magnificent natural wonders in the raw. To get more information about the Great Walks and other tramps, check ⓦ tramper.co.nz.

NORTH ISLAND

The Tongariro Northern Circuit (3–4 days; see page 290) Takes in magnificent volcanic and semi-desert scenery.

Waikaremoana Track (3–4 days; see page 344) A gentle circumnavigation of one of the country's most beautiful lakes.

The Whanganui River Journey (2–4 days; see page 312) Best explored by canoe and a series of highly atmospheric short walks.

SOUTH ISLAND

The Abel Tasman Coast Track (2–4 days; see page 432) Skirts beaches and crystal-clear bays, ideally explored by sea kayak.

The Heaphy Track (4–5 days; see page 444) Passes through the Kahurangi National Park, balancing subalpine tops and surf-pounded beaches.

The Kepler Track (4 days; see page 649) Renowned for ridge walks and virgin beech forest.

Milford Track (4 days; see page 659) The world-famous track accesses stunning glaciated alpine scenery and stupendous waterfalls.

Paproa Track and Pike29 Memorial Track (2-3 days; see page 469) The newest addition, running through Paparoa National Park and opening in 2019.

The Rakiura Track (3 days; see page 679) Follows the rainforest-bordered coast of Stewart Island and provides opportunities to see kiwi in the wild.

The Routeburn Track (3 days; see page 608) One of the country's finest walks, with quality time spent above the bushline.

---

be altered online subsequently if there is space left in the hut you want.

Should you wish to do a lot of tramping outside the Great Walks system, or on the Great Walks out of season, it's worth buying a **Backcountry Hut Pass** ($122 for a year; $92 for 6 months), which allows you to stay in most Standard and Serviced huts.

In winter (May–Sept) the huts on Great Walks are often stripped of heating and cooking facilities and downgraded to Standard status, so if you have a Backcountry Hut Pass you can use them, though possessing the pass or a ticket doesn't guarantee you a bunk; beds go on a first-come-first-served basis.

Camping is allowed on all tracks except the Milford. Rules vary, but in most cases you're required to minimize environmental impact by camping close to the huts, whose facilities (toilets, water and gas rings where available) you can use.

Equipment

Tramping in New Zealand can be a dangerous and/or dispiriting experience if you're not equipped for both hot, sunny days and wet, cold and windy weather. Conditions can change rapidly. The best tramps pass through some of the world's wettest regions, with parts of the Milford Track receiving over 6m of rain a year. It's essential to carry a good waterproof jacket. Keeping your lower half dry is less crucial and many Kiwis tramp in shorts. Early starts can involve wading through long, sodden grass, so a pair of knee-length gaiters can be useful. Comfortable boots with good ankle support are a must; take suitably broken-in leather boots or light-weight walking boots, and some comfortable footwear for the day's end. You'll also need a warm jacket or jumper, plus a good sleeping bag; even the heated huts are cold at night and a warm hat never goes amiss. All this, along with lighter clothing for sunny days, should be kept inside a robust backpack, preferably lined with a strong waterproof liner such as those sold at DOC offices.

Once on the tramp, you need to be totally self-sufficient. On Great Walks, you should carry **cooking** gear; on other tramps you also need a cooking stove and fuel. **Food** can be your heaviest burden; freeze-dried meals are light and reasonably tasty but expensive; many cost-conscious trampers prefer pasta or rice, dried soups for sauces, a handful of fresh vegetables, muesli, milk powder and bread or crackers for lunch. Consider taking biscuits, trail mix (known as "scroggin"), tea, coffee and powdered fruit drinks (the Raro brand is good), and energy-boosting spreads. All huts have drinking **water** but DOC advise treating water taken from lakes and rivers to protect yourself from giardia; see page 63 for more on this and water-purification methods.

You should also carry basic supplies: a first aid kit, blister kit, sunscreen, insect repellent; a torch (flashlight), candles, matches or a lighter; and a compass (though few bother on the better-marked tracks).

In the most popular tramping areas you will be able to **rent equipment**. Most important of all, remember that you'll have to carry all this stuff for hours each day. Hotels and hostels in nearby towns will generally let you leave your surplus gear either free or for a small fee.

Safety

Most people spend days or weeks tramping in New Zealand with nothing worse than stiff legs and a few sandfly bites, but **safety** is nonetheless a serious issue and deaths occur every year. The culprit is usually New Zealand's fickle **weather**. It cannot be stressed too strongly that within an hour (even in high summer) a warm, cloudless day can turn bitterly cold, with high winds driving in thick banks of track-obscuring cloud. Heeding the mountain weather forecast (posted in DOC offices) is crucial, as is carrying warm, windproof and waterproof clothing.

Failed **river crossings** are also a common cause of tramping fatalities. On Great Walks, rivers are always bridged, but elsewhere if you are confronted with something that looks too dangerous to cross, then it is, and you should wait until the level falls or backtrack. If the worst happens and you get swept away while crossing, don't try to stand up; you may trap your leg between rocks and drown. Instead, lie on your back and float feet first until you reach a place where swimming to the bank is feasible.

If you do get lost or injured, your chances of being found are better if you've left word of your intentions with a **friend** or with a **trusted person** at your next port of call, who will realize you are overdue. DOC make no attempt to track hikers so make your intentions clear to friends by using Ⓦ adventuresmart.org.nz. While on the tramp, fill in the hut logs as you go, so that your movements can be traced, and check in with the folk you told about the trip on your return.

Animals are not a problem in the bush, the biggest irritants being sandflies whose bites itch (often insufferably), or kea, alpine parrots that delight in pinching anything they can get their beaks into and tearing it apart to fulfil their curiosity.

Swimming, surfing and windsurfing

Kiwi life is inextricably linked with the beach, and from Christmas to the end of March (longer in warmer northern climes), a weekend isn't complete without a dip or a waterside barbecue – though you should never underestimate the ferocity of the southern **sun** (see page 62 for precautions). Some of the most picturesque beaches stretch away into salt spray from the pounding Tasman surf or Pacific rollers. **Swimming** here can be very hazardous, so only venture into the water at beaches patrolled by surf lifesaving clubs and always swim between the flags (see page 63). Sharks are occasionally seen at swimming beaches, so if you notice everyone heading for safety, get out of the water.

New Zealand's coastline offers great conditions for **surfing**, windsurfing and kite-boarding. At major beach resorts there is often an outlet renting dinghies, catamarans, canoes and stand-up paddleboards; in regions where there is reliably good surf you might also come across boogie boards and surfboards, and seaside hostels often have a couple for guests' use. For more information, see Ⓦ surf-2surf.co.nz.

Sailing

New Zealand's numerous harbours, studded with small islands and ringed with deserted bays, make **sailing** a favourite pursuit, which explains why New Zealand and Kiwi sailors have been so influential in the fate of the America's Cup. People sail year-round, but the summer months from December to March are busiest. Unless you befriend a yachtie you'll probably be limited to commercial yacht **charters** (expensive and with a skipper), more reasonably priced and often excellent **day-sailing trips**, or renting a dinghy for some inshore antics.

Scuba diving and snorkelling

The waters around New Zealand offer wonderful opportunities to **scuba dive** and **snorkel**. What they lack in long-distance visibility, tropical warmth and colourful fish they make up for with the range of diving environments. Pretty much anywhere along the more sheltered eastern side of both islands you'll find somewhere with rewarding snorkelling, but much the best and most accessible spot is the **Goat Island Marine Reserve**, in Northland, where there's a superb range of habitats close to the shore. Northland also has world-class scuba diving at the

Poor Knights Islands Marine Reserve, reached by boat from Tutukaka, and wreck diving on the *Rainbow Warrior*, from Matauri Bay, plus a stack of good sites around Great Barrier Island and White Island. On the South Island, there are wrecks worth exploring off **Picton** and fabulous growths of **black and red corals** relatively close to the surface, in the southwestern fiords near Milford.

For the inexperienced, the easiest way to get a taste of what's under the surface is to take a **resort dive** with an instructor. If you want to dive independently, you need to be PADI-qualified. For more information consult ⓦ divenewzealand.com.

Rafting

The combination of challenging rapids and gorgeous scenery makes **whitewater rafting** one of New Zealand's most thrilling adventure activities. Visitor numbers and weather restrict the main **rafting season** to October to May, and most companies set an **age limit** at 13. Take a swimming costume and an old pair of trainers, and after safety instruction you'll generally spend a couple of hours on the water.

Thrilling though it is, rafting is also one of the most **dangerous** of the adventure activities, claiming a number of lives over the years. Operators have a self-imposed code of practice, but there are still cowboys out there. It might be stating the obvious but fatalities happen when people fall out of rafts: heed the guide's instructions about how best to stay on board and how to protect yourself if you do get a dunking.

Canoeing and kayaking

New Zealand is a paddler's paradise, and pretty much anywhere with water nearby has somewhere you can rent either **canoes** or **kayaks**. Sometimes this is simply an opportunity to muck around in boats but often there are guided trips available, with the emphasis being on soaking up the scenery. The scenic **Whanganui River** is a perennial favourite.

Jetboating

The shallow, braided rivers of the high Canter-bury sheep country posed access difficulties for run-owner Bill Hamilton, who got around the problem by inventing the **Hamilton Jetboat** in the early 1960s. His inspired invention could plane in as little as 100mm of water, reach prodigious speeds (up to 80km/hr) and negotiate rapids

while maintaining astonishing, turn-on-a-sixpence manoeuvrability.

The jetboat carried its first fare-paying passengers on a deep and glassy section of the Shotover River, which is still used by the pioneering Shotover Jet. **Rides** last around thirty eye-streaming minutes, time enough for hot-dogging and as many 360-degree spins as anyone needs. **Wilderness trips** can last two hours or longer.

Bungy jumping and bridge swinging

For maximum adrenaline, minimum risk and greatest expense, **bungy jumping** is difficult to beat. Commercial bungy jumping was pioneered by Kiwi speed skiers A.J. Hackett and Henry Van Asch. They began pushing the bungy boundaries, culminating in Hackett's jump from the Eiffel Tower in 1987. He was promptly arrested, but the publicity sparked worldwide interest that continues to draw bungy aspirants to New Zealand's sites – some of the world's best, with bridges over deep canyons and platforms cantilevered out over rivers. The first commercial operation was set up just outside Queenstown on the 43m Kawerau Suspension Bridge. Its accessible location and the chance to be dunked in the river make this the most popular jump of many on both islands. For a bit of variety you could try a close relative of the bungy, **bridge swinging**, which provides a similar gut-wrenching fall accompanied by a super-fast swing along a gorge while harnessed to a cable.

Ziplines

New Zealand was slow off the mark installing **zipwires** or flying foxes through the trees, but is quickly catching up with sites – Waiheke Island, Taihape, Rotorua, Nelson and Queenstown. Some are just single lines across ravines, but most modern installations feature a sequence of lines with changeovers on platforms high in the trees.

Canyoning

The easiest way to get your hands on New Zealand rock is to go **canyoning**, which involves following steep and confined river gorges or streambeds down chutes and over waterfalls for a few hours, sliding, jumping and abseiling all the way. Guided trips are available in a handful of places, the most accessible being in Auckland, Thames, Queenstown and Wanaka.

MULTI-DAY TOURS

Tours included in this box involve taking part in one or other several of the activities featured in this section. Although New Zealand is an easy place to explore independently, tours offer specialist insight, logistical help and company along the way.

HIKING AND WILDLIFE

Active Earth Adventures ⓦactiveearthadventures.com. Suitable for anyone who is reasonably fit and wants to see things few other tourists will. Good-humoured and informative guides take small groups tramping, climbing, cycling, Nordic skiing and wilderness camping in virtually untouched country. Seven-night South Island hike, ski and cycling-trip NZ$2995.

Hiking New Zealand ⓦhikingnewzealand.com. Conservation-minded company offering everything from hiking trips around the far north of Northland (5 days; NZ$1750) to glacier hikes on the South Island (5 days; NZ$4100)

Kiwi Wildlife Walks ⓦnzwalk.com. Expertly run guided walks including Stewart Island, where they go kiwi spotting (4 days; from NZ$2495).

Ruggedy Range ⓦruggedyrange.com. Stewart Island-based company offering enthusiastic and entertaining trips visiting the unique wildlife (full day NZ$255).

CRUISES

Heritage Expeditions ⓣ0800 262 8873, ⓦheritage-expeditions.com. Several pricey but spectacular cruises each southern summer to New Zealand's subantarctic islands – Antipodes, Auckland, Campbell etc – plus the Australian Macquarie Island and even the coast of Antarctica. Prices from US$5000 for 8 days.

Real Journeys ⓦrealjourneys.co.nz. As well as their Milford Sound and Doubtful Sound trips, Real Journeys run remoter multi-day trips to Dusky Sound (5 days from NZ$2650).

CYCLING, HORSERIDING AND KAYAKING

Adventure South ⓦadvsouth.co.nz. This environmentally conscious company runs guided cycling and multi-activity tours around the South Island, with accommodation in characterful lodges or track huts. Their 5-day Otago Rail Track cycle costs from NZ$1795. All tours carry a single supplement.

Alpine Horse Safaris ⓦalpinehorse.co.nz. Multi-day rides in North Canterbury and the central South Island that follow old mining and farm tracks well away from civilization and most roads. They're intended for serious riders and start at $815 for 2 days including food and simple accommodation.

Natural High ⓦnaturalhigh.co.nz. A vast range of guided road and MTB trips from half a day to over two weeks, plus self-guided trips, bike rentals and even hire of cycle-friendly campervans.

New Zealand Sea Kayak Adventures ⓦnzkayaktours.com. Fully catered, guided sea-kayak camping tours around Northland catering to a wide range of abilities. Go for the Bay of Islands (3 days; NZ$830) or Whangaroa Harbour (3 days; NZ$850).

Pacific Cycle Tours ⓦbike-nz.com. Mountain-bike, road-bike and hiking tours round both islands with varying degrees of adventurousness, including a five-day cycling and wine-tasting trip (from $2195).

Pakiri Beach Horseriding ⓦhorseride-nz.co.nz. Multi-day tours through Northland's native bush and along clifftops, from one-day trots to the epic 5-day Warrior Trail.

Pedaltours ⓦpedaltours.co.nz. Guided road- and mountain-biking tours of both islands, including a 10-day ride around the Southern Alps (NZ$5295).

Mountaineering

New Zealand is better suited to **mountaineering** than rock climbing, though most of what is available is fairly serious stuff, suitable only for well-equipped parties with a good deal of experience. For most people the only way to get above the snowline is to tackle the easy summit of Mount Ruapehu, the North Island's highest point, the summit of Mount Taranaki, near New Plymouth, or pay for a guided ascent of one of the country's classic peaks. Prime candidates are New Zealand's highest mountain, Aoraki/Mount Cook (3754m), accessed from the climbers' heartland of Aoraki/Mount Cook Village, and the nation's most beautiful peak, the pyramidal Mount Aspiring (3030m), approached from Wanaka. In both cases networks of climbers' huts are used as bases for what are typically twenty-hour attempts on the summit.

Flying, skydiving and paragliding

Almost every town in New Zealand seems to harbour an airstrip or a helipad, and there's inevitably someone happy to get you airborne for half an hour's **flightseeing**. Helicopters cost around fifty percent more than planes and can't cover the same distances but score on manoeuvrability and the chance to land. If money is tight take a regular flight somewhere you want to go anyway. First choice here would have to be the journey from either Wanaka or Queenstown to Milford Sound, which overflies the very best of Fiordland.

In **tandem skydiving**, a double harness links you to an instructor, who has control of the parachute. The plane circles up to 12,000ft (around 2500m) and after you leap out together, you experience around 45 seconds of eerie freefall before the instructor pulls the ripcord. Higher jumps are also available.

Tandem paragliding involves you and an instructor jointly launching off a hilltop, slung below a manoeuvrable parachute, for perhaps ten to twenty minutes of graceful gliding and stomach-churning banked turns. **Tandem hang-gliding** and **parasailing** are also offered in a few places.

Skiing and snowboarding

New Zealand's **ski season** (roughly June–Oct) starts as snows on northern hemisphere slopes melt away, which, combined with the South Island's backbone of 3000m peaks makes New Zealand an increasingly popular international ski destination. Most fields are geared to the domestic downhill market, and the eastern side of the Southern Alps is littered with **club fields** sporting a handful of rope tows, simple lifts and a motley collection of private ski lodges. They're open to all-comers, but some are only accessible by 4WD vehicles, others have a long walk in, and ski schools are almost unheard of. A dozen exceptions are scattered throughout the country – **commercial resorts**, with high-speed chairs, ski schools, gear rental and groomed wide-open slopes. What you won't find are massive on-site resorts of the scale found in North America and Europe; skiers commute daily to the slopes from nearby après-ski towns and **gear rental** is either from shops in these or on the field.

The main **North Island ski-fields** are Turoa and Whakapapa, both on the volcanic Mount Ruapehu. The best combination of uncrowded runs, a party atmosphere and some of the most spectacular snow-dusted scenery you'll ever see is on the **South Island**. **The main commercial fields are:** Porters and Mount Hutt, both within two hours' drive of Christchurch; Coronet Peak and The Remarkables near Queenstown; and Treble Cone, Cardrona and the Snow Farm, all accessed from Wanaka.

For up-to-date skiing information, consult ⓦsnow.co.nz which lists snow, lift and terrain details of all the major fields and most of the smaller ones, plus has links to local accommodation and gear rental places.

Fishing

All around the coast there are low-key canoe, yacht and launch trips on which there is always time for a little **casual fishing**, but you'll also find plenty of trips aimed at more dedicated anglers. From December to May these scout the seas off the northern half of the North Island for marlin, shark, tuna and lots of smaller quarry. Regulations and bag limits are covered on the Ministry for Primary Industries website, ⓦmpi.govt.nz.

Inland, the **rivers** and **lakes** are choked with rainbow and brown trout, quinnat and Atlantic salmon, all introduced for sport at the end of the nineteenth century. Certain areas have gained enviable reputations: Lake Taupo is world-renowned for its rainbow trout; South Island rivers, particularly around Gore, boast the finest brown trout; and the braided gravel-bed rivers draining the eastern slopes of the Southern Alps bear superb salmon.

A national **fishing licence** ($127 for the year from Oct 1–Sept 30, $20/day) covers all New Zealand's lakes and rivers except for those in the Taupo catchment area, where a local licensing arrangement applies. They're available from sports shops everywhere and directly from Fish and Game New Zealand (ⓦfishandgame.org.nz), the agency responsible for managing freshwater sports fisheries. The website also lists bag limits and local regulations.

Wherever you fish, **regulations** are taken seriously and are rigidly enforced. If you're found with an undersize catch or an over-full bag, heavy fines may be imposed and equipment confiscated. The NZ Fishing Rules app is a handy reference. Other fishy websites include ⓦfishinginnewzealand.com and ⓦfishing.net.nz.

Horse trekking

New Zealand's highly urbanized population leaves a huge amount of countryside available for **horse trekking**, occasionally along beaches, often through patches of native bush and tracts of farmland. There are schools everywhere and all levels of experience are catered for, but more experienced riders might prefer the greater scope of full-day or even week-long wilderness treks (see page 53). We've highlighted some noteworthy places and operators throughout the guide, and there's a smattering of others listed at Ⓦ truenz. co.nz/horsetrekking.

Mountain biking

With the explosion of the New Zealand Cycle Trail network of bike routes (Ⓦ nzcycletrail.com), getting around the country by bike has never been easier or more pleasurable (see page 35). But several of the routes are more appropriate for **mountainbikers**, supplementing an already generous selection of off-road rides. The two big centres are **Rotorua**, principally for the tortuous pleasures of Whakarewarewa Forest (aka "The Redwoods"; see page 250), and **Queenstown**, where there's everything from relatively easy cross-country trails to extreme downhill and heli-biking. In between there are a couple of excellent rides at the top of the South Island. You can ride the whole 71km of the Queen Charlotte Track for most of the year, though the northernmost 26km is off limits in Dec, Jan and Feb. Riding the Heaphy Track is even more time constrained, but if you're considering being in New Zealand between May and September, inclusive, this is one you shouldn't miss.

Spectator sports

If God were a rugby coach almost every New Zealander would be a religious fundamentalist. News coverage often gives headline prominence to sport, particularly the All Blacks, and entire radio stations are devoted to sports talkback, usually dwelling on occasions when Kiwi underdogs overcome betterfunded teams from more populous nations.

Most major sports events are televised. Increasingly these are on subscription-only Sky TV, which encourages a devoted following in pubs.

Anyone with a keen interest in sport or just Kiwi culture should attend a rugby game. Local papers advertise games along with ticket booking details. **Bookings** for many of the bigger events can be made through Ticketek (Ⓦ ticketek.co.nz), although, except for the oversubscribed internationals and season finals, you can usually just buy a ticket at the gate.

Rugby

Opponents quake in their boots at the sight of fifteen strapping **All Blacks**, the national **rugby** team, performing their pre-match *haka*, and few spectators remain unmoved. Kiwi hearts swell at the sight, secure in the knowledge that their national team is always among the world's best, and anything less than a resounding victory is considered a case for national mourning in the leader columns of the newspapers – although, thanks to the All Blacks' dominance, this is relatively rare. The team won the **Rugby World Cup** for the third consecutive time in 2015. New Zealand is also leading the way with women's rugby, with an historic announcement in 2018 seeing the National Women's team – the Black Ferns – offered paid contracts for the first time.

Rugby is played through the winter, the season kicking off with the **Super 15 series** (mid-Feb to May) in which regional southern hemisphere teams (five apiece from New Zealand, South Africa and Australia) play each other with the top four teams going on to contest the finals series. Super 15 players make up the All Blacks team which, through the middle of winter, hosts an international test series or two, including the annual **Rugby Championship** (mid-July to Aug) against South Africa, Australia and Argentina. Games between the All Blacks and Australia also contest the **Bledisloe Cup**, which creates much desired bragging rights for one or other nation for a year.

The international season often runs over into the **ITM Cup**, a national provincial competition, played from the middle of August until the end of October. Throughout the ITM Cup season, teams also do battle for the right to hold the **Ranfurly Shield**, affectionately known as the "log of wood". The holders accept challenges at their home ground, and the winner takes all. Occasionally minor teams will wrest the shield, and in the smaller provinces this is a huge source of pride, subsequent defences of the shield prompting a surge of community spirit.

Domestic rugby ticket prices vary, depending on where you are in the ground, but start at around $15, while a similar seat for an international will start at $45. To find out more, visit the New Zealand Rugby Union's official website (Ⓦ nzrugby.co.nz).

Rugby league (W rugbyleague.co.nz and W nzrl. co.nz) has always been regarded as rugby union's poor cousin, though success at international level has raised its profile. New Zealand's only significant provincial team are the Auckland-based **Warriors**, who play in Australia's NRL during the March to early September season, with home games played at Mount Smart Stadium, where you can buy tickets at the gate. The top eight teams in the league go through to the finals series in September.

Cricket

Most visitors spend their time in New Zealand from October to March, when the stadiums are turned over to the country's traditional summer sport, **cricket** (W nzcnz). The national team – the **Black Caps** – hover mid-table in international test and one-day rankings but periodic flashes of brilliance, the odd unexpected victory over Australia, and the co-hosting of the 2015 **Cricket World Cup** keep fans interested. You can usually just turn up at a ground and buy a ticket, though games held around Christmas and New Year fill up fast and internationals sell out in advance. **Tickets** start at around $25–30 for an international, less for a domestic match.

Other sports

Other team sports lag far behind rugby and cricket, though women's **netball** (W netballnz.co.nz) has an enthusiastic following and live TV coverage of the Silver Ferns' international fixtures gets good audiences.

Although more youngsters play **soccer** than rugby, it was the New Zealand All Whites' participation in the 2010 World Cup that boosted the game's profile nationally. For domestic fixtures, see W nzfootball.co.nz. New Zealand's only represent-ative in the Australian A-League is the Wellington Phoenix (W wellingtonphoenix.com). The season runs from October to early April and home games are played at Westpac Stadium in Wellington; **tickets** (from around $40 for a domestic match) can be bought at the gate or on the team's website.

Auckland is a frequent midway point for round-the-world **yacht** races and has twice hosted the **America's Cup**. New Zealand's **Olympic** heritage is patchy, with occasional clutches of medals from rowing and yachting and a long pedigree of **middle-distance runners**. These days, however, multi-event champi-onships and endurance events like triathlons and Iron Man races seem to dominate.

Culture and etiquette

Ever since Māori arrived in the land they named Aotearoa, New Zealand has been a nation of immigrants. The majority of residents trace their roots back to Britain and Ireland, and northern European culture prevails with a strong Māori and Polynesian influence. New Zealand's policy of bi-culturalism gives Māori and Pakeha (white European) values equal status, at least nominally. In practice, the operation of Parliament and the legal system is rooted in the old country, the Queen continues as head of state and beams out from all coins and the $20 note, and, along with "God Defend New Zealand", "God Save the Queen" remains one of the country's two official national anthems.

That said, **Māori** are very much part of mainstream contemporary NZ society (see page 708). The racial tension that does exist mostly stays below the surface (aside from some issue-specific protests), and as a visitor you'll probably come away from New Zealand with the impression of a relatively tolerant society.

In the last couple of decades **Asian immigration** (principally from China and Korea, as well as the Indian subcontinent) has seen Asians make up around 12 percent of the population (with Māori comprising just under 15 percent) nationwide. In the Auckland region, though, this figure rises to over eighteen percent, making some form of tri-culturalism a possibility in the future.

Notwithstanding this mix, the archetypal **Kiwi personality** is rooted in the desire to make a better life in a unique and sometimes unaccommodating land. New Zealanders are inordinately fond of stories of plucky little Kiwis overcoming great odds and succeeding, perceiving the NZ persona to be rooted in self-reliance, inventiveness and bravery, tempered by a certain self-deprecating humour. Overachieving "tall poppies" are routinely cut down.

Sport is a huge passion; the country has consist-ently punched above its weight in international competition, especially on the rugby field. Despite a reputation for a rugby-playing, beer-swilling, male-dominated culture, Kiwis like to point out that they run an open-minded and egalitarian society, in everything from same-sex marriage and nuclear-free waters (see page 705), to the country's third female prime minister announcing her pregnancy in 2018. Broadly liberal social attitudes prevail, with Japanese whaling and genetic modification hot topics.

New Zealand's relationship with its larger neighbour, Australia, is a cause for endless entertainment on both sides of "the ditch" (the Tasman Sea). Kiwis and **Aussies** are like siblings: there are lots of scraps (mostly just good-natured ribbing), especially when it comes to sport, but they're the first to jump to each other's defence in everything from military conflict to pub brawls.

Etiquette

New Zealanders are refreshingly relaxed, low-key and free of pretension, and you're likely to be greeted with an informal "gidday!", "Kia ora!" (Hi) or "Kia ora, bro!" (Hi, mate). **Dress standards** are as informal as the greetings, and unless you're on business or have a diplomatic function to attend you can leave your suit and tie at home; even the finest restaurants only require smart-casual attire.

The legal **drinking age** is 18, but by law you may be asked to prove your age by showing ID, which must be either a New Zealand driver's licence or a passport (foreign driver's licences aren't accepted).

Smoking is increasingly outlawed. It's banned on all public transport and in public buildings and some outdoor areas – see Ⓦ smokefree.org.nz.

The Kiwi attitude to **tipping** is pleasingly uncomplicated. No tip is expected, though reward for excellent service in restaurants and cafés is appreciated.

Shopping

One of the most popular souvenirs from NZ is a curvaceous greenstone (jade) pendant, probably based on a Māori design. They're available all over the country, though it makes sense to buy close to the main source of raw material around Greymouth and Hokitika on the West Coast of the South Island. Cheaper items are manufactured from Chinese jade or inferior stones such as soapstone: for the genuine article, insist on NZ pounamu carved locally (see page 479).

A variation on this theme is the **bone pendant**. Several places around the country give you a chance to work a piece of cattle bone into your own design or something based on classic Māori iconography. With a little talent and application you should be able to whip up something to be

proud of in a few hours. Something similar can be made of iridescent paua shell, or you can simply buy ready-made pieces fashioned into anything from buttons to detailed picture frames.

Sheepskin and **wool** products are also big, as are garments that have at least partly been made from **possum fur** – many New Zealanders hate these pests. A quality possum-fur throw will set you back over $1000 but cushion covers come much cheaper. Sheepskins go for around $100.

There's plenty of outdoor clothing around, but look out for the Icebreaker (Ⓦ nz.icebreaker.com), Untouched World (Ⓦ untouchedworld.co.nz) and Glowing Sky (Ⓦ glowingsky.co.nz) brands of stylish merino-wool garments, which are fairly pricey but feel great, keep you warm and don't harbour nasty odours.

Some of New Zealand's top fashion designers are world-class. Garments by Karen Walker, Kate Sylvester, Trelise Cooper, Alexandra Owen, Zambesi and World are expensive but coveted and unique.

Travelling with children

New Zealand is a child-friendly place, and while other people's kids aren't revered in the way they are in Mediterranean Europe, if you're travelling with children you'll find broad acceptance.

Accommodation is well geared for families: family rooms are almost always available at motels and hostels, and holiday parks (campsites) typically offer self-contained units where the whole family can be together. The better holiday parks also have kids' play areas and often a swimming pool. To be more self-sufficient, consider renting a medium-sized **campervan** with its own shower and toilet, though the downside is that you'll have no escape.

Travelling around you'll find **public toilets** in most towns and anywhere tourists congregate – cleanliness standards are usually good.

Older kids can often join in adult **adventure activities**, though restrictions may apply. Bungy operators usually require a **minimum age** of 10, though this might rise to 12 or 13 for the bigger jumps. Whitewater rafting is typically limited to those 13 and over, though there are a few easier family-oriented trips. Similar restrictions apply to other activities – ask when you book. **Family tickets** are often available and usually cost about the same as two adults and one child.

Children are welcomed in most cafés and **restaurants**, and most will make a reasonable effort to accommodate you.

Living in New Zealand

New Zealand is the sort of place people come for a short visit and end up wanting to stay (at least for a few months). Unless you have substantial financial backing, this will probably mean finding some work. And while your earning potential in New Zealand isn't necessarily going to be great, you can at least supplement your budget for multiple bungy jumps, skydiving lessons and the like. Paid casual work is typically in tourism-linked service industries, or in orchard work.

For the last few years unemployment has remained relatively low and, providing you have the necessary paperwork, finding casual work shouldn't be too difficult, while better-paid, short-term **professional jobs** are quite possible if you have the skills. Employment agencies are a good bet for this sort of work, or simply look at general job-search websites such as ⓦseek.co.nz or the jobs section of ⓦtrademe.co.nz. The **minimum wage** for all legally employed folk over the age of 16 (other than 16- and 17-year-old new entrants or trainees) is $16.50 an hour. If you'd rather not tackle the red tape you can simply reduce your travelling costs by **working for your board** (though the Immigration Department still considers this to be work and you are legally an employee).

Working for board and lodging

A popular way of getting around the country cheaply is to **work for your board and lodging**, typically toiling for 4–6 hours a day. **FHiNZ** (Farm Helpers in New Zealand; ⓦfhinz.co.nz) organizes stays on farms, orchards and horticultural holdings for singles, couples and families; no experience is needed. Almost 350 places are listed in its booklet ($25; sold online) and accommodation ranges from basic to quite luxurious. The international **WWOOF** (originally Willing Workers on Organic Farms; ⓦwwoof.co.nz) coordinates over a thousand properties (membership, for one or a couple, with online access $40 or printed booklet $52),

mostly farms but also orchards, market gardens and self-sufficiency-orientated smallholdings, all using organic methods to a greater or lesser degree. Many backpacker hostels also offer work in exchange for a bed. They'll expect a minimum stay of around five nights, though much longer periods are common; you **book direct** (preferably a week or more in advance). There have been occasional reports of taskmasters; make sure you discuss what's expected before you commit yourself. Property managers are vetted but **solo women** may prefer placements with couples or families. Other organizations have fewer guarantees, though many are perfectly reputable.

A similar organization is the online **Help Exchange** (ⓦhelpx.net), which supplies a regularly updated list of hosts on farms as well as at homestays, B&Bs, hostels and lodges, who need extra help in return for meals and accommodation; you register online and book direct.

Visas and permits

Australians can work legally in New Zealand without any paperwork. Otherwise, if you're aged 18–30 (up to 35 for Canadians), the easiest way to work legally is through the **Working Holiday Scheme** (WHS), which gives you a temporary work permit valid for twelve months. An unlimited number of Brits, Irish, Americans, Canadians, Japanese, Belgian, Danish, Finnish, French, German, Italian, Dutch, Norwegian and Swedish people in this age bracket are eligible each year, plus various annual quotas for two dozen other nationalities on a first-come-first-served basis; apply as far in advance as you can. You'll need a passport, NZ$208 for the application, evidence of an onward ticket out of New Zealand (or the funds to pay for it), and a minimum of NZ$350 per month of your intended stay (or, depending on your country of origin, NZ$4200 in total) to show you can support yourself – work is not meant to be the main reason for your visit. Brits can apply for a 23-month stay, the last 11 months of which can be applied for in New Zealand as an extension. Working holiday-makers who can show they've worked in the horticulture or viticulture industries for at least three months may be eligible to obtain an extra three-month stay in New Zealand with a **Working Holidaymaker Extension** (WHE) permit. Applications are made through **Immigration New Zealand** (ⓣ0508 558 855, ⓦimmigration.govt.nz), which has details and downloadable forms on its website.

Some visitors are tempted to **work illegally**, something for which you could be fined or deported.

However, there is a variety of other visa options, including the Silver Fern visa for 20–35-year-olds, and visas for seasonal horticulture and viticulture work – contact the **Immigration Service** for details. The only other legal option is trying to gain resident status – not something to be tackled lightly.

Anyone working legally in New Zealand needs to obtain a **tax number** from the local Inland Revenue Department office (Ⓦ ird.govt.nz); without this your employer will have trouble paying you. The process can take up to ten working days, though you can still work while the wheels of bureaucracy turn. Inland Revenue will take 10.5 percent of your first $14,000 of earnings, 17.5 percent of the next $34,000, and higher rates above that. Many companies will also only pay wages into a New Zealand **bank account** – opening one is easy (see page 65).

Casual work

One of the main sources of casual work is **fruit-picking** or related **orchard work** such as packing or pruning and thinning. The main areas are Kerikeri in the Bay of Islands for citrus and kiwifruit, Hastings in Hawke's Bay for apples, pears and peaches, Tauranga and Te Puke for kiwifruit, Blenheim for grapes and Alexandra and Cromwell in Central Otago for stone fruit. Most work is available during the autumn **picking season**, which runs roughly from January to May, but you can often find something just as easily in the off season. In popular working areas, some hostels cater to short-term workers, and these are usually the best places to find out what's going.

Picking can be hard, physical work and **payment** is usually by the quantity gathered, rather than by the hour. When you're starting off, the poor returns can be frustrating, but with persistence and application you can soon find yourself grossing $130 or more in an eight-hour day. Rates vary considerably so it's worth asking around, factoring in any transport, meals and accommodation, which are sometimes included. Indoor packing work tends to be paid hourly.

Particularly in popular tourist areas – Rotorua, Nelson, Queenstown – **cafés**, **bars** and **hostels** often need extra staff during peak periods. If you have no luck, try more out-of-the-way locales, where there'll be fewer travellers clamouring for work. Unless you have good experience, bar and restaurant work only pays minimum wage and tips are negligible. Generally you'll need to commit to at least three months. **Ski resorts** occasionally employ people during the June to October season, usually in catering roles. Hourly wages may be supplemented by a lift pass and subsidized food

and drink, though finding affordable accommodation can be difficult and may offset a lot of what you gain. Hiring clinics for ski and snowboard instructors are usually held at the beginning of the season at a small cost, though if you're experienced it's better to apply directly to the resort beforehand.

In addition to local hostels and backpackers, handy **resources** include Ⓦ backpackerboard.co.nz and Ⓦ job.co.nz; for fruit picking and the like, check out Ⓦ seasonalwork.co.nz and Ⓦ picknz.co.nz.

Volunteering

A useful starting point is the online service from the UK-based **The Gapyear Company** (Ⓦ gapyear. com), which offers free membership plus heaps of information on volunteering, travel, contacts and living abroad. The Department of Conservation's **Conservation Volunteer Programme** (search at Ⓦ doc.govt.nz) provides an excellent way to spend time out in the New Zealand bush while putting something back into the environment. Often you'll get into areas most visitors never see, and learn some skills while you're at it. Projects include bat surveys, kiwi monitoring and nest protection, as well as more rugged tasks like track maintenance, tree planting and hut repair. You can muck in for just a day or up to a couple of weeks, and sometimes there is a fee (of around $50–200) to cover food and transport. Application forms are often available on the website. Programmes are in high demand and often book up well in advance, so it's worth applying before you reach New Zealand.

Travel essentials

Climate

The sunny summer months (October to April) are the most popular time for travellers visiting New Zealand, but winter offers great skiing and snowboarding and the days are often clear and bright, if chilly. The far north of the country is often dubbed the "winterless north", although even in this subtropical area, winters can be nippy. The far south is the coldest part of the country – if you're surfing you'll need a wetsuit year-round.

Costs

The strong Kiwi dollar and lingering effects of the global financial crisis means that New Zealand is no bargain, but with high standards of quality and service the country is still decent value for money.

Daily costs vary enormously, and the following estimates (in NZ dollars) are per person for two people travelling together. (With the prevalence of good hostels, **single travellers** can live almost as cheaply as couples, though you'll pay around thirty percent more if you want a room to yourself.)

If you're on a tight budget, using public transport, camping or staying in hostels, and cooking most of your own meals, you could scrape by on $70 a day. Renting a car, staying in budget motels, and eating out a fair bit, you're looking at more like $180 a day. Step up to comfortable B&Bs and nicer restaurants, throw in a few trips, and you can easily find yourself spending over $350 a day. Also, you can completely blow your budget on **adventure trips** such as a bungy jump or tandem parachuting, so it pays to think carefully about how to get the maximum bang for your buck.

The price quoted is what you pay. With the exception of some business hotels, the 15-percent Goods and Service Tax (**GST**) is always included in the listed price. GST refunds are available on more expensive items bought then taken out of the country – keep your receipts and carry the items as hand luggage.

Student **discounts** are few and far between, but you can make substantial savings on accommodation and travel by buying one of the backpacker or YHA cards (see page 39). **Kids** (see page 57) enjoy reductions of around fifty percent on most trains, buses and entry to many sights.

Crime and personal safety

New Zealand's rates of violent crime are in line with those in other developed countries and you'll almost certainly come across some grisly stories in the media. Still, as long as you use your common sense, you're unlikely to run into any trouble. Some caution is needed in the **seedier quarters** of the larger cities where it's unwise to walk alone late at night. One major safety issue is "**boy racers**" using city and town streets as racetracks for customized cars, leading to bystander fatalities. Although the police do take action, their presence is relatively thin on the ground so be careful when out late in city suburbs.

Always take precautions against **petty theft**, particularly from cars and campervans. When staying in cities you should move valuables into your lodging. Thieves also prey on visitors' vehicles left at trailheads and car parks. Campervans

AVERAGE MONTHLY TEMPERATURES AND RAINFALL

	Jan	Feb	Mar	Apr	May	Jun	July	Aug	Sep	Oct	Nov	Dec
AUCKLAND												
max/min (°C)	23/16	23/16	22/15	19/13	17/11	14/9	13/8	14/8	16/9	17/11	19/12	21/14
max/min (°F)	73/61	73/61	72/59	66/55	63/52	57/48	55/46	57/46	61/48	63/52	66/54	70/57
rainfall (mm)	79	94	81	97	112	137	145	117	102	102	89	79
WELLINGTON												
max/min (°C)	21/13	21/13	19/12	17/11	14/8	13/7	12/6	12/6	14/8	16/9	17/10	19/12
max/min (°F)	70/55	70/55	66/54	63/52	57/46	55/45	54/43	54/43	57/46	61/48	63/50	66/54
rainfall (mm)	81	81	81	97	117	117	137	117	97	102	89	89
CHRISTCHURCH												
max/min (°C)	21/12	21/12	19/10	17/7	13/4	11/2	10/2	11/2	14/4	17/7	19/8	21/11
max/min (°F)	70/54	70/54	66/50	63/45	55/39	52/36	50/36	52/36	57/39	63/45	66/46	70/52
rainfall (mm)	56	43	48	48	66	66	69	48	46	43	48	56
HOKITIKA												
max/min (°C)	19/12	19/12	18/11	16/8	14/6	12/3	12/3	12/3	13/6	15/8	16/9	18/11
max/min (°F)	66/54	66/54	64/52	61/46	57/43	54/37	54/37	54/37	55/43	59/46	61/48	64/52
rainfall (mm)	262	191	239	236	244	231	218	239	226	292	267	262
QUEENSTOWN												
max/min (°C)	21/10	21/10	20/9	15/7	11/3	9/1	9/0	11/1	14/3	18/5	19/7	20/10
max/min (°F)	70/50	70/50	68/48	59/45	52/37	48/34	48/32	52/34	57/37	64/41	66/45	68/50
rainfall (mm)	79	72	74	72	64	58	59	63	66	77	64	62

EMERGENCY PHONE CALLS

☏ 111 is the free emergency telephone number to summon the police, ambulance or fire service.

containing all your possessions make obvious and easy pickings. Take your valuables with you, put packs and bags out of sight and get good insurance. When setting out on long walks use a secure car park if possible, where your vehicle will be kept safe for a small sum.

Police and the law

If you get **arrested**, you are entitled to talk to a lawyer. One will be appointed if you can't afford one and you may be able to claim legal aid. It's unlikely that your consulate will take more than a passing interest unless there is something strange or unusual about the case against you.

The laws regarding **alcohol consumption** have traditionally been pretty lenient, though persistent rowdy behaviour has encouraged some towns to ban drinking in public spaces. Still, most of the time nobody's going to bother you if you fancy a beer on the beach or glass of wine at some wayside picnic area. The same does not apply to drink driving (see page 32), which is taken very seriously.

Marijuana has a reputation for being very potent and relatively easily available. It is, however, illegal, and although a certain amount of tolerance is sometimes shown towards personal use, the police and courts take a dim view of larger quantities and hard drugs, handing out long custodial sentences.

Prejudice

New Zealanders like to think of themselves as a tolerant and open-minded people, and foreign visitors are generally welcomed with open arms. Racism is far from unknown, but you're unlikely to experience overt **discrimination** or be refused service because of your race, colour or gender. In out-of-the-way rural pubs, women, foreigners – and just about anyone who doesn't live within a 10km radius – may get a frosty reception, though this soon breaks down once you get talking.

Despite constant efforts to maintain good relations between Māori and Pakeha, tensions do exist. Ever since colonization, **Māori** have achieved lower educational standards, earned less and maintained disproportionately high rates of unemployment and imprisonment. Slowly Māori are getting some restitution for the wrongs perpetrated on their race, which of course plays into the hands of those who feel that such positive discrimination is unfair.

Recent high levels of immigration from east Asia – Hong Kong, China and Taiwan in particular – have rapidly changed the demographics in Auckland, where most have settled. Central Auckland also has several English-language schools that are mostly full of Asian students. The combined effect means that in parts of Auckland, especially downtown, longer-established New Zealanders are in the minority. It is a sensation that some Māori and Pakeha find faintly disturbing. There's little overt racism, but neither is there much mixing.

Electricity

New Zealand operates a 230/240-volt, 50Hz **AC power supply**, and sockets take a three-prong, flat-pin type of plug. Suitable socket adaptors are widely available in New Zealand and at most international airports; and for phone chargers and laptops that's all you'll need. In most other cases, North American appliances require both a transformer and an adaptor, British and Irish equipment needs only an adaptor and Australian appliances need no alteration.

LGBT+

Homosexuality was decriminalized in New Zealand in 1986 and the **age of consent** was set at 16 (the same as for heterosexuals). It is illegal to discriminate against them and people with HIV or AIDS, and New Zealand makes no limitation on people with HIV or AIDS entering the country. Civil unions were legalized in 2005 and full marriage made it into the statute books in 2013.

Though there remains an undercurrent of redneck intolerance, particularly in rural areas, it generally stays well below the surface, and New Zealand is a broadly LGBT+-friendly place. The mainstream acceptance is such that the New Zealand Symphony Orchestra and Auckland Philharmonia composer, Gareth Farr, also performs as drag queen Lilith LaCroix. This tolerant attitude has conspired to de-ghettoize the LGBT+ community; even in **Auckland** and **Wellington**, the only cities with genuinely vibrant LGBT+ scenes, there aren't any predominantly LGBT+ areas and most venues have a mixed clientele. Auckland's scene is generally the largest and most lively, but the intimate nature of Wellington makes it more accessible and welcoming. Christchurch, Nelson and Queenstown also have small LGBT+ scenes.

The best source of on-the-ground information is the fortnightly LGBT+ newspaper *express* (Ⓦ gayexpress.co.nz), available free in LGBT+-friendly cafés and venues and almost any decent bookshop.

LGBT+ EVENTS

Auckland Pride Festival Ⓦ aucklandpridefestival.org.nz. See page 102.

Wellington Pride Festival Ⓦ wellingtonpridefestival.org.nz. End Feb to early March.

Winter Pride Ⓦ gayskiweekqt.com. Late Aug to early Sept. Aussie and Kiwi members of the LGBTQ community fly in to party up large at cabaret nights, a transsexual-hosted bingo night, live music gigs and yet more partying in venues around Queenstown. There's even time for skiing.

Vinegar Hill Summer Camp search for Vinegar Hill Gay Camping at Ⓦ facebook.com. Very laidback affair, with a couple of hundred gay men and women camping out, mixing and partying 5km north of the small town of Hunterville, in the middle of the North Island. Runs from Boxing Day to just after New Year. There's no charge (except around $5 for camping) and no hot water, but a large river runs through the grounds and everyone has a great time.

LGBT+ TRAVEL WEBSITES

Ⓦ **gaynewzealand.com** A virtual tour of the country with a gay and lesbian slant.

Ⓦ **gaynz.com** Useful site with direct access to gay, lesbian, bisexual and transgender information including a guide to what's on in the LGBT+ community and a calendar of events all over the country.

Ⓦ **gaytravel.co.nz** A LGBT+ online accommodation and travel reservation service.

Ⓦ **newzealandawaits.com** Lesbian-owned and -operated company that organises tours and recommends LGBT+ businesses around NZ.

Ⓦ **purpleroofs.com** Comprehensive listing for LGBT+-owned and LGBT+-friendly accommodation in NZ and beyond.

Health

New Zealand is relatively free of serious health hazards and the most common pitfall is simply underestimating the power of nature. **No vaccinations** are required to enter the country, but you should make sure you have adequate health cover in your travel insurance, especially if you plan to take on the great outdoors (see page 51 for advice on tramping health and safety).

New Zealand has a good **health service** that's reasonably cheap by world standards. All visitors are covered by the accident compensation scheme, under which you can claim some medical and hospital expenses in the event of an accident, but without full cover in your travel insurance you could still face a hefty bill. For more minor ailments, you can visit a doctor for a consultation (from around $65) and, armed with a prescription, buy any required medication at a pharmacy at a reasonable price.

Sun, surf and earthquakes

Visitors to New Zealand frequently get caught out by the intensity of the **sun**, its damaging ultraviolet rays easily penetrating the thin ozone layer and reducing burn times to as little as ten minutes in spring and summer. Stay out of the sun (or keep covered up) as much as possible between 11am and 3pm, and always slap on plenty of sunblock. Reapply every few hours as well as after swimming, and keep a check on any moles on your body: if you notice any changes, during or after your trip, see a doctor right away.

The sea is a more immediate killer and even strong swimmers should read our **surf** warning (see box opposite).

New Zealand is regularly shaken by **earthquakes** (see page 715), but, although Christchurch experienced major quakes in 2010 and 2011 and Kaikoura in 2016, most are minor and it is generally not something to worry about. If the worst happens, the best advice is to move no more than a few steps to stand in a doorway or crouch under a table. If caught in the open, keep your distance from trees and rocky outcrops to reduce the chances of being injured by falling branches or debris.

Wildlife hazards

New Zealand's wildlife is amazingly benign. There are no snakes, scorpions or other nasties, and only a few poisonous **spiders**, all rarely seen. No one has died from spider venom for many years, but if you get a serious reaction from a bite be sure to see a doctor or head to the nearest hospital, where antivenin will be available.

Shark attacks are also rare; you're more likely to be carried away by a strong tide than a great white, though it still pays to be sensible and obey any local warnings when swimming.

A far bigger problem is the country's **mosquitoes** and **sandflies**, although they're generally free of life-threatening diseases. The West Coast of the South Island in the summer is the worst place for these irritating insects, though they appear to a lesser degree in many other places across the country. A liberal application of repellent helps keep them at bay; for a natural deterrent, try lavender oil.

At the microscopic level, **giardia** inhabits many rivers and lakes, and infection results from drinking contaminated water, with symptoms appearing

SWIM BETWEEN THE FLAGS

The New Zealand coast is frequently pounded by ferocious surf and even strong swimmers can find themselves in difficulty in what may seem benign conditions. Every day throughout the peak holiday weeks (Christmas–Jan), and at weekends through the rest of the summer (Nov–Easter), the most popular surf beaches are monitored daily from around 10am to 5pm. Lifeguards stake out a section of beach between two red and yellow flags and continually monitor that area: **always swim between the flags**.

Before entering the water, watch other swimmers to see if they are being dragged along the beach by a strong along-shore **current** or **rip**. Often the rip will turn out to sea, leaving a "river" of disturbed but relatively calm water through the pattern of curling breakers. On entering the water, feel the strength of the waves and current before committing yourself too deeply, then keep glancing back to where you left your towel to judge your drift along the shore. Look out too for **sandbars**, a common feature of surf beaches at certain tides: wading out to sea, you may well be neck deep and then suddenly be only up to your knees. The corollary is moments after being comfortably within your depth you'll be floundering around in a **hole**, reaching for the bottom. Note that **boogie boards**, while providing flotation, can make you vulnerable to rips, and riders should always wear fins (flippers).

If you do find yourself in **trouble**, try not to panic, raise one hand in the air and yell to attract the attention of other swimmers and surf rescue folk. Most of all, don't struggle against the current; either swim across the rip or let it drag you out. Around 100–200m offshore the current will often subside and you can swim away from the rip and bodysurf the breakers back to shore. If you have to be rescued (or are just feeling generous), a large donation is in order. Surf lifeguards are dedicated volunteers, always strapped for cash and in need of new rescue equipment.

several weeks later; a bloated stomach, cramps, explosive diarrhoea and wind. The Department of Conservation advises you to purify drinking water by using iodine-based solutions or tablets (regular chlorine-based tablets aren't effective against giardia), by fast-boiling water for at least three minutes or by using a giardia-rated filter (obtainable from any outdoors or camping shop).

The relatively rare **amoebic meningitis** is another waterborne hazard, this time contracted from hot pools. Commercial pools are always safe, but in natural pools surrounded by earth you should avoid contamination by keeping your head above water. The amoeba enters the body via the nose or ears, lodges in the brain, and weeks later causes severe headaches, stiffness of the neck, hypersensitivity to light, and eventually coma. If you experience any of these symptoms, seek medical attention immediately.

Insurance

New Zealand's Accident Compensation Commission (Ⓦ acc.co.nz) provides limited medical treatment for visitors injured while in New Zealand, but is no substitute for having comprehensive **travel insurance** to cover against theft, loss and illness or injury.

Before paying for a new policy, it's worth checking whether you are already covered: some home insurance policies may cover your possessions when overseas, and many private medical schemes include cover when abroad. Students will often find that their student health coverage extends during the vacations and for one term beyond the date of last enrolment.

After exhausting the possibilities above, you might want to contact a specialist travel insurance company. Most policies exclude so-called **dangerous activities** unless an extra premium is paid. In New Zealand this can mean scuba diving, bungy jumping, whitewater rafting, windsurfing, surfing, skiing and snowboarding, and even tramping under some policies.

Many policies can exclude coverage you don't need. If you do take medical coverage, ascertain whether benefits will be paid as treatment proceeds or only after return home, and if there's a 24-hour medical emergency number. When securing **baggage cover**, make sure that the per-article limit will cover your most valuable possession. If you need to make a claim, you'll need to keep receipts for medicines and medical treatment, and in the event you have anything stolen, you must obtain an official statement from the police.

Internet

Free wi-fi is abundant in major centres – you can get online at all New Zealand public libraries, as well as some i-SITE visitor centres, accommodation, cafes and bars, though its seldom blindingly fast. There's also free wi-fi in the city centres of Auckland, Rotorua, Wellington and Dunedin.

Although wi-fi is increasingly widespread, you're going to struggle in **rural areas**. Your best bet will be in holiday parks, hostels, motels and hotels which might have hotspots accessible using your credit card or by buying access from reception. Rates vary considerably: an hour might cost $10 but you can often get a full 24-hour day for under $25. Organizations such as Zenbu (ⓦ zenbu.net.nz) allow you to store your purchased time for future use. Note that in New Zealand, there's often a kilobyte cap, so make sure your device isn't using up your kilobytes in automatic updates.

Some Spark phonebooths also double as wi-fi hotspots, and you'll also find Spark hotspots in public building across New Zealand, although you'll need a Kiwi or Australian mobile phone number to use the service – consider buying a mobile data pack.

Internet cafés may not be as common as they once were, but they are still to be found in town and city centres, and coin- or card-operated machines are sometimes available at **visitor centres**, backpacker hostels, motels and campsites, generally charging around $6 an hour. Most are set up with card readers, headsets and webcams, and often loaded with Skype and iTunes. At more expensive accommodation there'll often be a free-use computer, and laptop connections may be available.

Mail

Stamps, postcards, envelopes, packing materials and a lot more can be bought at **post offices**, which are open Monday to Friday 8.30am to 5pm, plus Saturday 9 or 10am to noon or 1pm in some large towns and cities. Red and silver **post boxes** are found outside post offices and on street corners, with mail collected daily.

Parcels are quite expensive to send overseas as everything goes by air; regular airmail takes up to ten days, while the more expensive courier services will deliver your package in less than six days.

One post office in each major town operates a **Poste Restante** (or **General Delivery**) service where you can receive mail; we've listed the major ones in town accounts. Most hostels and hotels will keep mail for you, preferably marked with your expected date of arrival.

Maps and GPS

Specialist outlets should have a reasonable stock of **maps** of New Zealand. **Road atlases** are widely available in bookshops and service stations; the most detailed are those produced by Kiwi Pathfinder, which indicate numerous points of interest and the type of road surface. Many car- and van-rental places have **GPS navigation systems**, usually for an additional $10–15 a day.

With a road atlas and our city plans you can't go far wrong on the roads, but more detailed maps may be required for tramping. All the major walks are covered by the **Park Map** series, complete with photos (around $19 from DOC offices and bookshops in NZ), while the larger-scale 1:50,000 Topo50 and 1:250,000 Topo250 (downloadable at ⓦ linz.govt.nz and sold in i-SITE visitor centres, book and outdoors shops and DOC offices) cover the whole country.

Money

The **Kiwi dollar** is divided into 100 cents. There are $100, $50, $20, $10 and $5 notes made of a sturdy plastic material, and coins in denominations of $2, $1 (both gold in colour), 50¢, 20¢ and 10¢. Grocery prices are given to the nearest cent, but the final bill is rounded up or down to the nearest ten cents. All prices quoted in the Guide are in New Zealand dollars, and at the time of writing the New Zealand dollar was about 2:1 against the British pound.

IMPORTANT PHONE NUMBERS

National directory assistance ☎ 018
International directory assistance ☎ 0172
Emergency services Police, ambulance and fire brigade (no charge) ☎ 111

Cards and ATMs

For purchases, visitors generally rely on **credit cards**, particularly Visa and MasterCard, which are widely accepted, though many hostels, campsites and homestays will only accept cash. American Express and Diners Club are far less useful. You'll also find credit cards handy for advance booking of accommodation and trips, and with the appropriate PIN you can obtain **cash advances** through 24-hour ATMs found almost everywhere. **Debit cards** are also useful for purchases and ATM cash withdrawals.

Banks

The major **banks** – ASB, ANZ, BNZ, Kiwibank (found in post offices), National Bank and Westpac – have branches in towns of any size and are open Monday to Friday from 9.30am to 4.30pm, with some city branches opening on Saturday mornings (until around 12.30pm). The big cities and tourist centres also have **bureaux de change**, which are typically open from 8am to 8pm daily.

Especially if you are working in New Zealand you may want to open a **bank account**. A New Zealand EFTPOS (debit) card can be used just about anywhere for purchases or obtaining cash. An account can usually be set up within a day; remember to take your passport.

Opening hours

New Zealand's larger cities and tourist centres are increasingly open all hours, with cafés, bars and supermarkets open till very late, and shops open long hours every day. Once you get into rural areas, things change rapidly, and core **shopping hours** (Mon–Fri 9am–5.30pm, Sat 9am–noon) apply, though tourist-oriented shops stay open daily until 8pm.

An ever-increasing number of **supermarkets** open 24/7 and small "dairies" (corner shops or convenience stores) also keep long hours and open on Sundays. **Museums** and sights usually open around 9am, although small-town museums often open only in the afternoons and/or only on specific days.

Public holidays and festivals are listed on page 47.

Phones

Given the near-ubiquity of mobile phones, and the prominence of FaceTime or Skype (or similar services) for international calling, most people don't have much need of **public payphones**, though they are still fairly widespread across New Zealand. Coin-operated phones are now rare, but all payphones accept major credit cards, account-based phone-cards and slot-in disposable PhoneCards sold at post offices, newsagents, dairies, petrol stations, i-SITE visitor centres and supermarkets.

Phone numbers

New Zealand **landline numbers** have only five area codes. The North Island is divided into four codes, while the South Island makes do with just one (☎ 03); all numbers in the Guide are given with their code. Even within the same area, you may have to dial the code if you're calling another town some distance away. **Mobile numbers** start with ☎ 021, ☎ 022, ☎ 027 or ☎ 029, and you'll come across **freephone** numbers which are all ☎ 0800 or ☎ 0508. Numbers prefixed ☎ 0900 are **premium-rated** and cannot be called from payphones.

International dialling codes

To call New Zealand from overseas, dial your international access code (☎ 00 from the UK, ☎ 011 from the US and Canada, ☎ 0011 from Australia, ☎ 09 from South Africa), followed by ☎ 64, the area code minus its initial zero, and then the number.

Phonecards and calling cards

For **long-distance and international calling** you are best off with pre-paid account-based **phonecards** that can be used on any phone. There are numerous such cards around offering highly competitive rates,

CALLING HOME FROM ABROAD

To make an international call, dial the international access code (in New Zealand it's 00), then the destination's country code, before the rest of the number. Note that the initial zero is omitted from the area code when dialling the UK, Ireland and Australia from abroad.
Australia 00 + 61 + area code.
Republic of Ireland 00 + 353 + area code.
South Africa 00 + 27 + area code.
UK 00 + 44 + area code.
US and Canada 00 + 1 + area code.

but be wary of the very cheap ones: they are often internet-based and the voice quality can be poor and delayed. Be warned, though, that public payphones have an additional per-minute charge for account-based phonecards, so try to use them from private phones whenever possible.

Mobile phones

New Zealand has four **mobile** providers: Spark (Ⓦ spark.co.nz), Vodafone (Ⓦ vodafone.co.nz), 2degrees (Ⓦ 2degreesmobile.co.nz) and Skinny (Ⓦ skinny.co.nz). All have excellent reception in populated areas but sporadic coverage in remoter spots.

If you're thinking of bringing your phone from home, check with your service to see if your phone will roam in New Zealand and check roaming costs, which can be excessive. Providing your phone is unlocked, you can also buy a New Zealand SIM card and pre-pay.

Time and seasons

New Zealand Standard Time (NZST) is twelve hours ahead of Greenwich Mean Time, but, from the last Sunday in September to the first Sunday in April, Daylight Saving puts the clocks one hour further forward (GMT+13). Throughout the summer, when it is 8pm in New Zealand, it's 6pm in Sydney, 7am in London, 2am in New York, and 11pm the day before in Los Angeles.

New Zealand follows Britain's lead with **dates**, and 1/4/2016 means April 1 not January 4.

Don't forget that the southern hemisphere **seasons** are reversed: summer is officially December 1 to February 28 (or 29), and winter is June 1 to August 31.

Tourist information

New Zealand promotes itself enthusiastically abroad through Tourism New Zealand (Ⓦ newzealand.com).

Many information centres, as well as some cafés, bars and hostels, keep a supply of **free newspapers** and **magazines** oriented towards backpackers – they're usually filled with promotional copy, but are informative nonetheless. *TNT* (Ⓦ tntdownunder.com) is about the best.

Visitor centres

Every town of any size has an official **i-SITE visitor centre**, staffed by helpful and knowledgeable personnel and sometimes offering some form of video presentation on the area. Apart from dishing out local maps and leaflets, they offer a

---

CONTACTS IN NEW ZEALAND

Access Tourism NZ Ⓦ accesstourismnz.org.nz. Informative advocacy blog.

Disability Resource Centre 14 Erson Ave, Royal Oak, Auckland ☎ 09 625 8069, Ⓦ drct.co.nz. General resource centre.

DPA Level 4/173–175 Victoria St, Wellington, NZ ☎ 04 801 9100, Ⓦ dpa.org.nz. Disability advocacy organization with useful links.

Enable New Zealand ☎ 0800 362 253, Ⓦ enable.co.nz. Organization assisting people with disabilities, though not specifically focused on travellers.

---

free booking service for accommodation, trips and activities, and onward travel, but only for businesses registered with them. Some (usually small) businesses choose not to register and may still be worth seeking out; we've mentioned them where relevant. In the more popular tourist areas, you'll also come across places representing themselves as **independent information centres** that usually follow a hidden agenda (ie commission), typically promoting a number of allied adventure companies. While these can be excellent, it's worth remembering that their advice may not be impartial.

Other useful resources are **Department of Conservation** (DOC; Ⓦ doc.govt.nz) offices and field centres, usually sited close to wilderness areas and popular tramping tracks, and sometimes serving as the local visitor centre as well. These are highly informative and well geared to trampers' needs, with local weather forecasts, intentions forms and maps as well as historic and environmental displays and audiovisual exhibitions. The website contains loads of detail on the environment and the latest conservation issues plus details of national parks and Great Walks.

Travellers with disabilities

Overall, New Zealand is disabled traveller-friendly. Many public buildings, galleries and museums are **accessible**, and many tour operators will make a special effort to help you participate in all manner of activities, such as swimming with dolphins or seals. However, restaurants and local public transport generally make few concessions.

Planning a trip

Independent travellers should advise travel agencies, insurance companies and travel companions of limitations. Reading your travel **insurance** small print carefully to make sure that people with a pre-existing medical condition aren't excluded could save you a fortune. Your travel agent can help make your journey simpler: airline or bus companies can better cater to your needs if they are expecting you. A **medical certificate** of your fitness to travel, provided by your doctor, is also extremely useful; some airlines or insurance companies may insist on it.

Accommodation

New accommodation must have at least one room designed for disabled access, and many pre-existing places have converted rooms, including most YHA hostels, some motels, campsites and larger hotels. Older buildings, homestays and B&Bs are the least likely to lend themselves to such conversions.

For listings, visit ⓦ tourism.net.nz/accommodation/accessible-accommodation, which has a searchable database of places that offer disability-friendly facilities.

Travelling

Few airlines, trains, ferries and buses allow complete independence. Air New Zealand provides aisle wheelchairs on international (but not domestic) flights, and the rear toilet cubicles are wider than the others to facilitate access; for more details search for "Special Assistance" on its website.

Other **domestic airlines** have poorer facilities. Inter-islander Cook Strait **ferries** have reasonable access for disabled travellers, including help while boarding, if needed, and adapted toilets. If given advance warning, trains will provide attendants to get passengers in wheelchairs or sight-impaired travellers on board, but moving around the train in a standard wheelchair is impossible and there are no specially adapted toilets; the problems with **long-distance buses** are much the same.

In cities there are some **taxis** specifically adapted for wheelchairs, but these must be pre-booked; otherwise taxi drivers obligingly hoist wheelchairs into the boot and their occupant onto a seat.

Women travellers

New Zealand is generally considered a safe country for women to travel alone and harassment is rare. In the unlikely event of a sexual assault, contact the police or RPE (Rape Prevention Education), ⓦ rpe.org.nz, which coordinates a series of sexual assault support centres across the country. You might also consider partly organizing your holiday through **Women Travel New Zealand** (ⓦ womentravelnz.com), which offers information, links to retreats, women-oriented tour operators and accommodation. Auckland's Women's Bookshop (see page 106; ⓦ womensbookshop.co.nz) is a handy resource and hosts literary events.

Auckland and around

AUCKLAND

1 Auckland and around

Auckland is New Zealand's largest city and, as the site of the major international airport, most visitors' first view of the country. Planes bank over the island-studded Hauraki Gulf and yachts with bright spinnakers tack through the glistening waters of the Waitemata Harbour towards the "City of Sails". The skyscrapered downtown is surrounded by the grassy humps of some fifty-odd extinct volcanoes, and a low-rise suburban sprawl of prim wooden villas surrounded by substantial gardens. Auckland has a modest small-town feel and measured pace, although even this can seem frenetic in comparison with the rest of the country. In fact, Auckland is one of the least densely populated cities in the world, the size of London and yet home to only 1.5 million inhabitants. It is also the world's largest Polynesian city. Around eleven percent of the population claim Māori descent while fourteen percent are families of migrants who arrived from other South Pacific islands during the 1960s and 1970s.

Nevertheless, the Polynesian profile has traditionally been confined to small pockets, and it is only in the last decade or so, as the second generation matures, that Polynesia is making its presence felt in mainstream Auckland life, especially in the arts.

Many visitors only stay in the city long enough for a quick zip around the smattering of key sights, principally the **Auckland Museum**, with its matchless collection of Māori and Pacific Island carving and artefacts. A better taste of the city is gleaned by ambling around the fashionable **inner-city suburbs** of Ponsonby, Parnell, Newmarket and Devonport, and using the city as a base for exploring the wild and desolate West Coast **surf beaches** and the **wineries**, all less than an hour from the city centre. With more time, head out to the **Hauraki Gulf islands**: craggy, volcanic Rangitoto, sophisticated Waiheke, bird-rich Tiritiri Matangi and chilled-out Great Barrier.

Auckland's climate is temperate and muggy, though never scorching hot, and the humidity is always tempered by a sea breeze. Winters are generally mild but rainy. The average daytime high is 23°C in January and February, and drops down to 14°C in July and August.

Auckland

AUCKLAND's urban sprawl smothers the North Island's wasp waist, a narrow isthmus where the island is all but severed by river estuaries probing inland from the city's two harbours. To the west, the shallow and silted **Manukau Harbour** opens out onto the Tasman Sea at a rare break in the long string of black-sand beaches continually pounded by heavy surf. Māori named the eastern anchorage the **Waitemata Harbour** for its "sparkling waters", which constitute Auckland's deep-water port and a focus for the heart of the city. Every summer weekend the harbour and adjoining Hauraki Gulf explode into a riot of brightly coloured sails.

Auckland is increasingly focusing on its **waterfront**, with former docks and fishing wharves now dotted with bobbing yachts and the rejuvenated surrounds converted to flashy restaurants and swanky apartments. This is very much the place to hang out, sucking life from **downtown Auckland**, which is fighting back with the superb **Auckland Art Gallery**.

RANGITOTO ISLAND

Highlights

❶ Auckland Art Gallery With an impressive $90 million refit, Auckland's Art Gallery now ranks as the best showcase for Kiwi art in the country. See page 79

❷ Auckland Museum The exemplary Māori and Pacific Island collection is the highlight of this landmark museum. See page 80

❸ Devonport Stroll the streets of this refined waterside suburb where Maungauika (North Head) provides wonderful harbour views. See page 86

❹ Otara Market Island print fabrics, veg stalls and a lot of life make this New Zealand's finest multicultural market. See page 90

❺ Karekare and Piha Swim, surf, go canyoning or simply laze on the black-and-gold sands of these wild, bush-backed beaches less than an hour from the city. See page 110

❻ Rangitoto Island Make a day-trip to this lava landscape draped in pohutukawa forest with great views back to the city. See page 116

❼ Great Barrier Island Step back in time to this laidback land of golden beaches, mountain bushwalks and hot springs. See page 125

❽ Tiritiri Matangi Enjoy close encounters with some of New Zealand's rarest birds amid regenerating bush on one of the Hauraki Gulf's prettiest islands. See page 131

HIGHLIGHTS ARE MARKED ON THE MAP ON PAGE 72

1

At the top of Queen Street lies **Karangahape Road**, an altogether groovier strip of cheaper shops, ethnic restaurants and more down-and-dirty clubs. To the east lies **The Domain**, an extensive swathe of semiformal parkland centred on the city's most-visited attraction, the **Auckland Museum**, exhibiting stunning Māori and Pacific Island artefacts.

Neighbouring **Parnell** forms the ecclesiastical heart of the city, with one of Auckland's oldest churches and a couple of historical houses. At the foot of the hill, **Tamaki Drive** follows the eastern waterfront past the watery attractions of Kelly Tarlton's aquarium to the city beaches of Mission Bay and St Heliers. West of the centre, the cafés, shops and bars of **Ponsonby Road** give way to Western Springs, home of the **Museum of Transport and Technology** (MOTAT) and the excellent **zoo**.

Across the Waitemata Harbour the seemingly endless suburbs of the **North Shore** stretch into the distance, though you're only likely to want to spend much time in the old waterside suburb of Devonport and perhaps the long golden beach at **Takapuna**.

Immediately south of the centre, two of Auckland's highest points, **Maungawhau** (Mt Eden) and **Maungakiekie** (One Tree Hill) with its encircling **Cornwall Park**, provide wonderful vantage points for views of the city. **Pah Homestead** presents more great art, but the main reason for heading further south is to visit Saturday's **Otara Market**.

HIGHLIGHTS

1. Auckland Art Gallery
2. Auckland Museum
3. Devonport
4. Otara Market
5. Karekare and Piha
6. Rangitoto Island
7. Great Barrier Island
8. Tiritiri Matangi

AUCKLAND & AROUND

Brief history

The earth's crust between the Waitemata and Manukau harbours is so thin that, every few thousand years, magma finds a fissure and bursts onto the surface, producing yet another volcano. The most recent eruption, some six hundred years ago, formed Rangitoto Island. The Rangitoto eruption was witnessed by some of the region's earliest **Māori inhabitants**, settled on adjacent Motutapu Island. Legend records their ancestors' arrival on the Tamaki isthmus, the narrowest neck of land. With plentiful catches from two harbours and rich volcanic soils on a wealth of highly defensible volcano-top sites, the land, which they came to know as **Tamaki Makaurau** ("the maiden sought by a hundred lovers"), became the prize of numerous battles over the years. By the middle of the eighteenth century it had fallen to **Kiwi Tamaki**, who established a three-thousand-strong *pa* (fortified village) on Maungakiekie ("One Tree Hill"), and a satellite *pa* on just about every volcano in the district, but who were eventually overwhelmed by rival *hapu* (subtribes) from Kaipara Harbour to the north.

The Europeans arrive

With the arrival of musket-trading **Europeans** in the Bay of Islands around the beginning of the nineteenth century, Northland Ngapuhi were able to launch successful raids on the Tamaki Māori, which, combined with smallpox epidemics, left the region almost uninhabited, a significant factor in its choice as the new capital after the signing of the Treaty of Waitangi in 1840. Scottish medic **John Logan Campbell** was one of the few European residents when this fertile land, with easy access to major river and seaborne trading routes, was purchased for £55 and some blankets. The capital was roughly laid out and Campbell took advantage of his early start, wheeling and dealing to achieve control of half the city, eventually becoming mayor and "the father of Auckland". After 1840, immigrants boosted the population to the extent that more land was needed, a demand which partly precipitated the **New Zealand Wars** of the 1860s (see page 697).

Loss of capital status

During the depression that followed, many sought their fortunes in the Otago goldfields, and, as the balance of European population shifted south, the capital moved to Wellington in 1865 and the city slumped further. Since then, Auckland has never looked back, almost continuously growing faster than the country as a whole and absorbing waves of migrants, initially from Britain, then, in the 1960s and 1970s, from the Polynesian Islands of the South Pacific. A steady stream of rural Māori has been arriving on Auckland's doorstep for over half a century, now joined by an influx of East Asians whose tastes have radically altered the city centre. Asians now comprise almost twenty percent of Greater Auckland's population, many of them inhabiting the high-rise apartments that pepper the city centre, and Korean, Thai, Malaysian, Chinese and Japanese restaurants are everywhere. Almost forty percent of Aucklanders were born overseas compared to an average of eighteen percent throughout the rest of the country.

The waterfront

Through much of the twentieth century, Auckland's city centre was cut off from its harbour frontage by working docks. As business gradually moved to the container port, the **waterfront** is finally getting a chance to shine.

The 1912 **Ferry Building** remains the nexus of the harbour ferries, whose history and social importance are covered at the nearby **Voyager** maritime museum. **Viaduct Harbour** and **Princes Wharf** were smartened up around the Millennium, though the torch has now moved a little west to the revitalized **Wynyard Quarter**.

GREATER AUCKLAND

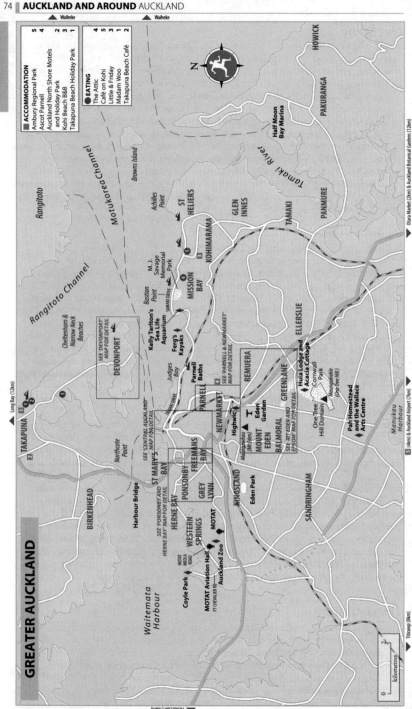

■ ACCOMMODATION	
Ambury Regional Park	5
Ascot Parnell	4
Auckland North Shore Motels and Holiday Park	2
Kohi Beach B&B	3
Takapuna Beach Holiday Park	1

● EATING	
The Attic	4
Café on Kohi	5
Little & Friday	3
Madam Woo	1
Takapuna Beach Café	2

N

Waiheke

Waiheke

Rangitoto Channel

Motukorea Channel

Rangitoto

Browns Island

Waitemata Harbour

HOWICK

PAKURANGA

Half Moon
Bay Marina

Tamaki River

ST
HELIERS

GLEN
INNES

Achilles
Point

KOHIMARAMA

TAMAKI

PANMURE

M. J.
Savage Memorial
Park

MISSION
BAY

Bastion
Point

ELLERSLIE

Kelly Tarlton's
Sea Life
Aquarium

Ferg's Kayaks

Judges Bay

Parnell
Baths

SEE 'PARNELL & NEWMARKET' FOR DETAIL

REMUERA

GREENLANE

Huia Lodge and
Acacia Cottage

Cornwall
Park

Manukau Harbour

*Maungakiekie
(One Tree Hill)*

SEE 'DEVONPORT' MAP FOR DETAIL

DEVONPORT

*Cheltenham &
Narrow Neck
Beaches*

TAKAPUNA

Long Bay (12m)

*Northcote
Point*

ST MARY'S
BAY

SEE 'CENTRAL AUCKLAND' MAP FOR DETAIL

PARNELL

NEWMARKET

Highwic

Eden
Garden

MOUNT
EDEN

*Maungawhau
(Mt Eden)*

BALMORAL

One Tree Hill Domain

Pah Homestead
and the Wallace
Arts Centre

Otara Market (2km) & Auckland Botanical Gardens (12m)

(4km) & Auckland Airport (7km)

BIRKENHEAD

Harbour Bridge

HERNE BAY

**SEE 'PONSONBY AND
HERNE BAY' MAP FOR DETAIL**

PONSONBY

FREEMANS
BAY

GREY
LYNN

WESTERN
SPRINGS

MOTAT
MEOLA
ROAD

MOTAT Aviation Hall

Coyle Park

Auckland Zoo

MOTAT

PT CHEVALIER RD

KINGSLAND

Eden Park

SANDRINGHAM

Henderson (10km)

Titirangi (8km)

0   1   2
kilometres

1

AUCKLAND'S VOLCANIC CONES

Within 20km of the centre of Auckland there are **fifty small volcanoes**, but on the whole the city hasn't been very respectful of its geological heritage. Even the exact number is hard to pin down, not least because several cones have disappeared over the last 150 years, mostly chewed away by scoria and basalt quarrying.

That might sound a Herculean feat, but almost all are under 200m high and many are pimples that only just poke above the surrounding housing. Early on, **Māori** recognized the fertility of the volcanic soils, and set up *kumara* gardens on the lower slopes, usually protected by fortified *pa* sites around the summit. Europeans valued the elevated positions for water storage – most of the main volcanoes have **reservoirs** in the craters.

It is only in the last few decades that volcanic features have been protected from development, often by turning their environs into parks – all or part of 37 of them have some form of protection. The council's "volcanic viewshafts" dictate that some summits can't be obscured from certain angles, and yet a few years ago the edge of one volcano was only just saved from removal for a motorway extension. Some seek UNESCO World Heritage Site status for the cones, but protection looks more likely to come from the 2014 transfer of ownership to the thirteen Māori tribes – the Tamaki Collective – with historic claims to the Auckland (Tamaki Makaurau) isthmus. Fourteen of the major cones are now under Māori ownership though Auckland Council will still maintain them.

Crucially, public access will be maintained. The volcanoes make wonderful **viewpoints** dotted all over the city, notably from central Auckland's Maungawhau and Maungakiekie, Devonport's Maungauika and the top of Rangitoto Island where you can also explore lava caves.

The oldest volcanoes erupted 250,000 years ago, though it is only 600 years since the last eruption, and the volcanic field remains active. No one knows when the next eruption will be, but it is unlikely to be through one of the existing volcanoes – meaning one day a new peak will emerge.

New Zealand Maritime Museum

Corner of Quay and Hobson sts • Daily 10am–5pm; guided tours Mon–Fri 10.30am & 1pm • $20, incl. heritage sailing $50 • ☎ 09 373 0800, ⓦ maritimemuseum.co.nz

New Zealand Maritime Museum pays homage to the maritime history of an island nation reliant on the sea for colonization, trade and sport. A short movie on an imagined Māori migration voyage sets the scene for a display of South Pacific outrigger and double-hulled canoes. Designs for fishing, lagoon sailing and ocean voyaging include the massive 21m-long *Taratai*, which carried New Zealand film-maker and writer James Siers over 2400km from Kiribati to Fiji in 1976. The creaking and rolling innards of a migrant ship and displays on New Zealand's coastal traders and whalers lead on to *Blue Water Black Magic*, a tribute to New Zealand's most celebrated sailor, **Sir Peter Blake**. Wins in the 1990 Whitbread Round the World Race and two America's Cups (1995 and 2000) are celebrated along with high-tech boat construction and an opportunity to work as a team at the helm and grinders of an interactive America's Cup yacht. Other highlights include an early example of the Hamilton Jetboat, which was designed for shallow, braided Canterbury rivers, and a fine collection of boat figureheads and maritime art.

Book ahead for **cruises** on the *Ted Ashby*, a 1990s replica of one of the traditional flat-bottomed, ketch-rigged scows that once worked the North Island tidal waterways, or *Breeze*, a replica of a nineteenth-century coastal trader.

Viaduct Harbour and Princes Wharf

Viaduct Harbour was a scruffy fishing port until it was smartened up for New Zealand's successful defence of the **America's Cup** in 2000. Bobbing yachts still dominate a waterfront lined with exclusive apartments, a lively cluster of restaurants and bars. More restaurants and bars flank **Princes Wharf**, which spears out into the harbour to the dramatically sited *Hilton* hotel.

1

Wynyard Quarter

Cross Wynyard Crossing pedestrian bridge from Viaduct Harbour or get the City Link bus from Queen St (W panuku.co.nz)

Further west, **Wynyard Quarter** successfully blends the still-operational fish market (W afm.co.nz) and Great Barrier Island ferry terminal with parks and a dozen or so nicely-sited restaurants. A "six pack" of old industrial silos has been retained

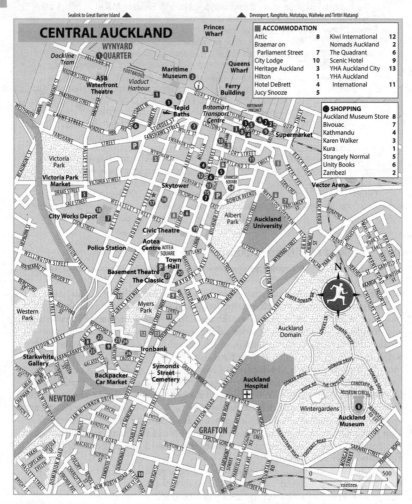

Sealink to Great Barrier Island ▲   ▲ Devonport, Rangitoto, Motutapu, Waiheke and Tiritiri Matangi

CENTRAL AUCKLAND

ACCOMMODATION			
Attic	8	Kiwi International	12
Braemar on		Nomads Auckland	2
Parliament Street	7	The Quadrant	6
City Lodge	10	Scenic Hotel	9
Heritage Auckland	3	YHA Auckland City	13
Hilton	1	YHA Auckland	
Hotel DeBrett	4	International	11
Jucy Snooze	5		

● SHOPPING	
Auckland Museum Store	8
Bivouac	7
Kathmandu	4
Karen Walker	3
Kura	1
Strangely Normal	5
Unity Books	6
Zambezi	2

● EATING					
Bellota	17	Federal		Misters	12
Bestie Cafe	24	Delicatessen	16	Ortolana	5
Better Burger	8	Food Alley	7	Ostro	4
Bombay Chinese	20	Grand Harbour	6	No. 1 Pancake	19
The Botanist	18	Jack Tar	1	Pok Pok	22
Cassia	10	Ima	11	Rasoi	23
Chuffed	13	Imperial Lane	10	Soul	3
Coco's Cantina	25	Mamak Malaysian	14	Sri Pinang	26
The Depot	16	Mexico	9	Tanuki's Cave	21
Ebisu	4	Mezze Bar	15	Wildfire	2

■ DRINKING & NIGHTLIFE			
1885 Britomart	4	Family Bar	9
Brew on Quay	2	Globe	6
Brothers Beer	7	O'Hagan's	1
Britomart Country Club	4	Shanghai Lil's	8
Cowboys	1	Sweat Shop Brew Kitchen	5
Galbraith's Alehouse	10	Xuxu	3

and provides a backdrop for the Friday-evening movies, and kids splash in the fountain. Catch it on a fine day and the whole area can be a delight.

The quarter is prettified by the **Dockline Tram**, on which restored 1920s trams make a pleasant enough 1.5km loop which doesn't take you anywhere you couldn't easily walk – and until mid-2019 it's only running on a short section of the track (for the latest see ⓦ aucklandtram.co.nz).

Downtown

Downtown Auckland spreads south from the waterfront along downbeat **Queen Street**, the main drag, largely sustained by banks and fairly dull shops. That said, there are still a couple of lovely Victorian shopping arcades along Queen Street – Queens Arcade at no. 34 and Stand Arcade at no. 233.

Either side is a grid of streets commemorating prime movers in New Zealand's early European history: the country's first governor-general, William Hobson; Willoughby Shortland, New Zealand's first colonial secretary; and William Symonds, who chivvied along local Māori chiefs reluctant to sign the Treaty of Waitangi.

Immediately east of Queen Street, restored old warehouses and a couple of new office blocks from the lively **Britomart Precinct**, home of many of the city's **top fashion shops**, but at its best in the evening when the restaurants and bars are packed.

Further south, spurn Queen Street in favour of the shops and cafés along O'Connell Street and High Street, heading for the kitsch beauty of the **Civic Theatre**, the **casino** and **Skytower**, and the superb **Auckland Art Gallery**. Wedged between the Art Gallery and the University, **Albert Park** makes a nice break from the concrete jungle.

Britomart Precinct

At the foot of Queen Street the neoclassical 1910 former post office has been transformed into the striking **Britomart Transport Centre** which goes some way to recapturing the majesty of train travel, though useful services are limited.

The transport centre opens out into the **Britomart Precinct**, a cluster of heritage buildings centred on **Takutai Square** with its fountain, lawns and scattered beanbags. Some hip new café, stylish bar or chic clothes shop seems to open every week; check out top Kiwi fashion at Karen Walker, World and Kate Sylvester.

Fort Street, High Street and Vulcan Lane

The waterfront once lapped at **Fort Street** (originally Fore Street), but progressive reclamation shifted the shoreline 300m to the north. Something of a backpacker ghetto (with three hostels and several bars catering to them), it also still has a few sleazy strip clubs. But Britomart's rejuvenation has spread south. Fort Lane, in particular, is packed with fun places and **High Street** and **O'Connell Street** are regaining some of the buzz they lost when everyone decamped to Britomart. Around the corner, **Vulcan Lane** was originally a street of blacksmiths, now replaced by bars and restaurants.

Civic Theatre

One of Queen Street's few buildings of distinction is the Art Nouveau **Civic Theatre**, on the corner of Wellesley Street. The talk of the town when it opened in 1929, the management went so far as to bring in a young Indian boy from Fiji to complement the ornate Moghul-style decor, all elephants, Hindu gods, a proscenium arch with flanking red-eyed panthers and star-strewn artificial sky. You may be able to stick your head in for a glimpse, but, sadly, the only way to see inside properly is to attend a performance (see page 105).

1

GUIDED AND SELF-GUIDED WALKS IN AUCKLAND

The most ambitious **walking** normally attempted by visitors to Auckland is a stroll through The Domain or a short hike up to one of the volcano-top viewpoints. More dedicated hikers can head to Rangitoto Island (see page 116) or pick off sections of the **Hillary Trail** (see page 109) out west in the hills of the Waitakere Ranges. Most of the West Coast tours (see page 110) also include some gentle walking.

SELF-GUIDED WALKS

Coast to Coast Walkway (16km one way; 4hr) The best of the city's sights are threaded together on this fine walk which straddles the isthmus. A route map can be downloaded free from ⓦ aucklandcouncil.govt.nz and the route is marked on the council's free and widely available *Explore Central Auckland* map. Either stop after Maungakiekie (12km; 3hr) and get the #304, #305 or #312 bus back to the city from Manukau Road or do the full walk and catch the train back from Onehunga.

North Shore Coastal Walk (23km one way) Free leaflet from visitor centres. The Devonport ferry wharf marks the southern end of the North Shore Coastal Walk (part of the tip-to-toe Te Araroa; see page 48) which follows the waterfront past the Navy Museum, close to Maungauika then up the coast past several pretty beaches with views of Rangitoto. If you've come over by ferry, consider following the walk as far as Takapuna (10km; 2–3hr) then getting the bus back to the city from there. Best either side of low tide when you can stick to the water's edge.

GUIDED WALKS

Auckland Walks ☎ 0800 300 100, ⓦ aucklandwalks.co.nz. Learn more about the city centre on these informative guided walks (daily 10am; 2hr; $45; booking essential) leaving the Harbour Information Centre at the Ferry Building, 99 Quay St.

Tamaki Hikoi ☎ 0800 282 552, ⓦ tamakihikoi.co.nz. Māori-led walks giving a Ngati Whatua perspective on Tamaki Makaurau. Choose from a tour of Maungawhau/Mount Eden (10am & 1.30pm; 1hr 30min; $50), Tamaki/Auckland and Takaparawhau/Bastion Point (2hr; $95),

or a ceremonial sunrise tour of Takaparawhau/Bastion Point with breakfast at the *marae*/tribal meeting house. All come with lots of stories and give a completely different perspective on Auckland and colonization.

TIME Unlimited ☎ 0800 868 463, ⓦ newzealandtours.travel. Māori-led city full-day tour ($295) explaining the significance to Māori of locations around the city. Their "Extra" package ($395) includes a guided tour through the Māori galleries at the Auckland Museum plus entry to the Māori Cultural Performance.

Skytower

Corner of Victoria and Federal sts • May–Oct daily 9am–10pm; Nov–April Mon–Thurs & Sun 8.30am–10.30pm, Fri & Sat 8.30am–11.30pm • $29 • ☎ 0800 759 2489, ⓦ skycityauckland.co.nz/attractions

At 328m, the **Skytower**, which sprouts from the **Skycity Casino**, is New Zealand's tallest structure and just pips the Eiffel Tower and Sydney's Centrepoint. You can admire the stupendous views over the city and Hauraki Gulf either from one of two observation decks (186m and 220m) or from the classy *Sugar Club* revolving restaurant.

SkyWalk

Daily 10am–6pm • $150; combined with SkyJump $290 • ☎ 0800 759 925, ⓦ skywalk.co.nz

The views from inside the Skytower are surpassed by those from the **SkyWalk** – if you dare to look around. At the 192m level you tentatively make a twenty-minute circumnavigation of the Skytower exterior on a metre-wide, handrail-free walkway with just a rope tether to steady the nerves. At first it is petrifying, but the guide will soon have you hanging over the edge trusting that tether with your life.

SkyJump

Daily 10am–6pm • $225; combined with SkyWalk $290 • ☎ 0800 759 586, ⓦ skyjump.co.nz

The **SkyJump** is a close relation of bungy jumping. You plummet 192m in a kind of ten-second arrested freefall at 80km per hour, with a cable attached to your back. You approach the ground frighteningly fast, but miraculously touch gently down onto the target platform.

Auckland Art Gallery

Corner of Kitchener and Wellesley sts • Daily 10am–5pm; tours 11.30am & 1.30pm • $20; free to New Zealand residents • ☎ 09 379 1349, Ⓦ aucklandartgallery.com

A 2011major restoration and expansion of **Auckland Art Gallery** garnered a slew of international architectural awards and made the country's best art gallery a whole lot better. The elaborate old mock-chateau galleries have been elegantly integrated with the superb new glass-cube atrium supported by kauri-wood columns that fan out to form an organic, forest-like canopy. The gallery feels open to the street and integrated with Albert Park behind, allowing everyone to see the atrium's keynote sculpture, which changes regularly. Park and atrium can both be seen from the excellent, smart but relaxed **café**.

There is a significant international collection, but the emphasis is on the world's **finest collection of New Zealand art**.

Europeans depicting Māori

Māori life romanticized through European explorers' eyes is best seen in a couple of contrasting but equally misleading views: Kennett Watkins' 1912 *The Legend of the Voyage to New Zealand*, with its almost biblical rendition of an imagined scene set on a still lagoon; and Charles Goldie's 1898 *The Arrival of the Māoris in New Zealand*, modelled on Géricault's *Raft of the Medusa* and showing starving, frightened voyagers battling tempestuous seas.

Much of the early collection is devoted to works by artists who remain highly respected by Māori for their accurate portrayal of their ancestors. **Gottfried Lindauer** emigrated to New Zealand in 1874 and spent his later years painting lifelike, almost documentary, portraits of *rangatira* (chiefs) and high-born Māori men and women, in the mistaken belief that the Māori people were about to become extinct. In the early part of the twentieth century, **Charles F. Goldie** became New Zealand's resident "old master" and earned international recognition for his more emotional portraits of elderly Māori regally showing off their traditional facial tattoos, or *moko*.

New Zealand art comes of age

It took half a century for European artists to grasp how to paint the harsh Kiwi light, an evolutionary process that continued into the 1960s and 1970s, when many works betrayed an almost cartoon-like quality, with heavily delineated spaces daubed in shocking colours.

Look out for oils by **Rita Angus**, renowned for her landscapes of Canterbury and Otago in the 1940s; **Colin McCahon**, whose fascination with the power and beauty of New Zealand landscape informs much late twentieth-century Kiwi art; and **Gordon Walters**, who drew inspiration from Māori iconography, to produce abstract art of strikingly graphic form. More recent acquisitions are strong on art by Māori artists. You'll usually find some of the excellent contemporary work by painter **Shane Cotton**, dark pieces by **Ralph Hotere**, and video by **Lisa Reihana**, whose epic, screen-based entry for the 2017 Venice Biennale turned more than a few heads.

Albert Park

East of Queen Street, the formal Victorian-style gardens of **Albert Park** were originally the site of a Māori *pa* before becoming Albert Barracks in the 1840s and 50s. Its oaks and Morton Bay figs are now thronged with sunbathing students and office workers, mostly unaware they're sitting atop a labyrinth of World War II air-raid shelters.

Karangahape Road

The southern end of Queen Street climbs to vibrant and grungy **Karangahape Road**, universally known as **K' Road**. Originally home to prosperous nineteenth-century

1

merchants, it became the heart of Auckland's Polynesian community in the 1970s, and was subsequently notorious for its massage parlours, strip joints and gay cruising clubs. For thirty years K' Road has been slated for a mainstream shopping renaissance, and while most of the strip joints and sex shops are gone, the atmosphere remains determinedly niche. There are few specific sights, but funky cafés, bars and vinyl music shops rub shoulders with colourful Indian- and Chinese-run stores along the road, and a handful of intriguing boutiques. While you're in the area, take a look in the contemporary Starkwhite gallery at no. 510 and the 1920s **St Kevin's Arcade**, which is packed with vintage clothing stores, chic brac-a-brac and breakthrough clothing designers. To the east, the **Symonds Street Cemetery** houses the somewhat neglected grave of New Zealand's first governor, William Hobson, tucked away almost under the vast concrete span of Grafton Bridge.

The Domain

The Domain is the city's finest park, draped over the low profile of an extinct volcano known as Pukekawa or "hill of bitter memories" (a reference to the bloodshed of ancient inter-tribal fighting) and furnished with mid-nineteenth-century accoutrements: a band rotunda, phoenix palms, formal flowerbeds and spacious lawns. In summer, the rugby pitches metamorphose into cricket ovals, and stages are erected in the crater's shallow amphitheatre for outdoor musical extravaganzas.

Auckland Museum

Auckland Domain • Daily 10am–5pm • $25, free to Auckland residents; Māori cultural performance daily 11am, noon & 1.30pm plus Nov–March 2.30pm, additional $20 • ☎ 09 309 0443, ⊕ aucklandmuseum.com • The museum is on the route of the Coast to Coast Walkway and city tour buses; the Inner Link bus stops on Parnell Rd, a 5min walk away

The imposing Greco-Roman-style **Auckland Museum** sits at the highest point of the Auckland Domain, and contains the world's finest collections of Māori and Pacific art and craft. Traditional in its approach yet contemporary in its execution, the museum was built as a World War I memorial in 1929 and has been progressively expanded, most recently with the **Auckland Atrium** entrance, a former courtyard capped with a copper dome and slung with a kind of upturned beehive of slatted Fijian kauri. More changes are underway and the museum will stay open while they increase public spaces and add galleries.

Several times a day a conch-blast that echoes through the building heralds the thirty-minute **Māori Cultural Performance** of frightening eye-rolling challenges, gentle songs and a downright scary *haka*.

Māori Court

As traditional Māori villages started to disappear towards the end of the nineteenth century, some of the best examples of carved panels, meeting houses and food stores were rescued and relocated here. The large and wonderfully carved **Hotunui** meeting house was built in 1878, late enough to have a corrugated-iron rather than rush roof. The craftsmanship is superb; the house's exterior bristles with grotesque faces, lolling tongues and glistening paua-shell eyes, while the interior is lined with wonderful geometric *tukutuku* panels. Outside is the intricately carved prow and stern-piece of **Te Toki a Tapiri**, a 25m-long *waka taua* (war canoe) designed to seat a hundred warriors, the only surviving specimen from the pre-European era.

Pacific Masterpieces

Exquisite Polynesian, Melanesian and Micronesian works to look out for include the shell-inlaid ceremonial food bowl from the Solomon Islands, ritual clubs and a wonderfully resonant slit-drum from Vanuatu. The textiles are fabulous too, with

designs far more varied than you'd expect considering the limited raw materials: the
Hawaiian red feather cloak is especially fine.

Pacific Lifeways
Daily life of Māori and the wider Pacific peoples is covered in the Pacific Lifeways room,
which is dominated by a simple yet majestic breadfruit-wood statue from the Caroline
Islands depicting **Kave**, Polynesia's malevolent and highest-ranked female deity.

Level 1
The middle floor of the museum comprises the **natural history galleries**, an unusual
combination of modern thematic displays and stuffed birds in cases. Displays such as
the 3m-high giant moa and an 800kg ammonite shouldn't be missed, but there's also
material on dinosaurs, volcanoes and a **Māori Natural History** display, which attempts
to explain the unique Māori perspective unencumbered by Western scientific thinking.
The middle floor is also where you'll find hands-on and "discovery" areas for kids.

Level 2
Halls of Memory occupies the entire upper floor and explores how New Zealanders'
involvement in war has helped shape national identity. The New Zealand Wars of
the 1860s are interpreted from both Māori and Pakeha perspectives and World War I
gets extensive coverage, particularly the Gallipoli campaign in Turkey, when botched
leadership led to a massacre of ANZAC – Australian and New Zealand Army Corps –
troops in the trenches. Powerful visuals and rousing martial music accompany newsreel
footage of the Pacific campaigns of World War II and Vietnam, with personal accounts
of the troops' experiences and the responses of those back home.

The Wintergardens and the Fernz Fernery
Auckland Domain • April–Oct daily 9am–4.30pm; Nov–March Mon–Sat 9am–5.30pm, Sun 9am–7.30pm • Free • ⓦ aucklandcouncil.govt.nz
The Domain's volcanic spring was one of Auckland's original water sources and was
used by the Auckland Acclimatization Society to grow European plants, thereby
promoting the rapid Europeanization of the New Zealand countryside. The spirit of
this enterprise lingers on in the lovely **Wintergardens**, a formal fishpond flanked by two
barrel-roofed glasshouses – one temperate, the other heated to mimic tropical climes.
Next door, a former scoria quarry has been transformed into the **Fernz Fernery**, a green
dell with over a hundred types of fern in dry, intermediate and wet habitats.

The inner east: Parnell and Newmarket
The Auckland Domain separates the city from established, moneyed **Parnell**. Once the
city's ecclesiastical heart, it was revived in the 1960s when eccentric dreamer **Les Harvey**
saved the dilapidated villas from the developers' wrecking ball. Through to the 1980s
Parnell was the only place in Auckland where you could shop on a Saturday (let alone
a Sunday) and while its long-standing reputation for chic clothes shops and swanky
restaurants has waned of late, the dealer art galleries remain.
    Parnell Road leads south past the cathedral becoming Broadway, the main drag of
Newmarket, lined with middle-of-the-road clothes shops. A few classier boutiques –
Teed, Kent, Osborne and Nuffield – hide among the backstreets.

St Mary's and the Holy Trinity Cathedral
Corner of Parnell Rd and St Stephens Ave • Daily 10am–3pm (4pm in summer) • Free • ☎ 09 303 9500, ⓦ holy-trinity.org.nz
At the southern end of Parnell Road stands one of the world's largest wooden churches,
St Mary's, built from native timbers in 1886 and almost 50m long. Inside, check out

1

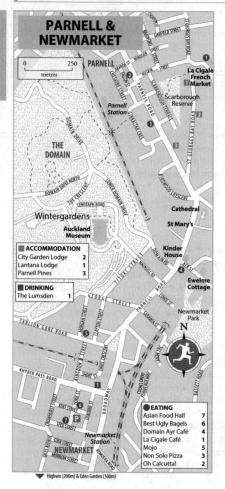

PARNELL & NEWMARKET

0   250
metres

PARNELL

La Cigale French Market

Scarborough Reserve

Parnell Station

THE DOMAIN

Wintergardens

Auckland Museum

ACCOMMODATION	
City Garden Lodge	2
Lantana Lodge	1
Parnell Pines	3

DRINKING	
The Lumsden	1

Cathedral

St Mary's

Kinder House

Ewelme Cottage

Newmarket Park

N

EATING	
Asian Food Hall	7
Best Ugly Bagels	6
Domain Ayr Café	4
La Cigale Café	1
Mojo	5
Non Solo Pizza	3
Oh Calcutta!	2

Newmarket Station

NEWMARKET

▼ Highwic (200m) & Eden Garden (500m)

the series of photos taken on the dramatic day in 1982 when the church was rolled in one piece from its original site across Parnell Road to join its modern kin.

The original Gothic chancel of the **Holy Trinity Cathedral** was started in 1959 then left half-finished until the early 1990s, when an incongruous, airy nave with a Swiss chalet-style roof was grafted on, supposedly in imitation of the older church alongside. Pop in to admire the stained-glass windows at the back symbolizing Māori and Pakeha contributions to society, and Māori artist Shane Cotton's panels along the side in unifying muted tones of red, brown and green. The massive cast-glass font is by internationally-renowned Kiwi artist Ann Robinson.

Kinder House

2 Ayr St, Parnell · Wed–Sun noon–3pm · Free · ☎ 09 379 4008, ⦿ kinder.org.nz

The Gothic flourishes of nearby St Mary's church show the influence of New Zealand's prominent ecclesiastical architect, Frederick Thatcher, who designed **Kinder House** for the headmaster of the new grammar school – a post filled by John Kinder, an accomplished watercolourist and documentary photographer. Built of rough-hewn volcanic rock from nearby Maungawhau, the house contains some interesting photos and reproductions of Kinder's paintings of nineteenth-century New Zealand.

Ewelme Cottage

14 Ayr St, Parnell · Sun 10.30am–4.30pm · $8.50 · ☎ 09 524 5729, ⦿ historicplaces.org.nz

For a glimpse of pioneer life in New Zealand, visit **Ewelme Cottage**, built in 1864 for the wonderfully named clergyman Vicesimus Lush, who lived further afield but built in town so that he could get his kids into a good school – some things never change. The appeal of the place lies not so much in the large kauri cottage itself but in its furniture and possessions, left just as they were when Lush's descendants finally moved out in 1968, the family heirlooms betraying a desire to replicate the home comforts of their native Oxfordshire.

Eden Garden

24 Omana Ave, Newmarket · Daily 9am–4pm · $10 · ☎ 09 638 8395, ⦿ edengarden.co.nz

Occupying a small former quarry hewn into the eastern flank of Maungawhau, **Eden Garden** is a remarkably manageable place with year-round interest in the form of ferns, tulips, roses, proteas, a small waterfall and Australasia's largest and widest collection of camellias, in bloom from April to October. Everywhere you look there are peaceful dells where you can sit awhile and listen to the birdlife, sustained by a visit to their very good café (daily 10am–3.30pm).

The waterfront: along Tamaki Drive

Tamaki Drive twists past 8km of waterfront immediately east of the city centre past Auckland's most popular city beaches – **Mission Bay**, **Kohimarama** and **St Heliers** – the undersea world of **Kelly Tarlton's** and a couple of headland viewpoints. During the summer, the waterfront is the favoured hangout of joggers and cyclists.

Kelly Tarlton's Sea Life Aquarium

23 Tamaki Drive, Okahu Bay, 6km east of the city • Daily 9.30am–5pm • $39, children $27 (under 3 free); get discounts on all tickets by booking online; Shark Cage snorkel $99 including entry • ☎ 0800 805 050, ⓦ kellytarltons.co.nz • Explorer Bus and city buses, #745, #756 and #769 from Tyler St in Britomart stop outside; Tarlton's free shuttle runs hourly on the half hour (9.30am–3.30pm) from opposite the Cloud, 152 Quay St

Kelly Tarlton's Sea Life Aquarium was opened in 1985 by Kiwi diver, treasure hunter and salvage expert Kelly Tarlton in some huge converted sewage tanks which, from 1910 until 1961, flushed the city's effluent into the Waitemata Harbour on the outgoing tides. Its pioneering walk-through acrylic tunnels have since become commonplace, but it is still a pleasure to stand on the moving walkway and glide through two tanks: one dominated by flowing kelp beds, colourful reef fish and twisting eels; the other with smallish sharks, all appearing alarmingly close in the crystal-clear water. If you want to get in among them, join one of the cage dives. Tanks in the **Stingray Bay** section feature specimens with a 2m wingspan. New Zealand is also home to six penguin species, but the gentoo and king penguins seen here reside much further south In the hands-on interactive turtle zone, kids can learn about the work the aquarium does rescuing and rehabilitating marine turtles.

Bastion Point

Grassy **Bastion Point** (Takaparawhau) has great views of the Hauraki Gulf and makes a wonderful picnic spot. It's topped by the **M.J. Savage Memorial Park**, the nation's austere Art Deco homage to its first Labour prime minister, who ushered in the welfare state in the late 1930s. More recently, Bastion Point was the site of a seventeen-month standoff between police and its traditional owners, the Ngati Whatua, over the subdivision of land for housing. The occupiers were removed in 1977, but the stand galvanized the land-rights movement, and paved the way for a significant change in government attitude. Within a decade, the Waitangi Tribunal recommended that the land be returned.

Mission Bay, Kohimarama and St Heliers

Tamaki Drive, 7km east of the city

Swimming conditions are best at half-tide and above at three pohutukawa-backed beach suburbs strung along Tamaki Drive. Just past the kayak and bike rental place, Fergs (see page 92), you reach **Mission Bay**, the closest of the truly worthwhile city **beaches**, where a grassy waterside reserve is backed by a lively row of cafés and restaurants. There are usually kayak and stand-up paddleboard rentals on the beach, and when the sea is shallow, kids make good use of the Sicilian marble **fountain** complete with its three bronze ornamental sea monsters gushing water.

1

Beyond Mission Bay there are similar but usually quieter café-backed beaches at **Kohimarama** (1km on) and **St Heliers** (1km beyond that).

West of the city centre

The suburbs of west Auckland developed later than their eastern counterparts, mainly because of their distance from the sea in the days when almost all travel was by ferry. The exceptions were the inner suburbs of **Ponsonby** and **Herne Bay**.

Sights are scarce until you get out to **Western Springs**, which, in the late nineteenth century, was the major water source for the burgeoning city of Auckland. The area is now home to a pleasant park flanked by the classy **Auckland Zoo** and the transport and technology museum known as **MOTAT**.

Ponsonby

Ponsonby Road has long been a byword for designer clothing, cafés and see-and-be-seen lunching for long-term residents and the overspill from the adjacent suburbs – the media luvvies stronghold of **Grey Lynn**, and **Herne Bay**, which with average property prices approaching $2 million is the priciest in the country. It's all a far cry from the 1960s when large numbers of immigrant Pacific Islanders made the area their home, followed a decade later by an influx of bohemians and artists.

Ponsonby Road itself is not especially beautiful, but the people sure are: musicians, media folk and the well-scrubbed Audi set congregate to lunch, schmooze and be seen in the latest fashionable haunt here. If it all sounds a bit too swanky, don't be deterred. Ponsonby retains a lively vibe with loads of places to eat that are no more expensive than many other areas of the city. The best names in Kiwi fashion are also here (see page 105).

Museum of Transport and Technology (MOTAT)

805 Great North Rd, Western Springs, 5km southwest of the city centre • Daily 10am–5pm • $19 • ☎ 0800 668 286, ⓦ motat.org.nz • Numerous buses including #18, #010, #030 from Britomart

While slightly run-down, the **Museum of Transport and Technology** (MOTAT) still manages to showcase New Zealand's vehicular and industrial past while keeping the kids entertained. The jumble of sheds and halls is centred on the restored Western Springs' **pumphouse** where the massive 1877 beam engine mostly sits grandly immobile, unless they find someone to fire up the boiler.

Appropriately for an agricultural nation there's an impressive array of tractors, including one Edmund Hillary took to the South Pole in 1958, the first overland party there since Scott and Amundsen 46 years earlier. Elsewhere there's a science-oriented, hands-on section, a Victorian village built around the original pumphouse engineer's cottage, and a shed full of trams that plied the city's streets from 1902–56.

Aviation Display Hall

One **tram** (every 15–30min; included in admission price) takes you 1km to MOTAT's impressive **Aviation Display Hall**, a hangar eco-designed with vast laminated wood beams. Star attractions are one of the few surviving World War II Lancaster bombers, early crop-dusting planes and fragile-looking things that took early tourists to the Fox and Franz Josef glaciers in the days before decent roads.

Auckland Zoo

Motions Rd, Western Springs, 5km southwest of the city centre • Daily 9.30am–5.30pm; check the website for Animal Encounters times • Adults $28.50, children $14; Animal Encounters free • ☎ 09 360 3805, ⓦ aucklandzoo.co.nz • Explorer bus stops here and numerous city buses including #030 from Britomart pass within 200m; there's also a zoo stop on the tramline between the two MOTAT sites

The **Auckland Zoo** is the best in the country, strong on spacious, naturalistic habitats and captive breeding programmes. The Tropics section threads its way among artificial islands inhabited by colonies of monkeys, you can walk through the wallaby and emu enclosure straight through to the new Tasmanian Devils' compound, and Pridelands has hippos, rhinos, giraffes, zebras and gazelles all roaming across mock savannah behind enclosing moats.

Six New Zealand environments – coast, islands, wetlands, forest, high country and nocturnal – are grouped as **Te Wao Nui**, beautifully designed with loads of sculptures, water features and clever deceits such as entering a free-flight aviary through what appears to be a high-country hut.

The North Shore

The completion of the harbour bridge in 1959 provided the catalyst for the development of the **North Shore**, previously a handful of scattered communities linked by ferries. By the early 1970s, the volume of traffic to the suburbs log-jammed

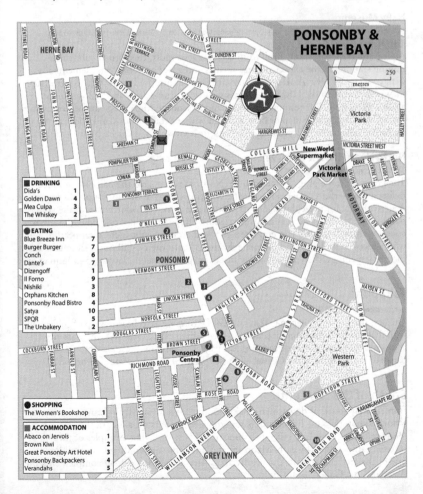

PONSONBY & HERNE BAY

0   250
metres

DRINKING
Dida's   1
Golden Dawn   4
Mea Culpa   3
The Whiskey   2

EATING
Blue Breeze Inn   7
Burger Burger   7
Conch   6
Dante's   7
Dizengoff   1
Il Forno   9
Nishiki   3
Orphans Kitchen   8
Ponsonby Road Bistro 4
Satya   10
SPQR   5
The Unbakery   2

SHOPPING
The Women's Bookshop   1

ACCOMMODATION
Abaco on Jervois   1
Brown Kiwi   2
Great Ponsonby Art Hotel   3
Ponsonby Backpackers   4
Verandahs   5

1

the bridge – until a Japanese company attached a two-lane extension (affectionately dubbed "the Nippon Clip-ons") to each side. The bridge and its additional lanes can now be seen at close quarters on the Auckland Bridge Climb (see page 92).

The peaceful maritime village of **Devonport** with its volcano-top harbour views makes a good target, set at the southern end of a long string of calm swimming **beaches**. Further north, try the more open and busier **Takapuna**, which has one of the most convenient all-tides swimming beaches and a few great places to eat.

Devonport

Devonport is one of Auckland's oldest suburbs, founded in 1840 and still linked to the city by a ten-minute ferry journey. The naval station was an early tenant, soon followed by wealthy merchants, who built fine kauri villas. The essence of Devonport's appeal is wandering the tree-fringed waterfront, up the volcanoes or along the **North Shore Coastal Walk** (see page 78) before grabbing fish and chips on Cheltenham Beach, then attending an aged cinema (see page 105).

Navy Museum

64 King Edward Parade, Torpedo Bay • Daily 10am–5pm; free guided tours Sat & Sun 10.30am & 2.15pm • Free • ☎ 09 445 5186, ⓦ navymuseum.co.nz

A pleasant 1km waterfront stroll from central Devonport, this former submarine mining station has the expected guns, medals and naval uniforms, supplemented with coverage of New Zealand's military involvement in the Battle of the River Plate in World War II to the HMNZS *Otago*'s visit to Mururoa Atoll in 1973 to protest against French nuclear testing. Try your hand at sending Morse code and don't miss the World War II Japanese map of New Zealand with a detail of Auckland; kids can try on uniforms. The on-site *Torpedo Bay Café* has great views across the harbour to the city.

North Head Historic Reserve

Daily 6am–10pm; vehicles 6am–8pm • Free

The grassy volcanic plug of **Maungauika** (North Head) guards the harbour entrance and makes a wonderful vantage point during yachting events or on any sunny afternoon. A strategic site for pre-colonial Māori, it was later co-opted to form part of the young nation's coastal defences. It is now operated by DOC and comes riddled with pillboxes, concrete tunnels linking gun emplacements and even an eight-inch "disappearing gun", which recoiled underground for easy reloading. Learn their significance from two short movies screenings, then explore along three intriguing walking loops (15–30min each).

Takapuna

From Devonport catch bus #813

The best thing about **Takapuna**, 5km north of Devonport, is its broad sweep of golden sand with that rarity for Auckland beaches, good swimming even at low tide. There are views across to Rangitoto, waterside camping (see page 97) and some great places to eat (see page 103). The North Shore Coastal Walk (see page 78) runs here from Devonport.

South of the city centre

Immediately south of downtown Auckland, the city's most lofty volcano, **Maungawhau** (Mount Eden), offers superb views, and its near-identical twin, **Maungakiekie** (One Tree Hill), has some of the best surviving examples of the terracing undertaken by early Māori inhabitants. The surrounding Cornwall Park is one of the city's best, while the nearby art gallery at **Pah Homestead** complements the Auckland Art Gallery beautifully.

Beyond Cornwall Park and Pah Homestead is **South Auckland**, neglected by most visitors, though the airport at Mangere is where most arrive. Arching around the eastern end of Manukau Harbour, it is the city's poorest sector and the less-than-flatteringly-depicted gangland setting of Lee Tamahori's film *Once Were Warriors*. It isn't a no-go zone, and is certainly worth a look on Saturday morning when Auckland's Polynesian community (along with almost every other immigrant community) plies its wares at **Otara Market**.

Further south again, the **Auckland Botanic Gardens** are a relaxing place to spend an hour before continuing out of town.

Maungawhau

2km south of the city centre • Bus #274, #277 to Mount Eden

At just 196m, **Maungawhau** (Mount Eden) is Auckland city's highest volcano. It is only a few metres higher then several other cones, and doesn't poke far above the surrounding suburban housing, but the summit car park affords extensive views all around. At the often-busy summit, take a walk around the cone rim for a more peaceful viewpoint. Alternatively, walk here on the Coast to Coast Walkway (see page 78).

One Tree Hill Domain

7km south of the city centre • Daily 7am–8.30pm (7pm in winter) • Free • Accessible off Manukau Rd, which can be reached on several buses from Stop 7055 close to the Civic Theatre

Auckland's most distinctive peak is **Maungakiekie** (One Tree Hill; 183m), topped by a 33m-tall granite obelisk and nine young totara and pohutukawa trees planted in 2016 (see page 91). The hilltop views are as good as those from Mount Eden and the surrounding **One Tree Hill Domain** makes this a more rewarding destination overall.

For a century, until just before the arrival of Europeans, the "mountain of the kiekie plant" was one of the largest *pa* sites in the country; an estimated 4000 people were drawn here by the proximity to abundant seafood from both harbours and the rich soils of the volcanic cone, which still bears the scars of extensive earthworks including the remains of dwellings and *kumara* pits. The site was abandoned and then bought by

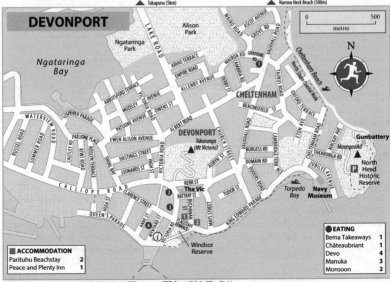

1

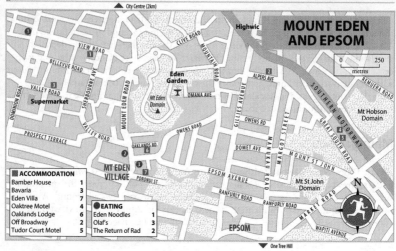

the Scottish medic and "father of Auckland", Sir John Logan Campbell, one of only two European residents when the city was granted capital status in 1840.

Cornwall Park

Off Green Lane West, 7km south of the city centre • Daily 7am–9pm (7pm in winter) • Free • ⓦ cornwallpark.co.nz

One Tree Hill Domain is almost entirely encircled by **Cornwall Park**, which Sir John Logan Campbell created from his One Tree Hill Estate and gifted to the people of New Zealand to commemorate the 1901 visit of Britain's Duke and Duchess of Cornwall. There are attractive formal areas, but large sections of the park are farmed, the grazing sheep and cattle making for an odd sight in the midst of a large modern city. Cornwall Park puts on its best display around Christmas, when avenues of pohutukawa trees erupt in a riot of red blossom.

Huia Lodge and Acacia Cottage

Green Lane Rd entrance • Huia Lodge daily 10am–4pm; Acacia Cottage daily 7am–dusk • Free • Huia Lodge ⓣ 09 630 8485

Cornwall Park's amenities are clustered around **Huia Lodge**, built by Campbell as the park caretaker's cottage and now containing displays on the park and the man. It also contains a **visitor centre**, which has free leaflets outlining the archeological and volcanic sites of the hill.

Immediately opposite Huia Lodge is the pit-sawn kauri **Acacia Cottage**, Campbell's original home and the city's oldest surviving building, built in 1841 and re-sited from central Auckland in 1920. Inside, the four simple rooms are furnished as they might have been in the 1840s.

Pah Homestead and the Wallace Arts Centre

72 Hillsborough Rd, 9km south of the city centre • Tues–Fri 10am–3pm, Sat & Sun 8am–5pm • Free • ⓣ 09 639 2010,
ⓦ tsbbankwallaceartscentre.org.nz • Bus #299 takes 30min from Queen St close to the Civic Theatre

One of the best reasons to stray south from the city centre is to visit **Pah Homestead**, an Italianate residence perched on a low hill overlooking the graceful, mature cedars and Moreton Bay fig trees of the surrounding **Monte Cecilia Park**. The house was completed in 1879 and despite spending time as a novitiate home and a boarding house, the wood panelling and elaborate ceiling bosses are original. However, it's the contents of

Pah Homestead that warrant the trip: an array of pieces from the seven thousand-work art collection housed in the **Wallace Arts Centre**. In the mid-1960s, Kiwi agribusiness magnate James Wallace began collecting works by emerging New Zealand artists and has continued to buy their best pieces (and commission more) as they've risen to become some of the country's most eminent. The result is a wide-ranging collection particularly strong on artists such as Toss Woollaston, Philip Trusttum and Michael Parekowhai. What's on show is constantly changing and typically superb, especially in September and October when the winners of the annual Wallace Arts Awards are on show. The *Pah Café* spills out onto the veranda, overlooking the sculpture garden.

Otara Market

Otara Town Centre, 18km southeast of the city centre • Sat 6am–noon, but liveliest 8–11am • ⓦ otarafleamarket.co.nz • Take East Tamaki Rd (Exit 444) off the southern motorway or catch the train to Otahuhu and then take bus #325 (50min)

On Saturday morning, **Otara Market** sprawls across the car park of the Otara Town Centre. Billed as the largest Māori and Polynesian market in the world, it sells Māori greenstone carvings and Māori sovereignty shirts (look for tees emblazoned with the words "*Tino Rangatiratanga*"), and Pasifika rhythms and reggae beats ringing out to the adjacent Community Hall, typically full of *kete* (woven baskets), tapa cloth and island-style floral print fabrics. But these days the diversity reflects the racial make-up of modern south Auckland, with Sikhs flogging gold bracelets next to Korean-language DVD vendors and lots of Chinese selling truckloads of cheap fruit and veg. There's plenty of low-cost **eating** here too, from coffee and pastries to wieners, goat curry, pork buns, whitebait fritters and even a classic Māori boil-up of pork bones, watercress, pumpkin and "fry bread".

Auckland Botanic Gardens

102 Hill Rd, Manurewa, 24km southeast of the city centre • Daily: April–Sept 8am–6pm; Oct–March 8am–8pm • Visitor centre & Café daily 8am–4pm • Free; free guided walk Wed 1pm • ☎ 09 267 1457, ⓦ aucklandbotanicgardens.co.nz

Southbound drivers might want to spend an hour or two just off the motorway at the extensive **Auckland Botanic Gardens**, which only opened in 1982. What was once farmland has a long way to grow, but already there's a beautiful rock garden, a children's garden, a great section of African plants, instructive sections on threatened New Zealand native species and, at the far northern end, bushwalks through native bush that form part of the Te Araroa pathway. There are great picnic spots, or visit *Café Miko*.

ARRIVAL AND DEPARTURE   AUCKLAND

As New Zealand's major gateway city, Auckland receives the bulk of **international arrivals**, a few disembarking from cruise ships at the dock by the Ferry Building downtown, but the vast majority arriving by air.

BY PLANE
Auckland International Airport The airport (ⓦ aucklandairport.co.nz) is 20km south of the city centre in the suburb of Mangere. There is no train service, but buses, collective minibuses and taxis run into the city.

Destinations Bay of Islands (4–5 daily; 50min); Blenheim (4 daily; 1hr 30min); Christchurch (20 daily; 1hr 25min); Dunedin (6 daily; 1hr 50min); Gisborne (5 daily; 1hr 5min); Great Barrier Island (6–8 daily; 40min); Napier/Hastings (6–8 daily; 1hr); Nelson (10 daily; 1hr 25min); New Plymouth (5 daily; 50min); Palmerston North (10 daily; 1hr 10min); Queenstown (6 daily; 1hr 50min); Rotorua (3–4 daily; 45min); Taupo (2–3 daily; 50min); Tauranga (9 daily; 40min); Wanganui (3–4 daily; 1hr); Wellington (20 daily; 1hr 5min); Whakatane (2–3 daily; 45min); Whangarei (3–4 daily; 40min).

AIRPORT INFORMATION
i-SITE There's a well-stocked international terminal office (daily 6am–10pm; ☎ 09 365 9925) with a free accommodation and travel booking service, plus courtesy hotel-booking phones.
Services There are several ATMs at both terminals, as well as foreign exchange offices at the international terminal that are open whenever flights arrive. Showers and left luggage facilities are also available.

AIRPORT TRANSPORT
Between terminals The international terminal is connected to the domestic terminal by a free shuttle bus

1

ONE TREE HILL

Sir **John Logan Campbell** is buried at the summit where a single totara tree originally gave **One Tree Hill** its English name. Settlers cut it down in 1852, and Campbell planted several pines as a windbreak, a single specimen surviving until the millennium. Already ailing from a 1994 chainsaw attack by a Māori activist avenging the loss of the totara, the pine's fate was sealed by a similar attack in 1999 and the tree was removed the next year. After sixteen years as "None Tree Hill" while Treaty of Waitangi grievances were redressed with the multiple *iwi* of Tamaki Mackaurau/Auckland, in 2016 a grove of nine young totara and pohutukawa trees were planted at the summit, as well as the kiekie plant after which **Maungakiekie** was given its Māori name.

(5am–10.30pm; every 15min), or you can walk in around ten minutes – follow the blue and white lines.

By taxi Expensive taxis wait outside both terminals. Expect to pay $80 into the central city, Ponsonby or Parnell; over $100 to Northcote or Devonport.

By bus The SkyBus (24/7 every 10–30min; $18 one way, $34 return; discount online ⓦ skybus.co.nz) is good value for solo travellers. It calls at both airport terminals then alternates between two fixed routes (along Mt Eden Rd or Dominion Rd) into the city (roughly 45min). The cheapest way into town is to take the #380 Airporter bus to Papatoetoe train station (every 30–40min; 30min; $3.50 from driver) then catch the train to central Auckland (frequent; 40min; $7).

By minibus Most travellers catch one of the shared, door-to-door minibuses that wait outside the terminals. Ask at the first in line and if they're not going to the part of town where you're staying they'll point you to one that is: you'll seldom have to wait more than 15min. Fares are $35 to downtown and $60 to Devonport; groups travelling to the same location get a significant reduction, adding only $8–11 per additional person.

To the airport For pick-up on departure call Super Shuttle (ⓣ 0800 748 885) or phone a taxi (see page 93).

BY TRAIN

Northern Explorer ⓣ 0800 872 467, ⓦ greatjourneysofnz.co.nz. The train from Wellington, National Park and Hamilton arrives at Auckland Strand station on Ngaoho Place in Parnell on Tues, Fri and Sun evenings. Southbound services run on Mon, Thurs and Sat.

Destinations Hamilton (3 weekly; 2hr 30min); National Park (3 weekly; 5hr 30min); Ohakune (3 weekly; 6hr);

Otorohanga (3 weekly; 3hr); Palmerston North (3 weekly; 8hr 30min); Wellington (3 weekly; 11hr 30min).

BY BUS

InterCity/Newmans, Great Sights and Northliner long-distance bus services arrive at the Sky City Coach Terminal. Other operators stop outside 172 Quay St, opposite the Downtown Ferry Terminal.

Bus companies Go Kiwi (ⓣ 07 866 0336, ⓦ go-kiwi. co.nz), daily to the Coromandel Peninsula with en route pick-ups at Auckland Airport, ideal if you want to head straight to Whitianga; InterCity/Newmans, Great Sights (ⓣ 09 583 5780, ⓦ intercity.co.nz) and NakedBus (ⓣ 0900 62 533, ⓦ nakedbus.com) all offer national coverage.

Destinations Gisborne (1 daily; 9hr 15min); Hamilton (25 daily; 2hr); Hastings (1 daily; 7hr 30min); Kerikeri (5–6 daily; 4hr 30min); Napier (1 daily; 7hr); National Park (1 daily; 6hr); New Plymouth (3 daily; 6hr–6hr 30min); Ohakune (1 daily; 6hr 45min); Paihia (7–8 daily; 4hr); Palmerston North (8 daily; 9–10hr); Rotorua (11 daily; 4hr); Taihape (6 daily; 7hr); Taupo (7 daily; 5hr); Tauranga (7 daily; 3hr 20min–5hr); Thames (4 daily; 1hr 45min); Waipu (5–6 daily; 2hr 15min); Waitomo Caves (1 daily; 3hr 30min); Warkworth (5–6 daily; 1hr); Wellington (7 daily; 11–12hr); Whangarei (6–7 daily; 2hr 50min); Whitianga (1 daily; 3hr).

BY BIKE

Northbound The Harbour Bridge is off limits so catch the Devonport Ferry or take the western route, possibly riding a suburban train as far as Waitakere (bike goes free; travel outside peak hours).

Southbound Cyclists heading south are better off following the Seabird Coast, avoiding the Southern Motorway, the main route south out of the city.

GETTING AROUND

You can get to many of the most interesting parts of Auckland on foot, notably along the Coast to Coast Walkway. Auckland's poor but improving public transport system is centred on the Britomart Transport Centre at the harbour end of Queen St – suburban trains pull in here while buses have various stops nearby. Out on the harbour, ferries connect the city to the inner suburb of Devonport and the islands. Taxis are best

contacted by phone (see page 93). Parking isn't a major headache, but drivers aren't courteous and you may be better off renting a car just before you leave the city.

BY TRAIN

Suburban trains Auckland's rail service is mostly of little interest to tourists. The main exception is the route from

1

AUCKLAND HARBOUR ACTIVITIES

Auckland is so water-focused that it would be a shame not to get out on the harbour at some point, either on a ferry to one of the outlying islands (see page 116), a **cruise**, a **dolphin and whale safari** or a **sea-kayaking** trip. You can also do a bridge climb and a bungy jump off the Harbour Bridge. For more activities nearby, see pages 110 and 107.

CRUISES AND SAILING

America's Cup Sailing ☎ 0800 397 567, ⓦ exploregroup.co.nz. Crew on old-style monohull America's Cup racing yachts *NZL41* (raced by Japan in the 1995 cup) and *NZL68* (used as a trial boat by New Zealand in 2007) from Viaduct Harbour. There's a chance to grind the winches or take the helm as you get a real sense of power and speed. $180 for a two-hour sail.

Auckland Harbour Cruise ☎ 09 367 9111, ⓦ fullers. co.nz. Fullers offer a 1.5hr cruise (daily 10.45am & 1.45pm; $40) that sails under the Harbour Bridge and past Rangitoto Island.

Explore Sailing ☎ 0800 397 567, ⓦ exploregroup. co.nz. Leisurely sailing trips (year-round at 10.30am & 3.15pm plus Nov–March 1pm; 1hr 30min; $99), plus a dinner cruise (6pm; 2hr 30min; $140). Also offers a great Waiheke Island deal with a return ferry trip and 3hr sailing while there (Dec–March daily 9am; 3hr; $85).

DOLPHIN AND WHALE WATCHING

Whale & Dolphin Safari Viaduct Harbour ☎ 0508 365 744 ⓦ whalewatchingauckland.com. There are stacks of common and bottlenose dolphins out in the Hauraki Gulf year-round, often forming huge pods in winter and spring when Bryde's whale and orca sightings increase. Daily educational and entertaining trips (4hr30min; $180) head out on a fast, 20m catamaran which also undertakes marine mammal research. If you don't see any marine mammals you can go again for free.

KAYAKING AND KAYAK FISHING

Auckland Sea Kayaks ☎ 0800 999 089, ⓦ aucklandseakayaks.co.nz. Great guided kayak tours

including an easy paddle over to Motukorea (Browns) Island (4hr; $135), a longer trip to Rangitoto with a summit hike (7hr; $175), a Rangitoto evening/night trip with sunset from the summit and excellent food along the way (7hr; $185), and a range of overnight trips including camping on Motuihe Island, where there are little spotted kiwi ($395).

Fergs Kayaks 12 Tamaki Drive, Okahu Bay ☎ 09 529 2230, ⓦ fergskayaks.co.nz. Offers guided trips 7km across the Waitemata Harbour to Rangitoto Island, hiking to the summit, then paddling back (departures 9.30am plus Mon–Fri 5.30pm, Sat & Sun 4pm; 6hr; $160). The later departure gives you a chance to paddle by moon or torchlight. Alternatively, opt for their 3km paddle to Devonport (9am; 3hr; $100), usually with a hike up North Head. Single sea kayaks ($25/hr), doubles ($40/hr), or slightly cheaper sit-on-tops are also available to rent; trips to Rangitoto and Devonport are not generally allowed for rentals.

AUCKLAND BRIDGE CLIMB AND BUNGY

Auckland Bridge Climb ☎ 0800 286 4958, ⓦ aucklandbridgeclimb.co.nz. Spend 1hr 30min (3 climbs daily; $130) strolling along steel walkways while harnessed to a cable as guides relate detail on the bridge's fulcrums, pivots and cantilevers, and guide you to the city views some 65m above the Waitemata Harbour. Free transport from the maritime museum.

Auckland Bridge Bungy ☎ 0800 286 4958, ⓦ bungy.co.nz. The place to go for an adrenalin rush, a 40m leap and a water touch (5 times daily; $165). There's free transport from the maritime museum and you get a free T-shirt.

the downtown Britomart Transport Centre to Parnell and Newmarket (every 10–20min; 10min).

BY BUS

Departures Most buses don't depart from the Britomart Transport Centre (see above) but from any of a couple of dozen stops along city streets within a 10min walk of there. It is confusing, so ask at Britomart or get the exact stop location from ⓦ at.govt.nz. The Link buses listed below are the most useful services.

Fares For buses other than the Link, AT HOP fares are: $1.90 to Parnell, Newmarket, Mount Eden, Ponsonby and

Kingsland; $3.30 to MOTAT, the Zoo, Mission Bay and St Heliers.

LINK SERVICES

City Link (Mon–Sat 6.30am–11.30pm every 7–8min; Sun 7am–11pm every 10min; $1; free to AT Hop card users using it to transfer between services). The red buses of this central city service travel the length of Queen St from K' Rd to Britomart Transport Centre then west to Wynyard Quarter.

Inner Link (Mon–Fri 6.30am–11pm, Sat & Sun 7am–11pm; every 10–15min; AT HOP fare $1.90). The single most useful route, with green buses continuously looping through the city, Parnell, Auckland Museum, Newmarket, K' Rd and Ponsonby; buy tickets on the bus.

Outer Link (Mon–Sat 6.30am–11pm, Sun 7am–11pm; every 15min; $1.90–3.40). Orange buses making a larger loop than the Inner Link and visiting Mt Eden, MOTAT and Herne Bay. Connects with the Inner Link in Parnell, the Auckland Museum, Newmarket and in Ponsonby.

OTHER BUS SERVICES

Night bus Journey planner at ⓦat.govt.nz. A series of secure night buses designed to get you home after a night out (Sat & Sun midnight–3.40am; normal fares apply).

Explorer Bus ☎0800 439 756, ⓦexplorerbus.co.nz. Get around the main sights on this commentated hop-on-hop-off bus with two intersecting circuits (9am–4pm; Nov–March every 15min; April & Oct every 20min, May–Sept every 30min; 24hr pass $45, 48hr pass $55, pay cash to the driver).

BY FERRY

The Waitemata Harbour was once a seething mass of ferries bringing commuters in from the suburbs, and ferries remain a fast, pleasurable and scenic way to get around. The main destinations are the Hauraki Gulf islands and Devonport; Rangitoto-bound and several Waiheke-bound ferries also stop at Devonport.

FERRY OPERATORS

Fullers ☎09 367 9111, ⓦfullers.co.nz. Auckland's principal ferry company runs ferries to Devonport, Rangitoto, Waiheke, Rotoroa and Tiritiri Matangi, plus a regular service across the Hauraki Gulf to Coromandel Town ($60 one way): for nondrivers it's a pleasant alternative to taking the bus via Thames.

Sealink ☎0800 732 546, ⓦsealink.co.nz. Car and passenger ferries to Waiheke and Great Barrier islands.

Destinations Coromandel (5–7 weekly; 2hr); Devonport (every 15–30min; 10min); Great Barrier (4–7 weekly; 2–5hr); Motutapu (every second Sun; 35min); Rangitoto (3–5 daily; 25min); Rotoroa Island (late Sept–early April 3–7 weekly; mid April–mid Sept Sat & Sun only; 1hr 15min); Tiritiri Matangi Island (5 weekly; 1hr 30min); Waiheke (every 30min; 35–45min).

BY CAR

With many sights accessible on foot or by public transport, a car isn't a huge advantage in the city centre, though you'll need one to explore the Kumeu wineries and surf beaches of the West Coast.

Car rental The international and major national companies all have depots close to the airport and free shuttle buses to pick you up; smaller companies are mostly based in the city or inner suburbs. In the central city, you'll find several close together on Beach Rd. The main international and local operators are listed in Basics (see page 33).

Buying a car For general advice, consult Basics (see page 34), then peruse the notice boards in hostels, or visit ⓦtrademe.co.nz and ⓦautotrader.co.nz. At Backpacker Car World, 15–19 East St (daily 9am–5pm; ☎09 377 7761, ⓦbackpackercarworld.com), just off K' Rd, where backpackers buy and sell directly to each other, there are also insurance and roadside deals. Alternatively, head to the Auckland Carfair, Ellerslie Racecourse, Greenlane (every Sun 9am–noon; ☎09 529 2233, ⓦcarfair.co.nz), which is well organized, with qualified folk on hand to check roadworthiness.

Driving On first acquaintance, Auckland's urban freeways are unnerving, but driving around Auckland by car isn't especially taxing if you avoid the rush hours (7–9am & 4–6.30pm). Inner-city streets are metered, which means that parking is best done in the multistorey car parks dotted around the city; we've marked the cheapest for short-term stays on our map (see page 76). Some are not open 24hr, so check the latest exit time.

BY TAXI

Taxi ranks are scattered around the city including along Queen St, at Viaduct Harbour and along K' Rd. Alternatively, call Discount (☎09 529 1000, ⓦdiscounttaxis.co.nz) which is cheap, or sustainability-oriented Green Cabs (☎0508 447 336, ⓦgreencabs.co.nz) whose hybrids are only a little pricier. From the city centre to Ponsonby should be $14–16.

BY BIKE

Routes Auckland's hills can make cycling a tiring and dispiriting exercise, compounded by motorists' lack of bike-awareness. However, a few areas lend themselves

AUCKLAND TRANSPORT INFORMATION AND TICKETS

For integrated information on Auckland's buses, trains and ferries consult **AT** (☎09 355 3553, ⓦat.govt.nz), which includes timetables and a journey planner. Alternatively, pick up the five free AT **public transport maps** from Britomart: the *Central Suburbs* region is the most useful.

You can pay cash for bus, train and ferry journeys, but it is much more convenient (and may end up cheaper) obtaining a stored-value tag-on-tag-off **AT Hop card** ($10 nonrefundable) from Britomart, train stations and Fullers ferry offices. Use it for individual journeys (at 10–15percent off the cash fare), or use a top-up machine to buy an **AT Hop day-pass** ($18 for 24hr from your first tag-on) which covers all trains and buses (including Waiheke Island buses) plus Devonport ferries, but not ferries to Rangitoto or Waiheke.

1

to exploration, most notably the delightful harbourside Tamaki Drive which follows the waterfront for 10km to the east of the city centre.

BIKE RENTAL

Adventure Capital 23 Commerce St ☏09 337 0633, ⓦadventurecapital.co.nz. Handy downtown location for low-grade mountain bikes ($35 4hr; $120/24hr) that are ideal for knocking about town, through parks and along the waterfront.

Adventure Cycles 9 Premier Ave, Western Springs ☏09 940 2453, ⓦadventure-auckland.co.nz.

Somewhat inconveniently sited west of the zoo, but a great resource for short-term bike rental (city bikes $15/day; mountain bikes $30/day) and touring bikes ($200/month). Call ahead to make sure they have what you want and for transport details. Mon, Thurs–Sat 7.30am–7pm.

Cycle Auckland Devonport Wharf ☏09 445 1189, ⓦcycleauckland.co.nz. A great selection (from $75/24hr), including road, touring, tandem, hybrid and kids' bikes, plus self-guided and guided tours. The people to talk to if you fancy more than just a meander around town.

INFORMATION

Tourist information i-SITE Auckland has two central visitor centres: 137 Quay St (daily 9am–5pm and sometimes later in summer; ☏09 365 9914, ⓦaucklandnz. com); and the more cramped branch inside the Sky City Casino (daily 9am–5pm; ☏09 365 9914, ⓦaucklandnz. com), on the corner of Victoria and Federal streets. Both stock leaflets from around the country including a number of advertisement-heavy free publications. The Devonport branch at Devonport Wharf (daily 9am–5pm; ☏09 365 9906, ⓦdevonport.co.nz) stocks maps and the free *Old Devonport Walk* leaflet outlining points of historic and architectural interest.

DOC office Inside the Quay St i-SITE (Mid-Oct–April Mon–Fri 9am–5pm, Sat & Sun 10am–4pm; May to mid-Oct Mon–Fri 9am–5pm; ☏09 379 6476, ⓔaucklandvc@doc. govt.nz). Great for hiking information, stocks DOC leaflets and does track bookings for the whole country although it specializes in the Auckland and Hauraki Gulf region.

Maps For most purposes you can get by with the maps in this guide and Auckland Tourism's *Explore* series of free maps available from i-SITE visitor centres, hotels and hostels.

Backpacker information Check the notice boards in hostels, where the adverts cover rides, vehicle sales and job opportunities.

ACCOMMODATION

With efficient door-to-door shuttle services into central Auckland there's little reason to stay at the **airport**, though Auckland is a place where you might choose to stay **outside the city centre**, particularly: Ponsonby, 2km west; Mount Eden, 2km south; Parnell, 2km east; and Devonport, a short ferry journey across the harbour. All are more peaceful than the city centre but still well supplied with places to eat and drink, and access is good on the Inner Link and Outer Link buses (see page 92). **Camping** involves staying further out and it's not really worth the hassle unless you've rented a campervan.

ESSENTIALS

Seasons From December to March you should book ahead. At other times it's less critical, and through the quiet winter

months (June–Sept) you'll be spoiled for choice and significant discounts on room rates can be had; it's worth asking.

Costs Room rates in Auckland are across the board a touch higher than in the rest of the country, though not unreasonably so.

CENTRAL AUCKLAND

International hotels (with high walk-up rates but good weekend and internet deals) brush shoulders with backpacker hostels, many with on-site travel services. Most downtown hostels cram in the beds and, with bars and clubs only a short stagger away, cater to a party crowd. Wherever you stay, you'll probably have to pay for parking.

Attic 15–31 Wellesley St W ☏09 973 5887, ⓦatticbackpackers.co.nz; map p.76. An ancient lift

---

FIRST-NIGHT CAMPING

If you're picking up a car or campervan near the airport after a long flight you may not fancy tangling with central city traffic. The closest appealing **campsite** is *Ambury Regional Park* (see page 97). There are also numerous tempting beachside spots only an hour or two from the airport, including: *Miranda Holiday Park* (see page 115); *Rays Rest Camping Reserve* (see page 115); *Muriwai Motorcamp* (see page 112); *Orewa Beach Top 10 Holiday Park* (see page 113); *Wenderholm Regional Park* (see page 114); *Piha Domain Motor Camp* (see page 111); and *Shakespear Regional Park* (see page 113). There are also places to park up your toilet-equipped campervan (see page 97).

takes you up to this friendly and well-managed, 94-bed backpackers atop a five-storey city hotel. Even the 12- and 10-bed dorms feel spacious, and the mixed and female-only smaller dorms (around $40) often have beds rather than bunks. Common areas include a quiet lounge and BBQ deck. Big dorms $\underline{$33}$, twins $\underline{$95}$

Braemar on Parliament Street 7 Parliament St ☎ 09 377 5463, ⓦ parliamentstreet.co.nz; map p.76. This very welcoming 1901 townhouse B&B in the heart of the city has retained its late Victorian feel. There's a large suite ($450), a smaller en-suite room and two rooms that share a bathroom (all baths are clawfoot), and breakfast is a major affair with dishes cooked to order. There's guest parking and a strong sustainability ethic. $\underline{$280}$

City Lodge 150 Vincent St ☎ 0800 766 686, ⓦ citylodge. co.nz; map p.76. YMCA-run tower block packed with en-suite rooms each with TV, fridge, tea & coffee. While there are no dorms or shared rooms, there are quads ($165; they don't put strangers together in the same room) and there's a decent communal kitchen/lounge. Weekly rates make it good for long stays. $\underline{$99}$

Heritage Auckland 35 Hobson St ☎ 0800 368 888, ⓦ heritagehotels.co.nz; map p.76. Top-class hotel partly fashioned from the original Farmers department store. Occasional bits of aged planking and wooden pillars in public areas augment the high standard fit-out and many rooms have views across the harbour or into the glassed-in atrium restaurant. The outside pool has great views over the city. $\underline{$365}$

Hilton Princes Wharf, 147 Quay St ☎ 09 978 2000, ⓦ hilton. com; map p.76. Fabulously sited on a wharf jutting into the harbour, this majestic hotel comes with a classy restaurant and the *Bellini* cocktail bar. The beautifully decorated rooms all have a terrace or balcony but it is worth paying the extra $80 for a good view. Valet parking $35 a day. $\underline{$380}$

★ **Hotel DeBrett** 2 High St ☎ 09 925 9000, ⓦ hoteldebrett.com; map p.76. The height of Auckland chic, this classy 25-room boutique hotel references its Art Deco origins while adding bold colours and mismatched but complementary furniture. Bathrooms are gorgeous, continental breakfast and wi-fi are included and guests have access to a lovely drawing room with honesty bar. Doubles $\underline{$330}$, suites $\underline{$440}$

Jucy Snooze 62 Emily Place ☎ 09 379 6633, ⓦ jucyhotel. com; map p.76. Budget hotel (by the cars and camper rental people) with decent value and surprisingly quiet (though garishly painted) rooms. Some are small and lack much natural light – the en suites with TV ($129) are considerably nicer. There's a small communal kitchen and lounge, and parking is available for $15/day. Wi-fi for only 30min/day. $\underline{$89}$

Kiwi International 411 Queen St ☎ 0800 100 411, ⓦ kiwihotel.co.nz; map p.76. Rambling 120-room budget hotel, where basic rooms have just a bed, hand basin, small desk and tea-making facilities: en suites add a TV ($99), or

go for an apartment with full cooking kit ($169). Limited off-street parking and a few rooms overlook Myers Park. Rates increase on Friday and Saturday nights. $\underline{$105}$

Nomads Auckland 16–20 Fort St ☎ 0508 666 237, ⓦ nomadshostels.com; map p.76. Classy conversion of a city office building into an upscale hostel with women-only dorms, rooftop kitchen and outdoor barbecue area. There's also a spa pool, sauna, good travel desk and the lively *Fort Street Union* bar, which offers very cheap meals to guests. Dorms have 6–12 beds and there are en-suite 4-shares ($37). Dorms $\underline{$25}$, en-suite doubles $\underline{$96}$

★ **The Quadrant** 10 Waterloo Quadrant ☎ 09 984 6000, ⓦ thequadrant.com; map p.76. Designer hotel chic without the high prices, this four-star place has a fresh appearance and great city and harbour views from the balcony of most of its 270 rooms. Most come with kitchenette and some have a washing machine and dishwasher. There's also a compact and intimate bar, a breakfast and lunch café, spa, sauna, plus a small gym. Studios $\underline{$220}$, one-bed apartments $\underline{$250}$

Scenic Hotel 380 Queen St ☎ 09 374 1741, ⓦ scenichotels.co.nz; map p.76. Good mid-range hotel with lobby areas restored to their Art Deco glory. Many of the hundred rooms have city views and/or full kitchens and there's a small fitness room. $\underline{$299}$

YHA Auckland City 18 Liverpool St ☎ 09 309 2802, ⓦ yha.co.nz; map p.76. This large, refurbished YHA has seven floors of mostly twin and double rooms – the upper ones with fine city views – plus four-shares ($42) and well-equipped common areas. No dedicated parking but 2Gb free wi-fi a day. Single-sex and mixed dorms $\underline{$38}$, doubles $\underline{$120}$

★ **YHA Auckland International** 5 Turner St ☎ 09 302 8200, ⓦ yha.co.nz; map p.76. This purpose-built 168-bed establishment comes with spacious single-sex dorms and four-shares ($35), en suites ($108), excellent cooking facilities, separate TV and quiet lounges, a travel centre and wi-fi (free 2Gb a day). There are even a few free parking spaces; book early. Dorms $\underline{$36}$, doubles $\underline{$120}$

PARNELL

Parnell is OK for B&Bs and hostels, is close to the Auckland Museum, has plenty of places to eat and drink and has good Inner and Outer Link bus connections.

Ascot Parnell 32 St Stephens Ave ☎ 09 309 9012, ⓦ ascotparnell.com; map p.74. Tranquil, comfortable Belgian-run B&B in a small, modern apartment block, with two mini-suites and a huge harbour suite. An enormous guest lounge with balcony overlooks the city and harbour, and there's a 12m pool, lift access from the secure parking, free wi-fi and computer, and airport pick-up (for a small fee). Try the signature savoury Flemish toast for breakfast. $\underline{$295}$, harbour suite $\underline{$375}$

City Garden Lodge 25 St George's Bay Rd ☎ 09 302 0880, ⓦ citygardenlodge.co.nz; map p.82. Friendly

1

TOP 5 ROOMS WITH A VIEW

Hilton see page 95
The Quadrant see page 95
Ascot Parnell see page 95
Peace and Plenty Inn see page 97
Takapuna Beach Holiday Park see page 97

backpackers in a large, well-organized villa originally built for the Queen of Tonga, and surrounded by lawns. Along with spacious dorms and some lovely doubles/twins there are little touches such as hot water bottles in winter and a barbecue to use. Dorms $28, doubles $89

Lantana Lodge 60 St George's Bay Rd ☎09 373 4546, ⓦlantanalodge.co.nz; map p.82. Clean and friendly hostel with a maximum of 25 guests, free local calls and a homely feel. Family rooms are $109. Dorms $27, doubles $75

Parnell Pines 320 Parnell Rd ☎09 358 0642; map p.82. Compact and simple hotel right in the heart of Parnell. Rooms are fairly small but there are some good views and kitchenettes are available. Off-street parking. $105

PONSONBY AND HERNE BAY

Ponsonby isn't especially close to the main sights, but its B&Bs and hostels are well-sited for the Ponsonby Rd café, bar and shopping strip. The Inner Link bus runs right along Ponsonby Rd.

Abaco on Jervois 59 Jervois Rd ☎0800 220 066, ⓦabaco.co.nz; map p.85. Stylish motel with off-street parking, unlimited free wi-fi, Sky TV and a/c in all rooms. Choose from compact studios, spacious rooms with cooking facilities and deluxe 2-bed suites with spa baths. $160, two-bed suite $250

Brown Kiwi 7 Prosford St ☎09 378 0191, ⓦbrownkiwi.co.nz; map p.85. Compact, home-away-from-home hostel in a restored Victorian villa on a quiet street close to the Ponsonby cafés. A patio and tiny garden is a relaxing oasis, and though daytime parking isn't great, there are good bus connections. Dorms $32, doubles $84

Great Ponsonby Art Hotel 30 Ponsonby Terrace ☎080 766 792, ⓦgreatpons.co.nz; map p.85. Welcoming boutique hotel based around a restored 1898 villa and boldly decorated in ocean tones and Pacific artworks. You can even choose your own breakfast. Luxurious en-suite rooms, and self-catering courtyard and garden studio units come with Sky TV and artsy books and magazines. $260

★**Ponsonby Backpackers** 2 Franklin Rd ☎09 360 1311, ⓦponsonby-backpackers.co.nz; map p.85. Well-managed hostel in a large villa perfectly sited just off Ponsonby Road. Does all the usual stuff, just better than most. Four-shares and the female-only dorm go for $35. Dorms $33, doubles $82

★**Verandahs** 6 Hopetoun St ☎09 360 4180, ⓦverandahs.co.nz; map p.85. Welcoming backpackers in a pair of grand 1905 villas overlooking a leafy park close to the Ponsonby Rd and K' Rd nightlife. The hostel has spacious 3-, 4- and 5-bed dorms with no bunks, twins and doubles some en suite), limited off-street parking and the main lounge favours piano and guitar over TV. Dorms $34, doubles $88

EPSOM

Epsom is a leafy, affluent suburb, close to the airport, Mount Eden and Newmarket's shopping area, but relatively far from most sights and beaches.

Oaktree Motel 104 Great South Rd ☎09 524 2211, ⓦoaktree.co.nz; map p.88. Upscale motel with modernized studios with a basic kitchen, and one-bed apartments. Some a/c. Studios $120, apartments $185

Off Broadway Motel 11 Alpers Ave ☎09 529 3550, ⓦoffbroadway.co.nz; map p.88. Business-oriented hotel with a/c, soundproofed en-suite studios and several one-bedroom suites with spa bath. There's undercover parking, a small gym, and breakfast can be served in your room. Studios $249, suites $339

Tudor Court Motel 108 Great South Rd ☎09 523 1069, ⓦtudor.co.nz; map p.88. Compact motel with small hotel-style rooms and slightly larger ones with kitchenettes ($179). HD TV with Sky including sport and movies. $159

MOUNT EDEN

Suburban Mount Eden is strong on hostels and B&Bs. The Outer Link bus runs close to all the places listed below.

★**Bamber House** 22 View Rd ☎09 623 4267, ⓦbamberhouse.co.nz; map p.88. Beautifully, well-managed hostel spread across a lovely old two-storey villa and a swish modern house in expansive grounds, plus several en-suite cabins ($100) that come with a kettle and fridge. There's a large lawn out front, as well as movie, games, pizza and poker nights. Dorms $32, doubles $85

Bavaria 83 Valley Rd ☎09 638 9641, ⓦbavariabandbhotel.co.nz; map p.88. The exuberant host has rejuvenated this eleven-room B&B in a quiet suburban villa. Rooms are airy and spacious and the king rooms ($180) have balcony views. With no TV in rooms guests are encouraged to use the big lounge (which does have TV) and deck area. Generous breakfasts are served. $150

Eden Villa 16 Poronui St ☎09 630 1165, ⓦedenvilla.co.nz; map p.88. You're always well looked after at this delightful, art- and antique-filled three-room villa in a quiet street just steps from the Mt Eden shops. One room opens out onto the sunny back garden where superb breakfasts are served on fine mornings. $250

Oaklands Lodge 5a Oaklands Rd ☎09 638 6545, ⓦoaklandslodge.co.nz; map p.88. This large Victorian house right by Mount Eden shops is well-managed and mostly comprises dorms with beds rather than bunks (three-shares $38). Good kitchen and lounge areas plus a packed schedule of film, pizza and curry nights through the busier months. Dorms $30, doubles $85

KOHIMARAMA
Kohi Beach B&B 72 Kohimarama Rd ☎09 521 1715, ⓦkohibedandbreakfast.com; map p.74. Lovely little German-Kiwi-run B&B a short walk from the beach, with a couple of clean, well-appointed rooms (one with sea views; $165), off-street parking and continental breakfast. $150

DEVONPORT
Devonport has a cluster of fine B&Bs, all close to the Devonport ferry and some reasonable cafés (though none of the city's really good restaurants).

★ **Parituhu Beachstay** 3 King Edward Parade ☎09 445 6559, ⓦparituhu.co.nz; map p.87. Helen and Lindsay will look after you at this LGBT+-friendly budget B&B homestay in the heart of Devonport that overlooks the harbour. There's just the one room, a private bathroom, access to a secluded garden and continental breakfast. No credit cards. $155

Peace and Plenty Inn 6 Flagstaff Terrace ☎09 445 2925, ⓦpeaceandplenty.co.nz; map p.87. There's a strong ethical bias to this beautifully presented, Victorian-styled B&B in a grand villa. Kauri floorboards lead through to a lovely veranda, past rooms filled with fresh flowers and stocked with sherry and port. They even put on afternoon teas at weekends ($45). $265

CAMPSITES AND HOLIDAY PARKS
There are several well-equipped motor camps within the city limits that are fine for campervans and offer bargain cabins, though without your own vehicle you'll end up spending a lot of money on buses. Ambury is the nicest spot to pitch a tent.

Ambury Regional Park Mangere, 6km north of the airport ☎09 366 2000; map p.74. Offers basic, flat sites (without power) in a field overlooking the Manukau Harbour – it's a great location for those wanting to rest up after flying into New Zealand. The adjacent farm park (with pigs, sheep, rabbits etc) has toilets and coin-operated showers. Call ahead in winter. Camping per person $15

Auckland North Shore Motels and Holiday Park 52 Northcote Rd, Northcote ☎0508 909 090, ⓦnsmotels.co.nz; map p.74. Well-appointed site with an indoor swimming pool, extensive BBQ areas and a range of apartments ($120) and motel units ($155). Located just off the northern motorway and only a 15min drive from the city centre – bus #922 from lower Albert St, City (and others) stop nearby. Powered tent and van sites $45

★ **Takapuna Beach Holiday Park** 22 The Promenade, Takapuna ☎09 489 7909, ⓦtakapunabeachholidaypark.co.nz; map p.74. Small, perfectly located caravan park that's neither very well equipped nor particularly spacious but you can't beat the views from the waterfront sites ($47). Frequent buses (#822, #839, #858, #879 etc) from lower Albert St in central Auckland. Book ahead as it is popular. Powered tent and van sites $42, kitchen cabins $135

EATING
Auckland has a huge range of places to eat, and standards are generally very high. Daytime cafés often morph into full-blown restaurants, with alcohol consumption becoming an increasingly significant activity, as the night wears on. Britomart and Ponsonby are the big eating destinations but there are plenty of good spots elsewhere. Many new and fashionable haunts don't take bookings, though they're happy to sell you a drink or call you as soon as a table is ready. Don't miss the La Cigale French Market (ⓦlacigale.co.nz) on Sat & Sun in Parnell and Sun only at the Britomart.

THE WATERFRONT
Fine summer days are a perfect time to venture down to the cafés, restaurants and bars of Princes Wharf, Viaduct Harbour and Wynyard Quarter. Some places are ostentatious and soulless, though the best (listed below) have great food and luscious vistas of super-yachts.

Grand Harbour 18 Customs St West ☎09 357 6889, ⓦgrandharbour.co.nz; map p.76. More opulent than most of the city's Chinese places and heavily patronized by the Chinese community, this bustling modern restaurant is popular for business lunches and

CAMPERVAN PARK-UPS
Auckland Council aids those who want to maximise their nights spent outside official campsites by allowing **self-contained campervans** to stay overnight at designated SCC parking areas for $8 per person. No facilities are provided. In summer (Oct–early April), there's a one-night limit though some places allow 2 or 3 nights in winter. Book (and pay) through ⓦauckландcouncil.govt.nz (search for SCC) where there's a full list of sites including most regional parks and a few appealing car parks in the Waitakere Ranges. We've also mentioned campervan parking in a few places in the text.

1

TOP 5 PLACES TO DINE IN STYLE

Bellota see page 99
The Depot see page 99
Orphan's Kitchen see page 101
Ortolana see page 98
Ostro see page 98

serves great *yum cha* (daily 11am–3pm). Daily 11am–3pm & 5.30–10pm.

Jack Tar North Wharf, Wynyard Quarter ☎ 09 303 1002, ⊛ jacktar.co.nz; map p.76. A great spot to soak up the afternoon sun overlooking the fishing boats. A beer and squid rings ($18) is perfect appetizer for pizzas ($18–$24), burgers (from $20.90) and pork belly with *kumara* mash ($32/50). Daily 8am–late.

Soul Viaduct Harbour ☎ 09 356 7249, ⊛ soulbar.co.nz; map p.76. An icon of Auckland's waterfront dining scene, *Soul* is perfect for slick, modern bistro meals or a glass of wine on the terrace overlooking the yachts. Go for mozzarella *fior di latte* ($19) followed perhaps by whole flounder with capers, lemon, parsley, macona almonds ($33). Daily 11am–10pm or much later.

Wildfire Princes Wharf ☎ 09 353 7595, ⊛ wildfirerestaurant.co.nz; map p.76. Flashy Brazilian barbecue restaurant with waterside tables that are perfect for a *caipirinha* cocktail. Their *churrasco* experience ($69.95) involves assorted tapas-style appetizers followed by a vast selection of meats and seafood marinated in herbs, roasted over manuka coals then carved off skewers at the table. Come early and you can drop the tapas for their *churrasco* special (Mon–Wed & Sun noon–3pm & 5–7pm, Thurs–Sat noon–3pm, $49.95). Daily noon–11pm or later.

BRITOMART PRECINCT

Waterside seating is traded for urban chic around the Britomart Precinct, home to some of the city's best dining and chic-est bars, lively day and night.

Better Burger 31 Galway St ☎ 09 303 2541, ⊛ betterburger.co.nz; map p.76. Nothing fancy, just a limited range of straightforward but delicious burgers such as the double cheeseburger, fries and shake combo ($13). Bring a beer from the *Britomart Country Club* next door. Daily 11am–10pm, later on Fri & Sat.

Cassia 5 Fort Lane ☎ 09 379 9702, ⊛ cassiarestaurant. co.nz; map p.76. Not a gloopy curry in sight as top chef Sid Sahrawat draws on his heritage to create magic with the freshest local ingredients and traditional Indian spices. Slink into this stylish basement for starters such as roasted beetroot with crème fraiche, black garlic and almonds ($18), followed by tandoori chicken, vindaloo, fennel ($34). Lunch Wed–Fri noon–3pm, dinner Tues–Sat 5.30–11pm.

Ebisu 116 Quay St ☎ 09 300 5271, ⊛ ebisu.co.nz; map p.76. Classy take on traditional Japanese *izakaya* dining effused with a few European ideas to produce a wonderfully modern combination. Try the ora king salmon with sauted shitake ($28), or small plates such as crisp soft shell crab ($25) and *agedashi* tofu ($16) and enjoy the bare brick decor of the old Union Fish Company premises. Reservation taken for lunch only. Mon–Fri noon–3pm & 5.30pm–late, Sat & Sun 5.30pm–late.

Ima 53 Fort St ☎ 09 377 5252, ⊛ imacuisine.co.nz; map p.76. A relaxed Israeli and Middle Eastern café, where everything they make is super-fresh, including the best falafel in town ($18.50). The Arab chicken *mesachan* (from $17) is also excellent. Brunch is served until 3pm at weekends. Daily 7am–3pm & 6–10pm.

★ **Imperial Lane** 7 Fort Lane ☎ 09 929 2703, ⊛ facebook.com/ImperialLane; map p.76. Industrial-chic café and bar with metal tables flanking a broad service ramp that links through to Queen St. Come for coffee and superb sandwiches and pastries during the day, and return later for drinks and hot dogs such as their Tijuana, stuffed with guacamole, chipotle and jalapeños ($11). Mon 7am–4pm, Tues–Fri 7am–9pm.

Mexico 23 Britomart Place ☎ 09 366 1759, ⊛ mexico. net.nz; map p.76. Kitsch Mexicana decor (all skulls, bullfighting and Frida Kahlo portraits) sets the tone for this fun joint where south-of-the-border staples are replaced by the likes of tacos with poached chicken ($7); *ceviche* with fresh coconut salad ($16); and *quesedillas* with cochinita pibil pork ($16). Kick off with a coriander and lime *agua frescas* ($4) or one of their sixty-odd tequilas then ease into the Mexican beer (from ¢8). No bookings. Daily noon–10pm or later.

★ **Ortolana** 33 Tyler St ☎ 09 368 9487, ⊛ ortolana.co.nz; map p.76. If you desire quality food, expertly presented and served but without fuss or pretension then *Ortolana* is the place for you. Fresh produce from their own farm and trusted suppliers is imaginatively combined into loosely Italian small and large plates like ashed Angus beef, summer squash and anchovy ($32) or crayfish ravioli ($29). The wine list is equally well thought out. Not exactly cheap, but great value for food of this quality. No bookings. Daily 7am–11pm.

Ostro 52 Tyler St ☎ 09 280 3789, ⊛ seafarers.co.nz; map p.76. Sexy brasserie and bar where the unfussy yet superb food is almost upstaged by the spectacular setting, with one entirely-glass wall overlooking the docks and harbour. Come for a meal here – perhaps roast harmony pork belly roll (for two to share; $90) – or just sip a killer cocktail ($15–18) on the more casual city side overlooking Britomart. Daily 7am–11pm.

CITY CENTRE

Away from the water, office workers dine at low-cost Asian restaurants and food halls while a couple of hubs meet the needs of more sophisticated tastes and deeper pockets. A short section of Federal Street at the foot of the Skytower comes packed with top-class places while some former council workshops have been transformed into the City Works Depot (⒲cityworksdepot.co.nz) on the corner of Wellesley and Nelson streets, where cafés, a bakery, a coffee roaster and a bagel shop surround a knot of architecture, design and media businesses.

★ **Bellota** 91 Federal St ☎09 363 6301, ⒲bellota. co.nz; map p.76. Fans of celebrated Kiwi chef Peter Gordon flock to the booths in this retro 1970s cave for his fusion take on Spanish tapas ($7.50–45), such as chorizo and serrano ham croquettes, blue cheese sauce. The name means "acorn", a reference to the acorn-fed pigs that feature on the menu (though there are plenty of veggie options). Daily 4–10.30pm or later.

Bombay Chinese 370 Queen St ⒲bombaychinese. co.nz; map p.76. The food court ambience only detracts a little from this excellent take on Indian-Chinese street food where $14 gets you a huge portion. Sample the legendary "chicken 65" with ginger, garlic, chillies and mustard seeds, and try the super-hot Death Valley chicken ($16) if you dare. Mon–Fri 10am–9pm, Sat & Sun 5–9pm.

★ **The Botanist** City Works Depot, 90 Wellesley St ☎09 308 9494, ⒲botanist.co.nz; map p.76. Creatives from surrounding media and design studios meet at this stylish concrete bunker, softened by bent-ply stools and plants that overflow from the attached florist. Gather around the communal table or perch at the counter and tuck into their passionfruit curd pancakes ($19) or salmon avocado bruschetta ($21). Quality wine and beers accompany Thai food some week night evenings. Mon & Tues 7am–7pm, Wed–Fri 7am–9pm or later, Sat & Sun 8am–2.30pm.

Chuffed 43 High St ☎09 367 6801, ⒲chuffedcoffee. co.nz; map p.76. An oasis of good coffee (cold-drip, batch brewed if you wish) tucked down an unlikely looking alley and even boasting a shaded terrace with outdoor fireplace. Delectable cabinet food is supplemented by house-made crumpets with ginger poached pear, vanilla cream and Canadian maple syrup ($16) or Philly cheese steak ($22). Licensed. Mon–Fri 7am–4pm, Sat 9am–4pm.

★ **The Depot** 86 Federal St ☎09 363 7048, ⒲eatatdepot.co.nz; map p.76. Waiters carrying plates of fresh oysters weave around stools clustered at high tables at this bustling, hip, industrially-styled bar and restaurant run by celebrity chef Al Brown. Quality wine comes by the carafe and the menu offers small plates of cumin-battered warehou tortillas ($18) and large dishes of crisp 'freedom farms' pork hock ($34). They don't take bookings, so add your name to the list and pop across to *Bellota* for a sherry while you wait. Daily 7am–around 11pm.

★ **Federal Delicatessen** 86 Federal St ☎09 363 7184, ⒲thefed.co.nz; map p.76. Brash and confident, this upscale licensed diner is celebrity chef Al Brown's take on

a 1950s New York Jewish deli. Slip into olive green booths or perch at the counter for crispy salmon latkes ($19), a delectable toasted Reuben ($22) and banoffee pie ($12.50). Aucklanders find the lack of espresso a little too authentic, but the bottomless filter coffee ($4) is decent. No bookings. Daily 7am–11pm or later.

Food Alley 9 Albert St ☎09 373 4917; map p.76. A spartan and inexpensive food hall, with over a dozen kitchens exhibiting a strong East Asian bias – *Indian Spice* is particularly good for its tasty biriyani and tikka masala dishes (most $11). Daily 10am–10pm.

★ **Mamak Malaysian** Chancery Square, 50 Kitchener St ☎09 948 6479, ⒲mamakmalaysian.co.nz; map p.76. The fabulously flaky *roti* are made on site at this quick-serve little restaurant known for its *roti* chicken curry ($15.50) but also good for Chinese-style salt and pepper squid ($9.50) and Malaysian tofu salad ($9). Add a *teh tarik* (tea made with condensed milk) for that true Malaysian experience. Licensed and also does takeaways. Tues to Sun 11.30am–3pm & 5–9.30pm.

★ **Mezze Bar** 9 Durham Lane East ☎09 307 2029, ⒲mezzebar.co.nz; map p.76. Relaxed, sepia-toned café and bar serving up predominantly Spanish, Moroccan and Middle Eastern dishes. Great for coffee and a slice of orange almond cake, tapas and meze (mostly $12–17) with sherry or Spanish wine, or dishes such as lamb tajine ($28) or chargrilled salmon Niçoise ($27). Mon & Tues 7am–10.30pm, Wed & Thurs 7am–11pm, Fri 7am–11.30pm, Sat 10am–11.30pm, Sun 10am–10.30pm.

Misters 12 Wyndham St ☎09 379 9939, ⒲misters. co; map p.76. Great little, mostly dairy- and gluten-free breakfast and lunch joint with a frequently changing menu which might include buckwheat griddle cakes with blueberries and coconut yoghurt ($10) or beef and pork-ball tabouleh ($14). Mon–Fri 7am–3pm.

No. 1 Pancake 10 Wellesley St, at Lorne St; map p.76. Bargain hole-in-the-wall serving Korean pancakes with delectable fillings such as pork, red bean, chicken and cheese, or sugar and cinnamon for $3–4.50 each. Mon–Fri 10am–7pm, Sat 11am–6pm.

Tanuki's Cave 319b Queen St ☎09 379 5151, ⒲sakebars.co.nz; map p.76. Excellent *yakitori* and sake bar in a cave-like basement setting, with a more formal restaurant above. Tuck into meaty skewers (around $5 each), octopus balls ($8) or order a *yakitori* set ($17) and wash it all down with sake or Japanese beer. Often busy; no reservations. Daily 5–11.30pm or later.

KARANGAHAPE ROAD AND AROUND

There's a relaxed vibe along Karangahape Road with laidback cafés, an abundance of low-cost international restaurants and a couple of smarter places moving in.

Bestie Cafe St Kevin's Arcade, 179 K' Rd ⒲bestiecafe. co.nz; map p.76. A hip café in a pretty 1920s arcade with

1

potted palms and a fab city view. Tuck into breakfast which might be crushed spiced lentils ($17.50) or flatbread with spicy chorizo ($19.50) or a simple lunch of tandoori fried chicken ($18). Also serves excellent coffee and cake. Mon–Fri 7.30–3pm, Sat & Sun 8.30am–3.30pm.

★ **Coco's Cantina** 376 K' Rd ☎ 09 300 7582, ⍟ cocoscantina.co.nz; map p.76. An offbeat and popular bistro that's Queen of the K' Rd. Its short, rustic-Italian menu might include arancini risotto balls ($13) followed by slow cooked belly pork ($33) or its signature spaghetti and meatballs ($31). The outside tables are great for people-watching, especially on Friday and Saturday nights. No bookings, so grab a glass of wine at the bar and wait your turn. Tues–Sat 5pm–midnight.

★ **Pok Pok** 261 K' Rd ☎ 09 963 9987, ⍟ pokpokthai.co.nz; map p.76. The place is nothing to look at, but the flavours at this modestly priced restaurant leave most Thai places for dead. The pulled chicken spring rolls ($10) are crispy and delicious, the *tom yum* prawn soup ($20) zings with galangal and lemongrass and you must leave room for the dark chocolate chilli mousse ($10) and the black sticky rice with coconut ice cream ($10). Licensed and BYO. Daily 5–10pm.

Rasoi 211 K' Rd ☎ 09 377 7780; map p.76. It feels almost like you're in South India at this budget vegetarian café that dishes up *dosas*, *uttappams* and *thalis* for $13–20; there's also an all-you-can-eat maharajah *thali* for $27. Great Indian sweets, too. Mon–Sat 11am–9pm.

Sri Pinang 356 K' Rd ☎ 09 358 3886; map p.76. A simple but ever-popular Malaysian restaurant where you can start with half a dozen satay chicken skewers and follow with dishes such as *sambal* okra, beef *rendang* or clay-pot chicken rice scooped up with excellent *roti*. Most dishes $15–24. BYO wine or beer from the shop across the road. Mon 5.30–10pm, Tues–Fri 11am–2.30pm & 5.30–10pm, Sat 5.30–11pm.

PARNELL AND NEWMARKET

Neither Parnell nor Newmarket are culinary hotbeds, but both have a respectable range of great places to eat, and Newmarket has got a whole lot trendier with the recent development of food businesses on and around Osborne Lane (⍟ osbornelane.co.nz).

Asian Food Hall Newmarket Plaza, 11 Kent St ☎ 09 529 1868; map p.82. A little slice of East Asia with Malaysian, Thai, Japanese and Chinese places all serving national staples for $10–17. *Laksa House* is particularly good for its *wat tan hor* (fried flat noodles; $12). Daily 10.30am–9pm.

Best Ugly Bagels 3a York St, Newmarket ☎ 09 529 5993, ⍟ bestugly.co.nz; map p.82. The coolest corner of Newmarket centres on this joint where wood-fired Montreal-style bagels are served up inside or out in their courtyard with its outdoor fire. Come early for their breakfast bagel or opt for classics like pastrami, swiss and habanero mustard ($13) or lox and cream cheese ($15). Mon–Fri 7am–3pm, Sat & Sun 8am–3pm.

★ **Domain Ayr Café** 492 Parnell Rd ☎ 09 366 4464, ⍟ facebook.com/domainayrcafe; map p.82. Join the communal table or tuck yourself away with a magazine at this modern organic and free-range café serving Fairtrade organic coffee, all made with organic milk. The recycled-paper menus include the likes of mushroom benny with grilled halloumi and poached egg ($18.50), bubble and squeak (with bacon $18.50) and great salads. Mon–Fri 6.30am–2.45, Sat & Sun 7.30am–2.45pm.

La Cigale Café 69 St George's Bay Rd, ⍟ lacigale.co.nz; map p.82. Hidden away on a Parnell backstreet is this lovely lunch spot that is especially lively at the weekends when it's host to a French market. Superb freshly made sandwiches, salads and quiche, plus plenty of French pastries. They usually open as a bistro on Wednesday evenings, too (three courses $50; see website). Mon–Fri 9am–4pm, Sat 8am–2pm, Sun 9am–2pm.

Mojo 110 Carlton Gore Rd ☎ 09 524 9619, ⍟ mojocoffee.co.nz; map p.82. A former car workshop has been transformed into this slick but welcoming café – one of a chain in Auckland – where great coffee and toothsome muffins supplement the likes of egg and minced beef cheek on rosemary sourdough, and Basque-style baked eggs with capsicum and smoked paprika piperade (both $17). Mon–Fri 7am–4.30pm, Sat 8am–4pm.

Non Solo Pizza 259 Parnell Rd ☎ 09 379 5358, ⍟ nonsolopizza.co.nz; map p.82. As the name says, not just pizza, but they do create wonderfully thin-crust concoctions with classic Italian toppings. Pasta and assorted *secondi piatti*, such as traditional Neopolitan *zuppa di pesce*, is served inside or on the intimate patio, tucked behind *Osteria*. Daily noon–10pm or later.

★ **Oh Calcutta!** 151 Parnell Rd ☎ 09 377 9090, ⍟ ohcalcutta.co.nz; map p.82. Bronzed statues of Shiva and Ganesh look down on diners in this curry restaurant that picks the best dishes from across the subcontinent – Malabar prawn cutlets with coriander and coconut cream ($26) or Kadhai paneer masala ($23) – and imbues them with wonderfully distinct flavours. Mon 5.30–10.30pm, Tues–Fri noon–10.30pm, Sat & Sun 5.30–10.30pm.

MOUNT EDEN AND DOMINION ROAD

Dining options in Mt Eden Village are getting better all the time while the strip along Dominion Road is home to one of the city's densest concentrations of cheap East Asian restaurants.

Eden Noodles 105 Dominion Rd ☎ 09 630 1899; map p.88. Go for the hand-pulled Dan Dan noodles with Sichuan sauce and crunchy pork at this ever-popular joint. Tues–Sun 11am–9.30pm.

★ **Olaf's** 1 Stokes Road, Mt Eden ☎ 09 638 7593, ⍟ olafs.co.nz; map p.88. Casual café that's best for superb baked goods like the rhubarb galette, ginger torte or a couple of Portuguese specialities – *pastel de nata* and *barquinhos de coco* (all under $5). Their breads (available by the loaf) work perfectly in their roast chicken ficelle ($13.50) and Reuben on rye ($14.50). Mon–Fri 6.30am–4pm, Sat & Sun 7am–5pm.

The Return of Rad 397 Mt Eden Rd, Mt Eden ☎09 631 5218, ⓦthereturnofrad.co.nz; map p.88. Hipster cool breaks out in Mt Eden at this great little café which, naturally, serves cold-drip single-origin coffee along with excellent espresso. Smart (often bearded) staff navigate the rough-brick and bare-bulb interior serving the likes of mushrooms with goat curd cheese and truffle oil ($17.50), pork *bánh mì* ($14.50) and fresh-squeezed juices and smoothies ($7). Mon–Sat 6.30am–4pm, Sun 8am–4pm.

TAMAKI DRIVE: OKAHU BAY AND MISSION BAY

Dining along Auckland's beach strip can be a hit-and-miss affair, but these spots are reliably good.

The Attic upstairs at 55 Tamaki Drive ☎09 521 0000, ⓦtheatticbar.co.nz; map p.74. Reliable spot for a beer or a cocktail, especially if you score a seat on the terrace overlooking the park and beach. The tap beer is boring but there are plenty of good wines by the glass and meals like pork ribs in Jack Daniels BBQ sauce ($29). Mon–Thurs 4–10pm, Fri noon–11pm or later, Sat & Sun 11am–11pm.

Café on Kohi 237 Tamaki Drive, Kohimarama ☎09 528 8335, ⓦkohicorner.nz; map p.74. A touch more formal than other Tamaki Drive cafés, and a dollar or two more expensive, but worth it for the best café food in these parts and great views across the beach to Rangitoto. The associated *The Store on Kohi*, around the corner in the same building, does superb pastries, savouries, gelati and coffee all to take away and eat on the beach. Daily 7am–4pm.

PONSONBY

Fashion-conscious foodies should make for Ponsonby, where devotion to style is as important as culinary prowess. But don't be intimidated; the food is excellent and competition keeps prices reasonable. There are stacks of excellent cafés (nowhere below par lasts long) so we've selected a few of the more unusual or tucked-away places. First stop should be Ponsonby Central, 136 Ponsonby Rd (ⓦponsonbycentral.co.nz), a dense knot of mostly excellent cafés, restaurants and food stores – including a crêperie, fish and chips, coffee roastery – that's always buzzing.

Blue Breeze Inn 136 Ponsonby Rd ☎09 360 0303, ⓦthebluebreezeinn.co.nz; map p.85. Hawaiian bar meets modern Chinese cuisine at this bustling Ponsonby Central darling where a rum cocktail is the perfect aperitif for the likes of tiger prawn and sesame dumplings ($12), stir-fried wagyu beef ($28) and roasted duck with hoisin sauce ($35). Daily noon–10pm or later.

Burger Burger Ponsonby Central, 136 Ponsonby Rd ☎09 360 8030, ⓦburgerburger.co.nz; map p.85. An oh-so-very-Ponsonby burger joint where the chicken burger (thigh meat with red pepper salsa; $13) comes with potato

skins and aioli and either a super-rich milkshake (organic milk, naturally) or champagne. Decadent and delicious – and available eat-in or takeaway. Mon–Thurs & Sun 11.30am–9.30pm, Fri & Sat 11.30–10pm.

Conch 115a Ponsonby Rd ☎09 360 1999, ⓦconch.co.nz; map p.85. Cult vinyl-heavy record store which is increasingly becoming a cool café and bar. It's perfect for a sidewalk coffee, or slip into a booth out back for Venezuelan flatbreads stuffed with pork *carnitas* and pickles or one of their wood-fired pizzas ($24) with a *caipirinha* or two. Mon–Thurs 4pm–late, Fri–Sun 8am–late.

Dante's 136 Ponsonby Rd ☎09 378 4443, ⓦdantespizzeria.co.nz; map p.85. They keep it simple with wonderful wood-fired pizza ($20–35) done the Neapolitan way – they've even got special certification from Naples – using only the freshest ingredients. Just a couple of starters and salad options and only three wines, all Italian, and Peroni on tap. Daily 10am–10pm.

Dizengoff 256 Ponsonby Rd ☎09 360 0108; map p.85. Buzzy breakfast and lunch café specializing in wonderful bagels, eggs with fried pastrami and other Jewish deli favourites, plus luscious chargrilled vegetables, all at reasonable prices. No alcohol. Mon–Fri 6.30am–4pm, Sat & Sun 6.30am–4pm.

Il Forno 55 Mackelvie St; map p.85. Simple daytime bakery and café, especially notable for its delectable made-on-the-premises cakes, pastries and coffee, but also doing fine sandwiches, rolls and cannelloni, lasagne and chicken schnitzel lunches (10.30am–1.30pm; $12). Daily 6.30–3pm.

Nishiki 100 Wellington St ☎09 376 7104, ⓦnishiki.co.nz; map p.85. Authentic, loud and busy *izakaya* (on the outskirts of Ponsonby, in Freemans Bay) with a vast menu of freshly cooked goodies. Try the pork belly skewers ($5), crispy *gyoza* ($7), okra tempura ($7) and made-to-order sushi. Licensed and BYO. Tues–Sun 6–10.30pm.

Orphans Kitchen 118 Ponsonby Rd ☎09 378 7979, ⓦorphanskitchen.co.nz; map p.85. Bright, fresh and imaginative restaurant where bookings are absent and tables often communal. By the time you read this the shared plates (around $25) almost certainly won't include smoked salmon with celeriac, black rice, apple and horseradish or braised venison shin with swede, feijoa and rainbow chard, but you get the idea. A well-thought-out wine list helps things along and they even open for only slightly less adventurous brunches. Mon 7am–2.30pm Tues–Fri 7am–2.30pm & 5pm–late, Sat 8am–2.30pm, 5pm–late, Sun 8am–2.30pm.

★ **Ponsonby Road Bistro** 165 Ponsonby Rd ☎09 360 1611, ⓦponsonbyroadbistro.co.nz; map p.85. Blackboard specials lend a relaxed ambience to this consistently good, casually sophisticated restaurant where pork, venison and prune terrine with pickled vegetables ($20) might be followed by chargrilled steak and chips ($33) or gourmet pizza ($25). Mon–Sat 4pm–late, plus lunchtime Fri.

1

★ **Satya** 17 Great North Rd ☎ 09 361 3612, ⓦ satya. co.nz; map p.85. This excellent South Indian place steps outside the usual range of curries with the likes of *bhel puri* ($8) followed by *murg badami* with almonds and marinated chicken ($22). Lunches from $10. Licensed & BYO. Mon–Sat noon–1.30pm & 6–9.30pm, Sun 6–9.30pm.

★ **SPQR** 150 Ponsonby Rd ☎ 09 360 1710, ⓦ spqrnz. co.nz; map p.85. Dimly lit and eternally groovy restaurant/bar with a strong LGBT+ following that's always popular for its quality Italian-influenced food. The crispy pizzas ($26) are superb and there's nothing the slightest bit shabby about the likes of roast snapper on saffron lime risotto ($36) or veal *scallopine* ($33). Many treat it more as a bar and venue for spotting actors and rock stars. Excellent cocktails and a wide range of wines (sold by the glass). Daily noon–11pm or much later.

The Unbakery 1a Summer St ☎ 09 555 3278 ⓦ littlebirdorganics.co.nz; map p.85. Not just an unbakery, this oh-so-fashionable café also uncooks breakfast and lunch using (mostly) raw organic ingredients. Expect the likes of raw corn taco with spiced Mexican mushrooms and cooked black beans ($18.50), a changing roster of flavoured kombucha, cold brewed filter coffee served on ice (with hazelnut milk if you wish) and delicious cakes from the counter. Daily 7am–4pm.

DEVONPORT

Bema Takeaways 87 Vauxhall Rd ☎ 09 445 4441; map p.87. On a nice evening it's hard to beat fish and chips or a straightforward burger on the adjacent Cheltenham Beach. Mon–Wed 4–8pm, Thurs–Sun noon–9pm.

AUCKLAND'S FESTIVALS

As befits a city of its size, Auckland has numerous festivals and annual events. These are some of the best.

JANUARY
Anniversary Day Massive sailing regatta on Auckland's Waitemata Harbour. Last Monday.
International Buskers Festival ⓦ auckland buskersfestival.co.nz. Buskers from around the world take over the city streets. Free. Late January.
Laneway Festival ⓦ auckland.lanewayfestival.com. One-day alt music festival held at Silo Park in Wynyard Quarter with class acts for NZ and abroad – Belle & Sebastian, Flying Lotus and Rackets in recent years. Last Monday.

FEBRUARY
Auckland Pride Festival ⓦ aucklandpride.org.nz. Highlight of the LGBT+ year with lavish gala-night opener, the Big Gay Out one-day festival (ⓦ biggayout. co.nz; second Sun) in Coyle Park, Point Chevalier, just west of the zoo, LGBT+ garden visits, the Pride Parade along Ponsonby Road (third Sat) and a big party to finish. Last 3 weeks.

MARCH
Round the Bays Fun Run ⓦ roundthebays.co.nz. Up to 70,000 people jog 9km along the Tamaki Drive waterfront. First Sunday.
Auckland Arts Festival ⓦ aucklandfestival.co.nz. Major annual international arts and culture festival at venues all over the city with everything from street performances to ballet. Held during two middle weeks of the month.
Pasifika ⓦ aucklandnz.com/pasifika. Twenty thousand people enjoy this free, two-day celebration

of Polynesian and Pacific Island culture – music, culture, food and crafts – at Western Springs Park. Free. Final weekend.
Easter Show ⓦ eastershow.co.nz. Family entertainment, Kiwi-style, with equestrian events, lumberjack show, wine tasting and arts and crafts, all held at the ASB showgrounds along Greenlane. Easter weekend.

MAY
International Comedy Festival ⓦ comedyfestival. co.nz. Three weeks of performances by the best from New Zealand and around the world; recent acts have included Sara Pascoe and Rhys Darby. End April to May.

JUNE
Matariki ⓦ matarikifestival.org.nz. The Māori New Year, marking the rising of Matariki (the Pleiades) in the winter sky, is marked by music, theatre and exhibitions throughout the month across the city.

JULY
Auckland International Film Festival ⓦ nzff.co.nz. The nationwide film tour usually kicks off in the city where it all started back in 1969. Tickets around $17. Late July to Aug.

DECEMBER
Christmas in the Park ⓦ coke.co.nz/christmas-in-the-park/. Free family music extravaganza in the Domain. Saturday night in mid-Dec.
Franklin Road Christmas Lights Residents decorate their houses with elaborate lights. 1–24 December. Free.

Châteaubriant 87a Vauxhall Rd ☎09 445 002, ⓦchateaubriant.co.nz; map p.87. This little piece of France blends a *boulangerie*, *charcuterie* and *fromagerie* in a tiled former butchers shop. Gather around the communal table for filled baguettes ($8), quiche Lorraine ($6.50) and éclairs or grab a baguette, free-range rotisserie chicken, cheese and pâté for a picnic at the beach. Tues–Thurs 7.30am–3.30pm, Fri–Sun 7.30am–4.30pm.

Devo 23 Wynyard St ⓦfacebook.com/devocoffee; map p.87. Tiny, unassuming place squeezed in next to a hardware store, dishing up top espresso and gluten-free muffins to go – or sit perched in the morning sun. Mon–Fri 5.45am–1pm, Sat & Sun 7am–2pm.

Manuka 49 Victoria Rd ☎09 445 7732, ⓦmanukarestaurant.co.nz; map p.87. Reliable restaurant specializing in pasta, wood-fired pizza (around $26) and the likes of chicken Caesar salad ($20) or seafood chowder ($17.50), but good at any time of the day for light snacks and salads or just for coffee and cake. Daily 7am–9pm or later.

Monsoon 71 Victoria Rd ☎09 445 4263, ⓦmonsoonthai.co.nz; map p.87. Value-for-money Thai/Malaysian place with tasty dishes such as fish and prawns in a red curry sauce ($23.50). Licensed & BYO. Mon–Wed 5–10pm, Thurs–Sat 5–11pm.

TAKAPUNA

★ **Little & Friday** 43 Eversleigh Rd, Belmont ☎09 489 8527, ⓦlittleandfriday.com; map p.74. Make the effort to visit this fabulous café and bakery that has gradually taken over a nondescript suburban strip-mall. Pies, tarts, pastries and cakes are all magic and they operate in the evenings as *Afterhours*, serving a choice of a pizza or a bistro-style dish (both change daily and cost $18–22: check the website for the week's line-up). Café daily 8am–4pm, Afterhours Tues–Sat 5–8pm.

Madam Woo 486 Lake Rd ⓦmadamwoo.co.nz; map p.74. The Auckland branch of this Queenstown darling replicates the original with its lively atmosphere and wide range of Southeast-Asian influenced dishes to die for. Half of foodie Auckland comes here for their famed hawker rolls (chicken, pork or eggplant; $14). Daily 11am–late.

Takapuna Beach Café 22 The Promenade ☎09 484 0002, ⓦtakapunabeachcafe.co.nz; map p.74. High prices are justified by the superb location and great food at this fairly formal café overlooking Rangitoto. Come for smashed eggs, with eggplant, capsicum and ricotta ($24) or wagyu beef burger hand cut truffle chips ($27), or just grab a coffee. The adjacent *Store* serves excellent takeaway coffee, pastries, gelato and some of the city's best fish and chips – perfect for a seawall sunset. Daily 6.30am–8pm.

DRINKING AND NIGHTLIFE

With 1.5 million people to entertain, there's always something going on in Auckland. One of the best ways to see local acts is to attend one of the free summer concerts held in The Domain and elsewhere under the Music in Parks banner (Jan–March; ⓦmusicinparks.co.nz), mostly on Friday, Saturday and Sunday afternoons.

ESSENTIALS

Listings and tickets Find out what's on at the Entertainment Guide section of the bFM radio station website ⓦ95bfm.co.nz or ⓦundertheradar.co.nz, which has links for ticket purchases.

LGBT+ Auckland Auckland has a fairly small but progressive and proactive LGBT+ scene largely woven into the café/bar mainstream of Ponsonby and K' Road, where strip clubs mingle freely with gay bars and cruise clubs. The best way to link into the scene is to pick up the free, monthly *exPress* magazine (ⓦgayexpress.co.nz), found in LGBT+-friendly shops, cafés and bars.

PUBS, BARS, CLUBS AND LIVE MUSIC

As elsewhere in the country, the distinction between eating and drinking places is frequently blurred. The places listed below concentrate on the drinking, though even basic pubs serve simple meals. Closing times are relaxed, with rowdier places staying open until 3am at weekends.

The clubbing torch currently burns brightest around Britomart and Viaduct Harbour, where you can join the nightly flow of young things meandering between venues. Unless someone special is on the decks or a band is playing, most clubs are free early in the week, charge $5–10 on Thursday and over $10 on Friday and Saturday. Lots of pubs and bars double as venues for live acts, employ DJs or put on some form of entertainment.

Many of the clubs have one area set up as a stage, and on any night of the week you might find top Kiwi acts and even overseas bands blazing away in the corner; a few pubs may also put on a band from time to time. Big acts from North America and Europe visit sporadically and tend to play only in Auckland, usually in the larger venues.

THE WATERFRONT

Cowboys 95 Customs St West ☎09 377 7778; map p.76. Faux-Western bar where the trick is to knock back a few bourbons or tequilas, help yourself to a cowboy hat and dance around to 1980s music. It might sound cheesy but everyone has a great time. Daily noon–midnight or later.

O'Hagan's 103 Customs St West ☎09 363 2106, ⓦohagans.co.nz; map p.76. Irish-themed pub spilling out onto the Market Square. Guinness, Kilkenny and English ales on tap, a good range of meals (pie and a pint $22.50), big-screen sports and live music on weekends. Daily 8am–10pm or later.

1

BRITOMART

1885 Britomart 27 Galway St ☎ 09 551 3100, ⓦ 1885. co.nz; map p.76. Ever-popular martini bar and club where there's almost always a DJ or two on the platters and cocktails are raised to a fine art. Befriend a member to get into the plush New York-clubby *Basement* bar. Wed–Sat 8pm–4am.

Brew on Quay 102 Quay St ☎ 09 302 2085, ⓦ brewonquay.co.nz; map p.76. Seek out one of the semi-private rooms or the rooftop deck in this historic former Wharf Police building where craft beer is king. Try the frequently changing roaster of guest tap beers with a 5-beer sample paddle ($22) or trawl the strong selection of wines, whiskies (including Japanese, Indian and NZ variants). There are quality pub meals (lunch specials $10, otherwise mostly $20) and live music at weekends. Daily 11am–11pm or later.

Britomart Country Club 31 Galway St ☎ 09 303 2541, ⓦ britomartcountryclub.co.nz; map p.76. Buzzing garden bar linked to *1885 Britomart*, and when it rains there's weather protection and cheaper beer. Coffee and fresh juices served during the day give way to shared jugs of Thai punch ($35) poured into jars and a menu of *kumara* fries, squid rings, burgers and sandwiches ($8–16). DJs most nights. Daily noon–midnight.

Xuxu Cnr Galway St & Commerce St ☎ 09 309 5529, ⓦ xuxu.co.nz; map p.76. Though it calls itself a dumpling bar (the prawn *har gao* and chicken potstickers are delicious) this is really an exotic little cocktail bar, perfect for that pre-dinner drink or late-night tipple. Mon & Tues 4pm–late, Wed–Fri noon–late, Sat 5pm–late.

CITY CENTRE

Brothers Beer 90 Wellesley St, ☎ 09 366 6100, ⓦ brothersbeer.co.nz; map p.76. Top-class beer and cider (plus a selected number of wines) at this casual City Works Depot brewpub with 18 beers on tap, including their own contributions. A 5-beer tasting paddle ($20 for Brothers, $25 for others) is a great starting point and the tables outside are a fine spot for one of their thin-crust pizzas. Daily noon–10pm.

Globe 229 Queen St, under Base Auckland hostel ☎ 09 357 3980, ⓦ globeauckland.wordpress.com; map p.76. Long, thin, noisy backpackers-get-drunk bar that's full most nights of the week. Nightly 6pm–late.

Sweat Shop Brew Kitchen 7 Sale St, Freeman's Bay ☎ 09 307 8148, ⓦ sweatshopbrew.co.nz; map p.76. Big, open semi-industrial space (a former garment factory, hence the name) and a massive deck that's ideal for sampling their house-brewed beers and a slab of pork or beef from their smokehouse grill. Daily 11.30am–10pm/late.

KARANGAHAPE ROAD AND NEWTON

Family Bar 270 K' Rd ☎ 09 309 0213, ⓦ facebook.com/FamilyBar; map p.76. Lively, predominantly LGBT+ bar

that welcomes all comers for drinks during the day and plenty of action at night – karaoke on Wed, DJs Thurs–Sat and drag shows from 1am on Fri and Sat nights. Daily 9.30am–4am.

★ **Galbraith's Alehouse** 2 Mount Eden Rd, Newton ☎ 09 379 3557, ⓦ alehouse.co.nz; map p.76. The closest Auckland gets to an English pub, with some of NZ's finest English-style ales brewed on site plus guest beers by other craft brewers and fifty-odd bottled varieties. Very good bar meals kick off with stuffed jalapeños ($12) and include burger and fries ($18), Thai red chicken curry ($20) and chargrilled Scotch fillet ($25). Tues–Sat noon–11pm, Sun & Mon noon–10pm.

Shanghai Lil's 335 Karangahape Rd ☎ 09 309 0213, ⓦ alehouse.co.nz; map p.76. Cocktail and piano bar with fabulous décor and dim lighting. There's comfy seating and a dance floor depending on your mood; it's LGBT+ friendly and with mellow music and swing jazz vibes. Wed–Sun 5pm–3am.

PONSONBY

★ **Dida's** 54 Jervois Rd ☎ 09 376 2813, ⓦ didas.co.nz; map p.85. The smart set flocks to this classy tapas bar and wine lounge, sinking into the leather sofas to choose from a fantastic wine selection and an array of delectable small plates such as snapper cakes ($12) or lamb *pincho* ($13). Daily noon–midnight.

Golden Dawn 134 Ponsonby Rd ☎ 09 376 9929, ⓦ goldendawn.co.nz; map p.85. Listen for the clamour or follow the cool folk to this quirky and unconventional, signage-free corner bar. The music (sometimes live) is always a treat, so grab a pre-dinner craft beer or wine and make yourself at home in the grungy courtyard. Stay for something from their small but considered menu or dine elsewhere and return when things hot up. Tues–Thurs 4pm–late, Fri & Sat 3pm–1am, Sun 3am–midnight.

Mea Culpa 175 Ponsonby Rd ☎ 09 376 4460; map p.85. There's a cosy feel to this tiny bar where you can sit outside on wrought-iron chairs on the Turkish rug. Tues & Wed 5pm–Midnight, Thurs 3pm–1am, Fri & Sat 3pm–3am, Sun 5pm–1am.

The Whiskey 210 Ponsonby Rd ☎ 09 361 2666; map p.85. Stylish bar with something of the feel of a groovy gentleman's club, all chocolate leather sofas and white brick walls hung with superb photos of Little Richard, the New York Dolls, Jimi Hendrix and more. Great cocktails ($17–20). Daily 5pm–3am.

NEWMARKET

The Lumsden 448 Khyber Pass Rd ☎ 09 550 1201, ⓦ thelumsden.co.nz; map p.82. This is a craft beer bar with a laidback pub-on-the-village-square vibe. Tables spill onto the outside patio, where live musicians play when the weather is fine. They also serve a mennu of above average traditional pub grub, with the likes of

pizza (around $24) and shared platters ($35–45). Daily 3pm–3am.

ENTERTAINMENT

Auckland's theatre, classical music and comedy scene seldom sets the world alight, though it is reasonably lively, and you'll usually have a choice of a couple of plays, comedy and dance or opera. See ⓦ theatrescenes.co.nz for reviews of the latest theatre productions.

Aotea Centre Aotea Square, Queen St ☏ 09 309 2677, ⓦ aucklandlive.co.nz. New Zealand's first purpose-built opera house (Kiri Te Kanawa performed on the opening night in 1990) and the Auckland home of the Royal New Zealand Ballet.

ASB Waterfront Theatre 138 Halsey St, Wynard Quarter ☏ 09 309 3395, ⓦ asbwaterfronttheatre. co.nz. This shiny new cultural space in the developing Wynyard Quarter is the state-of-the-art purpose-built home for the Auckland Theatre Company. It's a mid-size venue that hosts home grown talent and the best touring productions.

Basement Theatre Lower Greys Av (by Civic car park) ☏ 09 309 7433, ⓦ basementtheatre.co.nz. Exciting, edgy performance art theatre. *Basement Theatre* takes a cut of the door revenue rather than charging a fee and there's a real sense of collaboration and community – plus a cool bar. Note that it closes over Christmas and New Year. Tues–Sat 5pm–late.

Civic Theatre Corner of Queen & Wellesley sts ☏ 09 309 2677, ⓦ aucklandlive.co.nz. A lovely theatre that's worth visiting if there's anything at all on; it hosts July's International Film Festival along with musicals and visiting extravaganzas.

The Classic 321 Queen St ☏ 09 373 4321, ⓦ comedy. co.nz. Bar and comedy venue hosting top local names and touring acts. Shows are Mon–Sat with the best line-ups at weekends. $28 for the main acts, $15 for the regular late show (Fri & Sat at 10pm).

Q 305 Queen St ☏ 09 309 9771, ⓦ qtheatre.co.nz. This 2011 purpose-built theatre space is flexible enough to handle everything from Māori contemporary dance to cutting-edge plays and burlesque.

CINEMAS

Academy 44 Lorne St ☏ 09 373 2761, ⓦ academycinemas.co.nz. Dedicated art-house cinema with two screens tucked underneath the main library. Cheaper weekdays before 5pm, and $5 all day Wed.

Rialto 167 Broadway, Newmarket ☏ 09 369 2417, ⓦ rialto.co.nz. Handy 7-screener offering mainstream and slightly left-field fare. Cheap tickets before 5pm on Tues.

Silo Cinema ⓦ silopark.co.nz. Free open-air movies in the main plaza in Wynyard Quarter. Dec–March Fri at 9pm. Market stalls and bar open from 4.30pm.

The Vic 48 Victoria Rd, Devonport ☏ 09 446 0100, ⓦ thevic.co.nz. New Zealand's oldest cinema (built in 1912) has been revived with a programme of mainstream and artier new releases. Tickets are $15 (Tues $10) and Fullers do a $17 deal including return ferry trip from the city. Great for an evening out in Devonport.

SHOPPING

As New Zealand's biggest city, Auckland has its best range of shopping. For high-end fashion, the richest veins run through the Britomart Precinct and along Ponsonby Road with many of the top labels having shops in both locations. Newmarket also has a few notable names, plus a number of more mass-market outlets. Other names to look out for include: Deadly Ponies, Juliette Hogan, Kate Sylvester, Trelise Cooper, Twenty-seven names and World.

ARTS, CRAFTS AND SOUVENIRS

Auckland Museum Store ☏ 09 309 2580, ⓦ aucklandmuseum.com; map p.76. Excellent selection of everything from quality crafts through Kiwiana and classy homeware to books, prints and kids' toys. And every purchase goes to support the museum. Daily 10am–5pm.

Kura 95a Customs St West ☏ 09 302 1151, ⓦ kuragallery.co.nz; map p.76. Classy gallery focused on contemporary Māori art and design.

Everything from paua inlaid bookmarks and greenstone pendants to $2000 korowai feather cloaks and some wonderfully patterned carvings. Mon–Fri 10am–6pm, Sat & Sun 11am–4pm.

FASHION

Karen Walker 18 Te Ara Tahuhu Walking Street, Britomart ☏ 09 309 6299, ⓦ karenwalker.com; map p.76. New Zealand's biggest international brand as worn by Björk, Lady Gaga and many more. The clothes are cute-conservative and she also excels in eyewear and jewellery. Also in Newmarket, Ponsonby and Takapuna. Mon–Fri 10am–6pm, Sat & Sun 10am–5pm.

Strangely Normal 19 O'Connell St, downtown ☏ 09 309 0600, ⓦ strangelynormal.com; map p.76. Witty, modern take on Fifties men's style with some wonderfully bold patterned shirts. Mon–Fri 10am–6pm, Sat 10am–5pm, Sun 11am–4pm.

Zambezi 56 Tyler St, Britomart ☎09 303 1701, ⓦzambesi.co.nz; map p.76. Long-standing and quirky fashion label featuring a lot of black. There's also menswear at this store but not at their Ponsonby branch. Mon–Fri 10am–6pm, Sat 10am–5pm, Sun 11am–5pm.

BOOKSHOPS

Unity Books 19 High Street, downtown ☎09 307 0731, ⓦunitybooks.co.nz; map p.76. Probably the city's best independent bookshop. Mon–Fri 8.30am–7pm, Sat 9am–6pm, Sun 10am–6pm.

The Women's Bookshop 105 Ponsonby Rd, Ponsonby ☎09 376 4399, ⓦwomensbookshop.co.nz; map p.85. Excellent small shop with knowledgeable staff and plenty for men too. Mon–Fri 10am–6pm, Sat & Sun 10am–6pm.

OUTDOOR CLOTHING AND CAMPING

Bivouac 210 Queen St, downtown ☎09 366 1966, ⓦbivouac.co.nz; map p.76. Stocks the best range of quality outdoors gear. Also open similar hours at 312 Broadway, Newmarket. Mon–Thurs 9am–6pm, Fri 9am–7pm, Sat 9am–6pm, Sun 10am–6pm.

Kathmandu 151 Queen St, downtown ☎09 309 4615, ⓦkathmandu.co.nz; map p.76. Budget outdoor-clothing chain where there always seems to be a major sale on, so don't pay full price. Stores across Auckland and nationwide. Mon–Thurs 9am–6pm, Fri 9am–7pm, Sat & Sun 10am–5pm.

DIRECTORY

Consulates Australia Level 7, PWC Tower, 186–194 Quay St ☎09 921 8800, ⓦnewzealand.embassy.gov.au; Canada 9th floor, 48 Emily Place ☎09 309 3690, ⓦcanadainternational. gc.ca; Ireland Level 1, 5 High St ☎09 919 7450, ⓦireland. co.nz; UK Level 17, 151 Queen St ☎09 303 2973, ⓦgov.uk/ world/new-zealand; US Level 3, Citibank Centre, 23 Customs St East ☎09 303 2724, ⓦusembassy.gov.

Emergencies Police, fire and ambulance ☎111; Auckland Central police station, cnr Cook & Vincent streets ☎09 302 6400.

LGBT+ Helpline ☎0800 688 5463, ⓦoutline.org.nz. Operates Mon–Fri 10am–9pm, Sat & Sun 6–9pm.

Internet Libraries have free-use computers and wi-fi. There's also free wi-fi (1Gb/day) in Britomart's outdoor spaces.

Laundry Travellers Laundromat, 458 K'Rd ☎09 376 6062; daily 5am–9.30pm. Parnell Laundry, 409 Parnell Rd, ☎09 373 2680; Mon–Fri 8am–6pm, Sat 8am–5pm, Sun 9am–3pm.

Left luggage Sky City Bus Terminal, 102 Hobson St, has lockers (daily 7am–8pm; small $5 all day, large $8; ☎09 300 6130), and most of the larger hostels also have long-term storage for one-time guests at minimal or no charge. The airport also offers a left luggage service (opposite Quantas check-in), see ⓦbaggagestorage.com.au.

Library Central City Library, 44 Lorne St ☎09 377 0209, ⓦaucklandlibraries.govt.nz; Mon–Fri 9am–8pm, Sat & Sun 10am–4pm.

Medical treatment For emergencies go to Auckland City Hospital, Park Rd, Grafton ☎09 367 0000. The Travel Doctor, Level 1, 170 Queen St (Mon–Fri 9am–5pm; ☎09 373 3531, ⓦwww.traveldoctor.co.nz), offers vaccinations and travel health advice. CityMed, 8 Albert St (Mon–Fri 8am–5.30pm; ☎09 377 5525, ⓦcitymed.co.nz), has doctors and a pharmacy.

Pharmacy Medicines to Midnight, 160 Broadway, Newmarket (Mon–Sat 9.30am–midnight, Sun 10am–midnight; ☎09 520 6634, ⓦmedicinestomidnight.co.nz), is the most convenient late-closing pharmacy. Emergency departments of hospitals (see above) have 24hr pharmacies.

Post office The central city branch at 24 Wellesley St (Mon–Fri 9am–5.30pm; ☎0800 501 501) has poste restante facilities.

Swimming Central pools include the stylishly revamped, indoor Edwardian Tepid Baths at 100 Customs St West (☎09 379 4745), and the lovely open-air saltwater Parnell Baths on Judges Bay Rd (late Nov–Easter Mon–Fri 6am–8pm, Sat & Sun 8am–8pm; ☎ 09 373 3561). Check ⓦaucklandleisure.co.nz for these and others, or simply head for one of the beaches (see pages 83 and 86).

West of Auckland

Real New Zealand begins, for many, in **West Auckland**, where verdant hills and magnificent beaches replace tower blocks, suburbs and sanitized wharves. The suburban sprawl peters out 20km west of the centre among the enveloping folds of the **Waitakere Ranges**. Here, some of Auckland's finest scenery and best adventures can be had little more than thirty minutes' drive from downtown. Despite being the most accessible expanse of greenery for 1.5 million people, the hills remain largely unspoilt, with plenty of trails through native bush – though be aware that kauri dieback (a disease that kills most if not all the trees it infects; see page 716) has forced the closure of a number of tracks.

WEST COAST BEACHES: WALKS, TOURS AND ACTIVITIES

The West Coast's bush-clad hills, steep gullies and wild, open beaches are the setting for a bunch of activities including horseriding in the dunes, sand yachting and a couple of the best canyoning trips around.

HORSERIDING

Muriwai Beach Horse Treks Horse Park, Coast Rd ☎ 09 411 8948, ⓦ muriwaibeachhorsetreks.co.nz. Offers the chance to explore the beach, dunes and pine forests to the north (from $75/2hr). 1hr treks leave daily at 12.30pm, 2.30pm and in summer 4pm, but call ahead. See their website for longer day treks that start in the morning.

SURFING

Muriwai Surf School By the beach ☎ 021 478 734, ⓦ muriwaisurfschool.co.nz. Rents surf gear (board and wetsuit $30/2hr) and bodyboards ($10/hr), and conducts surf lessons (introductory $70, advanced $120).
Piha Surf School 138 Seaview Rd ☎ 09 812 8123, ⓦ pihasurfschool.com. Mike Jolly sells his own handcrafted longboards and a good range of secondhand boards from what is essentially

Piha's surf central. Whether you're a beginner or an advanced surfer you can book one-on-one (from $120/1hr 30min) or group lessons (from $70/1hr 30min).

CANYONING

AWOL Adventures ☎ 0800 462 965, ⓦ awoladventures.co.nz. About the most fun you can have in a wetsuit around Auckland is canyoning, a combination of swimming, abseiling, jumping into deep pools and sliding down rock chutes. AWOL run excellent trips in two canyons near Piha, with pick-ups at SkyCity in Auckland. In Piha Canyon the emphasis is on abseiling, particularly on their full-day trip ($215). The lower canyon is host to the half-day trip ($185) and night canyoning ($215; mostly in winter) with just a headtorch and glowworms for illumination. Bring your swimsuit, a towel and a pair of old trainers.

The soils around the eastern fringes of the Waitakeres nurture long-established **vineyards**, mainly around Kumeu and on hot summer days, thousands head over the hills to one of half a dozen thundering **West Coast surf beaches**, largely undeveloped but for a few holiday homes (known as *baches*), the odd shop and New Zealand's densest concentration of surf-lifesaving patrols.

GETTING AROUND   **WEST OF AUCKLAND**

By train Auckland's suburban trains make it to the outlying communities of Henderson and Waitakere but don't get you to the wineries or beaches.
By car The easiest access to the majority of the walks

and beaches is via the Waitakere Scenic Drive (Route 24), which winds through the ranges from the dormitory suburb of Titirangi, in the foothills past the informative Arataki Visitor Centre.

Kumeu and Huapai

Once a viticultural powerhouse, West Auckland has been eclipsed by bigger enterprises elsewhere. There is still some production, centred on the contiguous and characterless communities of **KUMEU** and **HUAPAI**, though much of the grape juice comes from Marlborough, Gisborne and Hawke's Bay.

As early as 1819 the Reverend Samuel Marsden planted grapes in Kerikeri in the Bay of Islands, ostensibly to produce sacramental wine. But commercial winemaking didn't get under way until Dalmatians turned their hand to growing grapes, after the kauri gum they came to dig ceased to be profitable. Many of today's businesses owe their existence to immigrant families, a legacy evident in winery names such as Babich, Nobilo, Selak and Soljan. The region's vines still produce Pinot Noir, Pinot Gris and superb Chardonnay. If you plan some serious tasting, designate a non-drinking driver or join Fine Wine Tours (see page 110).

1

By bus It's possible to get the bus to Kumeu and Huapai (#110 & change for #122; check ⓦ at.govt.nz for schedules) but you're lost without transport once you get there. Drive or take a wine tour.

Information The free *Kumeu Wine Country* booklet details almost a dozen wineries that can be visited.

EATING AND DRINKING

★ **Hallertau Brewbar & Restaurant** 1171 Coatsville Riverhead Hwy, off SH16 ☎ 09 412 5555, ⓦ hallertau.co.nz. Airy restaurant/bar and refreshing alternative to the wineries hereabouts. Sink a pint or two of their superb brewed-on-the-premises kolsch, pale ale, red ale, schwartzbier and cider, or try a tasting "paddle" of five ($12–16). Afterwards, tuck into light snacks ($14–16) or full meals such as wood-grilled gurnard, jerk spatchcocked chicken or hopped beef burger ($22–41). Daily 11am–midnight.

★ **The Riverhead** 68 Queen St, Riverhead ☎ 09 412 8902, ⓦ theriverhead.co.nz. Mangrovy tentacles of the Waitemata Harbour reach up to one of New Zealand's oldest taverns. Grab a beer and play pool in the public bar or head for the lounge bar for peri peri chicken nibbles ($18), beer battered fish and chips ($28) or pizza ($20)

under the oaks at high water. Mon–Fri 11am–10pm or later, Sat & Sun 10am–10pm or later.

THE WINERIES

Kumeu River 550 SH16, Kumeu ☎ 09 412 8415, ⓦ kumeuriver.co.nz. The Brajkovich family produces several of New Zealand's finest Chardonnays, all grown hereabouts. Generous tastings, including three single-vineyard varieties, make this an essential stop. Mon–Fri 9am–4.30pm, Sat 11am–4.30pm.

Soljans 366 SH16, Kumeu ☎ 09 412 5858, ⓦ soljans. co.nz. Quality winery making locally grown Pinot Gris and a fun sparkling Muscat. There are free tastings and a smart but casual café serving the likes of beer-battered fish ($26.50) or a Mediterranean platter for two ($55). Daily 9am–4pm.

Waitakere Ranges and the West Coast beaches

Auckland's western limit is defined by the bush-clad, 500m-high **Waitakere Ranges**, perennially popular with weekending Aucklanders intent on a picnic or a stroll, though a range of measures are in place to protect its ancient trees from the spread of kauri dieback. The western slopes roll down to the wild, gold-and-black-sand **West Coast beaches** of Whatipu, Karekare, Piha and Muriwai. A counterpoint to the calm, gently shelved beaches of the Hauraki Gulf, these tempestuous shores are pounded by heavy surf and punctuated by precipitous headlands threaded by moderate walks.

Brief history

The Kawerau a Maki people knew the region as **Te Wao Nui a Tiriwa** or "the Great Forest of Tiriwa", aptly describing the kauri groves that swathed the hills before the arrival of Europeans. By the turn of the twentieth century, diggers had pretty much cleaned out the kauri gum, but logging continued until the 1920s, leaving the land spent. The Auckland Council bought the land, built reservoirs and designated a vast tract as the **Centennial Memorial Park**, with 200km of walking tracks leading to fine vistas and numerous waterfalls that cascade off the escarpment.

Arataki Visitor Centre

300 Scenic Drive • May–Aug daily 10am–4pm; Sept–April daily 9am–5pm • ☎ 09 817 0077

The best introduction to the area is the **Arataki Visitor Centre**, entered past a striking *pou*, or guardian post created from a fallen kauri by Te Kawerau a Maki carvers. Duck into the ground-floor auditorium for the inspiring **movie** about the Waitakeres (12min; on demand; free) then head upstairs for more carvings and displays on the area. Outside, walkways forge into the second-growth forest: the ten-minute plant identification loop trail identifies a dozen or so significant forest trees and ferns; a longer trail (45min) visits one of the few mature kauri stands to survive the loggers. Arataki is also the place to pick up leaflets and maps for the numerous **short walks** in the ranges (see page 109). Up to five self-contained campervans can park here for one night, or two in winter (see page 97).

WAITAKERE WALKS AND THE HILLARY TRAIL

The Waitakeres have some beautiful walks to waterfalls, kauri trees and lookouts over the wild ocean but some of them are currently closed because of the devastating spread of kauri dieback and a **rahui** (a cultural restriction) has been placed on the ranges by the local Māori *iwi*, Te Kawerau a Maki. Arataki Visitor Centre is the place to go for information. The maps in several free leaflets – *Te Henga (Bethells Beach) and Cascade Kauri, Piha, Karekare and Anawhata* etc – are fine for most walks, though for the Hillary Trail you'll need the comprehensive *Waitakere Ranges Regional Park Recreation map* ($5).

WAITAKERE WALKS

The following walks are listed roughly from south to north.

Omanawanui Lookout Whatipu (1.6km; 3hr; 220m descent). Superb views of the Manukau Harbour and its churning bar are the main reason to tackle this ascent. There's a challenging ridgeline track which has some steep sections that you can continue further on, but this only works if you have someone to drop you off at the start.

Zion Hill–Pararaha Valley–Tunnel Point circuit Karekare (8km; 4hr; 200m ascent). This lovely loop at the south end of Karekare beach follows part of the old Pararaha Tramway to Whatipu visiting an old tunnel that proved too tight a squeeze for a large steam engine whose boiler still litters the shore.

Kitekite Falls Piha (2.8km; 1hr loop; 220m ascent). Starting at Glen Esk Rd car park, this fairly easy track passes the three-stage plunge of Kitekite Falls (totalling 40m), below which is a cool pool.

Lion Rock Piha (500m return; 20–30min; 60m ascent). An energetic climb to a shoulder two-thirds of the way up Lion Rock, best done as the day cools. The summit is out of bounds.

Tasman Lookout Track Piha (1.2km return; 30–40min; 40m ascent). From the south end of the beach this track climbs up to a lookout over the tiny cove of The Gap, where a spectacular blowhole performs in heavy surf.

Auckland City Walk (1hr loop; 1.5km; 50m ascent). Not a city walk at all but a delightful amble which threads its way from Falls Rd car park through native bush, alongside a peaceful stream and offers an adventurous side scramble up to a hidden waterfall.

THE HILLARY TRAIL

In honour of the 2008 passing of New Zealand's mountaineering hero, Sir Edmund Hillary, Auckland has linked a series of existing walking tracks through the Waitakere Ranges into the **Hillary Trail** (76km; 3–4 days; download map at ⓦhillarytrail.org.nz). Running from the Arataki Visitor Centre via Whatipu, Karekare, Piha and Te Henga to Muriwai, it gives a great sense of the region – regenerating rainforest, stands of kauri, rocky shores, black-sand beaches and historic remains. The highest point is only 390m but it is an undulating track and tougher than you might expect. Occasionally slippery, steep paths and unbridged streams can make it a good deal harder in winter, and in any season the last 27km day takes most people at least 10hr.

Nights are generally spent in primitive campsites ($5; book on ☏09 366 2000), though you can stay under a roof in Whatipu, Piha and Te Henga. The best source of on-the-ground information is the Arataki Visitor Centre (see page 108).

Whatipu

45km southwest of the city centre, at the north head of Manukau Harbour

Whatipu is the southernmost of Auckland's West Coast surf beaches and is located by the sandbar entrance to Manukau Harbour, the watery grave of many a ship. The wharf at Whatipu was briefly the terminus of the precarious coastal **Parahara Railway**, which hauled kauri from the mill at Karekare across the beach and headlands during the 1870s. The tracks were continually pounded by surf, but a second tramway from Piha covered the same treacherous expanse in the early twentieth century.

Over the last few decades, the sea has receded more than a kilometre, leaving a broad beach backed by wetlands colonized by cabbage trees, tall toetoe grasses and waterfowl.

1

WEST COAST TOURS

You'll need your own transport to do justice to the beaches and most of the ranges, unless you join one of the West Coast tours, or perhaps join a canyoning trip (see page 107). All trips pick up around central Auckland.

Bush & Beach ☎0800 423 224, ⓦbushandbeach. co.nz. Afternoon trips (12.30–5.30pm; $155) include a short bushwalk to waterfalls and kauri trees, and a visit to Piha beach and Arataki Visitor Centre.

Fine Wine Tours ☎0800 023 111, ⓦinsidertouring. co.nz. Phil Parker personally leads small-group, half-day tours ($199; $30 for optional beer tasting) including three Kumeu wineries, lunch and a visit to Muriwai. Also full-day wine tours to Kumeu ($269) with three wineries

and optional beer tasting, plus tours to Waiheke Island ($439 including classy lunch, premium tasting and ferry tickets).

TIME Unlimited ☎09 846 3469, ⓦnewzealandtours. travel. Personal service and a willingness to go the extra mile characterize these full-day small-group tours which include excellent bushwalking (matched to the group) along with the pounding surf of either Whatipu, Karekare or Piha beaches ($295).

It's a great, wild place to explore, particularly along the base of the cliffs to the north where, in half an hour, you can walk to the **Ballroom Cave**, fitted with a sprung kauri-wood dancefloor around 1900 that apparently still survives, buried by 5m of sand that drifted into the cave in the intervening years. For a longer walk try the track beyond the Omanawanui Lookout (see page 109).

ACCOMMODATION AND EATING WHATIPU

★ **Huia Foodstore** 1194 Huia Rd, Huia, 10km east of Whatipu ☎09 811 8113, ⓦhuiafoodstore.co.nz. On the way to Whatipu the last supplies are from this revamped take on a traditional Kiwi takeaway and café. There's fresh baking, superb espresso, jars of sweets along the walls and scooped ice cream. The takeaways are top notch (fish is freshest on Fri, Sat & Sun) and the waterside park across the road is a perfect spot to take them. Mon–Thurs 8am–4.30pm, Fri–Sun 8am–6pm; check website for reduced winter hours.

Whatipu Lodge ☎09 811 8860, ⓦwhatipulodge.

co.nz. This 1870 former mill manager's house is the only habitation at Whatipu and a great base to experience a wild area of New Zealand, just an hour's drive from Auckland. Twin and single rooms are simple, there's no mains electricity (it generates its own for limited hours) and no mobile phone coverage but there are communal cooking facilities, good hot showers, a tennis court and full-sized billiard table. Bring a sleeping bag or sheets and duvets. Booking is essential. Rooms are charged at $35 per person, but $45 for one-night stays. Camping $7.50, doubles $90

Karekare

Perhaps the most intimate and immediately appealing of the West Coast settlements is **KAREKARE**, 17km west of the Arataki Visitor Centre and accessed along Piha Road, with manuka, pohutukawa and cabbage trees running down to a broad beach and only a smattering of houses. In one hectic year, this dramatic spot provided the setting for beach scenes in Jane Campion's 1993 film *The Piano* and the inspiration for Crowded House's *Together Alone* album. The Karekare Surf Club patrols the beach on summer weekends, or there is a pool below **Karekare Falls**, a five-minute walk on a track just inland from the road. There is nowhere to stay here, and no facilities.

Piha

For decades **PIHA**, 20km west of the Arataki Visitor Centre and accessed along Piha Road, has been an icon for Aucklanders. A quintessential West Coast beach with a string of low-key weekend cottages and crashing surf, it lures a wide spectrum of day-trippers and the party set, whose New Year's Eve antics hastened in a dusk-till-dawn alcohol ban on holiday weekends. Despite the gradual gentrification of the old *baches* and the opening of the modern *Piha Café*, it is hanging onto its rustic charm.

1

The 3km beach is hemmed in by bush-clad hills and split by Piha's defining feature, 101m-high **Lion Rock**. With some imagination, this former *pa* site resembles a seated lion staring out to sea. The rock was traditionally known as Te Piha, referring to the wave patterns around it that resemble the bow wave of a canoe.

Most **swimmers** head for South Piha, where the more prestigious of two surf-lifesaving clubs hogs the best **surf**. *Piha Surf School* sells gear and you can book lessons with them. If battling raging surf isn't your thing, head for **Kitikite Falls**.

ARRIVAL AND DEPARTURE
PIHA

By shuttle Trippy offer a shuttle bus (daily year-round; $25 single, $40 return; ☎021 087 38350, ⊚trippy. co.nz); that runs from Base Backpackers at 9am – though you can pay an extra $5 for pick up. Return journeys are usually at 10.30am, 4pm or 6pm.

ACCOMMODATION

Up to five self-contained campervans can park at the end of Glen Esk Road for one night, or two in winter ($8 per person). Five more can stay at the end of Log Race Road.

Black Sands Lodge 54 Beach Rd ☎021 969 924, ⊚pihabeach.co.nz. A beach-chic style runs through these three tasteful *baches*: a beach cabin and two suites with big decks, French doors and quality furnishings and bedding. The genial hosts will also prepare romantic four-course dinners, served in your suite (around $140 a head, excluding wine). Cabin $140, suites $210

★ **Piha Beachstay** 38 Glenesk Rd ☎09 812 8381, ⊚pihabeachstay.co.nz. Excellent and peaceful backpackers sleeping just ten, uphill from the beach in a green valley. There's a huge garden and living area, and rooms (including one with en suite and bath at $120) that open onto sunny decks. Dorms $40, doubles $89

Piha Domain Motor Camp 21 Seaview Rd ☎09 812 8815. Classic Kiwi campsite, close to the beach with flat camping, fairly simple facilities (though there's a flash bathroom block) and some tiny but well-maintained cabins. Camping $15, powered sites $18, cabins $60

Piha Ocean Lookout 14a Log Race Rd ☎09 812 8207. Set high on a headland about 4km from Piha beach, this B&B has two rooms but they're only let to one party as they share a bathroom and mini-kitchen. There are great views from the lounge or deck where a lovely continental breakfast is served, and clifftop walks (including the Hillary Trail) run right by. $140

EATING AND DRINKING

★ **The Piha Café** 20 Seaview Rd ☎09 812 8808, ⊚facebook.com/thepihacafe. Piha's only real café, a casual but stylish rough-hewn timber place with plenty of seating inside and out. Plenty of good baking, fresh salads, counter food and a blackboard menu of seasonal dishes (mostly $15–25). The coffee's great and they even do takeaway pizzas ($19–25). Hours flexible and much reduced in winter. Licensed. Mon & Wed 8am–3pm, Thurs–Sat 8am–9.30, Sun 8am–5pm.

Piha Stores Seaview Rd ☎09 812 8844. Piha's central store has plenty of groceries and local produce, but they also sell homemade salads, pies and filled rolls (from $5), perfect for a picnic. The bread is also freshly made on-site and the coffee is awesome. Reduced hours in winter. Daily 7.30am–5.30pm.

Piha Surf Lifesaving Club 23 Marine Parade South, overlooking South Piha beach ☎09 812 8896, ⊚facebook.com/pihasurflifesaving. You can eat here, but it's really more of a spot to watch the sunset over the sea with a beer in hand. You have to be a member to eat here (or with one), but you can sign up on the spot. Oct–April Thurs–Sat noon–9pm, Sun noon–8pm

Cascade Kauri

3km along Falls Rd, accessed 1.5km along Te Henga Road off Scenic Drive • Daily: April–Sept 8am–7pm; Oct–March 8am–9pm • Free

The drive through the Waitakere Golf Club is an odd introduction to **Cascade Kauri**, a delightful patch of forest that's also known as the **Ark in the Park** (⊚arkinthepark. co.nz). Forest & Bird partly maintain this open sanctuary, its volunteers undertaking pest and weed control with superb results. The bush is looking great and North Island robins, kokako and whiteheads have all been reintroduced to the area. There are longer tracks, but the best introduction is the delightful **Auckland City Walk**, though be aware of ongoing track closures (see page 109).

1

Te Henga

TE HENGA (also known as Bethell's Beach), 27km northwest of the Arataki Visitor Centre, is similar to, but less dramatic than Karekare, Piha or Muriwai, and is correspondingly less visited, making it good for escaping the crowds in the summer. There are no shops, but there is a surf club and occasional café. If you fancy some freshwater swimming or just sliding down sand dunes, head to **Lake Wainamu**, reached on foot along a sandy streambed path (30min each way) from the car park, 1km back from the beach.

ACCOMMODATION AND EATING   TE HENGA

Up to five self-contained campervans can park at Cascade Kauri for one night, three in winter.

Bethells Beach Cottages 267 Bethells Road ☎09 810 9581, ⓦbethellsbeach.com. Located on a hill just behind the dunes, these three casually bohemian self-contained cottages have great sea views and a wonderfully relaxing tenor. Hot tub and holistic health treatments available. Bring everything you need to cook.

Discount for two or more nights. $330

The Bethells Café Main beach car park off Bethells Road ☎09 810 9387, ⓦfacebook.com/BethellsCafe. Good food (toasted sandwiches from $7.50), fresh smoothies and strong coffee are reason enough to stop by this caravan café, but it's more about the chilled vibe and occasional live music. Nov–March Wed–Sun 10am–6pm.

Muriwai

MURIWAI, 15km north of Piha and 15km southwest of Huapai, is the most populous of the West Coast beach settlements and has wonderful surf, and a long beach stretching 45km north to the heads of Kaipara Harbour.

Muriwai gannet colony

Muriwai's main attraction is at the southern end of the beach where a **gannet colony** (best seen late Oct to mid-Feb) occupies Motutara Island and Otakamiro Point, the headland between the main beach and the surfers' cove of Māori Bay. The gannets breed here before migrating to sunnier climes, a few staying behind with the fur seals that inhabit the rocks below. Gannets normally prefer the protection of islands, but this is one of the few places where they nest on the mainland, just below viewing platforms from where you get a bird's-eye view. Short paths lead up here from near the surf club and off the road to Māori Bay.

ACCOMMODATION AND EATING   MURIWAI

Muriwai Beach Campground 451 Motutara Rd ☎09 411 9262, ⓦmuriwaimotorcamp.co.nz. Renamed, revamped and reopened in 2017, this spacious campsite behind the dunes is shaded by pines. There are power sites, hot showers, kitchen, laundry and a lounge. Prices include two adults. Unpowered sites $20, powered sites $44, cabins $85.

Sand Dunz Beach Café 455 Motutara Rd ☎09 411 8558, ⓦfacebook.com/sanddunzbeachcafe. Good café with sandwiches and salads from the counter food, a standard range of breakfasts and lunches (mostly $16–20; served until 4pm or 5pm) and takeaway burgers and chips. Daily: April–Sept 7.30am–4pm (takeaways to 5pm); Oct–March 7.30am–7.30pm.

North of Auckland

Some 40km north of the city, Auckland's straggling suburbs merge into the **Hibiscus Coast**, centred on the suburban **Whangaparaoa Peninsula** and the anodyne beachside community of **Orewa**, now bypassed by the Northern Motorway. Immediately to the north, the hot springs at **Waiwera** herald the beach-and-barbecue scene of **Wenderholm Regional Park** and the classic old village of **Puhoi**.

Passing beyond Puhoi puts you into **Northland**; coverage of that region begins with Warkworth (see page 137).

Orewa and the Whangaparaoa Peninsula

The most striking of the Hibiscus Coast beaches is the 3km strand backed by **OREWA**, predominantly a retirement and dormitory town dominated by the twelve-storey Nautilus apartment block. It's a relaxing spot with plenty of good spots for swimming, kitesurfing and paddleboarding, but limited accommodation and eating options.

South of Orewa, the **Whangaparaoa Peninsula** juts out 12km into the Hauraki Gulf to Gulf Harbour Marina, launching point for trips to the delightful bird sanctuary of **Tiritiri Matangi** (see page 131).

Shakespear Regional Park

20km southeast of Orewa or 50km northeast of Auckland • Daily: April–Sept 6am–7pm; Oct–March 6am–9pm • Ferry to Gulf Harbour from Auckland's downtown Ferry Terminal Pier 4 then bus #988 from Laurie Southwick Pde

You can spend a few pleasant hours swimming, camping and birdwatching at **Shakespear Regional Park**, which envelops the tip of the Whangaparaoa Peninsula. This open sanctuary is protected by a predator-proof fence and, after extensive pest poisoning and trapping in 2011, bird numbers are on the up. Easy walks wander through regenerating bush where you might see red-crowned parakeets and bellbirds.

ARRIVAL AND ACTIVITIES   **OREWA**

By bus From downtown Auckland, catch bus #991X from Wellesley St near Hobson St.

Destinations Auckland (frequent; 1hr 25min).

SUP Shed 196 Centreway Rd ☎09 426 7873, ⓦsupshed.com. In summer months, this surf shop sets up at Orewa beach in front of the main carpark. Stand-up paddleboard rentals ($25/hr), kayaks $25/hr, surfboards $20/hr. One-hour lessons for $70 including board rental. Tues–Fri 10am–5pm, Sat & Sun 10am–3pm.

ACCOMMODATION

Orewa Beach Top 10 Holiday Park 265 Hibiscus Coast Hwy ☎09 426 5832, ⓦorewabeachtop10.co.nz. Large, high-standard and very popular campsite with kitchen cabins ($80) and tourist cabins ($120) shaded by pohutukawas backing Orewa Beach. Camping $20, cabins $64

Shakespear SCC Campground Whangaparaoa Rd ☎09 301 0100, ⓦaucklandcouncil.govt.nz. Flat shaded grassy area close to the beach for 20 self-contained campervans. Three nights max and booking online is essential. Prices are per person. $10

Te Haruhi Bay Campground Whangaparaoa Rd ☎09 301 0100, ⓦaucklandcouncil.govt.nz. Large camping area close to a great swimming beach. There's tap water, flush toilets, and space for tents and campervans. Booking essential. Prices are per person. $15

Villa Orewa 264 Hibiscus Coast Hwy ☎09 426 3073. Classy, whitewashed Greek-island-style B&B offering airy rooms with bold-coloured furnishings, beach-view balconies and delicious breakfasts. Dinner is available on request. $210

Waves 1 Kohu Rd, off Hibiscus Coast Hwy ☎0800 426 6889, ⓦwaves.co.nz. The town's fanciest motel is just steps from the beach, has underfloor heating and stylish decor. The premium rooms have the best views. $180, premium $230

EATING

Casa del Gelato 6 Moana Av ☎09 426 9219, ⓦfacebook.com/casadelgelatoorewa. Only the very best award-winning New Zealand ice cream is served at this cute spot. As well as cones and cups, there are smoothies (from

---

NORTHERN GATEWAY TOLL ROAD

To avoid paying the $2.30 **toll** for the final 5km of Auckland's Northern Motorway, come off at Silverdale and follow the coast road through Orewa – it'll only add ten minutes to your journey. Otherwise, pay online (ⓦtollingonline.nzta.govt.nz) either before or up to five days after your journey, or use the roadside service stations (though you'll be charged for paying by cash).

$7.50) and desserts (try the Freak Sundae for $13.50). Just a few indoor and outdoor tables. Mon & Sun 11am–6pm, Tues–Sat 11am–9pm.

Coast Bites and Brews 342 Hibiscus Coast Hwy ☎ 09 421 1016, ⓦ coastorewa.co.nz. Fun bar showcasing Deep Creek Brewing's excellent range of small-batch craft beers and serving up the likes of Thai steak tacos ($17.50) and surf-and turf platters ($36). Mon–Thurs & Sun 11am–11pm, Fri & Sat 11am–midnight.

Wenderholm Regional Park

SH1, 1km north of Waiwera • Daily: April–Sept 6am–7pm; Oct–March 6am–9pm • Free

Wenderholm Regional Park is bordered by the Puhoi River estuary and a sweeping golden beach backed by pohutukawa-shaded swathes of grass that's often packed with picnicking families on summer weekends. There are coin-op barbecues, cold showers and, three hours either side of high tide, the chance to rent sit-on-top **kayaks** (summer only) and muck about on the estuary. Walking tracks (20min–2hr) wind up to a headland viewpoint through nikau palm groves alive with birds that have repopulated the area from Tiritiri Matangi (see page 131).

ACCOMMODATION   WENDERHOLM

Wenderholm Camping SH1, 1km north of Waiwera ☎ 09 366 2000. Large *Schischka* campsite with flush toilets and potable water but little shade and no showers. It's a lovely green (and flat) spot beside the estuary (access only when park gates are open). Price per person. $15

Puhoi

A pale blue wayside crucifix marks the entrance to tiny **PUHOI**, 6km north of Waiwera, a bucolic place settled by staunchly Catholic Bohemian migrants who arrived in 1863 from what is now the Czech Republic. The land was poor, and settlers were forced to eke out a living by cutting the bush for timber. They stuck with it, though, and Mass is still held in the 1881 weatherboard Saints Peter and Paul **church**.

Puhoi Heritage Museum

77 Puhoi Rd • Daily noon–3pm • $3.50 • ☎ 09 422 0852, ⓦ puhoiheritagemuseum.co.nz

Most visitors to Puhoi get no further than the pub, but try to look in at the **Puhoi Heritage Museum**, in the former Convent School. The model of the village as it was in 1900 is a gem and really comes alive if you engage the interest of one of the volunteers on duty. Contact the museum if you're interested in a walking tour of Puhoi.

ACTIVITIES   PUHOI

Puhoi River Canoe Hire ☎ 09 422 0891, ⓦ puhoirivercanoes.co.nz. Rents kayaks for a gentle, unguided 2hr trip to or from Wenderholm, always going with the tide. $50; booking essential. Daily Sept–June.

EATING AND DRINKING

Puhoi Pub Puhoi Rd ☎ 09 422 0812, ⓦ puhoipub. com. Iconic 1879 Kiwi pub festooned with photos and pioneering paraphernalia including the horns of famed bullock teams that once helped clear the dense bush hereabouts. The drinks and food are barely average but tourists, motorbike groups and Auckland weekenders all enjoy chilling in the beer garden. Daily 10am–7pm, later at weekends.

★ **Puhoi Valley Café & Cheese Store** 275 Ahuroa Rd, 3km north ☎ 09 422 0670, ⓦ puhoivalley.co.nz. Pop in for free samples of the delicious cheeses, super-rich ice cream (the hokey pokey is locally famous) and sorbets such as forest berry, all made on the premises, but plan to stick around for something like an aged cheddar Welsh rarebit and bacon ($15) or a cheese platter ($18–45). It's all elegantly served inside or on the terrace overlooking lawns with bush-clad hills behind. Mon–Fri 10am–4pm, Sat & Sun 9.30am–4.30pm.

Southeast of Auckland

Most southbound travellers hurry along Auckland's southern motorway to Hamilton or turn off to Thames and the Coromandel Peninsula at Pokeno – either way missing out on the modest attractions of the **Firth of Thames**, a sheltered inlet of the Hauraki Gulf separating south Auckland from the Coromandel Peninsula. Its frequently windswept western littoral comprises land built up from successive deposits of shell banks; much has been converted to farmland but newer shell banks in the making can be seen, along with flocks of feeding birds, on what is known as the **Seabird Coast**.

Kaiaua

The tiny village of **Kaiaua** comprises little more than a pub, a fish and chip shop and a tiny marina where half a dozen boats squeeze in between the mangroves. It is like much of New Zealand was half a century ago.

Pukorokoro Miranda Shorebird Centre

283 East Coast Rd, 7km south of Kaiaua • Daily 9am–5pm, and often later in the summer • Free • ☎ 09 232 2781, ⊛ miranda-shorebird.org.nz

In the peak January-to-March season the modest **Pukorokoro Miranda Shorebird Centre** is often full of twitchers who can point you in the direction of the best hide (1hr return) and fill you in on the current hot sightings. Almost a quarter of all known species of migrating shore birds visit the region, and 30,000-strong flocks of **wrybill plover** avoid the northern winter by spending it at this internationally significant site. During the southern summer (Sept–March) you'll see arctic migrants – notably bar-tailed **godwits** and **lesser knots** – who fly 15,000km from Alaska and Siberia. Viewing is optimal two hours either side of high tide; the centre also has a good stock of natural history books and a sunny deck.

Miranda Hot Springs

Front Miranda Rd, 10km south of Kaiaua • Daily 9am–9pm • General entry $14, private spa $15/person for 30min, combo $24 each • ☎ 07 867 3055, ⊛ mirandahotsprings.co.nz

Just twenty minutes' drive short of Thames, the slightly alkaline **Miranda Hot Springs** is an open-air affair with an Olympic-size warm pool kept at 36–38°C, a cooler children's pool and private kauri spa tubs (40–41°C).

GETTING AROUND	SOUTHEAST OF AUCKLAND

By bike Cyclists will find that the coast road to the southeast is an excellent way into and out of Auckland, following Tamaki Drive from the city centre through Panmure and Howick to Clevedon and the coast.

ACCOMMODATION AND EATING

Kaiaua Fisheries 939 East Coast Rd, Kaiaua ☎ 09 232 2776. You can sit in at the small fish restaurant, but the real pleasure here is to order fish and chips to go (around $8), buy a couple of takeaway beers from the pub and sit by the water watching the world go by. Daily 9am–8.30pm.

Miranda Holiday Park Miranda Hot Springs ☎ 0800 833 144, ⊛ mirandaholidaypark.co.nz. Very high quality campsite with separate tent area, a wide range of cabins, a tennis court and delightful landscaped, hot mineral pools. Camping $23, cabins $149

Pukorokoro Miranda Shorebird Centre 283 East Coast Rd, 7km south of Kaiaua ☎ 09 232 2781, ⊛ miranda-shorebird.org.nz. Keen birders can stay here in 4–6-person bunk rooms or self-contained units. There's a good kitchen and a sunny veranda. Bring food and bedding (or rent for $5). Dorms $25, units $95

Rays Rest 5km south of Kaiaua. A line of campervans is normally parked on the shoreline where self-contained vans can stay for up to two nights. When it is full, some people camp outside the designated area (though you shouldn't). Public toilets are available in Kaiaua. **Free**

1 Islands of the Hauraki Gulf

Auckland's greatest asset is the island-studded **Hauraki Gulf**, a 70km-square patch of ocean to the northeast of the city. In Māori, Hauraki means "wind from the north" – though the gulf is somewhat sheltered from the prevailing winds and ocean swells by Great Barrier Island, creating benign conditions for Auckland's legions of yachties. Most just sail or fish, but those who wish to strike land can visit some of the fifty-odd islands, administered by the Department of Conservation, designated either for recreational use or as sanctuaries for endangered wildlife, requiring permits.

Auckland's nearest island neighbour is **Rangitoto**, a flat cone of gnarled and twisted lava that dominates the harbourscape. The most populous of the gulf islands is **Waiheke**, with sandy beaches and classy wineries. Wine was definitely verboten at nearby **Rotoroa Island**, once a Salvation Army detox centre and now open for day-visits.

Waiheke's sophistication is a far cry from laidback **Great Barrier Island** with its sandy surf beaches, hilly tramping tracks and exceptional fishing. The Department of Conservation's policy of allowing access to wildlife sanctuaries is wonderfully demonstrated at **Tiritiri Matangi**, where a day-trip gives visitors an unsurpassed opportunity to see some of the world's rarest birds.

Rangitoto and Motutapu islands

The low, conical shape of **Rangitoto**, 10km northeast of the city centre, is a familiar sight to every Aucklander. Yet few set foot on the island, missing out on a freakish land of fractured black lava with the world's largest pohutukawa forest clinging precariously to its crevices. Alongside lies the much older **Motutapu** or "sacred island", linked to Rangitoto by a narrow causeway.

A **day-trip** is enough to get a feel for Rangitoto, make the obligatory hike to the summit (from where there are magnificent views of the city and Hauraki Gulf) and tackle a few trails, but **longer stays** are possible if you manage to book one of the two *baches*, or you can pitch your tent at the simple campsite at Home Bay on Motutapu – though this is a 3hr walk from Rangitoto Wharf. There are frequent sailings to Rangitoto, but only one crossing to Motutapu every two weeks.

Brief history

Rangitoto is Auckland's youngest and largest **volcano**, its birth witnessed around six hundred years ago by Motutapu Māori, who apparently called the island "blood red sky" after the spectacle that accompanied its creation.

The government purchased Rangitoto for £15 in 1854, putting it to use as a military lookout point and a work camp for **prisoners**. From the 1890s, areas were leased for camping and unauthorized **baches** were cobbled together on the sites. Over 100 *baches* had sprouted by the late 1930s when legislation stopped any new construction. In recent years, the cultural value of this unique set of 1920s and 1930s houses has been appreciated and the finest examples of the remaining 34 are being preserved for posterity, their corrugated-iron chimneys and cast-off veranda-railing fence posts capturing the Kiwi make-do spirit.

Flora and fauna

Rangitoto's lack of soil and porous rock have created unusual conditions for **plant life**, though the meagre supply of insects attracts few birds, making it eerily quiet. Pohutukawa trees seeded first, given a head start by their roots, which are able to tap underground reservoirs of fresh water up to 20m below the surface. Smaller and fleshier plants then established themselves under the protective canopy. Harsh conditions have led to some strange **botanical anomalies**: both epiphytes and mud-loving mangroves are found growing directly on the lava, an alpine moss is found at sea level, and the

RANGITOTO SUMMIT WALK

The way to really appreciate Rangitoto Island is on foot, best along shady paths away from sun-baked black lava. A favourite is the **Summit/Coastal Loop Track** (12km; 5–6hr; 260m ascent) around the southeast of the island. Turn left just past the toilets at Rangitoto Wharf and follow signs for the **Kowhai Grove**, ablaze with yellow blooms in September. Turn right onto the coastal road from Rangitoto Wharf then left into **Kidney Fern Grove**, which is packed with unusual miniature ferns that unfurl after rain. From here, the well-worn **Summit Track** winds through patches of pohutukawa forest. Around three-quarters of the way to the summit, a side track leads to the lava caves (20min return) that probe deep into the side of the volcano. Further along the main track a former military observation post on the summit provides views out across Auckland city and the Hauraki Gulf.

Continue northwards to the east–west road across the island and follow it towards Islington Bay; from there, pick up the **coastal track south**, initially following the bay then cutting inland through some little-frequented forests back to Rangitoto Wharf.

pohutukawa has hybridized with its close relative, the northern rata, to produce a spectrum of blossoms ranging from pink to crimson. Successful eradication of wallabies, possums and even rats has allowed pohutukawa to rebound with vigour as DOC have introduced takahe, saddleback and whiteheads to Motutapu. Native parakeets (*kakariki*) have also self-introduced and bred here for the first time in a century.

Bach 38

Near Rangitoto Wharf • Open Sat & Sun Dec to Easter, rest of year by appointment • Free, donation appreciated • ☎ 09 445 1894, ⓦ rangitoto.org

Bach 38 has been restored to its 1930s condition by the Rangitoto Island Historic Conservation Trust. There's memorabilia rescued from various island *baches*, plus pohutukawa honey and summit certificates for sale. Several more *baches* are being preserved by the trust, though it is slow work.

Motutapu

The landscape of **Motutapu** is more typical rural New Zealand – grassy paddocks, ridge-top fencelines and macrocarpa windbreaks – but DOC's plan is to re-vegetate a third of the island with natives. It is early days yet and the only moderately mature section is the **Rotary Centennial Walkway** (2km one way; 40min) through bush first planted in 1994. Continue beyond the end of the walkway to see the remains of World War II gun emplacements, and long views of some beautiful coastline.

ARRIVAL AND DEPARTURE   RANGITOTO AND MOTUTAPU ISLANDS

By ferry Fullers (☎ 09 367 9111, ⓦ fullers.co.nz; 3–5 daily; $33 return) takes 25min to reach Rangitoto Wharf. Most crossings also call at Devonport. Catch the 7.30am ferry on Sat or Sun and the round-trip is just $23. Fullers also operate the infrequent ferry (35min) to Motutapu's Home Bay (every second Sunday departing 9.15am and returning 4.15pm; $35 return).

INFORMATION AND TOURS

Bio-security Check your shoes for seeds and your bags for stray mice – it does happen.

What to bring Apart from a couple of toilets there are no facilities on Rangitoto, so bring everything you need – including strong shoes to protect you from the sharp rocks, weather protection, water, food and a torch for exploring the lava caves.

Volunteering The Motutapu Restoration Trust (ⓦ motutapu.org.nz) runs volunteer day-trips (every second Sunday except for public holidays), typically involving 4–5 hours' weed busting and sapling planting. A ferry (see above) takes you direct to Home Bay.

Fullers Volcanic Explorer Tour Save yourself the slog and catch this tractor-drawn buggy tour (daily; 4.5hr; $68 including ferry) to the summit with full commentary; the final 900m is on foot along a boardwalk which includes 300 steps.

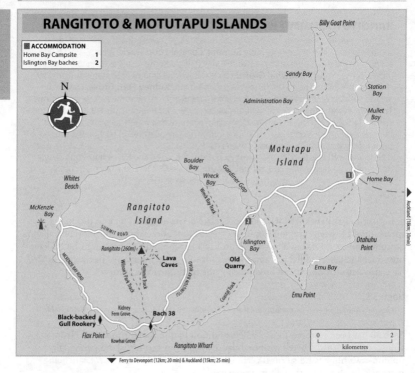

RANGITOTO & MOTUTAPU ISLANDS

ACCOMMODATION
Home Bay Campsite 1
Islington Bay baches 2

Billy Goat Point

Sandy Bay

Station Bay

Administration Bay

Mullet Bay

Motutapu Island

Boulder Bay

Wreck Bay

Gardiner Gap

Home Bay

Whites Beach

Wreck Bay Track

McKenzie Bay

Rangitoto Island

Auckland (18km; 30min)

SUMMIT ROAD

Rangitoto (260m)▲

Lava Caves

Islington Bay

Otahuhu Point

Wilson's Park Track

Summit Track

Old Quarry

Emu Bay

MCKENZIE BAY ROAD

Coastal Track

Emu Point

Kidney Fern Grove

Bach 38

Black-backed Gull Rookery

Flax Point

Kowhai Grove

Rangitoto Wharf

0   2
kilometres

▼ Ferry to Devonport (12km; 20 min) & Auckland (15km; 25 min)

ACCOMMODATION

Home Bay Campsite Eastern side of Motutapu ⓦdoc.govt.nz; map p.118. This primitive, but pleasant and spacious beachside DOC campsite has toilets and water, but no showers. Access is by Fullers ferry every other Sunday or a 3hr walk from Rangitoto Wharf. Booking is essential from Christmas to Jan. $\overline{\underline{8}}$

Islington Bay baches Eastern side of Rangitoto ⓦbookabach.co.nz; map p.118. *Bach* 78 and *Bach* 114 have been lovingly restored, with additional modern touches like solar lighting, gas cooking, a "chilly bin" (cool box) and chemical toilets. The secluded beachfront location is unbeatable. Access is a 1hr 30min walk from Rangitoto Wharf. Booking is essential from Christmas to Jan and there's a surcharge for more than 4 adults. $\overline{\underline{150}}$

Waiheke Island

Pastoral **Waiheke**, 20km east of Auckland, is the second largest of the gulf islands and easily the most populous, particularly when summer visitors quadruple its population of around 8000. The traffic isn't all one way, though, as fast and frequent ferry services allow islanders to commute to the city, a trend that has turned the western end of Waiheke into a suburb. But, with its chain of beautiful, sandy beaches along the north coast, a climate that's less humid than Auckland's and some great wineries, Waiheke is popular with international visitors in search of a peaceful spot to recover from jet lag or to idle away a day or two before flying home. The island is **busiest** on summer weekends and throughout January, when Aucklanders descend en masse and there's often live music.

People, cafés and restaurants mostly cluster around **Oneroa**. You can go for a swim here, but most people head elsewhere: to the almost circular **Enclosure Bay** for snorkelling, **Palm Beach** for swimming, and the more surf-oriented **Onetangi**. All over the island, the bays and headlands lend themselves to short, often steep walks, wineries tempt, and if you're still restless, there's kayaking or sailing.

Brief history

Waiheke Māori trace their lineage back to the Tainui canoe that landed at Onetangi and gave the island its first name, Te Motu-arai-Roa, "the long sheltering island". Waiheke, or "cascading waters", originally referred to a particular creek but was assumed by **Europeans** to refer to the entire island. Among the first **settlers** to set foot on Waiheke was Samuel Marsden, who preached here in 1818 and established a mission near Matiatia. The island then went through the familiar cycle of kauri logging, gum digging and clearance for farming. Gradually, the magnificent coastal scenery gained popularity as a setting for grand picnics, and hamper-encumbered Victorians, attired in formal dress, arrived in boatloads.

Development was initially sluggish, but the availability of cheap land amid dramatic landscapes drew painters and **craftspeople**; others followed as access from Auckland became easier and faster.

Oneroa and around

Most ferries arrive at **Matiatia Wharf**, a 2km uphill walk or bus ride from the main settlement of **ONEROA**, whose main street hugs a ridge-top from the library, community art gallery and cinema, past a bunch of cafés and restaurants. The sandy sweep of Oneroa Bay is a great spot to swim, but if the summer crowds get to you head to the eastern end where, at anything other than high tide, you can access some quieter nooks between the rocks. What passes for a main road on Waiheke winds southeast from Oneroa through the contiguous settlements of Little Oneroa, Blackpool and Surfdale to light-industrial **Ostend**, where there's a great **market** (Sat 7.30am–1pm; ⓦwaihekeostendmarket.co.nz).

Whittaker's Music Museum

2 Korora St • Daily: 1–4pm; performances Sat 1.30pm • Donation requested; performances $10 • ☎ 09 372 5573, ⓦ musicalmuseum.org

Oneroa's only real sight is this slightly eccentric museum full of flageolets, piano accordions, player pianos, xylophones and even a very well-restored 1896 Steinway and one owned by Paderewski. Incredibly, you're allowed to play most of them, and all are ably demonstrated during the occasional musical performances.

Palm Beach and Onetangi

Palm Beach is 4km east of Oneroa • Onetangi is 9km east of Oneroa

Palm Beach takes a bite out of the north coast, with houses tumbling down to a sandy beach separated by a handful of rocks from the nude bathing zone at its western end.

Waiheke's longest and most exposed beach is **ONETANGI**, popular in summer with surfers, board riders and swimmers, and the venue for beach horse races (ⓦonetangibeachraces.co.nz; usually early March) along with sandcastle building, tug-o-war and more.

Stony Batter Historic Reserve and Fort Stony Batter

Daily **Stony Batter** Historic Reserve 24hr • Free • **Fort Stony Batter** generally daily 10am–3pm but call ahead • Entry $8; guided tours $15; cash only • ☎ 021 043 8821

There's very little habitation east of Onetangi, just tracts of open farmland, vineyards and **Stony Batter Historic Reserve**, a mass of abandoned World War II defences at the northeastern tip of the island, 23km from Matiatia wharf. It is a twenty-minute walk from the car park to the site where you can wander around topside, or head into **Fort Stony Batter**, a labyrinth of dank concrete tunnels and gun emplacements built to protect Auckland from a feared Japanese attack during World War II. The attack never came and after the war the guns and equipment

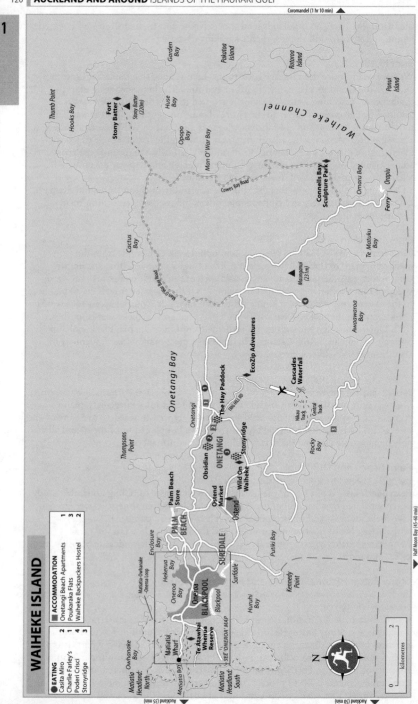

WAIHEKE ISLAND

● EATING	
Casita Miro	2
Charlie Farley's	4
Poderi Crisci	1
Stonyridge	3

■ ACCOMMODATION	
Onetangi Beach Apartments	1
Poukaraka Flats	3
Waiheke Backpackers Hostel	2

Coromandel (1 hr 10 min)

Waiheke Channel

Thumb Point
Hooks Bay
Garden Bay
Pakatoa Island
Rotoroa Island
Ponui Island

Fort Stony Batter
Stony Batter (220m)
Huse Bay
Opopo Bay
Man O'War Bay
Otapiu
Ferry
Omaru Bay
Te Matuku Bay

Cactus Bay
Cowes Bay Road
Man O'War Bay Road

Connells Bay Sculpture Park

Maunganui (231m)
Awaawaroa Bay

Onetangi Bay

Onetangi
The Hay Paddock
EcoZip Adventures
Cascades Waterfall
Trig Hill Rd
Nikau Track
Central Track
Rocky Bay

Thompsons Point

Obsidian
ONETANGI
Stonyridge
Wild On Waiheke
Ostend
Palm Beach Store
Ostend Market

PALM BEACH
SURFDALE
Putiki Bay

Enclosure Bay
Hekerua Bay
Oneroa Bay
Oneroa
BLACKPOOL
Blackpool
Surfdale
Huruhi Bay
Kennedy Point

Owhanake Bay
Matiatia-Owhanake-Oneroa Loop

Matiatia Wharf
Te Atawhai Whenua Reserve

SEE 'ONEROA' MAP

Matiatia Headland: North
Matiatia Bay
Matiatia Headland: South

Auckland (35 min)
Auckland (50 min)
Half Moon Bay (45–60 min)

N

0   2
kilometres

were removed. Bring or rent ($5) a torch to explore on your own, or join one of the guided tours that bring the place to life.

Connells Bay Sculpture Park

142 Cowes Bay Road, 20km east of Oneroa • Mid-Oct to mid-April daily on pre-booked guided tours only • $30 • ☎ 09 372 895, ⓦ connellsbay.co.nz

Book ahead and set a couple of hours aside to visit this wonderful, private contemporary **sculpture trail** typically guided in small groups by one of the instigators and owners, John and Jo Gow. As pasture has been turned into immaculate regenerating bush the Gows have commissioned the cream of New Zealand sculptors – Michael Parekowhai, Jeff Thompson, Chris Booth, Fatu Feu'u – to produce site-specific works, often the largest they've undertaken. The commissioning and development process comes alive with videos and working models, but the stars are the works themselves – a massive tree stump turned into what looks like an Easter Island *moai*, an organically sculpted steel wall and a stainless-steel limpet, fern and leaf delicately beautifying a small wetland.

ARRIVAL AND DEPARTURE

WAIHEKE ISLAND

By ferry Fullers (☎ 09 367 9111, ⓦ fullers.co.nz; roughly hourly 6am–10pm or later; 35min; $36 return, bikes free) operates from the Ferry Building in Auckland to Matiatia Wharf, just over 1km from the main settlement of Oneroa with times staggered so that in effect there is a ferry every half-hour. Sealink (☎ 0800 732 546, ⓦ sealink.co.nz) operates a car ferry from Half Moon Bay in Auckland's eastern suburbs to Kennedy Point, 4km south of Oneroa (roughly hourly; 45min; car only $174.50 return, each person $36.50 return, bikes free), or less frequently from Wynyard Wharf in Auckland. Foot passengers can use the summer-only shuttle bus between Kennedy Point and Oneroa (see timetable online).

INFORMATION

Visitor information There's a helpful office at Matiatia wharf (9.30am–1.30pm most days; ⓦ tourismwaiheke. co.nz). Pick up the free *Island of Wine* map and guide and the *Waiheke Art Map*, which details over 30 galleries and artists' studios you can visit.

Newspaper The weekly *Gulf News* ($2; ⓦ waihekegulfnews. co.nz) is published on Thursday and has details of what's on.

Services Free internet access is available at the community library, 131 Ocean View Rd (Mon–Fri 9am–

6pm, Sat & Sun 10am–4pm). There are a couple of banks on the main street.

Events The highlights of Waiheke's summer season are the annual Jazz Festival (Easter weekend; ⓦ waihekejazzfestival.co.nz) and, in odd-numbered years, the free Headland Sculpture on the Gulf (late Jan to mid-Feb; ⓦ sotg.co.nz) when the headland south of Matiatia and down to Church Bay is festooned with mostly wonderful, contemporary sculptures.

GETTING AROUND

By bus Ferry arrivals connect with Fullers Explorer hop-on-hop-off buses (see above) and the public bus service, which run to Onetangi via Oneroa, Surfdale and Ostend, and to Rocky Bay via Oneroa, Little Oneroa and Palm Beach. Tickets ($3.50/ cash single; $1.90/single with AT HOP card, $10 all day) are available on the bus.

By car Waiheke Car and Scooter Hire, Matiatia Wharf (☎ 09 372 3339, ⓦ rentmewaiheke.co.nz), rent scooters ($69/day) and cars (from $79). They charge by the calendar day, though if you get the vehicle back before 10am they'll only charge a $15 overnight fee for that day.

By bike Waiheke is constantly undulating, so you might want to rent an electric-assist bike from Bikes and Barbers at 108 Ocean View Rd (☎ 09 372 4428, ⓦ ecyclesnz.com). They have long-range ($60/day) models which will get you right round the island, just. Human-powered, sturdy mountain bikes ($40/day; $20/additional day) can be rented from Waiheke Bike Hire in the car park at Matiatia Wharf (☎ 09 372 7937, ⓦ waihekebikehire.co.nz).

By taxi Waiheke Express Taxis (☎ 0800 700 789, ⓦ waihekeexpresstaxis.co.nz).

ACCOMMODATION

Accommodation is generally plentiful except for the three weeks after Christmas and all summer weekends. While Oneroa is convenient for buses, restaurants and shops, many prefer the more relaxing **beaches** such as Palm Beach and Onetangi. There's often a two-night minimum at weekends.

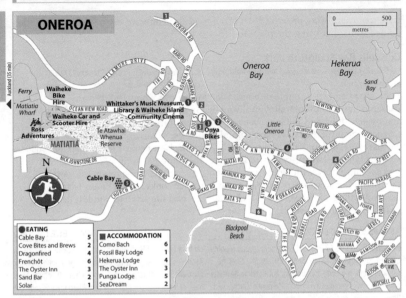

ONEROA

EATING	
Cable Bay	5
Cove Bites and Brews	2
Dragonfired	4
Frenchôt	6
The Oyster Inn	3
Sand Bar	2
Solar	1

ACCOMMODATION	
Como Bach	6
Fossil Bay Lodge	1
Hekerua Lodge	4
The Oyster Inn	3
Punga Lodge	5
SeaDream	2

ONEROA, LITTLE ONEROA AND BLACKPOOL

Como Bach 30 The Esplanade ⓦvisitwaiheke.co.nz; map above. One of the more convenient (and reasonably priced) holiday homes rented through this website, this small sunny beachfront house is priced for up to 4 people in two bedrooms. $325

Fossil Bay Lodge 58 Korora Rd, Oneroa ⓦfossilbay. net; map above. A very chilled collection of two-person huts and "glamping" tents 1km from town on an organic farm. Lovely communal spaces and lots of privacy, with a 5min walk to an all-but-private beach. Various cabins (one a single; $60). Two-night minimum (three Christmas–Jan). Cabins $85, tents $100

Hekerua Lodge 11 Hekerua Rd, Little Oneroa ⓣ09 372 8990, ⓦhekerualodge.co.nz; map above. Fun and often very lively backpackers peacefully set in the bush 10min walk from Oneroa. There's a small swimming pool, table tennis, a volleyball court often almost surrounded by tents (per person $20). Two-night minimum. Dorms $36, doubles $100

The Oyster Inn 124 Ocean View Road ⓣ09 372 2222, ⓦtheoysterinn.co.nz; map above. Like the namesake restaurant the three luxurious rooms here, right in the heart of Oneroa, are all white with an elegant stripped-back beachy feel. Breakfast and transfer to the ferry wharf are included. Two-night minimum at weekends. $335

★ **Punga Lodge** 223 Ocean View Rd, Little Oneroa ⓣ0800 372 6675, ⓦpungalodge.co.nz; map above. Delightful and hospitable B&B, well located in the bush close to Oneroa beach, with tea and muffins available from the helpful hosts. Accommodation consists of a range of comfortable and spacious en-suite doubles with verandas (breakfast included), and four self-catering apartments of different sizes. There's a free spa pool, and good-value off-season deals. They also run the nearby *Tawa Lodge*, which has well-priced shared-bathroom doubles ($115) and a very comfortable "cottage" with wonderful sea views ($285). Free wi-fi. Doubles $155, apartments $220

SeaDream 35 Waikare Rd ⓣ09 372 8991, ⓦseadream. co.nz; map above. These two comfortably appointed and very peaceful self-contained units are perfectly sited just steps from Oneroa's restaurants and with long bay views from the terrace. $200

ONETANGI

Onetangi Beach Apartments 5 Fourth Avenue ⓣ0800 663 826, ⓦonetangi.co.nz; map p.120. Only a road separates these upscale motel apartments from Onetangi beach. All are self-contained, with Sky TV and DVD players, access to a free sauna and spa pools, plus kayaks and paddleboards for rent. Apartments $190, "beachfront" $215

Waiheke Backpackers Hostel 421 Sea View Rd, Onetangi ⓣ09 372 7003, ⓦwaihekebackpackers. com; map p.120. Relaxed hostel on a headland just above Onetangi beach, with long views over the sea from the hammocks and beanbags on the lawn. Renovated and operated by Auckland council with 15 single bunk rooms,

1

WALKS ON WAIHEKE

Sometimes it is nice to feel like you've earned your extended winery lunch, or work it off afterwards. A series of leaflets (free from i-SITE visitor centres) expand on our suggested walks.

Matiatia Headland North (2–3hr loop; undulating). One of the island's finest walks visiting secluded beaches and windswept headlands, both peppered with some of New Zealand's finest modern mansions, many with sculptures visible in the grounds. Walk from Oneroa to Matiatia then complete the loop using the Te Atawhai Whenua Reserve (see below).

Matiatia Headland South (3–4hr loop; undulating). Easily combined with its northern counterpart, this walk follows the clifftops south of Matiatia and loops back passing close to three wineries open for tasting, including Cable Bay (see page 123).

Nikau Track (4km loop; 2hr 30min; 100m ascent). Starting at Whakanewha Regional Park this track runs past wetland and through mature native forest to the pretty tumbling Cascades Waterfall. Return via Central Track.

Onetangi Wine Trophy Trail (1–4hr). Short field and vineyard walk that's really an excuse to taste wine at *The Hay Paddock* (451b Seaview Rd) and *Obsidian* (22 Te Makiri Rd) and eat and taste at *Casita Miro* (see page 124). Park at *The Hay Paddock*, walk past *Casita Miro* to *Obsidian* then turn around and taste and dine on the way back. Open Nov–March 11.30am–3.30pm.

Te Atawhai Whenua Reserve (30min). Great bushwalk alternative to the roadside footpath when walking between the Matiatia ferry and Oneroa. Pick it up at the southern end of Matiatia beach.

---

a standard dorm and a couple of doubles, plus good bathrooms and an outside desk with barbecue. Dorms $\overline{33}$, doubles $\overline{85}$

ROCKY BAY

Poukaraka Flats ☎ 09 366 2000; map p.120. Attractively sited on a tidal bay in Whakanewha Regional Park, this is the island's only official campsite. It has flush toilets, potable water and free gas barbecues but no showers and the nearest bus stop is over 2km away. Self-contained campers can stay in the car park ($8) for a night in summer, 3 in winter. Reserve in Jan & Feb. Per person $\overline{15}$

EATING

To Aucklanders, Waiheke is all about long winery lunches, and we've listed some of the best, all also doing tastings. The bulk of the rest of the restaurants are in Oneroa, with additional spots at the various beaches. Live music mostly happens at weekends, with *Sand Bar* in Oneroa being a worthy bet.

ONEROA AND SURFDALE

★ **Cable Bay** 12 Nick Johnstone Drive, 1km west ☎ 09 372 5889, ⓦ cablebay.co.nz; map p.122. Starkly modern winery with magnificent views across the beanbag-dotted lawns to Auckland from two restaurants. The linen-tableclothed *Dining Room* has à la carte (mains around $38) showcasing fresh, seasonal produce from organic kitchen gardens, while the *Verandah* offers a Mediterranean-inspired sharing style menu. Wine tasting costs $10 for 4 tastings (their rosé and Syrah are superb) and the winery is an easy 15min uphill bushwalk from the Matiatia ferry terminal. Daily: tasting 11am–5pm; Verandah 11am–late; Dining Room noon–3pm & 6–10pm.

Cove Bites and Brews 149 Ocean View Rd ☎ 09 372 8209, ⓦ dcbrewing.co.nz; map p.122. Cruisy spot tucked beneath the viewing platform with a great sea view terrace that's perfect for sampling their Deep Creek Brewing Co beers and one of their "tasting paddles" ($34.50) laden with ribs, chicken wings, crispy prawns and dipping sauces. Mon–Fri 10am–11pm, Sat & Sun 8am–11pm.

Dragonfired Little Oneroa Beach ☎ 021 922 289, ⓦ dragonfired.co.nz; map p.122. Very Waiheke, this beachside caravan contains a wood-fired oven that's perfect for creating thin-based organic margherita pizza ($14, extra toppings $2.50 each) and polenta squares with salad ($16). Grab a drink from the nearby shop and head for the beach. Summer daily 10.30am–8pm, winter Sat & Sun 10.30am–8pm (weather dependent).

Frenchôt 8 Miami Ave, Surfdale ☎ 09 372 3400, ⓦ frenchot.com; map p.122. A welcome find, this traditional French bakery and crêperie where you can perch on stools overlooking the street or head to the spacious courtyard for a coffee and a *pain aux raisins*, *Petit Dej galette* ($19) or an apple, caramel and cinnamon crêpe ($12). The upstairs bistro serves classic French dishes such as canard confit and bouillabaisse (both around $32). Café Tues–Sun 8am–4pm, bistro Wed–Sat 6–10pm.

The Oyster Inn 124 Ocean View Rd ☎ 09 372 2222, ⓦ theoysterinn.co.nz; map p.122. Grab a people-watching spot on the veranda at this chic beach restaurant and bar, whose prices are pretty reasonable (for Waiheke). Local oysters ($5–6 each) might be followed by a crayfish

1

WAIHEKE ISLAND TOURS AND ACTIVITIES

Unless you've got transport, tours can be the most effective way to see something of the island, particularly the wineries.

TOURS

Ananda Tours ☎ 09 372 7530, ⓦ ananda.co.nz. Personalized wine, eco, art and scenic tours around the island from around $120/person (minimum numbers apply). Trips are timed to ferry arrivals; try the Gourmet's Food and Wine Tour ($185), particularly on Saturday, when they take in Ostend Market.

Fullers ☎ 09 367 9111, ⓦ fullers.co.nz. The ferry company runs a bunch of tours, all timed with boat arrivals. The Explorer Tour (daily year-round; $60/1 day or $90/2 days) includes a return ferry trip from Auckland and an hour-and-a-half hop-on-hop-off island tour. Their Wine on Waiheke tour (departing Auckland weekends 12.30pm; $140) has the same benefits but spends three hours visiting three top vineyards.

Hike Bike Ako ☎ 021 465 373, ⓦ waiheke islandMāori tours.com. Ako means "learn" in Māori and you'll certainly get a far greater understanding of both the Māori world and Waiheke's place in it on these academic-led tours (3hr 30min; $149) which combine easy walking, cruisy biking and a bit of wine tasting. They also offer an electric cycle tour ($199) and walking tour ($129). Trips start at the Matiatia ferry terminal.

KAYAKING

Ross Adventures ☎ 09 372 5550, ⓦ kayakwaiheke. co.nz. Guided paddling trips from Matiatia including half-day trips ($125), full-day trips with the wind behind you plus a shuttle back to your starting point ($195 including a good lunch), plus kayak rentals including sit-on-tops ($30 for 1hr), proper sea kayaks (from $110/half-day) and even kayaks set up for fishing ($90/half-day).

ZIPLINES

EcoZip Adventures 150 Trig Hill Rd, 2km south of Onetangi ☎ 09 372 5646, ⓦ ecozipadventures.co.nz. You get a great view right over Waiheke Island from the end of Trig Hill Road even before you enter EcoZip Adventures, where you're harnessed up and guided down a trio of increasingly steep and fast 200m-long ziplines. It is a pleasant way to spend a couple of hours, complete with a well-paced and informative bushwalk back to base. $119; includes free pick-ups from Matiatia Wharf. Daily 9am–5pm.

and watercress risotto ($28) or pan roasted market fish ($36). There's plenty of island wine and classic cocktails to help it down. Daily noon–10pm or later.

Sand Bar 153 Ocean View Rd ☎ 09 372 9458, ⓦ sandbar. co.nz; map p.122. Chic little bar, great for a cocktail on the deck as the sun goes down and frequently hosting DJs at the weekend. Tasty snacks like mushroom and pumpkin arancini ($14) and marinara beef meatballs ($12) provide an excuse to stay longer. Oct–April daily noon–10pm or later, May–Sept Tues–Fri 3–10pm or later, Sat & Sun noon–10pm or later.

★ **Solar** 139 Ocean View Rd ☎ 09 372 2133, ⓦ solarwaiheke.co.nz; map p.122. A chilled place to hang out and watch an endless parade of local characters call in for coffee or something from their menu of staunchly free-range and predominantly local and organic fare. Drop into a retro armchair or head out into the garden with sea views for Kiwi breakfasts (around $20), beef and bacon burger with fries ($24) and one of the Waiheke Island Brewing Co beers they have on tap. Mon–Thurs & Sun 8.30am–5pm, Fri & Sat 8.30am–8pm.

ONETANGI AND BEYOND

★ **Casita Miro** 3 Brown Rd ☎ 09 372 7854, ⓦ casitamiro.co.nz; map p.120. Come to sample their excellent wines (5 for $15) but mainly to dine on Iberian- and Mediterranean-inspired dishes like *harira* ($8), lamb and fig tajine with pistachio ($26), 18-month-aged serrano ham ($20) and Cloudy Bay clams with pearl barley and fino ($17). You've a choice of the rustic glass pavilion overlooking the vines or at the mosaic outdoor bar styled like Gaudí's Parc Güell. Both are delightful. Daily 11.30am–3pm plus Thurs–Sun 6–10pm.

Charlie Farley's 21 The Strand ☎ 09 372 4106, ⓦ charliefarleys.co.nz; map p.120. Casual licensed café serving the usual Kiwi breakfasts ($16–20) and the likes of squid with wasabi and lime mayo ($20) and fish of the day ($29), best served with a sundowner or two overlooking the sea. Free wi-fi. Mon–Fri 8.30am–10pm or later, Sat & Sun 8am–10pm or later.

★ **Poderi Crisci** 205 Awaawaroa Rd, Awaawaroa Bay, 7km southeast of Onetangi ☎ 09 372 2148, ⓦ podericrisci.co.nz; map p.120. Set a few hours aside to dine at this family-run vineyard restaurant at the far end of the island. The large kitchen garden is used to great effect in traditionally inspired, modern Italian dishes such as daily fish carpaccio ($19.50) and skewer

1

of lamb with sautéed artichokes ($34). The degustation dinners ($120–135 including wine matches) and the leisurely Sunday "long lunch" ($85) are exemplary. Also does wine tasting. Bookings highly recommended. Check website for winter hours; late Oct–Easter Mon–Wed & Sun noon–sunset, Thurs–Sat noon–11pm.

★ **Stonyridge** 80 Onetangi Rd ⊕ 09 372 8822, ⓦ stonyridge.com; map p.120. None of Waiheke's wineries is more highly regarded than *Stonyridge*, whose

organic, hand-tended vines produce Larose, one of the world's top Bordeaux-style reds. Vintages are often sold out (at over $350 a go) before they're even bottled, so there are limited cellar-door sales. Come for their public tour and tasting (Sat & Sun 11.30am; $15), to sample olive oil from some of NZ's oldest olive trees (though only from the 1980s), or for lunch in their Veranda Café overlooking the vines. You can also enjoy a casual alfresco lunch with tasting platters on their yoga deck. Daily 11.30am–5pm.

ENTERTAINMENT

Waiheke Island Community Cinema 2 Koroka Rd ⊕ 09 372 4240, ⓦ waihekecinema.co.nz. Screens

recent movies 3–4 times a day in a room full of old sofas.

Rotoroa Island

To cruise a fair bit of the Hauraki Gulf, swim off a gorgeous beach and experience something of Auckland's social history all in one compact day out, visit **Rotoroa Island**, off Waiheke's eastern tip. For over a hundred years this was a Salvation Army alcohol and drug rehab centre, off-limits except to detoxing residents; now it's something of an environmental restoration project, the residual grassland gradually being replanted with native saplings. The island has also been rendered pest-free and, in collaboration with Auckland Zoo, native species are being introduced, including tieke (saddleback), popokotea (whitehead) and, in summer, juvenile kiwi.

You can walk around the island in an hour or so, stopping off at beaches, headland viewpoints graced with sculptures and several buildings left from its working days: a chapel, diminutive jail and an 1860s-era schoolhouse. There's no food for sale but there are free barbecues, so take picnic supplies.

ARRIVAL AND INFORMATION

ROTOROA ISLAND

By ferry Fullers (⊕ 09 367 9111, ⓦ fullers.co.nz) ferries call in at Rotoroa (late Sept–early April 3–7 weekly; mid April–mid Sept Sat & Sun only; bookings essential; $52 return) on the way to Coromandel. The journey takes 1hr

15min, giving you about 5hr 30min on the island.
Information For information about your visit and a map of the island see ⓦ rotoroa.org.nz. The island's story is told in the superb Exhibition Centre (generally daily 10am–5pm).

ACCOMMODATION

Superintendent's House ⊕ 0800 768 676 ⓦ rotoroa. org.nz. Smart and well-equipped hostel-style accommodation in an old villa with great views. Bring a

sleeping bag or bedding and all your food. There are also three super-stylish homes sleeping 6–13. Dorms $\overline{\$35}$, homes $\overline{\$375}$

Great Barrier Island

Rugged and sparsely populated, **Great Barrier Island** (Aotea) lies 90km northeast of Auckland on the outer fringes of the Hauraki Gulf and, though only 30km long and 15km wide, packs in a mountainous heart which drops away to deep harbours in the west and golden surf beaches in the east. It's only a half-hour flight from the city but exudes a tranquillity and detachment that makes it seem a world apart. There is no mains electricity or water, no industry, no towns to speak of and only limited public transport.

Much of the pleasure here is in lazing on the **beaches**, ambling to the **hot springs** and striking out on foot into the **Aotea Conservation Park**, a compact and rugged chunk of deer- and possum-free bush between Port FitzRoy and Whangaparapara that takes up about a third of the island. In no time at all you can find yourself climbing in and out of little subtropical gullies luxuriant with nikau palms, tree ferns, regenerating

1

GREAT BARRIER ISLAND WALKS AND ACTIVITIES

A couple of days **hiking** in the Aotea Conservation Park is a great way to experience the Barrier: the i-SITE visitor centre's leaflets and maps will do for most hikers. Either tackle walks separately (see ⓦ doc.govt.nz/great-barrier-island) or piece together a loop using *Kaiaraara Hut* (see page 130) and the lovely modern *Mt Heale Hut* (see page 130). Shuttle operators offer trailhead transport from the airport or Tryphena.

BIKING

Paradise Cycles ☎021 1902865; ⓔparadisecyclesaotea@xtra.co.nz. There's enough worthwhile riding here to justify renting a bike for a day or two from this Whangaparapara-based company who deliver all over the island, run bike workshops, and are a mine of information. With one of their bikes, you can tackle the Te Ahumata Track, the Harataonga Coastal Track, Kowhai Track and Forest Road between Whangaparapara and Port FitzRoy. There are short rentals from $25, but the best deals are for multi-day rentals for several people.

KAYAKING

Rent kayaks from or Hillary Outdoors at Karaka Bay (double sea kayaks $80/day; ☎09 4290 762, ⓔgbi@opc.org.nz) or get in touch with *Currach Irish Pub* in Tryphena (see page 130).

FISHING AND SCUBA DIVING

Freedom Fishing Charters Medlands ☎09 429 0861, ⓦfreedomfishingcharters.co.nz. Ivan "Skilly" McManaway has been fishing the island for approaching fifty years and will take you out for $150 a head for half a day (minimum 2 people). He's also equipped for scuba diving, with gathering crayfish the main goal.

rimu and kauri, and onto scrubby manuka ridges with stunning coastal and mountain views. Many of the tracks follow the routes of mining and kauri-logging tramways. Tracks in the centre of the island converge on 621m **Hirakimata** (Mount Hobson), which is surrounded by boardwalks and wooden steps designed to keep trampers on the path and prevent the disturbance of nesting **black petrels**. If you're looking for more structure to your day, a few small-time tour and activity operators can keep you entertained (see page 126).

The vast majority of visitors arrive from Auckland between Boxing Day and the middle of January, many piling in for the New Year's Eve party at the sports club at Crossroads. The rest of the year is pretty quiet.

Brief history

Great Barrier is formed from the same line of extinct **volcanoes** as the Coromandel Peninsula and was one of the places first populated by **Māori**, who were occupying numerous *pa* sites when Cook sailed by in 1769. Recognizing the calming influence of Aotea on the waters of the Hauraki Gulf, Cook renamed it Great Barrier Island. From 1791, the island's vast stands of kauri were seized for ships' timbers, and kauri **logging** didn't cease until 1942, outliving some early copper mining and sporadic attempts to extract gold and silver. Logging and gum digging were replaced by a short-lived whale-oil extraction industry at Whangaparapara in the 1950s, but the Barrier soon fell back on tilling the poor clay soils and its peak population of over 5000 has now dropped to around 900.

Back to the land

Alternative lifestylers arrived in the 1960s and 1970s, and while 1970s idealism has largely been supplanted by modern pragmatism, **self-sufficiency** remains. People grow their own vegetables, everyone has their own water supply and wind-turbines and solar panels reduce the strain on diesel generators. **Agriculture** takes a back seat to **tourism**, however, and wealthy second-home owners are moving in.

Tryphena

Pretty **Tryphena** (Rangitawhiri) is the southernmost harbour, where the Great Barrier's main settlement is spread over four bays: **Shoal Bay** (where ferries arrive), **Mulberry Grove**, **Stonewall Village** (the largest settlement) and **Puriri Bay** (a short walk along the coast from Stonewall Village). Tryphena has good accommodation and places to eat, but activities are limited to swimming, renting a kayak and tackling a few short walks.

Medlands Beach

Most people head straight for **Medlands Beach** (Oruawharo), a long sweep of golden sand on the east coast broken by a sheltering island and often endowed with some of the Barrier's best (unpatrolled) surf. The pretty blue and white **St John's Church** looks suitably out of place, having only been moved here from the mainland by barge in 1986 before being dragged over the dunes.

Claris

Most flights arrive at **CLARIS** (Kaitoke), just north of Medlands, where the post office is called Pigeon Post in honour of Great Barrier's original airmail service, said to be the world's first. The story goes that when the SS *Wairarapa* was wrecked on the northwest coast of Great Barrier in 1898, the news took a sobering three days to get to Auckland. In response the island set up a **pigeon-gram** mail service that was used until 1908, when a telephone was installed.

Milk, Honey and Grain Museum

47 Hector Sanderson Rd • Open daily • Donation required • ☏ 09 429 0773

The **Milk, Honey and Grain Museum** does what it says on the box, thanks to a neatly organized collection of memorabilia, but also ranges far wider, covering odd aspects of the island's development. It's a worthwhile stop if the weather's bad.

Crossroads, Whangaparapara and the road north

Crossroads, 2km north of Claris, is just that – the junction of roads to Okupu, Port FitzRoy and Whangaparapara. The Whangaparapara road runs past the scant roadside remains of the **Oreville gold stamping battery** (unrestricted entry) and the start of a path to **Kaitoke Hot Springs**. At **WHANGAPARAPARA**, a short stroll around the bay brings you to the foundations of a whaling station built here in the 1950s.

   North of Crossroads, the Port FitzRoy road passes the lovely surf and swimming beach of **Awana Bay** and the roadside **Pinnacles Lookout** before reaching the start of a 1km return track to **Windy Canyon** (a narrow passage that gets its name from the eerie sounds produced by certain wind conditions).

Port FitzRoy

The harbour at **PORT FITZROY** remains remarkably calm under most wind conditions, a quality not lost on yachties who flock here in summer. They're served by a shop, burger bar and the *Port FitzRoy Boat Club*. Port FitzRoy also makes a good jumping-off point for tramps in the Aotea Conservation Park, though the huge Kaiaraara kauri dam that was once the main destination was swept away by floods in 2014.

Glenfern Sanctuary

Glenfern Rd • Guided tour by appointment $40 • ☏ 09 429 0091, ⓦ glenfern.org.nz

The northern shore of Port FitzRoy's harbour is formed by the Kotuku Peninsula, which since 2008 has been separated from the rest of the island by a 2km-long predator-proof fence forming the 2.3-square-kilometre **Glenfern Sanctuary**. Rats have been virtually eliminated, North Island robins have been reintroduced and other birdlife is slowly returning. Highly informative guided tours include a lovely kauri tree canopy walkway.

1

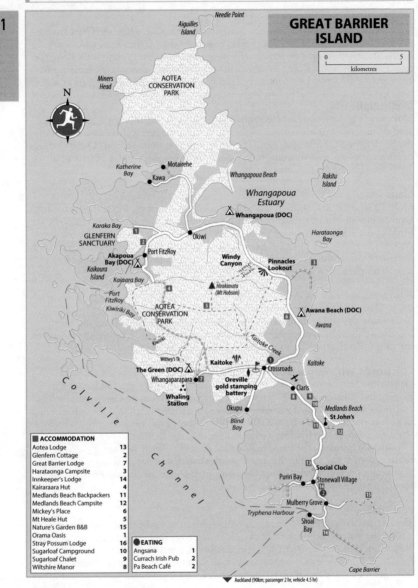

GREAT BARRIER ISLAND

0 — 5
kilometres

Needle Point

Aiguilles Island

Miners Head

AOTEA CONSERVATION PARK

N

Katherine Bay

Motairehe

Kawa

Whangapoua Beach

Rakitu Island

Whangapoua Estuary

Karaka Bay

Whangapoua (DOC)

GLENFERN SANCTUARY

Okiwi

Akapoua Bay (DOC)

Port FitzRoy

Harataonga Bay

Windy Canyon

Pinnacles Lookout

3

Kaikoura Island

Kaiaara Bay

Port FitzRoy

Kiwiriki Bay

4

Hirakimata (Mt Hobson)

5

AOTEA CONSERVATION PARK

6

Awana Beach (DOC)

Awana

Kiwiriki

Kaitoke Creek

Withey's Tk

Kaitoke

Crossroads

Kaitoke

The Green (DOC)

Whangaparapara

Oreville gold stamping battery

8   9

Claris

Whaling Station

Okupu

Blind Bay

10

Medlands Beach

St John's

11   12

13

Social Club

Puriri Bay

Stonewall Village

14
2

15

Mulberry Grove

Tryphena Harbour

Shoal Bay

16

Cape Barrier

Colville   Channel

ACCOMMODATION

Aotea Lodge	13
Glenfern Cottage	2
Great Barrier Lodge	7
Harataonga Campsite	3
Innkeeper's Lodge	14
Kairaraara Hut	4
Medlands Beach Backpackers	11
Medlands Beach Campsite	12
Mickey's Place	6
Mt Heale Hut	5
Nature's Garden B&B	15
Orama Oasis	1
Stray Possum Lodge	16
Sugarloaf Campground	10
Sugarloaf Chalet	9
Wiltshire Manor	8

● EATING

Angsana	1
Currach Irish Pub	2
Pa Beach Café	2

▼ Auckland (90km; passenger 2 hr, vehicle 4.5 hr)

ARRIVAL AND DEPARTURE

GREAT BARRIER ISLAND

BY FERRY

SeaLink ☎0800 732 546, ⓦsealink.co.nz. The sedate year-round car and passenger ferry leaves Brigham Street in Auckland's Wynyard Quarter for Tryphena (4–5 weekly; 4hr 30min) and Port FitzRoy (1 weekly; 4hr 30min). Return fares: passengers $105.50 ($153 in Dec & Jan); cars $359 ($454 in Dec & Jan); bikes $21.

BY PLANE

Claris Airport Most flights from Auckland International Airport arrive at Claris, the island's administrative centre and convenient for the best beaches at Medlands and Awana Bay.

INFORMATION

Visitor information An i-SITE visitor centre is at Claris Airport (daily Dec & Jan 10am–5pm; Feb–Nov Mon, Wed, Fri 10am–2pm, ☎0800 468 822, ⓦgreatbarrier.co.nz). Info on all things Barrier, including DOC huts, tracks and campsites.

Services There are no banks or ATMs on the island. Most places accept credit and debit cards, but bring plenty of cash. Mobile coverage is patchy at best; Tryphena and Port

AIRLINES

FlyMySky ☎0800 222 123, ⓦflymysky.co.nz. Flights from Auckland (3–4 daily; $89 if booked online 3 days ahead).

Barrier Air ☎0800 900 600, ⓦbarrierair.kiwi. Flights from Auckland (3–4 daily; $89 each way).

FitzRoy have reasonable Spark coverage (from Auckland) while Vodafone and 2Degrees pick up the island's only repeater around Claris, Medlands and Kaitoke. Internet access is limited but there's free wi-fi at the Claris Airport and free internet at the library, 75 Hector Sanderson Road, Claris (Mon–Fri 8.30am–5pm). Tryphena's *Curragh Irish Pub* has free wi-fi for customers and a few other places offer access.

GETTING AROUND

There is no public transport on the island but several on-demand shuttle buses generally meet all ferries and flights, though it's best to book in advance. It is often more convenient to rent a car, or even a bike, though the hills are steep and the more interesting roads are dusty in summer.

By shuttle bus Go Great Barrier Island (☎0800 997 222, ⓦgreatbarrierislandtourism.co.nz) run on-demand

shuttle services, as do GBI Shuttle Buses (☎09 429 0062, ⓦgreatbarrierisland.co.nz). From Tryphena, fares are around $20 to Medlands, $25 to Claris and $40 to Whangaparapara.

By rental car Aotea Rentals (☎0800 426 832, ⓦaoteacarrentals.co.nz) in Tryphena has cars from $60/day. GBI Rent A Car in Claris (☎09 429 0062, ⓦgreatbarrierisland.co.nz) has basic cars from $40/day.

ACCOMMODATION

Along with plush lodges and hotels, Great Barrier Island has some lovely **self-catering cottages**, many listed on ⓦgreatbarrierislandtourism.co.nz and ⓦgreatbarrier. co.nz. The owners often live close by and can arrange some meals. **Book well ahead** from Christmas to mid-January when the island is packed. There are numerous, simple DOC **campsites** ($10; book at peak periods; ⓦdoc.govt.nz), all with toilets, water and cold showers (except *The Green*) and marked on our map (see page 128).

TRYPHENA AND AROUND

Aotea Lodge 41 Medland Road, almost opposite Barrier Oasis Lodge ☎09 429 0628, ⓦaotealodge.com; map p.128. Three one- and two-bedroom self-contained units in pleasant grounds 600m inland from Tryphena Harbour. Rates are $40 higher for single nights but their ferry and car rental deals are worth exploring and there's free wi-fi. $130

★**Innkeeper's Lodge** Stonewall, Tryphena ☎09 429 0211, ⓦcurrachirishpub.co.nz; map p.128. The pick of the places around Tryphena – homely, small and welcoming, with a great pub and restaurant spilling out onto the veranda, all conveniently close to the shop. There are attractive rooms plus a single four-bed backpacker room that can be noisy with pub patrons leaving. Good-value flight, transport and accommodation packages available. Dorms $35, doubles $130

Nature's Garden B&B Rosalie Bay Rd ☎09 429 0494, ⓦnaturesgardenbandb.co.nz; map p.128. You'll need a vehicle to stay at this B&B on an organic, bio-dynamic macadamia orchard with lily ponds and native bush in the grounds. The three rooms all share a bathroom and living area. A delicious continental breakfast is included and there's internet access available. $130

Stray Possum Lodge 64 Cape Barrier Rd ☎0800 767 786, ⓦstraypossum.co.nz; map p.128. A little out on a limb, this bush-girt hostel has six- and eight-bed dorms, doubles, cabins and lovely self-contained chalets ideal for groups of up to six ($155). There's also a licensed restaurant which can serve bar meals or pizza (advance bookings only in winter). Linen $5 for your stay, or bring a sleeping bag. Camping $15, dorms $27, doubles $79

MEDLANDS

Medlands Beach Backpackers and Villas 9 Mason Rd ☎09 429 0320, ⓦmedlandsbeach.com; map p.128. Basic, low-key backpackers with small four-bed dorms, a few secluded private chalets and a couple of self-contained villas ($150) on a small farm a 10min walk from Medlands Beach – making it popular with surfers. There are bodyboards for guests' use, but there are no meals and no shops nearby, so bring your own food. Dorms $35, chalets $60

CLARIS, CROSSROADS AND AROUND

★ **Sugarloaf Chalet** Sugarloaf Rd, Kaitoke ☏ 09 429 0229; map p.128. A gorgeous, rustic-chic self-catering cottage with barbecue area, fire pit and solar power, just steps from a lovely beach and with a real outdoors flavour (complete with external shower and toilet). **$175**

Wiltshire Manor 47 Hector Sanderson Rd ☏ 021 138 7293 ✉ jacqui@islandaccommodation.co.nz; map p.128. Well-sited just 400m from the airport, this simple hostel is really just a basic house with one double and two twin rooms. **$70**

WHANGAPARAPARA

Great Barrier Lodge Whangaparapara Harbour ☏ 09 429 0488, ⌨ greatbarrierlodge.com; map p.128. This harbour-side lodge is pretty much all there is at Whangaparapara, and also serves as the local grocery and dive shop. Accommodation is in rooms with en-suite and kitchenette facilities (except garden rooms), and self-catering cottages and suites. The main building houses a bar/restaurant and cooked breakfasts are $22. **$195**

PORT FITZROY

Glenfern Cottage Glenfern Rd, Port FitzRoy ☏ 09 429 0091, ⌨ fitzroyhouse.co.nz; map p.128. Stay inside Glenfern Sanctuary at this wood-floored self-contained cottage sleeping up to ten, with views over the harbour and free access to the sanctuary and to canoes and a dinghy. Two-night min; $50-a-night discount for 3 nights or more. **$175**

Orama Oasis Karaka Bay ☏ 09 429 0063, ⌨ orama. org.nz; map p.128. Welcoming Christian camp that also operates as a waterfront holiday park, with bunkrooms ($33), lodges ($70) and self-contained cottages ($210). There's a swimming pool, basic shop and access to magnificent bushwalks, fishing and diving. Per person camping **$25**, cabins **$50**

CAMPSITES AND HUTS

Harataonga Campsite Harataonga; map p.128. Excellent, shady DOC site 300m back from the beach and very popular with families in the fortnight after Christmas. **$13**

Kaiaraara Hut Near Port FitzRoy ⌨ doc.govt.nz; map p.128. Longstanding 28-bunker huddled in the bush with a wood stove for heating. Book through DOC and take pots, utensils and all food. **$15**

Medlands Beach Campsite Medlands Beach; map p.128. Attractive DOC site beside an estuary and just over the dunes from an excellent beach. Very crowded for most of Jan but at other times you'll have it to yourselves. **$13**

Mickey's Place Awana ☏ 09 429 0140; map p.128. Hospitable but primitive campsite 25km north of Tryphena that's less well located than the nearby DOC site but has hot showers, toilets and a basic cookhouse. **$7**

Mt Heale Hut ⌨ doc.govt.nz; map p.128. Superb new 20-bunk hut set in a saddle below Mt Heale with great views across the Hauraki Gulf to Little Barrier Island. It's a 3–3hr 30min walk here. There's a gas cooking stove but take pots, utensils and food. Book online. **$15**

Sugarloaf Campground Sugarloaf Rd, Kaitoke; map p.128. A great private campsite overlooking the southern end of Kaitoke beach. It has water, toilets and showers. Ask about exploring the Mermaid Pool at low tide. **$12**

EATING

The limited number of stand-alone **restaurants** encourages lots of accommodation operators to offer meals, and those that don't will almost certainly have self-catering facilities. Restaurants often close early (or don't open at all) if business is slow, so **book ahead**. There are also **shops** in Tryphena, Claris, Whangaparapara and Port FitzRoy, where you can pick up picnic provisions.

Angsana 63 Grays Rd, just north of Crossroads ☏ 09 429 0272; map p.128. A quality Thai restaurant seems incongruous for the Barrier, but the island is a better place for it. The menu features all the Thai favourites (mains around $30) with friendly service. Oct–May Thurs–Sun 6–9pm.

Pa Beach Café 87 Blackwell Drive, Tryphena ☏ 09 429 0905; map p.128. This inexpensive daytime beach café is a gorgeous new addition to island life. Great coffee, homemade cakes and sandwiches, plus mouthwatering pies such as chicken, leek and pumpkin. Daily 8.30am–3pm.

DRINKING

Drinking tends to happen in bars attached to accommodation establishments or in the social clubs at Tryphena and Claris.

★ **Currach Irish Pub** Stonewall, Tryphena ☏ 09 429 0211, ⌨ currachirishpub.co.nz; map p.128. An Irish pub that's about as traditional as you can get on a South Pacific island – a lot of the paraphernalia came from the owner's grandmother's pub in County Kerry, which closed in 1950. There's Guinness plus local craft beers on tap and hot bar meals served in the evening (crumbed scallops and chips $27). There's also often live acoustic music, especially on Thurs when anyone is welcome to jam. Daily noon–10pm or later.

Tiritiri Matangi

Tiny **Tiritiri Matangi** island (roughly 2km by 1km) just off the tip of the Whangaparaoa Peninsula and 30km north of Auckland, is a wonderful "open sanctuary" where visitors are free to roam through the predator-free bush. Within a couple of hours, it's possible to see rarities such as takahe, saddlebacks, whiteheads, red-crowned parakeets, North Island robins, kokako and brown teals, though to stand a chance of seeing the little-spotted kiwi and tuatara, you'll have to stay overnight. **Northern blue penguins** also frequent Tiritiri and can be seen all year round, but are most in evidence in March, when they come ashore to moult, and from September to December, when they nest in specially constructed viewing boxes located along the seashore path west of the main wharf.

The standard loop along the east coast then back via the central Ridge Track passes **Hobbs Beach**, where you can swim from the island's only sandy strand.

Brief history

Tiritiri Matangi was first populated by the Kawerau-A-Maki **Māori** and later by Ngati Paoa, both of whom are now recognized as the land's traditional owners. They partly **cleared the island** of bush, a process continued by Europeans who arrived in the mid-nineteenth century to graze sheep and cattle. Fortunately, **pests** such as possums, stoats, deer and cats failed to get a foothold, so since farming became uneconomic in the early 1970s Tiritiri has been **reforested** with 300,000 saplings.

ARRIVAL AND DEPARTURE   TIRITIRI MATANGI

By ferry Fullers (daily Christmas to mid-Jan, 9am; rest of year Wed–Sun and public holidays, 9am; $75; ☏ 0800 360 3472, ⊚ fullers.co.nz) do day-trips giving five hours on the island.

INFORMATION AND TOURS

Tourist information ⊚ tiritirimatangi.org.nz.
Food There is no food on the island. Bring your own lunch.
Guided walks Ferry passengers can join a guided walk (1.5hr; $10) from the wharf, led by enthusiastic volunteers steeped in bird lore. They typically finish near the lighthouse at the modern interpretation centre.

ACCOMMODATION

Tiritiri Matangi Island Bunkhouse ⊚ doc.govt.nz/ tiritiribunkhouse. The island's only accommodation is this communal bunkhouse near the lighthouse. Book as far in advance as you can (months ahead for weekends), and bring a sleeping bag and food in sealed rodent-proof containers. **$30**

Northland

CAPE REINGA

Northland

Thrusting 350km from Auckland into the subtropical north, Northland separates the Pacific Ocean from the Tasman Sea. The two oceans swirl together off Cape Reinga, New Zealand's most northerly road-accessible point, which tourists often approach via the sands of Ninety Mile Beach. Kiwis regularly describe this staunchly Māori province as the "Winterless North", a phrase that evokes the citrus trees, avocado plantations, vineyards, warm aquamarine waters and beaches of white silica or golden sand. These attractions have increasingly made the upper reaches of the region a magnet for discerning tourists and holidaying Kiwis, keen to escape the hullabaloo of Auckland traffic. Increased tourism has, in turn, slowly brought back some prosperity and a more positive and welcoming attitude to a region once noted for its ambivalence to visitors.

Scenically, Northland splits down the middle. The **east coast** is a labyrinth of coves hidden between plunging headlands. Beaches tend to be calm and safe, with the force of occasional Pacific storms broken by clusters of protective barrier islands. There could hardly be a greater contrast than the long, virtually straight, **west coast** pounded by powerful Tasman breakers and broken only by occasional harbours. Tidal rips and holes make swimming dangerous, and there are few lifeguard patrols. Some beaches are even designated as roads but are full of hazards for the unwary – and rental cars aren't insured for beach driving, so don't risk it. Exploration of the undulating **interior** involves long forays down twisting side roads.

Beyond Auckland's extended suburbs, on the east shore, is the rural **Matakana Coast**, popular with yachties circumnavigating Kawau Island and snorkellers exploring the underwater world of the **Goat Island Marine Reserve**. The broad sweep of **Bream Bay** runs to the dramatic crags of Whangarei Heads at the entrance to Northland's major port and town, **Whangarei**. Off the coast here lie the **Poor Knights Islands**, one of the world's premier scuba spots with a multitude of unique dives around the islands. Tourists in a hurry tend to make straight for the **Bay of Islands**, a jagged bite out of the coastline that is steeped in New Zealand history and dotted with islands suitable for cruising, diving and swimming (some of the time) with dolphins. Everything north of here is loosely referred to as **The Far North**, a region characterized by the quiet remoteness of the **Whangaroa Harbour**, **Doubtless Bay**, and the **Aupori Peninsula**, which backs **Ninety Mile Beach** and leads to **Cape Reinga**.

The west coast is clearly discernible from the east, marked by the struggle out of economic neglect caused by the cessation of kauri logging and establishment of farming and tourism in its stead, both of which are finally beginning to alter the landscape and create a more positive atmosphere. First stop on the way back south from Ninety Mile Beach is the fragmented but alluring **Hokianga Harbour**, one of New Zealand's largest, with spectacular sand dunes gracing the north head. South of here you're into the **Waipoua Forest**, which is all that remains after the depredations of the kauri loggers – a story best told at the excellent Kauri Museum at Matakohe.

GETTING AROUND   NORTHLAND

By car With no trains and few airports, you'll most likely be driving around Northland. Road choices are limited to the state highways running up each side of the peninsula. These form a logical loop formalized as the Twin Coast Discovery Highway: there's no need to follow it slavishly, but the brown signs emblazoned with a dolphin and curling wave make a good starting framework.

WAIPOUA KAURI FOREST

Highlights

❶ **Matakana** Less than an hour's drive from Auckland, this affluent enclave with its buzzing Saturday farmers' market is surrounded by boutique wineries. See page 137

❷ **Poor Knights Islands** World-class scuba diving and snorkelling in caves, along walls and under rock arches, all abundant with beautiful and unusual sea life. See page 149

❸ **Bay of Islands** Sail, kayak and soak up the history and scenery of Northland's tourism hotspot and – if you're lucky – swim with dolphins. See page 151

❹ **Ninety Mile Beach and Cape Reinga** Journey the length of one of the country's

best-known beaches, stopping to sandboard giant dunes along the way, before taking in views of the Pacific Ocean and Tasman Sea meeting in a swirling mass. See page 174

❺ **Hokianga Harbour** Settle in to watch the sun set in a fiery rainbow of orange, fuchsia and indigo, or explore the wind-sculpted dunes that overlook this scenic, laidback harbour. See page 178

❻ **Waipoua Kauri Forest** Marvel at New Zealand's largest tree, the majestic 2000-year-old Tane Mahuta, and the other ancient kauri in the same stand. See page 182

HIGHLIGHTS ARE MARKED ON THE MAP ON PAGE 136

By bus The main bus line is InterCity (☎ 09 583 5780, ⓦ intercity.co.nz). Nakedbus (premium charged ☎ 0900 62533, ⓦ nakedbus.com) and Kiwi Experience (☎ 09 336 4286, ⓦ kiwiexperience.com) also run around the region and can be a very affordable option. Public bus services around Northland are provided by BusLink (ⓦ buslink.co.nz).

By plane Northland has a limited number of flights and since distances are relatively short you're unlikely to need them, except perhaps for flights from Kaitaia to Great Barrier Island with Barrier Air (☎ 0800 900600, ⓦ barrierair.kiwi) or a flightseeing trip from Paihia to Cape Reinga via the Bay of Islands (see page 159).

INFORMATION

Websites The Northland website is ⓦ northlandnz.com.
Tourist information The Far North region of Northland has regional i-SITE visitor centres in Whangarei, Paihia, Kaitaia and Opononi, as well as Warkworth.

Freedom camping Northland has designated free camping sites for self-contained campers (one night only). Pick up a leaflet from an i-SITE visitor centre (see above).

Brief history

Northland was the site of most of the early contact between Māori and European settlers, and the birthplace of New Zealand's most important document, the

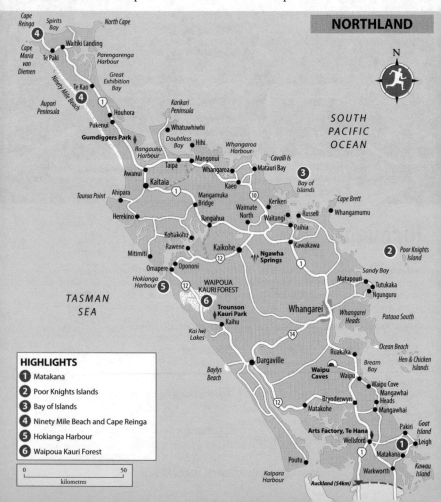

Treaty of Waitangi. Māori legend tells of how the great Polynesian explorer Kupe discovered the Hokianga Harbour and, finding the climate and abundance of food to his liking, encouraged his people to return and settle there. It was their descendants in the Bay of Islands who had the dubious honour of making the first contact with white men, as European whalers plundered the seas and missionaries sought converts. Eventually, the northern chiefs signed away their sovereignty in return for assurances on land and traditional rights, which were seldom respected.

As more fertile farmlands were found in newly settled regions further south, rapacious **kauri loggers** and **gum diggers** cleared the bush, and later, as extractive industries died away, pioneers moved in, turning much of the land to **dairy country**. Local dairy factories closed as larger semi-industrial complexes centralized processing, leaving small towns all but destitute, though the planting of fast-growing exotic trees and sporadic horticulture keep local economies ticking over.

The Matakana Coast to Bream Bay

Ⓦ matakanacoast.com

Around 50km north of central Auckland the city's influence begins to wane, heralding the **Matakana Coast**, a 30km stretch of shallow harbours, beach-strung peninsulas and small islands. Its individual character becomes apparent once you pass pretty **Warkworth** and head out either to **Kawau Island**, or up the coast to the village of **Matakana** and the snorkelling and diving nirvana of **Goat Island**.

The journey from Auckland to Warkworth has been made quicker, though less scenic, by the introduction of a 7km stretch of toll road ($2.30/car, payable online within five days). It's worth sticking to the old route though, if you have time, as there are great views via Orewa on the Hibiscus Coast Highway.

There's little to detain you on SH1 between Warkworth and Waipu as it passes the road junction at **Brynderwyn**, where SH12 loops off to Dargaville, the Waipoua kauri forest and the Hokianga Harbour. If you're heading north and want a scenic route, it's better to stay on the coast and follow **Bream Bay**, named by Cook when he visited in 1770 and his crew hauled in tarakihi, which they mistook for bream. There are no sizeable towns here, only the small beach communities of **Mangawhai Heads** and **Waipu Cove**, looking out to the **Hen and Chicken Islands**, refuges for rare birds such as the wattled saddleback.

Warkworth

The peaceful and slow-paced rural town of **WARKWORTH** only really comes to life in high summer when thousands of yachties moor their boats in the numerous estuaries and coves nearby. From the late 1820s for about a century, the languid stretch of river behind the town seethed with boats shipping out kauri: a boardwalk now traces its shores past the *Jane Gifford* (Ⓦ janegifford.org.nz), a rebuilt scow which once worked the tidal waterways and now runs occasional trips (1hr; $20).

Warkworth and Districts Museum

Tudor Collins Drive, 3km south of Warkworth off the SH1 • Daily 10am–4pm (3pm in winter) • $7 • Ⓦ warkworthmuseum.co.nz

Spend a few minutes at the **Warkworth and Districts Museum**, which explores the region's history through re-created rooms, and a 5m-long, 130-link chain carved from a single piece of kauri. The two ancient kauri outside mark the start of two well-presented twenty-minute boardwalk nature trails through the preserved bush of the **Parry Kauri Park** (9am–dusk; donation). A free leaflet at the museum's entrance explains the trees in detail.

2

GOAT ISLAND TOURS AND ACTIVITIES

The waters surrounding **Goat Island** have good visibility, making them perfect for snorkellers and scuba divers who can enjoy a lush world populated by kelp forest and numerous multicoloured fish, while deeper still are more exposed seascapes with an abundance of sponges. Because of the clarity of the water this is also an excellent spot for the less adventurous who want to observe from glass-bottom boats or kayaks.

Glass Bottom Boat ☎09 422 6334, ⓦglassbottomboat.co.nz. Tours depart from the beach (3 trips daily in winter, more in the summer; $30), last about 45min and are best in fine, calm weather. Phone ahead to check conditions and make bookings.
Goat Island Dive 142a Pakiri Rd, Leigh ☎09 422 6925, ⓦgoatislanddive.co.nz. A highly professional outfit that rents mask, snorkel and fins ($25), and wetsuits (from $15) plus offers a 2hr guided snorkel ($75). They also run scuba courses and trips to Goat Island Marine Reserve and beyond. They'll also rent scuba gear (full set from $90) if you want to go independently, assuming you have the relevant qualification. Open daily in summer, and on weekends in winter.

Brick Bay Sculpture Trail

Arabella Lane, 6km east of Warkworth off SH1 · Daily 10am–5pm, last entry 4pm · $12 · ☎09 425 4690, ⓦbrickbaysculpture.co.nz

For a combination of outdoor sculpture and striking architecture, try the **Brick Bay Sculpture Trail**. An hour wandering the 2km-long bush, vines and parkland trail past the art – 45-plus sculptures mostly by New Zealand artists and all for sale (and likely to remain so, given the prices) – gets you back to the predominantly glass café, where wine tastings, olive oil tastings and platters (for two) of local-ish produce ($32) may slow you down further.

Kawau Island

With a resident population of around seventy (plus lots of weekenders), **KAWAU ISLAND** is chiefly given over to holiday homes, each with its own wharf. Boats for the island leave from the wharf 8km east of Warkworth (see page 137).

Mansion House

Sept–May Mon–Fri noon–2pm, Sat & Sun noon–3.30pm · $4

The only sight of note on Kawau Island is the grand, kauri-panelled **Mansion House**, the former private home of George Grey – then doing his second stint as New Zealand's governor – and furnished much as it would have been in the late 1880s, including with Grey's writing desk.

Grey's pursuit of the Victorian fashion for all things exotic resulted in **grounds** stocked with flora and fauna from all over the world, such as Chilean wine palms and coral trees. He also brought in four species of **wallaby**, which have overtaken the island and have to be regularly culled. You might even see Australian kookaburras and a white peacock.

A path runs through the gardens to the tiny beach at **Lady's Bay** and on to a network of short tracks that weave through pine forest and kanuka scrub. The most popular destination is the ruins of the island's old **copper mine** (40min each way). The on-site **café** (see page 142) provides sustenance.

Matakana and around

Over the last decade or so, **MATAKANA**, 9km northeast of Warkworth, has transformed itself from an inconsequential crossroads to the heart of an aspiring **wine** region, and minor Slow Food centre. It is close enough to Auckland to attract weekenders who arrive for the **farmers' market** (Sat 8am–1pm) and stick around to visit the local boutique cinema (2 Matakana Valley Rd; ☎09 422 9833, ⓦmatakanacinemas.co.nz), browse the shops – which include a heritage butchers, a quality bookshop and a fancy deli (see page 142) – and stop in at the wineries.

Morris & James Pottery & Tileworks

2km west of Matakana at Tongue Farm Rd • Daily 9am–5pm; café/bar 9am–4pm; free tour daily 11.30am • Free • ☎ 09 422 7116, ⓦ morrisandjames.co.nz

The catalyst for the region's development was the **Morris & James Pottery & Tileworks**, which has been producing vibrant, handmade terracotta tiles and bright, large garden pots from local clay since the late 1970s. You can catch a free thirty-minute tour of the pottery and visit the café/bar.

Tawharanui Regional Park

10km southeast of Matakana, along Takatu Rd • Gates open daily 6am–dusk • Free

Tawharanui Regional Park has great beaches and swathes of regenerating bush, and makes for a pleasant spot to visit before leaving the Matakana area. Predators have been eradicated and native birds are returning to this designated **open sanctuary**: come to swim, snorkel, picnic and walk or bike the easy trails, but you'll have to bring everything with you. You can also camp here (see page 141).

Leigh and Goat Island

The village of **LEIGH**, 13km northeast of Matakana, holds a picturesque harbour with bobbing wooden fishing boats. Heading a further 4km northeast brings you to the **Cape Rodney–Okakari Marine Reserve**, usually known simply as **Goat Island** since the bush-clad islet is 300m offshore. In 1975, this became New Zealand's first marine reserve, with no-take areas stretching 5km along the shoreline and 800m off the coast. Some 40 years on, the undersea life is thriving, with large rock lobster, huge snapper and rays. Feeding has been discouraged since blue maomaos developed a taste for frozen peas and began to mob swimmers and divers. Easy beach access (from the road-end parking area), clear water, rock pools on wave-cut platforms, a variety of undersea terrains and relatively benign currents combine to make this an enormously popular year-round diving spot, as well as a favourite summer destination for families: aim to come midweek if you value tranquillity.

Pakiri

There's not much to **PAKIRI**, 10km north of Leigh, except for a beautiful, long, deserted white surf beach, backed by farmland, dunes and stands of mature pohutukawa trees that bloom with vibrant red flowers in December (hence their nickname: Christmas trees). This is a perfect setting for leisurely beachcombing, birdwatching, sunset gazing and **horseriding** (see page 141).

Mangawhai

Tiny **Mangawhai**, 40km north of Warkworth, is a commercial farm supply settlement that has transmogrified into a weekend village for holidaying Aucklanders. It has a few restaurants, a chic farmers' market at the weekends and access to the infinitely more scenic Mangawhai Heads.

Mangawhai Heads

On the coast 3km north of Mangawhai sits **Mangawhai Heads**, at the mouth of the Mangawhai Harbour, marked by holiday homes straggling over the hillsides behind a fine surf beach. Long a Kiwi summer-holiday favourite, Mangawhai Heads is relaxed outside the peak summer blitz and is chiefly of interest for the extraordinary views on the scenic **Mangawhai Cliffs Walkway** (2–3hr; year-round; at low tide you can return along the beach).

Mangawhai Museum

Molesworth Drive • Daily 10am–4pm • $12 • ☎ 09 431 4663, ⓦ mangawhai-museum.org.nz

The new **Mangawhai Museum** is home to exhibitions charting human habitation of the area around this natural harbour, stretching from Māori settlement to the present day – "from building ships to building sandcastles". Follow the strands of 11 different stories through the stingray-shaped contemporary building, discovering everything from the great Māori battle between the Ngapuhi and Ngati Whatua groups to the ongoing struggle to save the critically endangered Fairy Tern.

Waipu and around

An Aberdeen granite monument topped by a Scottish lion rampant dominates the quirky village of **WAIPU**, 25km north of Mangawhai. It's a nod to the nine hundred Scottish settlers who followed charismatic preacher, the Reverend Norman McLeod, here in the mid-1800s. On New Year's Day, Waipu hosts its **Highland Games** (ⓦ waipugames.co.nz), in which competitors heft large stones and toss cabers and sheaves in Caledonian Park.

Waipu Museum

36 The Centre • Daily 10am–4pm • $10 • ☎ 09 432 0746, ⓦ waipumuseum.com

The excellent **Waipu Museum** tells the tale of Scottish settlers and their journey via Nova Scotia where famine and a series of harsh winters drove them on to form a strict, self-contained Calvinist community. All is admirably illustrated, with everything from McLeod's old pocket watch to genealogical records that are regularly consulted by Kiwi Scots tracing their ancestry. Also worth a look are the various Caledonian-themed rotating exhibitions.

Waipu Caves

16km from town (signposted) via Shoemaker and Waipu Caves roads

Waipu Caves is a popular local excursion, and in among its many limestone formations is one of the longest stalagmites in New Zealand, in a 200m glowworm-filled passage. Obtain a free map from the visitor centre in the Waipu Museum, wear old clothes and good footwear, and take a couple of reliable torches. The cave is impenetrable after heavy rain; even when it's dry you'll get muddy, so use the cold shower, located on the wall away from the road, or the public toilets on the site.

ARRIVAL AND DEPARTURE   **MATAKANA COAST TO BREAM BAY**

WARKWORTH

By bus InterCity/Northliner and NakedBus buses stop outside the i-SITE visitor centre on Baxter St.

Destinations Auckland (4 daily; 1hr 20min); Whangarei (4 daily; 2hr).

KAWAU ISLAND

By boat All boats to Kawau Island leave from the wharf (parking $10/24hr) at Sandspit, a small road-end community on the Matakana Estuary, 8km east of Warkworth. Kawau Cruises (☎ 0800 111 616, ⓦ kawaucruises.co.nz) run one or two trips direct to Mansion House Bay daily ($55 return), which allow for roughly twice the time ashore as the Royal

Mail Run (see page 141), which also takes you to the island.

LEIGH AND GOAT ISLAND

By taxi Without your own vehicle, the only way to get to Leigh is via taxi from Matakana. Matakabs (☎ 0800 522743) cost around $40 one way.

WAIPU

By bus InterCity/Northliner and NakedBus drop off and pick up on request outside the Pear Tree gift shop, 13 The Centre (☎ 09 432 0046), which also acts as a ticket agent.

Destinations Auckland (4 daily; 2hr 30min); Whangarei (4 daily; 40min).

INFORMATION

WARKWORTH
Visitor information i-SITE, 1 Baxter St (Mon–Fri 9am–5pm, Sat & Sun 10am–3pm; ☎ 09 425 9081. The office can help with travel bookings and has free internet access.

MANGAWHAI
Useful website ⓦ mangawhai.co.nz

WAIPU
Visitor information 36 The Centre (daily 10am–4pm; ☎ 09 432 0746). Located in the museum, and run by volunteers.

TOURS AND ACTIVITIES

KAWAU ISLAND
Royal Mail Run ☎ 0800 111616, ⓦ kawaucruises.co.nz. Kawau Cruises (see page 140) operates the mail run service (daily 10.30am; 4hr; $68 return; $95 with BBQ lunch), delivering mail, papers and groceries to all the wharves on the island and giving you around an hour and a half ashore at Mansion House Bay – plenty of time to enjoy the native bush and beach, take a swim or have a look around the house before meeting the boat for the return. Lunch is served on board on the outward leg of the trip.

MATAKANA
Blue Adventures Omaha Watersports Centre, 5km east of Matakana ☎ 022 630 5705, ⓦ blueadventures.co.nz. Offers lessons for stand-up paddleboarding ($59/person/hr), wakeboarding ($99/person/2hr; minimum

three people) and kitesurfing (from $89/person/hr), plus they rent out equipment.
Matakana River Tours ☎ 021 046 9426, ⓦ matakanarivertours.co.nz. Hour-long tours from the wharf (just down the hill from the village) take in the beautiful tidal waterway as far as Sandspit Basin. Phil – who built the boat – shares stories along the way. Check online for sailing times and book ahead. $25/person.

PAKIRI
Pakiri Beach horse rides Rahuikiri Rd ☎ 09 422 6275, ⓦ horseride-nz.co.nz. The horse-riding part of this family business runs year-round and offers some stunning trips. Rides ($80/hr, $160/2hr, $270/half day, $365/full day with lunch) go along the beach, among the dunes, across streams and through a pohutukawa glade.

ACCOMMODATION

WARKWORTH
★ **Sandspit Holiday Park** 1334 Sandspit Rd ☎ 09 425 8610, ⓦ sandspitholidaypark.co.nz. Set among mature trees and situated next to the ferry landing for Kawau Island, the camp offers free use of canoes and paddleboats, safe swimming, proximity to surf beaches and an internet kiosk. Camping $23, cabins (4 people) from $90
Warkworth Country House 18 Wilson Rd, 300m north of Warkworth and Districts Museum (see page 137) ☎ 09 422 2485, ⓦ warkworthcountryhouse.co.nz. Two cosy en suites with their own private patio entrances that overlook an acre of well-tended garden, with a further acre of native bush full of birds nearby – recently taken over by new owners. $120

PAKIRI
Pakiri Beach Horse Rides Rahuikiri Rd ☎ 09 422 6275, ⓦ horseride-nz.co.nz. Has a range of wonderfully atmospheric accommodation: riverside backpacker cabins; self-contained, beachside *baches* for two with a bed, stove and loo; a family cabin for seven; and the luxurious Ngapeka four-bedroom beach house ($600, 2-night minimum stay) sleeping up to eight. They specialise in horse trekking (see page 141). Cabins $70, beachside cabins $155

MANGAWHAI
Coastal Cow Backpackers 299 Molesworth Drive ☎ 09 431 5246, ⓔ coastalcow@gmail.com. Hostel accommodation in a pleasant, modern house with all the usual facilities, run by a helpful and informative host and 5min from the estuary beach for swimming. Choose from either dorms or rooms, and be sure to make use of the deck and BBQ area. Dorms $30, rooms $90
Mangawhai Lodge 4 Heather St ☎ 09 431 5311, ⓦ seaviewlodge.co.nz. Comfy and contemporary self-contained apartments, plus two B&B rooms (one is en suite). All except the wheelchair accessible "Par 3" apartment on the ground floor have their own breezy balconies and distant sea views. Host Jeanette is a font of local knowledge. Double $195, apartment $250

TAWHARANUI REGIONAL PARK
Campsite ☎ 09 366 2000, ⓦ regionalparks.aucklandcouncil.govt.nz. Beautiful and very low key tents-only campsite with simple toilet blocks set back behind the sand dunes on the northern coast. There's also an All Modes campsite suitable for campervans (same cost). $15

2

WAIPU COVE

Camp Waipu 869 Cove Rd, Waipu Cove ☎ 09 432 0410, ⓦ campwaipucove.com. Beachside accommodation is extensive at the southern end of Bream Bay north of Lang's Beach, but packed in January. Most cabins are pretty basic but there are a few high-end self-contained options, plus a bunk house. Camp facilities are clean and there's access to the beach on foot. Camping $34, bunk house $45, self-contained units from $110

★ **Waipu Cove Cottages and Camping** 685 Cove Rd, Waipu Cove ☎ 09 432 0851, ⓦ waipucovecottages.co.nz.

Adjacent to *Camp Waipu*, this is a smaller establishment with a more exclusive feel and modern cottages ($155). The grounds contain well-spaced camping sites, plus there's free use of dinghies. Camping $42, cottage $155

WAIPU

Uretiti Beach campsite 6km north of Waipu, signposted on SH1. The wonderful long white beach at Uretiti is backed by a basic DOC camping area with running water, toilets, cold showers and an adjacent (and unofficial) naturist beach. $10

EATING AND DRINKING

The widely available *Matakana Wine Trail* leaflet details eighteen regional wineries and wine-related sites that offer tastings, mostly for a small charge.

WARKWORTH

You can eat well enough in town – there's a New World supermarket for those wanting to stock up – or at a price in the surrounding vineyards.

Ginger Café 21 Queen St ☎ 09 422 2298. Has good coffee and they bake their own bagels and bread (which they stuff with lots of goodies), as well as offering an impressive breakfast menu and veggie meals (mains around $20). They specialize in gluten- and dairy-free. Mon–Fri 6.45am–4pm, Sat & Sun 7.30am–4pm.

Quince Café 10 Elizabeth St ☎ 09 442 2555. A local favourite, serving up dishes such as lamb shanks with pea and lentil gravy and mint jelly pistachio mash (mains around $26). It's licensed, but you can also bring your own booze. Wed–Sun 9am–late.

★ **Tahi Bar** 1 Neville St ☎ 09 422 3674, ⓦ tahibar.com. Located in an alley opposite the i-SITE visitor centre, this craft beer bar stocks a great range of boutique NZ beers. They have a gorgeous courtyard to chill out in and host loads of live music. Tues, Weds, Thurs 3.30pm–late, Fri & Sat noon–late.

KAWAU ISLAND

Café Sandspit The wharf at Sandspit, 8km east of Warkworth ⓦ cafe-sandspit.co.nz. A pleasant, licensed café in a wooden shed offering passable nosh, specializing in seafood, such as chowder ($14.50), fish and chips ($24.50), and burgers ($19.50), and serving up post-cruise liquid restoratives. Daily 9am–5pm (reduced hours in winter).

Mansion House Bay Café ☎ 09 422 8903, ⓦ facebook.com/MansionHouseNZ. Licensed café open for lunches as well as snacks and light meals ($10–30), including the likes of all-day breakfast, seared beef on noodles, or seared salmon. Most people visit as part of one of the guided trips so lunch is your most likely option, but a water taxi from Kawau Cruises (see

page 140) will get you there and back for dinner. Open weekends and most days in summer; call ahead for exact hours.

MATAKANA

Black Dog Café 23 Matakana Valley Rd ☎ 09 422 9130. A local favourite for coffee, chocolate cake, breakfasts, big juicy burgers ($17), and bagels with a variety of good-quality fillings (from $6). Mon–Sat 6.30am–3.30pm, Sun 7am–3.30pm.

Matakana Market Kitchen 2 Matakana Valley Rd ☎ 09 423 0383, ⓦ matakanamarketkitchen.com. Expect classy and expensive dining at this designer restaurant with schist rock walls, wooden furniture and a big shiny bar. Dishes include avocado on toast ($16), brunches made with free-range eggs (from $17.50), and dinner mains such as scallop and snapper risotto ($29). Gluten-free options also available, plus a kids three course menu ($16). Daily 9am–late.

Plume 49a Sharp Rd ☎ 09 422 7915, ⓦ plumerestaurant. co.nz. A stylish, expensive vineyard restaurant with an open kitchen, serving classy dishes such as venison medallions with cassis juniper ($37.50) and tempura prawn tails with dipping sauce ($35). Weds & Thurs 11am–2pm, Fri 11am–2pm & 6pm–late, Sat 11.30am–3pm & 6pm–late, Sun 11am–3pm.

LEIGH AND GOAT ISLAND

Leigh Fish and Chip Shop 18 Cumberland St ☎ 09 422 6035. Legendary (locally) for tasty fish and chips, mussel fritters and gourmet burgers, this is a traditional takeaway serving fresh fish, mostly cooked to order with nothing on the menu over $15. April–Dec Thurs–Sun 11am–7pm, Fri & Sat 11am–8pm; Dec–Easter 11am–8pm, Fri & Sat 11am–9pm.

★ **The Leigh Sawmill Café** 142 Pakiri Rd ☎ 09 422 6019, ⓦ sawmillcafe.co.nz. This converted former sawmill is now a smart café/bar with an abundance of historic milling paraphernalia (closed Mon–Wed in winter) and is the premier gig venue in these parts. They do excellent gourmet pizzas ($25) and there is a good wine list, plus tasty beers from the excellent micro-brewery next door, which does takeaway sales. Live music is usually at weekends in the massive beamed area in front of the bar. Also has five spacious en-suite doubles, a self-contained cottage and two dorms. March–Dec Thurs noon–late; Fri–Sun 10am–late; Dec–Feb daily 10am–late.

MANGAWHAI AND MANGAWHAI HEADS

Bennetts Café 52 Moir St, Mangawhai ☎09 431 5500. Specializes in imaginative breakfasts and lunches such as pancakes with mixed berries, maple syrup and whipped cream ($15) and wagyu beef burger ($22) using quality ingredients in a pseudo-Tuscan setting. There's also a wonderful chocolatier just across the courtyard. Daily 8am–4pm.

★ **Frog and Kiwi** 6 Molesworth Drive, Mangawhai ☎09 431 4439. As the name suggests, the food here is of the Franco-New Zealand fusion variety. Particular treats include a bowl of coffee, snails and *sauté de lapin* (rabbit with Dijon mustard, gherkins and olives), and a six-course degustation menu (with drinks $116). Most dishes cost around $25. Licensed. Daily 8.30am–2.30pm & 6pm–late.

Ivy Bistro 198 Molesworth Drive, Mangawhai Heads, ☎09 431 4111. Atmospheric little bistro, much loved by locals, serving an ever-changing menu of contemporary dishes of locally sourced meat and fish (brunch from $12, main dishes from $22). Mon–Thurs & Sun 9am–2pm, Fri & Sat 9am–3pm, plus Weds–Sat 5.30–10pm.

Mangawhai Tavern 2 Moir St, Mangawhai ☎09 431 4505, ⓦmangawhaitavern.co.nz. This traditional Kiwi pub serving traditional Kiwi grub would have little to recommend it except a beautiful location were it not a world-famous (in Northland, at least) venue for live music. Every weekend, summer and winter, Kiwi favourites and touring international acts strut their stuff in front of up to 1200 whooping drinkers. Daily 11am–1am.

WAIPU

Pizza Barn 2 Cove Rd ☎09 432 1011. The tastiest fare is traditional pub food or pizza in Waipu's former post office. Well-priced lunches and dinners (mains $18–33) vie with pizzas sporting elaborate toppings. You can either eat in the cosy corrugated iron, timber and McLeod tartan bar, or the garden room, which is filled with surfboards and a massive stuffed fish. Take a minute to peek at the toilets, a veritable art installation of 1950s kitsch. Mid-Dec to mid-Feb daily 11.30am–9am, rest of year Mon–Wed 11.30am–9pm.

Whangarei

Despite its prime gateway location to Whangarei Heads' sweeping beaches and world-class diving around the Poor Knights Islands, Northland's capital, **WHANGAREI** (pronounced Fahn-ga-ray), has never had the wherewithal to slow down tourists on their mad dash up to the Bay of Islands. But things are changing. The newly developed **Town Basin marina** provides a focal point for visitors, with a few restaurants overlooking the sleek yachts dotted along the river and a landscaped boardwalk with sculptures by local artists along the water's edge. There are a series of easy walks within a few minutes of the town and out to Parihaka Scenic Reserve, the best of which are outlined in the free *Whangarei Central Walks* leaflet.

The Town Basin

Looking out over the water, the redeveloped **Town Basin**, a primarily pedestrian area between Lower Dent Street and the Hatea River, is an attractive hub of retail outlets and restaurants. Check out **Clapham's Clocks** (daily 9am–5pm; $8, tour included), a museum of some 1300 clocks ranging from mechanisms taken out of church towers to cuckoo clocks. The planned **Hundertwasser Art Centre with Wairau Māori Art Gallery** (ⓦyeswhangarei.co.nz) should also open here by mid-2020.

Whangarei Art Museum

The Hub, Dent St • Daily 10am–4pm • Donation optional • ☎09 430 4240, ⓦwhangareiartmuseum.co.nz

The **Whangarei Art Museum**'s galleries host travelling exhibitions and rotates work from its own excellent contemporary and historic collection. Worth seeking out are paintings by **E. Kate Mair**, one of the first Pakeha artists to paint Māori sympathetically despite being married to Captain Gilbert Mair, who spent a part of his career fighting them; sadly, of the two works held, neither is a Māori portrait. Also worth a look is the more familiar portrait of Harataori Harota Tarapata, painted by Goldie (see page 79) and presented to the gallery by former prime minister Helen Clarke, and a couple of Lindauer's (see page 79) skilfully executed portraits.

Kiwi North and Whangarei Native Bird Recovery Centre

SH14, 6km southwest of Whangarei • **Kiwi North** Daily 10am–4pm • $20, kids $5 • ☎ 09 438 9630, Ⓦ kiwinorth.co.nz • **Whangarei Native Bird Recovery Centre** Mon & Fri 1–4.30pm, Tues–Thurs 10am–4.30pm • Donation optional • ☎ 09 438 1457 • Ⓦ nbr.org.nz

Kiwi North consists of a fabulous kiwi house, which sits at the centre of a rejuvenated museum and the **Whangarei Native Bird Recovery Centre**, all in the same walled area, although the recovery centre is an independent entity.

The kiwi enclosure and museum

Undoubted pride of place – and alone worthy of the entry fee – goes to the specially designed and spacious **kiwi enclosure**, where you'll be transfixed by the glorious, long-beaked curmudgeons and a couple of morepork, as well as several Duvaucel's gecko, some skink and a couple of tuatara. A few paces up the hill, the **museum** has an intriguing selection of objects including a 200-year-old *waka*, a fine assortment of Māori cloaks, Hone Heke's (see page 160) musket, some revealing information on Ruapekapeka Pa – including some of the cannon balls from the battle (see page 150) – and photographic collections that include images of Māori and early settlers.

Heritage Park and Native Bird Recovery Centre

Surrounding the two central attractions is the **Heritage Park**, at the heart of which is the **Clarke Homestead**, a rare example of an original unrestored homestead, built in 1886 for Scottish doctor Alexander Clarke. Also of note are the restored **steam locomotives** running through the compound.

A must-see for all twitchers is the **Native Bird Recovery Centre**, which attempts to rehabilitate injured birds. This collection of walking and hopping wounded is a mixture of temporary and permanent residents, among which you are almost certain to find a talking tui.

Whangarei Falls

5km northeast of the town centre

A broad curtain of water cascades over a 26m-high basalt ridge into a popular swimming hole at **Whangarei Falls**. The nicest way to get here is to walk along a bushland trail, which winds up at a bridge overlooking the falls after following the Hatea River (1hr 30min one way) from the Parihaka Scenic Reserve on the opposite shore from the Town Basin; the i-SITE visitor centre has a route map.

A.H. Reed Memorial Kauri Park

Northeast of the town centre, 1.5km down Whareora Rd

The **A.H. Reed Memorial Kauri Park** holds shady paths that weave through native bush, passing 500-year-old kauri trees; look out for the ten-minute Alexander Walk, which links with a short, sinuous **canopy boardwalk** high across a creek before reaching some fine kauri. From the lower car park, it's possible to take the Elizabeth track and link up with the trail along the Hatea River to Whangarei Falls (30min one way).

Abbey Caves

6km east of the town centre on Abbey Caves Rd, accessed via Whareora Rd

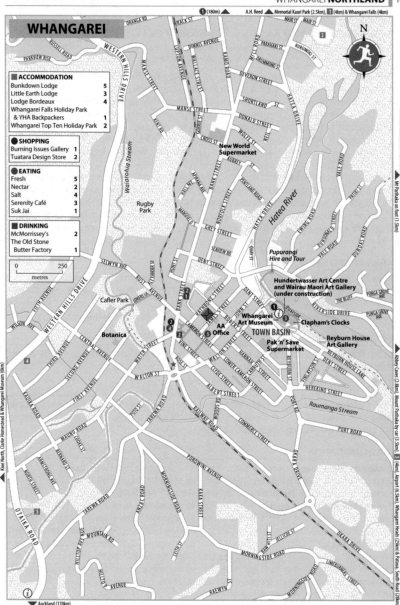

The fluted and weather-worn limestone formations of **Abbey Caves** have stalactites and stalagmites in abundance, as well as glowworms. Armed with a torch plus a moderate level of fitness you can explore them at leisure. A little scrambling is required to get into the first, Organ Cave, where you can walk a couple of hundred metres along an underground stream, although it's best avoided after heavy rain. Middle Cave and Ivy Cave are badly signposted but, once found, are worth exploring.

2

WHANGAREI AND AROUND TOURS AND ACTIVITIES

In and around Whangarei there are a number of tours and activities that introduce you to experiences and places that give you an insiders' knowledge of the district.

Loop de Loop Cycle Hire ☎022 0606 799, ⓦloopdeloop.co.nz. Conveniently located in the town basin opposite the children's playground, loop de loop offer mountain bikes from $10/hr plus tandems, city bikes and electric bikes. Kayaks for the inner harbour can also be hired for $10/hr.

Pacific Coast Kayaks ☎09 436 1947, ⓦnzseakayaking.co.nz. Organises kayak trips to Limestone Island ($110/half-day; leaves from the Onerahi Yacht Club) or along the Tutukaka coastline ($120/half-day; leaves from Tutukaka harbour), as well as more intrepid expeditions further afield.

Tu Tika Tours ☎021 507 826, ⓦtutikatours.co.nz.

One-of-a-kind Māori experience with Merv and Rangi and their *whanau* (family). They'll pick you up from accommodation around Whangarei and take you to their home for a welcome ceremony and morning tea, before taking you to sites they hold dear around town. The *hangi* for lunch is a real treat. $290/person (min two).

Whangarei Deep Sea Anglers Club Marina Rd, Tutukaka ☎09 434 3818, ⓦsportfishing.co.nz. Fishing for marlin, shark and tuna (Dec–April) can be done by taking a quarter-share of a charter game-fishing boat for the day, which will cost around $250–350. The club (daily 8am–6pm during fishing season) can provide a list of operators who run fishing charters.

ARRIVAL AND DEPARTURE
WHANGAREI

By bus InterCity/Northliner and NakedBus pull up on Bank St. Destinations Auckland (4 daily; 3hr); Paihia (4 daily; 1hr 15min); Warkworth (4 daily; 2hr).

By plane Whangarei Airport, which is served by Air New Zealand, is 5km east of town in Onerahi. Get into town on the City Link bus or with Kiwi Cabs (☎09 438 4444; around $25).

Destinations Auckland (3 daily; 40min).

GETTING AROUND

By bus Bank St is the hub of the skeletal local town bus service (City Link; ⓦcitylinkwhangarei.co.nz) that runs frequently on weekdays, slightly less so on Saturday, and not at all on Sunday.

INFORMATION

Tourist information There are two i-SITE visitor centres in Whangarei: 92 Otaika Rd, 2km south of town (Nov–Easter daily 9am–5pm; Easter–Oct Mon–Fri 9am–5pm, Sat & Sun 9am–4.30pm; ☎09 438 1079, ⓦwhangareinz.com); and a satellite branch in The Hub, within the Town Basin complex (same hours; ☎09 430 1188).

ACCOMMODATION

Bunkdown Lodge 23 Otaika Rd ☎09 438 8886, ⓦwww.bunkdownlodge.co.nz; map p.145. Ageing, low-key, small hostel with dorms and rooms in and around a pretty 1903 villa. There are two kitchens, a bath, piano, heaps of DVDs, and the owners go out of their way to help with local information. Linen rental $3. Dorms $29, rooms (linen included) $67

★**Little Earth Lodge** 85 Abbey Caves Rd ☎09 430 6562, ⓦlittleearthlodge.co.nz; map p.145. Tucked into a pastoral valley 7km northeast of Whangarei beside Abbey Caves, this hostel has three-bed shares and a range of singles, doubles and twins, some with garden views. There's also gear to hire to explore the caves, and free-range eggs – but be quick, as the latter get snapped up fast. Triples $96, doubles $78

Lodge Bordeaux 361 Western Hills Drive ☎09 438 0404, ⓦlodgebordeaux.co.nz; map p.145. Elegant modern motel with a summer-only heated outdoor pool. All rooms come with a/c, heated tile floors, spa bath and DVD players, and some have dishwashers. Studios $195, suites $230

Whangarei Falls Holiday Park & YHA Backpackers Ngunguru Rd at Tikipunga, 5km from town near Whangarei Falls (take bus #3 or #3A) ☎09 437 0609, ⓦwhangareifalls.co.nz; map p.145. On the edge of the countryside and within walking distance of the falls, this basic site has a small pool, hot tub, barbecue area and a comfy lounge. The cabins have kitchenettes provide good value for money. Camping $25, dorms $32, cabins (double) $86

Whangarei Top Ten Holiday Park 24 Mair St ☎09 437 6856, ⓦwhangareitop10.co.nz; map p.145. Small, tranquil and friendly site in a pretty setting 2km north of town with a range of accommodation. Camping $40, cabins (without linen) $75

EATING

Cafés and **restaurants** are spread around town and the Pak 'n Save supermarket is on the corner of Robert and Carruth sts. Also in town is a vibrant **growers market** (Sat 6–10am) in Water St, opposite the Shell station.

Fresh 12 James St ☎09 438 2921; map p.145. Airy, licensed café with a range of panini, pasta, frittata and salads – roasted vegetable and quinoa, for example – with lunch specials from $15–20. Mon–Fri 7.30am–4pm, Sat & Sun 8.30am–3pm.

Nectar 88 Bank St ☎09 438 8084, ⓌNectarcafe.co.nz; map p.145. Contemporary café/restaurant with big windows overlooking the town's rooftops, serving up classy breakfasts ($13–20) and healthy lunch dishes such as Thai salad ($16.50) and corn fritters ($15.50). Gluten free and vegan available. Mon–Fri 7am–2.30pm, Sat 8am–2.30pm.

★ **Salt** 4 Water St ☎09 430 0428, Ⓦfacebook.com/saltcafewhg; map p.145. The coolest coffee bar and café in town serves breakfast until 2.30pm (the vegan brekkie packs in garlic mushrooms, sourdough, spinach, hummus, grilled tomato and herb roasted potatoes for $18.50 – the delicious bacon and sausage version is $21). Lunch specials might include soft tacos ($18) or homemade fettucine ($17). Mon–Fri 7am–3pm, Sat 6.30am–1pm.

Serenity Café 6, 45 Quay St, Town Basin ☎09 430 0841, Ⓦserenitycafe.co.nz; map p.145. Pick of the Town Basin cafés, this local favourite serves excellent and generous breakfasts ($9–23), including a monster steak breakfast that would stop an All Black forward, and lunch dishes such as burgers ($14) and BLTs ($12). Mon–Sat 7am–3pm, Sun 8am–3pm.

★ **Suk Jai** 93 Kamo Rd ☎09 437 7287, Ⓦsukjai.co.nz; map p.145. Authentic Thai restaurant where attention to detail and good service complement tasty Thai favourites such as fish cakes ($7), *gang massaman* ($15.50) and *pad thai* ($14.50). Mon 5–10pm, Tues–Sat 11.30am–2.30pm & 5–10pm, Sun 5–10pm.

DRINKING

McMorrissey's 7 Vine St ☎09 430 8081, Ⓦmcmorrisseys.co.nz; map p.145. Irish bar that's primarily for drinking but also serves simple and hearty meals such as fish and chips, bangers and mash or stew (all around $20) to soak up the beer. Live music at weekends. Tues–Thurs & Sat 4pm–3am, Fri noon–3am.

The Old Stone Butter Factory 8 Butter Factory Lane ☎09 430 0044, Ⓦthebutterfactory.co.nz; map p.145. Whangarei's liveliest bar/restaurant caters to a slightly older crowd and serves the likes of tapas and stone-baked pizza ($14–17). There are often DJs and live acts, as well as more relaxed jazz evenings. Drinks run the gamut from Kiwi beers and wines to cocktails with names like Purple Death ($10). Tues–Sat 11am–late.

SHOPPING

Burning Issues Gallery 8 Quayside ☎09 438 3108, Ⓦburningissuesgallery.co.nz; map p.145. This town basin gallery has a studio at the back where you can watch glass-blowing and chat to the artist. Burning Issues sells pieces by mostly local artists who create handcrafted glass, ceramics, jewellery and sculpture. Daily 10am–5pm.

Tuatara Design Store 29 Bank St ☎09 430 0121, Ⓦtuataradesignstore.co.nz; map p.145. Small design store and gallery near the centre of town focusing on works by emerging Māori artists. The inventive shop stocks Māori-designed goods from contemporary clothing to fine jewellery and greenstone carving. Mon–Fri 9.30am–5.30pm, Sat 8am–3.30pm.

Around Whangarei

It's worth hanging around Whangarei to explore the surrounding area, particularly to the east and north of the town where craggy, weathered remains of ancient volcanoes abut the sea. Southeast of the town, **Whangarei Heads** is the district's volcanic heartland, where dramatic walks follow the coast to calm harbour beaches and windswept coastal strands; a kayak trip is a great way to get the best views. To the northeast, **Tutukaka** acts as the base for dive trips to the undersea wonderland around the **Poor Knights Islands**. Many **regional w**alks are described in DOC's *Whangarei District Walks* leaflet, available from the i-SITE visitor centre in Whangarei.

Whangarei Heads

Whangarei Heads, 35km southeast of Whangarei, is a series of small, residential beach communities scattered around jagged volcanic outcrops that terminate at Bream Head, the northern limit of Bream Bay. About the best way to see the area is from the sea, more specifically from the quiet, low viewpoint of a kayak, and one

2

SCUBA DIVING AT THE POOR KNIGHTS

The Poor Knights are a big draw for **scuba divers** (novices and experts) and snorkellers, primarily because of great visibility, the broad range of wildlife and the spectacular nature of the underwater environment. You'll get the most out of the area by scuba diving, as you'll be able to inspect the wildlife and scenery more closely.

Dive Tutukaka Marina Rd, Tutukaka ☎0800 288 882, ⓦ diving.co.nz. The largest, best and most flexible operator leaves from Tutukaka (with pick-ups from Whangarei available) several times a day from Nov–April, and usually offers at least one trip a day for the rest of the year. It has several boats, so you are typically with similarly skilled divers. Two-dive trips ($199; including gear $299) also carry snorkellers and sightseers ($199) and everyone can use the on-board kayaks. First-timers can try a Discover Scuba dive ($319 with full gear and one-to-one instruction). A five-day PADI open-water dive qualification costs $799.

---

of the most accessible trips is a paddle over to, or around, Limestone Island (see below).

Limestone Island

Just off the coast of Onerahi, a waterside suburb, **Limestone Island** (Matakohe) is a microcosm of New Zealand history. Now managed by DOC, it was originally home to part of the Ngaitahuhu *iwi*, and various tribes vied for control before European settlers established a flax pressing plant. Thereafter, settlers fleeing Hone Heke (see page 160) used the island as a refuge, before it became a farm and then a lime works until 1918. In 1989 it was gifted to the Whangarei District for ecological restoration. These days the process is well under way and fifty kiwi chicks have been raised on the island before being released on the mainland; there are interpretive boards at various sites across the island. Visiting the island (see below) – you can land on or circumnavigate it – is best done on an organized trip or with a DOC ranger.

Mount Manaia and around

For safe swimming stop at **McLeod Bay**, or continue until the road leaves the harbour and climbs to a saddle at the start of an excellent, signposted **walk** (3km return; 2hr–2hr 30min; 200m ascent) up the 403m **Mount Manaia**, crowned with five eroded pinnacles shrouded in Māori legend – the rocks are said to be Chief Manaia, his children and the last, facing away, his unfaithful wife. The pinnacles remain *tapu*, but you can climb to their base through native bush, passing fine viewpoints.

Beyond Mount Manaia, the road runs for 5km to **Urquharts Bay**, where a short walk (20min each way) leads to the white-sand **Smugglers Cove**.

ARRIVAL AND DEPARTURE   WHANGAREI HEADS

By bus City Link buses run (Mon–Sat; every hour) as far as Onerahi, a beachside community on the way to the Heads. If you want to get further on to the Heads you'll need a car.

ACCOMMODATION

★**Tidesong** Beasley Rd, Onerahi ☎09 436 1959, ⓦ tidesong.co.nz. Very welcoming B&B set in a peaceful spot on the mangrove-filled Taiharuru Estuary, a twitcher's paradise with 25 species on view in the extensive bush and gardens surrounding the property. On offer are a great-value self-contained apartment or smaller room, bikes to rent, a putting course round the gardens and the chance to take a guided ride in the estuary on a small sailing boat. Home-cooked meals are available and there's an outdoor pizza oven, which is also used for baking. Look out for a bit of family history in the hall – a picture of former prime minister Thomas McKenzie. Apartment $150, double $120

Treasure Island Motor Camp ☎09 436 2390, ⓦ treasureislandnz.co.nz. Treasured by in-the-know Kiwis as a secluded and picturesque spot with access to a gorgeous surf beach and good fishing. There's a kitchen, TV room and BBQ area, plus an on-site general takeaway and bakery (Dec–Feb) serving coffee and croissants. Camping $20

Tutukaka and around

Boats set out from tiny **TUTUKAKA** – set on a beautiful, deeply incised harbour 30km northeast of Whangarei – for one of the world's premier dive locations, the **Poor Knights Islands Marine Reserve**, 25km offshore.

Poor Knights Islands Marine Reserve

The warm East Auckland current and the lack of run-off from the land combine to create visibility approaching 30m most of the year, though in spring (roughly Oct–Dec) plankton can reduce it to 10–15m. The clear waters are home to New Zealand's most diverse and plentiful range of sea life, including a few subtropical species found nowhere else, as well as a striking underwater landscape of near-vertical **rock faces** and arches that drop almost 100m. One dive at the Poor Knights, the Blue Mao Mao Cave, was rated by Jacques Cousteau as one of the top ten dive sites in the world. The Poor Knights lie along the migratory routes of a number of **whale** species, so blue, humpback, Bryde's, sei and minke whales, as well as dolphins, are not uncommon sights on the way to the islands. The waters north and south of Tutukaka are home to two navy **wrecks**. The survey ship HMNZS *Tui* was sunk in 1999 to form an artificial reef, and it was so popular with divers and marine life that the obsolete frigate *Waikato* followed two years later.

ARRIVAL AND DEPARTURE   TUTUKAKA AND AROUND

By shuttle bus The only public transport from Whangarei to Tutukaka is with the Whangarei Coastal Commuter ($25 one way, $40 return, to coincide with dive times; $55 one way at other times; ☎021 901 408, ⓦcoastalcommuter. co.nz).

ACCOMMODATION AND EATING

★**Sands Motel** 48 Whangaumu St ☎09 434 3747, ⓦsandsmotel.co.nz. There's a retro feel to this establishment, with comfortable, well-equipped and spacious two-bedroom units beautifully set beside a nice beach 4km off the highway. It's quiet (but within the sound of the crashing waves) and well run with friendly hosts. 2-bed units **$150**

Schnappa Rock Café Marina Rd ☎09 434 3774, ⓦschnapparock.co.nz. The most notable of the restaurants around the harbour, this groovy bar-restaurant turns out a tempting range of meat and vegetarian dishes such as lamb back strap ($36) and mussels with Thai curry coconut sauce ($27.50), as well as bar snacks. It's buzzing with divers and serves good coffee. Book ahead for dinner in summer. Daily 8am–late.

★**Tutukaka Holiday Park** Matapouri Rd ☎09 434 3938, ⓦtutukaka-holidaypark.co.nz. An ever-expanding and improving site a 2min walk from the harbour that is very busy in Jan and Feb. It's also simply awash with pukeko (see page 718), who are not averse to panhandling. The self-contained cabins are spacious and the standard cabins adequate, while the en suites are great value. The camp kitchen and laundry are clean and well equipped. Camping **$22**, dorms **$27.50**, cabins **$120**

Matapouri and Whale Bay

MATAPOURI, 6km north of Tutukaka, is a lovely holiday settlement which backs onto a curving white-sand bay. At low tide, you can swim in safe, clear-blue rock pools (locally known as the **Mermaid Pools**) just above the sea. Bushy headlands separate Matapouri's beach from the pristine **Whale Bay**, signposted off Matapouri Road 1km further north and reached by a short bushwalk. There are virtually no facilities along this stretch, apart from a shop and takeaway at Matapouri.

North of Whangarei to the Bay of Islands

The roads that access the coast around Tutukaka and Matapouri rejoin SH1 at **Hikurangi** 16km north of Whangarei. About 6km further north you have a choice

> ## HUNDERTWASSER TOILETS
>
> The small town of **Kawakawa**, 15km north of Ruapekapeka, would be otherwise unremarkable if it wasn't known for being the home of the celebrated **Hundertwasser toilets** on the town's main drag, Gillies Street. These works of art were created in 1997 by the reclusive Austrian painter, architect, ecologist and philosopher, **Friedrich Hundertwasser**, who made Kawakawa his home from 1975 until his death in 2000, aged 71. The ceramic columns supporting the entrance hint at the interior's complex use of broken tiles, coloured bottles and found objects such as the old hinges on the wrought-iron doors. A steady trickle of visitors takes a peek in both the Gents and the Ladies after suitable warning.

of routes: both go to the Bay of Islands but approach from different directions: carry straight on and you go direct to Paihia with opportunities for side trips to the Māori redoubt of Ruapekapeka Pa, and the **Hundertwasser toilets** at Kawakawa; turn right along Old Russell Road and you twist towards the coast on the tar-sealed but narrow and winding back-road to Russell. The latter route is the most scenic way to approach the Bay of Islands, along a 70km narrow, winding road that takes about two hours. You can spin the drive out by admiring the wonderful coastline around the **Whangaruru Harbour**, stopping for swims in numerous gorgeous bays, and perhaps a short walk in the mixed kauri forest of the **Ngaiotonga Scenic Reserve**.

Ruapekapeka Pa

17km north of Hikurangi on SH1 then 5km east on a signposted unsealed road • Free

Ruapekapeka Pa is the site of the final battle in the War of the North in 1846, a grassy hilltop with a few earthworks, a commemorative wooden pole, one of the original cannons and stunning views of the surrounding countryside. Hone Heke's repeated flagpole felling in Russell (see page 160) precipitated nine months of fighting during which Māori learnt to adapt their *pa* defences to cope with British firepower. The apotheosis of this development is Ruapekapeka, the "Bat's Nest". Its hilltop setting, double row of totara palisades and labyrinth of trenches and interconnecting tunnels helped Hone Heke and his warriors defend the site, despite being heavily outgunned and outnumbered three to one. Signs explain the full story, and trench lines and bunkers are clearly visible.

Oakura

Leaving SH1, you travel through 14km of farmland along Old Russell Road before reaching Helena Bay, where's there's a gallery-café (see opposite), which is a good spot to stop for a bite (there's little else between here and Russell) before continuing north to **OAKURA**. Oakura itself is not much more than an island-studded bay backed by a gently curving beach and a cluster of holiday homes. Its primary appeal is that not a great deal ever happens, though there are plenty of places to swim and walk, and one decent place to stay (see page 151).

Whangaruru North Head Scenic Reserve

10km from Ngaiotonga

At Ngaiotonga, a sealed side-road runs through hilly farmland to the broad sweep of **Bland Bay** with great beaches on both sides of an isthmus. Continue beyond Bland Bay to reach **Whangaruru North Head Scenic Reserve**, with yet more lovely beaches, fine walks around the end of the peninsula and a DOC campsite (see page 151).

Rawhiti

Back on the coast road it is 7km north to a junction where you turn left for Russell (25km further) and continue straight on for the scattered and predominantly Māori village of **RAWHITI**, the start of the Cape Brett Track (see below). Just 1km along the Rawhiti road there's shorter, easier walking in the form of the **Whangamumu Track** (4km each way; 1hr; 150m ascent), a forest path that crosses the base of the Cape Brett Peninsula to a lovely beach. Here you can see the remains of a whaling station, which closed in 1940.

Following the Manawaroa Road back to the Russell Road and on toward Russell for 11km you'll come across a signposted side road to some fine stands of kauri. These can be visited on the **Twin Bole Track** (around 200m; 5min) and the **Kauri Grove Walk** (1km; 20min).

ACCOMMODATION   NORTH OF WHANGAREI TO THE BAY OF ISLANDS

Coast Road Farm Russell Rd, 12km north of Oakura ☎ 09 433 6894, ⓦ thefarm.co.nz. Along the Russell Road you can get involved with dairy farm life, ride horses ($50/1hr trek), go kayaking (free if you stay 2 nights), fishing ($10) and much more, while staying in the dorm room, one of three doubles (one en suite), one of four cabins, or camping. Meals are by arrangement.

Camping $\overline{\$15}$, dorms $\overline{\$20}$, doubles $\overline{\$80}$
Puriri Bay campsite Whangaruru North Rd, Whangaruru North Head Scenic Reserve ⓔ whangareiao@doc. govt.nz. DOC site overlooking Puriri Bay and Whangaruru Harbour, with 93 sites, running water, toilets and cold showers. The camp office is open 7.30am–8pm, and bookings are essential in the summer. $\overline{\$13}$

EATING AND DRINKING

The Gallery & Café Helena Bay Hill Old Russell Rd, Helena Bay ☎ 09 433 9616, ⓦ galleryhelenabay. co.nz. An imaginative gallery coupled with a great German-run daytime café with views across bush-clad hills down to Helena Bay. Stop for a coffee or a snack: schnitzel and strudel alongside more traditional Kiwi fare. Daily 9.30am–5pm (kitchen closes 3pm).

The Bay of Islands

THE BAY OF ISLANDS, 240km north of Auckland, lures visitors with its beautiful coastal scenery, scattered islands and clear blue waters. There are other equally stunning spots along the Northland coast, such as the Whangaroa and Hokianga harbours, but what sets the bay apart is the ease with which you can get out among the islands, and its pivotal history. This was the cradle of European settlement in New Zealand, a fact abundantly testified to by the bay's churches, mission stations and orchards. It's also a focal point for Māori because of the **Treaty of Waitangi** (see page 154), still New Zealand's most important legal document.

THE CAPE BRETT TRACK

Northland's best overnight tramp is the challenging but rewarding **Cape Brett Track** (20km each way; 6–8hr) which follows the hilly ridge along the centre of the peninsula with sea occasionally visible on both sides: a route outlined in DOC's *Cape Brett* leaflet. The former lighthouse keeper's house at the tip of the peninsula is now a DOC **hut** (23 bunk beds; $15; backcountry hut pass not valid) and the only place to **stay** on the track itself, in a fabulous location surrounded by sea and views out to the Hole in the Rock. There are gas cooking stoves but no utensils, and camping is not allowed.

The track starts in Rawhiti (see above) and crosses private land, so all walkers must pay a **track fee** ($40). The Russell Booking & Information Centre is the place to pay this, book the DOC hut and ask about secure parking in Rawhiti. You might also enquire about a **water taxi** from Russell to Rawhiti (around $170 for up to six people), Deep Water Cove, three-quarters of the way along the track ($190), or Cape Brett ($230; conditions permitting). Secure parking is available at *Hartwells* in Kaimarama Bay, at the end of Rawhiti Road, for a small fee.

2

THE BAY OF ISLANDS, WHANGAROA HARBOUR & DOUBTLESS BAY

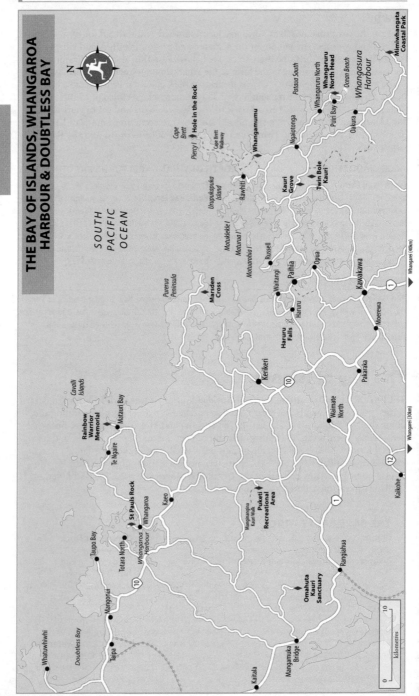

N

SOUTH PACIFIC OCEAN

Mimiwhangata Coastal Park

Whangaruru North
Whangaruru North Head
Potawa South
Ocean Beach
Whangasura Harbour
Putri Bay
Oakura

Hole in the Rock
Cape Brett
Piercyl
Cape Brett Walkway
Whangamumu
Ngaiotonga

Twin Boie Kauri
Kauri Grove

Urupukapuka Island

Rawhiti

Motukiekiel
Maturaa I.
Motuarohia I.
Motuwarohia I.

Russell

Opua
Paihia
Waitangi
Kawakawa

Whangarei (40km)

Purerua Peninsula

Marsden Cross

Haruru
Haruru Falls

Moerewa

Kerikeri

Cavelli Islands

Rainbow Warrior Memorial

Mataura Bay

Te Ngaire

10

Pakaraka

Waimate North

Whangarei (30km)

12

Kaikohe

St Pauls Rock

Whangaroa
Whangaroa Harbour

Kaeo

Mangapapaia Kauri Walk

Puketi Recreational Area

Taupo Bay

Totara North

10

1

Rangiahua

Mangonui

Doubtless Bay

Tapia

Omahuta Kauri Sanctuary

Whatuwhiwhi

Mangamuka Bridge

Kaitaia

10

0   kilometres

0

Perhaps surprisingly, much of your time in the Bay of Islands will be spent on the mainland, as there are no settlements on the islands. Most visitors base themselves in beachside **Paihia**, which is set up to deal with the hordes who come here for the various cruises and excursions, as well as being the closest town to the Treaty House at **Waitangi**. The compact town of **Russell**, a couple of kilometres across the bay (though still on the mainland) by passenger ferry, is prettier and almost equally convenient for cruises. To the northwest, away from the bay itself, **Kerikeri** is intimately entwined with the area's early missionary history, while **Waimate North**, inland to the west, was another important mission site and Mission House.

Brief history
A warm climate, abundant seafood and deep, sheltered harbours contributed to dense pre-European **Māori settlement** in the Bay of Islands, with many a headland supporting a *pa*. The bay also appealed to **Captain Cook**, who anchored here in 1769. Cook landed on Motuarohia Island at what became known as Cook's Cove, where he forged generally good relations with the inhabitants. Three years later the French sailor **Marion du Fresne**, en route from Mauritius to Tahiti, became the first European to have sustained contact with Māori, though he fared less well when a misunderstanding, probably over *tapu*, led to his death, along with 26 of his crew. The French retaliated, destroying a *pa* and killing hundreds of Māori.

Missionaries and treaties
Despite amicable relations between the local Ngapuhi Māori and Pakeha whalers in the early years of the nineteenth century, the situation gradually deteriorated. With increased contact, firearms, grog and Old World diseases spread and the fabric of Māori life began to break down, a process accelerated by the arrival in 1814 of Samuel Marsden, the first of many **missionaries** intent on turning Māori into Christians. In 1833, James Busby was sent to secure British interests and prevent the brutal treatment meted out to the Māori by whaling captains, but lacking armed backup or judicial authority, he had little effect. The signing of the **Treaty of Waitangi** in 1840 brought effective policing yet heralded a decline in the importance of the Bay of Islands, as the capital moved from its original site of Kororareka (now Opua, although many claim it was Russell), first to Auckland and later to Wellington.

Paihia and Waitangi
PAIHIA is the place where things kick off, mostly on the 2km-long string of waterside motels, restaurants and holiday homes lined with trip operators, backpacker hostels, party-oriented bars and hotels. Fortunately, Paihia's low-rise development is sympathetic to its three beautiful, flat bays looking towards Russell and the Bay of Islands, encircled by forested hills. A plaque outside the current **St Paul's Anglican Church** on Marsden Road marks the spot where, in 1831, the northern chiefs petitioned the British Crown for a representative to establish law and order. In 1833 King William IV finally addressed their concerns by sending the first British resident, James Busby. Busby built a house on a promontory 2km north across the Waitangi River in **WAITANGI** – the scene some seven years later of the signing of the **Treaty of Waitangi**, which ceded the nation's sovereignty to Britain in return for protection.

Paihia is primarily a base for exploring the bay, and there are no sights in town itself. Fans of mangroves and estuarine scenery can tackle the gentle **Paihia–Opua Coastal Walkway** (6km; 1hr 30min–2hr one way), which wanders along the wave-cut platforms and the small bays in between.

Waitangi Treaty Grounds
Tau Henare Drive

THE TREATY OF WAITANGI

The Treaty of Waitangi is the **founding document** of modern New Zealand, a touchstone for both Pakeha and Māori, and its implications permeate New Zealand society. Signed in 1840 between what were ostensibly two sovereign states – the United Kingdom and the United Tribes of New Zealand, plus other Māori leaders – the treaty remains central to New Zealand's **race relations**. The Māori rights guaranteed by it have seldom been upheld, however, and the constant struggle for recognition continues.

THE TREATY AT WAITANGI

Motivated by a desire to staunch French expansion in the Pacific, and a moral obligation on the Crown to protect Māori from rapacious land-grabbing by settlers, the British instructed naval captain **William Hobson** to negotiate the transfer of sovereignty with "the free and intelligent consent of the natives", and to deal fairly with the Māori. Hobson, with the help of James Busby and others, drew up both the English Treaty and a Māori "translation". On the face of it, the treaty is a straightforward document, but the complications of having two versions (see page 698) and the implications of striking a deal between two peoples with widely differing views on land and resource ownership have reverberated down the years.

The treaty was unveiled on February 5, 1840, to a gathering of some 400 representatives of the five northern tribes in front of Busby's residence in Waitangi. Presented as a contract between the chiefs and Queen Victoria – someone whose role was comprehensible in chiefly terms – the benefits were amplified and the costs downplayed. As most chiefs didn't understand English, they signed the Māori version of the treaty, which still has *mana* (authority or status) among Māori today.

THE TREATY AFTER WAITANGI

The pattern set at Waitangi was repeated up and down the country, as seven copies of the treaty were dispatched to garner signatures and extend Crown authority over parts of the North Island that had not yet been covered, and the South Island. On May 21, before signed treaty copies had been returned, Hobson claimed New Zealand for Britain: the North Island on the grounds of cession by Māori, and the South Island by right of Cook's "discovery", as it was considered to be without owners, despite a significant Māori population.

Māori fears were alerted from the start, and as the settler population grew and demand for land increased, successive governments passed laws that gradually stripped Māori of control over their affairs – actions which led to the New Zealand Wars of the 1860s (see page 697). Over the decades, small concessions were made, but nothing significant changed until 1973, when **Waitangi Day** (February 6) became an official national holiday. Around the same time, Māori groups, supported by a small band of Pakeha, began a campaign of direct action, increasingly disrupting commemorations, thereby alienating many Pakeha and splitting Māori allegiances between angry young urban Māori and the *kaumatua* (elders), who saw the actions as disrespectful to the ancestors and an affront to tradition. Many strands of Māori society were unified by the *hikoi* (march) to Waitangi to protest against the celebrations in 1985, a watershed year in which Paul Reeves was appointed New Zealand's first Māori Governor General and the **Waitangi Tribunal** for land reform was given some teeth.

Protests have continued since, as successive governments have vacillated over whether to attend the commemorations at Waitangi; cautious optimism greeted Prime Minister Jacinda Ardern's decision to stay an unprecedented five days in the Far North in 2018 and she was granted the right to speak from the *marae* (meeting house).

Crossing the bridge over the Waitangi River you enter the **Waitangi Treaty Grounds**, where in 1840 Queen Victoria's representative William Hobson and nearly fifty Māori chiefs signed the Treaty of Waitangi (see page 154).

Waitangi Visitor Centre and Treaty House

Tau Henare Drive • Daily March to late Dec 9am–5pm; late Dec to Feb 9am–6pm • Day pass $50 (includes 50min guided tour and cultural performance) • Māori Hangi and concert Nov–April Tues, Thurs, Fri & Sun 6–8.30pm • $110 (book ahead; includes a day pass) • ☎ 09 402 7437, Ⓦ waitangi.org.nz

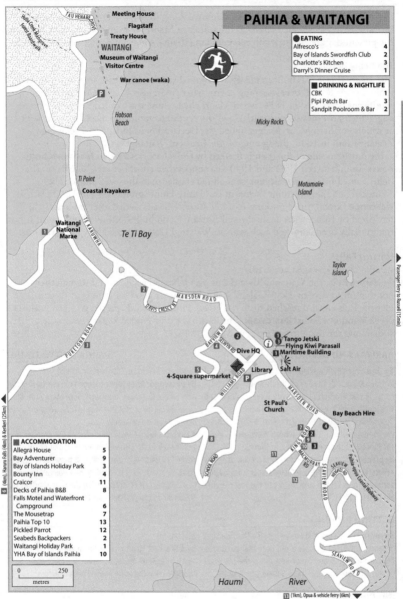

PAIHIA & WAITANGI

Meeting House
Flagstaff
Treaty House
WAITANGI
Museum of Waitangi
Visitor Centre

War canoe (waka)

Hobson Beach

Micky Rocks

Motumaire Island

Taylor Island

Ti Point
Coastal Kayakers

Waitangi National Marae

Te Ti Bay

MARSDEN ROAD

DAVIS CRESCENT

BAYVIEW RD

SELWYN RD

Dive HQ

Library

4-Square supermarket

WILLIAMS ROAD

MARSDEN ROAD

Tango Jetski
Flying Kiwi Parasail
Maritime Building
Salt Air

St Paul's Church

Bay Beach Hire

KINGS ROAD

MACMURRAY RD

SCHOOL ROAD

SEAVIEW ROAD

SEAVIEW ROAD

Paihia–Opua Coastal Walkway

Passenger ferry to Russell (15min)

(4km), Haruru Falls (4km) & Kerikeri (25km)

● EATING

Alfresco's	4
Bay of Islands Swordfish Club	2
Charlotte's Kitchen	3
Darryl's Dinner Cruise	1

■ DRINKING & NIGHTLIFE

CBK	1
Pipi Patch Bar	3
Sandpit Poolroom & Bar	2

■ ACCOMMODATION

Allegra House	5
Bay Adventurer	9
Bay of Islands Holiday Park	3
Bounty Inn	4
Craicor	11
Decks of Paihia B&B	8
Falls Motel and Waterfront Campground	6
The Mousetrap	7
Paihia Top 10	13
Pickled Parrot	12
Seabeds Backpackers	2
Waitangi Holiday Park	1
YHA Bay of Islands Paihia	10

0 — 250 metres

Haumi River

(1km), Opua & vehicle ferry (6km)

The **Waitangi Treaty Grounds** is the single most symbolic place in New Zealand for Māori and Pakeha alike, and a focal point for the modern nation's struggle for identity. You can easily spend half a day here, taking in the excellent **Museum of Waitangi** and its audiovisual presentation that sets the historical framework, Māori lively guided tour and a cultural performance in the traditional meeting house. Most people return in the evening for the **Māori Hangi and Concert**, an excellent contemporary approach to presenting Māori culture. After a traditional *hangi* in the *Whare Waka Café*, you're introduced to an extended family as the stories of Māori life from the arrival of Kupe to the present day are enacted with verve, mixing drama, song and dance with storytelling.

The Treaty House

The **Treaty House** was built in Georgian colonial style in 1833–34. Its front windows look towards Russell over sweeping lawns, where marquees were erected on three significant occasions: in 1834, when Māori chiefs chose the Confederation of Tribes flag, which now flies on one yardarm of the central flagpole; the meeting a year later at which northern Māori leaders signed the Declaration of Independence of New Zealand; and, in 1840, the signing of the Treaty of Waitangi itself.

The northern side of the lawn is flanked by the *whare runanga*, or **Māori meeting house**, built between 1934 and 1940 as a cooperative effort between all Māori. The richly carved interior panels represent all *iwi* (rather than the usual single tribe).

Housed in a specially built shelter in the Treaty House grounds is the world's largest **war canoe** (*waka*), the 35m-long *Ngatoki Matawhaorua*, named after the vessel navigated by Kupe when he discovered Aotearoa, and built from two huge kauri. It has traditionally been launched each year on Waitangi Day, propelled by eighty warriors.

Haruru Falls

4km west of Waitangi, accessed from the main road

At **Haruru Falls**, the Waitangi River drops over a basalt lava flow, and though they're not that impressive by New Zealand standards, there's good swimming at their base. Haruru Falls are also reached from the Treaty House grounds via the very gentle **Hutia Creek Mangrove Forest Boardwalk** (2hr return) or on a guided **kayak** trip up the estuary and among the mangroves (see page 159).

ARRIVAL AND DEPARTURE

PAIHIA AND WAITANGI

By bus InterCity/Northliner and NakedBus arrive on Marsden Rd, outside the Bay of Islands' main i-SITE visitor centre. A trial Mid North Link service connects Paihia and Waitangi Kaikohe to Kerikeri/Waipapa (w buslink.co.nz).
Destinations Auckland (4–6 daily; 4hr); Kaitaia (1 daily; 2hr 15min); Kerikeri (3 daily; 30min); Mangonui (1 daily; 1hr 50min); Whangarei (4–6 daily; 1hr 15min).
By plane Flights from Auckland arrive at the Bay of Islands airport (☎ 09 407 6133, w bayofislandsairport.co.nz), 22km northwest, near Kerikeri, and are met by the Super Shuttle bus ($60 to Paihia).

Destinations Auckland (8–10 daily; 45min).
By passenger ferry Foot passengers can use the frequent ferry service (Oct–May 7am–10pm; June–Sept 7am–8pm; every 30min or so; $7 one way, $12.50 return; 15min) between Paihia and Russell.
By vehicle ferry A small vehicle ferry runs between Paihia and Russell (daily 6am–10pm; every 15min or so; car & driver $13 each way, foot/additional passengers $1; buy ticket on board; 10min), crossing the Veronica Channel at Opua, 6km south of Paihia. Taking the ferry shortens the 100km drive between Paihia and Russell to 15km.

GETTING AROUND

By car Paihia isn't big, and everywhere is within walking distance, but if you do have a car, note that parking is tight in the high season; your best bet is the pay-and-display car park opposite the 4-Square supermarket on

Williams Rd.
By bike Rent good-quality mountain bikes from Bay Beach Hire (☎ 09 402 6078, w baybeachhire.co.nz; $15/hr, $50/day) at the south end of Paihia Beach.

INFORMATION

Tourist information An i-SITE visitor centre is at The Wharf, 101 Marsden Rd (daily 8am–5pm; ☎ 09 402 7345, w northlandnz.com).

Internet The public library (6 Williams Rd; Mon–Fri 9am–5pm, Sat 9am–1pm) has free wi-fi that they ask you to access from outside.

ACCOMMODATION

Paihia abounds in accommodation for all budgets, though rates can be stratospheric during the couple of weeks after

Christmas. B&Bs and homestays vary their prices less than motels, and hostels mostly maintain the same prices year-round. Kings Road is a veritable backpackers' village with a selection of generally good places, noisy in the height of summer.

★**Allegra House** 39 Bayview Rd ☎ 09 402 7932, ⓦ allegra.co.nz; map p.155. A choice of luxury B&B or self-contained apartment in a big, light and modern house at the top of a hill, and all with stupendous views right out over the Bay of Islands. All are a/c, sport their own balconies and have access to a hot tub in native bush. B&B $230, apartment $285

Bay Adventurer 26–28 Kings Rd ☎ 09 402 5162, ⓦ bayadventurer.co.nz; map p.155. Upmarket backpackers resort with apartments, an attractive pool, free bikes, kayaks and access to the nearby tennis courts (free in winter). It's particularly good for its doubles and fully self-contained studio apartments. Dorms (some female only) $22, doubles $65

Bounty Inn 42 Selwyn Rd ☎ 09 402 7088, ⓦ bountyinn. co.nz; map p.155. Pleasant, central yet quiet motel, 100m from the beach with ample parking. Rooms without cooking facilities, and fully equipped motel units all come lined in timber with a sundeck or balcony. $140

Craicor 49 Kings Rd ☎ 09 402 7882, ⓦ craicor-accom. co.nz; map p.155. A couple of excellent-value self-catering apartments, both spacious, well-kept and with limited sea views, plus an attractive double room. Continental breakfast can be supplied for $12. $180

Decks of Paihia B&B 69 School Rd ☎ 09 1402 6146, ⓦ decksofpaihia.co.nz; map p.155. Welcoming three-room B&B in a comfortable, tastefully decorated modern house with swimming pool set into a large, sunny deck high on the hill above Paihia. $195

The Mousetrap 11 Kings Rd ☎ 0800 402 8182, ⓦ mousetrap.co.nz; map p.155. Welcoming, nautically themed, wood-panelled hostel that sets itself apart from the other backpackers on this lively street. Rooms are scattered all over the site, there are three small kitchens, a BBQ area, free bike use and a decent sea view. Dorms $29, rooms $79

Pickled Parrot Grey's Lane, off MacMurray Rd ☎ 09 402 6222, ⓦ pickledparrot.co.nz; map p.155. One of Paihia's smaller, more relaxed hostels, tucked away in a peaceful spot with a lovely courtyard. Secluded tent sites ($16); four-

and six-bed dorms as well as singles, doubles and twins, all with free parking, bikes and tennis racquets. Dorms $28, doubles $74

★**Seabeds Backpackers** 46 Davis Crescent ☎ 09 402 5567, ⓦ seabeds.co.nz; map p.155. The best-value backpackers in town: grown-up accommodation with proper facilities in a one-time motel, with a gorgeous kitchen/living room area. *Seabeds* is run by a friendly professional with abundant local knowledge. Dorms $28, en-suite doubles $85

YHA Bay of Islands Paihia Corner of Kings and MacMurray rds ☎ 09 402 7487, ⓦ yha.co.nz; map p.155. Well-maintained and -run hostel with well-informed staff and a good kitchen, attracting a friendly mix of travellers and families. Most rooms and dorms are en suite. Dorms $25, rooms $99

CAMPSITES

Bay of Islands Holiday Park 52 Puketona Rd ☎ 09 402 6601 ⓦ bayofislandscampervanpark.co.nz; map p.155. Small, super-friendly site with modern toilets and showers ($2 for 4min), a pleasant BBQ area next to a lily pad pond and unlimited free wi-fi. It's a 15min walk to town. Camping per person $20

★**Falls Motel and Waterfront Campground** 336 Puketona Rd, 4km north of Paihia ☎ 0800 757 525, ⓦ falls.co.nz; map p.155. Fabulous location by the river with commanding views of Haruru Falls, offering riverside campsites and various sized units around a pool. There's a private beach, gas BBQ's to use, plus kayaks to rent. The wi-fi is limited and slow. Camping $22, studio $120

Paihia Top 10 SH11, 3km south of Paihia ☎ 09 402 7678, ⓦ paihiatop10.co.nz; map p.155. Small and peaceful, beautifully situated waterside site with a range of cabins and units, good kitchen and laundry, free wi-fi, plus bikes and kayaks for rent. Camping per person $40, cabins $75

Waitangi Holiday Park 21 Tahuna Rd, Waitangi ☎ 09 402 7866, ⓦ waitangiholidaypark.co.nz; map p.155. The closest campsite to Waitangi and a 20min walk to Paihia, this simple site has pitches overlooking the Waitangi River and four spacious kitchen cabins. Camping $22, cabins $8

EATING

Paihia's range of places to eat is plentiful but, with a few notable exceptions, all are sort of similar; competition keeps prices reasonable and many spots specialize in seafood.

★**Alfresco's** 6 Marsden Rd ☎ 09 402 6797, ⓦ alfrescosrestaurantpaihia.com; map p.155. Relaxed café and bar that's excellent for a coffee, breakfasts (including hot cakes stacked with bacon and maple syrup, $16.50), lunchtime salads and chowders (around $17) and some fine dining in the evening (mains from $27). Daily 7.30am–late.

★**Bay of Islands Swordfish Club** Marsden Rd ☎ 09 402 7773, ⓦ swordfish.co.nz; map p.155. Private club, overlooking the bay and welcoming visitors outside the peak summer season: just get the bar staff to sign you in. The great views are accompanied by ample, good-value food such as fish and chips or steak and chips (mains $20–35). "Swordy's" also has some of the cheapest drinks in town. Mon–Thurs 4pm–late, Fri–Sun 11.30am–2pm & 4pm–late.

2

BAY OF ISLANDS TOURS AND ACTIVITIES

Unless you get out onto the water you're missing the essence of the Bay of Islands. The majority of yachting, scuba diving, dolphin-watching, kayaking and fishing trips start in Paihia, but all the major **cruises** and bay **excursions** also pick up in Russell. From December to March everything should be booked a couple of days in advance. Hotels and motels can book for you; hostels can usually arrange a discount of around ten percent for backpackers.

The two main operators are Fullers Great Sights and Explore NZ/Dolphin Discoveries, both offering sightseeing, sailing and dolphin trips. There are also numerous **yachts** that usually take fewer than a dozen passengers and go out for around six hours: competition is tight and standards vary. Most operators give you a chance to **snorkel**, **kayak** and **fish**.

The Bay of Islands is excellent for **dolphin watching**; there's an eighty percent chance of seeing bottlenose and common dolphins in almost any season, as well as orca from May to October, and minke and Bryde's **whales** from August to January.

Your chances of **swimming with dolphins** are about 35–40 percent. Swimming is forbidden when there are juveniles in the pod, and only 18 people are allowed in the water with dolphins at any time. There's usually a money-back offer if you miss out (check when you book); your best chance is on a cruise with companies licensed to search for and swim with dolphins.

CRUISES, SAILING AND DOLPHIN ENCOUNTERS

Ecocruz ☎ 0800 432 627, ⓦ ecocruz.co.nz. A three-day sail (Oct–April; dorm bunk $725, double cabin $1700) on the *Manawanui*, which takes up to ten people around the bay, with the emphasis on appreciation of the natural environment. Excellent meals are included, along with use of kayaks, snorkel gear, fishing tackle and a good deal of local knowledge and enthusiasm. Book early.

Explore/Dolphin Discoveries ☎ 0800 397 567, ⓦ exploregroup.co.nz. The pioneers of dolphin swimming in this area operate a range of trips. Discover the Bay is a 4hr 30min cruise including a spin through the Hole in the Rock, a stop at Otehei Bay on Urupukapuka and dolphin viewing ($149); the Dolphin Discovery trip prioritizes getting in the water with bottlenose dolphins (4hr; $115); and the full-day (10hr) Dune Rider travels up to Cape Reinga along the "sand highway" of 90 Mile Beach ($150).

Fullers Great Sights ☎ 0800 653 339, ⓦ dolphincruises.co.nz. The Cream Trip (a.k.a. "Day in the Bay"; Oct–April daily; 7hr; $129) is the best all-round option, with a visit to the Hole in the Rock, a stop on Urupukapuka, a chance to get wet boom-netting and a look around as the boat delivers groceries and mail. You'll probably see dolphins and may have the chance to swim with them (for an additional $30) and you can extend your stay on Urupukapuka if you wish. There's also a dedicated dolphin cruise (2 daily; 3hr; $107).

Phantom ☎ 0800 224 421, ⓦ yachtphantom. com. Only ten can board this excellent, Russell-based ocean-racing sloop for six glorious hours around the bay ($110), relaxing on deck or taking the helm. Lunch included. Oct–April only.

R. Tucker Thompson ☎ 0800 882 537, ⓦ tucker. co.nz. Day-trips into the islands on a beautiful Northland-built schooner (daily Nov–April; 6hr; $149) with morning tea and freshly baked scones and cream before anchoring for a swim and BBQ lunch. Two-hour

Charlotte's Kitchen 69 Marsden Rd ☎ 09 402 8296, ⓦ charlotteskitchen.co.nz; map p.155. Right on the wharf, with gorgeous bay views, *Charlotte's Kitchen* has a bright contemporary feel and great service. Wood-fired pizza ($20–26), seafood (pan-fried market fish, $35) and steak (grass-fed Scotch fillet, $35) feature on the menu, plus it's a good spot for a sundowner. Live music Wednesday and Saturday. Mon–Fri 11.30am–late, Sat & Sun 8am–late.

Darryl's Dinner Cruise Paihia Wharf ☎ 0800 334 6637, ⓦ dinnercruise.co.nz; map p.155. Convivial and leisurely cruise (2hr 30min; $98) leaving from the wharf around 6.30pm and heading up the Waitangi River to Haruru Falls, where you tuck into prawns and mussels followed by T-bone steak, lamb and fish. There's a cash bar on board or BYO wine. If you catch it during a good sunset it's a great way to spend the evening. Trips are subject to minimum numbers.

DRINKING & NIGHTLIFE

CBK Maritime Building, Marsden Rd ☎ 09 402 8526, ⓦ cbk.nz/paihia; map p.155. It's all shiny tiles and taps at *CBK Paihia*, the latest pub-restaurant from this classy NZ

craft beer company. Right on the waterfront (with a little terrace), there's more than 60 different beers on offer (plus a decent wine and cocktail list), and a street food menu late-afternoon sails (Nov–March Wed, Fri & Sun; $65) including an antipasto platter are also available.

★ **The Rock** ☎ 0800 762 527, ⓦ rocktheboat.co.nz. Backpacker-style accommodation and group activities aboard a converted former car ferry, with a great range of ages and a real sense of kicking back. Board in the late afternoon and chug out to some gorgeous bays for fishing, swimming, snorkelling and night kayaking – which usually includes the chance to experience phosphorescence – and then feast on a big BBQ before a walk on an island the next day and 3pm arrival back at Paihia. Six-berth dorms ($268) and private cabins ($650) all have sea views. Dinner, breakfast and lunch included, but not drinks. Day cruise and shorter overnight tour also available.

KAYAKING

Coastal Kayakers ☎ 09 402 8105, ⓦ coastalkayakers. co.nz. Operates from near the bridge crossing to Waitangi. Runs a variety of trips including 2hr paddles in the bay ($95) or upstream to Haruru Falls ($75). Also offers kayak hire ($20/hr, $45 half-day).

FLIGHTS AND PARASAILING

Flying Kiwi Parasail Paihia Wharf ☎ 0800 359 691, ⓦ parasailnz.com. Offers ten- to fifteen-minute parasail flights from the back of a speedboat to a height of 1300ft, NZ's highest parasail. Single, tandem and triple parasails available (from $95).

Salt Air Marsden Rd, near the Maritime Building ☎ 09 4028 338, ⓦ saltair.co.nz. Runs chopper flights ($250/20min to the Hole in the Rock; $335/30min up the coast) along with awesome fixed-wing flights to Cape Reinga (see page 177). A new tour in conjunction with the Motu Kōkako Ahu Whenua Trust offers the chance to land atop the Hole in the Rock, with guided tour of the island with a Māori guide ($615).

Jet-Ski

★ **Tango Jetski Adventure** Paihia Wharf ☎ 0800 253 8754, ⓦ tangojetskitours.co.nz. The self-drive, speed-lover's way to see the seascape can cover a lot of ground in a relatively short period of time. Try the one-hour Island Blaster ($220).

SCUBA DIVING

Dive HQ Williams Rd ☎ 0800 107 551, ⓦ divenz.com. Will take you out in the Bay of Islands or to the wrecks of the *Rainbow Warrior* (see page 173) and the scuttled navy frigate *Canterbury*. Two-tank dives including gear cost $249 for those with Advanced Open Water certification or higher, $299 for those with Open Water status and $260 for the beginners' Discover Scuba Diving.

TRIPS FROM THE BAY OF ISLANDS

As the main tourist centre in Northland, the Bay of Islands acts as a staging post for forays further north, in particular for day-long bus tours to **Cape Reinga** and **Ninety Mile Beach** (see page 177) – arduous affairs lasting eleven hours, most of them spent stuck inside the vehicle. You're better off making your way up to Mangonui, Kaitaia or Ahipara and taking a trip from there, or taking Salt Air's fixed-wing Cape Reinga Flight (see above), which takes in the beach, Bay of Islands, and includes a field landing and short run to the cape itself.

Fullers Great Sights (see page 158) also runs Discover Hokianga (daily; 8hr; $129), another epic tour visiting the **Hokianga Harbour**, taking a Footprints Waipoua tour to the giant **kauri trees**, and taking a look at the **Kawiti Glowworm Caves**. Again you are better off getting closer independently and spending more time at the actual attractions.

with the likes of popcorn cauliflower ($12.90) and slow smoke BBQ chicken wings ($14.90) to choose from, "until hometime". Mon–Fri 9am–late, Sat & Sun 8am–late.

Pipi Patch Bar 18 Kings Rd ☎ 09 402 7111, ⓦ facebook.com/baseBayOfIslands; map p.155. Run by *Base Backpackers*, this place is busy with the beer pong crowd. There's a relaxed atmosphere during the day but at night the lights go down and the music cranks up. Daily 7am–2pm & 5pm–1am.

Sandpit Poolroom & Bar 16B Kings Rd ☎ 09 402 6063; map p.155. Another raucous backpacker bar on Kings Rd is *Sandpit Poolroom*; perfect for cheap beers, live sport on big screens and pool (8 large pool tables dominate the space). Daily 5pm–1am.

The islands

The Bay is aptly named, with six large, and around 140 small, islands. Many are subject to the DOC-led **Project Island Song** (ⓦ projectislandsong.co.nz), which aims to rid many of introduced predators and turn them into wildlife havens. Assorted birds have been reintroduced to many islands, notably **Urupukapuka Island**, which can be explored in a few hours using DOC's *Urupukapuka Island Archeological Walk* leaflet highlighting Māori *pa* and terrace sites.

Of the other large islands, by far the most popular is **Motuarohia (Roberton Island)**, where DOC manages the most dramatic central section, an isthmus almost severed by a pair of perfectly circular blue lagoons. Snorkellers can explore an undersea nature trail waymarked by inscribed stainless-steel plaques.

Other sights that often feature on cruise itineraries include the **Black Rocks**, bare islets formed from columnar-jointed basalt – these rise only 10m out of the water but plummet a sheer 30m beneath. At the outer limit of the bay is the craggy peninsula of **Cape Brett**, named by Cook in 1769 after the then Lord of the Admiralty, Lord Piercy Brett. Cruises also regularly pass through the **Hole in the Rock**, a natural tunnel through Piercy Island, which is even more exciting when there's a swell running.

ACCOMMODATION   THE ISLANDS

Urupukapuka Island ⓦ doc.govt.nz. This is the only island in the Bay of Islands that accommodates overnight guests, with DOC managing three basic sites: *Cable Bay*, with running water, showers and toilets, and *Sunset Bay*, with running water and toilets, are both on the south shore; *Urupukapuka Bay*, with running water, toilets and showers, is the island's easternmost campsite. Book your site well in advance. **$13**

Russell

The isolated location of **RUSSELL** – on a narrow peninsula with poor road but good sea access – gives this small hillside settlement an island ambience. In summer, however, the place is often full of day-trippers who pile off passenger ferries from Paihia and vehicle ferries from nearby Opua to explore the village's historic buildings, stroll along its quaint waterfront and stop in for a drink at *The Duke of Marlborough Hotel* – the original building on this site held New Zealand's first liquor licence.

Brief history

Modern-day Russell is a far cry from the 1830s when **Kororareka**, as it was then known, was a swashbuckling town full of whalers and sealers with a reputation as the "Hell Hole of the Pacific". Savage and drunken behaviour served as an open invitation to **missionaries**, who gradually won over a sizeable congregation and left behind Russell's two oldest buildings, the church and a printing works that produced religious tracts.

After the Treaty of Waitangi

By 1840, Kororareka was the largest settlement in the country, but after the signing of the Treaty of Waitangi, Governor William Hobson fell out with both Māori and local settlers and moved his capital progressively further south.

Meanwhile, initial Māori enthusiasm for the Treaty of Waitangi had faded: financial benefits had failed to materialize and the Confederation of Tribes flag that flew from Flagstaff Hill between 1834 and 1840 had been replaced by the Union Jack. This came to be seen as a symbol of British betrayal, and as resentment crystallized it found a leader in **Hone Heke Pokai**, Ngapuhi chief and son-in-law of Kerikeri's Hongi Hika. Between July 1844 and March 1845, Heke and his followers cut down the flagstaff no fewer than four times, the last occasion sparking the first **New Zealand War**, which raged for nearly a year, during which Kororareka was destroyed. The settlement rose from the ashes under a new name, Russell, and grew slowly around its beachfront into the tranquil village of today.

Pompallier

The Strand · Daily: May–Oct 10am–4pm; Nov–April 10am–5pm, access by guided tour only · $10 · ☎ 09 403 9015, ⓦ historicplaces.org.nz

Russell's most striking building is the fascinating **Pompallier**, the last survivor of Russell's Catholic mission, and once the headquarters of Catholicism in the western Pacific. Pompallier was built in 1842 as a printing works for the French Roman Catholic bishop Jean Baptiste François Pompallier. He had arrived three years earlier to find the Catholic word of God under siege from Anglican and Wesleyan tracts, translated into Māori. The missionaries built an elegant rammed-earth structure in a style typical of Pompallier's native Lyon. The press and paper were imported, and a tannery installed to make leather bookbindings. During the next eight years over a dozen titles of Catholic teachings were printed, comprising almost forty thousand volumes, which were some of the first books printed in Māori.

In a building now restored to its 1842 state, artisans again produce handmade books, all best understood on the **free tours**, which explain the production processes in each room. You can even get your hands dirty in what is New Zealand's only surviving colonial tannery.

Christ Church
Robertson Rd

New Zealand's oldest church, the cream, weatherboard **Christ Church** was built in 1836 by local settlers – unlike most churches of similar vintage, which were mission churches. In the mid-nineteenth century the church was besieged during skirmishes between Hone Heke's warriors and the British, leaving several still-visible bullet holes.

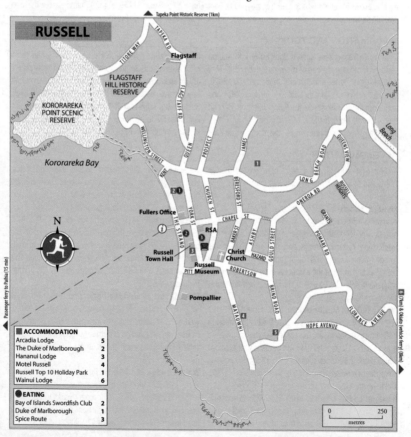

RUSSELL

▲ Tapeka Point Historic Reserve (1km)

Flagstaff

FLAGSTAFF HILL HISTORIC RESERVE

KORORAREKA POINT SCENIC RESERVE

Kororareka Bay

WELLINGTON STREET

TITORE WAY

TAPEKA RD

FLAGSTAFF RD

PROSPECT

QUEEN

JAMES

BERESFORD ST

LONG BEACH ROAD

QUEENS VIEW

Long Beach

RUSSELL HEIGHTS

LONG

ONEROA RD

GRANTS

POMARE RD

ROHANCE AVENUE

◀ Passenger ferry to Paihai (15 min)

N

KENT

YORK ST

THE STRAND

CHURCH ST

CHAPEL ST

BAKERS ST

ASHBY

GOULD STREET

HAZARD

ROBERTSON

BRIND ROAD

MATAUWHI

HOPE AVENUE

Fullers Office

ⓘ

RSA

Russell Town Hall

Russell Museum

PITT

Christ Church

Pompallier

ⓖ (7km) & Okiato (vehicle ferry) (8km) ▶

2 **1**

3

4

3

ACCOMMODATION

Arcadia Lodge	5
The Duke of Marlborough	2
Hananui Lodge	3
Motel Russell	4
Russell Top 10 Holiday Park	1
Wainui Lodge	6

● EATING

Bay of Islands Swordfish Club	2
Duke of Marlborough	1
Spice Route	3

0   250
metres

2

Russell Museum

2 York St • Daily: Jan 10am–5pm; Feb–Dec 10am–4pm • $10 • ☎ 09 403 7701, ⓦ russellmuseum.org.nz

The small **Russell Museum** shows a video telling the town's history and contains great exhibits, including an impressive one-fifth scale model of Cook's *Endeavour*, which called in here in 1769 and Māori artefacts such as the small family *waka* (canoe).

Flagstaff Hill and Tapeka Point Historic Reserve

30–40min return

At the end of The Strand, a short track climbs steeply to **Flagstaff Hill** (Maiki). The current flagpole was erected in 1857, some twelve years after the destruction of the fourth flagpole by Hone Heke, as a conciliatory gesture by a son of one of the chiefs who had ordered the original felling. The Confederation of Tribes flag, abandoned after the signing of the Treaty of Waitangi, is flown on twelve significant days of the year, including the anniversary of Hone Heke's death and the final day of the first New Zealand War. From Flagstaff Hill it's a further kilometre to the **Tapeka Point Historic Reserve**, a former *pa* site at the end of the peninsula – a wonderfully defensible position with great views and abundant evidence of terracing.

ARRIVAL AND DEPARTURE   RUSSELL

By ferry and car Most visitors reach Russell by ferry, but it's also accessible along a back road (see page 151). Foot passengers can take one of the frequent passenger ferries (Oct–May 7am–10pm; June–Sept 7am–8pm; every 30min or so; $7 one way, $12.50 return; 15min) between the main wharves in Paihia and Russell.

INFORMATION AND TOURS

Tourist information Russell Booking & Information Centre is located at the end of the wharf (daily Sept–May 7.30am–8pm; June–Aug 8.30am–4pm; ☎ 09 403 8020, ⓦ russellinfo.co.nz). Makes bookings for local trips and accommodation. Also stocks the *Russell Heritage Trail* and *Bay of Islands Walks* leaflets.

Tours Most of the bay's cruises and dolphin trips are based in Paihia but also pick up at Russell wharf (with prior reservation) around 15min later. Occasionally there are no pick-ups available, but you can catch the frequent, inexpensive passenger ferry between Paihia and Russell. Russell Mini Tours (☎ 0800 646 486, ⓦ russellminitours.com) offer a locals' view on the area's history and the town (six daily Oct–April, four daily May–Sept; $30).

ACCOMMODATION

Accommodation in Russell is much more limited than in Paihia and tends to be more upmarket, mostly B&Bs and lodges.

Arcadia Lodge 10 Florance Ave ☎ 09 403 7756, ⓦ arcadialodge.co.nz; map p.161. Stylish B&B in a historic wooden house encircled by decks on a quiet hill overlooking cottage gardens and the bay. Five of the wooden-floored suites and rooms (one not en suite) enjoy sea views and much of the produce is organic and grown in the garden, or locally. No under-15s. Two-night minimum in summer. Rooms $220, suites $290

★ **The Duke of Marlborough** 35 The Strand ☎ 09 403 7829, ⓦ theduke.co.nz; map p.161. The beating heart in the centre of the town, *The Duke of Marlborough's* ambience is of an old colonial hotel until you get into your room, at which point it becomes modern with a hint of romance. Some rooms have sea views ($360), others sundecks ($290), and there are a few cosy options with neither. $165

Hananui Lodge 4 York St ☎ 09 403 7875, ⓦ hananui.co.nz; map p.161. Well-run, modernized motel-style place by the water. The waterfront suites have the best views but even the standard lodges are comfortable, with sea glimpses, and all get spa access. There are also new apartments across the road with big TVs and a/c. Apartments $150, waterfront lodges $215

Motel Russell 16 Matauwhi Rd ☎ 0800 240 011, ⓦ motelrussell.co.nz; map p.161. Choose one of the comfortable, recently modernized units in an acre of well-tended subtropical garden full of birds surrounding this simple motel with an attractive pool. Studios $120, one-bedroom units $155

Russell Top 10 Holiday Park Long Beach Rd ☎ 09 403 7826, ⓦ russelltop10.co.nz; map p.161. Central, well-ordered and spotless campsite with tent and campervan sites and an extensive range of high-standard cabins (from $85) and motel units. Campervans $52, motel units $175

Wainui Lodge 92d Wahapu Rd, 7km south of Russell ☎ 09 403 8278, ⓦ wainuilodge-russell-nz.com; map p.161. Excellent, tiny two-room backpackers with morning birdsong and kayaking from its own mangrove-lined beach. Full kitchen. Dorms $29, doubles $68

EATING

Russell has a limited range of restaurants and prices are fairly high, but quality is good.

Bay of Islands Swordfish Club 25 The Strand ☎ 09 403 7857, ⓦ swordfish.co.nz; map p.161. Technically a private club, much the same as the one in Paihia (see page 157), so you just sign yourself in or get the bartender to do it. Always a winner for cheap beer, fish and chips, simple bar meals (mains around $25) in big portions, and great sunset views from the veranda. Daily 3pm–late.

★ **The Duke of Marlborough** 35 The Strand ☎ 09 403 7829, ⓦ theduke.co.nz; map p.161. Waterside bar seating, a pub bar at the back and a restaurant all serving a broad range of wine and beer. Best of all is the food, stunningly presented in imaginative combinations and generous portions. King on the menu is the 8hr cooked shoulder of lamb on the bone ($65 for two; dinner only), which melts in the mouth and could feed a coach party. The kitchen closes at 9pm. Daily 11.30am–10.30pm.

Spice Route 202/15 York St ☎ 09 403 7561, ⓦ spicerouteindian.co.nz; map p.161. The best Indian restaurant in the Bay of Islands is tucked away off York Street. The lengthy menu includes meat (think tender goat curry or sizzling chicken dopiaza) and veggie options (try the dal makhani) for under $20, and all the usual tandoori breads and chutneys. Mon–Wed 4.30–9.30pm, Thurs–Sat 11.30am–9.30pm, Sun 11am–10pm.

Kerikeri and around

KERIKERI, 25km north of Paihia, is central to the history of the Bay of Islands and yet geographically removed from it, strung out along the main road and surrounded by the orchards that form Kerikeri's economic mainstay. Two kilometres to the east of town, the thin ribbon of the Kerikeri Inlet forces its way from the sea to its tidal limit at **Kerikeri Basin**, the site chosen by Samuel Marsden for the Church Missionary Society's second mission in New Zealand – nearby **Waimate North** also has a mission house that has stood the test of time.

Kerikeri has always been a centre for **seasonal work** and in recent years it's earned itself a reputation for high-quality **craft shops** dotted among the orchards.

Kemp House & Gardens

246 Kerikeri Rd • Daily Nov–April 10am–5pm; May–Oct 10am–4pm; entry by guided tour only, minimum of four; call ahead for tour times, $10 combined ticket with Old Stone Store Museum • ☎ 09 407 9236, ⓦ historicplaces.org.nz

It was here, in 1821, that mission carpenters started work on what is now New Zealand's oldest European-style building, **Kemp House**, a restrained, two-storey Georgian colonial affair. The first occupants, missionary John Butler and his family, soon moved on, and by 1832 the house was in the hands of lay missionary and blacksmith James Kemp, who extended the design. Since the last of the Kemps moved out in 1974 it has been restored, furnished in mid-nineteenth-century style, and surrounded by colonial-style **gardens**.

Old Stone Store

246 Kerikeri Rd • Daily Nov–April 10am–5pm; May–Oct 10am–4pm • Free; upper floors $8 or $10 combined ticket with Kemp House & Gardens • ☎ 09 407 9236, ⓦ historicplaces.org.nz

Mission House guided tours start next door at the **Old Stone Store**, the only other extant building from the mission station and the country's oldest stone building. Completed in 1836 as a central provision store for the Church Missionary Society, it successively served as a munitions store for troops garrisoned here to fight Hone Heke, then a kauri-trading store and a shop, before being opened to the public in 1975.

The ground-floor **store** (free) sells some goods almost identical to those on offer almost 180 years ago, most sourced from the original manufacturers. You can still buy the once-prized Hudson Bay trading blankets, plus copper and cast-iron pots, jute sacks, gunpowder tea, old-fashioned sweets, and preserves made from fruit grown in the mission garden next door. The two **upper floors** admirably outline the history of Māori and European contact and the relevance of Kerikeri Basin, aided by old implements, including a hand-operated flour mill from around 1820, thought to be the oldest piece of machinery in the country.

From opposite the Old Stone Store, a path along the river leads to **Kororipo Pa**, which commands a hill on a prominent bend in the river from where local chief Hongi Hika launched attacks on other tribes using newly acquired firearms.

Rewa's Village

1 Landing Rd • ⓦ rewasvillage.co.nz, ☎ 09 407 6454 • Daily Nov–April 10am–5pm; May–Oct 10am–4pm • $5

A footbridge across the creek leads to **Rewa's Village**, a reconstruction of a fishing village where you'll get a better appreciation of pre-European Māori life. It comes complete with *marae*, weapons and *kumara* stores, as well as an authentic *hangi* site with an adjacent shell midden.

Kerikeri Basin Reserve

Opposite Rewa's Village

The **Kerikeri Basin Reserve** marks the start of a track past the site of Kerikeri's first hydroelectric station (15min each way) and the swimming holes at Fairy Pools

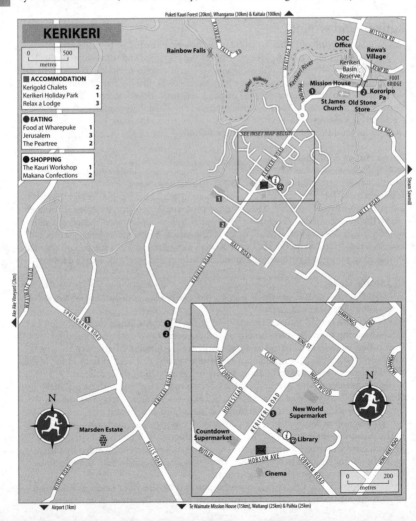

KERIKERI

Puketi Kauri Forest (20km), Whangaroa (30km) & Kaitaia (100km)

0 — 500 metres

ACCOMMODATION
Kerigold Chalets 2
Kerikeri Holiday Park 1
Relax a Lodge 3

EATING
Food at Wharepuke 1
Jerusalem 3
The Peartree 2

SHOPPING
The Kauri Workshop 1
Makana Confections 2

Rainbow Falls
DOC Office
Rewa's Village
Kerikeri Basin Reserve
FOOT BRIDGE
Mission House
Kororipo Pa
St James Church
Old Stone Store

Kerikeri River
Heritage Bypass
Mission Rd
Kzemp Rd
Pa Road

SEE INSET MAP BELOW
Steam Sawmill

Hall Road
Kerikeri Road
Inlet Road

Springbank Road
Waimate Road
Kerikeri Road
Bulls Road
Wiroa Road

Marsden Estate

Ake Ake Vineyard (2km)

N

Hawkings Cres
King St
Clark
Fairway Drive
Homestead
Kerikeri Road
Wedgwood
New World Supermarket
Countdown Supermarket
Library
Butler
Hobson Ave
Cobham Road
Kemp Road
Home Here Road
Cinema

N

0 — 200 metres

Airport (1km)
Te Waimate Mission House (15km), Waitangi (25km) & Paihia (25km)

WINERIES AROUND KERIKERI

Ake Ake Vineyard 165 Waimate North Rd ☎09 407 8230, ⓦakeakevineyard.co.nz. Organic vineyard producing intriguing wines (including Chambourcin, which has become a favourite with Northland grape growers) that's open for tastings ($8, or free with lunch) and for lunch or dinner (mains $27–35), including the likes of chargrilled venison steak and fish of the day. Customers can stroll the vineyard on a 1km trail. Tastings daily 10.30am–4.30pm; honk your horn if there's no one at the cellar door.

Marsden Estate Wiroa Rd ☎09 407 9398, ⓦmarsdenestate.co.nz. A medium-sized winery producing a broad variety of excellent reds and whites sampled through free tastings, or in larger quantities in the moderately priced lunch restaurant. Daily specials might include seared tuna niçoise or chargrilled steak (mains $20–36). Daily: Aug–May 10am–5pm; June & July 10am–4pm.

2

(35min each way) to the impressively undercut **Rainbow Falls** (1hr each way). The latter are also accessible off Waipapa Road, 3km north of the Basin.

Te Waimate Mission House

344 Te Ahu Ahu Rd, 15km southwest of Kerikeri • Nov–April Fri–Tues 10am–5pm; May–Oct Sat–Mon 10am–4pm • $10 • ☎09 405 9734, ⓦheritage.org.nz

Waimate North is home to the colonial Regency-style **Te Waimate Mission House**, New Zealand's second-oldest European building. Now virtually in the middle of nowhere, in the 1830s this was the centre of a vigorous **Anglican mission**. Missionaries were keen to add European agricultural techniques to the literacy and religion they were teaching the Māori, and by 1834 locally grown wheat was milled at the river, orchards were flourishing and crops were sprouting – all impressing Charles Darwin, who visited the following year. The house, built by converts from local kauri in 1832, has been restored as accurately as possible to its original design. Guided tours highlight prize possessions.

Puketi Kauri Forest

20km west of Kerikeri • Guided tours are offered by Adventure Puketi

The **Puketi Kauri Forest** comprises one of the largest continuous tracts of kauri forest in the north and there are a couple of easy walking tracks to explore. **Manginangina Kauri Walk** is a 350m boardwalk through lush forest that brings you to a stand of good-sized kauri, or, in the evening, stroll the 1.6km **Puketi Nature Trail** for the chance to see glowworms.

ARRIVAL AND DEPARTURE

KERIKERI AND AROUND

By plane Air New Zealand flights from Auckland arrive at the Bay of Islands airport (☎09 407 6133, ⓦbayofislandsairport.co.nz), 6km southwest of town and are met by the Super Shuttle bus ($12 into town).

Destinations Auckland (5–6 daily; 50min).
By bus InterCity/Northliner buses stop on Cobham Rd. Destinations Auckland (4 daily; 5hr); Kaitaia (1 daily; 1hr 45min); Paihia (4 daily; 30min).

INFORMATION AND TOURS

Tourist information There's no official visitor centre, but you can pick up leaflets inside the foyer of the library on Cobham Rd (Mon–Fri 8am–5pm, Sat 9am–2pm, Sun 9am–1pm), which also has free wi-fi.
DOC 34 Landing Rd (Mon–Fri 8am–4.30pm; ☎09 407 8474). Advises on local walks and more ambitious treks into the Puketi Kauri Forest (see page 165).
Seasonal work For most of the year it's possible to get seasonal work weeding, thinning or picking in the subtropical orchards among citrus, tamarillos, feijoas, melons, courgettes, peppers and kiwifruit. Work is most abundant from January to July, with so-called "silly season" from mid-March to mid-June. The best contacts are the managers of the hostels and campsites, many of whom also offer good weekly rates.
Adventure Puketi 476 Puketi Rd ☎09 401 9095, ⓦforestwalks.com. Runs a number of informative walks in Puketi Kauri Forest, one of which takes place at night (2hr; $80) with the hope of encountering kiwi, morepork and other night owls.

ACCOMMODATION

Kerikeri has a good selection of accommodation in all categories, particularly budget places – a consequence of the area's popularity with long-stay casual workers. Seasonal price fluctuations are nowhere near as marked as in Paihia, though it's still difficult to find accommodation in January.

KERIKERI AND AROUND

Kerigold Chalets 326 Kerikeri Rd ☎0800 537 446, ⓦkerigoldchalets.co.nz; map p.164. Modern, spacious and spotless one-bedroom stand-alone wooden chalets with kitchens and access to a communal pool and barbecue area. Courtesy car to the airport available on request. $200

★ **Kerikeri Holiday Park** Kerikeri Rd ☎0800 272 642, ⓦkerikeriholidaypark.co.nz; map p.164. Large, beautiful streamside site on the edge of town with a spacious camping area, well-equipped standard cabins and comfortable self-contained units. There's a covered BBQ area and the occasional sound of kiwi in the night. Camping per person $16, standard cabins $100, self-contained units $140

Relax A Lodge SH10, 5km west of Kerikeri ☎09 407 6989, ⓦrelaxalodge.co.nz; map p.164. Top-class rooms and cottages on an organic citrus orchard, with comfortable, shared-bathroom rooms in the lovely wooden house and gorgeous cottages scattered around the orchard. The owners speak German, there's an outdoor pool and free-range eggs are available. Doubles $55, cottages $110

PUKETI KAURI FOREST

Puketi Recreation Area Campsite Turn off SH10 at Pungaere Rd, 600m north of Waipapa and follow signs to the campsite ⓦdoc.govt.nz. A bog-standard DOC campsite in the Puketi Kauri Forest, with running water, long-drop toilets, cold showers, BBQs and picnic tables. No bookings; leave the fee in the honesty box. $6

EATING

★ **Food at Wharepuke** 190 Kerikeri Rd ☎09 407 8936, ⓦfoodatwharepuke.co.nz; map p.164. Stunning Thai-European fusion garden café serving high-quality nosh ($14–39) including crispy pork-belly salad, aged Angus eye fillet and *tom yum* with tiger prawns, to name but a few. Also plays some lounge-like live music to entertain diners. Three-course Thai banquet ($50) served every Friday. Tues–Sat 11am–3pm & 5–10pm.

Jerusalem Cobblestone Mall ☎09 407 1001, ⓦcafejerusalem.co.nz; map p.164. Small, friendly, licensed Israeli café beloved by Northlanders for its authentic, low-cost and wonderfully aromatic Middle Eastern dishes to eat in or take away, including falafel, *levivot* and *metuvlun* ($4–18). Mon–Sat 10am–late.

The Peartree 215 Kerikeri Rd ☎09 407 8479, ⓦthepeartree.co.nz; map p.164. With a fabulous setting by Kerikeri Basin this spot is best used for midday tipples or sun-downers, but if you're too lazy to get lunch or dinner elsewhere you can eat here in a semiformal atmosphere, inside or on the veranda. Typical menu items are twice-baked *kumara* soufflé and tempura-battered fish and chips (mains around $32). Daily: 10am–late (closed Tues & Wed in winter).

ENTERTAINMENT

Cathay Cinemas Hobson Avenue ☎09 407 4428, ⓦcathaycinemas.co.nz. Entertainment is thin on the ground in Kerikeri, so thank goodness for this lovingly restored cinema showing mainstream and more off-beat movies, with three screens and a licensed café.

SHOPPING

You could easily spend a couple of hours pottering around the **craft outlets** that dominate the Kerikeri hinterland, guided by the free and widely available *Kerikeri Art & Craft Trail* leaflet: most places are open daily from 9am–5pm.

The Kauri Workshop 500 Kerikeri Rd ☎09 407 9196; map p.164. Stocks anything you might hope to make from kauri, including spoons, bowls and carvings. Open daily.

Makana Confections 504 Kerikeri Rd ☎09 407 6800, ⓦmakana.co.nz; map p.164. Boutique shop produces handmade chocolates, which you can see being made and then, of course, sample. Daily 9am–5.30pm.

Matauri Bay to the Karikari Peninsula

North of the Bay of Islands everything gets a lot quieter. There are few towns of any consequence along the coast and it is the peace and slow pace that attract visitors to an array of glorious beaches and the lovely Whangaroa Harbour. The first stop north of Kerikeri is tiny **Matauri Bay**, where a hilltop memorial commemorates the Greenpeace flagship, *Rainbow Warrior*, which now lies off the coast. A sealed but winding back road continues north, offering fabulous sea views and passing gorgeous headlands and beaches before delivering you to **Whangaroa Harbour**, one of the most beautiful in Northland, and an excellent place to go sailing or kayaking. Further north is the idyllic surfing and fishing hideaway of **Taupo Bay**.

Continuing north brings you to the huge bite out of the coast called **Doubtless Bay**, which had two celebrated discoverers: Kupe, said to have first set foot on Aotearoa in **Taipa**; and Cook, who sailed past in 1769 and pronounced it "doubtless, a bay". Bounded on the west and north by the sheltering **Karikari Peninsula**, the bay offers safe boating and is popular with Kiwi vacationers. In January you can barely move here and you'll struggle to find accommodation, but the shoulder seasons can be surprisingly quiet, and outside December, January and February room prices drop considerably. Most of the bay's facilities cluster along the southern shore of the peninsula in a string of beachside settlements – **Coopers Beach**, **Cable Bay** and **Taipa Bay** – running west from picturesque **Mangonui**.

Matauri Bay

A high inland ridge provides a dramatic first glimpse of the long, Norfolk-pine-backed **MATAURI BAY**, 30km north of Kerikeri, and the **Cavalli Islands** just offshore. At the northern end of the main bay a well-worn path (20min return; 70m ascent) climbs to Chris Booth's distinctive **Rainbow Warrior Memorial**, which commemorates the Greenpeace flagship (see above), now scuttled off the Cavalli Islands. The memorial comprises a stone arch (symbolizing a rainbow) and the vessel's salvaged bronze propeller. Paihia-based dive operators (see page 159) run trips out to the wreck, which is based ten minutes offshore from Matauri Bay. The best visibility is in April; from September to November plankton sometimes obscure the view, but it's still pretty good.

Samuel Marsden Memorial Church
Matauri Bay Rd, just before the beach

Missionary Samuel Marsden first set foot in Aotearoa in 1814 at Matauri Bay, where he mediated between the Ngati Kura people – who still own the bay – and some Bay of Islands Māori, a process commemorated by the quaint wooden **Samuel Marsden Memorial Church**. The Ngati Kura tell of their ancestral *waka*, *Mataatua*, which lies in waters nearby. It was the resonance of this legendary canoe that partly led the Ngati Kura to offer a final resting place to the wreck of the *Rainbow Warrior* (see page 173).

Whangaroa Harbour

West of Matauri Bay, the virtually landlocked and sheltered **Whangaroa Harbour** is the perfect antidote to Bay of Islands' commercialism. The scenery, albeit on a smaller scale, is easily a match for its southern cousin and, despite the limited facilities, you can still get out on a cruise or to join the big-game fishers. Narrow inlets forge between cliffs and steep hills, most notably the two bald volcanic plugs, **St Paul and St Peter**, which rise behind the harbour's two settlements, **WHANGAROA** on the south side, and **TOTARA NORTH** opposite.

Brief history

Whangaroa Harbour was among the first areas in New Zealand to be visited by European pioneers, most famously those aboard the *Boyd*, which called here in 1809 to load kauri spars for shipping to Britain. A couple of days after its arrival, all 66 crew were killed and the ship burned by local Māori in retribution for the crew's mistreatment of Tara, a high-born Māori sailor who had apparently transgressed the ship's rules. A British whaler avenged the incident by burning the entire Māori village, sparking off a series of skirmishes that spread over the north for five years. Later the vast stands of kauri were hacked down and milled, some at Totara North. Even if you're just passing through, it's worth driving the 4km along the northern shore of the harbour to Totara North, passing the atmospheric remains of this historic community's last sawmills, which ceased operation in 2004.

Taupo Bay

A sealed 13km road from SH10 brings you to **TAUPO BAY**, a blissfully undeveloped holiday community with a smattering of beach shacks, and some of the best surfing and rock and beach fishing in Northland.

Mangonui and around

With its lively fishing wharf and a traditional grocery perched on stilts over the water there's an antiquated air to **MANGONUI**, strung along the sheltered Mangonui Harbour off Doubtless Bay. A handful of two-storey buildings with wooden verandas have been preserved, some operating as craft shops or cafés, but this is still very much a working village. To get a feel for the layout of Mangonui Harbour, take in the views at **Rangikapiti Pa Historic Reserve**, off Rangikapiti Road, between Mangonui and Coopers Beach.

Mangonui also makes a good base for organized trips to **Cape Reinga** and **Ninety Mile Beach** (see page 174).

Brief history

Mangonui means "big shark", recalling the legendary chief Moehuri's *waka* which was supposedly led into Mangonui Harbour by such a fish. But it was whales and the business of provisioning **whaling** ships that made the town: one story tells of a harbour so packed with ships that folk could leap between the boats to cross from Mangonui to the diminutive settlement of Hihi on the far shore. As whaling diminished, the kauri trade took its place, chiefly around Mill Bay, the cove five minutes' walk to the west of Mangonui.

Coopers Beach

While ships were repaired and restocked at Mangonui, barrels were mended a couple of kilometres west at **COOPERS BEACH**, a glorious and well-shaded sweep of sand backed by a beautiful stand of red-flowering pohutakowa trees and, less elegantly, by a string of motels. The beach is popular in January and at weekends, but at other times you may find you have it pretty much to yourself.

Cable Bay

About 3km west of Coopers Beach, the smaller swimming and surfing settlement of **CABLE BAY** is separated by the Taipa River from the beachside village of **TAIPA**. This pleasant stretch of pink coral sand is now the haunt of sunbathers and swimmers, but it's also historically significant as the spot where Kupe, the discoverer of Aotearoa in Māori legend, first set foot on land. There's a concrete memorial to him near the Shell station by the Taipa River.

The Karikari Peninsula

Doubtless Bay to the east and Rangaunu Harbour to the west are bounded by the crooked arm of the **Karikari Peninsula**, which strikes north swathed in unspoiled golden- and white-sand beaches. Outside Christmas to mid-February, they have barely a soul on them. Apart from the large and modern **Karikari Estate** golf resort, vineyard and winery, facilities remain limited, though there's the usual scattering of motels and cheap places to eat. There's no public transport, and without diving or fishing gear, you'll have to resign yourself to lazing on the beaches and swimming from them.

Puheke Beach

The initial approach across a low and scrubby isthmus is less than inspiring, but 10km along Inland Road, a side road leads to the peninsula's west coast and **Puheke Beach**, a gorgeous, dune-backed beach that's usually deserted. Another fine white strand spans the nearby hamlet of **RANGIPUTA**.

Tokerau Beach to Maitai Bay

The peninsula's main road continues to the community of **TOKERAU BEACH**, a cluster of houses and shops at the northern end of the grand sweep of Doubtless Bay. 1km further north, the road passes the golf course and **Karikari Estate winery** (ⓦkarikariestate.co.nz). However, the Karikari Peninsula saves its best until last: **Maitai Bay**, a matchless double arc of golden sand split by a rocky knoll, encompassed by a campsite (see page 170). Much of the site is *tapu* to local Māori, and you are encouraged to respect the sacred areas. A walking track (3.5km) runs out from here to the rugged headland and fantastic views over the sea, though the path can be dangerously slippery in wet weather.

ARRIVAL AND INFORMATION   MATAURI BAY TO THE KARIKARI PENINSULA

By bus There is little public transport so your own wheels are recommended if not essential. InterCity/Northliner buses serve the Mangonui waterfront, running once a day in each direction between Paihia and Kaitaia. By bus The Far North link (ⓦbuslink.co.nz) operates on weekdays between Mangonui and Kaitaia, with stops at Coopers Beach, Cable Bay and Karikari.

Destinations Kaitaia (1 daily; 55min); Paihia (1 daily; 2hr).

Tourist information 118 Waterfront Drive, Mangonui. The volunteer-staffed visitor centre (Nov–Easter daily 10am–4pm; Easter–Oct Tues–Sat 10am–3pm; ☎09 406 2046) can point you to accommodation, both here and along the coast, and has wi-fi.

TOURS AND ACTIVITIES

Northland Sea Kayaking ☎09 405 0381, ⓦnorthlandseakayaking.co.nz. Located on the northeastern flank of Whangaroa Harbour, this knowledgeable operator arranges local kayak trips in the summer ($90 half-day; no credit cards).

Whangaroa Big Gamefish Club ☎09 405 0399, ⓦwhangaroasportfishingclub.co.nz. The people you want to see if you want to go game fishing are listed on the website, or you can phone them, but don't just rock up to the bar and expect to go out that day. Charter rates

typically kick off at around $1000/day, with bait and ice costing extra. Expect mostly marlin off the Cavalli Islands and more modest edible domestic fish closer to shore.

Whangaroa Harbour Water Transport ☎027 680 5588, ⓦwhangaroawater.co.nz. Take a tour of the harbour (1hr 30min; $60) to learn about the area's history and get up close to marine life or arrange a water taxi to collect you at the end of the Wairakau Stream Track (Totara North to Lane Cove is 5.6km on foot; one-way water taxi $25).

ACCOMMODATION

WHANGAROA HARBOUR

★ **Kahoe Farms Hostel** SH10, 1.5km north of the Totara North turn-off ☎09 405 1804, ⓦkahoefarms. co.nz. A small and extremely hospitable backpackers on a working cattle farm with a dorm and rooms in a house with polished wood floors and more rooms (some en suite) in a separate villa on the hill behind. The Kiwi-Italian owners whip up superb home-made pizza, pasta and farm steak dinners, generous breakfasts and a fine espresso, plus you can hike a picturesque private trail to the nearby kauri dam. The daily InterCity/Northliner bus passes the farm and will drop up/pick up on request. Dorms $32, doubles $86

TAUPO BAY

Taupo Bay Holiday Park 1070 Taupo Bay Rd ☎09 406

0315, ⓦtaupobayholidaypark.co.nz. One of the few places worth staying at in the area, much beloved by Kiwi holiday-makers for its ample camping, good communal facilities and modern but no-frills cabins sleeping up to five. Camping $18, cabins $150

MANGONUI

★ **Beach Lodge** 121 SH10, Coopers Beach ☎09 409 0068, ⓦbeachlodge.co.nz. Five breezy yet elegant water-view apartments, on the beachfront at Coopers Beach and within the sound of the waves, each with its own deck, full kitchen and free use of kayaks and boogie boards. No under-8s. $395

Carneval 360 SH10, Cable Bay ☎09 406 1012, ⓦcarneval.co.nz. Perched high on a hill overlooking the sea is this relaxed, Swiss-run house with comfortable

2

spacious rooms and a stunning view of the coastline, plus a full Swiss breakfast if you can handle it. Rooms $200

★ **Driftwood Lodge** SH10, Cable Bay ☎ 09 406 0418, ⓦ driftwoodlodge.co.nz. Great lodge right beside the beach with views of the Karikari Peninsula from the broad deck where everyone gathers for sundowners and perhaps a BBQ. Accommodation is in fully self-contained units and there's free access to dinghies, kayaks and boogie boards. It's popular, so book well ahead. $285

Puketiti Lodge 10 Puketiti Drive, 7km south of Mangonui ☎ 09 406 0369, ⓦ puketitilodge.co.nz. There's a rural feel to this modern lodge with two en-suite rooms, sleeping up to four ($40/additional person), with long views to the coast. Everyone has access to the huge deck and well-equipped

kitchen and lounge. Nov–March only. Doubles $150

KARIKARI PENINSULA

Maitai Bay Campground Maitai Bay Rd ⓦ doc.govt.nz. Northland's largest DOC campsite has cold showers, toilets and drinking water, as well as campervan access. DOC rangers service the site daily in the high season. Ideal for birdlife and wildlife watching. Camping $13

Whatuwhiwhi Top 10 Holiday Park Whatuwhiwhi Rd, 18km off SH10 ☎ 0800 142 444, ⓦ whatuwhiwhitop10.co.nz. Within easy walking distance of a picturesque bay and beach, this is a quiet, basic and traditional Kiwi campsite with a spa pool and good communal facilities. It gets very busy in the summer. Camping $40, cabins $75

EATING AND DRINKING

MATAURI BAY

Matauri Top Shop Top of Matauri Bay Rd ☎ 09 405 1040. A combined store and good-value café, this is the only place to stop for a bite in town, serving sandwiches, rolls and ice cream (nothing over $12), as well as offering a few supplies for you to make up a picnic, which might be preferable. Daily 8am–late (9am public holidays).

MANGONUI

Committed drinking mostly happens at the *Mangonui Hotel*, which often has bands at weekends.

Little Kitchen 118 Waterfront Rd ☎ 09 406 1644. A cheerful licensed café with outdoor tables offering breakfasts (until 11.30am) and lunches along the lines of burgers, bagels or mussels (under $20). They also serve great coffee and a selection of cakes and pastries. Daily 8am–3pm.

Fresh & Tasty Inside the Mangonui Hotel, Waterfront Drive ☎ 09 406 0082. Rival chippy to neighbouring *Mangonui Fish Shop*, and much frequented by locals happy to trade location for lower prices (under $15), less waiting time and equally good tucker, plus roast dinners if you can't

stand fish. Open daily 11am–8pm.

Mangonui Fish Shop 137 Waterfront Drive ☎ 09 406 0478. Famed fish and chip restaurant idyllically set on stilts over the water, and a regular afternoon stop for returning Cape Reinga buses. Expect fresh-cooked fish, buckets of chips and some more healthy seafood-oriented salads and seafood chowder (all under £21). Licensed and BYO. Daily 8.30am–9pm.

★ **Waterfront Café** Waterfront Drive ☎ 09 406 0850. Decent café/bar with harbour views, good coffee, breakfasts, light lunches, a wide range of dinner mains including fine pizzas, seared scallops and fresh oysters (mains $30–38). Occasional live music. Daily 8am–late.

TAIPA

Bush Fairy Dairy 1195 Oruru Rd, Peria, 12km south of Taipa ☎ 09 408 5508. A hippie-style commune that hosts the Far Out Food Van (FOFV) Thursday to Saturday evenings, plus Sunday bazaars every few weeks throughout the summer (brimming with art, crafts, clothing, organic produce, plus standard dairy items). Call ahead for dates and times.

SHOPPING

Flax Bush 50 Waterfront Drive, Mangonui ☎ 09 406 1510, ⓦ flaxbush.co.nz. Carries reasonably priced woven

flax items and other locally made crafts; the deals on woven baskets (*kete*) are worth it. Mon–Sat 9.30am–4.30pm.

Kaitaia and around

KAITAIA, 40km west of Mangonui, is the Far North's largest commercial centre, situated near the junction of the two main routes north. It makes a convenient base for some of the best trips to Cape Reinga and Ninety Mile Beach (see page 177), far preferable to the longer trips from the Bay of Islands. As a farming service town there's not much to detain you, except for a rather fine museum – and if you're in the area around the third

weekend of March, you can catch competitors from around the world taking part in a series of running events on Ninety Mile Beach, including the **Te Houtaewa Challenge** (ⓦtehoutaewa.co.nz). If you have your own transport, you might want to base yourself at the magnificent beach in nearby **Ahipara** (see below), to sand-toboggan the giant dunes, surf or explore the old gum fields.

Brief history

A Māori village already flourished at Kaitaia when the first missionary, Joseph Matthews, came looking for a site in 1832. The protection of the mission encouraged European pastoralists to establish themselves here, but by the 1880s they found themselves swamped by the gum diggers who had come to plunder the underground deposits around Lake Ohia and Ahipara. Many early arrivals were young Croats fleeing tough conditions in what was then part of the Austro-Hungarian Empire, though the only evidence of this is a Serbo-Croat welcome sign at the entrance to town, and a cultural society that holds a traditional dance each year.

Museum at Te Ahu

Corner of Matthews Ave and South Rd • Mon–Fri 10am–4pm • Donation requested • ☎ 0800 920 029, ⓦ teahuheritage.co.nz

The best place to gain a sense of the area is the **Museum at Te Ahu**. The museum showcases the best of the extensive local archive including the massive anchor from the *De Surville*, wrecked in 1769, considered to be the first European object left in New Zealand. Look too for the copy of the twelfth- or thirteenth-century Kaitaia Carving (the original is in the Auckland Museum), a fine example of the transitional period during which Polynesian art began to take on Māori elements. The **Te Ahu Centre** also houses temporary exhibitions, a cinema and the local i-SITE visitor centre.

Ahipara

The southern end of Ninety Mile Beach finishes with a flourish at **AHIPARA**, 15km west of Kaitaia, a secluded scattered village that grew up around the now barren, but eerie and hauntingly beautiful, **Ahipara gum fields**. A hundred kilometres of sand recede into sea spray to the north, while to the south the high flatlands of the Ahipara Plateau tumble to the sea in a cascade of golden dunes. Beach and plateau meet at **Shipwreck Bay**, a surf and swimming beach with an underground following with surfers for its long tubes (sometimes 400m or more). The bay is named after the 1870 wreck of the *Favourite*, its paddle-shaft still protruding from the sand. At low tide you can pick mussels off the

---

AHIPARA TOURS AND ACTIVITIES

The **dunes** and **gum fields** are best approached on foot or via a guided quad bike tour. There have been access problems of late across Shipwreck Beach, due to disagreements between operators and the local *iwi*; check with the tour guides listed below for the latest information. Locals are trying to reopen a tide-dependent walking track from the bridge at Shipwreck Beach to the desolate gum fields – ask at the i-SITE visitor centre or Ahipara Adventure for the latest.

TOUR OPERATORS

Ahipara Adventure 15 Takahe St ☎ 09 409 2055, ⓦ ahiparaadventure.co.nz. Rents single-rider quad bikes ($115/hr) heading north of the settlement along the beach. They also rent surfboards ($40/half-day) and blokarts for use on the beach ($80/1hr).

Ahipara Horse Treks 11 Foreshore Rd ☎ 09 409 4122 or ☎ 027 333 8645. Saddle up for two-hour rides ($65) along the beaches and across some of the local farmland.

Tua Tua Tours ☎ 0800 494 288, ⓦ ahipara.co.nz/tuatuatours. Runs a variety of quad biking tours around the gum fields and dunes, including the chance to try sand-boarding. From $100.

FRENCH NUCLEAR TESTING IN THE PACIFIC

Claiming that nuclear testing was completely safe, the French government for decades conducted tests on the tiny Pacific atolls of **Mururoa** and **Fangataufa**, a comfortable 15,000km from Paris, but only 4000km northeast of New Zealand.

In 1966 France turned its back on the 1963 Partial Test Ban Treaty, which outlawed atmospheric testing, and relocated Pacific islanders away from their ancestral villages to make way for a barrage of tests over the next eight years. The French authorities claimed that "Not a single particle of radioactive fallout will ever reach an inhabited island" – and yet radiation was routinely detected as far away as Samoa, Fiji and even New Zealand. Increasingly antagonistic public opinion forced the French to conduct their tests underground in deep shafts, where another 200 detonations took place, threatening the stability of these fragile coral atolls.

In 1985, Greenpeace coordinated a New Zealand-based protest flotilla, headed by its flagship, the **Rainbow Warrior**, but before the fleet could set sail from Auckland, the French secret service sabotaged the *Rainbow Warrior*, detonating two bombs below the waterline. As rescuers recovered the body of Greenpeace photographer Fernando Pereira, two French secret service agents posing as tourists were arrested. Flatly denying all knowledge at first, the French government was finally forced to admit to what then Prime Minister David Lange described as "a sordid act of international state-backed terrorism". The two captured agents were sentenced to ten years in jail, but France used all its international muscle to have them serve their sentences on a French Pacific island; they both served less than two years before being honoured and returning to France.

In 1995, to worldwide opprobrium, France announced a further series of tests. Greenpeace duly dispatched *Rainbow Warrior II*, which was impounded by the French navy on the tenth anniversary of the sinking of the original *Rainbow Warrior*. In early 1996 the French finally agreed to stop nuclear testing in the Pacific.

volcanic rocks and follow the wave-cut platform around a series of bays for about 5km to the dunes – about an hour's walk – although most do it by quad bike or mountain bike.

ARRIVAL AND DEPARTURE
KAITAIA AND AROUND

By bus The daily InterCity/Northliner bus service pulls up behind the Te Ahu Centre on the corner of South Rd and Matthews Ave. The Far North link (ⓦ buslink.co.nz) operates a local service.

Destinations Ahipara (1–2 Mon–Fri; 30min); Kerikeri (1 daily; 1hr 40min); Mangonui (1–2 Mon–Fri; 1hr); Paihia (1 daily; 2hr 15min).

By plane Kaitaia's airport is 9km north of town, near Awanui, and is serviced by taxi shuttle (ⓣ 027 481 4962). Barrier Air (ⓣ 0800 900600, ⓦ barrierair.kiwi) operate scheduled services to Auckland and Great Barrier Island.

INFORMATION

Tourist information i-SITE visitor centres are at the corner of Matthews Ave and South Rd, in the Te Ahu Centre, Kaitaia (daily 8.30am–5pm; ⓣ 09 408 9450, ⓦ northlandnz.com). The office – one of three for the Far North region of Northland – stocks DOC leaflets such as *Kaitaia Area Walks* and *Cape Reinga and Te Paki Walks* and sells bus tickets. There's internet access at the library in the same centre (Mon–Fri 8.30am–5pm, Sat 8.30am–1pm).

ACCOMMODATION

Outside the post-Christmas peak, rooms are plentiful and prices are generally lower than at the coastal resorts to the east. Ahipara is a more appealing place to stay than Kaitaia, though there is little public transport (just a local bus to and from Kaitaia), and no supermarket or bank.

KAITAIA

★ **Beachcomber Lodge and Backpackers** 235 Commerce St ⓣ 09 408 1275, ⓦ beachcomberlodge. com. A welcoming, well-equipped and deceptively large hostel that's alive with folk headed for the Cape (tours pick up from the hostel). The doubles are spacious and there are a number of dorm rooms. You can also arrange seasonal work here. Dorms $30, doubles $70

Waters Edge 25b Kitchener St ⓣ 09 408 0870, ⓦ watersedgebandb.co.nz. An attractive B&B – owned by the last lighthouse keeper at Cape Reinga – in a modern suburban house with lush gardens, a pool and cosy rooms. Dinner can be provided here, too, but only by prior arrangement. **$120**

AHIPARA

Ahipara Bay Motel 22 Reef View Rd ☎09 408 2010, ⓦahiparabaymotel.co.nz. You'll have a choice of pleasant, older motel units, or six excellent luxury versions with tremendous sea and beach views. There's also a decent on-site restaurant – which is useful if you arrive late or on a Sunday. **$110**

★ **Ahipara Holiday Park** 164 Takahe St ☎09 409 4864, ⓦahiparaholidaypark.co.nz. The area's best camping option, just 300m from the sea, offering YHA discounts across the accommodation range, which includes good-value cabins, en-suite doubles as well as some well-equipped, self-contained cabins. Camping **$20**, cabins **$70**

Beach Abode 11 Korora St ☎09 409 4070, ⓦbeachabode.co.nz. The three well-appointed (and serviced) beachfront apartments here each come with free wi-fi, full kitchen, BBQ, deck, great sea views and a private path to the sand. Not recommended for children. Apartments **$160**

★ **Endless Summer Lodge** 245 Foreshore Rd ☎09 409 4181, ⓦendlesssummer.co.nz. Well-managed hostel in an atmospheric 1880 timber homestead with kauri floors, right across the road from the beach; choose from comfortable doubles, twins or two four-bed dorms. There's also a BBQ, free boogie boards, and surfboard rental; surfing instruction can be arranged. Dorms **$34**, doubles **$78**

EATING AND DRINKING

KAITAIA

★ **Beachcomber** 222 Commerce St ☎09 408 2010, ⓦbeachcomber.net.nz. Probably Kaitaia's best restaurant, serving a fairly standard range of meat and fish dishes (lunches $18–32; dinner mains from $30), which all come with a visit to the salad bar. Try the prawn, chilli and lemon pasta or the lamb rump with roasted garlic and herbs. Mon–Fri from 11am–2.30pm & 5–9pm, Sat 5–9pm.

Birdie's 14 Commerce St ☎09 408 4935. Great old-school café with inventive touches, which is open for breakfast until 3.30pm and serves huge portions of Kiwi food at modest prices (mains $15–25), including some rib-sticking chilli beef nachos and decent eggs Benedict. Daily 8am–3.30pm.

AHIPARA

Bayview Restaurant and Bar Ahipara Bay Motel, 22 Reef View Rd ☎09 408 2010, ⓦahiparabaymotel. co.nz. Decent (for these parts) licensed restaurant that benefits from sea views and serves traditional dishes, including seafood chowder ($12.50), lamb rump with mint sauce ($28.50) and fish of the day ($26). Daily 11.30am–11pm.

North Drift Café Takahe Rd ☎09 409 4093. Local café serving good coffee, cakes and snacks, as well as tasty all-day breakfasts (all under $20) and lunch options including Cajun chicken tacos ($16.50) and "nourish bowls" with smoked salmon or bacon ($22). Mon & Tues 8am–2.30pm, Wed–Sun 8am–late.

Ninety Mile Beach and Cape Reinga

Northland's exclamation mark is the **Aupori Peninsula**, a narrow, 100km-long finger of consolidated and grassed-over dunes ending in a lumpy knot of 60-million-year-old marine volcanoes. To Māori it's known as Te Hika o te Ika ("The tail of the fish"), recalling the legend of Maui hauling up the North Island ("the fish") from the sea while in his canoe (the South Island).

The most northerly accessible point is **Cape Reinga**, where the spirits of Māori dead depart this world. Beginning their journey by sliding down the roots of an 800-year-old pohutukawa into the ocean, they climb out again on Ohaua, the highest of the Three Kings Islands, to bid a final farewell before returning to their ancestors in Hawaiiki. The spirits reach Cape Reinga along **Ninety Mile Beach** (actually 64 miles long), which runs straight along the western side of the peninsula. Most visitors follow the spirits, though they do so in modern buses specifically designed for belting along the hard-packed sand at the edge of the surf – officially part of the state highway system – then negotiating the quicksands of Te Paki Stream to return to the road; for many, the highlight is **sandboarding** on a boogie board (or in a safer but less speedy toboggan) down the huge dunes that flank the stream. The main road runs more or less down the centre of the peninsula, while the western ocean is kept tantalizingly out of sight by the thin

GOING IT ALONE ON NINETY MILE BEACH

Rental cars and private vehicles are not insured to drive on Ninety Mile Beach and for good reason. Vehicles frequently get bogged in the sand and abandoned by their occupants. As there are no rescue facilities near enough to get you out before the tide comes in, and mobile phone coverage is almost nil, you could end up with a long walk. Even in your own vehicle, **two-wheel-drives** aren't recommended, regardless of weather conditions, which can change rapidly.

If you are determined to take your own vehicle for the 70km spin along the beach, seek local advice and prepare your car by spraying some form of water repellent on the ignition system – CRC is a common brand. Schedule your trip to coincide with a receding tide, starting two hours after high water and preferably going in the same direction as the bus traffic that day; drive on dry but firm sand, avoiding any soft patches, and keep your speed down. The main reason for this is the gutters and streamlets running over the beach, which pop up out of nowhere; they might look fairly insignificant but their banks can be surprisingly steep – you definitely don't want to negotiate one at high speed. **Slow down** too when turning on sand, otherwise your front wheels can dig in to any unexpectedly soft patches, flipping the vehicle over. Another hazard is pedestrians, should you encounter any, who won't be able to hear you coming from behind against the noise of the surf (even if it's far away); give them a wide berth. If you get stuck in a soft drift at any stage, don't sit there revving the engine – all that will happen is your rapidly spinning wheels will dig the car down into the sand. The first thing to do is to stop, then attempt to reverse out slowly in low range; if this doesn't work you need to dig out behind each wheel to make a ramp and try again. If you still have no luck, then deflate tyres to about 10psi, which will give the vehicle far more traction, and try once more.

There are several access points along the beach, but the only ones realistically available to ordinary vehicles are the two used by the tour buses: the southern access point at **Waipapakauri Ramp**, 6km north of Awanui, and the more dangerous northern one along **Te Paki Stream**, which involves negotiating the quicksands of a river – start in low gear and don't stop, no matter how tempting it might be to ponder the dunes.

pine ribbon of the **Aupori Forest**. The forests, and the **cattle farms** that cover most of the rest of the peninsula, were once the preserve of gum diggers, who worked the area intensively early last century.

Awanui

The eastern and western roads around Northland meet at **AWANUI**, 8km north of Kaitaia, Māori for "Big River" – though all you'll find is a bend in a narrow tidal creek that makes a relaxing setting for the daytime *Big River Café*.

Kauri Unearthed

229 SH 1F, 1km north of Awanui • Daily 8.30am–5.30pm; later in summer • Free • ☎ 09 406 7172, ⑩ ancientkauri.co.nz

Almost all buses to Cape Reinga stop at the **Kauri Unearthed**, a defunct dairy factory now operating as a sawmill, cutting and shaping huge peat-preserved kauri logs hauled out of swamps where they have lain for around 45,000 years. Unfortunately the workshop is closed to the public (the new owners hope to add viewing windows) and the emphasis is on the shop. Be sure to climb up to the mezzanine on the spiral staircase hewn out of the centre of the largest piece of swamp kauri trunk ever unearthed, a monster 3.5m in diameter.

Gumdiggers Park Ancient Buried Kauri Forest

171 Heath Rd, 3km off SH1 • Daily 9am–5pm (4pm in winter) • $12.50 • ☎ 09 406 7166, ⑩ gumdiggerspark.co.nz

The delightfully low-key **Gumdiggers Park Ancient Buried Kauri Forest** is the pick of the local attractions. It features an easy thirty-minute nature trail through shady

TE PAKI COASTAL TRACK

The **Te Paki Coastal Track** (48km one way; 3–4 days; constantly undulating) is spectacular and increasingly popular coastal hike starts at Kapowairua (Spirits Bay), heads west to Cape Reinga, continues to Cape Maria van Diemen, swings southeast to the northernmost stretch of Ninety Mile Beach, and then finally past the impressive dunes of Te Paki Stream. You need to be fit and self-sufficient: the only facilities are a couple of DOC campsites, and some ad hoc camping spots with no guaranteed water. Fresh water from streams is limited and you'll need mosquito repellent. Beware of **rip tides** on all the beaches hereabouts and bear in mind the wild and unpredictable nature of the region's weather. Arrange with one of the more local bus tours for pick-up.

manuka forest and includes a gum diggers' camp, holes that have been excavated to show the methods used for gum digging, huts illustrating the living conditions and a small kauri gum collection. There's a longer trail through the bush with information boards speculating on what knocked over the two giant kauri forests thousands of years ago: tidal wave, meteor or earthquake. Be sure to check out the monstrous section of a kauri dating back 100,000 years. The main southern entrance to Ninety Mile Beach, the **Waipapakauri Ramp**, is just south of the park's turn-off.

Houhora and Pukenui

The Aupori Peninsula's two largest settlements, 30km north of Awanui, are scattered **HOUHORA** and the working fishing village of **PUKENUI**, 2km to the south, where good catches are to be had off the wharf. At Houhora, a 3km side road turns east to **Houhora Heads**. A further 10km north is the turn-off for white sand **Rarawa Beach**, home to a great DOC campsite (see page 178).

Te Kao

The Māori Ngati Kuri people own much of the land and comprise the bulk of the population in these parts, particularly around **TE KAO**, 20km north of Houhora. Beside SH1, you'll spot the twin-towered Ratana Temple – one of the few remaining houses of the Ratana religion, which combines Christian teachings with elements of Māori culture and spiritual belief.

Parengarenga Harbour

12km north of Te Kao on SH1, then follow the Paua Rd

Straggling **Parengarenga Harbour** was the drop-off point for the limpet mines (delivered by yacht from New Caledonia) that were used in the 1985 sabotage of the *Rainbow Warrior*. Bends in the road occasionally reveal glimpses of the harbour's southern headland. In late February and early March, hundreds of thousands of bar-tailed godwits turn the silica sands black as they gather for their 12,000km journey to Siberia. Insect repellent is a must here.

Landing to Spirits Bay

The last place of any consequence before the land sinks into the ocean is **WAITIKI LANDING**, 21km from Cape Reinga. If you are heading to Spirits Bay this is your last chance to buy petrol and milk. From Waitiki Landing a dirt road twists 15km to the gorgeous and usually deserted 7km sweep of **Spirits Bay** (Kapowairua), where you'll find a DOC campsite (see page 178).

Te Paki

The main road (SH1) continues towards Cape Reinga. After 4km you pass a turn-off to the **Te Paki Stream entrance** to Ninety Mile Beach, where there's a small picnic area and parking, plus a twenty-minute **hike** to huge sand dunes ideal for **sandboarding** or **tobogganing**. Equipment can be rented at several places from Kaitaia northwards; and also by calling ahead to Ahikaa Adventures (☎09 409 8228, ⊚ahikaa-adventures. co.nz), who often rent boards ($15/hr; passport or driving licence required for deposit) from the Te Paki road end, right by the dunes.

2

Cape Reinga

The last leg to **Cape Reinga** (Te Rerenga Wairua: the "leaping place of the spirits") runs high through the hills before revealing magnificent views of the Tasman Sea and the huge dunes that foreshadow it. At road-end there's just a car park with toilets and an 800m-long interpretive trail to the Cape Reinga **lighthouse**, dramatically perched on a headland 165m above Colombia Bank, where the waves of the Tasman Sea meet the swirling currents of the Pacific Ocean in a boiling cauldron of surf. On clear days the **view** from here is stunning: east to the Surville Cliffs of North Cape, west to Cape Maria van Diemen, and north to the rocky **Three Kings Islands**, 57km offshore, which were named by Abel Tasman, who first came upon them on the eve of Epiphany 1643.

GETTING AROUND NINETY MILE BEACH AND CAPE REINGA

By car You can drive yourself along Ninety Mile Beach, although doing so is fraught with potential difficulties (see page 175).

By bus The Far North Link operates between Kaitaia and Pukenui on Thursdays only (⊚buslink.co.nz). There is no other public transport.

INFORMATION

Tourist information The nearest i-SITE offices are in Paihia (see page 156), Kaitaia (see page 173) and, if you're coming via Hokianga, in Opononi (see page 180). They should be able to answer all your questions, including those pertaining to Ninety Mile Beach and Cape Reinga.

Services As with the rest of rural Northland, there is a paucity of facilities here. You can refuel at Houhora; petrol isn't always available in Waitiki.

TOURS

Tours by bus loop up the Aupori Peninsula, travelling SH1 in one direction and Ninety Mile Beach in the other, the order being dictated by the tide. Trips start from Kaitaia, Mangonui and Paihia in the Bay of Islands. Those from Paihia are the most numerous but too long (11hr), most leaving daily at around 7.30am. They go via Kerikeri, Mangonui and Awanui in one direction and pass Kaitaia and the Puketi Forest in the other, with pick-ups along the way, but there is little time for sightseeing. A few operators offer a somewhat more personalized experience via tours in 4WD vehicles, usually for anywhere from two to six people.

Far North Outback Adventures Kaitaia ☎09 408 0927, ⊚farnorthtours.co.nz. Exclusive 4WD custom tours (8hr; $650 for up to two passengers; $700 for three to six passengers) that include morning tea and lunch. They go off the beaten track, taking in the white sands of Great Exhibition Bay to explore flora, fauna and archeological sites.

Harrisons Cape Runner Kaitaia ☎09 408 1033, ⊚ahipara.co.nz/caperunner. Bargain, basic coach tour (8hr; $50) including the Cape, beach, Kaitaia pick-up and a light lunch.

Sand Safaris Kaitaia ☎0800 869 090, ⊚sandsafaris. co.nz. Good-value tour (8hr; $55) that's similar to Harrisons but with Ahipara pick-ups (extra $5) and a Māori welcome. A light lunch is included.

Awesome NZ ☎0800 653 339, ⊚awesomenz.com. Cape bus trip ($130) from Paihia aimed at those with an adventurous spirit, with maximum sandboarding time and a walk in Puketi Kauri Forest. The cost of a dinner stop at Mangonui for fish and chips comes out of your own pocket.

Dune Rider ☎09 402 8681, ⊚explorenz.co.nz. Upscale Cape and beach trips ($150) from Russell, Paihia or Kerikeri, in a comfortable high-clearance bus with just 36 reclining seats.

Salt Air ☎0800 475 582, ⊚saltair.co.nz. Fly to the Cape, landing at Waitiki, then cover the last section to Cape Reinga by 4WD ($425). Includes refreshments at Tapotupotu Bay and sandboarding, as well as a 45min flight across the Bay of Islands.

ACCOMMODATION

There's sporadic accommodation along the Aupori Peninsula, ranging from some beautifully sited DOC campsites to motels, lodges and hostels. Most are reasonably priced, reflecting the fact that many visitors pass through without stopping; however, all are very busy immediately after Christmas.

PUKENUI

Rarawa Beach Campsite 10km north of Pukenui, 4km along a signposted gravel road ⓦdoc.govt.nz. The pure white silica sand at this shady, streamside DOC campsite is beautiful, and a great place for birdwatching and swimming in the lagoon – although abundant mosquitoes temper its paradisiacal appeal. Amenities include running water, toilets and cold showers. No bookings: first come, first served. $8

★ **Wagener Holiday Park** 3km south of Pukenui, off SH1 ⓣ09 409 8511, ⓦwagenerholidaypark.co.nz. A beautifully located, traditional, council-run campsite

with great-value accommodation under canvas or in cabins, all nestled among tall trees with great views of the sea and just 500m from the Houhora Wharf. Camping $34, cabin $65

SPIRITS BAY

Kapowairua (Spirits Bay) campsite Spirits Bay Rd, 16km on a gravel road from Waitiki Landing ⓦdoc.govt. nz. A simple DOC site with pitches in manuka woods, and campervan access. It has cold showers, running water and toilets, and is also ideal for fishing, swimming and walking. $8

CAPE REINGA

Tapotupotu Bay campsite Tapotupotu Rd, 3km south of Cape Reinga ⓦdoc.govt.nz. A serene DOC site with toilets, cold showers, running water and lots of mosquitoes in the summer. It's beautifully sited where the beach meets the estuary and is a popular lunchtime picnic stop for tour buses. $8

EATING

Houhora Tavern Saleyard Ave, just off SH1, Pukenui ⓣ09 409 8805, ⓦhouhoratavern.co.nz. New Zealand's northernmost pub, dating from the 1800s, with lawns beside the harbour and great views, although check ahead as it was up for sale at the time of writing. Basic meals that come with chips for the most part, as well as home-made pies and sausage rolls and decent coffee, all

for under $25. Daily 9am–11pm, meals 9am–4pm & 5–8pm.

★ **Pukenui Pacific Bar and Café** 816 Far North Rd (SH1), Pukenui ⓣ09 409 8816. Diners are often defeated by the huge burger known as PukuNui (Māori for "big stomach") at this good-value café/bar, the only takeaway north of Kaitaia (mains $10–25). Daily 7am–9pm.

Hokianga Harbour

South of Kaitaia, the narrow, mangrove-flanked fissures of the **Hokianga Harbour** snake deep inland past tiny and almost moribund communities. For a few days' relaxation, the tranquillity and easy pace of this rural backwater are hard to beat. From the southern shores, the harbour's incredible, deep-blue waters beautifully set off the mountainous **sand dunes** of North Head. The dunes are best seen from the rocky promontory of South Head, high above the treacherous Hokianga Bar, or can be reached by boat for sandboarding or the fantastic Sandtrails Hokianga tours. The high forest ranges immediately to the south make excellent hiking territory, and the giant kauri of the Waipoua Forest are within easy striking distance.

Note that there are **no banks** between Kaitaia and Dargaville, which is around 170km away to the south. The ATMs in Rawene and Omapere accept a limited range of cards so bring cash.

Brief history

According to legend, it was from here that the great Polynesian explorer **Kupe** left Aotearoa to go back to his homeland in Hawaiiki during the tenth century, and the harbour thus became known as Hokianganui-a-Kupe, "the place of Kupe's great return". Cook saw the Hokianga Heads from the *Endeavour* in 1770 but didn't realize what lay beyond, and it wasn't until a missionary crossed the hill from the Bay of Islands in 1819 that Europeans became aware of the harbour's existence. Catholics, Anglicans and Wesleyans soon followed, converting the local Ngapuhi, gaining their trust, intermarrying with them and establishing the well-integrated Māori and European communities that exist today. The Hokianga area soon rivalled the Bay of Islands in importance and notched up several firsts: European boat building began here in 1826; the first signal station opened two years later; and the first Catholic Mass was celebrated in the same year.

With the demise of **kauri felling** and **milling** (see page 182), Hokianga became an economic backwater, but over the last couple of decades, city dwellers, artists and craftspeople have started creeping in, settling in **Kohukohu** on the north shore, **Rawene**, a short ferry ride away to the south, and the two larger but still small-time settlements of **Opononi** and **Omapere**, opposite the dunes near the harbour entrance. Note though, that this is still the sort of place where businesses close at 7pm, taking your chance of a cooked meal with them.

Kohukohu

Heading south from Kaitaia, the hilly SH1 twists its way through the forested Mangamuka Ranges for 40km to reach **Mangamuka Bridge** from where an equally tortuous road heads to **KOHUKOHU**, a waterside cluster of century-old wooden houses. Four kilometres further east is Narrows Landing and the northern terminus of the **Hokianga Vehicle Ferry** (see page 180).

Village Arts Gallery
1376 Kohukohu Rd · Daily 10am–4pm · Free · ☎ 09 405 5827, ⓦ villagearts.co.nz

Check out the community-run **Village Arts Gallery**, which promotes Hokianga's artistic community, with exhibitions of sculpture, painting, photography, steampunk models and textiles at a much higher standard than you might expect for such a backwater.

Rawene

Delightfully situated **RAWENE** occupies the tip of Herd's Point, a peninsula roughly halfway up the harbour. Though almost isolated by the mudflats at low tide, Rawene's strategic position made it an obvious choice for the location of a timber mill, which contributed material for the town's attractive wooden buildings, some perched on stilts out over the water. Clendon Esplanade leads to the **Mangrove Walkway**, an ageing fifteen-minute return boardwalk through the coastal shallows with boards telling of intertidal life and the sawmill, which once operated here.

Clendon House
Clendon Esplanade · Nov–April Sat & Sun 10am–4pm; more extensive hours during school holidays · $10

Clendon House is Rawene's only significant distraction, and was the last residence of British-born US Consul James Clendon, a pivotal figure in the early life of the colony. Starting life as a ship-owner transporting convicts to Australia, Clendon settled in New Zealand, befriended local Māori and was instrumental in the negotiations which culminated in the Treaty of Waitangi. The house itself is mostly pit-sawn kauri construction. Downstairs, one room beside the veranda has been retained as the post office it once was.

Opononi and Omapere

The two small villages of **OPONONI** and **OMAPERE**, 20km west of Rawene, comprise little more than a roadside string of houses running seamlessly for 4km along the southern shore of the Hokianga Harbour, with great views across to the massive sand dunes on the north side. If you decide to break your journey in this area it will be because you want to explore the dunes, either on foot or by beach buggy (see page 180), or by viewing them from far away; the Arai te Uru Reserve is a wonderful viewpoint reached along Signal Station Road, 1km south of Omapere. It's also a great base to hook up with a guided tour of the Kauri forests to the south (see page 181) and you can learn about Hokianga's heritage at the small **museum** (Mon–Sat 10am–2pm; $2) in Omapere.

Waiotemarama Bush Walk

647 Waiotemarama Gorge Rd, 8km southeast of Opononi • 2.5km loop

Labyrinth Woodworks (see page 181) marks the start of the **Waiotemarama Bush Walk**, the best and most popular of the short walks in the district, running through a lovely fern-, palm- and kauri-filled valley. A ten-minute walk leads you to a waterfall with a small swimming hole, and after a further ten minutes you reach the first kauri.

ARRIVAL AND DEPARTURE   HOKIANGA HARBOUR

By bus To properly explore the Hokianga and Waipoua region you will need your own vehicle, though Intercity/Northliner do run some services through here. There's a link bus running between Omapere and Kerikeri, via Kaikohe and Rawene (Rawene by advance request only; Tues & Thurs Dec–March, rest of the year Thurs only; ⓦ nrc.govt.nz/hokianga).

By ferry Apart from a lengthy drive around the head of the harbour, the only way around the Hokianga is on the Hokianga Vehicle Ferry (car and driver $20 one way; campervan and driver $40; car passengers and pedestrians $2 each way), which shuttles from Narrows Landing, 4km east of Kohukohu on the northern shores, to Rawene in the south, a journey of 15min. Departures (around 7am–8pm) are on the hour southbound and on the half-hour northbound.

By bike Hokianga Harbour is the west coast destination of the Twin Coast Cycle Trail (2 days; ⓦ twincoastcycletrail. kiwi.nz) that starts out from Paihia in the Bay of Islands.

INFORMATION

Tourist information i-SITE visitor centre is at 29 SH12, just outside Opononi (daily: Nov–April 8.30am–5pm; May–Oct 9am–5pm; ☏ 09 405 8869, ⓦ hokianga.co.nz). The office has information for the Hokianga area and Waipoua Forest (see page 182), can book accommodation, and has internet access.

TOURS AND ACTIVITIES

Footprints Waipoua 334 SH12 ☏ 09 405 8207, ⓦ footprintswaipoua.co.nz. Runs excellent guided walks to the kauri trees in Waipoua Forest with a strong Māori spiritual component. The Twilight Encounter (4hr; $95) is the pick of the tours.

Hokianga Express ☏ 09 405 8872. Leaving from Opononi wharf from 10am daily, this boat service ($27) will drop you off at the dunes with sandboards (after a modicum of instruction) and pick you up a couple of hours later.

ACCOMMODATION

KOHUKOHU

★ **The Tree House** 168 West Coast Rd, 2km west of the car ferry terminus ☏ 09 405 5855, ⓦ treehouse. co.nz. Accommodation is scattered among the trees in two spacious dorms, double and twin cabins with sundecks and a well-equipped house bus in a macadamia orchard. Bedding is provided, towels are $3 to hire. Camping $20, dorms $32, cabins $88

RAWENE

Rawene Holiday Park 1 Marmon St, 1.5km from the ferry landing ☏ 09 405 7720, ⓦ raweneholidaypark. co.nz. A low-key site with hilltop harbour views, sheltered areas for tents and good-value, spacious, well-kept cabins in bush enclaves. The views from the swimming pool and shared kitchen are fabulous, especially at sunset. Camping $36, cabins $75

OPONONI AND OMAPERE

Copthorne Hotel & Resort SH12, Omapere ☏ 09 405 8737, ⓦ milleniumhotels.com. The best of the hotels in town, set opposite the dunes, with a solar-heated pool, nice bar and licensed restaurant and a range of accommodation including some beautifully appointed waterside rooms with all the usual big hotel touches. $240

★ **Globetrekkers Lodge** SH12, Omapere ☏ 09 405 8183, ⓦ globetrekkerslodge.com. Relaxing and very well-kept hostel with some harbour views. The five- and six-bed dorms and doubles are all spacious and airy. TV is intentionally absent and the evening BBQ usually brings everyone together. Dorms $29, doubles $75

★ **Hokianga Haven** 226 SH12, Omapere ☏ 09 405 8285, ⓦ hokiangahaven.co.nz. The owner only takes single-party bookings for her two attractively furnished beachside rooms with private bathrooms, opposite the harbour entrance with fabulous views of the dunes and the sea. Two-night minimum. $180

EATING AND DRINKING

KOHUKOHU

The Koke Cafe Kohukohu Rd ☎ 09 405 5808. This cute alfresco cafe serves up a friendly welcome, not to mention tasty breakfasts (try the toasted bagel with cream cheese, avocado and tomato; $12) and lunch and dinner (mussels served with fries or a warm roast pork sandwich with apple sauce are both under $12). It also has great coffee, cakes and cookies. Wed–Sun 8am–4pm, extended in summer.

RAWENE

★ **Boatshed Café** 8 Clendon Esplanade ☎ 09 405 7728, ⓦ facebook.com/boatshedcaferawene. A daytime, licensed establishment built out over the water, offering magazines to read on the sunny deck as you tuck into gourmet pizza slices or home-made muffins and soups, and espresso from just $5. Daily 8.30am–3.30pm.

OPONONI AND OMAPERE

Copthorne Hotel & Resort SH12, Omapere ☎ 09 405 8737, ⓦ milleniumhotels.com. The best dining hereabouts, in both the elegant *Bryers Room* restaurant (mains around $40) and the *Sands Bar* (mains around $30). Both have great views over the lawns and harbour to the sand dunes. Look out for dishes with a Māori influence, such as local seafood or *rawena* bread and butter pudding with *titoki* liqueur. Bryers Room 7.30am–late; Sands Bar 9am–late.

Opononi Hotel SH12, Opononi ☎ 09 405 8858, ⓦ opononihotel.com. Lively pub offering good-value eating, both bar food and à la carte. Try the surf and turf ($36). Regular Kiwi touring bands stop by in summer when 1200-odd people can crowd in. Daily 11am–11pm.

Opo Takeaways SH12, Opononi. Known locally as the best fish and chip takeaway, it also serves generous, well-stuffed burgers, mussel and paua fritters, battered sausages and other deep-fried delights. Fish is usually $4–6 a piece, depending on type. Daily 10am–7pm, until 9pm in summer.

SHOPPING

Hoki Smoki Signposted on SH12 1km south of Omapere. An excellent fish and seafood smokery – drop in and buy some to take on the road with you or for a picnic. It's only open for business if the sign is out.

Labyrinth Woodworks 647 Waiotemarama Gorge Rd, 8km southeast of Opononi ☎ 09 405 4581, ⓦ nzanity. co.nz. One of the region's better craft shops, with wares including carved kauri pieces and excellent woodblock prints. Pride of place, however, goes to the mind-bending puzzles in the puzzle museum, which include the smallest puzzles in the world, and a maturing hedge maze with an anagram problem that stumps many a visitor – it's great fun. Owner Louis has opened another outlet on Clendon Esplanade in Rawene. Daily 9am–5pm.

The kauri forests and around

Northland, Auckland and the Coromandel Peninsula were once covered in mixed forest dominated by the **mighty kauri** (see page 182), the world's second-largest tree. By the early twentieth century, rapacious Europeans had nearly felled the lot, the only extensive pockets remaining in the **Waipoua and Trounson kauri forests** south of the Hokianga Harbour. Though small stands of kauri can be found all over Northland, three-quarters of all the surviving mature trees grow in these two small forests, which between them cover barely a hundred square kilometres. Trails provide access to the more celebrated examples, which dwarf the surrounding tataire, kohekohe and towai trees.

Just south of the Trounson forest are the **Kai Iwi Lakes**, a trio of popular dune lakes that get busy in the summer season.

Brief history

This area is home to the **Te Roroa people** who traditionally used the kauri sparingly. Simple tools made felling and working these huge trees a difficult task, and one reserved for major projects such as large war canoes. Once the Europeans arrived with metal tools, bullock trains, wheels and winches, clear felling became easier, and most of the trees had gone by the end of the nineteenth century. The efforts of several campaigning organizations eventually bore fruit in 1952, when much of the remaining forest was designated the Waipoua Sanctuary. It's now illegal to fell a kauri

THE KAURI AND ITS USES

The **kauri** (*agathis australis*) ranks alongside the sequoias of California as one of the largest trees in existence. Unlike the sequoias, which are useless as furniture timber, kauri produce beautiful wood, a fact that hastened its demise and spawned the industries that dominated New Zealand's economy in the latter half of the nineteenth century.

The kauri is a type of pine that now grows only in New Zealand, though it once also grew in Australia and Southeast Asia, where it still has close relations. Identifiable remains of kauri forests are found all over New Zealand, but by the time humans arrived on the scene its range had contracted to Northland, Auckland, the Coromandel Peninsula and northern Waikato. Individual trees can live over two thousand years, reaching 50m in height and 20m in girth, finally toppling over as the rotting core becomes too weak to support its immense weight.

KAURI LOGGERS

Māori have long used mature kauri for dugout canoes, but it was the "rickers" (young trees) that first drew the attention of **European loggers** since they formed perfect spars for sailing ships. The bigger trees soon earned an unmatched reputation for their durable, easy-to-work and blemish-free wood, with its straight, fine grain. Loggers' ingenuity was taxed to the limit by the difficulty of getting such huge logs out of the bush. On easier terrain, bullock wagons with up to twelve teams were lashed together to haul the logs onto primitive roads or tramways. Horse-turned winches were used on steeper ground and, where water could be deployed to transport the timber, dams were constructed from hewn logs. In narrow valleys and gullies all over Northland and the Coromandel, loggers constructed kauri dams up to 20m high and 60m across, with trapdoors at the base. Trees along the sides of the valley were felled while the dam was filling, then the dam was opened to flush the floating trunks down the valley to inlets where the logs were rafted up and towed to the mills.

GUM DIGGERS

Once an area had been logged, the **gum diggers** typically moved in. Like most pines, kauri exudes a thick resin to cover any scars inflicted on it, and huge accretions form on the sides of trunks and in globules around the base. Māori chewed the gum, made torches from it to attract fish at night and burned the powdered resin to form a pigment used for *moko* (traditional tattoos). Once Pakeha got in on the act, it was exported as a raw material for furniture varnishes, linoleum, denture moulds and the "gilt" edging on books. When it could no longer be found on the ground, diggers – mostly Dalmatian, but also Māori, Chinese and Malaysian – thrust long poles into the earth and hooked out pieces with bent rods; elsewhere, the ground was dug up and sluiced to recover the gum. Almost all New Zealand gum was exported, but by the early twentieth century synthetic resins had captured the gum market. Kauri gum is still considered one of the finest varnishes for musical instruments, and occasional accidental finds supply such specialist needs.

THE FUTURE

In recent years the kauri have been further threatened by a new disease known as PTA or **kauri dieback** (🌐 kauridieback.co.nz) with symptoms including yellowed leaves, dead branches and resinous lesions close to the ground, eventually leading to the tree's death. The disease is transmitted through soil and water, so always keep to the tracks and boardwalks and clean your footwear after visiting a kauri forest.

except in specified circumstances, such as culling a diseased or dying tree, or when constructing a new ceremonial canoe.

Waipoua Kauri Forest

SH12, 15km south of Omapere

Heading south from the Hokianga Harbour area, you pass through farmland and arrive at Waimamaku. The highway then twists and turns through nearly 20km of mature kauri in the **Waipoua Kauri Forest**. Eight kilometres south of Waimamaku you reach a small car park, from where it's a three-minute walk to New Zealand's mightiest tree, the (estimated)

2500-year-old **Tane Mahuta**, "God of the Forest". A vast wall of bark 6m wide rises nearly 18m to the lowest branches, covered in epiphytes. A kilometre or so further south on SH12, a ten-minute track leads to a clearing where three paths split off to notable trees: the shortest (5min return) runs to the **Four Sisters**, relatively slender kauri all growing close together; a second path (30min return) winds among numerous big trees to **Te Matua Ngahere**, the "Father of the Forest", the second-largest tree in New Zealand – shorter than Tane Mahuta but fatter and in some ways more impressive. The third path, the **Yakas Track** (3km return; 1hr), leads to Cathedral Grove, a dense conglomeration of trees, the largest being the **Yakas Kauri**, named after veteran bushman Nicholas Yakas.

Trounson Kauri Park

Signposted off SH12, 7km down an unsealed side road

Trounson Kauri Park is a small but superb stand of kauri where the **Trounson Kauri Walk** (40min loop) weaves though lovely rainforest. In 1997, Trounson was turned into a "mainland island" in order to foster North Island brown kiwi survival. Numbers are up significantly, and you've a good chance of seeing them – along with weta and glowworms – if you stay over. A **tour** of the kauri stands is easy enough to do on your own, but *Kauri Coast Top 10 Holiday Park* offers a guided night walk (see below).

Kai Iwi Lakes

11km west off SH12, 20km south of Trounson

The **Kai Iwi Lakes** are a real change, with pine woods running down to fresh, crystal-blue waters fringed by silica-white sand. All three are dune lakes fed by rainwater and with no visible outlet. Though the largest, **Taharoa**, is less than 1km across, and **Waikere** and **Kai Iwi** are barely 100m long, they constitute the deepest and some of the largest dune lakes in the country. People flock here in the summer to swim, fish and waterski, but outside the first weeks in January you can usually find a quiet spot. Shallow and consequently warmer than the sea, they're good for an early-season dip.

ACCOMMODATION AND EATING   THE KAURI FORESTS AND AROUND

WAIPOUA KAURI FOREST

Morrell's Café 7235 SH12, Waimamaku ☎ 09 405 4545. The best café in the area cooks up all-day breakfasts (under $25), light meals such as gourmet burgers, wraps and salads (all under $12), mussel chowder ($10) and excellent coffee. Daily 9am–4pm.

TROUNSON KAURI PARK

★ **Kauri Coast Top 10 Holiday Park** Trounson Park Rd, off SH12 ☎ 09 439 0621, ⊚ kauricoasttop10.co.nz. A traditional Kiwi campsite with tidy communal areas, clean toilets and showers and well-tended campsites. There are also small but adequate basic cabins (add $10 for a kitchen) and roomy motel units. You can join the site's two-hour guided night walk ($30, non-guests $35) which explores

the kauri forest. Camping $44, cabins $90

Trounson Kauri Park Campground Signposted off SH12, 17km south of Waipoua Forest. A simple but popular DOC campsite with sites by a small stand of kauri, and equipped with kitchen, toilets, tap water and hot showers. No bookings: first come, first served. $15

KAI IWI LAKES

Kai Iwi Lakes ☎ 09 439 4757. Comprised of two locally run sites: the *Pine Beach* site on the gently shelving shores of Taharoa Lake, with running water, toilets and coin-operated showers; and the intimate but primitive *Promenade Point* site, with just long-drop toilets. *Pine Beach* has a shop selling the basics (summer only) and you can pay an extra $10 for a powered site. Camping $15

The northern Kaipara Harbour

South of the kauri forests are the muddy, mangrove-choked shores of the **Kaipara Harbour**, New Zealand's largest. The harbour once unified this quarter of Northland, with sailboats plying its waters and linking the dairy farming and logging towns on its shores. Kauri was shipped out from the largest northern town, **Dargaville**, though the fragile boats all too often foundered on the unpredictable Kaipara Bar. Many eventually washed up on **Ripiro Beach**, which just pips Ninety Mile Beach to the title of New Zealand's longest, running for 108km.

Dargaville and around

The unexciting dairying and *kumara*-growing town of **DARGAVILLE**, 30km south of Kai Iwi Lakes, was founded as a port in 1872, on the strongly tidal but navigable Northern Wairoa River, by Australian Joseph McMullen Dargaville. Ships came to load kauri logs and transport gum (see page 182) extracted by Dalmatian settlers who, by the early part of the twentieth century, formed a sizeable portion of the community.

Dargaville Museum

Harding Park, 2km west of town • Daily: April–Sept 9am–4pm; Oct–March 9am–5pm • $15 • ☎ 09 439 7555, ⓦ dargavillemuseum.co.nz

Two masts rescued from the *Rainbow Warrior* (see page 173) mark the surprisingly good **Dargaville Museum**. It contains extensive displays of artefacts recovered from the shifting dunes, which occasionally reveal old shipwrecks. The only pre-European artefact is the Ngati Whatua *waka*, which lay buried under the sands of the North Head of the Kaipara Harbour from 1809 until 1972, and is a rare example of a canoe hewn entirely with stone tools. A fine collection of kauri gum gives pride of place to an 84kg piece – reputedly the largest ever found – and there is an ancient heated oil Blackstone engine-powered gum washer that they occasionally run to the delight of visitors.

Woodturners Kauri Gallery & Working Studio

4 Murdoch St (SH12) • Daily 9am–dark • ☎ 09 439 4975, ⓦ thewoodturnersstudio.co.nz

At the western end of town, at the **Woodturners Kauri Gallery & Working Studio**, leading woodturner Rick Taylor demonstrates what can be done with the extraordinarily varied grains and colours of kauri, sells all manner of kauri products, and runs courses for those prepared to dedicate a day or more.

Baylys Beach and Ripiro Beach

14km west of Dargaville, along a minor road

BAYLYS BEACH is a conglomeration of mostly holiday homes on a central section of 100km-long **Ripiro Beach**, a strand renowned for its mobility, with several metres of beach often being shifted by a single tide, and huge areas being reclaimed over the centuries; the anchors or prows of long-lost wrecks periodically reappear through the sand. As elsewhere on the West Coast, tidal rips and holes make swimming dangerous and there are no beach patrols. Beach driving is no less fraught with danger and shouldn't be undertaken without prior local consultation; vehicles frequently get stranded. Nevertheless, it's a fine place for long walks, and spotting **seals** and **penguins** in winter.

ARRIVAL AND DEPARTURE   DARGAVILLE AND AROUND

There is no longer a bus service to Dargaville so you will need your own transport.

INFORMATION AND TOURS

Tourist information The tourist office (4 Murdoch St; ☎ 09 439 4975; daily 9am–6pm) can book accommodation and give advice.

The Kumara Box 503 Pouto Rd, just south of Dargaville ☎ 09 439 7018, ⓦ kumarabox.co.nz. Low-key introduction to and tour of a *kumara* farm, in the heart of *kumara*-growing country, full of charm, enthusiasm and ingenuity. After Ernie's 1hr show-and-tell ($20), a *kumara* train ($20) takes you around the grounds and past the smallest church in Northland. You can also arrange morning/afternoon tea or lunch which might include home-made *kumara* soup or a *kumara* muffin. Phone ahead.

ACCOMMODATION

★**Baylys Beach Holiday Park** 22 Seaview Rd, Baylys Beach ☎09 439 6349, ⓦbaylysbeach.co.nz. A well-run and tidy park with charming *bach*-style cabins just a short walk from the beach, good camping, clean cabins and some spacious units. You can rent quad bikes for a gentle putter up the beach to see the wind-crafted sand sculptures, and lines of burned kauri captured in sand banks. Camping $\underline{\$20}$, cabins $\underline{\$80}$

Dargaville Holiday Park 10 Onslow St, Dargaville ☎0800 114 441, ⓦdargavilleholiday.co.nz. A large traditional Kiwi campsite set in park-like grounds a 10min walk from town, with well-kept cabins and comfortable units. There's lots to keep the kids happy,

too, including the community swimming pool next door. Camping $\underline{\$18}$, cabins $\underline{\$70}$

Greenhouse Hostel 15 Gordon St, Dargaville ☎09 439 6342, ⓔgreenhousebackpackers@ihug.co.nz. Centrally located in a 1920s former school, this hostel is old-fashioned but clean and well run, with simple rooms, great-value doubles, bedding and a communal kitchen. Closed May–Aug. Dorms (no bunks) $\underline{\$28}$, doubles $\underline{\$70}$

★**Kauri House Lodge** 60 Bowen St, Dargaville ☎09 439 8082, ⓦkaurihouselodge.co.nz. Dargaville's grandest accommodation option is in an engagingly low-key yet vast kauri villa. The rooms are all en-suite, and there's a billiard room, library and swimming pool. $\underline{\$250}$

EATING AND DRINKING

★**Blah Blah Blah** 101 Victoria St, Dargaville ☎09 439 6300. A licensed café specializing in dishes featuring Dargaville's famed *kumara*; try the *kumara*, mussel and bacon chowder ($19.50). They also serve tasty coffee and a selection of home-made cakes, plus pizza ($21) great breakfasts. Tues–Sat 9am–late; kitchen closes at 9pm.

Shiraz 17 Hokianga Rd, Dargaville ☎09 439

0024, ⓦshiraz-nz.co.nz. Restaurant and takeaway specializing in north Indian dishes, seafood and pizza – not a combination forged in heaven but there isn't much in the way of competition in town so it can get quite busy. The curries are pretty fair and there is nothing on the menu more than $25. Try the tandoori or the Amritsari fish, but give the pizza a miss. Mon–Sat 11am–10pm.

Tokatoka Peak

SH12, 17km southwest of Dargaville

SH12 zips through flat farmland before reaching the knobby 180m **Tokatoka Peak**. Panoramic views unfold from the summit of this extinct volcanic plug, reached in ten breathless minutes from a trailhead 1km off SH12 near the *Tokatoka* pub.

Matakohe and the Kauri Museum

30km south of Tokatoka Peak, on SH12 · Kauri Museum 5 Church Rd · Daily 9am–5pm · $25, plus $5 guided tour · ☎09 431 7417, ⓦkaurimuseum.com

If there's one museum you must see in the north it's the **Kauri Museum** at tiny **MATAKOHE**. One of the best museums in the country, and deserving at least three hours, it explains the way the kauri's timber and its valuable gum shaped the lives of pioneers in Northland. The displays focus on the settlements around logging camps, the gum fields, and the lives of merchants who were among the few who could afford to buy the fine kauri furniture or beautifully carved gum on show. Diagrams show how even Tane Mahuta is tiny compared to the giants of yore, and the smell of the freshly sawn timber lures you to the replica steam sawmill. There is also a stunning collection of kauri furniture, boats and gum (in the basement).

ACCOMMODATION AND EATING   MATAKOHE

Gumdiggers Café Church Rd ☎09 431 7075. This café makes a welcoming spot to rest after your meanderings round the galleries. Daytime food includes gumdiggers' pasties, excellent wraps, pies, burgers, sandwiches, chips and cakes, with nothing over $20. Daily 9am–5pm.

Matakohe Holiday Park ☎0800 431 6431, ⓦmatakoheholidaypark.co.nz. A well-kept hillside campsite 500m beyond the museum offering great harbour views and a range of accommodation including decent well-spaced camping, and

cabins and comfortable motel units. Camping $\underline{\$40}$, cabins $\underline{\$65}$

★**Petite Provence** 703c Tinopai Rd, 9km south of Matakohe ☎09 431 7552, ⓦpetiteprovence.co.nz. A lovely Kiwi-French-run B&B amid rolling farmland with views of the Kaipara Harbour. Rooms are nicely decorated and comfortable, and wonderfully tasty evening meals ($45, BYO wine) are available. The host also makes beautiful, handcrafted metal and wood furniture, featured in some rooms, which is stunningly comfortable and quite captivating. $\underline{\$170}$

Waikato and the Coromandel Peninsula

WHANGANUI RIVER

Waikato and the Coromandel Peninsula

Named after New Zealand's longest river, the lush, culturally rich Waikato region stretches south from Auckland, and is home to countless dairy farms, peaceful rural towns and world-class surfing. Much of its appeal is tied to its extraordinary history of pre-European settlement and post-European conflict. It was on the west coast, at Kawhia, that the Tainui people first landed in New Zealand. And Kawhia was also the birthplace of Te Rauparaha, the great Māori chief who led his people down the coast to Kapiti Island and on to the South Island, to escape the better-armed tribes of the Waikato.

Approaching the region from the north, **Waikato** centres on the workaday provincial capital, **Hamilton**, which won't detain you long, but has enough to soak up a couple of days' exploration in the immediate vicinity. The nearby surfers' paradise of **Raglan** has world-class waves and some great places to stay, eat and unwind. Southeast of Hamilton on SH1, there's a genteel English charm to **Cambridge**, while at Matamata, **Hobbiton** tours are essential for *Lord of the Rings* and *The Hobbit* film fans.

South of the Waikato, the highlight is **Waitomo**, where fabulous adventure trips explore otherworldly glowworm-filled limestone caverns. The adjacent **King Country** took its name from the King Movement (see page 201), and was the last significant area in New Zealand to succumb to European colonization. Further south, you'll find the farming town of **Taumarunui**.

Northeast of Hamilton, across the dairy country of the **Hauraki Plains**, is the spa town of **Te Aroha**. Nearby **Paeroa** has walks in the **Karangahake Gorge**, once the scene of intensive gold mining. Jutting north, the only half-tamed **Coromandel Peninsula** is an area of spectacular coastal scenery, offering walks to pristine beaches and tramps in mountainous rainforest. The **west coast** has a more rugged and atmospheric coastline, and offers easier access to the volcanic hills and ancient kauri trees around. **Thames** and quaint **Coromandel**. On the east coast, **Whangamata** and **Whitianga** offer a plethora of water-based activities and long sandy beaches. Whitianga is also handy for **Hot Water Beach**, where natural thermal springs bubble up through the sand, and the crystalline **Cathedral Cove Marine Reserve**. Finally, at the base of the Coromandel Peninsula is the gold-mining town of **Waihi**.

Hamilton

On the banks of the languid green Waikato River, New Zealand's fourth-largest city, **HAMILTON**, functions as a regional hub rather than a major tourist destination, but it's within striking distance of some of the North Island's top spots, such as the surf beaches of Raglan and Waitomo Caves, as well as Auckland, 127km north. There's not much to detain you in town but it is worth devoting some time to the excellent **Waikato Museum** and the tranquil **Hamilton Gardens**, and there's a good nightlife scene thanks to the city's university. Consider also a stroll along the recently redeveloped riverside and a tour of the **Zealong** tea estate.

In mid-June, the **Fieldays festival** (⌨ fieldays.co.nz) is held at Mystery Creek Events Centre just outside the city. The largest agricultural field day in the southern hemisphere, it's a quintessentially Kiwi event with everything from sheep shearing to ploughing contests plus lots of other entertainment.

WAITOMO

Highlights

❶ Raglan Surf some of New Zealand's finest waves, kayak around the harbour or just soak up the laidback atmosphere of this bohemian town. See page 197

❷ Waitomo Abseil or blackwater raft into labyrinthine caves on some of the world's best adventure caving trips, often illuminated by a glittering canopy of glowworms. See page 203

❸ Te Aroha Rejuvenate in the geyser-fed hot soda springs in this charming Edwardian spa town at the foot of Mount Te Aroha. See page 210

❹ Kauaeranga Valley Hike past gold-mining remains as you work your way through a jagged landscape of bluffs and gorges to the Pinnacles overlooking both Coromandel coasts. See page 216

❺ Driving Creek Railway One man's passion for pots created this modern narrow-gauge railway, now moving passengers rather than clay through rich Coromandel bush to a wonderful viewpoint. See page 219

❻ Hot Water Beach Grab a shovel, find your spot, dig into the sand and then wallow in your own surfside hot springs. See page 226

HIGHLIGHTS ARE MARKED ON THE MAP ON PAGE 190

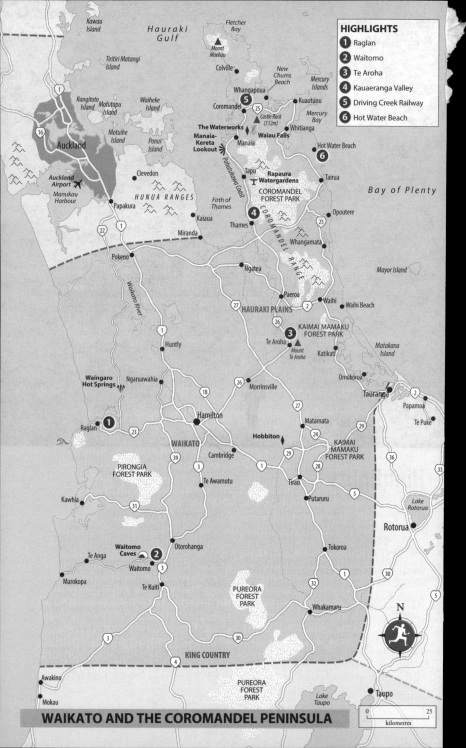

WAIKATO AND THE COROMANDEL PENINSULA

HIGHLIGHTS

1. Raglan
2. Waitomo
3. Te Aroha
4. Kauaeranga Valley
5. Driving Creek Railway
6. Hot Water Beach

Kawau Island

Haraki Gulf

Fletcher Bay

Mount Moehau

Tiritiri Matangi Island

Colville

New Chums Beach

Mercury Islands

Whangapoua

Coromandel

Castle Rock (512m)

Kuaotunu

Mercury Bay

Rangitoto Island
Motutapu Island

Waiheke Island

The Waterworks

Waiau Falls

Whitianga

Manaia-Kereta Lookout

Manaia

Hot Water Beach

Motuihe Island

Ponui Island

Auckland

Clevedon

Tapu

Rapaura Watergardens

Tairua

Auckland Airport

HUNUA RANGES

COROMANDEL FOREST PARK

Bay of Plenty

Manukau Harbour

Papakura

Firth of Thames

Thames

Opoutere

Kaiaua

Whangamata

Miranda

Mayor Island

Pokeno

Ngatea

Waikato River

Paeroa

Waihi

Waihi Beach

HAURAKI PLAINS

KAIMAI MAMAKU FOREST PARK

Te Aroha

Mount Te Aroha

Katikati

Matakana Island

Huntly

Ngaruawahia

Morrinsville

Omokoroa

Tauranga

Waingaro Hot Springs

Hamilton

Matamata

Papamoa

Te Puke

Raglan

WAIKATO

Cambridge

Hobbiton

KAIMAI MAMAKU FOREST PARK

PIRONGIA FOREST PARK

Te Awamutu

Tirau

Putaruru

Lake Rotorua

Kawhia

Rotorua

Otorohanga

Tokoroa

Waitomo Caves

Waitomo

Te Anga

Te Kuiti

PUREORA FOREST PARK

Whakamaru

Marokopa

KING COUNTRY

Awakino

PUREORA FOREST PARK

Lake Taupo

Taupo

Mokau

N

0   25
kilometres

Victoria Street

Most things of interest in Hamilton are on or just off the main drag, **Victoria Street**, which parallels the west bank of the tree-lined Waikato River. One of the more striking buildings is the 1924 **Wesley Chambers** (now *Hamilton City Oaks* hotel) on the corner of Collingwood Street, influenced by the buildings of boomtime Chicago. Diagonally opposite, a small open space is graced by a statue of the English-born *Rocky Horror Show* creator, **Richard O'Brien** – decked out as Riff Raff, the role he played in the film of the show – who spent his teens and early twenties in Hamilton watching late-night B movies at the cinema that once stood on this site. Opposite are public toilets decked out like Dr Frank-N-Furter's science lab.

Waikato Museum

1 Grantham St • Daily 10am–5pm • Free • ☎ 07 838 6606, ⓦ waikatomuseum.co.nz

Set in a modern building that steps down to the river, the excellent **Waikato Museum** takes an imaginative approach to local history but really excels with its section devoted to **Tainui culture**, much of it curated by the local Māori community. Of course, there are tools, ritual artefacts, woven flax and carvings, but the displays give a real sense of the living culture of the four main Tainui subtribes along with insights into tribal leaders, and there's frequently changing art. The magnificent *Te Winika* war canoe is housed beside a window where you can look out over the river at the mouldering hulk of the paddle steamer *Rangiriri*, which worked the river in early colonial times.

Hamilton Gardens

Cobham Drive (SH1), 4km southeast of the city centre • Daily: mid-April–mid-Sept 7.30am–5pm; late Sept–early April 7.30am–8pm; visitor centre 9am–5pm • Free • ☎ 07 838 6782, ⓦ hamiltongardens.co.nz • Take bus #10 (#17 on Sat & Sun) from the Transport Centre

From Memorial Park, a riverside path follows the bends in the river to the huge, unfenced **Hamilton Gardens**, with extensive displays of roses, tropical plants, rhododendrons, magnolias and cacti. Pick up a free map from the visitor centre then duck next door to the inner sanctum of the **Paradise Gardens Collection**, six beautiful enclosures each planted in a different style from around the world. Wander through an uninspiring archway to be dazzled by the stunning colours of the Indian Char Bagh Garden, stroll and smell the flowers in the English Garden and take in the idealized Chinese Scholar's Garden, complete with red pavilion where you can sit and catch a view of the Waikato River. A highlight is the American Modernist Garden, with aloe-and-grass mass plantings around a shallow pool, ringed with bright yellow loungers and a huge Marilyn Monroe screenprint.

The rest of the gardens are also well worth a stroll – even packing a picnic. The **Rose Garden** is especially popular, featuring a wide range of different colours and cultivars, arranged to tell the story of the development of the modern rose.

Zealong

495 Gordonton Rd, 13km north of the city centre • **Tours** 9.30am & 2pm: May–Oct Tues–Sun; Nov–April daily • **Camellia Teahouse** May–Oct Tues–Sun 10am–5pm; Nov–April daily 10am–5pm • Tours from $49 (bookings essential); signature tea from $45 for one • ☎ 07 853 3018, ⓦ zealong.com

The flat, low-lying sheep and cattle country of the northern Waikato seems an unlikely place to find rows of neatly tended *Camellia sinensis*, but in the late 1990s Taiwanese immigrant Vincent Chen pioneered growing tea in New Zealand – and very fine it is, too. At **Zealong** they concentrate on **oolong tea** (partly fermented, somewhere between green and black tea), best experienced as part of the hour-long **guided tour**. Alternatively, just drop into the fabulous *Camellia Teahouse* for a leisurely (and

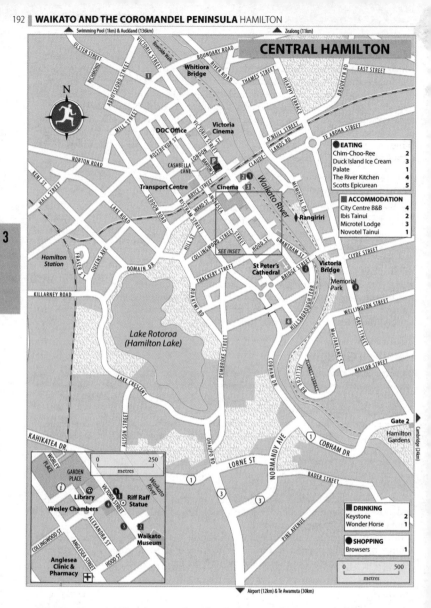

CENTRAL HAMILTON

Swimming Pool (1km) & Auckland (136km)
Zealong (11km)

EATING
Chim-Choo-Ree — 2
Duck Island Ice Cream — 3
Palate — 1
The River Kitchen — 4
Scotts Epicurean — 5

ACCOMMODATION
City Centre B&B — 4
Ibis Tainui — 2
Microtel Lodge — 3
Novotel Tainui — 1

DRINKING
Keystone — 2
Wonder Horse — 1

SHOPPING
Browsers — 1

Airport (12km) & Te Awamuta (30km)

informative) gourmet lunch, or settle in for the signature high tea with delicious savouries and exquisite cakes.

ARRIVAL AND DEPARTURE
HAMILTON

By plane Hamilton's airport (ⓦwww.hamiltonairport. co.nz) is 15km south of the city. Super Shuttle (☎0800 748 885, ⓦsupershuttle.co.nz) offers transfers for $25 one way.
Destinations Christchurch (4 daily; 1hr 45min), Palmerston

North (2 daily; 45min), Wellington (7 daily; 1hr 15min).
By train The station is on Fraser St in the suburb of Frankton, almost 2km west of the city centre. Bus #3 runs to the Transport Centre in town, where you can also buy train tickets.

Destinations Auckland (3 weekly; 2hr 20min); Wellington (3 weekly; 8hr 10min).

By bus The Transport Centre, 373 Anglesea St (Mon–Thurs 7am–6pm, Fri 7am–7pm, Sat 9am–5pm, Sun 9am–7pm), is the hub for local and long-haul buses. An office here sells tickets for InterCity and NakedBus.

Destinations Auckland (every 30min–1hr; 2hr); Cambridge (7 daily; 40min); Matamata (6 daily; 1hr);

New Plymouth (2 daily; 4hr 15min); Ngaruawahia (every 30min; 20min); Otorohanga (3 daily; 1hr); Paeroa (1 daily; 1hr 35min); Raglan (2–4 daily; 40min); Rotorua (5 daily; 1hr 30min); Taupo (9 daily; 2hr 30min-3hr); Tauranga (4 daily; 1hr 50min); Te Aroha (1 daily; 1hr 5min); Te Awamutu (3 daily; 30min); Te Kuiti (1 daily; 1hr 30min); Tirau (12 daily; 45min); Wellington (5 daily; 9hr 10min).

GETTING AROUND

By bus Buslt (☎0800 428 75463, ⓦbusit.co.nz) runs services around town and to Cambridge, Te Awamutu, Raglan and Paeroa from the Transport Centre. Pick up the free timetable there or at the i-SITE. One-way fares within

the city limits are $3.30 including free transfers for two hours.

By taxi There's a taxi rank at the Transport Centre, or call Hamilton Taxis on ☎0800 477 477.

INFORMATION

Visitor information i-SITE is at the corner of Caro and Alexandra streets (Mon–Fri 9am–5pm, Sat & Sun 9.30am–3.30pm; ☎07 958 5960, ⓦvisithamilton.co.nz).
DOC Level 5, 73 Rostrevor St (Mon–Fri 8.30am–4.30pm; ☎07 858 1000, ⓦdoc.govt.nz). Come here for hiking

information and hut passes.
Services Free wi-fi around Garden Place and free use of computers in the Central Library, 9 Garden Place (Mon–Fri 9.30am–8pm, Sat 9am–4pm, Sun noon–3.30pm; ☎07 838 6826).

ACCOMMODATION

City Centre B&B 3 Anglesea St ☎07 838 1671, ⓦcitycentrebnb.co.nz; map p.192. There's a relaxed, homey feel to the good-value rooms and studios with kitchenettes, which open out onto a courtyard garden with swimming pool. Minimum two-night stay. Doubles $90, studios $109

Ibis Tainui 18 Alma St ☎07 859 9200, ⓦibishotel. com/hamilton; map p.192. Conveniently central, this reliable mid-range hotel is in an eight-storey block. Many of the modern en suites have views of the river, as does the restaurant terrace. Wi-fi/internet access $10/day. $130

Microtel Lodge 140 Ulster St ☎07 957 1848, ⓦmicrotel. co.nz; map p.192. Compact and contemporary hostel with Sky TV in its private rooms (some of which are en-suite), plenty of singles, mixed bunkbed dorms, and some self-contained studios. Dorms $30, doubles $79

Novotel Tainui 7 Alma St ☎07 838 1366, ⓦnovotel. com; map p.192. Bang in the centre, this recently revamped *Novotel* is a fine choice, offering modern and spacious en suites (many with river views) plus an attractive restaurant and bar, and well-equipped gym. Wi-fi/internet access $10/day. $274

EATING

The city's food and drink scene is concentrated along the southern end of **Victoria Street** and around the corner on **Hood Street**, where places start off as cafés and become restaurants/bars as the day wears on. There's a night food market most Fridays and Saturdays (Fri at the corner of Te Rapa Rd & The Base Parade, Sat under Kmart on Bryce St; 5–11pm; ⓦhamiltonnightmarket.co.nz).

Chim-Choo-Ree 14 Bridge St ☎07 839 4329, ⓦchimchooree.co.nz; map p.192. A bare concrete floor and a cluster of 1930s and 1940s lampshades greet you at this bustling bistro. Nip in for a glass or two of wine or tuck into dishes like snapper sashimi, flat iron steak and olive gnocchi (mains $36–38). Alternatively, settle in for the six-course tasting menu ($100; $145 with wine). Mon–Fri 11.30am–2pm & 5pm–late, Sat 5pm–late.

Duck Island Ice Cream 300a Grey St ☎07 856 5948, ⓦduckislandicecream.co.nz; map p.192. This top-notch

ice cream parlour offers 26 inventive flavours – including white chocolate and miso, lemon poppy seed cheesecake, and toasted marshmallow – as well as cakes, ice cream floats and milkshakes. Mon–Wed & Sun 11am–7pm, Fri–Sat 11am–10pm.

Palate 20 Alma St ☎07 834 2921, ⓦpalaterestaurant. co.nz; map p.192. Hamilton's finest restaurant, done in a relaxed but professional style by people who really know what they're doing. The menu changes regularly, but expect mains ($34–40) like seared venison with pureed shitake mushrooms and truffle arancini. There's a good value two-course lunch, too ($25). Tues–Fri 11.30am–2pm & 5.30pm–late, Sat 5.30pm–late.

The River Kitchen 237 Victoria St ☎07 839 2906, ⓦtheriverkitchen.co.nz; map p.192. Sit in the window that opens out onto the street and try the breakfast of Spanish beans with smoked ham hock and poached eggs ($19) or some of the superb sandwiches and salads from the cabinet. Mon–Fri 7am–4pm, Sat 8am–4pm, Sun 8am–3pm.

★ **Scotts Epicurean** 181 Victoria St ☎ 07 839 6680, ⓦ scottsepicurean.co.nz; map p.192. A multi-award-winning café offering beautifully presented brunch dishes ($8–19.50) such as green eggs and ham, creative lunches like Sri Lankan sour chicken, delicious cakes and expertly made Allpress coffee. Sit out front, grab a booth or head to a hidden courtyard garden out back. Mon–Fri 7am–3pm, Sat & Sun 8am–4pm.

DRINKING

Hamilton's sizeable student population ensures there's a good bar and club scene, at least during term-time.

Keystone 150 Victoria St ☎ 07 839 4294, ⓦ keystonebar.co.nz; map p.192. Hamilton's Monteith's bar serves a wide range of draft and bottled beers (from $8), as well as a menu of pub grub-style meals (from $15) such as southern-fried chicken and sliders, and platters to share. Daily 11.30am–midnight.

Wonder Horse 232 Victoria St ☎ 07 839 2281; map p.192. Comfy sofas, board games, engaging staff, a sophisticated but not exclusive vibe, regular DJ sets and great cocktails (around $15) make a drink at *Wonder Horse* a must while you're in town. As an added bonus, it also stays open later than most of its competitors. Wed–Sat 5pm–3am.

SHOPPING

Browsers 298 Victoria St ☎ 07 839 1919, ⓦ browsersbooks.co.nz; map p.192. Every city deserves a bookshop like Browsers, which has a diverse, well-laid-out selection of secondhand fiction and non-fiction; Kiwi authors are particularly well represented. Mon–Wed 9.30am–5.30pm, Thurs & Fri 9.30am–9.30pm, Sat & Sun 10am–9.30pm.

Around Hamilton

Hamilton is a good base for exploring the Waikato region and its cluster of modest sights. Heading south from Auckland, the first place of real interest is the important Māori town of **Ngaruawahia**, though if you are headed for Raglan you may skip Ngaruawahia and follow the back roads past **Waingaro Hot Springs**. Art-lovers will want to nip east to the **Wallace Gallery** while Hobbit fans shouldn't miss **Hobbiton**, on the outskirts of Matamata. Southeast of Hamilton, Cambridge and Tirau are really just waystations on the route to Taupo, while to the south, **Te Awamutu** celebrates its Māori, Pakeha and Finn Brothers heritage.

Waingaro Hot Springs

Waingaro Rd, 40km northwest of Hamilton • Mon–Fri 9.30am–8.30pm, Sat & Sun 9.30am–9pm • $13 • ☎ 07 825 4761, ⓦ waingarohotsprings.co.nz

If you're working your way on the back roads between Auckland and Raglan consider stopping off at the old-fashioned (some might say dated) **Waingaro Hot Springs**, which offer a real slice of Kiwi family life with three hot-water pools and New Zealand's longest open hot-water slide.

Ngaruawahia

The Waikato and Waipa rivers meet at the historically and culturally significant farming town of **NGARUAWAHIA**, 18km northwest of Hamilton on SH1. Both rivers were important Māori canoe routes and the **King Movement** (see page 201) has its roots here. Home to the Māori king, the town was the scene of the signing of the Raupatu Land Settlement (1995), whereby the government agreed to compensate Tainui for land confiscated in the 1860s.

The Māori heritage is most evident on **Regatta Day** (the closest Saturday to March 17). Watched by the Māori king, a parade of great war canoes takes place along the two rivers, with events such as hurdle races at the **Turangawaewae**

Marae on River Road, off SH1 just north of the river bridge. The *marae* is only open to the public on Regatta Day; the rest of the year you can view it through the perimeter fence, which is made of the trunks of tree ferns interspersed with sculpted red posts and a couple of finely carved entranceways.

Wallace Gallery

167 Thames St, Morrinsville, 33km northeast of Hamilton • Tues–Sun: Oct–June 10am–4pm, July–Sept 10am–3pm • Free • ☎ 07 889 7791, ⓦ morrinsvillegallery.org.nz

The nondescript farming service town of Morrinsville seems an unlikely location for the small but classy **Wallace Gallery**, which is a rural offshoot of Auckland's Wallace Arts Centre (see page 88). It is housed in the town's mid-century former post office building where the old radiators have been put to imaginative use as doors and gallery seating. Changing exhibitions draw from the wider Wallace collection of contemporary New Zealand art.

Matamata

The dairy-farming and racehorse-breeding town of **MATAMATA**, 63km east of Hamilton, shot to prominence as the location of **Hobbiton** from the *Lord of the Rings* trilogy. Lifelike *Lord of the Rings* character **statues** have since been installed in the town centre but the only way to visit the Hobbiton location (on a working sheep farm 15km southwest of town) is on a tour.

Hobbiton Movie Set and Farm Tours

501 Buckland Rd, 16km southeast of Matamata • Tours daily every 15–30min • $79 • ☎ 07 888 9913, ⓦ hobbitontours.com • Drive straight there, get the free shuttle from Matamata i-SITE, or arrange a transfer (see website for details)

Between the filming of Peter Jackson's three *Lord of the Rings* films in the early 2000s and his return a decade later to shoot the two films of *The Hobbit*, there really wasn't much to see at Hobbiton. The set was mostly dismantled and early visitors just got to see a handful of hobbit-hole facades amid the rolling hills of a working sheep farm. Interiors for all films were done in Wellington.

Since the shooting of *The Hobbit* in 2011, however, almost all sets have been left intact. You can wander over a hillside of 42 hobbit-hole facades, all superbly rendered to look old and hobbit-like. Chimneys appear to have soot on them, the fake lichen on fences looks totally authentic and there's an orchard of apple and pear trees (one of which was turned into a plum tree for the filming to satisfy a single line in the book). Across the lake the film-makers have created two of New Zealand's very few thatched buildings, a water mill connected by a "stone" bridge to *The Green Dragon* inn. Die-hard fans will revel in the chance to wander around real-life Hobbiton, but the less ardent may find the whole experience overlong – and overpriced.

ARRIVAL AND INFORMATION   MATAMATA

By bus InterCity and NakedBus Auckland–Rotorua runs stop outside the i-SITE.

Destinations Auckland (3 daily; 3hr 10min); Hamilton (6 daily; 1hr); Rotorua (3 daily; 1hr); Tauranga (1 daily; 50min).

Visitor information i-SITE, 45 Broadway (Mon–Fri 9am–5pm, Sat & Sun 9am–2.30pm; ☎ 07 888 7260, ⓦ matamatanz.co.nz). Useful for Hobbit-related information and has internet access.

EATING

★ **Workman's Café & Bar** 52 Broadway ☎ 07 888 5498. Funky café with more of a free spirit than you would expect to find in a place such as Matamata. Great for coffee, cakes and snacks but also full meals (from $20) such as beef salad with baby beets. Wed–Sun 7.30am–10pm.

Cambridge

CAMBRIDGE, 24km southeast of Hamilton, was founded as a militia settlement at the navigable limit of the Waikato River in 1864, and today is surrounded by stud farms. Mosaics of Cambridge-bred winners are embedded in the pavements along the town's **Equine Stars Walk of Fame**; of these Zabeel stands out for having sired winners of prestigious races in Hong Kong, Dubai and Australia.

The town's collection of elegant **nineteenth- and twentieth-century buildings** is mapped on a heritage trail brochure (free from the i-SITE).

ARRIVAL AND INFORMATION   CAMBRIDGE

By bus InterCity and NakedBus stop on Lake St, 50m from the i-SITE, on their Auckland–Wellington routes. Buslt (☎ 0800 287 5463, ⓦ busit.co.nz) runs a local service (#20) from Hamilton that stops at 36 Victoria St.
Destinations Hamilton (7 daily; 40min); Matamata (2 daily; 30min); Tauranga (2 daily; 50min).

Tourist information i-SITE, cnr of Queen and Victoria sts (Mon–Fri 9am–5pm, Sat & Sun 10am–4pm; ☎ 07 823 3456, ⓦ cambridge.co.nz). Located in the former library building and has internet access.

EATING

The Deli on the Corner 48 Victoria St ☎ 07 827 5370. The pick of Cambridge's cafés is in the airy 1920s Triangle Building, with a nice little corner seat for two in the apex. The sandwiches, pies and wraps are excellent, as are brunch dishes ($12–20) such as creamy mushrooms on toast. Or just stop in for a coffee, a pear and ginger muffin, bread and butter berry pudding or ice cream. Mon–Fri 8am–4.30pm, Sat 8am–4pm, Sun 9am–3pm.

Tirau

Almost everyone seems to stop for a break in the farming settlement of **TIRAU**, 55km southeast of Hamilton, its highwayside strip completely taken over by corrugated iron. It kicked off with a corrugated-iron sheep housing a woolshop and followed with a sheepdog containing the **i-SITE**. The corrugated-iron constructions have attained iconic status and spawned a rash of sheet-metal structures and signs, including a biblical shepherd in the grounds of a church.

INFORMATION AND EATING   TIRAU

Visitor information i-SITE, SH1 (daily 9am–5pm; ☎ 07 883 1202, ⓦ tirauinfo.co.nz).

Te Awamutu

TE AWAMUTU, 30km south of Hamilton, is renowned for its musical and military history. The birthplace of fraternal Kiwi music icons Tim and Neil Finn, of **Split Enz** and **Crowded House** fame, "TA", as it's dubbed by locals, is surrounded by rolling hills and dairy pasture, and overlooked by Mount Pirongia. During the 1863 **New Zealand Wars**, Te Awamutu was a garrison for government forces and site of one of the most famous battles of the conflict, fought at the hastily constructed Orakau *pa*, where three hundred Māori held off two thousand soldiers for three days.

Immediately across the road from the i-SITE you'll find Te Awamutu's extensive **rose gardens** (open access; free), at their best between November and May. The i-SITE also holds the key to the 1854 garrison church, **St John's**, just across Arawata Street. Inside is a tribute from the British regiment, written in Māori, honouring Māori who crawled, under fire, onto the battlefield to give water to wounded British soldiers.

Te Awamutu Museum

135 Roche St • Mon–Fri 10am–4pm, Sat 10am–2pm • Free • ☎ 07 872 0085, ⓦ tamuseum.org.nz

The **Te Awamutu Museum** punches above its (admittedly modest) weight with interesting displays about European settlers and the New Zealand Wars, and a "*True Colours*" exhibit devoted to the Finn brothers, complete with home movies, newspaper clippings from the early days, an interview with the boys and assorted artefacts.

The room of Māori artefacts is notable chiefly for **Uenuku**, a 2.7m-high wooden representation of an important Māori god. It looks quite unlike almost any other Māori carving you'll see, something that supports the contention that it was made before 1500 AD. No one really knows why it spent decades (perhaps centuries) in a lake near Te Awamutu where it was found in 1906.

ARRIVAL AND DEPARTURE

TE AWAMUTU

By bus InterCity and NakedBus stop at the i-SITE. BusIt (⦿busit.co.nz) runs to Hamilton.

Destinations Hamilton (3–8 daily; 35min); Otorohanga (3 daily; 25min).

INFORMATION AND TOURS

Visitor information i-SITE, 1 Gorst Ave (Mon–Fri 9am–5pm, Sat & Sun 10am–4pm; ☎07 871 3259, ⦿teawamutuinfo.com). All the information you need, plus free showers.

Finn Tour Fans of the brothers Finn can take a self-guided jaunt around the (frankly fairly dull) places of significance from the brothers' formative years by buying the "Finn Tour" booklet ($5) from the i-SITE.

EATING AND DRINKING

Empire Espresso Bar 65 Sloane St ☎07 871 2095, ⦿facebook.com/empireespressobar. Smart little café in the entrance to a 1915 former cinema with great all-day breakfast ($14–24) like brioche French toast, plus lunch dishes with Moroccan, Mexican and Middle Eastern influences. If you just fancy a snack, try their passion fruit and macadamia macaroon. Tues–Fri 6am–2pm, Sat 6am–1.30pm, Sun 8am–1.30pm.

Fahrenheit 13 Roche St ☎07 871 5429, ⦿fahrenheitrestaurant.co.nz. Find a sunny afternoon seat on the terrace overlooking the main street for a beer and some tapas, or settle down later for dinner, where mains ($26–37) include crispy twice-cooked pork belly and slow-roasted shoulder of lamb. Sometimes open later than advertised. Tues–Sun 11am–10pm.

Raglan and around

It's easy to stay far longer than you intended in **RAGLAN**, 48km west of Hamilton and hugging the south side of the large and picturesque Whaingaroa Harbour. The town has a bohemian creative scene and a laidback spirit thanks to its **surfing** community – the waters here feature some of the world's best left-hand breaks. Cafés, restaurants, surf shops and boutiques line palm-shaded **Bow Street**, whose western end butts against the harbour, spanned by a slender footbridge where kids are always egging each other to jump off. Apart from wandering the foreshore, there are few sights as such, so you'll soon want to head 8km south of town to the surf beaches.

There's good **hiking** and **horseriding** both here and further south at **Bridal Veil Falls**. Sweeping views of Raglan Harbour and along the coast unfurl from the summit of **Mount Karioi** (755m), reached on a winding gravel-road loop around the Karioi Mountain. In January, the town hosts the **Sound Splash** (⦿soundsplash. co.nz) music festival and the **Raglan Arts Weekend** (check Facebook for info).

Brief history

The horizon to the south is dominated by **Mount Karioi**, which according to Māori legend was the ultimate goal of the great migratory canoe Tainui. On reaching the mouth of the harbour a bar blocked the way, hence the name Whaingaroa ("long pursuit"). The shortened epithet, Whangaroa, was the name used for the harbour

3

RAGLAN TOURS AND ACTIVITIES

There are great waves all around the country, but Raglan is New Zealand's finest **surfing** destination – the lines of perfect breakers appear like blue corduroy southwest of town. The best place for inexperienced surfers is the rock-free **Ngarunui Beach**, 5km south of Raglan. For the experienced, the main breaks, both around 8km south of town, are **Whale Bay** and **Manu Bay** (Waireki), which featured in the cult 1960s surf film *Endless Summer*.

For non-surfers, Raglan is mostly about doing not much at all, but there is plenty to keep you occupied. You really should spend some time on the water, particularly exploring the horizontally jointed **Pancake Rocks** forming low cliffs just across Raglan's Whaingaroa Harbour. Kayaking is a perfect way to see them at their best.

Inland, saddles are the way to go, either on horseback or mountain bike.

SURFING AND BOARD SPORTS

Raglan Surfing School Whale Bay ☎07 825 7873, ⓦraglansurfingschool.co.nz. The main surf school with rentals (half-day from $35) and assorted packages including starter lessons (3hr; group $89; private $149).

Raglan Watersports 7a Main Rd ☎07 825 0507, ⓦraglanwatersports.co.nz. Offers paddleboarding, kiteboarding and surfing lessons (from $80) and equipment hire.

EXPLORING THE HARBOUR

Raglan Backpackers ☎07 825 0515, ⓦraglanbackpackers.co.nz. Rent kayaks and paddleboards (from $15/hr) then launch them from right next to the hostel and explore the harbour, particularly the Pancake Rocks over the far side, easily reached in 15–20min.

Raglan Kayak ☎07 825 8862, ⓦraglaneco. co.nz. Offers kayaking and paddleboarding lessons for beginners/intermediates (from $55), runs guided tours (from $79) and has gear to rent (from $25/hr).

Wahine Moe Raglan Wharf ☎07 825 7873, ⓦraglanboatcharters.co.nz. Delightful 2hr sunset cruises ($49) on Raglan Harbour aboard a powerful cruiser. A sandwich is included and there's a bar on board. Operated Dec–March Thurs–Sun.

HORSERIDING

Extreme Horse Adventures Ruapuke, 20km southwest of Raglan ☎07 825 0059, ⓦwildcoast. co.nz. Offers horseriding trips through native bush and on to Ruapuke Beach (from $130/person).

CYCLING

Cyclery Raglan 24b Stewart St ☎07 825 0309, ⓦcycleryraglan.co.nz. There's great riding in the countryside all around Raglan (some of it quite challenging) and these guys know it well. They specialize in self-guided tours including bike rental (from $10/hr). Go for the Round Mt Karioi (45km), a sunset descent known as Ruapuke Thunder, or a two-day tour to some limestone caves with B&B in a nearby cabin.

until 1855, when it was renamed Raglan after the officer who led the Charge of the Light Brigade.

Raglan Museum

15 Wainui Rd • Daily 9.30am–6.30pm • $2 • ☎07 825 0556, ⓦraglanmuseum.co.nz

Accessed via the i-SITE, the **Raglan Museum** has modest displays on the area's history including the original telephone exchange and an apothecary chest. Alongside the usual run of old photos and paraphernalia, surf fans should check out the short film on 1970s attempts to use early computers to predict ocean wave patterns and hence the best day to head to the coast at a time when high petrol prices limited the transport options of impecunious surfers.

Old School Arts Centre

5 Stewart St • Mon–Fri 10am–2pm • ☎07 825 0023, ⓦraglanartscentre.co.nz

Raglan is home to dozens of artists and several galleries, notably the **Old School Arts Centre**, in a heritage building and run by the town's creative community. It has exhibitions, hosts a funky market with everything locally produced (second Sun of each month 10am–2pm; ⓦraglanmarket.com), screens new films (third weekend of the month), offers numerous workshops and publishes the free *Raglan Arts Trail* leaflet (also available from the i-SITE).

Te Kopua and Ocean beaches

The safest swimming beach is **Te Kopua**, in the heart of town, reached via the footbridge from lower Bow Street or by car along Wainui Road and Marine Parade. The black sand can make it look a little dowdy, but it's popular enough and there are barbecue sites and a children's play area.

Ocean Beach, just outside the town off Wainui Road on the way to Whale Bay, gives great views of the bar of rock and sand that stretches across the mouth of the harbour and is a fine picnic spot, but strong undertows make swimming unsafe. For Raglan's renowned **surf beaches**, see page 198.

Te Toto and Mount Karioi tracks

Both start 12km south of Raglan along Whaanga Rd • Te Toto 2km return; 1hr; 200m ascent on way back • Karioi 8km return; 5–6hr; 650m ascent; not to be attempted in bad weather

For a short walk head to **Te Toto Track** which heads down steeply from an obvious car park through coastal forest to the grassy margins of Te Toto Stream. From there it is easy enough to access the stony beach.

The same car park is the start of the much more arduous **Mount Karioi Track**, which follows a ridge through manuka with rapidly improving views along the coast. A walk through dense forest and a short descent using a ladder brings you to the final hand-over-hand ascent using fixed chains.

Bridal Veil Falls

20km southeast of Raglan

Bridal Veil Falls hides in dense native bush just off the Kawhia Road. Water plummets 55m down a sheer rock face into a green pool where rainbows appear in the spray in the sunshine. From the carpark it's a ten-minute walk down to the bottom of the falls; allow twice that for the walk back up.

ARRIVAL AND INFORMATION

RAGLAN

By bus The #23 Hamilton city BusIt (ⓦbusit.co.nz) bus arrives outside the i-SITE; during the summer some services head onto Manu Bay.
Destinations Hamilton (2–4 daily; 1hr).
By taxi Raglan Shuttle (☎07 825 8159, ⓦraglanshuttle.co.nz) provides a taxi service (including to/from Hamilton Airport); try to give them 24hr notice.

i-SITE 13 Wainui Rd (Nov–April Mon–Sat 9am–7pm, Sun 9.30am–6.30pm; April–Nov Mon–Fri 9.30am–5.30pm, Sat & Sun 9.30am–5pm; ☎07 825 0556, ⓦraglan.org.nz). Can help with booking accommodation, including holiday cottages and apartments.
Services There's free wi-fi inside (and outside) the library, 7 Bow St (Mon–Fri 9.30am–5pm, Sat 9.30am–12.30pm).

ACCOMMODATION

Bow Street Studios 1 Bow St ☎07 825 0551, ⓦbowstreet.co.nz. All seven one-bedroom apartments have harbour views from the upstairs bedroom and a subtropical terrace accessed from the kitchen/lounge. Everything is well thought out, including New Zealand art. There's also a pretty two-bedroom cottage dating back to 1874. Apartments $205, cottages $245
Harbour View Hotel 14 Bow St ☎07 825 8010, ⓦharbourviewhotel.co.nz. A stay at Raglan's centrepiece

old hotel comes with verandas overlooking the main street, pleasant rooms (including good value singles for $60 and large family rooms for $115 and an on-site sports bar and restaurant (see page 200). $80
Karioi Lodge 5 Whaanga Rd, Whale Bay ☎07 825 7873, ⓦkarioilodge.co.nz. Pleasant hostel in native bush 8km southwest of Raglan, with four-bed dorms and doubles and hillside campervan sites. Amenities include a communal kitchen, sauna, cheap bike rental, mountain tracks to

explore and free pick-up from Raglan. Also runs Raglan Surfing School. Camping $18, dorms $33, doubles $79

★ **Raglan Backpackers** 6 Nero St ☎07 825 0515, �🌐raglanbackpackers.co.nz. Wonderfully relaxed hammock-strewn hostel in the town centre, laid out across two adjoining buildings backing onto the estuary. There's free use of kayaks, bikes, golf clubs, fishing gear, spa and sauna. Also offers inexpensive surfboard rental ($30/day including board, wetsuit and transport) and lessons. Dorms $29, doubles $78

Raglan Kopua Holiday Park Marine Parade ☎07 825 8283, �🌐raglanholidaypark.co.nz. Central but somewhat raucous and crowded campsite with a wide range of cabins, 1km away by road from town and also accessible by a short footbridge. It is well sited next to Te Kopua, the harbour's safest swimming beach. Camping $24, cabins $70

★ **Solscape Eco Retreat** Wainui Rd, Manu Bay, 6km south of Raglan ☎07 825 8268, �🌐solscape.co.nz. Delightfully idiosyncratic accommodation is provided at this associate YHA: you can stay in a converted train carriage (a "caboose"), earth dome or even a tipi, among other options. Set on a hilltop with panoramic views, the resort has a strong environmental focus, with a solar water-heating system, solar lights, and vegetarian cuisine at the (excellent) in-house café-restaurant just three of the initiatives. There's a yoga studio, surf lessons, free pick-ups/drop-offs and a variety of eco courses. Camping $20, dorms $30, cabooses $80, tipis $80

EATING

One of Raglan's charms are the relaxed cafés that make for a great post-surf breakfast or laidback meal. Most places are around the intersection of Bow Street and Wainui Road, and generally run considerably shorter hours in winter.

Raglan Roast Food Department 45 Wainui Road ☎07 282 0248. Laidback pizza joint, based in the old dairy, with a pleasant terrace on which to sit and carve up the large inventive pizzas with friends ($20 upwards). Eat in or takeway. Daily 7am–8.30pm.

Harbour View Hotel 14 Bow St ☎07 825 8010, �🌐harbourviewhotel.co.nz. This reliable hotel/pub has a mix of pub grub – burgers, fish and chips, nachos, etc – steaks, and more inventive options like seafood chowder and herb-crusted snapper (mains $16–39), as well as good beer. Mon–Fri 11am–late, Sat–Sun 8am–late.

Orca Restaurant & Bar 2 Wallis St ☎07 825 6543, ⌐orcarestaurant.co.nz. Raglan's best restaurant, serving brunches, lunches, snacks and standout dinners ($17–34)

like 12-hour marinated beef cheeks and braised pork belly. The attached bar opens onto a deck overlooking the estuary, and has regular live bands. Bar stays open until 1am when busy. Daily 9am–midnight.

★ **Raglan Roast** Volcom Lane ☎07 825 8702, ⌐raglanroast.co.nz. Tucked down a laneway in the town centre, this daytime hole-in-the-wall spills out to a clutch of tables and roasts its knockout coffee (from $3.50) on site. There's a small selection of pastries and cookies. Daily 7am–5pm.

★ **The Shack** 19 Bow St ☎07 825 0027, ⌐theshackraglan.com. Contemporary café with a laidback vibe, a steady flow of interesting locals and an extensive range of imaginative brunch and lunch options, including avocado toast, chickpea and corn fritters, and cinnamon waffles ($11–21), plus smoothies, coffee and alcoholic drinks. Customers get 30min free wi-fi. Daily 8am–4pm.

DRINKING AND NIGHTLIFE

In addition to the option here, several of the restaurants double up as drinking spots: the *Harbourview Hotel* has a traditional pub feel, while the *Orca's* attached bar has sport on TV, a pool table, weekday happy hour (5-6.30pm), an open-mic night on the first Thursday of the month, and regular live bands.

Yot Club 9 Bow St ☎07 825 8968. Raglan's last-night scene is found here: there's frequent gigs and DJ sets, with the genres ranging from hip hop and reggae to rock and funk. For a free pick-up or drop-off, text 02 1103 4156. Wed–Sat 8pm–2am, Sun 4pm–midnight.

Kawhia

Far-flung **KAWHIA**, 55km south of Raglan and a similar distance northwest of Otorohanga, slumbers on the northern side of Kawhia Harbour but wakes up when its population of around five hundred people is joined by over four thousand holidaying Kiwis flocking to **Ocean Beach**, where **Te Puia Hot Springs** bubble from beneath the black sand. At peak time, many come to witness the annual **whaleboat races** (Jan 1), when 11m-long, five-crew whaling boats dash across the bay. The only other site of note is the modest **Kawhia Museum**.

The village centre is strung along Jervois Street, where there's a petrol station and a handful of combined shop/cafés.

THE KING MOVEMENT

Before Europeans arrived, Māori loyalty was solely to their immediate family and tribe, but wrangles with acquisitive European settlers led many tribes to discard age-old feuds in favour of a common crusade against the Pakeha. **Māori nationalism** hardened in the face of blatantly unjust treatment and increasing pressure to "sell" land.

In 1856, the influential Otaki Māori sought a chief who might unite the disparate tribes against the Europeans, and in 1858 the Waikato, Taupo and other tribes, largely originating from the Tainui canoe (see page 201), chose **Te Wherowhero**. Taking the title of **Potatau I**, the newly elected king established himself at Ngaruawahia – to this day the seat of the **King Movement**. The principal tenet of the movement was to resist the appropriation of Māori land and provide a basis for a degree of self-government. Whether out of a genuine misunderstanding of these aims or for reasons of economic expediency, the settlers interpreted the formation of the movement as an act of rebellion – despite the fact that Queen Victoria was included in the movement's prayers – and tension heightened. The situation escalated into armed conflict later in 1858 when the Waitara Block near New Plymouth was confiscated from its Māori owners. The fighting spread throughout the central North Island: the King Movement won a notable victory at Gate Pa, in the Bay of Plenty, but was eventually overwhelmed at Te Ranga.

Seeing the wars as an opportunity to settle old scores, some Māori tribes sided with the British and, in a series of battles along the Waikato, forced the kingites further south, until a crushing blow was struck at Orakau in 1864. The king and his followers fled south of the Puniu River into an area that, by virtue of their presence, became known as the **King Country**.

There they remained, with barely any European contact, until 1881, when **King Tawhiao**, who had succeeded to the throne in 1860, made peace. Gradually the followers of the King Movement drifted back to Ngaruawahia. Although by no means supported by all Māori, the loose coalition of the contemporary King Movement plays an important role in the current reassessment of Māori–Pakeha relations, and the reigning Māori King is the recipient of state and royal visits.

Brief history

Legends tell of the arrival of the **Tainui** in 1350, in their ancestral **waka** (canoe), and of how they found Kawhia Harbour so bountiful that they lived on its shores for three hundred years. Tribal battles over the rich fishing grounds eventually forced them inland, and in 1821, after constant attacks by the better-armed Waikato Māori, the Tainui chief, Te Rauparaha, finally led his people to the relative safety of Kapiti Island.

When the original *waka* arrived in Kawhia, it was tied to a pohutukawa tree, Tangi te Korowhiti, still growing on the shore on Kaora Street, near the junction with Moke Street, 800m west of the museum, and reached along the waterside footpath. The Tainui canoe is buried on a grassy knoll above the beautifully carved and painted **meeting house** of the **Maketu Marae**, further along Kaora Street at Karewa Beach, with Hani and Puna stones marking its stern and prow. The arrival of **European** settlers and missionaries in the 1830s made Kawhia prosperous as a gateway to the fertile King Country, though its fortunes declined in the early years of the twentieth century, owing to its unsuitability for deep-draught ships.

Kawhia Museum

Ommitti St • Nov–March daily 11am–4pm; April–Oct Wed–Sun noon–3pm• Free • ☎ 07 8710 0161

The small **Kawhia Museum** helps to bring to life the region's rich Māori heritage. Among the exhibits are some good carved pieces, a fine modern flax-and-feather cloak and an 1880s-era kauri whaleboat. It shares a building with the tourist information office.

Te Puia Hot Springs

Accessed 4km along the Tainui–Kawhia Forest Rd

It isn't easy to find **Te Puia Hot Springs**, and they're at their best an hour either side of low tide: check times and ask for detailed directions at the museum or any of the local stores. Park at the road-end car park and follow a track over the dunes to where you may find others have already dug shallow holes in the sand. Be warned: the black sand can scorch bare feet and dangerous rip tides make swimming unsafe.

ARRIVAL AND INFORMATION KAWHIA

By car There is no public transport to Kawhia, so you'll need your own wheels to get here.

Tourist information There's a small visitor centre inside the museum (Oct–March daily 11am–4pm; April–Nov Wed–Sun noon–3pm; ⓦ kawhiaharbour.co.nz). Ask about the summer harbour cruises.

ACCOMMODATION AND EATING

Quintessential eating Kawhia-style is fish and chips from one of the town takeaways, eaten on the wharf overlooking the harbour.

Kawhia Camping Ground 73 Moke St ☎ 07 871 0863, ⓦ kawhiacampingground.co.nz. Shady and fairly basic family campsite one block back from the beach with simple but adequate facilities, plus rustic cabins. Camping $18, cabins $50

Kawhia Beachside S-cape 225 Pouewe St (SH31) ☎ 07 871 0727, ⓦ kawhiabeachsidescape.co.nz. Water-side campsite where, a couple of hours either side of high tide, you can launch kayaks (from $10/hr). The cabins are a bit scruffy but the cottages are modern. Camping $20, cottages $135, cabins $75

The King Country

The rural landscape inland from Kawhia and south of Hamilton is known as the **King Country**, because it was the refuge of **King Tawhiao** and members of the **King Movement** (see page 201), after they were driven south during the New Zealand Wars. The area soon gained a reputation among Pakeha as a Māori stronghold renowned for difficult terrain and a welcome that meant few, if any, Europeans entered. However, the forest's respite was short-lived: when peace was declared in 1881, loggers descended in droves.

Tourist interest focuses on **Waitomo**, a tiny village at the heart of a unique and dramatic landscape, honeycombed by limestone caves ethereally illuminated by glowworms, and overlaid by a geological wonderland of karst. North of Waitomo is the small dairy town of **Otorohanga**, with a kiwi house and Kiwiana displays. To the south of Waitomo, **Te Kuiti** provided sanctuary in the 1860s for Māori rebel Te Kooti, who reciprocated with a beautifully carved meeting house.

From Te Kuiti, SH4 runs south to **Taumarunui**, with access to the Whanganui River and the start of the **Forgotten World Highway** (see page 300).

Otorohanga

Surrounded by sheep and cattle country some 30km south of Te Awamutu, **Otorohanga** celebrates all things archetypally Kiwi with street signs bearing kiwi-bird icons and a series of glassed-in shrines to **Kiwiana icons** along the **Ed Hillary Walkway**, off Maniapoto Street next to the ANZ bank. Exhibits include Marmite, pavlova, the farm dog and Hillary himself. A few more displays spill over onto Maniapoto Street.

Otorohanga Kiwi House

20 Alex Telfer Drive, off Kakamutu Rd • Daily: Sept–May 9am–4.30pm; June–Aug 9am–4pm; kiwi feeding daily 10.30am, 1.30pm & 3.30pm • $24 • ☎ 07 873 7391, ⓦ kiwihouse.org.nz

The **Otorohanga Kiwi House** is one of the country's best. Here the grumpy little bird's lifestyle is explained in the well-laid-out nocturnal enclosure, where you really feel close to the birds. Outdoor enclosures contain the lizard-like tuatara and most species of the New Zealand native bird, many in a walk-through aviary. You can catch a kiwi feeding session, and there are also guided twilight tours with plenty of explanation and a chance to see the birds at their most active.

ARRIVAL AND INFORMATION   OTOROHANGA

By train The station is centrally located on Wahanui Crescent.

Destinations National Park (3 weekly; 2hr 20min); Wellington (3 weekly; 9hr).

By bus InterCity and NakedBus both stop on SH3 in the middle of town.

Destinations Hamilton (3 daily; 1hr); Te Kuiti (1 daily; 35min); Waitomo (1 daily; 15min).

Visitor information i-SITE, 27 Turongo St (Oct–April Mon–Fri 9am–5pm, Sat 9am–1pm, May–Sept Mon–Fri 9am–5pm; ☎ 07 873 8951, ⓦ otorohanga.co.nz).

Services You can pick up free wi-fi from the library, adjacent to the i-SITE.

ACCOMMODATION AND EATING

★ **Origin Coffee Station** 7 Wahanui Crescent ☎ 07 873 8550, ⓦ origincoffee.co.nz. The old Otorohanga Railway Station is the venue for the best coffee (from $4) in town, directly imported from Malawi, where the owner, Roger, once grew the stuff. It is roasted on the premises to produce mild but complex flavours. There's also a small selection of cakes, biscuits and pastries. Mon–Fri 8.30am–4.30pm.

Otorohanga Holiday Park 20 Huiputea Drive ☎ 07 873 7253, ⓦ kiwiholidaypark.co.nz. Well-

equipped central campsite in the centre of town with modern facilities including a TV lounge and a children's playground. Staff can also book Waitomo tours. Camping $38, cabins $85

The Thirsty Weta 57 Maniapoto St ☎ 07 873 6699, ⓦ theweta.co.nz. Your best bet for a beer in the sun – or try one of their hearty meals, such as a pot of greenshell mussels with chilli and coconut ($21.50). There's live music on Friday nights. Daily 10am–1am.

Waitomo and around

Some 16km southwest of Otorohanga (8km west of SH3), **WAITOMO** is a diminutive village of under fifty inhabitants with an outsize reputation for incredible **cave trips** and magnificent **karst features** – streams that disappear down funnel-shaped sinkholes (Waitomo means "water entering shaft" in Māori), craggy limestone outcrops, fluted

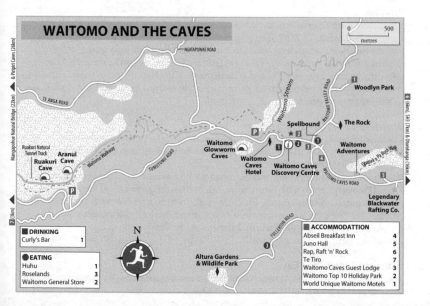

WAITOMO AND THE CAVES

0 ——— 500
metres

DRINKING
Curly's Bar   1

EATING
Huhu   1
Roselands   3
Waitomo General Store   2

ACCOMMODATTION
Abseil Breakfast Inn   4
Juno Hall   5
Rap, Raft 'n' Rock   6
Te Tiro   7
Waitomo Caves Guest Lodge   3
Waitomo Top 10 Holiday Park   2
World Unique Waitomo Motels   1

GLOWWORMS

Glowworms (*Arachnocampa luminosa*) are found across New Zealand, mostly in caves but also on overhanging banks in the bush where in dark and damp conditions you'll often see the telltale bluey-green glow. A glowworm isn't a worm at all, but the matchstick-sized larval stage of the fungus gnat (a relative of the mosquito), which attaches itself to the cave roof and produces around twenty or thirty mucus-and-silk threads or "fishing lines", which hang down a few centimetres. Drawn by the highly efficient chemical light, midges and flying insects get ensnared in the threads and the glowworm draws in the line to eat them.

The six- to nine-month larval stage is the only time in the glowworm **life cycle** that it can eat, so it needs to store energy for the two-week pupal stage when it transforms into the adult gnat that has no mouthparts. The gnat only lives a couple of days, during which time the female has to frantically find a mate in the dark caves (the glow is a big help here) and lay her batch of a hundred or so eggs. After a two- to three-week incubation, they hatch into glowworms and the process begins anew.

3

rocks, potholes and natural bridges caused by cave ceiling collapses. Below ground, seeping water has sculpted the rock into eerie and extraordinary shapes. The ongoing process of **cave creation** involves the interaction of rainwater and carbon dioxide from the air, which together form a weak acid. As more carbon dioxide is absorbed from the soil the acid grows stronger, dissolving the limestone and enlarging cracks and joints, eventually forming the varied caves you see today. Each year a further seventy cubic metres of limestone (about the size of a double-decker bus) is dissolved. Many of the caves are dazzlingly illuminated by **glowworms**, not in fact a worm but really an insect.

Only a fraction of the 45km of cave passages under Waitomo can be visited on **guided tours**. Operators lease access from farmers, so each offers the chance to explore different caves. The get-wet active caving trips are listed in the "Adventure caving" box (see page 206). In all cases, **heavy rain** can lead to cancellations if water levels rise too high. This happens perhaps ten days a year, so it pays to check weather forecasts and plan accordingly.

Brief history

Local chief **Tane Tinorau** introduced Waitomo's underground passages to English surveyor **Fred Mace**, in 1887. The pair explored further, building a raft of flax stems and drifting along an underground stream, with candles their only source of light. Within a year, the enterprising Tane was guiding tourists to see the spectacle. The government took over in 1906 and it wasn't until 1989 that the caves were returned to their Māori owners, who receive a percentage of all revenue generated and participate in the site's management.

Waitomo Caves Discovery Centre

I-SITE, 21 Waitomo Caves Rd • Daily: late Dec–mid-Jan 8.30am–6.45pm, mid-Jan–late Feb 8.30am–6pm, late Feb–early April 8.45am–5.30pm, early April–late Oct 8.45am–5pm, late Oct–late Dec 8.45am–5.30pm • $5, though free or discounted with many caving trips • ☎ 07 878 7640, Ⓦ waitomocaves.com

Your underground experience will be enhanced by a prior visit to the small **Waitomo Caves Discovery Centre** with informative exhibits on the geology and history of the caves, interactive displays on the life cycle of glowworms and **cave wetas** (prehistoric grasshopper-like creepy crawlies) and a free eighteen-minute multimedia show, screened on request. If you're worried about tight underground passages, test out your nerve (and girth) on the cave crawl.

Waitomo Glowworm Caves

39 Waitomo Caves Rd • Daily 9am–5pm plus summer twilight tours; 45min tours depart every 30min • $51; combination ticket available: with Aranui cave $76; with Ruakuri cave $91; all 3 caves $97 • ☎ 0800 456 922, Ⓦ waitomo.com

Bus tours all stop at Waitomo's original cave experience, **Waitomo Glowworm Caves**, 500m west of the i-SITE. Paved walkways and lighting pick out the best of the stalactites and stalagmites and there's a boat ride through the grotto, where glowworms form a heavenly canopy of ghostly pale-green pinpricks of light. The fairly steep price is offset by combos with Ruakuri and Aranui caves (see below), and a ten-percent online discount when booked 48 hours in advance. To avoid the crowds, take the first or last tour of the day.

Ruakuri and Aranui caves

Ruakuri Scenic Reserve, 3.5km west of the i-SITE • **Ruakuri** Tours daily 9am, 10am, 11am, 12.30pm, 1.30pm, 2.30pm & 3.30pm; 2hr with 1hr 30min underground • $74 • **Aranui** Tours daily 9.30am, 11am, 1pm, 2.30pm & 4pm; 1hr • $50 • ☎ 0800 782 587, ⓦ waitomo.com

You descend into a vast, theatrically lit void to access the "The Den of the Dogs" as **Ruakuri Cave**'s name translates. Waitomo's longest guided underground walking tour follows suspended walkways linking spectacular, subtly lit cavern passages as guides thread the practicalities of cave creation and the glowworm life cycle with Māori stories. The whole trip is wheelchair accessible.

The Glowworm Caves office also sells tickets for tours around the **Aranui Cave**, which, although only 250m long, is geologically spectacular, with high-ceilinged chambers and magnificent stalactites and stalagmites. You'll see cave wetas here but no glowworms.

Spellbound

10 Waitomo Caves Rd • Tours July–May 10am, 11am, 2pm & 3pm • 3hr • $75 • ☎ 0800 773 552, ⓦ glowworm.co.nz

For a gentle but impressive underground experience it is hard to beat **Spellbound**'s two-cave combo, starting off with a peaceful drift along a subterranean stream under a canopy of magnificent glowworms. The second cave has the pick of the limestone formations, a moa skeleton and expert explanation of the processes that create the weird forms and force the passages to cross a natural faultline.

Woodlyn Park

1177 Waitomo Valley Rd, 1km north of Waitomo • Show daily, typically at 1.30pm (check ahead; 1hr) • $28 • ☎ 07 878 6666, ⓦ woodlynpark.co.nz

Woodlyn Park hosts the entertaining **Billy Black's Kiwi Culture Show**, an offbeat look at the history of logging and farming, with loads of audience participation such as helping shear sheep or chop wood, always with a dollop of rural Kiwi humour. Even if this is normally the sort of thing you'd run a mile from, take a chance on this – it's good fun.

ARRIVAL AND DEPARTURE   WAITOMO

By train and bus The nearest trains, InterCity and Naked buses stop 15km away in Otorohanga, from where the Waitomo Shuttle ($15 one way; bookings essential; ☎ 0800 808 279) ferries people to Waitomo. Great Sights buses (run by InterCity) run daily to Waitomo on their Auckland–Rotorua run. The Waitomo Wanderer (☎ 0800 000 4321) runs daily from Rotorua (and Taupo by prior booking). Tickets available at the i-SITE.

Bus destinations Auckland (3 most days; 3hr); Otorohanga (1 daily; 15min); Rotorua (1 daily; 2hr 30min).

INFORMATION

i-SITE, 21 Waitomo Caves Rd, inside the Waitomo Caves Discovery Centre (see page 204). This mine of information acts as a booking agent for cave trips; pick up the free *Waitomo Caves* map, which shows local walks.

Services Though there is an ATM, there is no bank, petrol or supermarket at Waitomo; the nearest are 15km away at Otorohanga and Te Kuiti. The i-SITE has a post office and internet access.

ACCOMMODATION

Abseil Breakfast Inn 709 Waitomo Caves Rd, 400m east of the museum ☎ 07 878 7815, ⓦ abseilinn. co.nz; map p.203. Charge up the very steep drive to this relaxing and stylish B&B on top of a hill, with great views from the four individually styled rooms and the lovely BBQ deck. Your enthusiastic host will keep you

3

ADVENTURE CAVING

Waitomo excels at adrenaline-fuelled **adventure-caving trips**, which need to be booked in advance, especially in the period between November and January. Most involve getting kitted out in a wetsuit, rubber boots and a caver's helmet with lamp, and combine two or more adventure elements. Children under twelve (or under a minimum weight) are not usually allowed on adventure trips, and the wilder trips are for those sixteen and over.

Access to some caves is by **abseiling**. Some trips feature **cave tubing** (also known as blackwater rafting), generally involving wedging your derrière inside a rubber ring for a (usually) gentle float through a pitch-black section of cave gazing at a galaxy of glowworm light overhead.

★ **The Legendary Black Water Rafting Co** 585 Waitomo Caves Rd ☎0800 228 464, ⓦ waitomo. com. A range of trips in Ruakuri Cave, the easiest being the Black Labyrinth (3hr; 1hr underground; $138), which includes scrambling through the caves, an idyllic float through a glowworm-clad tunnel on a cave tube and two short jumps from underground waterfalls. The more adventurous Black Abyss (5hr; 2–3hr underground; $240) kicks off with a 35m abseil down a narrow *tomo* followed by an eerie flying-fox ride into darkness, some floating among glowworms and an exciting scramble back to the surface up two short waterfalls. If you'd rather not get wet, but still fancy working up some adrenalin, the Black Odyssey tour (5hr; $185) takes you through the caves on a series of high wires, featuring spider walks and flying foxes to really test that head for heights.

Rap, Raft 'n' Rock 95 Waitomo Caves Rd/ SH37, 8km east of the i-SITE, 1km from the junction with SH3 ☎0800 228 372, ⓦ blackwaterraftingwaitomo.co.nz. Budget, everything-in-one, small-group trips starting with a 27m abseil into a glowworm-filled cave explored partly on foot and partly floating on a tube, and ending with a rock climb out to the starting point (5hr; $250).

Waitomo Adventures Waitomo Caves Rd ☎0800 924 866, ⓦ waitomo.co.nz. Professional outfit offering five trips, including its signature Lost World (4hr; $405) – a glorious, spine-tingling 100m abseil into the gaping fern-draped mouth of a spectacular pothole, followed by a relatively dry cave walk before climbing out on a seemingly endless ladder. Cave junkies should go for the Lost World Epic (7hr; $580, including lunch underground and BBQ dinner above), where an abseil is followed by several "wet" hours, navigating upstream through squeezes, behind a small waterfall and into a glittering glowworm grotto. There's also an abseil-free cave tubing trip (4hr; $190), the active abseil-heavy Haggas Honking Holes (4hr; $275) and St Benedict's Caverns (3hr 30min; $215), a dry trip with abseils and a flying fox. Save twenty percent if you book more than 12hr ahead.

entertained, and the breakfasts (as you might expect) are a highlight. $180

Juno Hall 600 Waitomo Caves Rd, 1km east of Waitomo ☎07 878 7649, ⓦ junowaitomo.co.nz; map p.203. Cosy, well-equipped associate YHA hostel in a timber-lined building set on a low hill by a pool, BBQ deck and a tennis court, with the chance to hand-feed baby animals. Some powered sites ($19). Dorms $33, doubles $80

Rap, Raft 'n' Rock 95 Waitomo Caves Rd/SH37, 8km east of the i-SITE, 1km from the junction with SH3 ☎0800 228 372, ⓦ blackwaterraftingwaitomo. co.nz; map p.203. Homey backpacker digs attached to an adventure-caving operator with brightly painted ten-bed dorms, a cosy lounge, kitchen and sunny courtyard. Dorms $30, doubles $70

Te Tiro 9km west of Waitomo ☎07 878 6328, ⓦ waitomocavesnz.com; map p.203. Cosy self-contained cottages (sleeping up to five people) with fabulous views and a glowworm grotto. Breakfast goodies are included, but if you're cooking, bring food or something for the BBQ. $140

Waitomo Caves Guest Lodge 7 Te Anga Rd, 100m east of the museum ☎07 878 7641, ⓦ waitomocavesguestlodge.co.nz; map p.203. Eight comfortable, good-value rooms (some in cabins with good views) perched on a hillside in a lovely garden. There's no kitchen, but guests have use of a microwave and fridge-freezer. $110

Waitomo Top 10 Holiday Park 12 Waitomo Caves Rd ☎07 878 7639, ⓦ waitomopark.co.nz; map p.203. Well-equipped campsite in the heart of town, with lots of fairly new cabins of varying levels of comfort, plus a swimming pool and spa for soaking after your underground adventure. Camping $25, cabins $95

★ **World Unique Waitomo Motels** 1177 Waitomo Valley Rd, 1km north ☎07 878 6666, ⓦ woodlynpark. co.nz; map p.203. Ingenious accommodation on the site of Billy Black's Kiwi Culture Show (see page 205). Sleep in a Bristol freighter aircraft converted into two comfortable self-contained units; a 1914 railway carriage containing a three-room unit; two hobbit holes with circular entrances sunk into a hillside; and a converted World War II patrol boat; among several others. Book at least a month ahead for Dec–Feb. Self-contained campervans can park here for free. **$180**

EATING

★ **Huhu** 10 Waitomo Caves Rd ☎ 07 878 6674, ⍟ huhucafe.co.nz; map p.203. Classy restaurant with a short lunch menu including soup with soft, chewy *rewana* (Māori bread) with herb butter. Dinner dishes (from $30) include bacon-wrapped pork loin. King Country Brewing Company beer is on tap and there's a downstairs bar dedicated to these local brews. Reservations are recommended in the evenings. Daily noon–9pm.

Roselands 579 Fullerton Rd, 3km south of the i-SITE ☎ 07 878 7611, ⍟ roselands-restaurant.co.nz; map p.203. Fish or meat (or vegetarian options by prior arrangement) sizzles on the barbecue on the deck of this garden-set restaurant in a beautiful hillside location. Morning and afternoon teas are among the other options. Fixed-priced lunch/dinner buffet $36. Daily 8am–late.

★ **Waitomo General Store** 15 Waitomo Caves Rd ☎ 07 878 8613; map p.203. A modern take on the classic general store with groceries, organic meat and cone ice-cream, plus excellent coffee (from $4), great pies and a wide range of breakfasts. Daily 8am–3.30pm.

DRINKING

Curly's Bar School Rd ☎ 07 878 8448, ⍟ curlysbar. co.nz; map p.203. Almost everyone eventually ends up at this unreconstructed Kiwi pub, either for convivial boozing or good-value meals in the steak, seafood and burger tradition (mains mostly $15–30). Sport on the TV and occasional live music. Daily 11am–2am.

Mangapohue Natural Bridge
Te Anga Rd, 24km west of Waitomo

The finest free limestone sight hereabouts is the **Mangapohue Natural Bridge**, an easy fifteen-minute loop trail through forest to a riverside boardwalk leading into a narrow limestone gorge topped by a double bridge formed by the remains of a collapsed cave roof. It's especially dazzling at night when the undersides glimmer with constellations of glowworms. In daylight, don't miss the rest of the walk, through farmland past fossilized examples of giant oysters, 35 million years old.

Piripiri Caves and Marakopa Falls
Te Anga Rd, 4km west of Mangapohue Natural Bridge

A five-minute walk through a forested landscape full of weathered limestone outcrops brings you to **Piripiri Caves**. Inside the cavern you'll need a decent torch (and an emergency spare) to explore the Oyster Room, which contains giant fossil oysters, though there are no glowworms.

A kilometre or so on, a track (15min return) accesses one of the area's most dramatic waterfalls, the multitiered 30m **Marokopa Falls**, through a jungle-like rainforest of tawa, pukatea and kohekohe trees.

Te Kuiti

The "Shearing Capital of the World", **TE KUITI**, 19km south of Waitomo, greets visitors with a 7m-high statue of a man shearing a sheep at the southern end of Rora Street, and hosts the annual New Zealand **Shearing and Wool Handling Championships** in late March or early April; get details from the **i-SITE**.

At the south end of Rora Street on Awakino Road is a magnificently carved **meeting house**, Te Tokanganui-a-noho, left by Māori rebel Te Kooti in the nineteenth century in thanks for sanctuary.

INFORMATION   TE KUITI

Tourist office The i-SITE is on Rora St (Mon–Fri 9am–5pm,   Sat & Sun 10am–2pm; ☎ 07 878 8077, ⍟ waitomo.govt.nz).

EATING

Bosco Café 57 Te Kumi Rd (SH3), 1km north of town ☏ 07 878 3633. Pleasant café in an airy pine-and-plywood building, serving great coffee, smoothies, home-made pies and a range of breakfasts (from $10) and lunches. Daily 8am–5pm.

Mokau and around

Southwest of Te Kuiti, SH3 makes a beeline for the Tasman Sea and the small coastal town of **MOKAU**, noted for its run of whitebait from mid-August to November – and there are plenty of opportunities to sample it in the local cafés around this time. The highway then twists its way through tiny communities, sandwiched between spectacular black beaches and steep inland ranges. Opportunities for exploration focus on the wonderful **Whitecliffs Walkway**; eventually the scenery opens out onto the Taranaki Plains just north of New Plymouth.

Whitecliffs Walkway

47km south of Mokau; starts on Pukearuhe Rd, off SH3, 11km northwest of Mimi • 5km return; 4–7hr; flat

Though billed as a 4–7hr loop walk over the hills and back along the beach, it is the beach section that really makes the **Whitecliffs Walkway** special, and that's the walk described here. Start by the steep Pukearuhe boat ramp, then simply follow the beach north with the Tasman breakers sweeping up the beach towards high, off-white sandstone cliffs. Calm pools, boulder fields and the odd stream–crossing keep it interesting until you reach the **Te Horo Stock Tunnel**, an 80m-long passage bored through the cliff in the 1870s to allow stock to be driven along the beach, on up to the clifftops and then beyond to market. The tunnel itself is crumbling and is officially closed, though repairs are planned. Return along the beach or follow the Walkway signs back across the bush-clad hills following the route of a buried gas pipeline. If you want to do the whole thing rather than just the beach section, start 2hr before low tide.

EATING AND DRINKING   **MOKAU AND AROUND**

Mike's Organic Brewery 487 Mokau Rd (SH3), 48km south of Mokau ☏ 05 0846 4537, ✆ mikesbeer.co.nz. This craft brewery of international standing produces organic brews using rainwater – including Strawberry Blonde, made from organic strawberries. Buy to take away or sit in the garden over a beer flight (from $12). Daily 10am–5pm.

Taumarunui

Some 83km south of Te Kuiti, at the confluence of the Ongarue and Whanganui rivers, **TAUMARUNUI** is a little down on its luck. One of the last towns in New Zealand to be settled by Europeans, who arrived in large numbers in 1908, when the railway came to town, it has been in decline since the end of the 1990s' timber boom. Still, it is well located at the northern end of the Forgotten World Highway (with its associated cycle trail) and is a base for canoe trips on the Whanganui River (see page 310).

Raurimu Spiral

Visible from a signposted viewpoint 37km south of Taumarunui on SH4

Finding a suitable route for the railroad on its steep descent north towards Taumarunui from the area around the Tongariro National Park proved problematic, but surveyor R.W. Holmes' ingenious solution, the **Raurimu Spiral**, is a remarkable feat of engineering combining bridges and tunnels to loop the track over and under itself. Sadly, trains no longer stop at Taumaruni.

ARRIVAL AND INFORMATION   **TAUMARUNUI**

By bus Buses stop opposite the train station on Hakiaha St. Destinations Hamilton (1 daily; 2hr 40min); National Park (1 daily; 30min); Te Kuiti (1 daily; 1hr); Wanganui (1 daily; 2hr 40min).

Tourist information Located at the train station, the i-SITE (daily 8.30am–5pm; ☎ 07 895 7494) has a model train replica of the Raurimu Spiral, internet access, books accommodation and sells Whanganui National Park Hut and Camp passes.

ACCOMMODATION AND EATING

Jasmine's Thai Café 43 Hakiaha St (SH4) ☎ 07 895 5822, ⊕ jasminesthai.co.nz. If you're after a hit of spice, head to this great Thai restaurant for a nourishing red, green, yellow, jungle, massaman or penang curry (mains $16.50–22). Daily 8am–9pm.

Taumarunui Holiday Park SH4 3km east ☎ 0800 473 281, ⊕ taumarunuiholidaypark.co.nz. Small, well-run site wedged between the Whanganui River and a grove of native bush at the start of the riverside Mananui Walkway (3km). There are simple wood-lined cabins, a self-contained cottage sleeping seven and a play area. Camping $18, cabins $55

The Hauraki Plains

North of Hamilton and southeast of the Coromandel Peninsula, the fertile **Hauraki Plains** form a low-lying former swamp-turned-farming region that, in typically laconic Kiwi fashion, describes itself as "flat out and loving it". The Firth of Thames, the final destination for a number of meandering rivers, borders it to the north. The hub of the plains is **Paeroa**, not much in itself but handy for walks in the magnificent **Karangahake Gorge**, running almost to **Waihi**. The real gem hereabouts is **Te Aroha**, a delightful Edwardian spa town at the southern extremity of the plains, where you can hike Mount Te Aroha and soak afterwards in natural hot soda springs.

Paeroa

PAEROA, 73km northeast of Hamilton, is "World Famous in New Zealand" as the birthplace of **Lemon and Paeroa** (L&P), an iconic home-grown soft drink founded in 1907 using the local mineral water (though it is now made elsewhere by Coca-Cola). The L&P logo is emblazoned on shopfronts throughout town and there's a giant brown L&P bottle at the junction of SH2 and SH26.

ARRIVAL AND INFORMATION   PAEROA

By bus InterCity and NakedBus stop outside the Information Centre on their Auckland–Tauranga run. Services on Hamilton's BusIt network (☎ 0800 428 748, ⊕ busit.co.nz) go between Hamilton and Paeroa via Te Aroha, and from Coromandel to Hamilton via Thames, Paeroa and Te Aroha.

Destinations Auckland (3 daily; 2hr 20min); Hamilton (2 daily; 1hr 35min); Te Aroha (1 daily; 20min); Thames (3 daily; 30min).

Tourist information The Paeroa Information Hub (Mon–Fri 8.30am–4pm, Sat 9am–4pm, Sun 9am–3pm; ☎ 07 862 8636) is at 101 Normanby Rd.

EATING

L&P Café, Bar & Brasserie Corner of SH2 and Seymour St ☎ 07 862 7773, ⊕ lpcafe.co.nz. Sells L&P-flavoured ice cream as well as filling, and sometimes artfully presented breakfast, lunch and dinners, including good burgers ($17–22), salads, and mains like pork ribs. Mon & Tues 8am–5pm, Wed–Sun 8am–10pm.

Karangahake Gorge

Karangahake Gorge SH2, 8km east of Paeroa, was the scene of the Coromandel's first gold rush, though in this leafy cleft it's hard to envisage the frenetic activity that took place around the turn of the twentieth century. The steep-sided gorge snakes along SH2 as it traces the Ohinemuri River to Waihi.

The largest (though still tiny) settlement is **KARANGAHAKE**, where a car park marks the start of several excellent walks along the rivers and around old gold-mining ruins. They range from twenty minutes to several hours and are detailed in DOC's

Karangahake Gorge leaflet. Beyond, minuscule **Waikino** is the western terminus of the Goldfields Railway (see page 232).

Karangahake Tunnel Loop Walk

3km; 45min; mostly flat

At Karangahake, a pedestrian suspension bridge crosses the river to join a **loop walk**, heading upstream beside the Ohinemuri River, past remnants of the gold workings and the foundations of stamper batteries, hugging the cliffs and winding through native bush. You complete the loop by crossing the river and walking through a 1km-long tunnel (partially but adequately lit), where you can spot glowworms.

Karangahake Gorge Historic Walkway

To explore the length of the gorge, follow the **Karangahake Gorge Historic Walkway** that covers 7km of a former rail line right through the gorge as far east as the *Waikino Station Café*. One section is shared by the Karangahake Tunnel Loop Walk (see above) and the full length has been made suitable for **bikes** as part of the National Cycle Network and the Hauraki Rail Trail (⍟haurakirailtrail.co.nz).

Victoria Battery

The stumpy remains of the **Victoria Battery** mark the eastern end of Karangahake Gorge. The area's gold ore was processed here from 1897 until 1952, using up to 200 stamps to crush 800 tonnes a day, at one stage making it the largest such site in Australasia. Explanatory panels clarify the mysterious-looking concrete foundations. On Wednesdays, Sundays and public holidays (10am–3pm) you can ride a tram (Alfred is converted from a milk float) or visit the museum (⍟vbts.org.nz) at the top of the hill – ask one of the enthusiastic volunteers to demonstrate the stamper.

ACCOMMODATION AND EATING   KARANGAHAKE GORGE

★**The Falls Retreat** 25 Waitawheta Rd, opposite Owharoa Falls ☎07 863 8770, ⍟fallsretreat.co.nz. Sit in the shade under the trees or in the rustic cottage at this delightfully peaceful café and restaurant, which whips up thin-crust, wood-fired pizza and mains ($26–38) such as porchetta. There is also a pair of self-catering cottages ($150). Jan & Feb daily 11am–10pm; March–Dec Wed–Sun 11am–8.30pm.

Karangahake Winery Estate 23b Moresby St ☎07 862 8874, ⍟forbiddenfruitwine.co.nz. Formerly called *Ohinemuri*, this is a combined winery, restaurant and guesthouse. You can sample the wines (made here with

grapes grown elsewhere), tuck into café fare, and stay the night in one of the spacious double rooms ($120). Nov–Easter Monday daily 10am–6pm; rest of year Wed–Sun 10am–4pm.

Waikino Station Café SH2, 13km east of Paeroa ☎07 863 8640. The original Waikino train station (still served by the Goldfields Railway from Waihi) makes a superb setting for this good café with great old photos and a roaring fire in winter. Expect breakfasts, sandwiches and burgers ($11–20) plus cakes and coffee. Sometimes closes early if it's quiet. Mon–Fri 10am–3pm, Sat & Sun 9.30am–4pm.

Te Aroha

On the fringes of the Hauraki Plains, the small town of **TE AROHA**, 21km south of Paeroa, is home to New Zealand's only intact **Edwardian spa**. In a quiet way it is a delightful spot, hunkered beneath the imposing bush-clad slopes of the **Kaimai-Mamaku Forest Park**. The 952m **Mount Te Aroha** rears up immediately behind the neat little town centre, providing a reasonably challenging goal for hikers. The town itself is a good base for the relaxing Hauraki Rail Trail.

Everything of interest – banks, post office, library – is on or close to Whitaker Street, the old-fashioned feel enhanced by an old air-raid **siren** which sounds daily at 8am, 1pm (midday in winter) and 5pm: some people still measure their day by it.

Brief history

The town was founded in 1880 at the furthest navigable extent of the Waihou River. A year later, rich deposits of gold were discovered on Mount Te Aroha, sparking a full-scale **gold rush** until 1921. Within a few months of settlement, the new townsfolk set out the attractive **Hot Springs Domain**, 44 acres of gardens and rose beds around a cluster of **hot soda springs** which, by the 1890s, had become New Zealand's most popular mineral spa complex. Enclosures were erected for privacy, most rebuilt in grand style during the Edwardian years. The fine suite of original buildings has been restored and integrated with more modern pools fed by the springs and nearby **Mokena Geyser**.

Te Aroha Mineral Spas

Hot Springs Domain • Mon–Thurs & Sun 10.30am–9pm, Fri & Sat 10.30am–10pm • $19/person for 30min, minimum 2 people; advance bookings essential • ☎ 07 884 8717, ⓦ tearohamineralspas.co.nz

Te Aroha's centrepiece is the **Mineral Spas**, where the silky-smooth mineral waters of the Mokena Geyser are channelled into private, enclosed pools, usually kept at 40°C though you can adjust the temperature. Choose a king-size claw-foot slipper bath if you fancy adding aromatherapy oils; otherwise go for one of the six, bubbling cedar tubs, good for up to eight people. A half-hour soak in the hot, naturally carbonated water is plenty. Not only will your skin feel gloriously soft (don't shower directly afterwards), but it's claimed that the alkaline waters extract polluting heavy metals from your system and ease arthritis. Fear of people fainting and drowning means you're not allowed to bathe alone. Assorted pampering and massage treatments are also available.

Swim Zone Te Aroha

Hot Springs Domain • Mon–Fri 10am–5.45pm, Sat & Sun 10am–6.45pm • $6 • **Spa pool** Mon & Wed–Sun 11am–4pm • $18 • ☎ 07 884 4498, ⓦ swimzonepools.co.nz

There's a family feel to the outdoor **Swim Zone Te Aroha**, where regular town water is chlorinated and kept at around 32°C in the 20m-long main pool and around 38°C in the spa. There's also a toddlers' pool and, nearby, a free 36°C **foot-spa** that's perfect for a bit of pampering at the end of a Mount Te Aroha hike.

Mokena Geyser

Hot Springs Domain

Just uphill from the Mokena Spa Baths is the erratic **Mokena Geyser** (said to be the world's only hot soda geyser), which goes off roughly every forty minutes to a height of four metres – on a good day. Due to its spa-feeding duties it doesn't always spurt to an impressive height, so take a coffee and a book while you wait.

Te Aroha and District Museum

102 Whitaker St • Daily: Nov–Easter Monday 11am–4pm; rest of year noon–3pm • $5 • ☎ 07 884 4427, ⓦ tearoha-museum.com

An old sanatorium, just below the spa baths in front of the croquet lawn, houses the exhibit-packed town **museum**. Highlights include two finely decorated Royal Doulton Victorian lavatories, a chemical analysis of the local soda water, the remains of Pelton power station, and over three hundred pieces of souvenir porcelain.

St Mark's Anglican Church

Corner of Church and Kenrick sts • Often open during the day; call ahead • ☎ 07 884 9292

By the Boundary Street exit from the Domain you'll find the 1926 **St Mark's Anglican Church**, insignificant but for the incongruous 1712 organ, brought to New Zealand in 1926 and said to be the oldest in the southern hemisphere. Ask at the i-SITE about organ demonstrations.

3

Mount Te Aroha

Immediately east of the Hot Springs Domain

The town edges up onto the lower slopes of **Mount Te Aroha** (952m), which, legend has it, was named by a young Arawa chief, Kahumatamomoe, who climbed it after losing his way in the region's swamp while making for Maketu in the Bay of Plenty. Delighted to see the familiar shoreline of his homeland, he called the mountain Te Aroha, "love", in honour of his father and kinsmen. There are some great new mountain-bike tracks and enough **trails** to keep you entertained for a day or so; two of the best walks are Bald Spur Track and Summit Track.

Bald Spur Track

3km return; 1hr 30min; 900m ascent

The most rewarding short hike is the tramp to and from the Hot Springs Domain up through a lovely puriri and fern grove, climbing fairly steeply to a bench and lookout point known as Whakapipi or **Bald Spur**. With great views across the town and farmland beyond, it is particularly good before breakfast or towards sunset.

Summit Track

8km return; 4–6hr; 900m ascent

The thigh-burning **Summit Track** ascent builds on the Bald Spur walk, continuing steeply up into the Kaimai-Mamaku Forest Park and gradually getting rougher to the TV transmitter at the top. The reward (on a fine day) is a 360-degree view, as far as Ruapehu and Taranaki. Return by the same route or the longer **Tui Mine Track** (extra 1–2hr) via old mine workings.

ARRIVAL AND INFORMATION

TE AROHA

By bus Services on Hamilton's Busit network (☎0800 428 748, ⓦbusit.co.nz) stop at Kenrick St on SH26.
Destinations Hamilton (1 daily; 1hr 5min); Paeroa (1 daily; 20min).
Visitor information i-SITE is at 102 Whitaker St (Mon–

Fri 9.30am–5pm, Sat & Sun 9.30am–4pm; ☎07 884 8052, ⓦtearohanz.co.nz). This is New Zealand's oldest information centre (dating back to 1894), handing out local and DOC information along with leaflets on day-walks in the area. They can also advise on bike hire.

ACCOMMODATION

★**Aroha Mountain Lodge** 5 Boundary St ☎07 884 8134, ⓦarohamountainlodge.co.nz. Opt for comfortable rooms in a pair of villas right next to the Hot Springs Domain, or the lime green *Chocolate Box*, a cute self-contained cottage sleeping up to eight. Breakfast costs $20/person extra. Doubles $145, cottages $320
The Nunnery 16 Burgess St ☎07 884 4436, ⓦthenunnery.co.nz. Built in 1977 to house the Sisters of Mercy, this former convent is now a charming guesthouse, located closed to the town centre. The hosts are friendly

and the a/c rooms are clean and comfortable. Doubles $85, studios $110
Te Aroha Holiday Park 217 Stanley Rd, 3km south, off the road to Hamilton ☎07 884 9567, ⓦtearohaholidaypark.co.nz. Traditional site set among shady oaks, with a flying fox, mineral water rock pool (evenings only), large summer-only swimming pool and a haphazard range of mismatched buildings that have accumulated over the decades. Camping $35, cabins $60

EATING AND DRINKING

Ironique 159 Whitaker St ☎07 884 8489, ⓦironique.co.nz. This friendly all-rounder is a good bet all day – pop in for some good coffee ($4–5) and a slice of cake or pastry (try the lemon and raspberry muffins). Alternatively, you can head here for a beer (from $8). Mon & Tues 8am–4pm, Wed–Sun 8am–10pm.
Palace Hotel 165 Whitaker St ☎07 884 4536, ⓦpalacehoteltearoha.co.nz. Typical Kiwi pub, with international flags fluttering outside, live music on Fridays,

good beer and hearty main meals ($14–30), including decent pizzas. Mon–Thurs 9am–8pm, Fri & Sat 9am–late, Sun 11am–late.
★**Villa Nine** 9 Lawrence Avenue ☎07 884 9696. Although it describes itself as an "organic health shop", there's plenty for gluttons here, including ice cream-rich milkshakes and a raw "Snickers" cake, alongside the green juices, smoothies, salads and meals ($16–25) like asparagus and lemon frittata. Mon–Fri 8am–4.30pm, Sat 8am–4pm.

The Coromandel Peninsula

The Hauraki Gulf is separated from the Pacific Ocean by the mountainous, bush-cloaked **Coromandel Peninsula**, fringed with beautiful surf and swimming beaches and basking in a balmy climate.

Along the **west coast**, cliffs and steep hills drop sharply to the sea, leaving only a narrow coastal strip shaded by **pohutukawa** trees that erupt in a blaze of red from mid-November to early January. The beaches are sheltered and safe but most are only good for **swimming** when high tide obscures the mudflats. Most people prefer the sweeping white-sand beaches of the **east coast**, which are pounded by impressive but often perilous **surf**.

At the base of the peninsula, **Thames** showcases its gold-mining heritage and is the most convenient place from which to explore the forested **Kauaeranga Valley**'s walking tracks. Further north, **Coromandel town** offers the opportunity to ride the narrow-gauge **Driving Creek Railway** and is close to the scenic trans-peninsular 309 Road. For really remote country, however, head to **Colville** and beyond, to the peninsula's northern tip. The sealed SH25 continues east to **Mercury Bay**, centred on more populous **Whitianga**, near which you can dig a hole to wallow in the surfside hot springs that lure hundreds to **Hot Water Beach**, or snorkel in a gorgeous bay at **Cathedral Cove Marine Reserve**. Yet more beaches string the coast further south around **Whangamata** and **Waihi Beach**, which is separated from nearby **Waihi** by about 10km of farms and orchards.

If you're here between mid-November and early December you'll come across the **Pohutukawa Festival**, during which the whole peninsula marks the crimson blooms of these distinctive coastal trees with picnics, wearable art competitions and music.

Brief history

The peninsula is divided lengthwise by the **Coromandel Range** – sculpted millions of years ago by volcanic activity, its contorted skyline clothed in dense rainforest. Local Māori interpret the range as a canoe, with **Mount Moehau** (the peninsula's northern tip) as its prow, and Mount Te Aroha in the south as its sternpost. The summit area of Mount Moehau is sacred, Māori-owned land, the legendary burial place of Tama Te Kapua, the commander of one of the Great Migration canoes, *Te Arawa*.

Except for the gold-rush years, the peninsula largely remained a backwater, and by the 1960s and 70s, the low property prices in declining former gold towns, combined with the juxtaposition of bush, hills and beaches, lured hippies, **artists** and New Agers. Most eked out a living from organic market gardens, or holistic healing centres and retreats, while painters, potters and **craftspeople**, some very good, hawked their work. These days much of the peninsula is a more commercial animal: increasingly Aucklanders are finding ways to live here permanently or commute, and are converting one-time *baches* into expensive designer properties, raising both the area's profile and the cost of living.

VISITING THE COROMANDEL

As one of the North Island's main **holiday destinations**, the Coromandel Peninsula is frenetic from late Dec–Jan with little real relief until the end of March. Book as far ahead as you can. Numbers are more manageable for the rest of the year (though long weekends fill quickly), and in winter much of the peninsula is deserted, though the climate remains mild.

The issue of limiting **freedom camping** (see page 40) really came to a head on the peninsula and rules are stricter here than elsewhere – and enforced. You can only legally freedom-camp in a certified self-contained vehicle, and only in a very few places: search for freedom camping at ⓦ tcdc.govt.nz for the latest.

Thames

The Coromandel's gateway and main service hub, the historic former gold town of **THAMES** is packed into a narrow strip between the Firth of Thames and the Coromandel Range. It retains a refreshingly down-to-earth sense of community, and its range of accommodation, eateries, transport connections and generally lower prices make it a good starting point for forays further north.

Its gold legacy forms the basis of Thames' appeal and you can spend half a day visiting the several museums, though they're all volunteer-run and, frustratingly, open at different times – summer weekends are best. Fans of Victorian **architecture** can spend a happy couple of hours wandering the streets aided by the maps in two free leaflets – *Historic Grahamstown* and *Historic Shortland & Tararu*.

Inland, the industrial heritage is all about kauri logging in the **Kauaeranga Valley**, a popular destination for hikers visiting the Coromandel Forest Park and easily accessible from town.

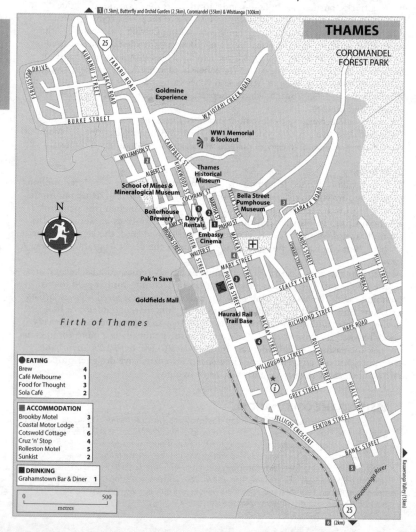

THAMES

COROMANDEL FOREST PARK

(1.5km), Butterfly and Orchid Garden (2.5km), Coromandel (55km) & Whitianga (100km)

Goldmine Experience

WW1 Memorial & lookout

Thames Historical Museum

School of Mines & Mineralogical Museum

Bella Street Pumphouse Museum

Boilerhouse Brewery

Davy's Rentals

Embassy Cinema

Pak 'n Save

Goldfields Mall

Firth of Thames

Hauraki Rail Trail Base

Kauaeranga Valley (13km)

Kauaeranga River

EATING	
Brew	4
Café Melbourne	1
Food for Thought	3
Sola Café	2

ACCOMMODATION	
Brookby Motel	3
Coastal Motor Lodge	1
Cotswold Cottage	6
Cruz 'n' Stop	4
Rolleston Motel	5
Sunkist	2

DRINKING	
Grahamstown Bar & Diner	1

0   500
metres

Brief history

Thames initially evolved as two towns: **Grahamstown** to the north and **Shortland** to the south. The first big discovery of gold-bearing quartz was made in a creek-bed in 1867, and by 1871 Grahamstown had become the largest town in New Zealand with a population of around 20,000 and over 120 pubs, only a handful of which remain today. Due to the reliance on machinery (rather than less costly gold-panning), gold mining tailed off during the 1880s and had mostly finished by 1913. Little of significance has happened since.

Goldmine Experience

Corner SH25 and Moanataiari Creek Rd • May–Aug Sat & Sun 10am–1pm; Oct–April daily 10am–4pm • $15 • ⓦ goldmine-experience.co.nz

The only way to really get a sense of what it was like to be a miner in Thames is to visit the **Goldmine Experience**, built around an informative forty-minute tour underground along a narrow horizontal shaft originally cut by hand by Cornish miners. Topside, gold ore is crushed and the gold extracted when a stamper battery kicks into deafening gear. You can also pan for gold and watch a great video of miners at work in the 1914 office building.

School of Mines & Mineralogical Museum

Corner of Cochrane and Brown sts • Jan & Feb daily 11am–3pm; March–Dec Wed–Sun 11am–3pm • $10 • ⓣ 07 868 6227, ⓦ thamesschoolofmines.co.nz

Adults with little or no mining experience flocked to Thames, and the more ambitious among them attended this **School of Mines**, which operated from 1886 until 1954 and was one of the most important in the country. Enthusiastic volunteers will show you around the ancient chemistry lab with its lovely precision balance and the public assay room where miners could bring their ore for quality assessment. Most of what's here has been on-site since the glory days, including the vast collection of geologic samples.

Bella Street Pumphouse Museum and Thames Historical Museum

Bella Street Pumphouse Museum Cnr of Bella St and Waiokaraka Rd • Sat & Sun 10am–3pm • $5 • ⓣ 07 868 8696, ⓦ bellastreetpumphouse.com Thames Historical Museum Corner of Cochrane and Pollen • Daily 1–4pm • $5

The vast machinery may be gone but this 1898 building, now the **Bella Street Pumphouse Museum**, remains largely unchanged from when its pump helped keep most of Thames' mines dry. Excellent models and photos help interpret its pivotal role. Just up the road is the **Thames Historical Museum**, which covers the town's social history. Rooms in the old schoolhouse are set up as old miners' huts, there are tales of logging days, and a nice 1925 Simplex movie projector.

Butterfly and Orchid Garden

115 Victoria St, just off SH25, 3.5km north • Sept–May daily 9.30am–4.30pm • $12 • ⓣ 07 868 8080

Spend a tranquil half-hour or so inside a tropical hothouse at the magical **Butterfly and Orchid Garden** amid the acrobatics of hundreds of butterflies. At any one time there are around twenty to thirty species here; because of the insects' short lifespan (roughly 2–3 weeks), the garden cycles through over a thousand of these exquisite winged creatures each month, about half imported as pupae, and half bred on-site.

ARRIVAL AND INFORMATION   THAMES

By bus NakedBus and InterCity buses stop outside the i-SITE, as do Go Kiwi shuttles.
Destinations Auckland (4 daily; 1hr 40min); Coromandel (2 daily; 1hr 20min); Tauranga (3 daily; 1hr 50min); Whitianga (3 daily; 2hr 15min).

Tourist information The i-SITE at 206 Pollen St (Nov–April Mon–Fri 8.30am–5pm, Sat & Sun 9am–4pm; May–Oct Mon–Fri 9am–5pm, Sat 9am–1pm, Sun noon–4pm; ⓣ 07 868 7284, ⓦ thamesinfo.co.nz) sells bus tickets.

GETTING AROUND

By bus *Sunkist* (see page 216) run a shuttle service to the Kauaeranga Valley road end.

By car Davy Rentals, 731 Pollen St (☎07 868 7153, ⓦ davyrentals.co.nz), has budget cars for $55–65/day and allows them onto the peninsula's roughest roads. *Sunkist also* has some RAV4s for rent.

By taxi Thames Taxis ☎07 868 3100 (Mon–Sat only).

ACCOMMODATION

Brookby Motel 102 Redwood Lane ☎07 868 6663, ⓦ brookbymotel.co.nz; map p.214. A short stroll to the centre of town, hidden away on a quiet residential street, this well-run, small-scale motel has half a dozen en-suite rooms, with mini kitchenettes, though relatively little free space. $\overline{\$115}$

Coastal Motor Lodge 608 Tararu Rd (SH25), 2.5km north of town ☎07 868 6843, ⓦ stayatcoastal.co.nz; map p.214. Well-equipped "cottage" family units and streamlined, spacious black A-frame chalets (all self-contained and designed for two) set in spacious grounds, some with views over the firth. Cottages $\overline{\$160}$, chalets $\overline{\$173}$

★ **Cotswold Cottage** 46 Maramarahi Rd, 3km south of town off SH25 ☎07 868 6306, ⓦ cotswoldcottage.co.nz; map p.214. This luxury B&B is in a restored 1920s villa on the outskirts of Thames. There are beautiful views of the adjacent river and hills, a guest spa, and three renovated en-suite rooms (one, the Neatherwood Suite, with a four-poster). The breakfast (included in the rates) is delicious, and evening meals are available on request. $\overline{\$185}$

Cruz 'n' Stop 309 Mary St ☎07 868 9833; map p.214. Basic, paved parking lot for campervans right in the centre of town with no dump station but with power hook-ups, a shower, toilets and a small lounge with TV and magazines. Per campervan $\overline{\$30}$

Rolleston Motel 105 Rolleston St ☎07 868 8091, ⓦ rollestonmotel.co.nz; map p.214. Classic 1970s motel (since remodelled) on a quiet backstreet. Each unit has its own little courtyard and everything is beautifully maintained, including the outdoor pool, hot tub and barbecue area. $\overline{\$115}$

Sunkist 506 Brown St ☎07 868 8808, ⓦ sunkistbackpackers.com; map p.214. Atmospheric 1860s former pub, with a wide balcony, hammocks in the garden, and slightly overpriced dorms and private rooms. InterCity buses stop out front on request; free pick-ups can be arranged from the bus station. Dorms $\overline{\$50}$, doubles $\overline{\$85}$

EATING

Brew 200 Richmond St ☎07 868 5558; map p.214. Casual daytime café that becomes gastropub at night. Their own Foundry Pale Ale goes nicely with the open steak sandwich with blue cheese ($21.50). Occasional live music and poetry readings. Mon 9am–3pm, Wed–Thurs 9am–9pm, Fri & Sat 9am–11pm, Sun 9am–3pm.

Café Melbourne 715 Pollen St ☎07 868 3159; map p.214. The ladies who lunch like the urban industrial vibe of this café, or maybe they're just here for the imaginative breakfasts ($10–22; options include a tasty feta, spinach and chive omelette), well-prepared flat whites, tempting cakes and pastries, and a selection of lunch/dinner options. Next door there's *Bite*, a great deli with fresh bread. Mon–Thurs 8am–5pm, Fri 8am–9pm, Sat & Sun 9am–4pm.

Food for Thought 574 Pollen St ☎07 868 6065; map p.214. This café has taken numerous awards for its home-made pies (there are no fewer than eighteen different versions; each around $5) and also has a mouth-watering range of cakes, plus excellent coffee. Mon–Fri 6am–3.30pm, Sat 6am–2pm.

★ **Sola Café** 720b Pollen St ☎07 868 8781; map p.214. Relaxed bohemian café serving cakes, stellar coffee, salads and vegetarian dishes, from breakfasts and frittatas to wraps and enchiladas (mostly around $15); some vegan and gluten-free options are available. There's courtyard seating out back, as well as out front. Daily 8am–4pm.

DRINKING

As well as the option listed here, *Brew* (see page 216) is an excellent spot for an evening (or, indeed, daytime) drink.

Grahamstown Bar & Diner 700 Pollen St ☎09 868 6008, ⓦ thejunction.net.nz; map p.214. Popularly known locally as the GBD, this bar-restaurant is good for a pint ($8.50–11) or pub grub such as pizzas, cheesy chips and gravy, and fish and chips. Mon–Fri 11am–9pm, Sat & Sun 8.30am–10pm.

Kauaeranga Valley

The steep-sided **Kauaeranga Valley** stretches east of Thames towards the spine of the Coromandel Peninsula, a jagged landscape of bluffs and gorges topped by **the Pinnacles**

(759m), with stupendous views to both coasts across native forest studded with rata, rimu and kauri. It's reached along the scenic and mostly sealed Kauaeranga Valley Road snaking 21km beside the river, providing access to some of the finest walks in the Coromandel Range. The road winds through regenerating bush containing scattered "pole stands" of young kauri that have grown since the area was logged a century ago: only a handful in each stand will reach maturity.

The ease of access to these tracks can lead hikers not to take them as seriously as other tramps, but in bad weather the conditions can be treacherous, so go properly prepared (see page 50).

Note that the soil-borne **kauri dieback** (see page 182) has been found in the Coromandel: be extra vigilant about cleaning your footwear before and after trips, especially if you've recently visited the Auckland or Northland forests (where it is widespread).

INFORMATION   **KAUAERANGA VALLEY**

DOC visitor centre 14km along Kauaeranga Valley Rd (Dec 26–April daily 8.30am–5pm; May–Dec 8.30am–4pm; closed in severe weather; ☎07 867 9080, ⊕doc.govt.nz). Superb visitor centre with great displays, big maps of the area and a 20min DVD on the history of logging. Pick up the *Kauaeranga Valley & Broken Hills Recreation* booklet that details walks or the 1:50,000 *Hikuai Topo50* map BB35; you can also buy hut tickets.

ACCOMMODATION

The DOC campsites (⊕doc.govt.nz) listed here are the best of eight very similar options, all dotted along Kauaeranga Valley Rd 14–23km east of Thames. The two huts are only accessible on foot on the Kauaeranga walks.

Crosbies Hut ⊕doc.govt.nz. This ten-bunk hut is best accessed on the Wainora–Booms Flat circuit. It comes equipped with mattresses and a wood store but no gas rings. If you're looking for a quieter alternative to the Pinnacles Hut, this is it. Book online; backcountry hut passes not valid. Per person $15

Pinnacles Hut ⊕doc.govt.nz. This large and relatively plush eighty-bunk place is one of the most popular of all DOC huts, especially on Saturday nights and during school holidays. It is beautifully sited atop the range, around a 3hr walk from the road end, and there's always a warden present. Book online; backcountry hut passes not valid. Per person $15

Shag Stream 14km along Kauaeranga Valley Rd from Thames. The nearest DOC campsite to Thames is a simple affair right by the DOC visitor centre. It's equipped with vault toilets and has access to stream water (which should be treated). Per person $13

Whangaiterenga 19km along Kauaeranga Valley Rd from Thames. Marginally the nicest of the roadside campsites and the only one with flush toilets. Water is gathered from the stream and should be treated. Per person $13

The Pohutukawa Coast

From Thames, SH25 snakes 58km north to Coromandel town, tracing the grey rocky shoreline of the **Pohutukawa Coast** (so called for its abundance of these blazing native trees) past a series of tiny, sandy bays, most with little more than a few houses and the occasional campsite.

Hills and sand-coloured cliffs rise dramatically from the roadside for the first 19km until you reach **Tapu**, where the **Tapu–Coroglen Road** peels off to the peninsula's east coast. It is a wonderfully scenic 28km run of narrow, unsealed yet manageable driving, leaving behind the marginal farmland on the coast and climbing over the peninsula's mountainous spine. You eventually drop down to Coroglen, linking with the main road between Whitianga and Whangamata.

Near the road's summit, an easily missed signpost points to the "**square kauri**", opposite a rough lay-by and just before a small bridge. Steep steps through bush (175m; 10min) lead to this 1200-year-old giant of a tree (41m high and 9m wide), whose unusual, angular shape saved it from loggers.

Rapaura Watergardens
586 Tapu–Coroglen Rd • Daily 9am–5pm • Oct–April $15, May–Sept $10 • ☎07 868 4821, ⊕rapaurawatergardens.co.nz

Even if you aren't driving the whole Tapu–Coroglen Road, it's worth making a detour 6km along to **Rapaura Watergardens**, a landscaped "wilderness" of bush and blooms, lily ponds and a trickling stream, threaded by paths, with philosophical messages urging you to stop and think. There are a few picnic areas, an excellent summer-only **café** and accommodation (see page 219).

Manaia-Kereta Lookout
SH25, 12km north of Tapu

The road lurches inland soon after Kereta, snaking over hills to the roadside **Manaia-Kereta Lookout** (206m), which has great views of the northern peninsula, the majestic Moehau Range and Coromandel Harbour. Beyond, the vertical cliffs of Great Barrier Island may be visible on a clear day. Along the rocky shoreline and blue-green Firth of Thames, SH25 continues for 23km before reaching Coromandel.

ACCOMMODATION   POHUTUKAWA COAST

Rapaura Watergardens 586 Tapu–Coroglen Rd ☎ 07 868 4821, ⓦ rapaurawatergardens.co.nz. Choose from an enchanting luxury cottage for two or a serene two- bedroom lodge lined with rimu. Once the day-visitors have gone you'll have the watergardens to yourself. Cottage **$185**, lodge **$295**

Coromandel

The peninsula's northernmost town of any substance is charming little **COROMANDEL**, 58km north of Thames, huddling beneath high, craggy hills at the head of Coromandel Harbour. The town and peninsula took their name from an 1820 visit by the British Admiralty supply ship *Coromandel*, which called into the harbour to obtain kauri spars and masts. A more mercenary European invasion was precipitated by the 1852 discovery of **gold**, near Driving Creek.

From the south, SH25 becomes Tiki Road and then splits into two: Wharf Road skirts the harbour while Kapanga Road immediately enters the heart of town, which is made up of photogenic wooden buildings, where you'll find supermarkets, petrol stations, a bank and a cluster of cafés and arty shops. A couple of blocks further on, it becomes Rings Road, before heading northwards out of town towards the main attraction, the **Driving Creek Railway**.

Driving Creek Railway and Potteries
380 Driving Creek Rd, 3.5km north of town • **Train trips** Daily: Oct–April 9am, 10.15am, 11.30am, 12.45pm, 2pm, 3.15pm, 4.30pm & 5.45pm; May–Sept 10.15am, 11.30am, 12.45pm, 2pm, 3.15pm & 4.30pm; 1hr return, booking advised • $35 • **Pottery** Daily 10am–4pm • Free • ☎ 07 866 8703, ⓦ drivingcreekrailway.co.nz

The ingenious **Driving Creek Railway** is the country's only narrow-gauge hill railway. It was built mostly by hand and is the brainchild of Barry Brickell, an eccentric local potter and rail enthusiast who wanted to access the clay-bearing hills. The track is only 381mm wide and climbs 105m over a distance of about 3km, rewarding you with spectacular views, extraordinary feats of engineering and quirky design; at the end of the line panoramas extend from a wooden lodge, the Eyefull Tower. The journey starts and ends at the **workshops**, where you can see various types of **pottery**: stoneware, bricks and earthenware items, and terracotta sculptures.

Long Bay Kauri Grove
Wharf Rd, 3km west of town • 40min loop

The attractive beach at **Long Bay** marks the start of a pleasing **walk** through a scenic reserve winding through bush to an ancient kauri tree and on to a small grove of younger ones. Beyond, at the junction with a gravel road, turn right to Tucks Bay to follow the coastal track back. The track starts 100m inside the *Long Bay Motor Camp* where a signpost marks the track.

ARRIVAL AND INFORMATION

COROMANDEL

By bus InterCity buses pull into the car park opposite the i-SITE.

Destinations Thames (1 daily; 2hr 40min via Whitianga); Whitianga (1 daily; 50min).

By ferry 360 Discovery (☎ 09 307 8005, ⓦ 360discovery. co.nz) operate a passenger ferry between Auckland and Hannafords Wharf, 7km south of Coromandel. The $60 one-way fare includes a bus into town.

Destinations Auckland (5 weekly; 2hr).

Information Centre 8 Kapanga Rd (daily 10am–4pm; ☎ 07 866 8598, ⓦ thecoromandel.co.nz). Carries DOC leaflets and Hot Water Beach tide times.

GETTING AROUND

By shuttle bus There are two tour and shuttle bus operators offering trips to the must-see spots and up north, so you can enjoy the view rather than worry about the road. Both also run trips ($115–130 return) for the Coromandel Walkway (see page 222), dropping off walkers at one end, and picking up at the other before returning to Coromandel. Coromandel Discovery starts at Fletcher Bay (☎ 0800 668 175, ⓦ coromandeldiscovery. co.nz). Coromandel Adventures starts at Stony Bay, which means you can tack on the Muriwai walk if you're still lively at the end (☎ 0800 462 676, ⓦ coromandeladventures.co.nz).

By taxi Coromandel Cabs will also drop you off for walks (☎ 07 866 8927, ⓦ coromandelcabs.co.nz).

ACCOMMODATION

Anchor Lodge 448 Wharf Rd ☎ 07 866 7992, ⓦ anchorlodgecoromandel.co.nz. Modern, well-run motel with heated pool, free spa and a wide range of accommodation, from a hostel section aimed at backpackers to luxury "spa apartments", as well as plenty of midway options. Dorms $31, doubles $75, apartments $330

Buffalo Lodge 860 Buffalo Rd ☎ 07 866 8960, ⓦ buffalolodge.co.nz. Artist Evelyne Siegrist's architect-designed home is perched high up in five acres of bush north of town, with dizzying gulf views from its three sun-drenched rooms (all with private deck). Not suitable for children. Closed May–Sept. $220

Coromandel Colonial Cottages Motel 1737 Rings Rd ☎ 07 866 8857, ⓦ corocottagesmotel.co.nz. Beyond the white picket fence are attractive, well-kept wooden cottages (some sleeping up to six people) neatly arranged in tranquil gardens. The motel is 1.5km north of town, and has a big solar-heated swimming pool, a playground and a BBQ area. $175

Coromandel Top 10 Holiday Park 636 Rings Rd ☎ 0800 267 646, ⓦ coromandeltop10.co.nz. Sprawling over 3.5 acres just north of town, this all-purpose spot combines camping and campervan facilities with a comprehensive range of cabins and apartments. Guests have access to the heated swimming pool, and there's bike rental. Camping $22, cabins $69, apartments $125

★ **Hush** 425 Driving Creek Rd ☎ 07 866 7771, ⓦ hushaccommodation.co.nz. These aren't any cabins: these are stylish *Hush* cabins (named "Have", "Hideaway", etc), with eating nooks, fridges, crisp cotton sheets and thoughtful touches like umbrellas. Each is discreetly nestled in native bush, so you'll be woken by tui and keruru before you make breakfast in the shared open-air kitchen. There's also the self-contained *Hush* house sleeping up to six people ($325). Cabin $140

Jacaranda Lodge 3195 Tiki Rd (SH25) ☎ 07 866 8002, ⓦ jacarandalodge.co.nz. Set in farmland 3km south of town offering B&B accommodation in five immaculate and thoughtfully styled rooms (most en-suite), a stellar collection of Kiwi films on DVD, and delicious breakfasts featuring juices and jams from the orchards outside. $155

Long Bay Motor Camp 3200 Long Bay Rd ☎ 07 866 8720, ⓦ longbaymotorcamp.co.nz. Laidback beachfront campsite 3km west of town with great sunset views, safe swimming, bushwalks and kayak rental ($10/hr). There are additional unpowered sites at the secluded Tucks Bay, a 1km drive through the bush or a 5min walk around the headland. Camping $28, cabins $65

Tidewater Tourist Park 270 Tiki Rd ☎ 07 866 8888, ⓦ tidewater.co.nz. Comfortable motel and attached associate YHA, 200m from town near the harbour, with BBQ area, free guest bikes and kayaks and spacious cabin-style apartments sleeping up to six people (from $150). You can pitch a tent too ($15). Dorms $30, doubles $60

Tui Lodge 60b Whangapoua Rd, just off SH25 ☎ 07 866 8237, ⓦ coromandeltuilodge.co.nz. Located a 10min walk south of town, this hostel is in a big rambling house surrounded by an orchard and tranquil garden with a large chill-out gazebo. Free perks include laundry, tea and coffee, fruit, a BBQ and bike use. Dorms $32, doubles $70

EATING

Coromandel Mussel Kitchen Corner of SH25 and 309 Rd, 4km south ☎ 07 866 7245, ⓦ musselkitchen. co.nz. This roadside café cultivates and cooks their own premium mussels: try the mussel pots ($26) served with a choice of sauces (tomato and basil, Thai green curry, or white wine, cream, and garlic) with sourdough bread to dunk. They also dish up mussel chowder, fritters and even spring rolls, plus regular café fare. Daily 9am–3pm.

Coromandel Oyster Company 1611 Tiki Rd (SH25), 5km south of town ☎07 866 8028, ⌨freshoysters. co.nz. Buy mussels, scallops and, of course, oysters fresh out of the water. They also serve up battered fish and seafood and chips (you can get a good feed for less than $10), as well as seafood chowder ($7). Daily 10am–5pm.

Coromandel Smoking Company 70 Tiki Rd ☎0800 327 668, ⌨corosmoke.co.nz. Great shop selling their own smoked fish and shellfish; they're particularly known for kahawai and mussels. A perfect spot to stop for picnic supplies. Daily 9am–5pm.

★ **Driving Creek Café** 180 Driving Creek Rd, 3.5km north of town ☎07 866 7066, ⌨drivingcreekcafe. com. Classic Coromandel: a laidback and welcoming

vegetarian (and mostly organic) café that's perfect for great coffee, sourdough raisin toast, buckwheat blinis with spiced plums, and tempeh wraps (dishes $5–20). There are beautiful hill views from the veranda, occasional acoustic music, and an attached secondhand bookshop. Tues–Sun 9am–5pm.

Peppertree 31 Kapanga Rd ☎07 866 8211, ⌨peppertreerestaurant.co.nz. Coromandel's finest dining option, serving either indoors – there's an open fire in winter – or in the garden. Pop in for dishes like tuna carpaccio ($16), crispy skin pork shank ($35) and peace and rhubarb crumble ($14). Daily 10am–9pm.

Umu 22 Wharf Rd ☎07 866 8618. Popular for its pizzas ($16.50–25) but worth returning for their imaginative meals, including pulled pork bao buns with tamarind dressing ($14.50), grilled lamb rump with crab apple jelly ($33.50), and coconut and black plum mousse ($13.50). There's sometimes live music in the evenings. Daily 8.30am–9pm.

3

DRINKING

Star and Garter 5 Kapanga Rd ☎07 866 8503, ⌨starandgarter.co.nz. Airy wood-lined 1873-built bar and covered beer garden in the centre of town, popular

with an urbane, mixed-age crowd for the full range of Monteith's brews (from $8) and wine specials. Daily 11am–1am.

Northern Coromandel Peninsula

The landscape at the tip of the Coromandel is even more rugged than the rest of the peninsula, its green hills dropping to apparently endless beaches, clean blue sea and frothing white surf. The roads are lined with ancient pohutukawa trees, blazing red from early November until January. It's virtually uninhabited and there are **few facilities** except for some superb basic camping; replenish supplies in Coromandel.

The only real settlement is **Colville,** little more than a post office, a petrol pump, a café and the **Colville General Store** where you can stock up on provisions before heading to points north. North of there the road turns to gravel, becoming narrower, rougher and dustier the further north you go. Three kilometres beyond Colville the road splits, the right fork heading east over the hills to **Stony Bay** and the southern end of the Coromandel Walkway. The left fork runs 35km north to **Port Jackson** with its excellent sandy crescent of beach and a DOC campsite and **Fletcher Bay** at the very tip of the peninsula, following the coast all the way. In fine weather, allow an hour to reach Fletcher Bay from Colville.

INFORMATION AND ACTIVITIES

NORTHERN COROMANDEL PENINSULA

Visitor information Before heading out, check on the road conditions at the Coromandel information centre (8 Kapanga Rd; daily 10am–4pm; ☎07 866 8598, ⌨thecoromandel.co.nz), fill up with petrol and be prepared to drive slowly and take your time. There's no hurry up here.

Horse trekking Colville Farm (2140 Colville Rd, 1.5km south of Colville ☎07 866 6820, ⌨colvillefarmholidays. co.nz) offers guided horse trekking with short rides on a sheep and cattle farm. Longer treks head into native bush or out along the beach ($50/hr; $180/5hr).

ACCOMMODATION

Accommodation is mainly limited to camping. To help deter illegal freedom camping, DOC has five waterside

campsites/hostels around the northern peninsula: three of the best are listed here. For the two weeks after

Christmas the campsites are full, but for most of the rest of the year you'll have this unspoilt area to yourself. Expect toilets, cold showers and little else.

Colville Farm Colville Rd, 1.5km south of Colville ☎07 866 6820, ⓦcolvillefarmholidays.co.nz. Great rural bolt-hole with spots for tents ($12; pay $2 extra to use the backpacker facilities), backpacker beds in a cottage, some "glamping" static caravans (from $50), a couple of rustic bush lodges and two self-contained houses with fabulous views ($120). Dorms $30, lodges $95

Fantail Bay campsite 22km north of Colville ⓦdoc.govt.nz. Beachfront DOC site surrounded by farmland. There's room for 100 people, sharing flush toilets, stream water and cold showers. Booking is essential in the summer. $13

Fletcher Bay Backpackers Fletcher Bay, 34km north of Colville ☎07 866 6685, ⓦdoc.govt.nz. Basic hostel in a superb location on a hill 400m from the beach overlooking the campsite. The four rooms have two bunk beds in each and bedding is provided. $25.50

Fletcher Bay campsite 34km north of Colville ⓦdoc.govt.nz. The most remote DOC site, with views across to Great Barrier and Little Barrier islands. It comes with flush toilets, stream water and cold showers, and, despite its 250-person capacity, booking is essential for the two weeks after Christmas. $13

Coromandel to Whitianga

The drive east from Coromandel to Whitianga can be done in under an hour, but you could easily stretch it out longer on either of two highly **scenic roads** that cross the mountains: the snaking **309 Road** (33km, of which 14km are gravel; no public transport) spends much of its time in the bush, twisting across the peninsula's spine and topping out at the 306m-high saddle before descending to Whitianga; the main **SH25** climbs through forested hills before zigzagging down to the coast past the deserted beaches of Whangapoua and Kuaotunu. Keep an eye out for Stu's pigs (about 3km along the 309). These friendly, free-roaming Captain Cookers, and the character who owns them, are local celebrities in Coromandel.

The Waterworks
471 The 309 Rd • Daily: Nov–April 10am–6pm; May–Oct 10am–4pm • $25 • ☎07 866 7191, ⓦthewaterworks.co.nz

Set at least a couple of hours aside to visit **The Waterworks**, 5km along the 309 Road, an eccentric garden carved from the bush where you can do fun stuff with water. The tone is set with a waterwheel built from construction helmets, teapots and gumboots. Play an elaborate form of pooh sticks on the raised waterway or try one of many devices designed to splash the unsuspecting. The highlight is a huge clock powered by jets: apparently it keeps remarkably good time unless the wind blows the pendulum off kilter. Have a snack in the café, and bring a swimsuit for a dip in the natural swimming hole. There's no electricity – everything's powered by the on-site spring (make sure you find it before you leave).

Castle Rock
100m past The Waterworks • 2km return; 40min–1hr 30min

THE COROMANDEL WALKWAY

If you're after more exertion than swimming, fishing or lolling about on the beaches, consider hiking from Fletcher Bay to Stony Bay (or vice versa) along the easy **Coromandel Walkway** (11km one way; 3hr). The walk starts at the far end of the beach in Fletcher Bay and first follows gentle coastal hills that alternate between pasture and bush, before giving way to wilder terrain as you head further south past a series of tiny bays. Several hilltop **vantage points** provide spectacular vistas of the coast and Pacific Ocean beyond. **Stony Bay** is a sweep of pebbles with an estuary that's safe for swimming. The DOC leaflet *Coromandel Recreation Information* briefly describes the walk and shows a map, but the path is clearly marked.

For information on how to reach the walkway via shuttle bus from Coromandel town, see page 220.

A rough access road to the north crosses a ford and climbs steeply for 3km to the trailhead for the track to **Castle Rock**, the most easily accessible peak on the Coromandel Peninsula. The climb gets steeper towards the final tree-root claw onto the 521m summit of this old volcanic plug, but your efforts are rewarded by fantastic views to both coasts: the Whangapoua Peninsula and the Mercury Islands on the east, and Coromandel and the Firth of Thames on the west.

Waiau Falls and the "Siamese" Kauri
309 Rd, 2.5km southeast of Castle Rock

Though of modest height, **Waiau Falls** still crash over a tiered rock-face into a pool below, making this a gorgeous spot to cool off right next to the road. Half a kilometre on, a car park heralds the easy bush track to the towering, magnificent **Kauri Grove** (1km return; 30min) and the so-called "**Siamese**" **Kauri** a little further; this is one of the best places in the country to appreciate their immense size.

Whangapoua and New Chums Beach
From Coromandel, SH25 traverses lush native forest, passing a couple of isolated but pretty beachside settlements with campsites. About 14km from Coromandel is the 5km turn-off to the secluded village and white-sand beach of **WHANGAPOUA**. At the end of the road (along the right fork into town) a pretty bushwalk over a headland brings you to **New Chums Beach** (accessible at low tide only; 4km return; 1hr), one of New Zealand's finest beaches.

Stargazers Astronomy Tours
392 SH25 • Advance booking essential • 1–1hr 30min • $50 • ☎ 07 866 5343, ⓦ stargazersbb.com

With so little light pollution the New Zealand night sky can be amazing, but to be really wowed let Alastair Brickell (cousin of the more famous Barry Brickell; see page 219) show you around the universe. He's got great kit, but it's his enthusiasm, humour and clear explanations that really delight. If you can't drag yourself away from the stars, stay the night (see page 223).

Kuaotunu
Continuing along SH25, about 30km from Coromandel, you descend to diminutive **KUAOTUNU**, beside a lovely white-sand beach. There's not much to it, but the village is an alluring spot with a few places to stay and a great pizza joint. From here, SH25 continues through farmland to Whitianga and Mercury Bay.

ACCOMMODATION   **KUAOTUNU**

Kuaotunu Bay Lodge SH25 ☎ 07 866 4396, ⓦ kuaotunubay.co.nz. Understated luxury is on offer at this modern house, which has amazing views from private decks. The en suites, and indeed everything else, are beautifully appointed. Two-night minimum stay Dec–March. **$310**

Kuaotunu Campground 33 Bluff Rd ☎ 07 866 5628, ⓦ kcg2008.co.nz. This is a decent campsite with kayak rental and an on-site fish and chip shop. The beach is just across the road, but few of the sites have great views.

Camping **$23**, cabins **$65**

Stargazers B&B 392 SH25 2km south of Kauotunu ☎ 07 866 5343, ⓦ stargazersbb.com. Only one booking a night at this beautiful home in the bush. Guests have their own separate lounge, breakfast is served on the spacious deck, and binoculars are provided to spot birds or stars. The owner has also restored the self-contained *Miner's Cottage* ($295; sleeping up to four people) down the hill, with modern bathrooms and the chance to spot glowworms. Minimum two-night stay. **$295**

EATING

★ **Luke's Kitchen** 20 Blackjack Rd, off SH25 ☎ 07 866 4480, ⓦ lukeskitchen.co.nz. Kuaotunu's only restaurant – fortunately, it's great. There's a bar, café, outdoor seating, and new gallery of local art. Come for a coffee and savoury

scone while you enjoy the view, a superb wood-fired pizza ($10–28), or beetroot falafel wrap ($13). Live music most summer evenings. Nov–March Mon–Fri 11am–9.30pm; Sat & Sun 9am–10pm; April–Oct Fri–Sun 8.30am–3pm.

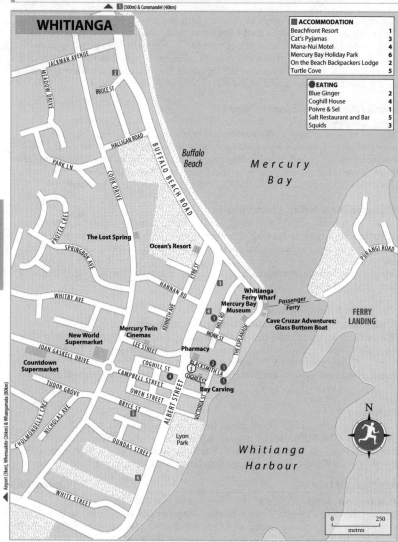

▲ 1 (500m) & Coromandel (40km)

WHITIANGA

■ ACCOMMODATION	
Beachfront Resort	1
Cat's Pyjamas	3
Mana-Nui Motel	4
Mercury Bay Holiday Park	6
On the Beach Backpackers Lodge	2
Turtle Cove	5

● EATING	
Blue Ginger	2
Coghill House	4
Poivre & Sel	1
Salt Restaurant and Bar	5
Squids	3

JACKMAN AVENUE

MEADOW DRIVE

BRUCE ST

HALLIGAN ROAD

PARK LN

COOK DRIVE

BUFFALO BEACH ROAD

Buffalo Beach

Mercury Bay

PROTEA CRES

SPRINGBOX AVE

The Lost Spring

Ocean's Resort

FYFE ST

PURANGI ROAD

Shakespeare Lookout, Hahei (15km); Cathedral Cove (17km) & Hot Water Beach (20km)

HANNAN RD

WHITBY AVE

KENNETH AVE

HILL RD

Whitianga Ferry Wharf

Mercury Bay Museum

Passenger Ferry

FERRY LANDING

Mercury Twin Cinemas

New World Supermarket

LEE STREET

MONK ST

THE ESPLANADE

Cave Cruzar Adventures; Glass Bottom Boat

JOAN GASKELL DRIVE

Pharmacy

Countdown Supermarket

COGHILL ST

COGHILL ST

BLACKSMITH LA

CAMPBELL STREET

ALBERT STREET

VICTORIA ST

Bay Carving

TUDOR GROVE

OWEN STREET

BRYCE ST

CHOLMONDELEY CRES

NICHOLAS AVE

DUNDAS STREET

Lyon Park

Whitianga Harbour

N

WHITE STREET

Airport (3km), Whenuakite (26km) & Whangamata (80km)

0 ——— 250 metres

Whitianga and around

Pretty **WHITIANGA** clusters where Whitianga Harbour meets **Buffalo Beach**, a long curve of surf-pounded white sand on the broad sweep of **Mercury Bay**. The town is a relaxed place to chill for a day or two, perhaps trying **bone carving** or pampering yourself at The Lost Spring **hot pools**. It also makes a central base from which to make **trips** to some of the Coromandel's top spots.

A short passenger ferry ride across the narrow harbour mouth to **Ferry Landing** opens up a bunch of **gorgeous beaches** such as Lonely Bay. They're often deserted out of season, though from December to February you'll have to work harder to find tranquillity. By taking a bus from Ferry Landing (or driving south via Whenuakite) you can access **Cathedral Cove**, a stunning geological formation with great swimming, and magical **Hot Water Beach**, where natural hot springs bubble up through the sand.

Offshore, the protected waters of **Te Whanganui-A-Hei (Cathedral Cove) Marine Reserve** offer superb snorkelling and scuba diving, where bottlenose **dolphins** and **orcas** are often seen. These, and an extraordinary array of volcanic island and sea caves, are the main focus of **boat** and **kayak trips** from Hahei and Whitianga.

Mercury Bay Museum

11 The Esplanade • Oct–June daily 10am–4pm, July–Sept Tues–Sun 10am–3pm • $7.50 • ☎ 07 866 0730, ⊛ mercurybaymuseum.co.nz

An old butter factory houses the **Mercury Bay Museum** with plenty on kauri logging, early settlers and big game fishing. The highlight is the coverage of early explorers, particularly Māori pioneer Kupe, who is thought to have landed near here up to a thousand years ago. Don't miss the moa or the reconstructed 1960s *bach*.

The Lost Spring

121a Cook Drive • Mon–Fri 9.30am–7pm, Sat 9.30am–9pm, Sun 9.30am–7pm • $40 for 1hr 30min, $70 for full day • ☎ 07 866 0456, ⊛ thelostspring.co.nz

A nondescript patch of suburban Whitianga is the unlikely location for **The Lost Spring**, a series of hot pools set among lavishly landscaped grounds, where cocktails are delivered by staff with frangipani flowers behind their ears. Ranging from 33°C–40°C, the pools combine spa kitsch with re-created natural bush splendour. You can dine at the classy on-site **restaurant** and should book ahead for all manner of decadent pampering opportunities.

Shakespeare Lookout

1.5km east of Ferry Landing and another 1km uphill • Free

The cliffs below **Shakespeare Lookout** apparently once resembled the Bard's profile, though it is hard to imagine today. It is better to admire the panoramic views from the lookout, which stretch east to Cooks Beach and across Mercury Bay, west to Buffalo Beach, and north towards Mount Maungatawhiri. Signposted tracks (2km one way; 30min) lead from the car park to the secluded Lonely Bay and on to the popular family holiday spot of **Cooks Beach**, also accessible from the main road 2km further east.

Hahei

The small beachside community of **HAHEI**, 6km east of Cooks Beach (10km by road), has a store, a few places to stay and eat, and is the launch site for boat, kayak and dive trips into **Te Whanganui-A-Hei (Cathedral Cove) Marine Reserve** (see page 226), also accessible via the Cathedral Cove Walk.

Cathedral Cove Walk

5km return; 1hr 30min; 300m ascent on the way back

Almost everybody does the **Cathedral Cove Walk**, a hilly coastal track from a car park on Grange Road. Although steep in places, the route affords great views out to sea. The reward is a perfect pair of beaches backed by white cliffs and separated by an impressive rock arch that vaults over the strand like the nave of a great cathedral.

COOK PLANTS THE FLAG

James Cook effectively claimed New Zealand for King George III, planting the British flag at Cooks Beach in November 1769. Cook spent 12 days anchored here – the longest he spent anywhere on his first voyage around Aotearoa – observing the **transit of Mercury** across the sun on November 9; in doing so he established the exact latitude and longitude of the land and named (or rather renamed) both Mercury Bay and, of course, Cooks Beach.

TOURS AND ACTIVITIES AROUND WHITIANGA AND MERCURY BAY

BONE CARVING
Bay Carving 5 Coghill St ☎021 105 2151, ⓦbaycarving.com. German carver Roland Baumgart offers short (around 2hr) carve-your-own sessions (from $55) based on set patterns using cattle bone blanks.

KAYAKING
Cathedral Cove Kayak Tours 88 Hahei Beach Rd, Hahei ☎0800 529 258, ⓦkayaktours.co.nz. Hahei Beach is the launch pad for professional, guided sea-kayak half-day trips ($115) to Cathedral Cove and the islands offshore, or the sea caves to the south (the Remote Coast Tour; also $115). Full-day trips ($190) combine the two, and they offer shorter but wonderful dawn and sunset trips (Dec–Feb only; $105).

BOAT TRIPS
All trips similar territory, between Whitianga and Hot Water Beach, including Cathedral Cove and its marine reserve.
Cave Cruzer Adventures Whitianga Wharf ☎0800 427 893, ⓦcavecruzer.co.nz. Boat tours past Shakespeare Cliff to Cathedral Cove and beyond. The Express tour departs 9am & 4pm (1hr–1hr 30min; $60); an extended and more leisurely variation departs 10am & 1pm (2hr–2hr 30min; $85).
Glass Bottom Boat Whitianga Wharf ☎07 876 1962, ⓦglassbottomboatwhitianga.co.nz. Two-hour trips ($95) with the chance to see what's below the surface. Departures daily at 10.30am & 1.30pm, and more in summer.
Hahei Explorer Hahei ☎07 866 3910, ⓦhaheiexplorer.co.nz. A rigid inflatable boat takes small groups on exhilarating hour-long sea-cave trips (2–4 departures daily; call ahead for times; $95), visiting Cathedral Cove and an amazing blowhole.

DIVING
Scuba diving and snorkelling in Cathedral Cove Marine Reserve and along the coast can be arranged through a couple of companies, both offering first-time dives and full instruction.
Cathedral Cove Dive 48 Hahei Beach Rd, Hahei ☎07 866 3955, ⓦhahei.co.nz/diving. Offers diving and snorkelling trips (from $95), PADI courses and equipment hire. Departures daily at 9am, 12.30pm & 3.30pm, and more in summer.

Steps bring you down onto **Mare's Leg Cove**, a gorgeous swimming beach with composting toilets offering a seat with a view. You need to walk through the arch to reach the second fine beach, **Cathedral Cove**. **Rockfalls** from the ceiling have made DOC jittery, so there are warning signs – and if the arch is roped off, stay well back.

To walk from Hahei Beach follow the step at the northern end of the beach: you'll reach the car park at the start of the walk in around twenty minutes.

Gemstone Bay and Stingray Bay
A short way along the Cathedral Cove Walk, a five-minute track descends to the rocky **Gemstone Bay**, great for snorkelling. DOC has set up buoys in different marine environments between 50m and 150m offshore with panels explaining the undersea wonders. Rent gear from Cathedral Cove Dive (see box below).

Stingray Bay, signposted further along the Cathedral Cove Walk, is a perfect cove of white sand that's often deserted when Cathedral Cove is packed.

Hot Water Beach
15km southeast of Whitianga, but over 30km by road

With the opportunity to dig your own hot pool in the sands next to the breakers, **Hot Water Beach** is understandably one of the most popular destinations on the Coromandel Peninsula. The hot springs which bubble up beneath the sand can only be exploited two hours either side of **low tide** (less in rough weather; check tide times at the Whitianga i-SITE). Wander 100m across the sands to the rocky outcrop that splits the beach in two, dig your hole and enjoy the hot water, refreshed by waves. You'll need a spade to dig your "spa": rent one from your accommodation, the local café or *Hot Waves Café* (see page 229) for $5, plus $20 deposit.

The springs have become so popular – up to five hundred people crowd the beach at peak times – that some prefer to come at night: bring a torch. The beach here has a dangerous **tidal rip**, so take care when swimming (see page 63). For accommodation and a café near the beach, see pages 228 and 229.

ARRIVAL AND INFORMATION

By plane Whitianga's small airport, 4km south of the town centre, was serviced by Sunair until 2017, when the airline was grounded for the second time. At the time of writing, there were no scheduled flights.

By bus NakedBus and InterCity buses drop off at accommodation around town and outside the i-SITE. To reach Tauranga, change at Thames (InterCity) or Ngatea (NakedBus).

WHITIANGA AND AROUND

Destinations Ngatea (1 daily; 2hr 45min); Thames (2 daily; 1hr 30min).

Visitor information The i-SITE is at 66 Albert St (Oct–April daily 9am–5pm, May–Sept Mon–Fri 9am–5pm, Sat 9am–4pm, Sun 9am–2pm; ☎ 07 866 5555, ☒ thecoromandel.com).

GETTING AROUND

By ferry A passenger ferry (☒ whitiangaferry.co.nz) between Whitianga Wharf and Ferry Landing ($5 single, $7 return) runs roughly every 10min; the crossing takes 3min.

By bus During the summer, Go Kiwi (☎ 07 866 0336, ☒ go-kiwi.co.nz) runs buses (5 daily; 45min) between Ferry Landing and Hot Water Beach, calling at Cooks Beach, Hahei and Cathedral Cove. Cathedral Cove Shuttles (☎ 027 422 5899, ☒ www.cathedralcoveshuttles.co.nz) is essentially an on-demand taxi service between Ferry

Landing, Cooks Beach, Hahei and Hot Water Beach.

By car Getting to Hahei and Hot Water Beach by car takes around half an hour: head 25km southeast on SH2 to Whenuakite and turn north onto minor roads.

By bike Hahei Beach Bikes (64 Lees Rd, Hahei ☎ 021 701093, ☒ haheibeachbikes.co.nz). Best call ahead to book – especially if you want meeting at Ferry Landing. You can also collect from *Hahei Holiday Resort* (see page 228). Bikes come with a spade (for Hot Water Beach) or storage box ($45/day).

ACCOMMODATION

Whitianga has plenty of accommodation, with further options around Hot Water Beach and Hahei. In addition to advance bookings in summer, be prepared for higher prices than on the rest of the peninsula (especially anywhere with a sea view) and minimum stays in peak periods.

WHITIANGA

Beachfront Resort 113 Buffalo Beach Rd ☎ 07 866 5637, ☒ beachfrontresort.co.nz; map p.224. Luxurious yet family-friendly motel, right on the beach, featuring a range of spacious apartments with private balconies (those with sea views cost $325). Guests can use the spa pool, BBQ, kayaks, and boogie boards. **$225**

Cat's Pyjamas 12 Albert St ☎ 07 866 4663, ☒ cats-pyjamas.co.nz; map p.224. Scruffy, basic and rather cramped hostel with fading facilities, though the location's central (a 2min walk from the centre and beach), there's a friendly, communal vibe, and prices for the dorms (6- to 12-bed; mixed and single sex available) and private rooms are low. Dorms **$26**, doubles **$66**

Mana-Nui Motel 20 Albert St ☎ 07 866 5599, ☒ mananui.co.nz; map p.224. A centrally located, comfortable motel with a dozen fully self-contained ground-floor apartments (some of which have two bedrooms), plus a swimming and spa pools. The owners are lovely. **$156**

Mercury Bay Holiday Park 121 Albert St ☎ 07 866 5579, ☒ mercurybayholidaypark.co.nz; map p.224. Award-winning resort, in a sheltered location about 700m from the town centre. There are campsites and self-contained chalets, plus a pool and free spades for Hot Water Beach. Camping **$18**, chalets **$140**

Oceans Resort 18 Eyre St ☎ 07 869 5222, ☒ oceansresort.co.nz; map p.224. Beside Buffalo Beach, this high-end resort has a selection of big, light apartments, with kitchens, living rooms and balconies, sleeping up to four people. There's a heated swimming pool, tennis court and private path to the beach. **$195**

★ **On the Beach Backpackers Lodge** 46 Buffalo Beach Rd ☎ 07 866 5380, ☒ coromandelbackpackers.com; map p.224. This associate YHA, a 10min walk north of town and just across from the beach, is Whitianga's best hostel. It offers mixed and female-only dorms, bright cottage-style private rooms (some en suite), and free use of kayaks, boogie boards, spades for Hot Water Beach, and fishing gear. Dorms **$28**, doubles **$80**

Turtle Cove 14 Bryce St ☎ 07 867 1517, ☒ turtlecove.co.nz; map p.224. A 5min walk from the beach and town, *Turtle Cove* has stylish dorms and rooms (some en suite) in the main building (note: the doubles next to the lounge can get noisy). Facilities include a pool table, dart board and free use of spades for Hot Water Beach; bike hire available. Dorms $26, doubles $79

HAHEI

Cathedral Cove B&B 14 Cathedral Court ☏021 722 402, ⓦcathedralcovebandb.co.nz; map p.228. With spades and torches for Hot Water Beach, umbrellas for the local beach, curvaceous pool, book exchange and much more besides, this top end, modern, sustainably minded guesthouse has pretty much everything. The four light and airy en suites are swish and very comfy. Breakfast is excellent, too. $325

★**The Church** 87 Beach Rd ☏07 866 3533, ⓦthechurchhahei.co.nz; map p.228. A delightful array of elegant studios and cottages in a tranquil garden setting; all face the sun, most have leadlight windows and some boast wood fires for the winter. Continental breakfast trays available (an extra $12/person). There's also an excellent restaurant (see page 229). Studios $140, cottages $220

Hahei Holiday Resort 41 Harsant Ave ☏07 866 3889, ⓦhaheiholidays.co.nz; map p.228. Located on half a kilometre of beachfront, an easy walk from Cathedral Cove and close to restaurants so popular with the buses, the options here

include powered sites right on the beach (2 people $45) and luxurious self-contained beachfront villas ($300), as well as cabins and cottages. Cabins $80, cottages $200

Tatahi Lodge 13 Grange Rd ☏07 866 3992, ⓦtatahilodge.co.nz; map p.228. Tranquilly set in bush and gardens, just footsteps from cafés and shops and with easy access to Cathedral Cove, your options here comprise self-contained timber-lined studios and cottages, airy backpacker accommodation, and a villa that sleeps up to seven ($300). Free spades for the beach. Dorms $32, studios $165

HOT WATER BEACH

★**Auntie Dawns Place** 15 Radar Rd ☏07 866 3707, ⓦauntiedawn.co.nz; map p.228. This hillside house overlooking the beach offers true Kiwi hospitality. The owners have been welcoming guests for decades, and the home brew (which is regularly shared) is as good as ever. There are two simple yet comfortable self-contained apartments for two, and a campsite, just a 3min walk along a hidden track from Hot Water Beach. Camping $20, apartments $120

Hot Water Beach Top 10 Holiday Park 790 Hot Water Beach Rd, Hot Water Beach ☏800 246 823,

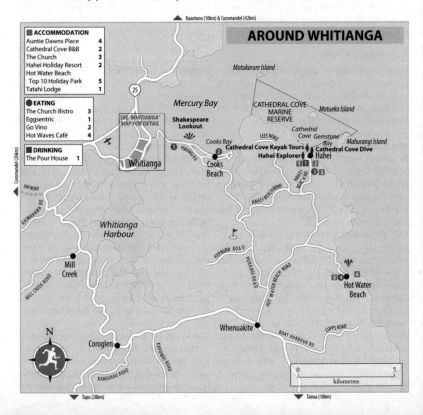

Kuaotunu (10km) & Coromandel (42km)

AROUND WHITIANGA

■ ACCOMMODATION
Auntie Dawns Place 4
Cathedral Cove B&B 2
The Church 3
Hahei Holiday Resort 2
Hot Water Beach
  Top 10 Holiday Park 5
Tatahi Lodge 1

● EATING
The Church Bistro 3
Eggsentric 1
Go Vino 2
Hot Waves Café 4

■ DRINKING
The Pour House 1

Motukorure Island

Mercury Bay

CATHEDRAL COVE MARINE RESERVE

Motukea Island

Cathedral Cove

Gemstone Bay

Mahurangi Island

Shakespeare Lookout

SEE 'WHITIANGA' MAP FOR DETAIL

Cooks Bay

Cathedral Cove Kayak Tours
Hahei Explorer
Cathedral Cove Dive
Hahei

Whitianga

Cooks Beach

LEES ROAD

HAHEI BEACH ROAD

309 ROAD

KAIMARAMA RD

Whitianga Harbour

Mill Creek

MILL CREEK ROAD

HEPBURN ROAD

PURANGI ROAD

HOT WATER BEACH ROAD

Hot Water Beach

N

Whenuakite

BOAT HARBOUR RD

CUPPS ROAD

Coroglen

KAPONGA ROAD

RANGIHAU ROAD

0   5
kilometres

Coromandel (26km)

Tapu (28km)

Tairua (10km)

Ⓦ hotwaterbeachtop10.co.nz; map p.228. Friendly owners and modern amenities, plus a sunny glassed-in guest lounge and an on-site shop serving fish and chips in summer. Family campers have a separate area to the under-25s, so the Kiwi Experience bus shouldn't disturb you. Camping $23, cabins $100, chalets $180

EATING

COOKS BEACH

Go Vino 19 Captain Cook Rd ☎07 867 1215, Ⓦ govino.co.nz; map p.228. Boasting its own philosophy ("KaiZen") and a cookbook, *Go Vino* has a seasonally changing menu of sharing plates ($14–22): expect dishes like octopus confit, duck sausage with spiced apple chutney, and mushroom risotto Scotch egg, as well as a Sunday roast ($25-30). Mon & Wed–Sun 11am–2pm & 6–10pm.

WHITIANGA

★ **Blue Ginger** 10 Blacksmith Lane ☎07 867 1777, Ⓦ blueginger.co.nz; map p.224. Great little eat-in or takeaway spot serving delectable morsels such as *banh mi* ($16), *poke* bowls ($24), and spicy sizzling Korean beef ($28); a vegan menu is available. Tues–Sat 11.30am–2pm & 5.30–10pm.

Coghill House 10 Coghill St ☎07 866 0592, Ⓦ cafecoghill.co.nz; map p.224. Relaxing café good for breakfast, lunch and snacks: try the BLOT (bacon, lettuce, caramelised onion and tomato focaccia sandwich; $15.50). Tues–Sun 8am–3pm.

Poivre & Sel 2 Mill Rd ☎07 866 0053, Ⓦ poivresel. co.nz; map p.224. Classy French gastronomy is on offer here – think garlic snails, côte de boeuf, and crème brûlée with a passion fruit macaron. The wine list combines Gallic and Kiwi vintages. Two courses $60, three courses $80. Tues–Sat 5–11pm.

Salt Restaurant and Bar Whitianga Marina Hotel, The Esplanade ☎07 866 5818, Ⓦ salt-whitianga. co.nz; map p.224. Beachy-chic lunch and dinner café/bar with decking onto the marina, serving mains ($32–38.50) like Bloody Mary linguine and slow-roasted shoulder of lamb. Live music sometimes in the summer. Mon–Thurs 4–10pm, Fri–Sun noon–11pm.

Squids 15/1 Blacksmiths Lane ☎07 867 1710; map p.224. Restaurant-wine bar, good for a few drinks and good-value dishes, such as the fish tacos ($16) or the smoked fish platter ($20). Mon–Fri 11.30am–2.30pm & 5.30–9pm, Sat & Sun 5.30–9pm.

FERRY LANDING

★ **Eggsentric** 1049 Purangi Rd, Flaxmill Bay, 1km west of Ferry Landing ☎07 866 0307, Ⓦ eggsentriccafe. co.nz; map p.228. Quirky place where the tables are scattered among the sculpture-strewn gardens and the colourful interior comes alive in the evenings with acoustic music and poetry readings, particularly on Fridays. Superb dishes include slow-roasted aubergine with a Mexican *mole* sauce, quiche of the day, and Thai fish cakes (mains $29–34). Bookings essential for dinner. Nov–April Tues–Sun 9am–10pm.

HAHEI

★ **The Church Bistro** 87 Beach Rd ☎07 866 3797, Ⓦ thechurchbistro.co.nz; map p.228. A wooden former Methodist church, trucked here from Taumarunui in the 1910s, is the lovely setting for this classy restaurant, which serves, ahem, heavenly food. The short but sweet menu (mains $30–35) features braised chicken pot pie, cassoulet and a passion fruit baked Alaska. The wines are excellent, too. Daily 3–10pm.

HOT WATER BEACH

Hot Waves Café 8 Pye Place ☎07 866 3887; map p.228. Stylish café with airy dining areas and an attractive garden setting, serving light meals such as burgers with parsnip chips, breakfast burritos, and excellent Allpress coffee (from $4). Regular quiz nights. Mon–Thurs & Sun 8.30am–4pm, Fri–Sat 8.30am–8.30pm.

DRINKING

HAHEI

The Pour House 7 Grange Rd ☎07 866 3354, Ⓦ coromandelbrewingcompany.co.nz; map p.228. Coromandel Brewing Company pub, offering their finest beer – from German-style pilsner to Belgian blonde beer

– alongside generous portions of burgers, fish and chips, and pizzas ($20–26). Keep an eye out for Max, the pub dog. Nov–April daily noon–late; May–Oct Mon–Fri 5–10pm, Sat & Sun noon–late.

Tairua

Diminutive and pretty **TAIRUA**, 22km south of Hot Water Beach and 44km from Whitianga, nestles between pine-forested hills and the estuary of the Tairua River.

Mostly popular with holidaying Kiwis, it's separated from the crashing Pacific breakers by two opposing and almost touching peninsulas: one is covered by the exclusive suburban sprawl of anodyne **Pauanui**; the other is crowned by the impressive volcanic **Mount Paku**, which can be climbed (10min ascent from car park, 30min ascent from beach) for spectacular views over the town, its estuary and beaches.

ARRIVAL AND INFORMATION   TAIRUA

By bus InterCity buses stop at the information centre. Destinations Thames (3 daily; 45min); Whitianga (1 daily; 45min).

By ferry A five-minute passenger ferry ride links Tairua and Pauanui (hourly 10am–4pm, more in summer; $10 return,

$5 one way). Check the latest schedules at the information centre.

Tourist information Tairua's information centre is at 223 Main St (Mon–Fri 9am–5pm, Sat & Sun 9am–4pm; ☎07 864 7575, ⊚tairua.co.nz).

ACCOMMODATION

Colleith Lodge 8 Rewa Rewa Valley ☎07 865 9152, ⊚colleithlodge.co.nz. Gorgeous, luxurious, eco-friendly guesthouse with a trio of rooms, each with king-sized beds, coffee machines, and private patios, as well as charming hosts, swimming pool, guest lounge with books and magazines, and sea views. **$575**

Opoutere

Around 20km south of Tairua, a 5km side road leads to **Opoutere**, a tiny harbourside retreat at the foot of a mountain with a gorgeous, wild sweep of white-sand **surf beach** backed by pines. The pohutukawa-fringed road hugs the shores of the Wharekawa Harbour where wetlands make good birdwatching spots, mudflats yield shellfish and the calm waters are good for kayaking.

Opoutere Beach

At the junction of Opoutere and Ohui roads, Opoutere Beach car park has a footbridge leading to two paths, both reaching the beach in ten minutes or so. The left fork runs straight through the forest to the usually deserted **beach**, while the right-hand track follows the estuary to the edge of the **Wharekawa Harbour Sandspit Wildlife Refuge**, where endangered New Zealand **dotterels** breed from November to March. Opoutere Beach can have a strong undertow and there are no lifeguards, so don't swim. It's an unofficial nudist beach, but even if you're clothed, be sure to bring repellent to guard against sandflies.

Mount Maungaruawahine
2km return; 40–50min

For a wider view over the estuary and the coastline, tackle the track up **Mount Maungaruawahine**, climbing through gnarled pohutukawa and other native trees to the summit where there are sweeping vistas of the estuary and out towards the coast. The summit track begins just before the gate to the *YHA* (see page 230).

ARRIVAL AND INFORMATION   OPOUTERE

By bus There's no regular bus service, but drop-offs can be arranged with Go Kiwi (see page 227).

Groceries You'll need to bring all your food as there is no shop, and lodgings offer only basic provisions.

ACCOMMODATION

Opoutere Coastal Camping 460 Ohui Rd, 700m beyond the YHA ☎07 865 9152, ⊚opouterebeach.co.nz. There's direct beachfront access from this well-maintained campsite in a secluded setting amid pines and pohutukawas. There are also rustic cabins (sleeping up to three) with great views, and some more sophisticated chalets (sleeping up to four; $160). Closed May–late Oct. Camping **$19**, cabins **$120**

YHA Opoutere 389 Opoutere Rd ☎07 865 9072, ⊚yha. co.nz. This traditional YHA beside the estuary occupies a 1908 schoolhouse and surrounding wooden buildings amid mature bush alive with the calls of native birds. There's free use of kayaks and the chance for nocturnal glowworm spotting. Look out for the kaka. Closed Sun–Thurs between May and late Oct. Dorms **$30**, doubles **$95**

Whangamata

The summer resort town of **WHANGAMATA**, 15km south of Opoutere, is bounded on three sides by estuaries and the ocean, and on the fourth by bush-clad hills. Voted the best beach in the country by *New Zealand Herald* readers in 2018, **Ocean Beach**, a 4km-long crescent of white sand, curves from the harbour to the mouth of the **Otahu River**. The sandbar at the harbour end has an excellent left-hand break that's sought after by **surfers**.

The main drag, Port Road, runs straight through the small town centre, linking it with SH25.

Wentworth Falls

Walk 10km return; 2hr • The track starts at the DOC campsite (see page 231) 5km down Wentworth Valley Rd, which is off SH25 about 2km south of town

One of the best ways to pass a couple of hours is to walk to **Wentworth Falls** in the Wentworth Valley which cuts into foothills of the Coromandel Range, 7km southwest of town. It is a lovely walk on well-maintained paths winding gradually uphill through regenerating bush past numerous small swimming holes. The route continues into the heart of the mountains, but most turn around at the pretty two-leap 50m falls, best viewed from a small deck.

ARRIVAL AND DEPARTURE   WHANGAMATA

By bus Go Kiwi (☎ 0800 446 549, ⓦ go-kiwi.co.nz) run from Auckland via Thames to Whangamata (change at Hikuai).

Destinations Auckland (1 daily; 3hr 10min); Thames (1 daily; 1hr).

INFORMATION AND TOURS

Visitor information The tourist office is at 616 Port Rd (Mon–Sat 10am–5pm, Sun 9am–2pm; Sun until 5pm Oct–March; ☎ 07 865 8340, ⓦ thecoromandel.com/whangamata).

Whangamata Surf Shop 634 Port Road ☎ 07 865 8252, ⓦ whangamatasurfschool.co.nz. Run by the parents of world champion surfer Ella Williams. Group

lessons cost from $70; board rental $20/hr.
Kiwi Dundee Adventures ☎ 07 865 8809, ⓦ kiwidundee.co.nz. Dedicated conservationist Doug Johansen ("Kiwi Dundee") runs a variety of day- and multi-day ecotours incorporating wildlife experiences and paths off the beaten track. Full-day trips cost around $250; book well in advance.

ACCOMMODATION

Breakers Motel 318 Heatherington Rd ☎ 0800 865 8464, ⓦ breakersmotel.co.nz. An impressive, modern motel with spacious rooms, many of which have spa pools and views over the marina. There's also a large swimming pool. **$185**
★ **Brenton Lodge** 2 Brenton Place ☎ 07 865 8400, ⓦ brentonlodge.co.nz. A garden-set retreat with sea views on the edge of Whangamata, with two beautifully decorated cottages (each sleeping two people) and two suites, as well as a sparkling swimming pool, spa, fresh flowers, home-made chocolates and delicious breakfasts. Doubles/cottages **$470**

Southpacific Motel Accommodation Corner of Port Rd and Mayfair Ave ☎ 07 865 9580, ⓦ thesouthpacific. co.nz. An immaculate motel (with full kitchens in some rooms) and conference centre. There's a café-bar, and guests have free use of kayaks, surfboards, and a nearby gym. **$140**
Wentworth Valley Campground Wentworth Valley Rd, 7km southwest of Whangamata ☎ 07 865 7032, ⓦ wentworthvalleycamp.co.nz. Chilled DOC-run campsite with streamside pitches, BBQ area, pool, and coin-operated hot showers, right by the start of the track to Wentworth Falls. Camping **$13**

EATING

Blackies Café 418 Ocean Rd ☎ 07 865 9834. Just a hop and a skip from the beach, behind the surf club, this café serves some of the best coffee – hot and iced ($4-7) – in town, as well as brunch, lunch and snack options. Mon–Wed 7am–3pm, Thurs 7am–4pm, Fri–Sun 7am–5pm.

Six Forty Six 646 Port Rd ☎ 07 865 6117, ⓦ sixfortysix. co.nz. Contemporary café/restaurant serving breakfasts, good coffee, and excellent fusion tacos featuring garlic prawns, falafel and Cajun chicken (from $18). Fri and Sat open later in summer. Daily 8am–4pm.

3

Waihi and around

SH25 and SH2 meet at the southernmost town on the Coromandel Peninsula, **WAIHI**, 30km south from Whangamata. The small town merits a quick stop to sample its gold mining, both past and present.

Gold was first discovered here in a reef of quartz in 1878, but it wasn't until 1894 that a boom began. Workers flocked, but disputes over union and non-union labour ensued, and the violent **Waihi Strike** of 1912 helped galvanize the labour movement and led to the creation of the Labour Party. Although underground mining stopped in 1952, extraction was cranked up again in 1987 in the open-pit but well-hidden Martha Mine. The open-pit mine has now wound down, with the focus now on tunnel mining.

Cornish pumphouse

In the last few years, the hollow concrete shell of a three-storey 1904 **Cornish-style pumphouse** has become the town's icon and most prominent feature. It once kept the mine dry by pumping 300 tonnes of water an hour, then languished in an increasingly precarious position on the edge of the open-cast mine. Then, over a period of three months in 2006, hydraulic rams slid the building 296m on teflon pads and steel runners to its current central location. The move was ostensibly to save the historic building, but also allowed the mine to expand into new territory.

Walk behind the Cornish pumphouse to the **mine viewpoint**, where you can peer 260m down into the abyss where 85-tonne dump trucks look like toys. For more pit views follow the **Pit Rim Walkway** (4km loop; 1hr), an almost level track which circumnavigates the mine past a number of explanatory panels and one of the huge dump trucks.

Waihi Arts Centre & Museum

54 Kenny St • June–Sept Mon & Thurs–Sun noon–3pm; Oct–May Mon, Sat & Sun noon–3pm, Thurs & Fri 10am–3pm • $5 • ☏ 07 863 8386, ⓦ waihimuseum.co.nz

Mining life, including the 1912 strike, is conjured up evocatively in displays at the **Waihi Arts Centre & Museum**. Check out the diorama of the Victoria Battery and the ants' nest-like model of the original fifteen-level-deep Waihi mine; only the uppermost eight levels have been chewed out by the current open-cast incarnation. There's also a small-scale stamper battery, a model of the Cornish pumphouse, a re-created gold mine tunnel, and a couple of **thumbs** preserved in formaldehyde. Miners once deliberately chopped off a thumb to get £500 compensation – enough to buy a small cottage they'd otherwise never be able to afford on miners' wages.

Gold Discovery Centre

126 Seddon St • Nov–April 9am–5pm; May–Oct 9am–4pm • $25 • ☏ 07 863 9015, ⓦ golddiscoverycentre.co.nz

The **Gold Discovery Centre** is well presented, if a little glossy, and has an emphasis on participation – try your hand with the pneumatic drill, set off dynamite, gamble at cards and pick up a gold ingot. There are also a fair few facts, and a great Lego model. Mine tours available (see page 233).

Goldfields Railway

End of Wrigley St • Mon–Fri 11.45am – timetables do sometimes change, so check the website; weekends, public holidays and school holidays daily 10am, 11.45am, 1.45pm & 3.30pm • $15 single, $20 return • ☏ 07 863 9020, ⓦ waihirail.co.nz

The 1930s' diesel engine of the **Goldfields Railway** runs scenic 6km rail trips west to Waikino in the nearby **Karangahake Gorge** (see page 209) along tracks built by a mining company. The return trip takes about an hour, provides attractive views of the Ohinemuri River and allows a few minutes at the far end to inspect the displays on local history. Hire a bike and cycle back.

Waihi Beach

The 9km-long golden-sand surf beach of **Waihi Beach**, 11km east of Waihi, is one of the safest ocean beaches in the country. Although the area has something of a suburban feel, there's an excellent campsite that justifies you making a detour off SH2.

ARRIVAL AND DEPARTURE

By bus InterCity and NakedBus buses on their Auckland–Tauranga runs stop outside the visitor centre in Waihi.

Destinations Auckland (5 daily; 2hr 40min); Tauranga (5 daily; 1hr).

INFORMATION AND TOURS

Information The i-SITE is at 126 Seddon St (daily: Oct–April 9am–5pm, May–Sept 10am–4pm; ☎07 863 6715, ⓦwaihi.org.nz), in the same building as the mine tour office and mining display.

Waihi gold-mine tours Pick-up from i-SITE (daily 10.30am & 12.30pm, plus extras during the summer; $36; ☎07 863 9015, ⓦwaihigoldminetours.co.nz). As a complement to the Discovery Centre, the mine company offers a 1.5-hour guided tour to the mine rim, and then to the other end of the 2.7km conveyor belt where the ore is processed. It's partly to demonstrate how environmentally friendly they are (dotterel nest at the waste dump), but even grown-ups will be thrilled by the size of the machinery here. Wear covered shoes, not sandals.

ACCOMMODATION AND EATING

★ **Bowentown Beach Holiday Park** 510 Seaforth Rd, Bowentown Beach ☎0800 143 769, ⓦbowentown. co.nz. A secluded site right at the southern end of the beach with lots of water activities available, modern showers, a TV lounge, plus bike and kayak rental for guests. Camping per site $51, cabins $85, apartments $175

3

EATING

The Porch Kitchen and Bar 23 Wilson Rd, Waihi Beach ☎07 863 1330, ⓦtheporchwaihibeach.co.nz. Now under new ownership, Waihi Beach's dining mainstay is good for everything from chilli hot chocolate and cake to a dinner of chicken breast with roast *kumara*. Mains around $30. May–Oct Mon–Thurs & Sun 8am–4pm, Fri & Sat 8am–11pm; Nov–April daily 8am–11pm.

Ti-Tree Café 14 Haszard St, Waihi ☎07 863 8668. Grab a coffee at this great little café with a wood-floored interior and a garden out back. Food spans the likes of pumpkin feta frittata ($16.50) and "world famous" chowder to evening wood-fired pizzas ($18–28). Occasional live music. Mon–Sat 6.30am–3pm, Thurs & Fri also 5.30–8.30pm.

Waitete Restaurant 31 Orchard Rd, 1.5km west of Waihi ☎07 863 8980, ⓦwaitete.co.nz. Combined restaurant, café and ice parlour that serves superb natural ice creams and fat-free sorbets (try the limoncello flavour) made in the small on-site factory. Lunch is a relaxed affair with burgers, omelettes and pan-fried fish, while dinner (mains $28–34) is more linen-and-candles formal and features the likes of prawn and shrimp risotto. Tues 6–11pm, Wed–Sun 11am–2.30pm & 6–11pm.

Katikati

South of Waihi, the coast begins to curl eastwards into the Bay of Plenty, leaving the bush-clad mountains behind to take on a gentler, more open aspect, with rolling hills divided by tall evergreen shelter belts that protect the valuable kiwifruit vines. In summer, numerous **roadside fruit stalls** spring up, selling ripe produce straight from the orchards, often at knockdown prices.

Some 20km after leaving Waihi you pass **KATIKATI**, an otherwise ordinary town but for the colourful and well-painted **murals** that have sprung up in the last couple of decades to catch passing traffic, many reflecting the heritage of the original Ulster settlers.

Rotorua and the Bay of Plenty

WHITE ISLAND

Rotorua and the Bay of Plenty

Southeast of the Waikato region, Rotorua is one of New Zealand's most popular tourist destinations – so much so, in fact, that it's been dubbed "Roto-Vegas". Here boiling mud pools plop next to spouting geysers fuelled by super-heated water, drawn off to fill hot pools in and around the city. Accessible Māori cultural experiences abound, with expert Arawa carvings and groups who perform traditional dances and *haka* before a feast of fall-off-the-bone meat and succulent vegetables cooked in a *hangi* underground steam oven. North of Rotorua, stretching from the Coromandel Peninsula in the east to the East Cape in the west, is the Bay of Plenty. As well as playing an important role in New Zealand's history, this coastline is strung with beaches and dotted with islands.

You smell **Rotorua** long before you see it. Hydrogen sulphide drifting up from natural vents in the region's thin crust means that a whiff of rotten eggs lingers in the air, but after a few hours you'll barely notice it. The odour certainly doesn't stop anyone from visiting this small city on the southern shores of **Lake Rotorua**: indeed, this is the North Island's tourist destination *par excellence*. The dramatic volcanic scenery around the city is striking for its contrast with the encroaching pines of the Kaingaroa Forest, one of the world's largest plantation forests, with serried ranks of fast-growing radiata (Monterey) relishing the free-draining pumice soils.

From the open-pit gold-mining town of Waihi, at the base of the Coromandel Peninsula, the **Bay of Plenty** sweeps south and east to **Opotiki**, traced along its length by the Pacific Coast Highway (SH2). The bay earned its name in 1769 from Captain Cook, who was impressed by the Māori living off its abundant resources and by the generous supplies they gave him – an era of peace shattered by the New Zealand Wars of the 1860s, when fierce fighting led to the establishment of garrisons at **Tauranga** and **Whakatane**.

The Bay of Plenty has the best climate on the North Island, making it a fertile fruit-growing region (particularly citrus and kiwifruit). Though popular with Kiwi holidaymakers, the coast has remained relatively unspoiled, offering great surf beaches and other offshore activities. The western bay is home to one of the country's fastest-growing urban areas, centred on Tauranga and the contiguous beach resort of **Mount Maunganui**. The east revolves around Whakatane, the launching point for boat excursions to actively volcanic **White Island**, as well as dolphin swimming and wilderness rafting on the Motu River.

Rotorua

Rotorua lies in one of the world's most concentrated and accessible geothermal areas, where 15m geysers spout among kaleidoscopic mineral pools, steam wafts over cauldrons of boiling mud and terraces of encrusted silicates drip like stalactites. Birds on the lakeshore are relieved of the chore of nest-sitting by the warmth of the ground; in churchyards tombs are built topside as digging graves is likely to unearth a hot spring; and many hotels are equipped with geothermally fed hot tubs. Throughout the region, sulphur and heat combine to form barren landscapes where only hardy plants brave the trickling hot streams, sputtering vents and seething fumaroles. There's no shortage of colour, however, from iridescent mineral deposits lining the pools: bright oranges juxtaposed with emerald greens and rust reds.

MĀORI MEETING HOUSE, ROTORUA

Highlights

❶ Kaituna River Give white-water rafting a go on this excellent short river, and hold on as you shoot over the spectacular 7m-high Tutea Falls. See page 244

❷ Māori cultural performance A delectable *hangi* feast wraps up an evening of chants, dance, songs and stories, and you'll come away with an insight into the Māori world-view. See page 248

❸ Wai-O-Tapu Luminous pools, bubbling mud and a spurting geyser make this the best of Rotorua's abundant thermal areas. See page 253

❹ Mount Maunganui Scale the peak of this extinct volcano for spectacular panoramic views of the beach town it gave its name to. See page 259

❺ Mataatua Wharenui Visit one of New Zealand's most beautiful Māori meeting houses, which was returned to its rightful home after more than a century. See page 264

❻ White Island Explore the otherworldly moonscape and sulphur deposits of New Zealand's most active volcano. See page 265

HIGHLIGHTS ARE MARKED ON THE MAP ON PAGE 238

But constant hydrothermal activity is only part of the area's appeal. The naturally hot water lured **Māori** to settle here, using the hottest pools for cooking and bathing, and building their *whare* (houses) on warm ground to drive away the winter chill. Despite the diluting effects of tourism, there's no better place to get an introduction into Māori culture.

Rotorua Lake's northern and southern boundaries are marked by two ancient villages of the Arawa subtribe, Ngati Whakaue: lakeshore **Ohinemutu** and inland **Whakarewarewa**. The original **Bath House** is now part of **Rotorua Museum**, set in the grounds of the very English **Government Gardens**. At the southern end of Rotorua, Māori residents still go about their daily lives amid the steam and boiling pools at **Whakarewarewa Thermal Village**, while the adjacent **Te Puia** offers the region's only natural geysers, plopping mud and a nationally renowned Māori carving school.

Beyond the city, Mount Ngongotaha rises up, providing the necessary slope for a number of gravity-driven activities at the **Skyline Rotorua**. In its shadow, **Rainbow Springs Kiwi Wildlife Park** provides a window into the life cycle of trout, and an excellent **Kiwi Encounter**, while **Agroventures** fills the prescription for adrenaline junkies.

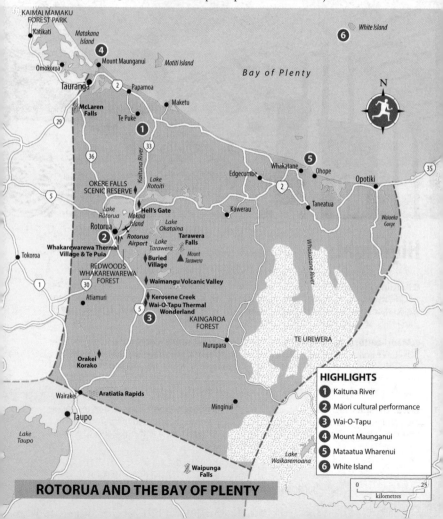

HIGHLIGHTS

1. Kaituna River
2. Māori cultural performance
3. Wai-O-Tapu
4. Mount Maunganui
5. Mataatua Wharenui
6. White Island

0 — 25 kilometres

ROTORUA AND THE BAY OF PLENTY

ROTORUA SAFETY

A continuing problem in and around Rotorua is **theft from cars**, with thieves targeting those parked near hostels, as well as cars left at trailheads, tourist attractions and other unguarded areas (Kerosene Creek is a particular hotspot for break-ins). Take any valuables into your room or ask to use a safe. The general rate of crime in Rotorua is also higher than the national average; keep your wits about you, but don't be paranoid.

Some of the region's finest geothermal areas lie outside the city – see page 249.

Brief history

The Rotorua region is the traditional home of the **Arawa** people. According to Māori history, one of the first parties to explore the interior was led by the *tohunga* (priest), **Ngatoroirangi**, who made it as far as the freezing summit of Mount Tongariro, where he feared he might die from cold. His prayers to the gods of Hawaiki were answered with fire that journeyed underground, surfacing at White Island in the Bay of Plenty, then at several more points in a line between there and the three Central North Island volcanoes. Ngatoroirangi was saved, and he and his followers established themselves around Lake Rotoiti ("small lake") and Lake Rotorua ("second lake").

In revenge for an earlier raid, the Northland Ngapuhi chief, **Hongi Hika**, led a war party here in 1823, complete with muskets traded with Europeans in the Bay of Islands. The Arawa retreated to Mokoia Island, in the middle of Lake Rotorua; undaunted, Hongi Hika and his warriors carried their canoes overland between lakes (the track between Lake Rotoiti and Lake Rotoehu still bears the name Hongi's Track) and defeated the traditionally armed Arawa. In the New Zealand Wars of the 1860s the Arawa supported the government. In return, colonial troops helped repulse **Te Kooti** and his people a decade later.

A few **Europeans** had already lived for some years in the Māori villages of Ohinemutu and Whakarewarewa, but it wasn't until Te Kooti had been driven off that Rotorua came into existence. **Tourists** began to arrive in the district to view the Pink and White Terraces, and the Arawa, who up to this point had been relatively isolated from European influence, quickly grasped the possibilities of tourism, helping make Rotorua what it is today. Set up as a **spa town** on land leased from the Ngati Whakaue, by 1885 the fledgling city boasted the Government Sanatorium Complex, a spa designed to administer the rigorous treatments deemed beneficial to the "invalids" who came to take the waters.

The city centre

With their juxtaposition of the staid and the exotic, **Government Gardens**, east of the town centre, are a bizarre vision of an antipodean little England. White-clad croquet players totter round sulphurous steam vents and palm trees loom over rose gardens centred on the Elizabethan-style **Bath House**, built in 1908. Heralded as the greatest spa in the South Seas, it was designed to treat patients suffering from just about any disorder – arthritis, alcoholism, nervousness – and offered ghoulish treatments involving electrical currents and colonic irrigation as well as the geothermal baths. The bathhouse limped along until 1963, although the era of the grand spas had come to a close long before. For a contemporary, altogether more luxurious version of the experience, head to the nearby **Polynesian Spa** or the **Spa at QE**.

The Rotorua Museum

Queens Drive, Government Gardens • Closed at time of research – check ahead • ⓦ rotoruamuseum.co.nz

The old bathhouse houses the wonderful **Rotorua Museum**, which was closed at the time of research after the building failed earthquake safety standards. If and when it

THE LOVE STORY OF HINEMOA AND TUTANEKAI

The Māori love story of **Hinemoa and Tutanekai** has been told around the shores of Lake Rotorua for centuries. It tells of the illegitimate young chief Tutanekai of Mokoia Island and his high-born paramour, Hinemoa, whose family forbade her from marrying him. To prevent her from meeting him they beached their *waka* (canoe), but the strains of his lamenting flute wafted across the lake nightly and the smitten Hinemoa resolved to swim to him. One night, buoyed by gourds, she set off towards Mokoia, but by the time she got there Tutanekai had retired to his *whare* (house) to sleep. Hinemoa arrived at the island but without clothes was unable to enter the village, so she immersed herself in a hot pool. Presently Tutanekai's slave came to collect water and Hinemoa lured him over, smashed his gourd and sent him back to his master. An enraged Tutanekai came to investigate, only to fall into Hinemoa's embrace.

re-opens, visitors will be able to explore spa's history, which is told through the "Taking the Cure" exhibit. Several rooms have been preserved in a state of arrested decay while an entertaining film re-creates some of the history of both the area and baths.

There's also a small but internationally significant **Te Arawa** display showcasing the long-respected talents of Arawa carvers who made this area a bastion of pre-European carving tradition. Meanwhile, extensive displays covering the dramatic events surrounding the **Tarawera eruption** include an informative relief map of the region, eyewitness accounts and reminiscences, a multimedia presentation and photos of the ash-covered hotels at Te Wairoa and Rotomahana, both now demolished. There's also a small but moving section on the **Māori battalion**, which served in World War II.

The Polynesian Spa

Hinemoa St, lake end • Daily 8am–11pm; spa therapies daily 10am–7pm • Adult pools $30; private pools $20 each/30min, lake view $30/30min; deluxe lake spa $50; family spa: $23 for adults, $10 for children; spa therapies from $159 • ☎ 07 348 1328, Ⓦ polynesianspa.co.nz

A mostly open-air complex landscaped for lake views, the **Polynesian Spa** comprises four separate areas. Most people head straight for the **Adult Pools**, a collection of seven pools (36–42°C) ranged around the historic Radium and Priest pools. These are off-limits, but the Priest water (claimed to ease arthritis and rheumatism) is fed into three of the pools. If you only want half an hour in the water, you're probably better served by the **Private Pools** where two or three of you can soak in a shallow rock-lined pool. For a little exclusivity opt for the adjacent **Lake Spa**, with landscaped rock pools along with private relaxation lounge and bar or book ahead for massages, mud wraps and general pampering. Kids are catered for in the **Family Spa**, with one chlorinated 33°C pool, a couple of mineral pools and a waterslide.

The Blue Baths

Queens Drive, Government Gardens • Daily: Nov–March 10am–6pm; April–Oct noon–6pm • $11 • ☎ 07 350 2119, Ⓦ bluebaths.co.nz

While the main bathhouse promoted health, the adjacent **Blue Baths** promised only pleasure when it opened in 1933. Designed in the Californian Spanish Mission style, this was one of the first public swimming pools in the world to allow mixed bathing. It closed in 1982, but later partly reopened to allow swimming in an outdoor pool (29–33°C) and soaking in two smaller pools (38–40°C). The water is fresh, not mineral. Most of the building is given over to private functions so it's often closed at weekends.

Spa at QE

1073 Whakaue St • Mon–Fri 9am–9pm, Sat & Sun 9am–7pm • Pool $14; treatments from $79 • ☎ 07 343 1665, Ⓦ qehealth.co.nz

The spirit of the original bathhouse lives on at the **Spa at QE**, where the emphasis is on therapeutic treatments. It has a clinical, slightly scruffy feel, but there's increasing sophistication in the areas devoted to pampering. Soak in a private pool filled with alkaline water from the Rachel Spring or book in for a soothing mud bath or an Aix massage – like being rubbed down while under a horizontal hot shower.

Ohinemutu

On the lakeshore, 500m north of Rotorua • $2 donation • ☎ 07 348 0189

Before Rotorua the principal Māori settlement in the area was at **Ohinemutu**. Ohinemutu remains a Māori village centred on its hot springs and the small half-timbered neo-Tudor **St Faith's Anglican Church** built in 1914 to replace its 1885

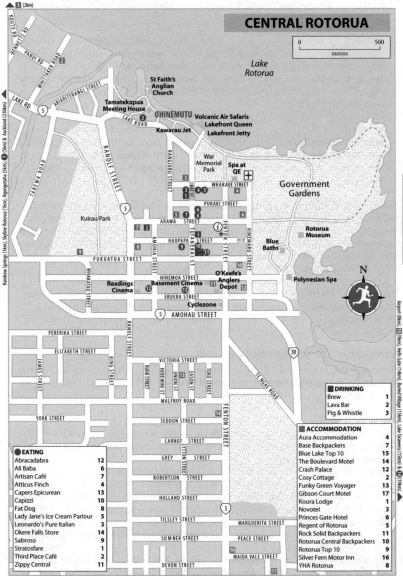

CENTRAL ROTORUA

0   500
metres

Lake Rotorua

St Faith's Anglican Church
Tamatekapua Meeting House
OHINEMUTU
Volcanic Air Safaris
Lakefront Queen
Lakefront Jetty
Kawarau Jet
LAKE ROAD

BENNETTS RD
DILLON RD
PANUI RD
WHITTAKER ROAD
ARIARITERANGI STREET
LAKE RD

TAREWA ROAD
RANOLF STREET

War Memorial Park
Spa at QE
Government Gardens

RANGIURU STREET
WHAKAUE STREET
PUKAKI STREET
ARAWA STREET
HAUPAPA STREET
FENTON STREET
HINEMARU STREET

Kuirau Park
AMOHIA STREET
PUKUATUA STREET
WHAKATUU STREET

Rotorua Museum
Blue Baths

HINEMOA STREET
O'Keefe's Anglers Depot
Readings Cinema
Basement Cinema
ERUERA STREET
Cyclezone
AMOHAU STREET

Polynesian Spa
Polynesian Spa

N

PERERIKA STREET
ELIZABETH STREET
JAMES STREET
KING STREET
RANOLF STREET
RUHI STREET
HEREWINI ST
UNION ST
EASON ST
TOKO STREET

VICTORIA STREET
MALFROY ROAD

TE NGAE ROAD

YORK STREET
SEDDON STREET
CARNOT STREET
GREY STREET
LYTTON STREET
ROBERTSON STREET
HOLLAND STREET
FENTON STREET

TILSLEY STREET
MARGUERITA STREET
SUMNER STREET
PEACE STREET
MAIDA VALE STREET
DEVON STREET

Whakarewarewa (1km) & Taupo (80km) ▼

■ **DRINKING**
Brew   1
Lava Bar   2
Pig & Whistle   3

■ **ACCOMMODATION**
Aura Accommodation   4
Base Backpackers   7
Blue Lake Top 10   15
The Boulevard Motel   14
Crash Palace   12
Cosy Cottage   2
Funky Green Voyager   13
Gibson Court Motel   17
Koura Lodge   1
Novotel   6
Princes Gate Hotel   3
Regent of Rotorua   5
Rock Solid Backpackers   11
Rotorua Central Backpackers 10
Rotorua Top 10   9
Silver Fern Motor Inn   16
YHA Rotorua   8

● **EATING**
Abracadabra   12
Ali Baba   6
Artisan Café   7
Atticus Finch   4
Capers Epicurean   13
Capizzi   10
Fat Dog   8
Lady Jane's Ice Cream Parlour 5
Leonardo's Pure Italian   3
Okere Falls Store   14
Sabroso   9
Stratosfare   1
Third Place Café   2
Zippy Central   11

LAKE ROTORUA AND MOKOIA ISLAND TOURS AND ACTIVITIES

Rotorua meets the water at the Lakefront Jetty, at the northern end of Tutaneka Street. This is the starting point for trips to **Mokoia Island**, 7km north of the jetty, a predator-free bird sanctuary where a breeding programme supports populations of saddlebacks and North Island robins (often spotted at the feeder stations) and kokako. The island is better known, however, for the story of **Hinemoa and Tutanekai** (see page 240); the site of Tutanekai's *whare* and Hinemoa's Pool can still be seen on guided island visits.

All sixteen lakes around Rotorua, but especially Lake Rotorua, given its proximity to the city, have a reputation for **trout fishing**. The angling is both scenic and rewarding, with waters stocked with strong-fighting rainbow trout.

CRUISES

Lakeland Queen Lakefront Jetty ☎0800 572 784, ⓦlakelandqueen.com. For a leisurely cruise on the lake, try the *Lakeland Queen*, a replica paddle steamer that runs a series of trips including meals (breakfast $44; lunch $55; coffee $29; dinner $59).

FISHING

O'Keefe's Anglers Depot 1113 Eruera St ☎07 346 0178. Has up-to-date information on lake and river conditions, and stocks the free *Lake Rotorua* *& Tributaries* leaflet published by Fish & Game New Zealand, explaining the rules of the fishery, and will provide contacts for fly-fishing guides, generally around $500 for a day. For information on fishing licences, see page 54. Mon–Fri 8.30am–5.30pm, Sat 9am–2pm.

Kawarau Jet Lakefront Jetty ☎07 343 7600, ⓦnzjetboat.co.nz. Runs high-octane spins around the lake ($85), parasailing ($69), and trips to Mokoia Island ($95) and the Manupirua Hot Springs ($125), which can only be accessed by boat. Daily 9am–5.30pm.

predecessor. Within, there's barely a patch of wall that hasn't been carved or covered with *tukutuku* (ornamental latticework) panels. The main attraction is the window featuring the figure of Christ, swathed in a Māori cloak and feathers, positioned so that he appears to be walking on the lake. Outside is the grave of Gilbert Mair, a captain in the colonial army who twice saved Ohinemutu from attacks by rival Māori, becoming the only Pakeha to earn full Arawa chieftainship.

At the opposite end of the small square in front of the church stands the **Tamatekapua Meeting House**, again beautifully carved, though the best work, some dating back almost two hundred years, is inside and inaccessible. Call for details of guided tours.

Whakarewarewa Thermal Reserve

Rotorua's closest geothermal attractions, **Te Puia** and the **Whakarewarewa Thermal Village**, share the **Whakarewarewa Thermal Reserve**, and lie around 3km south of the city centre.

Te Puia

Hemo Rd, around 4km south of the centre · Daily: April–Sept 8am–5pm, Oct–March 8am–6pm; hour-long guided tours on the hour (free) · $54; daytime guided tour, evening cultural show and *hangi* $163; a range of other activities are on offer – check the website for details · ☎07 348 9047, ⓦtepuia.com

Around two-thirds of the active thermal zone is occupied by **Te Puia**, a series of walkways past glooping pools of boiling mud, sulphurous springs and New Zealand's most geysers, the 7m **Prince of Wales' Feathers** and the granddaddy of them all, the 15m **Pohutu** ("big splash"). The latter performed several times a day until 2000, when it surprised everyone by spouting continuously for an unprecedented 329 days. It has since settled back to two to three times an hour, immediately preceded by the Prince of Wales' Feathers.

The geothermal wonders are certainly impressive, but Te Puia is also home to a **nocturnal kiwi house**, a replica of a traditional **Māori village** that's used on ceremonial occasions, and an **Arts and Crafts Institute** where skilled artisans produce flax skirts and enormous carvings. Pricey samples can be bought in the gift shop.

Whakarewarewa Thermal Village

17 Tryon St, 3km south of the centre • Daily 8.30am–5pm; free cultural performance at 11.15am and 2pm • $40 including an optional guided tour (hourly); $58 for entry, guided tour and a *hangi* (served noon–2pm) • ☎ 07 349 3463, Ⓦ whakarewarewa.com

The rest of the thermal area falls under the auspices of **Whakarewarewa Thermal Village**, a living village founded in pre-European times and undergoing continual, though sympathetic, modernization. The focus here is not on geysers but on how Māori interact with this unique environment. You can stroll at leisure around the village, attend the free **cultural performance**, and partake in a **hangi**. You can even buy corn cobs ($2) boiled in one of the natural cauldrons. Book via the website for a ten percent discount.

Northwest Rotorua

Aside from visits to the thermal areas, much of Rotorua's daytime activity takes place around the flanks of **Mount Ngongotaha**, 5–10km northwest of the centre, which is increasingly being overtaken by the city's suburbs.

Skyline Rotorua

185 Fairy Springs Rd, 4km northwest of the centre • Daily 9am–10pm • Gondola $30; gondola and luge packages from $42 • ☎ 07 347 0027, Ⓦ skyline.co.nz

At **Skyline Rotorua**, gondolas whisk you 200m up to the station on the mountain for views across the lake and town and for lunch or dinner in the buffet restaurant (see page 248). Once you're up above Rotorua you can zip around the hillside, trying out adventure activities including the **luge** and the adjacent **Zoom Zipline**, which whizzes down the side of Mount Ngongotaha for 383m. There are two parallel lines so you can zip with a friend, and at the end there's the chance to finish with a leap of faith, falling backwards off the 10metre-high **Quickjump** freefall.

Rainbow Springs Kiwi Wildlife Park

Fairy Springs Rd, 4km from the centre • **Wildlife Park** Daily 8am–9.30pm, until 10.30pm in summer • $40 • **Kiwi Encounter** Daily 10am–4pm; guided tour on the hour from 10am • ☎ 07 350 0440, Ⓦ rainbowsprings.co.nz

At the foot of Mount Ngongotaha lies **Rainbow Springs Kiwi Wildlife Park**, a series of pools where you can view massive rainbow, brown and North American brook trout. These are linked by nature trails which visit several free-flight bird enclosures, a tuatara, a talkative kea and a nocturnal kiwi house. Your ticket gives you access for 24 hours, so come back after dark when the trees and pools are colourfully lit and kiwi are out and about in a naturalistic enclosure with little separating you from the birds.

Also here is the excellent **Kiwi Encounter**, giving visitors an insight into the conservation work supporting the country's icon in the battle against extinction. A 30-minute guided tour demonstrates egg incubation and ends with a kiwi viewing.

Paradise Valley Springs

467 Paradise Valley Rd, 11km west of the centre • Daily 8am–5pm • $30 • ☎ 07 348 9667, Ⓦ paradisev.co.nz

Trout share billing with lions at **Paradise Valley Springs**, a patch of mature bush where manicured pathways weave between pools of trout, an attractive wetland area, a walk-in aviary with kea, and paddocks containing tahr, wallabies and wild pigs. An elevated boardwalk nature trail gives a great introduction to New Zealand's trees, but the big draw is the breeding pride of lions which are fed daily at 2.30pm. At times they have lion cubs which, between the ages of four weeks and one year, can be petted.

4

RAFTING, KAYAKING AND SLEDGING AROUND ROTORUA

Rotorua has a considerable reputation for its nearby **whitewater rivers**, which you can tackle aboard rafts, kayaks (usually tandems) or, more in-your-face, by "sledging" – floating down rapids clinging to a buoyant plastic sledge (really only suitable for strong swimmers). There's no shortage of operators willing to take you out (usually September–May); the most popular rivers are listed below, along with recommended outfitters.

Other options include renting kayaks or undertaking kayaking courses and guided trips on several of the larger lakes in the region, with the emphasis on scenic appreciation, soaking in hot pools and a little fishing. With more time and money, it's worth considering a multi-day wilderness rafting trip on the East Cape's Motu River.

RIVERS

Kaituna River Much of the hype is reserved for this Grade IV river, or at least the 2km section after it leaves Lake Rotoiti 20km north of Rotorua, which includes the spectacular 7m Tutea Falls (sledgers walk around the falls).

Wairoa River If you can get the timing right, this Grade IV+ river, 80km by road from Rotorua, on the outskirts of Tauranga, is the one to go for. It relies on dam-releases for raftable quantities of whitewater (Dec–March every Sun; Sept–Nov, April & May every second Sun). This is one of the finest short trips available in New Zealand, negotiating a hazardous but immensely satisfying stretch of water.

Rangitaiki River If your tastes lean more towards appreciation of the natural surroundings with a bit of a bumpy ride thrown in, opt for this Grade III river, which also shoots Jeff's Joy, a Grade IV drop that's the highlight of the trip.

OUTFITTERS

Kaitiaki Adventures 1135 Te Ngae Rd, 12km northeast of Rotorua ☎ 0800 338 736, ⓦ kaitiaki. co.nz. Rafting and sledging trips with a cultural dimension – explaining the significance of the river to Māori. Along with trips down the Kaituna (rafting $109; sledging $120) they do trips down the Wairoa (rafting $137.50). They also do trips on the gentler Rangitikei River (rafting $137.50 including hot pools).

Kaituna Kayaks 3G Trout Pool Rd, Okere Falls ☎ 07 362 4486, ⓦ kaitunakayaks.co.nz. Offers kayak lessons on the Kaituna River ($150/half day) and trips along the Kaituna to hot springs ($150), plus certification course for more experienced paddlers and multi-day holidays.

Raftabout Rotorua Airport ☎ 0800 723 822, ⓦ raftabout.co.nz. Runs trips down the Kaituna, the Wairoa and the Rangitikei on a raft (from $129), sledging adventures on the Kaituna ($129), plus a variety of combo deals with other adventure activities.

The Agrodome

Western Rd, Ngongotaha, 10km north of the centre • Daily 8.30am–5pm • tour $49; show $36; combo ticket $68 • ☎ 07 357 1050, ⓦ agrodome.co.nz

Just about every bus touring the North Island stops at the Agrodome, where the star attraction is an hour-long **sheep show**. Though undoubtedly corny, this popular spectacle is always entertaining: rams representing the nineteen major breeds farmed in New Zealand are enticed onto the podium, a sheep is shorn, lambs are bottle-fed and there's a sheepdog display. Afterwards, the dogs are put through their paces outside and you can watch a 1906 industrial carding machine turn fleece into usable wool. There's also a one-hour farm tour complete with honey tasting, a visit to an organic orchard, deer viewing and, between April and June, kiwifruit picking.

Agroventures

1335 Paradise Valley Rd, 10km from the centre • Daily 9am–5pm • Bungy jump $109; Swoop swing, Agrojet, Freefall Extreme and Shweeb one for $49, two for $79, all four $109; all four plus bungy $189 • ☎ 0800 949 888, ⓦ agroventures.co.nz

Adrenaline junkies can get a hit at **Agroventures**, where attractions include a 43m **bungy jump**, the **Swoop** swing ride, and the **Agrojet** where you're piloted around a short course at breakneck speed in a three-seater jetboat. The **Freefall Extreme** simulates a freefall skydive using a powerful vertical fan above which you hover (or at least try to). The **Shweeb** offers a chance to race recumbent bicycles encased in clear plastic fairings and slung from an overhead monorail. Either race the clock or your mates around the undulating track. It's nowhere near as geeky as it sounds, particularly if you can get two teams together. Assorted combo deals get you more bang for your buck.

Zorb

SH5, at Western Rd, 10km from the centre • Daily: May–Oct 9am–5pm; Nov–April 9am–7pm • Rides from $45 • ☎ 0800 227 474, ⓦ zorb.com

Another Kiwi-pioneered adrenaline ride is the **Zorb**. You dive into the centre of a huge clear plastic ball and roll down a 200m hill or the slower but wilder zigzag course; you can choose from wet and dry rides, the former being the more fun.

Rotorua Canopy Tours

SH5, at Western Rd, 10km from the centre • Daily 7.45am–4pm • $149 (3hr) • ☎ 0800 227 474, ⓦ canopytours.co.nz

For an adventure that gives something back, head out to the evergreen native forests of the Mamaku Plateau with **Rotorua Canopy Tours**. The three-hour ziplining tour runs through a beautiful tract of rare virgin native forest with platforms high in the rimu trees with the indigenous birds (listen out for robins and morepork) and zipwires swooping at great heights (up to 44 metres) over fern-packed gullies looked down upon by moss-covered trunks. The company have spent thousands in trapping to rid the forest of pests such as possums and rats, giving rare native birds a fighting chance and returning this gorgeous area to its former pre-European glory. Though the moa and Haast's eagle will never return, many native birds have, and future plans include fencing a large area to keep all pests out – and possibly reintroduce the kiwi.

ARRIVAL AND DEPARTURE   ROTORUA

By plane Rotorua's airport is 8km northeast of the centre on SH30 (ⓦ rotorua-airport.co.nz). Rotorua Taxi (☎ 07 348 1111) charges around $40 to the city centre; Grumpy's Tours & Transfers (see page 245) have airport transfers from $30.
Destinations Auckland (3 daily; 40min); Christchurch (3 daily; 1hr 40min); Wellington (3 daily; 1hr 10min).
By bus InterCity and NakedBus long-distance buses stop

outside the i-SITE on Fenton St.
Destinations Auckland (13 daily; 4hr); Gisborne (1 daily; 4hr 35min); Hamilton (5 daily; 1hr 30min); Opotiki (1 daily; 2hr 5min); Palmerston North (4 daily; 5hr 25min–6hr); Taupo (7 daily; 1hr 5min); Tauranga (4 daily; 1hr 35min); Turangi (4 daily; 2hr 5min); Waitomo (2 daily; 2hr 30min–4hr); Whakatane (1 daily; 1hr 30min).

GETTING AROUND

By bike Cyclezone (1299 Fenton St; ☎ 07 348 6610, ⓦ cyclezone.co.nz) has a range of bikes for hire (all come with helmets, repair kits and pumps), as well as trail maps. The I-SITE (see below) has a useful leaflet outlining ten mountain-biking routes around Rotorua (also see ⓦ riderotorua.com for more information).
By bus Cityride (☎ 0800 422 928, ⓦ baybus.co.nz) is

an urban bus system centred on Pukuatua St between Tutanekai and Amohia streets; its most useful services are #1 (to Skyline Skyrides, Rainbow Springs and the Agrodome) and #2 (to Te Puia); both run daily from roughly 6.30am–6.30pm every 30min (hourly on Sun, none on public holidays). Timetables are available at the i-SITE. Tickets are $2.70 each way, or $8.60 for a day-pass.

INFORMATION AND TOURS

Visitor information i-SITE, 1167 Fenton St (daily 7.30am–6pm, until 7pm in summer; ☎ 07 343 1730, ⓦ rotoruanz.com). Handles local, DOC and New Zealand-wide travel enquiries, and offers copies of the free weekly visitor's guide.
Grumpy's Tours & Transfers Call or book online; ☎ 07 348 2229; ⓦ grumpys.co.nz. Has entertaining tours to everywhere from Wai-O-Tapu ($80; see page 253) to Hawkes Bay ($1020 for up to six people) as well as tours around town.

Headfirst Call or book online; ☎ 0800 004 321; ⓦ travelheadfirst.com. Have tours to Waitomo ($175), Hobbiton ($119), and Wai-O-Tapu ($82), among others, as well as a range of shuttles.
Tim's Thermal Shuttle Call or book online; ☎ 0274 945 508; ⓦ thermalshuttle.co.nz. Runs to Waimangu, Wai-O-Tapu, Waitomo and Te Puia.

ACCOMMODATION

There's a wide range of accommodation, and many places have a **hot pool**, though genuine mineral-water pools

are less common. **Hostels** are all within walking distance of the city centre, while **motels** mostly line Fenton Street,

ROTORUA SCENIC FLIGHTS

The scenery around Rotorua is breathtaking from the air, particularly the region's volcanic spine centred on Mount Tarawera.

Volcanic Air Safaris Lakefront Jetty ☎ 0800 800 848, ⓦ volcanicair.co.nz. Offers all manner of options (from $165/person), including floatplane flights over Tarawera and Orakei Korako and helicopter flights to landings on White Island (see page 265).

which runs south towards Whakarewarewa. Competition is fierce and off-peak prices plummet. Although plentiful, **hotels** generally cater to bus-tour groups and have high walk-in rates. There are also numerous **B&Bs** in and around Rotorua: check out ⓦ rotoruabedandbreakfast.co.

CENTRAL ROTORUA

Aura Accommodation 1078 Whakaue St ☎ 07 348 8134, ⓦ aurarotorua.co.nz; map p.241. Formerly the *Havana Motor Lodge*, this quiet motel, close to the lakefront is a solid choice, with spacious grounds, a heated pool, two small mineral pools and free bike hire for guests. $168

Base Backpackers 1286 Arawa St ☎ 0800 227 396, ⓦ stayatbase.com; map p.241. Large, lively hostel that's a perennial favourite of the backpacker tour buses, with heated outdoor spa and swimming pool and the *Lava Bar* next door. Accommodation is in 4–8-bunk dorms (female-only ones available). Light sleeper should head elsewhere. Dorms $30, doubles $90

The Boulevard Motel 265 Fenton St ☎ 07 348 2074, ⓦ boulevardrotorua.co.nz; map p.241. Smartly appointed, well-run, family friendly motel with a range of room sizes and some of the best on-site mineral pools in town, as well as a heated swimming pool, and spa. $130

Crash Palace 1271 Hinemaru St ☎ 07 348 8842, ⓦ crashpalace.co.nz; map p.241. This is a hostel for real shoestring travellers, offering bargain basement, no frills dorms (4–10-bed; female-only available) and private rooms, as well as a hot tub, pool table, laundry service and a free barbecue in the summer. Dorms $20, doubles $70

★ **Cosy Cottage** 67 Whittaker Rd ☎ 07 348 3793, ⓦ cosycottage.co.nz; map p.241. Holiday park 2km from the centre with an extensive range of comfortable cabins, self-contained cottages, dorms and powered and tent sites, some geothermally heated. There's a swimming pool, a couple of pleasant mineral pools, naturally fed steam boxes for *hangi*-style cooking, city bikes and direct access to a lake beach where you can dig your own hot pool. Camping $43, dorms $22, cabins $80, cottages $120

Funky Green Voyager 4 Union St ☎ 07 346 1754, ⓦ funkygreenvoyager.co.nz; map p.241. Relaxed, eco-conscious hostel in a pair of suburban houses a 10min walk from the centre, with an easy-going communal atmosphere. Some doubles have en-suite bathrooms. Cooking facilities,

in particular, are excellent and there's a cosy TV-less lounge. Dorms $24, doubles $62

Gibson Court Motel 10 Gibson St ☎ 07 346 2822, ⓦ gibsoncourtmotel.co.nz; map p.241. Welcoming motel in a quiet area with ten one-bedroom units that are showing their age but are great value, particularly since most come with a private mineral-water pool in a secluded, leafy courtyard. $145

Novotel Lake end of Tutanekai St ☎ 07 3463 888, ⓦ novotelrotorua.co.nz; map p.241. In a great location close to the lakeshore, the *Novotel* is one of the best top-end hotels in town, with spacious, well-equipped en suites, some with views of the water. Highlights include a set of geothermal pools (free for guests), a heated swimming pool, gym, clutch of good restaurants/bars, and efficient service. $165

Princes Gate Hotel 1057 Arawa St ☎ 0800 500 705, ⓦ princesgate.co.nz; map p.241. Historic 1897-built wooden wide-verandahed hotel that's the sole survivor from the days when all of Hinemaru St was lined with places catering to folk taking the waters at the bathhouse. Lounges and bar are delightfully creaky (serving high tea), while the rooms and suites have been modernized, though remain rather twee. $196

★ **Regent of Rotorua** 1191 Pukaki St ☎ 0508 734 368, ⓦ regentrotorua.co.nz; map p.241. Accommodation at this revamped 1950s motel is in immaculate all-white studio suites that come with a pristine bathroom, stylish wallpaper and furnishings straight out of a style mag. You can lounge next to the heated outdoor pool, bathe in the mineral pool, work out in the small gym, or eat/drink in the attached restaurant-bar. $220

Rock Solid Backpackers 1410 Hinemoa St ☎ 07 282 2053, ⓦ rocksolidrotorua.co.nz; map p.241. Reliable, friendly hostel with clean and comfortable private rooms and mixed and female-only dorms, though the decor (grey features heavily) is rather gloomy. Facilities include a good kitchen, pool table and table tennis, while in the same building there's a climbing wall (visible from the hostel's communal areas) and a cinema (see page 249). Dorms $24, doubles $80

Rotorua Central Backpackers 1076 Pukuatua St ☎ 07 349 3285, ⓦ rotoruacentralbackpackers.co.nz; map p.241. Small, homey hostel, with beds rather than bunks in the 4- and 6-bed dorm rooms, plus private rooms, a spa pool, and pleasant communal lounge. Dorms $\underline{24}$, doubles $\underline{66}$

Silver Fern Motor Inn 326 Fenton St ☎0800 118 808, ⓦsilverfernmotorinn.co.nz; map p.241. This is a knockout modern motel with spacious, refurbished studios and one-bedroom units, all with spa pools, Sky TV, sunny balconies, oodles of space and helpful staff. There's a spa, and free bikes are available for guests to use. Studios $\underline{145}$, one-bedroom $\underline{185}$

YHA Rotorua 1278 Haupapa St ☎07 349 4088, ⓦyha. co.nz; map p.241. This sparkling, purpose-built, 180-bed hostel comes with spacious communal areas, including a big timber deck plus a well-equipped kitchen and exemplary eco credentials. There are 4-6-bed single-sex and mixed dorms (many without bunkbeds) and comfortable, en-suite private rooms. Good discounts for Rotorua activities, too. Dorms $\underline{29}$, doubles $\underline{84}$

CAMPING

Rotorua Top 10 1495 Pukuatua St ☎07 348 1886, ⓦrotoruatop10.co.nz; map p.241. This is the closest campsite to the city, with pitches for tents and campervans, simple cabins and motel rooms. Good facilities including a small outdoor pool and two hot tubs. Camping $\underline{58}$, cabins $\underline{175}$

AROUND ROTORUA

Blue Lake Top 10 723 Tarawera Rd, Blue Lake, 9km southeast of Rotorua ☎0800 808 292, ⓦbluelaketop10.co.nz; map p.241. A well-organized rural site, just across the road from Blue Lake, featuring a wide range of accommodation options, plus a games room and spa pool. Camping $\underline{45}$, doubles $\underline{175}$, cabins $\underline{80}$

Koura Lodge 209 Kawaha Point Rd, 5km north of central Rotorua ☎07 348 5868, ⓦkouralodge.co.nz; map p.241. Go for a lakeside room in the main building at this stylish, intimate lodge, which is equipped with secluded sauna and hot tub right on the water's edge, kayaks, tennis court and even a jetty for floatplanes. Understated rooms are tastefully furnished and well equipped, and there's a comfy guest lounge. $\underline{525}$

EATING

Head to the short strip at the lake end of **Tutanekai Street** (better known as "Eat Street" for the greatest concentration of international cuisine – from Korean to Tunisian – and a few quality restaurants). Most visitors spend one evening of their stay at a combined *hangi* and Māori concert in either a tourist hotel or, preferably, one of the outlying Māori *maraes*. Rotorua's **night market** takes place on Thursdays (5–9pm) on the section of Tutanekai Street between Haupapa and Hinemoa streets, with lots of food stalls plus arts and crafts.

Abracadabra 1263 Amohia St ☎07 348 3883, ⓦabracadabracafe.com; map p.241. Maghrebi music provides a suitable accompaniment in this loosely Moroccan café and restaurant strung with filigree lamps and divided into intimate rooms. Come for coffee and almond cake, brunch, tapas ($10–15), sharing platters, or dinner dishes such as seafood tagine (mains $27.50–32). Tues–Sat 10.30am–11pm, Sun 10.30am–3pm.

Ali Baba 1146 Tutanekai St ☎07 348 2983, ⓦalibabastunisiancuisine.co.nz; map p.241. This friendly Tunisian restaurant delivers the goods: succulent kebabs, well-spiced falafel, Middle-Eastern-style flatbread pizzas, and *kascrute* (a kind of baked kebab). It's good value, too, with dishes in the $9–18 bracket. Daily 11.30am–10pm.

Artisan Café 1149 Tutanekai St ☎07 348 0057, ⓦartisancaferotorua.com; map p.241. Breezy café, with interesting decor (for example, a delivery bike dangling from the wall), chilled-out tunes, excellent coffee ($4–7.50), breakfast and lunch options, and good cakes and pastries. Mon–Fri 7am–4pm, Sat & Sun 7.30am–4pm.

Atticus Finch Eat Street ☎07 460 0400, ⓦatticusfinch. co.nz; map p.241. This creative restaurant, named after the *To Kill a Mockingbird* lawyer, is the pick of the Eat Street options, serving modish "small" ($6–18) and "large" ($22–34) plates such as beer-braised beef shin with chipotle mayo, and chilli caramel jackfruit with refried beans. There's a good wine and beer selection, too. Daily noon–2.30pm & 5pm–late.

Capers Epicurean 1181 Eruera St ☎07 348 8818, ⓦcapers.co.nz; map p.241. Large, airy café/deli serving up wonderful breakfasts/brunches ($13–24) like sultana-and-apple bircher and lunch/dinners ($23–33) like harissa-spiced lentils. It's also a good spot for coffee and a cake. Daily 7am–9pm.

Capizzi 1198 Tutanekai St ☎07 347 0447, ⓦcapizzi. co.nz; map p.241. A narrow restaurant with a few tables out front and out back serving economical, thin-crust pizzas (slices from $5, whole pizzas from $15) to eat in or takeaway. Daily noon–9pm.

Fat Dog 1161 Arawa St ☎07 347 7586, ⓦfatdogcafe. co.nz; map p.241. Heaped portions of robust food are served at mismatched tables at this cheerful café/bar. Think stacked burgers ($19–23), copious breakfasts, lunch specials and great slabs of cake. Mon–Wed & Sun 7am–9pm, Thurs–Sat 7am–9.30pm.

Lady Jane's Ice Cream Parlour 1092 Tutanekai St ☎07 347 9340; map p.241. This award-winning Rotorua institution is a haven on a sunny day, with more than fifty ice cream flavours, including hokey pokey, white chocolate and raspberry, and *affogato*, plus frozen yoghurt, smoothies and ice coffees. Cones from $5. Daily 10am–10pm.

4

★ **Leonardo's Pure Italian** Eat Street ☎ 07 347 7084, ⓦ leonardospure.co.nz; map p.241. Widely regarded as the city's premier Italian restaurant. Hosts Leonardo and Yuka treat guests like friends and serve a limited but excellent range of expertly prepared Italian dishes, such as pappardelle with wild boar ragu, and – of course – tiramisu. Most mains $22–30. Daily 5–10pm.

Okere Falls Store 757a SH33, 15km northeast of town ☎ 07 362 4944, ⓦ okerefallsstore.co.nz; map p.241. A rambling beer garden (which hosts winter bonfire nights from 5–9pm on Friday, Saturday and Sunday) surrounds this fabulous gourmet and general store and café, while the big timber deck out front is also a choice spot for tucking into smashed avocado on toast, bratwurst and beetroot burgers (dishes $8–17). Mon–Wed & Sun 7am–7pm, Thurs–Sat 7am–9pm.

Sabroso 1184 Haupapa St ☎ 07 349 0591, ⓦ sabroso. co.nz; map p.241. Run by a Venezuelan-Kiwi couple, this Latin American restaurant's menu (mains $21.50–25.50) features Mexican tacos, Tex-Mex chimichangas, and Brazilian *moquecas* (a spicy prawn stew). As well as well-mixed margaritas and mojitos, they have a selection of Argentine and Chilean wines. Wed–Sun 5pm–late.

Stratosfare Skyline Rotorua ☎ 07 347 0037, ⓦ skyline.co.nz; map p.241. This buffet restaurant reclines at the top of the Skyline gondola (see page 243), ranging across the hillside with great views of Rotorua. Not to mention great steak and seafood cooked to order, abundant salads and a dessert buffet that will keep kids of all ages happy for hours. There's also wine from on-site winery Volcanic Hills. Lunch and gondola $64, dinner and gondola $85. Daily 11.30am–2pm & 5.30–10pm.

Third Place Café 35 Lake Road ☎ 07 349 4852, ⓦ thirdplacecafe.co.nz; map p.241. Buzzing café popular with locals and with views of the lake. Fill up with an all-day breakfast ($7–19.50) or call in for brunch of Moroccan chicken salad or toasted sarnie. Mon–Fri 7.30am–4pm, Sat & Sun 7.30am–3.30pm.

Zippy Central 1153 Pukuatua St ☎ 07 348 8288; map p.241. With green walls, orange seats, and a bust of Zippy (from the British children's TV show *Rainbow*), this café has a surreal feel. Beyond the decor, the goods are delivered: excellent coffee, tasty lunches (like Moroccan chicken salad: $17.50), and house-made cakes. Daily 7am–6.30pm.

DRINKING

There are several good bars (and several of the restaurants listed in "Eating" double up as drinking spots), but otherwise nightlife is fairly tame.

★ **Brew** Eat Street ☎ 07 346 0976, ⓦ brewpub.co.nz; map p.241. For the discerning beer drinker, this craft beer bar has the full range of their own Croucher Brewing productions on tap, as well as an ever-changing line-up of Kiwi craft brews (most beers around $10). There's also a menu of brunches, burgers, pizzas and bar snacks (chicken wings and the like). Mon–Fri 11am–late, Sat 10am–late.

Lava Bar Base Backpackers hostel (see page 246); map p.241. A pool table, discount drinks, budget meal deals and theme nights (eg Sunday pyjama party, Thursday ladies' night etc), are sure-fire winners with assorted backpackers, rafting guides and locals. Drinks around $10. Mon, Tues & Sun 5.30pm–2am, Wed–Sat 5.30pm–3am.

Pig & Whistle Corner of Haupapa and Tutanekai sts ☎ 07 347 3025, ⓦ pigandwhistle.co.nz; map p.241. Buzzing pub in a redbrick former police station with a garden bar, live bands Thurs–Sat, and good draft and bottled beers (from $7.50). There's also a wide range of hearty bar meals including fish and chips, served until 10pm. Daily 11.30am–late.

ENTERTAINMENT

Most visitors spend one evening of their stay at a combined *hangi* and Māori concert in either a tourist hotel or, preferably, one of the outlying Māori *maraes*.

HANGI AND MĀORI CONCERTS

Rotorua provides more opportunities than anywhere else to sample food steamed to perfection in the Māori earth oven or *hangi* and watch a Māori concert, typically an hour-long performance of traditional dance, song and chants. The bigger hotels all put on somewhat forced extravaganzas, so go for the "Māori experiences" here instead (daily, by reservation). All have buses picking up at hotels and hostels ready for a start around 6pm, then run for three to four hours. They follow largely the same format, giving instruction on *marae* customs and protocol

(see the "Experiencing Māori culture" box in Contexts, p.713) followed by a formal welcome, concert and *hangi*.

Mitai ☎ 07 343 9132, ⓦ mitai.co.nz. All the standard elements are very well done, the excellent *hangi* is cooked in the ground, plus the events are conveniently sited beside Rainbow Springs, giving a chance of a night-time walk through the bush past a beautiful clear spring which feeds a stream where a fully manned *waka* arrives in flaming torchlight. $116

Tamaki Māori Village ☎ 07 349 2999, ⓦ maoriculture. co.nz. You, and several busloads, are driven out to a specially built "Māori village" south of town for a spine-chilling welcome and tales of early Māori–European interaction. Everything is so professionally done that it is hard to quibble, but its popularity has become its biggest downfall and sightlines can be restricted. The *hangi* is good,

though, and the overall experience memorable. $130
Te Po ☎ 07 348 9047, ⓦ tepuia.com. Wear clean socks as it is shoes off (and men to the front) for the thoroughly professional performance in a traditional meeting house at Te Puia (see page 242). The *hangi* is top-class, and the night is rounded off with a tour of the geothermal valley, and hopefully a sight of a floodlit geyser performing. $112.50, combined with daytime entry to Te Puia $146.70

CINEMAS

Basement Cinema 1140 Hinemoa St ☎ 07 350 1400, ⓦ basementcinema.co.nz. Intimate, two-screen art-house theatre with a licensed café.
Readings Cinema 1263 Eruera St ☎ 07 349 0061, ⓦ readingcinemas.co.nz. The local multiplex showing the latest mainstream releases.

DIRECTORY

Library 1127 Haupapa St (Mon–Wed & Fri 9.30am–6pm, Thurs 9.30am–8pm, Sat 9.30am–4pm; ☎ 07 348 4177, ⓦ rotorualibrary.govt.nz). Unlimited free wi-fi and free use of computers for up to 30min.
Medical treatment For emergencies and urgent health

care go to Lakes Care, at Arawa and Tutanekai sts (daily 8am–10pm; ☎ 07 348 1000).
Pharmacy Lakes Care Pharmacy is at 1155 Tutanekai St (daily 8.30am–9.30pm; ☎ 07 48 4385).
Police 1190–1214 Fenton St ☎ 07 348 0099.

Around Rotorua

Many of the best attractions in the area lie outside the city itself but shuttles and tours (see page 245) mean that just about every combination of sights can be packed into a day, as well as all manner of **adventure activities** – from rafting to skydiving.

Travellers can quickly dispatch minor sights along the eastern shore of Lake Rotorua, leaving time for the seldom-crowded **Hell's Gate** thermal area and the opportunity to watch terrified rafters plunging over **Tutea Falls**. Rewards are more plentiful to the east and south especially around the shattered 5km-long massif of **Mount Tarawera**. During one cataclysmic night of eruptions in 1886 this chain split in two, destroying the region's first tourist attraction (the beautiful Pink and White Terraces), entombing the nearest settlement, Te Wairoa, now known as the **Buried Village**, and creating the **Waimangu Volcanic Valley**. It now ranks as one of the finest collections of geothermal features in the region alongside kaleidoscopic **Wai-O-Tapu Thermal Wonderland**, with its daily triggered **Lady Knox Geyser**, boiling mud, and brilliantly coloured pools. Other magnificent geothermal areas around Rotorua include **Kerosene Creek**, which has the best free hot pools hereabouts, and **Orakei Korako**, which offers a peaceful geothermal experience. Meanwhile, the **Whirinaki Forest Park** presents great hiking and biking opportunities on the road to Lake Waikaremoana (see page 343).

Okere Falls Scenic Reserve

Trout Pool Rd, off SH33, 21km from central Rotorua

SH33 continues north towards Tauranga. Signs 6km north point down Trout Pool Road to **Okere Falls Scenic Reserve**, which surrounds the popular rafting destination of the Kaituna River. From the first car park, 400m along Trout Pool Road, a broad, well-maintained track follows the river to a second car park (2.5km return; 40min–1hr) passing glimpses of the churning river below, and a viewing platform that's perfect for observing rafters plummet over the 7m **Tutea Falls**. From here, steps descend through short tunnels in the steep rock walls beside the waterfall to **Tutea Caves**, thought to have been used as a safe haven by Māori women and children during attacks by rival *iwi*. Afterwards refuel at the wonderful *Okere Falls Store* café (see page 248).

Hell's Gate

SH30, 14km northeast of the centre • Daily: Oct–March 8.30am–10pm; April–Sept 8.30am–8.30pm • Geothermal walk $35; Sulphurous Spa $25; mud bath $75 • ☎ 07 345 3151, ⓦ hellsgate.co.nz

Most traffic sticks to SH30, the route to **Hell's Gate**, the smallest of the major thermal areas, but also one of the most active. Its fury camouflages a lack of notable features, however, and the only real highlights are the bubbling mud of the Devil's Cauldron and the hot **Kakahi Falls**, whose soothing 38°C waters once made this a popular bathing spot (now off-limits). The real attraction here is the **Sulphurous Spa** where you can soak in the hot waters overlooking the park or sign up for mud-based treatments. There are a number of combination packages including transfers from Rotorua.

The northern lakes

Lake Rotoiti translates as "small lake", though it is in fact the second largest in the region, and is linked to Lake Rotorua by the narrow Ohau Channel. This passage, along with the neighbouring **Lake Rotoehu** and **Lake Rotoma**, traditionally formed part of the canoe route from the coast. A section of this route, apparently used on a raid by the Ngapuhi warrior chief Hongi Hika, is traced by **Hongi's Track** (3km return; 1hr), a pretty bushwalk which runs through to Lake Rotoehu.

Redwoods Whakarewarewa Forest

Access from the car park off Long Mile Rd, 5km south of the city centre off SH38 • Daily 24hr • Free; it's advisable to buy the waterproof trail map ($5) or book ($10) from the visitor centre (daily: summer 8.30am–6pm; winter 8.30am–5pm), the i-SITE or bike rental shops (see page 245) • Southstar Shuttles (ⓦ southstaradventures.com) operate a shuttle service to the top of the hill ($10)

The North Island's best accessible **mountain biking** lies fifteen minutes' ride southeast of central Rotorua, with large areas of the **Redwoods Whakarewarewa Forest**'s redwoods, firs and pines threaded by single-track trails especially constructed with banked turns and drops. Altogether there's around 70km of track, divided into over a dozen circuits graded from 1 (beginner) to 6 (death wish). The forest is also a great place to hike and horseride: ⓦ redwoods.co.nz has plenty of information on both.

Redwoods Treewalk

Long Mile Rd, 5km southeast of the city centre • Daily 9am–11pm • Day and night walks $25; $35 for both • ☎ 07 536 1010, ⓦ treewalk.co.nz

Inside the forest, and the brainchild of a German mechanical engineer, the **Redwoods Treewalk** allows visitors a bird's-eye view of these glorious trees. It consists of a 553m walkway, made up of interlinked suspension bridges and raised up to 12m above the forest floor. At night, a series of suspended lanterns dramatically illuminate the redwoods.

The Blue and Green lakes

Around 10km southeast of Rotorua, Tarawera Road reaches the iridescent waters of **Blue Lake** (Tikitapu) with its campsite, easy circuit walk (see box opposite) and safe swimming beach. A little further on, a ridge-top viewpoint overlooks both Blue Lake and **Green Lake** (Rotokakahi), whose name means "freshwater mussel lake", although because it's privately owned, no fishing or boating activity is allowed here. Tarawera Road then reaches the shores of Lake Tarawera 15km southeast of Rotorua.

The Buried Village and Lake Tarawera

Buried Village 1180 Tarawera Rd • Daily: Oct–Feb 9am–5pm, March–Sept 9am–4.30pm • $35 • ☎ 07 362 8287, ⓦ buriedvillage.co.nz

Just before the Tarawera lakeshore, the **Buried Village** kicks off with a **museum** that captures the spirit of the village in its heyday and the aftermath of its destruction, through photos, fine aquatints of the Pink and White Terraces

THE MOUNT TARAWERA ERUPTION

Volcanic activity provides the main theme for attractions southeast of Rotorua, most having some association with **Lake Tarawera** and the jagged line of volcanic peaks and craters along the southeastern shore, collectively known as **Mount Tarawera**, which erupted in 1886.

Prior to that eruption Tarawera was New Zealand's premier tourist destination, with thousands of visitors every year crossing lakes Tarawera and Rotomahana in whaleboats and *waka*, frequently guided by the renowned Māori guide Sophia, to the **Pink and White Terraces**, two separate fans of silica that cascaded down the hillside to the edge of Lake Rotomahana. Boiling cauldrons bubbled at the top of each formation, spilling mineral-rich water down into a series of staggered cup-shaped pools, the outflow of one filling the one below. Most visitors favoured the Pink Terraces, which were prettier and better suited to sitting and soaking. All this came to an abrupt end on the night of June 10, 1886, when the long-dormant Mount Tarawera erupted, creating 22 craters along a 17km rift, and covering over 15,000 square kilometres in mud and scoria. The Pink and White Terraces were shattered by the buckling earth, covered by ash and lava, then submerged deep under the waters of Lake Rotomahana.

The cataclysm had been foreshadowed eleven days earlier, when two separate canoe-loads of Pakeha tourists and their Māori guides saw an ancient *waka* glide out of the mist, with a dozen warriors paddling furiously, then vanish just as suddenly; the ancient *tohunga* (priest) Tuhoto Ariki interpreted this as a sign of imminent disaster. The fallout from the eruption buried five villages, including the staging post for the Pink and White Terrace trips, **Te Wairoa**, where the *tohunga* lived. In a classic case of blaming the messenger, the inhabitants refused to rescue the *tohunga* and it wasn't until four days later that they allowed a group of Pakeha to dig him out. Miraculously he lived, for a week.

In 2011, scientists discovered that rather than being completely destroyed, parts of the Pink Terraces appear to have survived the 1886 eruption (the White Terraces are thought to have been more likely to have been affected). The gas and hot water vents discovered on the lake floor indicate rare active underwater geothermal systems, which scientists are continuing to research.

and ash-encrusted knick-knacks. The Māori and European settlement here was larger than contemporary Rotorua until the Tarawera eruption when numerous houses collapsed under the weight of the ash; others were saved by virtue of their inhabitants hefting ash off the roof to lighten the load. From the museum, either opt for a free **guided tour** with period-costumed guides (available throughout the day; call for seasonal hours) or make your own way through the grounds.

What you see today is the result of 1930s and 1940s excavations plus some substantial reconstructions. The village itself is less an archeological dig than a manicured orchard: half-buried *whare* and the foundations for the *Rotomahana Hotel* sit primly on mown lawns among European fruit trees gone to seed, marauding hawthorn and a perfect row of full-grown poplars fostered from a line of fenceposts. Many of the *whare* house collections of implements and ash-encrusted household goods, and contrast starkly with the simplicity of other dwellings such as **Tohunga's Whare**, where the ill-fated priest lay buried alive for four days (see page 252). Look out too for the extremely rare, carved-stone *pataka* (storehouse) and the bow section of a *waka* once used to ferry tourists on the lake and allegedly brought to the district by Hongi Hika, when he invaded in 1823.

Access to the **Te Wairoa Falls** is included in the entry fee: head up a steep staircase and slippery boardwalk that leads up the hill alongside the falls, then climb up through dripping, fern-draped bush on the far side. If that's worked up an appetite, stop by the on-site café.

Tarawera Road ends 2km further on at the shore of **Lake Tarawera** with the mountain rising beyond. Contact staff at *The Landing* café if you fancy getting out on the water; in the warmer months, you can paddle sit-on-top kayaks ($25/hr).

Waimangu Volcanic Valley

587 Waimangu Rd, 5km east off SH5 • Daily: Jan 8.30am–6pm (last admission 4.40pm); Feb–Dec 8.30am–5pm (last admission 3.40pm) • Walking and hiking $38.50; 45min lake cruises $45; combo package $83.50 • ☎ 07 366 6137, ⊛ waimangu.co.nz

Head 19km south of Rotorua on SH5 towards Taupo and you'll soon reach the southern limit of the volcanic rift blown out by Mount Tarawera, the **Waimangu Volcanic Valley**. This is one of the world's youngest geothermal areas, created in 1886 when a chain of eruptions racked the Mount Tarawera fault line. Pick up the comprehensive self-guided walking tour leaflet at the visitor centre then head downhill along a streamside path, which cuts through a valley choked with scrub and native bush that has regenerated since 1886. This process has been periodically interrupted by smaller eruptions, including one in 1917 that created the magnificent 100m-diameter **Frying Pan Lake**, the world's largest hot spring. Massive quantities of hot water well up from the depths of the **Inferno Crater**, an inverted cone where mesmerizing steam patterns partly obscure the stunning powder-blue water and are stirred and swirled by breezes across the lake. The water level rises and falls according to a rigid 38-day cycle – filling to the rim for 21 days, overflowing for two then gradually falling to 8m below the rim over the next fifteen. Steaming pools and hissing vents line the path, which passes the muddy depression where, from 1900 to 1904, the **Waimangu Geyser** regularly spouted water to 250m (and occasionally to an astonishing height of 400m), carrying rocks and black mud with it.

The path through the valley ends at the wharf on the shores of Lake Rotomahana, where the rust-red sides of Mount Tarawera dominate the far horizon. From here, free buses run back up the road to the visitor centre and **cruises** chug around the lake past steaming cliffs, fumaroles, and over the site of the Pink and White Terraces.

Kerosene Creek

1km south of SH38 junction turn east from SH5 along Old Waiotapu Rd and follow the gravel 2km to the parking area

If you're looking for free, hot soaking in natural surroundings, make straight for **Kerosene Creek**, 27km south of Rotorua, a stream that's usually the temperature of a warm bath and plunges over a metre-high waterfall into a nice big pool. It's always open and sometimes attracts a party crowd at weekends. Camping in the area is banned and there have been thefts from vehicles in the car park – see page 239.

Wai-O-Tapu Thermal Wonderland

201 Waiotapu Loop Rd, just off SH5 • April-Oct 8.30am–5pm, last entry 3.45pm; Nov–March 8.30am–6pm, last entry 4.45pm • $32.50 • ☎ 07 366 6333, ⊛ waiotapu.co.nz

Wai-O-Tapu Thermal Wonderland, 10km south of Waimangu, is the area's most colourful and varied geothermal site. At 10.15am daily, the 10m **Lady Knox Geyser** is ignominiously induced to perform by a staff member who pours a soapy surfactant into the vent. If you miss the geyser your ticket allows you to come back next morning.

Everyone then drives 1km to the main site where an hour-long walking loop wends its way through a series of small lakes which have taken on the tints of the minerals dissolved in them – yellow from sulphur, purple from manganese, green from arsenic and so on. The gurgling and growling black mud of the **Devil's Ink-Pots** and a series of hissing and rumbling craters pale beside the ever-changing rainbow colours of the **Artist's Palette** pools and the gorgeous, effervescent **Champagne Pool**, a circular bottle-green cauldron wreathed in swirling steam and fringed by a burnt-orange shelf. The waters of the Champagne Pool froth over **The Terraces**, a rippled accretion of lime silicate that glistens in the sunlight.

As you drive back to the main road, follow a short detour to a huge and active **boiling mud pool** which plops away merrily, forming lovely concentric patterns.

Orakei Korako

494 Orakei Korako Rd • Daily: Oct–March 8am–4.30pm; April– Sept 8am–4pm • $36, shuttle-boat journey included • ☎ 07 378 3131, ⓦ orakeikorako.co.nz

Diverting from either SH1 (14km) or SH5 (21km) and about 60km southwest of Rotorua is the atmospheric thermal area of **Orakei Korako**, characterized by its belching fumaroles, gin-clear boiling pools and paucity of tourists. A short shuttle-boat journey across the Waikato River (on demand throughout the day) accesses an hour-long trail which visits Ruatapu Cave, once used by Māori women to prepare themselves for ceremonies – hence Orakei Korako, "a place of adorning".

Orakei Korako can also be reached by **jetboat** along the Waikato River with NZ Riverjet (☎0800 748 375, ⓦriverjet.co.nz), based beside SH5, at Tutukau Road, 44km south of Rotorua and almost 20km south of Wai-O-Tapu. Its Riverjet Thermal Safari (3hr; $179) includes a jetboat ride and entry.

Te Urewera National Park

Midway between Waimangu and Wai-O-Tapu, 25km south of Rotorua, SH38 spurs southeast through the regimented pines of the Kaingaroa Forest towards the jagged peaks of **Te Urewera** (see page 254), a vast tract of untouched wilderness separating the Rotorua lakes from Poverty Bay and the East Cape. The Kaingaroa Forest finally relents 40km on, as the road crosses the Rangitikei River by the predominantly Māori timber town of **MURUPARA**.

INFORMATION   **TE UREWERA NATIONAL PARK**

Te Urewera Area DOC 1km southeast of Murupara, on SH38 (Nov–April Mon–Fri 8am–5pm, Sat & Sun 9am–3pm; May–Oct Mon–Fri 8am–5pm; ☎ 07 366 1080). Has stacks of information on the park and Lake Waikaremoana.

Whirinaki Forest Park

Adjoining Te Urewera National Park to the southeast is the wonderful but little-visited **Whirinaki Forest Park**, around 30km south of Murupara, which harbours some of the densest and most impressive stands of bush on the North Island: podocarps on the river flats, and native beech on the steep volcanic uplands between them, support a wonderfully rich birdlife with tui, bellbirds, kereru and kaka. The forest is now protected, after one of the country's most celebrated environmental battles, and is a wilderness paradise for hikers and mountain-bikers.

You can sample some of the best of the forest on a stretch of the well-formed **Whirinaki Track** (4hr return) which passes magnificent podocarps, the Whaiti-nui-a-tio Canyon where the river cascades over an old lava flow, and Whirinaki Falls. Go as far as you like and turn back, but the track system continues, allowing tramps of up to five days.

INFORMATION AND TOURS   **WHIRINAKI FOREST PARK**

Tourist information DOC offices (the closest is at Murupara) in the region carry the *Ride Whirinaki* leaflet ($2), which details a couple of great mountain-bike rides in the area (2hr–2 days), but you'll need to have your own bike or rent one in Rotorua .

Whirinaki Rainforest Experiences ☎ 0800 869 255, ⓦ whirinaki.com. Explore Whirinaki Forest Park on a friendly and involving day-long guided tour ($155) that offers a Māori perspective on the forest and its history.

ACCOMMODATION

DOC If you're planning a multi-day tramp through Whirinaki you can either camp or stay in the basic DOC huts that pepper the park. For more details, check the DOC website (ⓦ doc.govt.nz). Camping $̲5̲, huts $̲1̲0̲

The Bay of Plenty

North of Rotorua, the **Bay of Plenty** occupies the huge bite between the Coromandel Peninsula and the East Cape, backed by rich farmland famous for its **kiwifruit orchards**. Its western end centres on the prosperous and fast-growing port city of **Tauranga** and its beachside neighbour **Mount Maunganui**. These amorphous settlements essentially form a single small conurbation sprawled around the glittering tentacles of Tauranga Harbour. A combination of warm dry summers and mild winters initially attracted retirees, followed by home-based small businesses and then digital nomads.

Both towns have a thriving **restaurant** and **bar** scene, and a number of boats help you get out on the water to **sail**, or **swim with dolphins**. On land, make for Tauranga's modern **art gallery**, or head inland to picnic beside the swimming holes at **McLaren Falls** or paddle to see **glowworms**. With all this, it comes as no surprise that the area is a big draw for Kiwi summer holiday-makers.

Heading southeast along the Pacific Coast Highway (SH2), the urban influence wanes, the pace slows and the landscape becomes more rural, with orchards gradually giving way to sheep country. You'll also find a gradual change in the racial mix, for the eastern Bay of Plenty is mostly **Māori** country; appropriate since some of the first Māori to reach New Zealand arrived here in their great *waka* (canoes). In fact, **Whakatane** is sometimes known as the birthplace of Aotearoa, as the Polynesian navigator **Toi te Huatahi** first landed here. Whakatane makes a great base for forays to volcanic **White Island** or the bird reserve of **Whale Island**. Further east, **Opotiki** is the gateway to the East Cape and to Gisborne, as well as trips on the remote and scenic **Motu River**.

Tauranga

Once you're through the protecting ring of suburbs, it's apparent that rampant development hasn't completely spoilt central **TAURANGA** ("safe anchorage" in Māori). Huddled on a narrow peninsula with city parks and gardens backing a lively waterfront area, it is the country's biggest port, with a burgeoning population (currently around 140,000). You can easily spend half a day here, checking out the art gallery, strolling along the waterfront or lingering in the shops, restaurants and bars in the compact **city centre**, concentrated between Tauranga Harbour and Waikareao Estuary. Come summer, though, you'll soon want to head over to Mount Maunganui (see page 259).

Brief history

In 1864 the tiny community of Tauranga became the scene of the **Battle of Gate Pa**, one of the most decisive engagements of the **New Zealand Wars**. In January, the government sent troops to build two redoubts, hoping to prevent supplies and reinforcements from reaching the followers of the Māori King (see page 202), who were fighting in the Waikato. Most of the local Ngaiterangi hurried back from the Waikato and challenged the soldiers from a *pa* they quickly built near an entrance to the mission land, which became known as Gate Pa. In April, government troops surrounded the *pa* in what was New Zealand's only naval blockade, and pounded it with artillery. Despite this, the British lost about a third of their assault force and at nightfall the Ngaiterangi slipped through the British lines to fight again in the Waikato.

In 2011, the area became the focus of attention when the MV *Rena* container ship grounded on the **Astrolabe Reef**, 20km northeast of Mount Maunganui. Images of crazily tilted stacks of containers on the back of the severely listing ship zipped around the world as rescue crews tried to save the local beaches and birds from the slick of leaking fuel oil. At the time of writing, the wreck remained on the reef, though a court case seeking its removal was ongoing.

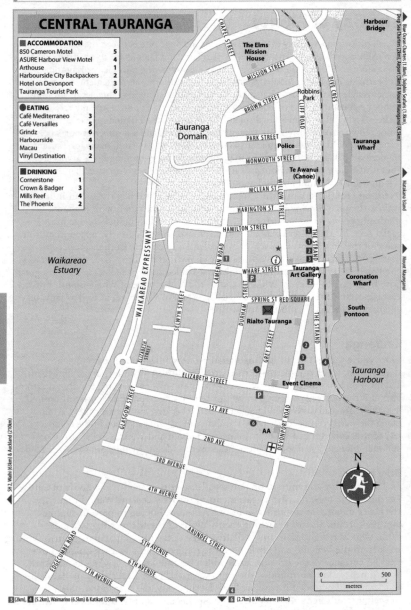

CENTRAL TAURANGA

Tauranga Art Gallery

108 Willow St • Daily 10am–4.30pm • Free • ☎ 07 578 7933, ⊕ artgallery.org.nz

After a determined fifteen-year campaign to give the city a contemporary cultural attraction, the **Tauranga Art Gallery** opened in 2007. A former bank building has been so transformed with layered metal sheets that it has been dubbed "the armadillo". There's no permanent display inside, but its series of clean-lined display spaces over two floors are a great blank canvas for excellent national and international travelling exhibitions.

Te Awanui and Robbins Park

A protective awning on the Strand shelters **Te Awanui**, the carved traditional war canoe that is still used on ceremonial occasions on the harbour. The Strand continues north to **Robbins Park**, a swathe of green adorned by a rose garden and begonia house with fine views of Mount Maunganui. This was the site of Monmouth Redoubt from the New Zealand Wars (see page 697).

The Elms Mission House

Mission St • Daily 10am–4pm • $15 • ☎ 07 577 9772, ⊛ theelms.org.nz

The Elms Mission House, at the northern end of town, is one of the country's oldest homes, built from kauri between 1835 and 1847 by the missionary, Archdeacon A.N. Brown, who tended the wounded of both sides during the **Battle of Gate Pa** (see page 255). The house has maintained its original form complete with dark-wood interior and a dining table at which Brown entertained several British officers on the eve of the battle, little suspecting that over the next few days he would bury them all. Other buildings in the beautiful grounds include a Fencible Cottage (given to retired British soldiers).

ARRIVAL AND DEPARTURE   TAURANGA

By plane The airport lies midway between Tauranga and Mount Maunganui (around 3km from each). Bus #2 goes to both towns but there are few evening services, so you may want to catch a cab: the fare to either is $15–20.
Destinations Auckland (6 daily; 35min); Christchurch (3 daily; 1hr 50min); Wellington (4 daily; 1hr 15min).

By bus InterCity and NakedBus long-distance buses stop outside the Tauranga i-SITE, as do Bayhopper (☎ 0800 422 928, ⊛ baybus.co.nz) services to/from Whakatane.
Destinations Auckland (8 daily; 3hr 35min–4hr); Hamilton (3 daily; 2hr); Napier (1 daily; 5hr 55min); Rotorua (4 daily; 1hr 30min); Taupo (4 daily; 2hr 45min); Thames (3 daily; 1hr 25min); Wellington (1 daily; 9hr 35min); Whakatane (Mon–Sat 1 daily; 2hr).

GETTING AROUND

Tauranga and Mount Maunganui are 6km apart, separated by the 3.5km-long Tauranga Harbour Bridge and an industrial estate linked to the Port of Tauranga.

By bus Bayhopper (☎ 0800 422 928, ⊛ baybus.co.nz) operates services around Tauranga and Mount Maunganui, covering most places in the immediate vicinity. Routes #1 and #2 run between Tauranga and Mount Maunganui (every 30min or so; 20–30min).

By taxi Try Tauranga Mount Taxis (☎ 0800 829 477, ⊛ taurangataxis.co.nz). There's a cab rank in Hamilton St (between the Strand and Willow St) in Tauranga. The fare between Tauranga and Mount Maunganui is around $30.

By bike Cycle Tauranga, *Harbour City Motor Inn*, 50 Wharf St (☎ 0800 253 525, ⊛ cycletauranga.co.nz), rent hybrids good for town and around ($20/2hr; $49/day).

INFORMATION

Visitor information i-SITE is at 95 Willow St (daily 8.30am–5pm; ☎ 07 578 8103, ⊛ bayofplentynz.com).
DOC 253 Chadwick Rd, Greerton, 6km south of central Tauranga (Mon–Fri 8am–4.30pm; ☎ 07 578 7677, ⊛ doc.govt.nz). They have details of charter operators for Mayor Island.

Services Free internet at the library, corner of Wharf and Willow sts (Mon, Tues, Thurs & Fri 9.30am–5.30pm, Wed 9.30am–7pm, Sat 9.30am–4pm, Sun 11.30am–4pm; ⊛ library.tauranga.govt.nz).

ACCOMMODATION

Tauranga has numerous hostels and motels within walking distance of the centre, and plenty more in the suburbs. Prices across the board are on the high side, though the plethora of motels lining 15th Avenue sometimes offer good deals during quiet periods of the year.
850 Cameron Motel 850 Cameron Rd ☎ 0800 850 123,

⊛ 850motel.co.nz; map p.256. The pick of the city's motels, around 3.5km south of the i-SITE, *850 Cameron Motel*'s large en suites have a touch more class than the norm. Facilities include a café on site and gym access. **$155**
ASURE Harbour View Motel 7 Fifth Ave East ☎ 07 578 8621, ⊛ harbourviewmotel.co.nz; map p.256. Quiet

KIWIFRUIT-PICKING

Tauranga is a major centre for **kiwifruit-picking**, a tough and prickly task that generally requires a commitment of at least three weeks. The picking season is late April to mid-June, but pruning and pollen collection also take place from mid-June to early September and again from the end of October to January. You're usually paid by the bin or by the kilo, so speed is of the essence. If this doesn't put you off, you'll find up-to-date information at the backpacker hostels, which will often help you arrange work.

and homey motel, with comfortable apartments, located just a 15min walk from town and a stone's throw from the bay. Free use of bikes and kayaks. Ideal for families. $175

★ **Arthouse** 102 Cameron Rd ☎07 975 0963, ⓦarthouse.co.nz; map p.256. As the name suggests, there's a distinct arty vibe to this hostel, with colourful decor and shabby-chic furnishings. There are 4- and 6-bed dorms (including a female-only one) and comfy private rooms, staff are friendly and well informed, and there's a small attached gallery and shop. Dorms $32, doubles $88

Harbourside City Backpackers 105 The Strand ☎07 579 4066, ⓦbackpacktauranga.co.nz; map p.256. Large hostel bang in the middle of the action. The waterfront views and tranquil atmosphere of the roof terrace make up for the basic dorms (4–8-bed; female-only available) and rooms and noise on Fri and Sat nights

(soundproofing from neighbouring bars and rooms at the rear of the building also help). Popular with workers who appreciate the management's good kiwifruit contacts. Dorms $31, doubles $86

Hotel on Devonport 72 Devonport Rd ☎07 578 2668, ⓦhotelondevonport.net.nz; map p.256. Modern hotel whose en suites are decorated in muted tones with black-and-white photos on the walls; most come with super-king-size beds and minibars, and some have balconies. Higher-priced rooms (from $250) have city and/or harbour views. $225

Tauranga Tourist Park 9 Mayfair St ☎07 578 3323, ⓦtaurangatouristpark.co.nz; map p.256. Some 4km south of the city centre, on a rather cramped site, this tourist park offers well-maintained powered and non-powered pitches to camp, no frills cabins, kitchen, small library and TV lounge. Camping $40, cabins $58

EATING

Most of Tauranga's cafés and restaurants are in the centre, notably along Devonport Road and the Strand. Fresh produce is sold at the Saturday-morning farmers' market (7.45am–noon; ⓦtaurangafarmersmarket.co.nz) at the Tauranga Primary School at 31 5th Ave.

Café Mediterraneo 62 Devonport Rd ☎07 577 0487, ⓦmedcafe.co.nz; map p.256. Also known as *The Med*, this popular café has good breakfasts, such as blueberry buttermilk pancakes, and tempting lunches ($9–22) including Caesar salads, open steak sandwiches, and sweetcorn fritters. Mon–Fri 7am–4pm, Sat 7.30am–4pm, Sun 8am–4pm.

Café Versailles 107 Grey St ☎07 571 1480, ⓦwww.cafe-versailles.net; map p.256. This award-winning, authentically French restaurant serves a wonderful range of traditional Gallic fare, including snails ($19), *boeuf bourguignon* (from $24.50) and duck *a l'orange* ($29.50), as well as conversation-stopping *crêpes suzette flambées* ($16.50). Mon–Sat 5pm–10pm.

Grindz 50 First Ave ☎07 579 0017; map p.256. Laidback Tardis-like neighbourhood café, with zingy flat whites ($4.50), cakes to die for, the biggest "mini" sausage rolls and plenty of veggie and vegan options. Mon–Fri 7am–4pm, Sat 8am–3.30pm, Sun 8.30am–3pm.

Harbourside 150 The Strand ☎07 571 0520, ⓦharboursidetauranga.co.nz; map p.256. Tucked under the rail bridge in a former dinghy storage shed, this fine-dining restaurant presents a short, stellar menu which might include half a dozen oysters with *yuzu kosho* ($24) followed by miso-glazed salmon ($24) or Chinese-style roast duck ($38). Daily 11.30am–2.30pm & 5–10pm.

Macau 59 The Strand ☎07 578 8717, ⓦdinemacau.co.nz; map p.256. Award-winning restaurant-bar with an inventive Pan-Asian menu (with the odd dish from beyond the region) designed for sharing. Highlights include the *takoyaki* octopus balls, the ramen, the tuna ceviche, and the *poke* bowl (dishes $10–33). Good drinks, too (happy hour daily 4-6pm). Daily 11.30am–11pm.

Vinyl Destination 52 Devonport Rd ☎0274 127628, ⓦvinyldestination.co.nz; map p.256. A radio station, record (CD and even tape) store, and coffee shop rolled into one. Grab one of the easy chairs, sip a coffee (from $3), scan the walls covered with classic album covers, concert posters and copies of Rolling Stone cover the walls, and nod along/endure (depending on your musical preferences) the rock soundtrack. Mon–Sat 9am–5pm, Sun 10am–5pm.

DRINKING AND NIGHTLIFE

Tauranga nights have two very different crowds – the early evening strollers and then the partygoers from 11pm

onwards. Summer revelry continues into the wee hours along the Strand. Mills Reef Winery (see page 262) is also within striking distance of the centre.

Cornerstone 55 The Strand ☎07 928 1120, ⓦcornerstonepub.net.nz; map p.256. The live music, mostly cover bands, starts around 10pm nightly in summer, and you should catch a few sessions per week at other times. Visit Sunday afternoons for jamming. Beer $7.50–12. Mon–Fri 10am–late, Sat & Sun 8.30am–late.

Crown & Badger 91 The Strand ☎07 571 3038, ⓦcrownandbadger.co.nz; map p.256. Relatively authentic British-style tavern with decent drinks (including Guinness) and pub grub like mini Yorkshire puddings stuffed with roast beef, bangers and mash, and the like ($18-24). DJs on Fri and Sat nights. Mon–Thurs & Sun 10.30am–10pm, Fri & Sat 10.30am–1.30am.

The Phoenix 67 The Strand ☎07 578 8741, ⓦthephoenixtauranga.co.nz; map p.256. This Monteith's Brewery bar is a good place to watch sport on TV (there are several screens), tuck into a thin-crust pizza ($24–29), or – of course – sample one of the wide range of craft beers. Mon–Fri 10.30am–1am, Sat & Sun 8.30am–1am.

ENTERTAINMENT

CINEMAS

Event Cinema 45 Elizabeth St ☎07 577 0288, ⓦeventcinemas.co.nz. Smart, multi-screen cinema showing mostly mainstream films.

Rialto Tauranga 21 Devonport Rd ☎07 577 0445, ⓦrialtotauranga.co.nz. Smaller than Event, but with a better range of independent and non-blockbuster films.

Mount Maunganui

Habitually sun-kissed in summer, Tauranga's neighbouring beach resort, **MOUNT MAUNGANUI**, huddles under the extinct volcano of the same name, a modest cone

4

ACTIVITIES AROUND TAURANGA AND MOUNT MAUNGANUI

The Tauranga and Mount Maunganui region is great for getting out **on the water**. Surfing is a big deal here, and plenty of places hire out gear and offer lessons. There's a full range of boats to take you cruising, fishing, sailing, swimming with dolphins and even out to Tuhua (Mayor Island). Tauranga Wharf has been overhauled, with a barge converted into a finger pier from which a number of trips depart. Others leave from Tauranga Bridge Marina, over on the Mount Maunganui side of the harbour.

DOLPHIN WATCHING

Dolphin Seafaris Tauranga Bridge Marina, 2.5km northeast of the i-SITE ☎0800 326 8747, ⓦnzdolphin.com. Five-hour trips ($150) in a powerful cruiser with committed anti-whaling crew; you can watch from the boat or get into the water and swim with the dolphins. Trips generally run Nov–May (weather permitting), leaving at 8am.

FISHING

Blue Ocean Charters Tauranga Bridge Marina, 2.5km northeast of the i-SITE ☎0800 224 278, ⓦblueocean.co.nz. Game fishing for marlin, tuna and kingfish (Dec–April), which involves chartering the boat (from $1450/day), but you can sometimes join an existing charter. Reef fishing for snapper and tarakihi goes for $120/person, plus $30 for tackle and bait.

Deep Star Charters 101 Te Awanui Rd, 2.7km northeast of the i-SITE ☎07 575 8917, ⓦdeepstarcharters.co.nz. Regular reef-fishing trips (from $80/day plus $30 for tackle and bait), plus overnight hapuku trips ($1500 for up to 10 people) which involve reef fishing in the morning then seeking hapuku, blue nose and bass around Mayor Island later on.

SURFING

Discovery Surf 167 Marine Parade, Mount Maunganui ☎027 632 7873, ⓦdiscoverysurf.co.nz. This is one of several outfits offering beginner and intermediate lessons ($89.50/2hr).

KAYAKING

Canoe & Kayak 5 MacDonald St, Mount Maunganui ☎07 574 7415, ⓦcanoeandkayak.co.nz. Budget, guided kayak trips ($59–99) taking you to visit Māori rock carvings and to encounter stingrays, among others. Also offers kayaking courses.

Waimarino 36 Taniwha Place, Bethlehem ☎07 576 4233, ⓦwaimarino.com. Offers kayak trips and guided ($105) or unguided ($75) explorations of the placid sections of the Wairoa River and the glowworm canyon on Lake McLaren ($130).

that's a visible landmark throughout the western Bay of Plenty. It was once an island but is connected to the mainland by a narrow neck of dune sand (a tombolo) now covered by "The Mount", as the town is usually known. The sprawl of apartment blocks, shops, restaurants and houses isn't especially pretty but is saved by the 20km-long golden strand of **Ocean Beach**, itself enhanced by a couple of pretty islands just offshore and lined by Norfolk pines. It's wonderful for swimming, surfing and beach volleyball, and there are good restaurants and bars nearby where everyone gravitates for sundowners. Naturally, it is a big draw for Kiwi holiday-makers, some of whom give it a party-town reputation, especially at New Year when the place can be overwhelming and accommodation hard to come by.

Exploring the Mount

Walking track 3km; 45min • Summit hike 2km one way; 1hr

The grassy slopes of the Mount (Mauao in Māori) rise 232m above the golden beach and invite exploration. A mostly level **walking track** loops around the base of the mountain, offering a sea and harbour outlook from under the shade of ancient pohutukawas. The base track links with a **hike to the summit** that is tough going towards the top but well worth the effort for views of Matakana Island and along the coast.

Hot Saltwater Pools

9 Adams Ave • Mon–Sat 6am–10pm, Sun 8am–10pm • Public pool $14; private spa, not including public pool $15.90/30min • ☎ 07 577 8551, ⓦ mounthotpools.co.nz

Wedged between the shopping strip and the Mount itself, the **Hot Saltwater Pools** harness deep geothermal groundwater to heat seawater, creating family-friendly open-air pools ranging from 33°C–39°C. Chlorination makes it feel more like a swimming pool, but after a stroll around the Mount a luxuriant soak is well deserved.

ARRIVAL AND INFORMATION   MOUNT MAUNGANUI

By bus The odd NakedBus service stops outside the *Pacific Coast Lodge*, but it is often more convenient to pick up buses in Tauranga.

By plane Mount Maunganui shares an airport with

Tauranga (see page 257).

Visitor information The i-SITE is in a cabin in the Phoenix car park on Maunganui Rd (daily 10.30am–4pm; ☎ 07 575 4471, ⓦ bayofplentynz.com).

ACCOMMODATION

Most accommodation is geared towards long-staying Kiwi holiday-makers, but you'll also find short-stay apartments and motels, as well as a couple of decent hostels.

Mount Backpackers 87 Maunganui Rd ☎ 07 575 0860, ⓦ mountbackpackers.co.nz; map p.263. A small hostel right in the thick of things, with tight, cell-like dorms (including one that sleeps sixteen) and private rooms, and low-cost surfboard rental ($20/4hr for board and wetsuit; staff can also put you in touch with teachers if you want a lesson or two). Dorms $28, doubles $82

Mount Maunganui Beachside Holiday Park 1 Adams Ave ☎ 0800 682 3224, ⓦ mountbeachside.co.nz; map p.263. An extensive, well-equipped campsite very close to the beach in a pleasant, terraced spot beside the hot saltwater pools, right at the foot of the Mount. Mostly

camping spots plus a few simple cabins and static caravans. Camping per site $65, caravans $90, cabins $130

Pacific Coast Lodge and Backpackers 432 Maunganui Rd ☎ 07 574 9601, ⓦ pacificcoastlodge.co.nz; map p.263. Vast hostel with spacious 4–8-person dorms and private rooms, plus a large kitchen and BBQ area. Nakedbus stops outside. The only downside is that it's about a 25min walk from the restaurants and the trendy end of the beach. Dorms $31, doubles $88

★ **Seagulls Guesthouse** 12 Hinau St ☎ 07 574 2099, ⓦ seagullsguesthouse.co.nz; map p.263. Clean, neat and immaculately maintained upscale backpackers with well-appointed kitchen, and bike and surfboard rental. Almost everyone gets a double or twin as there is just one three-bed dorm. Dorm $33, doubles $77

EATING

Mount Maunganui doesn't have Tauranga's selection or culinary hotspots, but there are plenty of places on the half-

dozen blocks of Maunganui Road that make up the centre, or on the waterfront strip by the Mount. There's also a farmers' market (Sun 9am–1pm; ⓦmountmaunganui.org. nz/markets) in the Phoenix car park on Maunganui Rd, and the Gourmet Night Market (Dec–mid-March Fri 5–10pm; ⓦgourmetnightmarket.co.nz in Coronation Park)

★ **Café Eighty-Eight** 88 Maunganui Rd ⓣ07 574 0384; map p.263. It is hard to go past the delectable selection of cakes at this excellent modern café with a cosy interior and small courtyard. Make the effort though for the great breakfasts ($12–20), the chunky sausage rolls, or the tasty chicken-and-pineapple burger. Daily 7am–4.30pm.

Deckchair Café 2 Marine Parade, under the Twin Towers ⓣ07 572 0942, ⓦdeckchaircafe.co.nz; map p.263. A great place to go for breakfast and morning coffee (when you can gaze across the beach to the ocean in the warming early sun), for lunch ($15–30) of chicken livers on toast or smoked salmon salad, or just drop in for a coffee (from $4). Daily 6.30am–4pm.

Fish Face 107 Maunganui Rd ⓣ07 575 2782, ⓦfish-face.co.nz; map p.263. Despite the playful name, this is a classy seafood restaurant-cum-wine bar, offering up dishes like Balinese king fish curry, spicy tamarind mussels, and spaghetti marinara (mains $16–29). Daily noon–9pm.

The General 19a Pacific Ave ⓣ02 1167 0691; map p.263. An appealing café-restaurant with a pared-back, vaguely Scandinavian feel in the furnishings and a wide-ranging menu that hops from decadent breakfast options like spiced granola with dates and coconut panna cotta ($13.50), healthy lunches, refreshing smoothies and juices, and a short list of alcoholic drinks (glass of prosecco $9). Mon & Wed–Sun 7.30am–3.30pm.

Pizza Library 314 Rata St ⓣ07 574 2928, ⓦthepizzalibrary.co.nz; map p.263. You may notice their quirky vehicles around town, and the names of the dishes ("Narnia", "The Bible", "Little Women", etc) are often mystifying, but this is seriously good pizza (from $15.50). Daily 11am–late.

DRINKING

Vaudeville 314 Rata St ⓣ07 575 0087, ⓦthepizzalibrary.co.nz; map p.263. A cast of grotesque statues and a set of seats that appeared to have been ripped out of a 1970s train stand outside the delightfully alternative *Vaudeville*, run by the people behind *Pizza Library*. It's a fun place to hang out, whether you want to gossip with the locals, enjoy an awesome cocktail (around $15) or grab some entertainment – it might be a singing poet, the resident pianist, or a fire-eater. Daily 4pm–late.

ENTERTAINMENT

CINEMAS
Bay City Cinemas 249 Maunganui Rd ⓣ07 577 0900, ⓦbaycitycinemas.co.nz. Mainstream films in a more laidback environment than the sister location in Tauranga.

Around Tauranga and Mount Maunganui

The fertile countryside inland from Tauranga and Mount Maunganui is backed by the angular peaks of the Kaimai-Mamaku Forest Park. Rivers cascade down the slopes and across the coastal plain, along the way creating **McLaren Falls** on the Wairoa River, which eventually reaches the sea near the adventure park of Waimarino.

Waimarino
36 Taniwha Place, Bethlehem, 8km west of town • Daily: Sept–April 10am–6pm, May–Aug Mon–Fri 10am–5pm • Day-pass $44 • ⓣ07 576 4233, ⓦwaimarino.com

The **Waimarino** adventure park sits beside a tidal section of the Wairoa River and is great for kids of all ages with opportunities to swim, work out on an outdoor climbing wall, plummet down New Zealand's only kayak slide, muck around in pedalos and get jettisoned off The Blob, a kind of massive cushion that lets you launch your mates sky high. They also run a variety of kayak trips (see page 259) and offer kayak rentals.

McLaren Falls
McLaren Falls Rd, off SH29, 18km southwest of Tauranga •Check the website for the latest info on water release dates • ⓦkaimaicanoeclub.org.nz

A dam normally diverts water away from the 15m **McLaren Falls**, but thanks to Kaimai Canoe Club the waters are released on selected Sundays, firing up the falls – check their website to be sure of the dates. The **Wairoa River** downstream then becomes the scene of frenetic activity as hundreds of **rafters and kayakers** congregate to run the Grade IV–V rapids (see page 244). On other days the place is the preserve of locals who flock here to soak in a series of shallow pools hewn out of the bedrock. A few minutes' rock hopping should secure you a pool to yourself; bring a picnic and sunscreen.

McLaren Falls Park

Daily Oct–April 7.30am–7.30pm, May–Sept 7.30am–5.30pm

Just upstream from McLaren Falls, 190 hectares have been turned into a pretty waterside park around **Lake McLaren**, most notable for its campsite (see page 262), the easy Waterfall Track through a glowworm dell, and excellent glowworm kayak tours (see page 259).

Papamoa Beach

Blokart Heaven 176 Parton Rd • Blokart $30/30min; drift kart $25/30min • ☎ 07 572 4256, ⍟ blokartrecreationpark.co.nz

Mount Maunganui's Ocean Beach stretches 20km southeast to **Papamoa Beach**, which is great for surfing and swimming away from the glitz of the Mount.

Papamoa is also home to the world's original purpose-built **blokart speedway track** at Blokart Heaven: think go-kart with a sail. With a fair wind, you can get up to 60km/hr; if there's no wind try a **drift kart** instead.

ACCOMMODATION   AROUND TAURANGA AND MOUNT MAUNGANUI

McLaren Falls Park McLaren Falls Rd, 11km south of Tauranga ☎ 07 577 7000, ⍟ tauranga.govt.nz. Simple grassy camp sites in a wooded, lakeside park (see above) with water, toilets and free showers. Camping __$10__
Papamoa Beach Top 10 Holiday Park 535 Papamoa Beach Rd ☎ 07 572 0816, ⍟ papamoabeach.co.nz. This

spotless site is located in the domain and right beside the beach at the eastern end of Papamoa. Everything is maintained to a very high standard and the beachfront villas ($380) are in a matchless location. Two-night minimum stay (except for campers). Camping __$52__, cabins __$105__

EATING AND DRINKING

Bluebiyou 559 Papamoa Beach Rd, Papamoa Beach ☎ 07 572 2099, ⍟ bluebiyou.co.nz. Smart and airy café/bar/restaurant with views over the dunes to the sea. Particularly nice for lunch, which might be pork belly with bacon-wrapped scallops ($22) followed by profiteroles ($16). You can also just drop in for a drink. Mon–Sat 10am–10pm, Sun 9am–10pm.

Mills Reef 143 Moffat Rd, Bethlehem, 6.5km southwest of Tauranga city centre ☎ 07 576 8800, ⍟ millsreef. co.nz; map p.256. Some 6.5km southwest of the city centre in the suburb of Bethlehem, this Art Deco-style winery has an excellent tasting room (glasses from $10); the Bordeaux and Syrah, in particular, are not to be missed. There's also a restaurant. Daily 10am–5pm.

Whakatane and around

Prettily set between cliffs and a river estuary, the 19,000-strong town of **WHAKATANE**, 90km east of Tauranga, sprawls across flat farmland around the last convulsions of the Whakatane River. It has had a turbulent history but is now a relatively tranquil service town with a couple of cultural attractions, and walks along the spine of hills above the town and to the viewpoint at **Kohi Point**.

It also makes a great jumping-off point for sunbathing at **Ohope Beach**, **swimming with dolphins**, visits to the bird sanctuary of **Whale Island** and cruises to volcanic **White Island**, which billows plumes of steam into the sky.

Brief history

The area has had more than its fair share of dramatic events. The **Māori** word *Whakatane* ("to act as a man") originated when the women of the *Mataatua* canoe were left aboard while the men went ashore; the canoe began to drift out to sea, but touching the paddles was *tapu* for women. Undeterred, Wairaka, the teenage daughter of a chief, led the women in paddling back to shore, shouting *Ka Whakatane Au i*

Ah au ("I will deport myself as a man"); a statue at Whakatane Heads commemorates her heroic act.

Apart from a brief sortie by Cook, the first Europeans were flax traders in the early 1800s. In March 1865, missionary **Carl Völkner** was killed at Opotiki and a government agent, **James Falloon**, arrived to investigate. Supporters of a fanatical Māori sect, the Hauhau, attacked Falloon's vessel, killing him and his crew. In response, the government declared **martial law**, and by the end of the year a large part of the Bay of Plenty had been confiscated and Whakatane was a military settlement. **Te Kooti** chose Whakatane as his target for a full-scale attack in 1869 before being driven back into the hills of Urewera.

Pohaturoa

Whakatane's defining feature is the large rock outcrop known as **Pohaturoa** ("long rock"). The place is sacred to Māori and the small park surrounding the rock contains carved benches and a black marble monument to **Te Hurinui Apanui**, a great chief who propounded the virtues of peace and is mourned by Pakeha and Māori alike. The site was once a shrine where Māori rites were performed, and the seed that grew into the karaka trees at the rock's base is said to have arrived on the *Mataatua* canoe.

Wairere Falls

The sea once lapped the cliffs that now hem in the town. Follow them around from Pohaturoa to the base of **Wairere Falls**, nestled in a sylvan cleft. Once the source of the town's water and motive power for mills, they're now free-flowing and an impressive sight after rain.

Te Koputu a Te Whanga a Toi (Whakatane Museum and Exhibition Centre)

49 Kakahoroa Drive • Mon–Fri 9am–5pm, Sat & Sun 10am–2pm • $5 suggested donation • ☎ 07 306 0509, ⊕ whakatanemuseum.org.nz

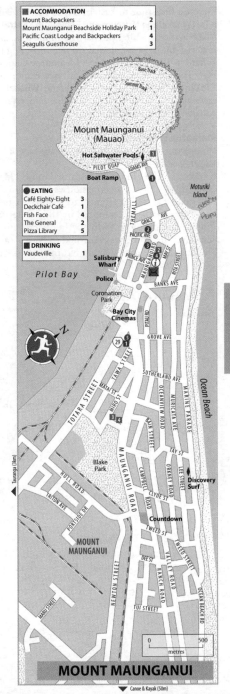

ACCOMMODATION

Mount Backpackers	2
Mount Maunganui Beachside Holiday Park	1
Pacific Coast Lodge and Backpackers	4
Seagulls Guesthouse	3

EATING

Café Eighty-Eight	3
Deckchair Café	1
Fish Face	4
The General	2
Pizza Library	5

DRINKING

Vaudeville	1

MOUNT MAUNGANUI

4

Devote a little time to Eastern Bay of Plenty's cultural focus, **Te Koputu a Te Whanga a Toi (Whakatane Museum and Exhibition Centre)**, a museum with exhibits on early Māori settlement after their arrival in the *Mataatua waka* (canoe). There's plenty of material on the post-colonial era too, including the local Māori rugby team that toured Britain in 1888, and the 1954 Melbourne Cup, won by locally raised horse, Rising Fast. There are three galleries, with new exhibitions every few months.

Te Whare Taonga o te rohe Whakatane (Whakatane Museum and Research Centre), nearby at 51-55 Boon Street, was due to open in late 2018 at the time of research, after a major revamp and expansion.

Mataatua Wharenui

105 Muriwai Drive • Daily: Dec–April Mon–Fri 9am–4pm; May–Nov 9.30am–3.30pm • Visitor centre free; guided tours from $49 • ☎ 07 308 4271, Ⓦ mataatua.com

Known as "The House That Came Home", **Mataatua Wharenui** is one of the finest (and largest) carved meetinghouses you'll see. Built here in 1875 by the Ngati Awa people as a final attempt to restore self-belief after all their land was sold or confiscated, it was removed in 1879 to represent New Zealand at the British Empire Exhibition in Sydney. After a long stint at London's Victoria and Albert Museum, the house was returned to New Zealand in 1925 and spent 70 years in Dunedin before finally being returned to its rightful Ngati Awa owners as part of

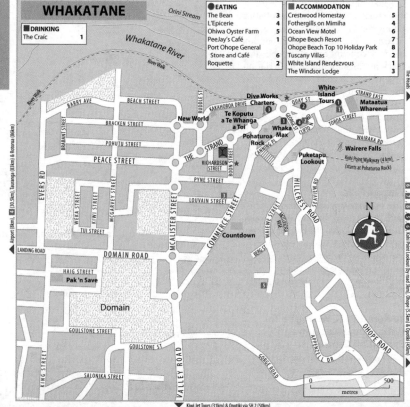

a Treaty of Waitangi settlement in 1996. Don't miss the brief but emotional film showing the house's history, before participating in the cultural tour. This is very intimate and engaging, greetings are given in Māori and English, and your guide will explain what some of the beautiful carvings of ancestors mean to them before the effective light show brings the images to life.

Kohi Point and Ohope Walk
5.5km one way; 2hr • Details in a free leaflet from the i-SITE

The best of the local walks starts in the centre of town and follows the Nga Tapuwae o Toi ("Sacred Footsteps of Toi") Walkway, which traverses the domain of the great chieftain Toi and continues to **Kohi Point**, giving panoramic views of Whakatane, Whale and White islands and Te Urewera. From Kohi Point, continue through Otarawairere Bay (no passage for an hour either side of high tide) and on to Ohope Beach, from where you can return to Whakatane by the Bayhopper bus (see page 257).

Whale Island
Access to the island itself is only by a limited number of guided tours (around $100/3hr)

Whale Island (Moutohora), 10km offshore from Whakatane, is a 2km-by-1km DOC-controlled haven where considerable efforts were made decades ago to eradicate goats and rats. Native bush is rapidly returning and the island has become a bird reserve and safe environment for saddlebacks, grey-faced petrels, sooty shearwaters, little blue penguins, dotterels and oystercatchers, as well as three species of lizard – geckos and speckled and copper skinks – and the reptilian tuatara; occasional visits are made by the North Island kaka and falcon, as well as fur seals. In the breeding season (May–Dec) over 100,000 muttonbirds return to the island, a spectacular sight made comical by their lousy landing skills.

White Island
Whakatane's star attraction is **White Island** (Whaakari), named by Cook for its permanent shroud of mist and steam. Roughly circular and almost 2km across, White Island lies 49km offshore, sometimes a rough ride. Neither this nor its seething volcanism deters visitors, who flock to its desolate, other-worldly landscape, with billowing towers of gas and steam spewing from a crater lake 60m below sea level. Smaller fumaroles come surrounded by bright yellow and white crystal deposits that re-form in new and bizarre shapes each day. The crystal-clear and abundant waters around the island make this one of the best dive spots in New Zealand.

Whaakari embodies the ongoing clash between the Indo-Australian Plate and the Pacific Plate that has been driven beneath it for the last two million years. This resulted in the upward thrust of super-heated rock through the ocean floor, creating a massive volcanic structure. Sulphur, for use in fertilizer manufacture, was sporadically mined on the island from the 1880s, but catastrophic eruptions, landslides and economic misfortune plagued the enterprise. The island was abandoned in 1934, and these days it is home only to 60,000 grey-faced petrels and 10,000 gannets. You can only land on the island via a guided boat (see page 266) or helicopter tour.

ARRIVAL AND DEPARTURE
WHAKATANE AND AROUND

By bus InterCity and NakedBus buses running along SH2 between Rotorua and Gisborne stop outside the i-SITE. The local Bayhopper (☎0800 422 928, ⊕baybus.co.nz) serves Tauranga, Ohope and Opotiki.

Destinations Gisborne (1 daily; 3hr); Ohope (Mon–Sat 7 daily; 35min); Opotiki (Mon & Wed 2 daily; 55min); Rotorua (1 daily; 1hr 30min); Tauranga (Mon–Sat 1 daily; 2hr).

By plane Whakatane airport is around 10km west of the centre, connected by the Dial-A-Cab shuttle (around $25; ☎0800 308 0222). Air Chathams (⊕airchathams.co.nz) has daily flights to Auckland.

Destinations Auckland (up to 3 daily; 45min).

INFORMATION AND TOURS

i-SITE (corner of Quay St and Kakahoroa Drive; Mon–Fri 9am–5pm, Sat & Sun 10am–3pm; ☎ 07 306 2030, ⓦ whakatane.com) is well-stocked with DOC leaflets and other information including local walks. Also offers rental bikes and free internet/wi-fi.

Dive Works Charters 96 The Strand ☎ 0800 354 7737, ⓦ whaleislandtours.com. Excellent dolphin and seal swimming trips (3–4hr; $160) around Whale Island and White Island, plus ecotours onto Whale Island ($120 with about 3 hours on the island) and diving and snorkelling trips.

Kiwi Jet Tours Matahina Dam boat ramp, Galatea Road, off Highway 30 ☎ 0800 800 538, ⓦ kiwijetboattours.com. Zoom around on the Rangitikei River with an ex-world champion jetboat racer, who will take you from the Matahina Dam, 25km south of Whakatane, to the beautiful Aniwhenua Falls via a number of modest whitewater sections ($120).

Port Ohope General Store and Café 311 Harbour Rd, Ohope ☎ 07 312 4707. This general store and café offers paddleboard classes ($45/75min), and has city bikes for hire.

White Island Tours The Strand East, White Island Rendezvous ☎ 0800 733 529, ⓦ whiteisland.co.nz. Book at least a couple of days in advance for the 5–6hr trip ($219) out to White Island, which offers two hours on the island – including standing on the edge of the crater (with a gas mask) amid pillars of smoke and steam looking down into the steaming crater lake. Whale Island is much closer to the mainland, so trips will often run when it's too rough to get to White Island; tours last about 3hr ($99) and are dependent on numbers, so book in advance. They run in the morning all year round; dusk trips operate May–Dec when hard hats are provided to protect you from crashing muttonbirds.

Services The library (49 Kakahora Drive; Mon–Fri 9am–5pm, Sat & Sun 10am–2pm) offers 30min free internet, and free wi-fi access.

ACCOMMODATION

Crestwood Homestay 2 Crestwood Rise ☎ 07 308 7554, ⓦ crestwood-homestay.co.nz; map p.264. Attractive, friendly B&B with a hilltop setting with scenic views to the islands and a 20min walk from the town centre. Dinner is available on request. The owner is a radio operator for the Whakatane Coastguard and is happy to show guests around its headquarters. $175

Fothergills on Mimiha 84 Mimiha Rd, 25km west of town ☎ 07 322 2224, ⓦ fothergills.co.nz; map p.264. If you have your own vehicle, this charming, out-of-town B&B is a great option, with welcoming hosts (the Fothergills, appropriately enough), impeccably maintained rooms, a beautiful garden, and a short walk to the beach. $160

Tuscany Villas 57 The Strand ☎ 07 308 2244, ⓦ tuscanyvillas.co.nz; map p.264. Top-of-the-line lodge in an ochre-shaded complex with a range of room and suites, all fitted out to a high standard with kitchenettes; some of the latter also come with a spa bath or hot tub. Doubles $152, suite $162

★ **White Island Rendezvous** 15 The Strand East ☎ 07 308 9588, ⓦ whiteisland.co.nz; map p.264. Opposite the wharf, *White House Rendezvous* oozes quality. Accommodation options include motel-style rooms, fancier en suites in the neighbouring villa, airy modern cabins and a renovated 1950s bungalow sleeping up to five people. Breakfast costs extra, unless you're staying in the villa. There's an excellent in-house cafe (see page 267), tasteful souvenir shop, and travel agency offering trips to White and Whale islands (see page 266). Doubles $119, cabins $150, bungalow $179

The Windsor Lodge 10 Merritt St ☎ 07 308 8040, ⓦ windsorlodge-backpackers.co.nz; map p.264. Whakatane has a severe lack of budget accommodation, so backpackers have limited choice. The *Windsor's* dorms and private rooms are drab, and can be cold in the winter, but are okay for a night if dollars are tight. Dorms $25, doubles $68

OHOPE

Ocean View Motel 18/2 West End, Ohope Beach ☎ 07 312 5665, ⓦ oceanviewmotel.co.nz; map p.264. Very relaxing motel at the western end of the beach, with safe swimming, bushwalks and free use of bikes, kayaks, boogie boards, surfboards, and laundry facilities. All of its apartments have sea views and sleep up to four people. $170

Ohope Beach Resort 307 Harbour Rd, 10km east of Whakatane ☎ 0800 464 673, ⓦ ohopebeachresort.net; map p.264. A collection of classy apartments with balconies and views across the water. Each is fully equipped with dishwasher, washing machine, and a/c. Shared facilities include a sauna, pétanque, gym, tennis court and three pools. $220

★ **Ohope Beach Top 10 Holiday Park** 367 Harbour Rd, 10km east of Whakatane ☎ 0800 264 673, ⓦ ohopebeach.co.nz; map p.264. High-end holiday park right behind Ohope Beach, with a pool complex including a waterslide and a free summertime kids' programme. Accommodation options include camping sites, cabins and apartments (the latter sleeping up to eight people). Camping $24, cabins $95, apartments $210

EATING

The Bean 72 The Strand East ☎ 07 307 0494, ⓦ thebeancafe.co.nz; map p.264. Laidback daytime café and coffee roastery, so you can be sure of a top espresso, long black or flat white hit ($4–6) to go with your breakfast, sandwich, bagel or cake Mon–Fri 7am–4pm, Sat 7am–3pm, Sun 8am–2pm.

L'Epicerie 128 Commerce St ☎ 07 307 1459, ⊛ lepicerie.co.nz; map p.264. Delightful French-run cafe-deli with a clear Gallic flair. The menu features crepes, croissants, pains au chocolat, and (when open for dinner) classics like boeuf bourguignon, as well as alcoholic drinks and Allpress coffee ($4.50–6). There are plenty of Gallic cheeses and baguettes to take away, too. Mon–Wed 8am–3.30pm, Thurs & Fri 8am–9pm, Sat 9am–9pm, Sun 9am–3pm.

★ **PeeJay's Café** 15 The Strand, inside White Island Rendezvous ☎ 07 308 9589, ⊛ whiteisland.co.nz; map p.264. A good spot for breakfast, snacks and lunch. If you're got an early boat ride, you may just want a decent espresso ($3.50); others should relax, try the mushroom and chorizo-slathered ciabatta ($16) or honey-toasted granola ($11). Daily 6.30am–4pm.

Roquette 23 Quay St ☎ 07 307 0722, ⊛ roquette-restaurant.co.nz; map p.264. A strong contender for Whakatane's best restaurant, *Roquette's* menu features dishes ($29–38) like braised pork belly with sticky plum sauce, pumpkin and mushroom gnocchi, and seafood pappardelle. Mon–Sat 10am–10pm.

OHOPE

Ohiwa Oyster Farm 11 Wainui Rd, 1km south of Ohope Beach on the road to Opotiki ☎ 07 312 4565; map p.264. Pick up inexpensive supplies of fresh seafood, including oysters from $1 each), mussels and smoked fish, from this shack beside Ohiwa Harbour, or tuck into some fish and chips at one of the picnic tables at the water's edge. Daily 9am–6.30pm.

Port Ohope General Store and Café 311 Harbour Rd ☎ 07 312 4707; map p.264. Licensed café overlooking the harbour and the surf. Go for breakfast, gourmet burger, pizza, or some great fish and chips (mains 266). Daily 7.30am–10pm.

DRINKING

The Craíc Whakatane Hotel, 79 The Strand ☎ 07 307 1670; map p.264. Atmospheric Irish pub furnished in mellow dark wood and serving inexpensive grub (from $16). Live bands, open-mic nights and plenty of opportunities to dance at the weekends. Sometimes open later than advertised. Daily noon–9pm.

4

Opotiki

The small settlement of **OPOTIKI**, 46km east of Whakatane (via the Ohope Road), is the easternmost town in the Bay of Plenty and surrounded by lush countryside and beaches. Opotiki also acts as the gateway to (and final supply stop for) the wilds of the East Cape and trips on the remote and scenic Motu River.

The town has few notable sights to delay your departure. From Opotiki, SH2 strikes inland to the more citified opportunities of **Gisborne** (see page 335), while SH35 meanders around the perimeter of the **East Cape** (see page 326), never straying far from its rugged and windswept coastline. Opotiki is about getting away from it all – out on the water, either fishing offshore, or exploring the rivers on kayaks, whitewater rafting or mountain biking along the Motu trails (⊛ motutrails.co.nz).

Opotiki Museum

123 Church St • Mon–Fri 10am–4pm, Sat 10am–2pm • $10 • ☎ 07 315 5193, ⊛ opotikimuseum.org.uk

All Opotiki's significant historic buildings cluster around the junction of Church and Elliot streets, including the **Opotiki Museum**, which occupies the whole block between Elliot and Kelly streets. Much of the content is typical small-town museum fare (agricultural implements, display rooms), boosted by the Tanewhirinaki Carvings, a fine collection of Māori sculptures from this area that spent many years as part of the Auckland Museum collection. After you leave, be sure to stroll along to the *Shalfoon & Francis* section at 129 Church St, a nostalgic 1890s-established grocery and hardware store that revels in its uncatalogued collections of old typewriters, biscuit tins and just about anything you might find in such a shop.

St Stephen's Church

Church St, opposite the museum • Mon–Fri 10am–4pm, Sat 10am–2pm; get key from the museum if it isn't open • Free

The innocent-looking white clapboard **St Stephen's Church** was once the scene of a notorious murder. In March 1865, following incitement by the Hauhau prophet Kereopa Te Rau, local missionary **Carl Völkner** was killed here. The case is far from clear-cut: it appears that Völkner had written many letters to Governor Grey espousing the land-grabbing ambitions of settlers, and local Māori claim Völkner was justly executed. Settlers used the story as propaganda, fuelling intermittent skirmishes over the next three years. Nip in and see the gorgeous *tukutuku* panels around the altar. Völkner's gravestone is slotted into the wall of the church around the back.

Hukutaia Domain

A welcome retreat into the bush is given by the small and unspoiled **Opotiki (Hukutaia) Domain**, with its understorey of nikau and a grand puriri tree thought to date from 500 BC and once used as a burial tree by local Māori. The bush also contains a good lookout over the Waioeka Valley and a series of short yet interesting rainforest tracks. To get here, head south from the centre of town on Church Street as far as the Waioeka River Bridge, cross it and bear left along Woodlands Road for 7km.

ARRIVAL AND DEPARTURE   OPOTIKI

By bus InterCity and NakedBus buses stop outside the *Hot Bread Shop Café* at the corner of Bridge and St John sts. Bayhopper (ⓦbaybus.co.nz) buses to Whakatane (Mon & Wed) and Potaka via Omaio, Te Kaha and Waihau Bay (Tues & Thurs) leave from the corner of Elliot and St John sts in the centre of town.

Destinations Gisborne (1 daily; 2hr); Potaka (Tues & Thurs 1 daily; 2hr); Rotorua (1 daily; 2hr 20min); Whakatane (Mon & Wed 2 daily; 1hr).

GETTING AROUND

By bike Travel Shop, 109 Church St (☎07 315 8881, ✉travelshop@xtra.co.nz). This travel agent rents bikes (including trail bikes), surfboards and kayaks (all $30/half day, $40/day) with drop-offs arranged.

INFORMATION AND TOURS

i-SITE/DOC The combined i-SITE and DOC office is at 70 Bridge St (Christmas–Jan daily 8am–5pm; Feb–Christmas Mon–Fri 9am–4.30pm; Sat & Sun 9am–1pm; ☎07 315 3031, ⓦopotikinz.com).

Marine Life Tours 16 Wharf St ☎027 350 4910, ✉admin@reaf.nz. As well as running kayaking and fishing trips, short tours of the Opotiki Community Reef, which the firm organised the construction of to maintain fish stocks.

Motu Trails Ltd ☎07 315 5864, ⓦmotucletrails. com. Ngaio and her team will do their best to ensure your ride matches your experience and enthusiasm. Hire bikes ($20/2hr) for the Pakihi track or Dunes trail. The shuttle to

Matawai costs $55/person (minimum numbers apply). They also have a bunkhouse (dorm $30) and secure parking near the centre of Opotiki. Contact by phone, via the website, or ask at the i-SITE.

Wet 'n' Wild Rafting 58 Fryer Rd, Hamurana ☎0800 462 7238, ⓦwetnwildrafting.co.nz. Offers a range of one- and multi-day trips (from $115) from Opotiki, including an adventurous 100km descent of the Motu River. In all cases transport and meals are provided; you can bring your own tent and sleeping bag or rent them from the company.

Services Free wi-fi or 30min on a terminal at the library, 101 Church St (Mon–Fri 9am–5pm & Sat 9am–1pm).

ACCOMMODATION

Beyond the Dunes 12 Wairakaia Rd, 5km east of town ☎021 123 0789, ⓦbookabach.co.nz/13241. Simple, modern, self-contained, pine-lined *bach* just over the dunes from a sweeping swimming beach. Two-night minimum stay during the summer. **$75**

Capeview Cottage Tablelands Rd, 8km southeast of town ☎07 315 7877, ⓦcapeview.co.nz. Very comfortable rimu-lined, self-contained cottage on a kiwifruit orchard, offering expansive coastal views, outdoor hot tub and a small library. The hosts are eco-minded and very knowledgeable about the area. **$150**

Colonial House B&B 123 Dickinson Rd, 7km west of town ☎07 230 5641. This attractive B&B boasts a kiwifruit orchard setting, a pair of elegant rooms with four-poster beds, games room with billiards table and perks like free laundry. Given the location, though, it's only really suitable for travellers with their own vehicle. **$160**

Ohiwa Beach Holiday Park 380 Ohiwa Harbour Rd, off SH2, 15km west of town ☎07 315 4741, ⓦohiwaholidays.co.nz. Gem of a campsite right on the beach, with good accommodation options for most budgets, safe swimming, glowworms, kayaks for rent and a "jumping pillow" – a cross between a bouncy castle and a trampoline, massively popular with kids (and a few adults). Camping **$20**, cabins **$75**, doubles **$130**

Opotiki Beach House 7 Appleton Rd, off SH2, 5km west of town ☎ 07 315 5117, ⓦ opotikibeachhouse.co.nz. This beachside hangout is one of the better budget options, with low-cost wood-panelled dorms and private rooms, though it could do with another bathroom or two. Guests have free use of kayaks and bodyboards. Dorms $26, doubles $60

EATING

Beyond the Bean Waiotahi Beach Rest Area on SH2, 6km west of town. Run by the same people who own *Beyond the Dunes* (see page 268), this coffee van serves fine espressos, long blacks and flat whites ($4–6), plus a small selection of home-made cakes and counter food. Mon 6.30am–noon, Tues–Fri 6.30am–2pm.

Hot Bread Shop Café 43 St John St ☎ 07 315 6795. This bakery-café is the place for yummy traybakes, pies, brunch and snacks ($4–10), as well as well-made coffees. Ideal for picnic fodder. Daily 5am–5pm.

Two Fish Café 102 Church St ☎ 07 315 5448. Appealing café with mismatched furniture and a dedication to quality, made-on-the-premises foods; stop in for breakfast ($10–22), a choice of delicious muffins (try raspberry and lemon) or quick bites such as chicken wraps. Good espressos, too. Mon–Fri 8am–3pm, Sat 8am–2pm.

DRINKING

1759 Masonic Hotel, 121 Church St ☎ 07 315 8284. Based at the *Masonic Hotel*, this Irish pub is a good place for a beer ($7.50–12), and huge, economical meals – steak, fish and chips, etc – are on offer in a raw brick backroom. Daily 10am–10pm.

The Waioeka Gorge route

From Opotiki, **SH2** strikes out south to **Gisborne**, 137km away. It's one of New Zealand's great scenic drives, dotted with tiny settlements, weaving up and down steep hills cloaked in bush. The route winds gingerly along the Waioeka River for 30km before tracing the narrow and steep **Waioeka Gorge** then emerging onto rolling pastureland and dropping to the plains around Gisborne, all arrow-straight roads through orchards, vineyards and sheep farms.

The **only petrol** along the route is at Matawai, but opening hours are limited: fill up in Opotiki or, if you're coming from the south, in Gisborne.

Waioeka Gorge walks

Break your journey on the first 72km stretch to Matawai by tackling one of the interesting **walks** on either side of the road. Check at the Opotiki i-SITE for details.

Central North Island

MOUNT TARANAKI

5 Central North Island

The Taupo, Taranaki and Whanganui regions contain some of New Zealand's star attractions, many the result of its explosive geological past. The inland section is dominated by three heavyweight features, notably Lake Taupo, the country's largest; spectacular Tongariro National Park; and the volcanic field that feeds colourful and fiercely active thermal areas. Towards the coast, meanwhile, is Mount Taranaki, a dormant, beautifully shaped volcano. The snow that falls on its summit subsequently works its way to the sea through tracts along the Whanganui River.

The region south of Rotorua is loosely referred to as the **Volcanic Plateau**, high country overlaid with a layer of rock and ash expelled two thousand years ago, when a huge volcano blew itself apart, the resultant crater and surrounds filled by expansive **Lake Taupo**. This serene lake, and the streams and rivers feeding it, have long lured anglers keen to snag brown and rainbow trout, while visitors flock to diverse sights and activities located near the thundering rapids on the Waikato River, which drains the lake. On the northeastern edge of the lake is the fast-growing resort town of **Taupo**, which offers travellers a beguiling array of outdoor activities. Just south of the lake is the smaller, tranquil town of **Turangi**, a favourite amongst trout fisherman. Alongside the even smaller settlements of **Whakapapa**, **National Park** and **Ohakune**, Turangi is also a popular base for exploring **Tongariro National Park**. Created in 1887 and home to three majestic volcanoes, the park is a winter playground for North Island skiers and a summer destination for hikers drawn by spectacular walking trails.

East of Ohakune the giant thumbprint peninsula of **Taranaki** is dominated by the symmetrical cone of **Mount Taranaki**, within **Egmont National Park**. At its foot, **New Plymouth** warrants a visit for its excellent contemporary art gallery and access to a multitude of **surf beaches**.

Inland from Egmont National Park, the farming town of **Taumarunui** is one of the main jumping-off points for multi-day canoe trips along the **Whanganui River**, through the heart of the verdant **Whanganui National Park**. The river bisects **Whanganui**, a small, creative city whose river port history can be relived on a restored paddle steamer. Some 60km south is the university city of **Palmerston North**, which lies at the centre of the rich farming region of **Manawatu**.

Taupo

The burgeoning resort town of **TAUPO**, 80km south of Rotorua and slap in the centre of the North Island, is strung around the northern shores of **Lake Taupo**, the country's largest lake, which is the same size as the island of Saint Lucia. Views stretch 30km southwest towards the three snowcapped volcanoes of the Tongariro National Park, the reflected light from the lake's glassy surface combining with the 360m altitude to create an almost alpine radiance. Here, the impossibly deep-blue waters of the Waikato River ("flowing water" in Māori) begin their long journey to the Tasman Sea, and both lake and river frontages are lined with parks.

For decades, Kiwi families have been descending en masse for a couple of weeks' holiday, bathing in the crisp waters of the lake, and lounging around holiday homes that fringe the lakeshore. But there's no shortage of things to see and do, from the spectacular rapids and geothermal badlands north of town to **skydiving** – this is New Zealand's freefall capital – and **fishing**. The Taupo area is a most fecund trout fishery, extending south to Turangi

HUKA FALLS

Highlights

❶ Lake Taupo Cruise, windsurf or kayak on New Zealand's largest lake, haul trout out of it, or approach at dizzying speed while skydiving. See page 272

❷ Huka Falls For volume and power alone – some three hundred tonnes of water per second plunging into a maelstrom of eddies and whirlpools – this is the country's finest waterfall. See page 282

❸ Tongariro Alpine Crossing Quite simply the best and most popular one-day hike in New Zealand, climbing over lava flows, crossing a crater floor, skirting active geothermal areas and passing emerald and blue lakes. See page 289

❹ Forgotten World Highway Take the slow road through pristine countryside and get your passport stamped at the self-declared village republic of Whangamomona. See page 300

❺ Egmont National Park Climb the conical summit of the North Island's second-highest peak, Mount Taranaki, or get great views of the mountain from the less committing Pouakai Circuit. See page 303

❻ Whanganui River Spend three chilled days canoeing in verdant canyons and tackling the gentle rapids of the country's longest navigable river. See page 315

HIGHLIGHTS ARE MARKED ON THE MAP ON PAGE 274

CENTRAL NORTH ISLAND

TASMAN SEA

North Taranaki Bight

Awakino

Mokau

Tongaporutu
**Whitecliffs
Walkway**

Taumarunui

Tangarakau
Gorge

Waitara

Urenui

New Plymouth

Oakura

3A

National Park

Inglewood

Whangamomona

TARANAKI

EGMONT
NATIONAL
PARK

WHANGANUI
NATIONAL
PARK

Cape Egmont
Lighthouse

Mount
Taranaki
(2518m)

Pungarehu

Stratford

Raetihi

Ohakune

Pipiriki

Opunake

Koriniti

Hawera

South Taranaki Bight

Bushy
Park

Oyster Shell
Cliffs

Patea

Aramoana

Whanganui

TASMAN SEA

N

Bulls

HIGHLIGHTS

1 Lake Taupo
2 Huka Falls
3 Tongariro Alpine Crossing
4 Forgotten World Highway
5 Egmont National Park
6 Whanganui River

Foxton

Waiterere

Levin

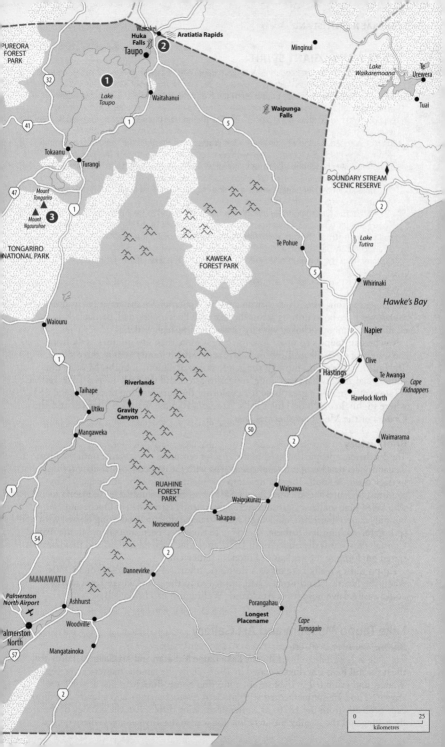

5

LAKE TAUPO: GIANT SPIRIT

Lake Taupo (616 square kilometres and 185m deep) is itself a geological infant largely created in 186 AD when the Taupo Volcano spewed out 24 cubic kilometres of rock, debris and ash – at least ten times more than was produced by the eruptions of Krakatoa and Mount St Helens combined – and covered much of the North Island in a thick layer of pumice. Ash from the eruption was carried around the world – the Chinese noted a blackening of the sky and Romans recorded that the heavens turned blood-red. As the underground magma chamber emptied, the roof slumped, leaving a huge steep-sided **crater**, since filled by Lake Taupo. It's hard to reconcile this placid and beautiful lake with such colossal violence, though the evidence is all around: entire beaches are composed of feather-light pumice which, when caught by the wind, floats off across the waters. Volcanologists continue to study the Taupo Volcano (currently considered dormant) and treat the lake as a kind of giant spirit-level, in which any tilting could indicate a build-up of magma below the surface that might trigger another eruption.

The local Tuwharetoa people ascribe the lake's formation to their ancestor, Ngatoroirangi, who cast a tree from the summit of Mount Tauhara, on the edge of Taupo, and where it struck the ground water welled up and formed the lake. The lake's full name is Taupo-Nui-A-Tia, "the great shoulder mat of Tia" or "great sleep of Tia", which refers to an explorer from the Arawa canoe said to have slept by the lake.

---

and along the Tongariro River, with an enviable reputation for the quality of its fish. Year-round, you'll see boats drifting across the lake with lines trailing and, particularly in the evenings, rivermouths choked with fly-casters in waist-high waders.

Nowhere in **Taupo**'s compact low-rise core is more than five minutes' walk from the waters of the Waikato River or Lake Taupo, which jointly hem in three sides. The fourth side rises up through the gentle slopes of Taupo's suburbs. Most of the commercial activity happens along Tongariro Street and the aptly named Lake Terrace.

Taupo also makes a great base for exploring the surrounding area (see page 281), where highlights include Huka Falls, Aratiatia Rapids, Wairakei Terraces and the Craters of the Moon geothermal area.

Brief history

The Tuwharetoa people had lived in the area for centuries, but it wasn't until the New Zealand Wars that Europeans took an interest with the Armed Constabulary trying to track down **Te Kooti**. They set up camp one night in June 1869 at Opepe, 17km southeast of Taupo (beside what is now SH5), and were ambushed by Te Kooti's men, who killed nine soldiers. Garrisons were subsequently established at Opepe and Taupo, but only Taupo flourished, enjoying a more strategic situation and being blessed with hot springs for washing and bathing. By 1877, Te Kooti had been contained, but the Armed Constabulary wasn't disbanded until 1886, after which several soldiers and their families stayed on, forming the nucleus of European settlement.

Taupo didn't really take off as a domestic resort until the prosperous 1950s, when the North Island's roads had improved to the point where Kiwi families could easily drive here from Auckland, Wellington or Hawke's Bay.

Lake Taupo Museum and Art Gallery

Story Place, Tongariro Park, off SH1 • Daily 10am–4.30pm • $5 • ☎ 07 376 0414, ⓦ taupodc.govt.nz

Set aside at least half an hour for the **Lake Taupo Museum and Art Gallery**, if only for the beautiful Reid Carvings, created in 1927–28 by the famous master carver Tene Waitere and exhibited in the form of a meeting house. They're as fine as you'll see anywhere and are supplemented with modern *tukutuku* panels and a lovely flax rain-cape probably from the 1870s or earlier. Interesting displays on the geology of the area, fly-fishing and the logging industry line the way to the Tuwharetoa Gallery ranged around the decayed hull of a 150-year-old 14.5m *waka*, found in the bush in 1967. Paintings around the room include two of Ngati Tuwharetoa chiefs by local polymath Thomas Ryan, who was also a lake steamer captain and an All Black. The watercolours show the unmistakeable influence of the artist's great friend Charles Goldie. Outside, the stunning **Ora Garden**, a 2004 Chelsea Flower Show winner, has been re-created in all its geothermal glory.

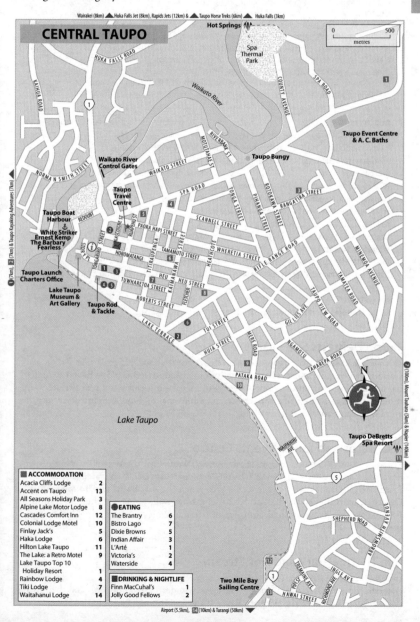

CENTRAL TAUPO

Wairakei (8km) Huka Falls Jet (8km), Rapids Jets (12km) & Taupo Horse Treks (6km) Huka Falls (3km)

Hot Springs
Spa Thermal Park

Waikato River

Taupo Event Centre & A. C. Baths

Waikato River Control Gates

Taupo Bungy

Taupo Travel Centre

Taupo Boat Harbour

White Striker
Ernest Kemp
The Barbary
Fearless

Taupo Launch Charters Office

Lake Taupo Museum & Art Gallery

Taupo Rod & Tackle

Lake Taupo

Taupo DeBretts Spa Resort

Two Mile Bay Sailing Centre

Airport (5.5km), (10km) & Turangi (50km)

ACCOMMODATION	
Acacia Cliffs Lodge	2
Accent on Taupo	13
All Seasons Holiday Park	3
Alpine Lake Motor Lodge	8
Cascades Comfort Inn	12
Colonial Lodge Motel	10
Finlay Jack's	5
Haka Lodge	6
Hilton Lake Taupo	11
The Lake: a Retro Motel	9
Lake Taupo Top 10 Holiday Resort	
Rainbow Lodge	4
Tiki Lodge	7
Waitahanui Lodge	14

EATING	
The Brantry	6
Bistro Lago	7
Dixie Browns	5
Indian Affair	3
L'Arté	1
Victoria's	2
Waterside	4

DRINKING & NIGHTLIFE	
Finn MacCuhal's	1
Jolly Good Fellows	2

5

TAUPO TOURS AND ACTIVITIES

Taupo offers a huge range of air-, land- and water-based activities to relieve you of your holiday money. There's great **mountain biking** around Taupo, much of it maintained by Bike Taupo (W biketaupo.org.nz). With great scenery and very competitive prices, Taupo is claimed to be the busiest tandem **skydiving** drop zone in the world; all operators offer jumps from 12,000ft (45 seconds of freefall) and 15,000ft (60 seconds of freefall).

Cruises visit striking, modern Māori **rock carvings** that can only be seen from the water at Mine Bay, 8km southwest of town. All cruise trips operate two or three times daily, weather permitting; they can be booked through the Taupo Charters Office (☎07 378 9794) at the boat harbour. Several **kayaking** trips also visit the carvings.

New Zealand's **fishing** rules dictate that trout can't be sold, so if you've got a taste for them you'll need to catch them yourself. The easiest way is to fish the lake from a charter boat. Rivers flowing into Lake Taupo are the preserve of fly-fishers. Boat operators supply tackle and will organize the mandatory Taupo District Fishing Licence ($20/24hr). The charters office also has a list of fishing guides (about $300/half day).

MOUNTAIN BIKING

Huka Falls Walkway A scenic ride best reached by heading north from Spa Thermal Park to Huka Falls (4km one-way) and on to Aratiatia Dam (additional 8km one way).

W2K This challenging single-track route (16km one way, with an additional 10km loop) starts at Whakaipo Bay, 20km west of Taupo, and finishes at Kinloch. Either plan to ride it both ways or arrange transport – it's around 40km by road.

Wairakei Forest Excellent loop riding: start by the Helistar Helicopter, 3km north of Taupo. Several companies offer tours and bike rental (see page 279).

SKYDIVING

Taupo Tandem Skydiving Airport ☎0800 826 336, W tts.net.nz. Skydiving trips (from $279) with this operator have been running since 1992; they pick you up in a stretch Hummer.

Skydive Taupo Airport ☎0800 586 766, W skydivetaupo.co.nz. Skydives (from $279) with expert instructors and free transfers in a limo from Taupo.

BUNGY JUMPING

Taupo Bungy 202 Spa Rd ☎0800 888 408, W taupobungy.co.nz. The river swirls right past one of New Zealand's finest bungy sites, cantilevered 20m out from the bank with a 47m drop and an optional dunking (bungy $169). Nov–March daily 9.30am–6.30pm; April–Oct Mon–Fri 9.30am–4pm, Sat & Sun 9.30am–5pm.

Taupo DeBretts Spa Resort

3km southeast on SH5 • Daily 8.30am–9.30pm • $22 • ☎07 377 6502, W taupodebretts.co.nz

Geothermal bathing is best at the family-oriented **Taupo DeBretts Spa Resort**, which has a couple of large outdoor pools filled with natural mineral water plus private mineral pools in a range of temperatures; an additional $7 buys as many descents as you like on the hot-water hydroslide.

A.C. Baths and Taupo Events Centre

A.C. Baths Ave • **Baths** Daily 6am–9pm • Swimming $8; private hot pools $10/person/30min • **Climbing wall** Timetable varies every month • Harness and shoes $10, plus $12 entry • A.C. Baths ☎07 376 0350, Events Centre ☎07 376 0350, W taupodc.govt.nz

Even without your own vehicle it's easy to reach the **A.C. Baths and Taupo Events Centre**, a sparkling sports hall and 12m climbing wall, alongside the longstanding **A.C. Baths**, a well-maintained complex of thermally heated swimming and hot pools.

Spa Thermal Park and Hot Stream

County Ave, 1km northeast of the centre • Daily 24hr • Free

A small, hot creek cascades through a series of wonderful soaking pools and then mixes with the cool waters of the Waikato River at the **Spa Thermal Park and Hot Stream**.

LAKE CRUISES

★**The Barbary** Harbour ☎07 378 5879, ⓦsailbarbary.com. Entertaining cruises (2hr 30min; $49), aboard a 1926 ketch allegedly once owned by Errol Flynn, including up-close viewing of the Māori rock carvings and the chance to swim. Thanks to its electric engine, this is the quietest boat on the lake.

Ernest Kemp Harbour ☎07 378 3444, ⓦernestkemp.co.nz. A replica 1920s steamboat that chugs to the carvings and back (2hr; from $35).

Fearless Harbour ☎022 189 1847, ⓦsailfearless. co.nz. Vaguely pirate-themed sailing trips on the comfortable *Fearless* (2hr; from $29) include a swimming stop at the Māori rock carvings and a drink served by the friendly skipper.

KAYAKING AND WATERSPORTS

Taupo Kayaking Adventures 876 Acacia Bay Rd ☎027 480 1231, ⓦtka.co.nz. Does half-day kayak trips to the carvings ($100), plus geothermal, evening and full-day paddles. Kayaks and paddleboards are also available to hire (from $20/hr).

2MileBay Watersports Centre Two Mile Bay ☎07 378 3299, ⓦsailingcentre.co.nz. Rents catamarans ($60/hr), windsurfing boards ($30/hr) and other sailboats (from $50/hr). Nov–March daily 9am–5pm, otherwise sporadically.

JETBOATING

Huka Falls Jet 200 Karetoto Rd ☎0800 485 2538, ⓦhukafallsjet.com. The peace at Huka Prawn Park (see page 282) is periodically shattered by one of this company's jetboats ($129) roaring along the river and doing 360-degree spins on the way to the base of Huka Falls.

Rapids Jet Rapids Rd, 3km beyond Aratiatia Dam ☎0800 727 437, ⓦrapidsjet.com. The North Island's only true whitewater jetboating run gives you plenty of bang for your buck (from $65/person), taking you down and up Nga Awapura rapids, during which the entire boat gets airborne. Listen closely to the safety spiel, hang on and prepare to get wet.

FISHING

White Striker Harbour ☎07 378 2736, ⓦtroutcatching.com. Has a good strike rate and a wealth of local knowledge. Their smallest charter holds up to eight ($140/hr).

Taupo Rod & Tackle 7 Tongariro St ☎07 378 5337, ⓦtauporodandtackle.co.nz. You can rent all manner of tackle here and pick your own spot to cast from – but average catches are much larger if you engage the services of a fishing guide.

HORSERIDING

Taupo Horse Treks Karapiti Rd ☎0800 244 3987, ⓦtaupohorsetreks.co.nz. Offers one-hour ($70) and two-hour ($140) jaunts through the pine forests around the Craters of the Moon.

The stream is around 400m along the riverside walkway which continues downstream (2.8km one way; 45min) to Huka Falls (see page 282).

ARRIVAL AND DEPARTURE   TAUPO

By plane Taupo's little airport (ⓦtaupoairport.co.nz), 10km south of the centre, has Air New Zealand flights to Auckland and Wellington.

Destinations Auckland (2 daily; 50min); Wellington (3 daily; 1hr).

By bus InterCity and Newmans buses stop at the Taupo Travel Centre bus station, 16 Gascoigne St (☎07 378 9005), in the middle of town. NakedBus stops outside the i-SITE on Tongariro St.

Destinations Auckland (7 daily; 5hr 15min); Hamilton (7 daily; 3hr); Hastings (3 daily; 2hr 30min); Napier (3 daily; 2hr); Palmerston North (5 daily; 3hr 50min); Rotorua (8 daily; 1hr–1hr 15min–1hr 15min); Taihape (6 daily; 1hr 55min); Tauranga (2 daily; 2hr 50min); Turangi (6 daily; 50min); Wellington (6 daily; 5hr 55min–6hr 20min).

GETTING AROUND

By shuttle For visiting the surrounding sights (and airport transfers), Shuttle 2U (daily 24hr; ☎07 376 7638) does a hop-on-hop-off circuit of all the main attractions and will even pick up from your accommodation.

By car Pegasus Rental Cars (☎0800 803 580, ⓦrentalcars. co.nz) generally have the best deals, from around $50/day.

By bike Most hostels have basic bikes for guests' use.

Taupo Kayaking Adventures (see page 279) have MTB bikes for $50/day, can arrange transport to trailheads, and offers guided tours. Pack & Pedal, 5 Tamamutu St (☎07 377 4346, ⓦpackandpedaltaupo.com), rents MTBs from $40/4hr, $60 all day.

By taxi Call Top Cabs (☎07 378 9250) or Taupo Taxis (☎07 378 5100).

5

INFORMATION

Visitor information The i-SITE is at 30 Tongariro St (daily: Nov–April 9am–5.30pm, May-Oct 9am-4.30pm; ☎0800 525 382, ⓦgreatlaketaupo.com). ⓦtaupo.info is a handy website, with sections on accommodation, eating and drinking, activities and more in and around Taupo.

ACCOMMODATION

Taupo maintains a high standard of accommodation for all budgets, but given its proximity to Tongariro National Park and host of events, it's worth booking ahead whatever the time of year. Much of the lakefront is taken up with **motels**, and grassy spots on the fringes of town are given over to **campsites**, while **hostels** are abundant in the centre.

Acacia Cliffs Lodge 133 Mapara Road ☎07 378 1551, ⓦacaciacliffslodge.co.nz; map p.277. Perched on Acacia Bay, 7km southwest of downtown Taupo and with beautiful lake views, this luxury boutique lodge has a cool, contemporary style and a strong environmental ethos. There are just four exemplary en suites, each with private terrace or garden; three of them overlook the water. **$650**

Accent on Taupo 310 Lake Terrace ☎0800 222 368, ⓦaccentontaupo.com; map p.277. Recently refurbished, this superior motel has super-king-size beds, timber decks, a spa, trampoline, BBQ and great lake views. Fantastic value for money. Doubles **$145**, cottages **$200**

All Seasons Holiday Park 16 Rangatira St ☎0800 777 272, ⓦtaupoallseasons.co.nz; map p.277. Situated 1.5km east of town, with thermal mineral pool, hedged tent sites scattered among cabins (which range from budget cells to spacious options with kitchenettes), plus hotel-style rooms. Camping **$25**, cabins **$46**, doubles **$128**

Alpine Lake Motor Lodge 141 Heu Heu St ☎0800 400 141, ⓦalpinelake.co.nz; map p.277. Modern motel with a wide range of well-equipped rooms: all have a/c (and underfloor heating for the winter) and DVD players; most have spa baths; some have kitchenettes and BBQs in their private courtyards. **$135**

Cascades Comfort Inn 303 Lake Terrace, SH1, Two Mile Bay ☎0800 996 997, ⓦcascades.co.nz; map p.277. Ideally situated with direct access to an attractive heated pool and the lake. Units are spacious with a full kitchen, a mezzanine sleeping area, a patio and a spa bath. **$139**

Colonial Lodge Motel 134 Lake Terrace ☎0800 353 636, ⓦcolonial.co.nz; map p.277. Double spas in the bathrooms, kitchenettes, and huge TVs are among the highlights of this efficiently run motel. Opt for one of the upstairs rooms, which open out onto a sunny balcony. **$180**

★**Finlay Jack's** 20 Taniwha St ☎07 378 9292, ⓦfinlayjacks.co.nz; map p.277. Formerly *Blackcurrant Backpackers*, this bright, contemporary YHA-affiliated hostel is a fine choice: clean and economical private rooms and 4–12-bed dorms (including female-only ones), switched-on staff, great lake views from the veranda, Netflix and Xboxes in the communal area and a friendly dog (Biggie in name, but not in stature). Dorms **$25**, doubles **$80**

Haka Lodge 56 Kaimanawa St ☎07 377 0068, ⓦhakalodge.com; map p.277. Formerly Taupo's YHA hostel, and recently renovated, *Haka Lodge* is a stylish backpacker option, with dorms (2–9-bed; female-only available) and private rooms that are a notch above what you might expect. The quality communal areas include a hot tub. Dorms **$28**, doubles **$89**

Hilton Lake Taupo 80 Napier–Taupo Hwy ☎07 378 7080, ⓦhilton.com; map p.277. This *Hilton* combines the beautifully restored 1889 original hotel with heritage rooms and distant lake views with a modern wing featuring suites and apartments. With the classy *Bistro Lago* (see page 281) and a hot springs next door, you've got all you need for a relaxed stay. Rates vary widely online, so shop around. **$260**

★**The Lake: a Retro Motel** 63 Mere Rd ☎07 378 4222, ⓦthelakeonline.co.nz; map p.277. Taupo's first ever motel has gone back to its roots, from its striking black exterior to rooms fitted out with funky 1960s and 70s decor (with touches like shag-pile rugs, red-leather and moulded white-plastic chairs and Noddy and Big Ears egg cups), most opening to black-and-white-furnished gardens. Doubles **$165**, suites **$185**

Lake Taupo Top 10 Holiday Resort 28 Centennial Drive, 2km northeast of town ☎0800 322 121, ⓦtaupotop10.co.nz; map p.277. Large, super-organized site with free activities including swimming pool, volleyball, tennis, games room, playground, giant chessboard and more. The bathrooms even have heated floors. Camping **$21**, cabins **$114**

Rainbow Lodge 99 Titiraupenga St ☎07 378 5754, ⓦrainbowlodge.co.nz; map p.277. Spacious, relaxed hostel spread over three buildings with a comfortable lounge, sauna, safe parking and bike rental. A stack of local information and little touches create a homey atmosphere. Dorms have six to nine beds (female-only ones available) and there are some particularly good-value en-suite doubles and twins with TV and patio. Free pick-ups from the bus station. Dorms **$25**, rooms **$64**

Tiki Lodge 104 Tuwharetoa St ☎0800 845 456, ⓦtikilodge.co.nz; map p.277. One of the better hostels in town, though not as characterful as its name suggests. Purpose-built, it has a spacious kitchen and 24-hour lounge area, plus a great balcony with lake views, and a spa. Perks include a free breakfast. Dorms **$23**, doubles **$80**

Waitahanui Lodge 116 SH-1 Kaimanawa St ☎07 378 7183, ⓦwaitahanuilodge.co.nz; map p.277. If you don't mind being based outside town, 13km south of central Taupo, try this anglers' favourite which has five self-contained cottages (sleeping 3–5 people), a fishing supplies shop, private boat ramp, breezy communal deck. Guests are also free to pick ingredients from the organic veg patch. Cottages $119

EATING

There's a year-round **food and craft market** on the first Saturday of the month on Redoubt Street (9am-1pm; ⓦ taupomarket.kiwi.nz).

The Brantry 45 Rifle Range Rd ☎07 378 0484, ⓦ thebrantry.co.nz; map p.277. Run by the Campbell sisters, this sophisticated restaurant serves inventive cuisine (mains $30–35), such as slow-cooked pulled lamb with barberry freekeh and spiced cauliflower, and sticky date pudding with fig-and-honey ice cream. The three-course meal ($55–60) is a great option. Reservations recommended. Tues–Sat 5.30–10pm.

Bistro Lago Hilton Lake Taupo (see page 280) ☎07 377 1400, ⓦ bistrolago.co.nz; map p.277. Taupo's finest dining in the beautifully modernized old wing of the hotel. Great service, immaculate presentation and delectable food that's similarly priced (fish and chips $36) to far inferior places. Three-course set menu from $78; high tea (Fri–Sun from 5pm) from $25. Daily 7am–11pm.

Dixie Browns 38 Roberts St ☎07 378 8444, ⓦ dixiebrowns.co.nz; map p.277. The pick of the lakeshore restaurants for a laidback lunch. High-quality mains ($29–47) include butter chicken, salmon and scallop stack, and perfectly-cooked steaks, and there's plenty of seating outside and friendly efficient service. Daily 6am–10pm.

Indian Affair 34 Ruapehu St ☎07 378 2295, ⓦ indianaffair.co.nz; map p.277. Smart, modern surroundings and the best Indian food in town. Highlights include the Goan fish curry, the goat balti and the *paneer makhani* (Indian cheese in a creamy tomato sauce). Mains $17–22. Daily 11am–2pm & 5–10pm.

★ **L'Arté** 255 Mapara Rd, Acacia Bay ☎07 378 2962, ⓦ larte.co.nz; map p.277. A pretty 8km drive around the head of Lake Taupo takes you to this rural sculpture gallery and garden of quirky mosaics, including some arranged as an outdoor living room. Great food (lunches ($15–20), such as corn fritter stacks layered with crispy bacon and avocado or pittas filled with marinated lamb and mint-and-yoghurt dressing, plus drinks, including Allpress coffee, are served inside or on a shady deck. Open most public holidays. Wed–Sun 8am–4pm.

Victoria's 127 Tongariro St ☎07 376 7310, ⓦ victorias.co.nz; map p.277. Take a booth for breakfast of smashed avocado on toast ($16) or come for a lunch of salt and pepper squid ($17). Either way you're sure to find the cakes cabinet a tempting finish. Mon–Fri 7.30am–3.30pm, Sat & Sun 8.30am–3pm.

Waterside 3 Tongariro St ☎07 378 6894, ⓦ waterside.co.nz; map p.277. Share one of the seafood platters ($44), tuck into a burger ($25–28) or opt for jerk-spiced venison fillet ($49) at this solid, if rather pricey, all-rounder. Daily 11am–late.

DRINKING AND NIGHTLIFE

Nightlife almost all happens along the westernmost block of **Tuwharetoa Street** through to the wee hours. Alternatively head out to **Wairakei Terraces** for a Māori cultural experience (see page 282).

Finn MacCuhal's 10 Tuwharetoa St ☎07 378 6165, ⓦ finns.co.nz; map p.277. Large Irish bar popular with both backpackers and locals; most come for the Guinness, but they also do good-value meals: try the hefty lamb shank pie ($26). They'll also cook your catch for you for $20. Daily 5pm–late.

Jolly Good Fellows 76–80 Lake Terrace ☎07 378 0457, ⓦ jollygoodfellows.co.nz; map p.277. The nearest Taupo gets to a British pub, not in style so much but for its excellent range of draught ales and lively community feel. Pub meals are also in the English tradition, with mains ($19–32) including bangers and mash, and beef and Guinness pasty. Lots of diners early on followed by revellers for the late shift. Nov–March daily 10am–late, reduced hours April–Oct.

DIRECTORY

Medical treatment Taupo Health Centre, 113 Heu Heu St (Mon–Fri 8am–5.30pm; ☎07 378 7060, ⓦ taupohealth.co.nz).

Pharmacy Unichem Mainstreet Pharmacy, at Tongariro & Heuheu sts (daily 8.30am–8.30pm; ☎07 378 2636).

Police 21 Story Place, by the museum and art gallery (☎07 378 6060).

Around Taupo

On the town's outskirts is a concentration of natural wonders, all within a few minutes of one another. Here you'll find boiling mud, hissing steam harnessed by the Wairakei

5

power station, and the clear-blue Waikato River, which cuts a deep swirling course north over rapids and through deep-sided gorges.

The majority of sights and activities are within 10km of Taupo, flanking the Waikato River as it wends its way north, and are accessible through Taupo's tour companies.

Huka Falls Road

Huka Falls Road loops off SH1 a couple of kilometres north of Taupo and passes the *Reids Farm* free campsite and *Huka Lodge* (one of New Zealand's most exclusive luxury retreats) en route to the first port of call, the magnificent **Huka Falls** (*hukanui*, or "great body of spray"). Here the Waikato, one of New Zealand's most voluminous rivers, funnels into a narrow chasm before plunging over a 9m shelf into a seething maelstrom of eddies and whirlpools; the sheer power of some three hundred tonnes of water per second makes it a far more awesome sight than the short drop would suggest. A footbridge spans the channel, providing a perfect vantage point for watching the occasional mad kayaker making the descent, usually on weekend evenings. The car park is only open until 6pm but you can park outside the barriers and walk in at any time.

Honey Hive
65 Karetoto Rd, off Huka Falls Rd • Daily 9am–5pm • Free • ☎ 07 374 8553, ⓦ hukahoneyhive.com

Continuing along Huka Falls Road, a large Russian helicopter marks the launch pad for Helistar flights (see page 278) en route to the cutaway hives and educational video at the **Honey Hive**, 1km further north, where you can buy products from jars of the sweet stuff through to skin-care products and meads and wines.

Huka Prawn Park
Karetoto Rd • Daily: Dec & Jan 9am–4pm; Feb–Nov 9.30am–3.30pm • $29.50 • ☎ 07 374 8474, ⓦ hukaprawnpark.co.nz

The new Taupo bypass road separates you from the Wairakei geothermal power station from where excess heat is channelled into the family-oriented **Huka Prawn Park**, large open ponds where tropical prawns are raised. Stroll around the ponds and nature walk, spend as long as you like fishing for prawns or combine the two. If learning about a day in the life of "Shawn the Prawn" doesn't fire your imagination, dine on some of Shawn's delicious little friends in the adjacent riverside restaurant.

Craters of the Moon
Karapiti Rd, off SH1 • Daily: Oct–March 8.30am–6pm, April–Sept 8.30am–5pm • $8 • ⓦ cratersofthemoon.co.nz

The Huka Falls loop road rejoins SH1 near Karapiti Road which runs west to **Craters of the Moon**, a lively geothermal area that sprang to life in the 1950s, after the construction of the Wairakei geothermal power station drastically altered the underground hydrodynamics. While it lacks geysers and colourful lakes, the area is so vigorous that you must wear closed footwear to walk the 3km of trails among roaring fumaroles and rumbling pits belching out a pungent rotten-egg stench.

The Wairakei Terraces
SH1, 3km north of Craters of the Moon • Daily 8.30am–5pm • Walkway $15; thermal pools $25 • ☎ 07 378 0913, ⓦ wairakeiterraces.co.nz

The Wairakei power station is supplied by shiny high-pressure steam pipes that cross under SH1, twisting and bending like a giant ball-bearing racetrack. The power of mineral-laden steam is harnessed nearby at **Wairakei Terraces**, where a vigorously boiling cauldron feeds an artificial cascade of silica terraces and pools. It mimics the process that created Rotorua's Pink and White Terraces. The hot pools here are adults only and a blissfully quiet place for a soak. At the time of writing, the **Māori cultural experience** had been suspended, though it may start up again in the future.

Aratiatia Rapids

2km downstream from Wairakei power station • Best seen Oct–March 10am, noon, 2pm & 4pm; April–Sept 10am, noon & 2pm

The Aratiatia Dam holds back the Waikato River immediately above the **Aratiatia Rapids**, a long series of cataracts that were one of Taupo's earliest attractions. In the 1950s, plans to divert the waters around the rapids were amended by public pressure, thus preserving them, though it's something of a hollow victory since they are dry most of the time, only seen in their full glory during three or four thirty-minute periods each day. Stand on the dam itself or at one of two downstream viewpoints, and wait for the siren that heralds the spectacle of a parched watercourse being transformed into a foaming torrent of waterfalls and surging pressure waves, before returning to a trickle. For jetboat rides, see page 279.

The Napier–Taupo Road

Travelling beyond the immediate vicinity of Taupo, SH1 hugs the lake as it heads southwest to Turangi (see page 285), while SH5 veers southeast along the **Napier–Taupo Road**, a twisting ninety-minute run through some of the North Island's remotest country. Much of the early part of the journey crosses the Kaingaroa Plains, impoverished land cloaked in pumice and ash from the Taupo volcanic eruption and of little use save for the pine plantations which stretch 100km to the north. The history of this route is traced by the **Napier–Taupo Heritage Trail**; pick up a free booklet from either town's i-SITE.

Opepe Historic Reserve

SH5, 17km southeast of Taupo

Many of the stops on the road to Napier are of limited interest, but be sure to call in at **Opepe Historic Reserve**, where, on the north side of the road, a cemetery contains white wooden slabs marking the graves of nine soldiers of the Bay of Plenty cavalry, killed by followers of maverick Māori leader Te Kooti in 1869.

Waipunga Falls

SH5, 35km southeast of Opepe Historic Reserve

The Waipunga River, a tributary of the Mohaka, plummets 30m over the picturesque **Waipunga Falls**, and continues beside SH5 through the lovely Waipunga Gorge, packed with tall native trees and dotted with picnic sites which double as **campsites** with no facilities but river water. The highway descends to the Mohaka River and *Mountain Valley Adventure Lodge* (see below). Beyond the Mohaka River, the highway climbs the Titiokura Saddle before the final descent through the grape country of the **Esk Valley** into Napier.

ACCOMMODATION **WAIPUNGA FALLS**

Mountain Valley Adventure Lodge 408 McVicar Rd, 5km south of SH5 ☎ 06 834 9756, ⓦ mountainvalley. co.nz. A little slice of rural New Zealand with a riverside bar and restaurant and the opportunity to fish the river (rod hire from $15), mountain bike (bike hire $30/full-day), go horse trekking (from $70), do some scenic rafting on Grade I–II stretches of the Mohaka River (from $109), or go clay pigeon shooting or paintballing. Accommodation includes campsites, a bunkhouse with dorms and private rooms, chalets and cottages. Camping **$12**, dorms **$32**, doubles **$16**, chalets & cottages **$100**

5

Tongariro National Park and around

New Zealand's highly developed network of national parks owes much to Te Heu Heu Tukino IV, the Tuwharetoa chief who, in the Pakeha land-grabbing climate of the late nineteenth century, recognized that the only chance his people had of keeping their sacred lands intact was to donate them to the nation – on condition that they could not be settled or spoiled. His 1887 gift formed the core of the country's first major public reserve, **Tongariro National Park**, which became a **UNESCO World Heritage Site** in 1991 due to its unique landscape and cultural significance. In the north a small, outlying section of the park centres on **Mount Pihanga** and the tiny **Lake Rotopounamu**, but most visitors head straight for the main body of the park, dominated by the three great volcanoes which rise starkly from the desolate plateau: the broad-shouldered ski mountain, **Ruapehu** (2797m); its squatter sibling, **Tongariro** (1968m); and, wedged between them, the conical **Ngauruhoe** (2287m).

Within the boundaries of the park is some of the North Island's most striking scenery – a beautiful mixture of semi-arid plains, steaming fumaroles, crystal-clear lakes and streams, virgin rainforest and an abundance of ice and snow. The more forbidding volcanic areas were used as locations for Mordor and Mount Doom in the *Lord of the Rings* trilogy. This all forms the backdrop to two supremely rewarding tramps, the one-day (7–8hr 19.4km) **Tongariro Alpine Crossing** and the three- to four-day **Tongariro Northern Circuit**, one of New Zealand's Great Walks. The undulating plateau to the west of the volcanoes is vegetated by bushland and golden tussock, while on the eastern side the rain shadow of the mountains produces the **Rangipo Desert**. Although this is not a true desert, it is still an impressively bleak and barren landscape, smothered by a thick layer of volcanic ash from the 186 AD Taupo eruption. **Mount Ruapehu** frequently bursts into life (most recently 1995, 1996 and 2007), occasionally emptying its crater lake down the side of the mountain in muddy deluges known as lahars. In 2011, Mount Ruapehu's Volcanic Alert Level was elevated to level 1 (signs of volcanic unrest), but at the time of writing it was not affecting visitors. Keep tabs on its status with DOC and the local i-SITE office.

The northern approach to the region is through **Turangi**, which – though it lacks the mountain feel of the service town of **National Park** and the alpine **Whakapapa Village**, 1200m up on the flanks of Ruapehu – makes a good base both for the Tongariro tramps and for rafting and fishing the Tongariro River. The southern gateway is **Ohakune**, a more aesthetically pleasing place than National Park but distinctly comatose outside the ski season. Heading south, the Army Museum at **Waiouru** marks the southern limit of the Volcanic Plateau, which tails off into the pastoral lower half of the region set around the agricultural town of **Taihape**.

Pretty much everyone comes to the park either to **ski** or to **tramp**, staying in one of the small towns dotted around the base of the mountains. Note that this region is over 600m above sea level, so even in the height of summer you'll need **warm clothing**.

ARRIVAL AND DEPARTURE   TONGARIRO NATIONAL PARK

By car In October 2017, parking restrictions were introduced in a bid to reduce congestion and overcrowding. There is now a four-hour time limit for private vehicles at the Mangatepopo Rd carpark, off SH47 – overstay and you'll be clamped. This leaves enough time for short walks, but if you want to do the whole crossing, you'll need to leave your vehicle in Ohakune, Turangi, National Park or Whakapapa and make use of the shuttle buses (see below).

By bus and shuttle bus A couple of InterCity bus routes pass through Tongariro National Park but most services are run by smaller companies, many associated with backpacker hostels. If you're staying in any of the towns listed below there'll be a choice of operators offering basically the same service (often with an early bus getting you to the trailhead before the masses). The larger, reliable operators are listed below: your accommodation and the various visitor centres can flesh out the options and make bookings. Companies generally charge $35–65 for combined Tongariro Alpine Crossing drop-off and pick-up.

INFORMATION AND TOURS

Equipment Any time of year, it's essential to take warm clothing and rain gear – and if you plan to scramble up and down the steep volcanic cone of Mount Ngauruhoe, take gloves and long trousers for protection from the sharp scoria rock. Water is also scarce on most tracks so carry plenty.

Safety The day-long crossing should not be underestimated: you need a reasonable level of fitness, should dress appropriately (sturdy hiking boots, water/windproof jacket and trousers, hat and gloves, and warm layered clothing), take a head torch, mobile phone, sunscreen and plenty of water (the water along the track is not drinkable), and give yourself plenty of time. You don't really need a guide for the crossing in summer, but in winter (June–Oct) they are essential. Several shorter, less challenging walks are possible – check ⓦ doc.govt.nz for more details.

Visitor information DOC leaflets from i-SITEs in Taupo and Turangi covering the tramps are informative and adequate for most purposes though map fans will want the region's *Parkmap* ($19).

Weather Mountain weather (ⓦ metservice.com) is extremely changeable, and the usual provisos apply. Even on scorching summer days, the increased altitude and exposed windy ridges produce a wind-chill factor to be reckoned with, and storms roll in with frightening rapidity. From the end of March through to late November there can be snow on the tracks, so check current conditions.

Adrift Outdoors 53 Carroll St, National Park ☎ 07 892 2751, ⓦ adriftnz.co.nz. National Park-based operator that offers a winter Alpine Crossing ($195) and a range of summer options (including short walks, if you don't fancy the full 7–8hr crossing). Hiking gear is available to rent.

Tongariro Expeditions ☎ 07 377 0435, ⓦ thetongarirocrossing.co.nz. Offers transfers (from $35 return) from National Park, Turangi and Taupo to the park.

Turangi

The small town of **Turangi**, 50km south of Taupo, was planned in the mid-1960s and built almost overnight for workers toiling away at the tunnels and concrete channels of the Tongariro Hydroelectic Power Scheme, which provides around seven percent of the nation's electricity. It's legendary among trout fishermen and is increasingly popular with whitewater rafters, but is otherwise is relatively quiet and a non-touristy alternative to Taupo, with Lake Taupo just 4km to the north.

Many people also stay in Turangi to hike the Tongariro Alpine Crossing, 40km to the southwest; the i-SITE (see page 286) has details of these and other walks in the area.

Tongariro National Trout Centre

SH1, 4km south of Turangi • Daily: Dec–April 10am–4pm; May–Nov 10am–3pm • $15 • ☎ 07 386 8085, ⓦ troutcentre.com

The massive amount of trout fishing around Turangi makes it essential that rivers are continually restocked from hatcheries such as the **Tongariro National Trout Centre**, set amid native bush between the Tongariro River and one of its tributaries, the Waihukahuka Stream. With an **aquarium** filled with native species such as eels, a chance to see fingerlings being raised and lots of material on water conservation, biodiversity protection and how to fish, it's a great place to spend an hour, especially if you've got kids in tow.

Tokaanu Thermal Pools

Mangaroa Rd, 5km west of Turangi • Daily 10am–9pm • $6; private pools $10/20min, including public pool access • ☎ 07 386 8575

If you want to wallow in hot water, head for **Tokaanu Thermal Pools** in tiny **Tokaanu**, which was the main settlement hereabouts in pre-European times. There's an open-air public pool and hotter, partly enclosed and chlorine-free private pools.

Volcanic Activity Centre

Inside the i-Site, Ngawaka Place • Daily: Oct–mid-June 9am–4.30pm, late June–Sept 8.30am–4pm • $12 • ☎ 0800 288 726, ⓦ volcanoes.co.nz

If you'd like to experience a 6.3 magnitude earthquake – the same strength as the one that hit Christchurch in 2011 – head to the **Volcanic Activity Centre**. As well as the earthquake simulator (you're strapped into a vibrating seat), there are displays on New Zealand's volcanic and geothermal makeup, with a particular focus on the Taupo region.

5

Tongariro River Loop Track

The pleasant **Tongariro River Loop Track** is well worth the hour it takes to complete, starting from the Major Jones footbridge at the end of Koura Street on the edge of town. It follows the true right bank of the river north past a couple of viewpoints and over a bluff, then crosses the river and returns along the opposite side.

ARRIVAL AND DEPARTURE   TURANGI

By bus InterCity and NakedBus buses drop off at the i-SITE visitor centre, Ngawaka Place. Tongariro Expeditions (see page 285) also stop when taking Taupo hikers to the Tongariro Alpine Crossing, although not if the weather is bad.
Destinations Auckland (5 daily; 6hr); Rotorua (4 daily; 2hr

5min); Taupo (6 daily; 50min); Wellington (6 daily; 5hr 35min). **Mountain Shuttle** ☎0800 117 686, ⓦ tongarirocrossing.com. Runs Tongariro Alpine Crossing and ski-field shuttles (from $30/one way) year-round. The earliest of the several crossing shuttles available is around 6–6.30am.

INFORMATION AND ACTIVITIES

i-SITE Ngawaka Place (daily; Oct–mid-June 9am-4.30pm, rest of year 8.30am–4pm; ☎0800 288 726, ⓦ greatlaketaupo.com/turangi-i-site). Offers a more personalized service than the busy offices in Taupo and Rotorua and sells bus tickets, Taupo fishing licences, maps, DOC tramping brochures and hut tickets. It also books accommodation, has wi-fi and offers access to the Volcanic Activity Centre (see page 285).
Rafting New Zealand 41 Ngawaka Place ☎0800

865 226, ⓦ raftingnewzealand.com. Award-winning local operator offering rafting trips (from $139) taking in everything from grade 2 to grade 5 rapids on the Tongariro, Mohaka and Wairoa rivers.
Tongariro River Rafting Atirau Rd ☎07 386 6409, ⓦ trr.co.nz. A good alternative to Rafting New Zealand, offering both gentle paddles suitable for families to wet-and-wild adventures (from $139).

ACCOMMODATION

Creel Lodge 183 Taupahi Rd ☎07 386 8081, ⓦ creel.co.nz. A rightly popular lodge with a focus on fishing surrounded by bird-filled grounds, *Creel Lodge* has a cluster of self-contained one- and two-bedroom units in grounds running down to the river edge with barbecue facilities. $140
Extreme Backpackers 26 Ngawaka Place ☎07 386 8949, ⓦ extremebackpackers.co.nz. This purpose-built hostel has clean, simply decorated dorms and private rooms set around a courtyard; there's a good atmosphere, but thin walls mean it can be noisy. Next door there's a climbing wall and a café. Dorms $26, double $64
★ **River Birches** 222 Tautahanga Rd ☎07 386 7004, ⓦ riverstonebackpackers.com. In a secluded location near the river, this boutique lodge is easily the most stylish place in town. There are just three rooms, all of which are spacious, tastefully decorated, and feature nice touches like honesty bars and huge bath tubs; two have private gardens, while the other has its own hot tub. There's also a self-contained, three-bedroom cottage (sleeping up to 7). If money's no object, *River Birches* is the place to stay. Doubles $700, cottages $950

Riverstone Backpackers 222 Tautahanga Rd ☎07 386 7004, ⓦ riverstonebackpackers.com. Appealing purpose-built boutique backpackers in a converted house with lots of communal living space, both inside and out, a well-equipped modern kitchen, and bike and walking-pole rentals. Dorms $35, doubles $76
Tongariro Holiday Park SH47 ☎07 386 8062, ⓦ thp.co.nz. The most convenient base for doing the Tongariro Alpine Crossing (see page 289), though somewhat scruffy, with simple cabins and camping pitches, a guest kitchen, and a games room. Staff can book transport with Tongariro Expeditions, who pick up and drop off here daily. Camping $44, cabins $65
Tongariro River Motel Corner of SH1 and Link Rd ☎0800 187 688, ⓦ tongariorivermotel.co.nz. Homey, comfortable motel that is hugely popular with anglers, partly for its rod racks and smoker, but mainly because of its "manager", a lovable boxer named Boof. The friendly owner is a good source of info on all things fishing, and there are free bikes to use. $115

EATING

Creel Tackle House & Cafe 183 Taupahi Rd ☎07 386 7929, ⓦ creeltackle.com. Based at *Creel Lodge* (see above), this fishing supplies shop doubles up as a café. As well as serving the best coffee (from $4) in town, it offers delicious

pastries, pies and cakes – try the raspberry almond slice or the pear tart. Daily 8am-4pm.
Hydro Eatery Corner of Ohuanga Rd and Pihuaga St ☎07 386 6612. This breezy, bustling café delivers a breakfast dishes ($12–20) like muesli, pancakes and

eggs Benedict, as well as sandwiches, wraps and salads for lunch, good coffee and refreshing smoothies. Daily 8am–3pm.

Oreti 88 Pukawa Rd, Pukawa ☎07 386 7070, ⓦoretivillage.co.nz. Based at the *Oreti Village Resort*, 8km northwest of Turangi on the shores of Lake Taupo, this romantic restaurant serves dishes like seared tuna with prawn ceviche, wild mushroom risotto, and coconut and lemongrass pannacotta (mains $29–36). July–May Wed–Fri & Sun 6–11pm, Sat 5–11pm.

Rust Shop 6, Town Centre ☎07 386 5947. Opened in late 2017 in the town's small shopping complex, *Rust* is a touch trendier than the other options in town. Gourmet venison, pulled pork and battered snapper burgers ($16–19), sharing platters and craft beers are on the menu. Wed & Sun noon–9pm, Thurs–Sat noon–11pm.

Tongariro Lodge 83 Grace Rd ☎07 386 7946, ⓦtongarirolodge.co.nz. Rump of lamb marinated in lavender, quinoa-stuffed peppers, and slow-cooked beef short rib are among the inventive mains ($26–39) at the restaurant of the *Tongariro Lodge*, which also has pricey but luxurious chalets and villas (from $299/double). Daily 6–10pm.

DRINKING

Turangi Tavern 277a Te Rangitautahanga Rd ☎07 386 6071. Classic Kiwi pub complete with Tab, beers on tap (around $8–10) and pub meals served from the counter. Try the BLT ($17) or fill up with bangers and mash ($18). Mon, Tues & Sun 11am–9pm, Wed 11am–10pm, Thurs–Sat 11am–2am.

Whakapapa

Tiny **WHAKAPAPA**, 45km south of Turangi on SH48, is the only settlement set firmly within the boundaries of Tongariro National Park and hugs the lower slopes of Mount Ruapehu. Approaching from the north, an open expanse of tussock gives distant views of the imposing *Chateau Tongariro* hotel, framed by the snowy slopes of the volcano behind and overlooked by the arterial network of tows on the Whakapapa ski-field.

Swarms of trampers use Whakapapa as a base for short walks or long tramps. The Tongariro Northern Circuit and the Round the Mountain track (see page 290) can both be tackled from here, but there are also easier strolls covered by DOC's *Walks in and around Tongariro National Park* leaflet (download at ⓦdoc.govt. nz). Three of the best of these are the **Whakapapa Nature Walk** (1km; 20–30min), highlighting the unique flora of the park; the **Taranaki Falls Walk** (6km; 2hr), which heads through open tussock and bushland to where the Wairere Stream plunges 20m over the end of an old lava flow; and the **Silica Rapids Walk** (7km; 2hr 30min), which follows a stream through beech forests to creamy-coloured geothermal terraces.

Ruapehu Crater Rim hike

5–8hr return • **From Iwikau Village car park** 15km return; 1000m ascent • **From top of Waterfall Express chairlift** 9km return; 650m ascent • Chairlift Nov–April, depending on weather, 9am–4pm • $30 return

There's much more of a vertical component to the **Ruapehu Crater Rim hike**, a tough, steep slog made worthwhile by the dramatic silhouettes of Cathedral Rocks and the views west to Mount Taranaki. The walk can be done from the car park at Iwikau Village but is much more appealing from the top of the Waterfall Express chairlift, thereby avoiding a long trudge through a barren, rocky landscape. From the top of the **chairlift** the route is unmarked, but from Christmas until the first snows, the ascent can usually be made in ordinary walking boots without crampons. Guided crater walks are also available (see below).

Iwikau Village

From Whakapapa, SH48 continues as Bruce Road 6km uphill to **Iwikau Village** (known locally as the "Top o' the Bruce"), an ugly jumble of ski-club chalets which from late June through to mid-October becomes a seething mass of wraparound shades and baggy snowboarders' pants. Outside the ski season, the village dies, leaving only a

5

MOUNT RUAPEHU SKI-FIELDS

Mount Ruapehu is home to the North Island's only substantial **ski-fields**, **Whakapapa** and **Turoa**, which attract around two-thirds of the nation's skiers. Every weekend from **late June to mid-October**, cars pile out of Auckland and Wellington (and everywhere in between) for the four-hour drive to Whakapapa, on the northwestern slopes of Mount Ruapehu, or Turoa, on the south side. Both have excellent reputations for pretty much all levels of skier and the orientation of volcanic ridges lends itself to an abundance of dreamy, natural half-pipes for snowboarding.

Mt Ruapehu (🌐 mtruapehu.com) manages both fields, sells lift passes (from $79/day) and rents gear (from $49). Several places in National Park, Ohakune and Turangi also offer competitive rates and a wide selection of equipment.

couple of **chairlifts** to trundle up to the shiny-new *Knoll Ridge Café*, from where you can take **guided walks** on the mountain.

ARRIVAL AND DEPARTURE

WHAKAPAPA

By bus The only services to Whakapapa are the daily shuttle buses from Taupo, Turangi and National Park, which drop off close to the DOC.

By car and shuttle No snow chains are available in Whakapapa, so you'll need to bring your own or use one of the shuttle services, which operate from accommodation in the area, or with the hourly-or-better mountain shuttle (☎ 0800 117 686).

INFORMATION

Visitor information DOC, SH48 (daily: Dec–Feb 8am–6pm; March–Nov 8am–5pm; ☎ 07 892 3729, ✉ tongarirovc@doc.govt.nz). Contains all the maps and leaflets you'll need, plus has extensive displays on the park, including the tiny Ski History museum and a couple of multimedia presentations (one for $3, both for $5) shown on demand – one on volcanism hereabouts, the other combining Māori legends surrounding Tongariro with impressive footage of the landscape through the seasons.

ACCOMMODATION

Chateau Tongariro SH48 ☎ 0800 242 832, 🌐 chateau. co.nz. Whakapapa's most prominent building is this 1929 brick edifice, with elegant public areas including a huge lounge with full-size snooker table and great mountain views; it's worth a visit for a Devonshire tea even if you're not staying. Guests have use of the highest nine-hole golf course in New Zealand, tennis courts, gym and a small indoor pool, and stay in fairly anodyne rooms modernized to international standards. If you're after space and good views you'll need one of the premium rooms (around $225), mostly in the new wing sympathetically added in 2004. The website has significant spring and autumn discounts. $125

Discovery SH47, 1.1km south of the SH48 turn-off ☎ 07 892 2744, 🌐 discovery.net.nz. A five-minute drive northwest of Whakapapa Village, this 10-acre site with views of the Tongariro volcanoes has a wide range of accommodation options including one-bedroom chalets with self-contained kitchen and bathroom. Camping $36, hut $60, chalet $195

Mangahuia Campsite Off SH47, close to the foot of the Whakapapa access road 🌐 doc.govt.nz. Simple streamside DOC campsite with toilets, running water, picnic tables and sheltered cooking area. Operates on a first-come, first-served basis; deposit fee at site registration stand. $13

Skotel 100m up the hill beside the Chateau Tongariro ☎ 0800 756 835, 🌐 skotel.com. Hotel with woodsy, three-bunk rooms, en-suite doubles, a sauna and a restaurant/bar. There are also some cabins with full cooking facilities, sleeping up to six ($225). Note that rates are hiked considerably in the ski season. Backpacker rooms $60, doubles $140

Whakapapa Holiday Park Opposite the DOC office ☎ 07 892 3897, 🌐 whakapapa.net.nz. The budget option, set in a pretty patch of beech forest with tent and powered sites, plus self-contained units with bathrooms ($130) and cabins without ($80). Camping $23, dorms $28

EATING

Fergusson's Café Opposite the DOC office, 🌐 chateau.co.nz/fergussons-cafe. Start your day at the *Chateau*'s cafe with egg-laden breakfasts, fill up on cheap snacks or tuck into filled (and filling) sandwiches for lunch (dishes $10–20). Daily 6am–6pm.

Pihanga Café & T Bar Chateau Tongariro ☎ 0800

242 832, ⓦ chateau.co.nz. The *Chateau's* budget option, serving pub-style meals ($20–32) that are a cut above: venison and ale pie, vegetarian *laksa*, and corned beef hash with a poached egg and bernaise sauce. Daily 11.30am–late.

Ruapehu Room Chateau Tongariro ⓣ 0800 242 832, ⓦ chateau.co.nz. If you want to reward yourself for the successful completion of a major tramp, it has to be the *Chateau's Ruapehu Room,* where elegant, high-quality à la carte meals are served (Chateaubriand for two, $85,

is the house dish), at à la carte prices (mains $30–43). You'll need to reserve ahead for dinner and Sunday lunch, and to dress for the occasion (no jeans or T-shirts). Mon–Sat 6.30–10am & 6.30–10pm, Sun 6.30–10am, noon–3pm & 6.30–10pm.

The Terrace Restaurant & Bar Skotel ⓣ 0800 756 835. The *Skotel's* terrace restaurant serves good-value bistro meals (mostly $25–35) spanning burgers and grilled polenta to porterhouse steak, and also has a lively bar. Daily 6pm–9pm.

DRINKING

Tussock Bar At the base of the village ⓣ 07 892 3809, ⓦ chateau.co.nz. The cheapest booze and grub ($23–27) is at the village pub, also run by the *Chateau*

Tongariro (see page 288), where the few locals tend to drink and catch sports on the big-screen TV. Daily 3pm–late.

Tramping in Tongariro National Park

Tongariro National Park contains some of the North Island's finest walks, all through spectacular and varied volcanic terrain. The **Tongariro Alpine Crossing** alone is often cited as the best one-day tramp in the country, but there are many longer possibilities, notably the three- to four-day **Tongariro Northern Circuit**. Mount Ruapehu has the arduous but rewarding **Crater Rim Hike** (see page 287) and the **Round the Mountain Track**, a circuit of Ruapehu offering a narrower variety of terrain and sights than the Tongariro tramps, but consequently less used; both are best accessed from Whakapapa.

Tongariro Alpine Crossing

19.4km; 6–8hr; 750m ascent • All shuttles drop off at Mangatepopo Rd End car park between 6–9am and pick up at Ketetahi Rd around 3–4.30pm

During the summer season (typically mid-Nov to April) the **Tongariro Alpine Crossing** is by far the most popular of the major tramps in the region, and for good reason. Within a few hours you climb over lava flows, cross a crater floor, skirt active geothermal areas, pass beautiful and serene emerald and blue lakes and have the opportunity to ascend the cinder cone of Mount Ngauruhoe. Even without this wealth of highlights it would still be a fine tramp, traversing a mountain massif through scrub and tussock before descending into virgin bush. On weekends and through the height of summer up to seven hundred people per day complete the Crossing: aim for spring or autumn and stick to weekdays. Another way to **avoid the crush** is to get the earliest possible shuttle, though you'll have to go at a fast pace to keep ahead of the crowds.

Mangatepopo car park to Mangatepopo Saddle

Almost everyone walks west to east, saving 400m of ascent. The first hour is gentle, following the Mangatepopo Stream through a barren landscape and passing the Mangatepopo Hut (with toilets). The track steepens as you scale the fractured black lava flows towards the **Mangatepopo Saddle**, passing a short side track to the **Soda Springs**, a small wildflower oasis in this blasted landscape. There are also toilets here, though bring your own toilet paper. The Saddle marks the start of the high ground between the bulky and ancient Mount Tongariro and its youthful acolyte, **Mount Ngauruhoe** (aka Mount Doom of *Lord of the Rings* fame) which fit walkers can climb (additional 2km return; 2–3hr; 600m ascent) from here and still make the shuttle bus at the end of the day. The two-steps-forward, one-step-back ascent of this 35-degree cone of red and black scoria is exhausting but the views

5

from the toothy crater rim and the thrilling headlong descent among a cascade of tumbling rocks and volcanic dust make it a popular excursion.

Mangatepopo Saddle to Ketetahi Hut

From the Mangatepopo Saddle, the main track crosses the flat pan of the **South Crater** and climbs to the rim of **Red Crater**, with fumaroles belching out steam, which often obscures the banded crimson and black of the crater walls. The track from here down to the **Emerald Lakes** is by far the toughest, steepest section of the descent and sees trepidatious trampers gingerly sliding down the scree slope while more gung ho hikers run down past them at a rate of knots. It's a relatively short section though and the colours around you get more vibrant still as you reach the Emerald Lakes at the bottom, where opaque pools shading from jade to palest duck-egg herald the start of the long but easy downhill hike. You'll make a short climb to the crystal-clear Blue Lake before sidling around Tongariro's **North Crater**, and enjoying the view over golden tussock slopes as you descend on well-made paths to **Ketetahi Hut**, a rest stop with views of Lake Rotoaira and Lake Taupo – and toilets.

Ketetahi Hut to Ketetahi car park

From Ketetahi Hut you make your final descent through cool streamside bush. This is a pleasant forested walk that comes as a relief to tired limbs, especially on hot days. Note, though, that there is a short (700m) section with a higher than average risk of lahars; no stopping is advised here so keep up the pace all the way to the car park on Ketetahi Road.

Tongariro Northern Circuit

42km; 3–4 days at a gentle pace • Whakapapa is the main point of access

If the Tongariro Alpine Crossing appeals, but you're looking for something more challenging, the answer is the **Tongariro Northern Circuit**, one of New Zealand's Great Walks. In summer (roughly Oct–April), the huts – Mangatepopo, Ketetahi, Waihohonu and Oturere – are classed as **Great Walk huts** and come with gas cooking stove but not pans or crockery. Campers can use the hut facilities. The circuit is usually done clockwise.

Whakapapa to Mangatepopo

9km; 2–3hr; 50m ascent

This section can be skipped by getting a shuttle to Mangatepopo car park. The track undulates through tussock and crosses numerous streams before meeting the Tongariro Alpine Crossing track close to Mangatepopo Hut. The track can be boggy after heavy rain but is usually passable.

Mangatepopo Hut to Emerald Lakes

6km; 3–4hr; 660m ascent

Follow the Tongariro Alpine Crossing (see p.300); you then have the choice of continuing on the Crossing to Ketetahi Hut (4km; 2–3hr; 400m descent) and returning to this point the next day, or continuing to the right. The track passes black lava flows from Ngauruhoe's eruptions in 1949 and 1954. From the top of Red Crater a poled route (to the left) leads to Tongariro Summit, while the main track continues on past the crater rim.

Emerald Lakes to Oturere Hut

5km; 1–2hr; 500m descent

There are spectacular views of the Oturere Valley, the Kaimanawa Ranges and the Rangipo Desert as you descend steeply through fabulously contorted lava formations from Red Crater's eruptions towards the desert and Oturere Hut.

Oturere Hut to Waihohonu Hut
8km; 2–3hr; 250m descent

You begin this leg by crossing open, rolling country over gravel fields – plant regeneration after volcanic eruptions is a lengthy process – before fording a branch of the Waihohonu Stream. You then descend into the beech forests before a final climb over a ridge brings you to the hut, where you can drop your pack and press on for twenty minutes to the cool and clear Ohinepango Springs.

Waihohonu Hut to Whakapapa
14km; 5–6hr; 200m ascent

The final day cuts between Ngauruhoe and Ruapehu, passing the Old Waihohonu Hut (no accommodation), which was built for stagecoaches on the old road in 1901. The path then continues alongside Waihohonu Stream to the exposed Tama Saddle and, just over 1km beyond, a junction where side tracks lead to Lower Tama Lake (20min return) and Upper Tama Lake (1hr return), both water-filled explosion craters, where you can swim, if you don't need your water warm. It is only around a two-hour walk from the saddle back to Whakapapa, so you should have time to explore Taranaki Falls before ambling back through tussock to the village.

Round the Mountain Track
71km; 4–5 days • Whakapapa is the main point of access

The challenging **Round the Mountain Track** loops around Mount Ruapehu and is most easily tackled from Whakapapa. The track can also be combined with the Northern Circuit to make a mighty five- or six-day **circumnavigation** of all three mountains.

National Park

The evocative moniker attached to **National Park**, 15km west of Whakapapa, belies the overwhelming drabness of this tiny settlement – a dispiriting collection of A-frame chalets sprouting from a scrubby plain with only the views of Ruapehu and Ngauruhoe to lend it grace. Comprised of a grid of half a dozen streets wedged between SH4 and the parallel rail line, the place owes its continued existence to skiers and trampers bound for the adjacent Tongariro National Park, and paddlers heading for **Whanganui River trips**. With limited accommodation at Whakapapa Village, visitors often stay here, using shuttle buses (see below) to get to the slopes and the tramps.

Tupapakurua Falls Track

When wind and rain tempt you to stay indoors, consider the **Tupapakurua Falls Track** (4–5hr return) which winds through the bush protected from the worst of the weather. It initially follows the gravel Fisher Road from near the train station then, at a small parking area after 2km (30min), you branch left onto a track to a bench seat (additional 20min) with great views west to Mount Taranaki. A further hour's walk brings you to a small canyon with views of the slender, 50m Tupapakurua Falls.

ARRIVAL AND DEPARTURE   **NATIONAL PARK**

By train Trains stop beside Station Road. Tickets can be bought at *Howard's Lodge* (see page 292).
Destinations Auckland (3 weekly; 5hr 30min); Ohakune (3 weekly; 35min); Palmerston North (3 weekly; 3hr 40min); Wellington (3 weekly; 5hr 30min).

By bus InterCity buses from Taumarunui, Turangi and Ohakune pull up nearby on Carroll Street close to the *National Park Hotel*. Tickets can be bought at *Howard's Lodge*). Numerous shuttle buses serve the trailheads in summer and ski-fields in winter. Try *Howard's Lodge, The*

5

Park and *YHA National Park Backpackers* (see page 293), who all run their own services.

Destinations Auckland (1 daily; 6hr).

INFORMATION

Tourist information National Park has no i-SITE but visitor information is available from the *Macrocarpa Café*.

Services There's an ATM in the petrol station on SH4 (generally daily 7.30am–7pm) and at *Schnapps Bar* (see page 293).

ACCOMMODATION

Howard's Lodge Carroll St ☏07 892 2827, ⓦhowardslodge.co.nz. Quality lodge where those in the en-suite rooms get access to a plusher kitchen and lounge. There's also a spa, and a wide range of rentals including mountain bikes, skis, snowboards, and hiking poles. Transport to the Tongariro Crossing is free on some rates and there's a two-night minimum stay. Dorms $19, doubles $55

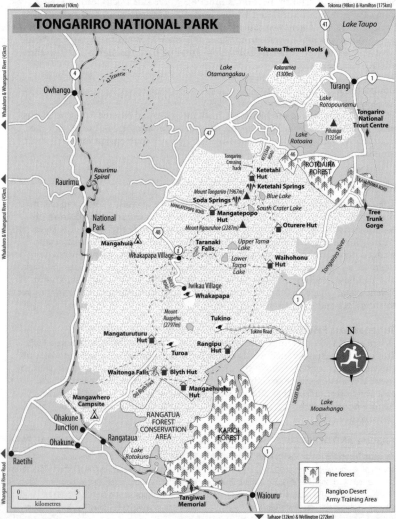

TONGARIRO NATIONAL PARK

Plateau Lodge Carroll St ☎0800 861 861, ⓦplateaulodge.co.nz. There's a relaxed ski-chalet feel to this wood-panelled lodge with a broad range of accommodation suitable for most budgets, including comfy en suite rooms ($120), plus a hot tub. Camping $40, dorms $30, doubles $78

Tongariro Crossing Lodge Carroll St ☎07 892 2688, ⓦtongarirocrossinglodge.co.nz. This quaint, colonially furnished lodge was once a stagecoach inn. Today it has a more intimate feel than most of the other lodges in town, with just six, cosy en-suite rooms. $189

YHA National Park Backpackers 4 Findlay St ☎07 892 2870, ⓦnpbp.co.nz. Fairly basic associate YHA with no frills dorms (6–8 beds; female-only options) and private rooms, as well as its own indoor climbing wall ($15, including harness and instruction). Dorms $26, rooms $62

EATING AND DRINKING

Macrocarpa Café 3 Waimarino Tokaanu Rd ☎07 892 2911. Busy café that serves as the village's post office, visitor centre and general gathering point, dishing up filling breakfasts (from $10), meals and snacks, plus lunch packs designed with trampers in mind. Daily 6am–8pm.

Schnapps Bar SH4 ☎07 892 2788, ⓦschnappsbarruapehu.com. A popular après-ski (or hike) joint, this big, orange pub near the entrance to town serves up mountainous burgers, huge fish and chips, and, the house favourite, braised lamb shanks in mint jus (mains $20–28). Breakfast is also served on weekends during winter, when, of an evening, there's often live entertainment, quizzes and sport on the big screen. If you've still got energy, there's also mini golf ($11). Daily noon–late.

★ **The Station** At the train station ☎07 892 2881, ⓦthestationcafe.co.nz. Based in the old railway station, this café-restaurant is worth a trip to National Park in its own right, thanks for its big cooked breakfasts, lunches such as seafood chowder, and exquisite evening meals. The latter include dill and lemon marinated salmon and grilled pork with a blue cheese sauce (most mains around $30), topped off with scrumptious desserts ($14) such as chocolate parfait (creamy frozen mousse with espresso jelly). On Sundays, they serve a hearty roast. Daily 9am–late.

Ohakune

Ohakune, 35km south of National Park, welcomes you with a giant fibreglass carrot, celebrating its position at the heart of one of the nation's prime market-gardening regions. This is easily forgotten once you're in town among the chalet-style lodges and ski-rental shops geared to cope with the influx of winter-sports enthusiasts who descend from mid-June to around the end of October for the ski season. Outside these months Ohakune has traditionally been quiet, but restaurants and bars are increasingly open year-round to cater to summer visitors here to **hike** the Old Coach Road, get bussed to the Tongariro Alpine Crossing or prepare for the Whanganui River journey (see page 312). There are numerous **walks** around Ohakune, most listed in the *Walks in and around Tongariro National Park* brochure (download from ⓦdoc.govt.nz)

ARRIVAL AND DEPARTURE   OHAKUNE

By train The Auckland–Wellington rail line passes through Ohakune Junction, at the town's northern edge. The train station is on Thames St.
Destinations Auckland (3 weekly; 6hr 30min); Wellington (3 weekly; 5hr 30min).

By bus InterCity buses on the Hamilton–Taumarunui–Whanganui run stop close to the i-SITE in Central Ohakune, 2km to the southwest of the train station.

Destinations Auckland (1 daily; 6hr 30min); Wellington (1 daily; 5hr 15min).

By shuttle bus Ruapehu Connexions (☎0800 462 824) provides transport around town, including a night shuttle during the ski season between Ohakune town centre and Ohakune Junction (daily 6pm until the last bar shuts; $5 one way).

INFORMATION, TOURS AND ACTIVITIES

i-SITE & DOC 54 Clyde St (i-SITE daily 8am–5pm; DOC hours vary but it's open at least Wed–Sun 9am–5pm; ☎06 385 8427, ⓦvisitruapehu.com).

CB 27 Ayr St ☎06 385 8433, ⓦtcbskiandboard.co.nz. Rents mountain bikes from $50/day. Ruapehu Connexions (see page 293) will take you and your bike to the top of the old Coach Road for $15.

5

Ruapehu Homestead 4km east of town on SH49 ☎027 267 7057, ⓦruapehuhomestead.kiwi.nz. If the area's more strenuous activities aren't to your taste, then let horses do the work on rides lasting from one to two and a half hours (from $60). Riders can choose from forest or open farmland routes.

ACCOMMODATION

Hobbit Motor Lodge 80 Goldfinch St ☎06 385 8248, ⓦthe-hobbit.co.nz. Situated midway between the town and Ohakune Junction, with motel-style amenities, including an outdoor spa. Bed down in dorms, basic through to en-suite private rooms, or self-contained units from $179. No *Lord of the Rings* link, despite the name. Dorms $30, doubles $60

LKNZ Lodge & Backpackers 1 Rata St, Ohakune Central ☎06 385 9169, ⓦlocalknowledgenz.com. Decent YHA-affiliated hostel with all manner of dorms (mixed and female-only), private rooms and facilities that include a café, hot tub, sauna and games room. The owners are enthusiastic, too. Dorms $30, doubles $65

Ohakune Top 10 Holiday Park 5 Moore St ☎06 385 8561, ⓦohakune.net.nz. A well-kept and centrally located campsite with a pleasant bush-girt setting and a range of basic cabins, some of which come with their own kitchens ($126). Camping $45, cabins $77

Powderhorn Chateau 194 Mangawhero Terrace, at base of Ohakune Mountain Rd, Ohakune Junction ☎06 385 8888, ⓦpowderhorn.co.nz. This hotel is housed in an immense log cabin, and boasts spacious, cosy rooms (the best come with balconies and forest views), plus a large indoor heated pool. $169

★ **Rimu Park Lodge** 27 Rimu St, Ohakune Junction ☎06 385 9023, ⓦrimupark.co.nz. One of the most comprehensive choices, this 1914 villa contains 6-bed dorms and doubles. Along with a hot tub, the grounds are dotted with simple cabins sleeping up to five people, two railway carriages ($230) fitted out as self-contained units with separate lounge and sleeping quarters, some classy modern apartments and a self-contained chalet. Dorms $32, doubles $80, cabins $110

The River Lodge 206 Mangawhero River Rd ☎06 385 4771, ⓦtheriverlodge.co.nz. Appealing lodge rooms and two cabins in a wonderfully peaceful parkland setting with mature native beech trees beside a small trout river. Well-appointed rooms (most with mountain views) are complemented by lounge areas, DVDs, books and games, and an outdoor spa pool. Look for signs 5km out on the road to Raetihi. $160

Station Lodge 60 Thames St ☎06 385 8797, ⓦstationlodge.co.nz. In the heart of the wintertime action at Ohakune Junction, this popular, well-equipped YHA hostel has everything from dorms to chalets, as well as great facilities including an outdoor spa and free town bikes, plus on-site mountain-bike, ski and snowboard rental. Dorms $28, doubles $70, chalets $220

EATING

The Blind Finch 29 Goldfinch St, central Ohakune ☎06 385 8076, ⓦtheblindfinch.co.nz. This gourmet burger joint has a range of creative concoctions – including tandoori chicken with mango chutney, teriyaki beef with coleslaw, and pork and crackling ($12.50–17), though you can also get a plain old cheeseburger if you wish. It turns into a bar later on, with over 25 craft beers, cocktails, and well-mixed G&Ts, and serves brunch at the weekend. Mon–Fri 4pm–midnight, Sat & Sun 9am–midnight.

Cyprus Tree 77 Clyde St, central Ohakune ☎06 385 8857, ⓦcyprustree.co.nz. Leather sofas and a roaring fire set the tone for this café/bar/restaurant doing a modern take on classic Mediterranean/Middle Eastern/North African dishes – aubergine tagine, cranberry and pistachio-stuffed chicken, and sumac-spiced rump of lamb (mains $24–34). Daily 5.30pm–late.

Matterhorn Powderhorn Chateau (see page 294). The chateau's fine-dining option has beamed ceilings and delivers superb food such as seared, spiced duck breast in a refined but relaxed atmosphere. Three-course set dinner from $65. May–Sept 7–9.30am & 6–10pm; Oct–April 7–9.30am.

Utopia 47 Clyde St, central Ohakune ☎06 385 9120. There's a European theme at this casual daytime spot for an extensive range of breakfasts, light lunches such as Portuguese-style sardines and the town's best espresso (most mains $10–20). Daily 8am–3pm.

DRINKING

Powderkeg Powderhorn Chateau (see page 294). With a woodsy après-ski feel, this casual (and usually jumping) brasserie/bar is always good for a bottled or draft beer ($9–22), including a huge array of craft options, as well as decent grub like cajun fish sliders and sesame chicken salad. Daily 7am–late.

The Desert Road

5

South of Turangi, SH1 sticks to the east of the Tongariro National Park running roughly parallel to the Tongariro River. This is the eerily scenic **Desert Road** (SH1), which traverses the exposed and barren Rangipo Desert – not a true desert (it gets too much rainfall), but kept arid by the free-draining blanket of volcanic ash and pumice. Road cuttings slice through several metres of the stuff, leaving a timeline of past eruptions. Snow can close the road in winter – keep tabs on the weather before you set out. The Desert Road and the roads flanking the western side of Ruapehu, Ngauruhoe and Tongariro meet at **WAIOURU**, an uninspiring row of service stations and tearooms perched 800m above sea level on the bleak tussock plain beside New Zealand's major **army base**, home to New Zealand's National Army Museum.

Tree Trunk Gorge

Tree Trunk Gorge Road leads down to the Tongariro River at a spot where it squeezes and churns through a narrow fissure known as **Tree Trunk Gorge**. Back on the highway you soon climb out of the pine forest for great views of the three volcanoes off to the west and the blasted territory ahead. It is a dramatic scene, somehow made even more elemental by the three lines of electricity pylons striding off across the bleak tussock towards Waiouru.

National Army Museum

SH1, at Hassett Drive, Waiouru • Daily 9am–4.30pm • $15 • ☎ 06 387 6911, ⓦ armymuseum.co.nz

Concrete bunkers house the **National Army Museum**, where the *Roimata Pounamu* ("Tears on Greenstone") **wall of remembrance** comprises water (symbolizing mourning and cleansing) streaming down a curving bank of heavily veined greenstone tiles while a recorded voice recites the name, rank and place of death of each of the roughly 33,000 New Zealanders who have died in various wars. The chronologically arranged exhibits are manageable in scale but detailed enough to give coverage of the campaigns, the affecting human stories behind them and the smaller details such as the display on the warrior flags Māori fought under during the New Zealand Wars of the 1860s. Accounts of the bungled Gallipoli campaign of World War I come complete with an instructive model of Anzac Cove. Nursing during World War II gets equal billing with coverage of POWs incarcerated not just in Germany but also Singapore as New Zealand's world focus begins to shift towards Asia, and eventually the Vietnam War. Allow around an hour and a half to take it all in.

There's also an interesting **discovery centre** for the kids, and the museum **café** is about the best around.

Taihape

In the 30km south of Waiouru you drop down off the volcanic plateau into the farming service town of **TAIHAPE** in the heart of the Rangitikei District. The main reason to stop is its proximity to the hilly country to the east, which hides one of New Zealand's most thrilling whitewater-rafting trips.

Taihape promotes itself as "New Zealand's Gumboot Capital" with a corrugated iron boot sculpture and an annual **Gumboot Day** (mid-March), a tongue-in-cheek celebration of this archetypal Kiwi footwear with a gumboot-throwing competition.

ARRIVAL AND DEPARTURE   TAIHAPE

By bus InterCity buses stop on Kuku St, around the corner from the Information Centre, while NakedBus stops at *Gumboot Manor* restaurant at the northern end of town.

Destinations Auckland (3 daily; 6hr 30min); Taupo (6 daily; 1hr 55min); Turangi (6 daily; 1hr 10min); Wellington (6 daily; 4hr 25min).

By train The train station is one block west of the Information Centre on Robin St.

Destinations Auckland (3 weekly; 7hr 50min); Wellington (3 weekly; 4hr 50min).

INFORMATION AND TOURS

Tourist information 90–92 Hautapu St (daily 9am–5pm; ☎ 06 388 0604, ⓦ taihape.co.nz). The Information Centre is inside the library; information on the region is also available at ⓦ rangitikei.com.

River Valley *River Valley* lodge ☎ 06 388 1444, ⓦ rivervalley.co.nz. Offers excellent horse-trekking

trips (from $129) that head over farmland, provide great views across the rugged country hereabouts, and last from two hours to four days. A range of rafting trips are also available.

ACCOMMODATION

★ **River Valley** Pukoekahu ☎ 06 388 1444, ⓦ rivervalley.co.nz. Visitors to the adventure lodge best known for its horseriding and rafting trips (see above) can camp ($18), stay in six-bunk dorms (linen provided), or the pleasant rooms. Kiwi Experience buses call nightly. There's a self-catering kitchen or straightforward low-cost meals and a bar. Everyone also has free access to pétanque and volleyball and (for a small fee) a wood sauna, an infrared sauna, a spa pool with river views, and massages in the summer. Dorms $31, doubles $169

Safari Motel 18 Mataroa Rd ☎ 06 388 1116, ⓦ safarimotel.co.nz. This uncluttered motel, located 1km north of town on SH1, offering up larger rooms with kitchenettes, as well as better-equipped one-bedroom apartments. Doubles $95, apartments $125

Taihape Motels Kuku St, at Robin St ☎ 0800 200 029, ⓦ taihapemotels.co.nz. The spotless rooms at this low-cost, centrally located motel have comfy queen- or king-size beds; there are also three holiday flats sleeping up to eight people. $80

EATING AND DRINKING

Brown Sugar Café Huia St ☎ 06 388 1886. Cottage-like café with a tempting blackboard menu of dishes like grilled brie and chicken, vegetable samosas and big Greek salads (dishes $12–24), plus decent coffee. Daily 8am–5pm.

Soul Food Café 69 Hautapu St ☎ 06 388 0176. Big

breakfasts ($12–24) – including pancakes, corn fritters and a "farmers brekkie" of mincemeat on grain toast with relish – are served all day at this popular spot; lunch could be an open steak sandwich or butter chicken. Mon–Wed 9am–4pm, Thurs–Sun 9am–8pm.

Mangaweka and the Rangitikei River

A DC3 aeroplane (and sign reading "Mangaweka International Airport") marks the dilapidated hamlet of **MANGAWEKA**, 24km south of Taihape on the SH1. This is the headquarters of the Mangaweka Adventure Company, which offers a number of **whitewater-rafting** and **kayaking** trips along the Grade V **Rangitikei River** one of the toughest whitewater-rafting rivers in the country with ten major rapids packed into a two- to three-hour run.

ACCOMMODATION AND ACTIVITIES

MANGAWEKA

Mangaweka Adventure Company SH1, Mangaweka village ☎ 0800 655 747, ⓦ mangaweka. co.nz. Offers a number of whitewater-rafting and kayaking trips including Rangitikei Grade V Gorge trips

(from $175), a couple of family-oriented rafting trips (from $90) and multi-day excursions. A lovely, simple campsite with some riverside pitches, cabins and private rooms, and a café. Camping $18, cabins $85

The Taranaki Peninsula

The province of **Taranaki** (nicknamed "The 'naki") juts out west from the rest of the North Island forming a thumbprint peninsula centred on **Mount Taranaki** (aka Mount Egmont), an elegant conical volcano rising 2500m from the subtropical coast to its icy summit. Taranaki means "peak clear of vegetation", an appropriate description of the upper half of "the mountain", as locals simply refer to it.

The mountain remains a constant presence as you tour the region, though much of the time it is obscured by cloud. The summit is usually visible in the early morning and just before sunset, with cloud forming through the middle of the day – the bane of summit aspirants who slog for no view.

Taranaki's vibrant provincial capital and largest city, **New Plymouth**, makes a good base for day-trips into the **Egmont National Park**, surrounding the mountain. It is also very convenient for short forays to the surfing and windsurfing hotspot of **Oakura**.

Rural Taranaki's attractions, including the **Surf Highway**, are best sampled on a one- or two-day loop around the mountain.

New Plymouth

The small but growing city of **NEW PLYMOUTH**, on the northern shore of the peninsula with an economy fuelled by the gas and oil industries, is the commercial heart of Taranaki and renowned New Zealand-wide for its concerts and arts festivals. **Port Taranaki**, at the edge of the city, serves as New Zealand's western gateway and is the only deep-water international port on the west coast. There's a strong **arts** and **gardens** bias to its attractions, though it is a pleasure just to walk around the town. Just offshore is the **Sugar Loaf Islands Protected Area**, a haven for wildlife above and beneath the sea.

Brief history

In the early nineteenth century few **Māori** were living in the area as annual raids by northern tribes had forced many to migrate with Te Rauparaha to Kapiti Island. This played into the hands of John Lowe and Richard Barrett who, in 1828, established a trading and whaling station on the Ngamotu Beach on the northern shores of the peninsula. In 1841, the **Plymouth Company** dispatched six ships of English colonists to New Zealand, settling at Lowe and Barrett's outpost. Mostly from the West Country, the new settlers named their community **New Plymouth**. From the late 1840s many Māori returned to their homeland, and disputes arose over land sold to settlers, which from 1860 culminated in a ten-year armed conflict, the Taranaki Land Wars. These formed part of the wider New Zealand Wars, and slowed the development of the region, leaving a legacy of **Māori grievances**, some still being addressed.

Govett-Brewster Art Gallery and the Len Lye Centre

42 Queen St • Daily 10am–5pm • Free • ① 06 759 6060, ⓦ govettbrewster.com

The not-to-be-missed **Govett-Brewster Art Gallery** is one of the country's finest contemporary art galleries. It showcases a huge permanent collection of works by Len Lye, housed in the eye-catching new **Len Lye Centre**, beside the original building.

Until fairly recently, the Christchurch-born sculptor, film-maker and conceptual artist (1901–80) was little known outside the art world, but his work is now earning well-deserved recognition. Lye developed a fascination with movement, which expressed itself in his late teens in early experiments in kinetic sculpture. His interest in Māori art encouraged him to travel more widely, studying both Australian Aboriginal and Samoan dance. Adapting indigenous art to the precepts of the Futurist and Surrealist movements coming out of Europe, he experimented with sculpture, batik, painting, photography and animated "cameraless" films (he painstakingly stencilled, scratched and drew on the actual film).

The gallery also a good art and design bookshop and an excellent café, *Monica's Eatery* (see page 302). Not to be missed.

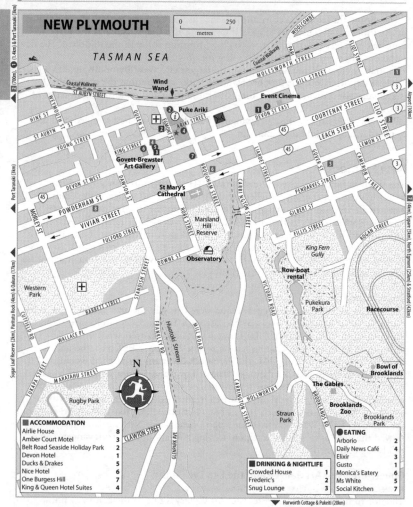

ACCOMMODATION
Airlie House	8
Amber Court Motel	3
Belt Road Seaside Holiday Park	2
Devon Hotel	1
Ducks & Drakes	5
Nice Hotel	6
One Burgess Hill	7
King & Queen Hotel Suites	4

DRINKING & NIGHTLIFE
Crowded House	1
Frederic's	2
Snug Lounge	3

EATING
Arborio	2
Daily News Café	4
Elixir	3
Gusto	1
Monica's Eatery	6
Ms White	5
Social Kitchen	7

Wind Wand

Arriving in the centre of New Plymouth, you can't miss the **Wind Wand**, a slender, bright-red, 45m-high carbon-fibre tube topped with a light globe that glows red in the dark and sways mesmerizingly in the wind. A smaller version was erected in Greenwich Village in 1962 but this wand wasn't constructed until 2000, taking advantage of advances in polymer engineering. Lye would probably have been disappointed with this single example: his vision was for a forest of 125 wind wands swaying together in the breeze.

Coastal Walkway

Landscaping and pathways stretch a couple of hundred metres either side of the *Wind Wand*, making a **waterfront park** that's pleasant for an evening stroll. More ambitious walkers and cyclists can follow the **Coastal Walkway** that stretches 3km west to the port and 7km east to Bell Block.

The best bet is to head 2km east to East End Reserve where there is bike rental (see page 301) and the *Big Wave Café*. Explore 2km further east as far as the Waiwhakaiho rivermouth, spanned by the stunning, 83m-long, white steel **Te Rewa Rewa Bridge**, said to be modelled on a curling wave but often likened to a whale's skeleton. In fine weather there's usually a coffee cart nearby.

Puke Ariki

1 Ariki St • Mon, Tues, Thurs, Fri 9am–6pm, Wed 9am–9pm, Sat & Sun 9am–5pm; Richmond Cottage Sat & Sun 11am–3.30pm • Free •
🕾 06 759 6060, ⓦ pukeariki.com

The city's hub is **Puke Ariki**, a combined i-SITE (see page 301), city **library**, **exhibition space** and interactive **regional museum**. The strength is in the temporary exhibitions, though there is an extensive gallery covering Taranaki Māori, along with volcanic rock carvings and woodcarvings in the unique local style. The museum site also encompasses **Richmond Cottage**, an 1854 stone dwelling built for local MP Christopher William Richmond, and moved to its current site in 1962.

St Mary's Cathedral

37 Vivian St • Free • 🕾 06 758 3111, ⓦ taranakicathedral.org.nz

The Frederick Thatcher-designed **St Mary's Church** is the oldest stone church in New Zealand. Built in 1845 along austere lines with an imposing gabled dark-wood interior, it finally became Taranaki's cathedral in 2010. The church contains a striking 1972 Māori memorial with carvings and *tukutuku* panels.

Pukekura Park and Brooklands Park

Parks Main entrances on Liardet St and Brooklands Park Drive • Daily dawn–dusk • Free • ⓦ pukekura.org.nz • **Gables** Sat & Sun 1–4pm •
Free • **Rowboats** Dec–Feb daily 11am–4pm & 7–10pm • $10 for 30min

Pukekura Park and Brooklands Park are effectively two sections of one large park – one of New Zealand's finest city parks and setting for both the Festival of Lights and WOMAD (see page 47). Pukekura is mostly semiformal, with glasshouses, a boating lake and a cricket pitch. The more freely laid out Brooklands occupies the grounds of a long-gone homestead and includes the **Bowl of Brooklands** outdoor amphitheatre, attracting big-name artists, as well as numerous mature trees, among them a 2000-year-old puriri and a big ginkgo. Nearby, a former colonial hospital from 1847 is now the **Gables**, containing an art gallery and small medical museum. Near the renovated Pukekura Teahouse you can rent **rowboats**.

Paritutu Rock

New Plymouth's port sprawls out from the foot of the 200m-high **Paritutu Rock**, 4km west of the city centre. A feature of great cultural significance to Māori and a near-perfect natural fortress, it still marks the boundary between Taranaki and Te Atiawa territories. You can ascend it from a car park on Centennial Drive, signposted off Vivian Street. It's a steep scramble (20–50min return) with a steel rope providing support, but the reward is a great view along the coast.

Sugar Loaf Islands Marine Protected Area

1hr boat trips • 2–3 daily, weather permitting • $40 • 🕾 06 758 9133, ⓦ chaddyscharters.co.nz

A few hundred metres off the north Taranaki coast, a cluster of rocky islands is the eroded remnant of ancient volcanoes, a sanctuary for rare plants, little blue penguins, petrels and sooty shearwaters. The surrounding waters form the DOC-administered **Sugar Loaf Marine Protected Area**, which harbours some 89 species of fish and a wealth of multicoloured anemones, sponges and seaweeds in undersea canyons. Humpback whales (Aug & Sept) and dolphins (Oct–Dec) migrate past, and the tidal rocks are populated by New Zealand's northernmost breeding colony of fur seals. Although the

THE FORGOTTEN WORLD HIGHWAY

For a taste of genuinely rural New Zealand, follow the **Forgotten World Highway** between Taumarunui (see page 208) and Stratford (SH43), a rugged 155m road that twists through the hills west of Taumarunui. All but a 12km stretch through the Tangarakau Gorge is sealed, but allow at least three hours for the journey, and be sure to fuel up beforehand as there's **no petrol** along the route. Much of the route is covered on the Whanganui National Park map (see page 311).

Leaving behind the farmland around Taumarunui, SH43 snakes through the sedimentary limestone of the **Tangarakau Gorge**, possibly the highlight of the trip, with steep bush-draped cliffs rising up above the river. At the entrance to the gorge, a small sign directs you along a short trail to the picturesque site of **Joshua Morgan's grave**, the final resting place of an early surveyor. At the crest of a ridge you pass through the dark, narrow **Moki Tunnel** before reaching Whangamomona.

A steady descent brings you alongside a little-used rail line that runs parallel to the road as far as tiny **Whangamomona**, 88km southwest of Taumarunui, with just ten residents. The population is boosted in late January of every odd-numbered year during celebrations of the village's independence, declared on October 28, 1989, after the government altered the provincial boundaries, removing it from Taranaki. The **republic** swears in a president and in full party mood hosts whip-cracking and gumboot-throwing competitions, amid much drinking, eating and merriment. Celebrations revolve around the 1911 *Whangamomona Hotel*, where year-round you can get your passport stamped or buy a Whangamomonian version ($1).

Leaving Whangamomona, SH43 climbs beside steep bluffs and passes a couple of saddles with views down the valley and across the **Taranaki Plains**. It then descends to flat dairy pasture, eventually rolling into **Stratford** as the permanently snowcapped Mount Taranaki looms into view, if the weather allows.

ACCOMMODATION AND EATING

Ohinepane campsite 21km west of Taumarunui, ⓦ doc.govt.nz. For a peaceful night beside the Whanganui River, stop at this grassy DOC campsite with water and long-drop toilets and possibly the company of canoeists stopping for their first night downstream from Taumarunui. $\underline{\$10}$

Whangamomona Domain Camp Whangamomona Rd ☎ 06 762 5822. Simple campsite in a peaceful setting with campervan hook-ups, basic cabins (bring your own bedding) and showers ($2), all an easy wander from the *Whangamomona Hotel*. Camping $\underline{\$15}$, cabins $\underline{\$30}$

Whangamomona Hotel Ohura Rd ☎ 06 762 5823, ⓦ whangamomonahotel.co.nz. Classic country pub/ hotel that has been refurbished without losing any of its character. Airy guest rooms share bathrooms and a continental breakfast is included. The hotel serves no-nonsense pub meals – steak and chips, burgers, pie and mash, etc (mains $18–35). $\underline{\$150}$

---

islands themselves are off-limits, Chaddy's Charters run entertaining **trips** around the reserve.

Tupare

487 Mangorei Rd, 6km southeast of the city centre • Daily 9am–8pm; house tours Oct–March Fri–Mon 11am • Free • ☎ 0800 736 222, ⓦ tupare.info

Taranaki's fertile volcanic soils and moist climate make for some great gardens, and there are few better than **Tupare**, developed since the 1930s. There's pleasure in just wandering round the maples, azaleas and rhododendrons, and learning a little of the history in the pretty **Gardener's Cottage**, but it all makes more sense when combined with a tour of the quirky **Arts & Crafts house** designed by prominent Kiwi architect James Chapman-Taylor.

Hurworth Cottage

906 Carrington Rd, 9km south of the city centre • Sat & Sun 11am–3pm and by appointment • $5 • ☎ 06 753 3593, ⓦ historicplaces.org.nz

The charming and historic **Hurworth Cottage** was built in 1856 for Harry Atkinson, four times prime minister of New Zealand and famous for advocating women's suffrage and introducing welfare benefits. The plain two-room cottage is the only one to have survived the New Zealand Wars of the 1860s and is now furnished as it would have been in the mid-nineteenth century. Check out the ancient charcoal graffiti, one section depicting a Māori warrior with full-face *moko*.

Pukeiti

2290 Carrington Rd, 23km southwest of the city centre • Daily 9am–5pm; café Wed–Sun 10am–4pm • Free • ☎ 0800 736 222, ⓦ pukeiti. org.nz

Carved out of the bush 370m up on the northern slopes of the Pouakai Range, **Pukeiti** are Taranaki's finest public gardens. They were established in 1951 by Douglas Cook, founder of Gisborne's Eastwoodhill Arboretum (see page 340), who needed a cooler, damper climate to grow New Zealand's largest collection of rhododendrons and azaleas. The result is a wild array of superb blooms, with bush paths linking up grassy avenues lined with fine specimens. The on-site *Founders Café* provides sustenance.

ARRIVAL AND DEPARTURE   NEW PLYMOUTH

By plane From the airport (ⓦ nplairport.co.nz, 12km northeast of town, Scott's Airport Shuttle Service can drop you anywhere in the city (from $20; ☎ 06 769 5974 or ☎ 0800 373 001, ⓦ npairportshuttle.co.nz). Shuttles meet all flights, but reserve ahead to guarantee a seat.
Destinations Auckland (6 daily; 45min); Wellington (2 daily; 55min).

By bus InterCity/Newmans and NakedBus stop at the bus station at 19 Ariki St, just along from the i-SITE.
Destinations Auckland (2 daily; 6hr 30min); Hamilton (2 daily; 4hr); Hawera (1 daily; 1hr 5min); Te Kuiti (1 daily; 1hr 15min); Whanganui (1 daily; 2hr 30min); Wellington (1 daily; 7hr).

GETTING AROUND

By bus CityLink (☎ 0800 872 287, ⓦ trc.govt.nz/bus-routes) run local services. The limited routes may be useful for Tupare and Oakura, but services are infrequent.

By bike Cycle Inn, 133 Devon St East (☎ 06 758 7418, ⓦ cycleinn.co.nz; Mon–Fri 8.30am–5pm, Sat 9am–4pm, Sun 10am–2pm) rent bikes from $20/day or $10/2hr.

INFORMATION AND TOURS

Visitor information i-SITE, 65 St Aubyn St, in the foyer of Puke Ariki (Mon–Fri 9am–6pm, Wed till 9pm, Sat & Sun 9am–5pm; ☎ 06 759 6060, ⓦ visit.taranaki.info). Excellent visitor centre with touch screens to access local

info, and plenty on Egmont National Park, including hut tickets.
Services The library, 1 Ariki St, has free internet access (Mon–Fri 9am–6pm, Wed till 9pm, Sat & Sun 9am–5pm).

ACCOMMODATION

New Plymouth has a range of modestly priced accommodation, as well as options close to the city at the surf beach town of **Oakura** (see page 307), or on the flanks of the mountain. Motels are strung along the approach roads into the city centre.
Airlie House 161 Powderham St ☎ 06 757 8866, ⓦ airliehouse.co.nz; map p.298. Attractive B&B in a large villa dating from the turn of the last century, with crisp modern decor. The "drawing room", with a bay-window seat, and studio apartment (with kitchen) are both en-suite, while the "garden room", overlooking the flowering front garden, has a private bathroom with a claw-foot bath. There are hundreds of DVDs and excellent breakfasts. $180

Amber Court Motel 61 Eliot Street ☎ 06 758 0922, ⓦ ambercourtmotel.co.nz; map p.298. Competitively priced, motel, just off the highway but easy walking distance to the city centre. Rooms are spacious with separate kitchen and bathroom, and there's an indoor swimming pool and laundry. $130
Belt Road Seaside Holiday Park 2 Belt Rd ☎ 0800 804 204, ⓦ beltroad.co.nz; map p.298. A scenic, seaside site that's a 25min walk along the coastal path from the city centre, with camping, motel rooms and cabins in a tidy area mostly sheltered from the otherwise exposed clifftop location. The three-night minimum stay in high season is an annoyance. Camping $23, doubles $150, cabins $75

5

Devon Hotel 390 Devon St East ☎0800 843 338, ⓦdevonhotel.co.nz; map p.298. A smart hotel, popular with business travellers, with a heated pool and spa, room service, buffet restaurant, free bikes and a range of rooms, including some spacious suites. Free use of an off-site gym. **$149**

Ducks & Drakes 48 Lemon St ☎06 758 0403, ⓦducksanddrakes.co.nz; map p.298. Choose to stay in the charming 1920s house (from $130), with a roomy kitchen and book-filled lounge, or the bright, airy hostel next door, opening onto a communal lawn. There's also a sauna ($5/person) and some tent sites ($25). Dorms **$32**, hostel rooms **$90**

★ **Nice Hotel** 71 Brougham St ☎06 758 6423, ⓦnicehotel.co.nz; map p.298. Despite the twee name, this is an excellent hotel. It's also very popular, so book well in advance to ensure you get one of the elegant en suites in this intimate *pied-à-terre*, with designer bathrooms, contemporary artworks and

luxurious fittings. The on-site restaurant, *Table* (dinner only; mains $35-42), is renowned for its French-accented cuisine. **$250**

One Burgess Hill 1 Burgess Hill Rd, 5km south of the city centre ☎06 757 2056, ⓦoneburgesshill.co.nz; map p.298. Set on a high promontory with great views across the cascading Waiwhakaiho River to a giant vertical garden of bush and tree ferns, these rooms and apartments (many with log fires) have state-of-the-art decor and furnishings including sleek self-catering kitchens and swish bathrooms. Doubles **$146**, apartments **$225**

★ **King & Queen Hotel Suites** Corner King and Queen sts ☎06 757 2999, ⓦkingandqueen.co.nz; map p.298. Modern boutique hotel offering classy en suites (some with private balconies and sea views), efficient service, onsite coffee shop and roastery, and an array of nice touches, including free macarons and hire bikes. **$209**

EATING

The majority of the cafés, restaurants, bars and clubs are on the so-called "**Devon Mile**", along Devon St between Dawson and Eliot sts. In recent times a second culinary hotspot has sprung up at Port Taranaki overlooking the water.

Arborio St Aubyn St, inside Puke Ariki ☎06 759 1241, ⓦarborio.co.nz; map p.298. A bustling, modern café-bar overlooking the *Wind Wand*, and a great spot throughout the day and night. Dishes include caramelised chicken breast with manchego galette ($36.50), thin-crust pizzas ($21-25; also available to takeaway), and porcini gnocchi with three-mushroom ragu ($27.90). Reservations recommended, as are seats on the outdoor terrace overlooking the water. Daily 9am-10pm.

Daily News Café Level 1 in the library, 1 Ariki St; map p.298. Inside the library, this small, serene café serves coffee (from $4), snacks and newspapers from around New Zealand and the world, so you're guaranteed something good to read. Daily 9.30am-3.30pm.

Elixir 117 Devon St East ☎06 769 9902, ⓦelixircafe.co.nz; map p.298. Chilled café plastered with posters of upcoming festivals and gigs, serving freshly baked muffins, panini, bagels and wraps, as well as delicious mains such as lemon and thyme chicken salad ($18.80). Mon 6.30am-4pm, Tues-Fri 6.30am-late, Sat 7.30am-late, Sun 8am-4pm.

Gusto Ocean View Parade, Port Taranaki ☎06 759 8133, ⓦgustotaranaki.co.nz; map p.298. This minimalist-chic harbour-view fine-diner, hidden away in a semi-industrial marina area, is a winner for its classy, contemporary fare. The economical set lunches ($30-33) and dinners ($52-70) include rolled pork

belly with sweet potatoes, and coconut crème brulee. Reduced hours in winter. Mon-Fri 10am-10pm, Sat 9am-10pm, Sun 9am-3pm.

★ **Monica's Eatery** 42 Queen St ☎06 759 2038, ⓦmonicaseatery.co.nz; map p.298. This airy café attached to the Govett-Brewster art gallery is a work of art in itself – specifically in the form of Sara Hughes' *The Golden Grain*, an installation piece that includes everything from the white banquettes and pie chart discs on the ceiling to the tables and crockery. None of it distracts from the excellent food and coffee, either, whether you opt for the blueberry cheesecake waffles ($15.90), or one of the set lunches (from $17.90) or dinners (from $30). Daily 6.30am-10pm.

Ms White 47 Queen St ☎06 759 2038, ⓦmswhite.co.nz; map p.298. Authentically Italian thin-crust pizzas ($13-19) and a healthy selection of over 40 craft beers (from $6.50) are the order of the day at this hip spot. Mon & Tues 4-9.30pm, Wed-Sun 11am-10pm.

★ **Social Kitchen** 40 Powderham St ☎06 757 2711, ⓦsocial-kitchen.co.nz; map p.298. This bistro serves some of the best food in town, in stylish surrounds. As well as a selection of small plates ($13-19) like sweetcorn churros and empanadas, the menu features expertly barbecued meat, fish and veg – served with the tangy Argentine dressing chimichurri – and slow-cooked ribs, shoulder of lamb, and 12-hour spiced goat (mains $30-58). Daily noon-late.

DRINKING AND NIGHTLIFE

Crowded House 93 Devon St East ☎ 06 759 4921, ⓦ crowdedhouse.co.nz; map p.298. Fairly formulaic downtown café-bar that's often busy, particularly if there's a big game on TV. Monteith's beers are on tap and you can eat well on dishes like a southern fried chicken and bacon burger ($19.90). Daily 10am–10pm.

Frederic's 34 Egmont St ☎ 06 759 1227, ⓦ frederics. co.nz; map p.298. This welcoming pub-style bar serves a range of craft beers (from $7) and ciders and a solid Kiwi-focused wine list. Generally a chilled atmosphere though things can get lively later in the week. Mon–Sun 11am–late.

Snug Lounge 134 Devon St West ☎ 06 757 9130, ⓦ snuglounge.co.nz; map p.298. This seductive Japanese-inspired cocktail bar offers inventive mixed drinks (cocktails $15–16), *sake* and plum wine, as well as a short food menu featuring *bao* buns, dumplings, wantons, and the like (dishes $7.5–20). Mon–Sat 4pm–late, Sun noon–11pm.

ENTERTAINMENT

Arthouse Cinema 73a Devon St West ☎ 06 757 3650, ⓦ nzcinema.co.nz. Independent and art-house films, which you can enjoy with a glass of wine.

Event Cinema 119–125 Devon St East ☎ 06 759 9077, ⓦ eventcinemas.co.nz. Screens mainstream Hollywood flicks.

New Plymouth Observatory Robe St, Marsland Hill Reserve, ✉ npstargazers@gmail.com. Members of the Astronomical Society volunteer to point out highlights in the night sky for visitors ($6). Tues: Nov–March 8.30–10pm; April–Oct 7.30–9.30pm.

Egmont National Park

Taranaki (Mount Egmont), a dormant volcano that last erupted in 1755, dominates the entire western third of the North Island. Often likened to Japan's Mount Fuji, its profile is a cone rising to 2518m, though from east or west the profile is disturbed by the satellite **Fantham's Peak** (1692m). In winter, snow blankets the mountain, but as summer progresses only the crater rim remains white. The mountain is the focal point for **Egmont National Park**, the boundary forming an arc with a 10km radius around the mountain, interrupted only on its north side where it encompasses the **Pouakai Range** and **Kaitake Range**, older, more weathered cousins of Taranaki.

According to Māori legend, the mountain-demigod Taranaki fled here from the company of the other mountains in the central North Island. He was firmly in place when spotted by the first European in the area, **Cook**, who named the peak Egmont after the first Lord of the Admiralty.

Surrounded by farmland, the mountain's lower slopes are cloaked in native bush that gradually changes to stunted flag-form trees shaped by the constant buffeting of the wind. Higher still, vegetation gives way to slopes of loose scoria (a kind of jagged volcanic gravel) – hard work if you're hiking.

Three sealed roads climb Taranaki's eastern flanks, each ending at a separate car park a little under halfway up the mountain from where the park's 140km of walking tracks spread out. **North Egmont** is the most easily accessible from New Plymouth but you can get higher up the mountain at **East Egmont**, and there are good short walks around **Dawson Falls**. The i-SITE in New Plymouth has extensive **information** on the park.

The Taranaki summit route

10km return; 7–10hr; 1560m ascent

From New Plymouth, the easiest access point to the park is tiny **Egmont Village**, 13km to the southeast on SH3. From here, the 16km sealed but winding Egmont Road runs up the mountain to **North Egmont** (936m), the starting point for the Pouakai Circuit, summit ascents and several easier walks.

Poled all the way, the route to the summit of Taranaki begins at North Egmont and initially follows the gravel Translator Road (the appropriately dubbed "Puffer") to *Tahurangi Lodge*, a private hut run by the Taranaki Alpine Club. A wooden

5

stairway leads to North Ridge, and after that you're onto slopes of scoria up the Lizard Ridge leading to the crater. Crossing the crater ice and a short scoria slope brings you to the summit and, hopefully, magical views over the western third of the North Island.

The upper mountain is off-limits to ordinary hikers in winter, but even during the hiking season **bad weather**, including occasional snow, sweeps in frighteningly quickly, and hikers starting off on a fine morning frequently find themselves groping through low cloud before the day is through. Deaths occur far too often: consult the **hiking advice** in Basics (see page 48), get an up-to-date **weather forecast** (ⓦmetservice.com/mountain/egmont-national-park) and obtain further information from the nearest DOC office or visitor centre in New Plymouth or North Egmont. Climb with at least one companion or a mountain guide, and leave a **record of your intentions** with your accommodation or at ⓦadventuresmart. org.nz.

Pouakai Circuit

Year-round, but expect snow from May–Sept; get advice from DOC before embarking • 24km loop; 2–3 days; track varies in altitude from 700–1300m

For exposed wetlands, subalpine tussock, steep fern-draped gullies, cliffs of columnar basalt and superb views of Taranaki make straight for this delightful loop tramp. Much of it is above the bushline, giving long views over the flatlands and the coast. It is steep in places and the tracks are never as groomed as the Great Walks, making the rewards well earned. There are two huts with camping outside (see page 306).

Veronica Loop Track

2.5km loop; 2hr; 200m ascent

A fairly stiff walk which initially climbs steps along a ridge through mountain forest and scrub past a monument to Arthur Ambury, a climber who died trying to save another man. Continue uphill (go past the sign that points you back downhill to the car park) to a great lookout with fine views of the ancient lava flows known as Humphries Castle, and beyond to New Plymouth and the coast, before retracing your steps and continuing with the loop. This is a good route for hikers with little time but plenty of energy.

East Egmont

East Egmont is accessed through Stratford (see page 307), from where Pembroke Road runs 14km west to the *Stratford Mountain House* hotel then a further 3km to a rugged and windswept spot known as **The Plateau**. At 1172m this is the highest road-accessible point on Taranaki's flanks. As well as being on the upper route of the Around the Mountain Circuit (see below), this acts as the wintertime parking area for the tiny **Manganui Ski Area** (ⓦskitaranaki.co.nz).

Curtis Falls Track

3.5km return; 2–3hr; 120m ascent

A fairly tough, short walk from the *Mountain House* hotel, crossing numerous deep gorges via steps and ladders, to the Manganui River Gorge, where you can follow the riverbed (no track or signs) to the base of a waterfall. This is part of the lower Around the Mountain Circuit.

Enchanted Track

3km oneway; 3hr return; 300m ascent

5

Park at the *Mountain House* hotel then hike up the road to The Plateau before heading south and cutting down onto the Enchanted Track, named for the fabulous views to the east. Note how the vegetation gradually changes as you descend.

Dawson Falls

Visitor centre Thurs–Sun & public holidays 9am–4pm

The most southerly access up Taranaki follows Manaia Road to **Dawson Falls** (900m), roughly 23km west of Stratford. Here you'll find the **Dawson Falls visitor centre** outside of which stands an impressive 8m-high *pou whenua* (carved pole) depicting famous Māori associated with the area.

Kapuni Loop Track

2km loop; 1hr; 100m ascent

A delightful walk through the twisted and stunted kamahi trees of the so-called "Goblin Forest", gnarled trunks hung with ferns and mosses. You soon reach Dawson Falls, where the Kapuni Stream plummets 17m over the end of an ancient lava flow. On the way back, call at the shed that houses the tiny **Dawson Falls Power Station**, a historic hydro plant built in 1935 to provide power for the *Dawson Falls Mountain Lodge* (see page 307).

Wilkies Pool Loop Track

2.3km loop; 1hr; 100m ascent

This walk from the Dawson Falls visitor centre heads uphill through more "Goblin Forest" to a series of pretty pools carved out by the Kapuni Stream. Take your time on the wet rocks and pause occasionally to appreciate the lush bush all around.

ARRIVAL AND INFORMATION   EGMONT NATIONAL PARK

By shuttle bus Taranki Tours (☎06 757 9888, ⓦtaranakitours.com) runs shuttle buses to/from New Plymouth, as well as guided tours and hikes.

North Egmont Visitor Centre End of Egmont Rd (daily 8am–4.30pm; ☎06 756 0990, ⓦdoc.govt.nz). This is the park's main information source, and has displays about the mountain, (not particularly detailed) maps of all the tracks for purchase, good viewing windows, weather updates and a decent café (daily 9am–4pm).

Mountain guides Several guides offer bushwalking, guided summit treks and a range of more technical stuff. They generally take up to six clients for summer hiking and summit attempts but perhaps only two for winter expeditions, rock climbing or instruction. Guiding rates are around $99/ per person for a half day (minimum four people). Try Top Guides (☎0800 448 433, ⓦtopguides.co.nz) or Adventure Dynamics (☎06 751 3589, ⓦadventuredynamics.co.nz).

ACCOMMODATION AND EATING

NORTH EGMONT

The Camphouse North Egmont ☎06 278 6523 or ☎06 756 9093, ⓦdoc.govt.nz. This large mountain hut, built in 1891, now operates as a basic but comfy hostel, with a heated communal lounge, full kitchen and hot showers. Check-in at the *Mountain Café*. Dorms $25

The Pouakai Circuit Hikers on the Pouakai Circuit have access to two huts: the 32-bunk Holly Hut and the 16-bunk Pouakai Hut. Both operate on a first come, first served basis and backcountry hut passes are valid. $15

Mountain Café North Egmont, inside the visitor centre. Warm café – the highest in Taranaki – with good views that's perfect for all-day breakfast ($15–23), soup, burgers or just a post-hike coffee. Dec–March 9am–3pm; April–Nov 10am–3pm.

EAST EGMONT

Stratford Mountain House Pembroke Rd, 14km west of Stratford ☎06 765 6100, ⓦstratfordmountainhouse.co.nz. Beautifully sited and revamped lodge 4km inside the national park boundary and 850m above sea level. Birds chirp in the bush outside the windows of the ten very comfortable rooms, all with spa bath. Alongside the spacious lounge there's a café and restaurant with fine views of the tip of Taranaki. Typical lunch dishes include lamb souvlaki ($18.50) while the quality dinner menu features items including feta, spinach and pumpkin parcels ($32.50). Room-only $175

DAWSON FALLS

Dawson Falls Mountain Lodge Dawson Falls ☎06 765 5457, ☯dawsonfalls.co.nz. Drive through a tunnel of native forest to reach this alpine-style lodge, which dates back to 1896, and find a dozen simple en-suite rooms and a cosy café-restaurant (daily 10am–3pm; the $55 three-course set dinner must be booked a day in advance). **$190**

Konini Lodge Dawson Falls ☎06 756 0990, ☯doc. govt.nz. Essentially a DOC-run oversized hikers' hut sleeping 38, with three- and eight-bed bunkrooms, hot showers and a kitchen equipped with stoves and fridges. Bring your own sleeping bag, towel, food, pans and eating utensils and be sure to clean up after yourself. **$25**

Stratford

Just over halfway between New Plymouth and Hawera, **STRATFORD** celebrates its name with a kitsch mock-Elizabethan **clock tower** (built in 1996 to hide the 1920s version), from which a life-size Romeo and Juliet emerge to mark the hour (at 10am, 1pm, 3pm and 7pm), accompanied by recordings of Shakespearean quotes. Every street name is a character from the bard's plays.

If you're bound for the central North Island, Stratford marks the start of the scenic **Forgotten World Highway** (see page 300).

ARRIVAL AND INFORMATION
STRATFORD

By bus Stratford offers direct access to the slopes of Mount Taranaki, particularly East Egmont and Dawson Falls. Eastern Taranaki Experience (☎06 765 7482, ☯eastern-taranaki.co.nz) runs 4WD mountain transport to The Plateau ($40–60 for a group of 1–5).

Visitor information The i-SITE is at Prospero Place, an alley opposite the clocktower (Mon–Fri 8.30am–5pm, Sat & Sun 10am–3pm; ☎0800 765 6708, ☯stratford. govt.nz).

The Surf Highway

The best route around Taranaki is the **Surf Highway** (SH45) from New Plymouth to Hawera, mostly travelling about 3km inland, with roads leading down to tiny uninhabited bays. It runs for only about 100km, but its beachy charms can consume half a day, longer if you want to surf its consistent glassy, even breaks. **Windsurfing** and **kiteboarding** are good too, with near constant onshore winds. Surf beaches are everywhere, but facilities are concentrated in the towns of **Oakura** and the quieter **Opunake**. Between the two towns is **Cape Egmont**, with its picturesque lighthouse.

Oakura

OAKURA is essentially a commuter suburb for New Plymouth, 17km away, wedged between the highway and the surf beach. It has managed to retain a hint of counter-cultural spirit thanks to its board-rider residents and a handful of funky **craft shops** and **cafés** that cluster along SH45.

Cape Egmont Lighthouse

At Pungarehu, about 25km southwest of Oakura, Cape Road cuts 5km west to the cast-iron tower of **Cape Egmont Lighthouse**, moved here in 1877 from Mana Island, north of Wellington. It perches on a rise on the westernmost point of the cape overlooking Taranaki's windswept coast, a great spot around sunset with the mountain glowing behind.

Opunake

Opunake, some 20km south of Cape Egmont, is a large village with a golden beach and little to do but swim, surf and cast a line. The beach is patrolled in summer (Jan daily 10am–6pm; Feb & March Sat & Sun 10am–5pm), and a couple of places offer surf rental and lessons (see p.308).

INFORMATION AND ACTIVITIES

Tourist information Oakura Library, 16 Donnelly St, Oakura ☎ 06 759 6060 (Mon, Wed & Fri noon–6pm, Tues, Thurs & Sat 9am–1pm). In the absence of a visitor centre, the library has the best local information.

Surf tuition Vertigo, 605 Main St, Oakura ☎ 06 752 7363, ⓦ vertigosurf.com. Offers stand-up paddle-board

THE SURF HIGHWAY

lessons starting with theory and finishing in the water, hopefully on two feet (from $65/hr), plus gear rental (from $20/hr). The Opunake Surf Co (aka Dreamtime Surf; ⓦ dreamtimesurf.co.nz), at the corner of Havelock and Tasman streets, also offers surfboard rental.

ACCOMMODATION AND EATING

OAKURA

Ahu Ahu Beach Villas 321 Ahu Ahu Rd ☎ 06 752 7370, ⓦ ahu.co.nz. The four gorgeous and luxurious self-contained villas here are fashioned from wharf piles, French clay tiles and all manner of salvaged architectural pieces. The three family villas sleep four and the studio sleeps a couple; all overlook the ocean. Meanwhile, their new *Oraukawa Lodge* has two bedrooms, two bathrooms, and sea views ($650). **$295**

Butlers Reef 1133 South Rd (SH45) ☎ 06 752 7765, ⓦ butlersreef.co.nz. This lively pub is the centre of Oakura action, with hearty meals such as beer-battered fish and chips ($18.90) and a range of burgers ($15.90–22), regular events and loads of concerts through the summer. There's also a bottle shop. Daily 11am–10pm.

Oakura Beach Holiday Park 2 Jans Terrace ☎ 06 752 7861, ⓦ oakurabeach.com. Perfectly sited campsite with ageing but still decent accommodation. Some

camping sites are just a couple of steps from the black-sand beach and there are cabins on a rise with awesome bay views. Camping per site **$44**, cabins **$75**

OPUNAKE

Opunake Beach Holiday Park Beach Rd ☎ 0800 758 009, ⓦ opunakebeachnz.co.nz. A golden beach with good surf pretty much right on your doorstep is the main lure of this welcoming campsite, which also has a selection of simple cabins. Camping per site **$44**, cabins **$80**

Sugar Juice Café 42 Tasman St ☎ 06 761 7062. Considerable care goes into everything at this brightly decorated, licensed café serving up huge breakfasts ($12–24) such as field mushroom, spinach, bacon and egg, an old-school counter selection of quiches, sausage rolls, and carrot cake, plus large pizzas. Daily 9am–4pm.

Hawera

Surrounded by gently undulating dairy country, **HAWERA** is the meeting point of the eastern and western routes around Taranaki. A service and administration centre for the district's farmers, Hawera is also home to the world's largest **dairy complex**, just south of town, which handles a fifth of the country's milk production, mostly gathered from the rich volcanic soils of Taranaki but also brought by rail from other parts of the North Island.

The town's main feature is the concrete former **Hawera Water Tower** (55 High St; Mon–Fri 8.30am–5.15pm, Sat & Sun 10am–3pm; $2.50), which was built in 1914 and soars 54m above town, offering fabulous views over South Taranaki; ask at the i-SITE for the key.

Morrieson's Café and Bar

58 Victoria St • Daily 11am–9pm or later

A working bar is an appropriate location for the town's ad hoc memorial to one of New Zealand's most celebrated authors, **Ronald Hugh Morrieson** (see page 729). He spent his entire life in Hawera, wrote well-observed and amusing Gothic novels about small-town life, and loved jazz (and a drink or three). The house where he once lived was demolished to make way for a *KFC*, but his fireplace and staircase were relocated here, the bar's tabletops are made of timbers salvaged from the house, a few of his books lie stacked on the mantelpiece, and there's a short biography of the man himself on the bar.

Elvis Presley Museum

51 Argyle St • Visits by appointment • No fixed entry fee, but a donation is expected • ☎ 06 278 7624, ⓦ elvismuseum.co.nz

Hawera resident Kevin Wasley loves Elvis Presley and, wanting to share that love around, opens up his garage-shrine, the **Elvis Presley Museum,** to the King. Call ahead and walk the ten minutes from the i-SITE to see thousands of rare recordings, photographs and memorabilia amassed since his boyhood spent trading goods with his Memphis-based pen pal. Much is from the 1950s era Kevin so admires – ask him and you'll hear a tale or two.

Tawhiti Museum and Bush Railway

401 Ohangai Rd, 4km northeast of Hawera • **Museum** Boxing Day–Jan daily 10am–4pm; Jan–May Fri–Mon 10am–4pm; June–Aug Sun 10am–4pm • $15 • **Bush railway** First Sun of the month, plus most public holidays; every Sun during school holidays • $6 • ☎ 06 278 6837, ⌨ tawhitimuseum.co.nz

Unique and ever-expanding exhibits at the absorbing **Tawhiti Museum and Bush Railway** explore the social and technological heritage of both Māori and Pakeha using a multitude of life-size figurines modelled on local people. Other highlights include a diorama of 800 miniatures depicting the 1820s musket wars; an extraordinary account of the 1860s New Zealand Wars, seen through the eyes of a deserter from the British Army who lived out his days with the Ngati Ruanui tribe; and a small-scale **bush railway** that trundles 1km through displays recounting Taranaki's logging history, as well as a good on-site café, *Mr Badger's*.

ARRIVAL AND INFORMATION   HAWERA

By bus InterCity and NakedBus services stop outside the i-SITE. Destinations New Plymouth (1 daily; 1hr 15min); Whanganui (1 daily; 1hr 20min).

i-SITE, 55 High St, at the base of the water tower (Mon–Fri 8.30am–5pm, Sat & Sun 10am–3pm; ☎ 06 278 8599, ⌨ southtaranaki.com).

ACCOMMODATION AND EATING

Il Chefs 47 High St ☎ 06 278 4444. Hawera's top restaurant places the emphasis on locally sourced ingredients and freshly prepared dishes. Lunch ($20–30) might be sweet and spicy pulled pork belly spring-rolls, while steak lovers shouldn't pass up a dinner of ribeye on garlic and rosemary fondant potato. Tues–Fri 11am–2pm & 5–11pm, Sat 5–11pm.

Marracbo Down the alley at 172 High St ☎ 06 278 5334. The pick of Hawera's cafés has a wide range of breakfasts, cakes and pastries, and more substantial mains (around $20). Mon–Thurs 8.30am–4pm, Fri & Sat 8.30am–10pm, Sun 9am–4pm.

Tairoa Lodge 3 Pouawai St ☎ 06 278 8603, ⌨ tairoa-lodge.co.nz. B&B in a gorgeous 1875 two-storey house set by a swimming pool in mature grounds on the edge of town. There are three tastefully appointed en suites in the main house, a pair of self-catering cottages sleeping up to four, and the more modern three-bedroom Gatehouse. Doubles $150, cottages $245, Gatehouse $275

Patea

Cutting through heavily cultivated farmland, SH3 splits **PATEA**, the only major community between Hawera and Whanganui. The township has a model of the Aotea canoe at the western end of the main street, commemorating the settlement of the area by Turi and his *hapu*; a good **surfing beach** at the mouth of the Patea River (unsafe for swimming); and a safe freshwater **swimming hole**, overlooked by the Manawapou Redoubt and *pa* site.

Museum of South Taranaki

127 Egmont St • Daily 10am–4pm • Donation • ☎ 06 273 8354

For an insight into the town, visit the **Museum of South Taranaki**, known as Aotea Utangunui in Māori. It features displays on the town and its freezing works (abattoir) that closed in 1982, spawning the creation of the Patea Māori Club, whose 1984 hit single *Poi-E* was imaginatively repurposed in Taika Waititi's 2010 film *Boy*. The original *Poi-E* video was shot around the town's Aotea canoe.

Check out the **Waitore artefacts**, early fifteenth-century wooden tools and carvings found in a local swamp between 1968 and 1978; the canoe prow, bow cover and bailer are the oldest wooden pieces found in New Zealand, their patterns showing clear Polynesian stylings predating the later, specifically Māori, patterns.

Bushy Park

791 Rangitatau East Rd, 47km southeast of Patea, 16km northwest of Whanganui • Oct–March Mon–Fri 10am–3pm, Sat & Sun 10am–5pm; April–Sept Sat & Sun 11am–4pm • $10 • ☎ 03 342 9879, ⊛ bushyparksanctuary.org.nz

A well-signposted side road runs 8km northeast off SH3 to **Bushy Park**, a charming historic homestead in native bush threaded by tracks. Encircled by a 5km fence, it's now a protected **bird sanctuary** with native birds including North Island robins, moreporks, saddlebacks, flocks of kereru and North Island brown kiwi.

Whanganui National Park

The emerald-green Whanganui River tumbles from the northern slopes of Mount Tongariro to the Tasman Sea at Whanganui, passing through the **Whanganui National Park**, a vast swathe of barely inhabited and virtually trackless bush country east of Taranaki. The park contains one of the largest remaining tracts of lowland forest in the North Island, growing on a bed of soft sandstone and mudstone (*papa*) that has been eroded to form deep gorges, sharp ridges, sheer cliffs and waterfalls. Beneath the canopy of broad-leaved podocarps and mountain beech, an understorey of tree ferns and clinging plants extends down to the riverbanks, while abundant and vociferous **birdlife** includes the kereru (native pigeon), fantail, tui, robin, grey warbler, tomtit and brown kiwi.

The best way to explore the Whanganui National Park is on a multi-day **canoe trip** into the wilderness mostly stopping at riverside campsites. The most popular exit point for canoe trips is the small settlement of **Pipiriki**, where jetboat operators run trips upstream to the **Bridge to Nowhere**.

If you're not taking a river trip, you can explore the **roads** that nibble at the fringes of the park: the Forgotten World Highway (SH43) provides limited access to the northwest, but only the slow and winding **Whanganui River Road** stays near the river for any length of time.

Brief history

At 329km, the Whanganui is New Zealand's longest navigable river. It plays an intrinsic part in the lives of local **Māori**, who hold that each river bend had a *kaitiaki* (guardian) who controlled the *mauri* (life force). The *mana* of the old riverside settlements depended upon the maintenance of the food supplies and living areas: sheltered terraces on the riverbanks were cultivated and elaborate weirs constructed to trap eels and lamprey.

European missionaries arrived in the 1840s, traders followed, and by 1891 a regular boat service carried passengers and cargo to settlers at Pipiriki and Taumarunui. In the early twentieth century **tourist-carrying** paddle steamers plied the waters to reach elegant hotels en route to the central North Island.

Failed settlements

European attempts to stamp their mark on this wild landscape have been ill-fated, however. In 1917 the **Mangapurua Valley**, in the middle of the park, was opened up for settlement by returned World War I servicemen, but, plagued by economic hardship, remoteness and difficulty of access, many had abandoned their farms by the 1930s. Although a concrete bridge over the Mangapurua Valley opened in 1936, after a major flood in 1942 the bridge was cut off, the three remaining families were ordered out, and the valley officially closed. Today, the only signs of

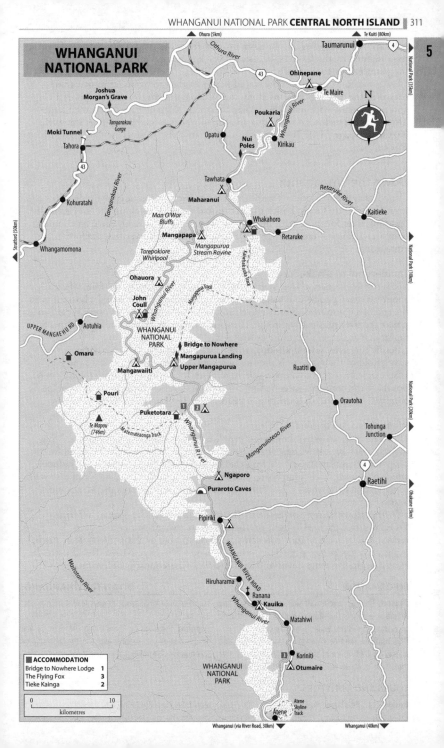

WHANGANUI NATIONAL PARK

ACCOMMODATION

Bridge to Nowhere Lodge	1
The Flying Fox	3
Tieke Kainga	2

0 ———————— 10
kilometres

habitation in the valley are the disappearing road, old fence lines, stands of exotic trees planted by the farmers, occasional brick chimneys and the bridge, now the poignant **Bridge to Nowhere**.

With the coming of the railway and better roads, the riverboat tourist trade ceased in the 1920s but farms along the Whanganui continued to support a cargo and passenger service until the 1950s; thereafter the wilderness reclaimed land. This attracted recluses and visionaries, the most celebrated being poet **James K. Baxter** (see page 314). The river was used extensively in Vincent Ward's 2005 film *River Queen*.

Down the Whanganui

Canoes, kayaks and jetboats work the river, tailoring trips to your needs. The rapids are mostly Grade I with the occasional Grade II, making this an excellent paddling river for those with little or no experience. That said, the river shouldn't be underestimated: talk to operators about variations in river flows before embarking.

Taumarunui to Whakahoro

The navigable section of river starts at Cherry Grove in **Taumarunui**, from where it's about two days' paddle to **Whakahoro**, essentially just a DOC hut and a boat ramp at the end of a 45km road (mostly gravel) running west from SH4. Between these two points the river runs partly through farmland with roads nearby, and throws up a few rapids that are larger than those downstream.

Beside the river, several kilometres southwest of Cherry Grove, a former stronghold of the *Hauhau* is the site of a couple of **nui poles**. In 1862 the Hau Hau erected a war pole, **Rongo-nui**, here, with four arms indicating the cardinal points of the compass, intended to call warriors to their cause from all over the country. At the end of hostilities, a peace pole, **Rerekore**, was erected close by.

Whakahoro to Pipiriki

Downstream from Whakahoro most people take three days to get to Pipiriki. Along the way you'll see the Mangapapa Stream Ravine, the **Man-o-war Bluff** (named for its supposed resemblance to an old iron-clad battleship) and the **Tarepokiore Whirlpool**, which once completely spun a river steamer. At Mangapurua Landing it's an easy walk to the **Bridge to Nowhere** (1hr 15min return), a trail that becomes the Mangapurua Track.

Further downstream you come to **Tieke Kainga** (aka Tieke Marae), a former DOC hut (see page 313) built on the site of an ancient *pa* that has been reoccupied by local Māori; you can stay or camp here or across the river at *Bridge to Nowhere Lodge* (see page 312), a terrific base for river activities. The last stretch runs past the **Puraroto Caves** and into Pipiriki, where most paddlers finish.

INFORMATION   **DOWN THE WHANGANUI**

Seasons The river is accessible year-round but paddling season is generally Oct–April, when all overnight river users must buy a Great Walks Ticket (see page 313).
DOC leaflets The free *Whanganui Journey* leaflet and map is the best source of practical information for river trips. Pick it up at visitor centres and DOC offices in

Taumarunui or Whanganui, or download it from ⓦ doc. govt.nz.
Supplies There are no shops along the river, so you need to take all your supplies with you: the nearest large supermarkets are in Taumarunui and Whanganui.

TOURS AND ACTIVITIES

Bridge to Nowhere Pipiriki ☎ 0800 480 308, ⓦ bridgetonowhere.co.nz. Popular and frequent jetboat

tours from Pipiriki, principally to the Bridge to Nowhere (4hr–4hr 30min; $140 return). They have an excellent

WHANGANUI RIVER ROAD MAIL TOUR

If you have neither the time nor inclination to spend a few days canoeing in the Whanganui National Park, consider taking the **Whanganui River Road Mail Tour** (daily; $65; ☎ 06 345 3475, ⓦ whanganuitours.co.nz/mail-run), a genuine mail-delivery service stopping frequently at houses along the way as well as points of interest. The trip starts early (accommodation pick-up can be arranged from Whanganui city) and doesn't return until mid- to late afternoon; there's a stop-off for morning tea, but it's worth bring some food with you, or taking the lunch option, as there's nowhere to buy refreshments en route. Canoeing from Pipiriki, trampers' transport and jetboating can also be arranged.

option allowing you to canoe the last 10km downstream to Pipiriki ($180) taking an hour or two. Also has Mangapurua mountain-bike options (see below).

Māori Blazing Paddles 985 SH4, 10km south of Taumarunui ☎ 0800 252 946, ⓦ blazingpaddles.co.nz. Good-value canoeing and kayaking tours, with prices including drop-off and pick-up (but not accommodation fees), with options ranging from one hour (from $65) to five days (from $190).

Whanganui Scenic Experience 1195 Whanganui River Rd ☎ 0800 945 335, ⓦ whanganuiscenicjet.com. A range of jetboat and canoeing tours including an eight-hour tour to the Bridge to Nowhere ($200). Also offers canoe rental.

Yeti Tours 3 Burns St, Ohakune ☎ 0800 322 388, ⓦ yetitours.co.nz. Ohakune-based guided trips on the river from two to six days ($420–895), including transport to launch points or for the tracks, a plethora of rental gear for self-guided trips (canoes/kayaks from $175 for two days, camping equipment packages from $35 for one person for two days) and lots of help and advice.

ACCOMMODATION

Bridge to Nowhere Lodge 20km upstream from Pipiriki ☎ 0800 480 308, ⓦ bridgetonowhere.co.nz; map p.311. The only comfortable accommodation beside the river is this boat-accessed lodge offering shared-bathroom doubles, twins and simple bunkrooms (bring a sleeping bag), all with great bush or river views. Either self-cater (bring all your food) or go for the home-cooked dinner, bed and buffet breakfast deal ($155/person); there's also a bar. Non-canoeists can get a package that includes a return jetboat (30min each way) transfer from Pipiriki, plus a Bridge to Nowhere tour, as well as accommodation and meals ($285). People taking packages get precedence for double rooms. Dorms $55, doubles $110

Great Walks Ticket ⓦ doc.govt.nz. Whanganui River canoeists stay at huts and campsites dotted along the riverbank. In summer (Oct–April) you must obtain a Great Walks Ticket, available online (where you can check hut and campsite availability and adjust your plans accordingly) or at DOC offices and i-SITEs for a small fee. The price depends on the number of places you book, and under-18s go free at both. Backcountry hut passes are valid in winter. Many operators offer canoe rental, transport and accommodation packages that include the Great Walks Ticket. Huts $32, camping $20, bunkrooms $10

Tieke Kainga 20km upstream from Pipiriki ⓦ doc. govt.nz; map p.311. Relaxing former DOC hut where you can stay in big sleeping huts for a small donation, or camp on terraces by the river (no alcohol allowed); if any of the Māori care-takers are about, you'll be treated to an informal cultural experience. You only have to pay to stay here between October and April – you also need to book in advance; the rest of the year it's free. Dorms $20

The Whanganui River Road

The outlying sections of the park to the south can be accessed along the **Whanganui River Road**, from either **Raetihi**, a small town on SH4 near Ohakune, or Whanganui (see page 315). The River Road hugs the river's left bank from the riverside hamlet of **Pipiriki** 79km downstream to **Upokongaro**, just outside Whanganui. It's a winding road and only fully sealed since 2014. Even in the best conditions the route takes a minimum of two hours.

Opened in 1934, the road is wedged between river, farmland and heavily forested outlying patches of the Whanganui National Park, and forms the supply route for the four hundred people or so who live along it. **Facilities** along the way are almost nonexistent: there are no shops, pubs or petrol stations, and only a handful of places to stay. If you don't fancy the drive, consider joining one of the Whanganui-based bus tours.

The road is detailed in the free *Whanganui River Road* leaflet (available from i-SITE and DOC offices and downloadable from ⓦwhanganui.com), which highlights points of interest and lists their distance from Whanganui.

Pipiriki

The southern reaches of the Whanganui National Park are accessed from Raetihi along the winding 27km Pipiriki–Raetihi Road, meeting the river at **PIPIRIKI**, 76km north of Whanganui. It is little more than a bend in the road, the finishing point for canoe journeys and the start of jetboat trips upstream. A couple of operators run snack bars that are open whenever there's enough business.

Hiruharama

HIRUHARAMA (Māori for Jerusalem), 13km south of Pipiriki and 64km north of Whanganui, was originally a Māori village and Catholic mission but is now best known as the site of the **James K. Baxter commune** that briefly flourished in the early 1970s. Baxter, one of New Zealand's most (in)famous poets, attracted hundreds of followers to the area. A devout Roman Catholic convert, but also firm believer in free love in his search for a "New Jerusalem", he became father to a flock of his own, the *nga moki* (fatherless ones), who soon dispersed after his death in 1972. The main commune house is situated high on a hill to the northeast of the church, and Baxter is buried just below. Ask for directions from the remaining Sisters of Compassion, who still live beside the 1892 **church** (from the north head up the first driveway, with a mailbox marked "The Sisters"), which features a Māori-designed and -carved altar.

Moutoa Island and Ranana

Moutoa Island, 59km north of Whanganui, was the scene of a vicious battle in 1864 when the lower-river Māori defeated the rebellious Hauhau warriors, thus protecting the *mana* of the river and saving the lives of European settlers downstream at Whanganui. A cluster of houses 1km on marks **RANANA** (London), where there's a Roman Catholic mission church that's still in use today.

Koriniti

The only real settlement of note in these parts is **KORINITI** (Corinth), 45km north of Whanganui, home to a lovely small church and a trio of traditional Māori buildings, the best being a 1920s **meeting house**, all down a side road. It's a private community, so while you can enter the church, the rest you should view from the road, unless you're invited into the compound. A *koha* of a couple of dollars is appropriate.

WHANGANUI OR WANGANUI?

Unlike the Whanganui National Park and Whanganui River, the city of **Whanganui** was long spelled without an "h". The pronunciation of both is the same, deriving from the local Māori dialect, pronouncing the "wh" prefix phonetically (as opposed to elsewhere in the country, where the "wh" is pronounced "f"). The spelling quirk results from a direct transcription of the Māori name (*whanga nui* translates as "big harbour"). Most locals opposed any streamlining of the spelling, but in 2009 authorities ruled that the "h" is optional. For consistency with the majority of current usage, the city spelling "Whanganui" is used in this guide.

Atene Viewpoint Walk and the Oyster Shell Cliffs
Atene 35km north of Whanganui • Oyster Shell Cliffs 8km south of Atene

The **Atene Viewpoint Walk** (5km return; 2hr; 100m ascent) affords great views of Puketapu, a hill that was once on a peninsula almost entirely encircled by the river. Riverboat owner Alexander Hatrick saw an opportunity to shave some time off his trips and blasted through the isthmus to leave the hill surrounded by a dried-out oxbow. The Viewpoint Walk comprises the first few kilometres of the **Atene Skyline Track** (18km loop; 6–8hr), making a wide loop following a gently ascending ridgeline that ends with a 2km walk along the road back to the start.

Further downriver are the **Oyster Shell Cliffs**, roadside bluffs with oyster-shell deposits embedded in them.

Aramoana
17km northwest of Whanganui

Soon the winding climb begins to the summit lookout of **Aramoana**, giving a last look at the river below. On a clear day you can enjoy views of the northeast horizon, dominated by Mount Ruapehu. From the junction of the River Road and SH4, it's 14km to Whanganui.

ACCOMMODATION   **THE WHANGANUI RIVER ROAD**

★ **The Flying Fox** Koriniti ☎ 06 342 8160, ⊕ theflyingfox.co.nz; map p.311. At this wonderfully remote and romantic hideaway, accessible only by boat or aerial cableway (prior booking essential; $5), an eclectic range of found objects and scavenged pieces of old buildings have been imaginatively combined to create a series of separate self-contained buildings that encourage outdoor living amid the organic gardens and bush. Wood-fired bush baths, solar-heated showers and odourless composting toilets add to the appeal. Browse through a fascinating range of books, old vinyl and CDs in the James K (self-catering, sleeping five), the Brewers Cottage (self-catering, sleeping three), the Glory Cart (modelled on a gypsy caravan; $120) Blackberry Patch trailer ($90), or camp. Camping $15, Brewers Cottage & James K $240

Whanganui

There's an old-fashioned charm to **Whanganui**, the slow pace mirroring the speed of the river that bisects it. Founded on the banks of the **Whanganui River**, New Zealand's longest navigable watercourse, Whanganui is one of New Zealand's oldest cities and was the hub of early European commerce because of its access to the interior, and coastal links with the ports of Wellington and New Plymouth. The river traffic has long gone and the port is a shadow of what it was, leaving a city that feels too big for its 43,000 people – it even has a small opera house. Still, it's a manageable place that exudes civic pride, both for its quality museums and well-tended streetscape. The low cost of living has seen a thriving **arts community** spring up here, and it's a pleasant place to idle away some time in the renowned **art gallery**, watch a **glass-blowing** demonstration or take a class, and to ride on a restored **river steamer**.

The cultural heart of Whanganui beats around Pukenamu, a grassy hill that marks the site of Whanganui's last tribal war in 1832. Now known as **Queens Park**, it contains three of the city's most significant buildings.

Brief history
When **Europeans** arrived in the 1830s, land rights quickly became a bone of contention with the local Māori population. Transactions that Māori perceived as a ritual exchange of gifts were taken by the New Zealand Company to be a successful negotiation for the purchase of Whanganui and a large amount of surrounding land. Settlement went ahead regardless of the misunderstanding, and

5

it was not until the **Gilfillan Massacre** of 1847 that trouble erupted – when a Māori was accidentally injured, his tribesmen massacred four members of the Gilfillan family. Further violent incidents culminated in a full-scale but inconclusive **battle** at St John's Hill. The next year the problems were apparently resolved by a payment of £1000 to the Māori. In the 1990s, the central Moutoa Gardens became the focus of renewed tensions, while the **spelling** of the city's name also creates divisions – see page 314.

Sarjeant Gallery

Queens Park • Daily 10.30am–4.30pm • Free, but donations welcome • ☎ 06 349 0506, Ⓦ sarjeant.org.nz

The gleaming hilltop **Sarjeant Gallery** is housed in one of Whanganui's most impressive buildings, a 1919 Oamaru stone structure boasting a magnificent dome that filters natural light into the exhibition space. Rotating quarterly exhibitions partly draw on the highly regarded permanent collection that is strong on both colonial and contemporary New Zealand art and photography. One artist to look out for is the underrated Edith Collier, a local painter whose career was overshadowed by that of her contemporary, Frances Hodgkins. All this is augmented by various strong touring exhibitions. At the time of writing, a major redevelopment plan had just been green-lit, with construction work due to start in 2019.

Much of the contemporary collection is the product of regular artist residencies at one of Whanganui's oldest buildings, the 1853 weatherboard **Tylee Cottage**, immediately to the north at the corner of Cameron and Bell streets.

The Quay Gallery, an offshoot of the Sarjeant, is upstairs at the i-SITE, and has quality exhibitions.

Whanganui Regional Museum

Watt St • ☎ 06 349 1110, Ⓦ wrm.org.nz

Southwest of the Sarjeant Gallery, the Veteran Steps lead towards the centre of the city past the **Whanganui Regional Museum**. Founded in 1892, it contains an outstanding collection of Māori artefacts and three impressive canoes, all displayed in the central court. Unfortunately, it was closed at the time of research because the building does not currently meet earthquake safety standards; check the website for the latest.

Moutoa Gardens

Moutoa Gardens, where the river kinks around the central city on Somme Parade, is little more than a small patch of grass imbued with history. Traditionally Māori lived at Moutoa during the fishing season, until it was co-opted by Pakeha settlers, who renamed the area Market Square. It was here that Māori signed the document agreeing to the "sale" of Whanganui, an issue revisited on Waitangi Day 1995, when simmering old grievances and one or two more recent ones reached boiling point. Māori occupied Moutoa Gardens, claiming it as Māori land, for 83 days. This ended peacefully in the High Court, but created much bitterness on both sides. By 2001 a more conciliatory atmosphere prevailed, and the government, city council and local *iwi* agreed to share management of the gardens.

Waimarie paddle steamer

1a Taupo Quay • Daily 11am • $45 • ☎ 06 347 1863, Ⓦ riverboats.co.nz

Whanganui's history is inextricably tied with the Whanganui River, and though commercial river traffic has virtually stopped, you can still ride the **Waimarie paddle steamer**. New Zealand's last surviving paddle steamer, it makes a two-hour run up a tidal stretch of the river. The huffing of the coal-fired steam engine and the slosh of the paddles make for a soothing background to an afternoon's sunning on deck, or you can retire to the wood-panelled saloon for scones and tea (or glass of wine).

Yarrow and Company of London built the *Waimarie* in 1899 to a shallow-draught design with a tough hull, making it suitable for river work. It was transported to New

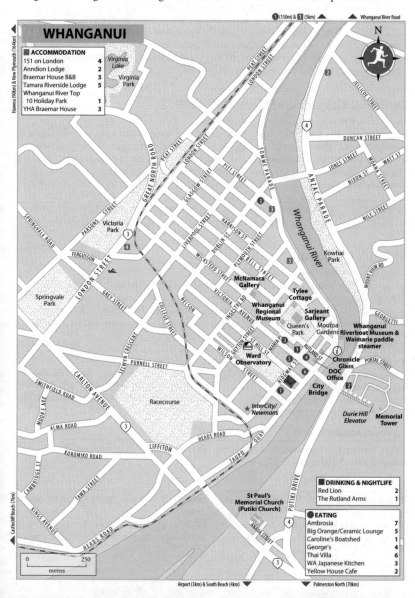

WHANGANUI

ACCOMMODATION
151 on London	4
Anndion Lodge	2
Braemar House B&B	3
Tamara Riverside Lodge	5
Whanganui River Top 10 Holiday Park	1
YHA Braemar House	3

DRINKING & NIGHTLIFE
Red Lion	2
The Rutland Arms	1

EATING
Ambrosia	7
Big Orange/Ceramic Lounge	5
Caroline's Boatshed	1
George's	4
Thai Villa	6
WA Japanese Kitchen	3
Yellow House Cafe	2

Zealand in kit form, then put to work on the Whanganui River, where it saw service during the pre-Great War boom in tourism, when thousands from all over the world came to travel up the Whanganui River and stay at the hotel at Pipiriki. In 1949 the *Waimarie* made her last voyage and three years later sank at her moorings. It wasn't until 1993 that the boat was salvaged, and it returned to the river in 1999.

Whanganui Riverboat Museum

1a Taupo Quay • Oct–April 10am–3pm • Free, but donations welcome • ☎ 06 347 1863, ⓦ riverboats.co.nz

The restoration of the *Waimarie* took place at the **Whanganui Riverboat Museum**, adjacent to the cruise departure docks and flanked by old warehouses and stores. Housed in an 1881 two-storey timber-framed building, the museum concentrates on the river and its history in relation to the town and includes the partly restored MV *Ongarue*, which worked the river from 1900 to 1957.

Durie Hill Elevator and Memorial Tower

Elevator Daily 8am–6pm • $2 each way • **Tower** Daily 8am–dusk • Free

City Bridge takes you from downtown to the east bank of the river and the **Durie Hill Elevator**. A Māori carved gateway here marks the entrance to a 213m tunnel, at the end of which a historic 1919 elevator carries passengers 66m up through the hill to the summit. At the top of the hill two excellent vantage points grant extensive views of the city, beaches and inland. The viewpoint atop the elevator's machinery room is the easy option, but the best views are 176 steps up at the top of the 33.5m-high **Memorial Tower**. Head back to town using the 191 steps to the river – it only takes about ten minutes, and provides additional satisfying views.

St Paul's Memorial Church

Anaua St • Often locked; contact the i-SITE for access • $2 donation

It's about 2km south along Putiki Drive to the small, whitewashed **St Paul's Memorial Church**, which contains magnificent Māori carvings adorned with paua, a painted rib ceiling (as in Māori meeting houses), two beautiful etched-glass windows and some intricate *tukutuku* panels. It's also known as "Putiki Church".

ARRIVAL AND DEPARTURE — WHANGANUI

By plane Flights from Auckland arrive at the airport (ⓦ whanganuiairport.co.nz), 7km southwest of the city; a taxi into town costs around $25.
Destinations Auckland (1–3 daily; 1hr).
By bus InterCity buses drop off at the Whanganui Travel Centre, 156 Ridgway St (☎ 06 345 4433).
Destinations Auckland (1 daily; 8hr 25min); Hamilton (1 daily; 5hr 55min); New Plymouth (1 daily; 2hr 30min); Palmerston North (4 daily; 1hr 30min); Taumarunui (1 daily; 2hr 40min); Wellington (2 daily; 4hr).

GETTING AROUND

By bus Tranzit buses (☎ 06 345 4433, ⓦ horizons.govt.nz) run a limited Mon–Sat bus service around the city.
By taxi Whanganui Taxis (☎ 0800 343 5555).

INFORMATION

Tourist information i-SITE, 31 Taupo Quay (Nov–April daily 9am–5pm; May–Oct Mon–Fri 9am–5pm, Sat & Sun 9am–4pm; ☎ 06 349 0508, ⓦ visitwhanganui.nz). Has free internet access and wi-fi, timetables for the local buses and sells Whanganui National Park hut and camping passes.
DOC 35 Taupo Quay (Mon–Fri 8am–5pm; ☎ 06 348 8475). Sells Whanganui National Park hut and camping passes.

5

ACCOMMODATION

151 on London 151 London St ☎ 0800 151 566, ⓦ 151onlondon.co.nz; map p.317. Contemporary motel, with a range of rooms (all with a/c, kitchenettes, and big TVs, though the decor is a little grey and drab), plus a small gym and an on-site café. **$130**

Anndion Lodge 143 Anzac Parade ☎ 0800 343 056, ⓦ anndionlodge.co.nz; map p.317. Professional combination of a quality hostel and a very comfortable motel spread between three houses. There are no dorms, just comfortable shared-bath rooms, en-suite rooms and one- and two-bedroom suites, all done out in slightly tacky black-and-crimson colour schemes. There is a communal kitchen, plus a lovely BBQ area, swimming pool, spa and sauna, courtesy city transport and a restaurant. **$79**

Braemar House B&B 2 Plymouth St ☎ 06 348 2301, ⓦ braemarhouse.co.nz; map p.317. Bathrooms are shared in this excellent-value guesthouse situated in a lovely 1895 homestead surrounded by lawns. Some rooms front onto a sun-drenched veranda and there's a YHA hostel out back (see below). Add $15–20 a head for breakfast. **$100**

Tamara Riverside Lodge 24 Somme Parade ☎ 06 347 6300, ⓦ tamaralodge.com; map p.317. A large, well-kept historic building with pretty gardens and a sociable vibe that makes it popular with younger backpackers. Offers free bikes, musical instruments, neat comfortable four-bed dorms (including a female-only one), some bargain singles (from $44) doubles and twins (some en-suite, $86), plus a balcony with a river view, and a trampoline in the large garden. Dorms **$29**, doubles **$62**

Whanganui River Top 10 Holiday Park 460 Somme Parade ☎ 0800 272 664, ⓦ wrivertop10.co.nz; map p.317. Well-tended site 6km northeast of the city centre, beside the river in the shade of giant trees, with a selection of camping sites and cabins, as well as a pool, and kayak and jet ski rental. Camping **$45**, cabins **$80**

YHA Braemar House 2 Plymouth St ☎ 06 348 2301, ⓦ braemarhouse.co.nz; map p.317. Welcoming hostel attached to *Braemar House B&B* with separate male and female dorms, private rooms out back, a kitchen and cosy lounge and a peaceful atmosphere. Dorms **$27**, doubles **$70**

EATING

The River Traders Market (Sat 9am–1pm; ⓦ therivertraders.co.nz) pops up every Saturday on Taupo Quay, behind the i-SITE, with a host of local artisans, producers and growers.

Ambrosia 63 Ridgway St ☎ 06 348 5524; map p.317. Great little deli stocking all manner of gourmet and artisan goodies from New Zealand and around the world, including organic meats, cheeses and Whanganui olive oil, plus top-notch bagels, pastries and excellent coffee ($4–6). Mon 8.30am–4pm, Tues–Fri 8.30am–5pm, Sat 9am–2pm.

Big Orange/Ceramic Lounge 51 Victoria Ave ☎ 06 348 4449; map p.317. Two names, same place: a buzzing café (*Big Orange*) transforms into a hip restaurant/cocktail bar *Ceramic Lounge*, where you might expect beetroot risotto or pork, anchovy and thyme ravioli (mains $26–40). Mon & Tues 7am–5pm, Wed–Fri 7am–9pm, Sat 8.30am–9.30pm, Sun 8.30am–5pm.

Caroline's Boatshed 181 Somme Parade ☎ 06 281 3377, ⓦ carolinesboatshed.co.nz; map p.317. Large gastro-pub with a lively atmosphere and plenty of crowd-pleasing dishes ($18-39) on the menu, including burgers, battered fish and seafood, chunky steaks, and "grazing platters" piled with tasty bites. Mon & Tues 10am–10pm, Wed 10am–10.30pm, Thurs 10am–11.30pm, Fri 10am–1am, Sat 9am–1am, Sun 9am–10pm.

George's 40 Victoria Ave ☎ 06 345 7937; map p.317. A local institution, this old-fashioned fish and chip shop has an attached dining room and also sells good-value wet fish. You can get a big feed for less than $10. Mon–Sat 8.30am–7.30pm, Fri to 8.30pm.

Thai Villa 17 Victoria Ave ☎ 06 348 9089; map p.317. Quality Thai place with all your favourite curries and stir-fries ($18–24) along with hot plate options such as Weeping Tiger, a dish of marinated beef and vegetables. Licensed and BYO. Tues–Sat 4.30–9.30pm.

★ **WA Japanese Kitchen** 92 Victoria Ave ☎ 06 345 1143, ⓦ facebook.com/JapaneseKitchenWA; map p.317. Feast on dishes ($10–25) like chicken katsu curry, teriyaki salmon, and gyoza dumplings at this authentic Japanese joint. For something a little different, try the *okonomiyaki* – deeply savoury seafood pancakes. The only downside is the early closing times at night. Tues–Fri 11.30am–2pm & 5–8.30pm, Sat & Sun 5–8.30pm.

Yellow House Cafe 17 Pitt St ☎ 06 345 0083, ⓦ yellowhousecafe.co.nz; map p.317. This bright yellow building is hard to miss, which is fortunate, as it's a real hit, with a menu featuring good coffee, lunches like Wagyu beef cheek pie ($18.50) and buttermilk fried chicken ($16.50), and copious high teas ($10-30 per person). Mon–Fri 8am–4pm, Sat & Sun 8.30am–4pm.

DRINKING

As well as the options listed here, *Ceramic Lounge* (see above) is an excellent spot for an evening drink.
Red Lion 45 Anzac Parade ☎ 06 348 4080, ⓦ redlioninn. co.nz; map p.317. Atmospheric pulse-of-the-town pub overlooking the river with meal deals and a lively atmosphere as the weekend approaches. Visit for happy hour on Friday or on Monday or Tuesday for $10 burger nights. Daily 11am–11pm.

The Rutland Arms Cnr Victoria Ave & Ridgway St ☎ 06 347 7677, ⓦ rutlandarms.co.nz; map p.317. Slap bang in the centre of the city this friendly pub is a relaxed place for a drink (beer from $8.50, glass of wine from $7.50) at any time of day. There's a simple menu of pub meals; combo deals featuring a meal and cinema ticket (see below) also available. Daily 9am–11pm.

ENTERTAINMENT

Embassy 3 Cinema 34 Victoria Ave ☎ 06 345 7958, ⓦ embassy3.co.nz. Mainstream films at Whanganui's only cinema, an Art Deco-style affair from the early 1950s.
Ward Observatory Hill St. Every clear Friday evening

you can look through the 24cm refractor at this wonderful 1901 observatory ($2 donation). To arrange a viewing outside of the hours listed here, contact the i-SITE. Oct–March Fri 8.30pm; April–Sept Fri 8pm.

Palmerston North and around

One of New Zealand's largest landlocked cities, **PALMERSTON NORTH** (as opposed to Palmerston near Dunedin, and known as "Palmy") is the thriving capital of the province of Manawatu, with around 84,000 residents, including a lively student population attending **Massey University**. After the arrival of the rail line in 1886, Palmerston North flourished, thanks to its pivotal position at the junction of road and rail routes, reflected today by some fine civic buildings, notably an excellent **museum** and **gallery** and a stunning **library**. Nonetheless, an unimpressed John Cleese famously claimed, "If you want to kill yourself but lack the courage, I think a visit to Palmerston North will do the trick." The town responded by naming the local rubbish dump after him.

The city's main cultural event, the Festival of Cultures (ⓦ festivalofcultures.co.nz), takes place around The Square in late March with a Friday-night lantern festival and a Saturday craft, food and music fair. Artists who recently played at WOMAD in New Plymouth often turn up on the bill.

The Square

Palmerston North centres on **The Square**, a smart, grassy expanse with an elegant clock tower. The adjacent **Te Marae o Hine**, or the Courtyard of the Daughter of Peace, is graced by a couple of 5m-high Māori figures carved by renowned artist **John Bevan Ford**. The Māori name is the one suggested for the settlement's central square by the chief of the Ngati Raukawa in 1878, in the hope that love and peace would become enduring features in the relationship between the Manawatu Māori and incoming Pakeha.

The most striking of the surrounding buildings is the **City Library**, a postmodern reworking of the original 1927 department store by Kiwi star architect, Ian Athfield.

Te Manawa

326 Main St • Mon–Wed & Fri–Sun 10am–5pm, Thurs 10am–7.30pm • Free • ☎ 06 355 5000, ⓦ temanawa.co.nz

The city's main cultural focus is **Te Manawa**, with well-laid-out galleries covering Māori heritage and life in the Manawatu once Europeans arrived. Some of the best material is in the Te Awa section, covering all aspects of the Manawatu River from geology and ecology to bug life (there's a weta cave) and a tank of native fish (effectively grown-up whitebait). The stunning carpet is an aerial view of the entire region. Throughout the galleries there's masses of hands-on stuff for kids.

The adjacent **Art Gallery** displays Pakeha and Māori art from its permanent collection, alongside touring exhibitions.

New Zealand Rugby Museum
Upstairs at Te Manawa • Daily 10am–5pm • $12.50 • ☎ 06 358 6947, ⓦ rugbymuseum.co.nz

Knock down a tackle bag, try to move a scrum machine or kick goals better than Piri Weepu at the small **New Zealand Rugby Museum**, where the interactive area is surrounded by an excellent decade-by-decade social history of rugby in New Zealand including games played by soldiers in Egypt during World War II. There's everything from old leather shoulder-pads and footage of the 1905 All Black "originals" tour, to cartoons lampooning rugby selectors and the coin tossed at the start of each Rugby World Cup final.

Manawatu Gorge
15km northeast of Palmerston North

Heading northeast from Palmerston North the skyline above the semirural town of **Ashhurst** is broken by the southern hemisphere's largest **wind farms**, draped across the Ruahine and Tararua ranges. These hills are separated by the Manawatu Gorge (Te Apiti in Māori), a narrow 10km-long defile through which a rail line, SH3 and the Manawatu River squeeze. The gorge can be explored on foot along the **Manawatu Gorge Track** (3–4hr one way; contact the i-SITE for gorge transport options), or you can see it on a jetboat tour (see page 279).

ARRIVAL AND DEPARTURE   PALMERSTON NORTH AND AROUND

By plane The airport (ⓦ pnairport.co.nz) is 3km northeast of the city. SuperShuttle (☎ 0800 748 885, ⓦ supershuttleco.nz) runs into town (around $20-25).
Destinations Auckland (7 daily; 1hr); Christchurch (4 daily; 1hr 15min); Wellington (3 daily; 30min).
By train The train station is on Matthews Ave, about 1500m northwest of the city centre.
Destinations Auckland (3 weekly; 8hr 50min); Hamilton (3 weekly; 6hr 30min); Wellington (3 weekly; 2hr 5min).

By bus InterCity buses stop at the Palmerston North Travel Centre, at the corner of Pitt and Main sts, while NakedBus stops outside the i-SITE.
Destinations Auckland (4 daily; 9hr 15min–9hr 45min); Hastings (2 daily; 3hr); Napier (2 daily; 3hr 30min); Paraparaumu (7 daily; 1hr 20min); Rotorua (4 daily; 5hr 5min–5hr 25min); Taupo (4 daily; 4hr–4hr 25min); Whanganui (4 daily; 1hr 30min); Wellington (9 daily; 2hr 30min).

GETTING AROUND

By bus A series of loop services runs from Main St, near the i-SITE, where you can pick up timetables.

By taxi Palmerston North Taxis (☎ 06 355 5333).

INFORMATION

Visitor information i-SITE, The Square (Mon–Thurs 9am–5.30pm, Fri 9am–7pm, Sat 9am–3pm, Sun 9am–7pm; 06 358 8414, ⓦ manawatunz.co.nz). Good for DOC leaflets and hut tickets plus showers. Parking is tricky here though.
Services Downtown Palmerston North has free wi-fi.

ACCOMMODATION

Palmerston North has more motels than you could ever imagine the town might need, so turning up and simply driving along Fitzherbert Avenue until you see one that takes your fancy is always an option.
Arena Lodge 74 Pascal St ☎ 0800 881 255 or 06 357 5577, ⓦ arenalodge.co.nz. *Arena Lodge* is a smart,

modern motel in a quiet location 1km west of the Square with a range of en-suite rooms, all with kitchenettes, some with barbecue areas and spa baths. $154
Palmerston North Holiday Park 133 Dittmer Drive ☎ 06 358 0349, ⓦ palmerstonnorthholidaypark. co.nz. Quiet (sometimes almost eerily so), shady

campsite with basic facilities, 2km south of the city centre and close to the Manawatu River. Camping per site $35, cabins $50

Primrose Manor 123 Grey St ⊕ 06 355 4213, ⓦ primrosemanor.co.nz. Five modern, spick-and-span en suites are on offer at the friendly, well-run *Primrose Manor*, which also offers guests the use of a communal lounge (with fireplace) and kitchen. $120

Railway Hotel Backpackers 275 Main St ⊕ 06 354 5037, ⓦ railwayhotel.co.nz. Just about the best of the city's limited selection of hostels, with cramped 3-bed single-sex dorms and slightly more spacious private rooms; the decor is decidedly dated, but it's not a bad choice. Dorms $35, doubles $79

★ **Rose City Motel** 120–122 Fitzherbert Ave ⊕ 06 356 5388, ⓦ rosecitymotel.co.nz. The pick of the motels along a street full of them, with contemporary and surprisingly spacious rooms with kitchens (some also have spa baths). Facilities include a squash court. $125

EATING

Thanks to its term-time student population, Palmerston North supports a vibrant restaurant scene, with almost everything of note close to the Square.

Aberdeen on Broadway 161 Broadway Av ⊕ 06 952 5570, ⓦ aberdeenonbroadway.co.nz. The perfectly cooked Aberdeen Angus cut ($36–44) served with choice of sauces, from blue cheese to green peppercorn, are the house speciality as this superior steakhouse. Good value set meals too ($48–60). Mon–Thurs 4.30–9.30pm, Fri 11.30am–10pm, Sat 5.30–10pm, Sun 5.30–9.30pm.

Barista 59 George St ⊕ 06 357 2614, ⓦ barista.co.nz. Much-lauded café-restaurant, known for its excellent coffee, plenty of brunch and lunch options, and dinner mains such as crispy confit duck leg with a warm black pudding, pear, walnut and rocket salad ($34). Theatre menus are available if you're heading to see a play at Centrepoint (see page 322). Daily 8am–11pm.

★ **Café Cuba** 236 Cuba St ⊕ 06 356 5750. Funky day/night café that's a local institution for breakfast, all-day brunch and lunch ($16.50–26) and dinners such as halloumi-and-aubergine stack ($24.90). Service is on point, and there's usually live music on Friday or Saturday nights. Licensed & BYO. Mon 7am–5pm, Tues–Sun 7am–9pm.

Café Express 41 The Square ⊕ 06 353 8440, ⓦ cafeexpress.net.nz. The perfect place to start the day in Palmy, overlooking the Square as it comes to life. Try the house-made baked beans on toasted ciabatta ($11.50), washed down with strong coffee, or visit at lunchtime for sake-and-ginger-glazed salmon ($24.60). Mon–Fri 7am–4pm, Sat-Sun 8am–4pm.

Yeda 78 Broadway Ave ⊕ 06 358 3978, ⓦ yeda. co.nz. Pan-Asian restaurant with a good line in the likes of deep-fried soft-shell crab ($14.90) and Hong Kong-style barbecued pork buns ($5.60). It doubles up as a cocktail bar (drinks from $8.50) in the evening. Daily 11am–9pm.

DRINKING

Brewers Apprentice 334 Church St ⊕ 06 358 8888, ⓦ brewersapprentice.co.nz. Lively, modern Monteith's pub with plenty of open-air drinking space, and a good range of quality pub meals (Wed is $15 steak night; $10 burgers on Fri). Live music on Fri nights. Mon–Thurs 4–10pm, Fri–Sun 11am–11pm.

The Fish Regent Arcade, 57 Broadway Ave ⊕ 06 357 9845. Cool little cocktail and wine bar (drinks from $7.50) with a short tapas menu to work your way through, as well as DJs on Thursday and Friday nights. Wed 4–11pm, Thurs 4pm–1am, Fri & Sat 4pm–3am.

ENTERTAINMENT

Centrepoint Theatre 280 Church St ⊕ 06 354 5740, ⓦ centrepoint.co.nz. New Zealand's only professional provincial theatre is a 135-seater with shows from April to Christmas.

Event Cinemas 70 Broadway Ave ⊕ 06 355 5335, ⓦ eventcinemas.co.nz. Predominantly screens mainstream films, though there are some art-house flicks.

Foxton and around

Horowhenua's most interesting town is **FOXTON**, 38km southwest of Palmerston North, where the old-style shop facades line the broad main street bypassed by SH1. Archeological evidence suggests there was a seminomadic **moa-hunter** culture in this area between 1400 and 1650, predating larger tribal settlements. **Europeans** (many of them Dutch) arrived in the early 1800s and settled at the mouth of the

Manawatu River, subsequently founding Foxton on a tributary. It quickly became the **flax-milling** capital of New Zealand, the industry only finally dying in 1985. A **historic walk** tells the tale through 28 plaques around town.

The long, sandy **Foxton Beach** is 5km away on the coast, where there's good surfing, safe swimming areas and abundant birdlife around the Manawatu river estuary.

Te Awahou Nieuwe Stroom

22 Harbour St • Mon–Fri 10am–5.30pm, Sat & Sun 10am–4pm • Free • ☎ 06 363 5571, ⓦ teawahou.com

Opened in 2017, **Te Awahou Nieuwe Stroom** is an impressive cultural complex with museums celebrating the area's Dutch and Māori heritage. The town's library and i-SITE are also found here, as are a café and some shops, and there are regular performances and exhibitions.

De Molen

Main St, next to Te Awahou Nieuwe Stroom • Daily 9am–4pm • Tours $5 • ☎ 06 363 5601

De Molen is a modern, full-scale **replica** of a classic seventeenth-century **Dutch windmill**. Self-guided tours visit the inner workings, and on three to four days a month you'll see it producing stoneground wholemeal flour. On the ground floor, you can buy Dutch groceries and the town's local soft drink, **Foxton Fizz**, in old-fashioned flavours such as creaming soda.

Flax Stripper Museum

Main St • Aug–May daily 1–3pm • $5 • ☎ 06 363 6846

A broad history of Foxton's flax industry is recounted in the **Flax Stripper Museum**, which shows examples of the handmade flax (*harakeke*) baskets and cloaks perfected by local Māori. But the real emphasis is on European operations, cultivating flax near swamps and on riverbanks in Manawatu and Horowhenua then exporting flax fibre around the country and abroad for binder twine, fibrous plaster and carpet.

Papaitonga Scenic Reserve

Off SH1, 23km south of Foxton

The main southbound road routes converge at the workaday town of **LEVIN**, the administrative centre of the Horowhenua region. Just south of town at the **Papaitonga Scenic Reserve**, a boardwalk leads to the Papaitonga Lookout (20min return) and great **views** of Lake Papaitonga. The surrounding wetlands provide a refuge for many **rare birds**, including the spotless crake, Australasian bittern and New Zealand dabchick.

ARRIVAL AND DEPARTURE   FOXTON

By bus InterCity buses pull in at the stop at 65 Main Street.   Wellington (3 daily; 1hr 45min).
Destinations Palmerston North (1 daily; 30min);

Eastern North Island

HAWKE'S BAY

Eastern North Island

A mountainous backbone from the tip of the East Cape runs parallel with the coast all the way down to Wellington. This unique geography means that the Eastern North Island has some of the sunniest skies in the country – great for tourism, but the bane of local sheep farmers who watch their land become parched, dusty and brown in summer. Increasingly, these pastures are being given over to viticulture, and the diverse landscapes of Hawke's Bay have become the country's second largest wine-producing areas. Historical links are strong, too – New Zealand's first wine makers came from a seminary just outside Napier, while further north Captain Cook first set foot in New Zealand at Gisborne, now a multicultural city with decent surfing beaches. Inland, spectacular Lake Waikaremoana lures in hikers for its draw-dropping lookouts and serene waterside trails. To the north, the East Cape is one of the least-visited parts of the country, where time virtually stands still and life is measured by the rhythm of the land.

Jutting into the South Pacific, the **East Cape** (sometimes known as Eastland) is an unspoiled backwater, strong in Māori culture and interspersed with tiny settlements tucked into secluded bays reminiscent of how Aotearoa once was. Here, the spiritual **Mount Hikurangi** looms over 1,700 metres high and is a sacred place to the local Māori tribes, where impressive carved statues stand proud on the hillside.

Equally remote, the scenic SH38 forges northwest from the small town of **Wairoa**, gateway to the wooded mountains of **Te Urewera** and beautiful **Lake Waikaremoana**. Encircled by the country's most underrated Great Walk, the lake is the focal point for many delightful tramping routes seldom busy even in the peak of summer.

Heading south on the SH2, the North Island's less-travelled secondary artery between Auckland and Wellington, you'll reach the contrasting **Hawke's Bay** region. This has long been dubbed "the fruit bowl of New Zealand", and its orchard boughs still sag under the weight of apples, pears and peaches. Its tourist hub is the quiet waterfront city of **Napier**, famed for its Art Deco buildings, though an even more scenic option is to stay nearer the bulk of the **wineries** in the countryside surrounding **Hastings**. With vineyards in such different locations – along the coast, cloaking hills and filling river valleys – it's no surprise that there's great range in the wine varieties in the region, though the intensely Chardonnays and subtler Syrah reds win the bulk of the awards. Here too you can traverse **Te Mata Peak** for its tranquil views overlooking the rolling farmlands, explore sweeping **beaches** around **Waimarama** or walk the wild picturesque coastline of **Cape Kidnappers**, where the world's largest gannet colony hangs out.

GETTING AROUND   **EASTERN NORTH ISLAND**

By bus InterCity (ⓦintercity.co.nz) run a daily service between Gisborne and Napier, and two heading south to Wellington via Palmerston North. ManaBus.com (ⓦmanabus.com) runs a twice-daily service from Napier and Hastings to Wellington also via Palmerston North.

East Cape

Skipped by the majority of travellers, the remote **East Cape** peninsula offers glimpses of a bygone era along the winding Pacific Coast Highway (SH35), which runs 330 kilometres

NAPIER

Highlights

❶ East Cape Drive the wild, seldom-visited East Cape coastline where Māori culture remains prevalent, and marvel at the spiritual sculptures atop Mount Hikurangi along the way. See page 326

❷ Wairoa Museum Visit the North Island's best little museum, which reveals the town's riverside identity and its passionate Māori heritage. See page 342

❸ Lake Waikaremoana Take in the stunning scenery of this majestic lake on short hikes or tackle the North Island's most breathtaking multi-day tramp. See page 343

❹ Napier Wander through the world's finest collection of small-scale Art Deco architecture to Napier's pine-shaded seafront promenade. See page 347

❺ Cape Kidnappers Come face-to-beak with residents of the world's largest mainland gannet colony on a tour or under your own steam. See page 353

❻ Vineyards Sip to your heart's content in Hawke's Bay wine country, or cycle to almost a dozen fine wineries around Havelock North. See page 356

HIGHLIGHTS ARE MARKED ON THE MAP ON PAGE 328

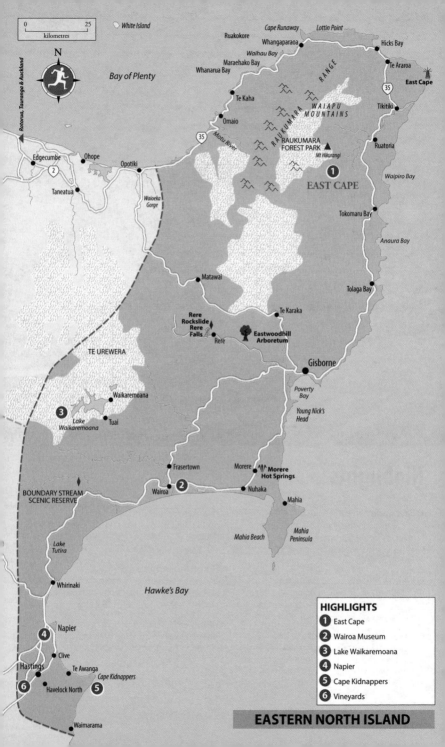

EASTERN NORTH ISLAND

HIGHLIGHTS

1. East Cape
2. Wairoa Museum
3. Lake Waikaremoana
4. Napier
5. Cape Kidnappers
6. Vineyards

EAST CAPE MANUKA OIL

Australian tea tree oil is famous for its antimicrobial qualities. The oil of the almost identical New Zealand **manuka** is generally just as good, but in 1992 manuka oil from the East Cape was found to have super-strong antibacterial and antifungal properties. The small factory at 4464 Te Araroa Rd, 2km west of Te Araroa (Oct–April Mon–Fri 8.30am–4pm, Sat & Sun 8.30am–2pm; May–Oct Mon–Fri 8.30am–4pm; ☎ 06 864 4824, ⓦ manukaproducts.co.nz), extracts the essential oils by steam distillation from the twigs of manuka trees grown in the surrounding hills. You can't tour the factory, but a wide range of manuka-oil soaps, medicinal creams and aromatherapy potions (all exported around the world) is sold in the shop/café where you can also sample manuka tea and buy local manuka honey.

between Opotiki and Gisborne. You'll notice a change of pace, epitomized by the occasional sight of a lone horseback rider clopping along the road. **Māori** make up a significant percentage of the population – over eighty percent of land tenure here is in Māori hands – and locals are welcoming, particularly once you take the time to chat with them.

The route along the west side of the Cape facing the calm Bay of Plenty has the prettiest scenery, hugging the rugged coastline much of the way. There are few places of specific interest though, and most come just to unwind on its **beaches** and **fish** in the tranquil waters.

By comparison, the route along the east side of the Cape between Gisborne and Hicks Bay is bland, cutting inland through hilly pastoral countryside and only touching the coast at a handful of bays. It's on this side however that you'll find the region's most interesting historical sites, **hiking** opportunities and Māori communities, and you're likely to find someone happy to take you **horse trekking**, either along the beach or into the bush.

Inland, the inhospitable **Waiapu Mountains** run through the area, encompassing the northeastern **Raukumara Range** and the typical native flora of the **Raukumara Forest Park**. The isolated and rugged peaks of **Mount Hikurangi** and **Mount Arowhana** provide a spectacular backdrop to the coastal scenery, but are only accessible through Māori land and permission must be sought.

GETTING AROUND   EAST CAPE

By car Although the road is sealed all the way around the East Cape, it twists in and out of the small bays so it can take a full eight hours to travel from Opotiki to Gisborne. Petrol pumps around the East Cape are found in most of the small towns along the east coast, but only at Waihau Bay on the west coast.

By bus Public transport is limited to infrequent buses and courier services, which also carry passengers. Tour company buses (see below) are also an option.

BUS COMPANIES

Bayhopper ☎ 0800 422 9287, ⓦ baybus.co.nz. Runs from Potaka (just west of Hicks Bay) to Opotiki and back on Tues and Thurs only. No booking needed; pay as you get on. If those don't quite suit, be polite and check where the driver lives – sometimes they might drop people off there at the end of their run.

Cooks Couriers ☎ 06 864 4711 or ☎ 02 137 1364. Runs from Hicks Bay to Gisborne and back (Mon–Fri only), and Te Araroa to Opotiki and back (Tues & Thurs only) stopping to pick up parcels and will drop off/pick up pre-booked travellers along the way.

INFORMATION AND TOURS

Tourist information There are no i-SITE offices around the East Cape, so you'll have to pick up information in the ones in Opotiki or Gisborne. Otherwise, there are informal visitor centres at Tolaga Bay Inn (daily 9am–7pm), Te Puia Springs (Mon–Fri 8am–4.30pm) and Te Araroa (Mon–Fri 10am–2pm), all along the east coast. The annual *Pacific Coast Highway* (ⓦ pacificcoasthighwayguide.co.nz) is a useful resource, though operators pay to be included.

Services There are no banks in the East Cape and the only ATM is inside the Four Square supermarket at Ruatoria (Mon–Sat 7am–6.30pm, Sun 8am–5pm). The only public place with free wi-fi is the *Uawa Café* in Tolaga Bay. Mobile phone coverage is limited to around Opotiki and most places between Te Araroa and Gisborne.

Stray ☎ 09 526 2140, ⓦ straytravel.co.nz. From Oct–April, Stray's hop-on, hop-off East Coaster pass (minimum

3 days; $295) covers the East Cape coastline departing Rotorua on Tuesday and Saturday, stopping overnight at Maraehako Bay and spending the next day visiting the East Cape Lighthouse and Tolaga Bay before journeying down to Gisborne. If you ask the driver you can get dropped off at any point along the route and be picked up on the next round.

ACCOMMODATION AND EATING

Accommodation Hostels are scattered along the route, with the occasional motel and B&B, but upmarket accommodation is almost non-existent.

Camping Campsites are an East Cape staple, and there are several good commercial sites. Free beachside camping is prohibited, but there are seven designated "freedom camping" sites along the east coast (Waipiro Bay, Tokomaru Bay, Kaiaua Beach, Tolaga Bay, Loisels Beach in Waihau, Pouawa Beach and Turihaua Beach, 15km north of Gisborne); there are also another three along the west coast (Hukuwai Beach, 3km north of Opotiki; Hoani Witi Reserve, Omaio; and the carpark at Maraetai Bay in north Te Kaha). While the west coast sites are free and open year-round, the east coast sites operate from mid-Sept to mid-April only and require a permit

($16 for two consecutive nights; $31 for ten; $66 for 28; valid for up to six people) available from the i-SITEs in Opotiki or Gisborne, direct from the Gisborne District Council at 15 Fitzherbert St or online at ⓦ gdc.govt.nz. If you're already in the Cape, permits can also be purchased Uawa Foodmarket, 51 Cook St, Tolaga Bay or at the council office in Te Puia Springs, cnr SH38 and Waipiro Rd. Fires are not allowed and campers must have an onboard or chemical toilet.

Eating Apart from a couple of pie shops, counter cafés and pub grub, there isn't anywhere on the East Cape that you'd describe as a real restaurant. Come prepared for self-catering or accept a diet of toasted sandwiches and fish and chips. Self-caterers will find limited grocery shopping, and most towns shut down by 5pm.

Opotiki to Whangaparaoa

The west coast road from **Opotiki** (see page 267) to **Whangaparaoa** is just over 110km long and generally sticks close to the coast, but frequently twists up over steep bluffs before dropping back down to desolate beaches heavy with driftwood. This section of the East Cape is where you'll spend most of your time at the beach with various aquatic activities on offer from kayaking to half-day fishing and dive trips – along with horseriding and biking to search out your own secluded cove.

Tirohanga and Maraenui

Leaving Opotiki, you first pass the town of **TIROHANGA**, which offers the last of the real swimming beaches for some distance. The Motu Trails **cycleway** (ⓦ motutrails. co.nz) passes along the coast here, making it a great base for exploring both the sand dune-backed coastline and inland forests. Heading north, the coastal road begins twisting over the rugged coast with several outstanding lookouts before reaching the tiny Māori settlement of **MARAENUI**. There are few places to stop though until you reach the **Motu River**, some 40km north of Opotiki, where you can pick up jetboat tours (ⓦ moturiverjet.com) from beside the bridge.

Te Kaha

Crossing the Motu River from Maraenui, a further 25km on is **TE KAHA**, a sleepy residential area with a few places to stay. It spreads for 7km along the highway above a beautiful crescent-shaped bay, with spectacular headlands and a deserted, driftwood-strewn beach that's safe for swimming. Te Kaha is the closest land to White Island (see page 265), 48km offshore.

Maraehako Bay

White Island remains in view as you continue for 16km from Te Kaha towards **Maraehako Bay**, where you'll find a pair of rock-fringed coves along the craggy headland. Still hugging the coast, the SH35 winds 13km to **Raukokore**, which is not really a place at all but the memorable site of a picture-perfect, white clapboard Anglican church built in 1895, which stands on a promontory framed by the ocean. Little blue **penguins** sometimes nest underneath the church, but you're unlikely to see them – though you may be able to smell their presence if you stand near the altar.

Waihau Bay

From Ruakokore it's 5km to **Waihau Bay**, another sweeping crescent of sand and grass that's ideal for swimming, surfing and kayaking, especially towards the northern end at Oruaiti, the prettiest beach in the entire region. The film director Taika Waititi thought it ideal too, and in 2010 he shot his film *Boy* in the area. The abundance of shellfish and flatfish here might encourage you to sling a line from the wharf beside the combined store, post office and petrol station.

Whangaparaoa

6

WHANGAPARAOA, 11km to the north of Waihau Bay, is the last settlement facing the Bay of Plenty. From here, the SH35 cuts inland, meandering through mountainous countryside for 45 minutes over to Hicks Bay on the east coast. There's not a great deal here other than a restored Pa site and a more recent larger-than-life tuatara wood carving.

ACCOMMODATION
OPOTIKI TO WHANGAPARAOA

TIROHANGA

Tirohanga Beach Motor Camp SH35 ☎ 07 315 7942, ⓦ tirohangabeachmotorcamp.co.nz; map p.333. Backing the long, sweeping beach and perfect for families, this well-organised holiday park has over 100 powered sites, a dozen cabins, a large playground plus bike hire to make use of the Motu Cycle Trail passing along the coast. Cabins $120, dorms $25, camping $20

MARAENUI

Oariki Coastal Cottage Pa Rd ☎ 07 325 2678, ⓦ bookabach.co.nz/6515, ✉ oariki@xtra.co.nz; map p.333. Relax in front of the log fire at the self-catering cottage, or enjoy B&B (en suite) at the main house. Either way, you'll be surrounded by native bush and overlook the sea. Ask about opportunities for fishing. Call ahead for directions and to arrange a three-course dinner ($35). Cottage $175, B&B $165

TE KAHA

Te Kaha Beach Resort 3 Hotel Rd, off SH35 ☎ 07 325 2830, ⓦ tekahabeachresort.com; map p.333. There's a very un-East Cape feel (apart from the dairy) to this modern, streamlined three-storey complex, which has apartment-style accommodation featuring state-of-the-art kitchens, as well as a pool, and a restaurant and bar with mesmerizing 180-degree ocean and coastal views. Studios $155

Tui Lodge 200 Copenhagen Rd ☎ 07 325 2922, ✉ tuilodge@yahoo.co.nz; map p.333. Set within three acres of gardens, this spacious and supremely tranquil B&B in a purpose-built lodge just inland from the *Te Kaha Beach Resort* has en-suite rooms and offers dinner by arrangement ($40). $175

MARAEHAKO BAY & AROUND

★ **Maraehako Bay Retreat** 8536 SH35, just north of the main settlement ☎ 07 325 2648, ⓦ maraehako.

co.nz; map p.333. Paradisiacal, rustic waterside hostel in a rocky cove with a safe, private swimming beach, free use of sit-on-top kayaks and the chance for fishing, diving, whale and dolphin watching and horse-trekking expeditions. The small double rooms and dorms feature large windows and wonderful sea views. Doubles $70, dorms $30

Maraehako Camping Ground SH35, accessed along a dirt track 100m north of the stream ☎ 07 325 2901; map p.333. Simple campsite covering the eastern end of stony Maraehako Bay, with toilets, gas-heated showers, kayaks for hire, a small store and plenty of space and trees to pitch under. Run by a welcoming Māori family related to the owners of *Maraehako Bay Retreat* on the other side of the stream. Camping $15

★ **The Homestead** 8523 SH35 at the northern end of Whanarua Bay ☎ 07 325 2071, ⓦ homesteadonthebay. co.nz; map p.333. An attractive B&B on a sunny clifftop setting with great views. There are only two bedrooms, which share a bathroom, and three-course dinners ($50 with wine) are available on request. $190

WAIHAU BAY

Oceanside Apartments Oruaiti Beach, 5km north of Waihau Bay ☎ 07 325 3699, ⓦ waihaubay.co.nz; map p.333. Two spacious self-contained units (one sleeping seven) just across the road from a safe, sandy beach. Try to catch your own supper by surfcasting for snapper and kahawai off the beach. Ask about the diving and fishing trips and kayak rental. Two-night minimum from Christmas–Easter. $135

Waihau Bay Lodge Orete Point Rd, Waihau Bay ☎ 07 325 3805, ⓦ thewaihaubaylodge.co.nz; map p.333. Modern weatherboard lodge with self-contained rooms next door to the historical Post Office and across the road from a sheltered bay. There's a decent restaurant serving a good fisherman's basket with oysters and scallops and hearty mixed grills. Units $195, doubles $70, camping $15

Hicks Bay to Gisborne

Rounding the top of East Cape, the SH35 starts its descent into the Gisborne region at **Hicks Bay**, which has a predominantly Māori feel. For the next 180km to Gisborne, the road cuts inland through native bush and pastoral country, offering only the occasional glimpse of the coast, emerging every so often into a handful of yawning bays with close-up views of the slate-grey rock shelves that characterize this coast.

Here, you can enjoy tranquil walks in and around **Tolaga Bay,** the region's largest settlement, hike the spiritual **Mount Hikurangi Trek** or head off road to visit the remote **East Cape Lighthouse**.

Hicks Bay

Guided 3hr walk visiting Māori sites, including a waterfall visit with Matakoa Cultural Tours · $50 · ☎ 02 188 5602 or ✉ amiph407@gmail.com

Tiny **Hicks Bay** (Wharekahika), 44km east of Waihau Bay, shelters between headlands and coastal bluffs and offers several short walks along from *Hicks Bay Motel* to a scenic lookout, pretty beaches and safe swimming at **Onepoto Bay** to the south. Another reason to stop is to visit some of the intriguing *pa* sites in the area, in varying states of repair, which were modified for musket fighting during the 1860 Hauhau uprising.

Te Araroa

Barely five kilometres to the south of Hicks Bay, the small village of **TE ARAROA** ("long pathway") was once the domain of the famous Māori warrior Tuwhakairiora and the legendary Paikea, who is said to have arrived here on the back of a whale. Ironically, the first Europeans in the area set up a **whaling station** not far from the present township. These days the settlement contains little more than a petrol pump, two stores and a takeaway selling fresh **fish and chips**. In the grounds of the local school on Moana Parade stands a **giant pohutukawa** tree – so giant that it's easy to believe the claims that it's New Zealand's largest.

East Cape Lighthouse

21km east of Te Araroa along an unsealed road · Follow the sign east along the foreshore

The mainland's easternmost point is marked by the **East Cape Lighthouse**. The dramatic coastal run from Te Araroa is along a cliff-clinging road that ends in a tiny car park. From there, climb 757 steps to the lighthouse perched atop a 140m-high hill – an atmospheric spot with views inland to the Raukumara Range and seaward towards East Island (a bird sanctuary), just offshore.

Tikitiki

From Te Araroa the SH35 cuts inland through 24km of sheep-farming country before reaching **TIKITIKI**, where you should take a peek inside the **Anglican church**, on a rise as you enter the town. It looks very plain from the outside, but within hides a treasure-trove of elaborate Māori design, *tukutuku* and carvings; unusually, the stained glass is also in Māori designs, and the rafters are painted in the colours of a Māori meetinghouse. The memorial to the war dead has a very long list for such a tiny community.

Ruatoria

Inland **RUATORIA**, signposted just off the main highway 19km south of Tikitiki, is the largest town in the East Cape (though that's not saying much), with a pub, bottle shop, groceries, and a serviceable daytime café as well as takeaways from the roadside *Kai Kart*.

Tokomaru Bay

Tokomaru Bay (or just "Toko"), 40km south of Ruatoria, is a gorgeous spot to idle for a day, exploring the steep green hills, rocky headlands and the broad expanse of **beach**, which is dotted with driftwood, pounded by surf and provides a good spot to swim.

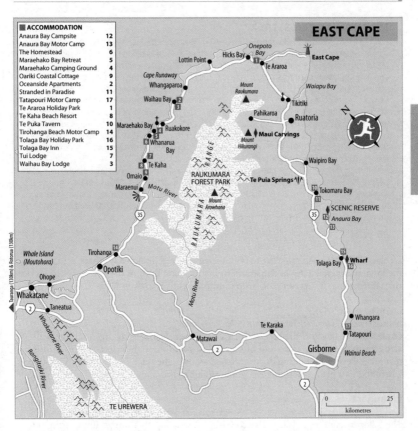

ACCOMMODATION

Anaura Bay Campsite	12
Anaura Bay Motor Camp	13
The Homestead	6
Maraehako Bay Retreat	5
Maraehako Camping Ground	4
Oariki Coastal Cottage	9
Oceanside Apartments	2
Stranded in Paradise	11
Tatapouri Motor Camp	17
Te Araroa Holiday Park	1
Te Kaha Beach Resort	8
Te Puka Tavern	10
Tirohanga Beach Motor Camp	14
Tolaga Bay Holiday Park	16
Tolaga Bay Inn	15
Tui Lodge	7
Waihau Bay Lodge	3

EAST CAPE

At the far northern end of the bay, a long wooden wharf and the ruined buildings of the abattoir and freezing works testify to the former prosperity of this once-busy port, which thrived until improved road transport forced the factory's closure in 1953.

Anaura Bay

Some 23km south from Tokomaru, a 7km-long sealed side road runs over the hill to rugged **Anaura Bay**, a prized **surf** spot with a broad sweep of sand and jagged headlands. At the north end of the bay (4km on a gravel road), the **Anaura Scenic Reserve** harbours a large area of mixed broadleaf bush noted for its large puriri trees and abundance of native birds. Starting near the end of the road, and signposted to the west by the reserve, the **Anaura Bay Walkway** (3.5km loop; 2hr) follows the course of the Waipare Stream into thick green bush, up a gently climbing valley and out into scrubland before turning back towards the bay and a lookout point with magnificent views.

Tolaga Bay

Tolaga Bay, 36km south of Tokomaru Bay, is the only place along the East Cape's east coast that feels like a viable seaside holiday town. Its eight-hundred-strong population is one of the better-serviced communities, and there's a clutch of cafés inside the historic *Tolaga Bay Inn*, which has an **information centre** and can put you in contact with locals for impromptu horseriding and other tours.

6

MOUNT HIKURANGI TREK

The 1754m-high **Mount Hikurangi**, 25km west of Ruatoria, is the North Island's highest non-volcanic peak and the first place on the New Zealand mainland to see the sunrise. It is sacred to the Māori as the place where Maui (see page 709) beached his *waka* after fishing up the North Island, and nine impressive **carvings** were installed at 1000m to celebrate the new millennium.

The remoteness of Hikurangi discourages most visitors from exploring the reserve, but there's a relatively easy **trek** to see the carvings of Maui Whakairo. It starts from the car park at Pahikiroa Station, and traverses farmland along the lower slopes of the mountain (15km return; 6hrs; 746m ascent. If the day-long trek is too daunting, you can reach the Maui carvings on a 4WD guided tour (4hrs; $300 for two) booked through the Ngati Porou (see below).). For those wanting to continue walking up to the summit, it's a more challenging 3–5hr hike with a steep scramble up scree for the final 200m.

Although the summit track can be achieved in one very long day from the bottom, it's really best done over two days with a night in the rustic Mt Hikurangi Hut ($15) 1 km beyond the carvings. The Ngati Porou are guardians of the land, so you'll need to contact Te Runanganui o Ngati Porou, 1 Barry's Ave, Ruatoria (Mon–Fri 8.30am–5pm, ☎ 02 186 4137, ✉ hikurangihutt@tronp.org.nz) for access permission and to pay hut fees.

Tolaga Bay's claim to fame is the 660m-long concrete **Tolaga Bay Wharf**, said to be the longest concrete jetty in the southern hemisphere. Built in the late 1920s to service coastal shipping, it juts out past steep sandstone cliffs into deep water.

Cooks Cove Walkway

1km south of town on Wharf Rd, near Tolaga Bay Wharf • 5.8km; 2hr 30min return

Cooks Cove Walkway is the best of Tolaga Bay's short walks, involving an initial walk across farmland then a steep and often muddy climb through bush rich with birdlife to a great viewpoint looking down to Cook's Cove. The track heads down to the cove, where there's a plaque marking the good captain's visit here in 1769.

Whangara

Guided introduction to the area, including a visit to *a marae*, with Tipuna Tours • $70 • ☎ 027 240 4493, ✉ annemcguire@gmail.com;

The 52km stretch from Tolaga Bay to Gisborne cuts mostly through uninspiring but prime farming land. It passes the turn-off to **Whangara**, where the film *Whale Rider* was shot, but, as there's no direct access, there's little to see from the lookout apart from a sweep of sand and an island, which is said to be the fossilized remains of the whale that the legendary Paikea rode from Hawaiki.

Tatapouri

At **Tatapouri**, a marine reserve with excellent reef snorkelling is accessible from the beachfront. For surfing and boogie boarding, choose between the sweeping sands of **Makorori Beach** – where freedom camping in the carpark is permitted year-round – or the famed breaks at **Wainui Beach**, just seven kilometres from the city centre.

ACCOMMODATION   **HICKS BAY TO GISBORNE**

TE ARAROA

Te Araroa Holiday Park 4814 Te Araroa Rd, SH35, 6km west of town ☎ 06 864 4873, ⊚ teararoaholidaypark. nz; map p.333. Landscaped campsite with six modern, self-contained units set 300 metres back from the beach with a handy shop and a caravan selling daily takeaways plus $10 Friday-night dinners. Units $130, camping $15

TOKOMARU BAY

★ **Stranded in Paradise** 21 Potae St ☎ 06 864 5870, ⊚ stranded-in-paradise.net; map p.333. A small, friendly spot with loft-style rooms, dorms for a maximum of three guests, composting toilets, a couple of superb tent sites and some amazing cabins (one of which is a single; $48), all perched on a hillside with great sea views. Borrow a fishing line, rent surfboards or a kayak ($20; free if you stay two nights or more) or ask them to arrange a horse trek with the local cop. Cabins$75, doubles $75, dorms $32, camping $18

Te Puka Tavern 153 Beach Road ☎06 864 5465, ⓦtepukatavern.co.nz; map p.333. Revitalised traditional Kiwi pub with accommodation and decent grub (daily 11am–11pm) such as a pan-fried tarakihi or steak and eggs ($25.50). They have four modern townhouse-style units with sea views. It is the only place in town for a drink, so it can get busy at weekends. $160

ANAURA BAY

Anaura Bay Campsite 886 Anaura Rd; map p.333.Very basic DOC site wonderfully set beside the beach immediately beyond the start of the Anaura Bay Walkway. There's water but no toilets (you'll need a chemical toilet or holding tank), though there is a dump station on-site from Dec–mid Jan. Closed May–Sep. $8

Anaura Bay Motor Camp ☎06 862 6380; map p.333. At the south end of the bay, superbly sited beside the beach. Facilities are in the former schoolhouse and there's a store selling essentials. Powered sites $20, camping $18

TOLAGA BAY

Tolaga Bay Holiday Park 167 Wharf Rd ☎06 862 6716, ⓦtolagabayholidaypark.co.nz; map p.333. Large beachfront campsite near the old wharf with barbecue area, laundry, kayak rental and a small store open Dec–Jan only. The views here are great and they have a dozen cabins, half of which front the beach. Cabins $60, powered sites $18, camping $16

Tolaga Bay Inn 12 Cook St ☎06 862 6856, ⓦtolagabayinn. co.nz; map p.333 Historic hotel with eleven guest rooms and cosy four-bed dorms, all with shared bathrooms. Doubles as the Bay's gathering place thanks to its bar and excellent café (daily 9am–7pm), serving muffins, coffee, and the likes of chicken ciabatta open sandwich ($18) or seafood chowder ($18). Also operates as an information centre for the local community with free internet. Doubles $80, dorms $25

TATAPOURI

Tatapouri Motor Camp 516 Whangara Rd (SH37) ☎06 868 3269, ⓦtatapouri.co.nz; map p.333. Sitting at the base of a beautiful headland 15min north of Gisborne, this spacious campsite has direct access to the beach and marine reserve. Family cabins $120, powered sites $22, camping $20

Gisborne

New Zealand's easternmost city, **GISBORNE**, known locally as Tairawhiti, is a historic yet youthful seaside town with a laidback vibe, popular with young families and surfers. The compact centre has broad, straight streets lined with squat weatherboard houses and shops, interspersed with expanses of parkland.

Brief history

Here, in October 1769, **James Cook** first set foot on the soil of Aotearoa, an event commemorated by a shoreside statue. He immediately ran into conflict with local Māori, killing several of them before sailing away empty-handed. He named the landing site **Poverty Bay**, since "it did not afford a single item we wanted, except a little firewood".

Early nineteenth-century Poverty Bay remained staunchly Māori and few Pakeha moved here, discouraged by both the Hauhau rebellion and Te Kooti's uprising. It wasn't until the 1870s that **Europeans** arrived in numbers to farm the rich alluvial river flats. After a decent port was constructed in the 1920s, sheep farming and market gardening took off, followed more recently by the grape harvest and the rise of plantation forestry. Today Gisborne's Māori and Pakeha population is almost exactly 50:50, and the city's endless sweep of beach makes it appealing to visitors in search of a little sun and surf.

Cook and Young statues

Young's and Cook's statues are both in the park on the western side of the river-mouth

Most of Gisborne's sights are connected in some way to the historical accident of James Cook's landing – and the dynamic between Māori and Pakeha cultures it engendered. The first of Cook's crew to spy the mountains of Aotearoa was 12-year-old surgeon's boy **Nick Young**. Cook rewarded him by naming the white-cliffed promontory, 10km south of Gisborne across Poverty Bay, on his chart as Young Nick's Head. Young's keen eyes are commemorated by a statue of a youth pointing (hopefully but none too certainly) at the cliffs. Nearby is a **statue of Cook** atop a stone hemisphere.

Cook's landing site and Kaiti Hill

Cook's landing site is on the eastern side of the river, on Kaiti Beach Rd • Kaiti Hill is accessed from either Queens Drive or Titirangi Drive

A grey obelisk on the eastern side of the river-mouth marks **Cook's landing site**. Behind, Titirangi Drive climbs the side of **Kaiti Hill** to Cook Plaza, a sculpture intended to represent Cook but dressed by its Italian artist in Italian uniform. Kaiti Hill's highest point has tremendous views across Poverty Bay to the cliffs of Young Nick's Head and a little further downhill, sweeping views over the city and marina.

Te Poho-o-Rawiri Meeting House

Queens Drive • Visits arranged by calling the caretaker at ☎ 06 868 5364 • Donation

On the eastern side of the Kaiti Hill lies **Te Poho-o-Rawiri Meeting House**, one of the largest in the country. The interior is superb, full of fine ancestor carvings interspersed with wonderfully varied geometric *tukutuku* (woven panels). At the foot of the two support poles, ancient and intricately carved warrior statues provide a fine counterpoint to the bolder work on the walls.

Tairawhiti Museum

10 Stout St • Mon–Sat 10am–4pm, Sun 1.30–4pm • $5 • ☎ 06 867 3832, ⓦ tairawhitimuseum.org.nz

Across the river at the **Tairawhiti Museum**, the permanent Watersheds exhibit charts the parallel and intertwining lives of Māori and Europeans on the East Coast. There's everything from a whalebone walking stick carved with Māori designs and coverage of Cook's arrival to the vibrant painting of early Ngati Porou leader Hinematioro by renowned painter Robyn Kahukiwa.

A maritime wing incorporates the original wheelhouse and captain's quarters of the 12,000-tonne *Star of Canada*, which ran aground on the reef off Gisborne's Kaiti Beach in 1912, along with exhibits on shipping, and a shrine to local surfing. Several disused buildings from around the region are clustered outside the museum, notably the six-room 1872 **Wyllie Cottage**, the oldest extant house in town, and the **Sled House**, built on runners at the time of the Hauhau uprising so that it could be hauled away by a team of bullocks at the first sign of unrest.

Toihoukura

80 Cobden St, near the corner of Gladstone Rd • Mon–Fri 8.30am–4.30pm • ☎ 06 869 0847, ⓦ facebook.com/www.eit.ac.nz • Free

A striking modern whale-tail sculpture heralds **Toihoukura**, a school of Māori visual arts and design where existing carvings are restored. Interpretations using modern materials and techniques are encouraged, and many vibrant and stunning pieces find their way into the public gallery. Most exhibits are for sale and would make meaningful souvenirs.

Harvest Cidery

91 Customhouse St • Mon–Fri 9am–4pm • ☎ 06 868 8300, ⓦ harvestcider.co.nz

The **Harvest Cidery** is Bulmer Harvest's smallest plant, where you can peer at operations through the glass wall. The guys here are friendly and they've been making cider, using apples from local orchards, for the last thirty years. The samples they dish out are splendid; try the zingy Thomas & Rose ciders (including refreshing watermelon and cucumber) or local ambrosia made from Manuka honey and laced with 24-carat gold leaf.

GISBORNE

EATING
Crawford Road Kitchen	6
Gisborne Farmers' Market	1
Muirs Bookshop Café	3
Off the Hook	7
Peppers Beachfront Bar & Café	5
Tatapouri Sports Fishing Club	4
Verve Café	2

SHOPPING
| Stone Studio | 1 |

ACCOMMODATION
Ahi Kaa	3
Flying Nun	2
The Green House	4
Knapdale Eco Lodge	1
Waikanae Beach Top 10 Holiday Park	5
YHA Gisborne	6

DRINKING
The Rivers	2
Smash Palace	1
Soho Bar	3

ARRIVAL AND DEPARTURE

GISBORNE

By bus NakedBus and InterCity buses converge on the i-SITE.

Destinations Auckland (1 daily; 9hr 25min); Hastings (1 daily; 5hr); Napier (1 daily; 4hr); Opotiki, via SH2 (1 daily; 2hr); Rotorua (1 daily; 5hr); Wairoa (1 daily; 1hr 30min); Wellington (1 daily; 9hr 55min); Whakatane (1 daily; 3hr).

By plane Air New Zealand operates direct flights connecting Gisborne with Auckland and Wellington.

Local operator Sunair (☎06 927 7021, ⍵sunair.co.nz) has flights to Rotorua, Hamilton and Tauranga. Gisborne airport is 2km west of the town centre, which can be reached by taxi for $20; try Gisborne Taxis (☎06 867 2222).

Destinations Auckland (4–5 daily; 1hr); Hamilton (Mon–Fri 2 daily; 1hr); Rotorua (Mon–Fri 2 daily; 45min); Tauranga (Mon–Fri 2 daily; 45min); Wellington (1–4 daily; 1hr 10min).

GETTING AROUND

By bike Most of the city is easily covered on foot, though Cycle Gisborne (☎06 927 7021, ⍵cyclegisborne.com) rent bikes and mountain bikes from $50/day, and also put together packages for guided or unguided spins round the wineries (from $130; see page 339). Bikes can be collected at the i-SITE.

INFORMATION AND TOURS

i-SITE 209 Grey St (daily: Mon–Fri 8.30am–5pm, Sat & Sun 10am–5pm; ☎06 868 6139, ⍵tairawhitigisborne. com). Offers free internet access, rents bikes on behalf of Cycle Gisborne (see above), can advise on freedom camping and provide information on DOC walks and hut passes.

Internet Internet terminals and free wi-fi at the library, 34 Bright St (Mon–Fri 9.30am–5.30pm, Sat 9.30am–1pm).

Free wi-fi in the CBD.

Gisborne Tours ☎021 204 1080, ⍵gisbornetours. nz. Long-time Gisborne resident, Nisbet Smith, offers a flexible itinerary five-hour scenic tour usually taking in three vineyards for tastings, one of which provides a platter of lunch, as well as visiting some historical and cultural sights along the way (daily 11.15am; $120; book in advance).

6

ACCOMMODATION

Despite the phenomenal number of motels – chiefly along the main strip, palm-shaded Gladstone Road, and the waterfront Salisbury Road – accommodation can be hard to come by during the month or so after Christmas.

★ **Ahi Kaa** 61 Salisbury Rd ☎ 06 867 7107, ⓦ ahikaa. co.nz; map p.337. This small family-run motel with studios and self-contained units stands out for its warmth of personality, as well as its great location across the road from the beach. The Māori owners may also be able to help organize a local village visit. Studios $125, units $150

Flying Nun 147 Roebuck Rd ☎ 06 868 0461, ⓔ yager@ xtra.co.nz; map p.337. This slightly scruffy, hippyish former convent, a 15min walk from town, is where Dame Kiri Te Kanawa first trained her voice. Some of the spacious dorms front onto broad verandas, and although doubles can be a little cramped, singles are good value. Spacious grounds include a BBQ area and games room. Cash only. Dorms $25, doubles $60

The Green House 9 Hinaki St ☎ 02 130 1375, ⓦ the-green-house.co.nz; map p.337. Quaint and cosy B&B in the suburbs, a 5min drive from the city centre, with just the one room and its own private bathroom. A homemade breakfast is served in the kitchen or, weather permitting, outside in the cottage garden. There's free use of bikes to explore. $120

Knapdale Eco Lodge 114 Snowsill Rd, Waihirere, 13km northwest of Gisborne ☎ 06 862 5444, ⓦ knapdale. co.nz; map p.337. Luxurious lodge in a tranquil semi-permaculture farm with chickens, deer and horses. The two rooms are both airy and cosy, and a dawn chorus from the nearby forest alerts you to the sumptuous breakfast. Gourmands should book one of the exquisite dinners ($95/person). Deluxe room $420, "Romance" room $495

Waikanae Beach Top 10 Holiday Park Grey St ☎ 06 867 5634, ⓦ gisborneholidaypark.co.nz; map p.337. Idyllically sited motor-park right by Gisborne's main beach and a 5min walk from town. Some of the comfortable cabins are en suite ($75), and there are also self-contained ($115) and motel units ($139). Camping $18, standard cabins $65

YHA Gisborne 32 Harris St ☎ 06 867 3269, ⓦ yha.co.nz; map p.337. Spacious, central hostel in a weatherboard homestead with a sunny deck, barbecue, a cheery paint job and staff switched on to the local surf hotspots. Guests can rent bikes, surfboards or wetsuits for $25/day. There are twins, doubles and one en suite. Ask nicely and the buses may drop you off outside. Dorms $26, rooms $58

EATING

Crawford Road Kitchen Gisborne Wine Centre, shed 3 Inner Harbour ☎ 06 867 4085, ⓦ crawfordroadkitchen. co.nz; map p.337. Showcases the Gisborne wine scene with a tasting flute ($15 for three samples) and offers advice on which cellar doors are open (they'll make appointments too). Or just buy a bottle of wine to enjoy overlooking the water with tasting plates to share (around $14) or a full-blown sumptuous meal such as mussels in ginger and coconut ($20). Tues–Sat 11am–9pm, Sun 11am–5pm.

Gisborne Farmers' Market Army Hall car park, cnr Fitzherbert and Stout Sts ⓦ gisbornefarmersmarket. co.nz; map p.337. A bustling market that's great for fruit and vegetables, as well as all manner of meats, cheeses, organic produce and baked goods. Sat 9.30am–12.30pm.

Muirs Bookshop Café 62 Gladstone Rd; map p.337. Airy café tucked above Gisborne's best bookshop, adjacent to the secondhand section. From a sun-drenched balcony that overlooks the main street, you can tuck into panini, salads, scrumptious cake; most menu items are under $12. Mon–Fri 8.30am–3.30pm, Sat 9am–3pm.

★ **Off the Hook** The Esplanade, at Crawford Rd ☎ 06 868 1644; map p.337. The best fish and chip takeaway in town serves cooked-to-order fresh fish, including snapper,

moki, trevally and terakihi ($15 with chips), all supplied fresh from its own boats. You can also buy from the fish truck at the farmers' market on Saturday. Mon–Wed 9am–6pm, Thurs & Fri 9am–7pm, Sat 11.30am–7pm .

Peppers Beachfront Bar & Café 40 Centennial Marine Drive ☎ 06 867 7696 ⓦ peppers.net.nz; map p.337. The meaty menu here is tasty although somewhat pricey at $39 for a main, but the main reason to come here is for the outstanding beachfront vistas. Make sure you book ahead to get one of the tables fronting the huge glass windows. Tues 11am–3pm, Wed–Fri 11am–late, Sat 9am–late, Sun 9am–3pm.

Tatapouri Sports Fishing Club 54 The Esplanade ☎ 06 868 4756; map p.337. Sociable club on the wharf with veranda seating for seafood, steaks or gourmet burgers (all under $30). Visitors just sign in: ask at the bar. Daily noon–2pm & 6pm–late.

★ **Verve Café** 121 Gladstone Rd ☎ 06 868 9095; map p.337. With rotating art exhibitions by up-and-coming local artists, this groovy but low-key daytime café and restaurant serves gorgeous, moderately priced food, from the famous chicken sandwiches ($18) to falafel, steak sandwiches and cakes (mains to $25). Mon–Fri 7.30am–5.30pm, Sat & Sun 8am–3pm.

DRINKING AND NIGHTLIFE

The Rivers Cnr Gladstone Rd and Reads Quay ☎ 06 863 3733, ⓦ therivers.co.nz; map p.337. Convivial Irish-type bar with Emerson's porter and a range of hearty meals

including steaks, pies, chicken and fish ($17–33) that's popular with families. Daily 11am–late.

★ **Smash Palace** 24 Banks St ☎ 06 867 7769,

ⓦthesmashpalace.co.nz; map p.337. Wonderfully oddball bar in a corrugated-iron barn, where overalls from the surrounding industrial area rub shoulders with suits. Food basically comprises bar snacks and lovingly made burgers including veggie variations and gluten-free buns ($11–17). There's live entertainment, too, from rock to heavy metal, mostly at weekends and in summer. Tues–Fri & Sun 3pm–late, Sat noon–late.

Soho Bar 2 Crawford Rd, Wharfside ☎06 868 3888, ⓦsohobar.co.nz; map p.337. Pretty standard (dark wood and mood lighting) bar that comes alive on Friday and Saturday nights when there are live bands and occasional DJs. The eclectic menu includes tapas. Tues–Fri 11am–late, Sat 9am–late.

ENTERTAINMENT

★ **Dome Cinema** The Poverty Bay Club, 38 Childers Rd ⓦdomecinema.co.nz. Fabulous, independent screen with bean-bag seating, a bar and an eclectic mix of must-see films, all shown in the old billiard room.

SHOPPING

Stone Studio 237 Stanley Road ☎06 867 3900, ⓦstonestudio.co.nz; map p.337. Family-run shop and studio where you can watch the two carvers at work. They only use New Zealand greenstone, and take commissions. Mon–Fri 8am–5pm, Sat 9am–2pm.

Around Gisborne

Winery visits, gentle walks and a smattering of specific attractions make a day or so spent in Gisborne's surrounds an agreeable prospect. Occupying a free-draining alluvial valley in the lee of the Raukumara Range and blessed with long hours of strong sun and cooling sea breezes, the wineries (ⓦgisbornewine.co.nz) have traditionally operated as a viticultural workhorse, churning out vast quantities of gluggable Chardonnay. Many give a personal touch if you call in advance, and a few open for regular tastings in summer. If you don't have a car, your best bet is to hire a **bike** or opt for a wineries tour (see below).

Bushmere Estate

166 Main Rd South, 6km northwest of Gisborne • Tastings Sept–May Wed–Sun 11am–3pm, April–Aug by appointment only; call ahead to check • ☎06 868 9317 • ⓦbushmere.com

With a reduced demand for Chardonnay, many smaller producers in the Poverty Bay region are now planting better cultivars (along with Viognier and Gewürtztraminer) and producing boutique wines. One such is **Bushmere Estate**, with a good café in a pretty vineyard setting; it's very popular with locals for Sunday lunch.

Millton

119 Papatu Rd, 11km southwest of Gisborne • Tastings daily 10am–4pm • ☎06 862 8680, ⓦmillton.co.nz

Millton is one of New Zealand's few organic wineries to apply biodynamic principles. The timing of planting, harvesting and bottling is dictated by the moon's phases to produce some delicious wines (especially Chardonnay, Chenin Blanc and Viognier) that, it is claimed, can be enjoyed even by those who experience allergic reactions to other wines. Buy a cheese or charcuterie platter to enjoy with your wine.

Tatapouri Reef

Tatapouri, 14km northeast of Gisborne • Reef walk $45; snorkel tour $70; advanced bookings only • ☎06 868 51530, ⓦdivetatapouri.com

Don waders on this guided ecology tour to explore **Tatapouri Reef** at low tide, where you can hand-feed stingrays, kingfish and octopuses, or try one of the snorkel with stingrays sessions.

Eastwoodhill Arboretum

Wharekopae Rd, 35km northwest of Gisborne • Daily 9am–5pm • $15 • ☎ 06 863 9003, ⓦ eastwoodhill.org.nz

A bottle of wine tucked under your arm and a groaning picnic hamper is the way to enjoy New Zealand's largest collection of northern hemisphere vegetation at **Eastwoodhill Arboretum**. It was the life's work of William Douglas Cook, who grew to love British gardens and parks while recuperating in England during World War I. Cook died in 1967, leaving over 3500 species – magnolia, oak, spruce, maple, cherry – brought together in an unusual microclimate in which both hot- and cold-climate trees flourish.

6

Rere Falls and Rere Rockslide

12km past Eastwoodhill Arboretum, accessed off Wharekopae Rd

The Wharekopae River plunges 10m over **Rere Falls**, where you can walk behind the curtain of water, but this is easily eclipsed by the **Rere Rockslide**, about 2km upstream, where the river cascades down a 20m-wide and 60m-long rock slope that is smooth enough to provide great sport. In summer there's little water and a lot of algae, making for a super-fast ride down to the pool at the bottom. Bring something to slide on – a boogie board, inner tube or old bit of plastic – and ask locals for advice and safety tips.

Gisborne to Napier

South of Gisborne, **SH2** leaves the Poverty Bay vineyards behind and traverses the hill country of the Wharerata State Forest before reaching **Morere**. From there it's just a short jaunt south before you can turn east and access the isolated beaches of the **Mahia Peninsula**. Continuing west on SH2 brings you to the quaint river town of **Wairoa**, from where you can access the magnificent inland environment of **Te Urewera** with its breath-taking lookouts and extensive hiking trails around **Lake Waikaremoana** (see page 343); or press on to Napier, 214km south of Gisborne and easily manageable in a day, stopping off to see endemic flora at the **Boundary Stream Scenic Reserve**.

Morere and Morere Hot Springs

SH2, 50km south of Gisborne • Daily 10am–6pm, later in summer if busy • $14; private pools extra $4 for 30min • ☎ 06 837 8856, ⓦ morerehotsprings.co.nz

Tiny **MORERE** is best known for the highly saline and pleasantly non-sulphurous waters – the result of ancient seawater, warmed and concentrated along a fault line – that well up along a small stream at the **Morere Hot Springs**. The immediate area is also one of the East Coast's last remaining tracts of native coastal forest, and grassy barbecue areas surrounding the pools form the nucleus of numerous trails that radiate out through stands of tawa, rimu, totara and matai; a short streamside walk (10min) takes you to the Nikau Plunge Pools, where soaking tanks are surrounded by nikau palm groves. Also consider the **Mangakawa Track** (3km; 2hr), which loops from the springs through gorgeous virgin bush up to a ridge-top beech forest.

ACCOMMODATION	MORERE
Morere Hot Springs Lodge SH2 ☎ 06 837 8824, ⓦ morerelodge.co.nz. A wonderfully relaxing spot with self-contained accommodation scattered around the well-kept grassy site, all on a working farm with a good swimming hole. Bring most supplies with you. Cabins __$100__, cottage __$120__	**Morere Tearooms & Camping Ground** Just west of Nuhaka on SH2 ☎ 06 837 8792, ✉ morere@extra.co.nz. A traditional Kiwi campsite surrounded by trees, with good tent sites, basic cabins and communal kitchen. Rush Munro's ice cream is available at the tearoom. Tearoom open Mon–Fri 8am–5pm, Sat & Sun 9am–5pm. Camping __$16__, cabins __$60__

CAPE KIDNAPPERS

Mahia Peninsula

At Nuhaka, 8km south of Morere, the highway flirts briefly with the sea before turning west to Wairoa. Nuhaka–Opoutama Road spurs east to the **Mahia Peninsula**, a distinctive high promontory that separates Hawke's Bay from Poverty Bay. The peninsula's main settlement, **MAHIA BEACH**, sits on the narrow neck of the peninsula and being leeward side offers calm **beaches** with safe bathing and boating and several beachfront freedom camping sites. Surfers make good use of the rougher windward side just 3km to the north. Outside the mad month after Christmas it makes a relaxing place to break your journey. If your timing is right, you might witness one of Rocket Lab's **satellite launches** from its high-security pad at the very tip of the peninsula. To find out about launch dates and vantage points contact the Wairua District Council.

ACCOMMODATION AND EATING — MAHIA PENINSULA

The Beach Café 43 Moana Drive St ☎ 06 837 5948, ⓦ facebook.com/thebeachcafemahia. Adjacent to the camping ground, this popular spot serves fish and chips, burgers and lasagne with nothing over $10. The local owners are a good contact for holiday home rentals in this beach community. Mon–Fri 4.30–7pm, Sat & Sun 10am–8pm.

Mahia Beach Holiday Park 43 Moana Drive, Mahia Beach ☎ 06 837 5830. Offers spacious camping and basic motel units spread out on grassland back from the beach, which gets absolutely stuffed in the summer. Camping $21, cabins $75, motel units $125

Sunset Point Bar and Grill Cnr Newcastle & Ratau Sts ☎ 06 837 5071. Mahia's only lively spot dishes out hearty meals such as steak, crayfish, and fish and chips ($17–35), and has a large beer garden. The bottleshop closes at 11pm, the kitchen at 8pm. Wed–Fri noon–late, Sat & Sun 11am–late.

Wairoa

For visitors, the sleepy farming community of **WAIROA**, 40km west of the Nuhaka junction, is best known as the closest town to Lake Waikaremoana (see page 343). Hugging the banks of the willow-lined Wairoa River a couple of kilometres from its mouth, historic Wairoa was once a merchant port where ships came safely upriver to load the produce of the dairy- and sheep-farming country all around. Today, this friendly, down-to-earth town offers the chance to break your journey and visit an intriguing museum or walk the historical path along the river to Whakamahia Beach (7km). If you want to visit Lake Waikaremoana, the town's accommodation can be used as a springboard for day-hikes, while the main street is the last chance for overnight trampers to stock up on camping supplies, food and petrol.

Wairoa Museum

142 Marine Parade • Mon–Fri 10am–4pm • Donation

The excellent **Wairoa Museum** evokes a picture of the town's more lively history through three small, carefully presented exhibit rooms crammed with fascinating stories. One of the key exhibits is the recovered Pai Marire flag, emblem of a Māori resistance movement during the Taranaki wars of the 1860s. Look out for the striking Lindauer portrait of government loyalist Ihaka Whaanga and a beautifully carved Māori statue from the early eighteenth century.

ARRIVAL AND INFORMATION — WAIROA

By bus InterCity buses pick up daily at the i-SITE.
Destinations Gisborne (1 daily; 1hr 30min); Napier (1 daily; 2hr 30min).

i-SITE Corner of SH2 and Queen St (Mon–Fri 8.30am–5pm, Sat & Sun 10am–4pm; ☎ 06 838 7440, ⓦ visitwairoa.co.nz). Knowledgeable staff can sell DOC hut tickets, arrange Lake Waikaremoana shuttle pick-ups and advise on freedom camping sites throughout the district.

Internet There's free wi-fi in the CBD.

GETTING AROUND

By bus The Big Bush Lake Waikaremoana Shuttle Service (☎ 06 837 3777) picks up on demand for the trip inland to the lake ($50/person, depending on numbers).

ACCOMMODATION

Wairoa has only a drab collection of roadside motels, but it does promote itself as a **motorhome-friendly** haven with plenty of freedom camping locations including along the town's riverbanks and at the stunning Whakamahia Beach Wildlife Reserve.

Riverside Motor Camp 19 Marine Parade ☎ 06 838 6301, ⓦ riversidemotorcamp.co.nz. Old-school but clean camping ground on a small, grassy patch overlooking the river just a 2min walk from town with powered sites, cabins and a very basic dorm with a small lounge and deck.

Camping $20, dorms $30, cabins $70
Whakamahia Lodge 4km south of Wairoa on Whakamahi Rd ☎ 02 731 3857, ⓦ whakamahialodge.co.nz. Delightful property perched on its own grassy hillside a short walk from the wild beach reserve and with panoramic ocean views. The three en-suite rooms are spacious, but there's a lot of hunting memorabilia that might put some people off; the hosts can arrange spearfishing, wild boar hunts or horseriding. $250

EATING AND DRINKING

★ **Café 287** 3km south of Wairoa on SH2 ☎ 06 838 6601. Roadside diner dishing up delicious home-cooked breakfasts, freshly ground coffee and healthy lunches plus dinners of fettuccini and steaks ($15–30). They also have three double rooms in a cabin ($110). Daily 7.30am–4pm.
Osler's Bakery & Café 116 Marine Parade ☎ 06 838 8299. Local institution run by the same family for five generations. Try the lamb and mint pie, which is one of a

dozen homemade gourmet pies all under $5, or be tempted by a tray-laden pastry cabinet ($3–$6). Mon–Fri 4.30am–4.30pm, Sat & Sun 6am–3pm.
Wairoa Club Inc 60 Marine Parade ☎ 06 838 7414. The place to come and fill up on massive steaks ($31), gourmet pizzas ($18) and cooked breakfasts ($15). They also serve local beer on tap and have country-style live music on weekends. Mon–Sat 9.30am–late, Sun 10.30am–late.

ENTERTAINMENT

The Gaiety Cinema & Theatre 252 Marine ⓦ gaietytheatre.co.nz. Refurbished historical theatre with a mix of Blockbuster movies, Māori films and live acts.

The annual Māori Film Festival is held here on the Queen's Birthday, the first Monday in June.

Te Urewera

Mighty **Te Urewera**, 65km northwest of Wairoa, once a government-managed National Park, became a formal legal entity in 2014, giving this pristine environment the same rights as a living person. Its development is now overseen by a guardian Board made up mostly of the original Tuhoe landowners, and access to the area remains open to visitors with their blessing.

Straddling the North Island's mountainous backbone, Te Urewera's 2120 square kilometres encompasses the largest untouched expanse of native bush outside Fiordland. Unusually for New Zealand, it is almost completely covered in vegetation; even the highest peaks – some approaching 1500m – barely poke through this dense cloak of primeval forest, whose undergrowth is trampled by deer and wild pigs and whose rivers are filled with trout. One road, SH38, penetrates the interior, but the way to get a true sense of the place is to hike, particularly the celebrated Lake Waikaremoana Track encircling **Lake Waikaremoana**, the "Sea of Rippling Waters" and the area's undoubted jewel. The lake's deep clear waters, fringed by white sandy beaches and rocky bluffs, are ideal for swimming, fishing and kayaking.

Habitation is sparse, but fifteen percent of Tuhoe people, the "Children of the Mist", still live here (the largest concentration around the village of **Ruatahuna**, 20km north of the lake). Most visitors make straight for the **visitor centre** on the lakeshore at Waikaremoana, where there's also a jetty and holiday park with a small store and petrol pump. Some 15km south, the quiet former hydroelectric development village of **Tuai** provides basic services and accommodation. Otherwise, you're on your own.

Lake Waikaremoana

Shrouded by bushland on the eastern edge of Te Urewera, **Lake Waikaremoana** fills a huge scalloped bowl at an altitude of 582m, precariously held back by the Panekiri

6

THE LAKE'S BIRTH: SCIENCE & LEGEND

Lake Waikaremoana came into being around 2200 years ago, when a huge bank of sandstone boulders was dislodged from the Ngamoko range, blocking the river that once drained the valleys. The Māori have a more poetic explanation for the lake's creation. Hau-Mapuhia, the recalcitrant daughter of Mahu, was drowned by her father and turned into a *taniwha*, or "water spirit". In a frenzied effort to get to the sea, she charged in every direction, thereby creating the protruding arms of the lake. Now two of those peninsulas, Whareama and Puketukutuku, have been fenced and predator-proofed, and kiwi have been successfully reintroduced.

and Ngamoko ranges. The lake environment is a hiker's paradise, with numerous short **walks** and trails to **lookouts**, as well as an exhilarating 46km walk hugging the western lakeshore between Onepoto and Hopuruhine.

The majority of **short walks** are between Onepoto and Aniwaniwa on the eastern perimeter of the lake, the only side skirted by a road, albeit unsealed in most parts. The pick of these are the Hinerau Track, which starts at the old visitor centre in Aniwaniwa (1km; 20min return; 50m ascent) and features the double-drop Aniwaniwa Falls; spectacular Lou's Lookout (1km; 45min return; 200m steep ascent), which boasts one of the most photogenic views of the lake; and the serene Lake Waikareiti Track (17km; 5-6hr; 300m ascent), where you can rent rowboats ($20/day). Around 9km south of the visitor centre on SH38 is the popular Onepoto Caves Track (4km; 2hr return) – bring a torch to explore inside the limestone caves.

The **Lake Waikaremoana Track** (46km) is a tranquil four-day hike, and among the most popular of New Zealand's "Great Walks" on the North Island. This hike is a gentle affair, with the exception of an exhausting climb over Panekire Bluff, and provides plenty of opportunities to fish, swim and listen to the plentiful birdlife.

Most walkers travel **clockwise** starting at a shelter by the lakeshore close to SH38 in Onepoto. The first day is the toughest, climbing up and over the challenging but panoramic Panekire. Those in the know seem to prefer walking **anti-clockwise** though, starting beside the Hopuruahine River on the northern edge of the lake. Walking anti-clockwise offers the most scenic views of the lake as you descend from Panekire Bluff; and as you'll make this descent on your last day you'll have a lighter load to carry. Travel to the **trailheads** either end of the Great Walk is generally by **water taxi** from the jetty near the visitor centre, where there's free parking although roads pass by both trailheads where you can park a car. If the Great Walk appears too long or daunting, there's no reason why you can't be dropped off by water taxi anywhere along the track for a **day-hike**, or even spend just the one night out on the track.

Camping throughout the fragile lake environment is prohibited outside of the five designated **campsites**. Note there's **no mobile phone coverage** on the walk except around Onepoto – hire a personal locator beacon at the visitor centre ($15 for one day; $40 for up to seven days).

Onepoto to Panekire Hut

9km; 4–5hr; 750m ascent; 150m descent track starts at a shelter by the lakeshore close to SH38, and climbs steeply past the site of a redoubt set up by soldiers of the Armed Constabulary in pursuit of Te Kooti. It then undulates along the ridge top, occasionally revealing fabulous lake views. Wonderfully airy steps up a rocky bluff bring you to the Panekire Hut, magnificently set on the brink of the cliffs that fall away to the lake far below; committed campers must press on to Waiopaoa, an exhausting 8hr walk from the start.

Panekire Hut to Waiopaoa Hut

7.5km; 3–4hr; 600m descent

Descending the western side of Panekire Bluff the trail rapidly loses height through an often muddy area where protruding tree roots provide welcome hand-holds.

Occasional lake views and the transition from beech forest to rich podocarp woodland make this an appealing, if tricky, section of track down to Waiopaoa Hut and campsite.

Waiopaoa Hut to Marauiti Hut

11km; 4–5hr; 100m ascent

The track largely follows the lakeshore, crossing grassland and then kanuka scrub before reaching the Korokoro campsite (1hr 30min from Waiopaoa Hut). A side track leads to the pretty 20m Korokoro Falls (45–60min return). Meanwhile, the main track climbs slightly above the lake past barely accessible bays, eventually reaching the Maraunui campsite and, after ascending the low Whakaneke Spur, descends to the waterside Marauiti Hut.

Marauiti Hut to Waiharuru Hut

6km; 2hr; 150m ascent

From the Marauiti Hut, the track crosses the bridge over the stream that runs into Marauiti Bay, passing the lovely white-sand Te Kopua Bay. It then climbs an easy saddle before dropping down to Te Totara Bay and follows the lake to Waiharuru Hut and campsite, the largest of the five huts with forty bunk beds.

Waiharuru Hut to Whanganui Hut

5.3km; 2–3hr; 100m ascent

It's a short hike across a broad neck of land to the Tapuaenui campsite and beyond. The track follows the lakeshore to the characterful old Whanganui Hut, the smallest of the huts with just eighteen bunk beds set in a clearing beside a stream.

Whanganui Hut to Hopuruahine

5km; 2–3hr; 50m ascent

The final leg of the hike is also the shortest and easiest. The track skirts the lake to the point where water taxis pick up (45min), then follows grassy flats beside the Hopuruahine River before crossing a suspension bridge.

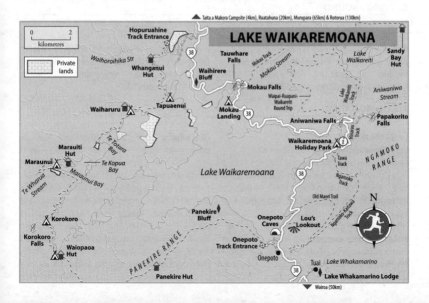

ARRIVAL AND DEPARTURE

LAKE WAIKAREMOANA

By car Lake Waikaremoana is approached most easily from Wairoa along SH38. This continues through to Murupara and Rotorua, but note that between Lake Waikaremoana and Murupara there is nearly 100km of tortuous gravel road; if you wish to travel this route, take local advice, grab the *Te Urewera Rainforest Route* leaflet and go slowly.

By bus The Big Bush Lake Waikaremoana Shuttle Service (☎06 837 3777, ⓦlakewaikaremoana.co.nz) services the lake from Wairoa, dropping off at the jetty beside the visitor centre.

INFORMATION

Equipment Each hut is supplied with drinking water, toilets and a heating stove, but a cooking stove, fuel and all your food must be carried. Campsites only have water and toilets.

DOC leaflets and maps Comprehensive walking information is covered in the *Lake Waikaremoana Track* leaflet, though map enthusiasts might like the two 1:50,000 Topo50 maps that cover the full circuit.

Pack transport Big Bush (☎06 837 3777; ⓦlakewaikaremoana.co.nz) can organize pack transport between most huts, allowing for a largely luggage-free walk, though this is only economical for groups of four or more.

Services The only place that has petrol between Wairoa and Murupara is the *Waikaremoana Holiday Park*.

Visitor information Te Urewera Visitor Centre is located within the wonderful Tuhoe Tribal Authority Building adjacent to the Waikaremoana Holiday Park (Tues–Sat 8am–4.30pm; ☎06 837 3803, ⓔteureweravc@doc.govt. nz) and can arrange hut bookings, maps and personal locator beacons.

Weather The winter months (June–Sept) can be cold and wet, making spring and autumn the best times to undertake the walk, though go prepared as it can snow at any point in the year.

TOURS

GUIDED HIKES

Walking Legends ☎0800 925 569, ⓦwalkinglegends. com. Offers four-day walks ($1490), led by enthusiastic and knowledgeable guides, with accommodation in the same DOC huts used by independent walkers. Trips depart from Rotorua, and excellent meals and wine are provided – all you need to carry is a day-pack. The longest day is around seven hours and there's usually enough time for a bit of trout fishing.

FISHING

David Dods 4939 Main Rd (SH38) ☎06 837 3988, ⓔfishdods@extra.co.nz. Lake Waikaremoana is one of the best places for brown trout in the world. Trips vary from $150 to $750 (for about five hours out including a lunch of smoked trout with wine). Also runs a beautiful B&B on the hillside overlooking Tuai Village.

GETTING AROUND

By car You can drive to the trailheads at either end of the Lake Waikaremoana Track, but there are occasional thefts and most people prefer to park free of charge at the *Waikaremoana Holiday Park* and take a water taxi out.

By bus and boat Big Bush (☎06 837 3777, ⓦlakewaikaremoana.co.nz) charge $50 for a joint drop-

off and pick-up package, and they'll also run a water-taxi service to anywhere else you might want to start or finish, enabling you to walk shorter sections by means of prearranged pick-ups from specified beaches. Alternatively, David Dods (see page 346) provides water shuttle services and scenic tours on the lake.

ACCOMMODATION

LAKE WAIKAREMOANA

Lake Whakamarino Lodge Tuai village, off SH38 15km south of the visitor centre ☎0800 837 387, ⓦlakelodge. co.nz. Converted construction workers' quarters wonderfully sited beside the trout-filled Lake Whakamarino. Accommodation is in basic rooms and more upmarket self-contained units; book ahead, as it fills up quickly. Dinner can be booked two days ahead for $32. Dorms $30, unit $140

Mokau Landing campsite SH38, 11km northwest of the visitor centre. A large, grassy DOC site that sits between the bush and the lake, with running water and toilets. Mokau Falls is just 1.5km away. $8

Ohuka Lodge 33 Ohuka Rd, just off SH38, half way between the visitor centre and Wairoa Town ☎06 837 3713, ⓦohukalodge.com. This private converted farmers' cottage has a modern interior with kitchen and two bedrooms. The rural setting here is blissfully tranquil and dissected by the Waikaretaheke River, good for fishing. $150

Waikaremoana Holiday Park SH38, adjacent to the visitor centre ☎06 837 3826, ⓦwaikaremoana. info. A well-organized establishment with camping sites fronting the lake, basic wooden cabins and newly built self-contained chalets sleeping up to five. A store and reasonably sized communal kitchen and dining room make this a great base for exploring the lake. Showers are available for non-guests ($5). Camping $\overline{\underline{\$36}}$, cabins $\overline{\underline{\$65}}$, chalets $\overline{\underline{\$130}}$

LAKE WAIKAREMOANA TRACK
DOC huts and campsites ⓦ doc.govt.nz. Panekiri, Waiopaoa, Marauiti, Waiharuru and Whanganui are all

Great Walk huts and must be booked in advance, as must the campsites; you can do so online, although you'll need to call in at the Te Urewera Visitor Centre to pick up your Great Walks Ticket. Your chances of getting a place are much better outside Christmas and Easter. Backcountry Hut Pass not valid. Under-eighteens free. Huts $\overline{\underline{\$32}}$, camping $\overline{\underline{\$14}}$

EATING

The nearest full-time restaurant is 55km away at *The Tavern* in tiny Frasertown, 8km east of Wairoa town, so you'll largely have to fend for yourself when it comes to food. There's a reasonable range of groceries at the *Waikaremoana Holiday Park*, and you

might get signed into the district club at Tuai which serves beer and snacks (ⓣ 06 837 3885). Meals are sometimes available on request at the *Lake Whakamarino Lodge* (two-course dinner $32), but you're better off relying on your own supplies.

Boundary Stream Scenic Reserve

Off SH2 at Tutira (43km north of Napier) inland onto Matahorua Rd and then 15km northwest along Pohakura Rd

From Wairoa south to Napier, the SH2 becomes considerably steeper and twistier, so take it slowly and allow at least an hour and a half. Make time to visit the wonderful **Boundary Stream Scenic Reserve**, a "mainland island" with great examples of a variety of environments from lowland to mountain forest. The reserve contains North Island brown kiwi, kereru, North Island kaka, shining cuckoo and, very occasionally, New Zealand falcon. There are several walks, including one to the Bell Rock viewpoint (5km return; 3hr) and, at the far end of the reserve, to **Shine Falls**, which crashes 58m down onto rocks surrounded by lush vegetation.

Napier

Laidback, seaside **NAPIER** is Hawke's Bay's largest city (population 60,000) and one of New Zealand's most likeable regional centres, thanks to its Mediterranean climate, affordable prices and the world's best-preserved collection of small-scale Art Deco architecture, built after the earthquake that devastated the city in 1931 (see below).

Thanks to the whim of mid-nineteenth-century Land Commissioner Alfred Domett, the grid of streets in the city's **commercial centre** bears the names of British literary luminaries – Tennyson, Thackeray, Byron, and more. Bisecting it all is the partly pedestrianized main thoroughfare of Emerson Street, whose terracotta paving and palm trees run from Clive Square – one-time site of a makeshift "Tin Town" while the city was being rebuilt after the earthquake – to the Norfolk pine-fringed **Marine Parade**, Napier's main beach.

Around the eastern side of Bluff Hill (Mataruahou), about 5km from the city centre, lies the original settlement site of **Ahuriri**, now home to a marina, fashionable restaurants, cafés and bars.

With a glut of seaside hotels and a decent array of restaurants, Napier does make a decent base from which to visit the gannet colony at Cape Kidnappers (see page 353) and the vat-load of **wineries** on the surrounding plains, although both Hastings and Havelock North (see page 356), just 20km further south, are closer to both.

Brief history

In 1769, James Cook sailed past **Ahuriri**, the current site of Napier, noting the sea-girt Bluff Hill linked to the mainland by two slender shingle banks and backed by a superb saltwater lagoon – the only substantial sheltered mooring between Gisborne and Wellington. Nonetheless, after a less-than-cordial encounter with the Ngati Kahungunu people he anchored just to the south, off what came to be known as Cape Kidnappers. Some thirty years later, when early whalers followed in Cook's wake, Ahuriri was all but deserted, the Ngati Kahungunu having been driven out by rivals

6

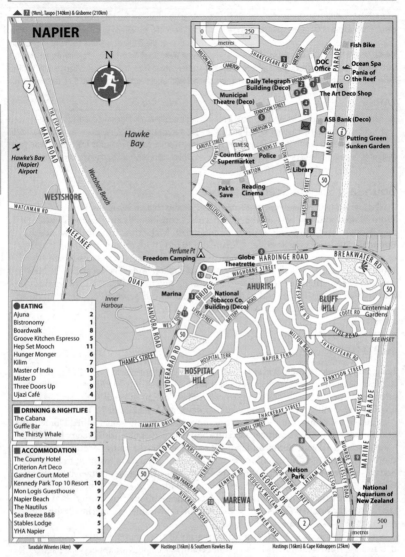

▲ 7 (9km), Taupo (140km) & Gisborne (210km)

NAPIER

Hawke
Bay

Hawke's Bay
(Napier)
Airport

WESTSHORE
WATCHMAN RD
MEEANEE

THE ESPLANADE
MAIN ROAD
Westshore Beach

QUAY

Inner
Harbour

Perfume Pt
Freedom Camping

Marina

PANDORA ROAD
BRIDGE ST
WEST QUAY
LEVER STREET
BATTERY

THAMES STREET

HYDERABAD RD

0   250
metres

SHAKESPEARE RD
MILTON RD
CAMERON
BROWNING
BREWSTER
BYRON
PARADE

**DOC
Office**

**Daily Telegraph
Building (Deco)**

**Municipal
Theatre (Deco)**

TENNYSON STREET
EMERSON ST
CARLYLE STREET
CLIVE SQ
DICKENS ST
DALTON STREET

**Countdown
Supermarket**   **Police**
STATION

**Pak'n
Save**   **Reading
Cinema**

WELLESLEY RD
MUNROE ST

Fish Bike

Ocean Spa
**Pania of
the Reef**

**MTG
The Art Deco Shop**

ASB Bank (Deco)

**Putting Green
Sunken Garden**

Library

MARINE PARADE
HASTINGS STREET
50

**Globe
Theatrette**
HARDINGE ROAD
WAGHORNE STREET
BREAKWATER RD

AHURIRI
**National
Tobacco Co.
Building (Deco)**

SHAKESPEARE RD
**BLUFF
HILL**
COOTE RD
CLYDE ROAD
Centennial
Gardens
50
SEE INSET

MILTON ROAD
SHAKESPEARE RD
NAPIER TERR

**HOSPITAL
HILL**
HOSPITAL TERR
TENNYSON STREET
HASTINGS PARADE

THACKERAY STREET
TAMATEA DRIVE
CARNELL STREET

TARADALE ROAD
ALPERS TERR
HERRICK STREET
KENNEDY RD
VIGOR BROWN STREET
GEORGES DR
DOUGLAS McLEAN AVE
LATHAM STREET
NELSON CR
WELLESLEY ROAD
NELSON ROAD

TOM PARKER AVE
RIVERBEND ROAD
BARKER ROAD

**Nelson
Park**

**National
Aquarium of
New Zealand**

MAREWA
50
2

0   500
metres

● **EATING**
Ajuna   2
Bistronomy   1
Boardwalk   8
Groove Kitchen Espresso 5
Hep Set Mooch   11
Hunger Monger   6
Kilim   7
Master of India   10
Mister D   3
Three Doors Up   9
Ujazi Café   4

■ **DRINKING & NIGHTLIFE**
The Cabana   1
Guffle Bar   2
The Thirsty Whale   3

■ **ACCOMMODATION**
The County Hotel   1
Criterion Art Deco   2
Gardner Court Motel   8
Kennedy Park Top 10 Resort 10
Mon Logis Guesthouse   9
Napier Beach   7
The Nautilus   6
Sea Breeze B&B   4
Stables Lodge   5
YHA Napier   3

Taradale Wineries (4km) ▼   ▼ Hastings (16km) & Southern Hawkes Bay   Hastings (16km) & Cape Kidnappers (25km) ▼

equipped with European guns. During the uneasy peace of the early colonial years,
Māori returned to the Napier area, which weathered the **New Zealand Wars** of the
1860s relatively unscathed. The port boomed, but by the early years of the twentieth
century all the available land was used up.

The earthquake

Everything changed in two and a half minutes on the morning of February 3, 1931, when
a 7.8 magnitude **earthquake**, one of the biggest in New Zealand's recorded history, rocked
the city. More than six hundred aftershocks followed over the next two weeks, hampering
efforts to rescue the 258 people who perished in the bay area, 162 of them in Napier
alone. Many of the wooden buildings survived, except for their chimneys; but the rest was

destroyed by fires that swept through unchecked – a sea breeze saved the Six Sisters on Marine Parade. The land twisted and buckled, finding a new equilibrium more than 2m higher, with 300 square kilometres of new land wrested from the grip of the ocean – enough room to site the Hawke's Bay airport and expand the city.

Napier embraced the opportunity to start afresh: out went the trams, telephone wires were laid underground, the streets were widened and, in the spirit of the times, almost everything was designed according to the precepts of the Art Deco movement. The simultaneous reconstruction gave Napier a rare stylistic uniformity that prevails even today, ranking it alongside Miami Beach as one of the world's largest collections of **Art Deco** buildings.

6

Marine Parade

Napier's most striking feature is **Marine Parade**, a dead-straight 2km of boulevard lined with stately Norfolk pines, bordered on one side by hotels, motels, B&Bs, hostels, shops and restaurants and by a dark grey stony beach on the other. The latter is Napier's main beach, but it's unsafe for swimming – better head 30km north to Waipatiki or 35km south to Waimarama or Ocean Beach (see page 357). A popular walking and cycling path links a string of attractions along the seaward edge of Marine Parade, starting by Napier's port at the northern end of town and passing the foot of Bluff Hill before arriving at the Ocean Spa.

Ocean Spa

42 Marine Parade • Mon–Sat 6am–10pm, Sun 8am–10pm • $10.70 • ☎ 06 835 8553, ⓦ oceanspa.co.nz

A large glass and concrete beachside complex, **Ocean Spa** houses a gym and salt-chlorinated, lido-style complex of hot pools (36–38°C) with bubbles, jets, spouts, steam room, sauna, massages ($40/30min), beauty treatments and a lap pool (26°C), all overlooking the sea. The long hours and warm waters make it a great place for a relaxed summer evening.

MTG

1 Tennyson St • Daily 10am–5pm • $10 • ☎ 06 835 7781, ⓦ mtghawkesbay.com

Opposite Pania (see page 350) stands **MTG**, the stylish Hawke's Bay museum and art gallery. It's light and spacious and has some good views across the town and bay. There's a moving permanent exhibition on the earthquake in the basement with stories from survivors (sailors were spooked by the appearance of a ghost ship thrown from the sea bed). The rest of the space is given to temporary exhibitions, with an emphasis on design and decorative arts.

National Aquarium of New Zealand

546 Marine Parade • Daily 9am–5pm; check website for various feeding times; behind-the-scenes tour daily by reservation • $21; animal close encounters $70; snorkelling with sharks $100/30min (incl. gear); scuba diving (qualified divers only) with sharks $82, or $127 with all gear • ☎ 06 834 1404, ⓦ nationalaquarium.co.nz

The **National Aquarium of New Zealand** is one of the finest in the country, with distinct marine environments from around the globe. The most spectacular section is the **ocean tank**, its walk-through tunnel giving intimate views of rays and assorted sharks, with which you can swim by arrangement. Hand feeding the fish happens at the **reef tank**, plus there are three daily feeding sessions in the pool for rescued little penguins, with live video feeds from their burrows and windows to watch them swimming. Non-aquatic sections include one for New Zealand's reptilian tuatara, and a nocturnal **kiwi house**.

Bluff Hill

The city centre's northern flank butts up against the steep slopes of **Bluff Hill**, a 3km-long hummock of winding streets, home to some of Napier's more desirable suburbs.

6

PANIA OF THE REEF

Just south of Ocean Spa (see page 349) is a bronze cast of the curvaceous **Pania of the Reef**, a siren of local Māori legend. **Pania** was a beautiful sea-maiden who would swim from the watery realm of Tangaroa, the god of the ocean, each evening to quench her thirst at a freshwater spring close to the base of Bluff Hill before returning to her people each morning. One evening, she was discovered by a young chief who wooed her and wanted her to remain on land. Eventually they married, but when Pania went to pay a farewell visit to her kin they forcibly restrained her in the briny depths and she turned to stone, forming what is now known as **Pania Reef**. Fishers and divers still claim they can see her with arms outstretched towards the shore.

The primary reason for negotiating the hill is the **Bluff Hill Domain Lookout** (daily 7am–dusk) at the northern summit, which offers views over the timber-laden Port of Napier and across Hawke's Bay to Mahia Peninsula.

Ahuriri

5km northwest of the city centre

Napier's European foundations are in harbourside **Ahuriri**. James Cook found shelter for the *Endeavour* in the estuary here and the fledgling town grew up around the harbour. When the industrial port moved round the headland Ahuriri languished, but in recent years the old wool stores and warehouses around the inner harbour (also known as the Iron Pot) and the waterfront strip stretching back to town, have been reborn as home to cavernous bars, cafés and restaurants, all buzzing from Thursday evening through the weekend.

ARRIVAL AND DEPARTURE — NAPIER

By plane Regular direct flights with Air New Zealand and Jetstar from Auckland, Wellington and Christchurch, as well as a Sounds Air (T 0800 505 005, W soundsair.com) service to Blenheim arrive at Hawke's Bay Airport, 5km north of town on SH2, where they are met by the Super Shuttle (T 0800 748 885, W supershuttle.co.nz), which charges $20 to get into town.

Destinations Auckland (11–15 daily; 1hr); Blenheim (4 weekly; 1hr); Christchurch (2–3 daily; 1hr 35min); Wellington (3–5 daily; 1hr).

By bus InterCity and ManaBus.com buses stop on Carlyle St by Clive Square.

Destinations Auckland (2 daily; 7hr 25min); Gisborne (1 daily; 4hr 50min); Hastings (5 daily; 25min); Palmerston North (2–3 daily; 2hr 45min); Rotorua (2 daily; 3hr 45min); Taupo (3 daily; 2hr); Wellington (2 daily; 5hr 25min).

GETTING AROUND

By bike Napier's central sights are easily covered on foot, but cycling along the 130km of paths in and around the city is a pleasant way to see the area; try Fish Bike, 22 Marine Parade (daily 9am–5pm; T 06 833 6979, W fishbike.co.nz), who rent out an assortment of bikes (including electric) from $40/day.

By bus The GoBay local bus services (T 06 835 9200, W hbrc.govt.nz/services/public-transport/bus-timetables) from Dalton St are of use primarily for visits to Hastings and Havelock North. In addition, the #13 stops by the Church Road and Mission Estate wineries.

By car Auto Rental (T 06 834 0045, W autorentalvehicles.co.nz) and Pegasus (T 06 843 7020, W rentalcars.co.nz) both have short-lease vehicles from $40/day.

By taxi Hawkes Bay Taxis (T 06 835 7777, W hawkesbaytaxis.nz).

INFORMATION AND TOURS

Visitor information i-SITE, 100 Marine Parade (daily 9am–5pm; T 06 834 1911, W hawkesbaynz.com). Can advise on tide times for gannet visits, has information about walks, can book travel and track/hut tickets.

Art Deco Walking Tours Art Deco Shop, 7 Tennyson St T 06 834 3111, W artdeconapier.com. Dedicated Deco buffs should meet at the Art Deco Shop for a guided walk around the city, which brings 1930s Napier to life through anecdotes and gives you the chance to check out the interiors of shops and banks (daily: 10am, 1hr, $19; or 2pm; 2hr; $21). There are additional evening tours in the busier months at 4.30pm (Oct–March; 2hr; $19). Alternatively, pick up the Art Deco Walk leaflet from the shop ($10) or download for free from their website, as it details a self-guided stroll (1.5km; 1hr 30min–2hr) around the downtown area.

Napier Māori Tours ☎021 077 0088, ⓦnapiertours. co.nz. A wholesome introduction into Māori culture, this guided walking tour around Otatatra *Pa*, a resurrected fortified village, explains some of the old ways of living with the land. Offers great views from the lookout, too. Bookings essential (min 2 people), 2hr tour without transport $95; half-day private tour with transport from Napier and lunch $430.

ACCOMMODATION

Apart from the usual shortage of rooms during the month or so after Christmas and the February festivals (see page 352), you should have little trouble finding accommodation in Napier. There are dozens of **motels** around town, and Marine Parade has low-cost backpacker **hostels**, plush **hotels** and classy **B&Bs**. There are four allocated **freedom camping** areas, all in car parks, the best being Perfume Point on the northern tip of Ahuriri off Nelson Quay or at the Te Awa Foreshore, a few kilometres south of the city centre.

The County Hotel 12 Browning St ☎06 835 7800, ⓦcountyhotel.co.nz; map p.348. One of the few 1931 earthquake survivors, this elegant, period-decorated business and tourist hotel (in the Edwardian former council offices) has only 18 luxurious rooms (some with clawfoot baths), a posh restaurant and tiny cocktail bar. Check for special offers. $285

★ **Criterion Art Deco** 48 Emerson St ☎06 835 2059, ⓦcriterionartdeco.co.nz; map p.348. Central, well-organized 60-bed hostel in an Art Deco building, formerly a hotel. The dorms (some single-sex) and doubles (some en suite) are good value and there are large communal areas (and a pool table), but a small kitchen. Continental breakfast included. Dorms $29, doubles $66

Gardner Court Motel 16 Nelson Crescent ☎0800 000 830, ⓦgardnercourtmotel.co.nz; map p.348. Old-school motel with a solar-heated pool and simple motel rooms at bargain prices. The place is made by the enthusiasm and friendliness of the long-term owners. $110

Kennedy Park Top 10 Resort 11 Storkey St, off Kennedy Rd ☎0800 457 275, ⓦkennedypark.co.nz; map p.348. This large, family-orientated suburban holiday park, 2km from the city centre, has acres of powered sites ($48 for two people), a pool, BBQ area, kids' playground, restaurant and a huge range of cabins. Basic cabins $63, units $121

★ **Mon Logis B&B** 415 Marine Parade ☎06 835 2125, ⓦmonlogis.co.nz; map p.348. Four rooms sharing a balcony with sea views in a century-old wooden house. The friendly and knowledgeable Gallic owner makes every effort to look after you and provides delicious breakfasts. $220

Napier Beach 10 Gill Rd, Bay View, 9km north of Napier ☎0800 287 275, ⓦnapierbeach.co.nz; map p.348. Welcoming, with a jazzy reception, wi-fi access and summer-only café, this beachfront campsite provides an antidote to *Kennedy Park's* gulag ambience. An extra couple of dollars gets a beach site with great views (usual rates: camping $22, powered sites $24), or splash out on a beach motel unit ($179). Cabins $84, units $159

The Nautilus 387 Marine Parade ☎0508 628 845, ⓦnautilusnapier.co.nz; map p.348. Art Deco-inspired motel in which all rooms offer sea views, a hot tub or spa bath, balcony and room service. There is also a small on-site restaurant. Studios $229, apartments $269

Sea Breeze B&B 281 Marine Parade ☎06 835 8067, ⓦseabreezebnb.co.nz; map p.348. Unique, seafront Victorian villa with three flamboyantly decorated themed rooms. The Asian Imperial and Turkish have en suites, while the Indian has its bathroom adjacent to the bedroom. Breakfast is self-service continental from the guest kitchenette and the communal lounge has sea views. $130

Stables Lodge 370 Hastings St ☎06 835 6242, ⓦstableslodge.co.nz; map p.348. Rooms ranged around a central courtyard give this 34-bed hostel an intimate feel and it's all pretty friendly and relaxed. Hammocks, a book exchange and a BBQ that takes the pressure off the small but well-equipped kitchen add to the communal atmosphere. Dorms $26, doubles $79

YHA Napier 277 Marine Parade ☎06 835 7039, ⓦyha. co.nz; map p.348. The rooms here are spread across three historic weatherboard houses overlooking the waterfront, and some have sea views, although the shared bathrooms are all quite tiny. There's a just-about-adequate kitchen and a sunny courtyard at the back with a BBQ. Dorms $32, doubles $69

EATING

Both Central Napier and the suburb of Ahuriri have decent eating options. There are two large, central **supermarkets** on Munroe St: Countdown (daily 7am–10pm) at no. 1, and Pak 'n Save (daily 7am–10pm) at no. 25.

Ajuna 53 Hastings St ☎06 835 6218; map p.348. Licensed café with outdoor tables on a busy street corner, popular with locals and travellers alike. Offers Mojo coffee, home-made quiches, veggie bakes, filos and wraps and delicious seafood chowder ($14.90), as well as other inexpensive breakfasts and lunches. Daily 6.30am–5pm.

Bistronomy 40 Hastings St ☎06 834 4309, ⓦbistronomy.co.nz; map p.348. This chic fine-dining restaurant has an evolving four seasons menu, ensuring the freshest local produce reaches your plate. There's a bit of everything here, mostly under $30, though the highlights are the tempting 20g cheese tasting plate ($35) and six-course chef's choice menu ($75). Wed & Thurs 5pm–late, Fri–Sun noon–late.

6

6

NAPIER FESTIVALS AND EVENTS

The Mission Concert ⓦ missionconcert.co.nz. An outdoor concert at the Mission Estate Winery featuring an internationally famous vocalist – past luminaries include the Dixie Chicks, Eric Clapton and Rod Stewart – and drawing crowds of around 25,000. Usually sometime between January and March.

Art Deco Weekend ⓦ artdeconapier.com. A celebration of all things Art Deco-related, featuring open-house tours, vintage cars, 1930s-dress picnics, silent movies and the like. Usually the third weekend in February.

★ **Boardwalk** 8 Hardinge Rd, Ahuri ☎ 06 834 1168, ⓦ boardwalknapier.co.nz; map p.348. From the outside it looks like a bog-standard beachside bar and café, with patio seating next to the pavement. But walk through to a lovely outdoor bar area and covered deck for the restaurant, both with great views across the sea. The menu's set by price ($21–34) and surprisingly reasonable given the view and vibe, though you could spend more on a "surf and turf" blow-out. Mon–Fri 10am–late, Sat & Sun 8am–late.

Groove Kitchen Espresso 112 Tennyson St ☎ 06 835 8530, ⓦ groovekitchen.co.nz; map p.348. Cool café with irresistible coffee and lovely food – try the "Jammin' salmon" ($19) made with hash cakes, spinach, fresh pesto and poached eggs, or the smoked fish pie ($9). There are random DJ nights during the busier summer months. Daily 8.30am–2pm.

Hep Set Mooch 58 West Quay, Ahuri ☎ 06 833 6332, ⓦ hepsetmooch.co.nz; map p.348. Gaudy, relaxed daytime café in a vast warehouse. Friendly staff serve a range of breakfasts including eggs benedict, great muffins and a healthy selection of salads, bagels and organic juices (nothing over $25). Mon & Wed–Sun 8am–3pm.

Hunger Monger 129 Marine Parade St ☎ 06 835 9736, ⓦ hungermonger.co.nz; map p.348. For seafood, this is the place. Beautifully presented and reasonably priced, with the likes of spicy fish tacos ($16) and fish tataki with artichoke puree ($26). There's even a $10 fish and chip takeaway. Mon & Tues 5pm–10pm, Wed–Sun 11am–11pm.

Kilim 193 Hastings St ☎ 06 835 9100, ⓦ facebook.com/kilimcafenapier; map p.348. BYO wine without corkage and cheap Turkish grub to eat in or take away make this a local favourite. Mains (around $20) include lamb *guvech*, grilled halloumi and spinach *borek*. Service is haphazard but

the staff are keen and the food is tasty and filling. Mon–Thurs & Sun 11am–9pm, Fri & Sat 11am–9.30pm.

Master of India 79 Bridge St, cnr Waghorne St, Ahuri ☎ 06 834 3440, ⓦ masterofindia.co.nz; map p.348. Atmospheric licensed curry house with ornate gilded decor and a broad menu of vegetarian options (under $16) as well as more unusual goat specialities ($21); takeaways available. Mon & Tues 5–9.30pm, Wed, Thurs & Sun 11.30am–2pm & 5–9.30pm, Fri & Sat 11.30am–2pm & 5–10pm.

★ **Mister D** 47 Tennyson St ☎ 06 835 5022, ⓦ misterd. co.nz; map p.348. Great ingredients prepared lovingly. If you eat meat, don't leave Napier without trying the bone-marrow ravioli ($26.50), while anyone with a sweet tooth should get their fix of homemade doughnut with filling to inject (custard, jelly or chocolate $7.50). Mon–Wed & Sun 7.30am–4pm, Thurs–Sat 7.30am–11pm.

Three Doors Up 3 Waghorne St, Ahuri ☎ 06 834 0835, ⓦ threedoorsup.co.nz; map p.348. A licensed fine-dining restaurant with a cosy atmosphere and affordable prices, hence very popular with the locals. Hearty meat dishes are popular, although some can be a little overloaded (scotch fillet with blue cheese and sherry mushroom) but everything is tasty (mains $28–40). Their neighbouring bar *The Four Doors Lounge Bar* (Wed–Sun) has live music on Friday evenings and Sunday afternoons. Daily 5.30pm–late.

Ujazi Café 28 Tennyson St ☎ 06 835 1490, ⓦ facebook. com/ujazicafe; map p.348. Napier's oldest café still retains its funky atmosphere and serves good breakfasts (including vegetarian) and lunch: homemade falafels and koftas or salads, strong Fairtrade coffee and particularly good custard squares; dishes $16–20. Daily 8am–5pm.

DRINKING AND NIGHTLIFE

It's rare to find anything really exciting in Napier, unless you hit town at **festival time** (see above), but a couple of the **bars** host **live music** at weekends.

The Cabana 11 Shakespeare Rd ☎ 06 835 1102, ⓦ cabana.net.nz; map p.348. Venue for travelling bands and shows that's the envy of many larger towns; a visit to Napier is not complete without at least poking your head through the door. Occasional cover charge applies, depending on the acts (usually $10). Thurs–Sat 8pm–1am; when events are scheduled also Mon–

Wed & Sun 8pm–midnight.

★ **Guffle Bar** 29a Hastings St ☎ 06 835 8847, ⓦ facebook.com/gufflebar; map p.348. Ultra-cool cocktail and wine bar, which serves the best drinks in town and has great tunes anytime, plus occasional movie classics and live music. Specialises in phenomenally good cocktails. Tues–Thurs 5pm–midnight, Fri 5pm–2am, Sat 6pm–2am.

The Thirsty Whale 62 West Quay, Ahuri ☎ 06 835 8815, ⓦ thethirstywhale.co.nz; map p.348. On weekends, this restaurant is the liveliest venue in town. Serves a great selection of beers on tap, including DB from Hawke's Bay and Black Dog from Wellington. The whole place is turned into a nightclub on weekends with two distinct areas: expect old-school tunes in the main bar area, and R&B in the smaller function room. Mon–Fri 11am–late, Sat & Sun 10am–late.

ENTERTAINMENT

Entertainment listings are covered in the Friday edition of *Hawke's Bay Today* newspaper.

Reading Cinema 154 Station St ☎06 831 0600, ⓦreadingcinemas.co.nz. Screens all the latest first-release mainstream films.

Globe Theatrette 15 Hardinge Rd, Ahuriri ☎06 833 6011, ⓦglobenapier.co.nz. Tiny cinema with leather seats showing a mix of mainstream and art movies.

Cape Kidnappers

After James Cook's ill-starred initial encounter with Māori at Gisborne (see page 335), he sailed south and anchored off the jagged peninsula known to the Ngati Kahungunu as Te Matua-a-maui, "the fishhook of Maui" – a reference to the origin of the North Island, which was, as legend has it, dragged from the oceans by Maui. Here, Māori traders noticed two young Tahitian interpreters aboard the *Endeavour*; believing them to be held against their will, the traders captured one of them and paddled away. The boy escaped back to the ship but Cook subsequently marked the point on his chart as **Cape Kidnappers**.

Neither Cook nor Joseph Banks, both meticulous in recording flora and fauna, mentioned any **gannets** on the peninsula's final shark-tooth flourish of pinnacles. However, a hundred years later, forty or so birds were recorded, and now there are over 5,000 breeding pairs – no visit to Napier and Hastings is complete without a visit to this, the world's most accessible mainland gannet colony (see box, page 355).

Hawke's Bay Wine Country

Napier and Hastings are almost entirely encircled by the **Hawke's Bay's Wine Country**, which has been one of New Zealand's largest and most exalted grape-growing regions since 1851 when French Marist missionaries planted the first vines. Largely the province of boutique producers, the rolling countryside is packed with citrus fruit and olive farms along with over seventy wineries, most with cellar doors and some with a restaurant, or at least the chance to picnic in landscaped grounds.

With a climatic pattern similar to that of the great Bordeaux vineyards, Hawke's Bay produces fine **Chardonnay** and lots of **Merlot**. **Cabernet Sauvignon** is also big but struggles to ripen in cooler summers. Many winemakers are now setting Hawke's Bay up to become New Zealand's flagship producer of **Syrah**, a subtler version of the Aussie Shiraz (though it is made from the same grape) that utilizes the original European name.

GETTING AROUND HAWKE'S BAY WINE COUNTRY

By car You can easily drive yourself around and visit the wineries, but taking a tour obviates the need to find a designated driver.

Wine tours At least half a dozen tours are on offer, most visiting four or five wineries over the course of a morning or afternoon. They're mainly Napier-based but will pick up in Hastings and Havelock North, usually for free. Self-guided bike tours are also available.

TOURS

Grape Escape ☎0800 100 489, ⓦgrapeescape.net.nz. Runs half-day trips ($90), visiting four to five wineries and tasting about thirty different wines – and some cheese. Picks up and drops off at accommodation in Napier, Hastings and Havelock.

On Yer Bike 12543 SH50, Hastings ☎06 650 4627, ⓦonyerbikehb.co.nz. A great alternative to the traditional tour, with an easy off-road bike route passing seven wineries in a 20km circuit. All-day bike rental (tandems available), route map and roadside support ($55).

Vince's World of Wine ☎06 836 6705, ⓦworldofwinetours.co.nz. Great fun, with an

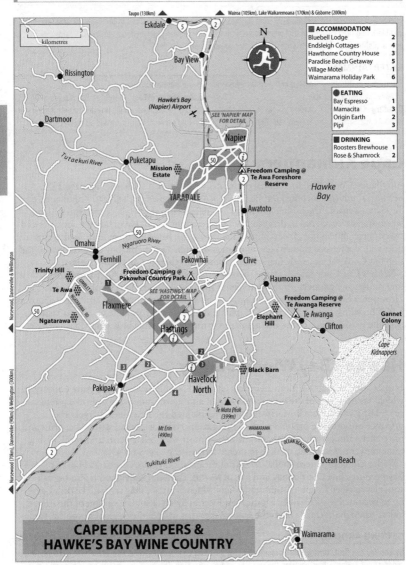

CAPE KIDNAPPERS &
HAWKE'S BAY WINE COUNTRY

entertaining, knowledgeable guide and a flexible schedule. A half-day trip fits in four to five wineries along with a gourmet food-board ($99) and will pick you up from Napier or Hastings.

INFORMATION

Wine leaflets The region's i-SITE offices carry the free *Hawke's Bay Food & Wine Map* leaflet, which can also be downloaded from the Hawke's Bay Winegrowers website (ⓦ hawkesbaywine.co.nz), outlining the local wineries, speciality stores and winery restaurants – for the pick of the cellar doors, see page 356.

Arts and crafts leaflets The free *Hawke's Bay Art Guide* (ⓦ hawkesbayartguide.co.nz) directs you to studios, workshops and galleries of painters, sculptors, potters and craftspeople in the region.

THE CAPE KIDNAPPERS GANNETS

Gannets are big birds that can live for up to thirty years. They're distinguished by their gold-and-black head markings and fearlessness around humans. The birds at Cape Kidnappers start nesting in June, laying their eggs from early July through to October, with the chicks hatching six weeks later. Once fledged, at around fifteen weeks, the young gannets embark on their inaugural flight, a marathon, as-yet-unexplained 3000km journey to Australia, where they spend a couple of years before flying back to spend the rest of their lives in New Zealand, returning to their place of birth to breed each year. It is thought that the birds mate for life, using the same or an adjacent nest each year, but recent observation indicates that adultery does occur – usually because of mistaken identity.

During the **breeding season** (July–mid-Oct), the cape is closed to the public. One of the three colonies, the Saddle, is reserved for scientific study and allows no public access. The remaining two colonies, Plateau and Black Reef, are open outside the breeding season, and at the former you will get within a metre or so of the birds. When pairs reunite, after a fishing or nest-material-gathering trip, you can get close enough to hear their beaks clack together in greeting.

VISITING THE GANNETS

There are three ways to visit the gannets – on foot and with two tours that can be booked through the Napier, Hastings or Havelock i-Sites – all starting from Clifton, 20km southeast of Napier, though the tours can pick you up for an additional cost. Most tours are tide-dependent and travel to the colony along the beach below rock-fall-prone 100m-high cliffs.

On foot (late Oct–April; roughly 6hr return). The most strenuous but least expensive way to get to the gannets is to walk the 11km along the beach from Clifton. No permits are needed, but you'll need to check tide tables and pick up the DOC's useful Guide to Cape Kidnappers leaflet from the Hastings or Napier i-SITEs or download a PDF version from the DOC website. You set off from Clifton about three hours after high tide; head back no more than ninety minutes after low tide. Once at the access point on the beach it's a strenuous 25min climb to the Plateau Colony across private land, though the track is well marked.

Gannet Beach Adventures ☏ 0800 426 638, Ⓦ gannets.com. The traditional gannet trip, aboard tractor-drawn trailers along the beach. The pace and approach give plenty of opportunities to appreciate the geology along the way and observe the birds at close quarters. Tours end near a DOC shelter from where it's a 25min uphill slog to the Plateau, where you'll have half an hour to admire the birds. For an extra $45 they'll pick you up from Napier, Havelock North or Hastings i-SITEs. Daily late Oct–early May; 4hr; $42.

Gannet Safaris ☏ 06 875 800 0888, Ⓦ gannetsafaris.com. If you don't fancy the uphill walk, want more time with the birds and the chance to see and learn about the spectacular *Summerlee Station* luxury accommodation complex, this is the tour for you. You travel overland by minibus, passing through *Summerlee Station*, and continue through some stunning scenery and great views to the colonies, where you have 55 minutes or so to gander at the gannets (3hr; $75, or $105 with pick-up from Napier or Hastings).

Hastings

Inland **HASTINGS**, 20km south of Napier, was once a rival to its northern neighbour as Hawke's Bay's premier city, buoyed by the wealth generated by the surrounding farmland and orchards. Napier's ascendancy as a tourist destination put Hastings firmly in second place, although its surrounding countryside is much more striking, especially around the hilly farming area and upmarket satellite suburb of **Havelock North**.

After the same earthquake that rocked Napier in 1931, Hastings embraced the Californian-inspired **Spanish Mission** style of Art Deco architecture: roughcast stucco walls, arched windows, small balconies, barley-twist columns and heavily overhung roofs clad in terracotta tiles. The finest examples can be seen in an hour or so, using the self-guided *Art Deco Hastings* walk leaflet ($1 from the i-SITE). If time is short, limit your wanderings to Heretaunga Street East, taking in the gorgeous bronzework and sumptuous lead lighting of the **Westerman Building** or, at the corner of Hastings Street, the **Hawke's Bay Opera House** – built fifteen years before the earthquake, but remodelled to create the region's finest Spanish Mission facade.

HAWKE'S BAY WINERIES

There are over seventy **wineries** in the entire region. Those listed below are recommended, either because they stand out for some particular reason other than wine tastings or because they make good lunch spots. You may find it cheaper to buy the same bottle of wine at a local supermarket than at the cellar door.

Napier's closest wineries are 8km to the southwest in among the residential suburb of **Taradale** but they don't have the same countryside appeal as those around **Hastings**. The most aesthetic vineyards sit in the cluster just east of **Havelock North** and along the coast at Te Awanga; while the fastest-growing wine district in Hawke's Bay is around **Fernhill**, 10km northwest of Hastings. Cellar door **opening hours** are generally daily 10am–5pm in summer, but they are sometimes closed on Monday, Tuesday and even Wednesday when things are quiet – if there's somewhere you must visit, phone first. The best of the winery restaurants are those at *Elephant Hill*, and *Te Awa*.

★ **Black Barn** Black Barn Rd, Havelock North ☎ 06 877 7985, ⓦ blackbarn.com. Designer winery complex with free cellar-door tastings, a lunch bistro and café (mains around $35) that also opens for dinner on Fridays, an art gallery and a growers' market. The amphitheatre hosts a number of outdoor events, including cinema, through the summer. Tastings daily 10am–4pm; bistro and café Nov–Mar Mon–Wed & Sun 10am–5pm, Thurs–Sat 10am–9pm; Apr–Oct Wed & Sun 10am–5pm, Thurs–Sat 10am–9pm; growers' market Dec–Feb 9am–noon.

Elephant Hill 86 Clifton Rd, Te Awanga ☎ 06 872 6060, ⓦ elephanthill.co.nz. Modern minimalistic winery on the coast with an award-winning restaurant/bar positioned for ocean views and open for lunch and dinner (mains around $40). Best known for its Chardonnay, Rose and Syrah; a tasting fee of $5 is redeemable on purchase of a bottle. Tastings: daily April–Oct 11am–4pm; Nov–March 11am–5pm.

Mission Estate 198 Church Rd, Taradale ☎ 06 845 9350, ☎ 06 845 9354 for restaurant bookings, ⓦ missionestate.co.nz. This is a former seminary, which produced sacramental wines in 1851 along with a little tipple for the Fathers. Today the estate owns several vineyards on different soil types in the region, plus two in Marlborough. All grapes are brought to the Mission to produce a variety of wines, so it's a great place to start. Tastings are $5 and include a wine glass as a gift. Lunch and dinner are served on the terrace or in the old seminary building; expect expertly presented classical dishes such as seared lamb rack ($39.50) and prosciutto-wrapped chicken ($33.50). Tastings Mon–Sat 9am–5pm, Sun 10am–4.30pm.

Ngatarawa 305 Ngatarawa Rd, Bridge Pa ☎ 06 879 7603, ⓦ ngatarawa.co.nz. Dependable small winery with educational tastings ($5 service charge) of quality tipples in a century-old racing stables overlooking attractive picnic areas and a pétanque pitch. Tastings daily 10am–5pm.

Te Awa 2375 SH50, Fernhill ☎ 06 879 7602, ⓦ teawa.com. This winery produces exceptional reds (Merlot and Cabernet Merlot) that are more aromatic and livelier than many of their Hawke's Bay rivals; tastings are $5, redeemable on cellar door purchase or dining. Treat yourself to lunch in one of New Zealand's finest winery restaurants, dining inside or out on dishes such as the charcuterie board ($46) or braised beef cheek with smoked beetroot purée ($29). Tastings daily 11am–4pm.

Both the city and Havelock North are handy bases for touring the wonderful Hawke's Bay Wine Country, with many of the vineyards within easy reach.

Te Mata Peak

2km south of Havelock North, accessed via Simla Rd and Te Mata Peak Rd • ⓦ tematapark.co.nz

Driving from Hastings south to Havelock North, the long ridge of limestone bluffs which make up the 399m **Te Mata Peak** loom into view. The ridge is held to be the supine form of a Māori chief, Rongokako, who choked on a rock as he tried to eat through the hill – one of many Herculean feats he attempted while wooing the daughter of a Heretaunga chief; according to legend, overcome with grief at her father's death, Rongokako's daughter threw herself off the peak.

Te Mata Peak Road winds up the hill to a wonderful vantage point that's especially picturesque at sunrise or sunset, and its panoramic views stretch over the fertile plains across Hawke's Bay and east towards Cape Kidnappers. There are several car parks within the area, the handiest being at Saddle Lookout almost at the top of Te Mata

EATING
Hawke's Bay Farmers' Market	1
Opera Kitchen	4
Rush Munro's	2
Sutto Café	3

ACCOMMODATION
| A1 Backpackers | 1 |
| Hastings Top 10 Holiday Park | 2 |

DRINKING
| Common Room | 1 |

Peak Road, where five moderate **walking tracks** meander along ridges around the summit and descend through groves of native trees (1–3hr return).

Ocean Beach and Waimarama
32km south of Hastings along Waimarama Rd; Ocean Beach accessed at the junction with Ocean Beach Rd

The beautiful surf-pounded **Ocean Beach** and **Waimarama** are the main swimming **beaches** for Hastings and Havelock North, and worth visiting just for the stunning countryside you pass through to get to them. Ocean Beach is slightly closer, around a thirty-minute drive south of Hastings, and is largely undeveloped save for the pretty Māori village beside its shore. Waimarama, a ten-minute drive further south, is slightly more developed with a couple of residential streets. Both beaches have expansive stretches of fine sand backed by sandstone cliffs – at Ocean Beach you can explore for 7km in either direction, making it perfect a long walk.

ARRIVAL AND DEPARTURE   HASTINGS

By bus Long-distance buses stop at Russell Street North, a few steps from the i-SITE. Local operator GoBay (☎ 06 878 9250) runs to Napier (Mon–Fri 30 daily, Sat & Sun 5 daily; 1hr) and Havelock North (Mon–Fri 15 daily, Sat & Sun 3 daily; 15mins) from the library (see page 350).
Destinations Auckland (2 daily; 7hr 55min); Gisborne (1 daily; 4hr 20min); Napier (5 daily; 25min); Palmerston North (2–3 daily; 2hr 20min); Rotorua (2 daily; 4hr 20min);

Taupo (3 daily; 2hr 35min); Wellington (2 daily; 5hr).
By plane Regular direct flights with Air New Zealand and Jetstar from Auckland, Wellington and Christchurch, as well as a Sounds Air (☎ 0800 505 005, ⓦ soundsair.com) service to Blenheim arrive at Hawke's Bay Airport, which is about 20km north of town on SH2. The airport is served by Super Shuttle (☎ 0800 748 885, ⓦ supershuttle.co.nz) charging $43 to Hastings ($45 to Havelock North); and Village Shuttle

6

(☎0800 777 796, ⊕villageshuttle.co.nz) who charge a few dollars less.

Destinations Auckland (11–15 daily; 1hr); Blenheim (4 weekly; 1hr); Christchurch (2–3 daily; 1hr 35min); Wellington (3–5 daily; 1hr).

By taxi Hastings Taxis (☎06 878 5055, ⊕hastingstaxis.co.nz).

INFORMATION AND ACTIVITIES

Visitor information Hastings i-SITE, 100 Heretaunga St East (Mon–Fri 9am–5pm, Sat 9am–3pm & Sun 10am–2pm; ☎0800 4278 4647, ⊕visithastings.co.nz), has wineries leaflets, a gift shop and keen staff will help with bookings and sell bus tickets. Havelock North's i-SITE (cnr Middle and Te Aute rds; Mon–Fri 10am–5pm, Sat 9am–4pm & Sun 9am–3pm; ☎06 877 9600, ⊕havelocknorthnz.com) can also help with bookings and rents bikes.

Fruit-picking work The fruit harvest begins in February and lasts three or four months, providing casual, hard-going, low-paid orchard work for those willing to thin, pick or pack fruit. The hostels are a good source of work and up-to-the-minute information though you'll be competing with locals and itinerant old fruit-picking hands; for more information on working in the region, see page 59.

Services Hastings Library, cnr Eastbourne and Warren streets (Mon 10am–6pm, Tues 9am–8pm, Wed–Fri 9am–6pm, Sat 10am–4pm, Sun 1–4pm) offers limited use of free wi-fi) and internet terminals. There's also free wi-fi in the CBD.

ACCOMMODATION

Availability of budget accommodation is affected by the fruit-picking season: from mid-February to May you'll struggle to find cheap rooms, so book well ahead. Limited **freedom camping** can be found at Pakowhai Country Park carpark on the northern outskirts of Hastings or otherwise at the oceanfront Te Awanga Reserve, a twenty-minute drive towards Cape Kidnappers. For more luxurious accommodation, head for Havelock North, where **B&Bs** and swanky **self-catering** predominate. If you've got your own transport and want to be by the beach, there are a couple of places to stay at Waimarama.

HASTINGS

A1 Backpackers 122 Stortford St ☎06 873 4285, ⊕a1backpackers.co.nz; map p.357. Less of a work-camp feel than Hastings' other backpackers, set in a well-kept peaceful villa whose helpful owner offers free local pick-up for two-night stays. The dorms are adequate but the doubles more comfortable. Off-street parking. Dorms $30, doubles $66

Bluebell Lodge 137 Longlands Rd East, 5km southwest of Hastings ☎06 876 5243, ⊕bluebell-cottage.co.nz; map p.354. Set in a pleasant orchard and offering a small studio room or larger self-contained cottages, one of them with two bedrooms ideal for families, all sharing the family grounds and swimming pool. Studio $159, cottages $179

Hastings Top 10 Holiday Park 610 Windsor Ave ☎06 878 6692, ⊕hastingstop10.co.nz; map p.357. Handy but uninspiring town campsite with tent sites, a range of modern units (the more expensive of which are quite swish) and good facilities, though it does get busy in the fruit-picking season. Camping $23, cabins $80, units $165

Hawthorne Country House 1420 Railway Rd South (SH2), 6km southwest of Hastings ☎06 878 0035, ⊕hawthorne.co.nz; map p.354. Elegant and welcoming B&B in a grand Edwardian villa surrounded by croquet lawns and farmland. The five en-suite rooms are decorated with understated elegance, while good breakfasts, afternoon teas and drinks with canapés all make for a relaxed atmosphere. $275

HAVELOCK NORTH

★**Endsleigh Cottages** 22 Endsleigh Rd, 3km southwest off Middle Rd ☎06 877 7588, ⊕endsleighcottages.co.nz; map p.354. The impeccably tidy cottages here come with claw-foot bathtubs and vintage furnishings, and each one has a cute veranda to enjoy the peaceful surroundings. Enclosed in beautiful gardens with a small orchard and plenty of native birdlife, the original bushman's cottage is the only of the three cottages here without a kitchen but does have a BBQ. Bikes are available for guests. Bushman's cottage $125, cottages $250

Village Motel Cnr Te Aute and Porter ☎06 877 5401, ⊕villagemotel.co.nz; map p.354. Centrally located motel run by friendly owners. The twelve studios have air conditioning and spa pools, but otherwise feels a bit empty; the larger apartments have good-sized kitchens. Breakfast is available for a fee. Studios $165, apartments $185

WAIMARAMA

★**Paradise Beach Getaway** 94 Harper Rd ☎06 874 6177 or ☎02 161 0167, ✉winward@xtra.co.nz; map p.354. This modern two-bedroom self-contained unit on the ground floor of a residential house is clean, comfortable and above all else excellent value. There's a private deck with BBQ (no ocean views), but a short path leads down to the stunning beach. $160

Waimarama Holiday Park Foreshore, Waimarama Rd ☎06 874 6735, ✉waimaramajetboattours@xtra.co.nz; map p.354. Old-school camping ground with almost half the sites occupied by seasonal fruit pickers. Basic facilities include a kitchen, laundry and hot showers, but its right on the beachfront. Powered sites $25, camping $23

EATING

For a town of its size, Hastings is relatively poorly supplied with good places to eat, though an ever-expanding selection of places in neighbouring **Havelock North** bumps up the quota, and lunches at the region's **wineries** are a good if pricey option (see page 356).

HASTINGS

Bay Espresso 141 Karamu Rd, 3km east of Hastings ☎06 876 5782, ⓦwww.bayespresso.co.nz; map p.354. A rustic café with plenty of garden seating that's a locals' weekend home-from-home. Superb coffee and breakfasts are supplemented by lunch specials ($14–20). If you're hungry, try the Orchardists Big Breakfast, which boasts chorizo and black pudding ($18.50). Mon–Fri 7am–4pm, Sat & Sun 8am–4pm.

Hawke's Bay Farmers' Market Hawke's Bay Showgrounds, Kenilworth Rd, ⓦhawkesbayfarmersmarket.co.nz; map p.357. On a fine Sunday morning, skip breakfast and head straight to this excellent market, where innumerable stalls introduce you to fresh local produce, coffee and pastries while a local musician or two entertains. It's held indoors in winter. Also at Clive Square in Napier (Sat 9am–1pm). Sun 8.30am–12.30pm.

Opera Kitchen 312 Eastbourne St East ☎06 870 6020, ⓦoperakitchen.co.nz; map p.357. Classy licensed café showcasing local produce through simple but delicious dishes (under $26) served in stripped-back surroundings. Worth checking out if just for the knitted hats they put on boiled eggs ($9.50 with Marmite soldiers). Mon–Fri 7.30am–4pm, Sat 9am–3pm.

Rush Munro's 704 Heretaunga St West ☎06 873 9050, ⓦrushmunro.co.nz; map p.357. A small ice-cream garden that's been packing in the locals for ninety years – even Bill Clinton once stopped in. For the retro experience go for the hokey pokey ice cream ($4.50). Mon–Fri 11am–5pm, Sat & Sun 10am–5pm.

Sutto Café 103-5 King St ☎06 878 4163; map p.357. With funky coloured outdoor seating and popular with local workers, *Sutto's* has the usual range of counter food plus some interesting specials such as Greek *spanakopita* ($12.20) or chicken and cranberry filo ($10.50). Mon–Fri 7am–4.30pm, Sat & Sun 8am–3pm.

HAVELOCK NORTH

Mamacita 12 Havelock Rd ☎06 877 6200, ⓦmamacita.co.nz; map p.354. Expect plenty of chaotic artwork, a punchy menu covering tacos and quesadillas and the customary jugs of margarita and sangria. Tues–Sun 4.30–10pm.

★ **Origin Earth** 393 Te Mata Rd ☎06 878 2786 ⓦoriginearth.co.nz; map p.354. This place specializes in homemade cheeses, crackers and chutney, and you can sample a whole variety of its produce with ten cheese sticks for $5 and a three-cheese sharing platter for two ($22). There's excellent freshly ground coffee too, and an imaginative menu from polenta pancakes to pulled pork and feta tortillas, all under $20. Daily 9am–3pm.

Pipi 16 Joll Rd ☎06 877 8993, ⓦpipicafe.co.nz; map p.354. Impressive in its pinkness, this casual and very popular café and pizza restaurant exudes casual style. Nothing matches but everything fits, and you help yourself from the drinks fridge and tell them what you've had when you pay. The food's great too, offering the likes of fishcakes with rocket and white bean mash ($23), great pizzas (from $16) and a slew of local wines. Tues–Sun 4–10pm.

DRINKING

★ **Common Room** 227 Heretaunga St East, Hastings ☎027 656 8959, ⓦcommonroombar.com; map p.357. Cosy wine bar with threadbare sofas and a straightforward admissions policy: "no idiots". Occasional DJs, but mainly ranges from live bands playing electronica to buskers with banjos. The whimsical kitchen whips up great small plates ($10) and steak burgers ($16). Wed–Sat 3pm–late.

Roosters Brewhouse 1470 Omahu Rd, Flaxmere 7km northwest of Hastings ☎06 879 5158; map p.354. Micro-brewery offering traditional natural brews, best enjoyed in the pleasant café or outdoors at the garden tables. There's free tasting of its English ale, lager and dark beers, and you can buy a flagon to take away – a wise move considering the prices elsewhere. Occasional live music. Mon–Fri 8.30am–7pm, Sat & Sun noon–7pm.

Rose & Shamrock 15 Napier Rd, Havelock North ☎06 877 2999, ⓦroseandshamrock.co.nz; map p.354. Popular for Sunday roasts with the agricultural and blue-rinse gangs, this fair attempt at a pub has 24 Irish, English and Kiwi beers on tap, plus well-priced bar meals ($19–28), including beef and Guinness pie or the fisherman's basket. Tripe nights, quiz nights and occasional live Irish folk music. Daily 10.30am–late.

ENTERTAINMENT

Focal Point 126 Heretaunga Street East ☎06 871 5418, ⓦhastings.focalpointcinema.co.nz. This cinema has three screens and mostly shows mainstream movies.

Hawke's Bay Opera House 101 Hastings St South ☎06 871 5000, ⓦhawkesbayoperahouse.co.nz. Although closed at the time of writing for extensive renovations, the opera house was due to re-open in late 2018.

Wellington and the south

WELLINGTON

Wellington and the south

Understandably, many people visiting New Zealand often reject its cities in favour of rural splendour – with the exception of Wellington. The urban jewel in the country's otherwise bucolic crown, Wellington is by far New Zealand's most engaging and attractive metropolis, a buzzing, compact cosmopolitan capital flanked by a stunning waterfront and surrounded by lush mountains. Beyond these mountains are the flats of Wairarapa, a farming district shaped by early European settlement with quaint market towns and boutique vineyards; while the dramatic coastline of Cape Palliser at the very southern tip of the North Island is a reminder of just how remarkable the countryside actually is. By contrast, the congested west coast, the main arterial route to Auckland, is peppered with ordinary commuter satellite suburbs and sandy beaches.

As New Zealand's underrated capital, **Wellington** is a beautifully laidback city where the **café culture**, culinary back alleys and multicultural nightlife speaks volumes about its friendliness. To the outside world, "Wellywood" is better known for its blustery rain and unexpected status as the global film industry's leading digital workshop (it burst into the limelight after the phenomenal success of the *Lord of the Rings* trilogy).

When the sun does come out, Wellingtonians like to remind everyone that there's no better place to live and work – **outdoor adventures** abound from cycle tracks in the mountains, forest hikes to lookouts bursting with birdlife, kayaks around the harbour and wonderful rural countryside that is so close by but feels a world away.

Extending northwest from the city, a succession of satellite towns hug the **Kapiti Coast** to Palmerston North. Paekakariki and **Paraparaumu** have the prettiest **beaches**, popular with both families and surfers and bustling on sunny weekends and summer holidays. Otherwise, there's nothing especially captivating along this coast other than the offshore **Kapiti Island**, a thriving nature reserve where you can spot kiwi and many other native birds along the island's tranquil walking tracks.

Directly north of Wellington, the ever-growing commuter towns of the **Hutt Valley** sprawl alongside the SH2, the most scenic of the two roads connecting Wellington with the north. Beyond Upper Hutt, the road twists and turns over the majestic Rimutaka Forest Range, descending eventually into the flat farming lands of the **Wairarapa**. Here, a string of market towns offer interesting museums and antique shops pervading its immigrant past, as well as the delightfully compact micro-vineyards around pretty **Martinborough**, all popular at weekends amongst the Wellington set. The remote coastal scenery of **Cape Palliser** on the southern tip of the island is a wild and whimsical spot for long, blistery seaside walks and where you can get close to **fur seals**.

Wellington

With a population of just over 200,000 (almost 500,000 in the wider region), **Wellington** is New Zealand's third most populous centre, but while Auckland grows more commercially important (and self-important in the eyes of its residents), Wellington reaches for higher ground as the nation's cultural capital: as the country's only city with a beating heart, it warrants a stay of at least a couple of days – more if you can manage it. Wellingtonians have cultivated the country's most sophisticated café society, microbreweries, nightlife and arts scene, especially in late summer when the city hosts a series of arts and fringe festivals (see page 385).

CUBA STREET

Highlights

❶ Cuba Street Stroll around this bohemian hub for people-watching, great cafés, boutique shops, hawker stalls and hip nightlife. See page 365

❷ Te Papa This striking national museum showcases New Zealand's natural and bicultural history along with the country's premier art collection. See page 368

❸ Parliamentary District New Zealand's political history unravels in this old quarter, with the original documents of the Treaty of Waitangi to the Beehive, home to the present government. See page 370

❹ Southern Walkway Wander through woodlands to the magnificent Mount Victoria lookout and along the Southern Walkway for an exceptional half-day hike to the Wellington coast. See page 377

❺ Kapiti Island A chunk of endemic New Zealand sits off the Kapiti Coast with soothing walking trails and exceptional fauna and flora offering a real opportunity to spot the elusive kiwi. See page 387

❻ Vineyards Cycle or walk around a compact collection of tiny vineyards specialising in Pinot Noir and Sauvignon Blanc, all amongst the quaint village of Martinborough. See page 390

❼ Cape Palliser Climb the 250 steps to the Cape Palliser lighthouse for sweeping views of this spectacular wild coastline and watch fur seas frolic around rocky bays. See page 392

HIGHLIGHTS ARE MARKED ON THE MAP ON PAGE 364 AND 366

Wedged between glistening Wellington Harbour (technically Port Nicholson) and the turbulent Cook Strait, tight surrounding hills restrict Wellington to a compact core, with much of the city centre built on land reclaimed from the sea. Distinctive historical and modern architecture spills down to the bustling waterfront with its beaches, marinas and restored warehouses, overlooked by Victorian and Edwardian weatherboard villas and bungalows that climb the steep slopes to an encircling belt of parks and woodland, a natural barrier to development. Many homes are accessed by narrow winding roads or precipitous stairways flanked by a small funicular railway to haul groceries and just about anything else up to the house. What's more, "Welly", as it's locally known, is New Zealand's **windy city**, buffeted by chilled air funnelled through Cook Strait, its force amplified by the wind-tunnelling effect of the city's high-rise buildings.

Brief history

Māori oral histories tell of the demigod **Maui**, who fished up the North Island, with Wellington Harbour being the mouth of the fish; and of the first Polynesian navigator, **Kupe**, discovering Wellington Harbour in 925 AD and naming the harbour's islands Matiu (Somes Island) and Makaro (Ward Island) after his daughters. Several *iwi* settled around the harbour, including the Ngati Tara people, who enjoyed the rich fishing areas and the protection the bay offered.

Both Abel Tasman (in 1642) and Captain Cook (in 1773) were prevented from entering Wellington Harbour by fierce winds and, apart from a few sealers and whalers, it wasn't until 1840 that the first wave of **European settlers** arrived. They carved out a niche on a large tract of harbourside land, purchased by the New Zealand Company, who set up their initial beachhead, named Britannia, on the northeastern beaches at Petone. Shortly afterwards, the Hutt River flooded, forcing the settlers to move around

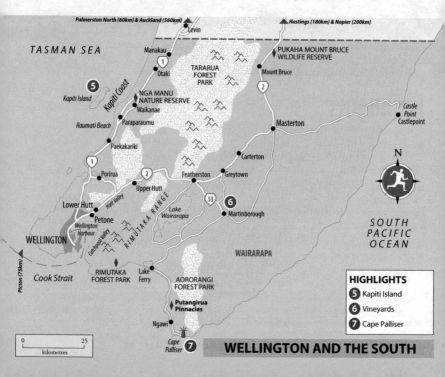

CITY TOURS

An ever-increasing number of clued-up local outfits offer entertaining and informative tours of the city; the best are listed below.

Flat Earth ☎0800 775 805, ⓦflatearth.co.nz. Upmarket outfit with a range of tours (from $175), including Wellington city highlights, nature and eco tours, as well as film tours.

Movie Tours ☎027 419 3077, ⓦadventuresafari. co.nz. Dedicated movie-theme tour options such as the half-day Wellington Movie Tour, including LOTR locations and Weta (daily; from $70).

Wellington Guided Tours ☎04 389 2161, ⓦwellingtonguidedtours.co.nz. Run by a local family, this more personalised tour visits the city's peripheral sights by minivan with the shorter 2hr30min tour

taking in two lookout stops and a scenic drive around Wellington's bays ($55) or the longer Wilderness Tour taking in both forest and coastal vistas ($120).

Wellington on Foot ⓦwellingtononfoot.co.nz. The most informal of the city's walking tours (Oct–Mar, Mon–Sat; 2hrs $25) with long-time locals exploring the hip areas of town and focusing on what it's like to live and grow-up in the city.

Zest Food Tours ☎ 04 801 9198, ⓦzestfoodtours. co.nz. Gourmet walking tours (daily; from $185) taking in coffee roasteries, chocolate producers, cheese and honey tastings and more.

the harbour to a more sheltered site known as Lambton Harbour (where the central city has grown up) and the relatively level land at Thorndon, at that time just north of the shoreline. They renamed the settlement after the Iron Duke and began **land reclamations** into the harbour, a process that continued for more than a hundred years.

In 1865, the growing city succeeded Auckland as the **capital** of New Zealand, and by the turn of the twentieth century the original shoreline of Lambton Harbour had been replaced by wharves and harbourside businesses, which formed the hub of the city's coastal trade; Wellington has prospered ever since.

The city centre

Central Wellington is easily walkable; the heart of the **city centre** stretches south from the train station to Courtenay Place along the backbone of the central business and shopping district, **Lambton Quay**. The main areas for eating, drinking and entertainment are further south around Willis Street, Courtenay Place, arty **Cuba Street**, and down to the waterfront at Queens Wharf with a bustling **promenade** alongside the harbour. From the central **Civic Square**, points of interest run both ways along the promenade, including the city's star attraction, **Te Papa**, the ground-breaking national museum.

Civic Square & City-to-Sea Bridge

A popular venue for outdoor events, **Civic Square** was extensively revamped in the early 1990s by New Zealand's most influential and versatile modern architect, **Ian Athfield**, who juxtaposed old and new, regular and irregular forms and incorporated artwork. The open space is full of interesting sculptures, including Neil Dawson's *Ferns* – metal fronds linked into a ball that appears to float above the square. Extending from the square leading to the waterfront is the broad **City-to-Sea Bridge**, decorated with Para Matchitt's timber sculptures of birds, whales and celestial motifs that symbolize the arrival of Māori and European settlers.

City Gallery Wellington

101 Wakefield St • Daily 10am–5pm • Donation optional • ☎04 801 3021, ⓦcitygallery.org.nz

At the heart of Civic Square the impressive 1939 Art Deco **City Gallery Wellington** hosts touring shows of national and international contemporary works through three exhibition spaces. All are free, but there's sometimes an entry fee for events at the auditorium. The stylish *Nikau Gallery Café* (see page 382) opens onto an external terrace.

CENTRAL WELLINGTON

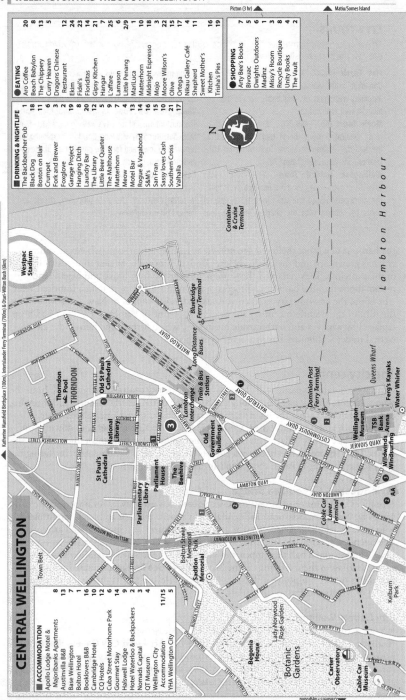

■ ACCOMMODATION

Apollo Lodge Motel & Majoribanks Apartments	8
Austinvilla B&B	13
Base Wellington	7
Bolton Hotel	1
Booklovers B&B	16
Cambridge Hotel	10
CQ Hotels	12
Cuba Street Motorhome Park	6
Gourmet Stay	14
Halswell Lodge	9
Hotel Waterloo & Backpackers	2
Nomads Capital	3
QT Museum	4
Wellington City Accommodation	11/15
YHA Wellington City	5

■ DRINKING & NIGHTLIFE

The Backbencher Pub	1
Black Dog	18
Boston on Blair	11
Crumpet	6
Fork and Brewer	3
Foxglove	2
Garage Project	19
Hanging Ditch	8
Laundry Bar	20
The Library	12
Little Beer Quarter	5
The Malthouse	4
Matterhorn	7
Meow	13
Motel Bar	16
Rogue & Vagabond	16
S&M's	16
San Fran	15
Sassy loves Cash	10
Southern Cross	21
Valhalla	17

● EATING

Aro Coffee	20
Beach Babylon	8
The Chippery	13
Curry Heaven	5
Dragons Chinese Restaurant	12
Ekim	24
Fidel's	23
Floriditas	14
Gipsy Kitchen	21
Hangar	7
L'affare	25
Lamason	6
Little Penang	2/9
MariLuca	1
Matterhorn	18
Midnight Espresso	3
Mojo	22
Moore Wilson's	15
Olive	15
Ortega	17
Nikau Gallery Café	11
Shepherd	
Sweet Mother's Kitchen	16
Trisha's Pies	19

■ SHOPPING

Arty Bee's Books	7
Bivouac	5
Dwights Outdoors	6
Madinz	1
Missy's Room	8
Recycle Boutique	4
Unity Books	3
The Vault	2

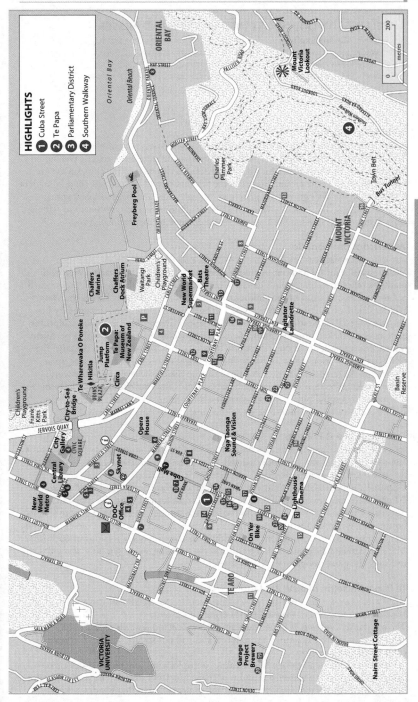

HIGHLIGHTS

1 Cuba Street
2 Te Papa
3 Parliamentary District
4 Southern Walkway

7

WELLINGTON TRANSPORT INFORMATION AND PASSES

The useful **Metlink Explorer** ($21) gives one day of unlimited bus and train travel throughout the Wellington region from 9am on weekdays and all day at weekends. You can buy the pass from bus drivers, train staff, Metlink ticket offices or Fix convenience stores.

For region-wide **train and bus information**, pick up the free *Metlink Network Map* or any of the individual timetables at the visitor centre or train station, or call Metlink (☎0800 801 700, ⓦmetlink.org.nz).

Wellington Museum

3 Jervois Quay • Daily 10am–5pm • Free; museum tour by appointment $12 • ☎ 04 472 8904, ⓦ museumswellington.org.nz

Tucked behind **Queens Wharf** in a Victorian former bond store is the eclectic **Wellington Museum**. The most useful area for visitors is a detailed chronicle of the city's key events meandering around the ground floor. On the first and second floors, Māori and immigrant influences on the city's growth are presented through audio and visual displays within eerily lit annexes. The Attic, the museum's newest addition, is a real mishmash of oddities from flying saucers to King Dick, a stuffed lion donated by the Wellington zoo.

Waterfront promenade

Water Whirler erupting hourly 10am–3pm (but not 2pm) and 6–10pm; 5–10min

Wellington's beautiful harbour manifests along a **waterfront promenade** dotted with **maritime relics** stretching from Queens Wharf in the north to the city's southern beach at Oriental Bay. In front of the children's playground at Frank Kitts Park is the **Water Whirler**, a kinetic sculpture spewing water in energetic gyrations and designed by Len Lye (see page 297). Heading south towards Te Papa, twenty-three inscribed **sculptures** are randomly tucked into the landscape, some quite hidden, each one with a pertinent quote connecting some of New Zealand's foremost authors and poets to the city. The pride of the collection is that of Katherine Mansfield who was born and grew up at Thorndon. At Taranaki Wharf, you won't miss the **Hikitia**, believed to be the world's oldest working steam-powered crane ship; beside it is the **Waterfront Jump Platform**, an 8.5-metre high spiral pipe staircase where the brave jump off into the harbour below. From here, it's a two-minute stroll on to the museum, Te Papa (see below).

Te Wharewaka O Poneke

Odlins Square, between the City-to-Sea Bridge and Te Papa • April–Sept Mon–Fri 8am–4pm, Sat & Sun 9am–4pm; Oct–March Mon–Fri 7.30am–9pm, Sat & Sun 8am–9pm • Free • **Walking tours** Mon–Fri 9am–3.30pm on demand, minimum 2 people. $30 for 1hr, $40 for 2hrs • ☎ 04 901 3333, ⓦ wharewakaoponeke.co.nz

Opposite the Hikitia, the purpose-built conference centre and gallery **Te Wharewaka O Poneke** contains two magnificent ceremonial *waka* (canoes) and the *Karaka Café*. There are three distinct "sheds": Wharewaka (*waka* house), Wharewaka Tapere (events house) and Wharekai (eating house) which features an extensive Māori menu including *hangi* for one ($22). Throughout the building are contemporary versions of traditional Māori design and carvings, which transform the building into a symbolic *waka* linked to Kupe, the great navigator of Māori legend.

Te Papa: Museum of New Zealand

55 Cable St • Daily 10am–6pm; guided tours daily: April–Oct 10.15am, noon & 2pm; Nov–March 10.15am, 11am, noon, 1pm, 2pm & 3pm; Māori Highlights Tour, daily 2pm • Free; tours $20 • ☎ 04 381 7000, ⓦ tepapa.govt.nz

The constantly evolving **Te Papa: Museum of New Zealand** rewards repeat visits – you can spend an entire day among the exhibits and still not see everything. A couple of **cafés** help sustain visitors.

This celebration of all things New Zealand occupies a striking purpose-built five-storey building on the waterfront and was opened in 1998 after extensive consultation with *iwi* (tribes). Aimed equally at adults and children (including hands-on kids' activities in dedicated "discovery" spaces), it combines state-of-the-art technology and dynamic exhibits. The museum is currently undergoing a five-year redesign project with one of the five floors likely to be closed for an extended period up to 2021.

The hub of Te Papa is **Level 2**, with its interactive display on earthquakes and volcanoes, where you can experience a realistic quake inside a shaking house, see displays on the fault line that runs right through Wellington, watch Mount Ruapehu erupt on screen and hear the Māori explanation of the causes of such activity. Level 2 provides access to the outdoor **Bush City**, a synthesis of New Zealand environments complete with native plants, caves and swing bridge.

The main collection continues on **Level 4**, home to the Māori section with cultural displays by different *iwi* along with modern interpretations of the land, history, trade and immigrants including Michel Tuffery's bullock made from corned beef cans. There's even an **active marae** with a symbolic modern meetinghouse quite unlike the classic examples found around the country, protected by a sacred boulder of *pounamu* (greenstone).

Level 5 is the home of New Zealand's **national art collection**, a changing display of works on paper, oils and sculpture representing luminaries of the New Zealand art world past and present; Colin McCahon, Rita Angus, Ralph Hotere, Don Binney, Michael Smither and Shane Cotton are just a few names to watch for.

Nairn Street Cottage

68 Nairn St • Sat & Sun noon–4pm; guided tours hourly noon–3pm • $8 • ☎ 04 384 9122, ⓦ museumswellington.org.nz

The twee **Nairn Street Cottage** is central Wellington's oldest building. Though dating from 1858 (two decades into Queen Victoria's reign), it's built in late Georgian style, and its decor gives the impression the family has just left for church and will be back for Sunday lunch.

Oriental Parade and around

Immediately east of Te Papa, **Waitangi Park** is named after a long culverted stream that has been restored to its natural course, creating a small urban wetland and home to a children's playground. At the end of Herd Street, the **Chaffers Dock** development incorporates cafés and an atrium where Wellington's Sunday-morning farmers' market sets up. The park marks the start of **Oriental Parade**, Wellington's most elegant section of waterfront. Skirting **Oriental Bay**, this Norfolk-pine-lined road curls past some of the city's priciest real estate and even flanks a **beach** installed here in 2003 with sand brought across Cook Strait from near Takaka. Apart from the Freyberg pool (see page 386) and a few restaurants, there are no attractions as such, but you can extend a stroll into a full afternoon by continuing to Charles Plimmer Park and joining the Southern Walkway (see page 377) to the summit of **Mount Victoria**.

Mount Victoria Lookout

At 196m, **Mount Victoria Lookout** is one of the best of Wellington's viewpoints, offering sweeping views of the city, waterfront, docks and beyond to the Hutt Valley, all particularly dramatic around dawn or dusk. The walk to the summit is best reached from the end of Majoribanks road from where it's a 20-minute hike along a well-maintained signposted trail zigzagging up through light forest. If you don't fancy the walk, you can also reach the summit on the #20 bus (Mon–Fri only) or by car following Hawker Street, off Majoribanks Street, then taking Palliser Road, which twists uphill to the lookout. The summit is not the only viewpoint though – walk east for 5 minutes to the radio tower with equally impressive views overlooking Evans and Lyall bays. A signed trailhead between the two lookouts leads down to Oriental Bay and makes for a fantastic loop-walk back to the city; or head south along the Southern Walkway, also signposted, for 10km to Lyall Bay, a gentle four-hour walk.

7

The Botanic Gardens

Entrances on Glenmore St, Salamanca Rd, Upland Rd and on the cable car • Bus #3 or #13 • Daily dawn–dusk; visitor Centre Mon–Fri 9am–4pm, Sat & Sun 10am–3pm summer only • Free

The easiest way to explore the **Botanic Gardens** is by taking the cable car to the top and walking back down to the city through numerous pockets of landscaped gardens, grassy lawns and native forests. The lookout at the top provides decent views over the city. Pick up the free map from the Cable Car Museum or Treehouse Visitor Centre, a five-minute walk from the main entrance on Glenmore Street.

Space Place at Carter Observatory

Tues & Fri 4pm–11pm, Sat 10am–11pm, Sun 10am–5.30pm; planetarium shows: Mon–Fri 11am, 12.30pm, 3pm, Sat & Sun 10.15am and then on the hour; night shows Tues & Sat 6pm, 7pm & 8pm (book ahead) • Exhibition $10; 45min planetarium shows (incl. exhibition) $18.50 • ☎ 04 910 3140, ⊛ museumswellington.org.nz

Two minutes' walk from the upper cable car terminus is the fabulous 1941 **Carter Observatory**, which has illuminating displays on the New Zealand angle on the exploration of the southern skies, from Māori and Pacific Island astronomy and astronavigation through to recent planet searches. Of particular note are a piece of moon rock you can touch and an exhibit explaining how the ancient Māori navigated the seas using the stars. The jaw-dropping planetarium shows include a live tour of the actual night's sky.

Lady Norwood Rose Garden and Begonia House

Begonia House • Daily April–Aug 9am–4pm, Sept–March 9am–5pm • Free

The star in the Botanic Garden's firmament is the fragrant **Lady Norwood Rose Garden**, where a colonnade of climbing roses frames beds of over three hundred varieties set out in a formal wheel shape. The adjacent **Begonia House** is divided into two areas: the tropical, with an attractive lily pond, and the temperate, which has seasonal displays of begonias and gloxinias in summer, changing to cyclamen, orchids and impatiens in winter.

The Parliamentary District

The northern end of Lambton Quay marks the start of **The Parliamentary District** – keep an eye out for the Kate Sheppard-themed pedestrian crossings. The district is dominated by the grandiose **Old Government Buildings**, which at first glance appear to be constructed from cream stone, but are really wooden. Designed by colonial architect William Clayton (1823–77) to mark the country's transition from provincial to centralized government, the intention was to use stone but cost-cutting forced a rethink. Today, Victoria University's Law Faculty occupies the building and you can only walk around the building's periphery, not inside.

The Parliament Buildings

Daily 10am–4pm • Free 1hr guided tours on the hour, bookings advisable • ☎ 04 817 9503, ⊛ parliament.nz

---

THE BIGGEST VIEW IN WELLINGTON

If the city panorama from Mount Victoria isn't enough for you, head west to the higher **Brooklyn Hill**, easily identified by its crowning 67m-high **wind turbine**. Fantastic views unfold across the city and south towards the South Island's Kaikoura Ranges as the giant propeller blades whirr overhead.

To reach the turbine by car, take Brooklyn Road from the end of Victoria Street and turn left at Ohiro Road, then right at the shopping centre up Todman Street and follow the signposts (the road up to the turbine is open only between 8am–5pm April–Sept and 7am–8pm Oct–March). Bus #8 runs up Willis Street in town to Karepa Street in Ashton – get off at Ashton Fitchett Drive, a 2km walk from the summit.

RIDING THE CABLE CAR

Even if you never use the rest of Wellington's public transport system, don't miss the short scenic ride up to the leafy suburb of Kelburn and the upper section of the Botanic Gardens on the **Cable Car** (Mon–Fri 7am–10pm, Sat 8.30am–10pm, Sun 8.30am–9pm; $4 one way, $7.50 return), installed in 1902. Its shiny red railcars depart every ten minutes from the lower terminus on Cable Car Lane, just off Lambton Quay, and climb a steep, one-in-five incline to the upper terminus on Upland Road where a café lies in wait; or you can take a little time enjoying the city views along several short walks around the summit. Adjacent to the terminus, the **Cable Car Museum** (daily: 9.30am–5pm; free) contains the historic winding room with the electric drive motor and a cat's cradle of cables. Two century-old cars are on display along with plenty of background on cable cars around the world. The best way back down to the City is by foot via the Botanical Gardens (20mins) ending up at Bolton Street in **The Parliamentary District**.

Visible across Lambton Quay are the **Parliament Buildings**, the seat of New Zealand's government, a trio of highly individual structures that nonetheless sit harmoniously together. Most distinctive is the modernist **Beehive**, a seven-stepped truncated cone that houses the Cabinet and the offices of its ministers. Designed by British (and Coventry Cathedral) architect Sir Basil Spence in 1964, it was finally completed in 1982, six years after Spence's death. The Beehive is connected directly to the Edwardian Neoclassical **Parliament House**, a grand authoritarian seat of government that stands in stark contrast to the Gothic Revival **Parliamentary Library**, all high church, pomp and whimsy.

Highlights of the hour-long guided tour include the decorative **Māori Affairs Select Committee Room** with its specially commissioned carvings and woven *tukutuku* panels from all the major tribal groups in the land, and the elegantly restored 1899 Victorian Gothic library. You're led through the Debating Chamber when Parliament's not sitting; when it is, check with your guide about watching proceedings from the public gallery.

National Library of New Zealand

70 Molesworth St • Mon–Sat 9am–5pm • Free • ☎ 04 4974 3000, ⓦ natlib.govt.nz

The main reason to visit the **National Library of New Zealand** is to see three of New Zealand's most historical documents proudly housed side by side in the stylish *He Tohu* enclosure sculptured from giant *rimu* trees. The best known of the documents is the original Māori-language **Treaty of Waitangi** (see pages 154 and 698) which barely survived a long spell lost in the bowels of the Old Government Buildings, suffering water damage and gnawing by rodents before it was rescued in 1908. Eight other sheets were carried by missionaries and officers to different parts of the country collecting Māori chiefs' signatures along the way, giving a sense of how haphazard the whole process of nationalisation was.

The other two documents are the 1835 Declaration of Independence of the Northern Chiefs, and the **1893 petition for women's suffrage**, put together by iconic suffragette, Kate Sheppard, who features on the $10 note. At this third attempt she managed to amass 32,000 signatures, a quarter of the adult female population, ushering in legislation which made New Zealand the first country to give women the vote.

Old St Paul's Cathedral

Corner of Mulgrave and Pipitea sts • Daily 9.30am–5pm • Free; guided tours $5 (45min) • ☎ 04 473 6722, ⓦ oldstpauls.co.nz

From 1866 to 1964 the modest **Old St Paul's Cathedral** operated as the parish church of Thorndon, but after the houses of the Parliamentary District were taken over by government departments and foreign delegations it was only saved from demolition by sustained public protest. Among the finest European timber churches in the country, its charming interior, lit by stained-glass windows, was crafted in early English Gothic style from native timbers that progressively darken with age.

KATHERINE MANSFIELD

Katherine Mansfield Beauchamp (1888–1923) is New Zealand's most famous short-story writer. During her brief life, she revolutionized the form, eschewing plot in favour of poetic expansiveness. Virginia Woolf claimed Mansfield's work to be "the only writing I have ever been jealous of".

Mansfield lived on Tinakori Road for five years with her parents, three sisters and beloved grandmother, and the place is described in some of her works, notably *Prelude* and *A Birthday*. The family later moved to a much grander house in what is now the western suburb of Karori until, at 19, Katherine left for Europe, where she lived until dying of tuberculosis in France, aged 34.

St Paul's Cathedral

Corner of Molesworth and Hill sts • Mon–Fri 8.30am–4.30pm, Sat 10am–4pm, Sun 7.30am–6.15pm; services daily • Free • ⓦ wellingtoncathedral.org.nz

Old St Paul's could hardly stand in greater contrast to its modern successor, **St Paul's Cathedral**. A mix of Byzantine and Santa Fe styles, it was designed in the 1930s by renowned ecclesiastical architect Cecil Wood of Christchurch. Queen Elizabeth II laid the foundation stone in 1954 but the cathedral wasn't complete until 1998. The distinctive pipe organ, built in London, was originally installed in Old St Paul's.

The Katherine Mansfield Birthplace

25 Tinakori Rd • Tues–Sun 10am–4pm • $8 • ☎ 04 473 7268, ⓦ katherinemansfield.com • Bus #14 stops on nearby Park St

A ten-minute walk north from the cathedrals through Thorndon gets you to the **Katherine Mansfield Birthplace**, a modest wooden house with small garden that was Mansfield's (see page 372) childhood abode. The house has a cluttered Victorian/Edwardian charm and avant-garde decor for its time, inspired by Japonisme and the Aesthetic Movement. There's more on the author's life and career in an upstairs room, with black-and-white photos and videos including the excellent *A Woman and a Writer*.

The suburbs

Wellington's suburbs are within easy reach of the city centre and contain the ground-breaking ecosanctuary **Zealandia: Te Mara a Tane**, complemented by a fine stand of native bush a few kilometres north at **Otari-Wilson's Bush**. A number of good walks thread through the greenery of the Town Belt, or take a scenic drive around the meandering coastline of the **Miramar Peninsula**, the hub of Wellington's film industry and with pretty seaside villages, walks and lookouts over the harbour and back towards the city.

Zealandia: Te Mara a Tane

Waiapu Rd • Daily: 9am–5pm;• $19.50; guided day tour 2hr $55, or night tour 2hr30min $85, including admission (book ahead) • ☎ 04 920 9200, ⓦ visitzealandia.com • Walk 2km from the Cable Car upper terminus, catch the free shuttle from the i-SITE visitor centre (from 9.30am, roughly every hour; 10min), or #3 bus from Lambton Quay or Willis St, #18 Cuba and Ghuznee St or #21 Cuba and Manners St.

Just 3km west of the city centre in the suburb of Karori is an oasis called **Zealandia**, named after the Zealandia microcontinent that broke away from the super-continent of Gondwana some 85 million years ago. Started in the late 1990s, the sanctuary is successfully restoring native New Zealand bush and its wildlife to 2.25 square kilometres of urban Wellington. As well as restocking the area with native trees, the trust has introduced native birds – the extremely rare flightless takake, saddlebacks, kakas and fantails – as well as the tuatara, a species of iguana that became extinct on the main island but re-introduced from Kapiti Island (see page 387).

You can walk much of the 32km of paths (some almost flat, others quite rugged) without seeing anyone, although the main trail from the visitor centre to the dam is

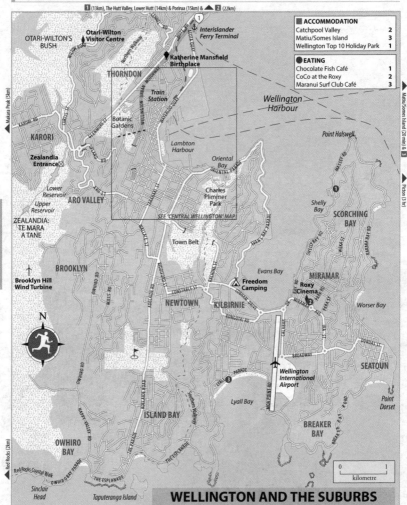

WELLINGTON AND THE SUBURBS

usually busier and takes around 90-minutes to walk. Feeding tables encourage some of the bolder birds towards the trail but otherwise it's a completely natural ecosystem and the forest resounds with birdsongs.

Otari-Wilton's Bush

160 Wilton Rd, 5km northwest of the city centre • Daily: dawn–dusk; visitor centre 9am–4pm • Free • Walk 3km from Zealandia or take the #14 bus from the Lambton Interchange (every 30min)

For a glimpse of New Zealand bush as it was before humans arrived, head to **Otari-Wilton's Bush**. The remains of the area's original podocarp-northern rata forest (including an 800-year-old rimu) were set aside in 1860 by one Job Wilton and form the core of the lush 0.8 square kilometres preserved here.

At the unstaffed visitor centre you'll find a map of the walks (all 30min–1hr), which initially follow a 100m **Canopy Walkway** of sturdy decking high in the trees across a gully.

"WELLYWOOD" AND WETA WORKSHOP

Wellington is the capital of **New Zealand's film industry**, which is centred on the Miramar Peninsula, some 12km southeast of the centre and employs around 3,000 people. During World War II, defence bases were set up here, and the large, long-abandoned buildings were prime for conversion into production company studios. The stunning natural setting has also been used as **locations** for numerous films including the *Lord of the Rings*, *King Kong*, and *The Hobbit*.

Peter Jackson still lives out this way, and his special effects and entertainment company, Weta, which he co-owns with Richard Taylor, Tania Rodger and Jamie Selkirk, has its base in Miramar. It's refreshingly low-key for the second largest **digital workshop** in the world that has worked on almost 100 blockbuster movies from Avatar to Blade Runner 2049.

Visit the workshop's **Weta Cave**, on the corner of Camperdown Road and Weka Street (daily 9am–5.30pm; free; ☎ 04 909 4100, ⊛ wetanz.co.nz; bus #2 from the city) – look for the King Kong footprint in the concrete out front – to watch an engaging twenty-minute film on their work, peek at the small museum, and browse hand-crafted figurines and limited-edition collectibles at its shop, which also sells LOTR or Hobbit movie location guides ($42).

To get the stories behind the sets, go on one of three intriguing **workshop tours** with a member of their crew ($25) including the Thunderbirds Are Go miniature set experience. Parking is difficult, so take Weta's *There and Back Again* tour ($65 including pick-up from the i-Site visitor centre, DVD introduction and some site-spotting en route), or a **movie tour** such as those listed on page 365.

To learn more about New Zealand's film industry – and to watch New Zealand films on demand for free – stop by **Nga Taonga Sound and Vision** (see page 385) in the city centre.

This leads to the **Native Botanic Garden**, laid out with plants from around the country, and the informative **Nature Trail** (30min), a good introduction to New Zealand forest plants.

Wellington Harbour

The sight of multicoloured sails scudding across the water should convince you Wellington is at its best when seen from the water. **Wellington Harbour** offers some water-based activities (see page 377), although few sailing opportunities for visitors – your best bet is to hop on the ferry to **Matiu/Somes Island** for a good look around.

Matiu/Somes Island

Dominion Post Ferry (3 services weekdays, 6 services weekends; 20min each way; $22 return; ☎ 04 499 1282, ⊛ eastbywest.co.nz). Call ahead to confirm departures

One of Wellington's best day-trips is to **Matiu/Somes Island**, in the northern reaches of the harbour. During the nineteenth century the island was a quarantine station for travellers carrying diseases such as smallpox; similarly, during both world wars, it became an intern for anyone in New Zealand considered even vaguely suspect – virtually all Germans, Italians and Japanese living in the country at the time.

In the early 1980s the islands conservation value was recognized, and it's now managed by DOC to oversee the revitalisation of **native species** and maintain the historic buildings. Already there are eight different reptiles, kakariki (the red-crowned parakeet), North Island robins, little blue penguins, the cricket-like giant weta and the ancient reptilian tuatara. Access is on the Dominion Post Ferry, which stops at the island on its cross-harbour journey to Days Bay, enabling you to explore the islands walking tracks for up to five hours (pack a picnic) before catching a ferry back to Wellington.

The Hutt Valley

34km northeast of the city centre along SH2 • Information from Upper Hutt Valley i-SITE, Arts & Entertainment Centre, Ferguson Dr; Mon–Fri 9am–4pm, Sat & Sun 9.30am–4pm; ☎ 04 527 2168, ⊛ huttvalleynz.com

At the northern end of the harbour commuter-land spreads along the **Hutt Valley**, the largest tract of flat land in these parts, accessible along SH2 and by suburban trains and buses. The original founding of Wellington is remembered in **Petone's Settlers Museum**, while nearby **Lower Hutt** has Wellington's closest campsite (see page 380), a great art gallery, and is on the way to the rugged **Rimutaka Forest Park**.

Petone Settlers Museum

The Esplanade, 2.5km east of the Petone train station • Wed–Sun 10am–4pm • Free • ☎ 04 568 8373, ⓦ petonesettlers.org.nz • Buses #81, #83, #84 or the orange Flyer (#91) from Courtenay Place and Lambton Quay

The suburb of Petone is the site of the first, short-lived European settlement in the Wellington region. The **Petone Settlers Museum**, in a striking old bathing pavilion built to commemorate the centenary of the arrival of the first British immigrants, and decorated with beautiful mosaics, tells the tale of the early Māori life in the region, the subsequent colonial settlement and relationships between the peoples.

The Dowse Art Museum

45 Laings Rd, 2km west of the Waterloo train station • Daily: 10am–5pm; café Mon–Wed 8am–4pm, Thurs & Fri 8am–8pm, Sat & Sun 9am–4pm • Free 20min tours Sat & Sun, 11am & 2pm • Donation optional • ☎ 04 570 6500, ⓦ dowse.org.nz • Bus #81, #83 or the orange Flyer from Courtenay Place and Lambton Quay

Six kilometres north of Petone sprawls **Lower Hutt**, home to the **Dowse Art Museum**, a progressive institution stunningly redeveloped by **Ian Athfield**. The well-conceived space is filled with travelling shows and occasionally challenging arts and crafts rotated from its permanent collection, as well as a decorative pataka (a raised outdoor pantry house). While there you'd be wise to visit the on-site licensed café, *Bellbird*.

Rimutaka Forest Park

Main entrance due south of Lower Hutt and 20km from Wellington along the Coast Rd • May–Sep 6am–6pm; Oct–April 6am–8pm • Pick up the *Catchpool Valley/Orongorongo Valley* leaflet from DOC in Wellington • No convenient bus service, so drive or arrange a lift/taxi

The **Rimutaka Forest Park** is popular among city-dwellers for its series of easy and short day-**walks** and cycle tracks in the attractive Catchpool Valley; there are also picnic and barbecue facilities, and a well-maintained DOC **campsite** (see page 380). From the signposted main entrance Catchpool Road winds a further 2km up the valley to the car park, the starting point for most of the walks. Keen hikers and campers will want to get as far as the braided Orongorongo River, from where a startlingly grand landscape opens out and there's a chance of spotting kiwis which are spreading throughout the forest here; there are six small DOC huts dotted along the river between 2–4hr walk from the Catchpool Valley carpark ($40-100 sole occupancy, must be pre-booked); or camping is free at Graces Stream.

ARRIVAL AND DEPARTURE   WELLINGTON

BY PLANE

Wellington International Airport (ⓦ wellingtonairport. co.nz), about 10km southeast of the city centre, is an important domestic hub, linking seventeen airports across New Zealand and handling international flights from Australia. Flying avoids the potentially choppy ferry crossing (see below), but you miss cruising through Marlborough Sound. The main airline operating out of Wellington is Air New Zealand with Jetstar also flying from Wellington to Auckland, Nelson and Dunedin. Local operator Sounds Air (☎ 0800 505 005, ⓦ soundsair.com) flies from Wellington to the South Island airports of Picton and Blenheim ($99 one way), Nelson ($120) and Westport ($199).

Destinations Auckland (24-26 daily; 1hr 5min); Blenheim (6–9 daily; 30min); Christchurch (13 daily; 1hr); Dunedin (2–4 daily; 1hr 15min); Gisborne (2–3 daily; 1hr 5min); Hamilton (4–6 daily; 1hr 10min); Invercargill (1 daily; 2hr 20min); Napier/Hastings (3–5 daily; 55min); Nelson (10–16 daily; 40min); New Plymouth (2–3 daily; 55min); Palmerston North (0–2 daily; 35min); Picton (4–8 daily; 25min); Queenstown (1 daily; 1hr 20min); Rotorua (2-3 daily; 1hr 10min); Taupo (1–2 daily; 1hr); Tauranga (3–4 daily; 1hr 15min); Timaru (2–2 daily; 1hr 20min); Westport (1–2 daily; 45min).

Getting to/from town Green Cabs (☎ 0800 464 7336) use hybrids; Wellington Combined Taxis (☎ 04 384 4444) are carbon zero-certified; both will cost about $35. The Airport Flyer bus (daily 6.35am–9.25pm; Mon–Fri every 10–20min, Sat & Sun 7am–8.45pm every 20–30min) costs $9 for the 15min journey to the city centre. Super Shuttle (☎ 0800 748

WELLINGTON ACTIVITIES

With its encircling wooded Town Belt, great city views from nearby hills and the temptation of watching seals along the southern coast, Wellington offers some excellent and easily accessible **walking**, while Wellington Harbour's brisk winds make it ideal for kitesurfing.

Starting from Charles Plimmer Park at the end of Oriental Parade, the **Southern Walkway** (11km; 4–5hr) offers excellent views of the harbour and central city (plus the option to take a dip in Island Bay), while the shorter **Red Rocks Coastal Walk** (4km each way; 2–3hr return) traces Wellington's southern shoreline from Owhiro Bay to Sinclair Head, where a colony of bachelor New Zealand fur seals takes up residence from May–Oct each year. Pick up free detailed leaflets from the i-SITE visitor centre (see page 379).

On a fine day there's little to beat **cycling** around the coastal roads that follow the bays east of the city. There is also stacks of off-road riding, much of it outlined in the *Mountain Biking in Wellington* leaflet (available free from the i-SITE visitor centre or download the PDF from ⓦwellington.govt.nz), which contains maps of key areas a short ride from the city. Highlights include the coastal track out to Red Rocks (see above) and the single-track trails around Mount Victoria (see page 369).

Other dry-land pursuits include quadbiking, in-line skating and climbing. Ferg's Kayaks (see below) rents **in-line skates** ($20/1hr; $25/2hr), perfect for use in nearby Frank Kitts Park or around Oriental Parade. Ferg's also offers an excellent and very popular **indoor climbing** wall ($21; shoes $4 each).

CYCLING AND QUAD BIKING

Makara Peak Mountain Bike Park 116–122 South Karori Rd, about 8km west of the city centre ⓦmakarapeak.org. Committed mountain-bikers should head to this two-and-a-half-square-kilometre area of forest and farmland centred on the 412m Makara Peak, up behind Karori. There's no entry fee and you'll have the run of some 40km of tracks suitable for all abilities.

Mud Cycles 424 Karori Rd, 2km short of the Makara Peak Mountain Bike Park ☎04 476 4961, ⓦmudcycles.co.nz. Rents hard tail ($35/half-day; $60/day) and full suspension mountain bikes ($50/half-day, $70/day). You can also rent for longer periods. Helmet and trail maps are included.

Wellington Adventures 1051 Coast Rd, Wainuiomata ☎0800 948 6386, ⓦwellingtonadventures.co.nz. If you have the urge to push the limit and rack up the kilometres with a few jaw-dropping views along the way, this is the outfit for you. They run one of the best value, most enjoyable and technically challenging quad-bike trips in the country. The views from the farm where it all kicks off are spectacular, but it keeps getting better as you head through a mixture of coastal scrub, farmland, forest, riverbed and beach (half-day $229, full day $329).

WATERSPORTS

Dive Wellington 432 The Esplanade, Island Bay ☎04 939 3483, ⓦdivewellington.co.nz. Scuba-diving charters to the frigate *Wellington*, scuttled a 5min boat ride off the coast in 21m of water in 2005 ($145 for two dives with gear rental), or just walk across the road and straight into the marine reserve ($40/day). There are options for people only qualified to 18m, and courses for all levels including beginners. One of the few activities that isn't weather or wind dependent.

Ferg's Kayaks Shed 6 Queens Wharf ☎04 499 8898, ⓦfergskayaks.co.nz. Rents SUPs ($40/2hr), single ($35/2hr) and double ($60/2hr) sit-on-top kayaks. They also run some fun guided trips, the best being the Lights at Night, a city-illuminated paddle round the bay with great views, lots of photograph opportunities and a light supper (6–9.30pm weather permitting; four or more $85 each, $105 each for 2; book at least three days in advance).

Wildwinds 36 Customhouse Quay ☎04 473 3458, ⓦwildwinds.co.nz. Offers a two-hour taster windsurf lesson ($110) or a series of two three-hour sessions ($295). There are also three-hour kite-surfing lessons ($195) but no rentals of any kind.

---

885 or ☎09 522 5100, ⓦsupershuttle.co.nz) charges from around $20 for the first person to a city centre destination, plus $5 for each extra person travelling to the same place.

BY FERRY

The Interislander terminal (☎0800 802 802, ⓦinterislander.co.nz) is 1km north of the train station; the Bluebridge terminal (☎0800 844 844, ⓦbluebridge.co.nz) is opposite the train station. Both companies offer year-round services across the Cook Strait to Picton (6–7 daily; 3hr). The crossing can be choppy, but does afford the chance to see the Marlborough Sounds. Both companies have different fare categories with varying flexibility – check the cancellation policy prior to booking. Interislander fares are around

$56–75 one-way for a single passenger, $177–260 for a car and driver, and $15 for bikes. Interislander's *Kaitaki*, *Kaiarahi* and *Aratere* ferries offer the Plus service ($55 extra, over-18s only), which includes private lounge, complimentary snacks and drinks including wine and beer, newspapers and internet. Get to the Interislander terminal on the free shuttle bus from the train station (by Platform 9) 50min before each sailing, or with the Interislander bus ($3) departing on Cambridge Terrace beside the *YHA* at 7.30am and outside Nomads on Wakefield a few minutes later for the 8.30am sailing (book through the hostels). Bluebridge fares are generally $53–73 one-way for a single passenger, $173–245 for a car (up to 5.5m) and driver, twin room bunk cabins cost an extra $40 and $10 for bikes. Car rental companies that permit their vehicles on the ferries include Ace, Apex, Maui (campervans only) and Jucy (see page 34).

BY TRAIN AND BUS

Train The main train station is on Bunny St. Kiwi Rail (☎0800 872 467, ⌨kiwirail.co.nz) operate the Auckland–Wellington *Northern Explorer* train (see page 31) which runs once daily, arriving from Auckland Mon, Thurs & Sat, and heading back Tues, Fri & Sun; the Wellington–Palmerston North *Capital Connection* commuter train runs weekdays only, stopping at Paraparaumu and Waikanae. Metlink (☎0800 801 700, ⌨metlink.org.nz) operate the local train network linking Wellington to the Kapiti Coast towns of Paekakariki, Paraparaumu and Waikanae, as well as to Upper Hutt and the main Wairarapa towns including Featherston and Masterton.

Destinations Auckland (Tues, Fri & Sun 1 daily; 11hr); Upper Hutt (every 30min; 45 min); Masterton (2–6 daily; 1hr 45min); National Park–Tongariro (Tues, Fri & Sun 1 daily; 5hr 20min); Otaki (Mon–Fri 1 daily; 1hr 10min); Hamilton (Tues, Fri & Sun 1 daily; 8hr 30min); Palmerston North (Sun–Fri 1–2 daily; 2hr); Paraparaumu (every 30min; 1hr).

Bus InterCity buses terminate at the train station, alongside Platform 9; ManaBus.com terminates opposite the train station on Bunny Street.

Destinations Auckland (5 daily; 11hr 15min); Napier (3 daily; 5hr 25min); New Plymouth (1–2 daily; 7hr); Palmerston North (12–14 daily; 2hr 15min); Paraparaumu (13–15 daily; 50min); Rotorua (4–5 daily; 7hr); Taupo (5–6 daily; 6hr).

BY CAR

From the north, both the SH1 through Porirua and SH2 (part of the grape-signed Classic New Zealand Wine Trail) via Lower Hutt turn into short urban motorways that merge, running scenically along the harbourside to the city centre. For details of parking, see below. Coming from or heading to the South Island, see page 377 for details of crossing Cook Strait.

GETTING AROUND

Wellington's local buses and trains are operated by Metlink (☎0800 801 700, ⌨metlink.org.nz). The Explorer ticket ($21) allows one day of unlimited travel on buses and trains (excludes Wairarapa line) after 9am weekdays or all day on weekends.

BY BUS

Wellington's extensive network of buses and trolley buses operates from Lambton Quay Interchange, just west of the train station. The bus network and timetable was due to be overhauled at the time of writing. Times and routes may vary from those shown for Wellington and its surrounds.

Bus tickets and passes All tickets and day-passes can be bought direct from the bus driver. One-way fares are $2 within the inner city, beyond which a zone system comes into operation: each extra zone costs an extra $1.50. A one-day BusAbout ticket ($9.50) allows unlimited travel around Wellington and the Hutt Valley after 9am weekdays and all weekend. For heavy use it's worth getting a Snapper stored value card on the first bus you board – it knocks off about twenty percent of the cost from each journey, although journeys are not discounted on the After Midnight fares. The After Midnight service (Sat & Sun hourly midnight–3am), designed to get the party crowd home safely, is centred on Courtenay Place and costs $6.50–13.

BY TRAIN

Suburban train services operate from the station on Bunny Street. Trains to the Hutt Valley (see page 375) and the Kapiti Coast (see page 386) leave the train station roughly every half-hour for Waterloo (for Lower Hutt; 20min; $5.50) and onto Upper Hutt (45min; $9); and Paraparaumu (1hr; $11.50). The Johnsonville line (Raroa; 20min; $5) provides handy access for hiking the Northern Walkway. You save a dollar or two when travelling outside peak hours (usually not before 9am or from 4–7pm).

Train tickets and passes A one-day Rover ticket ($14) gives you the run of the train network after 9am weekdays and all weekend. A three-day weekend Rover ($21) is valid from 4.30am Fri–midnight Sun. Bicycles are free. Tickets can be bought at the Metlink Service Centre at the main train station or on the train.

BY CAR

Making your way around the inner city is simple enough once you get used to the extensive one-way system.

Parking There is no free weekday parking in the city centre, but parking is free for up to 2hr at a time on Sat and all day Sun. Car parks are plentiful, council ones charging around $4/hr during weekdays (generally cheaper at night and on weekends), often with a one-day maximum of $15, assuming you park before 9am. The car park by the Te Papa museum is suitable for campervans, and there are several others nearby. If you don't want to move your vehicle all the time, some places charge $30–50 for a full 24hr.

Parking meters and coupon parking Most inner-city streets have parking meters (usually Mon–Thurs 8am–6pm & Fri 8am–8pm $3–$4.50/hr depending on street; otherwise free) that limit you to a 2hr stay during the metered hours and weekends 8am–6pm. Slightly further out you get coupon parking (Mon–Fri 8am–6pm) where the first 2hr are free, but to stay longer you have to display a coupon ($7.50 for all day), available from dairies and petrol stations. These areas are also free outside the set hours.

Car rental Wellington's electric car share initiative is run by Mevo, ⓦmevo.co.nz with cars available by the hour ($4) from Clyde Quay carpark near Te Papa and Queens Wharf carpark amongst others. Aside from the companies covered in Basics (see page 33), local firms offering daily deals include Rent-a-Dent, 24 Tacy St, Kilbirnie ☎04 387 9931, ⓦrentadent.co.nz; and Ace Rental Cars, Freight Drive,

Wellington Airport ☎0800 502 277, ⓦacerentalcars.co.nz. From time to time, but especially during summer, most rental companies offer free car or campervan rentals to return their vehicles back to Auckland, so ask around.

BY TAXI

You can hail one almost anywhere in town, but there are authorized stands at: the train station; on Whitmore St between Lambton Quay and Featherston St; outside the *James Smith Hotel* on Lambton Quay; off Willis St on the Bond St corner; at the corner of Courtenay Place and Taranaki St; and at the junction of Willis & Aro sts. Try Green Cabs (☎0800 464 7336) or Wellington Combined Taxis (☎04 384 4444).

BY BIKE

On Yer Bike (181 Vivian St ☎04 384 8480) has city bikes for $30 a day, mountain or road bikes for $40 a day, plus some good tips on where to go. For information on mountain bike rental and Makara Peak Mountain Bike Park, see page 377.

INFORMATION

i-SITE visitor centre 111 Wakefield, opposite Cuba St (Mon–Fri 8.30am–5pm, Sat & Sun 9am–5pm, public holidays 9am–4pm; ☎04 802 4860, ⓦwellingtonnz.com). Has all the usual leaflets and maps, plus the handy and free *Wellington: The Official Visitor Guide* booklet. The I-SITE visitor centre was hastily relocated after its old building was one of a handful

damaged during the 2016 earthquake; there's a possibility of another more permanent relocation in the near future.

DOC 18 Manners St (Mon–Fri 9am–5pm, Sat 10am–3.30pm; ☎04 384 7770). Has stacks of information on walks in the Wellington region and sells hut tickets and issues permits for Kapiti Island (both also available online).

ACCOMMODATION

Wellington has plenty of accommodation in the city centre, including some excellent backpacker hostels. B&Bs are becoming less common, but there are an increasing number of stylish self-catering serviced apartments. Breakfasting (or brunching) out is a quintessential Wellington experience, so you might not want a place where breakfast is included. Central motels are in short supply, but many business-oriented hotels offer good-value deals, especially on weekends. Freedom camping is allowed at the southern end of Marina carpark at Evans Bay, 2km southeast of the city centre, but some restrictions apply; check the Wellington City Council website (ⓦwellington.gov.nz) for information. Otherwise you can park overnight at the Cuba Street Motorhome Park (see page 380); or Base Backpackers (see page 379), both right in town but possibly noisy.

Apollo Lodge Motel & Majoribanks Apartments 49 Majoribanks St ☎0800 361 645, ⓦapollolodge.co.nz; map p.367. Appealing medium-sized renovated motel with modern rooms (some decorated in Edwardian style) 200m from Courtenay Place with off-street parking. Its adjacent apartments are well set up for longer stays; call ahead for prices. $150

★ **Austinvilla B&B** 11 Austin St, Mount Victoria ☎04 385 8334, ⓦaustinvilla.co.nz; map p.367. Two lovely and very private self-contained apartments in an elegant

villa, on a leafy street beside the Mount Victoria lookout trail and 10-minutes walk to the hub of Courtenay Place. One is a studio, the other with a separate bedroom and small garden – both have bathtubs, continental breakfast and off-street parking. Studio $205, one-bedroom $245

Base Wellington 21–23 Cambridge Terrace ☎04 801 5666, ⓦstayatbase.com; map p.367. Slick and lively 280-bed hostel converted from an office building in the nightlife district. Facilities include free daytime wi-fi, lockable cupboards, the *Basement* bar with DJs and even a carpark where they'll let you sleep in your campervan ($15/night) and use the hostel facilities. Women-only "Sanctuary" rooms ($4/night extra). Dorms $31, en suites $128

★ **Bolton Hotel** 12 Bolton St ☎04 472 9966, ⓦboltonhotel.co.nz; map p.367. Stylish independent hotel located around the corner from Parliament and named after a British cutter that docked here in 1840. Rooms are spacious, many with views over the Botanical Gardens. Each of the 19 floors displays unique artwork from Wellington artist Rita Angus and its restaurant, *The Artist*, is one of the few fashionable places to eat this side of town. Studios $229, suites $279

Booklovers B&B 123 Pirie St, Mount Victoria ☎04 384 2714, ⓦbooklovers.co.nz; map p.367. This classic bed and breakfast is within the literary host's Victorian home and

7

oozes charm. Of no surprise, the three en-suite guest rooms have books everywhere, and a full cooked breakfast is served any time within reason. Free off-street parking. $225

Cambridge Hotel 28 Cambridge Terrace ☏0800 375 021, ⌨cambridgehotel.co.nz; map p.367. Renovated 1930s hotel that operates partly as a backpackers and partly as accommodation for long-stay residents and workers. There's a popular, inexpensive locals' bar and restaurant, the four- to eight-bed dorms are spacious and the hotel rooms, while smallish, are good value. Dorms $26, en suites $99

CQ Hotels 223 Cuba St ☏04 385 2156, ⌨hotelwellington. co.nz; map p.367. Two hotels run to a high standard by the same family, and sharing the same facilities (swimming pool, café, bar, gym, restaurant, free wi-fi, charged-for off-street parking) in the heart of Cuba St. Rooms at the *Comfort* can be small but they are all en suite, while the *Quality* is more luxurious and includes lavish apartments with kitchenettes ($472). *Comfort* $156, *Quality* $234

Gourmet Stay 25 Frederick St ☏04 801 6800, ⌨gourmetstay.co.nz; map p.367. Small friendly hotel on a quiet street near the groovy end of town that uses every inch of space to squeeze in nine studios, three with shared bathrooms, and a family suite. There are also three rooms with tiny kitchens across the courtyard and a decent café. Studios $139, family suite $239, room with kitchen $252

Halswell Lodge 21 Kent Terrace ☏04 385 0196, ⌨halswell. co.nz; map p.367. Comfortable, central and welcoming establishment with simple but good-value hotel rooms (some with spa $180) and motel units in a lodge set back from the street. Free off-street parking. Rooms $119, motel units $160

Hotel Waterloo & Backpackers 1 Bunny St ☏04 473 8482, ⌨hotelwaterloo.co.nz; map p.367. Large hostel in the Art Deco *Waterloo Hotel*, convenient for train, bus and ferry arrivals. Dorms and rooms (some en suite) are adequate, and there's a cheap bar and a café in this once-grand hotel's former ballroom. Dorms $32, en suites $119

Nomads Capital 118 Wakefield St ☏0508 666 237, ⌨nomadsworld.com; map p.367. 180-bed hostel (with vertigo-inducing top bunks) with a bubbly atmosphere in the city centre with a backpacker bar/café *Blend*, tour desk, BBQ area and noticeboards. Women-only dorms available ($10 extra). Dorms $32, doubles $125

QT Museum 90 Cable St ☏04 802 8900, ⌨museumhotel. co.nz; map p.367. If the overt swagger of an artsy hotel is your thing, you'll love this place. Nicknamed the "Hotel de Wheels" for having been trundled across the street from the Te Papa construction site on rail tracks, there's a definite chic feel here with heaps of idiosyncratic artworks around the main reception which spills over to a grand, lethargic lounge

area with bar. Rooms are stylish, too, with gel beds and Bose sound systems. Rooms $259, apartments $329

Wellington City Accommodation 130 Abel Smith St ☏021 073 9232, ⌨wellingtoncityaccommodation.co.nz; map p.367. Two apartments close to bustling Cuba Street yet with a suburban charm. The quaint townhouse with two bedrooms and full kitchen can sleep ten whilst a modern studio beneath the owner's house has a kitchenette. Nearby on Tonks Grove, two renovated 1880 workers' cottages have a Queen bedroom with small kitchens. See their website for last minute half-price specials. Studio $150, cottage $185

★ **YHA Wellington City** 292 Wakefield St ☏04 801 7280, ⌨yha.co.nz; map p.367. This award-winning 320-bedder is one of the best – and greenest – hostels, right in the heart of the city with great harbour views from some of the upper-floor rooms. Spacious common areas include a foosball table and projector-screen TV room, well-equipped kitchens, bike storage, espresso bar, an info and travel desk and social events such as movie nights. Many of the doubles, twin, four- and six-share dorms have en suites. Dorms $33, rooms $99

CAMPSITES

Catchpool Valley Rimutaka Forest Park, 30km northeast of Wellington; map p.374. Pleasant drive-in DOC campsite beside the Catchpool stream with hot showers, toilets, water supply and barbecues. The 150 non-powered sites are scattered among tall trees. $13

Cuba Street Motorhome Park 25 Garrett Street ☏027 663 4411, ⌨cubastreetmotorhomepark.co.nz; map p.367. In the heart of town at the end of a side street, this tiny unmanaged powered site parking lot has spaces for just nine self-contained campervans. Pay at the machine. $29

★ **Matiu/Somes Island** map p.374. Twelve-person DOC campsite on the Matiu/Somes Island wildlife reserve (see page 375) in the middle of Wellington Harbour with great city views. There are flush toilets, tap water and a camp kitchen with gas oven, but you need to bring everything else. Book in advance through DOC or contact the Wellington i-SITE for more information. $13

Wellington Top 10 Holiday Park 95 Hutt Park Rd, Lower Hutt ☏0800 948 686, ⌨wellingtontop10.co.nz; map p.374. The capital's closest campsite, 15km north of Wellington on the harbour's northeastern shore. It's near beaches, shops and bushwalks and can be accessed on buses #81 and #83 from Courtenay Place and Lambton Interchange. There's a good range of accommodation, from camping ($50 per site) to motel units with Sky TV ($135). Kitchen cabins $90, self-contained units $120

EATING

Wellington has more places to eat per capita than New York and the standard is impressively high, whatever the budget. There's little need to venture much beyond the bounds

of the city centre, though a couple of reasons to stray are listed below. As the country's self-professed **coffee** capital (Wellington has nearly thirty independent roasteries),

BEANS AND BREWS

The Wellington **coffee scene** is now so established that budding baristas from across the globe come here to learn how to make the ultimate espresso or flat white. The capital is also home to **craft beer** giants Tuatara, plus an ever-changing raft of quirky newcomers (check ⓦcraftbeercapital.com for the latest listings and a brewery trail map, which you can also pick up from one of their 20 featured bars).

COFFEE

L'affare 27 College St ☎04 385 9748, ⓦlaffare.co.nz; map p.367. Try this two-hour class, which takes place every Thursday afternoon ($140), to improve your technique making espresso-based drinks at home. The cost includes a copy of *How to Make Really Good Coffee*.

Mojo Shed 13, 37 Customhouse Quay ☎04 385 3001, ⓦmojocoffee.co.nz; map p.367. A three-hour one-to-one ($175) where you'll learn what's needed for that perfect flat white. You can then move on to latte art ($175/2hr). They also run NZ's only City and Guilds barista course ($595/3 days).

CRAFT BEER

★ **Black Dog** 216 Cuba St ☎04 801 8491, ⓦblackdogbrewery.co.nz; map p.367. This up-and-coming microbrewery has loads of different experimental brews on the go but always stocks its impressive mango infused IPA. Tasting trays are $28 for eight beers with small plates to supplement costing $8–15. Daily 11am–late.

Garage Project 68 Aro St ☎04 384 3076, ⓦgarageproject.co.nz; map p.367. Queues now form at this old, barely modernized, petrol station to fill up bottles with delightful Venusian pale ale, or taste the chilli kick of Day of the Dead lager. Sun & Mon noon–7pm, Tues–Thurs noon–8pm, Fri & Sat 10am–9pm.

you'll find the good stuff served up everywhere from cosy spots through to the *très chic*. If you want to head off the beaten track, local neighbourhoods worth scouting out include Newtown and the Aro Valley. In the streets around **Courtenay Place** and **Cuba Street** there's a plethora of independent restaurants – from bohemian cafés through to award-winning establishments headed up by some of New Zealand's finest – and during the day many offer bargain lunch specials. The best of the cheap international food courts is the *Capital Market*, 151 Willis Street, while most pubs and bars (see page 383) serve impressive and generally inexpensive fare.

For **groceries** try *Moore Wilson's* or the three central *New World* supermarkets: at 68 Willis St; inside the railway station; and the largest, at the eastern end of Wakefield Street. Head down to the *Wellington Night Market* around Cuba Street on Friday and Saturday evenings for street food. Fresh produce markets are held every Saturday morning at *Thorndon Farmers' Market* outside Old St Paul's on Hill Street; with the largest being the Sunday morning *Harbourside Market* in the car park near Te Papa which combines food-trucks and artisan stalls.

CENTRAL WELLINGTON

★ **Aro Coffee** 90 Aro St ☎04 384 4970, ⓦarocoffee.co.nz; map p.367. The pick of a village-like cluster of cafés in weatherboard buildings in the Aro Valley, serving its own hand-blended coffee roasted on the premises, along with a short, smart menu of brunch fare such as their own baked beans with fried eggs and chorizo ($17). Their Mediterranean-influenced dinner menu includes light bruschettas for $16 and heartier feasts such as wild rabbit for

$26. Mon & Tue 7.30am–4pm, Mon–Fri 7.30am–10pm, Sat 9am–10pm, Sun 9am–5pm.

Beach Babylon Ground floor, 232 Oriental Parade ☎04 801 7717, ⓦbeachbabylon.co.nz; map p.367. Done out like a *bach*, and serving casual brunches to stylish dinners with a retro twist: chicken Kiev ($28), pan-fried polenta cakes ($25), fondue for two ($16) and banana splits ($10) for dessert. Good cocktails, too. Licensed and BYO. Daily 8am–late.

The Chippery 5 Majoribanks St ☎04 382 8713, ⓦthechippery.co.nz; map p.367. Fun and bustling little fish and chip shop selling the tastiest chips in the city (choice of five varieties from *kumara* to agria) matched with market fresh fish, which can also be bought wet, along with mushy peas ($3) or soft-shell crab burgers ($12). Delivery available too and there's a second location at 10 Murphy St in Thorndon. Mon–Thu Noon–8.30pm, Fri & Sat 11.30am–9pm, Sun 11.30am–8.30pm.

Curry Heaven 8 Bond St ☎04 472 0025, ⓦcurryheaven.co.nz; map p.367. There's nothing elaborate about this Indian restaurant with the focus squarely on its flavours, from the classic to the innovative, all cooked to perfection whether you like it subtly spicy or just barmy hot. Try the yoghurt and coconut infused Nawabi ($20), or if you don't mind things fiddly go for the hugely flavoursome goat on the bone ($21). Vegan and gluten-free options are plentiful and it's licensed or BYO. Mon–Fri 11.30am–2.30pm & 5pm–late, Sat 5pm–late.

Dragons Chinese Restaurant 25 Troy St ☎04 384 3288, ⓦwellingtondragons.co.nz; map p.367. This ordinary looking big square room is the long-standing favourite amongst the local community, especially for its sumptuous Yam Char (lunch and dinner) or sharing plates ($28). They do a great Peking duck ($68) although most mains from the 24-page menu are cheaper ($18–$30). Daily 11am–2.30pm & 5pm–10pm.

Ekim 257 Cuba St; map p.367. Van and hut selling milkshakes and burgers to take away or eat in their haphazard urban junkyard (occasional DJs and bands). There's an incredible six-veggie option if you don't want meat, and everything is transformed by Mike's secret sauce. Licensed. Daily 11am–9pm.

Fidel's 234 Cuba St 📞04 801 6868, 🌐fidelscafe.com; map p.367. At the offbeat southern end of Cuba St, this eternally cool, always busy café is plastered with revolution-era pictures of Castro, and extends into the barber's next door and into a sunny courtyard to the side. Come for locally roasted Havana coffee (Kahlua optional), margaritas, milkshakes, vegan muffins, or excellent-value meals (mains $14–26). Mon–Fri 7.30am–10pm, Sat 8am–10pm, Sun 9am–10pm.

Floriditas 161 Cuba St 📞04 381 2212, 🌐floriditas.co.nz; map p.367. This light, airy and stylish café is always busy, but if it's too packed you can visit its sister café *Loretta*, a few doors down. Wonderful breakfasts range from $11–24 and its limited but clever menu includes lunches such as gruyere frittata with mint salad ($18), dinners of grilled lamb skewers ($31.50) or the house speciality pastas ($20). Daily 7am–10pm.

Gipsy Kitchen 37 Jessie St 📞04 388 4455, 🌐bit.ly/GipsyKitchen; map p.367. Cosy hideaway with some pavement tables where you can snack on delicious homemade cakes and tarts over coffee with organic milk, or choose from a packed counter display where halloumi rolls, tasty quiches or spicy mushroom and bean burritos fight for your attention, all under $10. Daily 7am–3.30pm.

Hangar 119 Dixon St (cnr Willis) 📞04 830 0909; map p.367. Come for a long black or espresso and test your palate as each single-origin roast comes with a tasting card. There's also cold brew and drip coffee. Duck Benedict ($22) is their own take on eggs Benedict: braised duck served with hollandaise and kale. Licensed. Mon–Fri 7am–5pm, Sat & Sun 8am–5pm.

Lamason Cnr Lombard & Bond sts 📞04 473 1632; map p.367. Technically on the corner, but wander up Lombard St to this unprepossessing coffee bar hidden under a car park and run by friendly but madly obsessive coffee makers who specialize in smooth subtle vacuum pot and non-pressurised v60 filter coffee. Mon–Fri 7am–4.30pm, Sat 9.30am–3pm.

★**Little Penang** 40 Dixon St 📞04 382 9818, 🌐facebook.com/LittlePenang; map p.367. For good, cheap Asian food, this is the place for riotously flavoured counter food such as Mee Siam noodles or the tamarind spiced Papas curry, but you'll need to come early to get a seat. Combine any two dishes for lunch ($14.90) or dinner ($16.40); or snack on delicious BBQ pork buns ($3.90). There's a second outlet at 44 The Terrace, which isn't quite as buzzing but the food is just as good. No alcohol. Mon–Fri 11am–3pm & 5pm–9pm, Sat 11am–9pm.

MariLuca 55–57 Mulgrave St 📞04 499 5590, 🌐mariluca.co.nz; map p.367. High-quality, well-priced Italian food to meet Grandpa's Sicilian maxims: "meat makes meat, bread makes belly, wine makes dance". The menu varies seasonally, almost everything is cooked from scratch using mostly organic ingredients and the wine list extends beyond the horizon. Stop in while touring the Parliamentary District. Lunch Tues–Fri 11.30am–2.30pm; dinner Mon–Sat 5.30pm–midnight.

★**Midnight Espresso** 178 Cuba St 📞04 384 7014; map p.367. Looking like a bohemian artists' squat, with posters and flyers pinned to the community notice board, artwork and murals covering the walls, a pinball machine and frogger, this caffeine junkie's heaven serves Havana coffee along with lovely big breakfasts ($23), counter food and tasty hot dishes (many veggie or vegan), all under $18. Mon–Fri 7.30am–3am, Sat & Sun 8am–3am.

★**Moore Wilson's** Corner of Tory and College sts 📞04 384 9906; map p.367. Tucked under a parking station opposite the historic Thompson Lewis spring, this superb deli, charcuterie and bakery is the place to come for top-quality picnic supplies, including its own aged cheese. Fill your water bottle from the spring water fountain. Mon–Fri 7.30am–7pm, Sat 7.30am–6pm, Sun 8.30am–6pm.

★**Nikau Gallery Café** City Gallery Wellington, Civic Square 📞04 801 4168, 🌐nikaucafe.co.nz; map p.367. A stylish, contemporary daytime café with an airy setting and outdoor terrace, plus excellent coffee and a high-quality yet reasonably priced menu that makes the most of seasonal produce: try the goats cheese and mushroom salad ($16) with a home-made soda or a glass from their fine selection of wines. Mon–Fri 7am–4pm, Sat 8am–4pm.

Olive 170 Cuba St 📞04 802 5266, 🌐oliverestaurant.co.nz; map p.367. Elegant but relaxed bare-boards, licensed café that sticks mainly to organic produce and is popular with the locals. Great for coffee and cake throughout the day as well as brunches such as seared salmon and yoghurt ($24) and evening meals (mains $26–38) – try the mushroom pie. Tue–Sat 8am–late, Sun–Mon 8am–3pm.

★**Ortega** 16 Majoribanks St 📞04 382 9559, 🌐ortega.co.nz; map p.367. This self-titled "fish shack" has the feel of a classy neighbourhood bistro, and concentrates on superb seafood served with relaxed panache. Book for dinner (mains around $39), a dessert or just drop in for an Oloroso sherry at the bar. Tues–Sat 5.30pm–late.

Shepherd 1/5 Eva St 📞04 385 7274, 🌐shepherdrestaurant.co.nz; map p.367. One of the trendiest restaurants on the Wellington "to-dine" scene with funky décor and a small but carefully crafted locally inspired menu. Most mains are around $30 – try the clams in pork broth or coffee baked root vegetables but make sure you leave space for one of the rich doughnuts to end. Wed–Sun 5.30pm–late.

Sweet Mother's Kitchen 5 Courtenay Place 📞04 385 4444, 🌐sweetmotherskitchen.co.nz; map p.367.

Breakfast on beignets ($6), tuck into a Po' Boy baguette ($12.50), warm up with a bowl of gumbo ($16.50) or BBQ ribs with creole aioli ($25.50) and finish with a pecan and bourbon pie ($8.50). Rightly popular. Licensed. Sun–Thurs 8am–10.30pm, Fri & Sat 8am-late.

Trisha's Pies 32 Cambridge Terrace ☎04 801 5506; map p.367. A traditional Kiwi pie shop and a Wellington institution, serving a vast array of wonderful homemade pies. Particular favourites are the steak and cheese, pepper steak, steak and mushroom and veggie pies, all under $8 each. Mon–Sat 8am–3.30pm

THE SUBURBS

Chocolate Fish Café 100 Shelly Bay Rd, opposite Propeller Studio, Shelly Bay ⓦchocolatefishcafe.co.nz; map p.374. Located in the former Shelly Bay air force base, this shed-style café has transformed into a family hangout with indoor and alfresco seating plus a large grassy area overlooking the bay serving sandwiches hot off the grill

($10–20), and delicious home-made muffins, slices and biscuits. Licensed. Daily 8am–5.30pm.

★ **CoCo at the Roxy** 5 Park Road, Miramar ☎04 388 5555, ⓦcocoattheroxy.co.nz; map p.374. Classy bar and dining room in the grand foyer of *The Roxy* cinema (see page 385). The food (mains $16–28) almost manages to outshine its stunning surroundings. The focus is local seasonal ingredients with an exotic twist, like the Mongolian lamb ribs crème fraiche or the global Street Feast for two. Tues–Fri lunch 11.30am–3pm, dinner 5pm–late. Sat & Sun 9am–late.

★ **Maranui Surf Club Café** Maranui Surf Life Saving Club, The Parade, Lyall Bay ☎04 387 4539, ⓦmaranuicafe. co.nz; map p.374. Situated on the top floor, with a balcony overlooking the beach, sea and approaches to Wellington airport, this licensed café is an established locals' favourite, with colourful retro beachside decor, generous breakfasts, great salads and chocolate coconut cakes (all under $25). There are few better places to sit and watch the planes go by, particularly at weekends. Daily 7am–5pm.

DRINKING AND NIGHTLIFE

The distinction between bars and clubs is often blurred, with many bars hosting free live music and dancing in the evenings, especially at weekends. Cuba Street is home to some of New Zealand's best nightlife, with a huge array of late-night cafés, bars and clubs within walking distance of each other.

Wellington's LGBTQ scene is focused in the inner city, but for the most part it's woven seamlessly into the general café/bar mainstream. For the latest information, check out ⓦgaynz.com, or pick up the free, monthly *express* magazine (ⓦgayexpress.co.nz). The annual two-week long Wellington Pride Festival (ⓦwellingtonpridefestival.org.nz) opens late February with their long-standing main event, Out in the Park community fair.

The Backbencher Pub 34 Molesworth St, at Kate Sheppard St ☎04 472 3065, ⓦbackbencher.co.nz; map p.367. A convivial pub ambience, popular amongst MPs and civil servants, decorated with satirical cartoons. Try one of the dozen or more draught beers and the hearty pies ($24–30) named after current MPs. Daily 7am–11pm.

★ **Crumpet** 109 Manners St ☎04 803 3846, ⓦfacebook. com/crumpetbar; map p.367. This dainty retro bar serves tasty crumpets ($7) and sterling coffee, but the real reason to come is alcoholic reinvigoration. Try their gin shrubb ($12), or just tell one of the "brothers" what mood you're in, and they will create something wonderful to suit. Mon, Tues & Sun 1pm–1am, Wed–Sat 1pm–3am.

Fork and Brewer 14 Bond St ☎04 472 0033, ⓦforkandbrewer.co.nz; map p.367. Brave the unprepossessing staircase and you'll enter beer heaven – just smell the hops. With around thirty regularly changing beers and two ciders on tap, including their own, you'd better have a tasting tray (four beers/$15). Beers are matched to the decent pub grub if you're dining (most items under $25). Their

strongest beer is the malty Murder of Crows (9.8 percent), but they may have softer specials like the Raspberry & Lemon Berliner (3.7 percent) Mon–Sat 11.30am–late.

Foxglove 33 Queens Wharf ☎04 460 9410, ⓦfoxglovebar. co.nz; map p.367. Popular wine bar with some beers on tap too but most come for its prime location with a large sunny wrap-around veranda overlooking the harbour. There's a cosy lounge upstairs with comfy chairs and games boards for rainy days. The fine dining restaurant downstairs is a little pricey (mains around $33) but you can get tacos and burgers from the bar menu (under $20). Daily 11.30am–late.

Hanging Ditch 14 Leeds St ☎04 803 3566, ⓦfacebook. com/HangingDitchNZ; map p.367. Cosy cocktail bar and a good place to chat around comfy leather armchairs with hipster bartenders buzzing beneath emptied bottles hanging from the ceiling. Mon–Thurs 4.30pm–midnight, Fri–Sun 3pm–midnight.

Hawthorn Lounge 82 Tory St ☎04 890 3724, ⓦhawthornlounge.co.nz; map p.367. You'll have to keep an eye out for the inconspicuous staircase up to this cocktail bar, decked out with dark wood and classy upholstered chairs. Their drinks menu changes frequently, though the entertainingly daft names somewhat undermine the skilled mixology. Daily 5pm–3am.

★ **Laundry Bar** 240 Cuba St ☎04 384 4280, ⓦlaundry. net.nz; map p.367. Some come just for the spicy Sumatran steak burgers and to sip draft beer, but this funky little joint is one of the liveliest in town playing great dance music all night long with the sharpest DJ's and live music most weekends. Mon–Thurs & Sun 4pm–midnight, Fri & Sat 4pm–3am.

The Library Level 1, 53 Courtenay Place ☎04 382 8593, ⓦthelibrary.co.nz; map p.367. Ultra-cool book-lined

7

cocktail bar with separate rooms and a cornucopia of nooks and crannies where you can sip on excellent drinks and listen to the live music. Service can be famously slow. Mon–Thurs 5pm–late, Fri–Sun 4pm–late.

Little Beer Quarter 6 Edward St ☎04 803 3304, ⓦlittlebeerquarter.co.nz; map p.367. A suitably dingy bar where you can nibble beer-battered fries ($9) while you browse the craft beer menu. Mon 3.30pm–3am, Tues–Sat noon–3am, Sun 3pm–3am.

★ **The Malthouse** 48 Courtenay Place ☎04 802 5484, ⓦthemalthouse.co.nz; map p.367. In a lounge setting with low sofas, high stools and sleek glossy timber tables, this drinker's paradise has around thirty different brews on tap plus some 150 varieties by the bottle. The choice includes some of New Zealand's finest craft brews described in detailed tasting notes by top Kiwi beer commentator Neil Miller. There's a great selection of malt whiskies, too. Mon & Tues 3–11pm, Wed–Sun noon–3am.

Rogue and Vagabond 18 Garrett St ☎04 381 2321, ⓦrogueandvagabond.co.nz; map p.367. Its blackboard welcome entrance might look a bit tacky, but they dish up a great selection of craft beers, filling bar grub and there's live music (jazz, blues, funk) at least four nights a week. It overlooks Glover Park, which they've annexed with beanbags. Daily 11am–late.

S&M's 176 Cuba St ☎04 802 5335, ⓦscottyandmals. co.nz; map p.367. A stylish, alternative bar that is friendly and happening. Features DJs on Fri and Sat, plus the occasional live show on the corner stage, or private events downstairs. They'll order in food from *Midnight Espresso* (see page 382). Daily 5pm–late.

Southern Cross 39 Abel Smith St ☎04 384 9085, ⓦthecross.co.nz; map p.367. Cavernous family-friendly bar divided into some cosy spaces including a heated Balinese-style outdoor garden (and hot water bottles and blankets in winter). The charming local hosts organize everything from a book club (Mon) to music quiz nights (Thurs) and roast dinners (Sun), plus live music on Wednesdays and weekends. New

Zealand beers are well represented on tap, and the great pub grub is diverse (as well as the atmosphere) with steaks and Buddha bowls. Daily 9am–late.

CLUBS AND LIVE MUSIC VENUES

Live bands are a regular fixture across town, so check out the bars listed above as well as the clubs below, dedicated smaller venues or bigger halls such as the TSB Bank Arena and occasionally free concerts at the waterfront Frank Kitts Park or Civic Square. A good place to find out what's going on is to head to Rough Peel Music, 173 Cuba Street.

Boston on Blair 20 Blair St ☎04 384 9070, ⓦbostononblair.co.nz; map p.367. If you just want to dance to the latest hip-hop, this large lively club has local and international DJs and is a favourite amongst the city's Māori and Pacific Island crowd. Wed, Fri & Sat 9pm–4am.

Meow 9 Edward St ☎04 385 8883, ⓦmeow.nz; map p.367. Cosy retro club with antiques and fancy lampshades hosting local musicians playing anything from jazz to rap, and the occasional travelling bands too. Cover up to $20 when not free. Tues–Fri 4pm–late, Sat 6pm–late, Sun for live music only.

San Fran 171 Cuba St ☎04 801 6797, ⓦsanfran.co.nz; map p.367. The city's main indie, alternative rock and reggae venue, with a balcony looking out on the assorted life passing along Cuba St. First-rate Kiwi bands are occasionally joined by international acts. Most gigs $15–60, though some are free. Tues–Sat 5pm–late,.

★ **Sassy loves Cash** 24 Courtenay Place ☎04 384 8015, ⓦsassyloves.cash; map p.367. Cool, small, casual club with a frisky dance floor and a cute outdoor veranda to catch your breath. They serve great cocktails too. Free. Wed, Thurs & Sat 8pm–4am, Fri 6pm–4am.

Valhalla 154 Vivian St, ⓦvalhallatavern.com; map p.367. A lively, well-respected venue with a tradition of metal gigs plus everything from hardcore and goth to ukuleles, from emerging and established artists. Occasional cover $5–10. Wed–Sat 5.30pm–late (bands on at 8pm)

ENTERTAINMENT

Performing arts are strong in Wellington, which is home to several professional theatres, the Royal New Zealand Ballet, the New Zealand Symphony Orchestra and assorted opera and dance companies. In addition to its quota of multiplexes, Wellington also has a smattering of art-house cinemas: you can usually save a couple of dollars by going during the day or any time early in the week.

ESSENTIALS

Listings The best introduction is the *Wellington – What's On* booklet, free from the i-SITE visitor centre and from accommodation around the city. Extensive listings of exhibitions, events and community workshops can be found in the free weekly newspaper *The Wellingtonian*

(ⓦthewellingtonian.co.nz) available from New World supermarkets.

Tickets Book tickets direct at venues or, for a small fee, through Ticketek (☎0800 842 538, ⓦticketek.co.nz) which has an outlet at the Michael Fowler Centre, 111 Wakefield St.

THEATRES AND CONCERT HALLS

Bats Theatre 1 Kent Terrace ☎04 802 4175, ⓦbats. co.nz. Lively theatre (saved from demolition by Peter Jackson) that concentrates on developmental works served up at affordable prices (usually around $15), with discounts for YHA or Student card-holders.

Circa 1 Taranaki St, at Cable St ☎04 801 7992, ⓦcirca. co.nz. One of the country's liveliest and most innovative

WELLINGTON FESTIVALS

Whenever you visit Wellington there's a good chance there'll be some sort of festival happening. The visitor centre has full details; the following are the biggest occasions, listed chronologically.

Summer City Festival (@wellington.govt.nz) A council-sponsored series of free concerts, cultural events and performances around town. January–March.

Wellington Fringe Festival (@fringe.co.nz) Vibrant affair run as a separate and roughly concurrent event to the International Arts Festival, filling the inner city with street and indoor theatre. Usually held in late February or early March.

New Zealand International Arts Festival (@festival.co.nz) The country's biggest cultural event lasts a full month and draws top performers from around the world. Fashioned along the lines of the Edinburgh Festival, it celebrates the huge diversity of the arts: classical music, jazz and pop, opera, puppet shows, cabaret, poetry readings, traditional Māori

dance, modern ballet and experimental works. Most venues are in the city centre. Usually held in February and March in even-numbered years.

Wellington International Film Festival (@nzff. co.nz) The Wellington leg of the nationwide film tour screens less mainstream offerings at cinemas around town. Tickets around $18. Usually late July to early August.

Wellington on a Plate (@wellingtononaplate.com) Celebrates the capital's cuisine through tastings, talks and behind-the-stoves tours as well as discounted menus at top restaurants. Last two weeks of August.

World of WearableArt (WOW) (@worldofwearableart. com) Tickets go like hot cakes for this glorious spectacle of weird costumes which runs like a bizarre fashion show. Usually last two weeks of September.

7

professional theatres, which has fostered the skills of some of the best-known Kiwi directors and actors.

Michael Fowler Centre 111 Wakefield St @04 801 4231, @venueswellington.com Award-winning building showing touring comedy, classical music, and ballet.

Westpac Stadium Featherston St @04 473 3881, @westpacstadium.co.nz. Dubbed "the cake tin" by its detractors for its iron-clad design, this modern purpose-built stadium is the venue for rugby, cricket and football as well as occasional rock concerts.

CINEMAS

Lighthouse 29 Wigan St @04 385 3337, @lighthousecuba.co.nz. Plush modern cinema with three small screens, some rather fine pies and a programme mixing relayed theatre and opera, as well as mainstream and

art-house films.

Nga Taonga Sound and Vision 84 Taranaki St, at Ghuznee St @04 384 7647, @ngataonga.org.nz. Focusing entirely on New Zealand films and TV programmes with some free screenings and a massive archive library.

Reading Cinemas 100 Courtenay Place @04 801 4600, @readingcinemas.co.nz. Shows mostly mainstream movies with the option of going for their plush Gold Lounge seats (from $16.50) which come with an in-seat food and drink service.

The Roxy 5 Park Rd, Miramar @04 388 5555, @roxycinema.co.nz. Glorious 1930s style cinema with two screens, cocktail bar and restaurant, CoCo (see page 383). Check out the details, the bronze of Gollum, the light fittings, pillars, door pulls and toilets – a positive Weta dream for anybody who is a fan. Daily 9am–late.

SHOPPING

While High Street fashion, mostly along Lambert Quay and Willis Street, is not quite as expansive as in Auckland, boutique shops punch above its small size, with Cuba Street the place to head. For more affordable knickknacks visit the Wellington Underground Markets (Sat 10am–4pm; @undergroundmarket.co.nz) underneath Frank Kitts Park or find local artists selling out of shipping containers at the Pop-up Village (Nov–Mar & July, daily 10am–4pm weather permitting; @popupvillage.nz) on the waterfront at Taranaki Wharf near Te Papa.

ARTS, CRAFTS AND SOUVENIRS

Madinz 28 Waterloo Quay @04 473 2200, @madeinz. co.nz; map p.367. Specialising in corporate gifts with a New

Zealand flavour, this little art studio is a hidden gem for buying quality souvenirs from sculptures to display plates. Mon–Thurs 9am–4.30pm.

The Vault 2 Plimmer St @04 471 1404, @thevaultnz. com; map p.367. Stylish gift shop with lots of New Zealand-made contemporary jewellery and clothing, Māori prints and cards as well as unique decor for the home. Mon–Thurs 9.30am–5.30pm, Fri 9.30am–7pm, Sat 10am–5pm, Sun 11am–4.30pm.

FASHION

Missy's Room Old Bank Arcade, 233 Lambton Quay @04 472 2022, @facebook.com/missys.room; map p.367. Sourcing from local designers and using its own colourful materials, this independent store has a funky collection of dresses, accessories and jewellery. Mon–Thu 9am–6pm, Fri 9am–7pm, Sat 10am–4pm, Sun 11am–3pm.

Recycle Boutique 143 Vivian St ☎04 916 2020, ⌨thevaultnz.com; map p.367. Stylish secondhand outlet with some retro clothing too. Mon–Fri 9.30am–6pm, Sat 10am–5pm, Sun 11am–5pm.

BOOKSHOPS

Unity Books 57 Willis St ☎04 499 4245, ⌨unitybooks. co.nz; map p.367. Has the best selection of special interest and travel titles, plus more mainstream books. Mon–Thurs 9am–6pm, Fri 9am–7pm, Sat 10am–6pm, Sun 11am–5pm.

Arty Bee's Books 106 Manners St ☎04 384 5339, ⌨artybees.co.nz; map p.367. Offers a selection of secondhand books, antiquities, an excellent Māori collection and plenty of New Zealand focused books. Mon–Thurs 9am–7pm, Fri & Sat 9am–9pm, Sun 11am–7pm.

OUTDOOR CLOTHING AND CAMPING

Bivouac 39 Mercer St ☎04 473 2587, ⌨bivouac.co.nz; map p.367. National retailer with a wide range of camping equipment and active clothing. Mon–Thurs 9am–5.30pm, Fri 9am–6.30pm, Sat & Sun 10am–5pm.

Dwights Outdoors 35 Mercer St ☎04 499 1673, ⌨dwights.co.nz; map p.367. Long-standing family business with helpful staff selling mostly high-end brands. Mon–Fri 9am–5.30pm, Sat 9.30am–4.30pm, Sun 10am–4.30pm.

DIRECTORY

Automobile Association 342–352 Lambton Quay ☎04 931 9999.

Embassies and consulates Australia, 72–76 Hobson St, Thorndon ☎04 473 6411; Canada, 125 The Terrace ☎04 473 9577; UK, 44 Hill St ☎04 924 2888; US, 29 Fitzherbert Terrace, Thorndon ☎04 462 6000. For other countries, check online.

Emergencies Police, fire and ambulance ☎111. Wellington Central Police Station is on the corner of Victoria and Harris sts (☎04 381 2000).

Internet There's free wi-fi throughout the CBD and at many hotspots around Wellington's inner city. Otherwise, head to the Central Library (see below) for free internet and terminals; or for high speed access and business services try the 24hr Skynet Internet Café at 49 Manners St ($4/hr).

Laundry Agitator Laundrette 24 Elizabeth St ☎04 385 1999. Mon–Fri 8am–5.30pm, Sat 9am–5pm, Sun 10am–5.30pm.

Library Central Library, 65 Victoria St ☎04 801 4040. Mon–Fri 9.30am–8.30pm, Sat 9.30am–5pm, Sun 1–4pm.

Medical treatment For emergency treatment try the Accident & Urgent Medical Centre, 17 Adelaide Rd, Newtown, near Basin Reserve (daily 8am–11pm; ☎04 384 4944). Wellington Hospital is on Riddiford St, Newtown (☎04 385 5999).

Pharmacy Urgent Pharmacy, 17 Adelaide Rd, Newtown (Mon–Fri 9am–11pm, Sat, Sun & public holidays 8am–11pm; ☎04 385 8810), is open late.

Post office Several throughout the city centre; for poste restante go to 2 Manners St.

Swimming Freyberg Pool and Fitness Centre, 139 Oriental Parade (daily 6am–9pm; ☎04 801 4530), has a 33m indoor pool ($8.20 to swim), plus gym, spas, saunas, steam room, fitness classes and massage therapy. Thorndon Pool, 26 Murphy St (Oct–April Mon–Thurs 6.30am–8pm, Fri 6.30am–7pm, Sat & Sun 7.30am–7pm; $8.20) is a 30m heated outdoor pool near Parliament.

The Kapiti Coast

The narrow plain between the rugged and inhospitable **Tararua Range** and the Tasman Sea breakers is known as the **Kapiti Coast**, effectively part of Wellington's commuter belt, peppered with dormitory suburbs and golf courses. Still, it has sweeping beaches, a few minor points of interest and provides access to **Kapiti Island**, 5km offshore, a magnificent bush-covered sanctuary where birdlife thrives.

Paekakariki and around

At the southern extent of the Kapiti Coast, the village of **Paekakariki** has a tiny but vibrant beach community. Families should make straight for the 6.5-square-kilometre **Queen Elizabeth Park** (daily 8am–dusk), which has entrances at MacKays Crossings on SH1, and off the Esplanade in Raumati. At the former entrance is the **Tramway Museum** (Sat & Sun 11am–4.30pm; daily in Jan; tram rides $8; ☎04 292 8361, ⌨wellingtontrams.org.nz), which runs restored Wellington trams along 2km of track to the beach. The adjacent **Stables on the Park** (Daily 11am–3pm; horse treks and pony rides from $25; ☎027 448 6764, ⓦstablesonthepark.co.nz) offers horse treks and pony rides for kids.

Pataka Museum of Arts and Cultures

22km south of Paekakariki, corner of Norrie and Parumoana sts • Mon–Sat 10am–5pm, Sun 11am–4.30pm • Free • ☎04 237 1511, ⓦpataka.org.nz

Just 20km north of Wellington, the expanding satellite city of **Porirua** is worth a brief stop for the excellent **Pataka Museum of Arts and Cultures**, which hosts local and touring exhibitions by leading contemporary New Zealand artists, plus occasional Māori dance performances and a decent gift shop selling local arts and crafts.

ACCOMMODATION AND EATING   PAEKAKARIKI AND AROUND

Killara Homestay 70 Ames St, Paekakariki ☎04 905 5544, ⓦkillarahomestay.co.nz. The two guest rooms upstairs in this private beachfront house are for one group only to ensure privacy and good for families or couples. There's a spacious lounge with fridge and views to Kapiti Island. **$170**

★ **Moana Lodge** 49 Moana Rd, Plimmerton ☎04 233 2010, ⓦmoanalodge.co.nz. Friendly hostel set in a beautifully-sited Edwardian villa with sea views from many rooms and four-bed dorms. Dorms **$34**, doubles **$86**

Paekakariki Holiday Park 180 Wellington Rd, Paekakariki ☎04 292 8292, ⓦpaekakarikiholidaypark. co.nz. Very popular and well-appointed family holiday park on the southern fringe of QE Park with good access to a safe swimming beach. Camping **$18**, cabins **$70**

The Perching Parrot 5 Beach Rd, Paekakariki ☎04 292 8860. This decorative café serving excellent coffee and cakes is the heartbeat of the local community. The homemade soups ($12) are delicious or go for spinach and feta fritters ($20). Mon–Fri 7am–4pm, Sat & Sun 8am–4pm

Kapiti Island

Kapiti Island is one of the best and most easily accessible island **nature reserves** in New Zealand, a 15min boat ride offshore from Paraparaumu Beach. This magical spot, just 10km by 2km, was once cleared for farmland but is again cloaked in bush and home to birdlife that has become rare or extinct on the mainland. Much of New Zealand's bush is now virtually silent but here it trills to the sound of chirping birds – much as it did before the arrival of humans.

In 1824, famed Māori chief **Te Rauparaha** (original composer of the *haka*) captured the island from its first known Māori inhabitants and, with his people the Ngati Toa, used it as a base until his death in 1849. The island is considered extremely spiritual by Māori, and was designated a reserve in 1897.

Late January and February are the best months to visit, when the **birdlife** is at its most active, but at any time of the year you're likely to see kaka (bush parrots that may alight on your head or shoulder), weka, kakariki (parakeets), whiteheads (bush canaries), tui, bellbirds, fantails, wood pigeons, robins and a handful of the 300 takahe that exist in the world. Those staying overnight at the lodge (see page 388) might even spot one of the 1,400 nocturnal little spotted kiwis that live here.

The **North End** of the island (about a tenth of its total area) is also part of the Kapiti Nature Reserve, though it's managed and accessed separately. The **Okupe Lagoon** has a colony of royal spoonbills, and there are plenty of rare forest birds.

> **WALKING AROUND KAPITI**
>
> The island can be explored on two fairly steep **walking tracks**, the **Trig Track** and the **Wilkinson Track**, which effectively form a loop by meeting near the island's highest point, Tuteremoana (521m). There are panoramic views from the summit, though the widest variety of birdlife is found along the lower parts of the tracks – take your time, keep quiet and stop frequently (allow about 3hr for the round trip).

A wedge of sea between Kapiti Island and Paraparaumu has been designated a **marine reserve**, and its exceptionally clear waters make for great **snorkelling** around the rocks (bring your own gear, or rent it from the *Kapiti Nature Lodge*). You'll need your own gear for **scuba diving**, which is particularly good to the west and north of the island.

ARRIVAL AND INFORMATION   KAPITI ISLAND

By boat Kapiti Explorer (☎0800 433 779, ⑩kapitiexplorer. co.nz; 1hr guided walk $12) and Kapiti Island Nature Tours (☎0800 527 484, ⑩kapitiislandnaturetours.co.nz; 1hr guided walk $20) both run boat trips to the island from $75, taking 15min to cross over. Boats generally leave from Paraparaumu beach beside Kapiti Boating Club around 9am and return around 3.30pm. On the island you'll find toilets and a shelter at the landing point: take your own food and water, and bring back all rubbish

ACCOMODATION

★ **Kapiti Nature Lodge** Waiorua Bay ☎06 362 6606, ⑩kapitiisland.com. At the northern reserve end, private land owned by the descendants of Te Rauparaha is the setting for the island's only accommodation and the most rewarding way to experience Kapiti. There's a simple, comfortable lodge on its own beside the sea, sleeping up to six people and where meals are served for all guests; and two other "camping" areas up nearby valleys in amongst the bush and birds, one with five timber cabins and the other with two safari tents. Prices are per person include boat transfers, DOC permit, meals and a night-time Kiwi spotting walk. Cabins $384, tents $410, en-suite lodge $436

Paraparaumu

The burgeoning dormitory community of **PARAPARAUMU** (aka "Paraparam"), 7km south of Waikanae and 45km from Wellington, is the Kapiti Coast's largest settlement. It is primarily of interest as the only jumping-off point to Kapiti Island, which faces the long and sandy **Paraparaumu Beach**, 3km to the west along Kapiti Road. With safe swimming, accommodation and a few restaurants, this is the place to hang out.

ARRIVAL AND INFORMATION   PARAPARAUMU

By train The *Northern Explorer* and Wellington's Metlink commuter trains stop opposite the Coastlands shopping centre. Destinations Paekakariki (every 30min; 17min); Plimmerton (every 30min; 30min); Porirua (every 30min; 45min); Wellington (every 30min; 1hr 10min), Auckland (3 weekly; 8hr 45min).
By bus InterCity and NakedBus stop at the train station. Destinations Wellington (every 1hr; 1hr), Auckland (3 daily; 10hr 30min).

By plane Paraparaumu's airport (⑩kapiticoastairport. co.nz), midway between SH1 and the beach, is served by Air New Zealand and Air2There (⑩air2there.com). Destinations Auckland (1–2 daily; 1hr 10min); Blenheim (1–2 daily; 35min); Nelson (Fri & Sun; 45min).
i-SITE visitor centre 240 Main Rd, in the carpark of the Mediterranean Food Warehouse (Mon–Fri 9am–5pm, Sat & Sun 10am–4pm; ☎04 298 8195). Has local and DOC information and can help with permits for Kapiti Island.

ACCOMMODATION

Campers Campers in self-contained vans can park up opposite nos. 54, 62 & 69 Marine Parade beside Paraparaumu Beach.
Barnacles Seaside Inn 3 Marine Parade, Paraparaumu Beach ☎04 902 5856, ⑩barnacleseasideinn.co.nz. This rambling 1923 wooden hotel across the road from the beach has comfortable antique-furnished, shared bathrooms and dorms. Dorms $29, doubles $72
Kapiti Court Motel 341 Kapiti Rd ☎0800 526 683, ⑩kapiticourtmotel.co.nz. Beside the shops and a 2min walk from the beach, quiet with outdoor pool and pleasant twin- and king-bed rooms, some with self-contained kitchens. $120
Tudor Manor B&B 10 Tudor Ct, ☎04 298 3436, ⑩tudormanor.co.nz. Hosted by a welcoming and knowledgeable local couple, there are three spacious country-styled rooms in this quiet suburban cul-de-sac, and is a 10min walk to the boat launch for Kapiti Island and beach. There's a pool, too. $150

EATING AND DRINKING

Marine Parade Eatery 50 Marine Parade ☎04 892 0098. Hip café serving all day breakfasts from pickled pork hash to lentil and veggie bowls ($19) plus larger mains like seafood laksa or coconut poached chicken all under $25.

Mon–Thurs 7.30am–4pm, Fri 7.30am–8.30pm, Sat & Sun 7.30am–9pm.
D4 Raumati 9 Margaret Rd, Raumati Beach, 3km south of Paraparaumu Beach ☎04 892 0094, ⓦd4raumati.

co.nz. Popular outdoor garden with indoor dining too. Brunch menu is under $20 or the stonegrill plates under $30. Come for the Wednesday evening roast or Saturday high tea. Tues–Sat 9am–late, Sun & Mon 9am–4pm.

Waikanae

WAIKANAE, 7km north of Paraparaumu, is divided between the highwayside settlement and a beach community, 4km away along Te Moana Road, where the broad, dune-backed **beach** has safe swimming.

Nga Manu Nature Reserve

Ngarara Rd; Take Te Moana Road off SH1 for just over 1km and turn right at Ngarara Road; the sanctuary is a further 3km • Daily 10am–5pm • $18 • ☎04 293 4131, ⓦngamanu.co.nz

To see native wildlife in its more-or-less natural environment, stop at the **Nga Manu Nature Reserve**, a large man-made bird sanctuary with easy walking tracks and some picnic spots. A circular track (1500m) cuts through a variety of habitats, from ponds and scrubland to swamp and coastal forest, which attract all manner of birds. There is also a nocturnal house containing kiwi, morepork and tuatara, plus eels, fed at 2pm daily, and some walk-in aviaries where kea and kaka strut their stuff.

Southward Car Museum

Otaihanga Rd, 3km south of Waikanae • Daily: 9am–4.30pm • $18 • ☎04 297 1221, ⓦsouthwardcarmuseum.co.nz

With over 250 vehicles in a specially built showroom, the **Southward Car Museum** contains one of the largest collections of cars, fire engines and motorbikes in Australasia. As well as mundane models from the 1960s, 1970s and 1980s, there's no shortage of exotica, all in mint condition. Gems include Marlene Dietrich's Rolls-Royce, a 1915 Stutz Racer and a 1955 gull-winged Mercedes Benz.

The Wairarapa

Most of the **Wairarapa** region, lying north and east of Wellington's Rimutaka Range, is archetypal Kiwi sheep country. In recent years, however, the southern half of the region has increasingly benefited from free-spending weekenders from Wellington visiting the boutique hotels, innovative restaurants and many wineries surrounding **Martinborough**, the region's current wine capital. At the very southern tip of the island **Cape Palliser** is the ideal spot for blustery mind-clearing walks and dramatic coastal scenery.

North of Martinborough the SH2 cuts through the heart of the district, passing a succession of rural settlements, with **Greytown** its most appealing and **Masterton** the region's main commercial centre. From the latter a 50km tar-sealed road branches off to the laidback coastal settlement of **Castlepoint** where a decent beach for swimming and surfing makes it the only holiday spot to visit along the rugged and mostly inaccessible east coast. North of Masterton, the **Pukaha Mount Bruce National Wildlife Centre** provides a wonderful opportunity to witness ongoing bird conservation work along an otherwise unspectacular 200km stretch of road north to Hastings and Hawkes Bay.

Brief history

The establishment of New Zealand's earliest sheep station in the 1840s on rich alluvial lands close to present-day Martinborough paved the way for development by the progressive **Small Farm Association (SFA)**. This was the brainchild of Joseph Masters, a Derbyshire cooper and longtime campaigner against the separation of landowner and labourer, who sought to give disenfranchised settlers the opportunity to become smallholders. Liberal governor George Grey supported him and in 1853 suggested the SFA should persuade local Māori to sell land for the establishment of two towns – Masterton and Greytown.

Initially Greytown prospered, and it retains an air of antiquity rare among New Zealand towns, but the routing of the rail line favoured Masterton, famed chiefly today for the annual Golden Shears sheepshearing competition.

Martinborough

Little **MARTINBOROUGH**, 80km northeast of Wellington, has been transformed into a compact micro-vineyard region synonymous with some of New Zealand's finest reds. It's within easy striking distance of Wellington, and weekends see the arrival of the smart set to load up their shiny 4WDs at the cellar doors. On Mondays and Tuesdays much of the town simply shuts down to recover. Other busy times include **Toast Martinborough** (wtoastmartinborough.co.nz), a wine-oriented affair in November with international live acts; and the two **Martinborough Fairs** (first Saturday in February and March; wmartinboroughfair.org.nz) – huge country fêtes during which the central streets are lined with art and craft stalls.

Brief history

Martinborough was initially laid out in the 1870s by landowner John Martin, who named the streets after cities he had visited on his travels and arranged the core, centred on a leafy square, in the form of a Union Jack. For over a century the town languished as a minor agricultural centre until the **first four wineries** – Ata Rangi, Dry River, Chifney and Martinborough (all of which produced their first vintages in 1984) – reinvented it as the coolest, driest and most wind-prone of the North Island's grape-growing regions. With the aid of shelterbelts (strategically planted trees and hedges that splice the vineyards) the wineries produce some outstanding Pinot Noir, notable Sauvignon Blanc, rich Chardonnay and richly aromatic Riesling.

Martinborough Wine Village

6 Kitchener St • Daily: 9.30am–6pm • $2–5 per tasting • Walking tours with lunch $240, minimum 4 people • Bike hire $40 • ☎06 306 9040, wmartinboroughwinemerchants.com

Outside the festival times, your best starting point is the **Martinborough Wine Village**, predominantly a wine outlet but also offering free tastings from a different local winery every month, and a taste of fifteen other local wines "on tap". You can quaff a full glass at their seats in the square or join one of their passionate staff on its flexible Wine Walk tour going behind the scenes at some of the up-and-coming vineyards.

ARRIVAL AND INFORMATION   MARTINBOROUGH

By train and bus Metlink commuter trains (☎0800 801 700 wmetlink.org.nz) from Wellington stop at Featherston train station where Metlink bus #205 shuttles south to Martinborough, dropping off diagonally opposite the i-SITE visitor centre and at the Martinborough Wine Village. Alternatively bus #200 connects Masterton and Martinborough three times daily.

Visitor information i-SITE visitor centre, 18 Kitchener St

(Tues–Sat 9am–5pm, Mon & Sun 10am–4pm; ☎06 306 5010, wwairarapanz.com), carries loads of information on the surrounding vineyards, including the *Wairarapa Wine Trail* sheet. They also book accommodation and hire bikes.

Bike hire To rent a bike for a spin round the vineyards try the Martinborough Wine Village ($40/day), or Green Jersey (behind the i-SITE visitor centre ☎027 243 489, wgreenjersey.co.nz; $40/day).

ACCOMMODATION

Rooms are hard to find during festivals and on summer weekends: weeknights are often a happier hunting ground. **Martinborough Hotel** Memorial Square ☎06 306 9350, wmartinboroughhotel.co.nz. The attractively restored *grande dame* of Martinborough offers rooms upstairs in the old building with French doors opening onto a veranda, and more contemporary rooms set around the garden; all are serviced, well tended and spacious. There's also a good restaurant and a bar that's a bit of a gathering place for the local vineyard owners and farmers. **$200**

★**Martinborough Top 10 Holiday Park** 10 Dublin St West ☎0800 780 909, ⓦ mtop10.nz. Impeccably maintained and peaceful campsite adjacent to vineyards a 10min walk from the centre, with free unlimited wi-fi, pétanque, bike hire, tent sites separate from van hook-ups, and cosy cabins. The owner knows everything that's happening in town. Camping $42, cabins $80, motel units $139

The Old Manse 19 Grey St ☎06 306 8599, ⓦoldmanse.

co.nz. Boutique B&B in a wonderful old villa with five en-suite rooms all set amid vines on the edge of town. Double $180, suite (with clawfoot bath) $230

Straw House 22 Cambridge Rd ☎06 306 8577, ⓦthestrawhouse.co.nz. Cosy self-contained two-bedroom house built of straw bales, stylishly decorated and very comfortable. Breakfast goodies are generously provided and there's a decent discount for second and subsequent nights. $270

EATING

Lunch at a winery restaurant or a platter among the vines is an essential part of the Martinborough experience, though the town also caters to discerning diners with several restaurants charging moderate to high prices, in return for high-quality dishes.

Café Medici 9 Kitchener St ☎06 306 9965, ⓦcafemedici. co.nz. Busy breakfast and lunch café efficiently serving the likes of bruschetta ($17.50) or classic dinner mains of fish and chips or lamb tagine for under $30. There's jazz on Friday evenings. Daily 8.30am–4.30pm, plus Thurs–Sat 6.30pm–late in summer.

★**Circus Cinema Restaurant and Bar** 34 Jellicoe St ☎06 306 9442, ⓦcircus.net.nz. Wonderful coffee in the atmospheric bar, plus an unpretentious restaurant specialising in pizzas ($22–26) but with some other dishes like Vietnamese pho with chicken ($22) and

delicious desserts ($12–15). The place also happens to be a bijou HD cinema with two screens and a penchant for showing art-house classics. Sit watching the film, sipping your wine, and a tap on the shoulder announces your dessert. Mon–Wed & Fri–Sun 3pm–late.

The Grocer 3 Kitchener St. If you're looking to pack a picnic head to this gourmet specialist selling local produce such as olives, cheese and charcuterie. Feb–Nov Wed–Sun 10am–5pm, Dec & Jan daily 10am–4pm.

★**Pinocchio** 3 Kitchener St ☎06 306 6094. Wonderful, unassuming restaurant in a shady courtyard that produces classy evening meals (try confit duck leg on *kumara* gratin for $38) along with an expansive wine list from the local vineyards. Worth booking ahead. Wed–Sun 6pm–late; last reservations 8.30pm.

DRINKING

Martinborough Brewery 8 Ohio St ☎06 306 6249, ⓦmartinboroughbeer.com. Boutique brewery with beer

tasting room. Try their Black Nectar, an oyster stout made with the local water. Mon & Thurs–Sun 11am–7pm.

WINERIES

Over twenty **wineries** are accessible on foot or by bike, guided by the free and widely available *Wairarapa Wine Trail* sheet. During the summer, places generally open from 11am–4pm at weekends and have shorter hours midweek. Almost all charge $5 entry, sometimes refunded with any wine purchase.

Ata Rangi 14 Puruatanga Rd ☎06 306 9570, ⓦatarangi.co.nz. One of New Zealand's finest Pinot Noir producers also does the excellent Célèbre Merlot/Syrah blend and a couple of lovely steely Chardonnays. The tasting cellar is tiny and charges $5 for tastings. Dec–Feb daily noon–4pm, Mar–Nov Mon–Fri 1–3pm, Sat & Sun noon–4pm.

Margrain Vineyard Cnr Huangarua & Ponatahi rds ☎06 306 9292, ⓦmargrainvineyard.co.nz. Good-quality wine from the relaxed cellar door plus the great little *Vineyard Café* (generally open for lunch Wed–Sun) overlooking the vines with well-priced dishes (nothing over $20). The most entertaining tasting notes you will ever read. Tastings $5–10 (dependent on wines tasted), tour $35 (Tues–Sat 11.30am). Mon–Thurs 11am–3pm

Fri noon–4pm, Sat 11am–5pm, Sun 11am–4pm.

Muirlea Rise 50 Princess Street ☎06 306 9332, ⓦmuirlearise.co.nz. One of the original Martinborough vineyards and it remains one of the smallest, selling only through its cellar doors. Shawn, the owner, runs the place almost single-handedly, has great knowledge and loves to chat about the Pinot Noirs, his fortifieds and the wine business in general, making it a great place to start your journey. $5 service charge with tastings. Mon, Tues, Sat & Sun 11am–5pm.

Palliser 96 Kitchener St ☎06 306 9019, ⓦpalliser. co.nz. Pioneering winery which limits its impact on the environment while producing premium wines and running cooking classes. $5 information charge with tastings. Daily 10.30am–4pm.

7

Micro 14c Ohio St ☎06 306 9716. Unsurprisingly tiny wine bar with equally wee courtyard out the back that only serves small plates but somehow manages to squeeze in a couple of dozen craft beers as well as fine local wines. If they're not too busy, you can get a flight of wines to taste (Pinot Noir $25). Mon, Thurs & Fri 4pm–late, Sat & Sun 3–late.

Cape Palliser

Coast with the Post • Departs Featherstone Mon–Fri 8.30am • $85 includes picnic lunch • ☎027 430 8866, ⊛tothecoastwiththepost.co.nz

Cosmopolitan Martinborough stands in dramatic contrast to the stark, often windswept coast around **Cape Palliser**, 60km south, where the weather is renowned to be incredibly changeable. The southernmost point on the North Island, the cape was named in honour of James Cook's mentor, Rear Admiral Sir Hugh Palliser. With gentle walks around the stunning coastline between Ngawi and Cape Palliser and probable encounters with **fur seals** at close quarters, there's little else to do out here other than embrace nature, as swimming is unsafe and organised activities non-existent.

Putangirua Pinnacles
13km south of Martinborough

The Cape Palliser road twists through tranquil coastal hills until it meets the sea near the **Putangirua Pinnacles**, dozens of grey soft-rock spires and fluted cliffs up to 50m high, formed by wind and rain selectively eroding the surrounding silt and gravel. From the parking area, where there are BBQ areas and a DOC campsite (see below), allow a couple of hours to wander up the easy streambed to the base of the pinnacles, up to a viewpoint and then back along a pretty, ridge-top bush track.

Ngawi

Beyond the pinnacles, the sealed road hugs a wonderfully scenic stretch of rugged, exposed coastline for 15km to **Ngawi**, a small fishing village where all manner of colourful **bulldozers** grind out their last days, hauling sometimes massive fishing boats up the steep gravel beach. It's five kilometres further along a gravel road to the cape proper, where a resurgent **fur seal colony**, right beside the road, is overlooked by the century-old Cape Palliser **lighthouse**, standing on a knoll 60m above the sea at the top of a long flight of some 250 steps. It's easy enough to get within 15m of the seals, but they can become aggressive if they feel threatened, and move surprisingly quickly, given their bulk – keep your distance from pups or their parents will bite you, and don't get between any seal and the sea.

ACCOMMODATION AND EATING   CAPE PALLISER

Putangirua Pinnacles campsite Halfway between Lake Ferry and Cape Palliser. A view of the Cook Strait and a pebbly beach across the road are all you get at this DOC site that's within walking distance of the Pinnacles. It can get windy. There's tap water and toilets. Camping $8

Palliser Bay Beach House 34 Seaview Ave, Ngawi ☎027 485 9522, ⊛palliserbreak.com. This old-style holiday house on the hillside in Ngawi village offers good value for money and has great ocean views, a decent size lounge with kitchen and two bedrooms. It's a handy base for exploring the coast and walks to the lighthouse. $165

The Captains Table Cape Palliser Road, Ngawi ☎027 438 8007. Fresh home-made burgers, fish and chips and ground coffee sold from a caravan beside the public park in the centre of the village. Feb–Nov Fri 4pm–7pm, Sat 11am–7.40pm & Sun 11am–4pm; Dec & Jan daily 11am–8pm.

Waimeha Camping Village 2805 Cape Palliser Road, 3km north of Ngawi ☎06 307 8992, ⊛waimehacamping. co.nz. Brand new cabins and camping facilities beside a family farm backed by stunning hills and across the road from a grainy beach. The ten cabins can sleep up to four people, and the friendly owners have a small shop selling non-perishable foods and rent bikes. Camping $18, cabins $80

Greytown

Laid out in 1853, the genteel settlement of **GREYTOWN** lies in the heart of the Wairarapa, straddling the SH2 highway connecting Wellington and Napier. Once Wairarapa's main settlement, it declined when the railway bypassed the town and revived only when it became the favoured getaway for weekending Wellingtonians. The two-storey wooden buildings give the town a strong country Victorian feel and house assorted art galleries, "collectibles" shops, boutiques, excellent cafés and stylish B&Bs, as well as a great traditional butcher on 67 Main St.

Cobblestones Early Settlers Museum

169 Main St • June–Sept Mon & Fri 10am–4pm but daily during school holidays;,Oct–May daily 10am–4pm • $7 • ☎06 304 9687, ⓦcobblestonesmuseum.org.nz

Local historical buildings (one containing Schoc, a chocolate shop worth entering for the smell alone) have been re-sited here next to the original Greytown stables and surrounded by pleasant gardens. It's entertaining to wander round for an hour or two, peering through windows, trying to identify farm implements and admiring the room reconstructions. There's a **printing works**, and a smart new entrance building containing carriages and a *waka*.

ARRIVAL AND INFORMATION · GREYTOWN · 7

By train and bus Metlink commuter trains (☎0800 801 700 ⓦmetlink.org.nz) from Wellington stop at Woodside train station where the connecting Metlink bus #204 shuttles the 5km to Greytown village centre and onwards to Masterton.

Information 89 Main St, inside the library (staffed Fri 2–4pm, Sat & Sun 11am–3pm, otherwise unmanned Mon–Fri 9.30am–5pm). Neatly organized information and brochures on things to do locally.

ACCOMMODATION

Much accommodation is targeted at the smart set, but there's more choice for the budget traveller here than in Martinborough.

Greytown Camp Ground Kuratawhiti St ☎06 304 9387, ⓦgreytowncampground.co.nz. Basic campsite with two amenity blocks right next door to a large children's playground, the town swimming pool and tennis courts. $15, room $55

★ **Shy Cottage & Pequillo** 39 Main St ☎06 304 8387, ⓦshycottage.co.nz. Two self-contained historic cottages at the back of the owners' house and enclosed by pretty gardens. Both have small kitchens, quaint lounges and bedrooms with king-size beds; the Shy Cottage also has its own private deck with BBQ. $160

TurkeyRed 53 Main St ☎06 304 9569, ⓦturkeyredhotel. co.nz. Cheerfully decorated rooms upstairs in the old hotel with shared bathrooms, although each room has its own sink. Out back is a small, slightly cramped, backpackers. Dorms $35, doubles $80

EATING AND DRINKING

The town's dining leans towards the upmarket, though there are some good down-to-earth places as well.

★ **Cahoots Café** 97 Main St ☎06 304 8480. Not as cool and stylish as some of the newer competition, this small neighbourhood café serves great coffee and produces generous meals from a tiny kitchen. The staff welcome visitors and throw friendly abuse at their regulars. Mon–Fri 7am–4pm, Sat & Sun 8am–4pm.

Cuckoo 128 Main St ☎06 304 8992. Funky pizza and pasta joint serving the ever-popular Kiwi peppered with *kumara* and lamb chorizo ($21). If you still have room, tuck in to one of their cheesecakes. Wed–Fri 5–9pm, Sat & Sun noon–2.30pm & 5–9pm.

Salute 83 Main St ☎06 304 9825. Popular spot offering imaginative tapas ($11–18), such as *Porcini* duck risotto or *kumara* and pistachio falafels. Mon 5.30–8pm, Wed–Sat noon–9pm, Sun 11am–2.30pm.

Masterton and around

Though it is Wairarapa's largest town (population 16,000), workaday **MASTERTON**, crouched at the foot of the Tararua Range, is of only passing interest, with a commercial heart strung along the parallel Chapel, Queen and Dixon streets. On the town's eastern side **Queen Elizabeth Park** provides a pleasant opportunity to stroll through formal gardens.

Aratoi

Corner of Bruce and Dixon sts, opposite Queen Elizabeth Park • Daily 10am–4.30pm • Optional donation • ☎06 370 0001, ⓦaratoi.co.nz

GOLDEN SHEARS

The town's major event is the annual **Golden Shears** competition (🌐 goldenshears. co.nz), effectively the Olympiad of all things woolly, held on the three days leading up to the first Saturday in March. Contestants flock from around the world to demonstrate their prowess with the broad-blade handpiece; a top shearer can remove a fleece in under a minute, though for maximum points it must be done with skill as well as speed, and leave a smooth and unblemished, if shivering, beast. For a few bucks you can just walk in on the early rounds, but to attend the entertaining finals on Friday and Saturday nights you'll need to book well in advance.

This museum-gallery gives a good insight into the history of the Wairarapa region, with the evolving exhibition space housed in a former Wesleyan church relocated from the site of a nearby fast-food chain. Among the highlights are the **oldest Māori house site** (1180 AD) in New Zealand, part of an archeological exhibition based around findings at Omoekau, Palliser Bay. From the gallery collection the most interesting exhibits are early Lindauer portraits of local Māori (ask to see them if they're not on display) and a Barbara Hepworth copper and bronze from 1956.

Wool Shed (National Museum of Sheep and Shearing)

12 Dixon St • Daily: 10am–4pm • $8 • ☎ 06 378 8008, 🌐 thewoolshednz.com

An excellent museum on all things woolly; there's even weaving on Wednesdays. Housed in two century-old shearing sheds relocated from rural Wairarapa, it's filled with everything from sheep pens and shearing handpieces to pressed bales of wool stencilled with the marks of sheep stations, and a replica cloak from LOTR. Classic 1957 footage of Kiwi shearing hero Godfrey Bowen shows how it should be done, and there's usually footage of recent Golden Shears finals, perhaps showing the super-fast handiwork of David Fagan, New Zealand's five-time world champ and record-breaking sixteen-time Golden Shears winner.

Tararua Forest Park

Accessed from SH2, 25km west of Masterton • Hut bookings ☎ 06 377 0700, 🌐 doc.govt.nz

Draped over the hills to the west of town, the **Tararua Forest Park** offers excellent tramping through beech and podocarp forest to the subalpine tops, but be aware that the notoriously fickle weather in this area can be dangerous. Serious walkers should consider the **Powell–Jumbo Tramp**, a worthwhile twelve-hour circuit that can be broken down into two or more manageable days by staying at DOC **huts** ($15, advance bookings essential) evenly spaced along the route. The track starts at the backcountry hut-style *Holdsworth Lodge*. Day-trippers can undertake easy riverside walks (1–2hr) or head three hours across easy ground to the cosy Atiwhakatu Hut ($5), which has bunks.

ARRIVAL AND DEPARTURE   MASTERTON AND AROUND

By train Metlink (☎ 0800 801 700, 🌐 metlink.org.nz) runs commuter services from Wellington. The train station is a 15min walk from the centre at the end of Perry St; call Rideshop (☎ 06 377 4231) for a taxi.
Destinations Featherston (5 Mon–Fri, 2 Sat & Sun; 45min); Wellington (5 Mon–Fri, 2 Sat & Sun; 1hr 40min).

By bus InterCity buses (☎ 04 385 0520) run north to Palmerston North, stopping at 316 Queen St, a short walk from the i-SITE visitor centre; Metlink (☎ 0800 801 700) runs south to Martinborough.
Destinations Greytown (6 Mon–Fri, 3 Sat; 25min); Martinborough (1 Mon–Fri, 3 Sat; 1hr); Palmerston North (1 Tues–Fri; 1hr 35min).

INFORMATION

i-SITE visitor centre Corner of Bruce and Dixon sts (Mon–Fri 9am–4.30pm, Sat & Sun 10am–4pm; ☎ 06 370 0900, 🌐 wairarapanz.com). Enthusiastic staff can give information on local hikes as well as the usual services.

ACCOMMODATION

Cornwall Park 119 Cornwall St, 2km west of the town centre ☎06 378 2939, ⓦcornwallparkmotel.co.nz. A clean, peaceful old-style motel with a pool, spa and free wi-fi. It's all a bit dated-looking, but everything works perfectly well and units are undoubtedly great value. **$109**

Gallin Farmstay 143 Matapihi Rd St, 9km northeast of the town centre ☎06 370 4103, ⓦgallinfarmalpacas.co.nz. Set on an alpaca farm amongst stunning countryside with panoramic mountain views, the two modern en-suite guest rooms come with a gourmet breakfast including farm eggs and homemade jams. **$185**

Mawley Park Motor Camp 5 Oxford St ☎06 378 6454, ⓦmawleypark.co.nz. Masterton's best budget accommodation is this riverside spot, which offers decent flat campsites ($36) interspersed with trees, some new en-suite units and a range of the more traditional cabins and motel units. Cabins **$70**, en suites **$100**

EATING AND DRINKING

★ **Café Strada** 232 Queen St ☎06 378 8450, ⓦcafestrada.co.nz. The best eating and drinking option in town happens to be within the town's Regent Theatre (movie & meal deals available) providing tasty counter grub during the day and quality, moderately priced dinners (under $30) featuring dishes such as crispy-skinned South Island salmon. Licensed. Free wi-fi. Daily 7.15am–8.30pm.

Ten O'clock Cookie Bakery & Café 180 Queen St ☎06 377 4551, ⓦtenoclockcookie.co.nz. Large bustling café with fantastic cakes, croissants, fritters and 7-grain breads all served up in various forms but especially famous for its award-winning Shearer's Pie and pan-fried Halloumi ($17). Mon–Wed 7am–4.30pm, Thurs & Fri 7am–9.30pm, Sat 8am–9.30pm.

Entice At Aratoi, corner of Bruce and Dixon sts ☎06 377 3166, ⓦentice.co.nz. Licensed café at the museum-gallery serving delicious counter food including monster savoury muffins, gourmet pies and great coffee, with nothing over $23. Daily 8am–4pm.

Castlepoint

The 300km of coastline from Cape Palliser to Cape Kidnappers, near Napier is bleak, desolate and almost entirely inaccessible – except for **CASTLEPOINT**, 65km east of Masterton, where early explorers found a welcome break in the "perpendicular line of cliff". A lighthouse presides over the rocky knoll, which is linked to the mainland by a thin hourglass double **beach** that encloses a sheltered **lagoon** known as the Basin. Wairarapa families retreat here for summer fun and surfers ride the breakers, though when the weather turns it is a wonderfully wild bit of coastline. Unless you are a keen surfer, a day-visit will suffice; if you do decide to stay, take all your provisions with you.

ACCOMMODATION   CASTLEPOINT

Castlepoint Holiday Park & Motels 1 Jetty Rd ☎06 372 6705, ⓦcastlepoint.co.nz. Wonderfully situated, traditional Kiwi holidaymaker campsite, in the middle of nowhere and within earshot of the crashing waves. The broad range of reasonably kept accommodation also includes cottages and motel units ($140–180). Camping **$20**, kitchen cabins **$90**

Pukaha Mount Bruce National Wildlife Centre

SH2, 28km north of Masterton • Daily: 9am–4.30pm; check website for feeding and talk times • $20 • Guided tour daily 11am & 2pm ($45 incl. entry); night walks Sat 1.5hr/$55; behind the scenes $125 • ☎06 375 8004, ⓦpukaha.org.nz

Pukaha Mount Bruce National Wildlife Centre is one of the best places in the country to view endangered native birds, and is staffed by people engaged in bringing them back from the edge. Kokako, whio, kakariki, hihi, kiwi, takahe (a "rainbow couple") and more can be found in aviaries set along the trails through lowland primeval forest. The nocturnal **kiwi house** houses Manukura, a rare white kiwi, and there's also a **kiwi breeding facility** (ask about chicks). Beyond the aviaries, several thousand acres of forest have been set aside for reintroducing birds to the wild. Bring a packed lunch for the picnic area, or support the on-site café (no refunds if a kaka spills your coffee).

Marlborough, Nelson and Kaikoura

KAIKOURA

Marlborough, Nelson and Kaikoura

The South Island kicks off spectacularly in a blaze of indented bays and secluded hideaways along the northern coast, then descends in a sweep of golden beaches to an impressive array of national parks, sophisticated wineries and natural wonders. Despite discounted airfares from the North Island, many visitors still arrive by interisland ferry, striking land at Picton – drab in the winter, lively in the summer and looking out to the beautiful Marlborough Sounds. Here, bays full of unfathomably deep water lap at tiny beaches, each with its rickety boat jetty, and the land rises steeply to forest or stark pasture. South of **Picton**, slurp your merry way through Marlborough, New Zealand's most feted winemaking region centred on the modest towns of Blenheim and Renwick; a night or two in one of the rural B&Bs here and some time spent around the wineries will have you ready to explore further. To the west, lively Nelson is the springboard for forays into the wilds of Abel Tasman National Park, with the country's most gorgeous coastal tracks and dazzling golden beaches; while further north the relatively isolated Golden Bay offers peaceful times with uniformly decent weather. The curve of the bay culminates in a long sandspit that juts into the ocean – Farewell Spit, an extraordinary and unique habitat bordering Kahurangi National Park, through which the rugged and spectacular Heaphy Track forges a route to the West Coast.

The least visited of the region's well-preserved areas of natural splendour is the sparsely populated **Nelson Lakes National Park**, principally a spot for tramping to alpine lakes or fishing, though the nearby **Buller River** also attracts raft and kayak rats.

The more energetic activities of the national parks set you up nicely for a few days of ecotourism in **Kaikoura** where **whale watching** and **swimming with dolphins** and **seals** are the main draws.

The region's **weather** is some of the sunniest in the land, particularly around Blenheim and Nelson, which regularly compete for the honour of the greatest number of sunshine hours in New Zealand.

GETTING AROUND

By ferry and train Cross Cook Strait by ferry (see page 377) and link up with the region's only train, from Picton to Christchurch (Oct–April; 1 daily).

By bus Buses fill in the gaps, doing the Picton–Christchurch run via Kaikoura and to Blenheim and Nelson where there are connections for the Abel Tasman National Park and Golden Bay. The main operators running between Picton and Christchurch are Atomic Shuttles (☎03 349 0697, ⊚atomictravel.co.nz) and InterCity (☎09 583 5780, ⊚intercitycoach.co.nz).

The Marlborough Sounds

The **Marlborough Sounds** are undeniably picturesque, a stimulating filigree of bays, inlets, islands and peninsulas rising abruptly from the water to rugged, lush green wilderness and open farmland. Large parts are only accessible by sea, which also provides the ideal vantage point. The area is part working farms, including salmon or mussel farms, and

ABEL TASMAN NATIONAL PARK

Highlights

❶ The Queen Charlotte Track This beautiful multi-day hike is made all the more manageable by staying in great backpackers and B&Bs, and having your bags carried for you. See page 408

❷ Marlborough Wine Country No trip to this area is complete without supping Sauvignon Blanc in New Zealand's most famous wine region. See page 412

❸ Nelson A vibrant arts community, vineyards on the doorstep, a laidback atmosphere and great weather combine to make Nelson an essential stop. See page 417

❹ Abel Tasman National Park Crystal-clear water and golden beaches are rewards for hiking the lush Coast Track or kayaking the myriad inlets and islands. See page 430

❺ Farewell Spit tours Join an organized excursion to access the outer reaches of this unique place. See page 443

❻ Heaphy Track The huge range of dramatic scenery and final sense of achievement puts this Great Walk up with the best. See page 444

❼ Kaikoura Whale-watching along with dolphin and seal-swimming trips from this pretty town are the highlight of many a visitor's trip. See page 450

HIGHLIGHTS ARE MARKED ON THE MAP ON PAGE 400

part reserve – a mixture of islands, forested sections of coast and land-bound tracts. The Sounds' nexus, **Picton**, is the jumping-off point for **Queen Charlotte Sound** where cruises and water taxis provide access to the undemanding, varied and scenic **Queen Charlotte Track**. Heading west, Queen Charlotte Drive takes a scenic winding route to the small community of **Havelock**, New Zealand's green-lipped mussel capital; turn off to explore the spectacular vistas of Pelorus Sound and take the back roads or a boat to view the rich, swirling waters of French Pass, one of the world's great tidal bores.

Picton

Cook Strait ferries from Wellington arrive in **PICTON**, a small harbour and tourist town sandwiched between hills and Queen Charlotte Sound. Many people stop only

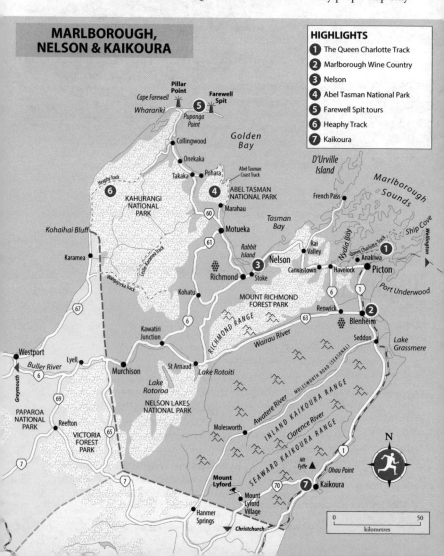

MARLBOROUGH, NELSON & KAIKOURA

HIGHLIGHTS
1. The Queen Charlotte Track
2. Marlborough Wine Country
3. Nelson
4. Abel Tasman National Park
5. Farewell Spit tours
6. Heaphy Track
7. Kaikoura

for a coffee, looking out over the water before pressing on, but Picton is the best base for exploring the **Queen Charlotte Track**, serviced by several water taxis, and a good spot for getting into the Sounds on **cruises and kayak trips**. The town itself has a few noteworthy attractions and it also makes a decent base for exploring the **wine region** around Blenheim, 25 minutes' drive to the south.

Brief history

There was a European settlement in the region as early as 1827 when John Guard established a whaling station, but Picton itself didn't come into being until the New Zealand Company purchased its site for £300 in 1848. Picton flourished as a port and **service town** for the Wairau Plains to the south but developed predominantly as the most convenient service port for Queen Charlotte Sound and travel between the islands.

The Edwin Fox

Close to the ferry terminal • Daily: Oct–May 9am–5pm; June–Sept 9am–3pm • $10

At its western end of Picton's phoenix-palm-lined waterfront, close to the ferry terminal, the hulk of the 600-tonne, Calcutta-built **Edwin Fox** is the world's oldest surviving merchant ship, the last of the vessels that brought migrants to New Zealand. This 1853 example operated as a troop carrier in the Crimean War, transported convicts to Australia and helped establish New Zealand's frozen meat trade before being beached at nearby Shakespeare Bay in 1967; she was later towed to Picton and raised onto the dry dock where she is today. A small but well-designed museum prepares you for the age-blackened hull of the last true "East Indiaman" clipper left in the world. Standing on the small part of the rebuilt lower deck gives a sense of what it must have been like to sail, but the best bit is in the large open hold, all heavy planking and teak ribs.

EcoWorld Aquarium and Wildlife Rehabilitation Centre

Next to the *Edwin Fox* • Daily: Dec–Feb 9.30am–7pm; March–Dec 9.30am–5.00pm; feeding at 11am & 2pm • $24 • ⓦ ecoworldnz.co.nz

EcoWorld offers an insight into the flora and fauna of the Marlborough Sounds with local marine life (including little blue penguins), small sharks and seahorses, a preserved giant squid plus tuatara, including babies, giant weta, and a breeding programme for yellow-crowned kakariki. It is best visited at feeding time. They also have the only cinema in town.

Picton Heritage and Whaling Museum

9 London Quay • Daily 10am–4pm • $5

At the end of the High Street, the **Picton Heritage and Whaling Museum** uses photos and whaling artefacts including a harpoon gun and carved whalebone (scrimshaw) to illustrate the working life of the Perano Whaling Station which operated from Queen Charlotte Sound until 1964. There are also displays of Māori *taonga*, general historical photos and artefacts.

National Whale Centre

London Quay • Tues–Sun 11am–6pm • Free • ⓦ aworldwithwhales.com

Formerly a virtual museum, this waterfront centre aims to share all aspects of current research on international biodiversity and cetacean protection. There's material on the history of Māori and Pakeha relations with whales, including a rundown of the local whaling industry, and an emphasis in the displays towards new technology and modern art.

ARRIVAL AND DEPARTURE   PICTON

By ferry Interislander ferry foot passengers disembark close to the town centre, while Bluebridge foot passengers and all vehicles disembark on the western side of town about 1km from the centre; Bluebridge operates a free shuttle bus to the i-SITE.

Destinations Wellington (6–9 daily).

By train Interislander ferry schedules work in with the summer-only Coastal Pacific train to Christchurch (one-way fares from $75).

Destinations Christchurch, via Blenheim and Kaikoura (daily Oct–April; 1 daily).

By bus Buses stop outside the Interislander ferry terminal

and again at the i-SITE.

Destinations Blenheim (8 daily; 30min); Christchurch (4–5 daily; 5hr–5hr 30min); Kaikoura (4–5 daily; 2hr 15min); Nelson (5 daily; 2hr).

By plane Picton airport, 9km south of town, is served by Soundsair (℡0800 505 005, ⒲soundsair.com). A bus ($7 one way) meets flights and runs into Picton.

Destinations Wellington (6 daily).

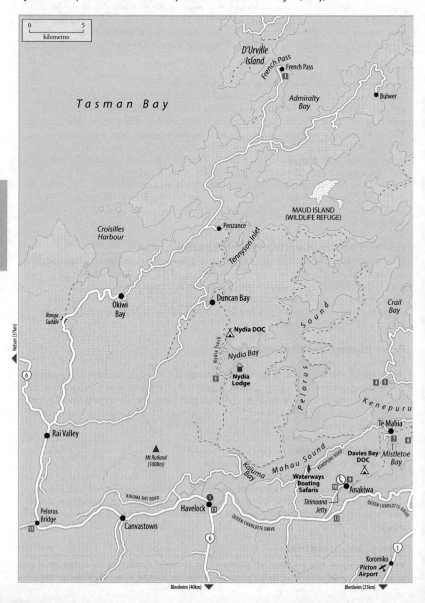

GETTING AROUND

By bus Ritchies (☎03 578 5467) and InterCity go to Blenheim. The half-hour run costs $14.

By mail bus It's possible to tag along in a minivan on the Rural Mail Bus Service (☎022 187 7532) serving remote spots linking postal centres in Havelock and Picton, along with the southern end of the Queen Charlotte Track at Anakiwa. There are several runs each day. Fares start at $15

By car Most major international and domestic car-rental companies have offices at the ferry terminal or in town. I-Site has pamphlet listing them.

By taxi A1 Picton Shuttles ☎022 018 8472 or ☎0800 A1PICTON, ⓦa1pictonshuttles.co.nz.Picton Shuttles ☎0800 252 520, ⓦpictonshuttles.nz.

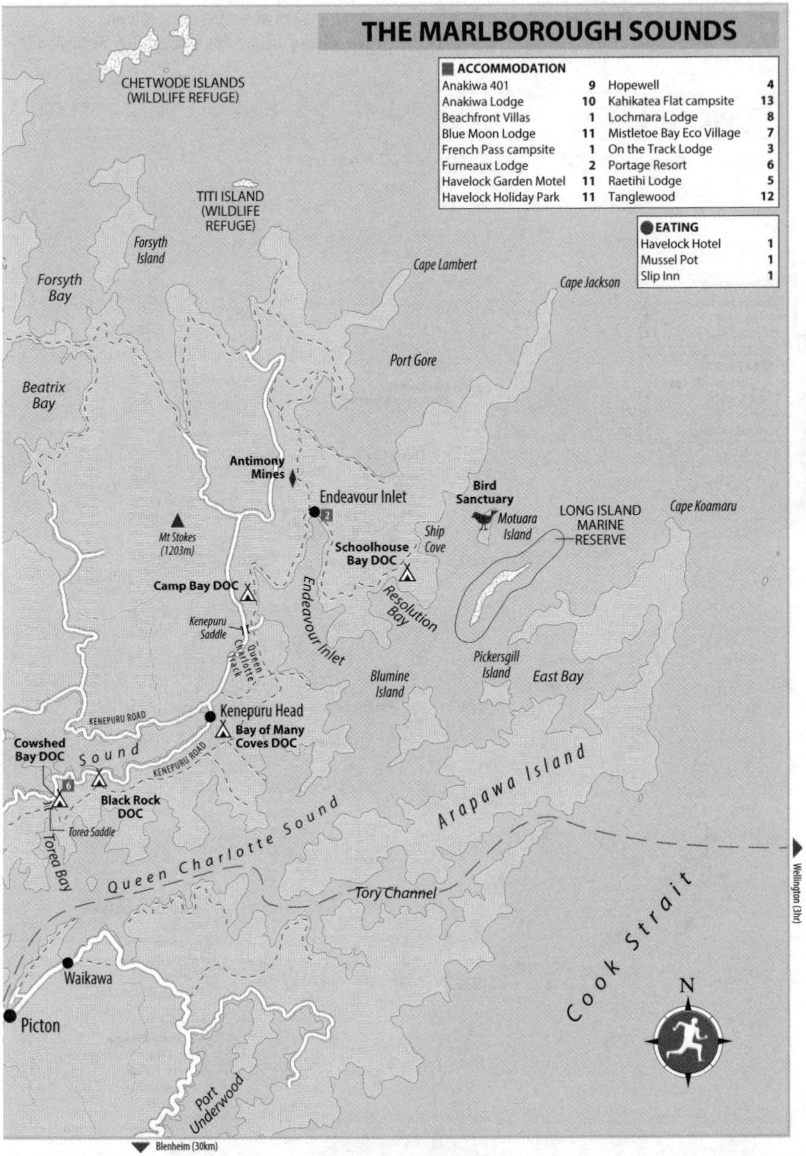
THE MARLBOROUGH SOUNDS
ACCOMMODATION
Anakiwa 401 9
Anakiwa Lodge 10
Beachfront Villas 1
Blue Moon Lodge 11
French Pass campsite 1
Furneaux Lodge 2
Havelock Garden Motel 11
Havelock Holiday Park 11
Hopewell 4
Kahikatea Flat campsite 13
Lochmara Lodge 8
Mistletoe Bay Eco Village 7
On the Track Lodge 3
Portage Resort 6
Raetihi Lodge 5
Tanglewood 12
EATING
Havelock Hotel 1
Mussel Pot 1
Slip Inn 1
CHETWODE ISLANDS (WILDLIFE REFUGE)
TITI ISLAND (WILDLIFE REFUGE)
Forsyth Island
Forsyth Bay
Beatrix Bay
Cape Lambert
Cape Jackson
Port Gore
Antimony Mines
Endeavour Inlet
Bird Sanctuary
Motuara Island
LONG ISLAND MARINE RESERVE
Cape Koamaru
Mt Stokes (1203m)
Ship Cove
Schoolhouse Bay DOC
Camp Bay DOC
Kenepuru Saddle
Queen Charlotte Track
Endeavour Inlet
Resolution Bay
Pickersgill Island
East Bay
Blumine Island
Kenepuru Head
Bay of Many Coves DOC
KENEPURU ROAD
Cowshed Bay DOC
Sound
Black Rock DOC
Torea Saddle
Torea Bay
Arapawa Island
Queen Charlotte Sound
Tory Channel
Wellington (3hr)
Waikawa
Picton
Cook Strait
N
Port Underwood
Blenheim (30km)

By water taxi A number of companies run services around the sound, as well as cruises (see page 406), including: Beachcomber Cruises (☎0800 624 526, ⓦbeachcombercruises.co.nz); Cougar Line (☎0800 504 090, ⓦcougarline.co.nz); Arrow (☎03 573 8229, ⓦarrowwatertaxis.co.nz).

INFORMATION AND ACTIVITIES

Visitor information The combined i-SITE and DOC agency is on the foreshore, a 5min walk from the ferry terminal (Mon–Fri 9am–5pm, Sat & Sun 8am–4pm5pm in summer; ☎03 520 3113, ⓦmarlboroughnz.com). It's packed with leaflets on the town and the rest of the South Island, including a free *Picton and Blenheim* map and DOC's free *Queen Charlotte Track* visitor guide. It also has large luggage lockers ($2/ half day $4/ full day or overnight)

Internet Free access during opening hours at the library, 67 High St (Mon–Fri 8am–5pm, Sat 10am–1pm, Sun 1.30–4.30pm), and free wi-fi in the centre of town.

Scuba diving GoDive Marlborough (66 Wellington St;

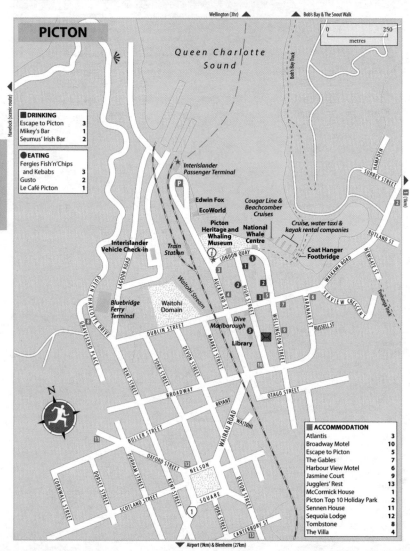

PICTON

Queen Charlotte Sound

0   250
metres

Wellington (3hr)
Bob's Bay & The Snout Walk
Havelock (scenic route)
Bob's Bay Track
Hampden
SURREY STREET
RUTLAND ST
NEWGATES ST
SEAVIEW CRESCENT
Timahaia Track

Interislander Passenger Terminal

Edwin Fox
EcoWorld

Cougar Line & Beachcomber Cruises

Picton Heritage and Whaling Museum

National Whale Centre

Cruise, water taxi & kayak rental companies

Coat Hanger Footbridge

Interislander Vehicle Check-in

Train Station

LONDON QUAY
AUCKLAND ST
HIGH STREET
WAIKAWA ROAD
WELLINGTON STREET
RUSSELL ST

QUEEN CHARLOTTE DRIVE
LAGOON ROAD
GRAVESEND PLACE

Bluebridge Ferry Terminal

Waitohi Domain
Waitohi Stream

Dive Marlborough

Library

DUBLIN STREET
YORK STREET
DEVON STREET
MARKET STREET
TARANAKI ST

BROADWAY
BRYANT
WAITOHI
OTAGO STREET

KENT STREET
BULLER STREET
OXFORD STREET
DURHAM STREET
NELSON
WAIRAU ROAD
DEVON STREET

CORNWALL STREET
DORSET STREET
SCOTLAND STREET
KENT STREET
YORK STREET
SQUARE
CANTERBURY ST

N

■ **DRINKING**
Escape to Picton	3
Mikey's Bar	1
Seumus' Irish Bar	2

● **EATING**
Fergies Fish'n'Chips and Kebabs	3
Gusto	2
Le Café Picton	1

■ **ACCOMMODATION**
Atlantis	3
Broadway Motel	10
Escape to Picton	5
The Gables	7
Harbour View Motel	6
Jasmine Court	9
Jugglers' Rest	13
McCormick House	1
Picton Top 10 Holiday Park	2
Sennen House	11
Sequoia Lodge	12
Tombstone	8
The Villa	4

▼ Airport (9km) & Blenheim (27km)

☎ 03 573 7831, ⊛ godive.co.nz) offers scuba discovery dives in the Double Cove fish reserve ($245), two-tank guided days ($295) and a 24hr guided wreck tour diving the *Mikhail Lermontov*, a Soviet cruise ship that became the southern hemisphere's largest diveable wreck when it hit rocks in 1986 ($360 including meals, gear, two guided dives and a night at the *Lermontov Lodge*). They also offer a range of dive courses and can organize trips off Kaikoura.

Winery tours Most tours of the Marlborough Wine Country pick up from Picton (see page 411).

ACCOMMODATION

Atlantis London Quay ☎ 03 573 7390, ⊛ atlantishostel. co.nz; map p.404. Central hostel, close to the ferry, with a variety of colourfully decorated dorms (including a cheap six-bunk room for just $20 if you have your own sleeping bag). Cosy doubles and free breakfast, dessert, movies and Art Deco powder room. Dorms $25, doubles $60

Broadway Motel 113 High St ☎ 0800 101 919, ⊛ broadwaymotel.co.nzl; map p.404. Attractive, relatively modern motel units with large windows and all the usual mod-cons, including Sky TV. Everything is clean and well kept and they have a good recycling policy. $119

Escape to Picton 33 Wellington St ☎ 03 573 5573, ⊛ escapetopicton.com; map p.404. Tiny, chic, boutique hotel finished to the highest standard, including freestanding baths in two of the three suites. . Rates vary widely so it pays to check the website. $350

The Gables 20 Waikawa Rd ☎ 03 573 6772, ⊛ thegables. co.nz; map p.404. Pleasant and welcoming B&B with three rooms in the house (two with en suite) and two self-contained cottages out back where breakfast is provided. Children and dogs welcome. Doubles $165, cottages $195

Harbour View Motel 30 Waikawa Rd ☎ 0800 101 133, ⊛ harbourviewpicton.co.nz; map p.404. Thirteen spacious and tastefully appointed self-contained units, each with a balcony and great views over the harbour. Guests are treated to a variety of well-kept clean units with a communal laundry and luggage storage if you're going on the Queen Charlotte Track. $165

★ **Jasmine Court** 78 Wellington St ☎ 0800 421 999, ⊛ jasminecourt.co.nz; map p.404. Top-of-the-line medium-sized motel with luxury units professionally run by a long-established couple prepared to go that extra mile. Plush renovated rooms include DVD and CD players, and some have spa baths and verandas. $165

Jugglers' Rest 8 Canterbury St ☎ 03 573 5570, ⊛ jugglersrest.com; map p.404. Small, very welcoming and relaxed shoes-off hostel about a 10min walk from the ferries, with spacious dorms and a couple of quiet rooms in the grounds. There's a strong recycling ethic and the vegetable garden is open to all. You can book breakfast of home-made jam and fresh bread. Closed June–Sept. Dorms $35, doubles $80

McCormick House 21 Leicester St ☎ 03 573 5253, ⊛ mccormickhouse.co.nz; map p.404. Situated in a half acre of native garden, this atmospheric Edwardian villa has an original rimu-panelled staircase, at the top of which are three luxurious, individually decorated rooms. The indulgent breakfasts are made from local produce, and there's a good stock of Kiwi movies and music in the lounge. $360

Picton Top 10 Holiday Park 78 Waikawa Rd ☎ 0800 277 444, ⊛ pictontop10.co.nz; map p.404. Centrally located campsite with swimming pool, children's playground, cabins (bedding $5) and motel-style self-contained units in a pleasant spot with sheltering trees. Camping $22, cabins $78, units $165

Sennen House 9 Oxford St ☎ 03 573 5216, ⊛ sennenhouse. co.nz; map p.404. Just a 10min walk from town, this gorgeous, grand 1886 villa has been tastefully converted into a B&B with three suites, all with limited kitchen facilities. A breakfast hamper and afternoon tea is supplied. $289

Sequoia Lodge 3a Nelson Square ☎ 0800 222 257, ⊛ sequoialodge.co.nz; map p.404. Very popular, well-organized hostel 7min walk from the town centre; free ferry pick-ups on request. Beds and bunks come with lights and side tables, and there's a separate, en-suite female dorm. Breakfast (May–Oct), bikes, spa, nightly pudding and ice cream and home cinema are all free. Dorms $28, doubles $82

★ **Tombstone** 16 Gravesend Place ☎ 03 573 7116 ⊛ tombstonebp.co.nz; map p.404. Wonderfully friendly, well-run hostel just across the road from Bluebridge ferry terminal (and alongside the town cemetery), an easy 10min walk into town. The modern, purpose-built accommodation has great views of the water and is carpeted and double-glazed. The barbecue area, piano, table tennis, gym machines, hot tub, bikes and freshly made hot scones with breakfast, come at no extra charge. Free shuttle for scheduled pick-ups and drop-offs. Dorms $31, doubles $84

The Villa 34 Auckland St ☎ 03 573 6598, ⊛ thevilla. co.nz; map p.404. Central associate YHA set in two houses, and a more modern cottage. When busy it is cramped, but there are all manner of free inducements such as bikes, outdoor spa (with rubber ducks) and apple crumble in winter. There's also a women-only six-bed dorm ($32). Dorms $28, doubles $74

EATING

★ **Gusto** 33 High St ☎ 03 573 7171; map p.404. Cosy and popular, this daytime café opens up onto the street and dishes up delicious breakfasts along with a blackboard lunch menu, home-made counter food, cakes and good coffee. 7am–2.30pm; closed Sat in winter.

Fergies Fish'n'Chips and Kebabs 83a High St ☎03 573 6115, ⓦfergies.nz; map p.404. Fish and chips, burgers and kebabs to eat in or take away, with good vegetarian options. Mon–Wed noon–8pm Thurs–Sat 11am–9pm, Sun 11am–8pm

Le Café Picton 14 London Quay ☎03 573 5588, ⓦlecafepicton.co.nz; map p.404. Bustling, popular and stylish café and bar with pavement seating just across from the Sounds, serving mouthwatering steaks with home-made chilli jam and all sorts of fresh seafood. Lunch mains $21.50–24.50, dinners $22–32. Bands play regularly in the summer. Daily 7.30am–late.

DRINKING AND NIGHTLIFE

Escape to Picton 33 Wellington St ☎03 573 5573, ⓦescapetopicton.com; map p.404. You can pop in to this former bank for a beer (the only Heineken on tap in the town) or bistro fare ($19.50–43.50) such as gourmet fish and chips. Live music on Fridays and Saturdays. Mon–Fri 10am–2.30pm & 5pm–late, Sat & Sun 10am–late.

Mikey's Bar 18 High St ☎03 573 5164; map p.404. Modern bar with very cheap food (all under $30, most around $15), two pool tables, gaming room and a barn-like nightclub out back where there's a variety of live music during the daytime and twilight hours. Daily 10.30am–11pm.

Seumus' Irish Bar 25 Wellington St ☎03 573 5050, wseumusirishbar.co.nz; map p.404. Cosy Irish bar, popular with backpackers for its inexpensive drinks and food. Free wi-fi and courtesy van. There's outdoor seating and live music most nights. Daily noon–1am.

Queen Charlotte Sound

Picton is a pretty spot, but you've barely touched the region's beauty until you've explored **Queen Charlotte Sound**. This wildly indented series of drowned valleys encloses moody picturesque bays, small deserted sandy beaches, headlands with panoramic views and cloistered islands, while grand, lumpy peninsulas offer shelter from the winds and storms, and solitude for the contemplative fisherman or kayaker. For a taste of these labyrinthine waterways, take one of the many **day-cruises** from Picton, but to really appreciate the tranquil beauty you're better off **kayaking** round the bays or **tramping** the Queen Charlotte Track. The relatively calm and warm waters of the Sounds also give the opportunity for **scuba diving**, checking out the rich marine life of the huge wreck of a Soviet cruise ship, the *Mikhail Lermontov* (see page 405).

Motuara Island

A couple of sights at the far end of Queen Charlotte Sound crop up on most itineraries, including the DOC-managed **Motuara Island**, a predator-free wildlife sanctuary that is home to the saddleback, South Island bush robin, bellbird and a few Okarito brown kiwi. All the birds are quite fearless and will rest and fly startlingly close to you. Throughout the island, little blue penguins take advantage of the nesting boxes provided, rather than build their own, and in spring (Oct–Dec), you can gently lift the top of the box and see the baby penguins.

Just across a channel from Motuara Island, **Ship Cove** marks the bay where Captain Cook spent a total of 168 days during his three trips to New Zealand. A large concrete monument – a disappointingly dull block surrounded by cannon – commemorates his five separate visits to the cove.

TOURS AND ACTIVITIES   QUEEN CHARLOTTE SOUND

Water taxis (see page 404) are always flitting about Queen Charlotte Sound, taking hikers to the Queen Charlotte Track, or delivering guests to swanky lodges and rustic hideaways. If you just want to get out on the water this may be all you need, but several companies also run excellent **cruises**.

CRUISES

Beachcomber Cruises ☎0800 624 526, ⓦbeachcomber cruises.co.nz. Although there are many other cruising options

for the Sounds, there is still something unique about the Rural Mail Runs, pulling up at a lonely wharf to deliver the post and odd supplies. The journey includes golden beaches with bush-clad shorelines and dolphins sometimes escort the boat. The downside is that you can't get off for a walk or jump off for a swim. The four-hour Magic Mail Run (Mon–Sat 1.30pm; 4hr; $99) leaves from Picton. Three routes are plied on different days of the week, but there's little to choose between them. In summer, all call into Endeavour Inlet, pass a salmon farm and allow fifteen minutes ashore at Ship Cove. Alternative postal routes explore Pelorus Sound from Havelock (see page 408). This operator also offers trips to Ship Cove (3hr; $81) and to Motuara Island (3hr; $87).

Cougar Line ☎0800 504 090, ⓦcougarline.co.nz. The direct competition to Beachcomber Cruises run similar trips, including a Ship Cove Cruise ($85) and scheduled as well as on-demand water taxi services.

E-ko Tours London Quay ☎0800 945 354, ⓦe-ko.nz. Some of the most sympathetic wildlife trips in the Sounds, including dolphin swimming (2–4hr; $165 to swim; $99 to watch) with dusky, common or bottlenose dolphins, as well as sightings of the endemic Hector's dolphins. To combine dolphin-watching with the Sounds' other sights, join their trips to either Motuara Island (45min, guided; $99) or Ship Cove (1hr unguided; $99), both of which can also be used as a drop-off for Queen Charlotte Track walkers. The Birdwatchers Expedition (daily 1.30pm; $99) gives you the chance to tick many New Zealand species off your list – if you're lucky you may get to see an extremely rare king shag.

Myths and Legends Eco Tours ☎03 573 6901, ⓦeco-tours.co.nz. Run by a sixth-generation local Pakeha and his Māori wife, who tour the bays in their 1930s kauri launch explaining the history and culture of the region ($200/4hr; $250/8hr and lunch; all tours have a two-person minimum).

Queen Charlotte Steam Ship Company ☎03 573 7443, ⓦsteamshipping.co.nz. A variation on the standard cruise, with hour-long cruises (on demand from Short Finger Jetty; $40) puttering about the Sound immediately adjacent to Picton in a 36ft, replica 1920 steel-hull steamboat.

KAYAKING

Visitors dashing straight to Abel Tasman National Park sadly overlook the breathtaking views to be had kayaking Queen Charlotte Sound, where other floating traffic is virtually nonexistent by comparison.

Marlborough Sounds Adventure Company London Quay ☎0800 283 283, ⓦmarlboroughsounds.co.nz. Friendly and professional outfit offering a huge range of guided kayaking trips including half-day paddles from Picton (Oct–April daily; 4hr; $95), a gentle one-day trip (7hr; $130), a two-day trip, initially guided then camping out by yourselves and paddling home the next day ($190); and a fully guided three-day trip in the outer sounds ($595). Rentals are $60 for one day, $100 for two, $135 for three.

Sea Kayak Adventures In the big green shed at the turn-off for Anakiwa ☎03 574 2765, ⓦnzseakayaking.com. Well-run, enthusiastic and intimate, with half-day ($90) and full-day ($125 with lunch) guided trips, a two-day guided and catered trip ($295) and various paddle and walk or bike options. These guys will help you experience the silence of the Sounds. Independent rentals are $60/day, $100/two days and $125/three days.

Queen Charlotte Drive

The 35km Queen Charlotte Drive between Picton and Havelock is a picturesque and spectacular back road, which slides past the flat plain at the head of Queen Charlotte Sound and climbs into the hills overlooking Pelorus Sound before descending to SH6 and Havelock itself. It is a slow and winding drive, but you may want to take it even slower by stopping to wander down to a couple of sheltered coves or up the **Cullen Track** (a 10min walk with spectacular views). With water taxis providing convenient access to fabulous out-of-the-way spots, it may seem a little perverse to try to see the Marlborough Sounds by car – doubly so when you start weaving your way around the slow, narrow roads – but ultimately it is well worth the effort as the views of turquoise bays, seen through the ponga, are magical.

Around 18km west of Picton, a narrow road heads north to **Anakiwa**, the southern end of the Queen Charlotte Track. Here you'll find a wharf used by water taxis taking hikers back to Picton, *Anakiwa Lodge* and *Anakiwa 401* (see page 409), the latter with its coffee caravan.

Kenepuru Road

A couple of kilometres further along Queen Charlotte Drive, **Kenepuru Road** cuts right and begins its 75km journey out along the shores of Kenepuru Sound. There are many picturesque bays and views along the way and the road provides access to several points along the Queen Charlotte Track, running past a handful of DOC campsites and several places to stay before ending at *Hopewell* backpackers.

THE QUEEN CHARLOTTE TRACK

The **Queen Charlotte Track** (70km one way; 3–5 days; open year-round) is a stunning walk partly tracing skyline ridges with views across coastal forest to the waters of Queen Charlotte and Kenepuru sounds. It is broad, relatively easy-going and distinguished from all other Kiwi multi-day tramps by the lack of DOC huts, replaced by some lovely **accommodation**. Access is generally by boat from Picton, and water taxis can **transport your bags** to your next destination each day. Boats call at numerous bays along the way, so less-ambitious walkers can tackle shorter sections, do day-hikes from Picton or take on the track as part of a guided walk.

INFORMATION, COSTS AND ACCESS

The Picton i-SITE can help organize your trip and has the free *Marlborough Sounds Visitor Guide* which contains info about the Queen Charlotte Track; check ⓦdoc.govt.nz or ⓦqctrack.co.nz for more information and updates on track conditions. Parts of the track cross private land and there is a **fee** for anyone over 15 hiking or biking these sections: Queen Charlotte Track Land Cooperative Passes are sold by Picton and Blenheim i-SITEs and a number of accommodations on the track. A one-day pass costs $10; a pass for up to five consecutive days is $18; an annual pass is $25.

Trampers normally **travel north to south** from Ship Cove to Anakiwa, using **water taxis** to drop them off and pick them up. Sections of the track are accessible from Kenepuru Road, but there is no public transport. There is no overnight parking at Anakiwa, although the Rural Mail Bus Service (see page 403) can take you there.

Water taxi companies (see page 404) all offer a standard package with drop-off at Ship Cove, bag transfers and pick-up at Anakiwa for $101–105 – pick whoever has the most convenient schedule. Bikes cost $5/journey, double kayaks $30.

GUIDED WALKS, COMBOS AND DAY-TRIPS

Marlborough Sounds Adventure Company (see page 407) offers **freedom walks** (4-day from $745; 5-day from $875; packed lunch each day), with nights spent at *Furneaux Lodge*, *Punga Cove Resort* and *Portage Resort*. Fully catered **guided walks** (4-day $1795; 5-day $2250) include a visit to Motuara Island and an optional day spent paddling. To pack in a day each of hiking, biking and paddling, go for the three-day Ultimate Sounds Adventure ($1060). Beachcomber Fun Cruises (see page 406) offer a series of one-day walks ($67–77), while the Cougar Line has walks from one to five hours ($80).

ACCOMMODATION

Booking is essential. Some smaller places don't accept debit or credit cards, so **take plenty of**

ACCOMMODATION   **KENEPURU ROAD**

★ **Hopewell** Double Bay, Kenepuru Sound ☎03 573 4341, ⓦhopewell.co.nz; map p.402. Gorgeous hostel in a dreamy setting where even a couple of nights isn't enough to fully appreciate the relaxing surroundings. The hosts are welcoming, there's a waterside hot tub, plus kayaks ($20), fishing, mountain bikes, the occasional free evening meal with *kai moana* and opportunities to visit the local mussel farm or go sailing. Access is either on a tortuous 2–3hr drive along Kenepuru Road, by a sequence of water taxis from Picton ($75/person each way) or water taxi from Temahia

($25/person each way): call the hostel for details. Closed May–Aug. Dorms $40, doubles $110

Raetihi Lodge Double Bay, Kenepuru Sound ☎03 573 4300, ⓦraetihilodge.co.nz; map p.402. New owners and recent renovation have transformed this small lodge with international beach chic. Borrow a fishing rod, SUP or kayak, go mountain-biking, play croquet on the lawn or have a relaxing massage before a gourmet dinner (mains $28–36). Hill-view room $280, sea view $390

Havelock and Pelorus Sound

The sleepy town of **HAVELOCK**, 35km west of Picton, is primarily of interest for cruising the stunning **Pelorus Sound**, an intricate maze of steep-sided bays, crescent beaches and sunken sea passages surrounded by forested peaks – the largest sheltered waterway in the southern hemisphere. Almost every bay has a farm for green-lipped mussels, making Havelock the world capital for these choice bivalves: you simply can't

cash. The six DOC **campsites** cost $6 and have water and toilets but only four have water taxi access. The accommodation below is listed from north to south, with hiking distances measured from Ship Cove.

★ **Anakiwa 401** 401 Anakiwa Rd, Km70 ☎03 574 1388, ⓦanakiwa401.co.nz; map p.402. Great, sparkling, renovated, self-catering guesthouse with hammocks in the garden, a small orchard, free kayaks, an espresso machine and a coffee caravan directly below (open afternoons). It makes a great base for walking the southern end of the track or just hanging out. There's a two-bed share, doubles, and a self-contained apartment sleeping four. Shared-room $50, doubles $100

Anakiwa Lodge 9 Lady Cobham Grove, Anakiwa ☎03 574 2115, ⓦanakiwa.co.nz; map p.402. Around 400m from the end of the track, this comfortable lodge sleeps fifteen, offers free use of kayaks and has a large luxury spa pool (small charge for dorm guests, free for those in private rooms). Dorms $35, doubles $136, family room $150

Furneaux Lodge Endeavour Inlet, Km14 ☎03 579 8259, ⓦfurneaux.co.nz; map p.402. One of the region's bigger lodges built in attractive grounds around a century-old homestead, with a convivial bar and an excellent restaurant. Rooms range from basic bunk rooms to self-contained cottages ($376). Phone available and free wi-fi in bar area. Hikers cabin (per person) $50, doubles $290

Lochmara Lodge Lochmara Bay, Km58 ☎03 573 4554, ⓦlochmaralodge.co.nz; map p.402. Beautiful ecolodge with its own café, bar, and sculpture trail overlooking Lochmara Bay. There's a new Underwater Observatory with stingrays to feed and touch tanks ($15pp). There are also free kayaks, a bathhouse ($60 for two for 1hr), and massage available Dec–March. All rooms are en-suite. The lodge is almost an hour's walk off the QCT or a 20min water-taxi ride from Picton ($50; Picton departures daily 9am, 12.15pm, 3.15pm). Closed June–Sept. Units $139, chalets $280

Mistletoe Bay Eco Village Mistletoe Bay, Km65 ☎03 573 4048, ⓦmistletoebay.co.nz; map p.402. Family-oriented, road-accessible rustic luxury in either the Whare (eight cabins with a communal kitchen), Vogel Cottage (sleeps six) or the backpackers and campsite ($36 per couple) with a camp kitchen and coin-op showers ($2). A small store sells basic items including meats, eggs and fresh coffee. Backpackers $30, Whare $80, Vogel Cottage $190

Portage Resort Kenepuru Rd, Km51 ☎0800 762 442, ⓦportage.co.nz; map p.402. Resort hotel with range of accommodation, swimming pool, restaurant and bar overlooking the Sound. There's a glowworm grotto on the property. It's a 30min walk from Torea Bay or get them to arrange a taxi. $225

Tanglewood 1744 Queen Charlotte Drive, Anakiwa ☎03 574 2080, ⓦtanglewood.net.nz; map p.402. Just four en-suite rooms in this family B&B, nicely surrounded by woodland (with some massive tree ferns next to the house) and popular with kereru. Spa pool in the garden and glowworm grotto out back. A 2min walk down to the beach. $195

leave without tucking into a plateful. Self-caterers can buy fresh mussels from the Four Square supermarket. The town's busy marina is worth an evening stroll.

Pelorus Mail Boat

Departs 10am daily Nov–April • $128; under-15s free • ☎03 574 1088, ⓦthemailboat.co.nz • Can pick up from Blenheim or Picton

To take in some of the Sound's remotest and most inaccessible bays, you can join the **Pelorus Mail Boat** as it delivers everything from mail, groceries, freight and even correspondence-school books to residents. The boat also stops at a secluded café, or you can bring your own packed lunch, and there's usually an opportunity to get off for a bush walk, sheep farm tour or even a swim in summer. The run can include a Greenshell Mussel Farm tour with gannets, blue penguins and dolphins among the wildlife usually spotted. The boat returns to Havelock around 4pm.

Pelorus Bridge Scenic Reserve

18km west of Havelock

The **Pelorus Bridge Scenic Reserve** is a gorgeous forested spot run through by the crystal-clear Pelorus River with abundant swimming holes and verdant bush enlivened by tui, bellbirds and rare native long-tailed bats. The place is understandably popular in summer; there's a revamped but still basic DOC camping area and a DOC office adjoining a modest daytime-only café.

The **walking tracks** in the reserve are well maintained, fairly flat and clearly marked and there's a swingbridge to add a little extra excitement: the **Totara Walk** (1.5km return; 30min) and **Circle Walk** (1km return; 30min) routes pass through the low-lying woodland for which the area is famous, while the **Trig K Track** (2.5km one way; 2hr), after a steady climb to 417m, offers stunning views of the whole area. For more of a river perspective, join Pelorus Eco Adventures barrelling down the river.

SH6 continues west past the turn-off to French Pass at the small settlement of **Rai Valley** and climbs the hills towards Nelson past Happy Valley Adventures (see page 420).

French Pass

Narrow winding roads head north from Rai Valley towards French Pass, a two-hour, 60km drive through pockets of bush locked in sheep country and pine plantations. After tantalizing glimpses of inaccessible bays and coves you're finally rewarded with French Pass itself, a narrow tidal channel between the mainland and D'Urville Island where nineteenth-century French explorer Dumont d'Urville was spun by tumultuous whirlpools and only barely made it through. If you're here at mid-tide it is easy to understand why these seething waters were so feared. The maelstrom is best seen from a couple of short tracks in **French Pass Scenic Reserve**, 1km before the road end at **FRENCH PASS**. This tiny settlement is little more than a wharf, a shop, DOC's basic **campsite** and *Beachfront Villas*.

ARRIVAL AND DEPARTURE   HAVELOCK AND PELORUS SOUND

By bus and water taxi Buses between Picton and Nelson all stop at Havelock, while local bus and water taxi operators offer services to Kenepuru and Pelorus sounds.

ACTIVITIES

Foxy Lady Cruises ☎027 438 9866, ⓦfoxyladycruises. co.nz. Bruce runs fishing charters ($180), Overnight Scenic Cruises ($299) and BBQ cruises ($165) aboard the 60ft *Foxy Lady* (sleeps nine).
Pelorus Sound Water Taxi and Cruises ☎0508 42835625, ⓦpelorussoundwatertaxis.co.nz.
A range of scenic tours, cruises and water taxi services, plus Nydia Track transfers ($35).
Pelorus Eco Adventures 48 Main Rd, Havelock ☎0800 252 663, ⓦkayak-newzealand.com. Trips down the Pelorus River in inflatable kayaks. It's a fun, undemanding trip with stops to explore the scenery, and imagine the famous Hobbit scene, before exiting at Totara Flats ($180).

ACCOMMODATION

HAVELOCK

Blue Moon Lodge 48 Main Rd ☎03 574 2212, ⓦbluemoonhavelock.co.nz; map p.402. Rooms are small but comfortable, and there are good communal facilities in this intimate hostel right in the centre of town, with friendly, helpful hosts. Dorms $37, doubles $84
★ **Havelock Garden Motel** 71 Main Rd ☎03 574 2387, ⓦgardenmotels.com; map p.402. Slightly older, fully self-contained units that are well kept and clean and set in a beautiful green garden with mature trees. The hosts are very helpful. Studio $125, motel units $140
Havelock Holiday Park 24 Inglis St ☎03 574 2339, ⓦhavelockholidaypark.kiwi; map p.402. Family- and pet-friendly traditional Kiwi campsite with good communal facilities and a good location near the centre of the community, just off Main Road. You'll need to book in the summer. Camping per site $34, cabins $60

PELORUS BRIDGE SCENIC RESERVE

Kahikatea Flat campsite ☎03 571 6019; map p.402. Basic DOC camping area that has a fabulously sited kitchen block, plus toilets, hot showers and tap water. $16

PELORUS SOUND

★ **On the Track Lodge** Nydia Bay, Pelorus Sound ☎03 579 8411, ⓦonthetracklodge.co.nz; map p.402. Right on the Nydia Track and only accessible by boat, foot or bike, but well worth visiting in its own right – you'll get a warm Kiwi welcome, scrumptious cakes, revamped accommodation in a yurt dorm, chalets or railway carriage, with endless hot water and wood-fired central heating. The spa bath, kayaks, fishing rods, and dinghies are all free. Home-cooked meals are available (mains $25), continental breakfast ($15), and they provide a generous packed lunch ($20). Dorms $60, doubles $140

MARLBOROUGH WINE-TASTING TOURS AND ACTIVITIES

Tastings and tours are the best way to experience the region. Don't be tempted to cram too many tastings into a day; most vineyards are more suited to leisurely sipping than whistle-stop guzzling. Most of the wineries will mail cases of wine anywhere in the world, but shipping costs and high import duties mean it seldom makes financial sense – better just drink the stuff on picnics and at BYO restaurants.

TASTINGS

Around 55 wineries have cellar-door **tastings** (mostly for a small charge, which is deducted from subsequent purchases). Some add a short tour, tack on a restaurant or even link up with outlets hawking olive oil, fruit preserves and the like. Most of the notable wineries are around Renwick or immediately north along Raupara Road, all listed on the free *Marlborough Wine Trail* sheet (along with their opening hours and facilities) and app (**W**wine-marlborough.co.nz).
Opening hours are generally 10am to 4 or 5pm daily, though much reduced in winter.

You're now ready for a day among the vines, preferably with lunch at one of the winery restaurants. Few wines are available for much under $20 a bottle, and wineries like to show off with their restaurants, so although it will almost certainly be a pleasurable experience it won't be cheap.

WINE TOURS

To avoid having to designate a driver, take an organized wine tour.

Highlight Wine Tours **☎**0800 494 638, **W**highlightwinetours.co.nz. A low-key locally owned and operated business, running afternoon ($70), half-day ($80) and full-day ($90, including lunch stop but not the cost of lunch) tours.

Marlborough Wine Tours **☎**03 578 9515, **W**marlboroughwinetours.co.nz. Offers some of the cheapest tours, including jaunts of three ($70), five ($95) and six hours ($120), with time for lunch at one of the wineries (not included).

Sounds Connection **☎**0800 742 866, **W**soundsconnection.com. Specializes in half-day tours visiting four or five wineries ($75), and also offers a full-day circuit of six or seven wineries ($99, excluding lunch).

Wine Tours by Bike **☎**03 572 7954, **W**winetoursbybike.co.nz. Relatively expensive bike rental ($45/5hr), but the cost includes accommodation pick-ups and they will come and rescue you if you have a mechanical breakdown.

NATURE TOURS

For a different cultural and geological perspective on the landscape, take an ecotour with Driftwood.

Driftwood Retreat and Eco-Tours **☎**03 577 7651, **W**driftwoodecotours.co.nz. With friendly and informative tour guides there are both kayak and van tours available ($200/4hr). The tree house retreat accommodation set in a beautiful wetland makes for an easy end to your day ($200). Pick-ups available from Blenheim (free) and Picton ($25).

FRENCH PASS

Beachfront Villas **☎**03 576 5204, **W**beachfrontvillas. co.nz; map p.402. Recently renovated beachfront accommodation in self-contained units, all with sea views and common dolphin sightings. B&B, with meals available on request. Closed June–Sept. **$230**

French Pass campsite map p.402. A basic sixteen-pitch DOC site with tap water, toilets and cold showers. Shop with basics just across the road. Booking required Dec 1–Feb 28. **$13**

EATING

Havelock Hotel 54 Main Rd, Havelock **☎**03 574 2412; map p.402. Serves simple cuisine for under $30, including steak and chips, fish and chips, burger and chips, plus mussel dishes. Mon–Fri 11am–2pm & 5pm–late, Sat & Sun 11am–late although kitchen closes at 9pm.

Mussel Pot 73 Main Rd, Havelock **☎**03 574 2824, **W**themusselpot.co.nz; map p.402. Popular for selfies with the outsize green-lipped mussels, and for the choice of steamed, smoked, marinated, grilled, battered or chowder-ed shellfish. Share a platter to taste the range ($46.80). Sept–June daily 10.30am–2.45pm & 5.15–8pm.

Slip Inn Havelock Marina **☎**03 574 2345, **W**slipinn. co.nz; map p.402. Marina-side establishment with big

8

windows and decks does good mussel dishes ($22.50 for a kilo in white wine sauce), plus slightly fancier dishes including the ubiquitous pizza ($28). It's also fine for coffee or a sundowner. Daily 8am–late.

The Marlborough Wine Country

In July 1972, Marlborough County Council Livestock Instructor, S.G.C. Newdick, wrote "Vineyards: in regard to these, as there is a glut on the market of grapes there does not appear to be any likelihood of vineyards starting up in Marlborough in the foreseeable future." In the intervening years **Marlborough Sauvignon Blanc** single-handedly put the New Zealand wine industry on the world map and made the Marlborough Wine Country the largest wine region, now producing almost seventy-seven percent of the national grape crop.

The gravel plains flanking the Wairau River, sheltered by the protective hills of the Richmond Range and basking in a New Zealand high of around 2500 hours of sunshine a year, are perfect for ripening the Sauvignon Blanc grapes, though Chardonnay and Pinot Noir grapes also grow well (guaranteeing tasty bubbly), as do olives.

Many local wineries go all out to attract visitors, using distinctive architecture, classy restaurants, art and gourmet foodstuffs. The profusion of weekend visitors from Nelson, Wellington and further afield has also spawned a number of smart B&Bs throughout the district, trying to out-luxury one another. If this is what you're after there's little need to bother with **Blenheim** itself, particularly since most of the vineyards are closer to the small, equally unremarkable town of **Renwick**, 10km to the west. The best of the local wineries are listed on page 415.

Blenheim

In the early 1970s, **BLENHEIM**, 27km south of Picton, was a fairly sleepy service town set amid pastoral land: now it is a fairly sleepy service town completely surrounded by

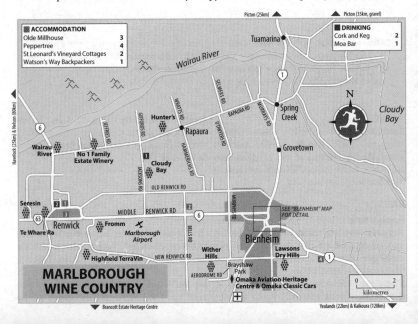

some of the most fecund and highly regarded vineyards in the land. Becoming a tourist hub for the region has developed a passable café culture, but most of the attractions of note are beyond its rather conservative town limits.

Omaka Aviation Heritage Centre

79 Aerodrome Rd, 4km southwest of town • Daily 10am–4pm • "Knights of the Sky" $25; "Dangerous Skies" $20; both exhibitions $39 • ⓦ omaka.org.nz

Easily the most diverting of Blenheim's sights is the **Omaka Aviation Heritage Centre**, located beside Omaka Aerodrome. Three large hangars contain two absolutely stunning exhibitions. "Knights of the Sky" features 21 World War I planes, some original and many still airworthy, others authentic replicas. Some are unique like the classic Curtis MF flying boat, and the German Halberstadt D.IV. Most of the exhibits are set in amazingly realistic dioramas created by film-maker Peter Jackson's Wingnut Films, with all mannequins by Weta Workshop. Check out the crash-landing scene depicting the shooting down and death of Manfred von Richthofen (The Red Baron), showing a group of Australian soldiers at the crash site souveniring his boots. The original fabric German cross from the plane is in a cabinet, along with his boots. Check out the flightsuit of Eddie Rickenbacker, America's top scoring ace of World War I, and personal effects of Herman Goering including his handwritten World War I logbook as well as the officer's cap he was wearing when he surrendered to US Forces in 1945. The newest addition here is the "Dangerous Skies" exhibition which focuses on World War II. Aviation buffs act as guides and truly enhance the visitor experience, so don't be shy to engage them. Every second Easter weekend, the museum puts on "Yealand's Classic Fighters", a must see airshow which alternates year by year with "Warbirds over Wanaka".

Omaka Car Collection

79 Aerodrome Rd, 4km southwest of town • Daily noon –4pm • $15; 14 and under free • ⓦ omakaclassiccars.co.nz

One man's obsession with automobiles, classics and otherwise, from the 1950s to the 1990s, plus a few spanky motorbikes. The collection totals around 150 exhibits, and all are roadworthy and ready to roll.

The Argosy

760 Middle Renwick Rd, at Caldwell • Daily 10am–6pm, 4pm in winter • $2

The *Argosy* is an Armstrong passenger and freight aircraft, the last of its kind in the world, which flew with the now defunct Safe Air Ltd, servicing the Chatham Islands. Board the plane for a look round and to watch the documentary, and sit in the cockpit to hear the recording of the night the plane encountered a UFO near Kaikoura.

Brayshaw Heritage Park and Marlborough Museum

New Renwick Rd, 2.5km south of Blenheim • Museum daily 10am–4pm • $10 (some vineyards give out complimentary vouchers)

The best bit of the **Brayshaw Heritage Park** is the **Marlborough Museum**, which has a small Māori collection and an interesting wine exhibit, covering the region's wine heritage, *terroir* and technology. The rest of the park is given over to old buildings, vehicles and equipment that usually come to life at weekends (the forge operates most Saturdays, as does the steam railway).

ARRIVAL AND DEPARTURE   MARLBOROUGH WINE COUNTRY

By train and bus Trains and long-distance buses stop at the Blenheim i-SITE at the rail station.
Train destinations Christchurch via Kaikoura (Oct–April, 1 daily); Picton (Oct–April 1 daily).
Bus destinations Christchurch (3 daily; 5hr); Nelson (1–2 daily; 1hr 50min); Picton (4 daily; 30min).

By plane The airport is 7km west of town. Marlborough Taxis (ⓣ 03 577 5511) charge $30 into town.
Destinations Auckland (3 daily; 1hr 25min); Christchurch (2–3 daily; 50min); Paraparaumu (1–2 daily; 25min); Wellington (11–13 daily; 25min).

8

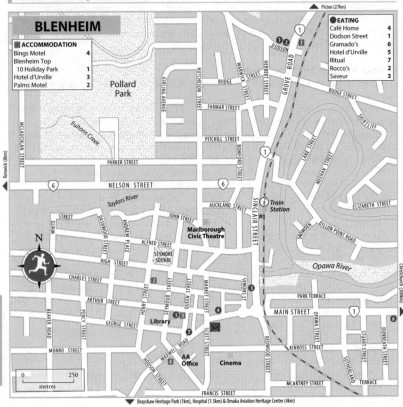

BLENHEIM

ACCOMMODATION

Bings Motel	4
Blenheim Top 10 Holiday Park	1
Hotel d'Urville	3
Palms Motel	2

EATING

Café Home	4
Dodson Street	1
Gramado's	6
Hotel d'Urville	5
Ritual	7
Rocco's	2
Saveur	3

GETTING AROUND

By bike Several hostels rent out bikes, or try Spokesman Cycles, 61 Queen St (☏ 03 578 0433; from \$40/day).

INFORMATION

i-SITE Opposite Blenheim train station, 8 Sinclair St (Mon–Fri 8.30am–5pm, Sat & Sun 9am–3pm; ☏ 03 577 8080, ⌨ marlboroughnz.com). Stocks an assortment of leaflets including the *Marlborough Wine Trail* map (free).

Internet Wi-fi is free in the centre of town and at the library, 33 Arthur St (Mon–Fri 9am–6pm, Sat 10am–1pm, Sun 1.30–4.30pm).

ACCOMMODATION

As befits a major wine region there's an abundance of high-priced luxury accommodation. Budget places mostly cater to seasonal workers, though there is one exceptional hostel in Renwick. During the first full week of February nearly all accommodation is booked far in advance for the festival season, so either plan well ahead or steer clear of the region.

BLENHEIM

Bings Motel 29 Maxwell Rd ☏ 03 578 6199, ⌨ bingsmotel.co.nz; map p.414. In the heart of Blenheim, this motel run by pleasant owners has a a range

of accommodation options includeing spacious one- or two-bedroom self-contained apartments, a separate male and female bunk room, also powered/non-powered caravan/campervan sites, casual laundry, shower and toilet facilities. Affordable ,clean and comfortable with plenty of off-street parking. **\$115**

Blenheim Top 10 Holiday Park 78 Grove Rd ☏ 0800 268 666, ⌨ blenheimtop10.co.nz; map p.414. Sited a little too close to the main road and railway line, but it is central and has all the expected facilities as well as pedal carts, electric bikes, good campsites and comfortable

THE WINERIES

Well known for its Sauvignon Blanc, the Wairau Valley's first commercial vines were planted by Montana Wines in the 1970s. Now more than 130 wineries operate in what has become the most appreciated wine-producing region in the country.

Brancott Estate 180 Brancott Rd, 5km south of Renwick on SH1 ☎ 03 520 6975, ⓦ brancottestate.com. A good starting point for your exploration of the region. Montana effectively kicked off the wine region in the early 1970s and now operates the country's largest winery, a favourite with coach parties. Try tastings ($6–16 free if you buy the tasting wine), a tutored Master of Sauvignon Blanc tasting (daily 11am, 2pm; $18), a vineyard cycle tour through the vines (booking essential (daily 11.30am; $35), or Falcon Encounter (Mon, Wed & Fri 11am weather permitting; $40). Also worth a look is the hilltop restaurant and heritage centre, where you can get good food and views. Restaurant daily 11.30am–3pm, cellar door daily 10am–4.30pm.

★ **Cloudy Bay** 230 Jacksons Rd ☎ 03 520 9197, ⓦ cloudybay.co.nz. Marlborough Sauvignon Blanc put New Zealand on the world wine map in the late 1980s and the Cloudy Bay Sauvignon became its flagship. It is still drinking so well today that they can't keep up with demand. This winery is huge on character with an elegant courtyard running out to a shady lawn with seductively comfy sofas. Delivery of the tasting experience is perfect too (CB Experience $10 for four wines). Some topnotch wines are for sale here, while the exquisite courtyard lunch restaurant, *Jack's Raw Bar*, offers fresh oysters served raw or in light tempura with wasabi mayo ($24/half-dozen), roasted nori and rice-crusted venison ($29), marinated tuna, salmon and roasted duck dishes and desserts to die for ($13). If you can only go to one vineyard for tasting, make it this one. Daily 10am–4pm.

Fromm Godfrey Rd ☎ 03 572 9355, ⓦ frommwineries.com. A vineyard that is turning winemakers' heads with a very hands-on approach, producing organic, predominantly red, wine, including an excellent Pinot Noir, a peppery Syrah, and a Malbec. Visit if you're serious about the subject and you'll taste a product that's a match for anywhere in the world ($5 six wines to $20 for the full range). Daily 11am–5pm (4pm in winter).

Highfield TerraVin Brookby Rd ☎ 03 572 9244, ⓦ highfield.co.nz. Easily recognizable by its Tuscan-inspired tower, which you can climb for excellent views, *Highfield* offers $5 tastings (free if you buy wine or eat in the Mediterranean-style restaurant (daily 11.30am–3pm). A self-contained apartment ($200) looks out over the vines. Summer daily: vineyard 10am–4.30pm, restaurant 11.30am–3pm; by appointment in winter.

Hunter's Rapaura Rd ☎ 03 572 8489, ⓦ hunters.co.nz. Jane Hunter is recognized as one of the world's top female winemakers. Drop by to taste ($5), visit the art gallery, stroll round the gardens or check out the wine shop and get a snack platter ($14.50) while you taste. Cellar door daily 9.30am–4.30pm.

★ **Lawsons Dry Hills** Alabama Rd ☎ 03 578 7674, ⓦ lawsonsdryhills.co.nz. Established vines produce stunning wines in this multi-award-winning winery, well worth visiting for the Pinot Noir, Pinot Gris, Gewürztraminer and Sauvignon Blanc if nothing else. Tastings are free. Cellar door daily 10am–5pm, closed weekends June–Aug.

No 1 Family Estate 196 Rapaura Rd ☎ 03 572 9876, ⓦ no1familyestate.co.nz. Home to the area's best-known and most accomplished maker of *methode traditionale* bubbly. Free tastings. Mon–Fri 10am–4.30pm, Sat & Sun 11am–4.30pm.

Seresin Bedford Rd ☎ 03 572 9408, ⓦ seresin.co.nz. Stylish winery with a distinctive primitivist "hand" logo perched on a rise overlooking the vines. Completely organic, biodynamic, estate-grown grapes interact with wild yeast to create world-class wines (try the Pinot Noir and their soft Chardonnay), and they produce some killer olive oil, jams and even soap. Free tastings. Daily 10am–4pm.

Te Whare Ra 56 Anglesea St, Renwick ☎ 03 572 8581, ⓦ twrwines.co.nz. Great little family-owned and -run vineyard where they still hand-pick and sort the grapes. Free tastings – try their Rieslings and brooding Syrah. Nov–March Mon–Fri 11am–4.30pm, Sat & Sun noon–4pm; April–Oct by arrangement only.

Wither Hills 211 New Renwick Rd ☎ 03 520 8284, ⓦ witherhills.co.nz. A striking, roadside winery that rises up concrete and tussock to form an impressive structure. Nip in for tastings ($5 refundable on bottle purchase) of the popular Chardonnay, Pinot Noir and Sauvignon Blanc (including the fine single-vineyard Rarangi). Daily Vine-to-Wine walks at 10am, 10.45am & 2.30pm(30min; $20). Wine blending sessions (1hr; $49) Vineyard daily 10am–4.30pm.

Yealands Awatere Valley ☎ 03 575 7618, ⓦ yealands.co.nz. Follow the white road to see one Kiwi bloke's vineyard vision, including 1500 "babydoll" sheep, gangs of chickens, and classical music piped to the vines that fill the valley to the sea. Great story, and the wine's decent too (free tastings, including a port style, and a Tempranillo). Daily 10am–4.30pm.

8

self-contained units and cabins ($82). Camping $40, units $150

Hotel d'Urville 52 Queen St ☎03 577 9945, ⓦdurville.com; map p.414. This former Public Trust building right in the centre of town has been turned into a chic and stylish boutique hotel with a classy bistro bar (Tues–Sat). The best – some say the only – place to stay in town, and a good place to eat and party, and check out the massive vault while you're there. Free guest wi-fi. $245

Palms Motel 78 Charles St, at Henry St ☎0800 256 725, ⓦblenheimpalmsmotel.co.nz; map p.414. Nicely decorated central motel with Sky TV and a range of units, most of which are spacious, and some of which come with spa bath. Cooked breakfast available ($19). $150

WINE COUNTRY

Olde Millhouse 9 Wilson St, Renwick ☎0800 653 262, ⓦoldemillhouse.co.nz; map p.412. Lovely three-room B&B set among cottage gardens where a continental breakfast can be served. There are complimentary bikes for guests (rental to non-guests), a spa pool and free airport transfers. $180

★ **Peppertree** 3284 SH1 ☎03 520 9200, ⓦthepeppertree.co.nz; map p.412. Luxurious

boutique B&B with just five individually styled, generous en suites in a sensitively restored Victorian home surrounded by landscaped gardens with their own orchard, vineyard (Chardonnay), olive grove, pétanque pitch, swimming pool, croquet lawn, and grand duck pond. The Swiss owners couldn't be more helpful. Breakfast includes Bircher muesli, home-made bread and conserves. $625

St Leonards Vineyard Cottages 18 St Leonards Rd ☎0276 861 636, ⓦstleonards.co.nz; map p.412. Five rustic self-contained cottages (sleeping 2–5), each with fully equipped kitchens, heat pumps and flatscreen Freeview TV. There's access to a heated pool in summer, complimentary bikes, barbecue areas and grounds amid the vines. Breakfast provisions are supplied, including home-laid eggs. $165 for two people, $50 each extra person

★ **Watson's Way Backpackers** 56 High St, Renwick ☎03 572 8228, ⓦwatsonswaylodge. com; map p.412. Easily Marlborough's best hostel: a very comfortable spot in the shade of large trees in a wonderful garden, with a public tennis court over the fence, snug rooms, made-up beds, easy access to the wineries, low-cost bikes, an outdoor spa bath, BBQ and owners who can't do enough for you. Closed Sept. Dorms $30, doubles $92

EATING

A few hours spent visiting vineyards should be accompanied by lunch at one of the wineries – especially *Hunter's*, *Herzog* and *Wairau River*. A few are also open in the evenings, but for dinner you may prefer to head into Blenheim.

BLENHEIM

★ **Café Home** 1c Main St; ☎03 5795040, ⓦcaféhome. co.nz map p.414. Primo espresso alongside fresh sandwiches, frittata slices and cakes in minimalist surroundings ($8–19). Mon–Fri 8am–5pm, Sat 9am–2pm.

Dodson Street 1 Dodson St ☎03 577 8348, ⓦdodsonstreet.co.nz; map p.414. Convivial bistro, wine and alehouse dishing up tasty pizzas ($19.50) and regular pub grub. Get a tasting tray, or have a Renaissance beer (brewed next door). Daily 11am–11pm.

★ **Gramado's** 74 Main St ☎03 579 1192 ⓦgramadosrestaurant.com; map p.414. Wonderfully unexpected Brazilian restaurant. The owners have adapted their recipes to take account of Kiwi tastebuds, so you can choose aged Wakanui steak and chips ($39.80), but if you go for the luscious *feijoada* ($36.90) you'll be presented with a range of different chillies to enhance and deepen your dish without blowing your socks off. The great customer care includes Saulo's mini wine tastings to ensure you happily

match your wine to your meal. Leave room for *pudim*. Tues–Sun 4pm–late.

Hotel d'Urville 52 Queen St ☎03 577 9945, ⓦdurville.com; map p.414. Classy restaurant in the town's grand old Public Trust building. Stylish modern decor and exemplary cuisine, making the best of seasonal produce (mains $34–39). Book in advance. Daily from 6pm.

★ **Ritual** 10 Maxwell Rd ☎03 578 6939; map p.414. Lively, licensed café with booths, serving delights such as herbivore burritos with tempeh and miso ($15), as well as delicious daily $10 "creations" in a bowl. Dinner mains are $20. Daily 7am–3.30pm.

Rocco's 5 Dodson St ☎03 578 6940; map p.414. Enjoyable, authentic Italian restaurant that could unabashedly sit on a New York or Rome street. For a blowout, order the awesome chicken Kiev alla Rocco – chicken breast filled with ham, garlic butter and cheese, all wrapped in a veal schnitzel. Fresh pasta is made daily. Licensed or BYO ($10). Mon–Sat 6pm–late.

Saveur 6 Symons St ☎03 577 8822, ⓦsaveur.co.nz; map p.414. Great café, bistro and patisserie with a terrace overlooking the Taylor River, serving superb lunches ($16–24) including hearty steak sandwich, bistro-style dinners ($22–354). Daily 7.30am–late.

8

DRINKING

RENWICK

Cork and Keg Inkerman St ☎03 572 9328, ⓦcorkandkeg.co.nz; map p.412. Friendly English-style local with traditional games like dominoes and a good selection of South Island craft beers including those from the local *Moa* stable. All-day pub meals $24–35. Mon–Thurs & Sun 10am–11pm, Fri & Sat 10am–1am.

Moa Bar 258 Jacksons Rd, a few kilometres northeast of town ☎03 572 5149, ⓦmoabeer.com; map p.412. Brilliant little modern bar serving at least twenty beers and two ciders from the *Moa* brewery, with lager, pale ale, IPA and Pilsner ABV. Try the Five Hop with a Renwick pie. $5 tastings. Daily 11am–6pm.

Nelson

The thriving city of **Nelson**, set on the coast in a broad basin between the Arthur and Richmond ranges, is beguiling. Modest rent and low rise, it is not much to look at, but the location – perfect for accessing Golden Bay and a raft of three national parks – warm climate, good beaches and a cluster of worthwhile wineries pulls in all manner of tourists and artists, and the city has become one of the most popular visitor destinations in New Zealand.

Within central Nelson itself the **Suter Gallery** and the lively **Saturday market** are good diversions, but you'll soon want to venture further, perhaps to **Tahunanui Beach** or the suburb of **Stoke** for the fascinating **World of WearableArt** museum. You can even do an **Abel Tasman day-trip** from town using early buses, which give you enough time for a water taxi ride and a few hours' walking along the Coast Track.

Brief history

Nelson is one of the oldest settlements in New Zealand. By the middle of the sixteenth century it was occupied by the Ngati Tumatakokiri, some of whom intercepted **Abel Tasman**'s longboat at Murderer's Bay (now Golden Bay) and killed four of his sailors.

By the time Europeans arrived in earnest, Māori numbers had been reduced by internecine fighting, the nearest pa site to Nelson being at Motueka. Land squabbles with the British colonists culminated in the **Wairau Affray** in 1843. Despite assurances from chiefs Te Rauparaha and Te Rangihaeata that they would abide by the decision of a land commissioner, the New Zealand Company pre-emptively sent surveyors south to the Wairau Plains, the catalyst for a skirmish during which Te Rangihaeata's wife was shot. The bereaved chief and his men slaughtered 22 Europeans in retaliation but the settlers continued their land acquisition after numbers were boosted by immigrants from Germany.

Christ Church Cathedral

Trafalgar St • Daily 9am–5pm (services permitting) • Donation requested

The glowering, grey-stone Christ Church Cathedral, perched on a small hill, unusually facing north (towards the sea), dominates the grid-pattern streets of Nelson. English architect Frank Peck's original 1924 design was gradually modified over many years not only due to lack of money but also worries about a proposed high steeple in a possible earthquake. World War II intervened further, and even now the cathedral tower still looks a bit like it's under construction. The interior is illuminated by dazzling stained-glass windows with ten particularly noteworthy examples in a small chapel to the right of the main altar.

Nelson Provincial Museum

Corner of Hardy and Trafalgar sts • Mon–Fri 10am–5pm, Sat & Sun 10am–4.30pm • $5 (locals free) • ☎03 548 9588, ⓦnelsonmuseum.co.nz

The **Nelson Provincial Museum** takes a fresh, multimedia approach to local exhibits and then draws strands from them to the rest of New Zealand and the wider world.

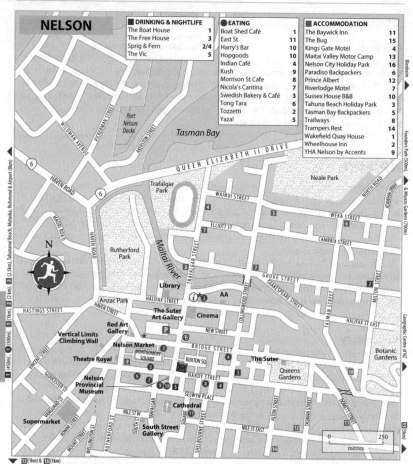

NELSON

DRINKING & NIGHTLIFE

The Boat House	1
The Free House	3
Sprig & Fern	2/4
The Vic	5

EATING

Boat Shed Café	1
East St	11
Harry's Bar	10
Hopgoods	10
Indian Café	4
Kush	9
Morrison St Cafe	8
Nicola's Cantina	7
Swedish Bakery & Café	3
Tong Tara	6
Tozzetti	2
Yaza!	5

ACCOMMODATION

The Baywick Inn	11
The Bug	15
Kings Gate Motel	4
Maitai Valley Motor Camp	13
Nelson City Holiday Park	16
Paradiso Backpackers	6
Prince Albert	12
Riverlodge Motel	7
Sussex House B&B	10
Tahuna Beach Holiday Park	3
Tasman Bay Backpackers	5
Trailways	8
Trampers Rest	14
Wakefield Quay House	1
Wheelhouse Inn	2
YHA Nelson by Accents	9

The Māori displays are each curated by the various local *iwi* with their choice of treasures from their own *marae*; witness the fine bone club, delicate flax and feather cloak, and interpretation of the designs in *tukutuku* panels. The death masks from the Maungatapu Murders near Canvastown highlight a grisly tale of robbery, murder and betrayal from 1866, and there's a collection of traditional Māori musical instruments whose sounds echo throughout the galleries. Upstairs, there's an exhibition on World War I and the locals it affected

The Suter Art Gallery

208 Bridge St · Daily 9.30am–4.30pm · Free entry, donation appreciated · W thesuter.org.nz

Situated just east of the city centre and sitting alongside the pretty Victorian Queens Gardens, the **Suter Art Gallery** is a blend of historical and contemporary architecture. Although the fully restored heritage gallery dates back to the late nineteenth century, the exhibitions displayed in it, and the recently opened modern spaces, can be from the Suter's collection or fresh from artists' studios. The complex includes a shop showcasing the types of locally handcrafted items for which Nelson is renowned – ceramics, jewellery and textiles – and there's a café backdropped by the Queen's Gardens and outdoor sculpture walk. A theatre screens films and has live performances.

Botanical Reserve

Accessed from the corner of Milton and Hardy Sts • Daily 24hr • Free

At the east end of Bridge Street is the **Botanical Reserve**, where New Zealand's first ever rugby game was played in 1870. The hill behind commands a good view over the town and is marked as the **geographical centre** of New Zealand.

Founders Park and Miyazu Gardens

87 Atawhai Drive • Daily 10am–4.30pm; Miyazu Gardens daily 8am–dusk • $7/$15 family; gardens free

About 1km north of the Botanical Reserve, **Founders Park** offers a re-created version of early colonial history through relocated and replica buildings all bursting with exhibits. Next door, the delightful Japanese-style **Miyazu Gardens** celebrate the relationship between Nelson and its sister city Miyazu. The gardens are a quiet oasis of reflective pools, ornamental cherry trees and traditional bridges.

Tahunanui Beach

4km northwest of central Nelson • Buses run here frequently along SH6 from the city

Haven Road (SH6) runs northwest out of central Nelson and, after 1km, becomes **Wakefield Quay**, a popular spot for strolling along the waterfront. Most conspicuous is the *Boat Shed Café* jutting picturesquely over the water. Continue 3km along SH6 to reach **Tahunanui Beach Reserve**, a long golden strand backed by grassland and drifting dunes. This is where Nelson comes to relax on sunny weekends, with safe swimming, a fun park, zoo and children's playgrounds.

World of WearableArt (WOW) and Classic Cars

95 Quarantine Rd • Daily 10am–5pm • $24 • ⓦ wowcars.co.nz

About 3km out of Nelson on SH6, follow signs off the roundabout to the **World of WearableArt and Classic Cars** for a unique theatrical experience. It is primarily a purpose-built showcase for the best designs from the annual WearableArt Show, a fashion show with a difference first put on by Suzie Moncrieff in Nelson in 1987 and now held annually in Wellington. Participants from around the world submit sculptures or pieces of art that can be worn as clothes – many made from unusual materials such as household junk, food, metal, stone, wood, even seaweed and tyres. The lighting, particularly UV sections, make the exhibits look amazing, and the human stories of the creators are told alongside. Attached is a stunning exhibition of vintage and classic cars from the past half-century, including the world's fastest Mini.

ARRIVAL AND DEPARTURE   NELSON

By plane Flights arrive at Nelson airport, 8km west of the centre. Super Shuttle (ⓘ 0800 748 885; $12.50 one person; $22.50 for two) meets most flights, or you can grab a taxi (ⓘ 03 548 8225; $35).

Destinations Auckland (9–13 daily; 1hr 25min); Christchurch (9–11 daily; 50min); Wellington (9 daily; 35min).

By bus Long-distance buses drop you near the centre of the city, within easy walking distance of most accommodation. Abel Tasman Coachlines pull in at 27 Bridge St, while the other companies all stop outside the i-SITE.

Destinations Blenheim (3–4 daily; 1hr 15min); Collingwood (1 daily; 3hr); Fox Glacier (1–2 daily; 10hr 30min); Franz Josef (1–2 daily; 9hr); Greymouth (1–2 daily; 6hr); Brown Hut, start of Heaphy Track (1 daily; 3hr 30min); Kawatiri Junction, for Nelson Lakes (1–2 daily; 1hr 5min); Motueka (3 daily; 1hr); Murchison (1–2 daily; 2hr); Picton (3–4 daily; 2hr 15min); Punakaiki (1–2 daily; 4hr 40min); Takaka (1 daily; 2hr 30min); Westport (1–2 daily; 3hr 30min).

GETTING AROUND

By bike The Crank Case, 114 Hardy St (📞 03 548 1666), rents bikes from $29/half-day depending on the type. Ask the guys about local tracks and rent a mountain bike for $50. A2B Ecycle, 12 South St (📞 021 222 7260, 🌐 a2b-ecycle. co.nz), have electric bikes for $40/half-day, $70/full-day.

By car Daily rates start at about $80, or $40/day for week-long rentals. Try: Nelson Car Hire, minimum three-day rental (📞 0800 283 545, 🌐 nelsoncarhire.co.nz); Apex (📞 03 546 9028); Hardy Cars (📞 03 548 1681); Rent-a-Dent (📞 03 546 9890); and Thrifty (📞 03 547 5563).

By taxi Nelson City Taxis 📞 03 548 8225.

By bus SBL buses (📞 03 548 3290, 🌐 nelsoncoaches. co.nz) run local routes to Tahunanui Beach and Stoke from the terminal at 27 Bridge St, while Abel Tasman Coachlines (📞 03 548 0285, 🌐 abeltasmantravel.co.nz) leaves Nelson at 7.30am daily in summer for Marahau ($21) via Motueka ($14), connecting with launch services deeper into the Abel Tasman National Park. Goldenbay Coachlines (📞 03 525 8352, 🌐 goldenbaycoachlines. co.nz) also run a service to Takaka ($38) in Golden Bay, with daily links service in season to the Heaphy Track and back to Nelson ($57).

INFORMATION

Visitor information i-SITE is at the corner of Trafalgar and Halifax streets (Mon–Fri 8.30am–5pm, Sat & Sun 9am–4pm; 📞 03 548 2304, 🌐 nelsonnz.com), where you'll also find the DOC (same hours; 📞 03 546 9339), which handles track bookings and dispenses invaluable info on all

national park tracks along the top-of-the-south – including Abel Tasman tide-tables.

Cycling information Check out 🌐 heartofbiking.org.nz on the Great Taste Trail, Dun Mountain, Canaan Downs and the cycleway to Abel Tasman National Park.

TOURS AND ACTIVITIES

Nelson is the sort of place where sunbathing and swimming at Tahunanui might be as active as you want to get, though there is no shortage of energetic diversions. In addition to the following, you might want to catch the Nelson Arts Festival (twelve days in mid-Oct; 🌐 nelsonartsfestival.co.nz), which includes theatre, music, readings and street entertainment, much of it free or for low cost. The city also hosts the Nelson Jazz & Blues Festival (four days in early Jan; 🌐 nelsonjazzfest.co.nz) at venues around the city.

QUAD BIKING AND THE SKYWIRE

Cable Bay Adventure Park 194 Cable Bay Rd, 17km northeast of Nelson off SH6 📞 03 545 0304, 🌐 cablebayadventurepar.co.nz. Explore up to 40km of track on a large forested farm, climbing hills, passing monstrous matai trees, stopping to learn a little about the forest and its stories and eventually reaching a high spot with expansive views of Cable Bay. The most popular trip is the Bayview Circuit (2hr; rider $135; passenger $35). Happy Valley Adventures also operates the Skywire ($85), a four-seater cable-car chair that swoops almost 1km across a forested valley at speeds of around 80kmph then back to the excellent hilltop café with its panoramic deck. The bird's-eye view is spectacular though many people find the return, with your back to the action, a little unnerving. Other options include horse trekking and paintball.

TANDEM PARAGLIDING

Nelson Paragliding 📞 03 544 1182, 🌐 nelson paragliding.co.nz. A hair-raising drive up the hill to the launch site reveals a spectacular landscape, before you run like hell then glide off into the quiet updraft for 15–20min of eerily silent flight. Tandem flights go for $220 and a half-day introductory lesson costs $250.

KAYAKING AND SAILING

Cable Bay Kayaks 📞 03 545 0332, 🌐 cablebaykayaks. co.nz. Paddling with this outfit – based near Happy Valley – makes a refreshing change from the mayhem around Abel Tasman. They do a half-day trip ($85) and a full-day tour ($145; bring your own lunch), which gives more time for exploring the caves of this beautiful and intricate coastline and doing a little snorkelling (gear provided).

Sail Nelson 📞 03548 5368 or 📞 0800 442441, 🌐 sailnelson.co.nz. Great, fully catered, five-day sailing courses (competent crew/yachtmaster;$1995) living aboard a 11m yacht, typically around D'Urville Island and Abel Tasman. Courses run on fixed dates for two to four people.

ROCK CLIMBING

Vertical Limits 34 Vanguard St 📞 03 777 0049, 🌐 verticallimits.co.nz. Indoor rock climbing is ideal for a wet day ($16 entry and harness, boulders only $10), and when the weather improves ask to join their full-day climbing trips. Mon–Fri 3–9pm, Sat noon–6pm, Sun noon–4pm.

ACCOMMODATION

There's a broad range of accommodation, much of it in the centre of town within reach of cultural diversions and nightlife. Classy **B&Bs** and excellent **hostels** are abundant,

and there are a couple of campsites close to town, but you may want to save your camping for the prettier areas around Motueka, the national parks or Golden Bay.

★ **The Baywick Inn** 51 Domett St ☎03 545 6514, ⓦbaywicks.com; map p.418. Lovely, renovated two-storey 1885 villa, overlooking the Maitai River with a luxuriously appointed cottage out back ($225 for a room, $450 to take as a self-catering unit). An enthusiastic welcome includes afternoon tea. Platters of local antipasti by arrangement ($50). $225

★ **The Bug** 226 Vanguard St ☎03 539 4227, ⓦthebug. co.nz; map p.418. Welcoming 46-bed hostel about 1km from the centre of Nelson adorned with VW Beetle paraphernalia. Along with free bikes, they have a hammock, table football and make a point of lacking a TV. Dorms $26, doubles $69

Kings Gate Motel 21 Trafalgar St ☎0800 104 022, ⓦkingsgatemotel.co.nz; map p.418. Close to the town centre with spacious, twelve comfortable and well-kept studios and units complete with full kitchens. Spa bath in honeymoon suite. There's also a pool. $158

Maitai Valley Motor Camp 472 Maitai Valley Rd ☎03 548 7729, ⓦmaitaivalleymotorcamp.co.nz; map p.418. Basic camping in a quiet, lovely wooded section beside the Maitai River (with good swimming holes), 7km southeast of Nelson. Camping $10, cabins $40, doubles $50

Nelson City Holiday Park 230 Vanguard Rd ☎0800 778 898, ⓦnelsonholidaypark.co.nz; map p.418. Small and well-managed campervan park with limited tent space but various grades of accommodation from simple cabins to more salubrious kitchen cabins and one-bed units. Camping per site $40, cabins $69, units $150

Paradiso Backpackers 42 Weka St ☎03 546 6703, ⓦbackpackernelson.co.nz; map p.418. A big hostel (650m to city centre) set in a converted villa with purpose-designed outbuildings, sleeping around 140. The solar-heated outdoor pool, spa, sauna and volleyball attempt to make up in shiny things what it lacks in space, peace and privacy; the slightly more expensive motel units next door offer more of the last two. Packed in the summer. Dorms $27, doubles $71

Prince Albert 113 Nile St ☎03 548 8477, ⓦtheprincealbert.co.nz; map p.418. Traditional neighbourhood pub providing backpacker accommodation. All rooms are en suite, there's a small courtyard with hammocks, and the owners are keen to make your visit fun. Free off-road parking, breakfast, bikes, and wi-fi allowance. Dorms $28, doubles $85

Riverlodge Motel 31 Collingwood St ☎0800 100, ⓦriverlodgenelson.co.nz; map p.418. One of the better motels in town, giving good value for money across a range of clean and comfortable units. All have Sky TV, access to a guest laundry, good showers and some have spa baths. Continental breakfast available. Studio $150, apartments $160

Sussex House B&B 238 Bridge St ☎03 548 9972, ⓦsussex.co.nz; map p.418. Charming, recently refreshed (new beds) five-room B&B in a central, 1880s villa featuring honey-coloured rimu floors and welcoming owner. All rooms are en-suite, except for one with a private bathroom, and two of the rooms open onto a veranda. The extensive continental breakfasts are great. $125

Tahuna Beach Holiday Park 70 Beach Rd, Tahunanui ☎0800 500 501, ⓦtahunabeach.co.nz; map p.418. Absolutely enormous, sometimes overwhelming, estuary-side campsite a 5min walk from Tahunanui Beach. Abundant facilities include mini-golf and kids' playground including pedal go-karts. Book far in advance for the summer. Camping $20, self-contained units $120

★ **Tasman Bay Backpackers** 10 Weka St ☎0800 222 572 ⓦtasmanbaybackpackers.co.nz; map p.418. Comfortable purpose-built hostel a few minutes from the town centre, with clean, spacious rooms (some en-suite) and enthusiastic, friendly management who ensure you always get more than you pay for. Free bikes, and free chocolate pudding nightly. Dorms $28, doubles $76

Trailways 66 Trafalgar St ☎03 548 7049, ⓦtrailways. co.nz; map p.418. Uniquely situated beside the tidal Maitai River, this central city hotel is only a 1min walk to Nelson's CBD. Forty-seven rooms with either riverside, poolside or city views and private balconies. Interconnecting family rooms also available. Super-friendly staff and the in-house Tides restaurant serves up superb dishes (lunches from $16, evening mains $26–38). Doubles $115, suites $186

Trampers Rest 31 Alton St ☎03 545 7477; map p.418. Lovely and cosy backpackers with only eight beds in comparatively small rooms. TV watching is by consensus only, there's a tuned piano, and the wee garden boasts a hammock, avocado tree and bike storage. There are also free bikes, and the owner, a real tramping enthusiast, is an absolute mine of information. Dorms $31, doubles $66

★ **Wakefield Quay House** 385 Wakefield Quay ☎03 546 7275, ⓦwakefieldquay.co.nz; map p.418. Great B&B with stupendous sea views over Haulashore Island and Nelson harbour out to the Abel Tasman. The house is up a steep rise from the busy road. Both rooms are beautifully turned out, drinks are served at 6pm, plus there's a tasty breakfast available. Minimum two-night stay. $349

★ **Wheelhouse Inn** 41 Whitby Rd ☎03 546 8391, ⓦwheelhouse.co.nz; map p.418. The bay views are magical from the picture windows of these five upgraded, nautically themed, self-catering apartments high on the hill, 2km west of central Nelson. All are very private and come with full kitchen, laundry, TV/DVD and BBQ, but you'll need to book well in advance. $180

★ **YHA Nelson by Accents** 59 Rutherford St ☎03 545 9988, ⓦaccentshostel.nz; map p.418. Purpose-built, this is the best hostel in Nelson, whose generous facilities include two kitchens, plenty of communal space, informed staff, table football, table tennis and an infrared sauna. There's a wide range of accommodation, including connecting rooms for families and two disabled-access units. Dorms $28, doubles $79

8

EATING

Nelson's enviable lifestyle is reflected in the broad choice of eating options within easy reach of the town centre. And when you tire of these, there's always fine food on the waterfront, at Mapua Wharf or at the wineries. Nelson's pubs and bars are also good for a quick snack.

Boat Shed Café 350 Wakefield Quay ☎03 546 9783, ⓦboatshedcafe.co.nz; map p.418. Fine views over Tasman Bay make this converted boat shed hanging out over the water a hit, but you also get fabulous fresh seafood and great concoctions from the best local producers. Perfect for romantic sunset dinners and relaxed lunches. Trust the Chef menu features four small courses ($70; add a dessert $82.50). Mon–Fri 10am–late, Sat & Sun 9.30am –late.

East St 335 Trafalgar Square East ☎03 970 0575; map p.418. Funky vegetarian café and bar, with outdoor seating, in the basement of a hostel. This helps guarantee generous portions and good value (everything under $24), occasional live music, and cheap drinks, so the clientele includes locals as well as backpackers. Daily noon–11pm.

★ **Harry's Bar** 296 Trafalgar St ☎03 539 0905, ⓦharrysnelson.nz; map p.418. Smooth cocktail bar and Asian restaurant, known these days primarily for good-quality, well-priced food, including particularly fine crispy duck, chilli salt squid, and kaffir lime tart. At weekends it can also get a bit lively after the plates are stacked. Tues–Sat 4pm–late.

Hopgoods 284 Trafalgar St ☎03 545 7191, ⓦhopgoods. co.nz; map p.418. Some of Nelson's finest dining is found in this airy restaurant with outdoor streetside tables. Locally sourced, organic produce informs a range of seasonal dishes fashioned by a perfectionist chef into traditional European-influenced gastronomy. Expect the likes of duck confit with chestnut polenta, parsnip, caramelized apple, prune and walnut ($40). Booking essential. Mon–Sat 5.30–9.30pm, also Fri 11.30am–2pm.

★ **Indian Café** 94 Collingwood St ☎03 548 4089; map p.418. The town's best curry house is set in a historic villa and dishes up all your favourites, plus one or two highly imaginative variations, for around $16–18, as well as offering a takeaway menu ($10–20). Mon–Fri noon–2pm & daily 5pm–late.

Kush 5 Church St ☎03 5394 793, ⓦkush.co.nz; map p.418. Funky, licensed coffee house named after the eponymous kingdom in Ethiopia thought to be populated by the world's first coffee drinkers. They may have calmed down the 1970s kitsch decor but not the coffee. There's a great selection of organic beans with each duty manager roasting their own *in situ*, keeping bug-eyed caffeine addicts fuelled on double shots. The counter food is simple but tasty, there's free wi-fi, they do legendary brunches on Sundays, and the notice board is full of local gossip. Mon–Thurs 7.30am–4pm, Fri & Sat 7.30am–2pm, Sun 9am–2pm.

Morrison St Cafe 244 Hardy St ☎03 548 8110, ⓦmorrisonstreetcafe.co.nz; map p.418. Smart café serving extremely good-quality brunches, lunches and snacks, with many dishes dairy or gluten free. Along with the liberal sprinkling of local art adorning the walls there is outdoor seating, newspapers and magazines, but don't let anything distract you from the food ($11–21), which is rightly popular with the natives, including home-made muesli, Nelson tasting platters and excellent coffee. Mon–Fri 7.30am–3.30pm, Sat & Sun 8.30am–4pm, public holidays 9am–3pm.

Nicola's Cantina 6 Church St ☎03 548 8761; map p.418. Short menu of Mexican standards (tacos, burrito, *quesadillas*, *huevos rancheros*). Everything is under $22 and there are some fun margarita cocktails. Tues–Sat 11–2pm & 5–9pm.

★ **Swedish Bakery & Café** 54 Bridge St ☎03 546 8685, ⓦtheswedishbakery.co.nz; map p.418. So small you could blink and miss it, but if you do you'll kick yourself. Swedish marzipan treats and sandwiches (including Swedish meatball and beetroot combos) sit beside some classic bakery favourites including genuine handrolled pastries and a passionfruit and lemon tart that is quite literally the taste of summer. Tues–Fri 8.30am–3.30pm, Sat 8am–2pm.

Tong Tara 142 Hardy St ☎03 548 8997, ⓦtongthai. co.nz; map p.418. Top traditional Thai, relaxed and well run and dishing up all your perennial favourites – including fiery *moo kum wan*, or local mussels *tom yum* – for around $22. BYO. Tues–Sun 11am–late.

Tozzetti 14 Vanguard St ☎03 539 4793; map p.418. Wonderful dine-in café and bakery serving freshly cut sandwiches, great pies, muffins, delicious cakes and stupendous bread (all under $15). Go early to get the pies – particularly the fish – and don't be surprised if you leave with more than you intended to buy. Tues–Fri 7am–4pm, Sat 7.30am–noon.

★ **Yaza!** Montgomery Square; map p.418. So hip it'll never need a replacement, this cool licensed café known for its home-made food is the epitome of laidback. They serve excellent breakfasts, lunches, coffees and the cheesiest cheese scones around (most items $5–20). Occasional evening entertainments too, including poetry, music and talks. Mon–Fri 8am–5pm, Sat 7am–4pm & Sun 8am–4pm.

DRINKING AND NIGHTLIFE

While most of its suburban neighbours retire early to sip cocoa, Nelson stays up and parties – at least on Friday and Saturday. For raucous boozing and some dancing head for Trafalgar Street or the half-dozen bars on Bridge Street between Trafalgar and Collingwood streets. Pubs and **bars** of all stripes often have **live music**, karaoke and DJ **nights**; pick up the *Star Times* gig guide flyer to find out **what's on**.

The Boat House 326 Wakefield Quay ☎03 548 7646; map p.418. Just down the road – on the Nelson side – from the more famous *Boat Shed Café*, with equally fine views over Tasman Bay is this private licensed club, set up in the 1980s to save the 1906 rowing club building – a large stilted boat shed and ramp hanging over the tide. Open to the public and now a highly regarded live-music venue (cover sometimes free but usually $10–20), it's a fabulously atmospheric place to enjoy a gig, a drink or some home-made, high-end bar food (mains $16–25). Wed–Fri 11am–2pm & Fri 5pm–late.

★ **The Free House** 95 Collingwood St ☎03 548 9391, ⓦthefreehouse.co.nz; map p.418. Brilliant pub in a former church fitted with hand pumps gives this place a perfect atmosphere for their selection of the best local microbrews. They do some food, but you can also ask at the bar and order in a curry from the *Indian Café*. Mon–Thurs 3–11pm, Fri 3pm–midnight, Sat noon–midnight, Sun noon–11pm.

★ **Sprig & Fern** 280 Hardy St ☎03 548 1154, ⓦsprigandfern.co.nz; map p.418. Central incarnation of this local institution, set in a double-fronted shop with a large outdoor courtyard at the back. Great beer on tap (tasting racks of six beers cost $16), good pub surroundings and dine-in menu. Popular with the locals, who come along for the chat, the pub quiz, live music several times a week and because it's slightly less expensive than most other bars in town, thanks to "true pint" serves. Daily 11am–midnight

Sprig & Fern 134 Milton St ⓦsprigandfern.co.nz/ taverns; map p.418. Suburban villa converted into a cosy bar with open fires and a selection of twenty locally brewed, award-winning Sprig & Fern beers – crisp pilsners, pale ales limited releases, porter and stout with a selection of local ciders. Local wines, locally roasted coffee and Nelson's own Proper Crisps too. Mon 2pm–late, Tues–Sun 11am–late.

The Vic 281 Trafalgar St ☎03 548 7631, ⓦvicbrewbar. co.nz; map p.418. Quality version of the Mac's brewery pubs that have sprung up all over the country, with a lively atmosphere, decent beer, good-value pub grub ($16–29) and mostly iffy live music (Fri & Sat) – with the occasional good band thrown in. Daily 11am–late.

ENTERTAINMENT

Nelson Theatre Royal 78 Rutherford St ☎03 548 3840, ⓦtheatreroyalnelson.co.nz. Beautifully restored "A"-listed theatre, with comfortable seats over two levels. Shows traditional touring productions, local dramatics and vaudeville/cabaret-style shows.

State Cinema 6 91 Trafalgar St ☎03 548 0808, ⓦstatecinemas.co.nz. Screens all the latest mainstream films plus a few eclectic ones.

DIRECTORY

Internet Free at the library plus at most cafés.
Library 27 Halifax St (Mon–Fri 10am–6pm, Sat 10am–1pm, Sun 1–4pm).
Left luggage Lockers at the i-SITE ($6/12hr) and Aurora ($5/day).
Medical treatment Nelson Region After Hours and Duty

Doctor, 96 Waimea Rd ☎03 546 8881 (daily 8am–10pm appointments from 8.30am).
Life Pharmacy Prices, corner of Hardy and Collingwood sts (Mon–Fri 8am–8pm, Sat 9am–8pm, Sun 10am–6pm).
Post office 209 Hardy St (Mon–Fri 8am–5.30pm, Sat 9am–1pm).

The road to Abel Tasman

A great part of Nelson's charm lies on its doorstep, particularly the excellent **wineries** to the west. Here the vines appreciate the combination of New Zealand's sunniest climate and either the free-draining alluvial gravels of the Waimea Plains or the clay gravels of the Moutere Hills. Wineries are interspersed with the **studios** of contemporary artists, many of whom exhibit in their own small **galleries**, showcasing ceramics, glass-blowing, woodturning, textiles, sculpture, installations, jewellery and painting.

Almost everywhere of interest is located on or just off the much straightened SH60, which runs north from Richmond towards Motueka through rural scenery and sea views. A couple of kilometres north along SH60, the Moutere Highway cuts left for **Upper Moutere** and an alternative route to Motueka, while Redwood Road turns right past the *Seifried* winery and on to the picture-book-pretty **Rabbit Island**, one of Nelson's most popular beaches, especially for picnics on weekends.

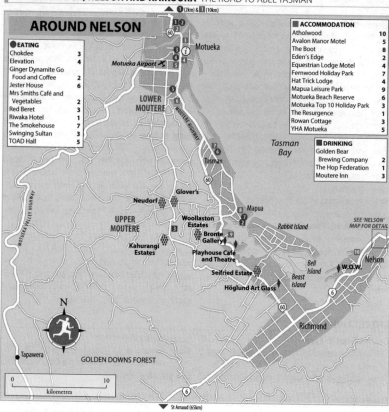

AROUND NELSON

● **EATING**
Chokdee	3
Elevation	4
Ginger Dynamite Go Food and Coffee	2
Jester House	6
Mrs Smiths Café and Vegetables	2
Red Beret	3
Riwaka Hotel	1
The Smokehouse	7
Swinging Sultan	3
TOAD Hall	5

■ **ACCOMMODATION**
Atholwood	10
Avalon Manor Motel	5
The Boot	8
Eden's Edge	2
Equestrian Lodge Motel	4
Fernwood Holiday Park	7
Hat Trick Lodge	4
Mapua Leisure Park	9
Motueka Beach Reserve	6
Motueka Top 10 Holiday Park	3
The Resurgence	1
Rowan Cottage	3
YHA Motueka	5

■ **DRINKING**
Golden Bear Brewing Company	2
The Hop Federation	1
Moutere Inn	3

You can sample the best of the region on an extended drive from Nelson to Motueka, but there's enough on offer to warrant spending a couple of leisurely days in the region. Equip yourself with the *Nelson Wine Guide*, *Nelson Craft Beer Trail*, *Art & Craft Nelson* and *Nelson's Creative Pathways* leaflets, all free and available from visitor centres. A few kilometres further north, **Motueka** is the most practical base and provides the most convenient access for trips into the Abel Tasman National Park.

Waimea Inlet and around

Artisans and craftspeople were well represented among the earliest European immigrants to Nelson. That tradition still dominates today, with studios, galleries and artistic retreats scattered all over this area.

Höglund Art Glass

52 Lansdowne Rd · Daily 10am–5pm · ☎ 03 544 6500, ⓦ hoglundartglass.com

Highway 6 runs 15km southwest of Nelson to Richmond where SH60 cuts straight north towards Motueka while its old route runs closer to the shores of **Waimea Inlet**. Roughly 5km along SH60, down a side road, **Höglund Art Glass** is an international-standard glass gallery displaying a vast array of Scandinavian-influenced work. The bold bright designs work best on bigger pieces with clean lines, but prices start around $49 before swiftly entering the stratosphere. A glass museum introduces you to the history and techniques of handblown glass manufacture through works by the Swedish owners Ola and Marie Höglund, and from December to April you can watch live glass-blowing.

Playhouse Café and Theatre

171 Westdale Rd • Summer Tues–Sun 11am–11pm; mainly only weekends in winter (check the website) • Cover charge for live music $5–15 • ☎ 03 540 2985, ⓦ playhousecafe.co.nz • The management offers free pick-up and drop-off from Mapua

Continuing north on SH60, follow the signs from the right-hand turn into Westdale Road and you'll end up at a curiosity worth at least an hour of your time. The straw-house **Playhouse Café and Theatre** is a live, licensed venue serving interesting daytime grub and hosting an extraordinary array of performances at night. Popular with live music acts, the grotto-like interior and Hundertwasser-esque decor plays host to lectures, talks, themed nights, plays, cabaret and travelling shows.

Bronte Gallery

122 Bronte Rd East • Daily 9am–5.30pm • ⓦ brontegallery.co.nz

Back on SH60, head north for Bronte Road East and signs to the **Bronte Gallery** about 1.5km off the highway. On display and for sale are highly individual works by internationally recognized ceramic artist Darryl Robertson and intriguing abstract oils by Lesley Jacka Robertson.

The Upper Moutere wine region

A rewarding day can be spent touring Nelson's wineries (see page 415). The free *Nelson Wine Guide* includes a map and lists opening hours, typically daily 10am to 4.30pm in summer. The region is centred on the village of **Upper Moutere**, where you'll find locally produced preserves, cheeses and the like inside the Old Post Office at Moutere Gold, 1381 Moutere Hwy (daily 10am–4pm, closed Sat & Sun in winter).

8

Mapua

On a sunny late afternoon, tiny **MAPUA**, a couple of kilometres off SH60 and some 34km from Nelson, is an idyllic spot to stop for a stroll and a bite or a drink, while the sun catches the boats moored in the picturesque Waimea Estuary with the pines of Rabbit Island as a backdrop. The historic waterfront area has been developed into a precinct of shops and restaurants and is particularly busy on weekends.

Rabbit Island

The Mapua Ferry, Mapua Wharf • Sept–May daily 10am–5pm (every hour); June–Aug Sat & Sun and school holidays 10am–4pm • $8 single; $12 return; $25 family • ☎ 03 540 3095 • Trail Journeys (ⓦ trailjourneys.co.nz) will rent you a bike for $47/day to explore the island

Before or after a munch in Mapua, take a ferry to **Rabbit Island** (Moturoa). The crossing involves a tour of the channel, and if you just go for the ride and don't disembark at the island it costs just $5. The ferry was introduced as part of the Nelson Tasman Cycle Trail, and there are 14km of cycle track round the island.

Motueka

The expanding town of **MOTUEKA**, 47km northwest of Nelson, is primarily used as a base for exploring the Abel Tasman National Park (see page 430): there's a complete booking service, a range of accommodation and places for renting hiking gear. Recently, the town has sprouted a few impressive attractions of its own, based largely around its airfield, mainly skydiving and with the chance to **fly** microlights and helicopters.

The name Motueka means "island of weka", a reference to the abundance of these edible birds, which provided sustenance for Māori. European settlers arrived in 1842 and established a horticulture industry based mainly around hops and later tobacco, since supplemented by pip fruit and grapes, which often need **seasonal workers**, particularly from December to March.

Motueka Quay

Motueka is strung along SH60, with quieter streets spurring off from the main highway. Head 1km down Old Wharf Road to reach **Motueka Quay** where the ghost of this once-busy port lingers among the scant remains of the old jetty. Here lies the rusting hulk of the Scottish-built *Janie Seddon* – named after the daughter of Richard Seddon, prime minister of New Zealand from 1893 until his death in 1906. The hulk provides a fantastic foreground for pictures of the seascape and a great backdrop for picnics, while one night-only freedom camping is permitted near the Public Wharf at the Motueka Beach Reserve (self-contained vehicles only).

Motueka District Museum

140 High St • Dec–March Mon–Fri 10am–3pm, Sat & Sun 10am–2pm; April–Nov Tues–Fri 10am–3pm, Sun 10am–2pm • Free admission, donations appreciated

The tiny **Motueka District Museum** delves into the area's history through a few Māori and European artefacts, as well as the *Motueka Carvings*, a modern four-panel frieze in the foyer that skilfully depicts the livelihoods that have traditionally sustained Tasman Bay.

ARRIVAL AND DEPARTURE   THE ROAD TO ABEL TASMAN

Buses do travel along the road to Abel Tasman, but they only stop in Motueka. For all other destinations, you'll need to have your own vehicle or join a guided tour, some of which combine the wineries and art galleries.

By bus Buses pick up and drop off on Wallace St in Motueka, close to the i-SITE.

Destinations Kaiteriteri (1 daily; 25min); Marahau (1 daily; 50min); Nelson (2 daily; 1hr); Takaka (1 daily; 1hr 10min).

INFORMATION & GETTING AROUND

The only i-SITE along the road to Abel Tasman is in Motueka, but you can also check in at the office in Nelson for information on the area before you begin your journey.

Visitor information Motueka's i-SITE (Wallace St; Dec–March Mon–Fri 8.30am–5.30pm, Sat & Sun 9am–5pm; April–Nov Mon–Fri 9am–5pm, Sat & Sun 9am–4.30pm; ☎ 03 528 6543, ⊛ abeltasmanisite.co.nz) has wi-fi ($5/24hr), a jobs notice board, and staff can assist in organizing Abel Tasman National Park and Heaphy Track trips with no booking fees. Full internet service but you can also get an hour's free wi-fi in the centre of Motueka.

By bike Trail Journeys, Mapua Wharf (☎ 03 540 3095, ⊛ trailjourneys.co.nz), rents a comprehensive range of bikes

($47/day); or try Wheelie Fantastic, Mapua Wharf (☎ 03 543 2245, ⊛ wheeliefantastic.co.nz; $40/day). Both companies can help plan routes and advise on the Taste Trail.

By tour Bay Tours Nelson (☎ 0800 229 868, ⊛ baytoursnelson.co.nz) offer a range of options, including afternoon winery trips (4 vineyards; $105) or full-day tours (3–4 wineries plus visits to artists; $238).

Tramping supplies You might be able to rent tramping gear from hostels. Coppins, 255 High St (Labour weekend to Easter Mon–Fri 8.30am–5.30pm, Sat 9am–4pm, Sun 10am–4pm; winter Mon–Fri 9am–5.30pm, Sat 9am–2pm; ☎ 03 528 7296), can sell you everything you need, including topo maps, and have great knowledge of the area.

TOURS AND ACTIVITIES

There are some great **hikes** around the Motueka area, but **airborne** activities such as skydiving and tandem paragliding are also very popular.

HIKING

In the hills to the west of Motueka is some of the best subalpine hiking in the north of the South Island, around

the 1795m Mount Arthur and the associated uplifted plateau, the Mount Arthur Tableland, all detailed in DOC's *The Cobb Valley, Mount Arthur and the Tableland* leaflet available from the Motueka i-SITE. Traditionally, few visitors have bothered coming up this way, so what company you find will mostly be Kiwis and wildlife.

The principal starting point is the Flora car park, 930m up

at the end of Graham Valley Road that leads off SH61 30km southwest of Motueka. A good 2–3hr loop heads up an easy path (1hr) to the Mount Arthur Hut (hut passes $15), from where the lowlands spread before you with Mount Arthur dominating the southern skyline. Continue along a ridge and down to Flora Hut (free) then back along a gravel road to the car park. The summit of Mount Arthur can be reached in three hours from the Mount Arthur Hut.

SKYDIVING

Skydive Abel Tasman, Motueka airport, 3km southwest of town ☎ 0800 422 899, ⓦ skydive.co.nz. Regarded as one of the ten best drop zones in the world, primarily because it offers jumps from 16,500ft (75 seconds freefall; $409), 13,000ft (50 seconds freefall; $319) and 9,000ft (35 seconds freefall; $269), which is currently longer than most companies, with a backdrop of stunning scenery.

HELICOPTER FLIGHTS, MICROLIGHTS AND TANDEM HANG-GLIDING

Nelson Tasman Air Queen Victoria St, Motueka airport, 3km southwest of town ☎ 0800 835 943, ⓦ tnthelicopters.co.nz. After a short briefing you take the controls of an R22 two-seater, entry-level helicopter (20min $250, 30min $350, 1hr $600), practising simple forward flight and hovering.

Tasman Sky Adventures College St, Motueka airport, 3km southwest of town ☎ 0800 114 386, ⓦ skyadventures.co.nz. Take the passenger seat in a microlight for some pulse-quickening thrills, buzzing above the region's glorious scenery (15min $105; 30min taking in parts of Abel Tasman National Park $205). They also offer tandem hang-gliding, towing the rig by microlight to a pre-appointed height before cutting you and your pilot loose (15min $195; 30min $330).

ACCOMMODATION

MAPUA

Atholwood 118 Bronte Rd East ☎ 03 540 2925, ⓦ atholwood.co.nz; map p.424. Luxurious accommodation next door to the Bronte Gallery, with comfortable rooms, a swimming pool, spa, mature gardens and bush running down to Waimea Inlet. B&B $600, self-contained $350

The Boot 320 Aporo Rd, 7km north of Mapua at Tasman ☎ 03 526 6742, ⓦ jesterhouse.co.nz/accommodation-stay-in-the-boot; map p.424. Attached to the *Jester House* café is *The Boot*, an enormous quirky red fairy-tale boot with a luxurious lounge area, romantic bedroom and a little garden patio. B&B $330

Mapua Leisure Park 33 Toru St ☎ 03 540 2666, ⓦ mapualeisurepark.co.nz; map p.424. A variety of accommodation options, some recently refurbished, including cabins and motel units (from $140), in wonderful surroundings. Stop in at the summer-only *Boat Shed Café* and bar. In Feb and March the place is clothing-optional, though plenty of non-nudists still visit. Beachside camping $26, kitchen cabins $106

MOTUEKA

Avalon Manor Motel 314 High St ☎ 0800 282 566, ⓦ avalonmotels.co.nz; map p.424. A well-equipped sixteen-unit motel with spacious and comfortable units that come with Sky TV, a well-tended garden, plus free movies. $140

★ **Eden's Edge** 137 Lodder Lane, Riwaka ☎ 03 528 4242, ⓦ edensedge.co.nz; map p.424. Located on an apple orchard 3km north of town, this purpose-built great-value hostel has a rural but very comfortable feel. There's a garden, pond, bike storage, nicely appointed rooms with en suites. $105

Equestrian Lodge Motel 2 Avelon Court (off Tudor St) ☎ 0800 668 782, ⓦ equestrianlodge.co.nz; map p.424. Well-kept upscale motel in a suburban area, only 5min walk from the centre of town, with comfy units backing onto a large grassy area with a heated pool. $170

Fernwood Holiday Park 519 High St South ☎ 03 528 7488, ⓦ fernwoodholidaypark.co.nz; map p.424. Small, traditional tree-lined site with swimming pool, TV room, aviary, organic veggie and herb garden, bike rental, small shop and strong recycling ethos. Camping $19, cabins $70

Hat Trick Lodge 25 Wallace St ☎ 03 528 5353, ⓦ hattricklodge.co.nz; map p.424. Conveniently located opposite the i-SITE, this purpose-built hostel has high standards, a spacious and well-equipped kitchen and lounge, and free gear storage, as well as a separate women's dorm and a family room with its own bathroom and kitchen. Dorms $28, rooms $70

Motueka Beach Reserve Wharf Rd, 4km southeast of town; map p.424. Council-run waterside parking for self-contained campervans only, with toilets and cold showers nearby, plus BBQs and picnic tables. Maximum one-night stay. **Free**

Motueka Top 10 Holiday Park 10 Fearon St ☎ 03 528 7189, ⓦ motuekatop10.co.nz; map p.424. Range of accommodation at this leafy site with well-kept facilities, including heated swimming pool, spa pool, bouncy playground pillow, just 1km north of the town centre. Camping per site $48, units $145

★ **The Resurgence** 574 Riwaka Valley Rd, 12km northwest of town ☎ 03 528 4664, ⓦ resurgence.co.nz; map p.424. A relaxing boutique lodge tucked away near the resurgence of the Riwaka River from below Takaka Hill. The attention to detail is staggering, from sound eco-credentials to the well-planned meals ($125). Facilities include an outdoor pool and spa, infrared sauna, gym and bushwalks. Rooms are in the house or cabins. $\overline{\$695}$

Rowan Cottage 27 Fearon St ☎03 528 6492, ⓦrowancottage.net; map p.424. Tastefully styled, small cottage with a lovingly tended garden that holds a self-contained guest room with a private entrance and en suite.

Continental breakfasts are available ($20) and everyone can use the barbecue. $\overline{\$130}$

★ **YHA Motueka** 310 High St ☎03 528 9229, ⓦlaughingkiwi.co.nz; map p.424. Friendly, central backpackers spread over three houses, with spacious dorms and rooms, a self-contained cottage ($130), plus plenty of outdoor seating, free bikes and kayaks (conditions apply), barbecues and free hot tub. Dorms $\overline{\$29}$, doubles $\overline{\$68}$

EATING

MAPUA

★ **Jester House** 7km north of Mapua at Tasman ☎03 526 6742, ⓦjesterhouse.co.nz; map p.424. A rewardingly quirky and thoroughly entertaining licensed daytime café popular for its tasty food, garden art and seating, rose arbours, giant chess set and tame eels to keep the kids entertained. The food is all home-baked and reasonably priced, and the coffee is strong. Daily 9am–5pm.

★ **The Smokehouse** Shed 2, Aranui Rd ☎03 540 2280, ⓦsmokehouse.co.nz; map p.424. Sells delicious manuka-smoked fish, widely acclaimed fish pâtés and lovely traditional fish and chips. Bring along a loaf of bread and have a picnic on a bench at one of the uncluttered ends of the wharf. Mon–Thurs & Sun 11am–7.30pm, Fri & Sat 11am–8pm.

MOTUEKA

Chokdee 109 High St ☎03 528 0318; map p.424. Reliable tasty Thai cuisine to eat in or take away, with all the usual soups, curries and noodle dishes at modest prices ($12–24.50). Licensed. Daily 11am–2pm & 5pm–late.

Elevation 218 High St ☎03 5286103; map p.424. Licensed café with the best food in town, including some great breakfasts, mains like steak and fresh fish of the day straight from the port – mains $26 - 34 range. Daily 8am–8pm.

★ **Ginger Dynamite Go Food and Coffee** 488 Main Rd, Riwaka ☎0211688736, ⓔgingerdynamitegogo@gmail.com; map p.424. After burning down in 2015, this business was resurrected out of two repurposed shipping containers 7km out of town. Best coffee, delicious award-winning pies and cakes plus great service make this an absolute must stop. Try the smoked

Fish Pie or a Steak 'n' Ale, both sensational. Sit among the 50s kitsch and pallet planters and have a paper cup of the fantastic coffee. Daily 8am–3pm.

Mrs Smiths Café and Vegetables 524 Main Rd, Riwaka; map p.424. The Smiths still grow their own veg to sell here, but now you can get breakfast, cake or a toasted sammie too (everything's under $20). Mon–Sat 7am–5.30pm, Sun 7am–4pm.

★ **Red Beret** 145 High St ☎03 528 0087; map p.424. Excellent café that draws in locals for a wide range of all-day breakfasts and lunches, from filo wraps and pasta dishes to gourmet burgers, steak sandwiches, excellent balsamic mushrooms ($16, $19.50 with bacon) and delicious monster slices of cake. Daily 7.30am–4.30pm.

Riwaka Hotel Main Rd, Riwaka ☎03 528 4750, ⓦriwakahotel.co.nz; map p.424. Traditional locals' bar with pub grub, which also books NZ's top bands and has a high-class restaurant tucked out back serving the likes of lamb cutlets with smoked paprika polenta ($33). Daily noon–late; restaurant 5.30pm–late but closed Mon & Tues April–Dec.

Swinging Sultan 172 High St ☎027 246 0680; map p.424. Kebab takeaway with just a couple of tables on the pavement, where you can tuck into chicken and beef kebabs or falafel ($9–12). Daily 8.30am–8pm.

★ **TOAD Hall** 502 High St, 3km south of town ⓦtoadhallmotueka.co.nz; map p.424. Organic fruit-and-veg vendor and café with a flower-filled garden that's perfect for imbibing delicious made-to-order ice cream, gourmet pies, bagels, great coffee and decent breakfasts. Can get ultra-busy in summer. Live music on Friday and Saturday summer evenings. Daily 8am–5pm, closes 10pm Thurs–Sun in summer.

DRINKING

UPPER MOUTERE

★ **Moutere Inn** 1406 Moutere Hwy ☎03 543 2759, ⓦmoutereinn.co.nz; map p.424. Established in 1850, the inn has claims as New Zealand's oldest pub and now expertly balances being a local boozer, brewer and shrine to fine beverages. Alongside the quality pub

snacks and main meals ($15–25) you can sip a tasting tray of four beers or a glass of wine – they have sixteen taps (including proper handpulls), around thirty different wines as well as thirteen single malts and six brands of tequila. Daily noon–9pm or later.

8

UPPER MOUTERE WINERIES

There are some great wineries in this region, well worth a visit.

★ **Glover's** Gardner Valley Rd ☎ 03 543 2698, ⓦ glovers-vineyard.co.nz. A wonderful small-output, one-man-and-his-cats winery run by the slightly eccentric winemaker owner, once renowned for tucking a Wagner CD into every package destined for overseas. Wagner usually plays in the background while you taste (free) European-structured wines crafted to produce highly tannic reds (Pinot Noir and Cabernet Sauvignon) and acidic whites (Sauvignon Blanc and Riesling) that stand up for themselves. Daily 10am–5pm.

Kahurangi 4 Sunrise Rd ☎ 03 543 2983, ⓦ kahurangiwine.com. Respected winery, offering tastings ($10 for four wines) from some of the South Island's oldest commercial vines (though that's only 1973), as well as the estate's own-brand olive oil. Daily 10am–4.30pm.

Neudorf Neudorf Rd, Upper Moutere ☎ 03 543 2643, ⓦ neudorf.co.nz. Relaxed winery in a low-slung wooden building covered by vines with simple outdoor seating in the shade of tall ancient trees. It is a lovely spot for tastings (free), some from the 30-year-old vines on site – splash out ($5, which is donated to charities) to sample the Moutere Chardonnay and the Pinot Noir, two of the country's best. Everything is available by the bottle and glass. Daily 11am–5pm; closed July & Aug.

Seifried Corner of SH60 and Redwood Rd ☎ 03 544 1600, ⓦ seifried.co.nz. The area's largest winery offering a wide range of wines to taste (five wines $6); try the Austrian Würzer and Zweigelt varietals, unique within New Zealand. The separately run restaurant fancies itself as fine dining, reflected in the high-end pricing. Daily 10am–4.30pm.

Woollaston Estates 243 Old Coach Rd ☎ 03 543 2817, ⓦ woollaston.co.nz. Swish, sprawling and fascinating, certified organic winery landscaped into the Moutere Hills with tussock-roofed buildings where operations are all gravity-fed. Try the restaurant, enjoy a platter ($48) or just a tasting ($5 at cellar door) with great views over the vines to the coast. A huge steel sculpture welcomes visitors and the art collections include works by relative Toss Woollaston. Daily 11am–4.30pm.

MAPUA

Golden Bear Brewing Company 501/6 Aranui Rd ☎ 03 540 3210, ⓦ goldenbearbrewing.com; map p.424. Top-class microbrews: elegant lagers and super-hoppy pale ales on tap at the bar with the brewing tanks as a backdrop, or enjoy the outside patio with a view over the water. They also dish up some Mexican food, burgers and ribs to soak up the brews. Hours can vary so check the website. Summer hours daily from noon.

MOTUEKA

The Hop Federation 483 Main Rd, Riwaka ☎ 03 528 0486 ⓦ hopfederation.co.nz; map p.424. A small craft brewery open for tastings and takeaways of their lovingly produced beers – the Red IPA and all-NZ hop Pilsner are real treats, not to mention their best sellers. Daily 11am–6pm.

ENTERTAINMENT

Gecko 23b Wallace St ☎ 03 528 9996, ⓦ geckotheatre. co.nz. Two small cinemas, two discount days (Tuesday and Wednesday), comfy seats and a mix of art-house and the mainstream.

State Cinema Old Wharf Rd ☎ 03 528 8648, ⓦ statecinemamotueka.co.nz. Screens all the latest mainstream films.

Abel Tasman National Park and around

ABEL TASMAN NATIONAL PARK, 60km north of Nelson, is stunningly beautiful with golden sandy beaches lapped by crystal-clear waters and lush green bush, interspersed with granite outcrops and inhabited by many birds. Deservedly it has an international reputation that draws large numbers of trampers, kayakers and day-trippers from November to March. But despite being New Zealand's smallest national park – barely 18km by 25km – the Abel Tasman absorbs crowds tolerably well and compensates with scenic splendour on an awesome scale.

Most visitors come to see the coastline. Some come to hike the **Abel Tasman Coast Track** with its picturesque mixture of dense coastal bushwalking, gentle climbs to lookouts and walks across idyllic beaches. Regular and abundant water taxis mean you can pick the sections to hike and get a lift back when you've had enough. Others come to **kayak**, spending leisurely lunchtimes on golden sands before paddling off in the late afternoon sun to a campsite or hut. Hiking and kayaking can be combined, and you might even tack on **sailing** the limpid waters to round off the experience. You can stay in the park, either at one of the DOC huts and campsites, or in considerably more luxury at an attractive lodge.

With **guided and advanced trip booking** you can be whisked from Nelson straight into the park, missing potentially fascinating nights in the surrounding gateway towns. **Motueka** (see page 425) is best for organizing your own trip, but most kayaks and water taxis leave from tiny **Marahau**, at the park's southern entrance. A few trips depart from diminutive **Kaiteriteri**, where there's plenty of accommodation and a gorgeous beach.

The park's northern reaches are accessed from **Takaka** (see page 438) where Abel Tasman Drive leads onto Wainui, Awaroa and **Totaranui**, all on the northern section of the Coast Track.

Brief history

Since around 1500, Māori made seasonal encampments along the coast and some permanent settlements flourished near the mouth of the Awaroa River. In 1642, **Abel Tasman** anchored two ships offshore from Wainui in Golden Bay and lost four men in a skirmish with the Ngati Tumatakokiri, after which he departed these shores. Frenchman **Dumont d'Urville** dropped by in 1827 and explored the area between Marahau and Torrent Bay, but it was another 23 years before **European settlement** began in earnest. The settlers chopped, quarried, burned and cleared until nothing was left but gorse and bracken. Happily, few obvious signs of their invasion remain and the vegetation has vigorously regenerated.

Natural history

Abel Tasman is full of rich and varied **plant life** with beech trees in the damp gullies and kanuka tolerating the wild and windy areas. **Bird** species include tui, native pigeons, bellbirds (their presence betrayed by a distinctive call), fantails that flutter close by feeding off the insects you disturb as you walk through the bush, and bobbing, ground-dwelling weka. Along the coast you might see the distinctive orange-beaked oystercatchers picking their way along the beaches and shags that dive to great depths for fish. Offshore, the **Tonga Island Marine Reserve** is famous for its **fur seal colony**, seabirds, and varied and bountiful fish.

Kaiteriteri

The tiny but often bustling resort settlement of **KAITERITERI**, 15km north of Motueka and just south of the Abel Tasman National Park, ranks high in the pantheon of Kiwi summer-holiday destinations and is consequently packed to its limited gills from Christmas through to late January. There's an understandable appeal, with a sandy arc of safe swimming beach looking out towards Tasman Bay where a couple of small rocky islands add perspective. With Marahau becoming too congested for some, Kaiteriteri has fashioned itself as an alternative embarkation point for cruises, water taxis and kayaking trips.

Marahau

About 8km north of Kaiteriteri, tiny **MARAHAU** is poised at the southern entrance to the Abel Tasman National Park. All the tours, water taxis and kayak operators not working out of Kaiteriteri or Motueka are based here, making this a very popular last or first night of civilization for park users.

The beach road runs through the settlement to the **park entrance**, marked by an unstaffed DOC display shelter with toilets alongside. A long boardwalk across marshland then leads into the national park.

Inside the national park

There are a plethora of **ways to explore** Abel Tasman National Park – no matter what combination of activities you'd like to try, there's almost bound to be an obliging operator. Relatively few people tramp the **Inland Track**, and most are keen to stick to the **Coast Track**, with its long golden beaches, and the constant temptation to snorkel in some of the idyllic bays. Unsurprisingly, the coast is where you'll find most of the **accommodation**, ranging from beachside campsites to swanky lodges. **Water taxis** take you virtually anywhere along the coast and as far north as the lovely beach at Totaranui. They usually give a commentary along the way, though there are also dedicated **cruises**, some visiting the seal colony on the **Tonga Island Marine Reserve** and **Split Apple Rock**, a large boulder that has split and fallen into two halves, like an upright, neatly cleaved Braeburn.

The intricate details of the coast are best explored by **kayak** (see page 434), either on a guided trip or by renting kayaks and setting your own itinerary. Better still, combine kayaking with walking a section of the Coast Track. Water taxi drop-offs and guided kayaking are banned in the section of park north of Totaranui, making this a much **quieter area** to hike and hang out.

Abel Tasman Coast Track

The **Abel Tasman Coast Track** (60km; 3–5 days) is one of the **easiest** of New Zealand's Great Walks, one for people who wouldn't normally think of themselves as trampers, but you should still get DOC's *Abel Tasman Coast Track* leaflet. Lack of fitness is no impediment as huts are never more than four hours apart (campsites 2hr) and you can use water taxis to skip some sections or just to pick the bits you fancy walking. In dry conditions you don't even need strong boots – trainers will do. All this makes the Coast Track extremely popular, especially from December to the end of February when some sections seem like a hikers' highway, although heading for the section north of Totaranui will often deliver a less frenetic experience.

The **route** traverses broad golden beaches lapped by emerald waters, punctuated by granite headlands and stacks silhouetted against the horizon, and zigzagging gentle climbs through valleys. The main planning difficulty is coping with the **tide-dependent** section across the Awaroa Estuary. Tide times will help you decide which way you're going to do the track – if there are low tides in the afternoon you'll probably want to head south, if they're in the morning, head north. Even at low tide you can still expect to get your feet wet. Before setting off you should also arrange your transport drop-offs and pick-ups with a water taxi or cruise company (see page 436). In winter (May–Sept) you can mountain bike from Totaranui up and over to Wainui Bay.

For accommodation along the track, see page 436.

Marahau to Anchorage

Direct access from Marahau makes this section (12.4km; 4hr) popular. The bush has large swathes of scrub, which isn't the most beautiful, but the beaches are unparalleled. The track follows a wooden causeway across the estuary to Tinline Bay before rounding a point overlooking Fisherman and Adele islands. As the track winds in and out of gullies the coastal scenery is obscured by beech forest and tall kanuka trees until you emerge at Anchorage, with its sprawling new hut, campsite and summertime offshore backpackers.

Anchorage to Bark Bay

8.7km; 3hr

Cross Torrent Bay two hours either side of low tide, or be prepared to skirt around the tidal Inlet (adding an hour) to reach the few dozen houses that constitute the settlement of **Torrent Bay**. Climb out of the bay through pine trees to the gorgeous Falls River, crossed by a 47m-long swingbridge. Bark Bay hut and campsites are 1hr ahead.

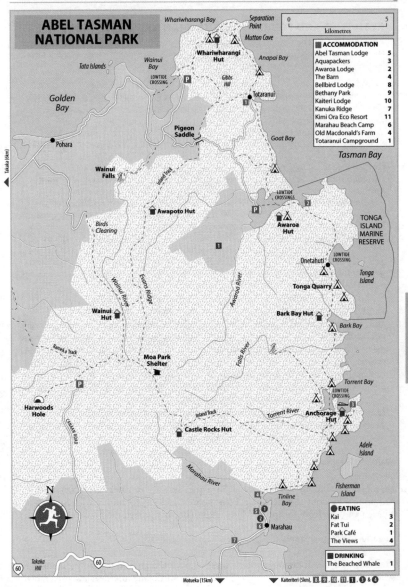

ABEL TASMAN NATIONAL PARK

0 ___ 5
kilometres

ACCOMMODATION

Abel Tasman Lodge	5
Aquapackers	3
Awaroa Lodge	2
The Barn	4
Bellbird Lodge	8
Bethany Park	9
Kaiteri Lodge	10
Kanuka Ridge	7
Kimi Ora Eco Resort	11
Marahau Beach Camp	6
Old Macdonald's Farm	4
Totaranui Campground	1

EATING

Kai	3
Fat Tui	2
Park Café	1
The Views	4

DRINKING

The Beached Whale	1

8

Bark Bay to Awaroa

11.5km; 4hr

After crossing (or skirting) Bark Bay Estuary, cut away from the coast to return at Tonga Quarry where there's a campsite and views out to Tonga Island and the Marine Reserve. You soon reach the beach at Onetahuti with its new walkway and bridge. The track then climbs to the Tonga Saddle and descends to Awaroa Inlet, its small settlement and a DOC hut with a campsite alongside; *Awaroa Lodge* is within easy walking distance (on the other side of the airstrip) and has a restaurant and bar.

ACTIVITIES AND TOURS IN ABEL TASMAN NATIONAL PARK

Although there are a number of operators offering activities such as **scuba diving**, **scenic cruises** and guided **walks**, one of the best ways to explore the park's more remote shores is by **sea-kayak**. Some of the best operators for these activities are listed below.

KAYAKING

It's hard to beat gently paddling along, exploring little coves (and possibly being accompanied by seals or dolphins), stopping on a golden beach for a dip and then continuing to a campsite where you can cool a beer in a stream.

Marahau, at the southern end of the park, is the kayaking hotspot for many operators. Most companies offer a broadly similar range of one- to five-day guided trips and freedom rentals. The stretch north of Marahau is known as the "Mad Mile", because that's where you'll see the largest concentration of paddlers, but congestion eases further north.

Guided trips typically combine paddling, water taxis, visiting seals and walking, while **multi-day** guided trips include all that plus accommodation, food and extra time to explore.

For **freedom rentals** you are typically given shore-based instruction then let loose in a double kayak. You are not allowed to venture north of Abel Head at the north end of the Tonga Island Marine Reserve nor paddle solo. Conditions are generally benign and suitable for relative beginners, though if you've any doubts about your ability, opt for a guided trip. Rental **prices** are around $80–100 per person for your first day, dropping to $120 for two days, and you can get one-way deals, catching a water taxi back ($200 for 3 days). Most companies have a range of camping **gear rental**, will store your vehicle while you're away and operate year-round, though the range of trips is reduced in winter.

ADVENTURE OPERATORS

Abel Tasman Canyons ☎ 0800 863 472, ⓦ abeltasmancanyons.co.nz. Get away from everyone else by abseiling, jumping, sliding and zip-lining down waterfalls. Torrent River ($269 with lunch and water taxis) is a great overall introduction (including an optional 8m jump) that can be combined with a night on an *Aquapackers* boat before walking and kayaking out. Advanced option Waterfall Creek up headwaters of the Awaroa River ($399) All gear provided.

Abel Tasman Charters ☎ 0800 223 522, ⓦ abeltasmancharters.co.nz. Operates two comfortable catamarans from near Kaiteriteri, with a flexible itinerary partly determined by the guests. Usually there's seal viewing, a visit to Split Apple Rock, and options to kayak, snorkel and spend time ashore. Minimum 6hr trip with delicious platter-style lunch included. Oct–April only ($285).

Abel Tasman Kayaks 273 Sandy Bay Rd, Marahau ☎ 0800 732 529, ⓦ abeltasmankayaks.co.nz. Guided

Awaroa to Totaranui

7.1km; 2hr 30min

You must cross the Awaroa Estuary (1.5hr either side of low tide) to reach Goat Bay then up to a lookout above Skinner Point before reaching Totaranui, with its great arc of beach and extensive campsite. Many hikers choose to finish their coastal walk here).

Totaranui to Whariwharangi

9.8km; 3hr 30min

After rounding the Totaranui Estuary, press on over and around rocky headlands as far as Mutton Cove then wander through alternating shrubland and beaches, preferably making a side trip to Separation Point with its lookout and fur seal colony. Continue to the hut at Whariwharangi, a converted historic homestead.

Whariwharangi to Wainui

5.5km; 1hr 30min

It is an easy walk to the road on the eastern side of Wainui Bay, where buses pick up, but it is also possible to cross Wainui Bay (2hr either side of low tide), or follow the road round the bay. If you follow the road, you can also take in the short hike up to the Wainui Falls, which heads off the road at the base of Wainui Bay.

kayak trip specialists based in Marahau offering half-day ($150) and full-day ($125–250) trips, plus a half-day seal sanctuary tour ($225) – all of which include a water taxi ride around much of the park. They also do catered overnight trips (from $499), and rent freedom kayaks (one-day rental $80).

Abel Tasman Sailing Adventures ☎ 0800 467 245, ⒲ sailingadventures.co.nz. Offers trips on one of three catamarans, combining sailing with walking, seal watching and kayaking, or you can just sail. They also do overnight trips ($98–218) and boat charters.

Abel Tasman Sea Shuttles ☎ 0800 732 748, ⒲ abeltasmanseashuttles.co.nz. Kaiteriteri-based water taxis and scenic cruises (half-day $45; full day $86), with cruise and walk options (from $66). Other options include drop-off and pick-up from *Awaroa Lodge and Café* ($79) and specialized guided kayak trips to Tonga and Adele islands.

Abel Tasman Aquataxi ☎ 0800 278 282, ⒲ aquataxi. co.nz. Water taxis from Marahau and Kaiteriteri, plus scenic cruises ($71–89).

★ **Golden Bay Kayaks** ☎ 03 525 9095, ⒲ goldenbaykayaks.co.nz. This highly recommended Tata Beach-based company is the only one to operate in the beautiful, quieter northern end of the park. Offers guided trips (half-day $90) and an unguided overnight trip ($90). Also rents double (half-day $100; full day $120) and sit-on-top kayaks ($40/2hr), plus stand-up paddleboards ($25/1hr, $35/2hr, $40/4hr).

Kahu Kayaks ☎ 03 527 8300, ⒲ kahukayaks.co.nz. Marahau-based kayak rentals and guided trips that often come in fractionally cheaper than the opposition. It offers the Swingers Delight ($175): a water-taxi ride to Torrent Bay, a walk to Bark Bay (2hr 30min), a water taxi to Obervation Beach and a 3hr guided kayak tour back to Marahau.

Kaiteriteri Kayaks ☎ 0800 252 925, ⒲ seakayak. co.nz. Guided trips from Kaiteriteri, including a half-day paddle to Split Apple Rock ($85); or a full-day with a water taxi ride to Onetahuti Beach, paddle to Tonga Island and the seals, lunch, and paddle to Anchorage Bay for water taxi pick-up ($205). Assorted combos also available. Accent on fun and getting close up to nature.

The Sea Kayak Company 506 High St, Motueka ☎ 0508 252 925, ⒲ seakayaknz.co.nz. Family-owned and operated Motueka-based business offering fourteen trip options ranging from half-day rentals to multiday excursions ($85– 750) with free hot showers, wi-fi, parking and transport from Motueka. Bus transfers from Nelson ($25)

Wilsons Abel Tasman ☎ 0800 223 582, ⒲ abeltasman.co.nz. Long-standing operator, offering all manner of trips including: a half-day Split Apple Rock kayak ($85); a five-day walking trip with three days walking and two days loafing at luxury beachfront lodges ($2100, all food included); cruises from Kaiteriteri to Totaranui and back on a spacious and stable catamaran (1–2 daily; 4hr; $78); and a Seals and Beach trip (6–8hr; $68), cruising around the Tonga Island seal colony with plenty of time to walk from Tonga Quarry to Medlands Beach and get in a swim.

8

The Inland Track

The strenuous **Inland Track** (41km; 3 days) between Marahau and Totaranui is far less popular than the Coast Track, and requires moderate fitness and decent tramping gear. The track can be combined with the Coast Track to make a six- to seven-day loop.

The route climbs from sea level to **Evans Ridge** past granite outcrops and views of the coast: highlights include the **Pigeon Saddle**, the moorlands of Moa Park and the moon-like Canaan landscape, with an optional side-trip to Harwood's Hole (see page 438).

Camping is not recommended on the Inland Track, but there are two, small, first-come, first-served **DOC huts** ($5; backcountry hut passes valid), with water and toilets but no cooking facilities.

ARRIVAL AND DEPARTURE   ABEL TASMAN NATIONAL PARK AND AROUND

Access into the park proper is generally on foot or by boat, but a couple of roads extend to the park entrances – principally Marahau in the south and Totaranui in the north.
By bus The best bus service in the region is ScenicNZ Abel Tasman coachlines (Nelson; ☎ 03 548 0285, ⒲ scenicnz.co.nz), which runs two times daily between Motueka, Kaiteriteri and Marahau. One service runs from Nelson (7.30am) for Motueka (1hr; $14 one way) and Marahau (1hr 50min; $20), connecting with launch services deeper into the park. Golden Bay Coachlines (☎ 03 525 8352, ⒲ goldenbaycoachlines. co.nz) connects Takaka and Motueka (12.15pm daily; $28) and Totaranui to Motueka ($38) and on to Nelson ($47).

GETTING AROUND

By water taxi Water taxis based in Kaiteriteri and Marahau give you the chance to walk a particular section of coast or simply ride to any of six beaches along the coast – Anchorage, Torrent Bay, Bark Bay, Onetahuti, Awaroa and Totaranui. Three main companies do two to five scheduled runs from the south of the park to Totaranui and back, charging virtually the same price – just book whichever is going the right way at the right time, or call Aquataxi (☎0800 278 282, ⓦaquataxi.co.nz). Typical one-way fares from Marahau are to Anchorage ($37), Torrent Bay ($37), Bark Bay ($42), Onetahuti ($44), Awaroa ($47) and Totaranui ($47).

INFORMATION

Abel Tasman National Park The main sources of information are the i-SITE offices in Nelson, Motueka and Takaka, all of which will book boats, kayaks, hut and camping tickets, transport and accommodation. There are also unmanned DOC display shelters at the Marahau and Totaranui park entrances, with tide times and safety precautions.

ACCOMMODATION

KAITERITERI

★ **Bellbird Lodge** 160 Sandy Bay Rd, Kaiteriteri ☎03 527 8555, ⓦbellbirdlodge.com; map p.433. Offers two comfortable suites, great views, first-class care and welcoming hosts, all in the family home where the peace and quiet is only shattered by the inconsiderate local birds. $350

Bethany Park 88 Martin Farm Rd ☎03 527 8014, ⓦbethanypark.co.nz; map p.433. Set slightly back from the beach (15min walk), convenient for the mountain bike tracks, and with a good choice of accommodation. Upgraded ablutions and kitchen blocks, water slide, and play areas. Camping/two people $30, en-suite cabins $78

Kaiteri Lodge Inlet Rd, just back from the beach ☎03 527 8281, ⓦkaiterilodge.co.nz; map p.433. Something between a motel and backpackers, with four-, six- and eight-bed dorms and en-suite doubles. It's the primary stop for all the tour buses, including Kiwi Experience, and is right by *The Beached Whale*. Dorms $30, en-suite rooms $160

Kimi Ora Eco Resort 99 Martin Farm Rd, signposted 1km back from the beach road ☎0508 546 4672, ⓦkimiora.com; map p.433. A genuine European spa complex, set in native bush, with an aqua centre including steam room, Finnish sauna, heated indoor and outdoor pools. You can just stay, but the emphasis is on fitness (the mountain-bike park skirts the property), therapy and indulgent massage sessions. Studio $195, suites $239

MARAHAU

★ **Abel Tasman Lodge** 295 Sandy Bay-Marahau Rd ☎03 527 8250, ⓦabeltasmanlodge.co.nz; map p.433. Tastefully refurbished studio and larger chalets scattered about the lawns, each with private deck, give a relaxed feel to this upmarket lodge with outdoor spa, sauna, and breakfast delivered to your room (on request). $185

The Barn Harvey Rd ☎03 527 8043, ⓦbarn.co.nz; map p.433. A lively backpackers near the park entrance with an outdoor fireplace and baths in the grounds. Well set up for campers with an outdoor cooking area, the site also has dorms, twins and doubles ($89), mostly in basic cabins. Camping $22, dorms $33

★ **Kanuka Ridge** 21 Moss Rd ☎03 527 8435, ⓦabeltasmanbackpackers.co.nz; map p.433. Peaceful hostel set on a hill back from the beach with a dedicated walking track, just one dorm, but several bush-backed rooms, plenty of birdsong, free bike rental, and the owner can direct you to great tracks and all manner of other cool stuff. Closed May–Sept. Dorms $33, doubles $72

Marahau Beach Camp Franklin St ☎0800 808 018, ⓦabeltasmancentre.co.nz; map p.433. Unpretentious, well-kept campsite with tent sites, backpackers accommodation and a variety of cabins ($75) on a site with good communal facilities (coin showers) and their own bus service to Nelson and Motueka. Camping $40, dorms $25

Old Macdonald's Farm Harveys Rd, by the park entrance ☎03 527 8288, ⓦoldmacs.co.nz; map p.433. Family-run farm with cabins, cottages and a self-contained studio ($80–150), plus camping and a huge wooded area next to a couple of swimming holes. There's also secure parking ($76/night), a well-stocked shop and gear storage. Camping $18, dorms $30

ABEL TASMAN NATIONAL PARK

Unlike many of New Zealand's national parks, Abel Tasman offers a range of accommodation, accessed either by boat or the Abel Tasman Coast Track. Most people stay at the four DOC huts, spaced around four hours' walk apart along the coast, while hardened trampers will want to camp at some of the nineteen DOC campsites strung along the coast, all either beside beaches or near the DOC huts (whose facilities you are not supposed to use). Bookings are required year-round for all huts and campsites and should be made at least a week in advance in summer, although at peak times these can be all booked out. Book online (ⓦdoc.govt.nz) or at an i-SITE. There are also private accommodation options and multi-day all-inclusive trips to consider; Wilsons (see page 435) run three- to five-day guided walking and kayaking holidays with comfortable accommodation at their two trackside lodges at Torrent Bay and Awaroa.

Huts These come with water, heating, good toilets, basic but comfortable bunks, but there are no cooking facilities: bring a sleeping bag, cooking stove, pans, utensils, food and a torch. Two-night maximum stay in summer. Oct–April $38, May–Sept $32

Campsites All eighteen DOC sites have a water supply and toilets, but it means carrying more gear and you'll need lots of sandfly repellent. Only the Anchorage and Bark Bay campsites allow campfires. Two-night maximum stay in summer for all campsites. $15

Aquapackers Anchorage ☎ 0800 430 744, ⓦ aquapackers. co.nz; map p.433. Relatively expensive backpacker accommodation in made-up dorms and doubles aboard a converted boat moored for the summer just off the beach in Anchorage Bay: there's a free ferry from beach to boat. The package includes BBQ dinner, basic breakfast, BYO drinks. It can feel cramped but the stillness of the park at night and sounds of lapping water make it worthwhile. Sept–May only. Dorms $85, doubles $245

Awaroa Lodge Awaroa ☎ 03 528 8758, ⓦ awaroalodge. co.nz; map p.433. Nestled in the bush with great wetland views, this wilderness lodge uses ingredients from its organic garden in its classy restaurant (mains around $28–36). Hikers, water-taxi users and casual visitors can drop in for a coffee or a drink by the enormous fireplace, there's even a pizza oven down past the garden which operates in summer, but it's also a great place to hang out and stay for a day or three. This establishment has gone through several incarnations but the latest is by far the most user friendly. Open all year round. Check website for off-season deals. $239

★ **Totaranui Campground** Totaranui ⓦ doc.govt.nz; map p.433. The only car-accessible accommodation on the Abel Tasman coast, this huge campsite (there's room for 850 people) is so busy in summer that it's online booking-only for Christmas to the end of January. A separate section for track hikers usually has space (one night only), though you might want to press on. $15

EATING

KAITERITERI

Kai Inlet Rd, at Kaiteriteri–Sandy Bay Rd ☎ 03 527 8507; map p.433. Beach views from the terrace and pretty decent meals (including Golden Bay clams), all ranging from $18–28. Daily 9am–10pm in summer, 9am–6pm in winter.

The Views 99 Martin Farm Rd ☎ 0508 546 4672, ⓦ kimiora.com; map p.433. The resort's restaurant serves tasty vegetarian dinners with a selection of local wines, beers and juices. Nov–Easter Mon–Sat 6–9pm.

MARAHAU

★ **Fat Tui** 11 Marahau Valley Rd, at Kahu Kayaks; map p.433. A van selling wonderful takeaway fish and chips

($10), salads and gourmet burgers ($13.50–16.50; try the Moroccan spiced lamb), all to restaurant standard. Sept–Dec Wed–Sun noon–8pm, Jan–April daily 8am–8pm.

★ **Park Café** 350 Sany Bay Kaiteriteri Rd ☎ 03 527 8270, ⓦ parkcafe.co.nz; map p.433. Located at the entrance to Abel Tasman National Park, this place is legendary among appreciative walkers emerging from the park. Famed for its signature beef goulash with potato gnocchi ($28), fantastic pizzas, wholesome lunches, good coffee, restorative beers and a range of delicious dinner mains ($19–36). Veggies/greens grown in the organic garden. Open mic Thursdays, live music most Saturday nights. Don't miss dessert ($12). Daily 8am–8pm (last meal orders).

DRINKING

KAITERITERI

The Beached Whale Inlet Rd ☎ 03 527 8114; map p.433. Fun, family-friendly bar specializing in tasty food

and live music. Summer daily 3–11pm; winter Mon, Wed, Fri & Sat 5–11pm.

Golden Bay

Occupying the northwestern tip of the South Island, **Golden Bay** curves gracefully around from the northern fringes of Abel Tasman National Park to the encircling arm of **Farewell Spit**, all backed by the magnificent Kahurangi National Park. With bush-clad mountains on three sides and waves lapping at the fourth, Golden Bay's inaccessibility has helped foster the illusion that if it is not a world apart it is certainly otherworldly.

Wainui Bay, just east of the main town of **Takaka**, is most likely the spot where Abel Tasman first anchored offshore, guaranteeing his place in history as the first European to encounter Aotearoa and its feisty inhabitants. The apparently isolating presence of **Takaka**

Hill keeps today's bayside communities from growing virally, though the area has attracted a cross section of immigrants, alternative lifestylers, craftspeople, businessmen and artists, which goes some way to explaining the population's perceived spirit of **independence**. The area has been particularly popular with German-speakers who constitute between three and four percent of the 5250 residents. Sunny, beautiful and full of fascinating sights, Golden Bay deserves a couple days of your time and has a knack of inducing you to stay longer.

Takaka Hill

Ngarua Caves Oct–April daily 10am–4pm • $20 • 45min guided tours on the hour

Unless you'd prefer to fly, the only way to get to Golden Bay is on SH60, a sealed but very winding road over **Takaka Hill** that skirts the inland border of the Abel Tasman National Park. Take your time and stop frequently at viewpoints with glorious mountain views and seascapes stretching from Nelson north to D'Urville Island. Expect short delays due to ongoing roadworks after damage from Cyclone Gita in early 2018

Atop Takaka Hill, some 20km north of Motueka, you can be guided through **Ngarua Caves**, a pleasing show cave with illuminated stalactite formations and skeletons of moa which fell through holes in the cave roof.

Harwoods Hole

Accessed along Canaan Rd, 500m north of Ngarua Caves

The twisting, unsealed Canaan Road runs 11km to a car park with access to **Harwoods Hole**, a huge vertical shaft 176m deep and over 50m in diameter, which links up to a vast Starlight Cave system below. The largest vertical shaft in the country is reached by an enchanting trail (5.8km return; 1hr 30min; mostly level) through beech forest that follows a dry rock-strewn riverbed, the lip has no viewing platform or guardrails, so don't go crashing about or you'll end up in it before you see it. About 30min along the trail, a side track (20min return) leads to a **clifftop viewpoint** with stunning views down towards the Takaka Valley and the coast. A spot beside Canaan Road 3km back from the car park was one of several sites in the area used by the **Lord of the Rings** crew and featured again in *The Hobbit* films.

Rameka Track

5km; 3hr one way; 750m descent

Mountain-bikers are spoilt for choice here, with the excellent new Canaan Downs tracks leading off from the road-end car park, and the clearly signposted **Rameka Track**, which follows one of the earliest surveyed routes down into the Takaka Valley. Along the way it includes Great Expectations, a section of single-track designed and built by Jonathan Kennett, co-author of New Zealand's mountain-bikers' bible (see page 730), on land being planted out in native trees. Find an amenable driver who can meet you at the bottom, thus avoiding the slog back up SH60 and Canaan Road.

Takaka and around

The small town of **TAKAKA**, almost 60km north of Motueka, is Golden Bay's largest settlement (pop 1500), and one that has increasingly set its cap at the summer tourists, while continuing to cater for the local farming community and barefoot crusties who emerge from their shacks and tipis to sell home-made crafts and natural healing services. Immediately north, **Te Waikoropupu Springs** emerges from its cavernous underground lair, while to the north stretches a considerable stretch of beautiful bay, running parallel to SH60 as it rolls into Collingwood and Farewell Spit. To the east, Abel Tasman Drive winds past the safe swimming beach at **Pohara** and a few minor sights before heading into the northern section of the Abel Tasman National Park (see page 430). Most of the action in Takaka takes place along Commercial Street (SH60 as it passes through town), where you can quickly get a handle on the spirit of the place by visiting **Golden Bay Organics** at no. 47, the *WholeMeal Café* at no. 60, and the **Monza Gallery** at no. 25.

Golden Bay Museum
73 Commercial St • Mon–Fri 10am–4pm, Sat & Sun 10am–1pm • Donation

The **Golden Bay Museum** has a detailed diorama depicting Abel Tasman's ill-fated trip to Wainui Bay in 1642 plus all manner of historic bits and bobs, from terrifying 1950s contact lenses to the skeleton of a pilot whale. There's coverage of local Māori and the area's industries, and some interactive displays.

Te Waikoropupu Springs
One sight not to miss, off SH60 4km north of Takaka, is **Te Waikoropupu Springs**, the largest freshwater springs in New Zealand, set amid old gold workings and regenerating forest. Vast quantities of fresh water (average 14 cubic metres per second and amongst the world's clearest) well up through crystal-clear vents, one creating the Dancing Sands (where the sands, pushed by the surging water, appear to perform a jig). They're an easy walk through remnant forest along an accessible track which takes in Fish Creek Springs, all part of this amazing artesian system where the water is kept underground for up to ten years (1km return, 30min).

Anatoki Salmon
230 McCallum Rd, 6km southeast of Takaka • Christmas–Feb daily 9am–6pm; March–Dec Mon–Sun 9.30am–4pm • Free • ☏ 03 525 7251, ⓦ anatokisalmon.co.nz

You can catch your own hatchery-raised fish at **Anatoki Salmon**. They'll provide you with tackle and you only pay for bait and what you catch ($24/kg of live Chinook or King salmon). They'll prepare your catch as sashimi, smoke or barbecue it; you can eat there or pop it in a pizza box and go somewhere more scenic. There's also a licensed café selling all things salmon-based if, weirdly, you have no luck.

Also on the premises is **Anatoki Tame Eels** (same entrance and hours), a quaint and engaging farm park whose stars are the Anatoki eels, who live wild in the river but have been fed here since 1914; put some eel food on a stick and the thick black eels will rise out of the water. Buy some animal feed and the llamas, donkeys, emus, piglets, rabbits and yak (among others) will love you. The *Eels Café* here serves great coffee and delicious treats.

Abel Tasman Drive
East of Takaka, **Abel Tasman Drive** threads its way past the small waterside settlement of Pohara before ending up at Wainui Bay where it branches off to Totaranui and Awaroa – all trailheads for the Abel Tasman Coast Track.

Rawhiti Cave
3hr return • Instruction sheet available from DOC

Up Packards Road, just off Abel Tasman Drive, is a signposted track, which can be perilously slippery in wet weather. From the car park cross the Dry River and follow the track up (1hr) to a viewing platform over **Rawhiti Cave**, its cavernous mouth hung with myriad pendulous stalactites, transparent stone straws and a discarded billy, now encrusted in rock deposited from the dripping ceiling. Wear hiking shoes, take a torch and spare batteries.

Grove Scenic Reserve
7km from Takaka • Unrestricted access • Free

From Takaka, follow signs to the wonderful **Grove Scenic Reserve**, a mystical place that could have been transplanted straight from Arthurian legend. Massive rata trees sprout from odd and deformed limestone outcrops, and a ten-minute walk takes you to a narrow slot between two enormous vertical cliffs where a lookout reveals expansive views of the coast and beaches around Pohara. Take your camera.

Tarakohe Marina

Espresso Ship Nov–May Tues–Sat 10am–4.30pm, but a bit random; check if the sign's out

Pohara, 10km east of Takaka, has a couple of places to stay and eat, a relaxing sandy beach and, just along the road at Tarakohe, a working **marina** opposite the jarring site of a former cement factory. Local boaties come to launch their boats amongst the moored fishing and pleasure boats moored here. Nesting boxes set all around the breakwater reclamation encourages little blue penguins to come ashore here so as not to cross the road to get inland.

Just round the corner is pretty Ligar Bay, where the golden sand starts, its little lagoon one of the best place to check out phosperesence on moonless nights in summer. Next is **Tata Beach** and further on a shortside leads to the carpark and trailhead for **Wainui Falls** (40min return), where Nikau palms shade the banks of the river, cross the swing bridge and just further on a curtain of spray swathes the rather lovely falls. Impressive country and great on a hot day under the jungle like vegetation. Palmville Café operates In the private garden alongside the carpark in summer. Great coffee and iced-chocolates, turkish-style toasted sandwiches and treats baked daily. Genuine kiwi hospitality here, and you're welcome to bring a picnic and sit on their lawn dominated by established palms. Open over summer (weather dependent) 10am-5pm.

Tui Community

The gravel Wainui Bay road runs past the **Tui Community,** a spiritual and educational trust started in Golden Bay in the early 1980s. Just past its main gate McShane Road ends at the northernmost access point to the Coast Track. Back a couple of km the weaving gravel Totaranui Road branches off to Awaroa Estuary, and the wonderful golden arc of **Totaranui Beach**. This is a common place to start or finish the Coast Track, right by the *Totaranui Campground* (see page 441).

ARRIVAL AND DEPARTURE · TAKAKA AND AROUND

By plane Golden Bay Air (**⊕** 03 525 8725, **ⓦ** goldenbayair. co.nz) fly from Wellington, Nelson and Karamea.
Destinations Karamea (1 daily; 30min); Nelson (1 daily; 30min); Wellington (1–4 daily; 50min).
By bus Golden Bay Coachlines (**⊕** 03 525 8352, **ⓦ** goldenbaycoachlines.co.nz) run from Nelson and continue north to Collingwood and the Heaphy Track, and east to Totaranui. Both drop off outside the Takaka i-SITE on SH60.
Destinations Collingwood (2 daily; 20min); Heaphy Track (1 daily; 1hr); Motueka (1 daily; 1hr 15min); Nelson (1 daily; 2hr 15min); Totaranui (1 daily; 1hr).

GETTING AROUND

By bike Most of the hostels in Takaka have free bikes for guests to get around the flat town, and The Quiet Revolution, 11 Commercial St (closed Sat afternoon & Sun; **⊕** 03 525 9555), rents bikes ($25/day road bikes; $45–65/day for full suspension off-road use) and sells the *Fat Tyre Fun* leaflet ($2), containing over a dozen great mountain-bike rides in Golden Bay.

INFORMATION

Golden Bay Visitor Centre SH60, as you enter Takaka from the south (daily 9am–5pm; **⊕** 03 525 9136, **ⓦ** goldenbaynz.co.nz). Handles bookings, hut tickets for the national parks and rental cars.
DOC 62 Commercial St (Mon–Fri 10.30am–12.30pm and 1.30–3pm, Dec–Easter 9am–4pm; **⊕** 03 525 8026). Has the information and expertise to meet your hiking, biking, fishing and ecology needs, including track forecasts and suggestions on getting away from the crowds.
Internet Free wi-fi for 1hr plus terminals at the Takaka Memorial Library, 3 Junction St (Mon–Thurs 9.30am–5pm, Fri 9.30am–6pm, Sat 9.30am–12.30pm; **⊕** 03 525 0059), and at Unlimited Copies 29 Commercial St. The Spark telephone booths at the northern end of the shops are wi-fii hotspots too.

ACCOMMODATION

Golden Bay is a popular holiday spot for both Kiwis and foreign visitors; as a result there is plenty of good-quality accommodation, from backpackers to swanky lodges. Camping ranges from the enormous DOC campsite at Totaranui to wayside spots where you can park your campervan overnight.

TAKAKA

Annie's Nirvana Lodge 25 Motupipi St ☎ 03 525 8766, ⓦ nirvanalodge.co.nz. Enthusiastically run associate YHA right in town with a homely atmosphere, two kitchens, nice garden with lots of seating and a record player, free bikes, and private rooms (including three attractive garden doubles). Dorms $\underline{$28}$, doubles $\underline{$66}$

★ **Autumn Farm Lodge** 3km south of Takaka, Central Takaka Rd off SH60 ☎ 03 525 9013, ⓦ autumnfarm.com. LGBTQ and naturist, straight-friendly establishment. Lodge rooms, cabins, dorm and campground. Communal facilities, huge gorgeous grounds and a pool. Reservations essential in summer. Camping $\underline{$25}$, dorms $\underline{$40}$, doubles $\underline{$70}$

Golden Bay Motel 132 Commercial St ☎ 0800 401 212, ⓦ goldenbaymotel.co.nz. Well-kept boutique motel with off-street parking, limited free wi-fi, and incredibly good-value, spacious, clean, comfy rooms about a 3min walk from the centre of town. Studio and motel units from $\underline{$125}$

Kiwiana 73 Motupipi St ☎ 03 525 7676, ⓦ kiwianabackpackers.co.nz. Beautifully kept and well-run hostel in a large villa where the Kiwiana theme runs to the labelling of the airy rooms. In the games room they have pool and table tennis. There's an outdoor BBQ/kitchen on the spacious deck in the well-tended garden, plus free bikes. Dorms $\underline{$30}$, doubles $\underline{$70}$

Mohua Motels SH60 ☎ 03 525 7222, ⓦ mohuamotels. co.nz. Modern self-contained motel apartments located at the entrance to the town. Everything you need located on your doorstep. $\underline{$125}$

★ **Shady Rest** 139 Commercial St ☎ 03 525 9669, ⓦ shadyrest.co.nz. Lovely central B&B in a historic former doctor's house with comfortable, wood-panelled rooms that are either en suite or have a private bathroom. A generous breakfast, solar-heated outdoor bath and a lovely garden that runs down to a peaceful creek make this a treat. $\underline{$150}$

AROUND TAKAKA

★ **Adrift** 52 Tukurua Rd, 17km north of Takaka ☎ 03 525 8353, ⓦ adrift.co.nz. Five gorgeous, self-contained cottages (and one studio) decorated in chic, modern style and all with direct access across lawns to the beach. All rooms have a sea view, making them perfect for a leisurely breakfast in bed. With double spa baths, and a small penguin colony on site

you may never want to leave. Studio $\underline{$230}$, cottages $\underline{$259}$

Golden Bay Hideaway 220 McShane Rd, Wainui Bay, 23km east of Takaka ☎ 03 525 7184, ⓦ goldenbayhideaway.co.nz. Wonderful spot, close to the northern end of the Abel Tasman Coast Track, comprising two eco-efficient houses and a "hippie house" (sleeping four), plus a beautifully crafted house truck. Great views, an outdoor bath and cook-your-own-dinner/breakfast supplies complete the package. Truck $\underline{$170}$, houses $\underline{$220}$

Laidback Lodge 23 Ironworks Rd, 13km north of Takaka ☎ 03 525 6244, ⓦ laidbacklodge.co.nz. A vibrant, kiwiana *bach* set in private natural surroundings looking out to Kahurangi National Park. Enjoy a bush bath under the stars before retiring to super-comfortable lodgings or stroll down to the *Mussel Inn* for a few beers. $\underline{$160}$

★ **Pohara Beach Top 10 Holiday Park** 809 Abel Tasman Drive ☎ 0800 764 272, ⓦ poharabeach.com. A popular, well-equipped traditional Kiwi beachfront holiday park with a broad range of accommodation including cabins (from $65), excellent communal facilities and very helpful owners. Camping $\underline{$28}$, motel $\underline{$140}$

★ **Sans Souci Inn** 11 Richmond Rd, Pohara Beach, 10km east of Takaka ☎ 03 525 8663, ⓦ sanssouciinn. co.nz. Endearing Swiss-run inn with a communal feel, set in a mud-brick building with sod roof and handmade floor tiles. The six rooms share one large bathroom with shower stalls, bath and composting toilets, though there's also a self-contained cottage sleeping four and an excellent restaurant (see page 442). Guests can use the kitchen or go for the delicious breakfasts. Closed July to mid-Sept. Doubles $\underline{$130}$, cottage $\underline{$160}$

★ **Shambhala** SH60, 16km north of Takaka at Onekaka ☎ 03 525 8463, ⓦ shambhala.co.nz. Welcoming shoes-off backpackers located 2km down a track almost opposite the *Mussel Inn*, from where free pick-up can be arranged. There's lovely native gardens, delightful BBQ/teahouse gazebo, beach access and a slightly spiritual bent, including free daily meditation sessions and yoga classes. Dorms ($35) are in the main house, or there are spacious twins and doubles with lovely sea views in a separate block, with solar-heated showers and composting toilets. Closed June–Oct. Camping $\underline{$20}$, doubles $\underline{$80}$

Totaranui Campground 26km east of Takaka. Large and popular beachside campsite within Abel Tasman National Park, with a shop, running water, toilets, picnic tables and cold showers. Book in advance. $\underline{$15}$

Waitapu Bridge 4km north of Takaka on SH60. Riverside freedom site for self-contained campervans only. Maximum two-night stay. $\underline{Free}$

EATING AND DRINKING

Takaka has some good places to eat and there are more a few kilometres out that justify the journey. Drinking and music are best in the *Wholemeal Café*, *Roots Bar*, *The Brigand* and the *Mussel Inn*.

TAKAKA

The Brigand 90 Commercial St ☎03 525 9636. Relaxed restaurant-bar serving open sandwiches, succulent ribs, and salmon (mains $2–34) – with lots of outdoor seating and live music several nights a week plus open mic on Thursdays. Daily 11am–late.

Dancing Sands Distillery 46a Commercial St (just up Hoddy Lane) in the town centre ☎03 525 9899, ⊛dancingsands.com. Takaka's town distillery creates fine vodka, gin and rum using spring water from the world's clearest springs. World-class whisky, a rum that beats most in the Caribbean, and extraordinary liqueurs and champagne infused from manuka honey. Mon–Fri 9am–5pm, Sat 10am–5pm.

Dangerous Kitchen 46a Commercial St ☎03 525 8686 for takeaway orders. Large, good-value café that's very popular with locals for watching the world pass by, or takeaway grub. Exotic pizzas ($17.50–35) are the mainstay, though they do tasty wraps, good breakfasts (under $20) and salads. Mon–Sat 9am–8.30pm (later in summer).

Kiwi Spirit Distillery 430 Abel Tasman Drive, 4km from town at Motupipi ☎03 525 8575, ⊛kiwispirits.co.nz. *Kiwi Spirit* recently moved to this large new site. Helped by one of the country's only female distillers, enthusiastic owner Terry Knight's aim has been to bottle some of Golden Bay's unique wild bounty. Using only purest water sourced from Takaka's deepest aquifer, their honey-infused Waitui Whisky and gold-bearing Vodka Juijui have been a big hit on the export market, as have their manuka honey and cider vinegar Bite Me tonic. But it may well be their extensive blue agave or tequiliana plantings (a sight in themselves) that will make these guys famous. Make sure you try their super-smooth Te Kiwi tequila, the only such spirit produced outside of Mexico. Daily 10am–4pm or by appointment.

★ **Roots Bar** 1 Commercial St. ☎03 5259592. Hang out around the open fire tucking into lovingly prepared Kiwi-style gourmet burgers ($18–20) and sipping Nelson-brewed Sprig & Fern beers and ciders as reggae, roots or drum 'n' bass music floats by. DJs and bands often play at the weekends until late (mostly free but occasional $10–25 cover charge). Tues–Sun 10am–late.

Takaka Infusion 30 Commercial St. The only German-run teahouse in the South Island, dishing up the best bread (the flour is freshly stone-ground) and pastries in the bay and thirty varieties of loose tea. A haven of tranquillity amid the small town bustle. Mon–Fri 9am–5pm, Sat 9am–3pm, 8am–6pm in summer.

TLC (The Little Café) 65a Commercial St ☎03 525 9077. Tiny coffee house with outdoor seating under a pin oak overlooking the main road, serving the best coffee in the bay and some counter nosh. Mon–Fri 9.30am–4pm.

★ **Wholemeal Café** 60 Commercial St. A Takaka institution that's endearingly sloppy at times, but it's always good value and makes a decent spot to hang out over a good coffee and large cake. Return for pizza, colourful and healthy salads, and assorted fish, meat and veggie dishes ($10–22) in the cavernous interior of this old picture theatre or on the deck out the side. Licensed. Daily 7.30am–4pm, later for events (such as Friday curry nights in winter) or concerts and during summer.

AROUND TAKAKA

★ **Mussel Inn** 1259 Takaka-Collingwood Hwy, 16km north of Takaka ☎03 525 9241, ⊛musselinn.co.nz. Do not miss this place – whether you want to eat, enjoy wine, cider or ale (they brew many varieties of their own, including the manuka-infused "Captain Cooker"), sit and read, play chess or soak up the lively atmosphere of a live band or local event. The building is adorned with Estuary Art and hand-hewn but comfortable, wooden furniture, with leafy shady surrounds to sit outside. You can always get a simple, fresh and wholesome meal (no fries); try a plate of their fresh steamed local mussels with garlic bread ($18), a pie, open burger (fish, meat or falafel) or some excellent cake. Cosy open fire in winter. Daily 11am–late, evening meals ($24.50–29) 6–9pm; closed Aug & Sept.

Penguin Café 822 Abel Tasman Drive, Pohara ☎03 5256126, ⊛penguincafe.co.nz. Spacious café/restaurant and bar that's worth the drive out from Takaka if only to sip a beer or coffee on the roadside deck which catches the sun most of the day, and has a water feature to keep the kids amused. Well-presented dishes include salmon and seafood pizza (mains $22–36). Mon 4pm–late, Tues–Sun 11am–late.

Sans Souci Inn 11 Richmond Rd, Pohara Beach, 10km east of Takaka ☎03 525 8663, ⊛sanssouciinn. co.nz. Simple licensed restaurant with a daily set menu of freshly prepared, imaginative food that can include Anatoki salmon, beef fillets and veggie options (around $38). There's also a choice of sumptuous desserts. Booking essential. Oct–Easter; dinner always served at 7pm unless specified.

★ **Toto's Cafe & Pizzeria** Totoranui Rd, Wainui Bay, 20km east of Takaka and 2km along a gravel road ☎03 970 7934 Earth-built pizza oven, cob café and gallery, with hydropower, amazing views and extremely fine pizza (small $12, large $22). You could also try the Anatoki smoked salmon, finished with fresh oregano from their flowerbed. A great place on a great day, but not quite enough shelter if the weather turns. Summer daily 10am–5pm; weekends only in winter.

ENTERTAINMENT

Village Theatre 32 Commercial St ☎03 525 8483, ⊛villagetheatre.org.nz. Small not-for-profit cinema screening arthouse movies and blockbusters. Check website for live performances too.

FAREWELL SPIT TOURS

The trip to Farewell Spit, some 22km north of Collingwood, is an iconic New Zealand journey and shouldn't be missed – if you do nothing else but this in Golden Bay your time will not have been wasted. At the time of writing, only one tour company merited inclusion.

Farewell Spit Eco Tours Tasman St, Collingwood ☎ 0800 808 257, ⓦ farewellspit.com. In operation since 1946, this outfit runs the Farewell Spit Eco Tour (6hr 30min; $155) which heads out along the sands of the spit to its historic lighthouse in a purpose-built 4WD. The trip comes with a bright commentary, peppered with local lore. During the day you'll see vast numbers of birds, seals (plus the occasional sea lion)and fossils, climb an enormous sand dune and maybe see the skeletons of wrecked ships if the sands reveal them. Their more eco-oriented Gannet Colony Tour (6hr 30min; $165) includes most of the above plus a 20min walk to the massive gannet colony towards the very end of the spit. Trips operate year-round with departure times dependent on tides: check the website. On both trips, light refreshments are provided.

Collingwood and around

Collingwood Museum and Aorere Centre • Daily 9am–6pm • Donation

Golden Bay's northernmost settlement of any consequence is laidback **COLLINGWOOD**, the base for tours to **Farewell Spit** (see above). The town occupies a strip of land wedged between the sea and Ruataniwha Inlet, a location which was briefly championed in the 1850s as the site for the nation's new capital; street plans were drawn up, but as the gold petered out, so did the enthusiasm. The details are spelled out in the diminutive **Collingwood Museum** and **Aorere Centre**, in adjoining buildings, the former a traditional museum, the latter using multimedia to present information on natural history and cultural heritage and links with various plaques around the town.

Devil's Boots

Aorere Valley runs southwest of Collingwood towards the start of the Heaphy Track. After 7km, call briefly at the **Devil's Boots**, huge bulbous limestone overhangs on either side of the gravel road that look like two feet protruding from the ground, with shrubby vegetation sprouting from their soles.

About 4km on, divert down to the end of Carter Road to the beginning of the lovely **Kaituna Track** (2hr return), a bushwalk past old gold workings to the river confluence at Kaituna Forks.

Langford's Store

Bainham, 18km southwest of Collingwood • Boxing Day–Easter daily 9am–6pm, other times Sat–Thurs 8.30am–4.30pm; closed July & Aug

The wonderful **Langford's Store** is a combined general store and post office built in 1928 by ancestors of the current owners, and seemingly little changed. Even the hand-cranked adding machine has been deemed too new-fangled so your bill will be tallied on paper. Be sure to stop for coffee and cake, or Devonshire tea – you can sit out back in the garden, or in the storeroom that's an absolute treasure trove of memorabilia. The friendly owners are worth visiting in themselves. Five kilometres further on is **Salisbury Falls**, a popular swimming spot.

ACCOMMODATION   COLLINGWOOD AND AROUND

Collingwood Motor Camp 6 William St, Collingwood ☎ 03 524 8149. Traditional but basic campsite, stuffed to the gills in the summer (make sure you book ahead) with a few wooden cabins ($55) and some much more swanky self-contained units. Camping per site $34, cabins $55

Collingwood Park Motel 1 Tasman St, Collingwood ☎ 0800 270 520, ⓦ collingwoodpark.co.nz. Good-value units on a small, modern, central site that backs onto the river estuary. They've also got a "pod" ($125/2 people). The rooms are comfortable, clean and run by friendly people. $130

Somerset House 12 Gibbs Rd, Collingwood ☎ 03 524 8624, ⓦ backpackerscollingwood.co.nz. A low-key backpackers with decent, clean and comfortable rooms in a house with reasonable communal facilities, sea and estuary

8

KAHURANGI NATIONAL PARK: THE HEAPHY TRACK

The huge expanse of Kahurangi National Park, 4520 square kilometres of the northwestern South Island, lies between the wet and exposed western side of the Wakamarama Range over to Mount Arthur in the east, and down to the limestone peaks of Mount Owen, the park's highest mountain. Over half New Zealand's native **plant species** are represented, as are most of its alpine plants, and the remote interior is a haven for wildlife, including rare carnivorous snails and giant cave spiders.

The park's extraordinary landscapes are best seen by walking the **Heaphy Track** (78km; 4–5 days), which links the Aorere Valley in Golden Bay with Kohaihai Bluff on the West Coast. One of New Zealand's Great Walks, it is appreciably tougher than the Abel Tasman Coast Track, though it compensates with beauty and the diversity of its landscapes – turbulent rivers, broad tussock downs, forests, and nikau palm groves at the western end. The track is named after Charles Heaphy who, along with Thomas Brunner, became the first European to walk the West Coast section of the park in 1846, accompanied by their Māori guide Kehu. Māori had long traversed the area heading down to central Westland in search of *pounamu* for weapons, ornaments and tools. During the off season (May–Nov) you can mountain-bike it in two to three days.

TRAILHEAD TRANSPORT

The western end of the track is over 400km by road from the eastern end, so if you leave gear at one end, you'll have to re-walk the track, undertake a long bus journey, or fly back to your base at Nelson, Motueka or Takaka. Track transport only runs from late October to mid-April: in **winter** everything becomes more difficult, requiring taxis to reach trailheads.

The **eastern end** starts at **Brown Hut**, 28km southwest and inland of Collingwood. Golden Bay Coachlines run there from Nelson (departing 3.15pm; $57), Motueka (4.30pm; $47), Takaka (9.15am; $35) and Collingwood (9.35am; $32). From the **west coast end** of the track, you'll arrive at the **Kohaihai shelter**, 16km north of Karamea. Even with the best connections you'll need to spend nights in both Karamea and Nelson before returning to Takaka. The operators listed below provide services that can help avoid this.

Adventure Flights ☎ 0800 150 338, ⊛ adventureflightsgoldenbay.co.nz. Flying gives you the chance to return to your car the same day you finish, as well as getting dropped off near Brown Hut at the start of the track. Pick-up and drop-off from either end ($220–270; bikes an extra $20).

Trek Express ☎ 0800 128 735, ⊛ trekexpress.co.nz. They'll run you from one of several start points to Brown Hut, pick you up at Kohaihai Shelter several days later, then run you back that evening ($115).

TRAIL INFORMATION AND GUIDED HIKES

Download DOC's *Heaphy Track* brochure, or buy one at an i-SITE. It includes a **schematic map** that is satisfactory for hiking, though it is helpful to carry the detailed 1:150,000 *Kahurangi Park* map ($19).

---

views, kayaks, free breakfast and free bikes. Arrange pick-ups or drop-offs for the Heaphy or Abel Tasman with the owners, who can also help with car rental. Dorms $32, doubles $78

Te Hapu Coastal Cottages 429 Te Hapu Rd, Collingwood 7073 ☎ 5248711, ⊛ tehapu.co.nz. Walking and exploring the karst landscape of this spectacular 1000-acre farm with eight beaches is a sublime wilderness coast experience. Extra special is being able to wander the expansive rock platforms with luxuriant rock pools at low tide. Three accommodation options (Chalet, Cottage, Shearing Shed Retreat), each in its own unique location, with fifteen beds in total. $130

Westhaven Retreat 336 Te Hapu Rd, Westhaven Inlet ☎ 03 524 8354, ⊛ westhavenretreat.com. Spectacular lodge on a working farm on a majestic coastal peninsula. Accommodation is in five luxurious Lodge Rooms and two spacious Luxury Lodge Suites, all with spectacular views out over the Tai Tapu Marine Reserve and Kahurangi National Park. Tariff includes full buffet breakfast, picnic lunch and activities. Afternoon tea with home-made afternoon cake or pastries, and four-course dinner. Heated indoor pool and spa. Luxury doesn't get much more remote than this. $900

EATING

Collingwood Tavern Tasman St, Collingwood ☎ 524 8160. A hangout for locals and also an excellent bistro where you can get great fish 'n' chips or meals ($16–24) to eat in the dining room or out in the covered veranda with

Bush and Beyond Guided Walks ☏ 021 0270 8209, 🌐 heaphytrackguidedwalks.co.nz. Guided walks along the track – and elsewhere in the park – are admirably handled by this ecologically caring operator, who runs multi-day trips ($1950).

ACCOMMODATION

Along the route, there are seven **huts** that **must be booked** and paid for year-round ($32; book online at 🌐 doc.govt.nz), with heating, water and toilets (mostly flush). All except Brown and Gouland Downs have cooking stoves, but you need your own pots and pans. There are also nine designated **campsites** that must be booked ($14) and are mostly close to huts, though you can't use hut facilities. There is a two-night limit in each hut or campsite. Take all provisions with you, and go prepared for sudden changes of weather and a hail of sandflies.

THE ROUTE

Ninety percent of hikers walk the Heaphy Track from east to west, thereby getting the tough initial climb over with on the first day and taking it relatively easy on subsequent days.
Brown Hut to Perry Saddle Hut (17km; 5hr; 800m ascent). A steady climb all the way along an old coach road, passing the Aorere campsite and shelter, and Flanagans Corner viewpoint – at 915m, the highest point on the track.
Perry Saddle Hut to Gouland Downs Hut (7km; 2hr; 200m ascent). It's a very easy walk across Perry Saddle through tussock clearings and down into a valley (passing the famed pole strung with discarded tramping boots) before crossing bridges over limestone ravines to the hut. This is a great little eight-bunk hut where you might hear kiwi.
Gouland Downs Hut to Saxon Hut (5km; 1hr 30min; 200m descent). Leaving Gouland Downs Hut you pass through an enchanted limestone section covered in beech forest festooned with moss and lichens. From here crossing Gouland Downs, a magnificent undulating area of tussock and scrublands with protruding rocky reefs.
Saxon Hut to James Mackay Hut (12km; 3hr; 400m ascent). Cross the grassy flatlands, winding in and out of small tannin-stained streams as they tip over into the Heaphy River below.
James Mackay Hut to Lewis Hut (12.5km; 3–4hr; 700m descent). If you have the energy it is worth pressing on to a haven of nikau palms – but sadly also less welcome sandflies.
Lewis Hut to Heaphy Hut (8km; 2–3hr; 100m ascent). It is possible to get from Lewis Hut to the track end in a day but it is more enjoyable to take your time and stop at the Heaphy Hut, near where you can explore the exciting Heaphy rivermouth: its narrow outlet funnels the river water, resulting in a maelstrom of sea and fresh water.
Heaphy Hut to Kohaihai (16km; 5hr; 100m ascent). This final stretch is a gentle walk through forest down the coast until you reach Crayfish Point, where the route briefly follows the beach. Avoid this section within an hour of high tide, longer if it's stormy. Once you reach Scott's Beach, you have only to climb over Kohaihai Bluff to find the Kohaihai Shelter car park on the other side – and hopefully your prearranged pick-up from Karamea.

superb views over Ruataniwha Inlet. Friendly staff make everyone welcome. Daily 10am–late.
Courthouse 11 Elizabeth St, Collingwood ☏ 03 524 8025. Small selection of counter food and some tasty specials (grilled halloumi with caper salsa; $18) in this tiny café, popular with locals and visitors alike. In the evenings they do gourmet pizza takeaways. Thurs–Tues 8am–4pm, plus Thurs & Sat 5pm–8pm.

Old School Cafe and Restaurant 1115 Collingwood-Puponga Main Rd ☏ 03 524 8457. The former school in this beachside settlement is now a café-bar and restaurant selling fine basic fare including steaks and pizza and a good selection of drinks. A nice place to hang out in the old classroom and sunny sheltered courtyard, with friendly owners. Thurs & Fri 4pm–late, Sat & Sun 11am–late.

The road to Farewell Spit

North of Collingwood the road skirts Ruataniwha Inlet, and, after 10km, passes *The Innlet* (see page 447). The road now follows the coast 11km to **Puponga**, at the northern tip of the South Island, where you can stay at the *Farewell Gardens*

NELSON LAKES HIKES

With 270km of track served by twenty huts there is no shortage of walking options. For **day-walks**, arm yourself with DOC's *Walks In Nelson Lakes National Park* booklet. The two **multi-day tramps** have their own leaflets supplemented by the 1:100,000 *Nelson Lakes National Park* map ($19). Blue Lake, now determined as the clearest water in the world, is an overnight trip from West Sabine Hut.

These are alpine tracks so **go equipped** with good boots, and warm, waterproof clothing – it can snow in almost any month up here – and crampons are likely to be needed from April to November. Both tracks start from the upper Mount Robert car park, 7km by road from St Arnaud. There've been some break-ins at the car park so remember the DOC centre will look after bags ($1/day). The following hikes are listed in approximate order of difficulty.

Bellbird Walk Kerr Bay, St Arnaud (10–15min loop; flat). Easy meander through beech forest alive with the sound of tui, bellbirds and fantails thanks to the Rotoiti Nature Recovery Project, an attempt to replicate the successful offshore island pest clearances by concerted trapping and poisoning. Several of these "mainland islands" have been set up across New Zealand since the late 1990s with considerable success. Visit in the early evening when the birds (even reintroduced great spotted kiwi) are particularly noisy and frisky.

Mount Robert Circuit (9km; 3–4hr loop; 600m ascent). An excellent loop around the visible face of Mount Robert starting at the Mount Robert car park, ascending the steep Pinchgut Track to the edge of the bush then traversing across to Bushline Hut ($15) before zigzagging down Paddy's Track to the start.

Angelus Hut Loop Mount Robert trailhead (28km; 2-day loop; 1000m ascent). One of the most popular overnighters, this loop follows the exposed Robert Ridge to the beautiful Angelus Basin with its shiny new hut (Oct–April bookings required $20, camping $10; May–Sept $15) and alpine tarn. Two common routes complete the loop: the steep Cascade Track and the Speargrass Track, a bad-weather escape.

Travers-Sabine Circuit (80km; 4–7 days; 1200m ascent). This major tramp is the scenic equal of several of the Great Walks, but far less crowded. The track probes deep into remote areas of lakes, fields of tussock, 2000m-high mountains and the 1780m Travers Saddle. At the height of summer its verges are briefly emblazoned with yellow buttercups, white daisies, sundew and harebells. The circuit requires a good level of fitness, but is fairly easy to follow with bridges over most streams. There are eleven huts ($15), all but three serviced ($5; tickets from DOC), and three campsites – fires are not allowed, so carry a stove and fuel.

Motor Camp. Around 2km on is Puponga Farm Park, a coastal sheep farm open to the public; check out the visitor centre for more information.

Farewell Spit

From Puponga Farm Park, there are great views right along **Farewell Spit** – named by Captain Cook at the end of a visit in 1770 – which stretches 26km east, often heaped with driftwood and tree trunks washed up from the West Coast. The whole vast sandspit is a **nature reserve** of international importance, with salt marshes, open mudflats, brackish lakes and bare dunes providing habitats for over a hundred **bird species**: bar-tailed godwit, long-billed curlew and dotterel all come to escape the Arctic winter, there are breeding colonies of Caspian terns, and large numbers of black swans. Sadly, the unusual shape of the coastline seems to fool whales' navigation systems and beachings are common, especially around January when hundreds of holidaymakers and locals come to help refloat them.

Short **walks** head to the outer beach (2.5km) and the inner beach (4km, as far as you're allowed to go); both provide good views of the spit, which is otherwise off-limits except on guided tours from Collingwood (see page 443).

Cape Farewell

Away from Farewell Spit, walks head through the farm park to **Cape Farewell** (the northernmost point on the South Island), the strikingly set **Pillar Point Lighthouse** and to wave-lashed **Wharariki Beach**. Here, rock bridges and towering arches are stranded just offshore, while deep dunes have blocked river-mouths, forming briny lakes and islands where fur seals and birds have made a home. Visit within a couple of hours of low tide to access some sea caves where the seals hang out. Nearby Fletcher's Beach, down a winding track, is a favourite hangout for extreme surfers.

INFORMATION AND ACTIVITIES

Tourist information The *Farewell Spit Café* (daily 9am–5pm; ☎03 524 8454), adjacent to Puponga Farm Park, acts as the visitor centre for Farewell Spit. You can also check ⓦdoc.govt.nz, and download the *Farewell Spit and Puponga Farm Park* leaflet for more information.

Cape Farewell Horse Treks ☎03 524 8031,

THE ROAD TO FAREWELL SPIT

ⓦhorsetreksnz.co.nz. Offers some of the most visually spectacular horseriding in the South Island. Trips don't actually go onto Farewell Spit, but visit Wharariki Beach (3hr; $160), Old Man Range (2hr 30min), Puponga Beach (90min; $80), , Puponga Beach/Old Man Range Combo (2hr 30min; $125) and Ultimate Combo (5hr; $240).

ACCOMMODATION

Farewell Gardens Motor Camp 37–39 Seddon St, Puponga ☎03 524 8445, ⓦfarewell gardens.co.nz. An idyllic little spot, located beside the sea at the base of Farewell Spit, with a variety of accommodation options for everyone from families to backpackers. Facilities include two camp kitchens, lounge, BBQ, free bikes and kayaks, and hot showers. Camping $18, two-bedroom apartment $160, en-suite cabin $85

The Innlet 839 Collingwood-Puponga Rd ☎03 524 8040, ⓦtheinnlet.co.nz. Excellent hostel with delightful garden cottages, several heated outdoor baths in the bush, and plenty of space for camping. Dorms $35, rooms $85

Westhaven Retreat Luxury Lodge 336 Te Hapu Rd ☎03 524 8354, ⓦwesthaven retreat.com. Luxury well-

appointed lodge in an unsurpassed setting atop a coastal peninsula with the Tasman Sea on one side and a marine reserve on the other. No neighbours for miles, the whole vast farm is yours to explore. With seven en-suite rooms, a spa and a 25m-long indoor heated swimming pool, this place oozes the European flair of the family who built and run it. The price includes all gourmet meals. $980

Wharariki Holiday Park Wharariki Beach, Cape Farewell ☎03 524 8507, ⓦwhararikibeachholidaypark. co.nz. Thirty tent sites, a backpacker lodge, cabins, plus a wide range of facilities that includes a communal kitchen, BBQ, hot showers (coin-op), laundry, and a coffee and snacks caravan (daily 9am–7pm in summer). Camping $18, cabins $80

8

Nelson Lakes National Park and around

Two glacial lakes characterize the **Nelson Lakes National Park,** around 120km southwest of Nelson, **Rotoiti** ("little lake") and **Rotoroa** ("long lake"), nestled in the mountains at the northernmost limit of the Southern Alps. Both are surrounded by tranquil mountains and shrouded in dark beech forest and jointly form the headwaters of the Buller River. **Tramping** is undoubtedly the main event and you could easily devote a week to some of the longer circuits, though the short lakeside walks are also rewarding.

The park's subalpine rivers, lakes, forests and hills are full of birdlife, but it has offered little solace to humans: Māori passed through the area and caught eels in the lakes, but the best efforts of European settlers and gold prospectors yielded meagre returns. Now, recreation is all, despite the sandflies.

St Arnaud

ST ARNAUD (pronounced Snt-AR-nard) is a speck of a place scattered around the north shore of Lake Rotoiti, with around a hundred residents but over four hundred houses, mostly used by holidaying Kiwis. The town is largely used as a base for anglers, kayakers and boaties. The lake is not only the venue for annual powerboat races but also vintage boat gatherings.

ARRIVAL AND DEPARTURE

By bus Access to the region is with Nelson Lakes Shuttles (☎03 547 6896, ⓦnelsonlakesshuttles.co.nz) who offer a service to and from Nelson (Dec–April, 4 a week; $45/

ST ARNAUD

person) and also connect St Arnaud with the Mount Robert car park and Lake Rotoroa.

GETTING AROUND

By water taxi Rotoiti Water Taxis (☎021 702 278, ⓦrotoitiwatertaxis.co.nz) operate on Lake Rotoiti from St Arnaud to the head of the lake and charge $100 for up to three people, then $30/person, if you fancy sections of hiking at the southern end of the lake. Scheduled services in summer and water taxi by arrangement to suit, along with scenic cruises around the lake by prior arrangement ($25–40/person; minimum charge $160, less for shorter look-arounds) and rents kayaks ($50/half-day) and canoes ($75/half-day).

INFORMATION

DOC are on View Rd (daily 8am–4.30pm extended to 5 in summer; ☎03 521 1806). Has all the hiking, biking, fishing and ecology information you could need as well as local accommodation and transport listings. If you're off on a hike, they'll store small baggage and valuables for $1 a day.

ACCOMMODATION AND EATING

★ **Alpine Lodge** Main Rd, opposite the Village Alpine Store ☎03 521 1869, ⓦalpinelodge.co.nz. Owned and managed by a family who are passionate about the Lakes. There's a good range of dorms, budget rooms ($75) and hotel rooms in wooden buildings, with an extremely popular licensed restaurant, bar and spa pool, only a 10min walk to Lake Rotoiti. The café provides strong coffee, home-made cakes, all-day snacks and dinners such as steak, fish and burgers. Closed June, and Mon/Tues in winter. Dorms $35, doubles $180

Kerr Bay campsite On the lakeshore, 500m from the Village Alpine Store. Simple DOC site with pay showers ($1), toilets, tap water, and cooking facilities. $18

Nelson Lakes Motels and Travers-Sabine Lodge SH63 ☎03 521 1887, ⓦnelsonlakes.co.nz. About 150m up the street from the Village Alpine Store. This is a modern purpose-built backpackers' lodge with double/twin/family rooms, large commercial kitchen, Sky TV and a wealth of information from friendly owners. Comfortable, fully self-contained log-built and contemporary motels are also part of the same complex. A 5min bush walk takes you down to the lake. Dorms $32, doubles $75, self-contained motels $135

St Arnaud Village Alpine Store 74 Main Rd ☎03 521 1854. The village hub sells petrol, alcohol, groceries – including fresh produce – and fish and chips (Fri & Sat). Mon–Sat 8am–6pm.

★ **Tophouse** Tophouse Rd, 8km northeast of St Arnaud ☎03 521 1269, ⓦtophouse.co.nz. Sitting by the fire in this earth-built former drovers' inn and stagecoach hotel decorated with Victorian furniture can make you feel like you've slipped back in time. Accommodation is either in shared-bathroom inn rooms or outside in fairly modern motel-style cabins. Morning teas and lunches by arrangement. Don't miss the country's smallest pub – six is a crowd – with excellent local beers. Cabins $135, B&B $150

West Bay Campsite 1.5km drive from St Arnaud. A basic DOC site with two separate camping areas with some forested pitches, plus tap water, cold showers and toilets. Closed May–Nov. $13

Lake Rotoroa

20km northwest of St Arnaud, approached along the Gowan Valley Rd

Pretty **Lake Rotoroa** feels a good deal more remote than the area around St Arnaud. The lake ends near a DOC **campsite**, from where there are a few short walks. Lake Rotoroa Water Taxis ☎03 523 9199 ply the length of the lake (3 persons $45 each; 4 persons or more $40; minimum water-taxi fee $160) to Sabine Hut on the Travers-Sabine Circuit.

Murchison

MURCHISON, 125km southwest of Nelson and 60km west of St Arnaud, is a small former gold and stagecoach town now favoured by hunting and fishing types as well as rafters and river kayakers. Numerous rivers feed the nearby Buller, providing excellent whitewater and plenty of opportunities for bagging trout. Once clear of Murchison, SH6 shadows the river through the Buller Gorge to the **West Coast** town of Westport.

Murchison museum

60 Fairfax St • Mon–Sat 11am–3pm • Donation

Everything of note is on SH6 (Waller St) or Fairfax Street, which crosses it, including the **Murchison Museum**. Housed in the 1911 former post office (60 Fairfax St), local history is sketched out in newspaper clippings, photographs and various oddities including Māori axe heads, gold-rush-era Chinese pottery and opium bottles.

ARRIVAL AND DEPARTURE   MURCHISON

By bus Buses stop at the west end of Waller St.
Destinations Greymouth (1 daily; 4hr); Nelson (1–daily;

2hr); Punakaiki (1 daily; 2hr 50min); Westport (1 daily; 1hr 30min) .

INFORMATION AND ACTIVITIES

Tourist information The Murchison Info Centre, 47 Waller St (☏ 03 5239350) stocks a range of leaflets and has enthusiastic helpers.
Services There are two ATMs in town, one at 32 Waller St, near the bus stop, the other in the Four Square supermarket.
Gold panning The town is one of the few places in the country with public gold panning. Pick up the *Recreational Gold Panning* leaflet at the museum. For gold pans ($10/15) and all the other equipment you'll need, head to H. Hodgson & Co at 46 Fairfax St (Mon–Fri 8am–5pm, Sat 10am–1pm, Sun 10am- 2pm)).
Day-walks When you're in St Arnaud, pick up DOC's *Murchison Day Walks* leaflet featuring the Skyline Walk

(3km return; 1hr 30min), which climbs through the native forest to the skyline ridge above Murchison with views of the confluence of the Buller, Matakitaki, Maruia and Matiri rivers. The track starts from the junction of SH6 and Matakitaki West Bank Rd.
Ultimate Descents 38 Waller St ☏ 0800 748 377, ⓦ rivers.co.nz. During early Sept–late May this operator runs sections of the Buller River (Grade III–IV; 4hr 30min; $160), spending at least two hours on the water. There are also gentler family trips (Grade II–III; 4hr 30min; $130). Check the website or phone for helicopter-access and multi-day trips on the Mokihinui and Karamea rivers (from $500).

ACCOMMODATION AND EATING

Commercial Hotel 37 Fairfax St ☏ 03 523 9696, ⓦ thecommercialhotel.co.nz. A transformed Kiwi pub that now concentrates more on eating than session-drinking. There's a zebra-striped dining room and a separate café with children's play area in the old vault. Everything's home-made, from the burgers and pies to the aioli. Closed Mon–Wed in winter, otherwise bar daily 2–10pm, café daily 9am–3.30pm, restaurant daily 5–8pm.
Cowshed Restaurant 37 Waller St ☏ 03 523 9523. Small BYO café out the back of the *Lazy Cow*, serving fresh, tasty lunches and pizzas ($20). Menu changes daily. Mon–Fri 10am–9pm.
Kiwi Park Motels & Cabins 170 Fairfax St, 1km south of town ☏ 03 523 9248, ⓦ kiwipark.co.nz. Family-run holiday park with farm animals to keep the kids entertained and a range of well-kept cabins as well as good communal facilities. Camping $38, self-contained motel units $145
Lazy Cow 37 Waller St ☏ 03 523 9451, ⓦ lazycow.co.nz. A cosy hostel in the centre of town with a lively atmosphere, clean and snug rooms, pizza oven and a spa bath. Dorms $32, doubles $90

Mataki Motel 34 Hotham St ☏ 0800 279 088, ⓦ matakimotel.co.nz. Clean and quiet motel clearly signposted about 1km from town, with comfortable and spacious rooms that are reasonably cosy. Some units have a full kitchen. $120
Murchison Lodge 15 Grey St ☏ 03 523 9196, ⓦ murchisonlodge.co.nz. Comfortable and convivial eco-conscious lodge with airy rooms, welcome drinks and a full breakfast with locally sourced produce. $170
Rivers Café 51 Fairfax St ☏ 03 523 9009, ⓦ riverscafemurchison.co.nz. Serves pretty good coffee and substantial main meals such as lamb shanks/fish of the day ($28.50) or big ribeye steak ($30) in comfortable, laidback surroundings. Licensed. Summer daily 8.30am–9pm; winter Mon–Thurs & Sat 9am–3pm, Fri 9am–7.30pm.
Riverside Holiday Park SH6, 1.5km east of town ☏ 03 523 9591, ⓦ riversidemurchison.co.nz. Simple campsite with lots of pitches, good communal facilities, a variety of well-kept, good-value cabins, a café and helpful owners. It's all located by the gurgling Buller River and is much frequented by kayakers and rafters. Camping per site $20, motel doubles $100

The road to the Kaikoura Coast

The 130km between the coast and the brooding Seaward Kaikoura Range from Blenheim to Kaikoura is one of the most spectacular coastal roads in New Zealand. Large sections including the main trunk rail link alongside got completely obliterated during the November 2016 Kaikoura Earthquake (magnitude 7.8), but it all got reinstated over 2017. Best to allow plenty of time for frequent stops to soak up the gorgeous scenery, not to mention eye-boggling new earthworks. Some of the coast was uplifted a massive 5m during this earthquake

Around 20km south of Blenheim a sign points inland towards **Molesworth Station** and Hanmer Springs. **Lake Grassmere**, 50km south of Blenheim, is a vast, shallow salt lake, which annually produces 70,000 tonnes a year of table salt. **Cyclists** may want to overnight 20km south of the salt works at *Pedallers Rest Cycle Stop*.

From Lake Grassmere, you're now following the coast, with grey gravel beaches all the way and accessible at various points. Almost 90km out of Blenheim, the rocky **Kekerengu Point** juts out and makes a great place to watch the crashing waves while stopping in at *The Store* for a bite to eat.

Ohau Point

Ohau Point, 35km south of Kekerengu Point, marks the best stretch of coastline – a wonderful rocky, surf-lashed strip that continues for around 30km to Kaikoura then 20km beyond. Ohau Point is home to the South Island's largest **seal colony** with dozens (if not hundreds) of seals lolling on the rocks not more than 20m away. Immediately before Ohau Point, Ohau Stream Walk (15min return) weaves through the bush to a nice waterfall and pool where in October and November seal pups can be seen playing in the pools during the day. Approach quietly, keep your distance (10m), and don't get between a seal and the water.

The coastline around here is also a perfect habitat for **crayfish**, which are sought by the locals and sold roadside, notably at Rakautara.

ACCOMMODATION AND EATING   THE ROAD TO THE KAIKOURA COAST

Nin's Bins Rakautara, 3km south of Ohau Point. Roadside caravan hawking delicious cooked crayfish for around $50–90. Daily, whenever they're in.

Pedallers Rest Cycle Stop 9km south of Ward, 1.5km off SH1 ☏ 03 575 6708, ✉ pedallers@ruralinzone.net. A small, friendly and comfy spot that's frequented by cyclists, but welcomes most everyone.

Linen is included and there's a small on-site shop. To get there, look for the water tank and sign beside the road. Dorms <u>$35</u>, camping <u>$20</u>

The Store Kekerengu Point ☏ 03 575 8600. A great spot to tuck into burgers ($21.50), fish and chips ($20), cakes and coffee. It's licensed, and is popular with the passing tour bus trade. Daily 8.30am–4.30pm.

Kaikoura

The small town of **KAIKOURA**, 130km south of Blenheim and 180km north of Christchurch, enjoys a spectacular setting in the lee of the Kaikoura Peninsula, wedged between the mountains and the ocean. Offshore, the seabed drops away rapidly to the kilometre-deep Kaikoura Canyon, a phenomenon that brings sea mammals in large and varied numbers. **Whale watching** and **swimming with dolphins** are big business here, and the presence of expectant tourists has spawned a number of eco-oriented businesses offering **swimming with seals**, **sea-kayaking** and hiking.

Brief history

Kaikoura got its name when an ancient **Māori** explorer who stopped to eat crayfish found it so good he called the place *kai* (food) *koura* (crayfish). Māori legend also accounts for the extraordinary coastline around Kaikoura. During the creation of the land, a young deity, Marokura, was given the job of finishing the region. First, he built the Kaikoura Peninsula and a second smaller peninsula (Haumuri Bluff). Then he set about creating the huge troughs in the sea between the two peninsulas, where the cold waters of the south would mix with the warm waters of the north and east. Realizing

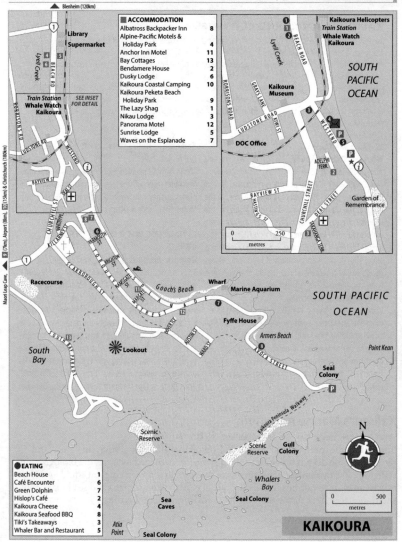

KAIKOURA

ACCOMMODATION
Albatross Backpacker Inn	8
Alpine-Pacific Motels & Holiday Park	4
Anchor Inn Motel	11
Bay Cottages	13
Bendamere House	2
Dusky Lodge	6
Kaikoura Coastal Camping	10
Kaikoura Peketa Beach Holiday Park	9
The Lazy Shag	1
Nikau Lodge	3
Panorama Motel	12
Sunrise Lodge	5
Waves on the Esplanade	7

EATING
Beach House	1
Café Encounter	6
Green Dolphin	7
Hislop's Café	2
Kaikoura Cheese	4
Kaikoura Seafood BBQ	8
Tiki's Takeaways	3
Whaler Bar and Restaurant	5

the depth of Marokura's accomplishment, the god Tuterakiwhanoa said that the place would be a gift (*koha*) to all those who see its hidden beauty – and it is still known to local Māori as Te Koha O Marokura.

The Ngai Tahu people harvested the wealth of the land and seas until Te Rauparaha and his followers decimated them, in around 1830. The first **Europeans** to settle were whalers who came in the early 1840s, swiftly followed by farmers. The trials and tribulations of their existence are recorded in the **Kaikoura Museum** and the more evocative **Fyffe House**. Kaikoura ticked on quietly until the late 1980s when whale watching really took off and put the place on the tourism map. Since then it has steadily expanded, becoming more commercial, though without losing its small-town feel.

KAIKOURA TOURS AND ACTIVITIES

Just 1km off the Kaikoura Peninsula the seabed plummets into the 1000m-deep Kaikoura Canyon, a network of undersea troughs that funnel warm subtropical waters and cold sub-Antarctic flows. This provides an unusually fecund habitat supporting an enormous variety of marine life, including fourteen species of whale. Marine mammals come for an easy meal, and tourists come to watch. You can expect to see gigantic sperm **whales** (year-round), **dolphins** (year-round), migratory humpback whales (June–July) and **orca** (Dec–Feb). Book well in advance, though rough seas often lead to **cancellations** so allow yourself a couple of days' flexibility.

WHALE WATCHING

Whale Watch Kaikoura The Whaleway Station, Whaleway Rd ☎0800 655 121, ⓦwhalewatch. co.nz. Kaikoura's flagship activity is conducted by this Māori-owned and -operated company. You meet at the office at the train station and are bused around to the new marina at South Bay where a speedy catamaran whisks you a few kilometres offshore (2hr 30min at sea; $150). There are typically one or two whale sightings along with dolphins and seabirds; if you see no whales there's an eighty percent refund. The office sells pills and bands to alleviate sea sickness – a wise investment, particularly for afternoon trips.

Wings Over Whales ☎0800 226 629, ⓦwhales. co.nz. An alternative to on-the-water viewing is aerial whale watching. This outfit offers 30min flights ($180). There's a shuttle service ($10/person each way) between the town and the airport. You're welcome to bring binoculars, but watch out for motion sickness when using them.

Kaikoura Helicopters ☎0800 455 4354, ⓦworldofwhales.co.nz. They offer a 30min and 40min flight (2 people $325/395 each), as well as other helicopter tours. There's an obvious advantage over planes as they can hover to get you the perfect view. Most sightings are 6–10km out.

SWIMMING WITH DOLPHINS AND SEALS

Dolphin Encounter 96 Esplanade ☎0800 733 365, ⓦdolphin.co.nz. Runs highly professional trips (daily 7.30am–5.30pm; swimming $175; watching $95), which you'll get the most out of if you're a reasonably confident swimmer; the more you duck-dive the more eager the dolphins will be to hear you humming through your snorkel – any tune will do. Don't get too carried away: dolphins have a penchant for swimming in ever decreasing circles until lesser beings are quite dizzy and disorientated. Book three to four weeks in advance for the Dec–Feb

Kaikoura Marine Aquarium

Wakatu Quay • Daily: summer 10am–5pm; winter 11am–4pm • $8 • ☎027 842 7860

Stocked by the local fishermen, who'll drop off anything interesting they find (and return it to the deep if it begins to seem stressed), managed by a marine biologist and staffed by local volunteers, this small site squeezes in a preserved giant squid and two touch tanks. Live exhibits usually include crayfish, octopus, paua and sea horses, plus there are permanent displays on the local environment and ecology.

Kaikoura Museum

96 Westend • Mon–Sun 10am–5pm • $125

Kaikoura Museum occupies a new purpose-built location opposite the i-SITE. Check out the early 1900s jailhouse, in use until 1980 and complete with padded cell, and the large rock containing the fossilized ribcage of a Cretaceous-period plesiosaur. Other highlights include the extensive marine and Māori collections and earthquake exhibition called "New Normal".

Fyffe House

62 Avoca St • Oct–April daily 10am–4pm; May–Sept Mon & Thurs–Sun 10am–4pm • $10 • ☎03 319 5835

Out on the peninsula, don't miss the town's oldest building, **Fyffe House**, an original whaler's cottage resting on whalebone foundations. The house began life as part of the peak season (though standbys do become available at short notice).

Seal Swim Kaikoura 58 Westend ☎ 0800 732 579, ⍇ sealswimkaikoura.co.nz. Swimming with fur seals is just as much fun as dolphin swimming (and some might say equally moving), as seals tend to be even more curious than dolphins. This operator offers shore-based trips ($80) and better, more flexible trips by boat (2hr 30min; $110). There's a fair bit of swimming involved so it helps if you've snorkelled before. Oct–May only.

BIRDWATCHING, SEA-KAYAKING AND SCUBA DIVING

Albatross Encounter 96 Esplanade ☎ 0800 733 365, ⍇ albatrossencounter.co.nz. Travel a kilometre or two offshore in a small boat for the chance to see some endangered seabirds (2–3 trips daily; 2–3hr; $125). Bait is laid to attract all manner of species – shags, mollymawks, gannets, petrels and several varieties of albatross come amazingly close. Relatively sheltered, so often runs when the big boats have to stay in.

Kaikoura Kayaks 19 Killarney St ☎ 0800 452 456, ⍇ kaikourakayaks.co.nz. Operates year-round and often runs trips when others don't because they can take you to sheltered spots. You'll learn most (and probably see more wildlife) on the half-day Seal Kayaking guided trips ($110), though suitably skilled paddlers can rent

kayaks ($50/half-day; $85/full day) or mess around on a sit-on-top ($40/2hr, $55/half day, $70 full day); rentals not available June–Aug.

Dive Kaikoura 13 Yarmouth St ☎ 03 319 6622, ⍇ divekaikoura.co.nz. Get a close look at temperate kelp forests, nudibranchs and sponges, plus the odd crayfish and seal on scuba-diving tours run by Go Dive, including guided trips from shore for certified divers (3hr total/$155, two tanks 4hr 30min/$215) and introductory dives for novices.

MĀORI CULTURE

Māori Tours Kaikoura ☎ 0800 866 267, ⍇ maoritours.co.nz. Offers emotionally engaging half-day tours ($130), guided by an ex-whale-watch boat driver and his family, that give a real taste of *Maoritanga* and the genuine hospitality it demands. Tours take in various local sights, storytelling, explanations of Māori ways and medicines, cultural differences, and involve learning a song, that you then surprise yourself by singing.

FLIGHTS

Pilot a Plane Kaikoura Airfield, SH1 ☎ 03 319 6579, ⍇ airkaikoura.co.nz. Aspiring fliers get to take off and then take the controls for 20min ($120). It's a great adrenaline buzz and comes with even better scenery. The company also runs various charter-plane whale-watching options.

Waiopuka Whaling Station that was founded by Robert Fyffe in 1842 and was originally an unprepossessing two-room cooper's cottage. Extended by George Fyffe in 1860, some rooms look now much as they did then, while others reflect the condition of the place when the last resident moved out in 1980. Avoca Street follows the edge of the peninsula round to a car park (the start of the Kaikoura Peninsula Walkway; see page 452) where fur **seals** often lounge on flat, sea-worn rocks watching the plentiful birdlife.

Māori Leap Cave

2km south of town on SH1 • 45min tours daily on the half-hour 10.30am–3.30pm • $15 • ☎ 03 319 5023

The sea-formed **Māori Leap Cave** is named after a Māori warrior who jumped to his death from the hills above the cave to escape capture by an enemy tribe. Stalagmites and stalactites sprout from the floor and ceiling of the cave, and translucent stone straws seem to defy gravity by maintaining their internal water level. There are also cave corals and algae that survive by turning darkness into energy.

ARRIVAL AND DEPARTURE KAIKOURA

By bus InterCity and Atomic buses on the Picton–Blenheim–Christchurch run all drop off on Westend, in the town car park near the visitor centre.

Destinations Christchurch (3–4 daily; 2hr 50min); Picton (3 daily; 2hr 15min).

By train The TranzCoastal train between Picton and Christchurch arrives at the station on Whaleway Station Rd.

Destinations Christchurch (Oct–April; 1 daily); Blenheim (Oct–April; 1 daily); Picton (Oct–April; 1 daily).

8

GETTING AROUND

By taxi Most places in town are within walking distance, though since the town is increasingly spread out you may find use for a taxi; try Kaikoura Shuttles ☎03 319 6166.

By bike Coastal Sport, 24 Westend (☎03 319 5028), bike rental charges $30 for a half-day and $40 for a full day.

INFORMATION

Visitor information The i-SITE is on Westend (daily 9am–5pm; ☎03 319 5641, ⓦ kaikoura.co.nz). Apart from regular i-SITE duties, the office also handles most DOC enquiries and stores luggage for $2.

Internet There's internet access at the library, Harakeke Mall, 134 Beach Rd ($6/hr).

ACCOMMODATION

There's a fair range of accommodation, most of it strung out along SH1 (Beach Road) immediately north of the centre, along the Esplanade or on the peninsula east of town.

★ **Albatross Backpacker Inn** 1 Torquay St ☎0800 222 247, ⓦ albatross-kaikoura.co.nz; map p.451. Cool converted post office and telephone exchange with brightly painted rooms, such as the cute Hobbit dorm, and a female-only four-bed dorm. Well-tended grounds and barbecue make it especially good on fine days and they love their music. Dorms $38, rooms $84

Alpine-Pacific Motels & Holiday Park 69 Beach Rd ☎0800 692 322, ⓦ alpine-pacific.co.nz; map p.451. This central, shaded park maintains high standards, offers a range of accommodation and has an outdoor pool and hot tubs. Camping per site $44, motel units $145

Anchor Inn Motel 208 Esplanade ☎0800 720 033, ⓦ anchorinn.co.nz; map p.451. Luxurious motel with tastefully decorated, self-contained units that come with every convenience (some with spa bath). $185, sea view $215

★ **Bay Cottages** 29 South Parade, South Bay ☎0800 556 623, ⓦ baycottages.co.nz; map p.451. Purpose-built self-contained motel-style units in a quiet spot 2km from the town centre on the south side of the peninsula. The owner is exceptionally lovely. $160

Bendamere House 37 Adelphi Terrace ☎0800 107 770, ⓦ bendamere.co.nz; map p.451. Five high-standard rooms, in the grounds of a large villa on the hill. There are great sea views, hearty breakfasts, a helpful owner, and it's all within walking distance of the town. Check website for specials. $260

Dusky Lodge 67 Beach Rd ☎03 319 5959, ⓦ duskylodge.com; map p.451. Well-organized hostel sleeping 120-plus with sauna, spa, swimming pool and a restaurant along with log fires and a big terrace. One level is devoted to deluxe en suites with flat-screen TVs and their own upscale lounge and kitchen. Popular with groups. Book for free pick-ups. Dorms $27, doubles $80

Kaikoura Coastal Camping SH1, 15km south of town ☎03 319 5348, ⓦ kaikouracamping.co.nz; map p.451. A string of appealing, family-oriented campsites, three of which are beachside. Main camp at Goose Bay. The northernmost, Paia Point, has no power, while the others have powered sites and showers. Paia Point $13, other sites $17

Kaikoura Peketa Beach Holiday Park 665 SH1, 8km south of Kaikoura ☎03 319 6299, ⓦ kaikourapeketabeach.co.nz; map p.451. Peaceful beachside campsite 7km south of Kaikoura that's popular with families and surfers who make use of the excellent waves on the doorstep. The surroundings are quiet (apart from the crashing of waves), there's lots of birdlife, and accommodation is in comfortable cabins. Mini golf, flying fox, wi-fi, and small shop on site. Camping $18, cabins $68

The Lazy Shag 37 Beach Rd ☎03 319 6662, ⓦ lazy-shag.co.nz; map p.451. Purpose-built hostel where guests' comfort is the priority. Rooms are warm and quiet, common rooms are spacious and well equipped, and all dorms, twins and doubles are en suite. Dorms $30, rooms $75

Nikau Lodge 53 Deal St ☎03 319 6973, ⓦ nikaulodge.com; map p.451. Four of the five en-suite rooms in this lovely, wooden, 1925 house have mountain or sea views, plus there's a hot tub and good breakfasts. Ground floor $220, with view $280

★ **Panorama Motel** 266 Esplanade ☎0800 288 299, ⓦ panoramamotel.co.nz; map p.451. There are superb views from the stripped-pine units with a chalet feel; you'll pay $25 extra for better views from the upper floor, and the whole shebang is run by a helpful owner. $175

Sunrise Lodge 74 Beach Rd ☎03 319 7444, ⓔ sunrisehostel@xtra.co.nz; map p.451. Small hostel, just a 2min walk from Whale Watch, offering a maximum of four to a room (no bunks), plus free bikes. Dorms $32, rooms $90

Waves on the Esplanade 78 Esplanade ☎0800 319 589, ⓦ kaikouraapartments.co.nz; map p.451. Luxurious two-bedroom motel-style apartments with balconies, sea views, full kitchen, laundry and access to a spa pool. Free use of bikes and sit-on kayaks. $280

EATING

Kaikoura is small but the steady flow of tourists helps keep a decent selection of cafés and restaurants alive. Prices are a little on the high side, especially if you're keen to sample the local crayfish, though you might prefer to buy them ready-boiled from the *kai* caravan north of town.

Beach House Café 39 Beach Rd ☎03 319 6035; map p.451. Kaikoura's cool set hangs out here, despite the dreadful service, imbibing coffee over extended breakfasts ($10–20) including eggs benedict, or lunches, which include seafood chowder and panini from the cabinet. Licensed. Daily 8.30am–4pm.

Café Encounter 96 Esplanade ☎0800 733 365; map p.451. Possibly the best coffee in town, at a licensed café perfect for treats before or after your dolphin swim, but well worth a visit in its own right – all the baking is done on the premises. Daily 7.30am–4.30pm.

Green Dolphin 12 Avoca St ☎03 319 6666, ⓦgreendolphinkaikoura.com; map p.451. Large windows and sea views, and food from a short contemporary menu that usually includes a half-crayfish (around $60), along with mains for half that price and a fab fish chowder. Daily: summer 5pm–late; winter 5–8.30/9pm.

★**Hislop's Café** 33 Beach Rd ☎03 319 6971, ⓦhislops-wholefoods.co.nz; map p.451. The pick of the cafés in Kaikoura, a lovely villa that's a must for coffee and cakes, inside or out, as well as wholefood meals (some vegetarian or gluten-free), tasty seafood and toothsome

daily fresh-baked bread. Wine by the glass, including vegan and organic varieties. Open for breakfast, lunch (salads and sandwiches) and dinner. Wed–Sun 8.30am–5pm.

Kaikoura Cheese 45 West End ⓦkaikouracheese.co.nz; map p.451. Lovely, prize-winning cheeses, such as *labneh* and authentic *fromage blanc*, as well as salami and other picnic essentials. Daily 9am–5pm.

Kaikoura Seafood BBQ Jimmy Armers Beach ☎027 376 3619; map p.451. Outdoor dining in its simplest form, at the beach. A few tables scattered roadside and a takeaway cart make a great setting for simple seafood, all served with salad and rice. Daily 10.30am–dusk.

Tiki's Takeaways 18 West End ☎03 319 5637; map p.451. Award-winning fish and crayfish dinners with unforgettably good chips – perfect for sunset on the waterfront or picnics. They also do surprisingly scrumptious chicken nuggets. Tues–Sat 5.30–8.30pm.

Whaler Bar and Restaurant 49–51 West End ☎03 319 3333, ⓦthewhaler.co.nz; map p.451. Monteith's bar serving cheap, generous grub (the best deal is their $18.50 porterhouse steak special), a range of ales and providing live music during the summer. Daily 3pm–late.

South from Kaikoura

South from Kaikoura, the SH70 slides inland past Mount Lyford ski-field to Hanmer Springs; while the SH1 heads along the coast for a delightful 20km, before cutting uneventfully through farmland to Christchurch. Hikers should consider putting three days aside for the Kaikoura Coast Walk while wine drinkers will want to stop in the **Waipara Valley**, 130km south of Kaikoura, where the junction with SH7 to Hanmer Springs marks the centre of one of New Zealand's fastest growing viticultural regions, with the focus on quality Pinot Noir and Riesling. As a wine destination it is very much in its infancy, but a dozen places offer tastings and several have restaurants. Some 10km to the south, burgeoning **Amberley** is the largest settlement between Kaikoura and Christchurch, 40km on.

EATING AND DRINKING   SOUTH FROM KAIKOURA

★**Black Estate** 614 Omihi Road, just off SH1, 8km north of the junction ☎03 314 6085, ⓦblackestate. co.nz. Welcoming slow-food restaurant in a modern shed perched on the hillside overlooking the vines. Expect confit duck leg with warm lentil and baby carrot salad ($38), best washed down with a glass of their pinot noir or riesling – all single vineyard, organic and biodynamically farmed. Tastings free with lunch. Daily 10am–5pm.

Little Vintage Espresso 20 Markham St, Amberley ☎03 314 9580. Virtually everything is made on-site at this welcoming locals' favourite. Drop in for a coffee and a cinnamon scroll, an iced chocolate served in a jar, or perhaps a breakfast burrito. Mon–Fri 7.30am-4pm, Sat 7.30am–2pm.

Pegasus Bay 4km south of the junction, then 3km east ☎03 314 6869, ⓦpegasusbay.com. One of the finest winery restaurants in the country with contemporary artworks the backdrop for diners tucking into the likes of wild venison with

black pudding and parsnip puree, oyster mushrooms, rhubarb and liquorice granola ($43). Each course has a recommendation from their superb wines (which can also be sampled). Winery daily 10am–5pm; restaurant Thurs–Mon noon–4pm.

★**Pukeko Junction Café & Deli** 458 Ashworths Rd (SH1), 6km south of Amberley ☎03 314 8834, ⓦpukekojunction. co.nz. Great wayside café. Sit out on the sunny patio and tuck into the likes of bacon and maple syrup pancakes ($19), lamb shank pie ($10), or exemplary fruit muffins ($4). Generous servings. The adjacent wine shop has Waipara wines to sample and buy. Tues–Sun 9am–4.30pm.

Waipara Springs 4km north of Waipara ☎03 314 6777, ⓦwaiparasprings.co.nz. The oldest surviving winery in the region, but that's only 1982. The family-oriented garden restaurant has wholesome fresh-baked bread to accompany the meals (mains $22–31; seafood platter for three $60). Tastings $6. Daily 11am–5pm.

The West Coast

GILLESPIE PASS

9 The West Coast

The Southern Alps run down the backbone of the South Island, both defining and isolating the West Coast. A narrow, rugged and largely untamed strip 400km long and barely 30km wide, the West Coast is home to just 33,000 people. Turbulent rivers cascade from the mountains through lush bush, past crystal lakes and dark-green paddocks before spilling into the Tasman Sea, its coastline fringed by atmospheric, surf-pounded beaches and backed by the odd tiny shack or, more often, nothing at all. But what really sets "the Coast" apart is the interaction of settlers with their environment. Coasters, many descended from early gold and coal miners, have long been proud of their pioneering ability to coexist with the landscape and their reputation for independent-mindedness and intemperate drinking. Stories abound of late-night boozing way past closing time, and your fondest memories of the West Coast might be chance encounters in the pub.

The boom-and-bust nature of the West Coast's mining has produced scores of ghost towns and spawned its three largest settlements – **Westport**, **Greymouth** and **Hokitika**. The real pleasure of the West Coast, though, lies in smaller places such as **Karamea**, on the southern limit of the Kahurangi National Park, **Reefton**, an inland town with an amazing goldmining past, or **Okarito**, by a tranquil lagoon. With the exception of a couple of decent museums and a handful of man-made sights, the West Coast's appeal is in its scenic beauty – the drive, either up or down the coast, is iconic, matching any great road trip in the world. The **Oparara Basin**, near Karamea, and the **Paparoa National Park**, south of Westport, hold some of the country's finest limestone formations, including huge arched spans and the famous Pancake Rocks, while in the Westland National Park the frosty white tongues of the **Franz Josef** and **Fox glaciers** spill down the flanks of the Southern Alps toward dense emerald bush and the sea.

Since this is New Zealand there's no shortage of **activities**, including thrilling fly-in **rafting** trips down the West Coast's steep rivers. The limestone bedrock makes for some adventurous **caving**, and there's plenty of **hiking**, with the Heaphy Track to the north, several excellent trails around Punakaiki and a stack of tramps around the glaciers.

Most people visit from November to April, but in **winter** temperatures are relatively mild, skies are more frequently cloud-free and pesky **sandflies** are less active. The West Coast never feels crowded but in the off season, accommodation is more plentiful, although some businesses close and excursions that require minimum numbers may be harder to arrange. Motels in particular can be slightly more expensive than elsewhere on the South Island, and the area's remoteness means that food prices tend to be somewhat higher – consider stocking up on basics beforehand.

GETTING AROUND

By car and bike The simplest and most rewarding way to see the West Coast is with your own vehicle. The wind and wet can make cycling a chore but the distances between towns aren't off-putting and accommodation is plentiful between the main settlements.

By train and bus Public transport is fairly restrictive; trains only penetrate as far as Greymouth, while bus services are scarce and only stop at places on the main road, SH6. However, with patience and forward planning it's possible to see much of interest, especially if you're prepared to walk from bus drop-off points. The main West Coast bus routes run from Nelson to Fox Glacier, and between Franz Josef and Queenstown. InterCity run daily services along both sectors, with Atomic piggybacking on the same service (though they do use their own fleet for a daily Greymouth–Christchurch run). While NakedBus runs daily services from

PANCAKE ROCKS

Highlights

❶ Karamea and the Oparara Basin Set a day aside to explore this remote area's caves harbouring moa bones, vast limestone arches and placid streams that are great for cooling off. See page 466

❷ Pancake Rocks Layered like a stack of pancakes, this geological curiosity is gorgeous at any time but it's especially spectacular when high seas set the blowholes into dramatic action. See page 470

❸ Greenstone shopping in Hokitika The South Island is famous for its *pounamu* – greenstone – and Hokitika is the best place to pick up this ultimate Kiwi souvenir. You can

even carve a piece yourself. See page 479

❹ Okarito The tiny settlement that inspired Keri Hulme's Booker Prize-winning novel *The Bone People* offers a rare opportunity to spot kiwis in the wild, and take a boat trip on the limpid, tannin-stained lagoon. See page 484

❺ Glacier adventures Hiking on and around icy glaciers is an awe-inspiring experience, and expeditions are run with great enthusiasm at both Fox and Franz Josef. See pages 486 and 489

❻ The Gillespie Pass Tramp Get into the West Coast's Great Outdoors on this great three-day tramp through the South Westland wilderness. See page 494

HIGHLIGHTS ARE MARKED ON THE MAP ON PAGE 460

HIGHLIGHTS

1. Karamea and the Oparara Basin
2. Pancake Rocks
3. Greenstone shopping in Hokitika
4. Okarito
5. Glacier adventures
6. The Gillespie Pass Tramp

THE WEST COAST

Queenstown to the glaciers, the company operates just three buses each week north of Franz Josef to Nelson.

Westport and around

Like a proud fly caught in amber, **WESTPORT** remains fixed in time, despite government money and the council's zealous desire to modernize. Diversions are scarce, except at the seal colony at **Cape Foulwind**, on the brain-clearing walk to the old lighthouse beyond or exploring the ghostly former coal towns of the **Rochfort Plateau**. Were Westport – once known as "Worstport" – not a transport interchange, few would stay in this workaday harbour as the temptations of the Heaphy Track and Karamea, 100km north, are too strong. However, time spent here is made tolerable by good-value accommodation, an engaging museum and some good adventure activities.

Brief history

Westport was the first of the West Coast towns, established by one **Reuben Waite** in 1861 beside the mouth of the Buller River, where he made his living provisioning Buller Gorge prospectors. When the miners moved on to richer pickings in Otago, Waite upped sticks and headed south to help found Greymouth. Westport turned to coal and engineers channelled the river to scour out a **port**. Although the coal and cement industry have now ceased to be major employers, Westport battles on as a seaport, with a respectable-sized fishing fleet and the odd cargo and cruise ship calling in.

Coaltown

Inside the i-SITE, 123 Palmerston St • Dec–March daily 9am–5pm; April–Nov Mon–Fri 9am–4.30pm, Sat & Sun 10am–4pm • $10 • ☏ 03 789 6658

Westport's coal-mining past is brought to life at **Coaltown**, where imaginatively presented and engaging exhibits concentrate on the Buller coalfield. Great films and photographs of the workings in their heyday are dramatically complemented by huge pieces of mine equipment, including a coal wagon on tracks angled at an unsettling forty-five degrees, a braking drum from the

Denniston incline, a mock mine tunnel and a host of smaller relics – early carbon monoxide detectors containing stuffed canaries and the like.

West Coast Brewery

10 Lyndhurst St • Mon & Tues 9.30am–5pm, Wed–Fri 9.30am–6pm; tours Mon–Fri 3.30pm • Tours $10 • ☎ 03 789 6201, ⓦ westcoastbrewery. co.nz

Before leaving town, check out the preservative- and chemical-free beers, ciders and ginger beer made at the **West Coast Brewery**. Originally famed for its signature Green Fern Organic Lager, the brewery now focuses on craft beers – including an English-style bitter – that are distributed nationwide. Tours include tastings of five brews, but if you don't have time for the full shebang, just turn up with an empty bottle and they'll fill it with your choice of ale.

The West Coast Bush Bath

114 Palmerston St • Mon–Fri 9am–5pm, Sat 10am–1.30pm • $40 for 1hr30min • ☎ 03 789 8828, ⓦ thesoapbox.co.nz

In true entrepreneurial West Coast spirit the owner of a soap shop has transformed his back block into **The West Coast Bush Bath**, where an open-air double bathtub is screened by bark and ferns imported from the bush outside town. Prices include soap or bubble bath plus glasses for wine, but you'll need to bring your own towel. After-hours access is possible, provided you book during the shop hours given above.

Cape Foulwind and the Tauranga Bay Seal Colony

12km west of town on Cape Foulwind Rd

Once again we have Captain Cook, battling heavy weather in March 1770, to thank for the naming of Westport's most dramatic and evocatively titled stretch of coastline, **Cape Foulwind**, its exposed headlands best explored on the undulating Cape Foulwind Walkway. It's perfect for sunset ambling between the old lighthouse, a replica of Abel Tasman's astrolabe and the **Tauranga Bay Seal Colony**, where platforms overlook a malodorous breeding colony of fur seals. The animals, at the southern end of the walkway, are at their most active and numerous from October to January, often numbering in the hundreds – a welcome recovery after the decimation wrought by 150 years of sealing. Don't be tempted by the beach at Tauranga Bay; the pretty cove's waters are treacherous – refreshment of a different kind is available at the *Bay House* restaurant.

ARRIVAL AND DEPARTURE

WESTPORT AND AROUND

By bus Karamea Express (☎ 03 782 6757), InterCity and NakedBus (ⓦ nakedbus.com) stop at the i-SITE; East-West (☎ 03 789 6251, ⓦ eastwestcoaches.co.nz) buses depart from the Caltex garage at 197 Palmerston St.

Destinations Christchurch (6 weekly; 4hr 30min); Greymouth (1–2 daily; 2hr 20min); Karamea (5–6 weekly; 2hr); Murchison (1–2; 1hr 30min); Nelson (1–2 daily; 4hr); Punakaiki (1–2 daily; 1hr 15min).

INFORMATION AND TOURS

Tourist information i-SITE, 123 Palmerston St (Oct–April daily 9am–5pm; May–Sept Mon–Fri 9am–4.30pm; Sat & Sun 10am–4pm; ☎ 03 789 6658, ⓦ buller.co.nz). In addition to housing the Coaltown museum, there's free wi-fi, and you can book your Heaphy Track (see page 465) tickets here for $5 (or book online for free).

Outwest Tours ☎ 0800 688937, ⓦ outwest.co.nz. Offers 4WD tours of near-ghost town Denniston (6hr; $130) and outback Mackley country full of fast-flowing rivers, deep gorges and many waterfalls (8hr; $160). There's also a trip into the remote country surrounding the Awakiri River (6hr; $150).

GETTING AROUND

By taxi Buller Taxis (☎ 03 789 6900), also Westport Shuttles (☎ 03 789 8294)

By bike Habitat Sports, 204 Palmerston St (☎ 03 788 8002,

ⓦ habitatsports.co.nz), rents quality mountain bikes (free airport service with bike rental) from $15/hr. Multi-day rentals available.

9

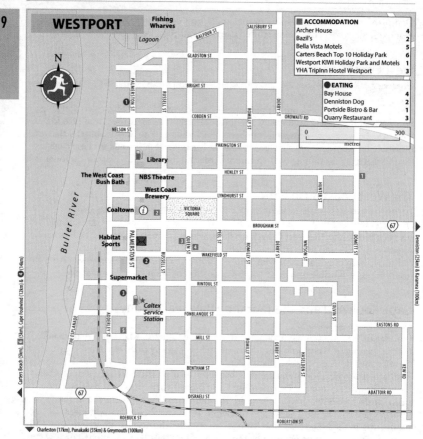

Charleston (17km), Punakaiki (55km) & Greymouth (100km)

ACCOMMODATION

Book ahead if you plan to visit in mid-February, when the town hosts the Buller Gorge Marathon.

Archer House 75 Queen St ☎03 789 8778, ⓦarcherhouse.co.nz; map above. A lovely 1890 villa with multiple antique-filled lounges, set in beautiful gardens, and retaining many ornate Victorian details including a wraparound veranda. Three en-suite rooms; rates include continental breakfast. **$245**

Bazil's 54–56 Russell St ☎03 789 6410, ⓦbazils.com; map above. Cheerful, busy backpackers with doubles, twins and a mass of dorms (some very cramped); there's a pleasant garden with a patch of lawn for tents, a TV room and a covered BBQ area. Surfing lessons available, and surf boards for rent along with electric bikes ($50/day). Dorms **$33**, doubles **$78**

Bella Vista Motels 314 Palmerston St ☎0800 235528, ⓦstaybellavista.co.nz; map above. A modern, business-like motel familiar from terracotta-and-cream *Bella Vista Motels* nationwide, with comfortable but bland rooms. Sky TV and limited cooking facilities available. **$130**

Carters Beach Top 10 Holiday Park 57 Marine Parade, Carters Beach, 5km west of town ☎0508 937 876, ⓦtop10westport.co.nz; map above. Spacious, fully equipped site, with cabins and comfortable motel units, situated a stone's throw from the beach and a 10min drive to the seal colony. Camping per site **$40**, cabins **$80**

Westport KIWI Holiday Park and Motels 37 Domett St ☎03 789 7043, ⓦwestportholidaypark.co.nz; map above. Smallish, low-key motor park partly hemmed in by native bush and surrounded by suburbia, a 10min walk from the town centre with its own eighteen-hole mini golf course. Camping per site **$36**, cabins **$80**

YHA TripInn Hostel Westport 72 Queen St ☎03 789 7367, ⓦtripinn.co.nz; map above. Friendly owners and an energetic refurbishment have breathed new life into this rambling historic home now a YHA Associate backpackers. Quiet and relaxed with a great deck, BBQ, well-equipped kitchen and TV room; there are camping spots in the garden. Quiet at night. Dorms **$33**, doubles **$80**

EATING

★ **Bay House** Tauranga Bay, 12km from Westport ☎ 03 789 4151 ⓦ bayhouse.co.nz; map p.462. If the seal colony isn't enough to lure you out here, this beautiful bungalow restaurant and café nestled into a bush-clad peninsula ought to do the trick. Big windows and a terrace with splendid views of the bay, plus an all-day menu of appetizing dishes like salmon bruschetta with horseradish cream, salsa verde, capers and dressed salad greens ($19.50), and seafood chowder with house bread ($20). Location and service make this a standout restaurant popular with visitors and locals alike. Wed–Sun 11.30am–8.30pm (last orders).

Denniston Dog 18 Wakefield St ☎ 03 789 8885, ⓦ dennistondog.co.nz; map p.462. The only café/bar that isn't just a pub with a percolator offers a good range of beers, coffee and some excellent light and main meals

($17–36) with thoughtful side dishes; slow-cooked pork belly comes with crispy potato, braised kumara, spinach and apple glaze, while juicy chicken breast comes with salad, fries and romesco sauce. Stone Grill menu as well. Limited vegetarian options. Daily 9am–late

Portside Bistro & Bar 13 Cobden St ☎ 03 789 7133, ⓦ portsidebistro.co.nz; map p.462. Full breakfast, lunch and dinner menu (mains $24–34) with everything made from scratch including all baking done daily. Great fish and chips too, along with a great range of beer, wine, spirits and cocktails. Daily 7.30am–late.

Quarry Restaurant 284 Palmerston St ☎ 03 789 5579; map p.462. Family-friendly, affordable restaurant with the option of dining outside. Free pool table in the bar, satellite sport on the big screen, great music and a fire make this a cosy place to spend an evening. Daily 5.30pm–9pm.

DRINKING AND NIGHTLIFE

Westport's pubs adhere to the West Coast tradition of after-work hours and spirited weekend drinking; head to the *Bay House* at nearby Tauranga Bay if you're looking for something a bit more sophisticated.

ENTERTAINMENT

NBS Theatre 105 Palmerston St ☎ 03 789 4219 ⓦ nbstheatre.co.nz. If the nightlife is too raucous elsewhere, head along to this modern two-screen cinema, which shows New Zealand and international films.

Reefton

Located beside the Inangahua River at the intersection of roads from Westport, Greymouth and Christchurch, **REEFTON** owes its existence to rich gold-bearing quartz veins known as **reefs**. These were exploited so heavily in the 1870s that some considered Reefton "the most brisk and businesslike place in the colony". It was also the first place in New Zealand, and one of the first in the world, to install electric street lighting powered by a hydro-electric generator. Unless you're a keen **angler** (there's excellent fly-fishing in these parts), once you've undertaken the town's historic walks and peeked at the museum you'll probably want to press on down the **Grey Valley**.

Town walks

Two walks link the specific points of interest around town. The elegiac, self-guided **Reefton Heritage Walk** (30min) meanders around Reefton's grid of streets visiting once-grand buildings; the route is outlined in a leaflet available from the i-SITE visitor centre. In the centre of town, on the corner of Walsh Street and Broadway, the so-called "Bearded Miners" entertain visitors at an old **miner's cottage** and smithy (daily, pretty much when they feel like it; donation) by firing up the forge and helping you pan for gold.

The pleasant **Bottled Lightning Powerhouse Walk** (40min), leading past the ruined generator that once powered Reefton's famous streetlights, is slightly more uplifting, perhaps because of its course along the Inangahua River – the signposted route starts at the Reefton Visitor Centre and heads up Broadway to a bridge over the Inangahua River. Return via Rosstown Road and main highway bridge.

Blacks Point Museum

Blacks Point, on SH7 towards Springs Junction • Oct–April Wed–Fri & Sun 9am–noon & 1–4pm, Sat 1–4pm • $5 • ☎ 03 732 8391

THE WET COAST

Although Coasters downplay it, no discussion of the West Coast would be complete without mention of the torrential **rainfall**, which descends with tropical intensity for days at a time; waterfalls cascade from rocks and the bush becomes vibrant with colour. Such soakings have a detrimental effect on the soil, retarding decomposition and producing a peat-like top layer with all the minerals leached out. The result is **pakihi**, scrubby, impoverished and poor-looking paddocks that characterize much of the West Coast's cleared land. The downpours alternate with abundant sunshine, while today's "gold rushes" occur during the springtime rush to catch **whitebait**, when fishermen swarm around the river-mouths trying to net this culinary prize on the rising tide.

The water for Reefton's original hydroelectric scheme was diverted 2km from town at Blacks Point, where the **Blacks Point Museum** occupies a former Wesleyan chapel. The museum charts the district's cultural and mining history and shows a DVD, on request, promoting the modern mining operation nearby. Outside, an ancient water-driven gold battery that once crushed quartz can be cranked into action with the insertion of a $2 coin.

ARRIVAL AND DEPARTURE

REEFTON

By bus East West Coaches (☏0800 142622, ⊛eastwestcoaches.co.nz) stop near the i-SITE on Broadway, Reefton's main street, on their Westport–Christchurch run. Destinations Christchurch (6 weekly; 4hr); Westport (6 weekly; 1hr).

INFORMATION

Tourist information i-SITE/DOC, 67–69 Broadway (Mon–Fri 9am–4.30pm, Sat 9.30am–2pm; Sun 9.30am–1pm; ☏03 732 8391, ⊛reefton.co.nz). The combined i-SITE and DOC office has internet access ($6/hr), informative displays on local industries and a small replica gold mine; gold-bugs can rent pans and shovels ($5/day, extra pans $2). Pick up a leaflet detailing Reefton's historic walks and former mining trails nearby, which have been converted to walking or mountain-biking trails.

Banks There is a branch of BNZ inside the i-SITE (Mon–Fri 9am–12.30pm and 1.30–4.30pm), and an ATM outside the same building.

ACCOMMODATION

The Old Bread Shop 155 Buller Rd ☏03 732 8420, ⊛reeftonbackpackers.co.nz. Cosy, unpretentious backpackers in a former bakery with loads of DVDs plus free internet terminals. Trev, the owner, holds fly-fishing lessons and can point guests to prime fishing locations on the surrounding rivers. No credit cards. Dorms $18, doubles $50

The Old Nurses Home 104 Shiel St ☏03 732 8881, ✉info@reeftonaccommodation.co.nz. Popular with domestic visitors, Reefton's rambling and faintly institutional former nurses' home offers smallish but pleasant twins and doubles with communal bathrooms. $90

Reef Cottage B&B Inn 51–55 Broadway ☏03 732 8440, ⊛reefcottage.co.nz. The fanciest place to stay in town, an ex-lawyer's cottage built in 1887, with four beautifully decorated Victorian- and 1920s-style doubles all with en-suite and an appealing café, where breakfast is included. $145

Reefton Domain Motor Camp 1 Ross St, at the top of Broadway ☏03 732 8477. This central campsite with popular local skatepark nearby has hook-ups and a grassy campsite beside the Inangahua River, close to the local swimming pool. Great place to meet some locals. Camping $15, doubles $25, cabins $50

Slab Hut Creek 1km off SH7, 8km south of Reefton. The primitive Slab Hut Creek DOC campsite is situated south down the Grey Valley and east off the SH7 in a former gold-mining area where you can try your luck fossicking. Great base for exploring Victoria Forest Park walks. $8

EATING

Alfresco's Eatery 16 Broadway ☏03 732 8513. Welcoming place serving mining-themed dishes including "Snowy Battery" (ribeye steak topped with crumbed mussels) and "Prohibition Pork" (hot sliced ham with pineapple sauce), plus equally aptly named pizzas, including the seafood-topped "Quartz Reef" (pizzas $15–22.50, mains $22.50–30). Daily lunch & dinner.

Reef Cottage Café 51–55 Broadway ☏03 732 8440. Warmed by an open fire, this timber cottage is an atmospheric spot for cooked breakfasts and light meals

including home-made soups, quiches and crispy bacon butties (dishes $6–18.50). Daily breakfast & lunch.
Shazzas Shack 54 Broadway ☎ 03 732 8458. Dependable calorie-rich fare from this chip shop includes a decent range of seafood (cod, John Dory and gurnard, plus crumbed shellfish), but they're best known for their burgers ($6–10). Mon–Wed & Fri noon–2pm & 4.30–8pm, Fri noon–2pm & 4.30–8.30pm, Sat noon–2pm & 4.30–8pm.

Westport to Karamea

The Karamea Road (SH67) runs north from Westport to Karamea, parallel to the coast and pinched between the pounding Tasman breakers and bush-clad hills. The journey takes almost two hours if you don't stop, passing through meagre but highly distinctive hamlets with barely a shop or pub. However, there are some interesting diversions – not least the coal towns around Westport such as **Denniston** – and great off-the-grid accommodation en route. North of the **Mokihinui River**, the road leaves the coastal strip, twisting and climbing over **Karamea Bluff** before descending again into a rich apron of dairying land, the surrounding hills cloaked in thick vegetation characterized by marauding cabbage trees and nikau palms. At the northern foot of the bluff, **Little Wanganui** marks the turn-off for the start of the **Wangapeka** (52km; 3–5days) and **Leslie–Karamea** (62km; 6–9 days) tracks, which traverse the southern half of Kahurangi National Park.

Charles Heaphy and Thomas Brunner explored the region in 1846, paving the way for the gold-miners, who arrived two decades later. Pioneers established themselves at **Karamea**, now the base for visiting the fine limestone country of the **Oparara Basin** and the final stretch of the **Heaphy Track**.

Note that there's little mobile phone coverage and **no fuel** between Westport and Karamea – and that the only fuel in Karamea itself is only available from the visitor centre during opening hours. Fill up before leaving Westport.

Denniston

Museum/visitor centre year-round by appointment 11am–3pm • Donation • ☎ 03 789 9755

Westport historically thrived on supplying inhospitably sited coal-mining towns where fresh vegetables were hard to grow and sheep reluctant to thrive. Foremost among these settlements was the now semi-ghost town of **DENNISTON**, 9km east of Waimangaroa off SH67, the setting for Jenny Pattrick's 2003 bestselling historical novel *The Denniston Rose*, located high on the Rochfort Plateau and once famous for its gravity-powered tramway. John Rochfort discovered the rich Coalbrook-Dale Seam in 1859 and the plateau was soon humming with activity, spurred on by the construction of an impressive, gravity-powered tramway in 1879, which transported a thousand tonnes of coal a day at a prodigious 70km/hr.

The region peaked at around 2500 inhabitants in 1910, but the accessible coal eventually played out in the late 1960s. Since then, houses have been carted off and the bush has engulfed what remains – a post office, a fire station, half a dozen scattered houses (three or four of them occupied) and a treasure-trove of industrial archeology centred on a gaunt winding derrick. There are great views in fine weather, but a blanket of cloud and damp fog adds a suitably ethereal, ghostlike quality.

Apart from these, the only real sight of note is the old schoolhouse, which has been turned into a small "Friends of the Hill" **museum** and **visitor centre**, containing historical photos and old mining machinery. It all comes alive when you talk to curator Gary James, who is usually happy to open up.

Granity

The tiny community of **GRANITY**, 12km north of Waimangaroa, makes for a good place to break your journey as you head further north on SH67. Stop off at *Miners on Sea*, 117 Torea St (☎ 03 7828664, ✆ minersonsea.co.nz), an authentic seafront pub built in 1892 to service the miners of Millerton and Stockton. Its *Tommy Knockers*

9

Restaurant and Café extends out almost to the seafront and offers appetizing, hearty fare (daily 11am–8pm).

Ngakawau and around

About 3km north of Granity a huge modern coal depot in **Ngakawau** signals the start of the **Charming Creek Walk** (5km one way; 2hr; 100m ascent), which follows an old railway, used for timber and coal extraction between 1914 and 1958. The first half-hour is dull, but things improve dramatically after the S-shaped Irishman's Tunnel, which has great views of the boulder-strewn river below and, after a swingbridge river crossing, the Mangatini Falls. From here to the picnic stop by the remains of Watson's Mills is the most interesting section of the walk and is as far as most people get (2–3hr return).

ACCOMMODATION   **WESTPORT TO KARAMEA**

GRANITY

Granity Sands Backpackers 94 Torea St ☎ 03 782 8558. Arty, eco-conscious backpackers footsteps from the beach, with board games, books, comfy sofas ranged around a huge fireplace, and rambling, rather overgrown gardens. Dorms $20, doubles $50

Miners on Sea 117 Torea St ☎ 03 782 8664. A small collection of chic modern cabins facing the sea; the four-star options are a little overpriced ($245), but their backpacker "pods" are far more reasonable, as long as you can face sharing facilities. $85

NGAKAWAU AND AROUND

Ngakawau's best accommodation is across the river, well north of the village.

Gentle Annie 15km north of Ngakawau on SH67 and 3km down a side road ☎ 03 782 1826, ⓦ gentleannie. co.nz. Relaxed, beautifully sited spot near the mouth of the Mokihinui River, beside Gentle Annie Beach. Spread-out accommodation ranges from flax-girt campsites (unlimited, no need to book) to well-equipped family cottages with sea views; the *Cowshed Café* (open seasonally, call for opening times) serves coffee and wood-fired pizzas, and there are bushwalks, a maze and kayaks for rent. Pet friendly. Camping $12, cottages $130

★ **The Old Slaughterhouse** 2km north of Hector, just off SH67 ☎ 03 782 8333, ⓦ oldslaughterhouse.co.nz. A relaxing wood-built hostel perched on the hillside (above a disused slaughterhouse) with vast ocean views, welcoming friendly hosts, good bushwalks and Hector's dolphins regularly playing in the surf below. It would be a crime to shatter the peace with TV, washing machines or hairdryers, so they don't – plus it saves their precious hydro-generated power. Limited internet. Access is via a steep 10min walk off SH67, though the owners will carry your bags on a quad bike. Dorms $40, doubles $88

Karamea and around

Despite its isolation, virtually at the end of the road (to continue any distance north you'd have to go on foot along the Heaphy Track), there's no shortage of things to do in **KARAMEA**, 100km north of Westport. The southern section of the **Kahurangi National Park** easily justifies a day or two and the **Oparara Basin** rewards exploration.

Back in 1874, this was very much **frontier territory**, with the Karamea River port providing the only link with the outside world. Settlers eked a living from **gold** and **flax**, barely supported by the poorly drained *pakihi* soils. They persevered, opening up the first road to Westport just in time for the 1929 Murchison **earthquake**, which silted up the harbour and cut the settlement's only road link for years. The most recent natural upheavals came in April 2014, when Cyclone Ita uprooted swathes of venerable beech and kahikatea trees in the surrounding hills.

The Oparara Basin

Kahurangi National Park's finest limestone formations lie 10km north of Karamea, and fifteen rolling kilometres inland from the Karamea–Kohaihai road in the **Oparara Basin**. This compact area of **karst** topography in a rainforest wonderland is characterized by sinkholes, underground streams, caves and bridges created over millennia by the action of faintly acidic streams on the jointed rock. The region is home to New Zealand's largest native **spider**, the harmless, 15cm-diameter *Spelungula cavernicola* (found only in caves around Kahurangi National Park), and to a rare species of ancient and primitive carnivorous **snail** that grows up to 70mm across and dines on earthworms. Tea-coloured rivers course gently over bleached boulders and, in faster-flowing sections, the rare **whio** (blue duck) swims for its supper. If your interest in geology is fleeting, the Oparara Basin still makes a superb place for day **walks** or a **picnic** – just make sure to bring some insect repellent.

Honeycomb Hill Caves

10km north of Karamea then 16km east along McCallums Mill Rd • Guided cave tours depart from the Upper Oparara Car Park at the far end of McCallums Mill Road daily 10am & 1.30pm; 2hr 30min; minimum two people • $95 • Transfers available from Karamea, $25 ☎ 03 782 6652, ⊛ oparara.co.nz

The Oparara Basin is home to the **Honeycomb Hill Caves**, which have become a valuable key to understanding New Zealand's fauna. The sediment on the cave floor has helped preserve the ancient skeletons of birds, most of them killed when they fell through holes in the roof. The bones of over fifty species have been found here, including those of Haast's eagle, the largest eagle ever known, with a wingspan of up to 4m.

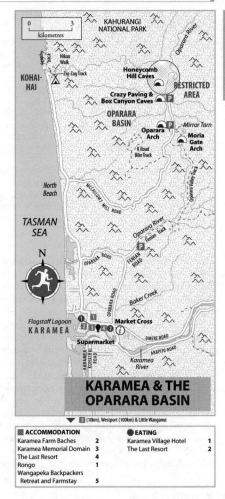

◼ ACCOMMODATION		● EATING	
Karamea Farm Baches	2	Karamea Village Hotel	1
Karamea Memorial Domain	3	The Last Resort	2
The Last Resort	4		
Rongo	1		
Wangapeka Backpackers Retreat and Farmstay	5		

The cave system can only be visited on the excellent and educational **Honeycomb Hill Caves Tour** which explores just some of the 15km of passages. It used to be possible to combine cave trips with the **Honeycomb Hill Arch Kayak Tour**, a gorgeous paddle through bush and under a broad limestone arch. These trips had been temporarily suspended at the time of research, after Cyclone Ita filled the river with tree trunks – it's worth checking to see if they have restarted.

Crazy Paving and Box Canyon caves

Accessed via a 5min track from the Upper Oparara Car Park

As is common in limestone areas, the watercourses alter frequently, leaving behind dry caves such as the **Crazy Paving** and more capacious **Box Canyon Caves** (about 10min return) near the Honeycomb Hill Caves. Both are good for spider- and fossil-spotting: take a torch and mind the slippery floors.

9

GOLD AND COAL

Captain Cook sailed up the West Coast in 1770, describing it as "an inhospitable shore … As far as the eye could reach the prospect was wild, craggy and desolate". Little here then for early European explorers such as Thomas Brunner and Charles Heaphy, who explored down the coast here in 1846–47, led by Kehu, a Māori guide. They returned without finding the cultivable land they sought, and after a shorter trip in 1861 Henry Harper, the first bishop of Christchurch, wrote, "I doubt if such a wilderness will ever be colonized except through the discovery of **gold**." Prophetic words – within two years reports were circulating of flecks in West Coast rivers and a year later Greymouth and Hokitika were experiencing gold rushes. The boom was soon over but modern mining techniques (and sky-high gold prices) have rendered the old goldfields profitable once more, and today there are active mines outside Reefton and Ross.

Coal eventually took gold's place and laid the foundation for more permanent towns; the West Coast still produces half the country's output. Recent decades, however, have seen a greater awareness of the Coast's fragile **ecosystems** – a situation that gave rise to tension between the Coasters and conservationists, leading to the government reassessing native timber felling and its impact on the area's unique environment.

Oparara Arch and Moria Gate Arch loop track

Signposted from the Oparara Car Park 3km before the caves

The two most spectacular examples of limestone architecture can be reached via beautiful, short bushwalks near the Oparara River. The largest is the **Oparara Arch** (2km, 50min return), a vast two-tiered rock bridge, its roof 43m high, inner sides 79m apart and overall 219m which erupts from the bush defying any attempt at photography. Also from the main car park there's the Moria Gate and Mirror Tarn loop track (4.1km; 1hr 30min). Smaller than the Oparara Arch, the **Moria Gate Arch** is very pretty and should not be missed. It is 19m high, 43m wide and fully deserving of its *Lord of the Rings* name given decades before the mania swept the land. A short cave scramble (a torch is handy but not essential) gets you to the sandy riverbank under the arch itself. The track carries on over the arch and after passing the turn-off to the Oparara Valley Track Mirror Tarn emerges, offering spectacular reflections of the surrounding rainforest. Continue on to the Mirror Tarn carpark where a short walk along the road takes you back to the main Oparara car park. Even if you don't complete the loop it's worth pressing on to a viewpoint just beyond the cave scramble, where there's a great view back to the rock formation.

Kohaihai River

At the end of the road, 17km north of Karamea

Visitors with no aspirations to tramp the full length of Heaphy Track can sample the final few coastal kilometres from the mouth of the Kohaihai River, where there's river (but not sea) swimming, a beautifully sited DOC **campsite** ($6) and an abundance of maddening sandflies (consider buying sandfly "armour" – close-weave mesh jackets, $39 from Westport's i-SITE). In the heat of the day, you're better off heading for the cool of the **Nikau Walk** (1km, 40min loop), which winds through a shady grove dense with nikau palms, tree ferns and magnificent gnarled old rata dripping in epiphytes. When it cools off, either continue along the Heaphy to **Scott's Beach** (6.5km, 2hr return), or return to the southern side of the Kohaihai River and the **Zig-Zag Track** (1.2km, 40min return), which switchbacks up to an expansive coastal lookout.

ARRIVAL AND DEPARTURE   **KARAMEA**

By bus Karamea Express minibus services ply the   ☏03 782 6757), picking up from accommodation in Karamea–Westport route (Mon–Sat; $35 each way;   Karamea around 8am, departing from Westport at

11.30am for the return journey. Karamea Connections (☎03 782 6767, ⓦkarameaconnections.co.nz) runs on demand to the Heaphy Track at Kohaihai ($15) and other nearby trailheads.

INFORMATION AND TOURS

Tourist information Market Cross, 2km east of the centre (Jan–April daily 9am–5pm; May–Dec Mon–Fri 9am–5pm, Sat & Sun 10am–1pm; ☎03 782 6652, ⓦkarameainfo.co.nz). Provides internet access ($2/30min) for booking Heaphy Track huts, among other things. The Heaphy Track is generally walked from north to south (see page 465). Pick up the DOC-produced *Karamea* leaflet, which has details of a dozen or so good walks nearby.

Karamea Outdoor Adventures Market Cross, just down from the information centre (☎03 782 6181, ⓦkarameaadventures.co.nz). Rents bikes, kayaks, inner tubes and "river bugs" (one-man dinghies with paddles worn like gloves) for exploring Flagstaff Lagoon and nearby rivers. Also does horseriding in the area. Check website for updates. Knowledgeable owner Sylvia Raikes can recommend suitable adventures for your stay.

ACCOMMODATION

Karamea Memorial Domain Waverley St (SH67), between The Last Resort and the Karamea Village Hotel ☎03 782 6069; map p.467. Basic site utilizing the showers and toilets of the town's sports field, with a kitchen, day-shelter and bunkroom. Showers for non-stayers cost $4 paid via honesty box, otherwise free. Camping $̶1̶3̶, communal bunkroom $̶1̶5̶

Karamea Farm Baches 17 Wharf Rd ☎03 782 6838, ⓦkarameafarmbaches.co.nz; map p.467. Seven quirky, colourful motel-style units that come equipped with full kitchens and spacious bedrooms. Run by the same people as *Rongo*. Dinner, bed and breakfast, seasonal produce available from their permaculture garden. $̶9̶9̶

The Last Resort 71 Waverley St (SH67) ☎03 782 6617, ⓦlastresortkaramea.co.nz; map p.467. Based around an imaginatively styled main lodge holding a restaurant and bar, with comfortable accommodation in five-bed dorms, simple but attractive lodge rooms (including a few cheaper rooms with shared bathrooms),

and attractive studios ($130) with basic kitchenettes. Dorms $̶3̶7̶, doubles $̶1̶0̶7̶

Rongo 130 Waverley St (SH67) ☎03 782 6667, ⓦrongo.nz; map p.467. Rainbow-painted, timber-floored hostel in grounds that house an organic veggie garden, a (very) rustic bush bath and a vibrant collie dog. Art and music play a big part in the hostel's daily life – it even runs a community radio station (107.5FM) out the back. Breakfast and dinner included, using produce from their permaculture garden. Singles $̶9̶0̶, twin/doubles $̶1̶8̶0̶

Wangapeka Backpackers Retreat and Farmstay 476 Wangapeka Valley Rd ☎03 782 6663, ⓦwangapeka.co.nz; map p.467. Cosy homestay on a working farm with native bush and welcoming, well-informed hosts, who will ensure you make the most of the beautiful surroundings. If you need to refuel post-tramp, consider going for a half-board deal (dorms with breakfast and dinner $55, doubles $125). Dorms $̶2̶0̶, doubles $̶7̶5̶

EATING

Karamea's eating options are limited; there's a small supermarket at Market Cross.

Karamea Village Hotel Waverley St, at Wharf Rd ☎03 782 6800, ⓦkarameahotel.co.nz; map p.467. Karamea's revamped pub is the best place to eat in town thanks to its enormous pub meals (mains $16–31), and especially, its good-value fish and chips ($10) and great whitebait patties ($16). Daily 10am–late.

The Last Resort 71 Waverley St (SH67) ☎03 782 6617, ⓦlastresortkaramea.co.nz; map p.467. Karamea's most formal dining (though that's not saying much) with good-value burgers and steaks (mains $20–36) and a couple of forays into more exciting territory with dishes like Thai chicken curry and duck confit. Tearoom staples available all day; evening bookings advised. Check out the 25m-long rimu log that holds the roof up. Daily 7.30am–late.

Paparoa National Park and around

South of Westport, SH67 crosses the Buller River and picks up the SH6, the main West Coast road. This stretch of coast is home to the Paparoa Range, a 1500m granite and gneiss ridge inlaid with limestone that separates the dramatic coastal strip from the valleys of the Grey and Inangahua rivers. In 1987, the coastal limestone country was designated the **Paparoa National Park**, one of the country's smallest and perhaps least appreciated. The highlight is undoubtedly **Pancake Rocks**, where crashing waves have forced spectacular blowholes through a stratified stack of weathered limestone. But to skip the rest would be to miss out

9

PAPAROA WALKS AND THE INLAND PACK TRACK

The best way to truly appreciate the dramatic limestone scenery of the Paparoa is on the region's walking trails. The longest and best of Paparoa's tramps, the **Inland Pack Track** (27km; 2–3 days), was seriously damaged by 2014's **Cyclone Ita**, closing the Bullock Creek to Fossil Creek section for months, but it's now been reopened. Check at the Punakaiki DOC office for the latest trail status and consider tackling one of the area's shorter walks if there are any inland closures which can happen during the summer season when cyclonic storm systems coming in off the Tasman are liable to hit this area.

INLAND PACK TRACK PRACTICALITIES

The Inland Pack Track starts beside the south bank of **Punakaiki River** (look for Waikori Rd), 800m south of the Punakaiki visitor centre. An alternative start is via the Pororari River Track car park, 1 km north of the visitor centre. DOC's *Inland Pack Track* leaflet provides enough information for the tramp; the 1:50,000 *Paparoa National Park* map is also very handy. Built in 1867 during the gold rush to avoid dangerous coastal travel, the track gives access to some of the finest features of Paparoa National Park.

The track is best walked south to north, which eliminates the risk of missing the critical turn-off up Fossil Creek. There are no huts along the way, just a massive rock **bivvy** known as the Ballroom Overhang at the end of a long first day. You're advised to carry a **tent** for protection from voracious sandflies, and to avoid a wet night in the open if the rivers flood. **Campfires** are permitted at the Ballroom Overhang, but DOC recommends carrying a stove as most of the usable wood has already been burned. Be sure to check the **weather** forecast with DOC and fill out an **intentions form**.

SHORTER WALKS

Punakaiki–Pororari Rivers Loop (12km; 3hr 30min; 100m ascent). A delightful route that follows the initial (open) stretch of the Inland Pack Track as far as the Pororari River, which is then followed downstream between some magnificent limestone cliffs to return to Punakaiki.

Fox River Cave Walk (10km; 2hr 30min; 100m ascent). This walk traces the last few kilometres of the Inland Pack Track from the Fox Rivermouth as far as the caves and returns the same way.

---

on a mysterious world of disappearing rivers, sinkholes, caves and limestone bluffs, which are best seen on the area's excellent **hiking trails**.

Māori often stopped while travelling the coast in search of *pounamu* (greenstone), and early **European explorers** followed suit seeking agricultural land. Charles Heaphy, Thomas Brunner and two Māori guides came through in 1846, finding little to detain them, but within twenty years this stretch was alive with **gold** prospectors at work on the black sands at **Charleston**.

Visitor services are centred on **Punakaiki** and Pancake Rocks, where bus passengers get a quick glimpse and others pause for the obligatory photos. A couple of days spent here will be well rewarded with a stack of wonderful walks, horseriding or canoeing up delightful limestone gorges.

Punakaiki and the Pancake Rocks

SH6, 32km south of Charleston

The **Pancake Rocks** and blowholes at **PUNAKAIKI** are often all visitors see of the Paparoa National Park, as they tumble off the bus opposite the twenty-minute paved loop track that leads to the rocks. Layers of limestone have weathered to resemble an immense stack of giant pancakes, the result of **stylobedding**, a chemical process in which the pressure of overlying sediments creates bands of varying durability. Subsequent uplift and weathering has accentuated this effect to create photogenic formations. The edifice is undermined by huge sea caverns where the surf surges in, sending spumes of brine spouting up through vast **blowholes**: visit at high tide when a good swell from the south or southwest sees the blowholes at their best.

Further examples of Paparoa's karst landscape are on show on a number of walks. At the **Punakaiki Cavern**, 500m to the north, you'll find a few glowworms (go after dark: torch essential), and, 2km beyond that, the **Truman Track** (30min return) runs down from the highway to a spectacular small beach hemmed in by rock platforms.

Apart from the rocks, there's good **swimming** in the Pororari and Punakaiki rivers, and at the southern end of Pororari Beach – where there's also decent **surfing**.

ARRIVAL AND INFORMATION
PUNAKAIKI

By bus North- and south-bound buses run by InterCity and NakedBus stop for half an hour opposite the Pancake Rocks, by the DOC/i-SITE, allowing enough time for a quick look.

Tourist information Punakaiki's DOC/i-SITE is on SH6 (daily: Dec–April 9am–6pm; May–Nov 9am–4.30pm; ☎ 03 731 1895, ⓦ doc.govt.nz). DOC's Paparoa National Park visitor centre is also an i-SITE, with displays on all aspects of the park, information on activities, walking maps, leaflets, and staff who can help with bookings.

Services Punakaiki has no fuel and no ATMs, so come prepared.

TOURS

Punakaiki Canoes SH6, 1km north of the Pancake Rocks ☎ 0800 271 383, ⓦ riverkayaking. co.nz. Friendly outfit renting kayaks ($40/2hr, then $5/hr thereafter) from their base beside the Pororari River; guided trips by arrangement (from $70).

Punakaiki Horse Treks SH6, 600m south of the Pancake Rocks ☎ 03 731 1839, ⓦ pancake-rocks. co.nz/horse. No experience is necessary for these horse treks, which see you riding into the Punakaiki Valley and stopping for refreshments before heading back to finish along the beach. Oct–April only (3hr; $180).

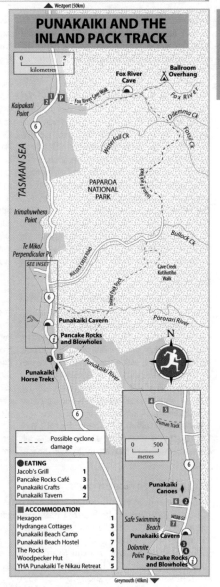

PUNAKAIKI AND THE INLAND PACK TRACK

▲ Westport (50km)

Fox River Cave

Ballroom Overhang

Fox River Cave Walk

Kaipakati Point

Dilemma Ck

Fossil Ck

Waterfall Ck

PAPAROA NATIONAL PARK

TASMAN SEA

Irimahuwhero Point

Bullock Ck

Te Miko/ Perpendicular Pt.

SEE INSET

BULLOCK CREEK ROAD

Inland Pack Track

Cave Creek Kotihotiho Walk

Punakaiki Cavern

Pororari River

Pancake Rocks and Blowholes

N

Punakaiki Horse Treks

Punakaiki River

Truman Track

- - - - Possible cyclone damage

0   500
metres

Punakaiki Canoes

● **EATING**
Jacob's Grill 1
Pancake Rocks Café 3
Punakaiki Crafts 4
Punakaiki Tavern 2

■ **ACCOMMODATION**
Hexagon 1
Hydrangea Cottages 3
Punakaiki Beach Camp 6
Punakaiki Beach Hostel 7
The Rocks 4
Woodpecker Hut 2
YHA Punakaiki Te Nikau Retreat 5

Safe Swimming Beach

WEBB ST

Punakaiki Cavern

Dolomite Point

Pancake Rocks and Blowholes

Greymouth (40km) ▼

0   2
kilometres

ACCOMMODATION

Hexagon 5825 SH6, Fox River (10min north of Punakaiki) ⓦ canopycamping.co.nz/hexagon; map p.471. The 20min walk to this one-room self-catering hut is worth it (the owner will take your gear in and out on his 4WD motorbike). This six-sided hut with heaps of character is off grid – light a fire under the outdoor bath and soak up the amazingly private location. **$190**

Hydrangea Cottages SH6 ☎ 03 731 1839, ⓦ pancake-rocks.co.nz; map p.471. Six gorgeous cottages set above the road, most with sea views. The real appeal, though, is the self-catering cottages themselves, all beautifully constructed with native timbers and local stone, several with outside bathtubs and private verandas. **$240**

Punakaiki Beach Camp 5 Owen St SH6 ☎ 03 731 1894, Ⓦ punakaikibeachcamp.co.nz; map p.471. Attractive, grassy campsite roamed by wekas and pukekos, with a range of tent sites and campervan hook-ups plus a handful of cabins. It's handily positioned close to the beach and *Punakaiki Tavern*. Cabins $68, camping $17, powered sites $20

★ **Punakaiki Beach Hostel** 4 Webb St ☎ 03 731 1852, Ⓦ punakaikibeachhostel.co.nz; map p.471. Cheery, timber beachhouse-style backpackers right by the sand with great communal areas, board games and a TV-free policy; you can buy home-made bread, muffins and a few essentials from their tuck shop. There's an assortment of room types (including one double in a fantastic house truck); comfy dorm beds come with reading lights and power points. Dorms $34, doubles $89

The Rocks Hartmount Place ☎ 03 731 1141, Ⓦ therockshomestay.com; map p.471. Welcoming homestay, with three comfortable en-suite rooms; it's worth paying a bit more for the "Sea Room" ($256) with its sea view, though the library and conservatory also have panoramic views. Rates include breakfast. No self-catering facilities. $216

Woodpecker Hut 5297 SH6, Woodpecker Bay, Fox River (5min north of Punakaiki) Ⓦ canopycamping. co.nz/woodpecker-hut; map p.471. Set on a coastal cliff property, these two small off-grid huts (one a bedroom, the other a lounge,) are joined by a covered self-catering kitchen. Soak in the cedar hot tub out front and take in the dramatic seascape. $290

YHA Punakaiki Te Nikau Retreat 19 Hartmount Place, 200m north of the Truman Track (10min to beach) and 3km north of the i-SITE ☎ 03 731 1111, Ⓦ tenikauretreat.co.nz; map p.471. Associate YHA hostel in a character rustic spot with buildings scattered around a hillside thick with nikau palms; most rooms have bathroom and kitchen facilities close by. Five self-contained cottages (there are dorms and attractive doubles plus some standalone cottages ($120); you can buy fresh bread, muffins and eggs on-site. Bookings essential. Dorms $32, doubles $85

EATING

Punakaiki has a limited supply of **eating** options. There's no shop for supplies, so bring everything if you're self-catering.

Jacob's Grill Punakaiki Resort SH6, 700m south of the i-SITE ☎ 03 731 1168, Ⓦ punakaiki-resort.co.nz; map p.471. Easily the swankiest place in Punakaiki, overlooking the sea, with elegantly presented fare such as scallops in white wine and cream sauce, followed by venison medallions with potato gratin (mains $28–39), though if they're busy you'll need to be staying at the resort to get a table. Daily lunch & dinner by reservation.

Pancake Rocks Café 4300 SH6, next to the i-SITE ☎ 03 731 1873; map p.471. Popular with the tour buses, this place serves "West Coast" breakfasts (bacon, eggs, sausages, hash browns and toast; $18.50), as well as good home-made pancakes, pies, sandwiches and cakes; their fluffy pancake stacks ($17.50), served all day and topped with fruit compote or bacon and maple syrup, are particularly good. Daily: summer 8am–10pm; winter 8am–4pm.

Punakaiki Crafts SH6, by the i-SITE; map p.471. Craft shop with a small café serving coffee, tea, cakes and slices. Daily 9am–4pm at least.

Punakaiki Tavern Corner of Owen St and SH6, 1km north of the i-SITE ☎ 03 731 1188, Ⓦ punakaikitavern.co.nz; map p.471. No-frills pub with good-value, simple, well-portioned meals ranging from vast cooked breakfasts to steaks, burgers, and bangers and mash (mains $18.50–26). Daily 8am–late.

Punakaiki to Greymouth

Punakaiki to Greymouth is a spectacular drive, pushed onto the sea cliffs by the intrusive ramparts of the Paparoa Range. Tragedy struck the area in 2010 when explosions rocked the Pike River coalmine, 46km north of Greymouth, trapping and killing 29 miners inside.

Photos aside, the only reasons to stop are to visit the **Barrytown knife maker**, 2662 Coast Rd/SH6, who will guide you through the intricacies of making your own blade, from hot steel to honed slicer, in a day ($160; around 9.30am–4pm; ☎ 0800 256433, Ⓦ barrytownknifemaking.com). Tiny **RAPAHOE**, 34km south of Punakaiki, has about the safest bathing beach on the coast and a reputation for gemstones. Follow the track to the excellent vantage point of **Point Elizabeth** (5km; 2hr return).

Greymouth and around

The Grey River forces its way through a break in the coastal Rapahoe Range and over two treacherous sandbars to the sea at **GREYMOUTH**, the West Coast's largest settlement. The drab, workaday town has few highlights but attracts a decent flow of visitors thanks to its position at the end of the line for the *TranzAlpine* Railway and as a convenient stop for drivers (an increasing number of people take the train from Christchurch and pick up a rental car here).

Greymouth, like Hokitika, has a reputation for high-quality greenstone carving. Once you've checked out the greenstone galleries and the brewery, and strolled along the waterfront, do what you came for and move on, particularly in winter when **The Barber**, a razor-sharp katabatic wind that whistles down the Grey Valley, envelops the town in thick icy fog.

Brief history

Greymouth began to take shape during the early years of the **gold rush** on land purchased in 1860 by James Mackay, who bought most of the West Coast from the Poutini Ngai Tahu people for £150. The town's defining feature is the river, which is deceptively calm and languid through most of the summer but awesome after heavy rains. Devastating **floods** swept through Greymouth in 1887, 1905, 1936, 1977 and 1988; since the town was last inundated a flood wall has successfully held back most of the waters.

Shades of Jade

16 Tainui St • Mon–Fri 9am–5pm, Sat & Sun 10am–2pm • ☎ 03 768 0794, ⓦ shadesofjade.co.nz

One of the town's jade gallery/shops well worth a visit is **Shades of Jade**, a charming spot where the local carver keeps the prices down, with traditional and modern designs in New Zealand *pounamu*. In addition to carved pieces there's a good selection of tumbled polished stones and pendants ($15–25), and a workshop in the store where the super-friendly owner is happy to show you stones and explain carving techniques.

History House Museum

27 Gresson St • Mon–Fri 10am–4pm, Sat 10am–2pm • $6 • ☎ 03 768 4028, ⓦ greydc.govt.nz

Despite presentation that owes much to the office photocopier, Greymouth's **History House Museum** does a good job of relating the Grey District's history, particularly prior to 1920, through maritime, gold- and coal-mining and timber-milling memorabilia and stacks of photos from the town's heyday. Take time to leaf through the books of newspaper articles and photographs that are piled in each room: stories of shipwrecks and claim-jumping that give a sense of just how recently Greymouth was a frontier town.

Monteith's Brewing Company

Corner of Turumaha and Herbert sts • Nov–April 11am–9pm, May to Oct 11am–8pm • Guided tours $25 • ☎ 03 768 4149, ⓦ monteiths.co.nz

Monteith's Brewing Company's shiny new brewery attracts a steady stream of beer aficionados. While locals come here for the excellent food and drink, it's possible to work up a thirst on a tour of the brewhouse, where the company's "Brewer's Series" craft ales are produced. The small production runs mean that you're unlikely to see the bottling plant in action, but there's a good chance of seeing the brewers at work on the morning tours. Take care though – the tour includes four 200ml glasses of beer, and even one glass of their *Doppelbock* could put you over the legal limit for driving.

Point Elizabeth Track

6km north of Greymouth • 5km return; 1hr30min

Choose a fine evening for this pleasant walk; the **Point Elizabeth Track** follows the coast through stands of nikau to a lookout, from where you may spot Hector's dolphins or fur seals. Double back from here, or continue another 3km to Rapahoe (see page 472)

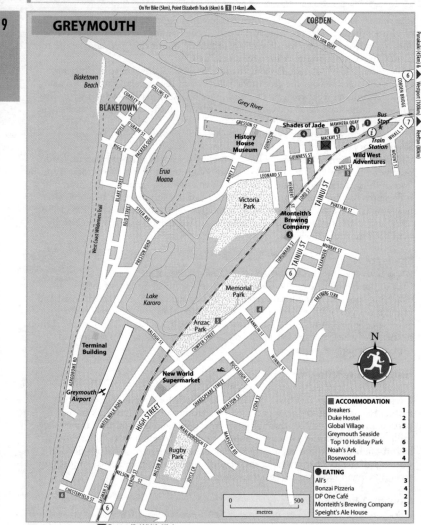

On Yer Bike (5km), Point Elizabeth Track (6km) & 1 (14km)

GREYMOUTH

COBDEN

Punakaiki (45km) & ► Westport (100km) ► Reefton (80km) ►

Blaketown Beach

BLAKETOWN

Grey River

Shantytown (9km) & Hokitika (40km)

ACCOMMODATION

Breakers	1
Duke Hostel	2
Global Village	5
Greymouth Seaside	
Top 10 Holiday Park	6
Noah's Ark	3
Rosewood	4

EATING

Ali's	3
Bonzai Pizzeria	4
DP One Café	2
Monteith's Brewing Company	5
Speight's Ale House	1

and pick up a bus from there back to town (2 daily). While it's not strictly necessary, the *Point Elizabeth Walkway* leaflet, available from Greymouth's i-SITE ($2), is a good guide to the walk's history and geography.

ARRIVAL AND DEPARTURE
GREYMOUTH

By train The *TranzAlpine* train (see page 519), Greymouth's only passenger service, stops at the Mackay St station.
Destinations Arthur's Pass (daily; 2hr 15min); Christchurch (daily; 4hr 20min).

By bus InterCity buses running south to Hokitika and Franz Josef, or north to Westport and Nelson, depart shortly after the arrival of the *TranzAlpine* train. Atomic,

InterCity and NakedBus all stop outside the railway station on Mackay St.
Destinations Arthur's Pass (2 daily; 1hr 30min); Christchurch (2 daily; 4hr 30min); Fox Glacier (1–2 daily; 3hr 45min–4hr 30min); Franz Josef (1–2 daily; 3hr–3hr 30min); Hokitika (3–5 daily; 45min); Murchison (daily; 4hr); Punakaiki (1–2 daily; 1hr); Westport (1–2 daily; 2hr 30min).

GETTING AROUND

By bike Greymouth's hostels all lend bikes to guests free of charge. Rentals are available from Mann Cycles (☎03 768 0255) on 37 Mackay St from $20/2hr.

By car Several major car rental companies have offices inside the i-SITE.

INFORMATION

Inside the train station on Mackay St (Mon–Fri 9am–5pm, Sat & Sun 9.00am–5pm; ☎03 768 5101, ⓦgreydistrict.co.nz). The combined i-SITE and West Coast Travel Centre has free wi-fi and provides the *West Coast* visitor guide plus a great street map of the town.

TOURS AND ACTIVITIES

Activities around Greymouth cover a wide variety of bases, with the newly-completed **West Coast Wilderness Trail** (ⓦwestcoastwildernesstrail.co.nz), a 132km-long (grade 2) cycle trail linking Ross, Hokitika and Greymouth -terrain includes dense rainforest, glacial rivers, lakes and expansive wetlands (allow 4 days).

On Yer Bike 511 SH6, Coal Creek, 5km north of Greymouth ☎0800 669372, ⓦonyerbike.co.nz. Offers adrenaline-charged activities on a private estate with quad bikes ($125/hr) and two-, four- and six-seat go-kart buggies, with free transport from Greymouth if you can't get out there.

Shantytown Rutherglen Rd, Paroa, 10km south of town ☎0800 742689, ⓦshantytown.co.nz. If you're travelling with kids, you might want to consider a visit to this re-created gold-rush village heritage park ($33) where activities include a steam train and panning for gold. Daily 8.30am–5pm.

Wild West Adventure Company 8 Whall St, Greymouth ☎03 768 6649, ⓦfun-nz.com. Runs some of the best activities in town, notably Taniwha Cave Rafting (5hr; 1hr 30min–2hr underground; $225), an undemanding caving trip where wetsuits and cavers' lamps are provided for a gentle float on inner tubes through a cavern lit by glowworms, which finishes with a warm-up soak in a hot tub. They also offer a more energy-intensive range of guided hikes and bike-rides, plus rafting trips and zipline/abseil adventures.

ACCOMMODATION

Greymouth has several great **backpackers** but few other standout places to stay. **Book** ahead around local events: the Kumara Races ($15, second weekend in Jan), the Coast to Coast Race (second weekend in Feb), Hokitika's Wildfoods Festival (second weekend in March) and the Around Brunner Cycle Race (third weekend in April).

Breakers 1367 SH6, Rununga, 14km north of Greymouth ☎03 762 7743, ⓦbreakers.co.nz; map p.474. Stunningly located beachfront B&B offering four rooms, two upstairs in the house, two in the garden. If you can't get enough of this wild coastline, this is your place. $285

Duke Hostel 27 Guinness St ☎03 768 9470, ⓦduke. co.nz; map p.474. As long as you can stand the purple-and-green paint job, this is an excellent hostel: smoothly organized in a central location with well-equipped doubles, comfortable beds and knowledgeable and helpful hosts who offer free soup nightly, as well as toast and jam each morning and complimentary wi-fi. Dorms $32, doubles $82

★ **Global Village** 42 Cowper St ☎03 768 7272, ⓦglobalvillagebackpackers.co.nz; map p.474. Light and spacious, well-equipped hostel backing onto parkland and a river. The rooms are imaginatively decorated in tribal themes with artefacts from around the world, the bathrooms have been decorated with large colourful mosaics, and there's a range of tempting activities: free bikes and kayaks, low-cost sauna, spa and small gym, and a BBQ out back most fine evenings. All beds are made up and there are some single-sex dorms and camping spots ($18). Dorms $32, doubles $80

Greymouth Seaside Top 10 Holiday Park 2 Chesterfield St ☎0800 867104, ⓦtop10greymouth. co.nz; map p.474. The more central and better of the two motor parks, right by the beach with the excellent facilities (adventure playground, games room, etc), expected of the Top 10 chain. Cabins $70, camping per site $51

Noah's Ark 16 Chapel St ☎03 768 4868, ⓦnoahsarkbackpackers.co.nz; map p.474. Large but homey hostel in a two-storey villa with great verandas and a spacious lounge with Sky TV. Rooms and dorms are lavishly decorated with animal themes and there are free bikes and a spa. Camping $21, dorms $32, doubles $82

★ **Rosewood** 20 High St ☎0800 185748, ⓦrosewoodnz. co.nz; map p.474. Appealing B&B in a beautiful two-storey 1920s home with wood panelling, leadlight windows and tasteful decor. Rooms are en suite or have private bathroom; rates include cooked breakfasts. $235

EATING

Greymouth's quiet centre has plenty of good cafés, but little in the way of proper restaurants – you may find yourself self-catering come dinnertime, whether you plan to or not.

Ali's 9 Tainui St ☎03 768 5858; map p.474. Unpretentious, licensed café serving snacks, lunches and dinners including Thai curries and tasty pasta

9

dishes ($18.50–29) plus snacks such as potato, spinach and feta fritters ($11.50). Tues–Sun 9am–9pm, Mon 9am–8.30pm.

Bonzai Pizzeria 31 Mackay St ☎ 03 768 4170; map p.474. Cheerful licensed restaurant (mains $14–28.50) with tearoom staples through the day, including delightfully squidgy cakes and vast quiches in addition to the deep-pan pizzas for lunch and dinner ($16/25). Daily 7.30am–9pm.

DP One Café 104 Mawhera Quay ☎ 03 768 4005; map p.474. Cool café, with local artists' work on the walls and pre-loved furniture, serving cooked breakfasts, filled bagels and salads ($8–18), along with good coffee, tea and smoothies. Daily 8.30am–8pm.

★ **Monteith's Brewing Company** Corner of Turumaha and Herbert sts ☎ 03 768 4149, ⓦ monteiths.co.nz; map p.474. Attached to the brewery itself, this popular café with indoor and outdoor seating serves an appealing range of tapas, peppered venison and blue cheese sliders, sticky baby back ribs and beer battered fries ($7–15), all of which can be paired with the brewery's ales. Daily 10am–8pm.

Speight's Ale House 130 Mawhera Quay ☎ 03 768 0667, ⓦ speightsalehousegreymouth.co.nz; map p.474. Cavernous restaurant/bar in a 1909 Edwardian Baroque former government building with a menu of hearty dishes (mains $16–32): whitebait patties, "great mates drunken steak" (rump steak) and Stewart Island battered blue cod – matched to beers from the Speight's range. Daily noon–late, food served until 9pm.

Blackball and around

Sleepy **BLACKBALL** is a former gold- and coal-mining village spread across a plateau at the foot of the Paparoa Range, 11km northeast of Stillwater. Today commuters and neo-hippies coexist with gnarled part-time hunters and prospectors. Blackball owes its existence to alluvial gold discovered in Blackball Creek in 1864, but gold returns quickly diminished and the town was sustained by its coal mines, which helped to stake the town's place in the nation's history as birthplace of the **labour movement** before the mines closed in 1964.

These days – apart from its famous salami (see page 477) – Blackball's rustic tranquillity is its main draw, along with excellent walking through the gold workings of Blackball Creek and up onto the wind-blasted tops of the Paparoa Range along the **Croesus Track**. There's a small information centre next to *Formerly The Blackball Hilton*, where you can pick up a free sketch map of the area.

Moana and Lake Brunner

From Stillwater, the sealed Arnold Valley–Lake Brunner road runs 55km southeast to link up with SH73 between Greymouth and Arthur's Pass. Roughly halfway the road passes **Lake Brunner**, a filled glacial hollow celebrated for its trout fishing. The village of **MOANA** on the north shore is popular with holidaying Kiwis but not brimming with diversions (or facilities). By late summer the lake is surprisingly warm and makes for good **swimming**, or you can stroll along a couple of easy paths. At the end of town, a slender swingbridge over the fledgling Arnold River leads to the riverside **Rakaitane Track** (45min loop) and the **Lake Side Track** (60min return), the latter with good mountain views.

ARRIVAL AND DEPARTURE   BLACKBALL AND AROUND

By train and bus The *TranzAlpine* train stops at Moana's lakeshore station on Ana St at 11.47am on its way to Greymouth, and again at 2.42pm on its return to Christchurch. Atomic Shuttles' (☎ 03 349 0697, ⓦ atomictravel.co.nz) daily Christchurch–Greymouth buses also stop here. With no regular public transport, you'll have to find your own way to and from Waiuta and Blackball.

ACCOMMODATION

Formerly The Blackball Hilton 26 Hart St, Blackball ☎ 03 732 4705, ⓦ blackballhilton.co.nz. The last of the mining-era hotels opened as the Dominion in 1910, and subsequently operated as the Hilton – ostensibly named after the former mine manager remembered in Hilton St nearby – until challenged by the international hotel chain of the same name. Apart from lively drinking with locals, the hotel offers a range of decent rooms with shared bathrooms; a continental breakfast is included. The pub serves coffee, lunches and dinner (mains $14

–36), which might include Blackball salami. **$110**
Hotel Lake Brunner 34 Ahau St, Moana ☎ 03 738 0083, ⓦ hotellakebrunner.co.nz. Block of swanky modern studio units overlooking the lake from Moana's main street, though not all rooms have lake views. The cheaper rooms have basic kitchenettes; there's a bar/restaurant on-site. Cabins **$29** per person, doubles **$85**

EATING

★ **Blackball Salami Co** 11 Hilton St, Blackball ☎ 03 732 4111, ⓦ blackballsalami.co.nz. For picnic supplies, call in at this excellent shop to feast on delicious venison sausages, chorizo, various salamis (of which 150 go to Antarctic bases every year) and other delectable morsels. Mon–Fri 8am–4pm, Sat 9am–2pm.
Station House Café 40 Koe St, Moana ☎ 03 738 0158, ⓦ lakebrunner.net. Opposite the railway station, this licensed restaurant/café opens onto a timber deck with umbrella-shaded tables and stunning lake and mountain views (weather permitting). It serves a tempting range of lunches and dinners (mains $29–35). Daily 10.30am–9pm in summer.

Hokitika and around

South of Greymouth, SH6 hugs a desolate stretch of coast with little of abiding interest until **HOKITIKA**, 40km away. "Hoki" is markedly more interesting than Greymouth, due to its location on a long, driftwood-strewn beach, some engaging activities – including Sock World, Hokitika's strangely seductive sock-making machine museum, and an atmospheric glowworm dell (about 1km north of the centre beside SH6) – and proximity to good bushwalks in the surrounding area, not least of which is the spectacular Hokitika Gorge.

Despite its long, windswept dark-sand beach, the town is primarily renowned for its crafts scene, and is something of an artists' enclave, with a slew of studios, galleries and shops where you can see weaving, carving (greenstone or bone) or glass-blowing in action or buy the high-quality results of the artists' labours.

Brief history

Like other West Coast towns, Hokitika owes its existence to the **gold rushes** of the 1860s. Within months of the initial discoveries near Greymouth in 1864, fields had been opened up on the tributaries of the Hokitika River, and Australian diggers and Irish hopefuls trekked to the West Coast to get their share. Within two years Hokitika had a population of 6000 (compared with today's 3850), streets packed with hotels, and a steady export of over a tonne of gold a month – a booming period evoked in Eleanor Catton's 2013 Booker Prize-winning novel, *The Luminaries*.

Despite a treacherous sandbar at the Hokitika river-mouth, the **port** briefly became the country's busiest, with ships tied up four deep along Gibson Wharf. As gold grew harder to find and more sluicing water was needed, the enterprise eventually became uneconomic and was replaced by dairying and the timber industry. The port closed in 1954, only to be smartened up in the 1990s for the town's Heritage Trail.

Hokitika Museum

Carnegie Building, 17 Hamilton St • Daily: summer 10am–5pm; winter 10am–2pm • $6 • ☎ 03 755 6898

Hokitika's leading role in the West Coast gold rushes rightly occupies much of the **Hokitika Museum**, with a fascinating film about the period showing on loop. There are also worthwhile displays on *pounamu* and the West Coast's whitebait fanatics, as well as plenty of period photographs depicting the dangers of crossing the Hokitika River bar and the difficulties of building the region's roads.

Sock World Hokitika

27 Sewell St • Daily 9am–5pm • Free • ☎ 03 755 7251, ⓦ autoknitter.com

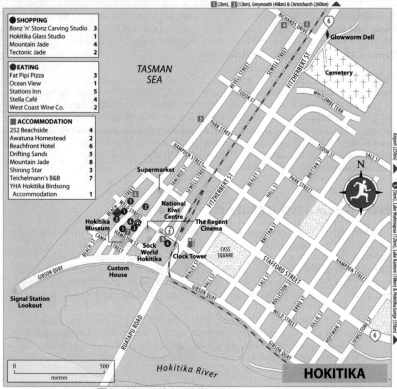

For an entirely different, charming and quirky experience pop into **Sock World Hokitika**, a working museum in a yarn store that houses a display of vintage knitting machines and a great range of woolly foot-warmers. The friendly, knowledgeable staff will give you a rundown on the largest collection of fully restored sock-knitting machines known to man, some capable of knocking up ten pairs an hour.

National Kiwi Centre

64 Tancred St · Daily: summer 9am–5pm; winter 9.30am–4.30pm; eel feeding 10am, noon & 3pm · $24 · ☎ 03 755 5251,
ⓦ thenationalkiwicentre.co.nz

Firmly on the tour bus circuit, the modest, privately run **National Kiwi Centre** holds a dimly lit nocturnal house which is just like being in the bush at night, where you can observe the small collection of kiwis scurrying about and sifting the leaf litter for insects. In the aquarium next door you can watch tuatara, a rare "living dinosaur", sunning themselves in summer, and finish off with feeding their giant long-finned eels.

ARRIVAL AND DEPARTURE   HOKITIKA

By plane Hokitika's tiny airport is 2km east of the centre, with regular flights to Christchurch (2–4 daily; 35min).
By car Fuel gets more expensive south along this coast, so fill up before leaving Hokitika.
By bus InterCity and NakedBus stop outside the i-SITE on Weld St.

Destinations Arthur's Pass (1–2 daily; 3hr 30min); Christchurch (daily; 5hr 30min); Fox Glacier (1–2 daily; 2hr 30min); Franz Josef (1–2 daily; 2hr); Greymouth (1–2 daily; 45min); Nelson (1–2 daily; 7hr); Punakaiki (1–2 daily; 1hr 45min); Ross (1–2 daily; 30min); Whataroa (1–2 daily; 1hr 30min).

INFORMATION AND TOURS

Tourist information i-SITE 36 Weld St (Dec–March daily 9am–6pm; April–Nov daily 9am–5pm; ☎03 755 6166, ⦻hokitika.org). Does DOC bookings and is your best source of information about the new Westland Wilderness Trail, a four-day, off-road cycle trail linking Greymouth and Ross.

Listings The *Hokitika Guardian*, available from the i-SITE and around town, has entertainment listings.

Services The banks on Revell St are the last before Wanaka, more than 400km to the southeast, although there are now two ATMs en route.

Tours Wilderness Wings (at the airport; ☎0800 755 8118, ⦻wildernesswings.co.nz) offer a number of scenic flights, including Grand Circle around the glaciers (35min; $285) and as far as Milford Sound (3hr; $975); two people minimum. Leaflets for the self-guided Hokitika Heritage Walk leaflet (50c) can be picked up at the i-SITE office; walks cover the town's historic landmarks, including the Gibson Quay area, a former riverside dock that makes for a pleasant evening stroll, the Signal Station Lookout, the 1897 Custom House and a reconstructed schooner, the *Tambo*, which stands as memorial to ships lost on the sandbar.

ACCOMMODATION

Accommodation in Hokitika is seldom hard to find, though you should book ahead during the Kumara Races (second weekend in Jan), for all of February including around the Coast to Coast race and during the Wildfoods Festival.

252 Beachside 252 Revell St ☎03 755 8773, ⦻252beachside.co.nz; map p.478. Old-fashioned motel and campervan park a block from the beach with a swimming pool and enclosed play area, with a row of dated but comfortable studios and a handful of basic cabins. The friendly owners have reams of information on activities in and around town. Powered sites $50, studios $110

★ **Awatuna Homestead** SH6, 13km north of Hokitika ☎03 755 6834, ⦻awatunahomestead.co.nz; map p.478. Welcoming B&B with four tasteful, comfortable rooms and one self-catering apartment. A relaxing spot with home-grown veggies, plenty of books, and a 10min walk to the beach. Evening meals by arrangement. 24hr advance notice. Doubles $300, apartment $390

Beachfront Hotel 111 Revell St ☎03 755 8344, ⦻beachfronthotel.co.nz; map p.478. With fifty rooms in two blocks, this is Hokitika's largest hotel. Rooms in the older block are rather average; the pick of the bunch are the modern first-floor rooms in the "Oceanview" building next door with full wall-windows and balconies just 50m from the water's edge. Doubles $190, ocean-view $285

★ **Drifting Sands** 197 Revell St ☎021 02665154, ⦻driftingsands.nz; map p.478. A sleekly designed "boutique hostel", with great beds, a coal-fire-warmed lounge and a pebbly path straight to the beach. If your tent can stand up to Hokitika's sea breezes, it's possible to camp in the garden ($18). Dorms $34, doubles $120

Mountain Jade 41 Weld St ☎03 755 5185, ⦻mountainjadebackpackers.co.nz; map p.478. Centrally located just across from the town's clock tower, this slightly tatty BBH hostel above the jade studio of the same name with cheap dorms and a couple of cramped but comfortable doubles out back, deck overlooks car

GREENSTONE

In Māori, the entire South Island is known as **Te Wahi Pounamu**, "the place of greenstone", with deposits found solely between Greymouth and Hokitika in the Taramakau and Arahura rivers, in Fiordland's Anita Bay – where the beautifully dappled *tangiwai* occurs – and the Lake Wakatipu region near Queenstown. When the Poutini Ngai Tahu arranged to sell most of Westland to James Mackay in 1860, the Arahura River, their main source of *pounamu*, was specifically excluded.

Greenstone's value has barely diminished. Mineral claims are jealously guarded, the export of greenstone is prohibited and no extraction allowed from national parks; penalties include fines of up to $200,000 and two years in jail. **Price** is heavily dependent on quality, but rates of around $100,000 a tonne are not unknown – and the sky's the limit when the stone is fashioned into sculpture and jewellery, although pendants can be picked up for as little as $15.

Hokitika is the main destination for greenstone shoppers; keep in mind that the larger **shops** and **galleries** are firmly locked into the tour-bus circuit so prices are kept high. Big shops are fine for learning about the quality of the stone and competence of the artwork but smaller places have more competitive deals. Buyers should ask about the origins of the raw material – insiders suspect that lots of greenstone sold in New Zealand is cheaper jade sourced overseas.

9

WILDFOODS FESTIVAL

In the last decade or so, Hokitika has become synonymous with the annual **Wildfoods Festival** (second Sat in March; advance tickets $35; ⓦ www.wildfoods.co.nz), when the population quadruples to celebrate bush tucker. Around fifty stalls in Cass Square sell delicacies such as marinated goat kebabs, smoked eel wontons, huhu grubs, "mountain oysters" (aka sheep's testicles) and, of course, whitebait, washed down with home-brewed beer and South Island wine. Also a great place to experience an authentic Māori *hangi*.

park and out to spectacular mountain views. Dorms $24, doubles $65

Shining Star 16 Richards Drive ☎ 03 755 8921, ⓦ accommodationwestcoast.co.nz; map p.478. There's no road between you and the beach at this neat, well-run site. The stylized geometric log cabins all have en suites; some also offer stunning sea views and cooking facilities, and there's a pet llama, sheep and a couple of likeable pigs, plus a playground. Beachfront chalets $185, camping per site $40, cabins $119

Teichelmann's B&B 20 Hamilton St ☎ 03 755 8232, ⓦ teichelmanns.co.nz; map p.478. Comfortable and well appointed, this history-filled central B&B has friendly hosts, a range of en-suite rooms and a romantic garden cottage with double spa bath overlooking a fern-filled courtyard. A hearty breakfast is served. Doubles $260, cottage $280

YHA Hokitika Birdsong Accommodation 124 Kumara Junction, SH6, 3km north of town ☎ 03 755 7179, ⓦ birdsong.co.nz; map p.478. The most long-lived of the local hostels, the brightly decorated rooms in this small, friendly laidback spot all feature a painting of the bird they're named after. There are discounts for YHA members, outdoor bathtubs and ocean views from upstairs. Dorms $35, doubles $89

EATING

★ **Fat Pipi Pizza** 89 Revell St ☎ 03 755 6373; map p.478. The locally famed pizzas here include "Greenpiece" (zucchini, spinach, mushrooms, feta, olives and roast red pepper pesto), and the whopping "Whitebait", topped with a quarter-pound of local delicacy whitebait folded into a beaten egg, with mozzarella, capers and lemon (all pizzas $20/26). You can takeaway, or eat-in – head to the back of the garden for a sea view with your dinner. Summer Mon & Tues 5–9pm, Wed–Sun noon–2.30pm & 5–9pm; winter Mon & Tues 5–8pm, Wed–Sun 12 noon–2.30pm & 5–9pm.

Ocean View 111 Revell St ☎ 03 755 8344; map p.478. *Beachfront Hotel* restaurant with tasty à la carte evening meals such as pork rack with crackling, garlic mash, potato, pear cider glaze and jus, plus there's a range of good-value light meals on offer (house smoked salmon and the like) with great sea views from window tables and the deck. Mains $19–39. Daily 7–10am & 5.30–9.30pm.

Stations Inn 7 Blue Spur Rd ☎ 03 755 5499, ⓦ stationsinnhokitika.co.nz; map p.478. Hokitika's only fine dining is to be had here, 5km east of town on an elevated terrace on the way to Lake Kaniere. The menu changes seasonally to show off choice Kiwi produce, with elegant dishes including things like braised rabbit in a pastry shell with *kumara* mash, house-cured Marlborough salmon with home-made rye bread, and great beef and lamb dishes (mains $28–45). Tues–Sat drinks from 5pm, dining 6pm–late.

Stella Café 84 Revell St ☎ 03 755 5432; map p.478. One of the town's most popular meeting spots, with great hot meals and coffee, though their cabinet food is somewhat uninspired. There's a climate-controlled room stocked with fancy cheese and chutney, plus stacks of magazines and an in-house beehive to keep you entertained. Cheese platters from $20. Daily 8.30am–4.30pm.

★ **West Coast Wine Co.** 108 Revell St ☎ 03 755 5417, ⓦ westcoastwine.co.nz; map p.478. Tiny bar in a wine shop with a delightful courtyard, where good wine, beer and cocktails are complemented by excellent coffee and supplemented by a short menu of sophisticated bar snacks (mostly $10). Their new "cellar door" setup is also now up and running at the *Fire House* at 11 Hamilton St. Wed & Thurs 3–8pm, Fri & Sat 3–10pm, Sun 2–6pm.

SHOPPING

Pick up a free city map from the i-SITE showing the locations of Hokitika's growing collection of art and craft shops, studios and galleries; **greenstone** in particular is big business. The places listed below allow you to go beyond mere shopping and to see artisans at work.

Bonz 'n' Stonz Carving Studio 16 Hamilton St ☎ 0800 214949, ⓦ bonz-n-stonz.business.site; map p.478. If you want to shape a piece of greenstone yourself, pop along to this excellent studio where you can learn to carve; the friendly and estimable Steve Gwaliasi guides you through the design and execution in what is a personal and very memorable experience (3–6hr; from $85). Nov–March

Mon–Sat 8am–5pm; April–Oct 9am–5pm.
Hokitika Glass Studio 9 Weld St ☎03 755 7775,
ⓦhokitikaglass.co.nz; map p.478. Glass-blowing is
another longstanding Hoki tradition, best seen on weekdays
at this studio, with a fine line in glass penguins, orca and
whales. Mon–Fri 9am–5pm, Sat 9am–4pm.
Mountain Jade 41 Weld St ☎03 755 8007,
ⓦmountainjade.co.nz; map p.478. One of the largest jade
workshops and galleries in the country, showing the entire
process from stone cutting through to polishing. Watch half a
dozen skilled carvers at work, with great staff interaction with

customers. Free workshop tours 9.30am & 2.30pm. Daily:
Oct–Feb 8am–8.30pm;March–Sept 8.30am–5pm.
Tectonic Jade 67 Revell St ☎03 755 6644,
ⓦtectonicjade.com; map p.478. One of the more
interesting jade shops around town, with a collection
of traditional and original designs in unusual types of
pounamu. There's a great café in-store too, though it's aimed
at refreshing potential buyers, rather than the general
public – purchases are rewarded with an excellent free
coffee. Sept–March daily 9am–5pm.

Lake Kaniere

Some of the best bush scenery and **walks** around Hokitika are inland where the
dairying hinterland meets the foothills of the Southern Alps. Minor roads (initially
following Stafford Street out of town) make a good 70km scenic drive, shown in
detail on DOC's **Central West Coast: Hokitika** leaflet ($2). The road passes the fishing,
waterskiing and tramping territory of **Lake Kaniere**, a glacial lake with fantastic
reflections of the mountains in the crystal water, several picnic sites and basic camping
at Hans Bay ($8) along its eastern side. The most popular walk is the **Kaniere Water
Race Walkway** (9km one way; 3hr 30min; 100m ascent), starting from the lake's
northern end and following a channel that used to supply water to the goldfields,
through stands of regenerating rimu.

Hokitika Gorge

Lake Kaniere's eastern-shore road passes the magical **Dorothy Falls**, with giant moss-
covered boulders in unearthly shades of green, and eventually loops westwards where
a side road leads to the dazzling **Hokitika Gorge**. A gentle path (1.2km; 30min return)
leads through glades of rimu and podocarp to a swingbridge over the exquisite
turquoise-coloured Hokitika River.

From Hokitika to the glaciers

The main highway snuggles in close to the Southern Alps for most of the 135km to the
glacier at Franz Josef. The journey through dairy farms and stands of selectively logged
native bush is broken by a series of small settlements – **Ross**, **Pukekura** and **Harihari**.
The most popular places to stop are **Whataroa**, to visit the **white heron** colony, and
Okarito, where the laidback charm of the hamlet's lagoon and **kiwi-spotting** trips may
give you pause.

Immediately **south** of Hokitika, it's less than 10km along SH6 to the **Mananui
Tramline** (12km return; 4hr; mainly flat; DOC leaflet from the Hokitika i-SITE $2),
which offers easy walking and cycling with picnic opportunities at a lakeside beach
– cyclists have the option of completing the loop around the lake. A further 2km
south along SH6 the **Mananui Bush Walkway** (20min return) leads through coastal
forest remnants to dunes and there's a particularly nice DOC **camping** spot at **Lake
Mahinapua**, accessed off SH6 1km south ($6). Those travelling with children may wish
to stop at the Westcoast Treetop Walk, a few kilometres further south, but the high
ticket prices will put off most.

Ross

At the village of **ROSS**, 26km south of Hokitika, a lake-filled hole is all that remains
of a massive opencast mine that sought alluvial **gold** until the deposit was exhausted

9

RAFTING THE WILD WEST COAST RIVERS

Kayakers and rafters visit New Zealand's West Coast to experience some of the country's most thrilling and scenic whitewater trips. Steep rivers spill dramatically out of the alpine wilderness, fed by the prodigious quantity of rain that guarantees solid flows most of the time. The steepness of the terrain means you're in constantly thrilling if not downright scary territory (generally Grade III–V).

ACCESS

Few upper reaches of the region's rivers had been kayaked or rafted until the 1980s, when access became possible by helicopter. Many rafting trips still require **helicopter access**, so costs are relatively high, and prices often depend on numbers – getting a group together can save you a packet.

BOOKING AND SEASONS

Though their popularity is increasing, trips are still comparatively infrequent and you should **book** as far in advance as possible. The main **season** is November to April, though rafting is generally possible from early September to late May, and there is a minimum age of 13 years (15 for some of the more frightening runs).

RIVERS

The **most commonly rafted rivers** are (from north to south) the Karamea (Grade IV–V), the Mokihinui (Grade IV), the Arahura (Grade IV), the Whitcombe (Grade V), the Hokitika (Grade III–IV), the Wanganui (Grade III), the Perth (Grade V) and the Whataroa (Grade IV).

OUTFITTERS

Eco Rafting Adventures Franz Josef ☎ 03 755 4254, ⓦ ecorafting.co.nz. Enthusiastic guides take small groups on wilderness rafting trips on the best rivers along the length of the West Coast, including the Whataroa River near Franz Josef. They organize drive-in rafting trips (from $90) but the heli-rafting (from $450) and overnight trips (from $450) are particularly popular.

Ultimate Descents 38 Waller St, Murchison ☎ 0800 748377, ⓦ rivers.co.nz. Specialists in rafting the top half of South Island, with everything from half-day (4hr) on the Buller River ($180) to one-day heli-rafting trips on the Karamea ($500) and two-day

trips on the Mokihinui ($900), among others.

★ **Wild Rivers Rafting** New Creek Rd, Upper Buller Gorge ☎ 0508 467 238, ⓦ wildriversrafting.co.nz. Super-exciting rafting adventures on the Earthquake Rapids section of the Buller River. Great commentary from enthusiastic guides Bruce and Marty. If you have a camera, the driver will follow the raft and take pictures of you from the road, no charge. 4hr total tour time/2hr on the river; $160

Wild West Adventures 8 Whall St, Greymouth ☎ 0508 286 877, ⓦ fun-nz.com. Offers a wide range of trips, from hardcore heli-rafting (from $485) to tamer trips (from $175), on most of the rivers listed above.

in 2004. The mining company has moved to a new site just south of town, but would dearly love to get at the gold-bearing gravels underneath the settlement itself. Leave time for the well-signposted **Water Race Walkway** (4km loop, 1hr) linking a clutch of historic buildings and the site of the area's first gold strike.

De Bakker Cottage

Bold St • Daily: Dec–March 9am–4pm; April–Nov 9am–2pm • Free

Though Ross had over 3000 residents at its gold-rush peak, things had slowed considerably by 1909, when a couple of diggers prospecting less than 500m from the current visitor centre turned up the largest gold nugget ever found in New Zealand, the 3.1kg "**Honourable Roddy**", named after the then Minister of Mines. The nugget was bought by the government and given as a coronation gift in 1911 to Britain's George V, who melted it down to make a tea service. A replica of the fist-sized lump resides in the 1885 **Miner's Cottage**, surrounded by period photos and Victorian bric-a-brac.

9

Pukekura

Bushman's Centre daily 9am–5pm • Free; museum $4 • ☎ 03 755 4144, ⓦ pukekura.co.nz

A giant model sandfly hangs from the eaves of the **Bushman's Centre**, in the two-house hamlet of **PUKEKURA**, 23km south of Ross. The centre's cobwebby **museum** takes a light-hearted approach to timber milling, live deer capture, possum trapping (with a few morose live examples) and harvesting sphagnum moss for East Asian orchid growers. The museum may not be to your taste, but the centre's **café** and the rest areas around pretty **Lake Ianthe**, 6km to the south, make good stops.

Harihari

Tiny **HARIHARI**, 23km south of Pukekura, was the marshy landing site of **Guy Menzies**, who flew solo from Sydney to New Zealand in 1931, becoming the first to do so. Menzies ended up landing upside down in the mud of La Fontaine swamp, 10km northwest of town. A replica of Menzies' plane resides near the southern entrance to town in **Guy Menzies Park**. You might also want to turn onto Whanganui Flat Road and drive 20km (partly gravel) coastwards past Menzies' landing site to the delightful **Hari Hari Coastal Walkway** (7.6km loop; 2hr 45min; negligible ascent), which runs past elaborate whitebaiting stands to the Doughboy Lookout (60m) with great views of the coast and the Southern Alps. After a short stretch of dramatic coastline you return though kahikatea forest and along the line of a tram track once used by loggers. Note that certain sections are only accessible for two hours either side of low tide.

Whataroa and the Waitangiroto Nature Reserve

SH6, 30km south of Harihari • White Heron Sanctuary Tours Oct–Feb 4 daily; 2hr 30min • $150; booking advised • ☎ 0800 523456, ⓦ whiteherontours.co.nz

From September to late February, graceful white herons (*kotuku*) arrive to breed at the Waitangiroto Nature Reserve near **WHATAROA**, the bird's only nesting site in the country. Sitting across the river in a two-storey hide, gazing on forty or so nesting pairs of herons and spoonbills going about the daily business of preening, fishing and mating is a truly memorable if slightly surreal experience that ends all too quickly. The only way to visit is with the professional **White Heron Sanctuary Tours**, with tours departing from their office in Whataroa. The trip includes a scenic jetboat ride on the pretty Waitangiroto River and about half an hour ogling the birds; binoculars are provided. Pick-ups from Franz Josef are available (enquire for prices).

Okarito

In 1642, Abel Tasman became the first European to set eyes on Aotearoa at **Okarito**, 13km off SH6 15km south of Whataroa, now a secluded hamlet dotted round the southern side of its eponymous lagoon. The discovery of gold in the mid-1800s sparked an eighteen-month boom that saw fifty stores and hotels spring up along the lagoon's shores. Timber and flax milling sustained the place once the gold had gone, but still the community foundered, leaving a handful of holiday homes, a few dozen permanent residents and a lovely beach and lagoon, used as the setting for much of Keri Hulme's prize-winning novel, *The Bone People*.

INFORMATION AND TOURS

Tourist information 4 Aylmer St, Ross (daily: Dec–March 9am–4pm; April–Nov 9am–2pm; museum $2; ☎ 03 755 4077). The visitor centre museum shows an interesting video (included in admission) on the 1865 gold rush and rents gold pans ($10); if you're after a sure thing, there's also on-site gold panning which includes a guaranteed strike ($13.50).

Okarito Kayaks 1 The Strand ☎ 0800 652748, ⓦ okarito. co.nz. Runs great-value guided kayaking trips (2hr; $100;

FROM HOKITIKA TO THE GLACIERS

minimum two people) and rents double kayaks (2hr $55; half-day $65; overnight rentals also available) for exploring the lagoon and its forested side-channels. Call first to check tide conditions, but plan to go out in the morning when the water is calmest and the birdlife abundant and active.

Okarito Kiwi Tours 53 The Strand ☎ 03 753 4330, ⓦ okaritokiwitours.co.nz. Wildlife of a different feather can usually be seen on these excellent, low-impact and good-value trips into the bush for kiwi spotting (3–5hr; $75). If it goes well you'll start shortly before dusk and catch a glimpse of some of the extremely rare Okarito brown kiwi. To maximize the already high (95 percent) success rate, wear quiet clothes (no noisy raincoats in particular) and sturdy boots. Bookings essential.

ACCOMMODATION AND EATING

PUKEKURA
Bushman's Centre Café ☎ 03 755 4144, ⓦ pukekura. co.nz. Serves a "roadkill menu" that includes rabbit, thar and hare. It's possible to stay across the road either in the campsite or double rooms with shared bathroom and kitchen facilities. A holiday house is available too. Café daily 9am–5pm. Camping $10, doubles $45

HARIHARI
Flaxbush Motel SH6 ☎ 03 753 3116, ⓦ flaxbushmotelsharihari.co.nz. What with the park and the coastal walkway you may decide to stay, in which case treat yourself to this very welcoming spot, which is a Noah's Ark for unwell and injured wildlife (including, at the time of research, an inquisitive peacock); all rooms have self-catering facilities. Doubles $100, cottage $120

OKARITO
While Okarito Nature Tours sell hot drinks (and particularly good coffee) from their offices, there are no proper cafés or shops in Okarito, so bring provisions.
Okarito Beach House & Royal Hostel The Strand ☎ 03 753 4080, ⓦ okaritobeachhouse.com. This huddle of buildings is Okarito's cosiest spot to stay, with comfy en-suite doubles and the "hutel" – a self-contained cottage – all decorated in beach-inspired style. Doubles $115, "hutel" $195
Okarito Community Campground Russell St. This grassy beachside campsite has a day-shelter, coin-operated hot showers, and fire pits – perfect for driftwood campfires. $15
The School House The Strand ☎ 03 752 0796, ⓦ doc.govt.nz. A memorial commemorating Okarito's settlers stands opposite this DOC-managed 1901 former schoolhouse. It sleeps up to twelve in single bunks (bring your own linen), and you'll need to book the entire place out to stay. There's a toilet and full kitchen, but you'll need to head to the campsite for showers. Closed June–Aug. $100

The glacier region

Around 150km south of Hokitika, two white rivers of ice force their way down to the thick rainforest of the coastal plain – ample justification for the region's inclusion in **Te Wahipounamu**, the South West New Zealand World Heritage Area. The glaciers form a palpable connection between the coast and the highest peaks of the Southern Alps. Within a handful of kilometres the terrain drops from over 3000m to near sea level, bringing with it **Franz Josef Glacier** and **Fox Glacier**, two of the largest and most impressive of the sixty-odd glaciers that creak off the South Island's icy spine, together forming the centrepiece of the rugged **Westland National Park**. Legend tells of the beautiful Hinehukatere who so loved the mountains that she encouraged her lover, Tawe, to climb alongside her. He fell to his death and Hinehukatere cried so copiously that her tears formed the glaciers, with Franz Josef known to Māori as Ka Riomata o Hinehukatere – "The Tears of the Avalanche Girl".

The area is also characterized by the West Coast's prodigious **precipitation**, with upwards of 5m being the typical yearly dump. These conditions, combined with the rakish angle of the western slopes of the Southern Alps, produce some of the world's fastest-moving glaciers; stand at the foot for half an hour or so and you're bound to see a piece peel off. But these phenomenal speeds haven't been enough to counteract melting, and both glaciers have receded more than 3km since Cook saw them at their greatest recent extent, towards the end of the Little Ice Age. Glaciers are receding worldwide, but the two here sometimes buck the trend by advancing from time to time, typically around five years after a particularly big snowfall in the mountains.

The glaciers were already in full retreat when travellers started to battle their way down the coast to observe these wonders of nature. They were initially named "Victoria" and "Albert" respectively but, in 1865, geologist Julius von Haast renamed Franz Josef after the Austro-Hungarian emperor, and following a visit by prime minister William Fox in 1872, the other was bestowed with his name.

9

Activity in the glaciers is focussed in two small **villages**, which survive almost entirely on tourist traffic. Both lie close to the base of their respective glaciers and offer excellent plane and helicopter **flights**, now often incorporated in guided **glacier walks**. With your own transport, it makes sense to base yourself in one of the two villages and explore both glaciers from there. If you have to choose one, Franz Josef has a wider range of accommodation and restaurants, while Fox is quieter.

Franz Josef Glacier

FRANZ JOSEF GLACIER (Waiau) is the slightly larger of the two glacier villages. Though the glacier is no longer visible from the edge of the village, the Southern Alps tower above and developers have done what they can to create an alpine character with steeply pitched roofs and pine panelling. It's an appealing place, and small enough to make you feel almost like a local if you stay for more than a night or two – something that's easily done, considering the beautiful surroundings.

In Franz Josef you can hike to, on or around the glacier, kayak on nearby Lake Mapourika or take a scenic flight over the mountains. While it was once possible to get up on the glacier on foot, these days the instability of the terminal ice means that most glacier walks start with a helicopter drop on firmer terrain higher up, and the glacier's airspace buzzes with activity on fine days. Options are more

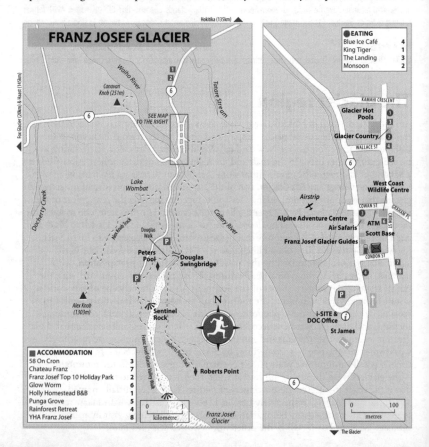

FRANZ JOSEF GLACIER

Hokitika (135km)

Waiho River

Canavan Knob (251m)

6

Tatare Stream

SEE MAP TO THE RIGHT

Fox Glacier (20km) & Haast (145m)

6

Docherty Creek

Lake Wombat

Alex Knob Track

Douglas Walk

Peters Pool

P

Douglas Swingbridge

Callery River

Alex Knob (1303m)

Sentinel Rock

Roberts Point Track

Franz Josef Glacier Valley Walk

N

Roberts Point

Franz Josef Glacier

ACCOMMODATION

58 On Cron	3
Chateau Franz	7
Franz Josef Top 10 Holiday Park	2
Glow Worm	6
Holly Homestead B&B	1
Punga Grove	5
Rainforest Retreat	4
YHA Franz Josef	8

0 ———— 1
kilometre

EATING

Blue Ice Café	4
King Tiger	1
The Landing	3
Monsoon	2

KAMAHI CRESCENT

Glacier Hot Pools

Glacier Country

WALLACE ST

6

West Coast Wildlife Centre

Airstrip

COWAN ST

GRAHAM PL

Alpine Adventure Centre

Air Safaris

ATM

Scott Base

Franz Josef Glacier Guides

CRON ST

CONDON ST

P

i-SITE & DOC Office

St James

6

0 ———— 100
metres

The Glacier

limited when poor weather sets in, though kayaking excursions and straightforward glacier valley walks often go ahead whatever the weather.

Glacier Hot Pools

63 Cron St • Daily 1–9pm; last entry 8pm • Main pools $28; private pool $95/45min for two people • ☎ 0800 044044, ⓦ glacierhotpools. co.nz

When the weather's wet, the best bet is a soak in the specially constructed **Glacier Hot Pools**. Artificially heated to 36°C, 38°C and 40°C respectively, the three public pools are covered in semi-porous canopies and surrounded by native bush, most of which has been transported to the site. Private pools come with cabana-type sheds containing showers. The pools' restorative qualities come into their own when you need to banish the aches of hiking or yomping about around the glacier; combo deals are available with Franz Josef Glacier Guides (see page 488).

West Coast Wildlife Centre

Corner of Cowan and Cron sts • Daily from 9am; call for seasonal closing times • $38, valid for 24hr; "backstage pass" $58 • ☎ 03 752 0600, ⓦ wildkiwi.co.nz

The enormous building that once housed the Hukawai Glacier Centre is now home to the state-of-the-art **West Coast Wildlife Centre**, where you can see New Zealand's rarest kiwis, the rowi and Haast tokoeka, as they scurry around in a dimly lit "nocturnal house". Part of Operation Nest Egg from approximately July to February, you'll also see chicks incubating and brooding if you stump up for the behind-the-scenes tour, which leaves at fixed times each day.

ARRIVAL AND DEPARTURE   FRANZ JOSEF GLACIER

By bus InterCity and NakedBus stop on the main road in the village (SH6; known here as Main Rd). Book tickets at Scott Base or the i-SITE.
Destinations Fox Glacier (4 daily; 30min); Greymouth (1–2 daily; 3hr 30min–4hr); Haast (2 daily; 2hr 30min–3hr 30min); Hokitika (1–2 daily; 1hr 45min–2hr 30min); Makarora (2 daily; 3–5hr); Queenstown (2 daily; 6hr–8hr 30min); Wanaka (2 daily; 5hr–6hr 30min).

GETTING AROUND

By shuttle bus Glacier Shuttles & Charters(☎ 0800 999739, ✉ glaciershuttlescharters@gmail.com) offer a scheduled shuttle service from Scott Base (or pick-up from your accommodation) to the glacier road-end (6 daily in summer; $12.50 return). Fox Bus (☎ 0800 369287) also run shuttle services on demand; the return trip Franz Josef to Fox Glacier costs $30, from Fox township to glacier $15.

INFORMATION

Tourist information i-SITE/DOC SH6 (daily: Nov–March 8.30am–6pm; April–Oct 8.30am–5pm; ☎ 03 752 0796, ✉ westlandnpvc@doc.govt.nz). The combined office has stacks of leaflets on hikes in the area and gets daily weather reports and glacier updates; check with them before starting any serious walks.
Services There is an ATM but no banks. Get online at Scott Base on SH6 (daily 9am–6pm; $4/hr).

TOURS AND ACTIVITIES

It's possible to walk to the glacier viewpoint independently, but to walk on the ice you'll need to take a guided trip. On any fine day the skies above Franz Josef are abuzz with choppers and light planes, which can make it rather noisy in the valley – kayaking trips further afield are a more tranquil experience.

WALKS

Glacier Valley Walk (6km return; 1hr 30min). This route is at the top of everyone's list of walks and starts at the car park 5km south of the village. The rough track crosses gravel beds left behind by past glacial retreats, giving you plenty of opportunity to observe small kettle lakes, the trim line high up the valley walls and a fault line cutting right across the valley (marked by deep gullies opposite each other). One of the best viewpoints is from the top of the glacier-scoured hump of Sentinel Rock, a 10min walk from the car park.
Douglas Walk (4km loop; 1hr). Reached from a car park halfway along the glacier access road, this circular walk passes through bush in various stages of regrowth to Peter's Pool, a serene kettle lake, and the Douglas Swingbridge.

9

Roberts Point Track (12km return; 5hr 30min; 950m ascent). One for more experienced trampers, the track leads from the Douglas Swingbridge past the Hendes Hut (a good lunch stop) to Roberts Point, high above the ice with stunning views. It's a bit of a slog and often slippery but well worth the effort.

Alex Knob Track (17km return; 8hr; 1000m ascent). Located on the other side of the glacial valley to the Roberts Point Track, this long but well-graded route climbs steadily above the glacier through several vegetation zones and offers more fine valley views; though long, it's less technical than the Roberts Point Track.

HIKING, HELI-HIKING AND ICE CLIMBING

Glacier Valley Eco Tours Scott Base (6 Main Rd) ☎0800 925 586, ⓦglaciervalley.co.nz. Runs a series of very informative nature tours that will see you hiking through the glacier valleys at Franz Josef and Fox (both 3hr; $75), climbing up onto the moraine, and exploring the glacier terminals. They also organize guided trips to Lake Matheson (3hr; $75), Okarito tours (3hr; $75), and the Lake Matheson-Fox glacier combo (9–12hr; $180).

Franz Josef Glacier Guides SH6 ☎0800 484337, ⓦfranzjosefglacier.com. This is the place to come if you want to get up onto the glacier itself – although the experience comes at price. Their most popular trip, the "Ice Explorer" (4hr; $469), starts with a quick helicopter ride to the upper part of the glacier, where you will spend up to 3hr exploring the icefield – hopefully finding tunnels to explore, deep blue crevices into which to stare and a general sense of wonder and otherworldliness – rounded off by a return flight and a soak at the hot pools. They also offer heli-hiking (3 daily; 3hr; $459) trips, with a longer scenic flight and a gentler walk, as well as adventurous heli-ice climbing tours 5hr; $699.

SCENIC FLIGHTS AND SKYDIVING

Safety demands that specific flight paths must be followed, limiting what can be offered and forcing companies to compete on price; ask for youth, student, YHA, senior or just-for-the-sake-of-it discounts, most readily given if you can band together in a group of four to six and present yourselves as a ready-to-go plane or chopper load. Most people go by helicopter, with all operators regularly landing on a snowfield high above the glacier where the rotors are left running – hardly serene. Planes give you a longer flight with greater range for less money while a ski-plane landing on a snowfield is very rewarding, particularly the silence after they switch the engine off.

Air Safaris 6 Main Rd ☎0800 723274, ⓦairsafaris.co.nz. For a slightly quieter experience than that offered by the helicopter operations around town, take a flight in one of Air Safari's turbo-prop flightseeing planes. Note that they don't do landings. Try their Grand Traverse (50min; $395).

Fox & Franz Josef Heliservices Alpine Adventure Centre, Main Rd ☎0800 800793, ⓦscenic-flights.co.nz. The cheapest operator hereabouts, offering one glacier and landing (20min; $245), two glaciers and landing (30min; $325), and two glaciers, landing and Mount Cook plus a quick nip across the main divide to see the Tasman Glacier (40min; $455).

Skydive Franz Scott Base ☎0800 458677, ⓦskydivefranz.co.nz. For the ultimate aerial adventure, book a tandem skydive – this is one of the few places in New Zealand where commercial tandem jumps from 19,000ft are permitted ($559); though lower drops are also available (9000ft $249; 13,000ft $319; 16,500ft $419).

KAYAKING

Glacier Country Kayaks 64 Cron St ☎0800 423262, ⓦglacierkayaks.com. Offers marvellous guided kayaking trips on the black waters of the kahikatea- and flax-fringed Lake Mapourika, 8km north of town (shuttle included). The most popular "Classic" trip (3 daily; 3hr; $115) is best in the calm of the morning, with loads of photo opportunities in sun and/or rain. You can also kayak across the lake and do a guided rainforest walk (4hr; $145). Deals are available if you wish to combine kayaking with a heli-hike or skydive.

ACCOMMODATION

With the region's popularity and a bus schedule that forces many people to overnight here, accommodation in Franz Josef is tight throughout the summer. Between November and March (and particularly February), you should aim to make **reservations** at least a week in advance, more for swankier places.

58 On Cron 58 Cron St ☎03 752 0627, ⓦ58oncron.co.nz; map p.486. Stylish units decorated with Italian fabrics and equipped with queen- or super-king-size beds; some rooms have spa baths. Guests have access to gas BBQs amid native bush gardens. Doubles $175, spa studios $200

Chateau Franz 8–10 Cron St ☎03 752 0738, ⓦchateaunz.co.nz; map p.486. A popular backpacker-oriented complex with bags of character; common areas are festooned with old photographs and memorabilia. The dorms, among the cheapest beds in town, were recently upgraded; double rooms are good value too. Free soup and popcorn, fun common areas and a lively events schedule complete the package. Dorms $31, doubles $125

Franz Josef Top 10 Holiday Park SH6, 1km north of town ☎03 7520735, ⓦfranzjoseftop10.co.nz; map p.486. High-spec rural campsite with a good range of tent and powered sites (on grass), cabins and units. Cabins $90, camping per site $51

Glow Worm 27 Cron St ☎ 0800 151027, ⓦ sircedrics.co.nz; map p.486. Small, homely hostel owned by the same crew as *Chateau Franz* with a well-equipped kitchen, six-bed dorms and nicer four-shares with their own bathrooms, plus comfy motel-style rooms. Free soup, popcorn and spa. Dorms $30, doubles $110

★ **Holly Homestead B&B** SH6, 1.5km north of town ☎ 03 752 0299, ⓦ hollyhomestead.co.nz; map p.486. Comfort in an attractive two-storey 1920s home with five en-suite rooms, one being a super deluxe king suite (one with bathtub). The owners give a warm welcome, there's a deck with mountain views and rates include a delicious full breakfast. The caveats: it's only suitable for those 12 and over and is closed outside summer (call for seasonal openings). $265

Punga Grove 40 Cron St ☎ 03 752 0001, ⓦ pungagrove.co.nz; map p.486. A choice of modern rooms ranging from nicely furnished doubles to vast two-bed apartments; the best, however, are the rainforest studios that back onto the bush and come with gas fires, underfloor heating and spa bath. $185, rainforest studios $210

Rainforest Retreat 46 Cron St ☎ 0800 873 346, ⓦ rainforestretreat.co.nz; map p.486. Sprawling twelve-acre complex comprising a hotel, backpackers and campervan park (sites from $23 per person), plus the adjoining *Monsoon* bar and restaurant. The backpacker rooms are popular with bus tours, while the (mercifully quieter) hotel rooms are styled after luxurious log cabins. Nineteen new deluxe rooms nestle into the rainforest, the sheer size of this place soaks it all up. There's also a spa and sauna. Dorms $30, doubles $160

YHA Franz Josef 2 Cron St ☎ 03 752 0754, ⓔ yhafranzjosef@yha.co.nz; map p.486. Modern, well-run hostel on the edge of town with the southernmost rooms overlooking bushland, where you'll hear a joyful dawn chorus. A spacious kitchen, clean comfortable rooms (some en suite), BBQ area and free sauna make it a decent choice. Dorms $32, doubles $125

EATING

Franz Josef's relatively remote location keeps prices high. Even if you're self-catering you can expect to pay over the odds for a limited stock of **groceries**.

Blue Ice Café Main Rd, between Cowan and Condon sts ☎ 03 752 0707; map p.486. The modern and airy restaurant downstairs serves imaginative and tasty mains ($20–36) and pizzas to take away or eat in the unreconstructed upstairs bar, where the free pool table and music draw in a lively crowd most nights. Owns the village Hummerzine. Daily 8am–9pm, bar until late.

★ **King Tiger** 70 Cron St ☎ 03 752 0060, ⓦ kingtiger.co.nz; map p.486. Decorated with photographs of Mahatma Gandhi and Mao Zedong, the menu (and decor) at this atmospheric "Eastern Eating House" sprawls from India to China by way of Bangkok, but the Indian dishes are the stars, with delicious and reasonably priced curries – none over $20 – making it a great change from the norm. Daily 7.30am–late.

The Landing Main Rd, at Cowan St ☎ 03 752 0229, ⓦ thelandingbar.co.nz; map p.486. Popular, swish-looking café/bar, with loads of outdoor seating (replete with blankets, ranks of patio heaters and a fire pit), serving substantial mains ($19.50–42) including a decent range of vegetarian options and lighter meals such as steamed mussels in white wine. Pizzas $19.50–35.50. Daily 7.30am–late.

Monsoon 46 Cron St ☎ 0800 873346, ⓦ rainforest retreat.co.nz; map p.486. Convivial spot at the *Rainforest Retreat*, serving Kiwi comfort food – think stuffed chicken with roast potatoes and coleslaw. Pizza and gourmet burgers too. From around 9pm, the serious business of drinking takes over (its motto: "it rains, we pour"). Daily 4.30pm–late.

Fox Glacier

The village of **FOX GLACIER** (Weheka), 24km south of Franz Josef, is scattered over an outwash plain of the Fox and Cook rivers, and services the local farming community and passing sightseers. Everything of interest is beside SH6 or Cook Flat Road, which skirts the scenic Lake Matheson on the way to the former gold settlement and seal colony at Gillespies Beach. The foot of the glacier itself is around 7km to the southeast.

ARRIVAL AND DEPARTURE   FOX GLACIER

By bus InterCity and NakedBus buses stop by Fox Glacier Guides in the centre of the village.

Destinations Franz Josef (4 daily; 30min); Greymouth (1–2 daily; 4hr); Haast (2 daily; 2hr 30min); Hokitika (1–2 daily; 3hr); Makarora (daily; 4hr); Nelson (1–2 daily; 11hr); Queenstown (2 daily; 7hr 30min); Wanaka (2 daily; 5–6hr).

9

GETTING AROUND

By shuttle bus Fox Glacier Shuttles & Tours (📞0800 369287) goes to the glacier ($15 return) and Lake Matheson ($18 return). They also go to Gillespies Beach (price on demand, depending on numbers) and Franz Josef for a very reasonable $30 return.

INFORMATION

Tourist information DOC, SH6 (Mon–Fri 10am–2pm; 📞03 751 0807, ✉foxglacier@doc.govt.nz). The office has displays concentrating on lowland forests and glaciation; visit to get advice on conditions around the glacier valley.

TOURS AND ACTIVITIES

Fox Glacier suffered from major ice collapses in 2014, which saw several ice-based tours suspended indefinitely – the best way to get onto the ice these days is to fly. The Fox Glacier airfield and helipads are quieter than those at Franz Josef, but a similar range of flights is on offer; Mount Cook is closer here, meaning that flights over the mountain here are shorter, and slightly cheaper.

WALKS

Don't miss the Fox Glacier just because you've already seen Franz Josef; the approaches are different and their characters distinct, the Fox Valley being less sheer but with more impressive rockfalls. Check the DOC's *Glacier Update* (posted at Fox Glacier Guides and the DOC office) before heading up the valley to check that the roads and trails around the glacier are open.

Te Weheka Walkway/Cycleway While drivers speed up the imaginatively named Glacier Access Road, it's possible for energetic types to walk or bike between the village and glacier; a broad gravel path connects the two, winding through dripping rainforest for 4km before joining the road for the last stretch, which is occasionally rerouted as "dead" ice under the roadway gradually melts.

Minnehaha Walk (1km; 20min loop). Branching off from Te Weheka Walkway is this short flat path through lush bush that's alive with glowworms after dark.

Fox Glacier Valley Walk The walk to the edge of the glacier begins from the car park at the end of Glacier Access Road. The rough 1.3km path (1hr) leads over a series of landslips and creeks before climbing steeply up to a viewpoint with great views over the glacier's icy snout.

River Walk (2km; 30min). Halfway along the Glacier Access Road, this walk crosses a historic swingbridge to the Glacier Valley Viewpoint on Glacier View Road, which runs 3km along the opposite side of the Fox River.

Chalet Lookout Walk (4km; 1hr 30min return; 150m ascent). From the Glacier Valley Viewpoint, this route climbs relatively moderately for stupendous glacier and mountain views, passing the former site of The Chalet, a hut where Victorian tourists could lunch looking down at the terminal ice – sadly, both the hut and the ice below are no more. The path ends with an unbridged crossing of Mills Creek, which often floods the track after heavy rainfall, periodically closing it.

Lake Matheson Circuit (4.5km; 1hr 30min). It's difficult to imagine a New Zealand calendar or picture book without a photo of Mount Cook and Mount Tasman mirrored in Lake Matheson, 5km northwest of town along Cook Flat Road. A well-signposted boardwalk through lovely native bush encircles the lake, which was formed by an iceberg left when the Fox Glacier retreated 14,000 years ago, giving everyone a chance for that perfect image, especially those who venture out for sunrise. The *Matheson Café*, by the Lake Matheson car park, serves superb food.

Peak Viewpoint About 5km beyond Lake Matheson on the road to Gillespies Beach, Peak Viewpoint is ideal for fabulous fine-day views of the top of the Fox Glacier and the snowcapped mountains.

Walks from Gillespies Beach A 20km drive from Fox Glacier Village along Cook Flat Road brings you to Gillespies Beach, a former gold-mining settlement with a small cemetery and a simple DOC campsite. From the campsite an excellent walk threads north parallel to the beach, past the scant remains of a 1940s gold dredge (30min return); to Gillespies Lagoon (1hr 15min return), a short Miners' Tunnel (1hr 40min return) and an often muddy track continues to the Galway Beach Seal Colony (3.6km return, 3hr 30min), a winter haul-out for New Zealand fur seals.

GLACIER HIKING, HELI-HIKING AND ICE CLIMBING

Fox Glacier Guides 44 Main Rd (SH6) 📞0800 111600, 🌐foxguides.co.nz. A smaller concern than the outfits operating on Franz Josef Glacier, Fox Glacier's recent instability meant that at the time of writing, the tours available were either gentle walks around the terminal face (2hr; $69) or full-on heli-adventures (heli-hiking, 4hr, $450; heli-ice climbing, 8–9hr, $575499), flying up and over any unsafe sections. They offer an Extreme option too.

SCENIC FLIGHTS AND SKYDIVING

Fox & Franz Josef Heliservices Inside Fox Glacier Guides 📞0800 800793, 🌐scenic-flights.co.nz. Besides

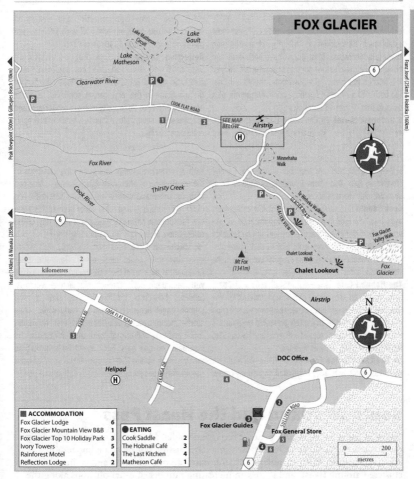

FOX GLACIER

ACCOMMODATION

Fox Glacier Lodge	6
Fox Glacier Mountain View B&B	1
Fox Glacier Top 10 Holiday Park	3
Ivory Towers	5
Rainforest Motel	4
Reflection Lodge	2

● EATING	
Cook Saddle	2
The Hobnail Café	3
The Last Kitchen	4
Matheson Café	1

similar deals to those on offer in Franz Josef, here there's also the option to fly-by Mount Cook's west face (30min; $325).

Skydive NZ ☎0800 751 0080, ⑩skydivefox.co.nz. Flying out of Fox Glacier's tiny airstrip, with tandem skydives from 9000ft ($249), 13,000ft ($299) and 16,500ft ($399).

ACCOMMODATION

Fox's range of places to stay is limited; **book** as far ahead as you can and be prepared for resort prices. The basic, free DOC **campsite** at Gillespies Beach is popular in summer.

Fox Glacier Lodge Sullivan Rd ☎0800 369800, ⑩foxglacierlodge.com; map p.491. A pine-lined alpine chalet with attractively furnished en-suite rooms (where a buffet breakfast is included), a range of self-contained apartments and campervan hook-ups outside. Camping per site $30, doubles $255

Fox Glacier Mountain View B&B 1 Williams Drive, 2km off SH6 ☎03 751 0770,

⑩foxglaciermountainview.co.nz; map p.491. Welcoming, modern B&B with three en suites and a separate self-contained studio in its own grounds on the edge of town with great mountain views. The decor is slightly dated, but rooms and beds are very comfortable, and a full breakfast is included. $195

Fox Glacier Top 10 Holiday Park Kerrs Rd ☎03 751 0821, ⑩top10.co.nz; map p.491. Comprehensive motor camp with ranks of powered sites, spacious studio units, and great mountain views. Camping per site $52, studio units $130

Ivory Towers Sullivan Rd ☎03 751 0838, ⓦivorytowerslodge.co.nz; map p.491. Fox's most established backpackers is friendly, clean(ish) and colourfully decorated. Most dorms have both beds and bunks, while the pleasant doubles share the bathrooms. The kitchen has plenty of elbow room, there's a sauna, spa bath and a TV room for those rainy afternoons, plus bikes to rent. Dorms $32, doubles $86

Rainforest Motel 15 Cook Flat Rd, 200m off SH6 ☎03 751 0140, ⓦrainforestmotel.co.nz; map p.491. Log cabins with attractive and well-priced studios and one-bedroom units, all with kitchens and plenty of space. Studios $130, units $145

Reflection Lodge 141 Cook Flat Rd, 1.5km off SH6 ☎03 751 0707, ⓦreflectionlodge.co.nz; map p.491. So named because of the glorious reflection of the mountains in the large garden pond, this romantic homestay offers just three pretty rooms in comfortable and spacious surroundings, plus it's run by a family of helicopter enthusiasts. $230

EATING

Self-catering supplies are available at the Fox General Store (daily 8am–8pm) from a surprisingly wide range at unsurprisingly elevated prices.

Cook Saddle SH6 ☎03 751 0700, ⓦcooksaddle.co.nz; map p.491. A local favourite, this Western-inspired, all-wood saloon dishes out massive portions of good-quality food (mains $18–32) from lentil loaf to pork spare ribs, served at tealight-lit tables. There's regular live music in the summer and a pool table. Daily noon–late.

The Hobnail Café 44 Main Rd (SH6) ☎03 751 0825; map p.491. In the alpine-chalet surroundings of Fox Glacier Guides, this café has a better-than-average selection of cabinet food, plus hearty, nicely presented breakfasts – their bubble and squeak topped with eggs and bacon ($16) is particularly good. Daily 8am–4pm.

★ **The Last Kitchen** Corner of Sullivans Rd and SH6 ☎03 751 0058; map p.491. Situated on a sunny corner with an attractive interior and interesting variations of the usual suspects, often with Asian accents – blue cod with coriander and cashew pesto with wok-fried veg ($27), for example – and a full liquor licence, this place hits the spot and has more atmosphere than most of the competition. Mains $21–34. Daily 11.30am–late.

★ **Matheson Café** Cook Flat Rd ☎03 751 0878, ⓦlakematheson.com; map p.491. Fantastic café/restaurant at the start of the walk around Lake Matheson, with mountain views through big picture windows. Fabulous breakfasts ($8.50–21.19.50) such as the salmon bagel Benedict reward an early walk, while lunches include a particularly fine lamb burger. Afternoon coffee and cake will coincide with the sun catching the mountains on fine days. Book ahead for summertime evening meals (mains $24–36) such as slow-cooked lamb shoulder with pea purée. Nov–March daily 8am–9pm.

South Westland and the Haast Pass

South of the glaciers, the West Coast feels even wilder. Many visitors do the run from the glaciers to Wanaka or Queenstown in a day, missing out on some fine remote country. Facilities aren't completely absent: many accommodation and eating places are clustered around **Haast**, and there's an increasing number of other pit stops along the way. There wasn't a road through here until 1965 and the final section of tarmac wasn't laid on the Haast Pass until 1995.

SH6 mostly runs inland, passing the start of the hike to the **Welcome Flat Hot Springs** and through moss-clad rimu forests as far as **Knight's Point**, where it returns to the coast along the edge of the Haast Coastal Plain, whose stunning **coastal dune systems** shelter lakes and some fine stands of soaring kahikatea. The plain continues south past the scattered township of Haast to the site of the short-lived colonial settlement at **Jackson Bay**. From Haast, SH6 veers inland over the Haast Pass to the former timber town of **Makarora**, not strictly part of the West Coast but moist enough to share some of its characteristics and a base for the excellent **Gillespie Pass** Tramp.

Bruce Bay

One place you might like to break your journey is **Bruce Bay**, where the road briefly parallels a long driftwood-strewn beach perfect for an atmospheric stroll. Recently tour bus drivers have been stopping long enough for their occupants to erect small cairns or etch their names on the rocks – though at least the former are quickly obliterated by high tide or good wind.

Paringa River and Lake Paringa

SH6, 17km south of Bruce Bay

Where SH6 crosses the **Paringa River** a plaque marks the southern limit of Thomas Brunner's 1846–48 explorations. Buses stop nearby at the *Salmon Farm* on SH6 for an overpriced snack or lunch. A better bet is to pick up some delicious hot or cold smoked salmon to take away and continue 8km south to the northern shores of trout-filled **Lake Paringa** and DOC's simple but beautifully sited *Lake Paringa campsite* ($8).

The Monro Beach Walk

SH6, 19km south of Lake Paringa • 5km; 1hr 30min return

The **Monro Beach Walk** leads through lovely fern-filled forest to a rocky spot of shoreline where you might see rare **Fiordland crested penguins**, particularly in early morning and late afternoon. They're mainly around during the spring breeding season, but occasionally reappear between January and March, when they come ashore to moult – though even in the absence of penguins the scenery and serenity justify taking the walk.

Knight's Point and Ship Creek

Knight's Point is on SH6, 23km south of Lake Paringa

The highway finally returns to the coast at **Knight's Point**, where a roadside marker commemorates the linking of Westland and Otago by road in 1965. Ahead lies the **Haast Coastal Plain**, which kicks off at the tea-coloured **Ship Creek**, ten winding kilometres ahead, where a picnic area and information panels by a beautiful, long, surf-pounded beach mark the start of two lovely twenty-minute walks: the **Kahikatea Swamp Forest Walk**, a wheelchair-accessible loop upriver through swampy kahikatea (white pine) forest, and the **Dune Lake Walk** along the coast to a dune-trapped and reed-filled lake – the latter an opportunity to see how forests have gradually colonized the sandy coastal plain.

From Ship Creek it's only another 15km to the 750m-long Haast River Bridge, the longest single-lane bridge in the country, immediately before Haast Junction.

Haast

Haast is initially a confusing place, with three tiny communities all taking the name: **Haast Junction**, at the intersection of SH6 and the minor road to Jackson Bay, **Haast Beach**, 4km along the Jackson Bay Road, and **Haast Township**, the largest settlement, 3km along SH6 towards Haast Pass and Wanaka.

ARRIVAL, INFORMATION AND TOURS   HAAST

By bus InterCity and NakedBus stop outside the *Fantail Café*, but you really need your own vehicle to get around.
Tourist information The DOC Visitor Centre is at the corner of SH6 and Jackson Bay Rd, Haast Junction (daily Nov–April 9am–6pm; May–Oct 9am–4.30pm; ☏ 03 750 0809, ✉ haastvc@doc.govt.nz). Informative displays on all aspects of the local environment, plus the 20-minute *Edge of Wilderness* film (shown on demand; $3). Local

information is also available at ⓦ haastnz.com.
Supplies Fuel is available in Haast Junction (24hr) and Haast Beach, and there's a small supermarket (with the only ATM) in Haast Township.
Waiatoto River Nature Safaris 1975 Haast–Jackson Bay Rd ☏ 0800 538723, ⓦ riversafaris.co.nz. Jetboat safaris (3 daily, Oct to late April; $199, 1 daily in winter leaves 11am) comprising a 2hr wilderness ride up

9

GILLESPIE PASS: THE WILKIN AND YOUNG VALLEYS CIRCUIT

This tramp over the 1501m Gillespie Pass links the upper valley of the Young River with that of the **Siberia Stream** and the **Wilkin River**. The scenery is a match for any of the more celebrated valleys further south, but is tramped by a fraction of the folk on the Routeburn or the Greenstone tracks.

Since a landslip dammed the north branch of the Young River in 2007, the valley has been open to trampers only on the condition that they avoid the entire river valley in the event of heavy rain, in case the potentially unstable dam gives way. Check at the DOC office if you're unsure whether to tackle it or not.

DOC's *Gillespie Pass, Wilkin Valley Tracks* leaflet ($2) has all the detail you need for the walk, though the Topo50 *Makarora* and *Mount Pollux* **maps** are useful. The route can be divided up into smaller chunks, using planes and jetboats, but the full circuit (58km) takes three days – more likely four if you make the worthwhile side-trip to Lake Crucible.

ACCESS AND ACCOMMODATION

All the **huts** ($15; no advance booking) in the Wilkin and Young valleys are equipped with mattresses and heating (but not cooking) stoves; hut **tickets** and backcountry hut **passes** are available from the DOC office in Makarora. The walk is typically done up the Young Valley and down the Wilkin and starts with a crossing of the braided Makarora River; if you don't fancy getting your feet wet or if you lack river-crossing experience, take a jetboat to the start, or use the **Blue-Young Link Track**, an extension of the Blue Pools Track, which crosses the river via a swingbridge 9km north of Makarora, adding 2hr and 7km to the first day's walk.

At the other end, it's a good idea to prearrange a jetboat **pick-up** from Kerin, unless you want to take your chances with river crossings or a stand-by backflight out of Siberia Valley.

THE ROUTE

Day 1: Young and Makarora rivers confluence to Young Hut (20km; 6–7hr; 500m ascent) The Young Valley is signposted on the left of SH6, 2.5km north of Makarora. Cross the stile and follow orange poles to the confluence of the Young and Makarora rivers.Once you're across the Makarora, the track traces the true left bank of the Young River through beech forest to Young Forks, where there is a campsite (free). After the bridge, the track follows the South Branch, climbing steeply (100m), before traversing a series of unstable slips to reach Stag Creek. From here it's a steady climb up through forest to the Young Hut (20 bunks).

Day 2: Young Hut to Siberia Hut (12km; 6–8hr; 700m ascent, 1000m descent) You've another strenuous day ahead, first up to the tree line overlooked by the 2202m Mount Awful, apparently named in wonder rather than horror. Then it's over the Gillespie Pass, a steep and lengthy ascent eventually following snow poles to a saddle; it'll take four hours to reach this fabulous, barren spot with views across the snowcapped northern peaks of the Mount Aspiring National Park. Grassy slopes descend steeply to Gillespie Stream, which is followed to its confluence with the Siberia Stream, from where it's a gentle, undulating hour downstream to Siberia Hut, staffed by a warden in the summer. Keen trampers might tag on a side-trip to Lake Crucible (4–5hr return) before cantering down to the hut. You can spend two nights at Siberia Hut and do the Lake Crucible side-trip on the spare day.

Lake Crucible side-trip (14km; 6–7hr return; 500m ascent) From the Siberia Hut, follow the true left bank of the Siberia Stream a short distance until you see Crucible Stream cascading in a deep gash on the far side. Ford Siberia Stream and ascend through the bush along the path that enters the forest on the true left of Crucible Stream. It is hard going, and route-finding among the alpine meadows higher up can be difficult, but the deep alpine lake tucked under the skirts of Mount Alba and choked with small icebergs is ample reward. Planes fly in and out of the Siberia Valley airstrip, and you can take your chance on "backloading" flights out.

Day 3: Siberia Hut to Kerin Forks (7km; 2–3hr; 100m ascent) Enter the bush at the southern end of Siberia Flats on the true left bank of Siberia Stream and descend away from the stream then zigzag steeply down to the Wilkin River and the Kerin Forks Hut (10 bunks), where many trampers prearrange to be met by a jetboat. If it has rained heavily, fording the Makarora lower down will be impossible, so don't forgo the jetboat. The alternative is to walk from Kerin Forks to Makarora (15km; 4–5hr; 100m ascent, 200m descent), following the Wilkin River's true left bank, then crossing the Makarora upstream of the confluence.

the Waiatoto River from its estuary into the heart of the mountains, with the emphasis on appreciating history and scenery.

ACCOMMODATION AND EATING

Haast gets busy between Christmas and late February so it pays to book ahead. Opening hours at Haast's eating establishments can vary.

Collyer House B&B Jacksons Bay Rd, 13km south of Haast Junction ☎03 750 0022, ⍟collyerhouse.co.nz. Welcoming luxury accommodation with four modern en suites, all with distant sea views and sizeable cooked breakfasts. **$250**

Fantail Café Marks Rd, Haast Township ☎03 750 0055. Friendly but workaday tearoom spread across several rooms. Serves breakfasts (including bacon butties, $10), whitebait patties ($15), cakes, sandwiches and coffee. Daily 8am–3pm.

Hard Antler Bar Marks Rd, Haast Township ☎03 750 0034. Locals' favourite, with antlers hanging from the rafters, ample bar meals (mains $20–34) including a hearty venison casserole, and $6 beers. Daily 11am–9pm.

Heritage Park Lodge Marks Rd, Haast Township ☎03 750 0868, ⍟heritageparklodge.co.nz. The pick of places to stay in the township, this well-tended motel offers spacious and comfortable studios with pure-wool blankets, some with self-catering facilities. **$95**

Wilderness Accommodation Haast Township ☎03 750 0029, ⍟wildernessaccommodation.co.nz. Good-value spot combining a backpacker hostel with a series of motel studio units, all with access to a plant- and board game-filled lounge and kitchen. Something of a character, the owner is knowledgeable about the area and rents scooters – ideal for getting out to Jackson Bay. Dorms **$35**, doubles **$90**

The road to Jackson Bay

A modest number of inquisitive tourists make it 50km south of Haast to the fishing village of Jackson Bay. Leaving Haast Junction, the canopies of windswept roadside trees bunch together like cauliflower heads down to and beyond **Haast Beach**, 4km south, where there's a small shop and fuel.

Hapuka Estuary Walk and around

Opposite the *Haast Beach Holiday Park*, the **Hapuka Estuary Walk** (1km, 20min loop) follows a raised boardwalk over a brackish lagoon and through kowhai forest that gleams brilliant yellow in October and November. Sand dunes support rimu and kahikatea forest, and there are views out to the **Open Bay Islands**, once a major sealing area – it's now a **wildlife sanctuary** and breeding colony for fur seals and Fiordland crested penguins. Turn off after crossing Arawhata Bridge and follow the road for 3km to the easy one-hour return walk around **Lake Ellery**.

Jackson Bay

JACKSON BAY, 50km south of Haast on the Haast–Jackson Bay Road, is a former sealing station tucked into the curve of Jackson Head, which protects it from the worst of the westerlies. In 1875 it was chosen as the site of a town to rival Greymouth and Hokitika. Assisted migrants – Scandinavians, Germans, Poles and Italians – were expected to carve a living from tiny land allocations, with limited and irregular supplies. Sodden by rain, crops rotted, and people soon left in droves; a few stalwarts stayed, their descendants providing the core of today's residents, who eke out a meagre living from lobster and tuna fishing.

Try the **Wharekai Te Kou Walk** (1.6km, 40min return) across the low isthmus behind Jackson Head to Ocean Beach where you may see New Zealand fur seals. The **Smoothwater Track** (9.4km, 3–4hr return) traces an old settlers' track to the Smoothwater River, before following the river out to secluded Smoothwater Bay.

EATING AND DRINKING   JACKSON BAY

The Cray Pot ☎03 750 0035. There are no facilities in Jackson Bay, except for this rustic diner in an old railway carriage. It sells crayfish when they're in, and dishes up fantastic fresh-cooked fish and chips, seafood chowder and the like (mains $15–36) along with mugs of tea or coffee. It's a great place to get away from the incessant sandflies and gaze at the sea-tossed fishing boats through fake leadlight windows. Seasonal openings can vary, check their board up the road as you drive in. Mid-Sept to April noon–4pm, though sometimes as late as 7pm.

Haast Pass

From Haast it's nearly 150km over the **Haast Pass** (lower than both Arthur's Pass and Lewis Pass) to Wanaka – a journey from the rain-soaked forests of the West Coast to the parched, rolling grasslands of Central Otago. Ngai Tahu used the pass as a greenstone-trading route and probably introduced it to gold prospector Charles Cameron, the first Pakeha to cross through in 1863; he was closely followed by the more influential **Julius Von Haast**, who modestly named it after himself.

The road starts beside the broad **Haast River**, which, as the road climbs, narrows to a series of churning cascades through the **Gates of Haast** – this stretch of the SH6 was closed for months in 2013 after a landslide destroyed the road, tragically sweeping two Canadian tourists and their campervan into the river below. Check the weather forecast before you leave – mountain weather can change quickly and this is unforgiving terrain, with patchy or completely nonexistent mobile phone coverage. Numerous short and well-signposted walks, mostly to waterfalls on tributaries, spur off at intervals. The most celebrated are the **Thunder Creek Falls**, the roadside **Fantail Falls**, and the **Blue Pools Walk**, where an aquamarine stream issues from a narrow, icy gorge; swim if you dare. This is magnificent and wild country, and it's great area to linger awhile, **camping** in one of the DOC's toilets-and-water sites ($8/person): *Pleasant Flat*, 45km from Haast, or *Cameron Flat* 10km short of Makarora.

Makarora

Comprising a smattering of buildings, the hamlet of **MAKARORA**, midway between Haast and Wanaka, lies on the northern fringe of Mount Aspiring National Park. If

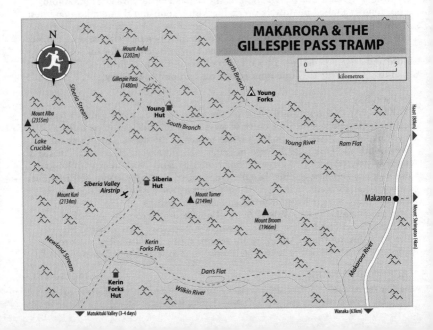

you're aching for the comforts of Wanaka and Queenstown there's little reason to stop, but casual hikers and keen trampers with a few days to spare should consider tackling the local walks.

In the nineteenth century the dense **forests** all about and the proximity of Lake Wanaka made Makarora the perfect spot for marshalling cut logs across the lake and coaxing them down the Clutha River southeast to the fledgling North Otago **gold towns** of Clyde and Cromwell. The 1964 creation of the national park and the beginning of the southern link highway through this wilderness in the 1960s paved the way for Makarora's increasing importance as the main northern access point to a region of majestic beauty, alpine vegetation and dense beech-filled valleys.

There are a couple of **short walks** close to Makarora. The **Makarora Bush Nature Walk** (15min loop) starts near the DOC office, and branching off it is the **Mount Shrimpton Track** (6km return; 5hr; 900m ascent), which climbs steeply up through silver beech to the bushline, offering fabulous views over the Makarora Valley.

INFORMATION AND TOURS   MAKARORA

Tourist information DOC, SH6 (Dec–Feb daily 8am–5pm; occasionally staffed at other times; ☎03 443 8365, ✉mtaspiringgvc@doc.govt.nz). The office has information, maps and hut tickets for tramps, and advice on the Gillespie Pass Tramp.

Siberia Experience ☎0800 345666, ⓦsiberia experience.co.nz. The 4hr Siberia Experience tour ($395) includes a fixed-wing flight into the remote Siberia Valley, a 3hr tramp to the Wilkin River and a jetboat ride back to Makarora; the same deal but with an extended flight of an extra 25min is $495.

Wilkin River Jets ☎0800 538945, ⓦwilkinriverjets.co.nz. Operates jetboat taxis to and from the Gillespie Pass trailheads ($25 to the Young River Mouth minimum three people, $110 from Kerin Forks, minimum five people), in addition to a range of standard jetboat trips and helicopter-hike-jetboat combos.

ACCOMMODATION AND EATING

Boundary Creek SH6. At the head of Lake Wanaka right by the lakeshore, this peaceful campsite has plenty of sheltered grass and gravel sites, along with toilets and tank water; it's basic but idyllically situated. __$8__

Makarora Tourist Centre SH6 ☎03 443 8372, ⓦmakarora.co.nz. Makarora's epicentre is this friendly jack-of-all-trades. The shop (daily: summer 8am–7pm; winter 8am–5pm) sells fuel and basic groceries, and there's a wood-beamed café/bar (daily 8am–late) serving breakfast, sandwiches and buffet lunches, plus basic steak, chicken and veggie evening meals (daily 5.30–8.30pm; mains $20–30). There's also camping ($12) and a range of good-value accommodation in A-frame huts. En-suite dorms __$39__, doubles __$70__

Christchurch and Canterbury

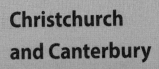

AKAROA

Christchurch and Canterbury

The Canterbury region is one of the most varied and visually stunning areas of New Zealand, with expansive pasturelands wedged between snowy mountains and a rugged coast. The main hub is the nation's third city, Christchurch, tragically devastated by the 2011 earthquake but now re-emerging as a dynamic metropolis of contemporary design, street art and chic restaurants. Inland, Canterbury's defining feature is the icy sawtooth ridge of the Southern Alps that peaks at New Zealand's loftiest summit, 3754m-high Aoraki/Mount Cook.

Southeast of Christchurch, the hilly **Banks Peninsula** sticks out into the South Pacific, indented with numerous bays and harbours, culminating in the picturesque "French village" of **Akaroa**. To the northwest, forested **Lewis Pass** provides access to the tranquil spa town of **Hanmer Springs** before passing the more rustic hot pools at **Maruia Springs**. Further south, both road and rail head through the spectacular **Arthur's Pass National Park**, with its abundance of hiking trails.

Southwest of Christchurch, roads lead across the Canterbury Plains towards **Methven**, the base for **Mount Hutt**-bound skiers and summertime walkers exploring **Mount Somers** – often dry when Arthur's Pass is wet and enveloped in cloud.

The southern half of the region spills into the sun-scorched grasslands of **Mackenzie Country**, an area renowned for the unearthly blues of its glacier-fed lakes, **Tekapo**, **Pukaki** and **Ohau**. **Aoraki/Mount Cook Village**, huddled at the foot of the mountain, is the starting point of numerous hikes, glacial lake trips and heli-trekking and heli-skiing. Yet further south, the road toward Wanaka and Queenstown passes through New Zealand's gliding capital, **Omarama**, before heading over the dramatic Lindis Pass, while on the coast, the up-and-coming destination of **Timaru** lies close to a series of important Māori rock painting sites.

Christchurch

The South Island's largest city, **CHRISTCHURCH** (Otautahi in Māori) was devastated by an **earthquake** that struck on 22 February 2011, killing 185 people. Much

---

THE FIRST FOUR SHIPS

Neighbouring Lyttelton had already been established as a whaling port in the 1830s when the **First Four Ships** arrived in December 1850, conveying the 773 "Canterbury Pilgrims" eager to found a new settlement at the southern end of Pegasus Bay. The *Charlotte Jane*, *Randolph*, *Sir George Seymour* and *Cressy* were sent by the **Canterbury Association**, formed in 1849 in London by Edward Wakefield (who had already helped to establish the Wellington colony) and John Godley (a graduate of Oxford's Christ Church College), and sponsored by the Church of England (the Archbishop of Canterbury was president). The association had the utopian aim of creating a middle-class, Anglican community in New Zealand in which the moralizing culture of Victorian England could prosper. By the end of 1851 there were some 3000 British settlers in the area, but the millenarian aspirations upon which the city was founded soon faded as people got on with the exhausting business of carving out a new life in unfamiliar terrain – **wool** rapidly became the main export on which the new city's fortunes grew. Nevertheless, the association's ideals had a profound effect on the cultural identity of the city, and descent from those who came on the First Four Ships still carries social cachet among members of the Christchurch elite.

CHRISTCHURCH

Highlights

❶ Christchurch rebuild Take in a creative blend of coffee shops, art galleries and contemporary architecture. See page 506

❷ Akaroa and Summit Road Traverse the top of the Banks Peninsula on this panoramic road to Akaroa, where you can swim with dolphins. See page 525

❸ Hiking Arthur's Pass Soak up the Southern Alps scenery from the highest mountain pass on the island. See page 538

❹ Skiing or biking Mt Hutt South Island's premier ski field offers plenty of fun in the winter, as well as an extensive bike park in the warmer months. See page 543

❺ Rafting Rangitata Experience New Zealand's best whitewater rafting, through the Rangitata River Gorge. See page 545

❻ Tekapo stargazing Allow yourself to be mesmerized by the ultra-clear night skies visible from atop Mount John. See page 548

❼ Aoraki/Mount Cook Tramp the spectacular trails around New Zealand's tallest peak, or take a closer look at the incredible Tasman Glacier. See page 551

❽ Gliding Omarama Float majestically over the Southern Alps from New Zealand's gliding capital in Omarama. See page 552

HIGHLIGHTS ARE MARKED ON THE MAP ON PAGE 502

of the city centre was subsequently demolished, and the former genteel, English Victorian architecture of Christchurch has largely disappeared. Though some key historical sights have been restored, what is rising in its place is a stylish showcase of contemporary design, with glass and steel towers, lavish street murals and pedestrian-friendly parks and promenades. For anyone that visited the city before the quake, the transformation will seem startling. Much of the centre is likely to remain a vast construction site well into the 2020s – indeed, the Christchurch rebuild has attracted

CHRISTCHURCH AND CANTERBURY

HIGHLIGHTS

1 Christchurch rebuild
2 Akaroa and Summit Road
3 Hiking Arthur's Pass
4 Skiing or biking Mt Hutt
5 Rafting Rangitata
6 Tekapo stargazing
7 Aoraki/Mount Cook
8 Gliding Omarama

CHRISTCHURCH PASS

Four of Christchurch's most popular activities – riding the tram, touring the Botanic Gardens, riding the Gondola and punting on the Avon – are included in the **Christchurch Pass**, available for $86 ($25 for children 5–15) at ⓦchristchurchattractions. nz or at 109 Worcester St (Shop 13; ☎03 366 7830), in Cathedral Junction; the pass saves you around $25 if you do all four. You can visit the attractions on different days, and the pass includes free shuttle transport to the Gondola.

10

so much investment analysts regard it as major spur to New Zealand's economic growth since 2014.

Not everything has changed: strolling (or **punting**) through the **Botanic Gardens** combines well with the fabulous Victorian gem of **Canterbury Museum** and a visit to the nearby Neo-Gothic **Arts Centre**. But what's special is the new stuff. Significant new buildings include the wonderful **Cardboard Cathedral**, the huge developments along the **Cashel Street Mall** and the **New Central Library**, but throughout the CBD you'll stumble across curiosities curated by community-minded groups such as **Gap Filler** (ⓦgapfiller.org.nz) and **Rekindle** (ⓦrekindle.org. nz), from the **Dance-O-Mat** (a coin-operated dancefloor) and Super Street Arcade to mini golf holes and sculpture installations. In the coming years, Christchurch looks set to become one of the world's most fascinating cities.

The city centre

Cathedral Square has always been the heart of Christchurch, with ChristChurch Cathedral as its focal point – it's still the place in the city where you can feel the magnitude of the 2011 earthquake destruction most keenly. The cathedral will remain in ruins for some time and the Italianate 1879 **Chief Post Office** remains boarded up, its future uncertain (a resolution on the building's insurance was still pending at the time of research). New projects look set to change things radically, however, with the new **Distinction Christchurch** hotel, **Christchurch Convention Centre** (Whare Rūnanga) and **Tūranga (New Central Library)** complete by 2019. Some of the square's monuments have endured, notably Neil Dawson's 18m-high *Chalice* sculpture, erected in 2000 to mark the Millennium and Canterbury's 150th anniversary. The popular **Friday Street Food Market** (Fri 11am–9pm) is likely to continue in some form in the square despite the new development.

ChristChurch Cathedral

Cathedral Square • Currently closed • ⓦcathedralconversations.co.nz, ⓦrestorechristchurchcathedral.co.nz

Half-ruined and virtually abandoned after the 2011 earthquake, the fate of the Gothic Revival **ChristChurch Cathedral** was confirmed only in 2017, when the Anglican Church finally decided to save the building. The main sticking point was the estimated $104 million cost of a restoration – a new building would have been much cheaper (the cathedral's insurance payout was only $42 million). Local enthusiasts launched a vocal campaign to save the cathedral, and at the time of research it looked like a combination of government money and private donations would be enough to complete the project. The **new cathedral** will probably blend Victorian and contemporary design, but is unlikely to be completed before 2025.

The original church was conceived in 1858 by George Gilbert Scott (architect of London's St Pancras Station) who had intended it to be built of wood. The design was later adapted by English-born architect **Benjamin Mountford**, reworked in stone and completed in 1904. Mountford was largely responsible for creating Christchurch's pre-quake architectural identity, fashioning volcanic "bluestone" and creamy Oamaru limestone into his English neo-Gothic creations.

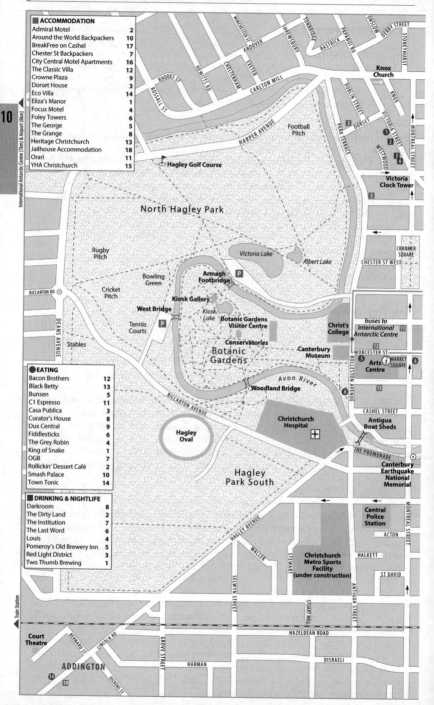

ACCOMMODATION

Admiral Motel	2
Around the World Backpackers	10
BreakFree on Cashel	17
Chester St Backpackers	7
City Central Motel Apartments	16
The Classic Villa	12
Crowne Plaza	9
Dorset House	3
Eco Villa	14
Eliza's Manor	1
Focus Motel	4
Foley Towers	6
The George	5
The Grange	8
Heritage Christchurch	13
Jailhouse Accommodation	18
Orari	11
YHA Christchurch	15

EATING

Bacon Brothers	12
Black Betty	13
Bunsen	5
C1 Espresso	11
Casa Publica	3
Curator's House	8
Dux Central	9
Fiddlesticks	6
The Grey Robin	4
King of Snake	1
OGB	7
Rollickin' Dessert Café	2
Smash Palace	10
Town Tonic	14

DRINKING & NIGHTLIFE

Darkroom	8
The Dirty Land	2
The Institution	7
The Last Word	6
Louis	4
Pomeroy's Old Brewery Inn	5
Red Light District	3
Two Thumb Brewing	1

International Antarctic Centre (7km) & Airport (8km)

10

Train Station

Knox Church

Victoria Clock Tower

CRANMER SQUARE

CHESTER ST WEST

buses to International Antarctic Centre

Christ's College

WORCESTER ST

Arts Centre

MARKET SQUARE

North Hagley Park

Rugby Pitch

Victoria Lake

Albert Lake

Bowling Green

Armagh Footbridge

Cricket Pitch

Kiosk Gallery

West Bridge

Kiosk Lake

Botanic Gardens Visitor Centre

Tennis Courts

Conservatories

Botanic Gardens

Canterbury Museum

Stables

RICCARTON RD

DEANS AVENUE

RICCARTON AVENUE

Avon River

Woodland Bridge

CASHEL STREET

Antigua Boat Sheds

Hagley Oval

Christchurch Hospital

THE PROMENADE

Canterbury Earthquake National Memorial

Hagley Park South

Central Police Station

ACTON

HALKETT

ST DAVID

Christchurch Metro Sports Facility (under construction)

HAGLEY AVENUE

WALTER

SELWYN STREET

STEWART

STUART MILL

ANTIGUA STREET

MONTREAL STREET

HAZELDEAN ROAD

Court Theatre

ADDINGTON

BERNARD ST

LINCOLN RD

GROVE STREET

HARMAN

DICKENS ST

DISRAELI

Hagley Golf Course

Football Pitch

HARPER AVENUE

CARLTON MILL

RHODES ST

HEWITTS RD

ROSSALL ST

CHELTENHAM

EXETER

ANDOVER

WINCHESTER ST

SHREWSBURY

TONBRIDGE

RASTRICK

PAPANUI RD

DUBLIN STREET

PARK TERRACE

DORSET

KNOX

VICTORIA STREET

WESTWOOD

MONTREAL STREET

OXFORD

DERBY STREET

STONEYHURST

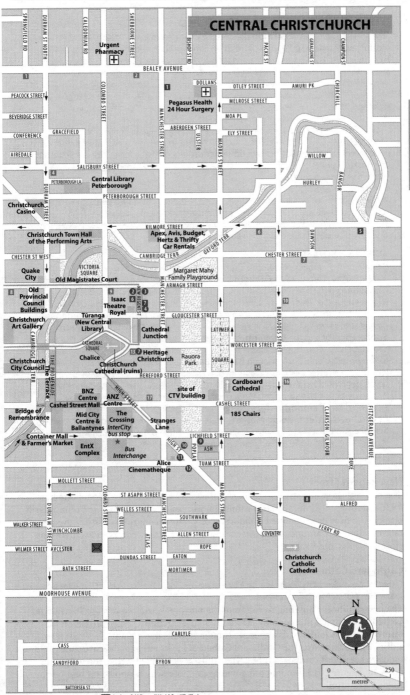

CENTRAL CHRISTCHURCH

10

SPRINGFIELD RD
DURHAM ST NORTH
CALEDONIAN RD
SHERBORNE STREET
BISHOP ST RD
PACKE ST
GERALDINE ST
CHAMPION ST

Urgent Pharmacy

BEALEY AVENUE

PEACOCK STREET

BEVERIDGE STREET

DOLLANS
Pegasus Health
24 Hour Surgery

OTLEY STREET
AMURI PK
MELROSE STREET
MOA PL
ELY STREET

CHURCHILL

CONFERENCE
GRACEFIELD

AIREDALE

COLOMBO STREET
MANCHESTER STREET
ABERDEEN STREET
ULSTER
MADRAS STREET

WILLOW
HURLEY
BANGOR

SALISBURY STREET

PETERBOROUGH LA.

Central Library Peterborough

PETERBOROUGH STREET

DURHAM STREET

Christchurch Casino

KILMORE STREET

Christchurch Town Hall of the Performing Arts

Apex, Avis, Budget, Hertz & Thrifty Car Rentals

CAMBRIDGE TERR

OXFORD TERR

CHESTER STREET

DAWSON

CHESTER ST WEST

Quake City

VICTORIA SQUARE

Old Magistrates Court

Margaret Mahy Family Playground

ARMAGH STREET

Old Provincial Council Buildings

Isaac Theatre Royal

REGENT ST

GLOUCESTER STREET

BARBADOES STREET

Christchurch Art Gallery

Tūranga (New Central Library)

Cathedral Junction

LATIMER

WORCESTER STREET

Christchurch City Council

CATHEDRAL SQUARE

Chalice

Heritage Christchurch

Rauora Park

SQUARE

THE PROMENADE
The Terrace

CAMBRIDGE TERR

ChristChurch Cathedral (ruins)

HEREFORD STREET

Cardboard Cathedral

BNZ Centre

Cashel Street Mall

ANZ Centre

HIGH STREET

site of CTV building

CASHEL STREET

185 Chairs

Bridge of Remembrance

Mid City Centre & Ballantynes

The Crossing

Stranges Lane

CLARKSON
GILMOUR
FITZGERALD AVENUE

Container Mall & Farmer's Market

EntX Complex

InterCity bus stop

Bus Interchange

Alice Cinematheque

LICHFIELD STREET

HIGH ST
POPLAR
ASH

TUAM STREET

DUKE

MOLLETT STREET

ST ASAPH STREET

WELLES STREET

QUILL

SOUTHWARK

MADRAS STREET

WILLIAMS

COVENTRY

ALFRED

FERRY RD

WALKER STREET

WINCHCOMBE

AVCESTER

WILMER STREET

BATH STREET

DURHAM STREET

COLOMBO STREET

ATLAS

ALLEN STREET

ROPE

EATON

DUNDAS STREET

MORTIMER

Christchurch Catholic Cathedral

MOORHOUSE AVENUE

N

CARLYLE

CASS

SANDYFORD

BYRON

BATTERSEA ST

0   250
metres

▼ Academy Gold Cinema (200m) & Port Hills (5km)

10

THE EARTHQUAKES AND THE REBUILD

The absence of really big **earthquakes** around Christchurch in the latter half of the twentieth century put everyone off their guard, so the 7.1 magnitude quake that hit the city at 4.35am on September 4, 2010, was unexpected. A few chimneys were dislodged but there was no major damage and no one was killed, but unfortunately the 6.3 magnitude aftershock that hit at lunchtime on **February 22, 2011**, was a very different story. Though it was weaker, this one was far shallower (5.95km deep versus 11km in 2010) and centred only 6.7km away (as opposed to 37.9km previously). It completely devastated the city centre and killed 185 people. More than seven thousand people were injured.

Outside the centre, the older, wealthier western suburbs were built on good land and withstood the quakes fairly well, but much of the housing in the eastern suburbs was built on reclaimed swamp that was prone to **liquefaction**: ground that became like quicksand during the quake. Foundations sank, roads buckled and drains gushed a mixture of ground water and waste from broken sewers.

In the aftermath, a three-square-kilometre zone enclosing much of the CBD was sealed off for buildings to be demolished and streets made safe; it took over **two years** for what was left of the centre to be reopened to the public. The government installed heavy-hitting Gerry Brownlee as minister with responsibility for the Canterbury Earthquake Recovery Authority (CERA), which was charged with the **rebuild**.

MOVING FORWARDS

Despite broad-ranging powers the city's reconstruction was frustratingly slow. In 2016, CERA was replaced by **Ōtākaro Limited** (ⓦ otakaroltd.co.nz) and **Regenerate Christchurch** (ⓦ regeneratechristchurch.nz), tasked with spurring overall redevelopment. By early 2019 the newly landscaped Victoria Square, Tūranga (New Central Library), Arts Centre, Christchurch Town Hall of the Performing Arts and the ambitious **Promenade** project (see page 507), should all be complete. The massive **Christchurch Metro Sports Facility** and the **Convention Centre** on Cathedral Square are slated for completion by 2020; the East Frame area of parks and residential development is unlikely to be complete until 2026 (though **Rauora Park** opened in 2018) and the new cathedral will take even longer. Private development has also been speeding up, with lots of fancy hotels opening downtown, new stylish South Island headquarters for Vodafone and PWC, shopping malls and entertainment complexes along Cashel Street (see page 507) and iconic **151 Cambridge Terrace**, designed by local architects Jasmax. A revamped **Christchurch International Market** should be open on Tuam Street by 2019, while **Science Alive!** (ⓦ sciencealive.co.nz) plans to reimagine the old Christchurch Court House complex as a $50 million science centre, to be open by 2019.

New Regent Street

The first real shopping street to reopen in the CBD was little **New Regent Street**, a 1930s Spanish Mission-style strip running north–south along which the tram merrily clanks. The neat pastel-painted buildings look pretty incongruous with all the shiny new development around, but make your way here for the centre's most interesting cluster of cafés and bars.

Cardboard Cathedral

234 Hereford St, overlooking Latimer Square • Nov–March Mon–Sat 9am–7pm, Sun 7.30am–7pm; April–Oct Mon–Sat 9am–5pm, Sun 7.30am–5pm • ⓣ 03 366 0046, ⓦ cardboardcathedral.org.nz

The first significant building to rise from the post-quake rubble was the **Transitional Cathedral**, designed pro bono by Japanese "disaster architect" Shigeru Ban on the former site of St John's parish church. Though it looks like a giant silver tent from a distance it's known as the **Cardboard Cathedral** for its elegant superstructure of 98 industrial-strength cardboard tubes. The 700-seat light-filled wedge threw open its doors in August 2013, sending out a message of hope which rippled far beyond the Anglican faithful.

Aside from the superstructure, massive paper tubes also form the cross behind the altar and the front of the pulpit. The walls are made from shipping containers, with timber and steel shoring everything up and clear polycarbonate sheeting as weatherproofing. The overall effect is far more beautiful than it might sound, and the building is intended as more than a short-term fix, with an estimated fifty-year design life.

185 Chairs and the CTV Building site

The devastated area surrounding the Cardboard Cathedral is slowly being developed into parks and gardens, but one block south on Cashel Street (at Madras St) lies Peter Majendie's **185 Chairs**, perhaps the most poignant **memorial** to those lost in the February 2011 quake. The 185 white-painted armchairs, stools, office chairs, etc have been adopted by the community, who replace a chair if one is stolen and whitewash the lot to mark each anniversary. Across the street lies the former site of the **Canterbury Television (CTV) building**, which collapsed in the earthquake killing 115 people (including 71 foreign students learning English, mostly young folks from China and Japan); the site is being developed as a series of gardens (including a central grove of cherry trees), in part to commemorate the victims.

Cashel Street Mall

Pedestrian **Cashel Street Mall** has been transformed in recent years, with a spate of stylish new shopping centres largely replacing the shipping containers that constituted the Re:START development after the quake. Subsequently dubbed the **Container Mall**, the eye-catching assortment of boutiques, cafés and food carts at Cashel and Oxford Terrace was formally closed at the start of 2018, but many of the vendors (and most likely some of the containers and food trucks) will be folded into the new **Farmers Market** complex being developed here. **The Crossing** (ⓦ thecrossing.co.nz) opened on Cashel Street in 2017, with high-end stores, a striking white-framed car park design and Paul Dibble's 2008 sculpture *Sleepwalker*, a bronze representation of Maui, the Polynesian mythological figure. Nearer the river, **The Terrace** (ⓦ theterrace.co.nz) features a series of stylish contemporary properties linked by laneways and first-floor air bridges, filled with bars and restaurants. One block over on Lichfield and Colombo, the **EntX** (Entertainment Central Christchurch) development (ⓦ entx.co.nz) will feature even more restaurants, a deluxe Hoyts Cinema and shops by 2019.

Bridge of Remembrance

The western end of Cashel Street Mall is framed by the stately arch dubbed the **Bridge of Remembrance**, built in 1924 overlooking the Avon River to commemorate locals who died in World War I (the names of those lost in subsequent conflicts were added later). Just to the north on the other side of the river, the **Park of Remembrance** features a bronze statue of **Henry Nicholas**, a local soldier who was awarded the Victoria Cross before being killed in action in 1918. White crosses symbolizing the war dead are usually arranged in rows in the park on key anniversaries.

The Promenade

One of the most ambitious of the city's post-quake projects, **The Promenade** has transformed the once busy thoroughfare of Oxford Terrace into a 2km pedestrian-only mall on the east bank of the **Avon River**, snaking through the heart of the city north and south of the Bridge of Remembrance. Art works and installations along both riverbanks include thirteen **Ngā Whāriki Manaaki**, Māori woven mats of welcome, printed on stone mosaic tiles and commemorating the Ngāi Tahu heritage of the region.

Canterbury Earthquake National Memorial
Promenade at Montreal St • Daily 24hr • ⓦ canterburyearthquakememorial.co.nz

10

CHRISTCHURCH BY TRAM

One of the city's biggest tourist attractions is its old **tramway**, only reinstalled in 1995 but with rolling stock largely made up of lovingly restored originals built between 1908 and 1925. Today, the driver-commentated trams weave a circuit past the Arts Centre, New Regent Street, Cashel Street Mall and Cathedral Square (every 15–20min; Sept–March 9am–6pm; April–Aug 10am–5pm; ☎ 03 366 7830, ⊕ christchurchattractions.nz). The $25 ticket allows you to get on and off all day, and children 15 and under are free (maximum of three per adult). There's even a **restaurant tram** (daily: March–Oct 7–9.30pm, Nov–Feb 7.30–10pm; $109), which does the circuit as you dine, leaving from Cathedral Junction.

Dedicated in 2017, the poignant **Canterbury Earthquake National Memorial** lines the south (east) bank of the Avon River near Montreal Street. The 111m-long wall is lined with marble panels inscribed with the names of those who lost their lives in the 2011 earthquake.

Antigua Boat Sheds

2 Cambridge Terrace • Daily: Oct–April 9am–5.30pm; May–Sept 9am–5pm (Boat Shed Café daily 7am–5pm) • Paddleboat $25/30min for two; single kayak $12/hr; double kayak $24/hr; rowboat $35/hr • ☎ 03 366 5885, ⊕ boatsheds.co.nz

You can explore the Avon River further from the **Antigua Boat Sheds** by renting a paddleboat, canoe or rowboat. If you'd rather lie back and enjoy it all, go punting instead, or just grab a coffee at the *Boat Shed Café*.

Christchurch Art Gallery

Corner of Worcester Blvd and Montreal St • Mon, Tues & Thurs–Sun 10am–5pm, Wed 10am–9pm • Free • ☎ 03 941 7300, ⊕ christchurchartgallery.org.nz

Completed in a dynamic contemporary style in 2003, the **Christchurch Art Gallery** survived the 2011 earthquake largely unscathed. Today the gallery is again one of New Zealand's best, its stylish spaces featuring primarily exhibitions of modern work that tend to change every three to six months. The permanent collection of around 6000 works of art features in a series of thematically arranged galleries on the first floor. Items rotate, but the sensitive Māori portraits of **Charles Goldie** should be displayed somewhere, along with the Modernist work of **Colin McMahon** and **Laura Herford**'s poignant *Little Emigrant*. **Rita Angus**' *Cass* depicts a lone customer on the platform of a desolate station (now on the *TranzAlpine* route), while **Bill Hammond**'s primordial works are liberally scattered with iconic bird-headed humanoids. The gallery's small European and British collection features mostly minor paintings from lesser-known eighteenth- and nineteenth-century artists – the likes of William Havell, Alfred East and Charles Eastlake – but contain some real gems nonetheless, notably *Among the Sandhills* by **Adrian Stokes**.

Centre of Contemporary Art

66 Gloucester St • Tues–Sun 10am–5pm • Free • ☎ 03 366 7261, ⊕ coca.org.nz

Aficionados should stroll around the back of the Art Gallery to the **Centre of Contemporary Art** (CoCA), which hosts changing exhibits from some of New Zealand's most lauded contemporary painters and sculptors, from **Ruth Watson** to Paemanu **Ngāi Tahu** artists.

Quake City

299 Durham St N, at Armagh St • Daily 10am–5pm • $20 • ☎ 03 365 8375, ⊕ canterburymuseum.com/whats-on/quake-city

To capture a sense of Christchurch's spirit during the city's darkest hours, visit Canterbury Museum's **Quake City**. Of course all the stats are here, but it is really about the human stories, the dead, the helpless and the helpers who stepped up when the need was greatest. Sobering TV reports, footage of the 2011 earthquake in process and emotional testimony from eyewitnesses make for a moving experience. A chilling long-distance photo taken seven minutes after the quake shows the city centre enshrouded in dust clouds. Huge spires, bells and statuary from the collapsed Anglican and Catholic cathedrals are displayed, and there's a more hopeful section on the long-term recovery effort.

The Arts Centre

301 Montreal St • Great Hall daily 10am–5pm; Central Art Gallery Tues–Sun 10am–5pm • Free • ☎ 03 366 0989, ⓦ artscentre.org.nz

The Gothic Revival heritage of Christchurch lives on at the **Arts Centre**, filling an entire block once occupied by former University of Canterbury buildings. Designed by Benjamin Mountfort and established in the 1870s, the site became one of the largest conservation projects undertaken in New Zealand after the 2011 quake, with most of the 23 heritage-listed buildings gradually opening after major repairs. Its leafy courtyards are once again becoming the city's cultural heart with performance and exhibition spaces, studios, an arts cinema, the **i-Site information centre** and an increasing roster of boutique galleries, shops and cafés. The principal feature of the **Great Hall** of 1882 is its stained-glass Memorial Window (erected in 1938), highlighting key figures "in the service of humanity" from Shakespeare to Captain Cook. The old library (1915) now serves as the **Central Art Gallery**, with revolving exhibitions from leading contemporary New Zealand artists.

Rutherford's Den

2 Worcester Blvd • Wed–Sun 10am–5pm (last entry 4.30pm); also Mon & Tues 2.30–5pm during school term • $20; students $15 • ⓦ rutherfordsden.org.nz

Housed in the venerable Clock Tower Building (1877), **Rutherford's Den** honours Nobel Prize-winning atomic nucleus discoverer **Ernest Rutherford** (1871–1937), whose work led to the invention of television, radio, sonar and telephones (he's also commemorated on the $100 banknote). Inside, hands-on exhibits bring to life the great man's work in the actual rooms where Rutherford studied in the early 1890s. Born near Nelson, New Zealand, Rutherford spent his later career in Canada and the UK, and was awarded the Nobel Prize in 1908. Grab a coffee or a snack in the on-site *Bunsen* café (see page 519).

Teece Museum of Classical Antiquities

3 Hereford St • Wed–Sun 11am–3pm (often closed between installations/exhibitions) • Free • ⓦ arts.canterbury.ac.nz/logie

Occupying the Old Chemistry Building (1910), the **Teece Museum of Classical Antiquities** showcases the University of Canterbury's Logie Collection of artefacts from ancient Greece, Rome, Egypt and the Near East. Exhibits rotate, but highlights include the "Logie Cup", a decorative Greek chalice from 525 BC, a rare Etruscan wine jug from the late seventh to early sixth century BC, and an incredibly precious Egyptian linen fragment from 300 BC, inscribed with Egyptian hieratic.

PUNTING THE AVON

Perhaps nothing links Christchurch with its genteel English roots like **punting**, popular since the early 1900s and stereotypically associated today with lazy afternoons on the rivers of Oxford and Cambridge. In an effort to avoid some of the on-water shenanigans that actually go on in England, it's not possible to "do it yourself" in Christchurch. Instead, **Avon River Punting** (2 Cambridge Terrace ☎ 03 366 0337, ⓦ christchurchattractions. nz) offers professional punters (don't ever compare them to gondoliers), nattily dressed in blazers and straw boaters, to gently pole you along the river for half an hour (daily: Oct–March 9am–6pm; April–Sept 10am–4pm $28), through the Botanic Gardens from the Antigua Boat Sheds. In the summer, tours also run from Mona Vale (see page 511).

THE CRUSADERS

Don't leave Christchurch without seeing one of the world's most successful rugby union teams, the **Canterbury Crusaders** (aka BNZ Crusaders; ⓦ crusaders.co.nz), based at **AMI Stadium** in Addington since the 2011 quake. The Crusaders have won the **Super Rugby** trophy a record eight times (including 2017). Games usually run from February to early August – see the website for schedules and ticket prices.

10

Canterbury Museum

Rolleston Ave, at Worcester Blvd • Daily: Oct–March 9am–5.30pm; April–Sept 9am–5pm • Free • ⓣ 03 366 5000, ⓦ canterburymuseum.com

Benjamin Mountford's 1870 neo-Gothic **Canterbury Museum** takes a broad-ranging trawl through the history of the province and beyond – blending old-fashioned displays with more innovative galleries, the museum is surprisingly big and lots of fun, with enough inside to fill half a day.

The ground floor begins with dioramas of New Zealand's first inhabitants hunting moa, fishing and leaving their marks inside caves, setting the scene for the superb **Māori collection** containing fine examples of carving, greenstone objects and weaving. You can also stroll along a replica of a Christchurch shopping street circa 1870 to 1901 and view a beautifully presented Victorian decorative arts section (topped by the Costume Gallery). No one minds the regional connection being stretched by **Fred and Myrtle's Paua Shell House**, a shrine to kitsch Kiwiana modelled on a house in Bluff (see page 674) where the famed Fluteys plastered their home with polished paua shells (it eventually became a tourist attraction). After their deaths the contents were shipped here and reassembled.

Upstairs Canterbury's links to **Antarctica** are explored through a flimsy, unreliable motor tractor from Shackleton's 1914–17 expedition and a Ferguson tractor that became the first vehicle to cross the Pole as part of Edmund Hillary's push in 1958. Up here you'll also find a "Discovery" section for kids ($2), rather dry displays of dinosaurs, stuffed birds and geological wonders, and a much more intriguing **Egyptian mummy** exhibit, identified as Tash pen Khonsu, a woman who died around 150 BC. The thought-provoking "**Living Canterbury**" gallery tackles local contemporary issues and the filming of cult movies such as *Goodbye Pork Pie*, adjacent to a small Asian art gallery and a shrine to local speedway hero **Ivan Mauger** (who won a record six World Championships). Recover in the café on the top floor, which sports handsome views of the Botanic Gardens.

Christ's College

33 Rolleston Ave, at Gloucester St • Tours mid-Oct to April Mon–Fri 10am (1hr 20min) • $10 • ⓣ 03 366 8705, ⓦ christscollege.com

Established in 1850, **Christ's College** is today one of New Zealand's elite private schools (modelled on posh English schools such as Eton), with around 620 pupils. The campus certainly looks the part, with a gorgeous quad that seems transplanted from Oxford and suitably neo-Gothic halls and embellishments throughout. The informative **tours** are the only way to get inside.

Botanic Gardens

Main entrance on Rolleston Ave • Daily: April–Sept 7am–6.30pm; Oct & March 7am–8.30pm; Nov–Feb 7am–9pm • Free • Tours $20

The **Botanic Gardens** have helped Christchurch live up to its "Garden City" moniker since 1863, and its mature collection of indigenous and exotic plants and trees is unrivalled on the South Island. From summer to autumn, perennials give a constant and dazzling display of colour; the herb garden, containing a variety of culinary and medicinal plants, exudes aromatic scents; and, from December, the **Rose Garden** blooms with over 250 varieties. Above all, though, it's just a great place to hang out on a sunny day. On the other side of the Avon River, the gardens are encompassed on three sides by **Hagley Park**, which sprawls over two square kilometres immediately west of the city centre.

Visitor Centre and ilex Café
Daily: Sept–May 9am–5pm; June–Aug 9am–4pm • Free • ☎ 03 941 7590

Long, white and strikingly modern, the **Visitor Centre** contains an airy café (*ilex*), gift shop and plant nursery greenhouses where everything is visible as you stroll past. The centre's small exhibition "Christchurch, the Garden City" explores how the totara and kahikatea forests of the Canterbury Plains were transformed by Māori into flax, kumara and raupo (reed) beds, then by Pakeha into farms and English gardens that struggle to cope with the drying summer winds. There's also a bizarre Edwardian travel case for plants, a sort of mini-greenhouse.

The Conservatories
Daily 10.15am–4pm • Free

Just beyond the Visitor Centre lie the **Conservatories**, historic greenhouses crammed with tropical plants year-round. Neoclassical **Cunningham House** dates from 1924 and features an upper gallery for a better view of the foliage; it's connected to the smaller Townend House, tiny Garrick House (full of cacti) and Gilpin House, home to a collection of orchids and carnivorous plants.

The suburbs

Beyond the open expanse of **Hagley Park**, the sylvan pleasures of **Mona Vale** and the historic **Riccarton Bush** lead you west towards the airport and the enlightening **International Antarctic Centre**. For laidback beach life, head to the Pacific Ocean suburb of **Sumner**.

Mona Vale
40 Mona Vale Ave, Fendalton • Daily: grounds 7am–dusk; Homestead 9am–late afternoon • Free • ☎ 03 341 7450, ⓦ monavale.nz • Bus #29 stops near the Fendalton Rd entrance

A picnic hamper and a bottle of rosé are the perfect accompaniment for a visit to **Mona Vale**, compact and oh-so-English gardens that flank the languid Avon River. Majestic displays of roses, fuchsias, magnolias and rhododendrons are set around the 1890s English Arts and Crafts **Homestead**, now a top-notch restaurant, café and events venue.

Riccarton Bush
16 Kahu Rd, Riccarton, 3km west of the city centre • Daily dawn–dusk • Free • Bus P runs close by on Riccarton Rd

Five hundred-year-old kahikatea trees rise up 25m in **Riccarton Bush**, a remnant of Canterbury's original forest saved from the axe by the Scottish brothers **William** and **John Deans**, who came here to farm in 1843 (seven years before the city was founded). Protected by a predator-proof fence, the park is threaded by a concrete loop path (20–30min) with signs interpreting the various species. On Saturdays the place comes alive with the **Farmers' Market**.

Deans Cottage
Daily 6am–9pm • Free

The tiny black-pine **Deans Cottage** was built for the Deans brothers within a few months of their arrival in 1843, making it the oldest structure in Canterbury (John

CHRISTCHURCH FARMERS' MARKET
The historic grounds of Riccarton House host the city's weekly Farmer's Market (Sat 9am–1pm; ☎ 03 348 6190, ⓦ christchurchfarmersmarket.co.nz), boasting more than eighty stalls. You can buy local produce direct from growers, bakers and brewers, as well as local Hummingbird coffee, ready-to-eat gourmet pies, posh porridge, Goan specialities, bagels, flowers, craft beers, oak-smoked salmon and stripped jerky. Come hungry.

actually died here in 1853). The cottage was moved to the entrance to Riccarton Bush in the 1970s and is furnished as it would have been when the brothers lived here.

Riccarton House

Tours Mon–Fri & Sun 2pm; 1hr; $18 • Sat 10am–noon, every 30min (30min); $8 • ☎ 03 341 1018, ⍟ riccartonhouse.co.nz

John Deans' wife Jane and their son John were largely instrumental in the construction of the grand Victorian **Riccarton House**, next door to Deans Cottage. Started in 1856 on land leased from Ngāi Tahu, the building was twice extended and substantially restored in period style after the quakes to produce the grand, three-storey weatherboard homestead you see now – essentially Christchurch's founding

10

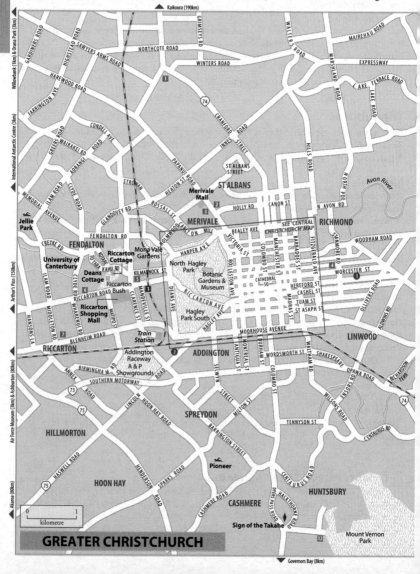

GREATER CHRISTCHURCH

family home. Take one of the guided heritage **tours** to really get a sense of the stoicism required of both men and women in carving out a life here.

International Antarctic Centre

38 Orchard Rd, a 10min walk from the airport – follow the penguin footsteps • Daily 9am–5.30pm • $59 ($29 children 5–15); discount if bought online • Penguin feedings at 10.30am, 1pm & 3.30pm • ☎ 03 357 0519, ☜ iceberg.co.nz • Free shuttle bus runs hourly from outside Christ's College on Rolleston Ave (daily: Oct–March 9am–3pm; April–Sept 10am–3pm; last bus back 4pm).

Christchurch airport is the launchpad for flights to US and New Zealand research bases in Antarctica, and if you're interested in all things polar you could easily spend half a day at the **International Antarctic Centre**; it may be pricey but the

10

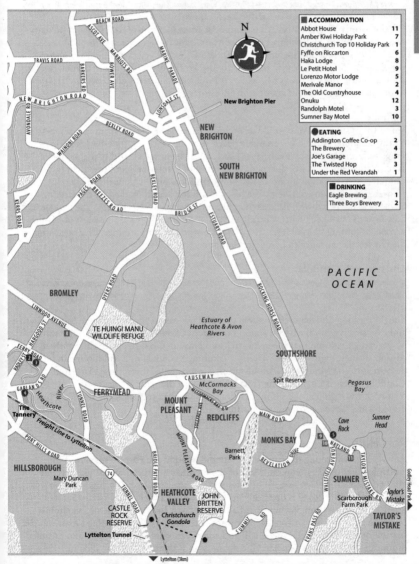

■ ACCOMMODATION	
Abbot House	11
Amber Kiwi Holiday Park	7
Christchurch Top 10 Holiday Park	1
Fyffe on Riccarton	6
Haka Lodge	8
Le Petit Hotel	9
Lorenzo Motor Lodge	5
Merivale Manor	2
The Old Countryhouse	4
Onuku	12
Randolph Motel	3
Sumner Bay Motel	10

● EATING	
Addington Coffee Co-op	2
The Brewery	4
Joe's Garage	5
The Twisted Hop	3
Under the Red Verandah	1

■ DRINKING	
Eagle Brewing	1
Three Boys Brewery	2

exhibits are dynamic and well presented. Don't miss the little blue penguins (which you can see being fed) and the Antarctic Storm, where you don a down jacket to endure a (fairly tame) simulated storm and accompanying -18°C Antarctic chill. Another highlight is *Beyond the Frozen Sunset*, a beautifully filmed HD video (17min) with great chopper footage of the limitless wastes of ice. Your ticket also includes access to the entertaining 4D theatre show, and unlimited goes at the ten-minute **Hägglund Ride** (every 20min), on which a five-tonne tracked polar buggy is put through its paces over an obstacle course.

10

Air Force Museum of New Zealand

45 Harvard Ave, Wigram, 7km west of the city centre • Daily 10am–5pm; 45min tours daily 11am, 1.30pm & 3pm • Free; flight simulators $6/5min • ☎ 03 343 9532, ⓦ airforcemuseum.co.nz • Bus Y from the city centre to Main S Rd in Wigram (550m from museum)

On the former Wigram RNZAF base, the **Air Force Museum of New Zealand** presents two dozen aircraft including a Dakota converted for use on Queen Elizabeth's state visit in 1953, and a Spitfire among several World War II veterans. Flight simulators will keep the (big) kids happy, particularly the World War II Mosquito as it engages in combat in the Norwegian fjords, while enthusiastic volunteer guides conduct assorted tours, including one of the restoration and storage hangars.

Sumner

Some 13km southeast of central Christchurch (reached on bus P from the city centre; 45min), **Sumner** is the city's premiere beach suburb, a Norfolk pine-backed strip of shops restaurants, cafés, wine bars and surf shacks fronting a broad patch of golden sand. Named after Dr J.B. Sumner, Archbishop of Canterbury and president of the Canterbury Association in the 1850s, Sumner took a big hit from the quakes but recovered faster than elsewhere. The focus is still the beach, marked by the striking **Cave Rock**, peppered with little cavities like an enormous Swiss cheese. The best **surfing** is at **Taylor's Mistake**, a narrow beach and small community 4km southeast of Sumner named, according to local lore, after a captain who ran aground here after mistaking the bay for the entrance to Lyttelton Harbour.

Christchurch Gondola

10 Bridle Path Rd, Heathcote, 10km southeast of the city centre • Daily 10am–5pm • $28 • ☎ 03 384 0310, ⓦ christchurchattractions.nz • Shuttle departs the Canterbury Museum 9.30am, 10.30am, 11.30am, 1pm, 2pm, 3pm & 4pm; $10 return (free with Christchurch Pass); or bus #28

The 945m-long **Christchurch Gondola** provides the easiest access to stupendous views and easy strolls from the 448m summit of **Mount Cavendish**, part of the crater wall of the extinct volcano that formed Lyttelton Harbour. Go early to see the Southern Alps in the best light. Alternatively try a combined gondola ride and mountain bicycle descent with the Mountain Bike Adventure Company ($70; see page 516). Your Gondola ticket also includes the **Time Tunnel** ride, a dramatic reconstruction of the history of the region at the summit station, and you can refresh at the *Red Rock Café* or more formal *Gondola Restaurant* on site.

Port Hills

An evening drive along the panoramic **Summit Road** of the **Port Hills** is one of the great pleasures of Christchurch. Most of the road has now been re-opened to traffic after post-quake repairs, save for one key section: the 2km stretch below the Gondola to Mount Pleasant Road is open only to foot and bike traffic. In addition, **Sumner Road**, which runs from Summit Road along the coast to the east side of Lyttelton is closed to all traffic for the foreseeable future. The ridge-top Summit Road itself was the passion of public-spirited Liberal MP and conservationist Harry Ell who also dreamed of fourteen rest stations between Christchurch and Akaroa. When he died in 1934, only four had been built. Drive over **Dyers Pass Road** (between the city and Governors Bay) and you'll pass the best of these, the **Sign of the Takahe**, a Gothic-style baronial house that was restored to its pre-quake glory in 2017 – it should be open as a classy restaurant by the end of 2019.

ARRIVAL AND DEPARTURE

CHRISTCHURCH

BY PLANE

Christchurch Airport (03 358 5029, christchurchairport.co.nz) is 10km northwest of the city centre. It has ATMs, foreign-exchange booths, unlimited free wi-fi, a Vodafone kiosk (daily 8am–6pm & 10pm–2am) to get your mobile up and running and an i-SITE desk (daily 8am–6pm; 03 741 3980) in the international arrivals hall. There's also left luggage at Luggage Solutions at the check-in hall, ground floor (suitcase or backpack $15 for one day, $30 overnight; daily 4.30am–6.30pm; 03 358 8027, luggagesolutions. co.nz). They also do bike boxing for $30.

Destinations Auckland (2 daily; 1hr 20min); Blenheim (1–3 daily; 50min); Dunedin (6 daily; 1hr); Hokitika (2–4 daily; 40min); Invercargill (4–6 daily; 1hr 25min); Napier/Hastings (2 daily; 1hr 30min); Nelson (4–6 daily; 50min); Palmerston North (2–3 daily; 1hr 10min); Queenstown (4 daily; 1hr); Rotorua (3 daily; 1hr 45min); Wellington (12 daily; 1hr).

TO/FROM AIRPORT

By bus The #29 bus runs direct between the airport and the city (every 30min; 40min journey; $8.50) while the Purple Line (every 30min; 55min journey; $8.50) takes a more circuitous route past the university, along Riccarton Road and through Hagley Park.

By shuttle Steve's Airport Shuttles (0800 101 021, steveshuttle.co.nz; first person $23, additional person $5) operates a frequent door-to-door service. They pick up at most accommodation when heading to the airport; book the evening before.

By taxi Taxis between the airport and central Christchurch charge $50–65 (15–20min) on the meter.

BY TRAIN

Two very scenic passenger trains operate from the Christchurch train station (0800 872 467) on Troup Drive, off Whiteleigh Ave in Addington, 4km southwest of Cathedral Square. The summer-only Coastal Pacific (with panoramic viewing windows) runs to Picton (1 daily; 5hr 15min) via Kaikoura (3hr) and meets ferries to the North Island, but note that this line was damaged by the 2016 earthquakes and will be out of action until 2019 (see greatjourneysofnz.co.nz). The *TranzAlpine* does day-returns to Greymouth.

Destinations Arthur's Pass (1 daily; 2hr 15min); Greymouth (1 daily; 4hr 30min); Moana (1 daily; 3hr 45min).

BY BUS

Most long-distance buses drop off and pick up at 72–78 Lichfield St, in front of the Bus Interchange in the heart of the city; the InterCity office (Mon–Thurs & Sat 6.30am–5pm, Fri & Sun 6.30am–5.30pm) just inside the terminal sells tickets for most of the services listed below; some services also run from Rolleston Ave, outside Canterbury Museum.

Destinations Akaroa (2 daily; 1hr 30min–2hr); Aoraki/Mt Cook (1 daily; 5hr 20min); Arthur's Pass (2 daily; 2hr 25min); Blenheim (2–3 daily; 4hr 45min–5hr 30min); Dunedin (5 daily; 6hr); Geraldine (3 daily; 2hr); Greymouth (3 daily; 4hr 50min); Hanmer Springs (5 daily; 2hr 10min); Hokitika (1 daily; 6hr 55min); Mt Hutt (June–Oct 1 daily; 2hr 15min); Kaikoura (2–3 daily; 2hr 30min); Lyttelton (every 15–30min; 35min); Methven (1–3 daily; 1hr 30min); Oamaru (4 daily; 4hr 10min); Picton (2–3 daily; 5hr–5hr 30min); Queenstown (3–4 daily; 7–11hr); Tekapo (3 daily; 3hr 30min); Timaru (5 daily; 2hr 30min); Twizel (3–4 daily; 5hr).

BUS COMPANIES

Akaroa French Connection 0800 800 575, akaroabus.co.nz. To Akaroa daily at 9am (returning at 4pm) from Canterbury Museum, Rolleston Ave; stops at Little River, Hilltop Tavern and Barry's Bay Cheese Factory for cheese tasting.

Akaroa Shuttle 0800 500 929, akaroashuttle. co.nz. To Akaroa Oct–April daily 8.30am (returning 3.45pm), with pick-ups at Rolleston Ave and Lichfield St.

Atomic Shuttles 03 439 0697, atomictravel.co.nz. South to Timaru, Oamaru and Dunedin; west to Greymouth; inland through Geraldine and Twizel to Queenstown; and services north to Kaikoura, Blenheim and Picton. Main stop on Lichfield St.

Hanmer Connection 0800 242 663, hanmerconnection.co.nz. Christchurch to Hanmer Springs daily at 9am, returning 4.30pm. Picks-up at various stops, including Rolleston Ave and Lichfield St.

Hanmer Shuttle 03 315 7418, hanmertours. co.nz. Hanmer Springs to Christchurch (8am) and back (1pm) daily. Pick up at the airport and on Colombo St (at Bealey Ave).

InterCity/Newmans 03 365 1113, intercity.co.nz. North to Kaikoura, Blenheim, Picton and Nelson; south to Timaru, Oamaru, Dunedin and Invercargill; and inland to Tekapo, Aoraki/Mount Cook and Queenstown. Daily 8.30am bus to Queenstown leaves from Rolleston Ave; otherwise all services depart Lichfield St.

10

10

Kaikoura Express ☎ 0800 500 929, ⓦ kaikouraexpress. co.nz. Departs Christchurch daily 8.30am for Kaikoura, returning at 4.30pm, with stops at main hotels downtown, and on Lichfield St (airport pick-up for extra $15).

Methven Travel ☎ 0800 684 888, ⓦ methventravel. co.nz. Daily from the city and airport to Methven; mid-Oct to June Mon, Wed, Fri & Sun 1 daily (check the website for times); July to mid-Oct 3 daily (1 from airport only). Pick-ups on Rolleston Ave.

Snowman Shuttles ☎ 0800 684 888, ⓦ snowmanshuttles.co.nz. Daily from the city (7am) to Mt Hutt June to mid-Oct (ski season), returning 4pm. Bus stop on Lichfield St.

West Coast Shuttle ☎ 03 768 0028, ⓦ westcoastshuttle.co.nz. Once-daily run from Greymouth (7.30am) to Christchurch then back in the afternoon (2.15pm). Bus stop on Lichfield St.

GETTING AROUND

BY BUS

Bus station Most of the local Metro bus services run from the new Bus Interchange (or "Central Station") on Colombo St south of Lichfield St (Mon–Sat 7am–7pm, Sun 9am–7pm; ☎ 03 366 8855, ⓦ metroinfo.co.nz), including #28 (Lyttelton), #29 and P (airport, Riccarton and Sumner). The website has good route planning. You'll find several places to eat, Metro maps, an ATM and lockers ($2 coin only; maximum 24hr) inside the terminal. Taxis line up on Lichfield St.

Fares and cards With the exception of trips to and from the airport ($8.50), the fare anywhere in the city's zone one, including Sumner and Lyttelton, is $4. If you're here for a few days, save money by buying a Metrocard from the Bus Interchange ($10 fee plus min $10 top-up). Standard fares drop to $2.55 (including to the airport), and once you've paid for two fares on a certain day subsequent journeys are free. Transfers (free) allow you to travel in one direction for up to 2hr (not including the airport).

BY CAR AND TAXI

Driving in Christchurch remains straightforward despite the quakes, with road closures well signposted.

Parking Most central spaces are metered (free on public holidays). There's convenient parking in the centre of Hagley Park (Armagh St entrance); it's free for the first hour and all day at weekends.

Vehicle rental There are dozens of car and van rental places in Christchurch, mostly based at the airport.

Taxis Try Blue Star (☎ 03 379 9799) or Gold Band (☎ 03 379 5795).

BY BIKE

Antigua Boat Sheds Bike Hire 2 Cambridge Terrace ☎ 03 366 5885, ⓦ boatsheds.co.nz. Pootle around town for 2hr ($15) or a full day ($30).

The Vintage Peddler Studio 7, 75 Peterborough St ☎ 03 365 6530, ⓦ vintagepeddler.co.nz. Retro bikes for gentle peddling from $30 for 4hr ($35 for full day).

INFORMATION

Visitor information The i-SITE is inside the Arts Centre at 28 Worcester Blvd (daily 8.30am–6pm; ☎ 03 379 9629, ⓦ christchurchnz.com). It will handle bookings for much of the South Island.

TOURS AND ACTIVITIES

BUS TOURS

Discover Christchurch Tours (☎ 0800 141 149, ⓦ hasselfree.co.nz) offers circuits of the city in an open-top double decker bus. Choose from the Christchurch Hop On Hop Off Tour (tickets valid 24hr; buses depart daily 10am–5pm: every 30min Nov–April; hourly May–Oct; $35; children under 15 free), which features two lines (red and blue) visiting the main central city sights; and the Discover Christchurch Tour (1 daily at 9am, Canterbury Museum; 3hr 45min; $69), which adds Sumner and the Port Hills.

HIGH COUNTRY TOUR

Alpine Safari ☎ 0800 427 753, ⓦ hasslefree.co.nz. A great alternative to a full day on the *TranzAlpine* train, spending 10hr jetboating the Waimakariri River, going off-road in a 4WD across a high-country sheep and cattle

station and returning by the *TranzAlpine* from Arthur's Pass ($449).

SEGWAY AND BIKE TOURS

Christchurch Bike Tours ☎ 0800 733 257, ⓦ chchbiketours.co.nz. The 2hr Rebuild Bike Tour (daily 10am & 2pm; $50) is supplemented by a Saturday-morning tour (10am) to the Christchurch Farmers' Market ($50; 2hr) or the Gourmet Bike Tour (4hr; $165; daily 9am & noon), which includes lunch somewhere intriguing.

Mountain Bike Adventure Company ☎ 03 377 5952, ⓦ cyclehire-tours.co.nz. Bike rental company specializing in gondola-assisted downhill rides. Your ticket ($70) gets you a gondola ride, time to look around then either a 16km road ride or a MTB off-road descent. Book ahead.

Urban Wheels ☎03 942 8834, ⓦurbanwheels.co.nz. Segway tours with all the advantages of a bike but faster, more fun and geekier. Go for the Rebuild Zone Tour or the Combo Tour (both daily 9.30am, 10.30am, 1.30pm; 2hr; $109), which wraps in Hagley Park and Mona Vale.

ADVENTURE SPORTS/ADRENALINE SPORTS

Adrenalin Forest 105 Heyders Rd, Spencerville ☎03 329 8717, ⓦadrenalin-forest.co.nz/christchurch. Take on seven high-ropes courses through the forest, up to 20m off the ground, with a range of difficulties and a 3hr maximum ($43; children under 18 $28). Oct–April daily 10am–2.30pm; May–Sept Wed–Sun 10am–2pm.

Ballooning Canterbury ☎0508 422 556, ⓦballooningcanterbury.co.nz. A romantic and tranquil way to get airborne, with early-morning flights over Christchurch's surrounds and spectacular views from mountains to the coast ($395).

Crate Escape 196 Armagh St ☎021 0291 0169, ⓦcrateescape.co.nz. Get confined with a group of friends in a room full of hidden clues, locks and puzzles for one hour from $20 per player depending on group size.

Flip Out Trampoline Park 230 Maces Rd, Bromley ☎03 384 8244, ⓦflipout.co.nz/christchurch. Kids and adults alike enjoy bouncing away at this trampoline and foam pit arena, with a "standard jump" from $16 (1hr). Mon–Sat 9am–9pm, Sun 9am–7pm.

ACCOMMODATION

Christchurch is slowly replacing accommodation lost in the quakes, with a spate of new hotels (the elegant *Distinction Christchurch* in Cathedral Square should be open in 2019). As a fallback there are plenty of **motels**, the majority strung out along Papanui Road to the northwest of the city centre, and Riccarton Road to the west of Hagley Park. Most **campsites** are within walking distance of a bus stop and **freedom camping** is permitted in self-contained campervans. All the options listed below have free parking unless otherwise stated.

CENTRAL CHRISTCHURCH

Admiral Motel 168 Bealey Ave ☎03 379 3554, ⓦadmiralmotel.co.nz; map p.504. Great-value motel with a BBQ, picnic tables and kids' play area in the flowering gardens, plus spotless rooms. $116

★ **Around the World Backpackers** 314 Barbadoes St ☎03 365 4363, ⓦaroundtheworld.co.nz; map p.504. Well-run, compact hostel with dorms and two comfy doubles. There's cheap bike rental ($25/day), hammocks and BBQ in the garden and laundry ($4 per wash and dryer). Dorms $34, doubles $85

BreakFree on Cashel 165 Cashel St ☎03 360 1064, ⓦbreakfree.com.au/on-cashel; map p.504. Budget, quirky accommodation in the heart of the city, with compact but stylish contemporary rooms equipped with Samsung smart TVs (with wireless keyboards) and mood lighting. Free wi-fi only up to 500MB – $10/day thereafter. Breakfast from $19.50, parking $15/day. $96

Chester St Backpackers 148 Chester St East ☎03 377 1897, ⓦchesterst.co.nz; map p.504. With just thirteen beds this is the city's smallest hostel and feels more like a shared house with comfy, colourful doubles, a three-bed share and a self-contained cottage ($190). There's limited off-street parking and a pleasant garden with BBQ; the owner also has a range of campervans for sale. Share $36, doubles $76

City Central Motel Apartments 252 Barbadoes St ☎03 379 0540, ⓦcitycentral.co.nz; map p.504. Modernized motel with flatscreen-TV-equipped, stylish rooms. It's on a busy intersection but the windows are double-glazed. Breakfast $12. $135

The Classic Villa 17 Worcester Blvd ☎03 377 7905, ⓦtheclassicvilla.co.nz; map p.504. It's hard to miss this pink, Victorian townhouse (built 1899), and hard to beat its central location; the rooms range from luxurious suites ($569) to cosy single rooms ($199), with decent continental breakfast, and coffee/tea included. $289

Crowne Plaza 764 Colombo St ☎03 741 2800, ⓦcrowneplaza.com; map p.504. Opening in 2017, the former Forsyth Barr office tower is now the city's biggest business hotel, with extremely well equipped rooms, great views and parking $15/day (breakfast usually $33 extra). $240

★ **Dorset House** 1 Dorset St ☎03 366 8268 or ☎0800 367 738, ⓦdorset.co.nz; map p.504. Spacious hostel in an artfully renovated 1871 house, with firm beds (no bunks) and even bathrobes to rent. There's Sky TV and a pool table in a huge lounge fitted with stained-glass windows. Dorms $34, doubles $84

★ **Eco Villa** 251 Hereford St ☎03 595 1364, ⓦecovilla.co.nz; map p.504. This comfortable boutique hotel near the Cardboard Cathedral offers eight individually designed rooms (using lots of recycled materials), shared kitchen, garden (full of organically grown produce available to guests) and outdoor baths. Hot-water heat pumps, solar-powered energy and grey-water reuse add to the ecofriendly ethos. Free rental bikes. Breakfast $20. $160

Eliza's Manor 82 Bealey Ave ☎03 366 8584, ⓦelizas.co.nz; map p.504. Luxury B&B in a grand 1861 house with eight rooms, all period furnished, and with heat-pump temperature control. It's worth splurging on the more spacious Heritage rooms ($375). Breakfast included, plus high tea served for $40. $275

10

10

Focus Motel 344 Durham St North ☎3 943 0800, ⊛focusmotel.com; map p.504. Stylish, central motel with modern studios and larger units, some with spa baths and all fitted out with leather sofas, classy bed linen with foliage prints and kitchen facilities. $205

Foley Towers 208 Kilmore St ☎03 366 9720, ⊛backpack.co.nz/foley.html; map p.504. A Christchurch backpacking original from the mid-1980s, built around a couple of old houses, which manages to maintain an intimate feel thanks to attentive staff, attractive gardens and an abundance of doubles and twins (en-suites from $78). Laundry ($2) and dryer ($3) available. Dorms $31, doubles $72

The George 50 Park Terrace ☎0800 100 220, ⊛thegeorge.com; map p.504. Splurge on one of the country's finest urban boutique hotels, renovated with considerable panache. There's great art, a cool bar and the chic *Pescatore* restaurant overlooking Hagley Park. $445

The Grange 56 Armagh St ☎03 366 2850, ⊛thegrange. co.nz; map p.504. Classy six-room B&B in a Heritage-listed Victorian home (1874), which has a modern eight-room motel annexe out the back with studios and larger apartments all opening onto a sheltered courtyard. Studios $150, B&B $199

★**Heritage Christchurch** 28–30 Cathedral Square ☎03 983 4800, ⊛heritagehotels.co.nz; map p.504. This iconic hotel, opened in 1913 in a grand Italian High Renaissance style, is once again top digs on Cathedral Square, with luxurious suites (all with full kitchens and lounges) and all the extras: posh restaurants and bars, health club, lap pool, jacuzzi and sauna. Valet parking $20/day. $275

Orari 42 Gloucester St ☎03 365 6569, ⊛orari.net.nz; map p.504. An informally run and art-adorned B&B in a large 1893 home. Ten bright, sunny rooms all have artworks and private bathrooms (one with a tub). Rates include wine on arrival and a full breakfast. $220

YHA Christchurch 35 Hereford St ☎03 379 9536, ⊛yha.co.nz; map p.504. This spic-and-span 120-bed YHA in a well-maintained weatherboard building comes with an abundance of four-shares ($43–48), six-bed dorms (including female only) and rooms (some en suite; from $149) plus spacious lounges for reading and TV. Free wi-fi up to 2GB/day. No parking. *YHA Rolleston House* is around the corner at 5 Worcester Blvd. Dorms $45 (members $40), doubles $99 (members $89)

ADDINGTON

★**Jailhouse Accommodation** 338 Lincoln Rd ☎03 982 7777, ⊛jail.co.nz; map p.504. This Victorian Gothic prison (operational from 1874 till 1999) has been imaginatively transformed into an atmospheric hostel with double and twin-bunk rooms plus some bunk-free dorms, all kauri-floored. Staff are super-helpful and the pool table

is free. A couple of cells have been left as they were. The Orange bus drops off at the door. Dorms $35, doubles $90

MERIVALE

Merivale Manor 122 Papanui Rd ☎03 667 1554, ⊛merivalemanor.co.nz; map p.512. Luxurious accommodation based around the 1882 manor with three period-furnished suites and several studio apartments. The spa studios in a separate building have more modern stylings and everything is self-contained and supplied with cereals, milk, bread and spreads – though there are plenty of good breakfast places nearby. Studios $189, suites $249

Randolph Motel 79 Papanui Rd ☎03 355 0942, ⊛randolphmotel.co.nz; map p.512. Excellent modern motel in grounds overshadowed by a huge copper beech tree. Rooms are extremely well equipped with cooking facilities, TV/DVD, stereo and in-room laundry. Deluxe rooms come with double spa baths and there's even a small gym. $170

RICCARTON

Fyffe on Riccarton 208 Riccarton Rd ☎03 341 3274, ⊛fyffeonriccarton.co.nz; map p.512. All rooms at this stylish motorlodge have super-king-size beds, double-glazed windows, DVD players and coffee plungers; higher-priced executive studios also have spas. $155

Lorenzo Motor Lodge 36 Riccarton Rd ☎03 348 8074, ⊛lorenzomotorlodge.co.nz; map p.512. Quality linens and passes to the gym across the road are among the highlights of this smart motel, which has good-sized studio units plus suites with double spas. Breakfast is $15. $150

PORT HILLS

★**Onuku** 27 Harry Ell Drive, Cashmere, 7km south of the CBD ☎03 332 7296, ⊛onukubedandbreakfast. co.nz; map p.512. Welcoming B&B in a stylish modern house high in the Port Hills, with fab views of the city and access to hiking trails and mountain biking. Rooms are simple but tasteful with comfy beds and there's a full breakfast to set you up for the day. $140

EASTERN CHRISTCHURCH AND SUMNER

Abbott House 104 Nayland St, Sumner ☎03 326 7034, ⊛abbotthouse.co.nz; map p.512. Attractively restored 1870s villa set a block back from the beach, with studios with kitchenette, or suites with large lounge, kitchen and laundry. Both have TV/DVD, private entrances and continental breakfast ingredients supplied. Studios $120, suites $140

Haka Lodge 518 Linwood Ave, Woolston ☎03 980 4252, ⊛hakalodge.com; map p.512. Chilled 1970s house that compensates for its poor location with small numbers, an enticing fire in the lounge, a rich veggie garden, doubles with balconies and even a two-bedroom apartment. Free public parking nearby. Dorms $\overline{\$33}$, doubles $\overline{\$70}$

★ **Le Petit Hotel** 16 Marriner St, Sumner ☎ 03 326 6675, ⓦ lepetithotel.co.nz; map p.512. Boutique B&B with French-themed decor and breakfast (served alfresco in fine weather), airy rooms with balconies or terraces, and satellite TV. $\overline{\$169}$

★ **The Old Countryhouse** 437 Gloucester St, Linwood ☎ 03 381 5504, ⓦ oldcountryhousenz.com; map p.512. Top-end, peaceful hostel fashioned from a trio of spacious, wood-floored villas (just outside the CBD), each with their own kitchen and lounges and some en-suite doubles ($118). There's loads of space, free herbs and lemons, solid tables and bunks made by the owners, a spa pool and sauna. Usually two-night minimum stay required. Take bus #60. Dorms $\overline{\$36}$, doubles $\overline{\$96}$

Sumner Bay Motel 26 Marriner St, Sumner ☎ 03 326 5969, ⓦ sumnermotel.co.nz; map p.512. Stylish motel a block from the beach, with a range of studios and one- and two- bedroom apartments all with a balcony or courtyard, Sky TV and DVD player. $\overline{\$160}$

CAMPING

Amber Kiwi Holiday Park 308 Blenheim Rd, Upper Riccarton ☎ 03 348 3327, ⓦ amberpark.co.nz; map p.512. Spacious, grassy site just 4km southwest of the centre with all the expected facilities and en-suite motel units ($148). Free wi-fi, but only 200MB/day. Handy for the train station; take bus #80 from the city. Camping per site $\overline{\$42}$, en-suite cabins $\overline{\$94}$

Christchurch Top 10 Holiday Park 39 Meadow St, Papanui ☎ 0800 396 323, ⓦ christchurchtop10.co.nz; map p.512. Situated 6km north of central Christchurch on SH74, this large campsite, close to supermarkets and restaurants, has a full range of facilities including self-contained chalets ($140), motel units (from $140) and a heated indoor pool. Free wi-fi in public areas. Catch the Blue bus from the city. Camping per site $\overline{\$39}$, cabins $\overline{\$78}$

EATING

As the rebuild hits its stride the culinary scene is rapidly shifting back to the city – as the new developments around Cashel Street, The Terrace and The Promenade come online there should be more and more choices in the centre. The **Friday Street Food Market** (Fri 11am–9pm) in Cathedral Square should continue in some form, featuring everything from *Malaysian-style noodles* and Chinese dumplings, to German dishes and Mexican tacos.

CENTRAL CHRISTCHURCH

★ **Bacon Brothers** 181 High St ☎ 021 287 4375, ⓦ baconbrothers.co.nz; map p.504. This burger specialist with the enticing name (which started as a stall at the Farmers' Market) knocks out an incredible spread of bacon, beef, veggie and chicken burgers ($12– 15), from a classic BLT to "Mike the Milkman" (chicken, cranberry, brie, bacon, lettuce, avocado and tomato) and even bacon and banana pancakes. Add deep-fried cauliflower as a side ($7). Mon–Fri 7.30am–4pm, Sat & Sun 8am–4pm.

Black Betty 165 Madras St ☎ 03 365 8522, ⓦ blackbetty.co.nz; map p.504. The best café in this part of town, all plywood and polished concrete with punchy coffee and the likes of slow-cooked pork belly with crispy potato cake and poached egg for brunch ($20.50). Limited free wi-fi. Mon–Fri 7.30am–4pm, Sat & Sun 8am–4pm.

Bunsen 2 Worcester Blvd ☎ 03 260 2272; map p.504. Inside the old Clock Tower building at the Arts Centre, this coffee shop pays homage to the chemistry experiments that once took place here (Rutherford's Den

---

THE TRANZALPINE

One of the most popular day-trips from Christchurch is the tourist-oriented *TranzAlpine* **train** through the Southern Alps to Greymouth on the West Coast (4hr 30min each way; book well ahead for non-changeable half-price fares; $179–219 each way; ⓦ greatjourneysofnz. co.nz/tranzalpine). It's a gorgeous 231km journey with braided river valleys, nineteen tunnels and open tussock country all seen from the train's large viewing windows and open-sided observation car. There's a pause at the beech-forest high point of Arthur's Pass before descending through the 8.5km-long Otira Tunnel that burrows under the 920m pass itself.

A good strategy for those with a vehicle is to catch the train at Darfield, 45km west of Christchurch, allowing a later start (9am) in return for missing Christchurch's industrial suburbs (the price is the same, though). It's also worth considering alighting at Moana (12.05pm) for a relaxed three-hour lakeside lunch before boarding for the return journey (3pm). It beats a hurried snack in Greymouth (also the same price).

The train leaves Christchurch at 8.15am daily, stops in Greymouth for one hour, then departs at 2.05pm for a Christchurch arrival at around 6.30pm. The trip can also form part of a high-country tour (see page 516).

10

CHRISTCHURCH CRAFT BREWERS

Beer aficionados should visit local craft brewers such as **Two Thumb** (352 Manchester St, ⓦtwothumb.com; Wed & Fri 3–6pm), **Three Boys Brewery** (592 Ferry Rd, Woolston, ⓦthreeboysbrewery.co.nz; Mon–Wed 8am–4.30pm, Thurs & Fri 8am–6pm, Sat 11am–4.30pm) and **Eagle Brewing** (55 Riccarton Rd, ⓦeaglebrewing.nz; Mon–Fri 11am–6pm, Sat noon–5pm), which sell and bottle their fresh ales on site, and offer tastings (but are not really bars).

is next door), featuring wooden tables and cosy nooks, plus outdoor seating and a selection of delicious cakes, pastries and light meals. Mon–Fri 8am–4pm, Sat & Sun 9am–4pm.

★ **C1 Espresso** 185 High St ☎03 379 1917, ⓦc1espresso.co.nz; map p.504. Fab licensed café in the grand 1930 former High St post office with a coffee roaster in the old vault. Get a potent coffee fix, breakfast on corn, kale and coriander fritters ($17.90) and return later for their trio of sliders ($20) delivered by pneumatic tube. Daily 7am–10pm.

★ **Casa Publica** 180 Armagh St, at New Regent St ☎03 366 1389, ⓦcasapublica.co.nz; map p.504. Hip Latin American-themed restaurant, which also offers over 160 types of rum and live music in the evenings (smooth soul and jazz Mon; 1980s Sat; live Latin guitar Sun). The varied menu features dishes inspired by Peru (ceviche $12.50), Mexico (tacos $10) and Brazil (*feijoada* stews and meaty *espetadas* from $33), plus Cuban sandwiches ($15) and grilled corn ($6). Daily 11am–3pm.

Curator's House 7 Rolleston Ave ☎03 379 2252, ⓦcuratorshouse.co.nz; map p.504. Fine Spanish dining from Barcelona-born chef Albert Alert in this gorgeous old English Tudor Revival-style home from 1920. Mains ($33–41) include a sumptuous *cordero asado* (slow-roasted alpine lamb shoulder) and traditional *paella*, and there's a substantial tapas menu ($7–20), including mushroom and parmesan cheese croquettes and Cloudy Bay clams cooked in white wine. Opt for the garden seating in fine weather, overlooking the Avon River and Botanic Gardens (the house was built for the curator of the latter). Daily 11.30am–3pm & 5.30–10pm.

Dux Central 10 Poplar St ☎03 6919 1436, ⓦduxcentral.co.nz; map p.504. Hip restaurant and bar complex that's a great place to mingle with fashionistas and local movers and shakers, dine on the justly celebrated crispy fried chicken ($16) and pulled-pork burgers ($19.50) or sample one of 200 or so craft beers (from $8). The Upper Dux terrace, amidst ivy-trailing exposed beams, is fabulous in the sunshine. DJs spin late nights. Daily 11am–3am.

Fiddlesticks 48 Worcester Blvd ☎03 365 0533, ⓦfiddlesticksbar.co.nz; map p.504. Sleek modern restaurant opposite the Art Gallery, with a contemporary New Zealand menu and popular outdoor terrace, packed at lunchtime. Dine on roasted cauliflower ($14), Akaroa salmon ($33), Canterbury lamb shoulder ($33) or lamb

sandwich for lunch ($23.50). Mon–Fri 8am–late, Sat & Sun 9am–late.

★ **The Grey Robin** 8 New Regent St ☎03 379 7822, ⓦthegreyrobin.co.nz; map p.504. Relatively newcomer to the Regent Street mall, opening in 2017, this plush fine-dining restaurant sports just sixteen seats (tables and communal bench). Owner Glenda Clark (a veteran of the *MasterChef* TV series) crafts changing five- ($79) and seven-course ($129) tasting menus only (think duck breast slices with crunchy Savoy cabbage and orange sauce, juicy beef ribeye with onions four ways and white chocolate mousse with toffee apple sauce). Tues–Fri 4pm–late, Sat 2pm–late.

King of Snake 145 Victoria St ☎03 365 7363, ⓦkingofsnake.co.nz; map p.504. The dark and intimate interior of this frequently packed joint makes you think bar, and so it is, but the Asian fusion menu is superb, from the stir-fried cumin lamb ($32.50) to the Penang beef-cheek curry ($34.50) and lime pudding with coconut milk ($14.50). Mon–Fri 11.30am–late, Sat & Sun 4pm–late.

OGB 28 Cathedral Square ☎03 377 4336, ⓦogb.co.nz; map p.504. The elegant contemporary restaurant and bar in the *Heritage Christchurch* ("Old Government Buildings") features oak tables, stylish rimu light shades and a changing seasonal menu that might include venison with juniper and black pepper ($18), North Canterbury lamb rump ($34) and falafel burgers at the bar ($22). Also does lavish breakfast plates ($12–17). Daily 6.30am–1am.

Rollickin' Dessert Café 35 New Regent St ☎03 365 4811, ⓦrollickin.co.nz; map p.504. Best sweet treats in town, from its house-made organic gelato and sorbets (including "pops lemon pie" and peanut butter and jelly flavours), to the addictive banoffee pie. Check out the Chocolate Tap, where you can add a "shot" of chocolate sauce to your gelato. Daily 11am–10pm.

★ **Smash Palace** 172 High St ☎03 366 5369, ⓦthesmashpalace.co.nz; map p.504. Juicy burgers ($11–15) served from an old bus (with outdoor and indoor seating), along with wedges ($8), Nepalese dumplings ($10–18) and the house Bodgie beers. Thursday Bike Nights attract vintage motorbike enthusiasts and lots of real bikes to admire. Mon–Thurs 3pm–late, Fri & Sat noon–late, Sun noon–8pm.

ADDINGTON

★ **Addington Coffee Co-op** 297 Lincoln Rd ☎03 943 1662, ⓦaddingtoncoffee.org.nz; map p.512.

Wonderful indie café in a former mechanics workshop that withstood the quakes. Sink into old sofas and try their Jailbreaker coffee, perhaps with fishcakes ($20) or a mushroom medley ($19). They redistribute seventy percent of their profits back to the local community and to some of their favoured Fairtrade coffee and cacao suppliers, and you can even clean your smalls while you dine (see page 522). Mon–Fri 7.30am–4pm, Sat & Sun 9am–4pm.

Town Tonic 335 Lincoln Rd ☎03 338 1150, ⓦtowntonic. com; map p.504. Bustling open-kitchen café and restaurant from Jamie Bennett, with a changing menu featuring fresh, mostly locally sourced ingredients. Dinner mains ($36–38) might include Cloudy Bay clams and chorizo in a spicy tomato sauce, and there is an "honest" menu of vegan options ($16–24) such as orange and star anise poached fennel with quinoa. Specials included curry and drink for $35 (Wed evenings). Mon 7.30am–4pm, Tues & Wed 7.30am–9pm, Thurs–Sat 7.30am–1am, Sun 9am–3pm.

EASTERN CHRISTCHURCH AND SUMNER

★ **The Brewery** 3 Garlands Rd, Woolston ☎03 389 5359, ⓦcasselsbrewery.co.nz; map p.512. Flagship for *Cassels & Sons* awesome craft ales ($8–10), made on site using a wood-fired, copper-domed kettle. A few jars perfectly accompany wood-fired pizza ($20–26), spice-crusted chicken ($26.50) or beer-battered fish and chips ($26.50). Quiz night Monday and DJs or live music later in the week. Daily 7am–10pm or later.

Joe's Garage 19 Marriner St, Sumner ☎03 962 2233, ⓦjoes.co.nz; map p.512. Funky Queenstown-based café chain, alive with folk getting their caffeine jolt from great espresso while huddled over a laptop (free wi-fi) or tucking into dishes such as the *jose* burrito (with bacon, egg, spinach, house-made beans and smashed spuds; $16.80), beef burger and handcut chips ($17.80) or Thai beef salad ($21.80). Pizzas ($17.50–23) are available in the evenings. Mon & Tues 7am–4.30pm, Wed–Sun 7am–10pm.

The Twisted Hop 616 Ferry Rd, Woolston ☎03 943 4681, ⓦthetwistedhoppub.co.nz; map p.512. CBD refugee (12min walk from *Haka Lodge*, p.518), now settled in the 'burbs and serving their own hand-pumped English-style beers alongside tasty pub food such as bangers and mash ($23) and bao sliders (pork belly buns; $18). Quiz nights, and occasional live music. Mon–Fri 3–10pm or later, Sat noon–11pm & Sun noon–9pm.

★ **Under the Red Verandah** 29 Tancred St, Linwood ☎03 381 1109, ⓦutrv.co.nz; map p.512. Everything is made on-site at this earthquake-survivor that's always popular with the lunching set. Sit in the partly recycled building on the original site or out in the courtyard for great counter food – broccoli and blue cheese tart, *spanakopita* and chicken and mushroom pie (each $10, $15.50 with salad) – or lunches like a corn fritter stack with bacon ($24). Mon–Fri 7.30am–4pm, Sat & Sun 8.30am–4pm.

10

DRINKING AND NIGHTLIFE

Despite a quick rebound after the quake, Christchurch nightlife hit hard times in 2017, with several bars and live venues closing; as well as the slow rebuild, contributing factors include higher rents in new buildings, ongoing roadworks in the centre and tougher liquor and drink-driving laws. Check the following spots are still open before heading out.

Darkroom 336 St Asaph St ☎03 974 2425, ⓦdarkroom. bar; map p.504. Studenty bar and music venue mostly showcasing new and up-and-coming local bands. Thurs 7pm–1am, Fri & Sat 5pm–3am.

The Dirty Land 131 Victoria St ☎03 365 534, ⓦthedirtyland.co.nz; map p.504. Grab a Frangelico sour and settle into a booth in this lively but relaxed and intimate bar where the food is all brought through from the kitchen of *Mexicano's* next door: think pulled pork tacos and tuna tostadas ($6–8). Daily 4pm–3am.

The Institution 28 New Regent St ⓦtheinstitution. co.nz; map p.504. Cosy cocktail and craft beer bar (five taps rotate), with friendly staff, quirky decor, blackboards to scribble on and old school desks. Tues–Thurs 4–10pm, Fri & Sat 2pm–late, Sun 2–10pm.

The Last Word 31 New Regent St ☎03 928 2381, ⓦlastword.co.nz; map p.504. Sample over 200 single malts and blends (from Wales, Sweden and India as well as the usual sources) at this cosy whiskey and cocktail bar. Mon–Wed 4pm–midnight, Thurs & Fri 4pm–2am, Sat 2pm–2am.

Louis 123 Victoria St ☎03 377 3614, ⓦlouisbar.nz; map p.504. This elegant champagne and oyster bar features Louis XV-themed mirrors and an ornate Italian-made crystal chandelier centrepiece, with sixteen champagnes to choose from and oysters in various styles from $4.80 each. Tues, Wed & Sun 11am–11pm, Thurs–Sat 11am–1am.

★ **Pomeroy's Old Brewery Inn** 292 Kilmore St ☎03 365 1523, ⓦpomspub.co.nz; map p.504. There's an English pub feel to this solid brick place that serves its own Pomeroy's craft beers, alongside other New Zealand brews (fifteen regular taps). There are also excellent whiskies, and wines to accompany the great pub food: chicken and pork terrine ($18), aged ribeye with duck-fat chips ($38) and fish and chips with pea puree ($24.50). Live bands play several nights a week. Pub Tues–Thurs 3pm–late & Fri–Sun noon–late; restaurant Tues–Thurs 3–10pm, Fri–Sun noon–10pm.

Red Light District 123 Victoria St ⓦredlightdistrict.nz; map p.504. Edgy cocktail bar themed as a secret Chinese opium den (you have to enter through the drycleaners). It's not as pretentious as it sounds, with stylish decor and top-notch cocktails. Wed–Sun 4pm–1am.

10

ENTERTAINMENT

Court Theatre Bernard St (off Lincoln Rd), Addington ⓣ 03 963 0870, ⓦ courttheatre.org.nz. Christchurch's premier theatre, now in this warehouse space with a large main stage and studio. There are usually door sales, so just turn up, or at weekends, go along to the improv comedy show "Scared Scriptless" (Fri & Sat 10.15pm; $20). Box office Mon–Thurs 9am–8.15pm, Fri 9am–10.15pm, Sat 10am–10.15pm.

Isaac Theatre Royal 145 Gloucester St ⓣ 03 366 6326, ⓦ isaactheatreroyal.co.nz. Musicals, ballets,

pantomime and live music all get an airing at this magnificent theatre dating from 1908, which was rebuilt with support from Sir Ian McKellen. Little except the proscenium arch, an elaborate ceiling dome and the brick-and-Oamaru stone facade are original, but ornate new plasterwork and modern comforts haven't stripped its spirit. Outside on the back of the building, check out Owen Dippie's wonderful *Ballerina* mural. Box office Mon–Fri 10am–5pm.

DIRECTORY

Banks and exchange Most banks now have branches (with ATMs) in the centre, including ANZ at 127 Cashel St (Mon–Sat 9am–4.30pm) and BNZ (Mon–Fri 9am–4.30pm) at 111 Cashel St.

Laundry The Addington Coffee Co-op (see page 520) laundry at 297 Lincoln Rd offers washing for $3 (powder included) and drying ($2/20min; coins only). Mon–Fri 7.30am–4pm, Sat & Sun 9am–4pm.

Left luggage Most hostels offer a left-luggage facility at usually no more than $5/day; the i-Site will also keep bags for you ($5 per bag for half a day or $10 for a full day, up to 5pm). There's also storage at the airport.

Medical treatment For a doctor at any time call or visit Pegasus Health's 24 Hour Surgery (ⓣ 03 365 7777, ⓦ 24hoursurgery.co.nz; no appointment necessary), 401

Madras St, near Bealey Ave (fees range $85–190 to see a doctor). Christchurch Hospital (ⓣ 03 364 0640) is at the corner of Oxford Terrace and Riccarton Ave.

Pharmacy Urgent Pharmacy, 931 Colombo St, at Bealey Ave (Mon–Fri 6am–11pm, Sat & Sun 9am–11pm).

Police Central Police Station, 62 St Asaph St (ⓣ 03 363 7400), will eventually move to the new Justice Precinct, south of Lichfield St between Durham and Colombo sts (slated to take place before 2021).

Post office At the time of research discussions were under way to establish a new post office in the centre; until then the South City Lotto & PostShop at 555 Colombo St (Mon–Fri 8.45am–5.45pm, Sat 9am–7pm, Sun 10am–4pm) offers most services.

Banks Peninsula

Jutting out into the sea south of Christchurch like a giant thumb, the rugged, fissured landscape of **Banks Peninsula** provides a dramatic contrast with the flat Canterbury Plains surrounding it. When James Cook sailed by in 1769 he mistakenly charted it as an island and named it after his botanist. In fact it's the first of two drowned volcanic craters. The first forms Lyttelton Harbour, a deep-water anchorage 12km south of Christchurch around which the small town of **Lyttelton** tumbles down towards the water. The shore of the second is graced by the picturesque, ecotourist-town of **Akaroa**, its refined tone lent a gentle Gallic influence by its French founders. Elsewhere on the peninsula, a network of narrow, twisting roads winds along the crater rims and dives down to quiet bays once alive with whalers, sealers and shipbuilders, and now a summer playground for Christchurch residents and tourists.

Lyttelton

A working port town, **LYTTELTON** took a big hit from the 2010 and 2011 quakes, losing much of its infrastructure and historic sites – not least the town's nineteenth-century **Timeball Station** (the tower of the Victorian landmark should be rebuilt and reopened in 2019; see ⓦ timeball.co.nz for the latest). The shattered buildings have long been removed, but permanent businesses have returned to the main drag, **London Street**, and Lyttelton's alternative, indie vibe has emerged stronger than ever. A new site for **Lyttelton Museum** is being planned (see ⓦ lytteltonmuseum.co.nz), while another poignant symbol of recovery, **St Saviour's at Holy Trinity**, was consecrated in 2015. The Anglican church (at 17 Winchester St) is an artful reconstruction of St Saviour's

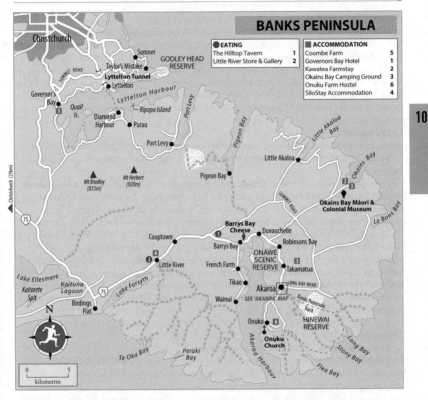

BANKS PENINSULA

● EATING

| The Hilltop Tavern | 1 |
| Little River Store & Gallery | 2 |

■ ACCOMMODATION

Coombe Farm	5
Governors Bay Hotel	1
Kawatea Farmstay	2
Okains Bay Camping Ground	3
Onuku Farm Hostel	6
SiloStay Accommodation	4

10

(built in 1885 and transported in pieces over from Christchurch), on the site where the Church of the Most Holy Trinity (an 1860 Lyttelton original) collapsed after the quakes. The original bell tower remains, detached in the church garden.

Torpedo Boat Museum

19/32 Park Terrace; signposted from Charlotte Jane Quay, about 2km southwest of the town centre • Dec–April Tues, Thurs, Sat & Sun 1–3pm; May–Nov Sat & Sun 1–3pm • $5 • ☎ 03 328 9093, ⬚ lytteltonheritage.co.nz

To get a sense of Lyttelton's maritime importance, visit this small museum in an old powder magazine building from 1874. As fears of Russian expansion spread around the western Pacific in the nineteenth century, New Zealand responded in 1883 by purchasing four British-made torpedo boats, with one to protect Lyttelton Harbour. Designed to charge up to an invading ship, detonate a torpedo below the waterline then scarper before it could be attacked itself, the boat was never used, but its restored remains are here along with an entertaining 36-minute video.

LYTTELTON FARMERS' MARKET

Lyttelton's beloved **Farmers' Market** takes over London Street between Canterbury and Oxford streets every Saturday (10am–1pm) – cars are banned and the live music is always good. Stalls sell all manner of fresh produce, as well as a range of tempting snacks, from bacon butties and gourmet meat pies to Belgian waffles, freshly baked cookies and pure fruit ice pops.

10

Steam Tug Lyttelton

No.2 Wharf · Cruises generally Christmas–April Sun 2.30pm · 90min · $25; booking required · ☎ 03 328 8954, ⓦ tuglyttelton.co.nz

To experience a piece of living history, go for a cruise on this beautiful antique boat, the older of just two steam tugs still operating in the country. Built in Glasgow in 1907, it was immediately put to service towing Shackleton's *Nimrod* to the heads on his way to Antarctica. The tug was decommissioned in 1970 but is maintained in full working order by impassioned volunteers who take trips around the harbour. The boiler room is particularly impressive: all burnished brass and oily pistons.

Quail Island

Black Cat Cruises visit the island Oct–April daily 10.20am from B Jetty in Lyttelton (extra sailing at 12.20pm Dec–Feb); return boat at 3.30pm (extra sailing at 12.30pm Dec–Feb) · $30 return, includes map; cash only · ☎ 03 384 0621, ⓦ blackcat.co.nz/quail-island-adventures

Set in mid-harbour, unspoiled **Quail Island** (Ōtamahua) was, from 1875, a quarantine station for people and animals heading to Christchurch; in the early days of Antarctic exploration Shackleton, Scott and American Commander Byrd quarantined and trained their dogs and ponies here before venturing towards the South Pole. Between 1906 and 1925 a small leper colony operated here, but since 1975 the island, barely 1km across, has been a recreational reserve offering beautifully wild scenery, easily absorbed on a day-trip hiking and swimming: pack food, plenty of drinking water and rain gear. Two circular **walking tracks** (1hr and 2hr 30min) start from the island's wharf and visit the **Heritage Centre** (an old farmhouse with panels on the history and ecology of the island), two safe **swimming beaches** (Walkers and Whakamaru) and a replica leprosy patients' hut along with several shipwrecks that can be seen at low tide.

Diamond Harbour

Ferries every 30–60min (8min) · $6.50 each way · ⓦ diamondharbour.info

In bright sunlight the water sparkles like a million gems at **DIAMOND HARBOUR**, directly across the water from Lyttelton. The passenger **ferry** is a pleasant way to get out on the water, and there are a couple of good cafés a five-minute uphill walk from the Diamond Harbour wharf. Alternatively, opt for the more energetic hike up **Mount Herbert** (at 919m the highest point on the Bank Peninsula), for sensational views of the harbour (allow 4–5hr round-trip).

ARRIVAL AND INFORMATION
LYTTELTON

By bus The quickest way from Christchurch to Lyttelton is through the 1.97km Lyttelton Tunnel (opened in 1964 and still New Zealand's longest road tunnel). The #28 bus from central Christchurch leaves every 20–60min ($4), takes about 30min and stops on Norwich Quay.

Tourist information Lyttelton Harbour Information Centre, 20 Oxford St (Mon–Sat 10am–4pm, Sun 11am–3pm; ☎ 03 328 9093, ⓦ lytteltonharbour.info).

EATING

Freemans Dining Room 47 London St ☎ 03 328 7517, ⓦ freemansdiningroom.co.nz. This beloved restaurant offers dinner (Wed–Sun), breakfast on Saturday and lunch at weekends, with a range of superb pizzas ($24–27), charcuterie boards ($24) and amazing desserts ($13.50). Wed–Fri 3pm–late, Sat 9am–late, Sun noon–late.

Glamour Cake/Lyttelton Bakery 8 Norwich Quay ☎ 03 328 9004. The *Glamour Cake* counter inside the otherwise humdrum *Lyttelton Bakery* knocks out gourmet cheesecake slices, "freak" shakes and cakes, but is best known for owner Bree Scott's high-rise doughnuts ($7–10) in flavours such as salted-caramel brandy snap, lemon meringue and Nutella

(get there before noon for the best selection). Tues–Sat 7.30am–2.30pm.

★ **Lyttelton Coffee Co** 29 London St ☎ 03 328 8096, ⓦ lytteltoncoffee.co.nz. The 2014 return of this Lyttelton institution to its original site brought joy to faithful locals, and it remains the best place to soak up the town's hip indie vibe. Great coffee ($3.50) and café food, a panoramic terrace overlooking the port and always something interesting cranking out of the bank of 1970s hi-fi speakers (mains $12–21). Mon–Fri 7am–4pm, Sat & Sun 8am–4pm.

Roots 8 London St ☎ 03 328 7658, ⓦ rootsrestaurant.co.nz. Foodie heaven where nose-to-tail meat cuts and locally foraged ingredients are artfully combined into exquisite small dishes. All meals are degustation ($105 for five courses, $145 for eight courses, $195 for twelve courses) and they'll explain what they've made when it arrives. Tues–Thurs 6–9pm, Fri & Sat noon–2.30pm & 6–9pm.

★ **Sherpa Kai** 10 Oxford St ☏ 210 850 8886. Let's hope this justly popular Nepalese food stall endures (or moves to a bricks-and-mortar joint) – Darjeeling native Thendup Sherpa's aromatic, tasty beef curries, dhal, vegetable thaali

and Tibetan beef *momos* (dumplings), which you can enjoy on the outdoor tables next to the *British Hotel*, are sublime (items $10–15). Tues–Thurs 10am–4pm, Fri & Sat 10am–9pm, Sun 9am–3pm.

Spooky Boogie 54 London St ☏ 021 161 0426. One of the town's quirkier cafés, with sensational coffee and cookies but also vinyl records (!), books and wacky art and gifts. Mon–Fri 8am–4pm, Sat 8.30am–4pm, Sun 9am–4pm.

10

DRINKING AND NIGHTLIFE

Lyttleton was key to the musical renaissance that emerged after the 2011 quakes, with local rock and alt-folk artists such as The Eastern, Delaney Davidson, Marlon Williams (frontman of The Unfaithful Ways) and Tiny Lies all performing at *Wunderbar*; live music remains a mainstay of the local scene.

★ **Hell Fire Club** Oxford St and Norwich Quay ☏ 021 134 7907, ⓦ facebook.com/hellfireclublyttelton. This notorious Art Deco landmark reopened as a bar and club in 2017 – it was originally the rough-and-tumble *British Hotel*, where Robert Scott downed whiskeys before heading to Antarctica, and a blood stain still remains on the ceiling from a knife fight between Russian sailors. Today

the open fireplace makes a more welcoming space for live music, open poetry nights and a DJ on Fridays. Wed 5pm–midnight, Thurs & Fri 5pm–2am, Sat 11am–2am, Sun 3pm–midnight.

★ **Wunderbar** 19 London St ☏ 03 328 8818, ⓦ wunderbar.co.nz. An iron fire escape behind the supermarket leads to this idiosyncratic late-night drinking-hole and club, with decor ranging from crushed velour to a gruesome doll's-head lightshade. The deck overlooking the docks is great for a peaceful drink away from the clamour within, which might be open mike (Tues), poetry, live bands (Wed–Sat), stand-up comics or film-noir evenings. Mon–Fri 5pm–late, Sat & Sun 1pm–even later.

Little River and Duvauchelle

Some 53km from Christchurch on SH75, the small community of **LITTLE RIVER** makes for an obvious pit stop on the winding journey to Akaroa, with some enticing accommodation and attractions. **Little River Gallery** (daily 9am–5pm; ⓦ littlerivergallery.com) offers a whimsical array of local arts and crafts (and coffee), while **Barry's Bay Cheese** (daily 9am–5pm; ⓦ barrysbaycheese.co.nz), 15km further on in neighbouring **DUVAUCHELLE**, offers fabulous cheeses sourced from local (Banks Peninsula) cows.

ACCOMMODATION
LITTLE RIVER

★ **SiloStay Accommodation** Christchurch-Akaroa Rd (SH75) ☏ 03 325 1977, ⓦ silostay.kiwi.nz; map p.523. This is perhaps one of the most bizarre accommodation options in New Zealand (from the owners of Little River Gallery); eight units each sleeping two people, fashioned out of actual corrugated grain silos, with custom kitchenette sinks to fit the curved walls; ecofriendly wood pellet boilers power the complex. Satellite TVs and iPod docks included. **$230**

Akaroa

The small waterside town of **AKAROA** ("Long Harbour" in Māori), on the eastern shores of French Bay (aka Akaroa Harbour), 85km from Christchurch, comes billed as New Zealand's **French settlement**. Uniquely for New Zealand, the first settlers did come from France and some of their architecture survives, the street names they chose have stuck, croissants are served in the town bakeries and there's a well-used *pétanque* court, but that's about as French as it gets. Still, it is an enchanting, laidback place, strung along the shore in a long ribbon easily seen on foot. There's even a small **beach** that attracts plenty of weekenders. The smattering of ecotourism activities includes a unique **dolphin swim** (Hector's dolphins, the world's smallest species, are relatively abundant here), "**NightSUP**" (illuminated paddle-boarding at night), **penguin and seal viewing** and easy access to the **Banks Peninsula Track**. Two-thirds of its houses are *baches* (holiday homes), leaving only around 650 permanent residents.

10

Note that Akaroa's daytime peace is regularly shattered by the arrival of **cruise ships** (mostly **late Oct to early April**, with up to 4000 passengers per ship), which spend the day at anchor while passengers get bussed to Christchurch, go dolphin watching or just mooch around the galleries and shops.

Brief history

The site of Akaroa was originally the domain of the Ngāi Tahu paramount chief, Temaiharanui. In 1838, successful French whaler **Jean Langlois** traded goods with the Ngāi Tahu for what he believed to be the entire peninsula, then returned to France to encourage settlers to populate a new French colony. However, unbeknown to the French, in February 1840 the South Island Māori chiefs signed the **Treaty of Waitangi** with the British (see page 698). Alerted to the French plans, the British sent one Captain Owen Stanley on the **HMS Britomart** to raise the British flag in Akaroa, just days before the French warship *Aube*, led by Commodore **Charles François Lavaud** arrived, and a month before the clueless settlers on the *Comte de Paris* sailed into the harbour on August 16, 1840. Lavaud's colonists decided to stay, which meant that the first formal settlement under **British sovereignty** was comprised of 57 French and six German settlers. The spot where they supposedly came ashore is marked by a **plaque and French flagstaff** on Beach Road. France did not formally recognise Britain's claim to the Banks Peninsula until 1846. The biennial **French Fest** re-enacts the 1840 arrival over three days (usually in Oct).

Akaroa Museum

71 Rue Lavaud • Daily: Oct–April 10.30am–4.30pm; May–Sept 10.30am–4pm • Free • ☎ 03 304 1013, ⓦ akaroamuseum.org.nz

The **Akaroa Museum** begins with several interesting Māori artefacts and a twenty-minute film account of the remarkable history of settlement on the peninsula, backed up by a display illustrating the differences between the English version of the Treaty of Waitangi and a literal English translation of the Māori-language document. Other exhibits deal with the peninsula's whaling history and fascinating albums full of photographs of the original French and German settlers.

The museum incorporates the town's former 1880 **Court House** and the early 1840s **Langlois-Eteveneaux Cottage**, possibly part-constructed in France before being shipped over, and now filled with nineteenth-century French furniture.

The Giant's House

68 Rue Balguerie • Daily: Nov–Dec 24 noon–3pm; Dec 26–April noon–5pm; May–Oct 2–4pm • $20 • ⓦ thegiantshouse.co.nz

Don't miss **The Giant's House**, home of sculptor **Josie Martin** (the house dates from 1881), and a working testament to her art since 1993. Every room, the garden and even the drive to the garage have become a canvas on which she can display her talents. Mosaics, concrete figures and sculpted seats tucked away in garden nooks all have an overriding spirit of fun. In summer there's a small café and Josie exhibits her art from a gallery.

French Cemetery

The tiny **French Cemetery** at the northern end of town is reached by a curving road or shorter (but steeper) footpath that leads from Rue Pompallier into the L'Aube Hill Reserve. Dating from 1842, this was the first consecrated burial ground in Canterbury; the cemetery was sadly neglected until 1925, when the bodies were reinterred in a grassy central plot marked by a single monument.

Akaroa Lighthouse

Beach Rd • Mon–Sat 12.30–3.30pm, Sun 1.30–4.30pm • $2.50 • ⓦ akaroa.com

The local Lighthouse Preservation Society moved the **Akaroa Lighthouse** from Akaroa Heads to its present location in 1980 (it dates from 1880), and today it's possible to view the rare, six-sided 8.5m wooden structure up close.

ARRIVAL AND DEPARTURE

AKAROA

By car From Christchurch, the main route to Akaroa is SH75. Beyond Little River, the road becomes extremely winding and steep in parts (allow 1hr 30min from the city in total). You can also branch off SH75 at the *The Hilltop Tavern* and follow the long and incredibly scenic Summit Road along the top of the crater rim to Akaroa.

By bus From Christchurch: Akaroa Shuttle (Oct–April daily 8.30am, returning 3.45pm; ☎ 0800 500 929, ⓦ akaroashuttle. co.nz), with pick-ups at Rolleston Ave and Lichfield St; Akaroa French Connection (daily at 9am, returning at 4pm); ☎ 0800 800 575, ⓦ akaroabus.co.nz); with pick-up outside Canterbury Museum. Both drop off beside the Akaroa Adventure Centre.

INFORMATION

Tourist information Akaroa Adventure Centre, 74a Rue Lavaud (daily 9am–5pm; ☎ 03 304 7784, ⓦ akaroaadventurecentre.co.nz) is a commercially run visitor centre promoting the town, selling walking maps

10

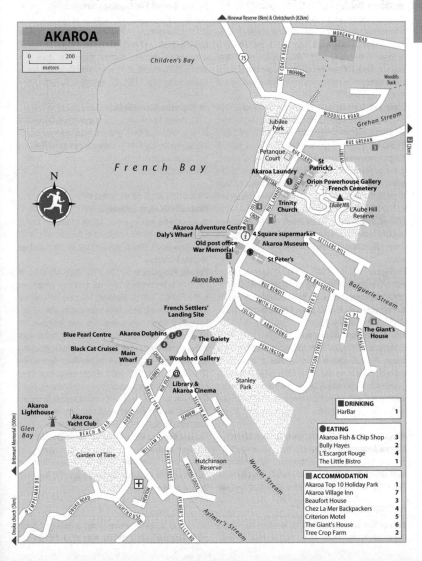

AKAROA

DRINKING
HarBar — 1

EATING
Akaroa Fish & Chip Shop — 3
Bully Hayes — 2
L'Escargot Rouge — 4
The Little Bistro — 1

ACCOMMODATION
Akaroa Top 10 Holiday Park — 1
Akaroa Village Inn — 7
Beaufort House — 3
Chez La Mer Backpackers — 4
Criterion Motel — 5
The Giant's House — 6
Tree Crop Farm — 2

and gently pushing their own adventure activities. It shares space with the post office, and has pack storage ($5/day).

Services There's a BNZ bank (Mon–Fri 9.30am–4.30pm) with an ATM at 73 Rue Lavaud, across the street from the Akaroa Adventure Centre. Akaroa Library, 2 Selwyn Ave (Mon–Fri 10am–4.30pm, Sat 10am–1pm), has free wi-fi that spills over to the adjacent cinema café (there are also free wi-fi zones along the bayfront). The Akaroa Laundry on Rue Pompallier operates 10am–2pm (closed Wed & Sat), but the coin-operated laundromat machines are accessible daily 8am–8pm.

TOURS AND ACTIVITIES

SWIMMING WITH DOLPHINS AND HARBOUR CRUISES

★**Akaroa Dolphins** 65 Beach Rd ☎ 0800 990 102, ⊛ akaroadolphins.co.nz. Small numbers and boats give a more intimate feel to these 2hr harbour cruises (daily: Oct–April 10.15am, 12.45pm & 3.15pm; May & Sept 10.15m & 12.45pm, June–Aug 12.45pm; $80). They visit all the same places as Black Cat (see below), usually see dolphins and put an emphasis on the region's history, Māori heritage and spotting sea birds.

Black Cat Cruises Main Wharf, Beach Rd ☎ 03 304 7641, ⊛ blackcat.co.nz. Experienced operator offering 3hr dolphin-swimming trips (Dec–March 6.30am, 8.30am, 11.30am & 1.30pm; Sept–Nov, April & May 11.30am & 1.30pm; swimming $160, spectators $89; partial refunds if the dolphins don't show). Having cruised out to the dolphins, they watch their behaviour to check that it is okay to get in the water. Their 2hr harbour cruises (year-round at 11am & 1.30pm, plus mid-Dec to mid-March 3.40pm; $79) use large boats to visit the mouth of the harbour via a beautiful high-walled volcanic sea cave, colonies of spotted shags and cormorants, and caves where blue penguins reside.

EcoSeaker ☎ 0800 326 794, ⊛ ecoseaker.co.nz. Intimate, boutique dolphin-swimming operation taking out just six swimmers at a time in a rigid inflatable with over 2hr on the water. Oct–April 10.30am daily from Daly's Wharf. $165 to swim, $80 to watch.

Fox II Sailing Adventures ☎ 0800 369 7245, ⊛ akaroafoxsail.co.nz. With its red sails catching the breeze, this 1922 kauri-built ketch makes an atmospheric and ecofriendly alternative to the other cruises ($80). They generally head out towards Akaroa Heads and will often see dolphins and seals. Late Dec to May daily at 10.30am and 1.30pm from Daly's Wharf.

KAYAKING, SUP BOARDING AND BIKING

Akaroa Adventure Centre 74a Rue Lavaud ☎ 03 304 7784, ⊛ akaroaadventurecentre.co.nz. Offers stand-up paddleboard rental (1hr for $20, 4hr for $45) and bike rental (1hr $15), with the option of a drop-off high above town and a cruisey 13km downhill ride back ($65). Kayaks $20/hr or $60/day, paddleboats (for two) $20 for 30min, $20/hr.

Akaroa Guided Sea Kayaking Safaris meets outside The Green Café at 37 Rue Lavaud ☎ 021 156 4591, ⊛ akaroakayaks.com. Provides small-group guided kayaking trips, with swimming and a good chance of encountering dolphins. Harbour Highlights Safari (1hr 30min; $155) departs at 11.30am, with the longer Scenic Cruiser Safari (3hr; $130) also departing 11.30am. Nov–April only.

★**Nightsup Akaroa Safaris** 58 Rue Lavaud ☎ 027 243 3243, ⊛ nightsupakaroa.co.nz. Stand-up paddleboarding at night ($80; 1hr 30min), with LED lights under the boards lighting up the bay floor – a magical experience. Departs just before sunset daily. Also offer SUP lessons for $50. Mid-Nov to April only.

PENGUIN AND SEAL VIEWING

Akaroa Seal Colony Safari ☎ 03 304 7255, ⊛ sealtours.co.nz. A/c 4WD vehicles depart Akaroa Information Centre to view fur seals, on the eastern tip of the peninsula. Tours (Oct–April daily 9.30am & 1pm; $60) last 2hr 30min and are limited to six people.

Pohatu Penguins ☎ 03 304 8542, ⊛ pohatu.co.nz. If you want to see penguins close up, don't miss these tours to the Flea Bay farm on the Banks Peninsula Track, where Shireen and Francis Helps have been looking after white-flippered penguins (aka Australasian Little Penguins) for decades. Their Evening Tour (2–3hr; $75) starts before dusk and gives you plenty of chance to see penguins returning from their day fishing. On their daytime Nature Tour option (2hr; daily 1.30pm; $65) you'll see the penguins in their nesting boxes and learn plenty about a working sheep farm. Both tours run Sept–April, and only on request in winter, when you are less likely to see penguins. To see penguins (and probably Hector's dolphins) from the water take their kayaking trips (4hr; daily at 8am; $75; noon; $90; 8am tour Oct–April only). All trips involve pick-up from Akaroa and a scenic drive down a 4WD track to the farm; there are cheaper options if you can drive yourself to the farm, but the road is 4WD-only and steep.

ACCOMMODATION

Akaroa Top 10 Holiday Park 96 Morgan's Rd, off the Old Coach Rd ☎ 03 304 7471, ⊛ akaroa-holidaypark. co.nz; map p.527. Sprawling across a terraced hillside overlooking the harbour and the main street, this site has

HIKES AROUND AKAROA

For those who lack the time or inclination to tackle the **Banks Peninsula Track**, there are equally rewarding shorter walks. There's further information at ⓦ bankspeninsulawalks.co.nz; detailed maps can be purchased at the Akaroa Adventure Centre.

Skyline Circuit (10km; 4hr return) The best of Akaroa's walks circumnavigates the hills above the town via the Purple Peak Track, which gives access to the bush of Hinewai Reserve.

Beach Road–Glen Bay–Red House Bay (5km one way; 1hr 15min) Stroll along waterfront Beach Road towards Glen Bay and the Akaroa Lighthouse. Continue towards Akaroa Head for about 15min and you'll come to Red House Bay, the scene of a bloody massacre in 1830, when the great northern chief Te Rauparaha bribed the captain of the British brig *Elizabeth* with flax to conceal his Māori warriors about the vessel and then to invite his unsuspecting enemies (led by Te Maiharanui) on board, where they were slaughtered. Te Rauparaha and his men then feasted on the victims on the beach.

Onuku Road (5km one way; 1hr 15min) Follow this inland road to Onuku, where you'll find the *Onuku Farm Hostel* and Onuku Marae with the pretty little nineteenth-century Onuku church.

10

modern facilities, including a swimming pool and self-contained family units ($135). Camping $40, cabins $72

Akaroa Village Inn 81 Beach Rd ☎03 304 1111, ⓦ akaroavillageinn.co.nz; map p.527. A rambling complex with probably the widest range of accommodation in town, a variety of decors and lots of self-catering apartments, several with two bedrooms and some good harbour views, including the Old Shipping Office ($239). Studio units $185, apartments $259

★ **Beaufort House** 42 Rue Grehan ☎03 304 7517, ⓦ beauforthouse.co.nz; map p.527. Gracious B&B in a fine old home with five antique-decorated rooms, each with en suite or private bath (two with deep tubs). There's a sumptuous guest lounge and breakfast is a major affair often finished with a coffee on the veranda. To top it all off, they even have their own small vineyard, the Pinot Noir and Chardonnay usually sampled with canapés on arrival. $395

Chez La Mer Backpackers 50 Rue Lavaud ☎03 304 7024, ⓦ chezlamer.co.nz; map p.527. High-quality budget accommodation in a homely 1871 house complete with a serene garden, hammock and outdoor cooking area. The staff are helpful, and offer free use of bikes and fishing rods and useful maps of local walks and points of interest. Some en suites ($86). Dorms $34, rooms $76

★ **Coombe Farm** 18 Old Le Bons Track, 4km north of Akaroa ☎03 304 7239, ⓦ coombefarm.co.nz; map p.523. Though there is a guest lounge stacked with books and DVDs, the farmhouse kitchen is the social hub of this delightful B&B on a working farm. Two very spacious rooms in the farmhouse plus the rustic Shepherd's Hut, with private outdoor bath and shower on the deck overlooking the stream. Make breakfast at your leisure with a hamper supplied. Be sure to take the 5min streamside bushwalk right by the house or a more ambitious hike up to a waterfall. Closed June–Sept. Hut $180, rooms $200

Criterion Motel 75 Rue Jolie ☎0800 252 762, ⓦ holidayakaroa.com; map p.527. Assiduously managed, modern motel with spacious rooms each with underfloor heating, double glazing and a balcony. Top-floor rooms ($225) have the best harbour views. Late checkouts make this a good deal. Units $162

The Giant's House 68 Rue Balguerie ☎03 304 7501, ⓦ thegiantshouse.co.nz; map p.527. Stay in a living art gallery (see page 526) built in and around this 1881 house. The large rooms (some en-suite) are all wildly decorated as, say, a boat bed or a greenhouse conservatory. A delicious continental breakfast is served and there are big reductions for multi-night stays. $300

★ **Onuku Farm Hostel** 6km south of town on the Onuku Rd ☎03 304 7066, ⓦ onuku.co.nz; map p.523. On a hillside sheep farm above the bay, this wonderfully secluded spot centres on the cosy main house where there are doubles (some with a view $80) and dorms (including a six-bunk girls-only en-suite). No TV but free wi-fi. Outside there's a hammock-strung campsite ($12.50 per person) and another basic dorm ($20) equipped with outdoor kitchens and showers, plus several stargazers – rather like wooden tents (BYO sleeping bag; $20 per person), some with magnificent views. There are walks all around, the hostel runs summer dolphin-swimming trips ($110 for guests; max six), and encourages fishing and mussel collecting. Free pick-up around 12.30pm from Akaroa. Cash only. Closed May–Sept. Dorms $30, rooms $70

Tree Crop Farm 2km up Rue Grehan ☎03 304 7158, ⓦ romanticretreatsakaroa.com; map p.527. The four "love shacks" are the only place to stay if you're looking for the sort of rustic romance that secluded candle-lit cabins hung with mirrors and supplied with outdoor fire-heated bush baths offer. It's not for everyone but is a unique experience. The surrounding "farm" is more managed wilderness with tracks throughout. $250

10

EATING

Akaroa has some outstanding places to eat, though many places cut back their hours, or even close completely, during winter. For self-catering, try the old-fashioned Akaroa Butcher & Deli (@akaroabutchery.co.nz), 67 Rue Lavaud, which makes its own sausages and also stocks Barry's Bay cheeses and local olive oil. There's a Four Square Supermarket (Mon–Thurs & Sun 8am–6.30pm, Fri & Sat 8am–7pm) next to Akaroa Adventure Centre on Rue Lavaud.

Akaroa Fish & Chip Shop 59 Beach Rd ☎ 03 304 7464; map p.527. Decent fish and chips on the bayfront, with indoor and outdoor tables and deliciously crisp fish dishes ($15–18.50) wrapped in paper (the blue cod and kumara chips is good, but the fresh fish of the day is your best bet). Mon–Thurs & Sun 11am–7.30pm, Fri & Sat 11am–8.30pm.

Bully Hayes 57 Beach Rd ☎ 03 304 7533, @bullyhayes.co.nz; map p.527. Named after the eponymous 1800s American pirate who frequented the waters hereabouts, this busy place cooks up big breakfasts and casual lunches, and serves sensational seafood platters (including Akaroa salmon, of course) as well as fancier evening fare like truffle-butter roasted chicken (most mains $35–42). Daily 8am–9pm or later.

L'Escargot Rouge 67 Beach Rd @lescargotrouge.co.nz; map p.527. "Parisian" breakfast choices at this chic spot include a combo that includes a baguette, coffee, croissant and pain au chocolat ($19.50), plus *croque monsieur* (brioche with Dijon mustard, ham and cheese; $9.20). During the day there's a tempting selection of deli-style counter food (dishes $5–10). Daily 7am–3.30pm.

★ **The Little Bistro** 33a Rue Lavaud ☎ 03 304 7314, @thelittlebistro.co.nz; map p.527. A classic restaurant whose thirty seats are packed so tight you eat elbow to elbow. Wonderfully convivial, they use locally sourced produce to dish up the likes of free-range pork rack ($38) or whole Lyttelton sole ($35), washed down with mostly Canterbury wines. For afters, try their take on an Eton mess ($15.50). Tues–Sat 5.30–10pm.

DRINKING AND NIGHTLIFE

HarBar 83 Rue Jolie ☎ 03 304 8889, @facebook.com/harbarakaroa; map p.527. This bayside bar in a former women's restroom is the perfect spot to watch the sun go down, craft beer in hand. As the evening cools huddle around the deck fireplace and grab something from their tapas menu ($4.50–15). Daily 11am–10pm.

★ **The Hilltop Tavern** 5207 Christchurch Akaroa Rd (SH75) ☎ 03 325 1005, @thehilltop.co.nz; map p.523. Magical views 450m down to Akaroa Harbour are the big draw to this excellent pub roughly halfway between Little River and Akaroa. In summer, chairs on the deck and bean bags on the grass are full of people tucking into nachos ($20) or wood-fired pizzas ($24–26), supping on local craft beers or spooning quality ice cream. Weekends bring folk from far and wide for top local bands: check the website. Self-contained campervans can stay overnight in the car park. Daily 10am–late (May–Aug Mon–Wed noon–6pm, Thurs–Sun 10am–late).

ENTERTAINMENT

Akaroa Cinema Corner of Rue Jolie and Selwyn Ave ☎ 03 304 7678, @cinecafe.co.nz. For non-blockbuster movies, check out this boutique cinema, which plays art, foreign, classic and new films. Buy a glass of wine or coffee from the foyer *Ciné Café* and take it in with you. Tickets $15.

Around Akaroa: the bays

A day is well spent exploring east from Akaroa via the **Summit Road**, which traces the 600m-high Akaroa crater rim. From here, roads twist down from the open tops (ablaze with gorse in November) to gorgeous bays with deserted beaches and the remains of once thriving towns where a school or store just about hangs on. With few interconnecting roads, exploring the region is likely to take longer than you might expect.

Verdant **LE BONS BAY** 19km northeast of Akaroa is a small peaceful community with a number of holiday homes ranged behind an unspoiled sandy **beach**, framed by two sides by cliffs. Head here for moody walks along the bay and safe swimming.

OKAINS BAY (25km from Akaroa via the Summit Rd) has a tiny permanent population but swells with Christchurch family holiday-makers in January. The village lies 2km inland from the beach and placid lagoon formed by the **Opara Stream**, excellent for swimming and boating, but the museum is the real reason to visit.

Okains Bay Māori and Colonial Museum

1146 Okains Bay Rd • Daily 10am–5pm • $10 • ☎ 03 304 8611, @okainsbaymuseum.co.nz

Set in and around the old town cheese factory, local collector Murray Thacker has amassed one of the most remarkable collections of Māori artefacts in the South Island at his **Okains Bay Māori and Colonial Museum**, including a great collection of *hei tiki* (a pendant with a design based on the human form) in different styles. There's also a "god stick" dating back to 1400, a war canoe (*waka*) from 1867 and a beautiful meeting house with fine symbolic figures carved by master craftsman John Rua. European-style outbuildings include a "slab" stable and cottage constructed from large planks of totara wood. The history of the early European pioneers of Okains Bay (many of whom intermarried with the local Māori) is painstakingly created – the first Thacker arrived in the 1850s.

10

ACCOMMODATION
OKAINS BAY

Kawatea Farmstay 1048 Okains Bay Rd ☎ 03 304 8621, ⓦ kawateafarmstay.co.nz; map p.523. Century-old homestead set in lush gardens bordered by 5km of scenic coastline, with welcoming hosts, three rooms and a romantic loft. Dinners are available on request. **$130**

Okains Bay Camping Ground 1357 Okains Bay Rd ☎ 03 304 8789, ⓦ okainsbaycamp.co.nz; map p.523. Tranquil, year-round campground right at the end of the road, on the beachfront, with toilets, washing facilities, coin-operated showers and excellent kitchens. Camping **$12**

North Canterbury

The mountains of **North Canterbury** are traversed by SH7, following an ancient Māori and early Pakeha trade route. A side road leads to the spa town of **Hanmer Springs**, a popular base for summer walks and winter sports. Some 60km further west, SH7 climbs the **Lewis Pass** before dropping down to the steaming thermal waters of **Maruia Springs**.

Hanmer Springs

Around 125km from Christchurch, a spur road (SH7A) branches off SH7 to **HANMER SPRINGS**, 9km further along at the edge of a broad, fertile plain snuggled against the Southern Alps foothills. Rainwater seeps through fractures in the rock of the Hanmer Range, absorbing minerals before being warmed by the earth's natural heat – a process that takes almost two centuries – before surfacing as Hanmer's famous **hot springs**. Everything centres on oak-lined **Amuri Avenue**, which runs past the springs, the i-SITE, shops, and the shady central park that gives the town its quiet, sheltered feel.

Hanmer Springs Thermal Pools and Spa

42 Amuri Ave • Pools daily 10am–9pm; spa daily 10am–7pm; café daily 10am–8.30pm • Pools $24; towel rental $5; waterslides $10; private pools $32/person for 30min (minimum 2 people, includes general entry) • Pools ☎ 03 315 0000, spa ☎ 03 315 0029; ⓦ hanmersprings.co.nz

Whatever the weather, it's a pleasure to wallow at this open-air complex where you can soak in twelve landscaped thermal pools ranging from 33°C to 42°C, or cool off in two freshwater swimming pools kept at 29°C. Add in three waterslides (one that swirls you around what looks like a giant toilet bowl), half a dozen private pools and the *Garden House Café* and you could stay all day. It's at its best in the evening when the crowds thin and the sun sets. Next door, the stylish **spa** offers pampering treatments including a good range of massages (from $90).

ARRIVAL AND DEPARTURE
HANMER SPRINGS

By bus Two companies, Hanmer Connection (☎ 03 382 2952, ⓦ hanmerconnection.co.nz) and Hanmer Tours & Shuttle (☎ 03 315 7418, ⓦ hanmertours.co.nz), run buses between Christchurch and Hanmer, where they arrive and depart from a stop just north of the springs.

To reach Kaikoura, you'll need to return to Amberley and catch a northbound bus from there; at the time of writing there was no public transport over the Lewis Pass to Nelson.
Destinations Christchurch (2 daily; 2hr).

10

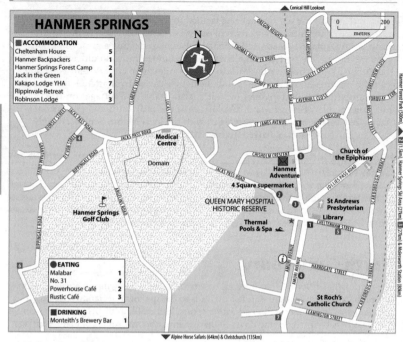

ACTIVITIES

Hanmer has plenty to keep you entertained, most conveniently in the **Hanmer Forest Park**, where hiking and biking trails wind through groves of black pine, Douglas fir and assorted deciduous trees.

SKIING

Hanmer Springs Ski Area Off Clarence Valley Rd, 17km north of town, and is generally open mid-July to Sept (daily lift rates from $60; ☎ 027 434 1806, ⓦ skihanmer.co.nz). Tiny ski resort with just one rope tow and New Zealand's longest Poma-style lift, with one beginner run, six intermediate and five advanced runs. The access road is notoriously dicey, so take the **shuttle bus** ($40 return) operated by Hanmer Adventure (see page 532), where you can also rent ski gear; snow chains are essential if you fancy driving yourself. On the mountain, *Robinson Lodge* (see page 533) has gear rentals and basic accommodation.

HIKING

Conical Hill (2km return; 1hr; 150m ascent). A short, steep and rewarding walk along a switch-backed forest trail to a hilltop pavilion with great views over Hanmer and the surrounding hills.

Waterfall Track (2.5km return; 2hr 30min; 400m ascent). An attractive walk through beech forest that climbs fairly steeply to the 41m-high Dog Stream Waterfall. The path starts from a car park well inside the Forest Park; follow Jollie's Pass Road out of town, after 2km turn left onto McIntyre Rd, then follow the road to its end.

BIKING

Hanmer Adventure 20 Conical Hill Rd ☎ 0800 368 7386, ⓦ hanmeradventure.co.nz. Rents out bikes ($60/day) to explore the forest's gravel roads and twisting singletrack. Alternatively, the centre can transport you to the top of Jacks Pass for their self-guided "Twin Passes" ride, a largely downhill trail with a small ascent over Jollies Pass ($125, including a hot pools pass).

BUNGY JUMPING, RAFTING AND JETBOATING

Hanmer Springs Attractions 839 Hanmer Springs Rd ☎ 0800 661 538, ⓦ hanmerspringsattractions.nz. The Waiau Ferry Bridge (8km southwest of town) is a base for all manner of activities including scenic 2hr rafting trips along the Grade II Waiau River (70–90min rafting, with a jetboat ride back to base; $169), jetboat rides through the steep-sided Waiau River Gorge (30min; $125), bungy jumps ($169 including T-shirt) from a 35m platform, and quad biking (2hr; $169), with combo packages available. Book online or visit their office in Hanmer (daily 9am–5.30pm).

HORSERIDING

Alpine Horse Safaris Waitohi Downs, Hawarden, 65km south of Hanmer ☎03 314 4293, ⓦalpinehorse.co.nz. Short rides are available (2hr for $85, half-day for $125) but this is really a place for serious three- to twelve-day cross-country trips (from $1225) across high country stations and even down to Tekapo, staying in musterers' huts and eating around camp fires. Check online for schedules

INFORMATION

Tourist information i-SITE, 40 Amuri Ave, next to the hot pools (daily 10am–5pm; ☎03 315 0020, ⓦvisithanmersprings.co.nz). Helpful for local information and bookings, and to obtain the excellent *Hanmer Springs Walks* and *Hanmer Springs Mountain Bike Tracks* leaflets ($3 each).

Services The i-SITE contains a small BNZ branch with ATM (Mon–Fri 10am–2pm); there's another 24hr BNZ ATM outside the Four Square supermarket at 12 Conical Hill Rd.

10

ACCOMMODATION

Hanmer has a good spread of accommodation but as a popular weekend getaway it's worth booking ahead year-round. Aside from the campsite, *Hanmer Backpackers* and *Jack in the Green* offer camping.

★ **Cheltenham House** 13 Cheltenham St ☎03 315 7545, ⓦcheltenham.co.nz; map p.532. The best B&B in town, with four large, gracious rooms in a 1930s house with a billiards room, plus two cottages in the lovingly tended garden. Evening drinks and spa included; an excellent breakfast is served in your room. They also have two modern self-contained four-bedroom villas. B&B doubles $245, villas $330

Hanmer Backpackers 41 Conical Hill Rd ☎03 315 7196, ⓦhanmerbackpackers.co.nz; map p.532. Heart-warmingly cosy A-frame chalet-style hostel bang in town with a snug, book-filled, TV-free lounge, hot water bottles, spotless facilities, sociable BBQ patio and lots of free treats such as plunger coffee. Dorms $33, doubles $76

★ **Jack in the Green** 3 Devon St ☎03 315 5111, ⓦjackinthegreen.co.nz; map p.532. Relaxed and tastefully decorated hostel, with spacious rooms in a couple of converted houses and chalets a 10min walk from the centre, plus a large garden with a giant swing-sofa. There's plenty of space for tents and campervan parking, and bunk-free dorms. Dorms $32, doubles $76

Kakapo Lodge YHA 14 Amuri Ave ☎03 315 7472, ⓦkakapolodge.co.nz; map p.532. Large, sun-filled associate YHA hostel with modern, roomy dorms and a communal balcony; there's a log-burning stove and a tuck shop in the lobby. Self-catering motel units also available ($115). Dorms $33, doubles $76

Rippinvale Retreat 68 Rippingale Rd ☎03 315 7139, ⓦhanmersprings.net.nz; map p.532. Upmarket B&B on the edge of town with just two suites, both beautifully furnished and each with private courtyard and fresh flowers. Breakfast, a gourmet affair with largely home-grown and organic ingredients, is served in your room and there's a spa pool and outdoor fireplace in the grounds. $355

Robinson Lodge Hanmer Springs Ski Area ☎027 434 1806, ⓦskihanmer.co.nz; map p.532. In season, ski-field visitors can sleep in the simple dorm accommodation (four bunkrooms and four family rooms), with shared hot showers. Bring all your food and a sleeping bag with you – there are cooking facilities on site, and the lodge supplies sheets and pillows. $30

CAMPING

Hanmer Springs Forest Camp 243 Jollies Pass Rd, 2km east of town ☎03 315 7202, ⓦhanmerforestcamp.co.nz; map p.532. A community campsite backing onto the Hanmer Forest Reserve with no powered sites, but plenty of well-maintained budget cabins, plus space for tents. Camping $14, cabins $52

EATING

Malabar 5 Conical Hill Rd ☎03 315 7745, ⓦmalabar.co.nz; map p.532. Modern fusion restaurant with an adventurous menu featuring modern twists on dishes from Asia and the subcontinent such as Canterbury lamb *rogan josh* ($33.50) and Cantonese double-caramelized pork belly ($34). Mon–Fri & Sun 5–9.30pm, Sat noon–2.30pm & 5–9.30pm.

★ **No. 31** 31 Amuri Ave ☎03 315 7031; map p.532. With the kitchen producing beautifully presented, modern Kiwi dishes, and local wines taking pride of place on the wine list, this is fine-dining, Hanmer Springs-style. Mains include Angus beef fillet with black garlic and mushroom glaze ($39.50), and there are vegetarian options available. Daily 5–11pm.

★ **Powerhouse Café** 8 Jack's Pass Rd ☎03 315 5252, ⓦpowerhousecafe.co.nz; map p.532. Funky modern café in a 1926 building that once housed a diesel generator, serving Hanmer's best coffee, mouth-watering and often gluten-free counter food, decadent versions of brunch classics including French toast and kedgeree ($19.50–20.50), and filling lunches such as steak sandwiches ($26) and *coq au vin* ($28). Daily 7.30am–2pm.

Rustic Café 8 Conical Hill Rd ☎03 315 7274; map p.532. Great little tapas restaurant with small plates of tasty treats; pan-fried chorizo with roasted capsicum, prawns in coconut panko and halloumi bruschetta ($11 each) all feature. Thurs & Fri 9.30am–9.30pm, Sat & Sun 8am–10pm.

10

DRINKING

Monteith's Brewery Bar 47 Amuri Ave ☎ 03 315 5133, ☎ mbbh.co.nz; map p.532. The town's liveliest bar, all timber and river stones fireplaces, with sport on TV and Monteith's on tap, serving reliable meals such as warm Morrocan lamb salad ($27.50) and pumpkin gnocchi with blue cheese sauce ($24). Daily 9am–10pm or later.

Maruia Springs

SH7, 75km west of Hanmer Springs • Daily 8am–9pm • Pools $40; towel rental $6 • ☎ 03 523 8840, ☎ maruiasprings.co.nz

Some 77km to the west of Hanmer Springs, and 8km beyond 907m-high Lewis Pass, SH7 continues to **Maruia Springs**, a blissful riverside spa with Japanese-style men's and women's bathhouses, private spas and natural-rock outdoor **hot pools**, whose steaming mineral-enriched waters range from black to milky white.

ACCOMMODATION   MARUIA SPRINGS

Maruia Springs Resort ☎ 03 523 8840, ☎ maruiasprings.co.nz. Simple but well-equipped rooms opening to shared or private balconies overlooking the garden and mountains, the hotel's electricity generated by the nearby Maruia River. Access to the springs is included and the restaurant serves good Japanese and European dishes (breakfast $12–21; dinner mains $29–39.50). **$169**

Central Canterbury

The **Central Canterbury** region directly west of Christchurch encompasses the transition from the flat Canterbury Plains to the rugged and spectacular Southern Alps further south. Both the *TranzAlpine* train and **SH73** (promoted as the Great Alpine Highway) from Christchurch to **Arthur's Pass** and the West Coast thread across the plains beside the braided Waimakariri River before climbing up through the Torlesse Range and dropping into a beautiful upland region hemmed in by bare-topped hills.

Alternatively you can head south along **Inland Scenic Route 72**, where the region is primarily known for the winter resort town of **Methven**, which serves the ski slopes of **Mount Hutt**. In summer, an array of activities includes skydiving, jetboating and some wonderful **hiking** around Mount Somers.

Springfield

From Christchurch the SH73 is virtually flat for 65km west to **SPRINGFIELD**, a lowland village that's the main base for four nearby **ski-fields** (see page 537), and high-speed boat trips in the clear waters of the narrow **Waimakariri River**.

INFORMATION AND ACTIVITIES   SPRINGFIELD

Tourist information The *Station 73 Café* (see page 536) acts as an ad hoc information centre.

Rubicon Valley Horse Treks ☎ 03 318 8886, ☎ rubiconvalley.co.nz. Offers some of the best-value horse trekking around, from a gentle farm ride (1hr; $55) to a mountain trail ride following a musterers' trail (minimum two people; 4hr 30min; $285). Heritage-minded visitors can opt for a stagecoach ride and cream tea combo ($50).

Pick-ups in Springfield.

Waimak Alpine Jet Rubicon Rd ☎ 03 385 1478, ☎ alpinejet. co.nz. Shallow braided sections, the narrow Waimakariri Gorge, 360-degree spins and a good deal of local lore make these jetboat trips excellent value for money. The route partly follows the *TranzAlpine* train line. Advance bookings essential. The Canyon Safari (1hr; $120) is the one to go for, but the Adventure Tour (30min; $90) covers the essentials.

ACCOMMODATION AND EATING

Kowai Pass Reserve Campground Domain Rd (1.5km south from Springfield, just off SH73) ☎ 03 318 4887.

Basic and peaceful with powered and standard sites in a sheltered spot with coin-operated showers. Sign in with the

10

caretaker signposted on the opposite side of the road. $10 per site; $20 with power hook-ups

★ **Smylies** 5653 West Coast Rd (SH73) ☎ 03 318 4740, ⓦ smylies.co.nz. Welcoming Japanese/Kiwi-run associate YHA and motel with free Japanese baths (daily in winter, on request in summer), a wood-fire-warmed lounge and comfy but creaky rooms. Delicious Japanese- or Kiwi-style evening meals ($27) and continental or cooked breakfasts (from $15), plus ski rental, winter shuttle services, and bouldering mat rental are also available. Dorms $38, doubles $90

★ **Station 73 Café** King St, signposted 500m off SH73

☎ 03 318 4000. A slice of ginger crunch and a cuppa seems just about right in this simple but well-kept café in the Springfield train station with mountain views and walls lined with railway ephemera. They also serve toasted sandwiches, gourmet pies, locally renowned "Tranz Alpine" muffins and good espresso. Daily 8.30am–3pm, later in summer.

Yello Shack Café SH73 ☎ 03 318 4880. This cheery café (next to the giant Springfield Donut sculpture) serves wood-fired pizzas on weekend evenings; the rest of the time the menu is focused on tasty cabinet food and home-made pies, washed down with good coffee (though it's fully licensed too). Daily 8am–4pm.

Kura Tawhiti (Castle Hill Conservation Area)

Once over 939m Porter's Pass, SH73 drops down into the Castle Hill basin, hemmed in by the ski-field-draped Craigieburn Range. The grassy lower slopes are peppered by clusters of grey limestone outcrops up to 30m high that have become a magnet for **world-class bouldering** and a regular stop for top international rock-climbers.

Boulderers make for scattered locales such as **Flock Hill** (where large portions of *The Lion, the Witch and the Wardrobe* were filmed), Spittle Hill and Quantum Field, but everyone else stops at **Kura Tawhiti**, often known as **Castle Hill** for its resemblance to a ruined fort. This is a place of spiritual significance to Māori – certain boulders are off limits – and home to Castle Hill buttercups and other rare flora; an area has been cordoned off for the plants' protection. From a parking area, a number of easy paths wind among the rocks and tussock-covered hills. Allow an hour or bring a picnic and stay for the afternoon.

Cave Stream Scenic Reserve

Some 6km north of Kura Tawhiti on SH73, **Cave Stream Scenic Reserve** nestles among limestone outcrops with views of the Craigieburn and Torlesse ranges and offers a rare opportunity for an unguided **walk/wade** exploration of a **limestone cave**. Cave art, signs of seasonal camps and the discovery of an ancient wooden-framed flax backpack and other artefacts over 500 years old indicate that Māori visited the area extensively. Today the cave provides a home for large but harmless **cave harvestman** spiders – only found here and in one other cave on South Island.

The cave "walk"

The 594m cave traverse takes about an hour: take a companion, dress warmly, be sure to carry at least two good torches each (the cave is pitch dark) and have something dry to change into afterwards. After entering at the downstream end, you wade through a deep pool. If the water is above waist-high, fast-flowing, foaming or discoloured, do not attempt the walk. As you work your way upstream there are only two major obstacles apart from the dark and cold; a 1.5m rockfall about halfway through that funnels the waterflow and can be quite hard to climb, and a 3m waterfall at the very end. The latter (within sight of the cave exit) is negotiated by climbing a ladder of iron rungs embedded in the rock and crawling along a short, narrow ledge while holding onto an anchored chain.

ACCOMMODATION	CAVE STREAM SCENIC RESERVE

Craigieburn Shelter campsite 5km north of Cave Stream Scenic Reserve on gravel road (signposted off SH73). A small and pretty DOC site beside a stream with long-drop toilets, tank water (which you'll have to treat), a day-use shelter and a healthy population of sandflies. $8

Flock Hill Lodge SH73, 10km north of Cave Stream Scenic Reserve ☎03 318 8196, Ⓦflockhill.co.nz. Accommodation on a high-country sheep station that's handy if you're bouldering, skiing or tramping hereabouts, set in a gorgeous spot that's popular for weddings. Backpacker bunkrooms sleep four (linen $10 extra) with a separate kitchen/dining room and coin-op internet, plus tent sites, double rooms and attractive wood-panelled self-contained cottages ($170). All options are self-catering. Dorms $35, doubles $90

Craigieburn ski-fields

The majestic **Craigieburn Range** runs along the south banks of the Waimakariri River, harbouring four basic ski-fields (generally open July–Sept), easily accessed from SH73 between Springfield and Arthur's Pass. **Porters Ski Area** (Ⓦskiporters.co.nz) is the closest (33km west of Springfield), with beginner and intermediate facilities as well as advanced runs, café and bar, a lodge and equipment rentals. **Broken River Ski Area** (Ⓦbrokenriver.co.nz), 11.5km northwest of Cave Stream, offers steep chutes, off-piste soft-snow skiing, snowboarding and three rustic lodges (with craft beer and cider on tap at *Palmer Lodge*), attracting more experienced skiers. Some 12.5km northwest from Cave Stream Scenic Reserve, **Mount Cheeseman Ski Area** (Ⓦmtcheeseman.co.nz) is a family-friendly resort primarily targeted at learners and intermediate skiers (with rentals and two lodges). **Craigieburn Valley Ski Area** (Ⓦcraigieburn.co.nz), 12.5km north from Cave Stream, also attracts experienced skiers with its longer runs, incredible views, uncrowded slopes (with narrow, steep chutes and wide open powder bowls) and access to backcountry skiing, but you'll need your own gear. Many of the resort lodges open in **summer** for **hikers** and **mountain bikers** – check the websites for details.

Arthur's Pass National Park

The most dramatic of the three Southern Alps crossings links Christchurch with Greymouth, via **Arthur's Pass**, traversed by a scenic railway and the equally mesmerizing SH73. The pass is surrounded by the 950-square-kilometre **Arthur's Pass National Park**, a remarkable alpine landscape with some superb easy walks and tough tramps. The park centres on diminutive **Arthur's Pass Village**, nestled along SH73 at 737m above sea level in a steep-sided, forest-covered U-shaped valley. Because the park spans the transition zone between the soggy West Coast and the much drier east, Otira, just west of the pass, gets around 6m of rain a year, while Bealey, 10km to the east, gets only 2m. Consequently, Arthur's Pass Village is often shrouded in mist, providing a moody contrast with the rich vegetation of the slopes above. The village offers a slim range of lodging and even more limited eating; stock up beforehand if you're planning to spend time in the area. Nights are often chilly and snow occasionally blocks the pass itself, 4km west of the village and, at 920m, almost 200m higher. It's marked by an obelisk dedicated to the civil engineer **Arthur Dudley Dobson**, who heard about the route from local Māori, and surveyed it in 1864. Immediately west of the pass, the road drops away dramatically across the **Otira Viaduct**, a huge concrete gash completed in 1999 to span the tumbling river below. Side streams carry so much water that one is diverted over the roadway in a kind of artificial waterfall. A small lookout provides the best view.

ARRIVAL AND DEPARTURE — ARTHUR'S PASS

By train The *TranzAlpine* stops just south of the village centre; reach the platforms through the underpass opposite the DOC offices.

Destinations Christchurch (1 daily; 2hr 30min); Greymouth (1 daily; 2hr).

By bus West Coast Shuttle (☎03 768 0028, Ⓦwestcoastshuttle.co.nz) runs a daily service from Greymouth to Christchurch and back, stopping in Arthur's Pass around 9.10am on the eastbound journey, mid-afternoon (4.45pm) on the westbound. Atomic Shuttles (☎03 349 0697, Ⓦatomictravel.co.nz) does the same journey in reverse, setting out from Christchurch. Both companies stop outside the Arthur's Pass Store/Mountain House Lodge.

Destinations Christchurch (1 daily; 2hr 30min); Greymouth (1 daily; 1hr 15min).

10

INFORMATION

Arthur's Pass National Park Visitor Centre SH73 (daily: Nov–April 8am–5pm; May–Oct 8.30am–4.30pm; ☏ 03 318 9211, ⓦ arthurspass.com). Excellent information centre with extensive displays on wildlife, plants, geology and local history; you can watch a video about the trail blazed by the stagecoaches and the railway on request ($2). The latest weather report is posted outside.

Services There is a single ATM in the Arthur's Pass Store which accepts most major cards; the store also operates the only petrol pump between Springfield and the West Coast.

ACCOMMODATION

Good-value accommodation is strung out along the main road; book ahead in high season (Dec–March).

Alpine Motel 52 Main Rd (SH73) ☏ 03 318 9233, ⓦ apam.co.nz; map p.539. A short walk south of the village these six aged but well-kept chalet-style motel units come with kitchen, DVD players and electric blankets. There are discounts in low season and wi-fi is free. **$130**

The Bealey SH73, 10km southeast of Arthur's Pass Village ☏ 03 318 9277, ⓦ bealeyhotel.co.nz; map p.539. High on a knoll, this historic hotel has motel-

---

WALKS AND TRAMPS AROUND ARTHUR'S PASS

Apart from a few easy walks around Arthur's Pass Village, the national park is substantially more rugged than most in New Zealand, making it suitable only for moderately to highly experienced trampers.

SAFETY, INFORMATION AND EQUIPMENT

All multiday walks involve some route finding (bring a compass) and unbridged river crossings; make adequate preparations (see page 50), and record your intentions through ⓦ adventuresmart.org.nz. The free *Tramping in Arthur's Pass National Park* leaflet is useful, downloadable from ⓦ doc.govt.nz. You'll also need 1:50,000 topographic maps, available for sale ($9 each) or rent ($2.50 for 1–3 days; $5 for 4–12 days; plus $20 deposit) at the visitor centre, where you can also get $1 photocopied maps of most of the overnight tramping routes), 230g gas canisters ($8) and gear storage ($1/item/day).

ACCESS AND ACCOMMODATION

West Coast Shuttle and Atomic (see page 515) can arrange to drop-off or pick-up from trailheads, if given advance notice. Overnight hikes involve camping or staying in **DOC huts** that can't be booked. Obtain hut tickets from the DOC office in Arthur's Pass or use a Backcountry Hut Pass.

SHORT WALKS

Devil's Punchbowl (2km return; 1hr; 100m ascent). The village's most popular short walk, following an all-weather climb and descent to the base of a 131m waterfall, crossing two footbridges and zigzagging up steps.

Dobson Nature Walk (1km return; 30min). Easy graded walk at the crest of Arthur's Pass with panels explaining subalpine herbs, tussock and shrubs, best seen Nov–Feb when they're in bloom. The nature walk can be reached on foot along the Arthur's Pass Walking Track.

Arthur's Pass Walking Track (6.8km return; 3hr; 200m ascent). A lively bushwalk that links the village to the Dobson Nature Walk and Arthur's Pass. The pretty path winds through beech forest, passing Bridal Veil Falls and Jack's Hut, a green corrugated-iron cabin once used by roading crews during the coaching days, en route.

DAY-WALKS AND MULTI-DAY TRAMPS

Avalanche Peak Track (5km return; 6–8hr; 1100m ascent). Strenuous day-hike that offers wonderful views of the surrounding mountains. Parts of the route are exposed; it should only be attempted by well-equipped, experienced trampers in reasonable weather. The best way is going up the spectacular Avalanche Peak Track and making a circuit by returning on the Scotts Track.

Casey Saddle to Binser Saddle (RG10: 40km; 2 days; 400m ascent). Moderate loop with great views as you cross easy saddles on well-defined tracks through open beech forest, camping overnight (the Casey Hut burnt down in 2015).

Mingha–Deception (RG6: 25km; 2 days; 400m ascent, 750m descent). A great (but demanding) overnighter that traces the route used for the mountain-run stage of the arduous Coast to Coast race. The Mingha Valley to Goat Pass section is marked, but the trail down the Deception Valley is unmarked and involves 20–30 river crossings, so watch the water levels. Stay at either the Goat Pass Hut (20 bunks; $15) or the Upper Deception Hut (6 bunks; free) and ponder how mad you'd have to be to run the route competitively.

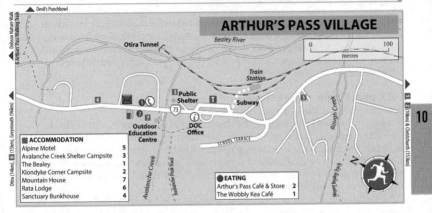

ACCOMMODATION

Alpine Motel	5
Avalanche Creek Shelter Campsite	3
The Bealey	1
Klondyke Corner Campsite	2
Mountain House	7
Rata Lodge	6
Sanctuary Bunkhouse	4

EATING

Arthur's Pass Café & Store	2
The Wobbly Kea Café	1

style cabins with great views of the upper reaches of the Waimakariri River. The restaurant/bar is filled with memorabilia of the hotel's early role as a stop-off point for Cobb & Co stagecoaches and of claimed moa sightings hereabouts in recent decades (hence the life-size moa sculptures that dot the grounds). Lodge rooms <u>$75</u>, motel units <u>$150</u>

★ **Mountain House** 84 Main Rd (SH73) ☎03 318 9258, ⊕trampers.co.nz; map p.539. This BBH and associate YHA hostel has the widest range of beds in the village. The neat main hostel is supplemented by a pair of four-bedroom, self-contained 1920s railway workers' cottages ($360) and, in summer (normally Dec–March), the owner opens the "Historic Lodge", an original 1950s YHA hostel with bags of old-school character. More upmarket tastes are catered to by two comfortable motel units with kitchenettes, queen beds and satellite TV ($165). Powered sites are also available ($22). Dorms <u>$33</u>, doubles <u>$92</u>

Rata Lodge SH73, Otira, 15km north of Arthur's Pass Village ☎03 738 2822, ⊕rata-lodge.co.nz; map p.539. Spacious and chilled forest-girt BBH hostel on the western edge of the national park. There's a four-bunk dorm, two en-suite doubles with TV, and a little bush walk

with glowworms. Bring food to self-cater. Dorms <u>$34</u>, doubles <u>$90</u>

Sanctuary Bunkhouse 126 Main Rd (SH73) ☎0274 662 755, ⊕thesanctuary.co.nz; map p.539. Unstaffed dorm-style bunk accommodation with just eight dorm beds (sleeping bags required). There are adequate kitchen facilities and a day-room, patchwork quilts on the beds and a home-made glass-roofed bathroom for stargazers. Coin-operated hot showers, 24hr internet and laundry facilities are open to the public; payment for everything is via honesty box. Dorms <u>$27</u>

CAMPING

Avalanche Creek Shelter Campsite Main Rd (SH73) ☎03 318 9211; map p.539. DOC site that's not much more than a patch of grass and a gravel parking lot for campervans directly opposite the DOC office. There's potable water, toilets and a day-use shelter. First come, first served, cash only. <u>$8</u>

Klondyke Corner Campsite SH73, 8km southeast of Arthur's Pass village ☎03 318 9211; map p.539. Basic, grassy DOC site set between the highway and the river with great views, a long-drop toilet and river water (which should be treated). <u>Free</u>

EATING

Arthur's Pass Café & Store 85 Main Rd (SH73) ☎03 318 9235, ⊕arthurspasscafe.co.nz; map p.539. The best place to fuel up for a hike or replenish afterwards. It offers breakfasts ($7–23.50), pies, sandwiches ($7–9.50) and excellent coffee, along with limited groceries and ATM. Daily 8am–5pm, later in summer.

The Wobbly Kea Café 108 Main Rd (SH73) ☎03 318 9101, ⊕wobblykea.co.nz; map p.539. The village linchpin for steaming hot chocolate and coffee, imaginative lunches, and hearty dinners; the $32.50 pizzas are big enough for two modest appetites. Also doubles as a bar hosting occasional live gigs. Daily 10am–8pm.

Methven

A hundred kilometres west of Christchurch, **METHVEN** is Canterbury's winter-sports capital and the accommodation and refuelling centre for the busy **Mount**

10

Hutt ski-field during the June to October **ski season**. Outside those months it can be pretty quiet, though summer visitors often base themselves here to explore **Rakaia Gorge** and **Washpen Falls** to the north, and **Mount Somers** to the south. It's not a big place but the small centre has banks, post office, medical centre, supermarkets and sports supplies.

NZ Alpine & Agriculture Encounter

Methven Heritage Centre, 160 Main St • Daily 9am–5pm • $12.50 • ☎ 03 302 9666

Methven celebrates its position at the intersection of plains and mountains in this interactive museum focussing on winter sports and agriculture. A full-size combine harvester emphasizes the historic importance of arable farming (which is proudly unsubsidized in New Zealand) and seed-growing in the mid-Canterbury region, while the cross-section of a model cow celebrates the big bucks that dairying has been bringing in since the 1990s.

A collection of historic skis and some great old film footage herald a section on the development of the Mount Hutt ski-field in the 1970s, including a replica of the hut used by Willi Huber to winter on the mountain in 1972 while assessing its skiing potential – two mice kept him company through the lonely snowy months. There's also a live beehive to examine, a fun hydraulic excavator simulation, a section on World War I and homage paid to one Henry Wigley, who "invented" the ski plane down here in 1955.

ACTIVITIES

Braided Rivers Fishing Guides ☎ 03 741 1338, ⓦ salmonfishingguide.co.nz. Professional fishing guide, Ben Haywood, leads salmon and trout fishing trips (from $675, all-inclusive) on the Rakaia and Waimakariri rivers.

Mt Hutt Helicopters 38 McMillan St, Methven ☎ 03 302 8401, ⓦ mthutthelicopters.com. Scenic helicopter flights above the patchwork quilt of the Canterbury Plains and the magnificent Southern Alps – especially magical in winter. The trips range from $85 for a quick 6min zip over the Mt Hutt Ski Area, to 1hr 15min flights over the Alps ($645) and 2hr 15min jaunts around Mt Cook ($1340). Hangar location 880 Forks Rd, Alford Forest.

Skydiving Kiwis Ashburton Airport, Seafield Rd, Ashburton, 35km south of Methven ☎ 0800 359549, ⓦ skydivingkiwis.com. Very professional outfit with an excellent safety record, offering magical mountain views from tandem jumps (from $235).

ARRIVAL AND INFORMATION

METHVEN

By bus Methven Travel (☎ 0800 684888, ⓦ methventravel. co.nz), with its office inside Methven Heritage Centre, runs buses from Christchurch (3–4 weekly in summer; 3 daily in ski season; 90min; $45 one way). Methven Travel and Snowman Shuttles (☎ 0800 766962, ⓦ snowmanshuttles. co.nz) also serve the ski-field.

i-SITE Methven Heritage Centre, 160 Main St (Oct–May Mon–Fri 9am–5pm, Sat & Sun 11am–3pm; June–Oct daily 8.30am–5.45pm; ☎ 03 302 8955, ⓦ midcanterburynz. com). Visit for information, free wi-fi, plus a "snow desk" run by Mt Hutt staff in ski season.

Services Love Laundry (☎ 027 629 5475) on the Mall features a 24hr coin-operated laundry ($6 for a wash or dry). The post office is at 129 Main St (Mon–Fri 8am–5pm).

Ski and bike rental Alpine Sports, 87 Main St (May–Oct daily 7.30am–7pm; ☎ 03 302 8084, ⓦ alpinesports. co.nz), rents and sells skis and other equipment. Big Al's, at the corner of Forest Drive and Main St (Nov–May Tues–Fri 9am–1pm & 3–5.30pm, Sat 9am–1pm; June–Oct daily 7.30am–7.30pm; ☎ 03 302 8003, ⓦ bigals. co.nz), rents skis, boards and bikes (hardtail $45/day; full suspension $59/day), with information on an easy town loop and the Mt Hutt Bike Park.

ACCOMMODATION

Outside the June–October ski season prices drop significantly from the winter prices shown below.

Abisko Lodge & Campground 74 Main St ☎ 03 302 8875, ⓦ abisko.co.nz; map p.541. Dependable, central establishment incorporating a campsite, en-suite doubles and cosy self-contained apartments ($205), complete with sauna and hot tub (fee charged). Camping per site $42, doubles $145

Big Tree Lodge 25 South Belt ☎ 03 302 9575, ⓦ bigtreelodge.co.nz; map p.541. Laundry and wi-fi are free at this homely snowboarder-run hostel. Rooms in the main house share a kitchen and bathrooms, while the pleasant three-bed cottage is self-contained ($130).

Dorms $40, doubles $85

The Lodge 1 Chertsey Rd ☏03 303 2000, ⓦthelodgenz. com; map p.541. Generously sized contemporary rooms at very decent prices, some with spa baths, and a popular on-site bistro and bar (see *The Dubliner* below). $125

Mount Hutt Bunkhouse 8 Lampard St ☏03 302 8894, ⓦmthuttbunkhouse.co.nz; map p.541. Comfortable but well-worn BBH backpackers that's spread over two adjacent houses with a large garden (including volleyball court), BBQ and log fires. Dorms $32, doubles $80

Skibo House 82 Forest Drive ☏03 302 9493, ⓦmethvenmthutt.co.nz; map p.541. Friendly B&B in a modern house where most rooms have great mountain views, though they share a bathroom. Excellent breakfasts include Bircher muesli, and eggs and bacon, and there's an outdoor hot tub. B&B $120, self-contained units $140

EATING

The Blue Pub 2 Barkers Rd ☏03 302 8046, ⓦthebluepub.co.nz; map p.541. Popular with the après-ski crowd, this 1918-built cobalt-painted hotel has a lively bar hosting bands and weekend DJs. The restaurant dishes up hearty meals such as lamb shank with honey swede mash ($30) and Dry Creek venison, fennel and date sausages ($24). Daily 11am–10pm or later.

Café 131 131 Main St ☏03 302 9131; map p.541. Airy wood-floored Art Deco café that's perfect for people-watching over Methven's best coffee. There's an array of cakes (try the cookies-and-cream slice), all-day breakfasts, filling, inexpensive lunches (BLT and fries $17) and free wi-fi. Daily 7.30am–5pm.

The Dubliner 116 Main St ☏03 302 8259, ⓦdubliner. co.nz; map p.541. Bistro fare, with great pizzas (small $19, large $26) and a few warming Irish dishes, including Irish stew ($28.50), served in the old post office, with original safe. Daily 4.30pm–midnight; closed Mon outside ski season.

★ **Primo & Secundo** 38 McMillan St ☏03 302 9060; map p.541. Wonderfully quirky café in an antique/vintage clothing/junk shop (everything is for sale), serving breakfast ($11–16) all day, along with good coffee, delectable home-made cakes and meals including savoury crêpes and shepherd's pie (lunch specials from $15). There's outside seating in the back. Daily 7am–5pm.

Thai Chilli Corner of Main Rd and Forest Drive ☏03 303 3038; map p.541. Enjoy authentic Thai dishes to a soundtrack of old- school tunes in purple-painted surroundings. The short menu is prepared and served with care – try their *pad thai* and green curry – and nothing is over $23, but the $25 daily buffet ($10 for take-away) is good value in ski season. Daily 4–9pm in ski season; closed Mon & Sun rest of year.

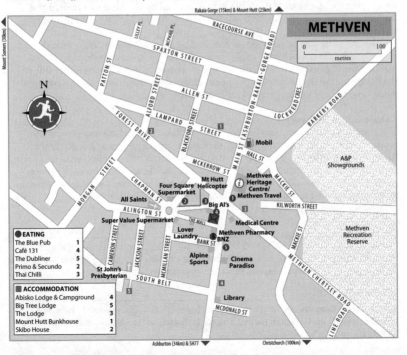

ENTERTAINMENT

Cinema Paradiso 112 Main St ☏ 03 302 1957, ⓦ cinemaparadiso.co.nz. Wonderful bijou digital cinema, with a licensed bar and two tiny rooms showing a roster of art-house flicks and new releases (tickets $12). Movies Wed–Sun 10am–8pm.

Washpen Falls

590 Washpen Rd (off SH77), near Windwhistle, 25km northeast of Methven • Self-guided walk $10 • ☏ 03 318 6813, ⓦ washpenfalls.co.nz

One of the area's lesser-known gems, the private family farm of **Washpen Falls** offers a wonderfully diverse meander through native bush and farmland. The **walking track** heads up to a point, and offers spectacular views of the Canterbury Plains. Along the way there's a canyon formed by an ancient volcano (used by Māori to trap moa), great examples of native-bush regeneration and, of course, the cascading falls. The office (a corrugated-iron shed) has leaflets outlining the track's highlights, including spots where parts of the 2015 movie *Z for Zachariah* was filmed. The loop walk is short but steep in places; set aside 2hr and take a picnic.

Rakaia Gorge

The opaque waters of the Rakaia River spill onto the Canterbury Plains from **Rakaia Gorge**, 16.5km north of Methven, created by an ancient lava flow and now lined in many places with regenerating forest. **Māori history** tells how a *taniwha* (water spirit) lived nearby, hunting and eating moa; his possessions, because of his status as a spirit, were *tapu*. One wintry day, while the *taniwha* was away searching for a hot spring, a demon in the form of the northwest wind flattened his property. Once he'd righted the damage, the *taniwha* gathered boulders to block the demon's path, so narrowing the Rakaia River and forcing the demon to blow through the rocky gorge to reach the plains. The heat generated by all this effort melted the mountain snow, and the *taniwha*'s drops of perspiration became crystals in the riverbed.

Today the gorge can be explored on foot and by jetboat (see page 532), with the single-lane **Rakaia Gorge Bridge** (SH77) over the Rakaia River, completed in 1882, marking the beginning of the scenic bit – you can stop at parking areas either side of the bridge to take in the views of the mountains and startling aquamarine waters, but you'll need to head up the gorge to really appreciate its beauty.

Rakaia Gorge Walkway

The *taniwha*'s sweaty work can be seen from the **Rakaia Gorge Walkway** (10km; 4hr return) which starts from a car park on the eastern bank of the river just across the **Rakaia Gorge Bridge** and winds up the wooded riverbank before emerging onto a high gorse-lined track formerly used by ferrymen. This path follows the rim of the gorge, passing hardened lava flows of rhyolite, pitchstone and andesite, and a former coalmine to the upper gorge lookout, forming a loop at its far end. The less committed can walk as far as the lower gorge lookout (3.4km, 1hr return).

ACTIVITIES   RAKAIA GORGE

Discovery Jet Rakaia Gorge Bridge, SH77 ☏ 0800 538 2628, ⓦ discoveryjet.co.nz. Great-value, high-octane jetboating to the top of the Rakaia Gorge. Go for the full 45min trip ($99), or opt for a 15min spin ($45) with a drop-off at the Rakaia Gorge Walkway and walk back – take a picnic to make an afternoon of it.

ACCOMMODATION

Rakaia Gorge Campsite SH77, 16km north of Methven. Peaceful campsite high on the west bank of the Rakaia Gorge Bridge with views out across the plains. Equipped with toilets (year-round), hot showers (mid-Oct to April), and pedestrian access to the river. **$10**

Mount Hutt ski-field and bike park

25km northwest of Methven • Lift pass $95; ski/board rental $48 • ⊕ 03 308 5074, ⓦ nzski.com

Since it opened in 1973, **Mount Hutt** is widely regarded as one of the best and most varied ski-fields in New Zealand, with a vertical rise of 683m, a choice of runs for all talents and, generally, the longest season (roughly June–Oct). All this is served by triple-, quad- and six-seater chairlifts, and plenty of snowmaking. Rentals are available on the mountain, but there's no accommodation, so most people **stay** in Methven, from where there are **shuttle buses** (2–3 daily; $20 return; 45min; ⓦ methventravel. co.nz); buy a ticket on board or from the i-SITE, from where the shuttles depart.

In the summer much of the mountain transforms into **Mt Hutt Bike Park** (ⓦ bikemethven.co.nz), with over 30km of trails, from family-friendly cross-country loops to downhill and single-track trails with technical descents. A full list of trail routes is available at ⓦ trailforks.com or at the i-SITE and *Big Al's* in Methven.

10

Mount Somers

The 1687m **Mount Somers** rises from the flatlands above the villages of **Staveley**, 21km southwest of Methven on Inland Scenic Route 72, and **Mount Somers**, 9km further south. The mountain is encircled by the **Mount Somers Track**, which is conveniently in the rain shadow of the Southern Alps and is often above the bushline – when it's raining in Arthur's Pass and Mount Cook is clagged in, there's still a chance you'll be able to get some hiking in here. The terrain, gentle by South Island standards, incorporates patches of beech forest and open tussock pocked by outcrops of rock. Large areas of low-fertility soil subject to heavy rainfall turn to bog, and as a result you'll find bog pine, toatoa, mountain flax and maybe even the rare whio (blue duck). **Climbing Mount Somers** itself is strenuous but straightforward day-hike, involving a 4.7km climb (one-way; 3hr 30min–5hr depending on fitness level) from the Sharplin Falls car park. In winter the climb is for experienced mountaineers only.

INFORMATION AND ACTIVITIES   MOUNT SOMERS

Information The Staveley Village Store and Mount Somers Store have good local information.

Staveley Horse Treks 191 Flynns Rd, 2km from Staveley towards Sharplin Falls ⊕ 027 203 3444, ⓦ staveleyhorsetreks.co.nz. Bruce Gray runs some of the South Island's cheapest horse treks across Mt Somers' flanks (from $40/hr; advance bookings essential).

ACCOMMODATION AND EATING

STAVELEY

★ **Staveley Village Store** 2 Burgess Rd ⊕ 03 303 0859. A local store in the best tradition (it dates from 1876): a place for great coffee, the famed cinnamon brioche, tasty breakfasts and lunches, ice cream, limited groceries and eight different kinds of superb Staveley Sausage rolls, including leek and mushroom and cheese and pineapple. Daily 9am–4pm; closed Mon in winter.

MOUNT SOMERS

Mt Somers Domain Camping Ground Hoods Rd, 1km off S Inland Scenic Rte 72 ⊕ 021 176 0677. Cheap camping next to the local swimming pool and a historic musterers' hut with a basic toilet and shower block (showers $1), and a small kitchen and lounge. Camping per site $20
Mount Somers Holiday Park 87 Hoods Rd, 1km off Inland Scenic Rte 72 ⊕ 03 303 9719, ⓦ mountsomers.

co.nz. Comfortable tree-filled area with powered sites, simple cabins (with linen for rent) and fully made-up en-suite cabins ($90). Camping $20, simple cabins $60
Mount Somers Store 59 Pattons Rd ⊕ 03 303 9831. Another classic country store selling DOC hut tickets, ice cream, pies, sausage rolls and a reasonable range of groceries; there are two fuel pumps outside. Mon–Sat 8am–6pm, Sun 9am–5pm.

Stronechrubie 8 Hoods Rd, at Inland Scenic Rte 72 ⊕ 03 303 9814, ⓦ stronechrubie.co.nz. Beautiful modern self-contained chalets in a lovely rural setting, as well as the only real restaurant in these parts: expect local beef ($40) or Clevedon coast oysters ($25) and an excellent wine selection. Good-value dinner and bed-and-breakfast packages make it popular at weekends. Book for meals Wed–Sat 6.30–10pm, Sun noon–2pm. $120

10

MOUNT SOMERS TRACK

The strenuous but exhilarating **Mount Somers Track** (26km loop; 2–3 days; 1000m ascent) makes a subalpine loop round the mountain, passing abandoned coal mines, volcanic formations and a deep river canyon.

The **entire loop** is best tackled anticlockwise from Staveley. However, roads meet the loop in the west at Woolshed Creek (13.5km from Mount Somers village) and in the east at Sharplin Falls car park (4km from Staveley on Flynns Rd), so if you don't fancy the whole thing you can **walk either half** and get your vehicle shuttled.

TICKETS AND EQUIPMENT

Buy **DOC hut tickets** ($15 for each hut) before you start at the stores in Staveley or Mount Somers, or from i-SITEs or DOC offices; there is no booking system for the huts. You'll need to carry a cooking stove, pots and all your food; all water should be treated. Marker poles point the way adequately in most conditions but the rolling country on top of the hills is subject to disorientating fog, so bring a map and compass.

TRANSPORT

Staveley Horse Treks (see page 543) will shuttle your car for $30. After dropping you at the Woolshed Creek trailhead, they keep your vehicle safe near Sharplin Falls car park ready for your emergence from the wilds. Methven Travel (☎03 302 8106) operates a shuttle service from Methven to the Woolshed Creek or Sharplin Falls car parks ($50 and $30 respectively for one person, one-way, plus $20 for each extra person).

THE ROUTE

Sharplin Falls car park to Pinnacles Hut (5.2km; 3hr; 470m ascent). Note that the 500m Sharplin Falls Track, which branches off the main route just 500m beyond Sharplin Falls car park, is now permanently closed due to the ongoing risk of rock fall (meaning the falls viewpoint is now inaccessible). Beyond here the route climbs steadily through beech forest, reaching the tree line at *Pinnacles Hut* (19 bunks), nestled below rock monoliths frequently used by climbers.

Pinnacles Hut to Woolshed Creek Hut (6.2km; 3hr; 265m ascent). Climb towards the 1170m saddle, across treeless tussock with open views into the mountains and back to the plains. On the descent, take the 5min side trip to the Water Caves, where a stream courses below a rockfall of house-sized boulders. It is then only 10min to the modern *Woolshed Creek Hut* (26 spaces on sleeping platforms), a good place to stay a couple of nights, spending the intervening day exploring the little valleys and canyons hereabouts.

Woolshed Creek Hut to the Sharplin Falls car park (13.5km; 8hr; 400m ascent). The tramp around the mountain's south face feels quite different with incredible views across the Canterbury flatlands towards the distant coast. The terrain is a mix of high-country scrub (somewhat exposed at times) and beech forest. Soon after leaving the hut, the Howden Falls side track is worth a quick look. You then climb a ridge before traversing tussock-covered flats, passing a day-shelter at about the halfway point. After a steep climb up through beech forest you begin the long descent, first on a ridge with great views then down into the bush to Sharplin Falls car park.

Peel Forest and Rangitata Gorge

The tiny hamlet of **PEEL FOREST**, 12km west of Inland Scenic Route 72 and 45km south of Mount Somers, is the hub of **Peel Forest Park**, one of the eastern South Island's last remaining patches of original native bush, with rare strands of ancient forest trees – including lowland totara and matai – which can be seen from the **walking tracks** that thread through the bush. Come for easy walks, horse trekking and the superb **whitewater-rafting** trips through the **Rangitata Gorge**.

ACTIVITIES

PEEL FOREST

Peel Forest Horse Trekking ☎0800 022536, ⓦ peelforesthorsetrekking.co.nz. Runs excellent treks that range from a stroll along (and occasionally through) the river (1hr; $65) to a full-day trek up Mt Peel (6hr; $320 including lunch), plus multi-day trips and accommodation.

Rangitata Rafts Rangitata Gorge Rd, 13km north of Peel Forest ☎ 03 696 3735, ⓦ rafts.co.nz. This highly professional outfit runs some of New Zealand's best whitewater-rafting trips on the Grade IV–V high-sided gorge section of the Rangitata River. Trips (Oct–May daily noon; $215) include two hours on the water – plus lunch and a barbecue dinner. Transport from Christchurch (add 2hr 30min at either end) costs just $24 extra. Book well in advance.

ACCOMMODATION AND EATING

Peel Forest Café and Bar 1202 Peel Forest Rd ☎ 03 696 3567, ⓦ peelforest.co.nz. Focal point for the village; the café serves pizzas ($17–19), burgers ($16.50) and pastries, while the bar offers cold beers, snacks and live music most weekends. Café daily 9am–4.30pm (closed Mon June–Sept); bar Wed–Sun 6pm–late.

Peel Forest Campground Peel Forest Rd ☎ 03 696 3567. A lovely wooded DOC-run campsite set beside the Rangitata River, with tent and powered sites and four simple "eco-cabins". Closed late April to late Sept; booking required Dec–March. Camping $18, cabins $50

Geraldine

The prosperous farming town of **GERALDINE**, 50km south of Mount Somers and 35km north of Timaru, rewards a brief stop to browse its smattering of **craft shops**, **galleries**, and **food stores** specializing in gourmet picnic ingredients such as local cheeses, pickles, jams, wine and chocolates. It's perhaps best known in New Zealand for being the home of the creative Linton family, recognized by the Guinness Book of Records as having the "World's Largest Jersey" and in 2012 the "World's Largest Steel Mosaic," a 64m-long **tableau of the Bayeux Tapestry** made entirely from tiny pieces of spring steel broken from the patterning discs of industrial knitting machines. Since 2016 the mosaic has been in tour in the UK (it's unlikely to return to New Zealand before 2019), while the whopping 5.5kg **Giant Jersey** is on display at the Kiwi Country Complex.

ARRIVAL AND INFORMATION GERALDINE

By bus InterCity/Newmans stop at the Kiwi Country Complex, while Atomic pick ups and drop off on Cox Street, just off the main road (Talbot St/SH79), as do Budget Shuttles (☎ 03 615 5119, ⓦ budgetshuttles.co.nz) on their Christchurch to Timaru run.
Destinations Aoraki/Mount Cook (1 daily; 2hr 50min); Christchurch (4 daily; 2hr 20min–2hr 45min); Queenstown (3 daily; 6hr–8hr 30min); Timaru (1 daily; 30min).

i-SITE Inside the Kiwi Country Complex (daily 8am–6pm; ☎ 03 693 1101) at 38 Waihi Terrace, the northern continuation of Talbot St (SH79).

ACCOMMODATION

Geraldine TOP 10 Holiday Park & Motel 39 Hislop St ☎ 03 693 8147, ⓦ geraldinetop10.co.nz. Well-tended, tree-filled campsite with the usual range of cabins and self-contained units ($86) where guests can rent cheap bikes ($5/hr) for knocking about town. Camping per site $37, cabins $52

Rawhiti Backpackers 27 Hewlings St, 1km southwest of the centre ☎ 03 693 8252, ⓦ rawhitibackpackers. com. Peaceful BBH hostel in an artistically decorated 1924 former maternity hospital, with spotless rooms and common areas, and expansive gardens. Dorms $36, doubles $82

EATING AND ENTERTAINMENT

Geraldine Cinema 74 Talbot St ☎ 03 693 8118, ⓦ geraldinecinema.co.nz. Wonderful reinvented movie house with sofas, beanbags and cosy duvets in winter (movies $12). It occasionally plays host to live bands and even opera. Typically open Wed–Sun.

The Running Duck 1 Peel St, at SH79 ☎ 03 693 8320, ⓦ therunningduck.co.nz. Retro burger bar in the old Peel St petrol station (themed around a *bach*, a modest Kiwi holiday home), with delicious burgers ($8–19),

equally tasty shakes ($6) and decent coffee. Mon, Wed & Thurs 8am–4pm, Fri 8am–8pm, Sat & Sun 9am–4pm.
Verdé Café Deli 45c Talbot St (SH79) ☎ 03 693 9616. Housed in a secluded rose-clambered cottage set back from the main road, the classy options here span a great selection of counter food plus a tempting brunch menu: think pea, asparagus and halloumi paella, or salmon on a feta potato cake (both $18). Daily 9am–4pm.

10

Mackenzie Country

The Canterbury Plains and the central South Island's snow-capped peaks frame the **Mackenzie Country**, a dramatic region of open sheep-grazed grasslands that shimmer golden brown year-round. It is all beautifully set off in November and December by strands of purple, pink and white **lupins** – regarded as weeds by farmers but much loved and photographed nonetheless.

Light reflected from microscopic rock particles suspended in glacial meltwater lends an ethereal opaque hue to the region's mesmerizingly blue, **glacier-fed lakes**, notably Tekapo, Pukaki and Ohau, which form part of the **Waitaki hydro scheme**. At 700m above sea level, the region has some of the **cleanest air** in the southern hemisphere, and on a good day the sharp edges and vibrant colours make this one of the best places to stargaze and photograph the Southern Alps, particularly around **Tekapo**.

Tekapo

The **Cass** and **Godley** rivers feed into the 83-square-kilometre **Lake Tekapo**, which in turn spills into the winding **Tekapo River** across the Mackenzie Basin. Glacial flour – ultra-fine particles of rock – suspended in the water gives the lake water its milky turquoise hue. On Lake Tekapo's southern shore, the burgeoning village of **TEKAPO** revolves around a roadside ribbon of cafés and gift shops. Its name derives from the Māori *taka* ("sleeping mat") and *po* ("night"), suggesting that this place has long been used as a stopover. It still is, with visitors keen to spend a sunny afternoon picnicking on the lakeshore, enjoying the sunset from a hot pool then stargazing after dark.

Church of the Good Shepherd

Pioneer Drive • Daily 9am–5pm • Donation

Everyone's first stop in Tekapo is the tiny lakeside **Church of the Good Shepherd**, an enchanting little stone chapel built in 1935 as a memorial to the Mackenzie Country pioneers. Behind the rough-hewn Oamaru stone altar, a window perfectly frames the lake and the surrounding mountains. Fifty metres to the east, the **Collie Dog Monument** was erected in 1968 by local sheep farmers to honour the dogs that make it possible to graze this harsh terrain.

Tekapo Springs

6 Lakeside Drive • Daily 10am–9pm • pools only $27, with steam and sauna $31; waterslide $25; tubing $12.50/hr; skating $18; towels $5 • ☎ 03 680 6550, ⓦ tekaposprings.co.nz

To simply unwind, head to the outdoor **Tekapo Springs** complex which combines beautiful, state-of-the-art hot pools – each subtly shaped like a local lake, with heated alpine water ranging from 36°C to 40°C – with a day-spa (massages from $55 for 30min). Less soothingly, there's also a waterslide in summer (Dec–Feb), an ice rink in winter (April–Sept), and tubing year-round (on snow in winter, carpet in summer).

University of Canterbury Mount John Observatory

2km on foot, 9km by road northwest of Tekapo • Summit access and café daily 9am–6pm (July–Sept 10am–5pm) • Cars $8 (pay at the kiosk on Mt John Access Rd) • ☎ 03 680 6960, ⓦ earthandsky.co.nz

Minimal light pollution presents perfect conditions for observing the night skies (Tekapo falls inside the **Aoraki Mackenzie International Dark Sky Reserve**), and the 1000m summit of Mount John, immediately northwest of Tekapo, has sprouted the **University of Canterbury Mount John Observatory**. There are two excellent hikes up here (see page 548) and great reward in the form of *Astro Café*, though the star attraction is the range of **observatory and night sky tours**. Weather conditions occasionally close the access road and café – keep an eye out for the sign at the start of the Mount John Summit walk. Note that you can drive or hike to the summit yourself during café operating hours only; for the night tours you must take the shuttle bus from Tekapo (the observatory is not open during the day).

ARRIVAL AND DEPARTURE

TEKAPO

By bus Buses linking Christchurch and Queenstown stop in the village centre on SH8; InterCity/Newmans at the car park next to the *Lake Tekapo Tavern*, Atomic outside the Four Square Supermarket. The Cook Connection (☏0800 266526, ☏cookconnect.co.nz), for Aoraki/Mount Cook,

also picks up from the *Lake Tekapo Tavern* car park, plus the *Tekapo Holiday Park*.

Destinations Aoraki/Mount Cook (2 daily; 1hr 20min–2hr 15min); Christchurch (3 daily; 3hr 45min); Queenstown (3 daily; 4–7hr 30min); Twizel (3 daily; 40min–1hr 10min).

INFORMATION

Information Kiwi Treasures & Info Centre (daily: 10am–6pm in summer, 9.30am–5pm in winter; ☏03 680 6866, ☏laketekaponz.co.nz) is on SH8 in the centre of town.

Services Tekapo's sole ATM (ANZ), on the main road (SH8) outside *Reflections* restaurant, accepts most major cards.

ACTIVITIES

SKIING

Mount Dobson 28km east of Tekapo on SH8 then 15km north along a gravel road ☏03 685 8039, ☏mtdobson. co.nz. Renowned for its powder snow, long hours of sunshine and uncrowded fields, Mt Dobson's four beginner, six intermediate and four advanced runs cater for all levels. There's a platter lift, T-bar and a triple chair, and a weekend and holiday shuttle connects to Fairlie; check online for schedules. Lift pass $82.

Roundhill 32km northwest of Tekapo along Lilybank Rd ☏03 680 6977, ☏roundhill.co.nz. Families flock to this relaxed field where you'll find one long T-bar and two learner tows plus the world's longest (1.4km) and steepest rope tow, giving a total vertical of 783m – the greatest in the country. Most of the terrain is gentle and undulating, though the rope tow gives access to four black runs. Lift passes $84.

HIKING

Mt John Summit (2km one way; 1hr; 300m ascent). Short, sharp ascent from Tekapo Springs along a switchbacked path that leads through larch forests full of birds.

Mt John Lakeshore & Summit (6km one way; 3hr; 300m ascent). A stroll north along the lakeshore then gradually up a long breezy ridge to the summit with even longer views.

SCENIC FLIGHTS

Air Safaris Lake Tekapo Airport, SH8, 4km west of Tekapo ☏03 680 6880, ☏airsafaris.co.nz. Take the "Grand Traverse" (50min; $370), which swoops across the Main Divide to the West Coast, providing views of the Franz Josef and Fox glaciers, the Tasman and Muller glaciers and Aoraki/Mount Cook – luckily every seat is a window seat.

Tekapo Helicopters SH8, 7km west of Tekapo (office on main road in Tekapo) ☏0800 359835, ☏tekapohelicopters.co.nz. Various flights (20–60min; prices from $235), all including a snow landing: the most popular flight, the "Mount Cook Adventure", sees you landing on the Liebig Dome, which is covered in snow year-round (40min; $400).

HORSERIDING

Mackenzie Alpine Horse Trekking Balmoral Station, Godley Peaks Rd (800m north of SH8) ☏0800 628269, ☏maht.co.nz. From 1hr ($80) to 3hr 30min ($180) guided horserides through dramatic alpine scenery. Operates Nov–April.

ACCOMMODATION

Most accommodation in Tekapo is on the expensive side, with the few budget options often oversubscribed – book ahead. Note that the excellent **YHA Lake Tekapo** should be open in spanking-new premises by the end of 2018 – check ☏yha.co.nz for the latest.

The Chalet Boutique Motel 14 Pioneer Drive ☏03 680 6774, ☏thechalet.co.nz. Seven beautiful individually decorated, self-contained apartments, some overlooking the lake, in a pretty spot 100m along the lakeshore from the Church of the Good Shepherd. Free laundry. **$190**

Lake Tekapo Motels and Holiday Park 2 Lakeside Drive ☏03 680 6825, ☏laketekapo-accommodation. co.nz. Situated 1km from the village at Lake Tekapo's southwest corner, this large, well-run holiday park overlooks the lake, and offers a wider-than-usual range of accommodation from dorms (housed in the formerly separate *Lakefront Lodge Backpackers*), camping sites ($46), cabins and motel rooms ($170). Free wi-fi to 100MB/day only. Bike rental available ($25/half-day). Dorms **$37**, standard cabins **$110**

10

10

OBSERVATORY TOURS

Book early if you don't want to be shunted onto an extra-late tour (there are departures as late as 1.30am in summer), and **dress warmly**: they equip you with enormous red parkas and feed you hot chocolate but it can still be cold. Check in at the **Earth And Sky Village Office** (☎03 680 6960, ⊛earthandsky.co.nz) at the western car park in the centre of Tekapo, beside the supermarket; a free shuttle bus takes you to the hilltop. Tours usually go ahead even if it's cloudy; you will only qualify for a refund if your tour is cancelled due to wind or rain.

Observatory Night Tour (daily after nightfall, approx 8pm in winter, 10pm in summer; 2hr; $150). Easily the most popular tour, you'll get to look through the largest telescopes available (up to 61cm) at whatever's up: the Southern Cross, the Large Magellanic Cloud, nebulae, and perhaps the glorious Jewel Box. They'll show you how to get the best star photos, and if the night is cloudy you'll delve into the life of an astronomer and the work being done by the universities of Canterbury and Nagoya.

Twilight Tour (daily at dusk, summer only; 2hr; $150). If you can't face the late finish of the night tour, go for this option where you'll get a (hopefully) great sunset followed by telescope viewing of the darkening sky.

Cowan's Observatory Star Tour (nightly after dark on clear nights, summer only; 75min; $95). A cheaper tour that doesn't visit Mt John but conducts viewing from a telescope on a hill away from the (admittedly minimal) lights of Tekapo. This is the only tour that offers a full refund if it is cloudy.

★ **Tailor Made Tekapo Backpackers Hostel** 11 Aorangi Crescent ☎03 680 6700, ⊛tekapohostelnz.com. A 5min walk uphill from the bus stop and shops, this friendly BBH hostel lacks views but does have cheerful, comfy rooms and bunk-free dorms, plus well-kept grounds and free-range chickens. Free wi-fi (500MB/day). Dorms $36, doubles $95

EATING AND DRINKING

Astro Café Mt John summit ☎03 680 6960, ⊛earthandsky.co.nz. With stupendous lake and mountain views, this café atop Mt John serves cakes, sandwiches, soup (from $10) and stellar espresso. Daily 9am–6pm (July–Sept 10am–5pm).

★ **Kohan** 6 Rapuwai Lane (just off SH8) ☎03 680 6688, ⊛kohannz.com. The surroundings are functional, but there's a great view and superb Japanese food that won't break the bank; the bento boxes start from $28.50, venison *tataki* (seared slices) is $20 and the signature salmon *don* (sashimi salmon and salmon caviar on rice) costs $22. BYO & licensed. Mon–Sat 11am–2pm & 6–9pm, Sun 11am–2pm.

Reflections SH8 ☎03 680 6234, ⊛reflectionsrestaurant. co.nz. Local salmon, lamb and beef all get a run on the wide-ranging menu at this reliable restaurant that opens out to a terrace at the lake's edge. Try the double beef burger ($23) or salmon with crushed potato and pickled red onions ($31). Free wi-fi. Daily 7am–9pm or later.

Run 76 SH8 ☎03 680 6910, ⊛run76laketekapo.co.nz. Classy store selling gourmet deli goods and housing the village's best daytime café; come here for good coffee, baked treats and hot meals – try the Mackenzie High Country Breakfast ($22). Daily 7.30am–4pm (window open till 6pm for take-away coffee).

Twizel

TWIZEL (rhymes with bridle), 60km southwest of Tekapo, began life in 1968 as a construction village for people working on the **Waitaki hydro scheme**. The town was due to be bulldozed flat after the project finished in 1983. Some think this would have been a kinder fate for the planned community, but enough residents wanted to stay that their wishes were granted, and it's now a low-key summertime base for forays to Aoraki/Mount Cook (a 45min drive away), scenic Lake Ohau and gliding at Omarama.

Before 2015, Twizel's main attraction was the **Kaki/Black Stilt visitor hide**, which allowed an insight into the DOC's Kakī Recovery Programme; the site has been closed since then due to damage caused by heavy snow (check Twizel i-Site for the latest).

ARRIVAL AND DEPARTURE   TWIZEL

By bus Atomic and InterCity/Newmans buses stop at the Twizel Bus Shelter across from the Four Square Supermarket. Cook Connection runs to Aoraki/Mt Cook via Glentanner.

Destinations Aoraki/Mt Cook (2–3 daily; 50min–1hr); Christchurch (3 daily; 5hr 15min–8hr); Omarama (3 daily; 20min); Queenstown (3 daily; 3hr 10min).

INFORMATION AND TOURS

Tourist information Marketplace (Mon–Fri 8.30am–5pm, Sat 10.30am–2.30pm; ☎ 03 435 3124, ⓦ twizel.info).
Services The post office, ANZ bank (Mon–Fri 9am–4.30pm) and ATM (24hr) are all in the Marketplace Shopping Centre.
OneRing Tours Mackenzie Country Inn, corner of Ostler and Wairepo sts, Twizel ☎ 03 4350 073, ⓦ lordoftheringstour.com. This outfit gets you out of

unlovely Twizel onto the gorgeous surrounding plains which were used for filming the battle scenes on the Pelennor Fields (daily at 8.15am, 1hr 30min with breakfast; $109; 10am & 2.30pm, 2hr; $89); there's also the Laketown Hobbit Film Tour of Lake Pukaki (12.15pm; 1hr 30min; $119, includes picnic lunch). Closed June–Aug (private tours still offered).

ACCOMMODATION

Twizel has a good range of accommodation but its proximity to Aoraki/Mount Cook means it's essential to book ahead from Christmas to at least the end of February. All the options below offer free wi-fi.
Aoraki Lodge 32 Mackenzie Drive ☎ 03 435 0300, ⓦ aorakilodge.co.nz. Tasteful and welcoming B&B in the centre of town with four en-suite rooms, all with separate access, and a pretty rose-filled garden. $230
Mountain Chalet Motels Wairepo Rd ☎ 03 435 0785, ⓦ mountainchalets.co.nz. Great-value collection of light-filled, self-contained A-frame chalets and an adjacent lodge offering worn but comfortable backpacker accommodation.

Breakfast is $12. Dorms $35, chalets $162
★ **Omahau Downs** SH8, 2km north of town ☎ 03 435 0199, ⓦ omahau.co.nz. Lovely combination of four modern en-suite doubles with fine Aoraki/Mt Cook views (and spectacular night skies), and three self-catering cottages set on a working family-run farm. Closed June–Aug. Doubles $160, cottages $170
Twizel Holiday Park 122 Mackenzie Drive ☎ 03 435 0507, ⓦ twizelholidaypark.co.nz. Large and fairly typical campsite with powered sites plus a sprinkling of cabins, cottages ($130) and en-suite rooms ($110) on the northern edge of town. Powered campsites $40, basic cabins $60

EATING AND DRINKING

★ **Poppies Café** 1 Benmore Place ☎ 03 435 0848, ⓦ poppiescafe.com. Elegant wine-red space with polished concrete floors and shelves of gourmet deli goods, serving classy café fare, as well as beautifully cooked lunches such as venison cannelloni ($19.50) and bean burritos ($17.50), with lots of organic produce straight from the owners' garden. The dinner menu offers the similar dishes at higher prices. Daily 8am–9pm.

Shawty's 4 Market Place ☎ 03 435 3155, ⓦ shawtys. co.nz. Restaurant and bar where tasty breakfasts and sizeable lunches are served with care in the casual interior or overlooking the village green. Dinners include a range of meat and fish dishes (mains $28–37), from a delicious smoked salmon chowder to lamb rack crusted in macadamia and a classic sticky date pudding ($12). Mon 8.30am–3pm, Tues–Sun 8.30am–9pm.

Lake Ohau and Ohau Snow Fields

Narrow Lake Ohau Road runs 25km west of Twizel to idyllic **Lake Ohau**, secluded among beech forest with distinctive natural features including kettle lakes (small depressions left when blocks of glacial ice melt) and terracing on its banks that reflects the light of summer sunsets. Northwest of the lake, the **Ohau Forests** are crisscrossed by numerous tracks (30min–4hr), outlined in DOC's *Ruataniwha Conservation Park* leaflet, available from *Lake Ohau Lodge*. In winter (July–Sept), the **Ohau Snow Fields**, 9km west of the *Lodge* (lift pass from $90; ☎ 03 438 9885, ⓦ ohau.co.nz) are in full swing. This small, high-country ski-field has reliable powder snow and uncrowded slopes, with beginner runs, and a range of groomed and off-piste intermediate and advanced runs. Equipment rental and lessons are available on-site.

ACCOMMODATION AND EATING   LAKE OHAU

Lake Ohau Lodge Lake Ohau Rd ☎ 03 438 9885, ⓦ ohau.co.nz. Though popular on summer tour-bus itineraries, this 62-room hotel is saved by its wonderful setting and super-peaceful evenings. There's no self-catering, but guests and visitors can book ahead for breakfast (continental $18; cooked $24) and dinner ($48)

from a set menu, or drop by for a drink at the well-stocked bar. The lodge also has petrol, powered campsites at the back (campers can use all lodge facilities), and organizes a ski-shuttle service (daily in season 9.15am; $30 return). No TVs or phone reception; wi-fi is $2 for 10MB, $4 for 20MB and $5 for 50MB. Camping per site $20, doubles $118

10

THE ALPS 2 OCEAN CYCLE TRAIL

Stretching over 300km from the Southern Alps to the Pacific Ocean, the **Alps 2 Ocean Cycle Trail** (w alps2ocean.com) is the longest continuous trail in New Zealand's nationwide **Nga Haerenga** network (see page 36). The entire trail is signposted and rideable – even by penny-farthing, as one intrepid group from Timaru proved in 2013.

Cyclists can start either from Mount Cook Village (with a helicopter hop to cross the Tasman River; $250 for one, or $125 each for two people; w heliworks.nz) or from Lake Tekapo. The two trails meet at Lake Pukaki, before looping around Lake Ohau and heading southeast past a series of lakes and dams that form the Waitaki hydro scheme, threading through the wine country around Kurow and reaching the coast at Oamaru.

It's most comfortable to tackle the frequently bumpy trail on mountain bike. Anyone with a reasonable level of fitness can ride the trail, with the eight stages averaging 30–40km each. Several local operators provide bike hire, portering and transport along different sections of the track, but it's straightforward enough to do the trail independently – just make sure you know how to fix a puncture.

CYCLE RENTAL AND SUPPORT

Cycle Journeys 3 Benmore Place, Twizel ☎ 03 377 2060, w cyclejourneys.co.nz. Offers a wide range of services that run the gamut from guided multi-day rides to shuttles, luggage portering ($15/section per 15kg) and bike rental (from $48/day).

The Jollie Biker 193 Glen Lyon Rd, Twizel ☎ 03 435 0517 w thejolliebiker.co.nz. Run by a local cyclist and specializing in the first half of the trail from Aoraki/Mt Cook to Omarama, services include bike ($50/day) and pannier ($5/day) rental, various transport options and all-inclusive packages, plus they own two wee holiday cottages in Twizel (from $150).

Omarama

SH8 traverses tussock and sheep country 30km south from Twizel to the junction settlement of **OMARAMA** (Māori for "place of light"), best known for the **Clay Cliffs** just outside town and its wonderful conditions for **gliding**.

Omarama Hot Tubs

29 Omarama Ave (SH8) • Daily 11am–10pm • Hot tubs $98 for two for 90min; hot tub & sauna $160 for two (2hr); towel rental $5 • ☎ 03 438 9703, w hottubsomarama.co.nz

There are no hot springs at **Omarama Hot Tubs**, just chemical-free mountain water heated in ten exquisitely landscaped private outdoor tubs overlooking the mountains. Though it feels very open, no one can overlook your idyll. Further relaxation is available in the massage rooms, starting from $60 for 30min.

Big Rooster Antiques & Collectables

18 Chain Hills Hwy (SH83) • Sept–mid-June Mon 9am–5.30pm, Tues–Thurs 9am–5pm, Fri–Sun 9am–6pm • Free • ☎ 03 438 9757, w bigrooster.co.nz

Behind the quirky Western-style frontage lies **Big Rooster Antiques & Collectables,** a fascinating movie-museum-cum-collectables-shop. Come to browse the secondhand books, old hand tools, ceramics, jewellery and classic cars (model and full-sized) but mostly to ogle the random collection of original props and costumes from TV shows such as *Xena: Warrior Princess*, the 1990s cult fantasy shot in New Zealand.

Clay Cliffs Scenic Reserve

15km from Omarama; turn west off the SH8, 5km north of town • Open access • $5 per car

A rough side-road leads to the **Clay Cliffs Scenic Reserve** where the braided Ahuriri River provides a picturesque backdrop to eerie badlands of bare pinnacles and angular ridges separated by narrow ravines and canyons. The rock formations were created when a 100m uplift caused by the Ostler Fault exposed layers of gravel and silt that have weathered at different rates. A stony path winds along the bottom of the cliff, with smaller tracks snaking up to the rocks themselves.

ARRIVAL AND INFORMATION

By bus Buses stop at the Merino Country Crafts car park, 7 Chain Hills Hwy (SH83) from Christchurch (3 daily; 5hr 40min–8hr 15min); Queenstown (3 daily; 2hr 30min); and Twizel (3 daily; 20–30min).

OMARAMA

Tourist information Omarama Hot Tubs (daily 11am–10pm; ☏ 03 438 9703) has a small information centre and does hotel and transport bookings. Hot showers are available for $7/person. See also ⊛ discoveromarama.co.nz.

10

ACCOMMODATION AND EATING

Ahuriri Bridge Campsite SH8, 3km north of Omarama. A pretty and peaceful, willow-shaded DOC campsite beside the Ahuriri River that's perfect for tenters and those in campervans. Comes with long-drop toilets and river water. **Free**

★ **Ahuriri Motels** 85 Clay Cliff Lane ☏ 03 438 9451, ⊛ ahuririmotels.co.nz. Well-run complex on the eastern edge of town, with powered sites ($36 for two people; closed June–Aug) and unusually spacious twin- and triple-bedded backpacker rooms, nicely decorated common areas plus a handful of self-contained motel units and the comfiest beds around. Dorms (closed June–Aug) **$38**, motel units **$115**

ASURE Sierra Motels 8 Omarama Ave (SH8) ☏ 03 438 9785, ⊛ omarama.co.nz. Popular with cyclists on the Alps-to-Ocean trail, this friendly motel has fourteen well-maintained units all with Sky TV, kitchenette or full kitchen, plus its own fishing tackle shop. **$145**

★ **Buscot Station** 1.5km east of SH8 on a gravel road (turning 9km north of town) ☏ 03 438 9646, ⊛ bbh.

co.nz. Peaceful working farm, in a higgledy-piggledy homestead surrounded by vegetable patches. Most rooms overlook the valley; there's a single ten-bed dorm. They'll arrange pick-ups if you book ahead. No wi-fi. Cash only. Dorms **$26**, doubles **$94.50**

Ladybird Hill 1 Pinot Noir Court ☏ 03 438 9550, ⊛ ladybirdhill.co.nz. Off SH8 on the western edge of town, the "Hill" includes a vineyard, fishponds where you can hook your own salmon and eat it as sashimi ($59/fish), and a licensed restaurant. The menu covers manuka-smoked salmon (from $27) and panko-crumbed hoki fillets ($20). Wed & Sun 10am–4pm, Thurs–Sat 10am–late.

The Wrinkly Rams 24–30 Omarama Ave (SH8) ☏ 03 438 9751, ⊛ thewrinklyrams.co.nz. Licensed local landmark that offers Omarama's best café- and pub-style fare, along with live sheep shearing shows (30min; $25). Expect quality steaks (from $38), tasty soups ($12–13) and excellent lamb shank ($28). Mon & Thurs–Sun 6.30am–8pm, Tues & Wed 6.30am–4.30pm.

Aoraki/Mount Cook National Park

New Zealand's highest mountain, the spectacular 3754m **Mount Cook** is increasingly known by its Māori name, **Aoraki**, meaning "cloud piercer" – with the two names often run together as Aoraki/Mount Cook. It dominates the 700-square-kilometre **Aoraki/Mount Cook National Park**, which was designated a UNESCO World Heritage Site in 1986. With 22 peaks over 3000m, the park contains the lion's share of New Zealand's highest mountains, easily accessible on walks to great viewpoints, as well as 27km-long **Tasman Glacier**, fed by icefalls tumbling from the heavily glaciated surrounding ranges. Mount Cook itself was named in honour of the English sea captain in 1851. It was first summited in 1894 but, due to the peak's sacredness to Māori, climbers are now asked not to step on the summit itself.

The **weather** here is highly changeable, often with a pall of low-lying cloud liable to turn to rain, and the mountain air is lung-searingly fresh. On windy days, an atmospheric white dust rises from the plain at the base of the mountain.

Aoraki/Mount Cook Village

The only habitation in the national park is tiny **AORAKI/MOUNT COOK VILLAGE**, sitting at 760m and encircled by a horseshoe of mountains topped by Aoraki/Mount Cook itself. Almost everything is run by *The Hermitage* hotel (which operates the Sir Edmund Hillary Alpine Centre) or DOC (who run a fascinating visitor centre). Mostly, though, you'll be wanting to get outdoors.

10

> ## GLIDING OMARAMA
>
> Prevailing westerly winds rising over the Southern Alps create a unique airflow across the Mackenzie Country's flatlands, making Omarama New Zealand's **gliding capital**. Based at Omarama Airfield (in the centre of town), **Glide Omarama** (☎ 03 438 9555, ⓦ glideomarama. com) lets you take the front seat on spectacular two-seater glider flights (30min for $358; 1hr for $488; 2hr 30min for $782), with a chance to take the controls and get great views of Aoraki/ Mt Cook on a good day.

Aoraki/Mount Cook National Park Visitor Centre
1 Larch Grove Rd · Daily 8.30am–5pm (May–Sept closes 4.30pm) · Free · ☎ 03 435 1186

Not just somewhere to register your intentions, get tramping and weather info and to buy maps, but also a window on the region's wondrous natural and social history, the **Aoraki/Mount Cook National Park Visitor Centre** is a complement to what's on show at the Sir Edmund Hillary Alpine Centre. Set an hour aside to delve into displays spread across two floors exploring climate, glacier dynamics, climbing history, and to flick through four sobering volumes filled with memorials to those who have perished in these mountains. There are wonderful photographs of Victorian climbers posing with their ice axes, a helpful relief model of the mountains, and histories of the mountain huts. Outside, the old six-bunk **Empress Hut**, relocated from the slopes above, gives a sense of mountain life that isn't much changed today.

Sir Edmund Hillary Alpine Centre
Next to The Hermitage · Daily 8am–8pm (May–Sept closes 7pm) · $20 · ☎ 03 435 1809, ⓦ hermitage.co.nz

The history of *The Hermitage* hotel and its place in Kiwi climbing history is told in the **Sir Edmund Hillary Alpine Centre,** a small museum that also showcases the development of the region and the climbing life of its namesake, including a replica of the tractor Hillary used to get to the South Pole in 1956. It is interesting enough but the emphasis is on a state-of-the-art **3D theatre** and **planetarium** which plays a continuous roster of shows, such as: *Mount Cook Magic in 3D*, which whizzes you through the geographical, cultural and sporting evolution of the mountains using a blend of authentic footage and computer graphics; *Hillary on Everest*; and *Primeval New Zealand*, revealing the surprising origins of New Zealand's most iconic animals.

Tramping and walking in Aoraki/Mount Cook National Park

Scenic **walks** in the park range from gentle day-hikes on the fringes of the village to spectacular alpine treks – **climbing Mount Cook** itself is a technically challenging and expensive proposition undertaken by expert mountaineers with specialist guides, usually over six days. DOC's *Walking and Cycling Tracks in Aoraki/Mount Cook National Park* leaflet ($1) lists eleven excellent day-treks (10min–6hr), which can be extended by those with relevant experience. Steer clear of the glaciers unless you know what you're doing, or are in the company of someone qualified.

Governors Bush Walk
1hr return from the village; 2km

The easiest of the local walks, this trail leads through a small strand of silver beech with abundant birdlife. You gradually climb to a lookout with views back towards Aoraki/ Mount Cook. It is sheltered enough to make it viable in poor weather.

Blue Lakes and Tasman Glacier View
1km return; 40min; 100m ascent

A fairly gentle walk with good views of the lower sections of the Tasman Glacier, which is 600m deep at its thickest point, 3km across at its widest and moves at a rate of 20cm a day. The walk starts at the Blue Lakes car park, 8km drive up the Tasman Valley Road, but you'll need your own vehicle as there are no shuttles.

Red Tarns Track

4km return from the village; 2hr; 300m ascent

This excellent and very achievable walk has one short, steep section but rewards with some pretty pools coloured by the red pond weed that gives them their name. From here uninterrupted views stretch across the village towards Aoraki/Mount Cook and along the Tasman Valley.

Kea Point Track

2hr, 7km return from the village or 1hr, 3km return from Whitehorse Hill Campground; 200m ascent

For great views with relatively little effort, follow this path through gentle grasslands to a viewpoint on the moraine wall of the Mueller Glacier. Here you can look down into Mueller Lake, up the valley to the Hooker Glacier and above you to the hanging glaciers and icefalls of Mount Sefton.

Hooker Valley Track

9km return from Whitehorse Hill Campground; 3hr; 200m ascent

You don't really need to do all of this popular and superb there-and-back hike; just go as far as you want, perhaps to the Alpine Memorial with views of the western side of Aoraki/Mount Cook or across a series of swingbridges to Hooker Lake at the base of the Hooker Glacier. Allow an extra hour if you start from and return to the village.

Mueller Hut Route

10.4km return from the village; 6–8hr; 1000m ascent

This challenging route leaves the Kea Point Track just before its arrival at the glacier and climbs steeply westwards up the Sealy Tarns Track. From the tarns, the route to the hut is marked by orange triangles guiding you up the final assault on loose gravel to a skyline ridge and the modern *Mueller Hut* (see page 556). At 1800m the views are quite startling and you're engulfed by almost perfect silence, interrupted only by the murmur of running water and squawking kea. The track requires crampons, ice axes and winter mountaineering experience in the colder months but is generally ice-free from December to mid-April. At any time of year, consult DOC's *Mueller Hut Route* leaflet ($2).

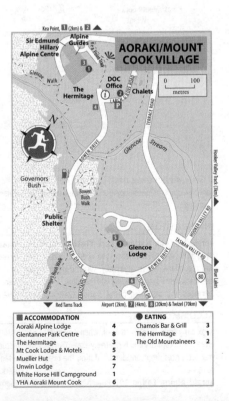

ARRIVAL AND DEPARTURE
AORAKI/MOUNT COOK

By bus Intercity/Great Sights makes daily runs from Queenstown and Christchurch to Aoraki/Mt Cook, while the Cook Connection (☎0800 266526, ⌨cookconnect.co.nz; Oct–May only) links Aoraki/Mt Cook with Twizel and Tekapo. All bus services call

■ ACCOMMODATION		● EATING	
Aoraki Alpine Lodge	4	Chamois Bar & Grill	3
Glentanner Park Centre	8	The Hermitage	1
The Hermitage	3	The Old Mountaineers	2
Mt Cook Lodge & Motels	5		
Mueller Hut	2		
Unwin Lodge	7		
White Horse Hill Campground	1		
YHA Aoraki Mount Cook	6		

10

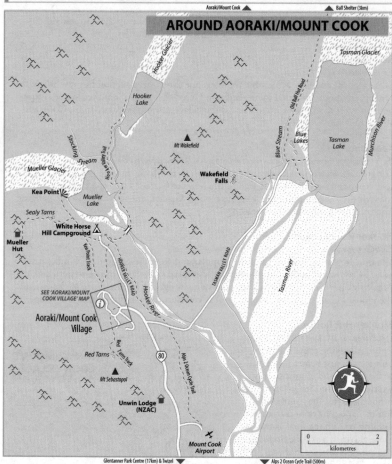

Aoraki/Mount Cook ▲

▲ Ball Shelter (3km)

AROUND AORAKI/MOUNT COOK

Hooker Glacier

Tasman Glacier

Hooker Lake

Mt Wakefield ▲

Old Ball Hut Road

Blue Stream

Blue Lakes

Tasman Lake

Murchison River

Mueller Glacier

Stocking Stream

Hooker Valley Trail

Wakefield Falls

Kea Point

Mueller Lake

Sealy Tarns

White Horse Hill Campground △

TASMAN VALLEY ROAD

Tasman River

Mueller Hut

Kea Point Track

HOOKER VALLEY ROAD

Hooker River

SEE 'AORAKI/MOUNT COOK VILLAGE' MAP

ⓘ

Aoraki/Mount Cook Village

Red Tarns

Red Tarns Track

80

Alps 2 Ocean Cycle Trail

N

Mt Sebastopol ▲

Unwin Lodge (NZAC)

0   2
kilometres

Mount Cook Airport

Glentanner Park Centre (17km) & Twizel ▼

▼ Alps 2 Ocean Cycle Trail (500m)

at *Glentanner Park Centre*, *Unwin Lodge* and *YHA Aoraki Mt Cook* on request, before dropping off at the car park near *The Hermitage*.

Destinations Christchurch (1 daily; 4hr 55min); Queenstown (1 daily; 4hr 5min); Tekapo (1–2 daily; 1hr 15min–1hr 30min); Twizel (2–3 daily; 45min–1hr).

INFORMATION

Aoraki/Mt Cook National Park Visitor Centre See page 552. All the information you need on walks, huts and the village – plus, unusually, you can register your intentions here if you're heading into the wilds.

Services The unstaffed petrol station (24hr) accepts most international credit cards (if your card isn't accepted, you can call *The Hermitage* from the station and they'll help out for a $5 fee). There's no bank or ATM. Very basic groceries are available from *The Hermitage*, *YHA* and *Alpine Lodge*.

ACCOMMODATION

Book early from October to April, when Aoraki/Mt Cook often fills to capacity and is relatively expensive for what you get; prices drop considerably during the rest of the year.

Aoraki Alpine Lodge 101 Bowen Drive ☎03 435

1860, ⓦaorakialpinelodge.co.nz; map p.553. Decent accommodation, with twins and doubles, a lounge with a fantastic view, a fully equipped kitchen and a barbecue deck. Free wi-fi (1GB per stay). Doubles $169, family rooms $234

Glentanner Park Centre SH80, 18km south of the village ☎03 435 1855, ⊛glentanner.co.nz; map p.553. Well-equipped site with sheltered camping, a ten-bed dorm (linen provided) and cabins with views of the mountains and Tasman Valley, a panoramic sheltered barbecue area and a café. Free wi-fi (30min only). Camping $22, dorms $40, cabins ("basic unit") $135

AORAKI/MOUNT COOK TOURS AND ACTIVITIES

As long as the weather plays ball, it would be hard to be bored around Aoraki/Mount Cook Village. As well as cruising or paddling a glacier lake you can hike to spectacular viewpoints, ride horses and off-road vehicles through mountain scenery or spend an hour gazing at the night sky.

Scenic flights offer glimpses of areas you could never dream of reaching on foot. Book a few days ahead, but be prepared to be flexible as flights are cancelled in high winds or poor visibility. The peak season is November–March, but in winter (June & July) the weather is often clearer and the views more dramatic.

There are no developed ski-fields in the Aoraki/Mount Cook area, but choppers open up the Tasman Glacier and surrounding mountains for guided **heli-skiing and heli-snowboarding** during the **season** (July–Sept or Oct).

TASMAN GLACIER

Glacier Explorers The Hermitage ☎03 435 1641, ⊛glacierexplorers.co.nz. Spend an eerie hour chugging around on Tasman Lake among detached icebergs with views of the Tasman Glacier ice face. Trips incorporate a shuttle from the *Hermitage Hotel* and a half-hour moraine walk before the boat ride. Trips run early Sept to late May (3–7 daily; 2hr 30min; $170).

Southern Alps Guiding Old Mountaineers Café ☎03 435 1890, ⊛mtcook.com. There's a real sense of being dwarfed by icebergs when you're at water level on unique and fascinating paddling trips aboard outrigger-stabilized kayaks with enthusiastic guides on Tasman Lake (daily; 4–6hr; $250). Trips run early Oct–April. The same outfit organizes various skiing and heli-skiing trips to the Tasman Glacier ($565; 4 runs from $1150).

GUIDED HIKING, MOUNTAINEERING AND SKIING

Alpine Guides 98 Bowen Drive ☎03 435 1834, ⊛alpineguides.co.nz. The main resource for experienced climbing guides and rental equipment such as crampons and ice axes ($12/item/day). There are daily heli-hiking trips (3hr; $565), mountaineering courses (9 days; $3560), winter ski touring and custom private guiding up Mt Cook (from $5900). Daily 8am–5pm.

Alpine Recreation ☎03 680 6736, ⊛alpine recreation.com. Professional guiding company best known for its high-altitude trek across Ball Pass ($1240) which involves a three-day alpine crossing reaching 2222m at Kaitiaki Peak, close to Aoraki/Mt Cook and two nights staying in the comfortable, private *Caroline Hut*.

SCENIC FLIGHTS

Helicopter Line Glentanner Park, 20km south of the village ☎0800 650651, ⊛helicopter.co.nz. Offers several scenic helicopter trips with opportunities to hover along the valley walls and peaks, or view the tumbling blocks of the Hochstetter Icefall; all trips include brief snow landings. Choose from the Alpine Vista (20min; $245), Alpine Explorer (35min; $375), Mountains High (40min; $460) or Mt Cook and Glaciers (50min; $640), which circumnavigates Aoraki and heads over to the West Coast before flying the length of the Tasman Glacier.

Mount Cook Ski Planes & Helicopters Aoraki/Mt Cook Airport ☎0800 800702, ⊛mtcookskiplanes. com. Flights from $299 for 25min in a helicopter, up to the Grand Circle (65min; $589), a plane or helicopter loop around Aoraki, briefly crossing the Main Divide, hugging the immense valley walls and then landing on the silent Tasman Glacier to wander on the breathtaking footprint-free snow.

OFF-ROAD 4WD TOURS

Tasman Valley 4WD Tours The Hermitage ☎0800 686600, ⊛hermitage.co.nz. The Hermitage operates this good rainy-day alternative (year-round; 2–5 trips daily; 90min; $49) involving riding around the Tasman moraine in an eight-wheeler Argo, stopping at otherwise inaccessible viewpoints.

STARGAZING

Big Sky The Hermitage ☎0800 686800, ⊛bigskystargazing.co.nz. A brief planetarium primer is followed by an outdoor examination of the southern sky through binoculars or telescope. Departures after dark year-round (2hr; $90).

10

10

The Hermitage 89 Terrace Rd ☎03 435 1809, ⓦhermitage.co.nz; map p.553. Vast hotel and restaurant complex, currently enjoying its third incarnation since the first premises opened in 1884. Rooms and suites in the high-rise main building (many with fine views; add $100) are supplemented by the *Mt Cook Lodge & Motels* units. Free wi-fi in *Snowline Lounge* and *Sir Edmund Hillary Café*, otherwise $5/day; breakfast usually $30 extra (B&B packages available). **$290**

Mt Cook Lodge & Motels ☎03 435 1653, ⓦmtcooklodge.co.nz; map p.553. This *Hermitage*-owned collection of budget accommodation merges the former Mt Cook backpackers hostel with motel and lodge units, with the *Chamois Bar* on site. Quad dorms (all en suite) mostly lack the views and balconies enjoyed by the en-suite doubles and the private units with their own kitchens ($179). Dorms **$40**, doubles **$150**

Unwin Lodge 5355 Mount Cook Rd (SH80) ☎027 523 5360, ⓦalpineclub.org.nz/product/unwin-lodge; map p.553. Alpine Club hut that gives priority to NZAC members and climbers but is open to all, with simple bunkroom accommodation and a massive common area with kitchen – you'll need to bring your own linen and

food, but laundry ($2 per wash) and wi-fi ($5 for 250MB) are available. **$30**

★ **YHA Aoraki Mt Cook** 1 Bowen Drive ☎03 435 1820, ⓦyha.co.nz; map p.553. Excellent if slightly cramped 76-bed hostel in a cosy log-cabin style building with modern well-kept facilities (and solar panels), free evening saunas and a fairly well-stocked shop. Free wi-fi (2GB/day). Discounts for YHA members. Dorms **$40**, doubles **$140**

CAMPING AND HUTS

Mueller Hut map p.553. Only hikers tackling the Mueller Hut Route (see page 553) will want to stay the night at this 28-bunk serviced hut, which can be booked online in summer. Sign in at the visitor centre before you head up here to register into their intentions system. Bookings mandatory mid-Nov to April. Hut **$36**, camping **$15**

White Horse Hill Campground Hooker Valley Rd, 2km north of the village; map p.553. A serene and informal first-come-first-served DOC camping area under Mount Sefton with stony ground and treated water in summer. Accessible by road or a 30min walk from the village along the Kea Point Track. Cash only. **$13**

EATING AND DRINKING

Chamois Bar & Grill Mt Cook Lodge & Motels ☎03 435 1653; map p.553. Straightforward boozing bar with pretty ordinary pub meals such as fish and chips ($22.50), steaks (from $28.50) and pizza ($22). Daily 5.30–9pm.

The Hermitage 89 Terrace Rd ☎03 435 1809, ⓦhermitage.co.nz; map p.553. The hotel has dining for every taste with the *Sir Edmund Hillary Café & Bar* serving light meals from an Aoraki/Mount Cook-view terrace. The *Alpine Restaurant* serves all-you-can-eat buffets for breakfast (continental $20, cooked $30), lunch ($33) and dinner ($63), while the *Panorama Room* offers swanky à la carte dining with matchless views (mains such as Aoraki salmon and lamb back strap $32.50–39.50), with priority given to hotel guests.

Lastly, the *Snowline Lounge* has deep leather sofas and magic views. Daily: Sir Edmund Hillary Café & Bar 8.30am–5pm; Alpine Restaurant 6.30–10am, noon–2pm & 6–9.30pm; Panorama Room 6–9.30pm; Snowline Lounge 3pm–late.

★ **The Old Mountaineers** 3 Larch Grove ☎03 435 1890, ⓦmtcook.com; map p.553. A little pricey, but undoubtedly the best place to hang out, with a log fire, real mountain-lodge feel, comfy chairs with wonderful mountain views, vintage mountain photos on the walls and outstanding café-style meals including organic burgers ($26) and "Sir Edmund Hillary's" pork sausages ($34), plus great coffee, beer and wine. Daily 10am–8pm (June–Sept daily 11am–8pm).

Timaru

Heading south from Christchurch, SH1 forges straight across the **Canterbury Plains**, connecting small farming service towns, many grown rich from the region's intensive dairy farming, to the 29,000-strong port city of **TIMARU** (from *Te Maru*, Māori for "place of shelter"). The city was overlooked by tourists until relatively recently, but its museum, art gallery and **rock art centre** are each worth an hour or so and there's evening **penguin viewing** nearby. Once a popular seaside resort, Timaru still packs people in around New Year and boasts of some iconic Kiwi foods and beers.

Te Ana: Ngai Tahu Māori Rock Art Centre

2 George St • Daily 10am–3pm • 1hr guided tour $22; 3hr guided tour of centre and Opihi Rock Art site Nov–April 2pm $130 (including transport and refreshments; book ahead) • ☎03 684 9141, ⓦteana.co.nz

Although seeing the rock art *in situ* is a wonderful experience, there's fuller context at the **Te Ana: Ngai Tahu Māori Rock Art Centre**, which occupies the 1876 volcanic "bluestone" Landing Service Building. Aerial shots give a sense of location, photos by Fiona Pardington (who has Ngāi Tahu roots) show off the paintings themselves, and displays illustrate what life was like at the time they were created. There's even a modern version of the sort of bulrush canoe used to get around the area, and the appropriation of Māori forms is explored through 1960s and 1970s matchboxes, ashtrays and peanut butter jars emblazoned with rock art designs.

South Canterbury Museum

4 Perth St • Tues–Fri 10am–4.30pm, Sat & Sun 1–4.30pm • Free • ☎ 03 687 7212, ⓦ museum.timaru.govt.nz

Most come to the small **South Canterbury Museum** to see the flimsy replica of the 1902 **aircraft** used by Temuka lad **Richard Pearse** in his attempt to notch up the world's first powered flight, some months in advance of the Wright brothers. His plane was technically far ahead of that of his rivals, but Pearse himself did not believe his flight – a rather desperate 100m, followed by an ignominious plunge into gorse bushes – was sufficiently controlled or sustained to justify this claim. Elsewhere, the gallery covers the life of local Māori (who lived a much more hunter-gatherer lifestyle than their northern kin), and the whaling station that occupied Patiti Point in the late 1830s and early 1840s.

Aigantighe Art Gallery

49 Wai-iti Rd • Tues–Fri 10am–4pm, Sat & Sun noon–4pm • Free • ☎ 03 688 4424, ⓦ facebook.com/aigantigheartgallery

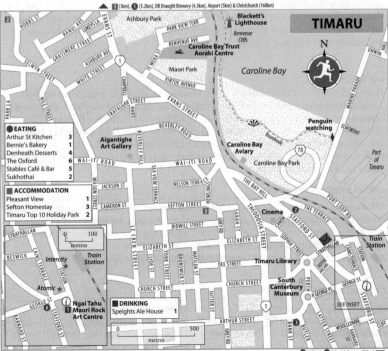

MĀORI ROCK ART

Around five hundred years ago, Māori moa hunters traversed the South Canterbury and North Otago coastal plain, leaving a record of their sojourn on the walls and ceilings of open-sided limestone rock shelters. There are more than three hundred **rock drawings** around Timaru, Geraldine and Fairlie; the faded charcoal and red ochre drawings depict a variety of stylized human, bird and mythological figures and patterns. The best of the cave drawings can be seen in the region's museums, notably Timaru's **Te Ana Māori Rock Art Centre** and the North Otago Museum in Oamaru. Around 95 percent of those remaining *in situ* are on private land and are often hard to make out, and what is visible is often the misguided result of nineteenth-century repainting. The best destination is **Te Manunui (aka Frenchman's Gully)** near Pareora Gorge, where moa and a stylized birdman figure can be seen under a limestone ledge. You can get to the Māori paintings (open access) from gravel Frenchman's Gully Road, 32km west of Timaru via SH1, Pareora River Road and then Craigmore Valley Road.

This grand 1908 Edwardian mansion known as Aigantighe (Gaelic for "at home"; their sign's suggested pronunciation is "egg-and-tie") retains many of its original features but now operates as the excellent **Aigantighe Art Gallery**. The diverse and rotating permanent collection includes four major works by native son **Colin McCahon**. Other artists to look out for are Frances Hodgkins, C.F. Goldie and the prolific landscape Realist, Austen Deans.

DB Draught Brewery

Sheffield St, Washdyke (6km north of the centre) • Shop Mon–Fri 8.30am–4.30pm; tours Mon–Sat 1pm • Tours $20 • ☎ 03 687 4230, ⓦ db.co.nz

Locals take a lot of pride in iconic DB Draught beer (crafted here since the 1930s, but owned by Heineken today), and tours of the **DB Draught Brewery** offer insights into the brewing process, from fresh raw ingredients through to the high-speed bottling line and ending with a tasting session.

Caroline Bay

The broad sweep of **Caroline Bay** is much loved by locals, though the looming port cranes detract somewhat. From Boxing Day it hosts the annual two-week **Caroline Bay Carnival** (ⓦ carolinebay.org.nz) centred around a big New Year's Eve fireworks display. At other times, stroll the beach **boardwalk** past the wooden 1878 **Blackett's Lighthouse** to Dashing Rocks; or, around sunset, find a place along Marine Parade to watch small numbers of **blue penguins** waddle to their nests in the rocks. Follow the posted instructions to avoid disturbing them.

ARRIVAL AND DEPARTURE   TIMARU

By bus InterCity buses stop outside the train station (not served by passenger trains); Atomic buses stop outside the visitor centre on George St.
Destinations Christchurch (4 daily; 2hr 25min–2hr 40min); Dunedin (4 daily; 2hr 50min–3hr 25min); Oamaru (4 daily; 1hr 10min).

By plane Timaru's Richard Pearse Airport is 13km north of the town centre on Falvey Rd. Contact Timaru Taxis in advance to get into town (around $40; ☎ 03 688 8899, ⓦ timarutaxis.co.nz).
Destinations Wellington (2–3 daily; 1hr 10min).

GETTING AROUND

By bus Timaru's Metro bus service (☎ 03 688 5544, ⓦ metroinfo.co.nz/timaru) has a flat rate of $2.40 for all journeys around the city, and $4.80 to Temuka. Tickets are sold in the visitor centre.

By bike Rent bikes from The Cyclery, 106 Stafford St (Mon–Thurs 7.45am–5.30pm, Fri 7.45am–6pm, Sat 9.30am–3pm; ☎ 03 688 8892, ⓦ thecyclery.co.nz), for $35/day.

INFORMATION

Tourist information The Visitor Centre is at 2 George St, inside the Rock Art Centre (Mon–Fri 10am–4pm, Sat & Sun 10am–3pm; ☎03 687 9997, ⓦsouthcanterbury.org.nz).

Services Timaru Library at 56 Sophia St (Mon, Wed & Fri 9am–8pm, Tues & Thurs 9am–6pm, Sat 10am–1pm, Sun 1–4pm; ☎03 687 7202) has free computers and wi-fi.

ACCOMMODATION

Pleasant View 2 Moore St ☎03 686 6651, ⓦpleasantview.co.nz; map p.557. A stylish, modern house with two en-suite rooms, one of which has great views over Caroline Bay and the docks, plus free wi-fi and a living area for all guests. $135

★**Sefton Homestay** 32 Sefton St ☎03 688 0017, ⓦseftonhomestay.co.nz; map p.557. Great-value B&B in a lovely 1920s house set in leafy grounds. One room is an en suite, while the other is equally attractive with a private guest bathroom fitted with a deep tub. There's a dedicated guest lounge and discounts for cyclists. $130

Timaru Top 10 Holiday Park 154a Selwyn St ☎0800 242 121, ⓦtimaruholidaypark.co.nz; map p.557. Well-kept, very high standard holiday-park offering a range of accommodation, close to the golf course and within walking distance of Māori Park. Camping per site $40, cabins $73

EATING

As well as being the home of iconic **May's pies**, Timaru is also known for the **Denheath Custard Square**, a delicious, creamy tart originally concocted in Pleasant Point (19km inland from Timaru) and now available at the Denheath Desserts factory shop, 3 Mill St, Parkside (just of High St), and various cafés in town.

Arthur St Kitchen 8 Arthur St ☎03 688 9449, ⓦarthurstkitchen.co.nz; map p.557. Pastel green walls make a backdrop for displays of local art in this relaxed café with plenty of outdoor seating, front and back. Come for the C4 Coffee and cake, something from their pretty standard breakfast menu or lunches from the counter. Mon–Fri 7am–5pm, Sat 9am–3pm.

Bernie's Bakery 187 Hilton Hwy (SH1), Washdyke (6km north of the centre) ☎03 683 9078, ⓦbernies. nz; map p.557. This modern bakery and café is now the official home of the legendary May's mince pie, made in Timaru since 1914, as well McGregor's mutton pie (from Palmerston), gourmet sausage rolls and a host of tempting pastries and cakes. Mon–Fri 5am–5.30pm, Sat & Sun 5am–6pm.

★**The Oxford** Stafford and George sts ☎03 688 3297, ⓦtheoxford.co.nz; map p.557. Timaru's premier fine-dining restaurant features an elegant bar, casual brasserie and more formal dining room, all offering an eclectic bistro-style menu; think crumbed lemon sole fillets ($19.50), cauliflower and cashew curry ($18.50) and Stewart Island salmon ($19). Mon & Wed–Fri 11am–late, Sat & Sun 9.30am–late.

★**Stables Café & Bar** 253 Beaconsfield Rd, 4km southwest of town ☎03 684 5617, ⓦfacebook.com/stablescafeandbar; map p.557. Delightful country café with seating in and around converted farm buildings hung with farm implements. Kids will love the (live) chickens, donkeys and budgies and everyone appreciates the excellent coffee and cakes; the menu extends to ribeye with chips and salad ($22). Wed–Fri 9am–4pm, Sat & Sun 9am–5pm.

Sukhothai 303 Stafford St ☎03 688 4843; map p.557. Decent Thai restaurant serving old favourites (most mains $19–28), plus $15 lunch specials. Daily 11.30–3pm & 5–10pm.

DRINKING

Speights Ale House 2 George St ☎03 686 6030, ⓦspeightsalehousetimaru.co.nz; map p.557. Popular, cavernous bar in the historic Landing Service Building, offering generous pub-style meals including its signature lamb shanks ($25.90), wild venison on polenta mash ($33.90) and home-made pork belly pie ($24.90). Daily 11.30am–late.

10

Otago

YELLOW-EYED PENGUIN, MOERAKI

Otago

Few regions in New Zealand offer such a rich and varied experience as Otago. The vibrant Gothic harbourside city of Dunedin is a seat of learning and culture, influenced by the country's oldest university and thriving Scottish immigrant traditions. Once outside the region's main city, however, nature takes precedence over man-made sights. On Dunedin's doorstep, the windswept Otago Peninsula is a phenomenal wildlife haven, fringed with opportunities to spot yellow-eyed and little blue penguins, fur seals and albatross. The big-sky landscapes of the Maniototo Plain spread out to the west of quirky Oamaru, also famed for its accessible penguin colonies, before descending into the heart of Otago with its gold-mining heritage, vineyard-covered hills and blissfully unhurried atmosphere. Wedged between the emerald beech forests and plunging cliffs of Fiordland and the snowcapped peaks of the Southern Alps, buzzing Queenstown lures adrenaline junkies with its bungy jumps, canyon swings, ski-fields and party vibe. Near neighbour Wanaka is its slightly more restrained cousin, draped around the placid waters of its eponymous lake.

Otago is shaped by its rivers and lakes. Meltwater and heavy rains course out of the mountains into the 70km lightning bolt of **Lake Wakatipu**, from which Queenstown and its environs get the moniker, the **Wakatipu Basin**. The lake drains east through the Kawarau River, which carves a rapids-strewn path through the Kawarau Gorge. Along the way it picks up the waters of the Shotover River from the goldfields of Skippers, riddled with the detritus of its nineteenth-century gold rushes, before it meets the mighty Clutha River, surging down from **Lake Wanaka**, in **Cromwell**. Just south of here, cyclists converge in **Clyde** and **Alexandra** to pedal along the famed **Otago Central Rail Trail** through the Maniototo to **Middlemarch**, from where the scenic **Taeiri Gorge Railway** winds its way through a ruggedly beautiful gorge to **Dunedin**. Villages south of Alex including sleepy **Lawrence**, Otago's first gold rush town, have a decidedly frontier feel.

Northwest of Queenstown, the raw, pristine landscapes surrounding the tiny lakehead town of **Glenorchy** make it easy to see why so many scenes from *The Lord of the Rings*, *The Hobbit* and other Hollywood blockbusters have been filmed here over the years.

Oamaru and around

The former port town of **OAMARU**, 85km south of Timaru, is one of New Zealand's most alluring provincial cities, and a relaxed place to spend a day or two. The most immediate attraction is the presence of both blue and yellow-eyed **penguin colonies** on the outskirts of town, but Oamaru itself has a well-preserved **Victorian Precinct**, a dense core of grand civic and mercantile buildings built of the distinctive cream-coloured local limestone that earned it the title "The Whitestone City".

The best times to visit Oamaru are from November to January when penguins are in their greatest numbers, and for the **Victorian Heritage Celebrations** (ⓦvhc.co.nz), in November, when the streets of the Victorian Precinct become a racetrack for

WANAKA

Highlights

❶ Dunedin Tour the vibrant street art and the growing number of hip cafés that are adding to Dunedin's increasingly cool status See page 573

❷ Otago Peninsula Whether you choose to paddle, cruise or drive around this stunning coastline, you'll get up close to all sorts of wildlife See page 586

❸ Queenstown adrenaline Test your nerve on giant swings, jetboat down the turquoise Shotover River, ski down mountains and more in New Zealand's adventure capital. See page 595

❹ The Routeburn Track Lush forest and

alpine scenery combine to make this one of New Zealand's best tramps. See page 608

❺ Wanaka Café hop, head out for a hike, or scale a waterfall in this relaxed lakefront town with something for everyone. See page 617

❻ Central Otago wineries More than twenty Central Otago wineries offer tastings, particularly of sublime Pinot Noir, in the world's most southerly wine-growing area. See page 631

❼ Otago Central Rail Trail Absorb the rural pleasures of the Maniototo region on a gentle three-day cycle ride, best combined with a go on the Taieri Gorge Railway. See page 634

HIGHLIGHTS ARE MARKED ON THE MAP ON PAGE 564

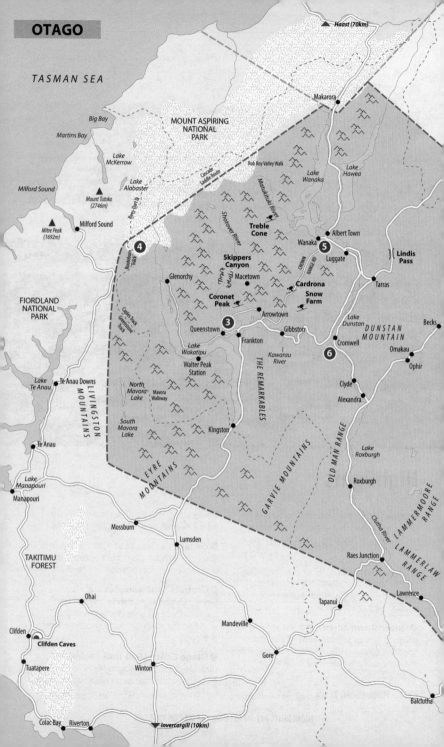

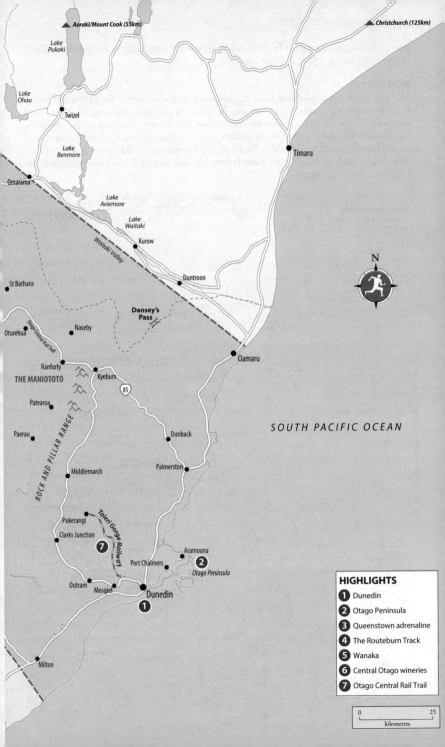

Aoraki/Mount Cook (55km)

Christchurch (125km)

Lake Pukaki

Lake Ohau

Twizel

Lake Benmore

Timaru

Omarama

Lake Aviemore

Lake Waitaki

Waitaki Valley

Kurow

St Bathans

Duntroon

Dansey's Pass

Oturehua

Otago Central Rail Trail

Naseby

Ranfurly

Kyeburn

Oamaru

THE MANIOTOTO

85

Patearoa

Paerau

Dunback

SOUTH PACIFIC OCEAN

ROCK AND PILLAR RANGE

Middlemarch

Palmerston

Pukerangi

Clarks Junction

Taieri Gorge Railway

7

Outram

Mosgiel

Port Chalmers

Aramoana

2

Otago Peninsula

1

Dunedin

Milton

N

HIGHLIGHTS

1 Dunedin

2 Otago Peninsula

3 Queenstown adrenaline

4 The Routeburn Track

5 Wanaka

6 Central Otago wineries

7 Otago Central Rail Trail

0   25
kilometres

penny-farthings, cheered on by local residents in Victorian attire. A few rebels hold a competing race on 1970s Raleigh 20s.

Brief history

The limestone outcrops throughout the area once provided shelter for Māori and later the raw material for ambitious European builders. As a commercial centre for gold-rush prospectors, and shored up by quarrying, timber and farming industries, Oamaru grew prosperous. The port opened for **migration** in 1874, although many ships foundered on the hostile coastline. After this boom period Oamaru declined, times evocatively recorded in work by local writer **Janet Frame**. It's only in recent years that the town has begun to come alive again.

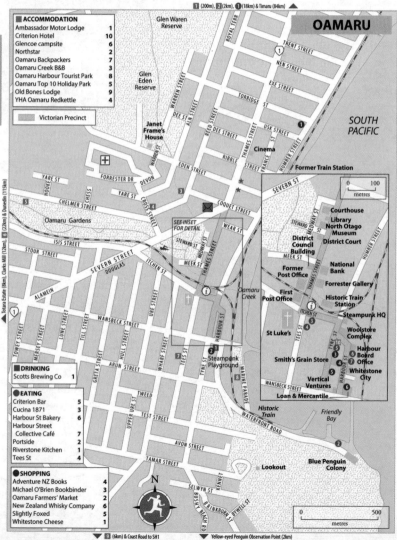

OAMARU

◼ ACCOMMODATION	
Ambassador Motor Lodge	1
Criterion Hotel	10
Glencoe campsite	6
Northstar	2
Oamaru Backpackers	7
Oamaru Creek B&B	3
Oamaru Harbour Tourist Park	8
Oamaru Top 10 Holiday Park	5
Old Bones Lodge	9
YHA Oamaru Redkettle	4

Victorian Precinct

◼ DRINKING	
Scotts Brewing Co	1

● EATING	
Criterion Bar	5
Cucina 1871	3
Harbour St Bakery	6
Harbour Street Collective Café	7
Portside	2
Riverstone Kitchen	1
Tees St	4

● SHOPPING	
Adventure NZ Books	4
Michael O'Brien Bookbinder	3
Oamaru Farmers' Market	2
New Zealand Whisky Company	6
Slightly Foxed	5
Whitestone Cheese	1

OAMARU WHITESTONE

The key to Oamaru's distinctive look is **whitestone**, which is still quarried on the outskirts of town. This "free stone" is easily worked with metal hand tools when freshly quarried but hardens with exposure to the elements. While keeping the prevailing Neoclassical fashion firmly in mind, the architects' imaginations ran riot, producing deeply fluted pilasters, finely detailed pediments and elegant Corinthian pillars topped with veritable forests of acanthus leaves. Oamaru was given much of its character by architect **R.A.** and by the firm **Forrester and Lemon** who together produced most of the more accomplished buildings between 1871 and 1883. Oamaru stone is still used in modern buildings such as the Waitaki Aquatic Centre in Takaro Park.

The town centre

Thames Street is the more formal face of Oamaru's **Victorian Precinct**, home the majority of civic buildings. One side packs in the 1906 Opera House, the Palladian Courthouse, the classically proportioned Athenaeum building (now home to the North Otago Museum), the First Post Office and the Former Post Office, whose tower was added by the architect's son, Thomas Forrester, in 1903. Opposite stand two fine buildings by R.A. Lawson: the imposing **National Bank** has perhaps the purest Neoclassical facade in town; while its grander neighbour now operates as the **Forrester Gallery**.

North Otago Museum

60 Thames St • Mon–Fri 1–4.30pm • Free • ☎ 03 433 0852, ⓦ northotagomuseum.co.nz

The colonnaded 1882 Athenaeum building houses the **North Otago Museum**, home to a modest selection of displays on North Otago history, Oamaru stone and early Māori rock art. The building was once a subscription library where local novelist Janet Frame spent much of her teenage years; her typewriter is still here as the centrepiece of a display on her life and works. Most displays have been downsized in the lead-up to a $6 million redevelopment of the Forrester Gallery site expected to open in 2019, which will incorporate the North Otago Museum and the Waitaki District Archive.

First Post Office

There's something a little incongruous about the Italianate **First Post Office** at 12 Thames St built in 1864 and predating all the other whitestone architecture. It's the town's only remaining example of the work of Australian-born architect W.H. Clayton, who designed Dunedin's All Saints' Church and Edinburgh House before being appointed the country's first – and only – Colonial Architect.

Forrester Gallery

9 Thames St • Mon–Fri 10.30am–4.30pm, Sat & Sun 1–4.30pm • Free • ☎ 03 433 0853, ⓦ forrestergallery.com

R.A. Lawson's Neoclassical bank building now houses Oamaru's premier **art gallery**, which runs an impressive programme of touring exhibitions of contemporary and traditional art. There's almost always something fascinating, supplemented by selected works from its own collection. Look out for works by iconic Kiwi artist Colin McCahon and local painter Colin Wheeler, whose cityscapes are dominated by the colour of Oamaru stone.

Tyne and Harbour streets

South of Thames Street you nip down Itchen Street into Oamaru's original commercial quarter, full of whitestone solidity. Gentrification is taking its time, but this is rapidly becoming the place to hang out, perhaps grabbing a coffee or a beer in between browsing the shops, art galleries and minor museums. Try to come at weekends when there's more happening.

Tyne Street kicks off with the Woolstore Complex and the *Criterion Hotel*, followed by Oamaru's elegant old **Union Offices**, built in 1877. The adjacent **Smiths Grain Store**, built in 1882 by stonemason James Johnson, is considered to be the most ornamental of its kind in the country.

Harbour Street runs parallel to Tyne Street and is lined by more rejuvenated mercantile buildings. The 1876 Venetian Renaissance-style **Harbour Board Office** was one of the first public buildings designed by the prolific Forrester and Lemon. The street ends at the massive 1882 **Loan & Mercantile** wool and grain store, once the largest in New Zealand.

Steampunk HQ

1 Itchen St • Daily 10am–5pm • $10 • ⓦ steampunkoamaru.co.nz

This wonderfully oddball museum has made Oamaru New Zealand's steampunk capital. Outside is a pimped, rakishly perched steam engine which (for $2) provides steam-belching, lights-flashing entertainment; inside is a world – somewhere between dystopian and phantasmagorical – that a modern Jules Verne or H.G. Wells might have created. Much of it is essentially junk reimagined with a welding torch: compressors, divers' helmets, old cathode ray tubes, skulls and much more form a bizarre synthesis of pseudo-Victorian mechanical-style overlaid with retro-futurism. Don't miss the Infinity Portal Experience or the two short movies. Steampunk even informs the design of a **kids' playground** and café at the harbour end of Wansbeck Street.

Woolstore Complex and the Oamaru Auto Collection

1 Tyne St • Gift shop and Oamaru Auto Collection daily 9.30am–5pm; galleries Sun 10am–4pm; Casa Mia café Tues–Sun 8am–3pm • Auto Collection $10; galleries free • ⓦ thewoolstorecomplex.co.nz

The **Woolstore Complex** houses a café, gift shop, and, upstairs, a floor of galleries and boutiques. Motorsport enthusiasts won't want to miss the **Oamaru Auto Collection**, with some thirty vintage, classic and historic vehicles which might include an Audi Quattro in rally trim and a 1970s Skoda 110 that successfully competed in New Zealand's forest rally stages. With the complex up for sale at press time, the future of the collection is uncertain.

Whitestone City

12 Harbour St • Daily 9.30am–5pm • $20 • ☎ 03 433 0852, ⓦ whitestonecity.com

Occupying a former grain store, **Whitestone City** brings Victorian-era Oamaru to life via a series of interactive exhibits arranged to resemble a colonial town – barber shop, schoolroom, medical dispensary, general store and all. The museum's "please do touch" philosophy makes it great fun for kids, but few adults can resist a spin on the world's first penny-farthing carousel. Passionate staff dressed in period clothing add to the experience of being immersed in living, breathing late nineteenth-century Oamaru.

Janet Frame House

56 Eden St • Nov–April daily 2–4pm • $5 • ☎ 03 434 2300, ⓦ jfestrust.org.nz

The **Janet Frame House** was the modest childhood home of one of New Zealand's greatest writers: "I wanted an imagination that would inhabit a world of fact, descend like a shining light upon the ordinary life of Eden Street…" Restored to 1930s style, you can explore it, get some insight from the custodian and listen to a marvellous recording of the author reading an extract from *Owls Do Cry*, about the very sofa you'll be sitting on. Fans of her work may also want to follow the **Janet Frame Trail** (free leaflet available from the i-SITE), taking you to locations used in varying degrees of disguise in her books.

The penguin colonies

Oamaru is unique in having both yellow-eyed and blue **penguin colonies** within walking distance of the town centre. It is usually possible to see both colonies in one evening, since the yellow-eyes tend to come ashore earlier than the blues. Penguins are timid creatures and easily distressed, so keep quiet and still, and do not approach within 10m of the birds. Once disturbed, the penguins may not return to their nests for several hours, even if they have chicks to feed.

Blue Penguin Colony

2 Waterfront Rd, 1.5km southeast of the town centre • Daily 10am–2hr after dark • Day viewing $15; evening viewing $30; premium evening viewing $45; 15 percent discount for seniors, students etc • ☏ 03 433 1195, ⓦ penguins.co.nz

Blue penguins (a.k.a. little penguins, fairy penguins or korora) are the smallest of their kind. They're found all around the coast of New Zealand, and along the shores of southern Australia, but are most easily seen around Oamaru. Some even nest under waterside buildings, and if you happen to be near the shoreline just after dark you'll probably see a few waddle past. More formal and informative viewing takes place at the **Blue Penguin Colony**. Visit during the day and you can hopefully see birds on their nests, but you're likely to get far more from an **evening viewing** in the 350-seat grandstand. During the breeding season (June–Dec) you'll see chicks – and hear them calling to their parents out at sea, hunting for food. When the parents return around dusk, travelling in groups known as rafts, they climb the steep harbour banks and cross in front of the grandstand to their nests.

In the peak season (Nov to mid-Feb) you might see nearly three hundred penguins in a night, though this might drop to a dozen or so in March, June and August. If the standard experience seems a bit of a circus, step up to the evening **premium** viewing, where you get more comfortable seats closer to the action, and approach through the penguin colony itself.

Yellow-eyed penguin colony

Bushy Beach, reached along Bushy Beach Rd

The much larger **yellow-eyed penguins** nest in smaller numbers (at last count there were only a small handful of nesting pairs here following a deadly outbreak of avian diphtheria in 2016) but keep more sociable hours, usually coming ashore in late afternoon or early evening; they're best seen between October and February. The birds mainly arrive 2km south at **Bushy Beach** where cliff-side viewpoints enable you to see them making their way across the beach in the morning and early evening (the beach is closed daily from 3pm to 9am). For the best chances of seeing one, be here at least an hour before sunset. And don't forget your zoom lens. If you're walking, allow 45 minutes from the centre of town.

ARRIVAL AND DEPARTURE   OAMARU

By bus InterCity and NakedBus drop off at the corner of Eden and Thames sts on their Christchurch–Dunedin runs. Oamaru-based Coastline Tours (☏ 03 434 7744, ⓦ coastline-tours. co.nz) run to Dunedin and will drop off in Moeraki.

Destinations Christchurch (3–4 daily; 4hr); Dunedin (4–5 daily; 2hr); Moeraki (1 daily; 40min); Timaru (3–4 daily; 1hr).

INFORMATION AND ACTIVITIES

Visitor information i-SITE, 1 Thames St (daily 9am–5pm; ☏ 03 434 1656, ⓦ visitoamaru.co.nz), stocks useful free leaflets to self-guided walking tours.

Services There's free wi-fi at the i-SITE and at the Oamaru Public Library, 62 Thames St (Mon–Wed & Fri 9.30am–5.30pm, Thurs 10am–5.30pm, Sat 10am–12.30pm).

The Town Bike 47 Thames St (Thurs–Sun 10am–6pm;

☏ 03 434 3078, ⓦ townbike.co.nz) rents electric bikes (from $35/2hr).

Vertical Ventures 4 Wansbeck St (Thurs–Sun 10am–6pm; ☏ 021 894 427, ⓦ verticalventures.co.nz) Runs all-inclusive eight-day ($2995) and four-day ($1900) tours on the Alps to Ocean trail as well as day rides (from $95) and mountain-bike rental ($45/day).

ACCOMMODATION

Finding accommodation is seldom difficult, but it pays to book a day or two ahead from December to March.

Ambassador Motor Lodge 296 Thames St ☏ 0800 437 214, ⓦ ambassadoroamaru.co.nz; map p.566.

Well-kept and fairly central motel with a range of units including some with spa baths ($165). The freshly baked muffins presented on arrival are a nice touch. $159

Criterion Hotel 3 Tyne St ☏ 03 434 6247, ⓦ criterionhotel.

11

co.nz; map p.566. This whitestone 1877 hotel is the only place you can stay in the Victorian Precinct. Simple (mostly bathless; $50 extra for en suite) rooms above the bar (noisy at weekends) come with a breakfast room where you self-serve cereal and toast. <u>$100</u>

Glencoe campsite Tulliemet Rd, 2km west of Herbert, itself 22km south of Oamaru; map p.566. Very pleasant and grassy DOC campsite that's fairly handy for Moeraki Boulders and has a track leading down to a swimming hole in the river. In Herbert, take Ord St then follow signs to Glencoe Domain. <u>$8</u>

Northstar 495a SH1 ☎ 03 437 1190, ⓦ northstarmotel. co.nz; map p.566. Revamped motel 3km north of the centre with tastefully furnished, self-contained units and its own good restaurant (mains around $30) also open to non-guests. <u>$160</u>

★ **Oamaru Backpackers** 24 Reed St ☎ 03 434 1190, ⓦ oamarucreek.co.nz; map p.566. One of the best new hostels on the South Island, this central, repurposed house has six beautifully furnished themed rooms with various bed configurations including the "Penguin Colony" dorm with sturdy custom-made bunks and privacy curtains, and the metal-toned "Steampunk" single ($80). All but the en-suite "Quarry Room" ($110) share two bathrooms. There's a big lounge and a light-filled sunroom, and guests can help themselves to an edible garden. Dorms <u>$30</u>, doubles <u>$80</u>

Oamaru Creek B&B 24 Reed St ☎ 03 434 1190, ⓦ oamarucreek.co.nz; map p.566. Warm, friendly homestay B&B in a former maternity home dating from

1901, with spacious rooms, mostly en suite, great breakfasts and sociable owners who will try to put you on the right trail to a good time. <u>$170</u>

Oamaru Harbour Tourist Park Esplanade ☎ 03 434 5260, ⓦ oamaruharbour.co.nz; map p.566. Hardstand campervan parking and tent sites close to the waterfront, with power and access to a full kitchen and hot showers. Unlimited wi-fi costs $2 per site. Camping per site <u>$40</u>

Oamaru Top 10 Holiday Park 30 Chelmer St ☎ 03 434 7666, ⓦ oamarutop10.co.nz; map p.566. In a lovely sheltered setting close to Oamaru Gardens with a good range of accommodation including self-contained units ($135). Kids facilities include a playground, kangaroo jumper, mini-golf and a trampoline. Camping per site <u>$40</u>, cabins <u>$80</u>

Old Bones Lodge 468 Beach Rd, Kakanui ☎ 03 434 8115, ⓦ oldbones.co.nz; map p.566. Purpose-built, upscale backpackers on the coast nearly 7km south of town (follow Wharfe Rd) with just eight shared-bath doubles and twins with underfloor heating opening onto a spacious, comfortable and TV-free lounge/kitchen. Guests receive $10 off the use of the six private outdoor hot tubs (usually $90 per two people; $105 for three), and campers enjoy access to all facilities. Doubles <u>$100</u>, camping <u>$25</u>

YHA Oamaru Redkettle 2 Reed St ☎ 03 434 5008, ⓦ yha.co.nz; map p.566. The wi-fi signal doesn't stretch past the cramped kitchen and the shower curtains don't offer much privacy but the central location of this small hostel occupying an old house is convenient for forays into the Victorian Precinct on foot. Dorms <u>$30</u>, doubles <u>$66</u>.

EATING

Most of Oamaru's **eating and drinking** takes place on and around Thames Street. If you're planning an outing to Moeraki Boulders, don't miss dining at the fabulous *Fleur's Place* (see page 573); heading north, try lunch at the *Riverstone Kitchen*.

Criterion Bar Criterion Hotel, 3 Tyne St ☎ 03 434 6247, ⓦ criterionhotel.co.nz; map p.566. With the tenor of a Victorian English pub there's a long wooden bar, some good old-fashioned Emerson's Bookbinder or local Craftwork beer plus filling, inexpensive food spanning bangers and mash to fresh Aoraki salmon on flatbread with basil pesto, spinach and cream cheese. Mon–Fri 11am–10pm, Sat & Sun 10am–10pm or later.

Cucina 1871 1 Tees St ☎ 03 434 5696; map p.566. Fusing local produce with the culinary traditions of Spain, Italy, and beyond, this smart restaurant might see you start with braised lamb empanadas and capsicum relish ($18) followed by gnocchi with roasted pumpkin, lemon *labneh*, roasted pumpkin seeds, crispy chickpeas, kale, pesto and parmesan ($22) topped off with a selection of Whitestone cheeses ($15). Daily 5–10pm.

Harbour St Bakery 1871 4 Harbour St ☎ 03 434 0444; map p.566. Grab a pastry or a tasty gourmet pie to go

($6.50) from this tiny bakery. A wee warning: the owner doesn't believe in tomato sauce. Daily: Dec–March 9am–5pm; April–Nov 10am–4pm.

Harbour Street Collective Café 8 Harbour St ☎ 03 434 3246, ⓦ facebook.com/harbourstreetcollective; map p.566. An atmospheric spot for breakfast, coffee and cake, or a light meal by day, this huge café is the place to be on Friday and Saturday nights when there's live music. Mon–Thurs 7am–6pm, Fri 7am–1pm, Sat 8.30am–10pm, Sun 8.30am–6pm.

Portside 2 Waterfront Rd ☎ 03 434 3400; map p.566. The deck of this casual, airy harbourside restaurant opposite the Blue Penguin Colony is a worthy spot for a sundowner or a hearty pre- or post-penguin-viewing seafood meal. 11am–9pm or later; closed Wed.

★ **Riverstone Kitchen** 1431 SH1, 19km north of Oamaru, 66km south of Timaru ☎ 03 431 3505, ⓦ riverstonekitchen.co.nz; map p.566. Some of the finest meals around are served in an uncluttered country setting with its own produce-filled gardens. Lighter fare dominates the lunch menu (spanning deep-fried courgette flowers with Clevdon buffalo Persian feta, $22, to seared squid with tamarind, chilli, green papaya and roasted peanuts, $25) while heartier bistro dishes such as seared venison with sauteed potatoes, purple broccoli and beetroot jam ($36) tempt a dinner reservation. Mon & Sun 9am–5pm, Thurs–Sat 9am–5pm & 6–10pm.

★ **Tees St** 3 Tees St ☎ 03 434 7004, ⓦ teesstreet.com; map p.566. There's no hint of the Victorian-era drapery that once inhabited this light, modern café where you might brunch on an acai and mango bowl with home-made granola, banana, coconut yoghurt and fresh fruit ($16) or mouth-watering spiced crispy chicken tacos ($20). Soft-brew and espresso coffees, both superb. Mon–Fri 7am–3pm, Sat & Sun 7.30am–3pm.

DRINKING

Scotts Brewing Co 1 Wansbeck St ☎ 03 434 2244, ⓦ scottsbrewing.co.nz; map p.566. Oamaru's original brewery pumps out some fine beers, including a gluten-free option (fill a bottle to take away for $15 or stick around to work your way through a tasting flight of five brews for the same price) but it also dishes up the tastiest pizzas in town (around $23), best enjoyed on the sunny deck. Daily 10am–10.30pm or later.

SHOPPING

Adventure NZ Books 7 Harbour St ☎ 03 434 7756, ⓦ facebook.com/adventurebooksoamaru; map p.566. If the collection of rare, new and out-of-print books about travel and adventure stocked here don't inspire the explorer in you, the furnishings – including a small yacht – might. Daily 10.30am–4.30pm.

Michael O'Brien Bookbinder 7 Tyne St ☎ 03 434 9277, ⓦ bookbinder.co.nz; map p.566. Watch Michael binding and restoring rare books among the old printing and letterpress machines in the atmospheric old Union offices. New hand-made books are available in various sizes and qualities ($30–720), some leather-bound. If you're captivated, ask about their one-day bookbinding courses ($175). Mon–Fri 2–5pm or by appointment.

Oamaru Farmers' Market Corner of Wansbeck and Tyne sts ⓦ oamarufarmersmarket.co.nz; map p.566. Two dozen stalls, a coffee cart and live music bring the Historic District to life. Sun 9.30am–1pm.

New Zealand Whisky Company 14 Harbour St ☎ 03 434 8842, ⓦ thenzwhisky.com; map p.566. When New Zealand's southernmost whisky distillery closed in 1997 almost 500 barrels of the good stuff were left in a bondstore in Oamaru's Historic District. Supplies are dwindling but you can still buy a wonderfully diverse range of single malts and blends dating back to 1987, some costing up to $400. Sample individually ($8 a dram) or in flights of four ($30). Daily 10.30am–4.30pm.

Slightly Foxed 11 Tyne St ☎ 03 434 2155, ⓦ slightlyfoxed. co.nz; map p.566. A wonderful range of quality secondhand and classic books, plus a case of Janet Frame first editions. Mon–Sat 10am–5pm, Sun 10am–4pm.

Whitestone Cheese 3 Torridge St ☎ 03 434 8098, ⓦ whitestonecheese.co.nz; map p.566. This cheese factory has a licensed shop-café offering free samples of its daily specials along with a six-cheese tasting platter ($14.50) which usually includes Whitestone's famed soft, creamy Windsor Blue. Factory tours run Monday to Friday at 10am (1hr; $30). Tours including cheese tasting with beer- or wine-matching ($45) can also be arranged. Mon–Fri 9am–5pm, Sat & Sun 10am–4pm.

Totara Estate

SH1, 8km south of Oamaru • Sept–May daily 10am–4pm • $10 • ☎ 03 433 1269, ⓦ totaraestate.co.nz

Set aside an hour to look around **Totara Estate**, the birthplace of the New Zealand meat industry. Until the early 1880s New Zealand was a major wool exporter with surplus meat, while Britain's burgeoning industrial cities starved. The solution came in 1882 when the three-masted *Dunedin* was refitted with coke-driven freezers and filled with UK-bound lamb from Totara Estate. The estate is now a grassy historic park whose solid whitestone buildings contain a small museum along with a harness room, stables, granary barn and blacksmith's forge. The foundations and partial remains of the original slaughterhouse form the basis of a modern reconstruction that gives an idea of what work was like here.

Clarks Mill

SH1, 13km south of Oamaru • Late Oct–April Sun 1–3pm, machine operating last Sun of the month at 2pm; Jan–March Thurs & Sun 10am–1pm, machine operating 2pm Sun, and last Sun of the month at 1pm, 2pm & 3pm • $10; $15 when machinery operating • ☎ 03 433 1269, ⓦ historicplaces.org.nz

Time it right and you can combine Totara Estate with the farm's four-storey **historic flour mill**, the only remaining, originally water-powered mill in the country. The waterwheel has long gone but otherwise not much has changed since 1866 when its completion finally brought flour to a land drowning in wheat; previously flour had to be imported from Australia. Just touring the belts, pulleys, elevators and wooden chutes with the custodian is wonderfully evocative and informative, but nowhere near as much as when everything is coaxed into flapping and creaking life.

Moeraki Boulders

SH1, 38km south of Oamaru and 3km south of Hampden • Access to the boulders is either by a 300m walk along the beach from a DOC parking area, or via a shorter private trail ($2 in the honesty box at any hour), though it's free for patrons of the adjacent café (daily: 9am–5pm)

The large, grey spherical **Moeraki Boulders** lie partially submerged in the sandy beach at the tide line, about 2km before you hit Moeraki village. Their smooth skins hide honeycomb centres, which are revealed in some of the broken specimens. They once lay deep in the mudstone cliffs behind the beach and, as these were eroded, out fell the smooth boulders, with further erosion exposing a network of surface veins. The boulders were originally formed around a central core of carbonate of lime crystals that attracted minerals from their surroundings – a process that started sixty million years ago, when muddy sediment containing shell and plant fragments accumulated on the sea floor. They range in size from small pellets to large round rocks (some almost 2m in diameter), though the smaller ones have all been souvenired over the years, leaving only those too heavy to shift.

Māori named the boulders Te Kaihinaki (food baskets), believing them to have been washed ashore from the wreck of a canoe whose occupants were seeking *pounamu*. The seaward reef near Shag Point was the hull of the canoe, and just beyond it stands a prominent rock, the vessel's petrified navigator. Some of the Moeraki Boulders were *hinaki* (baskets), the more spherical were water-carrying gourds and the irregular-shaped rocks farther down the beach were *kumara* from the canoe's food store. The survivors among the crew were transformed at daybreak into hills overlooking the beach.

Moeraki village

The picturesque and tranquil fishing village of **MOERAKI** offers boulder access along the beach (they're 2km to the north) and a chance to see yellow-eyed penguins up close. Drive to the white wooden **Katiki Point** lighthouse (1km off SH1 then 4km along a mostly unsealed road) then follow signs down a path which leads to a hide, overlooking the beach where yellow-eyed penguins emerge after a hard day's fishing (from around 3.30pm to nightfall), and fur seals loll.

A second path leads to a *pa* site, its importance explained on a panel nearby.

ARRIVAL AND DEPARTURE   MOERAKI VILLAGE

By bus Most bus services don't stop in Moeraki. From Oamaru use Coastline Tours (☏ 03 434 7744, ⓦ coastline-tours.co.nz) which will drop you in the centre on its Oamaru–Dunedin run (Mon–Fri only) and pick you up about 6hr later on the way back north.

ACCOMMODATION

Moeraki Beach Motels Corner of Cleddy and Haven sts ☏ 03 439 4862, ⓦ moerakibeachmotels.co.nz. Just 100m from the beach, all four of these light-filled, two-bedroom, self-contained units face the bay, and can sleep up to five guests. Units $\underline{115}$

Moeraki Boulders Kiwi Holiday Park 2 Lincoln St, Hampden, 6km north of Moeraki ☏ 03 439 4439, ⓦ moerakibouldersholidaypark.co.nz. Welcoming campsite just steps from the beach: you can walk along it to Moeraki Boulders in 30min. There are plenty of grassy campsites, a nice range of roofed accommodation (cabins $70, apartments and motel units $110), good showers and an undercover BBQ area. Camping $\underline{15}$, dorms $\underline{28}$

Moeraki Village Holiday Park 114 Haven St ☏ 03 439 4759, ⓦ moerakivillageholidaypark.co.nz. Well located above the boat harbour and just a 50m walk to the beach, this campsite has a range of accommodation options, including motel units ($120). Camping per site $\underline{35}$, cabins $\underline{70}$

Three Bays 39 Cardiff St ☎03 439 4520, ⊛threebays. co.nz. A delightful self-contained unit set high on the hill with great long views over the town towards the Moeraki Boulders and ocean. Unit $170

EATING

★**Fleur's Place** The Old Jetty ☎03 439 4480, ⊛fleursplace.com. Renowned restaurateur Fleur Sullivan lets the freshness of the fish do the talking at her marvellously rustic corrugated-iron shack by the water that attracts sophisticates from Dunedin (plus the likes of Gwyneth Paltrow and Rick Stein). Try the platter for two ($79) with five types of fresh-off-the-boat fish accompanied by tartare sauce served in an abalone shell.

Dinner bookings are essential and this could be your chance to sample muttonbird ($31). Most mains $36–45. Wed–Sun 10.30am–11pm.

Moeraki Tavern 144 Haven St ☎03 439 4705, ⊛moerakitavern.com. If you missed out on a table at *Fleur's* or simply fancy a beer, the local tavern is a scenic spot for a pub meal (mains $16.50–41) and an ale or two on the sunny deck overlooking the bay. Daily 11am–11pm.

Shag Point and the Matakaea Scenic Reserve

Just over 10km south of Moeraki village, a side road runs 3km to the windswept promontory of **Shag Point** and the **Matakaea Scenic Reserve**, where the rocks are often slathered with fur seals and a viewing platform allows distant views of yellow-eyed penguins, best before 9am and after 3pm.

Dunedin and around

The "Edinburgh of the South", **DUNEDIN** was founded by Scottish settlers in the 1840s and within decades had become the commercial centre for the gold-rush towns of inland Central Otago. This left an enduring legacy of imposing **Gothic Revival architecture** fashioned from volcanic bluestone and creamy limestone. Today its population of around 127,000 is bolstered by 18,000 full-time students from the **University of Otago** – New Zealand's oldest seat of learning – who contribute to a strong **arts scene** and a vibrant **nightlife**, during term time at least.

Although Dunedin spreads out into the suburb-strung hills and surf beaches, the city has a compact and manageable heart, centred on **The Octagon**, from where you can sample both the city's Gothic architecture and the delights of **Speight's Brewery**, while a short walk to the south will land you in the once run-down **Warehouse District**, now a canvas for street artists rapidly filling with creative businesses and hip cafés. North of the Octagon, the **Botanic Garden** climbs toward the viewpoint on **Signal Hill**, from where you can look down to **Otago Harbour**. Local buses get you quickly to **Baldwin Street**, the world's steepest, and to the sandy beaches of **St Clair** and **St Kilda**, the former with good surfing and a cluster of cool cafés. On Dunedin's outskirts, **Port Chalmers** hangs onto a slightly bohemian, rough-around-the-edges feel, repaying a quick visit by combining it with the nearby Orokonui Ecosanctuary.

Brief history

From around 1300 AD, **Māori** fished the rich coastal waters of nearby bays, travelling inland in search of moa, ducks and freshwater fish, and trading with *iwi* further north. Eventually they formed a settlement near the harbour's mouth, calling it Otakou (pronounced "O-tar-go") and naming the headland at the harbour entrance after their great chieftain, Taiaroa – today a *marae* occupies the Otakou site. By the 1820s European whalers and sealers were seeking shelter in what was the only safe anchorage along this stretch of coast, unwittingly introducing foreign diseases. The local Māori population was decimated, dropping to a low of 110, but subsequent intermarriage bolstered numbers.

The New Zealand Company selected the Otago Harbour for a planned **Scottish settlement** as early as 1840 and purchased land from local Maori, but it wasn't until 1848 that the first migrant ships arrived, led by Captain William Cargill and the

Reverend Thomas Burns, nephew of the Scottish poet Robert Burns. The arrival of English and Irish settlers soon made the Scots a minority, but their national fervour had already stamped its distinct character on the town – Dunedin takes its name from the Gaelic translation of Edinburgh, with which it shares its street and suburb names.

In 1861, a lone Australian prospector discovered **gold** at a creek near present-day Lawrence, about 100km west of Dunedin. Within three months, diggers were pouring in from Australia, and as the main port of entry Dunedin found itself in the midst of a gold rush. The port was expanded, and the population trebled in three years making the city briefly New Zealand's largest. The newfound wealth spurred a building boom that resulted in much of the city's most iconic architecture, including the university.

By the 1870s gold mania had largely subsided, but the area sustained its economic primacy through **shipping**, railway development and farming. Decline began during the early twentieth century, when the opening of the Panama Canal in 1914 made Auckland a more economic port for British shipping. In the 1980s, the improvement in world gold prices and technological improvements re-established **mining** in the hinterland. New Zealand's largest gold-mining operation is located an hour's drive north of Dunedin at Macraes' vast open-pit mine.

The city centre

Dunedin's central focal point is **The Octagon**, laid out in 1846 and ringed by a blend of well-preserved buildings and modern additions. The sloping site is presided over by a **statue of Robert Burns**, symbol of Dunedin's Scottish origins. On summer days when cruise ships are in port, the area hosts **market** stalls selling local crafts (9am–4pm). The Octagon is dominated by the 1880 **Municipal Chambers**, a grand structure with an Italianate clock tower, all constructed from limestone on a base of Port Chalmers breccia. It's a fine example of the handiwork of Scottish architect **Robert A. Lawson**, whose influence can be seen in many of Dunedin's public buildings.

Dunedin Public Art Gallery

30 The Octagon • Daily 10am–5pm • Free • ☎ 03 477 3240, ⓦ dunedin.art.museum

Although **Dunedin Public Art Gallery** was founded in 1884 – making it the country's oldest gallery – its current incarnation dates from 1996 when six Victorian buildings, were elegantly refurbished to create a light, modern split-level space. In the foyer a spiral staircase from the department store that once occupied the site winds up to Neil Dawson's *Cones*, five of them chasing each other across the ceiling. The gallery hosts a great rotating collection of early and contemporary pieces from New Zealand and further afield, along with temporary exhibits. There's a children's play-space on the foyer level.

St Paul's Cathedral

Daily 10am–4pm • Free

Beside the Municipal Chambers rise the twin white-stone spires of **St Paul's Cathedral**, one of Dunedin's finest buildings and the seat of Anglican worship in the city. The stone-vaulted Gothic Revival nave, entirely constructed from Oamaru stone, was consecrated in 1919. The vaulted ceiling is the only one of its kind in New Zealand, and much of the stained glass in the impressive windows is original. The Modernist chancel and large organ were added in 1971.

Regent Theatre

17 The Octagon • ☎ 03 477 8597, ⓦ regenttheatre.co.nz

Across The Octagon, directly opposite St Paul's, a fine 1876 facade announces the **Regent Theatre**, originally a hotel, then a cinema and finally a theatre. The theatre hosts international shows and the Royal New Zealand Ballet, as well as live music. Inside,

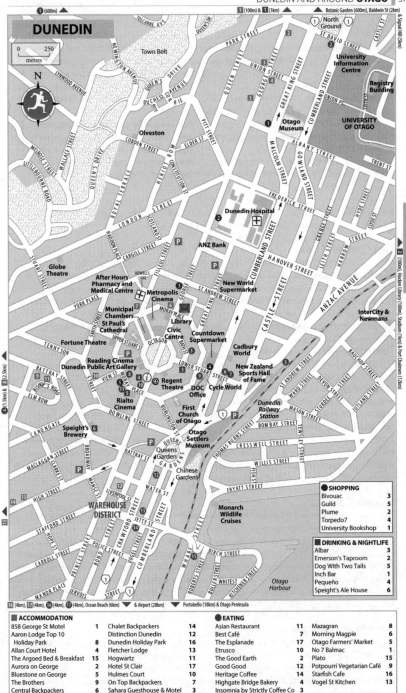

DUNEDIN

0 — 250
metres

N

11

1 (600m) ▲
1 (100m) & 1 (1km) ▲
▲ Botanic Garden (600m), Baldwin St (2km)
& Signal Hill (5km)
2 (100m), Hocken Library (100m), Stadium (1km) & Port Chalmers (12km)
1 (1.5km) & 2 (2.5km)
16 (4km), 17 (4km), 16 (4km), 17 (4km), Ocean Beach (6km)
& Airport (28km)
Portobello (18km) & Otago Peninsula

Town Belt

Olveston

Globe Theatre

Dunedin Hospital

ANZ Bank

After Hours Pharmacy and Medical Centre

New World Supermarket

Metropolis Cinema

Municipal Chambers
St Paul's Cathedral

Library

Civic Centre

Countdown Supermarket

Cadbury World

Fortune Theatre

Reading Cinema
Dunedin Public Art Gallery

Regent Theatre

New Zealand Sports Hall of Fame

DOC Office

Cycle World

Rialto Cinema

First Church of Otago

Dunedin Railway Station

Speight's Brewery

Queens Garden

Otago Settlers Museum

Chinese Gardens

WAREHOUSE DISTRICT

Monarch Wildlife Cruises

Otago Museum

University Information Centre

Registry Building

UNIVERSITY OF OTAGO

InterCity & Newmans

Otago Harbour

● **SHOPPING**

Bivouac	3
Guild	5
Plume	2
Torpedo7	4
University Bookshop	1

■ **DRINKING & NIGHTLIFE**

Albar	3
Emerson's Taproom	2
Dog With Two Tails	5
Inch Bar	1
Pequeño	4
Speight's Ale House	6

■ **ACCOMMODATION**

858 George St Motel	1	Chalet Backpackers	14	
Aaron Lodge Top 10 Holiday Park	8	Distinction Dunedin	12	
Allan Court Hotel	4	Dunedin Holiday Park	16	
The Argoed Bed & Breakfast	15	Fletcher Lodge	13	
Aurora on George	2	Hogwartz	11	
Bluestone on George	5	Hulmes Court	10	
The Brothers	9	On Top Backpackers	7	
Central Backpackers	6	Sahara Guesthouse & Motel	3	

● **EATING**

Asian Restaurant	11	Mazagran	8
Best Café	7	Morning Magpie	6
The Esplanade	17	Otago Farmers' Market	5
Etrusco	10	No 7 Balmac	1
The Good Earth	2	Plato	15
Good Good	12	Potpourri Vegetarian Café	9
Heritage Coffee	14	Starfish Cafe	16
Highgate Bridge Bakery	4	Vogel St Kitchen	13
Insomnia by Strictly Coffee Co	3		

DUNEDIN FESTIVALS

Arts Festival Dunedin ⓦ artsfestivaldunedin.co.nz. Biennial mid- to high-brow arts festival with opera, plays and plenty of music. Late September to early October every even year.

Cadbury Jaffa Race The 2018 closure of Dunedin's Cadbury factory also signalled the end of the city's annual Cadbury Chocolate Festival, but its key event, the Jaffa chocolate race down Baldwin Street, is expected to continue. Mid-July.

Craft Beer & Food Festival ⓦ dunedinbeerfest.org.nz. One-day festival held in Forsyth Barr Stadium with over ninety stalls offering more than four hundred brews, with plenty of tasty food to soak up the suds. November.

Fringe Festival ⓦ dunedinfringe.org.nz. Eleven-day arts and culture festival with street performers, short films, comedy and exhibitions. Generally takes place in mid-March.

New Zealand International Film Festival ⓦ nzff.co.nz. The Dunedin leg of the nationwide cinema festival features the usual mix of oddball and pre-release mainstream movies, all shown at the Regent and Rialto cinemas. Early to mid-August.

11

elaborate nineteenth-century plasterwork and marble staircases are juxtaposed with 1920s stained-glass windows and geometric balustrades.

First Church of Otago

415 Moray Place • Heritage Centre: Oct–May Mon–Fri 10am–4pm, Sat 10am–2pm; June–Sept Mon–Sat 10.30am–2.30pm • Free

The 60m-high stone spire of the **First Church of Otago** is visible throughout the city. Robert A. Lawson's neo-Gothic building is generally recognized as the most impressive of New Zealand's nineteenth-century churches, with particular praise given to the wooden gabled ceiling and, above the pulpit, a brightly coloured rose window. Behind the altar, the **Heritage Centre** explores the history of the church and its prime movers.

Toitu Otago Settlers Museum

31 Queens Gardens • Daily 10am–5pm • Free • ☎ 03 477 5052, ⓦ toituosm.com

A $38 million revamp in 2012 transformed the **Toitu Otago Settlers Museum** into one of Dunedin's most worthwhile attractions. The collection narrates two centuries of colonial and social history with artefacts ranging from whaling boats to washing machines. The transport-related displays are particularly strong, and the entire experience is enhanced by the museum's innovative use of technology and plenty of hands-on exhibits.

The museum complex is composed of three buildings: the original neo-Georgian brick heritage building, a 1939 Art Deco former bus depot and the dramatic glass-walled entrance foyer containing *Josephine*, a restored 1872 double-ended Fairlie steam engine, New Zealand's oldest locomotive.

Chinese Gardens

Corner of Rattray and Cumberland sts • Daily 10am–5pm • $9; audioguides free • ☎ 03 477 3248, ⓦ dunedinchinesegarden.com

Dunedin's **Chinese Gardens** opened in 2008, the culmination of a major project marking the contribution of the Chinese gold-miners and their descendants to the life of the city. It is one of a handful of classical Chinese gardens outside China and everything – from the 970 tonnes of limestone used in construction to the pavilions with their flying eaves – was shipped here from Shanghai. Ranged round a contemplative pond, it seems a world away from the surrounding city, a sensation only deepened by the opportunity to drink tea, eat steamed buns and play Go in the gardens' teahouse.

Dunedin Railway Station

Impossible to miss thanks to its towers, turrets and minarets, the resplendent **Dunedin Railway Station** on Anzac Avenue took over twenty years to build on reclaimed swampland; it was finally completed in 1906. The walls of its exquisitely preserved **foyer** glisten with green, yellow and cream majolica tiles made especially for New Zealand Rail by Royal Doulton, and the mosaic floor consists of more than 700,000 tiny squares of porcelain. On the upstairs balcony, two stained-glass windows depict approaching trains, their headlights gleaming from all angles.

The station no longer sees regular passenger services, though it is the terminus for the Taieri Gorge Railway (see page 580).

New Zealand Sports Hall of Fame
Daily 10am–4pm • $6 • ☎ 03 477 7775, ⓦ nzhalloffame.co.nz

The railway station's upper floor houses a hagiographic collection of memorabilia relating to the 170 members of the **New Zealand Sports Hall of Fame**. The objects are taken from disciplines ranging from yachting to sheep shearing, with – as you'd expect – an excellent section on rugby that includes the likes of an arm guard used by revered player Colin Meads to play a test match with a broken arm.

Cadbury World
280 Cumberland St • Daily 9am–4.30pm • Visitor Centre $5; 1hr tours every half-hour 9am–3pm; $22 • ☎ 0800 223 2879, ⓦ cadburyworld.co.nz

Dunedin's Cadbury factory may have closed its doors in 2018, but its adjacent chocolate-themed amusement park of sorts is set to live on in a big way. A $7million redevelopment due to be completed in late 2018 will see **Cadbury World** reopen in the nearby Castle Street Old Dairy, with features to include a "magic elevator" and the chance to make your very own block of chocolate. Until then, you can tour the original attraction with its "chocolate waterfall" and displays on the history of chocolate, or simply pop into the Visitor Centre for a goodie bag of Cadbury treats (included with entry fee).

Speight's Brewery
200 Rattray St • Oct–March noon, 2pm, 4pm, 5pm, 6pm & 7pm; April–Sept noon, 2pm & 4pm • $29; bookings essential • ☎ 03 471 9050, ⓦ thealehouse.co.nz

New Zealand's "liquid gold", Speight's Gold Medal Ale, has been brewed in Dunedin since the late 1880s, and remains one of the country's biggest-selling beers. Sample it and five other brews at the end of the **Speight's Brewery Tour**, an informative 90min meander around one of New Zealand's oldest breweries, established in 1876. Much of the recently refurbished brewery building dates from 1940, while the red-brick chimney (topped by a stone beer barrel) is visible from across the city.

Beside the tour entrance is a **spigot** fed by the same sweet-tasting artesian water that is used to brew the beer. Locals stop regularly to fill water bottles.

North of the centre

North of the centre, **Olveston** gives a taste of Dunedin life from its heyday, a topic treated more formally in the **Otago Museum**. The **Botanic Garden** climbs up towards the lookout on **Signal Hill**, from where you can look down to **Otago Harbour**, a sheltered inlet 22km long and no wider than a river in places. The harbour is protected from the ocean by the wildlife-rich **Otago Peninsula**.

Olveston
42 Royal Terrace, 15min walk northwest of The Octagon • Daily 9.30am, 10.45am, noon, 1.30pm, 2.45pm & 4pm for 1hr guided tours only; bookings recommended • $20.50 • ☎ 03 477 3320, ⓦ olveston.co.nz

Dunedin's showpiece historic home is **Olveston**, a fine Edwardian four-storey manor built around 1906 for Jewish businessman and collector, David Theomin. The last-surviving family member, his daughter Dorothy, lived there until her death in 1966, after which the house was bequeathed to the city. It remains just as she left it: you could easily imagine her walking in as you tour the house, which is an eclectic treasure-trove of art and antiques. The family were passionate about travel, art and music, and their tastes are reflected in everything from Arts and Crafts fireplaces, English oak panelling and Venetian glassware to Japanese and Delft porcelain.

Otago Museum

419 Great King St • Daily 10am–5pm; guided tours daily 11am, 1pm, 2pm & 3pm • Free; guided tour $15; Tuhura science centre including Tropical Forest $15; Planetarium $10; add $2 for shows • ☎ 03 474 7474, ☯ otagomuseum.govt.nz

The absorbing **Otago Museum**, and its fascinating **Southern Land, Southern People gallery** gives you a full introduction to life and natural history in the southern half of the South Island. Everything is knitted neatly together, with a discussion on climate illustrated by a Māori flax rain cape, and coverage of the region's fish, calling on the experience of whitebaiters.

Elsewhere look out for the **Animal Attic**, a deeply Victorian display of macabre skeletons and stuffed beasts – the chickens have even escaped to roost among the rafters. The **Pacific Cultures gallery** contains some excellent exhibits from Polynesia and Melanesia, and there's a decent collection of Māori artefacts in the **Tangata Whenua gallery**. Added in 2017, the **Tuhura science centre** includes a state-of-the-art **Planetarium** domed theatre screening 360°shows, and the renovated **Tropical Forest** is a great place to escape a cold Dunedin day among a thousand butterflies.

University of Otago

Campus accessed from the corner of Cumberland and Union sts • Information centre: Mon–Fri 9am–4.30pm, Sat 10.30am–3pm

New Zealand's oldest university, the **University of Otago** was founded by Scottish settlers in 1869. Based on the design of Glasgow University, it quickly expanded into a complex of imposing Gothic bluestone buildings, foremost among them the **Clocktower** building. The best bits are concentrated along Leith Street; for a more thorough look, follow the self-guided walk detailed in the *University Tour* booklet (available from the i-SITE and university information centre). Note that if your visit falls in the summer holidays (Dec–Feb) you'll miss the usual studenty vibe.

Hocken Library

90 Anzac Ave • Mon–Sat 10am–5pm; tours Wed 11am & 2pm (no booking required) • Free • ☎ 03 479 8868, ☯ library.otago.ac.nz/hocken

The **Hocken Library** is the university's extensive research facility, open to the public and built around an impressive New Zealand and Pacific collection assembled in the late nineteenth century by Dr Thomas Morland Hocken, a Dunedin physician and one of the country's first historians. The collection is housed in an Art Deco former butter factory where there are fascinating temporary exhibitions on the first floor, and free behind-the-scenes tours on Wednesdays at 11am and 2pm.

Dunedin Botanic Garden

2km north of The Octagon along Great King St • Sunrise–sunset • Free • Information centre & Winter Garden daily 10am–4pm; Alpine House daily 9am–4pm • ☎ 03 477 4000

The serene **Dunedin Botanic Garden** was established in 1863 at the foot of Signal Hill. Split in half by Lindsay Creek, the gardens' visitor facilities are centred in the flat **Lower Garden**. The steep **Upper Garden** contains an arboretum filled with now-mature trees planted in the nineteenth century to learn which species would flourish here for forestry purposes. Further up the hill there's also a sprawling rhododendron dell and an aviary, home to native birds as well as a garrulous flock of parrots.

The lower half of the Botanic Garden holds the steamy **Winter Garden**, its glasshouses filled with a profusion of tropical plants. Outside you can stroll through formal rose and herb gardens, and the expansive parklands that insulate the garden from the surrounding city. A volunteer-run information centre sits between the tea kiosk and the Winter Garden.

Signal Hill

Signal Hill Rd, 8.5km northeast of The Octagon • #11 Opoho bus from George St; get off at the last stop and walk up the road

The 393m summit of **Signal Hill**, just east of the Botanic Garden, is crowned by a scenic reserve with magnificent views over Dunedin and the upper harbour from the Centennial Memorial. Constructed to commemorate the century of British sovereignty (1840–1940) that followed the signing of the Treaty of Waitangi, the memorial is flanked by two powerful bronze figures symbolizing the past and the future. Embedded in the podium is a tribute to Dunedin's namesake: a chunk of the rock upon which Edinburgh Castle was built.

Baldwin Street

4.5km north of the city centre; follow Great King St until it becomes North Rd then look for road signs • #8 Normanby from George St runs past the foot of Baldwin St

Dunedin rejoices in the world's steepest street, the dead-straight **Baldwin Street**, which, with a *Guinness Book of Records*-verified maximum gradient of 1 in 2.86, has a slope of almost 19 degrees. The views from the top aren't bad, but the highlight is walking up, something achieved in about five minutes, under the bemused gaze of residents. As part of Dunedin's now-defunct Chocolate Carnival, the street has hosted the annual Cadbury Jaffa Race since 2002, which sees thousands of giant Jaffas (tangerine-coloured candy-coated chocolate balls) rolled downhill for charity.

Ocean Beach and around

The contiguous suburbs of **St Clair** and **St Kilda**, 5km south of the city centre, back onto **Ocean Beach**, a long, wild sweep of sand enclosed by two volcanic headlands. The St Clair end is excellent for surfing; further east, St Kilda is your best for swimming. Both ends are served by frequent buses from The Octagon.

St Clair Hot Salt Water Pool

The Esplanade • Oct–late March Mon–Fri 6am–7pm, Sat & Sun 7am–7pm • $6.50 • ☏ 03 455 6352

St Clair beach meets the cliffs at its western end beside the 25m **St Clair Hot Salt Water Pool**, the last open-air pool of its kind in the country. Filled with seawater heated to 28°C, it has a real community feel with all sorts of folk down for their constitutional. The pool's small café has the best views along the beach.

St Kilda and Tomahawk Beach

About 1km east of the saltwater baths, St Clair merges into **St Kilda**, where the beach is reasonably safe for swimming as long as you keep between the flags; it is patrolled in summer. At the beach's eastern end, a headland separates Ocean Beach from the smaller **Tomahawk Beach** (not safe for swimming), at low tide often dotted with horses and buggies preparing for trotting races.

Tunnel Beach

Buses #33 and #50 stop on Middleton Rd in Corstorphine; from the corner of Stenhope Crescent it's a 30min walk to the start of the track

Nearly 5km south of St Clair (by road), a narrow tunnel through the sandstone cliffs leads to a spectacular secluded beach. Hand-cut in the 1870s by John Cargill, son of Captain William Cargill (founder of the Otago settlement) to allow the Cargill families to bathe away from the prying eyes of St Clair, the tunnel entrance is reached by an easy fifteen-minute walk from the **Tunnel Beach** car park, off Blackhead Rd. Best visited at low tide, the beach is an eminently romantic spot. Keep an eye out for fossils and mysterious graffiti, and be mindful of unpredictable currents if you're planning a swim.

ARRIVAL AND DEPARTURE   DUNEDIN

By plane Dunedin Airport is 21km southwest of town on SH1 then 7km along SH86. Shuttle buses, including Super Shuttle (☏ 0800 748 885, ☏ supershuttle.co.nz; $25 for 1, $40 for 2), drop off at city-centre accommodation. A taxi is about $90.

11

Destinations Auckland (4 daily; 1hr 50min); Brisbane (3 weekly; 3hr 35min); Christchurch (7 daily; 1hr); Wellington (3 daily; 1hr 40min).

By train Dunedin has no main-line passenger trains, just the scenic Taieri Gorge Railway (see page 580).

By bus Dunedin is a regional hub for bus services. InterCity/Newmans (7 Halsey St) runs to Christchurch via Oamaru and Timaru, Queenstown via Alexandra and Cromwell, Wanaka and Te Anau via Gore. Atomic also runs to Queenstown and Ritchies (☎ 03 443 9120, ⓦ ritchies.co.nz) run from Dunedin Railway Station to Wanaka, while NakedBus (630 Princes St) goes to Christchurch and Invercargill. Catch-A-Bus South (☎ 03 479 9960, ⓦ catchabussouth.co.nz) operate a door-to-door service between Dunedin, Gore and Invercargill; Knightrider (☎ 03 342 8055, ⓦ knightrider.co.nz) runs to Christchurch and Invercargill.

Destinations Alexandra (3–5 daily; 3hr); Balclutha (2–4 daily; 1hr); Christchurch (7 daily; 6hr); Cromwell (5–6 daily; 3hr 30min); Gore (3–5 daily; 3hr); Invercargill (4–5 daily; 3hr 30min); Lawrence (3–4 daily; 1hr 30min); Oamaru (5–7 daily; 2hr); Queenstown (5 daily; 4–5hr); Te Anau (daily; 4hr 30min); Wanaka (2 daily; 4hr 45min).

GETTING AROUND

By bus The city has an efficient bus system (generally Mon–Fri 6.30am–11pm, Sat & Sun limited services; ⓦ orc.govt.nz). Buses are numbered and change numbers depending on which direction they're travelling in; fortunately routes are more usually identified by their destination. The most useful is the Normanby–St Clair run (#8), which goes from the beach right through the city, past the Botanic Garden, to the foot of Baldwin St. Fares are zoned: the central city is Zone One ($2.60), Portobello is Zone Four ($10.20). You'll save around twenty percent with a GoCard ($5 for the card and $10 minimum top-up; purchase from the i-SITE or directly from bus driver). All buses pass through the centre of town, stopping at different stands around The Octagon, or along Princes and George sts.

By car Dunedin operates a one-way system running north–south through the city affecting Cumberland, Castle, Great King and Crawford sts.

Parking Parking is seldom a problem, with inexpensive meters and restricted zones in the centre and free long-term street parking outside the downtown core.

Car rental The international agencies are complemented by good home-grown companies including Hirepool, 66 Cumberland St (☎ 03 471 9747, ⓦ hirepool.co.nz), and Ace at Dunedin Airport (☎ 0800 502 277, ⓦ acerentalcars.co.nz).

By taxi Call Dunedin Taxis (☎ 03 477 7777).

By bike Cycle World, 67 Stuart St (☎ 03 477 7473, ⓦ cycleworld.co.nz), rents road and mountain bikes from $35/half-day or $50/day, as well as full-suspension bikes ($100/day). Dunedin Bike Hire (☎ 0800 480 680, ⓦ ibikehire.co.nz) rents out electric ($80/day) and standard bikes (from $40/day), with free delivery and pick-up. The city is developing a network of cycle trails and lanes; the only section currently rideable takes you to St Leonard, about halfway to Port Chalmers.

INFORMATION

Tourist information i-SITE, 50 The Octagon (Nov–March Mon–Fri 8.30am–6pm, Sat & Sun 8.45am–6pm; April–Oct Mon–Fri 8.30am–5pm, Sat & Sun 8.45am–5pm; ☎ 03 474 3300). Handles transport, accommodation and tours, and stocks the informative *Dunedin Walks* leaflet ($5 or downloadable free via ⓦ dunedin.gov.nz) which details 28

THE TAIERI GORGE RAILWAY

The scenic Taieri Gorge Railway (☎ 03 477 4449, ⓦ dunedinrailways.co.nz) stretches 116km northwest from Dunedin through rugged hill country. Constructed between 1879 and 1921, the line once carried supplies a total of 235km from Dunedin to the old gold-town of Cromwell. Commercial traffic stopped in 1990, and much of the route was turned into the Otago Central Rail Trail (see page 634), but the most dramatic section – through the schist strata of the Taieri Gorge – continues to offer a rewarding rail journey at any time of year.

The air-conditioned train is made up of a mix of modern steel carriages with large panoramic windows and nostalgic, **refurbished 1920s wooden cars**. Storage is available for backpacks and bicycles, and there's a licensed snack bar on board.

In summer there are usually two trains a day from Dunedin's railway station to **Pukerangi**, a lonely wayside halt near the highest point of the track (250m) (Oct–April daily except Fri & Sun 9.30am & 2.30pm; $91 return, $61 one way; 4hr return), with the train continuing beyond Pukerangi for 38km to the old gold town of **Middlemarch** twice each week (Oct–April Fri & Sun, 9.30am; $115 return, $77 one way; 6hr return). In winter a 9.30am service runs to Pukerangi (Mon–Sat) with the Sunday service continuing to Middlemarch; check online for the latest timetables.

walks around the city. Free wi-fi.

DOC 50 The Octagon (☎03 474 3300). Combined with the i-SITE, it has the same opening hours.

Website Dunedin has a good promotional website, ⓦdunedinnz.com, filled with information on events and things to do in the city.

TOURS AND ACTIVITIES

Dunedin's guided and self-guided **walks** are a great way to get to know another side of the city. On the city fringes, there's **surf** at St Clair and forested **mountain-bike** trails on the Signal Hill Reserve, just 3km northeast of The Octagon. Half- and full-day biking routes are listed in the free *Fat Tyre Trails* leaflet (available at most bike shops or download it from ⓦdunedin.gov.nz), with some of the trails accessible from the city centre.

TOURS AND WALKS

City Walks ☎0800 925 571, ⓦcitywalks.co.nz. Guided heritage walks around Dunedin's historic centre (Mon–Sat 10.30am & 1.30pm; 2hr; $30). An abridged version of the morning tour runs each afternoon, enlivened by a snack of whisky and haggis. (Mon–Sat 4pm; 1hr; $30).

Dunedin Literary Walking Tours ☎027 444 4788, ⓦliterarytours.nz. Local creative writer and playwright Beverly Martens leads explorations of the city's literary heritage at Otago University (2hr; 2pm Tue, Thurs & Sun; $35) and in the inner city (90min; daily 10.30am; $25).

Dunedin Segway Tours ☎0800 734 929, ⓦdunedinsegwaytours.com. Learn about Dunedin's colonial past on a 1hr zip around the centre ($69), or opt for more in-depth 90min–3hr tours ($89–159).

Hair Raiser Tours ☎0800 428683, ⓦhairraisertours. com. Entertainingly spooky walking tours such as the Crime Walk (Mon–Fri 10.30am; $35), the Ghost Walk (daily: Oct–March 8pm; April–Sept 6pm; $35) and a graveyard tour of the city's Northern Cemetery (daily: Oct–March 9.30pm; April–Sept 8pm; $35).

Street Art Trail ⓦdunedinstreetart.com. Pick up a map from the i-SITE and head off on this self-guided walk around Dunedin's excellent street art works, many by renowned international artists including Belgium's ROA and Britain's Phlegm. The trail, thoughtfully bracketed by excellent cafés and restaurants, winds from the Octagon down into the Warehouse District, where the city's street art is concentrated.

SURFING

Esplanade Surf School Eastern end of the Esplanade, by the St Clair Surf Rescue Station ☎0800 484 141, ⓦespsurfschool.co.nz. Cool-water surfing lessons with wetsuit and board supplied (group lessons $60/90min; private lessons $120/90min); equipment rental is available too ($40/2hr for board and wetsuit).

MOUNTAIN BIKING

Offtrack ☎0800 633 872, ⓦofftrack.co.nz. Brilliant half-day guided rides on the Otago Peninsula ($99) and Dunedin's finest singletrack ($80) plus scenic day-rides in the Catlins ($199) and a tough-but-fun day trip ($250) on the Dunstan Road in the Maniototo.

ACCOMMODATION

There's a broad choice of accommodation in Dunedin, most of it near the city centre. If you prefer something more rural, consider the **Otago Peninsula**. **Freedom camping** is allowed in Dunedin City Council car parks all over the region (with the exception of prohibited zones on the Otago Peninsula) provided you are self-contained and legally parked, and there are no more than three campervans in a 50m radius.

CENTRAL DUNEDIN

858 George St Motel 858 George St ☎03 474 0047, ⓦ858georgestreetmotel.co.nz; map p.575. An attractively designed modern motel based on Victorian townhouses, with thirteen big, luxurious units and larger suites with their own kitchens. Studios $160, suites $190

Allan Court Motel 590 George St ☎03 477 7526, ⓦallancourt.co.nz; map p.575. Central and well-kept 1980s-built motel with spacious rooms, mostly one- and two-bedroom apartments, recently refitted bathrooms and nice touches such as Sky TV and a little welcome basket of goodies on arrival. $138

★ The Argoed Bed & Breakfast 504 Queens Drive ☎03 474 1369, ⓦargoed.co.nz; map p.575. If you don't mind a 15min walk to the centre, consider this delightful B&B set in a stately R.A. Lawson-designed home. Choose from three beautifully renovated rooms, one of which is en suite ($250), with a sumptuous cooked breakfast served in the dining room or plant-filled conservatory. There's also a well-stocked library, and a baby grand in the drawing room should you fancy tickling the ivories. $150

★ Aurora on George 678 George St ☎0800 737 378, ⓦauroradunedin.co.nz; map p.575. The calming blue-green hues of the aurora borealis are tastefully reflected in the smart studios and suites of the former *Cargills Hotel*, which reopened as the *Aurora* in 2016 following an extensive renovation. Amenities include a gym, coin-operated laundry, café, and Thai restaurant, *Buddha Stix*, with most rooms overlooking a peaceful central garden. $155

Bluestone on George 571 George St ☎03 477 9201, ⓦbluestonedunedin.co.nz; map p.575. Fifteen classy studio apartments with state-of-the-art kitchens, stylish bathrooms (most with spa baths), in-room laundries and tasteful decor. If you manage to prise yourself from the sumptuous beds there's even a small gym, courtyard and lounge. $230

★ **The Brothers** 295 Rattray St ☎ 03 477 0043, ⊕ brothershotel.co.nz; map p.575. Fifteen-room boutique hotel tastefully converted from a 1920s Christian Brothers' residence. Pared-down contemporary decor, with many of the compact rooms opening onto verandas with splendid city views; one is in the former chapel. A welcome glass of wine is served by the delightful owners in the spacious, sunny lounge each evening, which has even better views. A good continental breakfast is included. $170

Central Backpackers 243 Moray Place ☎ 0800 423 687 ⊕ centralbackpackers.co.nz; map p.575. Efficiently run 42-bed BBH hostel with a friendly cat, Mr Gizmo. Along with a TV lounge with Netflix and an included continental breakfast, there are backpack-size security lockers and fast wi-fi. Dorms $22, doubles $76

Chalet Backpackers 296 High St ☎ 03 479 2075, ⊕ chaletbackpackers.co.nz; map p.575. Light fills the rooms at this 1904 hospital-turned hostel with pleasing harbour views, decent kitchen, comfy singles ($50), doubles and dorms, plus a pool table, piano and several common areas. It's a bit shabby, but the chilled vibe makes up for it. Dorms $25, doubles $76

Distinction Dunedin 6 Liverpool St ☎ 03 471 8543, ⊕ distinctionhotels.co.nz; map p.575. Dunedin's newest hotel, located in the 1937 Chief Post Office building, is perfectly positioned for Warehouse District wanderings. Smart rooms come with all the mod cons, including a microwave and a washer/dryer, and there's a restaurant on-site if you prefer to eat in. $259

Fletcher Lodge 276 High St ☎ 03 477 5552, ⊕ fletcherlodge.co.nz; map p.575. Attention is devoted to guests' comfort at this elegant lodge set in an English baronial-style home built in 1924 for leading Kiwi industrialist Sir James Fletcher. The five rooms are complemented by an adjacent pair of well-appointed (but kitchen-less) apartments. Facilities include a spa pool and oak-panelled guest lounge. Doubles $335, apartments $650

★ **Hogwartz** 277 Rattray St ☎ 03 474 1487, ⊕ hogwartz. co.nz; map p.575. Welcoming BBH hostel in the former Catholic bishop's residence close to the centre of town. The dorms are bunk-free, some rooms have city views and it has all the facilities you'll need – from a laundry service to a TV room to a good kitchen. The former coach house and stables have

also been renovated into a handful of attractive self-contained studios (from $106). Dorms $32, doubles $74

Hulmes Court 52 Tennyson St ☎ 03 477 5319, ⊕ hulmes. co.nz; map p.575. The style of this pair of houses (one Edwardian, the other a grander 1860 Victorian affair) is a bit higgledy-piggledy but the price is right. Just a short climb from The Octagon with big, individually themed rooms (several en suite; $195), off-street parking and continental breakfast served in the sunny drawing room. $135

★ **On Top Backpackers** Corner of Filleul St and Moray Place ☎ 0800 668 672, ⊕ ontopbackpackers.co.nz; map p.575. Large, super-central, purpose-built hostel with a lively atmosphere aided by the bar and pool hall downstairs. Along with slightly cramped six- to eight-bed dorms there are a number of doubles (some en suite; $89), plus mini-cinema, BBQ terrace and a bright, open-plan kitchen/common room. A basic continental breakfast is included. Discounts for YHA and BBH cardholders. Dorms $27, doubles $66.

Sahara Guesthouse & Motel 619 George St ☎ 03 477 6662, ⊕ dunedin-accommodation.co.nz; map p.575. Pragmatic rather than romantic, the rooms at this 1863 guesthouse largely share facilities (some en suites at $83), though the standard motel units ($119) have their own bathrooms and kitchenettes and there are some comfortable newish deluxe studios ($164). Off-street parking. $72

ST CLAIR

Hotel St Clair 24 Esplanade ☎ 03 456 0555, ⊕ hotelstclair.com; map p.575. This modern, stylish 26-room hotel has four spacious room types, all with minibar and most with bathtubs and ocean views. The cheapest sea-view rooms fill up quickly; book in advance. $234

CAMPSITES AND HOLIDAY PARKS

Aaron Lodge Top 10 Holiday Park 162 Kaikorai Valley Rd, 2.5km west of the city centre ☎ 0800 879 227, ⊕ aaronlodgetop10.co.nz; map p.575. A sheltered, fairly spacious and well-tended site in the hills, with the Top 10 chain's usual wide range of accommodation options and on-site entertainment. Camping, per site $32, cabins $68

Dunedin Holiday Park 41 Victoria Rd ☎ 03 455 4690, ⊕ dunedinholidaypark.co.nz; map p.575. Lying alongside St Kilda Beach, this well-appointed park is a 5min drive from the city centre. There's a wide range of accommodation available if the weather precludes camping, plus a playground. Camping $22, cabins $57

EATING

Dunedin enjoys a pretty decent range of eating options, from cafés to fine restaurants, most of which are concentrated around The Octagon and along George Street, and increasingly, in the Warehouse District. Interesting outliers can be found in suburban Roslyn and beachy St Clair. For staples, visit the Countdown supermarket at 309 Cumberland St.

CENTRAL DUNEDIN

Asian Restaurant 43 Moray Place ☎ 03 477 6673; map p.575. Nothing flash, but convenient for a quick, cheap pan-Asian feed. The MSG-free menu spans all the classics, with most mains around $12. Licensed and BYO. Mon–Sat noon–2pm & 5–10pm or later, Sun 5–10pm.

★ **Best Café** 30 Lower Stuart St ☏ 03 477 8059; map p.575. Wonderfully time-warped Dunedin stalwart where mains are served with bread, curled butter and no frills to a soundtrack of golden oldies. The menu covers eight species of fresh fish, served with chips and coleslaw (one piece for $11–19; two pieces for $16–26), with Bluff oysters and whitebait patties in season. Licensed and BYO. Mon–Thurs 11.30am–2.30pm & 5–8pm, Fri & Sat 11.30am–2.30pm & 5–8pm or 9pm, Sun 11.30am–2.30pm on cruise ship days.

Etrusco First floor, 8 Moray Place ☏ 03 477 3737, ⊛ etrusco. co.nz; map p.575. Good value and popular Italian-run pizza and pasta restaurant (medium dishes $15–20; large $20–30) located in an elegant corner of the Edwardian Savoy building complete with twinkling chandeliers and green Ionian columns. There's often live piano, and a roaring fire in winter. Daily 5.30–10pm or later.

The Good Earth 765 Cumberland St ☏ 03 471 8554; map p.575. Near the university, this predominantly organic and Fairtrade café can whip up dairy and/or gluten-free versions of its menu items spanning organic muesli with poached Central Otago stone fruits and yoghurt ($10) to free-range chicken on preserved lemon couscous with organic salad ($16). Mon–Fri 7am–5pm, Sat & Sun 8am–5pm.

Good Good 22 Vogel St ☏ 027 332 2404, ⊛ goodgood.co.nz; map p.575. When you're hankering for a good burger, look no further than the beef, chicken and mac 'n' cheese varieties (all $15) served out of a caravan window in this fun warehouse conversion. It's tucked behind the Dunedin-made chocolate shop and café, Ocho. Wed–Sun 11.30am–2pm & 5–9pm.

Heritage Coffee Corner of Vogel and Jetty sts ☏ 03 470 1043, ⊛ heritagecoffee.co.nz; map p.575. One of the newest openings in the Warehouse District, this huge, beautifully fit-out café will set you up for the day with delicious house-made crumpets (from $13.50), fresh juices and smoothies ($8.50) baked treats, tasty salads and more, best enjoyed in a cosy leather booth or outside at a sunny pavement table. Mon–Fri 7.30am–3pm.

Insomnia by Strictly Coffee Co 23 Bath St ☏ 03 479 0017, ⊛ strictlycoffee.co.nz; map p.575. If not the best coffee in town then in company with it, sold by the cup or the kilo in this tiny-looking café set in a century-old former stamp-makers' shop. Enjoy the great crusty rolls and wraps in the street-art covered courtyard. Mon–Fri 7.30am–4pm.

Mazagran 36 Moray Place ☏ 03 477 9959; map p.575. If immaculate espresso is your goal head straight for this tiny café where everything is roasted on the premises. The barista decides which blend to use every morning and you can buy a dozen styles of freshly roasted beans. Mon–Fri 8am–5pm, Sat 10am–2pm.

★ **Morning Magpie** 46 Stuart St ☏ 03 477 6563; map p.575. The mismatched furniture, quirky art pieces and 1970s-era curios combine to create an eminently cosy vibe at this central café, where excellent house-roasted coffees, organic Dunedin teas, pastries, hand-rolled bagels (from $7) and more substantial brunch dishes including *huevos rancheros* ($17) are served on vintage crockery. Mon–Fri 7am–4pm, Sat 8am–3.30pm, Sun 8am–3pm.

Otago Farmers' Market Dunedin Railway Station car park ⊛ otagofarmersmarket.org.nz; map p.575. Every Saturday morning the station car park comes alive with up to 75 fruit, veg, food and drinks vendors from around the district at this always-popular market. An excellent choice for brunch on the run. Saturday 8am–12.30pm.

★ **No 7 Balmac** 7 Balmacewen Rd ☏ 03 464 0064, ⊛ no7balmac.co.nz; map p.575. The trek up to Māori Hill is well worth the effort to dine at this smart suburban café-restaurant, which turns out superb modern Kiwi bistro dishes, most cooked on its Texan-wood grill. Mon–Fri 7am–10pm, Sat 8.30am–11pm, Sun 8.30am–5pm.

Plato 2 Birch St ☏ 03 477 4235, ⊛ platocafe.co.nz; map p.575. Dunedin's seafood connoisseurs make their way across the overpasses and railway tracks to fill this excellent bistro in a 1960s former seafarers' hostel – a low rectangular room lined with shelves of quirky *tchotchkes*. The menu changes constantly, but expect sophisticated flavours – even humble fish and chips ($34) is dressed up with a kelp crust and finished with lemon butter. Lunch Wed–Sat noon–2pm; brunch Sun 11am–2pm; dinner daily 6–10pm or later.

Potpourri Vegetarian Café 97 Stuart St ☏ 03 477 9983, ⊛ potpourrivegetariancafe.co.nz; map p.575. You don't need to be veggie to appreciate this established vegetarian café where the bare brick walls are decorated with botanical etchings. Delicious seed-and-fruit slices and muffins complement cheap light meals (falafel rolls $6.50) and more filling dishes such as vegetarian nachos ($14). Mon–Fri 8am–3.30pm, Sat & Sun 9am–3pm.

★ **Vogel St Kitchen** 76 Vogel St ☏ 03 477 3623, ⊛ vogelstkitchen.nz; map p.575. A giant fish swallowing a flotilla of Māori *waka* by UK street artist Phlegm marks the entrance to this huge, exposed-brick restaurant, one of Dunedin's hippest. There's a great breakfast menu with lots of veg options, wood-fired sandwiches ($13.90) and pizzas ($23.90) for lunch, and Supreme coffee throughout the day. Fully licensed with Emerson's on tap. Mon–Thurs 7.30am–3pm, Fri 7.30am–4pm, Sat & Sun 8.30am–4pm.

ROSYLN

★ **Highgate Bridge Bakery** 300 Highgate ☏ 03 474 9222; map p.575. Known to locals as "The Friday Shop" for its limited opening hours, this plain-looking bakery sells superb pastries, tarts, quiches and gourmet prepared meals. Get here early: Albert Roux-trained chef, Jim Byars, shuts up shop when he's sold out, which can happen as early as 9am. Prices from $5.50 for a small quiche. Fri 6am–5pm.

ST CLAIR

The Esplanade 2 Esplanade ☏ 03 456 2544, ⊛ esplanade.co; map p.575. This stylish Italian café and

11

11

RUGBY IN DUNEDIN

There's no surer way to get a real taste of Dunedin in party mode than to attend a **rugby match** at the 30,000-seater Forsyth Barr Stadium (@forsythbarrstadium.co.nz) at 130 Anzac Ave, 2km east of The Octagon. The city is proud of having the world's only fully roofed, natural-turf stadium, but its $200 million construction (in time for the 2011 Rugby World Cup) was controversial and put huge strains on local ratepayers. Highlanders Super 15 games are held here regularly during the season (Feb–July) and there are occasional All Black Games (generally May–Oct). For fixtures and ticket sales visit the websites of the Highlanders (@thehighlanders.co.nz) and the All Blacks (@allblacks.com), or pop into the Champions of the World store, 8 George St (Mon–Fri 9am–6pm, Sat 10am–5pm, Sun 11am–4pm; @03 477 7852).

restaurant has a good range of brunch options, but the full menu (from 11am) is the real star, featuring well-executed Italian classics from antipasti ($8–19) to rich pastas and crispy wood-fired pizzas ($21–26). Go on, start with an Aperol spritz ($12). Daily 8am–late.

Starfish Cafe 7/240 Forbury Rd @03 455 5940, @starfishcafe.co.nz; map p.575. Bright and buzzing local favourite split over two levels with a cracking brunch menu spanning smashed avocado with poached eggs, tomato and chilli on toast ($18.50) to a free-range chicken salad ($25). Good coffee and smoothies, with beer and wine available too. Mon, Tues & Sun 7am–5pm, Wed–Sat 7am until late.

DRINKING AND NIGHTLIFE

Like all good university cities, drinking is taken seriously here. A number of the city's dozens of **pubs** and **bars** serve all manner of brews from Dunedin's premier micro-brewery, Emerson's. Local **bands** play at weekends at the places below, although once the students head home for the summer holidays (late Nov to early March) the dance floors can look forlorn.

Albar 135 Stuart St @03 479 2468; map p.575. A local favourite, this tiny Scottish-themed bar has a good selection of whiskies, European and Kiwi bottled beers and a couple of local craft brews on tap. The cosy booths are a great place to hole up in winter, while the pavement tables fill quickly during the warmer months. Mon–Sat 11am–late, Sun noon–late.

Dog With Two Tails 25 Moray Place @03 477 4198, @dogwithtwotails.co.nz; map p.575. It's a great spot for a wholesome brunch or a light lunch, but this eclectic café and bar really comes into its own of an evening when it hosts everything from live bands to trivia nights, art exhibitions to open-mic nights. Mon & Sun 8am–3pm, Tues–Fri 8am–midnight, Sat 9am–midnight.

★ **Emerson's Taproom** 70 Anzac Drive @03 447 1812, @femersons.co.nz; map p.575. If you're a fan of the beer you can now drink it straight from the source at the excellent new taproom and restaurant attached to the local brewery. Sink into one of the leather couches in the huge, industrial-styled space and work your way through the sixteen beers on tap, complemented by a great menu of bar snacks (around $10), sharing plates (around $13) and hearty mains (around $30). They even do brunch. Daily 10am–late.

Inch Bar 8 Bank St @03 473 6496, @facebook.com/inch-bar; map p.575. For a change from the downtown vibe, head for this intimate neighbourhood watering hole with speciality beers (including Emerson's and Tuatara on tap), a tasty tapas menu, and regular live acts. Daily 3–10pm or later; closed Mon in winter.

★ **Pequeño** Down the alley beside 12 Moray Place @03 477 7830, @pequeno.co.nz; map p.575. All low lighting, leather sofas and banquettes around the fire. Excellent wine and cocktails (mostly South American-style), Emerson's on tap and regular jazz bands add to the makings of a good night. Tues, Wed & Sat 7pm–late, Thurs 6pm–late, Fri 5pm–late.

Speight's Ale House 200 Rattray St @03 471 9050, @thealehouse.co.nz; map p.575. Spacious Speight's-owned pub right by the brewery with good beer and food served in rural-kitsch surrounds. Daily 11.30am–late.

ENTERTAINMENT

In addition to its festivals, Dunedin has a lively year-round theatre scene. Public recitals are held from time to time by the University of Otago's music department.

CINEMAS

MetroCinema, Town Hall Building, Moray Place @03 471 9635, @metrocinema.co.nz. With only 53 seats this is a delightful place to watch art-house and more commercial movies for just $12 before 5pm weekdays, and $14 at other times. Popcorn is out, but you're welcome to take your coffee in with you.

Reading Cinemas 33 The Octagon @03 974 6700, @readingcinemas.co.nz. Multiplex screening all the latest mainstream films, with a fully licensed bar.

Rialto 11 Moray Place @03 474 2200, @rialto.co.nz. Beyond its fabulously retro façade, the Rialto has six stadium-style cinemas screening Hollywood blockbusters, plus occasional art-house releases.

THEATRES

Fortune Theatre 231 Stuart St ☎ 03 477 8323, ⓦ fortunetheatre.co.nz. Converted from a neo-Gothic church, the Fortune divides its programme between new works by Kiwi playwrights, fringe theatre, popular Broadway-style plays and occasional musicals. Tickets around $45. Closed Jan to early-Feb.

Globe 104 London St ☎ 03 477 3274, ⓦ globetheatre. org.nz. This small and intimate venue features contemporary plays, classical drama and experimental works. Tickets $22.

Regent 17 The Octagon ☎ 03 477 8597, ⓦ regenttheatre.co.nz. The city's largest and most ornate theatre, hosting musicals, ballets, touring plays, comedians, the New Zealand Symphony Orchestra, Dunedin's Southern Sinfonia and the New Zealand International Film Festival.

SHOPPING

Outdoorwear chain Bivouac (ⓦ bivouac.co.nz) and biking chain Torpedo7 (ⓦ torpedo7.co.nz) also have outlets in Dunedin.

Guild 45 Moray Pl ⓦ guilddunedin.co.nz; map p.575. Peruse the wares of the region's best emerging designers in the one place at this cute boutique. Staffed by the designers themselves, it stocks clothing, accessories and homewares for men and women designed by twelve permanent retailers and an ever-changing array of pop-up designers. Mon–Sat 10am–5pm.

Plume 310 George St ☎ 03 477 9358, ⓦ plumestore. com; map p.575. Top womenswear store (with some menswear) run by Margi Robertson, founder of top Kiwi label Nom*D. Everything from Workshop to Comme des Garçons along with local labels Zambesi and, naturally Nom*D. Mon–Fri 9am–5.30pm, Sat 10am–4pm.

University Bookshop 378 Great King St, opposite the Otago Museum ☎ 03 477 6976, ⓦ unibooks.co.nz; map p.575. Comprehensive independent bookshop covering two floors, with the bargains located upstairs. Mon–Fri 8.30am–5.30pm, Sat & Sun 10am–4pm.

DIRECTORY

Banks and foreign exchange The major banks are clustered on George and Princes sts, all with ATMs. On Saturday try the ANZ, corner of George and Hanover sts, which is open 10am–2pm.

Internet Dunedin Public Library, corner of John and Stewart sts (Mon–Fri 9.30am–8pm, Sat & Sun 11am–4pm; ☎ 03 474 3690), has free wi-fi and computers for use; also has newspapers.

Medical treatment Dunedin Hospital, 201 Great King St (☎ 03 474 0999); emergencies only. After-hours doctors are available at Dunedin Urgent Doctors, 18 Filleul St (☎ 03 479 2900, ⓦ dunedinurgentdoctors.co.nz).

Pharmacy After-hours service at Urgent Pharmacy, 95 Hanover St (daily 10am–10pm; ☎ 03 477 6344).

Post office 310 Moray Place (Mon–Fri 9am–5.30pm, Sat 9am–1pm).

Port Chalmers

Container cranes loom over the small, quirky town of **PORT CHALMERS**, 13km northeast of Dunedin and reached along the winding western shore of Otago Harbour. Arranged on hills around a container port and cruise-ship berth, the town has a vibrant artistic community, with the **Hotere Sculpture Garden**, legacy of the late painter and sculptor **Ralph Hotere** (a long-time resident of Port Chalmers) perched at the end of Constitution Street. The whole place has a delightful lost-in-time feel, with many fine nineteenth-century buildings along George Street, the main drag, and a modest amount of renovation has made way for a few cool shops and cafés. Along with the portside **Port Chalmers Maritime Museum**, two late Victorian churches vie for attention amid the cranes: the elegant stone-spired Presbyterian **Iona Church** on Mount Street, and the nuggety bluestone Anglican **Holy Trinity**, on Scotia Street, designed by Robert A. Lawson.

Orokonui Ecosanctuary

600 Blueskin Rd, 6km north of Port Chalmers • Daily 9.30am–4.30pm; 1–2hr guided tours daily at 11am & 1.30pm; bookings essential • $19; 1hr tour $35; 2hr tour $50 • ☎ 03 482 1755, ⓦ orokonui.org.nz

Modelled on the Zealandia attraction in Wellington, the **Orokonui Ecosanctuary** is a welcome addition to the pantheon of wildlife activities within easy reach of Dunedin. The striking eco-designed visitor centre is packed with information and the café offers wonderful views of the valley, but the real treats are just the other side of the 8.7km predator-exclusion fence, protecting three square kilometres of regenerating bush, containing reintroduced native birds, **tuatara** and skinks. You can take a self-guided walk through the sanctuary along a number of well-marked trails (including one long path down the valley that leads to the country's tallest tree, a huge blue gum tree), but will learn and probably see more on a **guided tour** with the freedom to roam afterwards. Either drive here (30min from Dunedin) or come on a wildlife tour (see page 590), as no public buses visit.

ARRIVAL AND INFORMATION

PORT CHALMERS

By bus The #14 bus runs from Dunedin to Port Chalmers, leaving from stands 4 and 5 on Cumberland St, dropping you off on George St, Port Chalmers' main thoroughfare, about 30min later.

Tourist information Port Chalmers Library, 20 Beach St (Mon–Wed & Fri 9.30am–5.30pm, Thurs 9.30am–8pm, Sat 11am–2pm; ☎03 474 3690), has local leaflets and free internet.

ACCOMMODATION

★ **Billy Browns** 423 Aramoana Rd, Hamilton Bay, 5km north of Port Chalmers ☎03 472 8323, ⓦbillybrowns. co.nz; map p.589. Quirkily designed lodge isolated on a working sheep farm, in an area where you probably wouldn't stay were the accommodation not so brilliant. It has stunning views, a log fire and stacks of vinyl, with a continental breakfast included. The lodge sleeps just eight (including one four-bed bunk room; $250), so book ahead. Doubles $150

EATING

As well as the places to eat listed below you'll find several scenic picnic spots dotted along Peninsula Beach Road, just around from the harbour.

Carey's Bay Historic Hotel 17 MacAndrew Rd, 1km north of town ☎03 472 8022; map p.589. Pub in an 1874 Bluestone building specializing in seafood; try the *poisson cru* ($15.50) or work your way though platters laden with scallops, mussels, squid and prawns ($28.50–48). Daily 11am–10pm.

The Galley 36 George St ☎03 4728 528, ⓦthegalley

cafe.co.nz; map p.589. The sunny outdoor patio (complete with fireplace) is a fine spot to sip a coffee or a glass of wine. Soak it up with their famous seafood chowder ($20) or a wood-fired pizza (around $26). Tues & Wed 8.30am–3pm, Thurs–Sun 8am–late.

Union Co Café 2 George St ☎021 158 5165; map p.589. With sun streaming through the windows, this baby-blue corner café is a top spot for a flat white or a light breakfast (cheddar and posh ham bagel; $8). The cabinet of baked goods is particularly veggie- and vegan-friendly. Daily 8am–3pm.

The Otago Peninsula

The 35km-long crooked finger of the **OTAGO PENINSULA**, running northeast from Dunedin, divides Otago Harbour from the Pacific Ocean. With sweeping views of the harbour, the sea and Dunedin against its dramatic backdrop of hills, the peninsula offers outstanding year-round **wildlife viewing** that's probably the most condensed and varied in the country and best accessed on an organised tour.

The prime wildlife viewing spots are concentrated at the peninsula's tip, **Taiaroa Head** (less than an hour's drive from Dunedin), where cold waters forced up by the continental shelf provide a rich and constant food source. The majestic **royal albatross** breeds here in the world's only mainland albatross colony. Also concentrated on the headland's shores are **penguins** (the little blue and the rare yellow-eyed) and **southern fur seals**, while the cliffs are home to other seabirds including three species of **shag**, **muttonbirds** (sooty shearwaters) and various species of gull. New Zealand **sea lions** sometimes loll on beaches, while offshore, orca and **whales** can occasionally be seen. Apart from wildlife spotting there's appeal in the beautiful woodland gardens of **Glenfalloch**, the exemplary grounds of **Larnach Castle** and several **scenic walks** to spectacular viewpoints and unusual land formations created by lava flows.

The main hub for **accommodation** and eating is **Portobello** (see page 590).

Larnach Castle

145 Camp Rd, Company Bay • Daily: Oct–March 9am–7pm; April–Sept 9am–5pm • Castle and gardens $31; gardens only $13.50 • ☎ 03 476 1616, ☻ larnachcastle.co.nz • Take bus #18 from Stand 5 on Cumberland St to Broad Bay, from where it's a steep 2km walk (allow 40min)

At **Company Bay**, Castlewood Road runs 4km inland to the 1871 Gothic Revival **Larnach Castle**, which sits high on a hill commanding great views across the harbour to Dunedin. More Scottish château than fort, this sumptuous residence was designed by Robert A. Lawson for Australian-born banker and politician William Larnach (note the Queenslander-style verandas). Materials were shipped to Dunedin from all over the world then punted across the harbour and dragged uphill by ox-drawn sleds, the whole thing taking thirteen years to build.

William Larnach later took his own life in New Zealand's Houses of Parliament, and his son sold the castle in 1906. After years of neglect the property, which is reputed to be haunted, was rescued by the Barker family in the late 1960s and has since been progressively restored while remaining their home. Check out the concealed spiral staircase in the corner of the third floor, which leads up to a terraced turret.

The castle's manicured grounds, divided into nine **gardens**, are of national importance and quite beautiful; keep an eye out for the handful of *Alice in Wonderland* statues, such as one of the Cheshire cat hiding in an ancient Atlas cedar tree.

The excellent café (daily 9.30am–4.30pm) in the former ballroom makes the perfect lunch stop; you can also stay overnight (see page 590).

Glenfalloch Garden

430 Portobello Rd, 10km east of Dunedin • Daily 8am–dusk • Donation appreciated • ☎ 03 476 1006, ☻ glenfalloch.co.nz

"Hidden Valley" in Gaelic, **Glenfalloch Garden** contains a sizeable tract of mature garden and bush, surrounding a homestead built in 1871 and a fantastic restaurant (see page 591). Between mid-September and mid-October the garden – recognized as a "Garden of National Significance" – is ablaze with rhododendrons, azaleas and camellias.

Fletcher House

727 Portobello Rd, 15km northeast of Dunedin • Sat & Sun 11am–4pm • 30min guided tours $10 • ☎ 03 478 0180, ☻ fletchertrust.co.nz

As you head along Portobello Road towards the tip of the peninsula, devote a few minutes to **Fletcher House**, a small Edwardian villa built by James Fletcher, founder of the Fletcher construction conglomerate. Built entirely of native wood, with rimu ceilings and floors, in 1909, it became the family home of the Broad Bay storekeeper and has now been lovingly restored to its original state. Visits are by guided tour on demand; simply turn up and join the next one.

Penguin Place

45 Pakihau Rd, off Harington Point Rd, 3km south of Taiaroa Head • 1hr30min tours daily Oct–March 10.15am–late afternoon & April–Sept 3.45pm; bookings essential • $54 • ☎ 03 478 0286, ☻ penguinplace.co.nz

The wonderful **Penguin Place** penguin-conservation project gives you the rare privilege of entering a protected nesting area of around 25 yellow-eyed penguins. Tours held during the day in summer (when it's rare to see the penguins) have a broad focus on flora and fauna in the reserve, but from 5.15pm it's all about the penguins, with carefully controlled and informative tours beginning with a talk on penguins and their conservation followed by a visit to the onsite penguin rehab facility. Groups then head to the beachside colony where well-camouflaged trenches lead to several hides among the dunes. These allow extraordinary proximity to the penguins and excellent photo opportunities. Proceeds from the tours are used to fund the penguin rehabilitation centre and habitat restoration projects. You can also **stay** overnight (see page 590).

11

Taiaroa Head

The world's only mainland albatross colony occupies **Taiaroa Head**, a wonderland of wildlife that also served as a fortified outpost against threats imagined and real.

The Southern Hemisphere's sole mainland colony of royal albatross can be spied in flight all year round from anywhere on the headland, and a short signposted walk from the Royal Albatross Centre car park leads to a **cliff-edge viewing area** with spectacular views of a spotted shag colony.

Royal Albatross Centre

1260 Harington Point Rd • Daily 10.15am–dusk • Free; albatross tour 60min, $50; unique tour 90min, $55; bookings recommended • ☎ 03 478 0499, ⓦ albatross.org.nz

To see interesting displays on local wildlife and history (or just to grab a coffee) head into the **Royal Albatross Centre**. You can buy tickets here for the excellent **Albatross Tour**, which includes an introductory film and time to view the birds from an enclosed area in the reserve (binoculars provided), where there is also closed-circuit TV of the far side of the colony. The **best months** for viewing are generally January and February, when the chicks hatch, and April to August, when parent birds feed their chicks. By September the chicks and adults are ready to depart and new breeding pairs start to arrive. If you're hoping to grab a snack before penguin-viewing, be mindful that the café closes an hour before sunset.

Fort Taiaroa

30min guided tour 11.30am & hourly on demand noon–8pm • $25 • ☎ 03 478 0499, ⓦ albatross.org.nz

The Royal Albatross Centre is the starting point for tours around **Fort Taiaroa**, a historic warren of tunnels and gun emplacements originally built in 1885 when an attack from Tsarist Russia was feared, and re-armed during World War II. The main attraction is the restored Armstrong Disappearing Gun, which was raised by a hand-pumped water ram and used its recoil to swing back into the gun pit. The fort is accessed through a web of tunnels beneath the albatross colony and can be visited on a stand-alone basis, or as part of the centre's Unique Taiaroa tour.

Pilots Beach

Blue Penguin Encounter: nightly at dusk • $35 • ☎ 03 478 0477, ⓦ bluepenguins.co.nz

For many summers, visitors after a free wildlife encounter have headed down to **Pilots Beach**, on the western side of Taiaroa Head (follow the footpath to the shore from the Royal Albatross Centre car park), where southern fur seals loll on the shore in daytime and over a hundred little blue penguins come ashore around dusk.

While it's still possible to walk down to the beach in daylight, evening access is only possible on an authorized **Blue Penguin Encounter** tour, comprising a short guided walk from the Albatross Centre (where tickets are sold) down to a couple of low-impact viewing platforms among the sand dunes. Watching the penguins arrive in great rafts before waddling up the beach in surprisingly noisy fashion is the best night out you'll have on the peninsula.

Natures Wonders Naturally

Taiaroa Head, 1.5km past the Albatross Centre • Daily 10.15am until 1hr before sunset for 1hr tours • $99 • ☎ 0800 246 446, ⓦ natureswonders.co.nz

The peninsula road ends at **Natures Wonders Naturally**, a headland farm which endlessly enthusiastic owner, Perry Reid, has turned into one of the finest opportunities to see wildlife up close. There's no animal feeding or nesting boxes, just wild animals sometimes literally within arm's reach. The 8WD argos used to transport you around the 6km of often-steep farm tracks seem a little incongruous (and noisy) but get you to a fabulous viewing spot for cliff-dwelling spotted shags, in among a fur seal colony and to a hide above a beach where blue and yellow-eyed penguins waddle up to their sand-dune nests at just about any time of day. The tour can also be conducted by coach ($45).

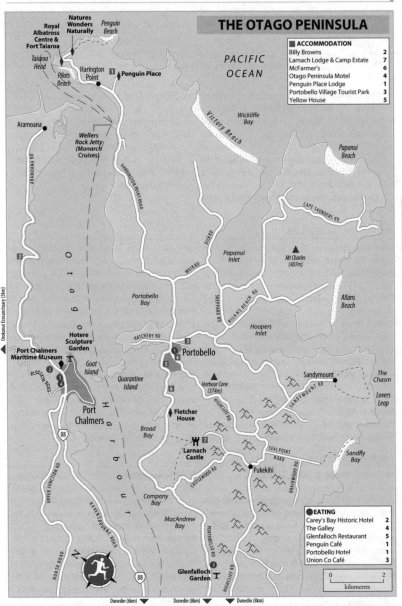

THE OTAGO PENINSULA

PACIFIC OCEAN

■ **ACCOMMODATION**

Billy Browns	2
Larnach Lodge & Camp Estate	7
McFarmer's	6
Otago Peninsula Motel	4
Penguin Place Lodge	1
Portobello Village Tourist Park	3
Yellow House	5

● **EATING**

Carey's Bay Historic Hotel	2
The Galley	4
Glenfalloch Restaurant	5
Penguin Café	1
Portobello Hotel	1
Union Co Café	3

0 — 2 kilometres

Dunedin (6km) ▼   Dunedin (8km) ▼   ▼ Dunedin (8km)

ARRIVAL AND INFORMATION

By car The peninsula is best accessed with your own wheels, either via Portobello Rd, which snakes along the western shoreline, or the inland Highcliff Rd, which winds up and over the hills.

By bus The #18 Peninsula bus (13–21 daily) runs along the coast road to Portobello (35min) from Stand 5 outside

THE OTAGO PENINSULA

the New World supermarket on Cumberland St, with 3–5 services continuing to Harrington Point, within 2km of Taiaroa Head.

Tourist information Pick up the free *AtoZ Dunedin Guide* from the Dunedin i-SITE.

11

OTAGO PENINSULA WALKS

The *Dunedin Walks* leaflet ($5 at Dunedin's i-SITE or downloadable for free at ⓦdunedin.gov.nz) briefly describes eight walks on the peninsula (including the two below), most of them well defined but pretty steep in places. The weather here can turn cold or wet very quickly, even on the sunniest days, so come prepared.

The Chasm and Lovers Leap (2.5km; 1hr; closed Sept & Oct for lambing). Wonderfully accessible peninsula walk, forming an easy loop which crosses farmland to sheer cliffs that drop 200m to the sea, where you'll see collapsed sea caves and rock faces of layered volcanic lava flows. The track begins from the end of Sandymount Road, 8km south of Portobello (a 25min drive from Dunedin).

Sandfly Bay (3km return; 90min). Pleasant walk across farmland then down the dunes to the beach, a fantastic place to watch yellow-eyed penguins come ashore in the late afternoon (keep well away and crouch down if you see one). Make for the colony at the south end where there's a hide and, in summer, a DOC ranger to make sure people don't disturb the birds. Start at the end of Seal Point Rd, 7km southwest of Portobello.

TOURS AND ACTIVITIES

4 Nature Tours ☏03 472 7647, ⓦ4nature.co.nz. Nature and wildlife oriented tours focused on the western side of Otago Harbour, such as their Ecosanctuary and Wading Birds Tour (4–5hr; $130) visiting Orokonui.

Elm Wildlife Tours ☏0800 356 563, ⓦelmwildlifetours.co.nz. Excellent, ecologically minded, guided bus tours (usually 6–6hr 30min; $105) leave Dunedin in the afternoon and visit a private conservation area where you'll see yellow-eyed penguins and fur seals, along with a host of other species. Trips can include a Royal Albatross Centre tour ($165), an hour-long Monarch Cruise ($158), or everything combined (8hr; $233). Children and students save $10 on all trips.

Monarch Wildlife Cruises & Tours 20 Fryatt St, Dunedin ☏0800 666 272, ⓦwildlife.co.nz. A converted fishing boat with licensed galley is put to good use running short cruises around Taiaroa Head (Oct–March 5 daily; April–Sept 1–2 daily; 1hr; $54) from the Wellers Rock jetty, near the tip of the Otago Peninsula. This can be combined with a trip to the Royal Albatross Centre ($93) or Penguin Place ($97). If you're not planning to drive out along the peninsula, opt for the Wildlife Tour (summer 8.30am & 3.30pm; winter 1pm; 4hr; $92), which leaves from the wharf in Dunedin, cruises around Taiaroa Head then drops you at Wellers Rock, returning to Dunedin by bus. Larnach Castle combos are also available.

Wild Earth Adventures ☏03 489 1951, ⓦwildearth.co.nz. For an often magical perspective on the coast and its wildlife, take a sea-kayaking tour around Taiaroa Head or Portobello (both 4hr; $115), spending around two hours on the water. There's also a Twilight Tour (Oct–March; 3–5hr; $115), with wildlife and wonderful sunsets.

ACCOMMODATION

★ Larnach Lodge & Camp Estate Larnach Castle ☏03 476 1616, ⓦlarnachcastle.co.nz; map p.589. Cosy up in the converted stables, containing six shared-bath rooms, or in *Larnach Lodge's* twelve grander themed rooms, some of which have great harbour views. Just outside the grounds, *Camp Estate* has five sumptuous rooms ($510) in a modern house designed like a Scottish manor house, with long harbour views and in-room fireplaces. All room rates include castle admission, breakfast and the chance to book a three-course dinner in the castle's grand dining room ($70/person plus wine). Stables **$160**, lodge **$300**

McFarmer's 774 Portobello Rd ☏03 478 0389, ⓔmcfarmers@xtra.co.nz; map p.589. Homely, environmentally aware harbourside accommodation with a cosy backpacker lodge, plus a two-bedroom cottage (from $120). It's a peaceful spot with no wi-fi, phone or TV; admiring the scenery and watching the lambs is the order of the day. Occasional winter closures. Single **$35**, doubles **$70**

Otago Peninsula Motel 1724 Highcliff Rd, Portobello ☏03 478 0666, ⓦotagopeninsulamotel.co.nz; map p.589. A small, comfortable modern motel in the heart of Portobello. All six room types have a fridge, microwave, cooktop, and harbour views, and some also have spa baths. Doubles **$150**

Penguin Place Lodge 45 Pakihau Rd ☏03 478 0286, ⓦpenguinplace.co.nz; map p.589. On the hill above Penguin Place, this simple, comfy backpackers has harbour views from many of its colourful doubles and twins. You can rent bedding ($5/stay/bed) or use your own; check-in before 6pm. No wi-fi. Doubles per person **$35**

Portobello Village Tourist Park 27 Hereweka St, Portobello ☏03 478 0359, ⓦportobellopark.co.nz; map p.589. Modest campsite with simple but spotless facilities, and a range of sleeping options including upscale apartments (from $115) with bathroom, TV and kitchenette. BYO or rent linen for cheaper rooms ($5/person/day). Camping **$18**, doubles **$65**

Yellow House 822 Portobello Rd, 1km southwest of Portobello ☎ 03 478 1001, ⌨ yellowhouse.co.n; map p.589. Classy lemon-hued B&B with one beautiful airy room and the "starry suite" with a glass roof and spa bath in its own wing. There are fine harbour views, two cats and an excellent full breakfast made with eggs laid on the property. Double $230, suite $285

EATING

Glenfalloch Restaurant 430 Portobello Rd, MacAndrew Bay ☎ 03 476 1006, ⌨ glenfalloch.co.nz; map p.589. German chef Hannes Bareiter has transformed the gardens' former *Chalet* restaurant into one of Dunedin's most sophisticated, its short lunch and dinner menus featuring creative uses of the best seasonal local produce. The two-course weekday lunch special ($38) is a good deal. Daily 9.30am–3.30pm, Thurs & Fri 5.30pm–10.30pm.

Penguin Café 1726 Highcliff Rd, Portobello ☎ 03 478 1055, ⌨ penguincafe.net.nz; map p.589. While the interior is rather plain, this café serves excellent Mazagran coffee and a wide range of teas, cakes, penguin-shaped biscuits and hot dishes including pies and toasties ($8–15). Free wi-fi. Daily: summer 8am–4pm; winter 9am–4pm.

Portobello Hotel 2 Harington Point Rd, Portobello ☎ 03 478 0759; map p.589. Classic Kiwi pub across from the water where you can tuck into the likes of beer-battered blue cod with salad and chips ($23) or a haloumi salad ($21) at outdoor tables or in the dining conservatory. Daily 11.30am–10pm or later.

11

Queenstown

New Zealand's premier resort town, **QUEENSTOWN** is superbly set by deep-blue Lake Wakatipu and hemmed in by craggy mountains. The peak summer and winter crowds can be off-putting for some, but it's difficult to blame the hordes for being drawn to a place with so much to offer. Queenstown is well worth using either as a base from which to plan lengthy forays into the surrounding countryside, or as a venue for sampling all manner of adventure activities. The most prominent of these is undoubtedly **bungy jumping** at three of the world's most gloriously scenic bungy sites, visited either in isolation or as part of a package, perhaps including **whitewater rafting** and **jetboating** on the Shotover River.

Visitors after a more sedate experience opt for easy **walks** around lakeshore gardens and to hillside viewpoints; **lake cruises** on the elegant TSS *Earnslaw*, the last of the lake steamers; a **gondola ride** to Bob's Peak, which commands magnificent mountain vistas; and **wine tours** around some of the world's most southerly vineyards (see page 599). **Milford Sound** is also easily visited from Queenstown (see page 654).

From mid-June to early October, Kiwi and international skiers arrive to carve up **Coronet Peak** and **the Remarkables**, two fine ski-fields within 45 minutes of Queenstown, particularly during the annual **Queenstown Winter Festival**, in late June.

The lakefront and town sights

On a warm day there's nothing better than chilling out by the lakeside. Every fine afternoon the grassy reserve beside Marine Parade is alive with people sunbathing, eating fish and chips with a beer and maybe even taking a chilly dip, though the summer peak water temperature around 11°C deters most. Watch the afternoon parasailers, then stick around as the sun sets over the mountains and the *TSS Earnslaw* steams towards Walter Peak for the last time that day.

Marine Parade continues east to **Queenstown Gardens**, an attractive parkland retreat that covers the peninsula separating Queenstown Bay from the rest of Lake Wakatipu.

Central Queenstown has relatively little to show for its gold-rush past, though the waterfront **Eichardt's Hotel** at 2 Marine Parade was Queenstown's original pub catering to gold prospectors, parts of it dating back to 1871. Until the mid-1990s you could still prop up the rough bar here over a few beers, but it is a now a super-expensive boutique hotel (with a suitably posh bar). Opposite is a statue of Queenstown founder, William Rees, with a ram.

Just along the street, **Williams Cottage** is the oldest house in Queenstown, retaining many original 1864 features and now operating as a design shop.

North of town, along Brecon St, you'll find Queenstown's **cemetery** – the final resting place of pioneers Nicholas von Tunzelmann (who opened up the first pastoral lease in the area), hotelier Albert Eichardt and Henry Homer, discoverer of the Homer Saddle on the Milford Road.

Kiwi Birdlife Park

Brecon St, at the base of Bob's Peak • Daily: Oct–April 9am–6pm; May–Sept 9am–5pm; conservation show daily 11am, 1.30pm & 4pm; kiwi feeding 10am, noon, 2pm, 3pm & 5pm • $49 for two consecutive days, including audioguide • ☎ 03 442 8059, ⓦ kiwibird.co.nz

Preserving New Zealand's native fauna is what drives this family-owned wildlife park, which is set among a compact knot of mixed native and exotic bush, laced with paths, ponds and lawns interspersed with walk-in aviaries and reptile houses. The focus is on breed-for-release programmes co-managed with the Department of Conservation which see some of New Zealand's rarest birds and reptiles – kiwi, whio (native blue ducks), pateke (brown teal), buff weka and Otago skinks – raised until they can look after themselves in the wild.

Be sure to time your visit around **kiwi feeding** in the nocturnal houses and the hugely entertaining thirty-minute **Conservation Shows** when kakariki (native parakeets), kereru (wood pigeons) and tuatara come out to play. If you miss one of these "Encounters" your ticket lets you return another day.

TSS Earnslaw

Steamer Wharf • Daily early July to mid-May; 1hr 30min • cruise only $65 • ☎ 0800 656 501, ⓦ realjourneys.co.nz

The coal-fired 1912 **TSS Earnslaw**, the last and largest of the lake steamers, is one of Queenstown's most enduring images. Wherever you are, the encircling mountains echo the deep blast of its horn as the beautifully restored relic glides surprisingly smoothly away from Steamer Wharf.

Burnished brass and polished wood predominate even around the gleaming steam engine, which is open for inspection. Crowds usually cluster around the piano at the back of the boat for a jolly singsong.

Walter Peak High Country Farm

Cruise and farm tour $80 • Cruise, farm tour and BBQ lunch $105 • Cruise, dinner and farm show $130 • Cruise and horseriding mid-Sept to April $133 • Guided cycling Nov–April $235 • Guided electric trail biking $159 • ☎ 0800 656 501, ⓦ realjourneys.co.nz

The *Earnslaw* cruises all head to **Walter Peak High Country Farm**, a tourist enclave nestling in the southwestern crook of Lake Wakatipu with various activities which can be added to your cruise.

Most people take the **farm tour** – an entertaining if sanitized vignette of farm life, with demonstrations of dog handling and sheep shearing. This comes with tea and truly excellent scones on a lakeside terrace surrounded by a beautifully manicured garden, or you can upgrade to a superb **BBQ lunch** with meats grilled to perfection and lots of imaginative salads. The **Evening BBQ** is much the same deal with the meal followed by a sheep shearing (or similar) demo. There's also a taste of **horse riding** plus tea and scones, and a **cycling tour** including a picnic lunch.

Bob's Peak

Accessed from the end of Brecon St • Daily: gondola 9am–10pm; luge 10am–dusk; mountain biking 9am–7pm (Sept–early May) • Gondola $35 return; with two, three or five luge rides $49/$52/$56; with mountain biking half-day pass $70, full day pass $95 • ☎ 03 441 0101, ⓦ skyline.co.nz

For easy access to superb views of Queenstown, Lake Wakatipu, the Remarkables and Cecil and Walter peaks, head up to **Bob's Peak** whose conifer-clad slopes rise immediately behind the town. The sedate **Skyline Gondola** whisks you up 450m,

Frankton (5km), Airport (6km), Arrowtown (20km) & Milford Sound (290km)

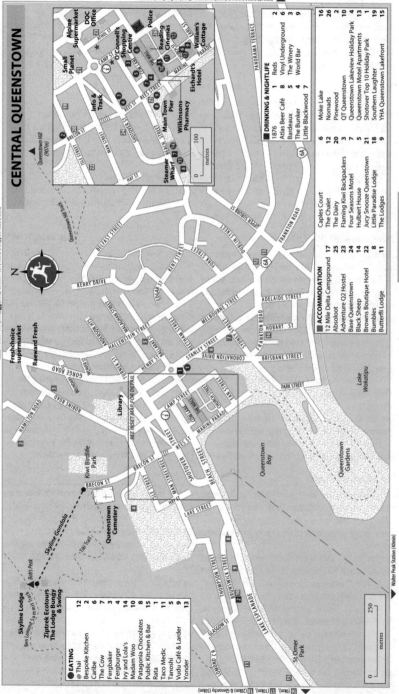

CENTRAL QUEENSTOWN

CENTRAL QUEENSTOWN (inset)

Alpine Supermarket
DOC Office
Small Planet
O'Connell's Shopping Centre
Police
Reading Cinemas
William's Cottage
Info & Track
Eichardt's Hotel
Wilkinsons Pharmacy
Main Town Pier
Steamer Wharf

0 — 100 metres

Queenstown Hill (907m)
Queenstown Hill Track

N

PANORAMA TERRACE

BELFAST STREET
KERRY DRIVE
EDGAR STREET
KENT STREET
YORK STREET
DUBLIN STREET
MELBOURNE STREET
ADELAIDE STREET
FRANKTON ROAD
HOBART ST
STANLEY STREET
BRISBANE STREET
CORONATION DRIVE
HENRY STREET
6A
PARK STREET

Library
Freshchoice supermarket
Raeward Fresh
HAMILTON ROAD
ROBINS ROAD
GORGE ROAD
GORGE ROAD
MANNERS STREET
HENDERSON HTS
HALLENSTEIN STREET
BALLARAT STREET
BEETHAM STREET
SYDNEY STREET

Kiwi Birdlife Park
Queenstown Cemetery
BRECON ST
Skyline Gondola
Tiki Trail

SEE INSET MAP FOR DETAIL

CAMP STREET
MALL
REES STREET
BEACH STREET
MARINE PARADE
CHURCH LANE
CHURCH STREET

Skyline Lodge
Ziptrek Ecotours
The Lodge Bungy & Swing
Ben Lomond (9.5km) via mtn track
Bob's Peak

Queenstown Bay
Lake Wakatipu
Queenstown Gardens

BRECON ST
ISLE STREET
MAN STREET
SHOTOVER STREET
HAY ST
LAKE STREET
THOMPSON STREET
BRUNSWICK STREET
LAKE ESPLANADE
GLASGOW ST
EDMOND C.R.
St Omer Park

Walter Peak Station (40min)

Arthur Point (5km), [2] (6km), Coronet Peak (16km) & Skippers Road (16km)

[16] (9km), [17] (10km), [18] (28km) & Glenorchy (50km)

0 — 250 metres

11

● EATING

@ Thai	12
Bespoke Kitchen	2
Caribe	6
The Cow	7
Fergbaker	3
Fergburger	4
Ivy and Lola's	14
Madam Woo	10
Patagonia Chocolates	8
Public Kitchen & Bar	15
Rata	1
Taco Medic	11
Tanoshi	5
Vudu Cafe & Larder	9
Yonder	13

▣ DRINKING & NIGHTLIFE

1876	2
Atlas Beer Café	8
Bardeaux	5
The Bunker	4
Little Blackwood	7
Reds	1
Vinyl Underground	6
The Winery	3
World Bar	9

▣ ACCOMMODATION

12 Mile Delta Campground	17
Absoloot	25
Adventure Q2 Hostel	23
Base Queenstown	24
Black Sheep	14
Browns Boutique Hotel	22
Bumbles	8
Butterfli Lodge	11
Caples Court	6
The Chalet	12
The Dairy	20
Flaming Kiwi Backpackers	3
Four Seasons Motel	7
Hulbert House	5
Jucy Snooze Queenstown	21
Little Paradise Lodge	18
The Lodges	11
Moke Lake	16
Nomads	26
Pinewood	2
QT Queenstown	10
Queenstown Lakeview Holiday Park	4
Queenstown Motel Apartments	13
Shotover Top 10 Holiday Park	1
Southern Laughter	19
YHA Queenstown Lakefront	15

depositing you at the Skyline Complex, base for a number of activities including **luge carting** and **mountain biking**. Bob's Peak-based activities such as **bungy jumping**, **swinging** and **tandem paragliding** don't include the gondola ride in their prices. If you'd rather save money and get some exercise, follow the steep **Tiki Trail** (1hr; 450m ascent) up through the trees.

Ziptrek Ecotours

Tours run several times daily • 2hr Moa tour $139; 3hr Kea tour $189 • ☎ 0800 947 8735, ⓦ ziptrek.co.nz

One way to get down from Bob's Peak is with **Ziptrek Ecotours**, which combines a zip-line (flying fox) adventure through the Douglas firs with informative briefings on the local environment and ecological awareness. It's soft adventure, though thrill-seekers will get a kick out of learning to zip upside down. You can also opt to plunge into darkness on a twilight tour (offered June–Aug).

The **Moa** uses the first four lines (up to 240m in length) and finishes a short walk from the gondola top terminal. The **Kea** adds two longer and steeper zip lines and finishes near the bottom terminal of the gondola. Wear closed shoes, and either walk up the Tiki Trail or pay extra for the gondola ride.

ARRIVAL AND DEPARTURE
QUEENSTOWN

By plane Queenstown's airport (ⓦ queenstownairport. co.nz) is at Frankton, 7km northeast of the city. As well as domestic flights, you can get here from eastern Australia with Air New Zealand, Qantas, Jetstar and Virgin Australia. Most flights are met by the door-to-door Super Shuttle ($20 for one person; $26 for two). You can also get into town using Ritchies (see page 580). Queenstown Taxis (☎ 03 450 3000) charge around $35 for the ride into town. Most major car rental companies have offices at the airport or nearby.

Destinations Auckland (12 daily; 1hr 50min); Christchurch (4 daily; 1hr); Wellington (1 daily; 1hr 45min).

By bus Buses arrive close to the junction of Camp and Shotover sts from where it's less than 100m to the i-SITE and barely a 15min walk to most hotels and hostels.

Bus services Atomic runs to Christchurch and Dunedin;

InterCity/Newmans operates the most extensive services to all major destinations, and Ritchies is handy for Arrowtown and Wanaka. NakedBus runs up the coast to Aoraki/Mt Cook and Franz Josef, and also to Oamaru. Trampers are well served by Tracknet (☎ 0800 483 262, ⓦ tracknet.net), who run fairly frequently to Te Anau, Milford Sound and the Milford Track, the Routeburn Track and Invercargill; and Info&Track (☎ 0800 462 248, ⓦ infotrack.co.nz) who serve Glenorchy, the Rees–Dart, Greenstone/Caples and Routeburn tracks.

Destinations Alexandra (4 daily; 1hr 30min); Aoraki/ Mount Cook (2 daily; 4–5hr); Arrowtown (19 daily; 30–40min); Christchurch (3–4 daily; 7–8hr); Cromwell (12 daily; 1hr); Dunedin (4 daily; 4–5hr); Franz Josef Glacier (2 daily; 7–8hr); Glenorchy (3–5 daily; 1hr); Invercargill (3–4 daily; 3hr); Te Anau (8 daily; 2hr 15min); Tekapo (3–4 daily; 3–4hr); Wanaka (8 daily; 1hr 30min).

GETTING AROUND

Everywhere you are likely to want to go in central Queenstown can be reached **on foot**. Most activities take place out of town but operators run courtesy buses to the sites, usually picking up centrally or from accommodation en route.

By bus Ritchies (☎ 03 443 9120, ⓦ ritchies.co.nz) operates from O'Connells Mall on Camp St. The most useful service goes from Queenstown to Frankton (every 15–20min) and on to the airport. From Arthur's Point there's a service to Arrowtown (hourly between 6.05am–10.05pm), via Queenstown and Frankton. With the purchase of a GoCard ($5 plus $10 minimum top-up, purchase from driver), all fares are $2. One-way fares from Queenstown without a GoCard are: airport ($10), everywhere else ($5).

By car Parking can be tight in the centre of town, and the free all-day spots in surrounding streets fill

up fast. Numerous car-rental companies around town and at the airport offer good deals: look for advertised rates.

By taxi There are taxi ranks on Camp St, at the top end of the Mall, and on Shotover St. Alternatively, book with Blue Bubble Taxis (☎ 03 450 3000) or Green Cabs (☎ 0800 464 7336).

By bike One of the best ways to explore the area is by bike, with the Queenstown Trail (ⓦ queenstowntrail. co.nz) alone offering a network of 120km of easy riding trails.

By Segway A great way to get your bearings and have a little fun is to take one of the tours run by Segway on Q (☎ 0800 734 386, ⓦ segwayonq.co.nz) which covers a lot of ground on its 1hr tour ($89), and throws in a few more anecdotes and history on its 2hr jaunt ($139).

INFORMATION

i-SITE Corner of Camp and Shotover sts (daily: Nov–April 8.30am–9pm, May–Oct 8.30am–8pm; ☎03 442 4100, ⓦqueenstowninformation.co.nz). There are numerous visitor-centre-cum-booking offices along Shotover St, all with products to push, but only the i-SITE offers impartial advice and bookings for just about everything.

DOC 50 Stanley St (daily: Nov–April 8.30am–5.30pm; May–Oct 8.30am–4.30pm; ☎03 442 7935, ⓦdoc.govt. nz, ✉queenstownvc@doc.govt.nz). The place to go for all tramping, Great walks and national parks information.

Destination Queenstown ⓦqueenstowninformation. co.nz The local tourism department's website is a handy planning resource, with itinerary ideas and comprehensive information on activities, accommodation, dining and more.

Left luggage Queenstown airport has luggage lockers ($7–15 for each 24hr period).

ACTIVITIES AND TOURS

They don't call Queenstown the world's adventure capital for nothing. Top of many people's lists is bungy jumping (see page 595) or getting wet in the Shotover and Kawarau rivers (see page 598). There's also a massive range of biking options (see page 597) and the rest of the tours and activities are covered below.

With so many activities on offer, it's tempting to be frugal elsewhere and blow the budget in Queenstown, but in reality most activities here are more expensive than in other parts of the country. To get the most action for the least money, check out one of the numerous **combo deals** such as the Awesome Foursome ($725), combining the 134m Nevis Bungy, the Shotover Jet, a helicopter flight and rafting the Shotover.

BALLOONING

Sunrise Balloons ☎03 442 0781, ⓦballooningnz. com. Gorgeous daybreak flights climbing as high as 2000m to gawp at the stunning mountains before landing for champagne and pastries (3–4hr including around 1hr flight time; daily year-round, weather permitting; $545).

BUNGY JUMPING AND SWINGING

Even visitors who had no intention of parting with a large wad of cash to dangle on the end of a thick latex strand find themselves bungy jumping in Queenstown: magnificent scenery and zealous promotion get to most people. The sport's commercial originator, AJ Hackett, runs three local jumps, as well as a giant swing. This presents an alternative to bungy jumping but still includes that stomach-in-your-mouth free fall sensation, with the bonus of a massive swoop through the air on the end of a rope. Bragging T-shirts and swing caps are included and your feat will be recorded in all manner of formats you can opt to purchase post-jump.

The Ledge Bungy + Swing AJ Hackett ☎0800 286 495, ⓦbungy.co.nz. Launching yourself off a 47m bungy platform in the pines near the top of the Skyline gondola feels like you are diving out over Queenstown. A special harness allows for a variety of jump styles, even a backflip if the mood strikes you. The same site hosts the Ledge Swing. Walk the Tiki Trail to the site (free) or pay for the Skyline gondola. Bungy $205; swing $165.

Kawarau Bungy + Zipride AJ Hackett ☎0800 286 495, ⓦbungy.co.nz. It may only be a modest 43m but this is the original commercial bungy site and the only place around Queenstown where you can do a water touch. They also operate a Zipride (three interconnected zip lines). Either self-drive or jump on one of the free "Bungy Bus" shuttles

---

QUEENSTOWN'S GOLD RUSH

In 1862, Thomas Arthur and Harry Redfern struck gold at what is now **Arthur's Point**, on the Shotover River 5km north of Queenstown. Word spread that prospectors were extracting over 10kg a day, and within months thousands were flocking from throughout New Zealand and Australia to work what was soon dubbed "The Richest River in the World".

The mother lode resided under **Mount Aurum**, with tributaries of the Shotover carrying the ore down to the goldfields. Initially all a miner needed was a pick and shovel, a pan, and preferably a special wooden box known as a "rocker" for washing the alluvial gravel. Within a couple of years, however, ever more ingenious schemes were needed to extract fresh gold, with landslides triggered and tunnels bored.

As mining continued in Skippers Canyon, gold was found in what is now **Arrowtown**, the last of New Zealand's major gold towns. Within a few years returns had dwindled, and as traders saw profits diminishing, Chinese miners were co-opted to pick over the tailings (discarded bits of rock and gravel) left behind by Europeans. The miners left behind a landscape littered with perilous shafts and scattered bits of mysterious-looking machinery. For decades these just rusted elegantly as sheep farming and fruit growing became the mainstays of the economy. Now they have become one of the focal points for the tourism industry.

11

from Queenstown (a 2hr 30min round trip). Bungy $205, Zipride $50.

The Nevis Bungy + Swing AJ Hackett ☎0800 286 495 ⓦbungy.co.nz. It might no longer be the world's highest jump, but at a massive 134m with eight seconds of free fall, the Nevis Bungy still offers one hell of a thrill. Jumpers launch from a partly glass-bottomed gondola strung way out over the Nevis River, a tributary of the Kawarau 32km east of Queenstown. Access is via private property so spectators have to fork out $50, though this does give you a ride out to the launch gondola and a great view. The adjacent Nevis Swing carves a 300m arc. The Bungy Bus also services the Nevis site: allow a 4hr round trip. Bungy $275; swing $210; swing and bungy combo $385.

Shotover Canyon Swing & Canyon Fox 37 Shotover St ☎0800 279 464, ⓦcanyonswing.co.nz. A direct competitor to AJ Hackett's smaller and more distant swing, with a 60m fall in a huge (109m radius) sweeping arc over the Shotover River – if staff aren't too busy, you may be able to jump with all manner of "toys" from bikes to chairs. High above the swing, the fox, which begins with a 5m free fall, opened in 2016. Spectators can come along for $20 and you'll only need to set aside 2–2hr 30min for one activity, or 3.5hr for both. Up ten departures daily. Swing $229; fox $169; $299 for both.

CANYONING

Canyoning Queenstown 39 Camp St ☎03 441 3003, ⓦcanyoning.co.nz. Swim across pools, slide down rocks and jump off cliffs in narrow canyons, protected only by a wetsuit, helmet and climbing harness. Queenstown Adventurer (Oct–April 1–4 daily; 4hr; $199) explores Twelve Mile Delta just out of town. For a bit more commitment, go for the Routeburn Explorer (Oct–April 1 daily; 8hr; $329) which involves walking the first 30min of the Routeburn Track then launching yourself into a water-sculpted, narrow canyon full of jumps and slides.

CYCLING AND MOUNTAIN BIKING

Queenstown is now a fully fledged biking hotspot with everything from gentle rides along smooth lakeside paths and supreme cross-country single-track to gondola-assisted downhill mayhem and glorious guided heli-biking. All the bike shops in Queenstown (and a couple more in Arrowtown) are staffed by keen riders who will point to the best the region has to offer.

Alta 8 Duke St ☎03 442 4994, ⓦalta.co.nz. High-end bike rental offering hardtails (half-day $35, full-day $55), and downhill ($89/$139) models.

Around the Basin Bike Tours ☎0508 782 9253, ⓦaroundthebasin.co.nz. Rents hardtail bikes (half-day $35/full-day $55) and offers drop-off and pick-up bike shuttle services to points along the Queenstown Trails (from $65 including bike rental). Great for one-way rides, say from Queenstown to Arrowtown or Gibbston (both $80).

Charge About Queenstown ☎0800 324 536, ⓦchargeabout.co.nz. Tackle the Queenstown Trail on an ebike (half-day $79, full-day $119) or opt for the half-day package (bike rental, water-taxi ride and a burger lunch at the Hilton; $129) or the full-day package (bike rental, water-taxi ride and a shuttle transfer back to Queenstown from the Gibbston wineries; $169). A handful of recharge stations allow you to grab a coffee while the bike tops up.

Cycle de Vine ☎0800 328 897, ⓦm.queenstown-trails. co.nz. Gentle 4hr guided tours along the Queenstown Trail on retro cruisers with a picnic snack and little Gibbston wine tasting. $155.

Heli Bike NZ ☎0800 328 897, ⓦhelibikenz.com. Guided heli-bike specialist offering a variety of super-scenic heli-biking tours using trails that criss-cross the surrounding mountains (Nov–May, 2–3hr from $399) and two single-track mountain-biking options in the Central Otago high country (Oct–May; 5hr; from $179).

Outside Sports 9 Shotover St ☎03 441 0074, ⓦoutsidesports.co.nz. Major bike-rental operation with everything from hardtails (half-day $39; full-day $59) through full suspension (half-day $59; full-day $95) to serious downhillers (half-day $85; full-day $129) and high-spec demo modelss (half-day $105; full-day $149).

QBT ☎0800 2453 8294, ⓦqueenstownbiketaxis.co.nz. Bike shuttle service mainly aimed at downhillers and cross-country MTBers. Kick off with the 9am and 1pm departures to Coronet Peak for the Rude Rock, Zoot and Skippers combo ($80).

Rabbit Ridge 1820 SH6, Gibbston ☎03 442 6910, ⓦrabbitridge.co.nz. Family-oriented bike park with 40km of trails, bike rentals and shuttles back to the top. Access is just $10 a day. Daily 9am–5pm.

Revolution Tours ☎0800 274 334, ⓦrevolutiontours. co.nz. Experience backcountry riding on a deluxe four-day three-night trip on the western side of Lake Wakatipu and up to Paradise, with short riding days, and nights in homesteads. $1849.

Station 2 Station ☎0800 264 536, ⓦsoutherndiscoveries.co.nz. Self-guided tour including a cruise to Mt Nicholas Farm on the *Spirit of Queenstown*, with a leisurely 2hr 30min cycle through gentle rolling farmland to Walter Peak Farm before the *Earnslaw* departs for your return journey to Queenstown. Epic views. Daily $89; with bike rental $139.

Torpedo 7 Corner of Camp and Shotover sts ☎03 409 0409, ⓦtorpedo7.co.nz/queenstown-bike-rental; map p.575. Decent rental bikes at modest prices: hardtail (half-day $39; full-day $59); full suspension (half-day $59; full day $89); downhill (half-day $79; full-day $119). Gondola combo deals cut prices further.

Vertigo 4 Brecon St ☎0800 837 8446, ⓦvertigobikes. co.nz. Downhill and cross-country experts offering bike taxis, skills clinics, rental of quality hardtails (half-day $39, full-day $59), freeride ($79/$109) and downhill bikes

IT'S RAINING. WHAT CAN WE DO?

If the weather turns foul and you don't fancy the virtual reality rides and haunted house along Shotover Street, then try these:

Alpine Aqualand 33 Joe O'Connell Drive, Frankton ☏03 450 9005, ⓦsportrec.qldc.govt. nz. Indoor pool with hydroslides, a lazy river and a 39°C hot pool. $8; hydroslide pass $5. Mon–Fri 6am–9pm, Sat & Sun 8am–8pm.

Caddyshack City 25 Brecon St ☏03 442 6642. Indoor minigolf. $19.50. Daily 10am–6.30pm.

Game Over Red Oaks Drive, Frankton ☏03 441 3139. Indoor entertainment complex offering go karting (14-lap race, $39), and laser tag (one mission

$19, two missions $29). Daily 10am–7pm.

Onsen Hot Pools 160 Arthur's Point Rd ☏03 442 5707, ⓦonsen.co.nz. Romantic, elegant artificially heated tubs on a hillside overlooking an achingly picturesque bend of the Shotover River. A 1hr session costs $47.50 each for two or $38 each for four. You can now also upgrade your package to include a massage ($216 each for two) after your soak. Book ahead, and get the free shuttle from Shotover St. Daily 10am–11pm.

11

($99/$139). Also offers a "gravity shuttle" service including three hours of shuttle runs on Coronet Peak trails ($69 with own bike; $148 including bike rental).

HORSERIDING

Ben Lomond Horse Treks ☏0800 236 566, ⓦnzhorsetreks.co.nz. Backcountry horseriding for those with a little experience. Great scenery and fun riding on trips ranging from an easy trek around Moke Lake (1hr 30min; $99) to the gold-mining heritage of historical gold mining sites (2hr 30min–3hr; $190). Free Queenstown pick-up and drop-off. Daily Oct–April.

JETBOATING

There are strong arguments for spending your jetboating dollar on better-value wilderness trips elsewhere, but Queenstown does offer the following excellent options.

Dart River Adventures ☏0800 327 853, ⓦdartriver. co.nz. Excellent and very popular jetboating (3hr from Glenorchy; 6hr from Queenstown; $259 from either town), picking routes through braided riverbeds amid grand snowcapped mountains on the edge of Mount Aspiring National Park. Their Funyak Safari (7hr from Glenorchy; 9hr from Queenstown; $379) adds in a rapid-free downstream paddle in inflatable canoes with a buffet lunch stop at the beautiful Rockburn Chasm.

Shotover Jet Corner of Camp and Shotover sts ☏0800 802 804, ⓦshotoverjet.com. Courtesy buses take you out to Arthur's Point, 5km north of Queenstown, where super-powerful jetboats thrust downstream along the Shotover Canyon. Perilously close shaves with rocks and canyon walls plus several 360-degree turns and periodic dousings guarantee that a 25min trip is enough for most (daily 8.30am–5pm; $149). Allow 1hr.

Skippers Canyon Jet ☏0800 226 966, ⓦskipperscanyonjet.com. A great way to combine exploring the Skippers Road (see page 604) with jetboating among the ancient gold workings of the upper Shotover

River. Trips (2–3 daily; 3hr) cost $149. For an extra $46 you get to add in the best of their scenic tour, with exclusive access to Winky's Museum and the Sainsbury Gold Claim.

SCENIC, OFF-ROAD AND 4WD TOURS

Lord of the Rings Tours ☏0800 568759, ⓦlordoftheringstours.co.nz. Locations, costumes, filming gossip and a stack of locations are blended in tours around Queenstown (3hr 30min for $170 or 7hr for $299), up the lake to Glenorchy (6hr; $299), or covering the region by road and helicopter (7hr; $1650).

Nomad Safaris 37 Shotover St ☏0800 688 222, ⓦnomadsafaris.co.nz. Easily the biggest 4WD tour operator, Nomad runs Land Rover trips into Macetown (see page 613), Skippers Canyon (see page 604) and offers *LOTR* trips visiting filming sites around Queenstown (4hr; $195) and Glenorchy (4hr 15min; $195), as well as a full-day option combining both destinations (9hr 30min; $395). Nomad will also let you get behind the wheel for some real off-roading (4hr 30min; $330).

Off Road Adventures 61a Shotover St ☏0800 633 7623, ⓦoffroad.co.nz. Not just pootling along in a line of quad-bikes, this is serious off-road fun on a variety of terrains. Packages range from straightforward, family-oriented quad-bike trips (1hr ride time; $199) to the tougher Adventure Tour (1hr 30min; $269), taking quad bikes on steep trails on an 11,000-acre high-country station, with stacks more adrenaline and scenic options. Also offers dirt-bike tours (1hr 30min; $289).

PARAGLIDING, HANG-GLIDING AND SKYDIVING

A fine day with a little breeze is all it needs to fill the skies above Queenstown with tandem paragliders descending from Bob's Peak. You get longer flights 10km northeast of town from Coronet Peak down to the Flight Park on Malaghans Road. New Zealand's first indoor skydiving wind tunnel, iFly Queenstown, is due to open sometime in 2018.

11

LORD OF THE RINGS AND THE HOBBIT TOURS

Queenstown and the surrounding area boast the country's highest concentration of *Lord of the Rings* and *The Hobbit* **film locations** – some instantly recognizable, others so digitally manipulated you'll need to stand there with a still from the film to work out just what was and wasn't used. Just about anyone who runs adventure trips around the Wakatipu Basin will tag "as seen in *The Lord of the Rings*" or "venturing into Middle-Earth" in their promotional material, but if you really want to stand where Frodo stood, check out the companies listed under Off-Road and 4WD Tours (see page 597), Jetboating (see page 597) and Scenic Flights (see page 598).

Extreme Air ☎ 021 156 3256, ⊕ extremeair.co.nz. If feeling the wind beneath your winds becomes addictive, learn how to paraglide or hang-glide properly. Day-courses from $250.

G Force Paragliding ☎ 0800 759 688, ⊕ nzgforce.com. Book in advance if you want to fly at a particular time, but otherwise just get yourself to the top station of the gondola and wait your turn. How many acrobatic manoeuvres are executed during the 10–15min you're airborne is largely down to you, your jump guide and the conditions. If you don't see anyone in the air during the main operating times, don't bother with the gondola ride, as the weather's probably being uncooperative. Daily 9am–5pm or later. $239; at 9am $219, both excluding gondola.

NZone 35 Shotover St ☎ 0800 376 796, ⊕ nzoneskydive. co.nz. Queenstown isn't the cheapest place to go tandem skydiving, but the fabulous views over Lake Wakatipu and the jump site at the foot of the Remarkables do compensate considerably. Jumps from 9,000ft ($299), 12,000ft ($349) and 15,000ft ($449). Allow 3hr 30min.

Skytrek 45 Camp St ☎ 0800 759 873, ⊕ skytrek.co.nz. Experienced tandem operators flying paragliders (20min flight; $220) and hang-gliders (20min flight; $235) from the top of Coronet Peak during the summer months. In winter they paraglide from the top of Coronet Peak ski lifts ($225).

WHITE-WATER RAFTING

Rafting action mostly takes place on the **Shotover River** (Grade III–V) with rapids revelling in names such as The Squeeze, The Anvil and The Mother-in-Law. The 14km rafted section flows straight out of the mountains and its level fluctuates considerably. In October and November, snowmelt ensures good flows and a bumpy ride; by late summer low flows can make it a bit tame for hardened rafters, though it is still scenic and fun for first-timers. The upper reaches of the Shotover are much tamer (Grade I–II), ideal for family rafting.

Family Adventures ☎ 0800 472 384, ⊕ familyadventures. co.nz. A dramatic drive into Skippers Canyon is followed by an hour and a half floating in rafts down the mostly calm (Grade I–II) waters of the upper Shotover River past gold-mining relics. Great for kids but equally enjoyable for those without. You don't even need to paddle. Daily Sept–April; 5hr total; adults $189; kids (ages 3–17) $120.

Queenstown Rafting 35 Shotover St ☎ 0800 723 8464, ⊕ rafting.co.nz. Although there appear to be three whitewater-rafting companies in town, all rafts are in fact operated by Queenstown Rafting, which runs trips on the Shotover River either driving in along the Skippers Road (half-day; $229), or more quickly by chopper ($339). In winter it's too cold for most people and all runs are shorter heli-access trips. Rafting tours on the tamer (Grade II–III) Kawarau River (half-day; $229) also run year-round (without heli), and three-day rafting trips on the Grade III–IV Landsborough River ($1899), a fly-in, raft-out wilderness trip with camping beside the river, depart on Fridays (mid-Nov to March).

Serious Fun River Boarding ☎ 0800 737 468, ⊕ riversurfing.co.nz. Bodyboard a 7km section of the Grade II–III Kawarau River twice (daily Sept–June $225), or opt for a single run on a custom-designed sledge (Daily Dec–March, $225), followed by a picnic. Allow 4hr 30min, with around 1hr 30min in the river, for both options.

SCENIC FLIGHTS

Numerous companies offer scenic flights, either fixed-wing or in a helicopter. Adventure combos often link the activities with a chopper flight, and both modes are used to reach Milford Sound. If neither of these satisfies, consider a stand-alone flight.

Air Milford ☎ 03 442 2351, ⊕ airmilford.co.nz. Milford Sound flight specialists with all sorts of options including the classic fly/cruise/fly (4hr; $510).

Glenorchy Air ☎ 03 442 2207, ⊕ glenorchyair.co.nz. The main company which flew *LOTR* cast and crew around. As well as flightseeing trips to Milford Sound and to Aoraki/Mt Cook and the Fox/Franz Josef Glaciers, options include the Two Ring Tour (2hr 30min; $395), flying past *LOTR* locations.

Heliworks ☎ 0800 464 354, ⊕ heliworks.co.nz. These folks did the chopper flying for the cast and now run a wide range of *LOTR* scenic flights, starting at $540 per person for a 45min whip around Middle Earth. Stacks of other scenic flights, too.

VIA FERRATA AND ROCK CLIMBING

Climbing Queenstown ☎ 027 477 9393, ⊕ climbingqueenstown.com. Choose from a half-day ($179) or full-day ($299, summer only) climbing trip that can be tailored for novice through to expert climbers. Climbing-related skills courses, as well as other guided activities including alpine walks, mountaineering and snowshoeing are also available.

Via Ferrata Queenstown 39 Camp St ☏03 441 3003, ⊕viaferrata.co.nz. Get a sense of rock climbing on via ferrata (daily 9.15am & 1.30pm; 4hr; $189), a system originally used in Europe to move troops quickly across mountainous terrain during the two world wars. Suitably harnessed up, you make your own way up a trail of steel rungs drilled into a series of cliff faces just above Queenstown. Previous experience isn't necessary.

WINE TOURS

Appellation Central Wine Tours ☏03 442 0246, ⊕appellationcentral.co.nz. To really learn about the area's wines and winemakers, join these informative and fun small-group tours calling at wineries in Gibbston and around Bannockburn and Cromwell. Tours include a half-day option

(11.30am–4.30pm; $199) visiting four wineries with a platter lunch, an afternoon tour (1–5pm; $159) with three tasting sessions and a light afternoon tea, and a full-day gourmet experience (9.30am–4.30pm; $269) including four wineries, cheese and chocolate tasting, and lunch at Wild Earth (see page 630). Private tours and combos are also available.

Queenstown Wine Trail ☏03 441 3191, ⊕queenstownwinetrail.co.nz. Run by a local family who know the region inside out, the company offers an afternoon tour (1.30–5.30pm; $165) including tutored tastings at three Gibbston wineries and a shared cheeseboard and a full-day tour (10am–6pm; $289) including five tastings and a gourmet lunch at Mt Difficulty in Bannockburn. Those with less time who still want lunch may prefer the Food & Wine Tour (12.30–5pm; $189) including a wine-matched lunch and tastings at two wineries. Custom tours are also available.

ACCOMMODATION

Queenstown has the widest selection of places to stay in this corner of New Zealand, but such is the demand in the middle of summer or at the height of ski season, that rooms can be hard to come by and prices high. Reserve several days ahead from Christmas to the end of February, longer if you're particular about where you stay. Accommodation at both ends of the spectrum is excellent, with abundant **boutique lodges**, classy **hotels** and budget **hostels**, on top of an ever-growing number of Airbnbs. Things are tougher in the middle where there are few modestly priced, convenient **motels** and **B&Bs**. Some hotels offer good deals in what passes for Queenstown's off-season (essentially May & Oct). Almost everywhere is close to the centre, though you might fancy staying out towards Glenorchy or even in **Arrowtown**.

CENTRAL QUEENSTOWN

Absoloot 50 Beach Rd ☏03 442 9522, ⊕absoloot. co.nz; map p.593. Lively hostel right in the centre with a lounge and some rooms sporting excellent lake views. Dorms are six- and four-bunk; the latter come with en suite, fridge and TV. Doubles and queens ($140) also have a microwave. There's an on-site laundry, and the hostel hosts a Friday pizza night, bar crawls ($25), and offers ski and bike storage. Dorms $33, doubles $115

Adventure Q2 Hostel 5 Athol St ☏03 927 4625, ⊕adventureq2.co.nz; map p.593. Opened in 2016, this super-central sister hostel to the longstanding *Adventure Queenstown Hostel* has all the mod cons (including a lift, a/c and personal device-charging stations), and hosts activities every night of the week. Dorms $31, doubles $130

Base Queenstown 47–49 Shotover St ☏03 441 1185, ⊕stayatbase.co.nz; map p.593. Massive, 300-plus-bed hostel with a busy booking desk and 24hr reception. The kitchen is a bit small but the youth-orientated hostel has its

own restaurant/bar, *Loco*, which thumps until late. Dorms have secure lockers, a toilet and shower, women can stay in the Sanctuary section ($35) and there are also en-suite doubles and twins with TV ($130). Wi-fi is free during the day, but costs from $4 between 7pm–7am. Dorms $33, doubles $95

Black Sheep 13 Frankton Rd ☏0800 743 3778, ⊕blacksheepbackpackers.co.nz; map p.593. Long-established hostel in a converted motel with a great deck with a barbecue and a spa pool. Most dorms are six-bed, and there's a relaxed atmosphere (no drinking after 8.30pm). A good choice if you're driving, with plenty of parking. Dorms $39, doubles $110

Browns Boutique Hotel 26 Isle St ☏03 441 2050, ⊕brownshotel.co.nz; map p.593. Close to town and yet in a peaceful setting, all ten rooms at this classy lodge have great views from their small balconies across town to the Remarkables. Everything is beautifully appointed, including the luxurious guest lounge with an open fire and the terrace where a wonderfully presented breakfast is served in summer. $400

Bumbles Corner of Lake Esplanade and Brunswick St ☏03 442 6298, ⊕bumblesbackpackers.co.nz; map p.593. Among the best hostels in town, and nicely set just across the road from the lakefront, offering great views from most rooms and common areas. There's a spacious kitchen, BBQ area, off-street parking, and a couple of free cruiser bikes. Dorms $35, doubles $76

Butterfli Lodge 62 Thompson St ☏03 442 6367, ⊕butterfli.co.nz; map p.593. Million-dollar views from a small house high on the hillside overlooking the lake. It's a bit of a slog up from town but the bunk-free BBH hostel, with guest kitchen and barbecue, is intimate and friendly. Book early; two-night minimum. Dorms $34, doubles $69

Caples Court 20 Stanley St ☏0800 282 275, ⊕caplescourt.co.nz; map p.593. All nine rooms at this comfortable, central hotel have fridge and microwave, and

11

most also come with private patio and views over the town and/or lake. Two-night minimum at busy times. Doubles $165, lake view $230

★ **The Chalet** 1 Dublin St ☎ 03 442 7117, ⦿ chaletqueenstown.co.nz; map p.593. Swiss cottage from the outside, stylish boutique B&B within, this quiet seven-roomer is a great choice. Furnishings are high quality but understated, all rooms have little balconies and some overlook the lake and onto the mountains. Undoubtedly one of the best around. $270

The Dairy 10 Isle St ☎ 03 442 5164, ⦿ thedairy.co.nz; map p.593. There's a refined air to this thirteen-room boutique hotel with delightful common areas hung with quality New Zealand artworks (several original). The rooms (some with bathtubs) are well appointed and tastefully decorated in modern styles. Breakfast is served in the original dairy (corner shop). Pay the extra few dollars for one of the seven rooms with a lake view. $435

Flaming Kiwi Backpackers 39 Robins Rd ☎ 0800 555 775, ⦿ flamingkiwi.co.nz; map p.593. Lockers with charging sockets inside, and free cruiser bikes, tea and coffee, and international calls to 21 countries give a sense of the attention to detail at this central hostel which discourages partying (after 10.30pm is quiet time). There are also three kitchens, and good off-street parking. Dorms $37, doubles $86

Four Seasons Motel 12 Stanley St ☎ 03 442 8953, ⦿ queenstownmotel.com; map p.593. Upgraded downtown motel with off-street parking, good kitchens, sparkling new bathrooms, mountain views, a spa pool and one of the very few outdoor motel swimming pools in town (unfortunately beside the main road). $230

Hulbert House 68 Ballarat St ☎ 03 442 8767, ⦿ hulberthouse.co.nz; map p.593. Set in a beautifully restored Victorian villa, this six-room B&B is fabulously OTT, with brightly wallpapered rooms, antique-style tiled bathrooms and sumptuous furnishings. Pre-dinner drinks and canapés add to the luxe factor. Check booking websites for much cheaper rates. $925

★ **Jucy Snooze Queenstown** Corner of Camp and Memorial sts ☎ 03 927 4204, ⦿ jucysnooze.co.nz; map p.593. The camper company's hotel arm expanded to Queenstown in 2018, complete with pod-style dorm rooms offering an extra degree of privacy for just a few bucks more than you'll pay for a dorm bed elsewhere. Each pod in the four-, eight- and twelve-bed rooms comes with a built-in locker, charging points, a storage net, a privacy blind and a fan. There's also a disabled/family room ($230), and a rooftop lounge, café and bar. Dorms $44, doubles $170

The Lodges 8 Lake Esplanade ☎ 0508 473 737, ⦿ thelodges.co.nz; map p.593. Renovated lakeside apartments (from studios to three-bedroom) with kitchen, laundry and parking. Most have good lake views. Studios $199

Nomads 5 Church St ☎ 03 441 3922, ⦿ nomadsqueenstown.com; map p.593. Massive, modern hostel right in the heart of things, built to a high standard. The kitchen is piddly and the biggest dorms sleep twelve, but there are four-shares ($37) and stylish en-suite double rooms with Sky TV and fridge. There's a free sauna, a pool table, and spacious lounges. However, no alcohol is allowed on the premises. Dorms $29, doubles $130

Pinewood 48 Hamilton Rd ☎ 0800 746 396, ⦿ pinewood.co.nz; map p.593. An extensive collection of new and older renovated self-contained buildings (all surrounded by lawns) a 7min walk from the centre, this mountain biker-friendly hostel has a spa bath with views ($10/30min) and en suites ($175) that collectively have their own kitchen and lounge areas. Also has a restaurant/lounge that can be booked for groups. Dorms $45, doubles $100

★ **QT Queenstown** 30 Brunswick St ☎ 03 450 3450, ⦿ qhotelsandresorts.com; map p.593. Opened in late 2017, the Queenstown outpost of the quirky Australian boutique hotel chain has a fabulously fun alpine vibe (cue snowflake-printed carpets and room numbers marked by mini-gondolas). Beautifully furnished with New Zealand-made textiles and ceramics (and mini-bar options including Merino wool socks), most rooms have lake views. $489

Queenstown Motel Apartments 62 Frankton Rd ☎ 0800 661 6683, ⦿ qma.co.nz; map p.593. Well-managed and good-value motel close to town with four renovated units and eighteen newer ones, all pale wood, bold colours and tasteful artworks. There's a strong environmental stance, with energy-saving light bulbs, double glazing and recycling bins in the kitchenettes. Over 18s only. Units $175

Southern Laughter 4 Isle St ☎ 0800 5284 4837, ⦿ sircedrics.co.nz; map p.593. Split over three buildings, this rabbit warren of a hostel has a wide variety of rooms (some sharing separate kitchen facilities), free soup, and a hot tub. Off-street parking available. Dorms $32, rooms $80

★ **YHA Queenstown Lakefront** 88 Lake Esplanade ☎ 03 442 8413, ⦿ yha.co.nz; map p.593. Fresh from a $12 million facelift in 2016, this flagship YHA has it all, from in-room lockers large enough to fit your backpack to personal bed lamps and charging points, and an enormous kitchen and dining area with lake views. There's also a TV room, a lounge, and plenty of bathroom facilities. It's a pleasant, 7min walk to the centre along the lakefront. Dorms $34, doubles $104

TOWARDS GLENORCHY

Little Paradise Lodge Meilejohn Bay, 28km along Glenorchy Rd ☎ 03 442 6196, ⦿ littleparadise.co.nz; map p.593. Eccentric, alternative and charming guesthouse close to the lake amid Little Paradise Gardens (see page 606). The Swiss owner has lined the walls with stone and timber patterns including a frieze depicting New Zealand wildlife. Most of the furniture is handcrafted, goatskins cover the floor and the toilet cistern is a fish

SKIING IN QUEENSTOWN

The closest ski resorts to Queenstown, Coronet Peak and The Remarkables, are run by the same company, with lift tickets that can be used at either resort. A handful of Queenstown outdoorwear stores offer gear rentals in-season (early June to late Sept or early Oct). You can drive to both resorts (snow chains essential) or take a shuttle bus.

Coronet Peak ☎ 03 442 4620, ⓦ nzski.com. Opened in 1947, Coronet Peak, 18km north of Queenstown, was New Zealand's first true ski destination. Known for its range of terrain for all abilities and great snowmaking facilities, the resort also offers night skiing ($62). Single day pass $119. **The Remarkables** ☎ 03 442 4615, ⓦ nzski.com.

The resort, 28km east of Queenstown, occupies three mountain basins tucked in behind the wrinkled face of The Remarkables. It's best known for learner and intermediate terrain, but there are some good advanced runs and decent off-piste (if there's good cover, take the Homeward Run back down to the access road). Single day pass $119.

tank. Accommodation is in a twin room ($110 for single occupancy; $155 for two people), two shared-toilet doubles and an en-suite chalet ($195). Doubles $190

CAMPING AND HOLIDAY PARKS

Freedom camping is restricted (see page 608) but the Queenstown district has a few compact campsites with attendant cabins and several simple DOC sites that get pretty busy in Jan, Feb and March.

12 Mile Delta Campground 11km west of Queenstown towards Glenorchy ⓦ 12miledelta.co.nz; map p.593. Hosted, lakeside DOC camping with room for 100 tents or vans, plus vault toilets, a solar shower and tap water amid regenerating scrub. Not the prettiest but good mountain views and lake access. No bookings. $13

Moke Lake 6km towards Glenorchy then 4km up Moke Lake Rd ⓦ 12miledelta.co.nz; map p.593. The pick of the DOC sites in a quiet and beautiful mountain-girt setting

with fifty non-powered sites, a cooking shelter, tap water and vault toilets. No bookings. $13

Queenstown Lakeview Holiday Park 45 Brecon St ☎ 0800 482 735, ⓦ holidaypark.net.nz; map p.593. Vast, high-standard site that sprawls over the base of Bob's Peak with grassy (though not well-shaded) tent and van sites plus kitchen-less en-suite studios, fully self-contained units ($235) and relatively luxurious apartments ($255), many with great mountain views. Free wi-fi in reception only for campers. Camping per site $55, cabins $92

Shotover Top 10 Holiday Park 70 Arthur's Point Rd, 6km north of Queenstown ☎ 0800 786 222, ⓦ shotoverholidaypark.co.nz; map p.593. Fairly spacious, family-oriented holiday park an easy drive or frequent bus ride (or complimentary shuttle) from town with a range of sleeping options including self-contained cabins ($139) and daily-serviced motel units sleeping six ($230) plus a well-equipped kitchen and dining area. Camping per site $55, cabins $99

EATING

Queenstown rivals only Dunedin for Otago's best range of eating options, many people making the most of the town's climate and spilling out onto the pedestrianized streets and along the waterfront, where you can sit and watch the *Earnslaw* glide in. **Breakfast** and **snack** places generally close by 5pm, though some serve early **dinners**, while many restaurants double as bars as the evening wears on.

@Thai Third Floor, 24 Church St ☎ 03 442 3683, ⓦ atthai.co.nz; map p.593. Flavours zing around your mouth with every bite at this Thai restaurant that does all your curry and noodle favourites wonderfully. Also dishes up the likes of prawn and squid glass noodle salad ($24) and *choo chee* – deep-fried blue cod topped with creamy red curry paste and kaffir lime leaves ($30). 4pm–midnight; closed Tues.

★**Bespoke Kitchen** 9 Isle St ☎ 03 409 0552, ⓦ bespokekitchen.co.nz.co.nz map p.593. Tucked up behind the centre near the Skyline gondola station, this light and airy café offers one of the best brunch menus in town (including inventive vegan options like cinnamon-

spiced pancakes, blackcurrant chia jam, roast apple, maple pumpkin seeds and whipped coconut, $19) along with a tempting array of baked treats and gourmet sandwiches. The indoor fireplace makes it a cosy spot in winter, with punters spilling onto the outdoor terrace during the warmer months. Daily 7.30am–5pm.

Caribe 36 The Mall ☎ 03 442 6658; map p.593. Sunny beats surge out from this Latin kitchen and takeaway with some casual seating. Try Mexican favourites and Venezuelan *arepa*, maize flatbreads ($5–12) best stuffed with chicken and avocado or slow-cooked pork belly (both $10). Daily 11am–10pm.

The Cow Cow Lane ☎ 03 442 8588; map p.593. Be prepared to share a table at this longstanding stone-built pizzeria offering straightforward pasta dishes ($25–29) and traditional pizzas (from $31 for a 14-inch). Daily noon–midnight.

Fergbaker 40 Shotover St ☎ 03 441 1206; map p.593. *Fergburger's* next-door sister doles out everything from gourmet pies (from $6) to delectable breads, blueberry

11

11

Danishes, jalapeño bagels and chocolate éclairs. Everything to go including the espresso. Daily 6.30am–4.30am.

Fergburger 42 Shotover St ☎03 441 1232, ⓦfergburger.com; map p.593. If you can face the queue (it moves faster than it looks), most would agree the iconic burger bar's variations on meat (or non-meat) in a bun (from $11.90) are worth the wait. Limited inside seating. Daily 8am–5am.

Ivy and Lola's 88 Beach St ☎03 441 2155, ⓦivyandlolas.com; map p.593. Busy lakeside restaurant and bar that catches plenty of daytime sun. With a more interesting menu than most, it's a good option for an Indonesian-style poached chicken salad with pickled pineapple and satay dressing for lunch ($21.90) but it's also a nice place to while away the afternoon over a beer or wine. Daily 8am–11pm.

★ **Madam Woo** 5 The Mall ☎03 442 9200, ⓦmadamwoo.co.nz; map p.593. Contemporary Malaysian hawker fare meets Queenstown sophistication at this hip central restaurant, so popular it has spawned four additional outlets across New Zealand since the original opened here in 2013. A table full of shared plates should definitely include prawn and coriander dumplings ($11), turmeric chicken satay skewers ($14) and stir-fried pork belly with spiced crackling crumble ($19). Finish off with salted coconut and mango ice cream ($7). Daily 11am–11pm.

Patagonia Chocolates 50 Beach St ☎03 442 9066, ⓦpatagoniachocolates.co.nz; map p.593. Relaxed lakeview café notable for rich hot chocolate drinks (ginger, lavender, chilli), luscious cakes, delectable gelato (from $5) and hand-made chocolates. There's a second outlet at 2 Rees St. Mon–Thurs 9am–6pm, Fri–Sun 9am–8pm.

Public Kitchen & Bar Steamer Wharf ☎03 442 5969, ⓦpublickitchen.co.nz; map p.593. It's all about locavore dining from shared plates (small around $16, large $28) at this smart-casual restaurant where tables spill out onto the lakeshore terrace. Expect the likes of venison *osso buco* with roast pumpkin puree ($32), cider-roasted pork belly with caramelized pear ($26) or baked flounder with fennel and orange $32). Daily 11am–11pm.

Rata 43 Ballarat St ☎03 442 9393, ⓦratadining.co.nz; map p.593. Contemporary top-end restaurant by celebrity chef Josh Emett set in a semi-industrial room. Dine on fairly complex modern New Zealand dishes such as Merino lamb with panzanella and charred aubergine puree ($42). Almost thirty wines (many Central Otago) by the glass. The set

lunch (daily noon–3pm; two courses $28, three courses $38) is good value. Daily noon–11pm.

★ **Taco Medic** 3 Searle Lane ☎03 442 8174, ⓦtacomeidc.co.nz; map p.593. This food truck-turned-fully-fledged taqueria will medicate your hunger with its excellent menu of gluten-free tacos ($7) including "the fisherman" (Oaxacan spice rubbed fish with red slaw, citrus tartare, picked onions and coriander) and "the producer" (garlic and thyme black bean, sweet roasted pumpkin and goat feta). Don't forget to try the home-made salsas. Daily 11am–10pm.

Tanoshi Cow Lane ☎03 441 8397, ⓦtanoshi.co.nz; map p.593. Sleek *Tanoshi* is one of Queenstown's better Japanese restaurants, specialising in tapas-style dishes spanning grilled scallops with wasabi mayo to crispy fried pork with smoked sauce (both $15). You can also opt for ramen, udon and bento meals ($13–15), and there's Kirin beer on tap. Daily noon–midnight.

Vudu Café & Larder 16 Rees St ☎03 441 8370, ⓦvudu.co.nz; map p.593. Adorned with a big photo of Queenstown in the 1950s, this vintage industrial-styled café does great smoothies and coffees, plus the likes of grilled halloumi and poached eggs, smashed pea and endamame, oven-dried tomatoes and crispy kale ($20), a vegan quinoa bowl ($18) and lots of baked goodies. Limited lakeside seating. Daily 7.30am–6pm.

Yonder 14 Church St ☎03 409 0994, ⓦyonderqt.co.nz; map p.593. Housed in a historic stone cottage, the menus at this cute new café-bar (under the same management as *World Bar* next door) draw from all corners of the globe. Try a kimchi bowl ($15) for brunch, share a pulled-lamb flatbread ($23) for dinner, or simply relax on the terrace over a well-brewed coffee or a "hard lemonade" cocktail ($12). An indoor function area hosts yoga, live music and more. Daily 7.30am–1.30am.

GROCERIES

For groceries, try the Alpine Supermarket, 6 Shotover St (daily 7am–10pm); Fresh Choice, 64 Gorge Rd (daily 7am–11pm); or the more gourmet Raeward Fresh, 53 Robins Rd (Mon–Sat 8am–6.30pm, Sun 10am–6pm). In Remarkables Park, directly south of the airport in Frankton, there's also the big New World Wakatipu supermarket (1/12 Hawthorne Drive; daily 7.30am–10pm) and Remarkables Market (off Hawthorne Drive; late Oct–early April Sat 9am–2pm; ⓦremarkablesmarket.co.nz), a farmers' market-style affair with loads of good food, arts and crafts.

DRINKING AND NIGHTLIFE

Queenstown claims to have more watering holes per capita than anywhere else in the country, with a bar to suit just about every type of punter on the planet.

1876 45 Ballarat St ☎03 409 2178, ⓦ1876.co.nz; map p.593. Lively pub in the town's original stone courthouse building with lots of streetside tables in the

sun, and some of Queenstown's cheapest drink deals. Snack on small plates including topped fries ($12) and grilled halloumi ($13), or share three plates for $30. DJs play Wed–Sun. Daily noon–3am.

★ **Atlas Beer Café** Steamer Wharf, Beach St ☎03 442 5995, ⓦatlasbeercafe.com; map p.593. Cosy, old-school bar popular with locals, who come here as much for the relaxed vibe as the whopping 22 craft beers on tap from labels including Emerson's, Altitude, Moa and Parrotdog. The tapas (from $8) are equally good but it's Atlas' signature rump steak, chips and salad ($19.90) that really flies out the door. Some of your beer money goes to support the local mountain-bike club. Daily 10am–2am.

Bardeaux 5 Eureka Arcade ☎03 442 8284, ⓦgoodgroup.co.nz; map p.593. Seductive little cocktail bar, with big leather sofas, a roaring fire and a broad selection of excellent whisky and wine. Relaxed early on, but picks up big time after 11pm. Daily 4pm–4am.

The Bunker Cow Lane ☎03 441 8030, ⓦthebunker.co.nz; map p.593. A stylish upstairs cocktail bar with a cosy fire, and DJs spinning house beats Thurs–Sat. Daily 5pm–4am.

★ **Little Blackwood** 5 Eureka Arcade ☎03 441 8066, ⓦlittleblackwood.com; map p.593. Blink and you'll miss this skinny wood-panelled bar spilling onto Steamer Wharf, which has a great little cocktail menu showcasing house-made syrups (cocktails $15–18) alongside its craft beer and wine (mostly Central Otago) offerings. All drinks are best enjoyed over a platter of Gibbston cheeses and locally cured Zamora meats (from $25). Daily 2pm–2am.

Reds 38 Lake Esplanade ☎03 450 1336, ⓦqthotelsandresorts.com; map p.593. With spectacular views towards The Remarkables, this huge, sunny bar housed in the new *QT Queenstown* hotel is the place to go for a smart evening drink, especially if you have a soft spot for quirky signature cocktails ($19). Daily 4pm–2am.

Vinyl Underground 12b Church St ☎021 736 581; map p.593. Intimate subterranean club under *World Bar* with DJs or live music (rock, hip-hop, dubstep), fun staff and a pool table. Mon–Sat 8pm–3am.

The Winery 14 Beach St, ☎03 409 2226, ⓦthewinery. co.nz; map p.593. If you don't have time to head out to the wineries in Gibbston or Bannockburn, call in to try over eighty wines dispensed by vending machines. Try what you fancy in sample (mostly $2–5), half-glass ($5–18) or full-glass quantities ($10–35), then hang out on the leather chairs, perhaps while snacking on a cheeseboard ($24–38). Whiskies are dispensed in the same manner. Daily 10.30am–10pm.

★ **World Bar** 12 Church St ☎03 450 0008, ⓦtheworldbar.co.nz; map p.593. After burning to the ground in 2013, *World Bar* is back in a big way with a hip earthy-industrial fit-out, a cosy beer garden, a huge dance floor, and a relaunched menu of its famous teapot cocktails. A very reasonably priced food menu ($16 for nachos that will feed two) is served until 9.30pm, and there's always a band on Friday nights. Daily 11am–2.30am.

ENTERTAINMENT

There's no theatre, but you will find a smattering of small art galleries dotted throughout the centre. Find out what's on in the free entertainment monthly *The Source* (ⓦsourcemag.nz).

Kiwi Haka Bob's Peak Complex ☎03 441 0101, ⓦskyline.co.nz. This half-hour Māori concert performance takes place daily at 5.15pm, 6pm, 7.15pm & 8pm ($77, including gondola ride). Reservations essential.

Reading Cinemas 11 The Mall ☎03 442 9990 ⓦreadingcinemas.co.nz. Mainstream movies. Head to Arrowtown (see page 612) if you're after something more arty.

DIRECTORY

Banks and exchange All major banks have a branch and ATM around the centre.

Internet Queenstown has free wi-fi hot-spots in The Village Green, The Mall, Earnslaw Park and Beach St, with 1GB of access per device per day. Most info centres along Shotover St also have free wi-fi. MCinternet, upstairs in O'Connell's Shopping Centre, 30 Camp St (daily 8.30am–11pm), has rows of computers and cheap internet.

Library 10 Gorge Rd (Mon–Fri 9am–5.30pm, Sat 10am–5pm); ☎03 441 0600.

Luggage storage/transfer Many lodgings will hold gear for you while you're away from Queenstown, especially if you're staying on your return. Info&Track, 37 Shotover St (☎0800 462 248, ⓦinfotrack.co.nz), charge $5/item/night (day storage $3). Track walkers wanting to transfer extra luggage can engage Info&Track, who work with Tracknet (☎0800 483 262, ⓦtracknet.net) to get bags from Queenstown to Te Anau ($15 a bag) or Milford Sound ($30).

Medical treatment Queenstown Medical Centre, 9 Isle St (☎03 441 0500), and Lakes District Hospital, 20 Douglas St, Frankton (☎03 441 0015).

Outdoor gear Info&Track (see page 607) rents gear such as packs ($7/day), sleeping bags ($9), camp stoves ($5) and tents ($12). Brother-store Small Planet (15 Shotover St ☎03 442 5397, ⓦsmallplanetsports.com) carries new and used gear, including snowboards, ski gear, climbing, camping and tramping stuff and books – all at good prices and with competitive buy-back deals. Some staff are guides and all are experienced outdoors people, and, if you've got something to get rid of, they'll hawk it for a 25-percent cut. The company also rents out tents ($12/day), climbing harnesses ($8/day), crampons ($10/day), and a pack/probe/shovel/transceiver kit ($10/day).

Pharmacy Wilkinsons Pharmacy, corner of The Mall and Rees St (daily 8.30am–10pm; ☎03 442 7313).

Police 11 Camp St (☎03 441 1600).

Post office 13 Camp St (Mon–Fri 9am–5pm, Sat 10am–2pm). Has poste restante facilities.

Around Queenstown

The commercial pressures of Queenstown drop away as soon as you leave, especially when heading west towards **Glenorchy** via **Moke Lake**, and onwards to the famous **Routeburn Track**. There's more rugged exploration east of Queenstown beside the churning **Shotover River**, once the scene of frenetic gold mining, and now rafting trips, jetboating, mountain-bike rides and 4WD tours. The Shotover rises in the Richardson Mountains north of Queenstown and picks up speed to surge through its deepest and narrowest section, **Skippers Canyon**, and into the Kawarau River downstream from Lake Wakatipu. The Skippers Road, which follows the Shotover River only in its upper reaches, branches off Coronet Peak Road 12km north of Queenstown. It is approached along Malaghans Road through **Arthur's Point**, 5km north, where the parabolic concrete Edith Cavell Bridge spans the Shotover River. The Shotover Jet performs its antics in the gorge below, and Shotover rafting trips finish here.

Nestled by the Arrow River, just a few kilometres northeast of the lower Shotover, quaint **Arrowtown** offers some good walks, a great museum, and a smattering of gold-rush-era buildings-turned cafes perfect for whiling away an afternoon (or two). Just beyond, the wineries of **Gibbston** tempt an afternoon (at least) of tastings.

Skippers Road

North of Queenstown, off Coronet Peak Rd

Rental vehicles are not insured on the treacherous **Skippers Road**, a narrow, winding ribbon of dirt track that locals tend to hare around, leaving little space for oncoming traffic. That's a shame, because it accesses a wonderful area of gold-rush relics that are well worth exploring. You'll get a bit of flavour of the area on Shotover rafting and Skippers Canyon Jet trips (see page 597), since both start up this way, but a full exploration is better covered on a historically oriented 4WD tour (see page 597).

From the start near Coronet Peak, Skippers Road descends numerous hairpin bends to the river, then shadows it, negotiating **Pinchers Bluff**, where the road was cut from a near-vertical cliff face, to what remains of Skippers township. There are no shops, cafés or much else along the whole route.

The road wends its way upstream to the 1901 **Skippers Bridge**, the first high-level bridge to be built over the Shotover, and consequently the only one to survive the winter floods, which had swept away past efforts.

Just over the bridge you'll find the remnants of **Skippers township**, which once had a population of 1500, though they all legged it once the gold ran out. The **old schoolhouse** has been restored and there are ruins of a few more buildings scattered around, making it a bleak, haunted place.

Glenorchy and around

The town of **GLENORCHY** is picturesquely sited on the delta where the Rees and Dart rivers flow into Lake Wakatipu. It makes a perfect retreat from Queenstown, 46km to the southeast, though for many it is simply a staging post for some of the finest **tramping** in New Zealand – a circuit of the Rees and Dart rivers, the **Routeburn Track** and the **Greenstone** and **Caples tracks**. While a fair number of tourists pass through each day (many to ride the Dart River Jet Safari), Glenorchy itself remains tiny, with just a petrol station, a post office, a couple of pubs and cafés and limited accommodation; though if even this is too much, consider a rustic cabin in **Paradise**, 18km north, or aim for **Kinloch**, a self-contained retreat just 3km from Glenorchy by water but 26km by road.

11

When you arrive you'll recognize the place instantly if you've seen the 2013 mini-series *Top of the Lake* directed by local resident Jane Campion. Glenorchy is gloriously and gloomily portrayed as the fictional village of Laketop and virtually the entire series was shot on location in Glenorchy and Queenstown. The mountain and lake surroundings may be less recognizable but provide the backdrop for numerous top-end car adverts and Hollywood movies as well as the expected Jackson/Tolkien scenes. If you need to see specific shooting sites, join the Queenstown-based LOTR trips run by Nomad Safaris (see page 598).

Moke Lake

6km towards Glenorchy from Queenstown then 4km up the partly dirt Moke Lake Road

The gorgeous-looking **Moke Lake** comes surrounded by mountains, and if the DOC campsite (see page 607) and adjacent Ben Lomond Horse Treks (see page 597) are not too busy it can be a supremely peaceful picnic spot that feels a million miles away from the bustle of Queenstown. Come January the water is usually warm enough for swimming and if you bring you own gear there's good kayaking and fishing. Fans of Jane Campion's *Top of the Lake* series will recognize this as the location for the women's commune scenes.

Little Paradise Gardens

Glenorchy Rd, 30km west of Queenstown • 9am–5pm or later; if the sign is out they're open • $15, including tea or coffee and a biscuit • ☎ 03 442 6196, ⊕ littleparadise.co.nz

A delightful, semi-wild haven tended by Swiss owner Thomas Schneider, who has a fine sense of the oddball. Full of roses, lilies, daffodils, plum trees and any plant that takes Schneider's fancy, the place is almost always a riot of colour, but there's nothing sterile or formal here, just grassy paths weaving past the frog and lily pond, a stream threading among concrete sculptures in yoga positions and the home-made fountain sundial. It stands right on the 45th parallel, equidistant from the equator and the South Pole.

Paradise Trust

1771 Paradise Rd, Paradise • Year-round open entry by donation • ☎ 03 442 9956, ⊕ paradisetrust.co.nz

Designed and built in 1883 by William Mason, New Zealand's first government architect and later Dunedin's first mayor, this historic homestead was eventually bequeathed to the not-for-profit **Paradise Trust** by then-owner David Miller in 1998 in hopes of saving it from developers. Just 1km north of Diamond Lake, the picturesque grounds make a lovely picnic spot and a great base for a number of day walks. Rebuilt in 2016 following a devastating fire, the homestead offers boutique accommodation, while those who really want to switch off can opt to bed down in one of eight rustic cabins scattered around the heavily forested property (see page 607).

ARRIVAL AND INFORMATION   GLENORCHY

By car and bus It is a beautiful drive from Queenstown to Glenorchy and you can continue from there to the major trailheads (which all have parking areas). But many hikes end a long way from where they start so it makes sense to leave your vehicle in either Queenstown or Glenorchy and use shuttle buses to get to the trailheads.

Bus destinations Dart trailhead (1–2 daily; 40min); Greenstone/Caples trailhead (3 daily; 50min); Queenstown (5 daily; 1hr); Rees trailhead (2 daily; 40min); Routeburn Shelter (3 daily; 30min).

Tourist information Nothing very formal but ask for advice at the *Trading Post* (café 13 Mull St; ☎ 03 442 7084, ⊕ glenorchytradingpost.co.nz).

TOURS AND ACTIVITIES

Dart River Adventures 45 Mull St ☎ 0800 327 853, ⊕ dartriver.co.nz. Excellent jetboating (3hr; $259) and "funyak" safaris (7hr; $379) on the Dart River, as well as horseriding in *LOTR* territory (1hr $140, 2hr $180).

Glenorchy Journeys ☎ 0800 495 687, ⊕ glenorchyjourneys.co.nz. Glenorchy-based operator

linking all the trailheads to Glenorchy and Queenstown at very competitive prices.

High Country Horses Priory Rd, 10km north of town ☎ 03 442 9915, ⊕ high-country-horses.co.nz. Glenorchy has always been a horsey town, and the scenery is matchless. Join the Rees River Trail ride (2hr 30min riding;

$185) with a couple of river crossings and lots of *LOTR* locations, or the more committing Mountain High, River Deep (5–6hr riding; $375) which adds a climb into the mountains and a gold mine. Trips run all year.

Info&Track ☎0800 462 248, ⍟infotrack.co.nz. The main tramp trailhead operator running between Queenstown and Glenorchy ($27 each way; $15 for bikes) and continuing to the trailheads for the Dart ($52),

Greenstone/Caples ($54), Rees ($54) and Routeburn ($49). Their Routeburn Track loop package costs $123. Scheduled services run late-Oct until early May, with on-demand services outside the Great Walks season.

Kinloch Lodge ☎03 442 4900, ⍟kinlochlodge.co.nz. Runs a boat from Glenorchy (Dec–March Mon–Sat at 12.30pm and on-demand for groups of two or more; $15/person each way).

ACCOMMODATION

Aside from Glenorchy, consider staying around the lake at Kinloch, an excellent, peaceful retreat close to the trailheads for the Greenstone, Caples and Routeburn tracks – there's also a campsite at the start of the latter.

GLENORCHY

Bold Peak Lodge Corner of Mull and Argyle sts, Glenorchy ☎03 442 9968, ⍟boldpeak.co.nz. Comfortable renovated rooms with fridge, tea- and coffee-making facilities, and on-site café/restaurant. Ask for the pitched-roof rooms upstairs which are lighter and have better views. $155

Camp Glenorchy 42 Oban St, Glenorchy ☎03 409 0051 ⍟theheadwaters.co.nz. Glenorchy's accommodation mainstay has been redeveloped into an ultra energy- and water-efficient complex of multi-room cabins, pricey but stylish four-bed bunk-rooms, and powered sites ($55), all with access to a shared kitchen, dining room and BBQ. Dorms $60, doubles $195

Glenorchy Lake House 13 Mull St, Glenorchy ☎03 442 4900, ⍟glenorchylakehouse.co.nz. Central two-room lodge with sumptuous fittings and bedding, deep baths, a spacious lounge with mountain views and a big hot tub outside. With a supplied breakfast tray, guests have the place to themselves. Reception is in *The Trading Post* next door, and dinner is available at *Kinloch Lodge*, with boat transport across the lake ($30/person return). $295

Mrs Woolly's Campground 60 Oban St, Glenorchy ☎021 0889 4008 ⍟theheadwaters.co.nz. Run by the same folks behind *Camp Glenorchy* next door, *Mrs Woolly's* offers tent sites and motorhome hook-ups along with a handful of luxury glamping tents, including coffee and fresh pastries delivered to your tent from the attached Mrs Woolly's General Store, where you can pick up dinner supplies for cooking in the ample camp kitchen. Camping per site (two people) $35, glamping double $160,

Precipice Creek 48 Nereus Way, Rees Valley, 6km north of Glenorchy ☎03 409 0960, ⍟experienceglenorchy. co.nz. For spectacular views from gorgeous en-suite rooms

separate from the main house visit this B&B with all the comforts you might expect, plus a delicious home-made breakfast. Along with their Labrador, Jacques, the Czech-Kiwi hosts also work with the Wakatipu Search & Rescue service. $300

Sylvan campsite 23km northwest of Glenorchy near the start of the Routeburn. Very pleasant DOC campsite beside the burbling Route Burn with BBQ pits, picnic tables and flush toilets. Camp in the shade of beech trees, and don't miss the easy walk to Lake Sylvan. $13

KINLOCH

Kinloch campsite A small, scenic lakeside DOC campsite opposite *Kinloch Lodge*, with a toilet, BBQ area, picnic table and tap water (which should be treated). For $5 you can take a shower at the lodge. $13

★ **Kinloch Lodge** 862 Kinloch Rd, 26km by road from Glenorchy ☎03 442 4900, ⍟kinlochlodge.co.nz. Enthusiastically run, the original 1868 Heritage Lodge houses small but comfortable Victorian-styled rooms ($175) with shared bathrooms and a cosy lounge. Rooms around a pleasant lawn constitute the adjacent *Wilderness Lodge*, a self-catering associate YHA section with bunks and neat rooms named after New Zealand birds. Two luxurious, eco-friendly "EcoScapes" studios ($395) round out the sleeping options. There's bike rental ($10/hr, $50/day), fishing rod rental ($15/day), guided kayak trips and transport to the track ends. They also run Routeburn and Greenstone/Caples track transfers ($27/$22). Dorms $39, doubles 105

PARADISE

★ **Paradise Trust** 1771 Paradise Rd ☎03 442 9956, ⍟paradisetrust.co.nz. Switching off is mandatory at the eight century-old cabins (sleeping up to eight) dotted around this historic property, as all are off the grid; see the website to check if you need to bring your own linen, gas bottle or firewood. Heritage-listed Miller House ($500) and The Annexe ($300) sleep eight and four respectively, and have more creature comforts. Double cabins $50

EATING

You can pick up basic meal supplies at Mrs Woolly's General Store, but self-caterers are better off doing a supermarket shop in Queenstown.

Glenorchy Café (aka The GYC) 25 Mull St ☎03 442 9978. Convivial café in the former post office with lots of cosy nooks, a bar and plenty of outdoor seating.

FREEDOM CAMPING AROUND QUEENSTOWN AND ARROWTOWN

Freedom camping is **banned** in Queenstown and Arrowtown and along much of the lakeshore around Queenstown, with "No Freedom Camping Zone" signs clearly posted on the approaches to built-up areas. Outside these areas, certified self-contained campervans can generally stay a maximum of two nights. For more information, visit ⓦ qldc.govt.nz. The free Rankers camping app (ⓦ rankers.co.nz) is also a terrific resource. If you camp inside a banned area or freedom camp with a vehicle without wastewater facilities you may well get hit with a $200 instant fine.

There are still great spots to stop, though in summer you may want to arrive early to grab a prime position. Here are some good places to try:

Glenorchy Road Numerous small wayside parking areas line the road along Lake Wakatipu to Glenorchy, though you'll need to go at least 8km out of Queenstown to be legal.

Lake Hayes Reserve Space for a handful of vans on the northeastern shore of Lake Hayes off the Arrowtown–Lake Hayes Road.

Shotover River East parking area Shotover Delta Rd. Gravel parking area off Tucker Beach Rd for 4–5 vans beside the broad lower reaches of the Shotover River. Close to SH6, though this is fairly quiet at night.

11

Fuel up before tackling the Routeburn with a GYC full breakfast ($19.50), or try the soup of the day ($12) for lunch. Gourmet pizzas are served on summer Saturday evenings, with plenty of home-made treats available all day, every day. Daily 10am–4.30pm, until 10pm Sat in summer.

★ **Kinloch Lodge Restaurant** ☎ 03 442 4900, ⓦ kinlochlodge.co.nz. The heart of the lodge, this cosy spot with a lake-view deck serves a great range of breakfasts, with the likes of slow-cooked wild venison stew ($29) and a ploughman's platter ($22) on the menu

for lunch. Dinner (by reservation, two courses $49, three courses $59) showcases local produce in hearty dishes including Cardrona Merino lamb with roast vegetables, with Kinloch rosemary baked cheesecake to finish. Daily 8–9.30am & noon–8pm.

The Trading Post 13 Mull St ☎ 03 442 7084, ⓦ facebook.com/glenorchytradingpost. Organic Fairtrade coffee, restorative fruit smoothies ($8.50) and delectable chocolate blackcurrant brownies ($6.50) are just the ticket at this friendly little café/shop. Eat in or out on the grass. Daily 8.30am–4pm.

The Routeburn Track

The fame of the 32km-long **Routeburn Track** (ⓦ doc.govt.nz/routeburntrack)– one of New Zealand's Great Walks – is eclipsed only by that of the Milford Track, yet arguably it is superior, with better-spaced huts, more varied scenery and a route mostly above the bushline, away from sandflies. Straddling the spine of the Humboldt Mountains, the Routeburn provides access to many of the southwestern wilderness's most archetypal features: forested valleys rich with birdlife (including the rare yellow-headed mohua) and plunging waterfalls are combined with river flats, lakes and spectacular mountain scenery. It is regarded as a moderate three-day tramp and anyone who can carry a backpack for five or six hours a day should be fine. That said, the track passes through subalpine country, and snowfall and flooding can sometimes close it, even in summer (heli-transfers, bookable through the DOC for $95, are often available at these times). The **main hiking season** is between October and late April, though the track stays open all year. In **winter** the Routeburn becomes a much more serious undertaking, with the track often snowbound and extremely slippery, the huts unheated and the risk of avalanche high. Return day-trips from Routeburn Shelter to Routeburn Falls Hut and from The Divide to the Lake Mackenzie Hut are much better bets.

Some say it's a little easier to hike the Routeburn Track eastwards from The Divide to Glenorchy. If you walk from Glenorchy and don't fancy driving nearly 300km back to Queenstown from The Divide, you can make a three- to five-day **Routeburn combo** loop via the Greenstone or Caples tracks.

Routeburn Shelter to Routeburn Falls Hut
8.8km; 2hr 30min–4hr; 550m ascent

The first 6.5km follows Route Burn steadily uphill on a metre-wide track, though it's never strenuous. You will already have experienced a wide variety of scenery – river flats, waterfalls and open beech forest – by the time you reach the **Routeburn Flats Hut** and nearby campsite, the latter superbly sited on the edge of wide alluvial flats. Only a few tents are permitted and campers can make use of an open fireplace and a small shelter.

Hut users are better off making the first day a little longer and tackling the steeper and rougher 2.3km-long leg to the magnificently sited **Routeburn Falls Hut**, perched on the bushline above a precipice with eastward views looking back to Routeburn Flats and Sugar Loaf (1329m).

Routeburn Falls Hut to Lake Mackenzie Hut
11.3km; 4hr 30min–6hr; 300m ascent, 350m descent

Most of this long, exposed section is spent above the bushline among the subalpine snow tussock of the Harris Saddle (1255m) and passing through bog country, where sundews, bladderworts and orchids thrive. You might even catch sight of chamois around the saddle. The track climbs gradually enough to the **Harris Saddle Shelter** (2–3hr), which has toilets; on a clear day, drop your pack here and climb up to the 1515m summit of **Conical Hill** (2km return;1hr 30min–2hr return; 260m ascent) for superb views down into the Hollyford Valley and along it to Martin Bay and the Tasman Sea.

Continuing from the shelter, you cross from Mount Aspiring National Park into Fiordland National Park and skirt high along the edge of the Hollyford Valley, before switchbacking down through silver beech, fuchsia and ribbonwood to **Lake Mackenzie Hut** (fifty bunks). The campsite is a short way from the hut, near the lake.

Lake Mackenzie Hut to The Divide
12km; 4–5hr 30min; 300m net descent

The track continues for 8.6km along the mountainside through a grassy patch of ribbonwood, known as The Orchard, and past the cascading Earland Falls to the **Howden Hut** at the junction of the Greenstone and Caples tracks (the latter handy for turning the tramp into a five-day Glenorchy-based circuit).

The final stretch initially climbs for twenty minutes to a point where you can make a one-hour excursion to Key Summit for views of three major river systems – the Hollyford, the Eglinton and the Greenstone. From the **Key Summit** (919m) turn-off, the track descends through silver beech to the car park and shelter at The Divide.

ARRIVAL AND DEPARTURE   THE ROUTEBURN TRACK

By bus You can drive to the Routeburn Shelter trailhead, but unless you're doing a day-walk it makes sense to use the trailhead buses. These drop off at Routeburn Shelter at around 9.45am, 2pm and, in peak season, 6.15pm, providing the flexibility to hike to either Routeburn Flats hut or, if you catch the first bus, continue to Routeburn Falls hut. Routeburn Shelter drop-offs cost $22 from Glenorchy and $49 from Queenstown. At The Divide (the western end of the Routeburn Track) catch one of the several buses running between Te Anau and Milford Sound. The best bet is Tracknet (☎0800 483 262, ⊛tracknet.net), with services to Te Anau (10.10am, 1.30pm, 3.15pm & 5.45pm; $41) and to Milford Sound (8.30am, 11am & 2.45pm; $39).

By car For two or more people wanting to walk the

Routeburn and return to Queenstown it may be cheaper and more convenient to use EasyHike (☎0800 327 944, ⊛easyhike.co.nz; $295/vehicle), which will drive your vehicle from Routeburn Shelter to The Divide so it's there for you when you finish – they then run the Routeburn to get back to their own vehicle.

Buckley Transport ☎03 442 8215, ⊛buckleytransport. co.nz. Track transport getting you to Routeburn Shelter by 9.15am for an early start ($45 from Queenstown; operates all year if at least three people book). Also runs a service to and from the far end of the Routeburn Track to Queenstown (arrives at The Divide at 11am, departs at 2pm; $80 one way) and offer a pick-up-and-drop-off Routeburn package for $115. Operates all year if at least five people book.

11

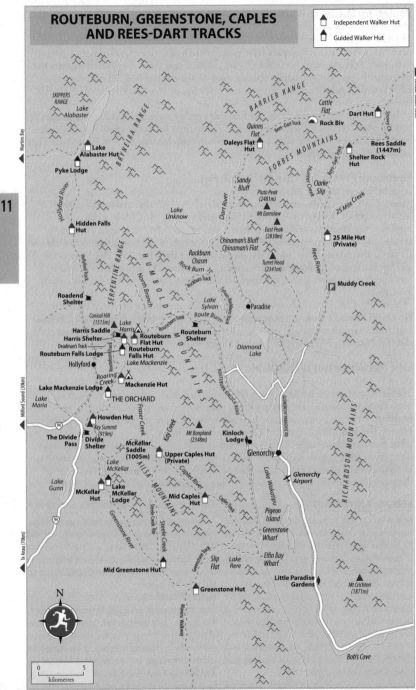

ROUTEBURN, GREENSTONE, CAPLES AND REES-DART TRACKS

Independent Walker Hut

Guided Walker Hut

SKIPPERS RANGE

Lake Alabaster

BARRIER RANGE

Cascade Saddle Route

Martins Bay

Lake Alabaster Hut

Pyke Lodge

BATEIREA RANGE

Cattle Flat

Dart Hut

Quinns Flat

Rees-Dart Track

Rock Biv

Stony Ck

Daleys Flat Hut

FORBES MOUNTAINS

Rees Saddle (1447m)

Shelter Rock Hut

Hollyford River

Sandy Bluff

Pluto Peak (2481m)

Clarke Slip

Reeds-Dart Track

Hidden Falls Hut

Lake Unknow

Mt Earnslaw

Hunter Creek

25 Mile Creek

Hollyford Track

SERPENTINE RANGE

HUMBOLDT

North Branch

Dart River

East Peak (2830m)

25 Mile Hut (Private)

Chinaman's Bluff
Chinaman's Flat

Rockburn Chasm

Rock Burn Jn

Rockburn Track

Turret Head (2341m)

Rees River

Muddy Creek

Roadend Shelter

Conical Hill (1515m)

Lake Harris

Routeburn Track

Lake Sylvan

Sylvan-Rockburn Track

Route Burn

Paradise

Harris Saddle
Harris Shelter

Deadman's Track

Routeburn Falls Lodge

Hollyford

Routeburn Flat Hut

Routeburn Falls Hut

Lake Mackenzie

Routeburn Track

Routeburn Shelter

MOUNTAINS

Diamond Lake

ROUTEBURN-KINLOCH ROAD

Milford Sound (30km)

Lake Maria

Roaring Creek

Mackenzie Hut

Lake Mackenzie Lodge

THE ORCHARD

Fraser Creek

Kay Creek

Mt Bonpland (2348m)

GLENORCHY-PARADISE RD

Howden Hut

Key Summit (919m)

The Divide

Divide Shelter

The Divide Pass

94

McKellar Saddle (1005m)

Upper Caples Hut (Private)

Caples River

Kinloch Lodge

Glenorchy

Glenorchy Airport

RICHARDSON MOUNTAINS

Lake Gunn

Lake McKellar

McKellar Hut

Lake McKellar Lodge

AILSA MOUNTAINS

Caples Track

Mid Caples Hut

Pigeon Island

Greenstone Wharf

Lake Wakatipu

Te Anau (70km)

Greenstone River

Steele Creek Rte

Steele Creek

Greenstone Track

Mid Greenstone Hut

Slip Flat

Lake Rere

Elfin Bay Wharf

Little Paradise Gardens

Mt Crichton (1871m)

Greenstone Hut

Mavora Walkway

Bob's Cove

N

0   5
kilometres

Mavora Lakes

INFORMATION AND TOURS

Information The DOC in Queenstown will have the latest weather forecast and track conditions, or check ⓦ doc. govt.nz/routeburntrack. DOC's *Routeburn Track* brochure is adequate but the 1:40,000 *Routeburn, Greenstone and Caples* NewTopo map ($23) is better. Note that the DOC does meals, hot showers and two nights in lodges equipped with duvets and a pay bar. Rates are for a four-share shared-bath room (Dec–March $1520; Nov & April $1375) or private en-suite room ($1950/$1800). The pace is fairly leisurely and

not track trampers' whereabouts: let someone know your intentions through ⓦ adventuresmart.org.nz.

Ultimate Hikes ☏ 0800 659 255, ⓦ ultimatehikes. co.nz. Walk the track in guided comfort with excellent interpretation, return transport from Queenstown, all walkers only carry their personal effects (no food or camping equipment). They also offer the shorter Routeburn Encounter day-walk (Nov–late April daily; 10hr; $179) and extended combinations with the Greenstone and Milford tracks.

ACCOMMODATION

Booking There's a compulsory booking system for the huts and campsites during the tramping season, which guarantees you a bed and allows people to stay up to two nights in a particular hut. Book three months ahead if you need a specific departure date or are part of a large group. It's easiest to book online (ⓦ doc.govt.nz/routeburntrack) from around early May for the following season, though it is also possible to book at DOC visitor centres, in person or by phone. If the track is closed due to bad weather or track conditions, full refunds are given but new bookings can only be made if there is space. Changes can be made to existing bookings ($10 fee) at least three days before you start if space allows, and only if you enquire at a DOC office in person.

Huts The four huts along the track are equipped with flush toilets, running water (which should be treated), and gas rings: you'll need to carry your own pans, plates and food. During the main Oct–late April season the huts are staffed by a warden, and neither the Backcountry Hut Pass nor individual Backcountry Hut Tickets ($5 each) are valid. Outside the main season the huts are unheated, have no gas or running water (though there is a coal fire) and cannot be booked, but the Backcountry Hut Pass and tickets are valid. Dorms per person/ night Oct–late April $65, per person/night in winter $15

Camping A limited number of campsites with pit toilets and water exist close to the Routeburn Flats and Lake Mackenzie huts; campers are not allowed to use hut facilities. $20

11

Greenstone and Caples tracks

The **Greenstone Track** (36km; 2–3 days)and **Caples Track** (27km; 2 days) run roughly parallel to each other. Both are easy, following gently graded, parallel river valleys where the wilderness experience is moderated by grazing cattle from the high-country stations along the Lake Wakatipu shore. The Greenstone occupies the broader, U-shaped valley carved out by one arm of the huge Hollyford Glacier. The Caples runs over the subalpine McKellar Saddle and down the Caples Valley, where the river is bigger and the narrow base of the valley forces the path closer to it.

The Greenstone and Caples can be done as a loop from Greenstone car park, 6km south of *Kinloch Lodge*, but more commonly people combine the Routeburn Track with either the Greenstone or the Caples: both are described here as a follow-up to the Routeburn. The tracks are open year-round. In **winter**, the lower-level Greenstone and Caples tracks make a less daunting prospect than the Routeburn: the McKellar Saddle is often snow-covered but at least all huts have a wood-burning stove.

ARRIVAL AND INFORMATION

By car There's a car park near Greenstone Wharf which is useful if you're planning a Greenstone and Caples loop.

By bus If you're combining with the Routeburn you'll want to use the trailhead buses. Info&Track ($37 to Glenorchy, $54 to Queenstown) and *Kinloch Lodge* ($15) both call by at noon while Glenorchy Journeys ($35/55) visit at 10am, noon and 4pm. Book ahead if you're coming off the track

GREENSTONE AND CAPLES TRACKS

and hope to be picked up.

Information Use DOC's *Greenstone and Caples Tracks* leaflet, together with the 1:40,000 *Routeburn, Greenstone and Caples* NewTopo map ($23). Queenstown DOC will have the latest weather forecast and track conditions, or check ⓦ doc.govt.nz. Let someone know your intentions through ⓦ adventuresmart.org.nz.

ACCOMMODATION

Booking No reservations are necessary at any time of the year for DOC-managed Mid Caples, McKellar and Greenstone Huts. The Upper Caples and Mid Greenstone Huts need to

be booked online in advance (Wsouthernlakesnzda.org.nz; $25).

Huts All huts (two on the Caples, three on the Greenstone) are heated by wood-burning stoves but there are no gas rings (or cooking utensils) in the DOC huts so you'll need a cooking stove as well as pots and food. The Backcountry Pass is valid at the DOC huts, or bring backcountry hut tickets. $\overline{\underline{\$15}}$

Camping Campers are encouraged to camp next to the DOC huts and use the outside facilities. Free camping is allowed in both valleys along the fringes of the bush, at least 50m away from the track and not on the open flats. $\overline{\underline{\$5}}$

Rees–Dart Track

The **Rees–Dart Track** (63km; 3–4 days) forms a Glenorchy-centred loop and is the toughest of the major tramps in the area, covering rugged terrain and requiring four to eight hours of effort each day. It follows the standard Kiwi tramp formula of ascending one river valley, crossing the pass and descending into another, but adds an excellent side trip to the Cascade Saddle (10km each way). The second day is the shortest but one of the toughest, scaling the 1471m Rees Saddle. The hike is straightforward enough between December and April, but in winter the Rees–Dart is really only for mountaineers.

11

ARRIVAL AND INFORMATION REES–DART TRACK

By car You can drive to the Rees trailhead at Muddy Creek car park, 20km north of Glenorchy, and to the Dart trailhead at Paradise car park, 24km north of Glenorchy. A 4WD road continues to Chinaman's Flat car park, 30km north of Glenorchy.

By bus Convenient shuttle buses run from either Queenstown or Glenorchy (see page 604), and bus timetables make it easiest to tramp up the Rees and down the Dart. Info&Track will get you to the Rees trailhead around 10am and pick up from Chinaman's Flat car park at 2pm ($108 for both from Queenstown, $74 from

Glenorchy). Glenorchy Journeys drop at the Rees at around 8am & 10am and picks up at Chinaman's Flat car park at 2pm and 4pm ($35 each way to/from Glenorchy, $110 to/ from Queenstown).

Information The DOC in Queenstown will have the latest weather forecast and track conditions; check ⓦ doc.govt.nz. DOC's *The Rees–Dart Track* leaflet is fine but the detailed 1:40,000 *Rees–Dart Track* NewTopo map ($23) adds contours. Let someone know your intended hiking route and dates through ⓦ adventuresmart.org. nz.

ACCOMMODATION

Huts The three huts (first come first served) provide heating stove but no gas rings. Bring all cooking gear. Hut wardens are present from Nov–April. The Backcountry Pass is valid, or bring backcountry hut tickets. $\overline{\underline{\$15}}$

Camping Permitted anywhere along the track (free), except for the fragile, subalpine section between Shelter Rock Hut and Dart Hut. Trampers are encouraged to camp outside the huts where you can use the toilets. $\overline{\underline{\$5}}$

Arrowtown and around

ARROWTOWN, at the confluence of the Arrow River and Bush Creek 23km northeast of Queenstown, still has the feel of an old gold town, though on busy summer days its lingering authenticity is swamped by the tourists prowling the sheepskin, greenstone and gold of its souvenir shops. Nonetheless, the town is very much a living community, with grocers' shops, pubs, a great range of accommodation and superb places to eat. Arrowtown has a permanent (and increasingly wealthy) population of around 2500, but in summer, when holiday homes are full and tourists arrive in force, it comes close to regaining the 7000-strong peak attained during the **gold rush**.

The best way to appreciate Arrowtown is to stay on after the crowds have gone. If you're visiting from Queenstown and not sleeping overnight, consider coming for lunch, spend the afternoon hiking, swimming in the river or biking up to the former mining settlement of **Macetown**, then catch a movie and dinner, making sure you get the last bus back (at 10.02pm).

If you can, visit in late April when the town is at its best, the trees golden and the streets alive during the week-long **Autumn Festival** (ⓦ arrowtownautumnfestival.org.nz), with all manner of historic walks, street theatre and hoedowns.

Brief history

In August 1862, a shearer employed by William Rees known as Jack Tewa or **Māori Jack**, discovered gold on the Arrow River. He wasn't particularly interested in gold mining but word soon spread to those who were, particularly the American **William Fox** who soon dominated proceedings, managing to keep his claim secret while recovering over 100kg of ore. Jealous prospectors tried to follow him to the lode, but he gave them the slip, on one occasion leaving his tent and provisions behind in the middle of the night. The town subsequently bore his name until Fox's gave way to Arrowtown. The Arrow River became known as the richest for its size in the world – a reputation that drew scores of Chinese miners, who lived in the now partly restored **Arrowtown Chinese Settlement**. Prospectors fanned out over the surrounding hills, where brothers Charley and John Mace set up **Macetown**, now abandoned.

Avenue of Trees

Twin rows of sycamores and oaks, planted in 1867, have grown to overshadow the tiny miners' cottages along the photogenic **Avenue of Trees**, Arrowtown's defining image. The sixty or so period cottages are unusually small and close together, the chronic lack of timber undoubtedly being a factor. The sheltering hills give Arrowtown parched summers and snowy winters, thrown into sharp relief by autumn, when the deciduous trees planted by the mining community cast golden shadows on a central knot of picturesque miners' cottages. A few have been turned into boutique businesses and cafés.

Lakes District Museum

49 Buckingham St • Daily 8.30am–5pm • $10 • ☎ 03 442 1824, Ⓦ museumqueenstown.com

Artefacts found during the 1983 Chinese Settlement dig are displayed inside the excellent **Lakes District Museum**, which covers the lives of the gold-miners and their families, with a particular emphasis on the Chinese community. Opium smoking remained legal in New Zealand until 1901, some twenty years after games of chance – *fantan* and *pakapoo* – were proscribed. You'll also find displays on the quartz-reef mining used at Macetown and on one of the country's earliest hydro schemes, which once supplied mining communities in Skippers and Macetown with power, but the most interesting section of the museum for many is the basement, which houses a gold rush-era brewery, a bakery, a print room and a school room.

Arrowtown Chinese Settlement

Western end of Buckingham St • Open entry • Free

This string of mostly restored buildings hugging a narrow willow-draped section of Bush Creek is easily the best preserved of New Zealand's Chinese communities, and provides an insight into a fascinating, shameful episode in the country's history. Many of the buildings were intended as temporary retreats – with tin, sod and timber the principal materials – only becoming permanent homes as miners aged. Little was left standing when an archeological dig began in 1983, and many of the dwellings languish in a state of graceful decay, fleetingly brought back to life by interpretation panels.

The best-preserved Chinese building is **Ah Lum's Store**, built in 1883 for Wong Hop Lee and leased from 1909 to 1927 to Ah Lum, one of the pillars of the Chinese community in its later years. By this time integration was making inroads: Ah Lum sold European as well as Chinese goods, and operated an opium den and bank.

Macetown

15km north of Arrowtown, accessed on foot (3–4hr each way), bike (2–4hr return) or high-clearance 4WD vehicle (2hr return)

As gold fever swept through Otago in the early 1860s, prospectors fanned out, clawing their way up every creek and gully in search of a flash in the pan. In 1862, alluvial gold was found at Twelve Mile, sparking the rush to what later became known as **Macetown**,

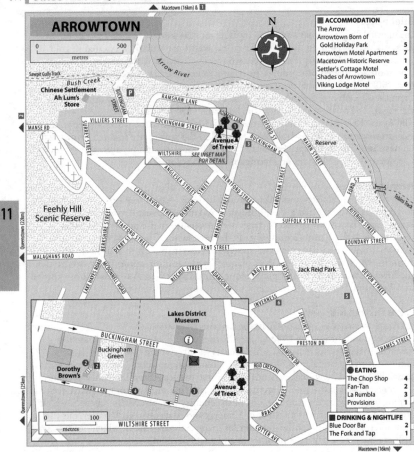

now an abandoned historic reserve and a popular destination for mountain-bikers, horse-riders and trampers.

At its peak, Macetown boasted a couple of hotels, a post office and a school, but when the gold ran out it couldn't fall back on farming in the way that Arrowtown and Queenstown did and, like Skippers (see page 604), it died. All that remains of the town are a couple of stone buildings – the restored schoolmaster's house and the bakery. The surrounding creeks and gullies are littered with the twisted and rusting remains of gold batteries, making a fruitful hunting ground for industrial archeology fans.

The 4WD road includes 23 fords of the Arrow River and, on first acquaintance, the place isn't massively exciting. But the grassy plateau makes a great (and free) camping spot. Indeed, arriving for a couple of days with a tent and provisions is the best way to experience Macetown's unique atmosphere.

ARRIVAL AND GETTING AROUND   ARROWTOWN AND AROUND

By bus Ritchies (☎ 03 443 9120, ⌨ ritchies.co.nz) operates services throughout the Wakatipu basin. The #2 runs from Arrowtown to Arthur's Point via Queenstown at least once every hour (6.02am–10.02pm). Trips everywhere but the

airport are $5 in cash, or $2 with a GoCard ($5 for the card, $10 minimum top-up).
Destinations Queenstown (19 daily; 30–40min).

By bike Arrowtown Bike Hire, 59 Buckingham St (☎ 0800 224 473, ⓦ arrowtownbikehire.co.nz) offer hardtails (half-day $42, full day $52) that are fine for use on the Queenstown Trail network. A ride to Gibbston is perfect and they'll do van pick-ups ($50) if you overdo it at the wineries and don't want to ride back. The

workshop-based Arrow Bikes, 4/9 Bush Creek Rd (☎ 03 409 8140, ⓦ www.arrowbikes.co.nz) rent hardtails (half-day $25, full-day $40) and full-suspension bikes (half-day $50, full-day $80). They'll also deliver to your Arrowtown accommodation.

INFORMATION, TOURS AND ACTIVITIES

Information centre 49 Buckingham St, inside the Lakes District Museum (daily 8.30am–5pm; ☎ 03 442 1824, ⓦ museumqueenstown.com and ⓦ arrowtown.com). Pick up the free *Historic Buildings of Arrowtown* booklet, the informative *Arrowtown Chinese Settlement* booklet ($4) and the detailed *Macetown and the Arrow Gorge* booklet ($4). It also has free wi-fi and 10min of free internet access. Arrowtown's website (ⓦ arrowtown.com) is packed with helpful information.

Gold panning Rent a pan ($3 for as long as you want from the Lakes District Museum) and try your luck along the Arrow River, or be assured of a fleck or three by dipping your pan in the salted troughs at *Dudley's Cottage*, 4 Buckingham St, beside the Chinese Settlement ($10 a go).

Guided walks The Lakes District Museum is the starting point for Arrowtown Time Walks (on demand; $20; ☎ 03 428 2843, ⓦ arrowtowntimewalks.com), giving an

entertaining look at the town's social history. There's a visit to the old gaol and a chance to follow in the footsteps of Nelson Mandela, who visited in 1999. The museum itself also runs on-demand walking tours ($100 for the guide plus $10 per person; ☎ 03 442 1824, ⓦ museumqueenstown. com) which includes museum entry. Both tours run for 1hr 30min.

Nomad Safaris ☎ 0800 688 222, ⓦ nomadsafaris. co.nz. Major operator running trips from Queenstown (4hr 30min; $295) heading up the Arrow River, crossing it more than twenty times on the rough road into Macetown. Arrowtown pick-ups available.

Walking ⓦ nomadsafaris.co.nz. There are some great walks to be had around Arrowtown; nine are detailed in the *Wakatipu Walks* brochure, downloadable for free from the DOC website. There's also a signposted map with walks marked on it in the Arrowtown Chinese Settlement car park.

11

ACCOMMODATION

Most of Arrowtown's accommodation is of a high standard and is usually less busy than in Queenstown. There is currently no hostel, though the holiday park has budget rooms.

The Arrow 63 Manse Rd ☎ 03 409 8600, ⓦ thearrow. co.nz; map p.614. Delightful architect-designed hotel that has a perfect blend of historic stone cottage (where wine is served each evening) and modern chic rooms with polished concrete floors. Big windows reveal views of the hills, appreciated each morning as your breakfast is delivered to your room. **$395**

Arrowtown Born of Gold Holiday Park 12 Centennial Ave ☎ 03 442 1876, ⓦ arrowtownholidaypark.co.nz; map p.614. Spacious campsite with a modern kitchen and ablutions block and tennis court, and handy for the nearby community swimming pool. Backpacker-style lodge rooms sleep four ($69; bring own top sheet and duvet or rent from them) and there are self-contained studios and two-room apartments($155) sleeping up to five. Room rates are for two people; add $20 for each extra adult. Camping per site **$40**, studios **$135**

Arrowtown Motel Apartments 48 Adamson Drive ☎ 03 442 1833, ⓦ arrowtownmotel.co.nz; map p.614. Choose from twelve tastefully furnished units sleeping up to five, most with kitchenettes, in this fully renovated 1970s motel. There's a guest laundry, and the Queenstown bus stops outside. Studios **$169**, one-bedroom unit **$189**

Macetown Historic Reserve 15km up a serious 4WD road from Arrowtown; map p.614. A grassy DOC-run campsite among gold-town remains sheltered by low stone walls and willow, sycamore and apple trees. Facilities are limited to long-drop toilets, and you'll have to get your water from a stream. **Free**

Settler's Cottage Motel 22 Hertford St ☎ 03 442 1734, ⓦ seettlerscottagemotel.co.nz; map p.614. Step back into olden-day Arrowtown in one of these sweet, white-picket-fenced cottages furnished in old-world style. There's also a guest laundry, a BBQ, and a kids' playground, and all rooms have a microwave. Studios **$180**, two-bedroom cottage **$299**

★ **Shades of Arrowtown** 9 Merioneth St ☎ 03 442 1613, ⓦ shadesofarrowtown.co.nz; map p.614. Tastefully decorated modern motel set in leafy surrounds in the heart of town. There's a good range of units sleeping up to four (most with kitchenette or full kitchen), plus a self-contained cottage that also sleeps four. The shaded front lawn houses BBQ facilities and picnic tables. Units **$145**, cottage **$250**

Viking Lodge Motel 21 Inverness Crescent ☎ 0800 181 900, ⓦ arrowtownvikinglodge.co.nz; map p.614. One of Arrowtown's best-value motels, featuring an outdoor pool and a cluster of one- and two-bedroom A-frame chalets with well-equipped kitchens and Sky TV. There's also a children's play area featuring a trampoline. **$160**

11

EATING

★ **The Chop Shop** 44 Buckingham St ☎03 442 1116; map p.614. Tucked away at the back of an alley this hip café brings five-star quality to brunch. Sure you can get eggs, but try the likes of braised pork belly *bao* buns with pickled cucumber ($24) or spicy *nasi goreng* with prawns and free-range chicken ($25). Daily 8am–3pm.

Fan-Tan 54 Buckingham St ☎03 442 0885, ⓦfantan. co.nz; map p.614. In a nod to the gambling game favoured by Arrowtown's gold rush-era Chinese community, this industrial-styled Asian fusion restaurant is a great new addition to the local dining scene, with a short menu of dishes perfect for sharing, from pork and *puha gyoza* ($16) to wok-seared squid with sambal green beans and crispy onions ($24). Daily 11am–11.30pm.

La Rumbla, 54 Buckingham St ☎03 442 0509, ⓦfacebook.com/larumbla.arrowtown; map p.614.

They've hit on a winning combination at this casual tapas-style place: beautifully prepared food served as generous shared plates at reasonable prices. Add in cocktails, well-priced wines and occasional DJs and live music and it's hard to beat. Tues–Sun 4–10pm or later.

Provisions 65 Buckingham St ☎03 442 0714, ⓦprovisions.co.nz; map p.614. Delightful little café in a historic miner's cottage with a sunny terrace and fruit tree-shaded garden. Mouth-watering counter food (mostly using their own range of chutneys, vinegars and sauces) is supplemented by an all-day brunch menu featuring the likes of chilli-scrambled eggs with hot smoked Marlborough salmon ($23.50) and exotic "brunch bowls" ($21). Licensed. Daily 8am–5pm.

DRINKING AND NIGHTLIFE

Blue Door Bar 18 Buckingham St ☎03 442 0130, ⓦbluedoorbar.co.nz; map p.614. Stylish, cool bar in a 140-year-old cellar with a log fire. The intimate cocktail tenor often gives way to Wednesday-night jam sessions when punters pack the alley outside, where there's a new outdoor bar to keep them hydrated. Daily 5pm–1.30am.

The Fork and Tap 51 Buckingham St ☎03 442 1860, ⓦtheforkandtap.co.nz; map p.614. Locals' favourite,

in a stone-built 1865 former bank and spilling out into the shady garden bar. Craft beers and an excellent selection of Central Otago wines will complement lunchtime salads, sandwiches and platters. Quality pub dinners include blue cod, chips and salad ($28.50), pizzas ($25) and wild rabbit and mushroom hotpot ($27). Irish music sessions Wednesdays from 6.30pm, and live music on Sunday afternoons in summer. Daily 11am–11pm.

ENTERTAINMENT

Dorothy Brown's 18 Buckingham St ☎03 442 1964, ⓦdorothybrowns.com. Watch mainstream and more arty films from stupendously comfortable seats in the main theatre of this wonderful two-screen independent cinema

and you can take your wine and snacks in with you. The smaller theatre, "the den", is a tad more cramped. Tickets $18.50.

Gibbston

After the **Kawarau River** flows out of Lake Wakatipu, it picks up the waters of the Shotover River before plunging into **Kawarau Gorge**, southeast of Arrowtown. The picturesque valley is a major destination for Queenstown's whitewater rafting, sledging and bungy operators, but **GIBBSTON** also has an enviable reputation for its wineries. More than half a dozen have cellar doors open for tasting, and a couple have good restaurants. You can drive to them all, but it's more fun to visit by bicycle from Arrowtown or Queenstown, or on an organised wine tour from the latter (see page 599).

EATING AND DRINKING
GIBBSTON

The following wineries all have tastings, and all but Peregrine have on-site restaurants. If you prefer beer, make a stop at the Gibbston Tavern (6 Coal Pit Rd), which turns out great wood-fired pizzas ($25-28).

Akarua Wines & Kitchen by Artisan 265 Arrowtown-Lake Hayes Rd ☎03 442 1090, ⓦakaruaandartisan. com. The Bannockburn winery now has a cellar door attached to an excellent new restaurant just off SH6. Come for an indulgent breakfast or linger over a gourmet lunch

showcasing the finest New Zealand produce (including the likes of cedar-wood Mt Cook salmon with herb creme fraiche, crackling, lemon and charred zucchini; $36.50). If you don't have time to eat, you can still pop in for a wine tasting (five wines for $5). Daily: restaurant 9am–5pm, cellar door 11am–5pm.

★ **Amisfield & Kitchen** 10 Lake Hayes Rd ☎03 442 0556, ⓦamisfield.co.nz. One of New Zealand's defining dining experiences, Amisfield specializes in haute tasting menus that change daily, with three to five courses for lunch ($75/95), and a whopping seven for dinner ($140). Naturally, you can opt to pair each course with the best drops from Amisfield's Cromwell winery. Alternatively, stop in to the cellar door to sample five wines for $10. Daily: restaurant noon–8pm, cellar door 10am–6pm.

Gibbston Valley 1820 Gibbston Valley Hwy (SH6) Rd ☏ 03 442 6910, ⓦ gibbstonvalley.com. It can be a bit of a circus these days, but then Gibbston's original winery does have the region's only "wine cave". Tour the cave and taste three wines for $17.50 (five tours daily), or opt for a standard cellar door sampling (four wines for $15). There's a good restaurant and a cheesery on-site offering complimentary tastings. Daily: restaurant noon–3pm, cellar door and cheesery 10am–6pm.

Kinross 2300 Gibbston Valley Hwy (SH6) Rd ☏ 0800 131 101, ⓦ kinrosscottages.co.nz. A boutique guesthouse (studio cottage from $275), bistro and cellar door representing five local, small-production wineries (Coal Pit, Domaine Thomson, Hawkshead, Valli and Wild Irishman) *Kinross* is a good option if you only have time to visit one winery (sample five wines for $15). Restaurant daily 8am–4pm, Mon, Wed & Sat also 5pm–8pm, cellar door daily 10am–6pm or later.

Peregrine 2127 Gibbston Valley Hwy (SH6) Rd ☏ 03 442 4000, ⓦ peregrinewines.co.nz. Take a turn through the barrel room after tasting four wines for free at this ultra-modern winery. Pinot Noir is the star, though Peregrine also produces five superb whites, a rose, and a method traditionelle sparkling (following the method developed in the Champagne region of France). Cellar door daily 11am–6pm.

11

Wanaka and around

Some people have begun to describe it as a "mini Queenstown," but while pretty **WANAKA** (pronounced evenly as Wa-Na-Ka), is certainly getting busier these days, it remains an eminently manageable place, with the tenor of an overgrown village and a feeling of light and spaciousness – an excellent place in which to chill out for a few days. There's no beating the setting, draped around the southern shores of **Lake Wanaka** at the point where the hummocky, poplar-studded hills of Central Otago rub up against the dramatic peaks of the **Mount Aspiring National Park**.

Founded in the 1860s as a service centre for the local run-holders and itinerant gold-miners, the town didn't really take off until the prosperous middle years of the twentieth century, when camping and caravanning Kiwis discovered its warm, dry summer climate. Though still only home to around 7500 people, it is now one of New Zealand's fastest-growing towns, with developments popping up everywhere. But although central Wanaka is a pleasant place to café cruise or relax on the foreshore, there are no sights as such aside from That Wanaka Tree, and you'll need to head out of town for museums, micro-breweries, vineyards and adventure activities.

During the winter months, Wanaka's relative calm is shattered by the arrival of skiers and snowboarders eager to explore the downhill **ski-fields** of **Treble Cone** and **Cardrona**, and the Nordic terrain at the **Snow Farm** (see page 624).

Lake Wanaka and surrounding sights

One of the real pleasures of Wanaka is spending time simply chilling out on the waterfront, a kilometre or so of grassy reserve-backed soft-gravel beach with wonderful mountain views. In summer it is full of people sunbathing, swimming out to the pontoon, picnicking, feeding the ducks and renting various watercraft such as kayaks, pedalboats and stand-up paddleboards.

Wanaka Tree

Tucked in a gentle curve of Roys Bay, off the Wanaka-Mount Aspiring Road, a small, twisted willow that appears to grow out of the lake's surface is perhaps **New Zealand's most photographed tree**. Having germinated in a fencepost more than eighty years ago when the level of the lake was lower, the picturesque tree found Instagram fame several years back, and at just about any time of the day you're bound to find a handful of tree-botherers lining up the perfect shot for a #thatwanakatree hashtag.

WANAKA

0 500 metres

Albert Town (1km), 3 (1km), Hawea (10km) & Haast Pass (80km)

7 (5km), Transport and Toy Museums (6km) & Warbirds and Wheels (6km)

Lake Wanaka

Ruby Island

Bremner Bay

Eely Point

Beacon Point–Clutha Outlet Track

That Wanaka Tree

Glendhu Bay Track

Mount Iron Track

Mt Iron

Puzzling World

Tititea/Mt Aspiring National Park Visitor Centre

Pembroke Park

Cinema Paradiso

Wanaka Medical Centre

Lakeland Wanaka/Deep Canyon

Wanaka Rock

Library

Supermarket

0 50 metres

SEE INSET BELOW FOR DETAIL

Rippon Vineyard (2km), 5 (11km), Glendhu Bay (11km), Treble Cone (20km), Cardrona (24km) & Mt Aspiring National Park (50km)

Ruby's Cinema (200m), Base Camp Wanaka (200m), Cardrona (26km) & Queenstown (70km)

Waterfall Creek (4km)

● EATING

Alchemy	11
Big Fig	8
Bistro Gentil	1
Brownston St Food Trucks	12
Francesca's Italian Kitchen	6
Kai Whaka Pai	9
Kika	10
Ode	5
Relishes	7
Sasanoki	3
Soul Food Organics	4
Urban Grind	2
White House Café & Bar	13

■ ACCOMMODATION

Albert Town Campground	3
Altamont Lodge	6
Base Wanaka	13
Clearbrook	8
Glendhu Bay Lakeside Holiday Park	5
Lime Tree Lodge	7
Matterhorn South	14
Lake Outlet Holiday Park	2
Peak Sportchalet	1
Te Wanaka Lodge	12
Wanaka Bakpaka	4
Wanaka Lakeview Holiday Park	11
Wanaka Springs Lodge	10
YHA Wanaka Purple Cow	9

■ DRINKING & NIGHTLIFE

Cork Bar	4
LaLaLand	3
Maude Tasting Room	2
Rhyme & Reason Brewery	1

Rippon Vineyard

246 Mount Aspiring Rd, 3km west of town • Daily 11am–5pm • ☎ 03 443 8084, ⓦ rippon.co.nz • Drive from Wanaka or walk in 40min alongside the lakeside Glendhu Bay Track, then uphill through the vines

One of Central Otago's oldest wineries, established in 1982, offers tastings of its interesting biodynamic wines in a stupendously scenic setting. Views from the hilltop tasting room sweep down across the vines towards the lake with the mountains behind. Following the trend of most Central Otago wineries, Pinot Noir is the star, but be sure to try Rippon's Riesling and the rare Osteiner Riesling hybrid. Donations for tasting sessions go towards the vineyard's native habitat restoration programme.

Stuart Landsborough's Puzzling World

188 SH84, almost 2km east of town • Daily: Nov–April 8.30am–5.30pm; May–Oct 8.30am–5pm • $18 for the maze or the illusion rooms, $22.50 for both • ☎ 03 443 7489, ⓦ puzzlingworld.co.nz

A line of monkey puzzle trees heralds **Stuart Landsborough's Puzzling World**, with its complex wooden "Great Maze" comprising 1500m of dead-end passageways packed into a dense labyrinth. Your mission is to reach all four corner towers, either in any order (30min–1hr) or in a specific sequence (at least 1hr), then find your way out again. Much of the rest of the place delights in optical illusions, including the "Hall of Following Faces", with arrays of moulded images of famous people – Einstein, Mother Teresa etc – whose eyes appear to follow you around the room. Great fun for travellers with kids.

National Transport and Toy Museum

891 Wanaka–Luggate Hwy (SH6), 9km southeast of town • Daily 8.30am–5pm • $18; family $43 • ☎ 03 443 8765, ⓦ nttmuseum.co.nz

Hangars full of everything from 500 Barbie dolls and Meccano sets to jet fighters, an impressive *Star Wars* collection, and an astonishing hoard of cars, trucks and bikes are preserved by Wanaka's dry climate at the **National Transport and Toy Museum**. Some machines are well-kept examples of stuff still puttering around New Zealand roads, but there's also exotica such as a Centurion tank, Velocette and BSA bikes, a yellow-fur-covered Morris Minor and the Solar Kiwi Racer, an aluminium and glass-fibre bullet-shaped car powered by solar panels on its roof.

Warbirds & Wheels

11 Lloyd Dunn Ave, Wanaka Airport, 9km southeast of town • Daily: Nov–April 9am–5pm; May–Oct 9am–4pm • $20 • ☎ 03 443 7010, ⓦ warbirdsandwheels.com

The year-round face of the Warbirds Over Wanaka festival (see page 622), **Warbirds & Wheels** displays several warplanes in half a hangar, among them a Strikemaster training plane, a World War II Hurricane and a Skyhawk that did service in the New Zealand Air Force until 2001. The museum honours the festival's colourful founder, aircraft owner and originator of the 1980s live-deer-capture industry, **Sir Tim Wallis**.

The other half of the hangar houses more than thirty classic cars and motorcycles, and you can usually see restoration going on in the workshop.

The Cardrona Valley

The discovery of gold at Arrowtown in 1862 quickly brought prospectors along the Crown Range and into the **Cardrona Valley**, where gold was discovered later that year. Five years on, the Europeans legged it to new fields on the West Coast, leaving the dregs to Chinese immigrants, who themselves had mostly drifted away by 1870.

Tiny **CARDRONA**, 24km south of Wanaka, comprises little more than a few cottages, a long-forgotten cemetery, a fantastic distillery, the *Cardrona Hotel* and the similarly ancient former post office and store.

South from here, the road twists over the **Crown Range Road** (SH89), the quickest and most direct route from Wanaka to Queenstown, though it is sometimes snowbound in winter and trailers are discouraged. Nonetheless, on a fine day the drive past the detritus of the valley's gold-mining heyday is a rewarding one, with views across bald, mica-studded hills to the tussock high country beyond. At the 1076m pass, a great **viewpoint** overlooks Queenstown and Lake Wakatipu, before it switchbacks down towards SH6, Arrowtown and Queenstown.

Cardrona Distillery

2125 Cardrona Valley Rd, Cardrona • Daily 9.30am–5pm • ☎ 03 443 1393, ⓦ cardronadistillery.com

Built of schist stone and surrounded by a fragrant rose garden, the world's southernmost whisky distillery has already been winning awards for its rosehip gins while its first batches of single malts await their bottling in 2025. Stop by for a free tasting of the family-owned distillery's vodka, gins and artisan liqueurs, or sign up for a full tour (1hr 30mins; $25). Eventually, the reception building will house a museum. If you don't have to drive straight back to Wanaka, consider sampling the house spirits in a cocktail ($15), best enjoyed on the front lawn with a cheese board ($27.50).

The Matukituki Valley and Mount Aspiring National Park

The **Matukituki Valley** is Wanaka's outdoor playground, a 60km tentacle reaching from the parched Otago landscapes around Lake Wanaka to the steep alpine skirts of Mount Aspiring, which at 3033m is New Zealand's highest peak outside the Aoraki/Mount Cook National Park. Extensive high-country stations run sheep on the riverside meadows, briefly glimpsed by skiers bound for Treble Cone, rock climbers making for the roadside crags, and trampers and mountaineers hot-footing it to the **Mount Aspiring National Park**.

The park is one of the country's largest, extending from the Haast Pass in the north, where there are tramps around Makarora (see page 496), to the head of Lake Wakatipu in the south, where the Rees–Dart Track and parts of the Routeburn Track fall within its bounds. The pyramidal Mount Aspiring forms the centrepiece of the park, rising with classical beauty over the ice-smoothed broad valleys and creaking glaciers. It was first climbed in 1909 using heavy hemp rope and without the climbing hardware used by today's mountaineers, who still treat it as one of the grails of Kiwi mountaineering.

Travelling along the unsealed section of the Mount Aspiring Road beside the Matukituki River, you don't get to see much of Aspiring, as Mount Avalanche and Avalanche Glacier get in the way. Still, craggy mountains remain tantalizingly present all the way to the **Raspberry Creek**, where a car park and public toilets mark the start of a number of magnificent tramps (see page 623) into the heart of the park.

ARRIVAL AND DEPARTURE	WANAKA AND AROUND
By bus Buses all stop outside the log cabin at 100 Ardmore St. Ritchies (☎ 03 443 9120, ⓦ ritchies.co.nz) links to Dunedin and Queenstown, some with connections stopping at Cromwell. InterCity/Newmans also run services to Queenstown, and pass through on their Queenstown–	Cromwell–Franz Josef run. NakedBus also does a daily run to Queenstown **Destinations** Cromwell (4 daily; 45min); Dunedin (2 daily; 4hr 30min); Franz Josef Glacier (2 daily; 7hr); Queenstown (11 daily; 1hr 30min).

GETTING AROUND

Wanaka is compact and you can walk everywhere in the centre. Most accommodation is less than fifteen minutes away on foot, but you may want transport for longer excursions. **By bike** Many hostels and B&Bs have knockabout bikes for guests' use but for serious riding you'll want to visit the bike rental places. Outside Sports, 17 Dunmore St	(daily 8am–7pm longer in midwinter and summer in peak season); ☎ 03 443 7966, ⓦ outsidesports.co.nz) have road ($30/4hr, $50/day), hardtails ($30/$50), full-suspension ($60/$90) and downhill ($120) models. Racers Edge, 99 Ardmore St (daily: summer 9am–6pm; winter 7.30am–7pm; ☎ 03 443 7882, ⓦ racersedge. co.nz), rents hardtails ($30/half-day, $50/full) and full-

suspension bikes ($50/$70). Both also operate ski rental and tuning services in winter.

By bus Ritchies (see page 580) run the 55km along Mount Aspiring Rd to the national park's main trailhead at Raspberry Creek twice daily from Oct–April. Bookings essential. $40 one-way or $60 return (with stops at Roy's Peak, Diamond Peak and Glendhu Bay; $15). KT sightseeing (☎0800 272700, ⓦktsightseeing.co.nz) charge $50 return

to the Rob Roy Glacier track, and $40 one-way to the Mt Aspring Hut Track and to the Cameron Flat Track, departing Wanaka at 9am.

By car Wanaka Rentacar, 2 Brownston St (☎03 443 6641, ⓦwanakarentacar.co.nz), have the cheapest range of vehicles, starting at around $45/day, with unlimited kilometres for longer rentals.

By taxi Yello! (☎0800 443 5555).

INFORMATION

Information i-SITE, 103 Ardmore St (daily: Dec–March 8.30am–5.30pm or later; April–Nov 9am–5pm; ☎03 443 1233, ⓦlakewanaka.co.nz). The DOC Tititea/Mt Aspiring National Park visitor centre is at the corner of SH84 and Ballantyne Rd, 500m east of central Wanaka (Nov–April daily 8am–5pm; May–Oct Mon–Fri 8.30am–5pm, Sat 9.30am–4pm; ☎03 443 7660, ✉mtaspiringvc@doc.govt.nz).

Gear rental Outside Sports (17 Dunmore St; ☎03 4437966, ⓦoutsidesports.co.nz) stocks the gamut of outdoor adventurewear and offers rentals including backpacks ($10/day), sleeping bags ($10), waterproof jackets and pants ($10/$8) hiking boots ($8), trekking poles ($5) and cooking stoves ($5).

TOURS AND ACTIVITIES

Magnificent scenery, clear skies and competitive prices make Wanaka an excellent place to get airborne, and with a beautiful lake and a number of decent rivers there's plenty of opportunity for getting wet in style. Most accommodation and numerous agents around town handle **bookings**, or you can contact the activity operator direct.

CANYONING

Deep Canyon 100 Ardmore St ☎03 443 7922, ⓦdeepcanyon.co.nz. Experienced guides take small groups into narrow canyons following a creek downstream with heaps of jumps, rockslides and abseils. Warm, protective clothing helps ease the sense of vulnerability, and the day is rounded off with a bush picnic. First-timers should opt for Niger Stream (8hr; $260), down a gorgeous stream with plenty of jumping into deep pools. Abseiling experience ensures you get the best from Big Nige (8hr; $320), which covers the same territory as the Niger Stream trip but starts further upstream with some big rappels. Even more adventurous trips are also possible.

ROCK CLIMBING AND MOUNTAINEERING

Aspiring Guides ☎0800 754 868, ⓦaspiringguides. com. Professional mountaineering with five-day heli-in/walk-out ascents of Mt Aspiring (Oct–April; $5250) as well as excellent seven-day Summit Weeks ($3450) where you get a guide to help tackle whatever peaks or learn whatever skills you need.

Basecamp Wanaka 50 Cardrona Valley Rd ☎03 443 1110, ⓦbasecampwanaka.co.nz. Two climbing experiences in one. Inside is the child-oriented Clip 'N Climb ($20/hr; kids $10–16; bring trainers), where an auto-belay system allows you to climb against the clock, do a face-to-face race, or climb in the dark with UV-lit holds. The superbly sculpted outdoor wall ($21; includes harness) is pretty

close to climbing on real rock. Lessons available. Mon–Fri 10am–8pm, Sat & Sun 10am–6pm.

Wanaka Rock 99 Ardmore St ☎022 015 4458, ⓦwanakarock.co.nz. Wanaka's dry, sunny climate is ideal for rock climbing, and these guys run full-day introductory courses involving top-roping, seconding and abseiling for a minimum of two people (half-day $203 each; full-day $293), a day trip for more advanced climbers ($293), and offer private guiding ($553/day).

Wildwire Wanaka ☎0800 9453 9473, ⓦwildwire. co.nz. Criss-crossing a stunning waterfall near the access road up to Treble Cone, this Via Ferrata is up there with the world's best – not to mention the most scenic. You can choose to climb partway (around 1hr 30min; $189) or half-way (around 3hr; $249) and return to the base via a steep track, or continue to the top (around 5hr; $495), with a heli-transfer back down. No climbing experience is required, though only those with a decent level of fitness should attempt full "Lord of the Rungs" ascent, which includes two small overhangs. A brilliant day out.

SKYDIVING AND PARAGLIDING

Skydive Lake Wanaka ☎0800 786 877, ⓦskydivewanaka.com. A 10–15min scenic flight can be combined with 25–60 seconds of free fall on a tandem skydive ($299 from 9000ft; $349 from 12,000ft; $449 from 15,000ft), with views of Mt Cook on clear days. Free pick-ups from Queenstown.

Wanaka Paragliding ☎0800 359 754, ⓦwanakaparagliding.co.nz. A gentle but spectacular approach to viewing the tremendous scenery is a tandem flight from high on Treble Cone ski-field down to the lakeside (800m descent) with 15–20min in the air. Trips ($239) take 2hr from Wanaka and transport is included. Self-drive and save $30.

11

11

WANAKA FESTIVALS

From air shows to arts and music festivals, Wanaka has one of the most packed festival calendars in the country. Keep in mind that local accommodations can book out well in advance of the most popular events, so plan ahead.

Tuki Festival (W tukifestival.nz). Formerly known as the Rippon Festival, this one-day February rock, roots and reggae fest with a top Kiwi line-up is now held at the scenic Glendhu Station. Tickets around $119.

A&P Show (W wanakashow.co.nz). Town meets country at Wanaka's lakefront showgrounds in March with everything from calf-wrangling demos and biggest pumpkin competitions to the perfect Victoria sponge. Heaps of food, drink and fun.

Warbirds Over Wanaka (W warbirdsoverwanaka. com). Wanaka Airport plays host to New Zealand's premier air show – three days of airborne craft doing their thing watched by over 50,000 people. Day tickets from $60. Easter every even-numbered year.

Festival of Colour (W festivalofcolour.co.nz). A biennial celebration of visual art, dance, music, theatre and the like, with top Kiwi acts, including the symphony orchestra, performing all over town. Lots of free stuff, or buy tickets for individual performances. April in odd-numbered years.

Wanaka Beer Fest (W facebook.com/ wanakabeerfestival). Sample the latest beers from Wanaka's craft breweries (at last count, there were five) as well as those of a handful of guest breweries from around the country at this newish festival held every December. Tickets $30.

Rhythm & Alps (W rhythmandalps.co.nz). Huge crowds attend this two-day music festival leading up to New Years Eve in the Cardrona Valley. Loads of big acts (Tash Sultana and Fat Freddy's Drop in 2017); on-site camping logistics that get better by the year. $227 ($322 with camping).

SCENIC FLIGHTS

Scenic flights from Wanaka to Milford Sound tend to be a few bucks more expensive than those from Queenstown, but they do spend half an hour more flying over a wider range of stunning scenery, including Mount Aspiring, the Olivine Ice Plateau and the inaccessible lakes of Alabaster, McKerrow and Tutoko. Most local accommodation receives daily bulletins on Milford weather and flight conditions.

Alpine Helicopters ☎ 03 443 4000, W alpineheli.co.nz. Get a quick bird's-eye view of Wanaka (20min; $230) or blow the budget on a Milford Sound flight with one landing (1hr 30min–2hr; $995) or two landings (2hr 30min–3hr; $1295). Plenty more options available.

Southern Alps Air ☎ 0800 345 666, W southernalpsair. co.nz. Excellent Milford Sound flight/cruise/flight combo (4hr total; $540) plus scenic flights around Mt Aspiring (50min; $290) and transport deals to link to their Siberia Experience and Blue Pools trips in Makarora.

BIKING

Wanaka has several shops renting bikes, which may also be able to supply off-road trail maps produced by Bike Wanaka, the local MTB club (downloadable for free at W bikewanaka. org.nz). Pick of the local biking routes detailed in the *Wanaka Outdoor Pursuits* brochure include the excellent Upper Clutha River Track and the beautiful, gentle Beacon Point–Outlet Track (see page 623).

Cardrona Mountain Bike Park ☎ 03 443 8880, W cardrona.com. The resort's new "chondola" uplifts riders (and bikes) to the access point for over 25km of mountain-bike trails threading down the mountain from beginner to advanced (Dec–March daily 10am–4pm, until 8pm Fri; half-day $69, full-day $89, Fri 4–8pm $35). Rent a bike in town or on the mountain (downhill bike full-day $119), or try your hand at mountain karting ($99 for 2hr cart and lift) instead.

Wanaka Bike Tours ☎ 03 443 6363, W wanakabiketours.co.nz. Dedicated guided riding company offering escorted rides along the Lakeside and Clutha tracks ($299), backcountry rides ($299) and even heli-biking (various options from $650).

CRUISES, KAYAKING, RAFTING AND JETBOATING

Eco Wanaka Adventures ☎ 0800 926 326, W ecowanaka.co.nz. A wonderfully informative and scenic cruise (daily 9am & 1.30pm; 4hr; $245) across Lake Wanaka to Mou Waho island nature reserve and its population of buff weka. The nature walk highlight is "high tea" overlooking the island's picturesque lake-within-a-lake, and you can even plant a tree, helping Mou Waho's regeneration.

Go Jets Wanaka ☎ 0800 465 387, W gojetswanaka. co.nz. Wanaka's newest jetboating operator combines the typical thrills and spills with an interesting primer on the Clutha's gold rush history as you zoom towards the surging waters of "Devil's Nook" (1hr 30mins; $125).

Lakeland Wanaka 100 Ardmore St ☎ 03 443 7495, W lakelandwanaka.com. Offers all manner of waterborne activities, from a gentle lake cruise (1hr; $85) to jetboating (1hr; $119). Also rents kayaks ($20 per person/hr) and assorted aquatic toys.

Paddle Wanaka ☎ 0800 926 925, W paddlewanaka. co.nz. Kayak and stand-up paddleboard (SUP) specialists renting from the beach ($20 per person/hr), and running no-experience-necessary kayak trips on the lake (half-day $135, full-day $295 including picnic lunch) and down the Clutha River (4hr; $189). Various SUP tours include SUP yoga (1hr; $35) and a SUP adventure down the Clutha (3hr; $174).

Pioneer Rafting ☎03 443 1246, ⓦecoraft.co.nz. Rafting on the Grade II Upper Clutha (daily Sept–April), where half- and full-day trips involve bobbing along choppy water with emphasis on appreciating the scenery and gold panning. Suitable for families, trips are run free of charge to prospective donors to the company's river conservation projects.

Wanaka River Journeys ☎0800 544 555, ⓦwanakariverjourneys.co.nz. Great-value half-day jetboating tours (1–2 daily; 4hr; $239) which thunder up the Matukituki River, providing great views of Mt Aspiring, the Avalanche Glacier, Mt Avalanche and the rest, with a knowledgeable guide and a bushwalk. Also offers pack-rafting (full-day; $355) and heli-combo options.

FISHING

Lake Wanaka and nearby lakes and rivers are popular territory for Quinnat salmon and brown and rainbow trout fishing. There's a maximum bag of six fish per day and you'll require the sport fishing licence ($20/ day, $127 for the season for Kiwis, $165 for foreigners; ⓦfishandgame.org.nz), obtainable online or from tackle shops such as Southern Wild, 10 Helwick St (☎03 443 8094, ⓦsouthernwild.nz), which rents fishing rods and lures ($25/day). For all sorts of fishing instruction, there's a decent list of local guides on the New Zealand Professional Fishing Guides Association website (ⓦfishandgame.org.nz).

HORSERIDING

Waterfall Equestrian Centre 22 Wanaka-Mt Aspiring Rd ☎272 109 098, ⓦwaterfallequestrian.com Gentle rides through Rippon Vineyard with a stop for tasting (1hr 30min; $100). Very civilized.

11

WALKS AROUND WANAKA

There are some great walks and more serious hikes around Wanaka. No special gear is required, just robust shoes, wet-weather gear, sun protection and DOC's *Wanaka Outdoor Pursuits* leaflet ($3.50, downloadable free from the DOC website), which has a good map. The **Outlet Track** (3km each way; 1hr each way; mostly flat) is a great option for an undemanding riverbank wander (or ride). If you prefer a bit more of an incline, try the **Mount Iron Track** (4.5km return; 1hr 30min; 240m ascent), the most accessible of Wanaka's hilltop walks which takes you through farmland and the bird-filled manuka woodland of the Mount Iron Scenic Reserve.

WALKS IN THE MATUKITUKI VALLEY

The more serious tramps in the Matukituki Valley are covered in the DOC's *Matukituki Valley Tracks* and *Dart & Rees Valleys* leaflets ($2 each or downloadable free from ⓦdoc. govt.nz): get hold of the *Aspiring Flats* topo50 map ($9 from DOC) if you like contour lines. The routes are manageable for fit and experienced trampers, but the climatic differences in the park are extreme – the half-metre of rain that falls each year in the Matukituki Valley does not compare with the six metres that fall on the western side of the park, so go prepared. The hikes start at the Raspberry Creek car park, about an hour's drive from Wanaka.

The most manageable walk is the **Raspberry Creek to Aspiring Hut** (9km one way; 2hr–2hr 30min; 100m ascent). It's a popular and mostly pastoral day-walk starting along a 4WD track which climbs from the Raspberry Creek car park beside the western branch of the Matukituki River, only heading away from the river to avoid bluffs en route to Downs Creek, from where you get fabulous views up to the Rob Roy Glacier and Mount Avalanche. Brides Veil Falls is a brief distraction before the historic Cascade Hut, followed 20min later by the relatively luxurious stone-built Aspiring Hut (NZAC; 38 bunks; $30, with gas, no bookings), a common base camp for mountaineers off to the peaks around Mount Aspiring. There's camping ($5) near the hut, but facilities (including toilets) are not available to campers.

Alternatively try the **Rob Roy Valley Walk** (10km return; 3–4hr; 300m ascent). This justly popular there-and-back hike is shorter and steeper than the walk to Aspiring Hut and more spectacular, striking through beech forest to some magnificent alpine scenery, snowfields and glaciers. Eco Wanaka Adventures (☎0800 926 326, ⓦecowanaka.co.nz) run an all-day guided trip here including a picnic lunch ($295).

11

WINTER IN WANAKA

In June Wanaka gets geared up for winter, with summer sports instructors morphing into lift operstors, and frequent shuttle buses running up to the ski-fields. If you plan to drive up there you'll need snow chains, which can be rented at petrol stations in Wanaka. The bike rental shops (see page 622) all switch to ski rental, starting at as little as $25/day for budget skis or a snowboard, boots and poles.

DOWNHILL AND CROSS-COUNTRY SKIING

Cardrona Alpine Resort Reached by a 12km unsealed access road branching off 24km south of Wanaka, near Cardrona ☎ 0800 440 800, ⓦ cardrona.com. Predominantly family-oriented field sprawled over three basins on the southeastern slopes of the 1934m Mount Cardrona. Expect an abundance of gentle runs, four terrain parks and two pipes. There are three learner tows, quads, a new "chondola," and a maximum vertical descent of 600m. Non-drivers can catch shuttles from Wanaka and Queenstown. There's limited accommodation on the mountain in luxury, fully self-contained studios for two ($350), or two- and three-bedroom apartments which sleep up to ten ($699). Single-day lift pass $115. Late June to early Oct.

Snow Farm Across the valley from Cardrona, 24km south of Wanaka, then 14km up a winding dirt road ☎ 03 443 7542, ⓦ snowfarmnz.com. With so many Kiwi skiers committed to downhill, it comes as a surprise to discover a cross-country ski area. At $40 for access to the field and $30 for ski rental for a full day, it's an inexpensive way to get on the snow, negotiating the 55km of marked Nordic trails. July–Sept.

Treble Cone 22km west of Wanaka, accessed by a 7km unsealed road ☎ 03 443 7443, ⓦ treblecone. co.nz. More experienced skiers tend to frequent the steep slopes here. Its appeal lies in its range of uncrowded runs spectacularly located high above Lake Wanaka, and a full 700 vertical metres of skiing with moguls, powder runs, gully runs and plenty of natural and created half-pipes. Three groomed trails make it accessible for beginners and snowboarders will have a ball. Morning buses leave from Wanaka, and a shuttle bus takes skiers from the start of the access road on Mount Aspiring Road up to the tows. Backcountry tours are also available from Treble Cone, with Aspiring Guides (☎ 03 443 9422, ⓦ aspiringguides.com; $275). Single-day lift pass $135. Late June to early Oct.

HELI-SKIING AND CATSKIING

Heli-skiing is not cheap, but there's no other way of getting to runs of up to 1200 vertical metres across virgin snow on any of seven mountain ranges. Cat-skiing typically guarantees more runs.

Harris Mountains Heli-Ski ☎ 03 442 6722, ⓦ heliski.co.nz. Offers over 400 different runs on 200 peaks – mainly in the Harris Mountains between Queenstown's Crown Range and Wanaka's Mt Aspiring National Park. Strong intermediate and advanced skiers get the most out of the experience, where conditions are more critical than at the skifields, but on average there's heli-skiing seventy percent of the time, typically in four- to five-day weather windows. Of the multitude of packages, "The Classic" ($1045) is the cheapest option, with four runs (extra runs $110).

Soho Basin Next to Cardrona Alpine Resort ☎ 03 450 9098, ⓦ sohobasin.com. With no lifts, cat-skiing is the name of the game at this private resort opened in 2015, with a full day including an alpine hut lunch by *Amisfield* ringing in at $685 a head. The resort is also open to those with their own ski touring gear for a $5 donation.

4WD TRIPS

Ridgeline Adventures ☎ 0800 234 000, ⓦ ridgelinenz. com. Get a sense of how a high-country station operates on Wild Hills Safari (4h; $249) which takes you high up onto remote farmland with long views over Lake Wanaka. Photography tours and chopper and jetboat combos also available.

ACCOMMODATION

For a diminutive place, Wanaka has a great range of accommodation, particularly luxury lodges. You should have no problem finding a bed, except during the peak months of January, February, July and August, and during events when **booking** is essential and prices rise. **Freedom camping** is not allowed in town or along the lakefront.

Altamont Lodge 121 Mount Aspiring Rd ☎ 03 443 8864, ⓦ altamontlodge.co.nz; map p.618. For hostel prices without the dorms or backpacker vibe, head for this tramping-slash-ski-lodge with a pine-panelled alpine atmosphere, communal cooking and lounge areas, a spa pool, drying rooms, spacious lawns with BBQ facilities, and a guest laundry. Twins, doubles and triples are fairly functional, with shared bathrooms. $99

Base Wanaka 73 Brownston St ☎03 443 4291, ⓦstayatbase.co.nz; map p.618. Purpose-built hostel in the heart of town; the kitchen is cramped but there's also a bar serving budget meals. The smart rooms feature upscale women-only dorms ($35). Tends to attract a youngish crowd. Dorms $29, doubles $100

Clearbrook 72 Helwick ☎0800 443 441, ⓦclearbrook.co.nz; map p.618. Afternoon sun streams in to the studios, one- and two-bedroom apartments at this classy motel with tastefully decorated luxury units ranged along the gurgling Bullock Creek. All units have TV/DVD, full kitchen with dishwasher, laundry and balconies with mountain views. All are great value including the separate three-bedroom townhouses sleeping up to eight ($500). Doubles $200

Matterhorn South 56 Brownston St ☎03 443 1119, ⓦmatterhornsouth.co.nz; map p.618. Combined hostel and budget lodge, with an appealing backpacker section featuring dorms of various sizes and a teeny standalone double ($75). The more upmarket lodge section has modern, en-suite doubles and family rooms (from $105) with TV and fridge, and access to an excellent kitchen and comfortable lounge. Dorms $30, doubles $80

Peak Sportchalet 36 Hunter Crescent, 2km north of town ☎03 443 6990, ⓦpeak-sportchalet.co.nz; map p.618. Purpose-built, certified enviro-friendly self-contained studio and two-bedroom chalet in a peaceful part of town, run by a charming German couple who provide a buffet breakfast ($15 extra). There's an individual touch to the decor, bathrooms get under-floor heating and everywhere is super-insulated. The studio is great for couples; the chalet for a family or two couples. Studio $160, one-bedroom chalet $200

★ **Lime Tree Lodge** 672 Ballantyne Rd, 9km east of Wanaka ☎03 443 7305, ⓦlimetreelodge.co.nz; map p.618. Removed from the bustle of town, this stylish B&B has four rooms and two suites with all the amenities you could wish for, from fluffy robes to fresh baking, afternoon aperitifs to complimentary evening transfers into Wanaka. There's also a swimming pool, a cosy lounge with an open fireplace, and even a heli-pad. $395

★ **Te Wanaka Lodge** 23 Brownston St ☎03 443 9224, ⓦtewanaka.co.nz; map p.618. Welcoming thirteen-room lodge built around a large walnut tree. Comfortable rooms all have private entrances and Sky TV, and rooms 9, 10, 11 and 12 also come with views. A cedar hot tub shares the peaceful garden with a delightful small cottage room. There's a hearty breakfast served around a communal table, complimentary afternoon tea, and even an honesty bar with a good wine selection. The owners are highly knowledgeable about all things outdoors. $240

Wanaka Bakpaka 117 Lakeside Rd ☎03 443 7837, ⓦwanakabakpaka.co.nz; map p.618. Beautifully maintained low-key BBH hostel in a converted house a 5min walk from town, with great lake and mountain views (doubles with views are $94), a peaceful atmosphere, summer BBQs and bike rental ($19/day). Plenty of room for sitting out in the afternoon sun. Dorms $31, doubles $76

Wanaka Springs Lodge 21 Warren St ☎03 443 8421, ⓦwanakasprings.com; map p.618. Classy, purpose-built, boutique bed and breakfast in a quiet area with comfortable, beautifully decorated rooms, stylish communal areas, and a spa pool in the native garden. The hosts have good local knowledge. Small discounts for two-night stays or longer. $400

★ **YHA Wanaka Purple Cow** 94 Brownston St ☎03 443 1880, ⓦyha.co.nz; map p.618. Large and inviting hostel where dorms (up to six beds) and rooms all come with their own bathroom. Also several en-suite doubles, some with lake view ($125). Sit and gaze at the fabulous lake view through the big picture windows, play pool (free), watch the nightly movie or rent a bike. There's also an ample kitchen, a nice BBQ area and a guest laundry. Dorms $33, doubles $102

CAMPSITES AND HOLIDAY PARKS

Albert Town Campground SH6, 6km northeast of Wanaka; map p.618. Open, informal camping area on the banks of the swift-flowing Clutha River with tap water and flush toilets. There's plenty of shade but it gets very busy for four weeks from Boxing Day. $10

Glendhu Bay Lakeside Holiday Park Camp 1127 Mount Aspiring Rd, 12km west of Wanaka ☎03 443 7243, ⓦglendhubaymotorcamp.co.nz; map p.618. Beautifully situated family campsite with numerous pitches strung along the lakeshore, cabins sleeping up to five, a house sleeping ten ($275), a bunkhouse sleeping 21 ($375) and fabulous views across to Mount Aspiring. Facilities include a communal kitchen, coin-operated showers, a guest laundry, a playground, and a boat ramp. Camping per site $34, cabins $50

★ **Lake Outlet Holiday Park** 197 Lake Outlet Rd, 6km from Wanaka ☎03 443 7478, ⓦlakeoutlet.co.nz; map p.618. Spacious and stunningly sited campsite at the point where Lake Wanaka becomes the Clutha River, in a great position for strolls along the lake or river frontage. Along with tent and powered sites there are simple cabins (some with a lounge) and a cottage sleeping 6 ($250). Rent a bike ($20 for 3hr) and ride the Outlet Track. Camping $18, cabins $55

Wanaka Lakeview Holiday Park 212 Brownston St ☎03 443 7883, ⓦwanakalakeview.co.nz; map p.618. The closest campsite to town is a 5min walk from the centre and has tent and powered sites, cabins and a self-contained flat ($100). Camping $20, standard cabins $60

11

EATING

Skiers and the healthy influx of summer tourists have contributed to the growing proliferation of places to eat and drink around town.

Alchemy 151 Ardmore St ☏03 443 2040, ⓦalchemywanaka.nz; map p.618. There's a relaxed, Scandinavian feel to this pastel-toned café, a buzzy spot for brunch (try the "green eggs and ham" pesto scramble; $17) or a smart-casual evening meal (from 4pm), with a good range of small plates (from salt and pepper squid with wasabi mayo to mini beef Yorkshire puddings; both $16), and a short selection of mains. Daily 8am–11pm.

Big Fig 105 Ardmore St ☏03 443 5023, ⓦbigfig.co.nz; map p.618. A fantastic healthy takeaway option, *Big Fig* serves slow food fast: simply choose your plate size (a medium gets you one meat dish and four salads; $18), make your selections (from pomegranate beef cheek to lamb shwarma, with around ten wonderfully inventive salads to choose from), and grab a table or get it to go. Daily around noon–9pm.

Bistro Gentil 76a Golf Course Rd ☏03 443 2299, ⓦbistrogentil.co.nz; map p.618. Classy modern French restaurant with an elegant interior (hung with contemporary New Zealand art) and a terrace with long views towards the lake and mountains. Expect New Zealand produce cooked *à la française* including the likes of Cardrona Merino lamb rump with lamb shoulder croquette, sunchokes, hazelnut and rosemary jus ($45). Self-serve wine dispensers let you sample a good range before committing to a full glass. Tues–Sat 5–9pm.

Brownston St Food Trucks Brownston St; map p.618. More than half a dozen food trucks are scattered along Brownston St, with most occuypying a semi-permanent base at the top end of the street. If you don't want to dine in, you can grab a *Francesca's* pizza ($20) to go here, or perhaps opt for a flavour-packed burrito from *Burrito Craft* ($10). There's also a dumplings truck and a coffee/hot chocolate stand, with some bench seating. Daily around noon–9pm.

★ **Francesca's Italian Kitchen** 93 Ardmore St ☏03 443 5599, ⓦfransitalian.co.nz; map p.618. Always busy with folk tucking into bowls of its famed polenta fries with truffle oil ($9) and wonderful pizzas ($20–25), this modern take on a traditional Italian joint artfully also turns super-fresh ingredients into starters like Cloudy Bay clams with chilli, garlic, Prosecco and black garlic butter ($16). Reservations recommended. Daily noon–3pm & 5–9pm or later.

Kai Whaka Pai Corner of Ardmore and Helwick sts ☏03 443 7795; map p,618. Wanaka's liveliest daytime eating spot is a favourite with locals who come for hearty all-day breakfasts, good coffee and baked counter treats. On summer evenings the emphasis is on beer and wine, seated at tables on the street perhaps eating an open steak sandwich ($22) or thin-crust pizza ($23). Wanaka Beerworks "Brewski" is on tap along with a rotating selection of local brews. Daily 7am–11pm.

★ **Kika** 33 Dunmore St ☏03 443 6536. ⓦkika.nz; map p.618. One of just seven Otago restaurants named among New Zealand food bible *Cuisine* magazine's top 100 in 2017, *Kika*'s tapas-style menu showcasing local produce and fresh, sustainable ingredients is a real winner. Perhaps start with a *piccolo* dish such as charred asparagus, tarragon and pancetta with smoked macadamia ($15) before sharing a *grande* portion of lamb shoulder with preserved lemon, rosemary and chilli ($55). Alternatively, allow the staff to select the best dishes of the day for you ($62 per person). Daily 5.30pm–late.

★ **Ode** 33 Ardmore St ☏03 443 6394. ⓦodewanaka. com; map p.618. Conscious dining is taken to a new level at this new restaurant that does magical things with organic, ethical, seasonal and sustainable ingredients. Dinner is by set menu; go with the standard three-course "trust the chef" option ($55), or blow out on the weekly-changing eight-course ($89) option. With 24hrs' notice, you can even have a thirteen-course degustation ($199; Wed–Sat). Terrific value, with a wine list that matches *Ode*'s dining philosophy. Mon–Sat 6–10pm or later.

Relishes 99 Ardmore St ☏03 443 9018, ⓦrelishescafe.co.nz; map p.618. Long-standing Wanaka favourite that serves a great breakfast menu alongside the likes of citrus and chilli-marinated prawns, vegetable noodle salad, vermicelli, peanuts and *nam jim* dressing ($21) for lunch, and Alexandra Boer goat loin, cauliflower hummus, cumin-spiced puy lentils, olives, tomatoes, and sumac brown butter yoghurt for dinner ($34). Daily 7.30am–10pm or later.

Sasanoki 26 Ardmore St ☏03 443 6474; map p.618. Eat in or take away from this modest Japanese kitchen, serving excellent *otsumami* (Japanese tapas; $7–16.50), udon and ramen noodles ($24), *donburi* $23–33) and bento meals ($29.50). Mon–Fri 11.30am–2.30pm & 5.30–9pm, Sat 5.30–9pm.

Soul Food Organic 74 Ardmore St ☏03 443 7885; map p.618. There's cute courtyard seating out the back of this café and wholefood shop specializing in vegetarian, dairy- and gluten-free dishes. Drop by for excellent plunger coffee and bliss balls ($5), wholesome breakfasts ($10–20), winter soups, salads and tasty juices and smoothie combinations such as raw cacao, almond milk, date and banana ($10). Mon–Fri 8am–6pm, Sat & Sun 8am–4pm.

Urban Grind 73 Ardmore St ☏03 443 6748, ⓦurbangrind.co.nz; map p.618. Start the day with a bacon and egg butty ($12.50) or a Japanese pancake with roast pork belly and a fried egg ($20.50) in this modern exposed-brick café illuminated by oversized pendant lights. Blue cod sliders ($18) and chicken *bao* buns ($18) work as an appetizer for thin-crust pizza ($19.50–24) washed down with a local beer or a jug of Pimms ($19). Daily 7.45am–11pm.

White House Café & Bar 33 Dunmore St ☎ 03 443 9595; map p.618. Set on the bottom floor of an Art Deco house that could be in Santorini, this quirky family restaurant and bar serves delicious, loosely Mediterranean-influenced dishes (mains around $40) with an inventive list of bruschetta to start such as beetroot and blue cheese ($15). There's a good, all-Kiwi wine list, and leave room for dessert, which might be ginger loaf with figs and blue cheese. Tues–Sat 6–10pm or later.

DRINKING AND NIGHTLIFE

★ **Cork Bar** 14 Helwick St ☎ 03 443 2224, ⓦ facebook. com/corkbar.co.nz; map p.618. With more than fifty gins, more than sixty whiskies, ten beers on tap and Wanaka's most extensive wine list, this great new bar has all bases covered. There's often live music in the intimate courtyard, which has a retractable roof to keep punters comfortable year-round. Daily 3pm–2.30am.

LaLaLand Level 1, 99 Ardmore St ☎ 03 443 4911, ⓦ facebook.com/lalalandwanaka; map p.618. Mixology reaches its Wanaka apotheosis at this cute little cocktail bar. Come for a sundowner on the deck overlooking the lake or stick around until it really kicks off. Daily 4pm–2.30am.

Maude Tasting Room 76a Golf Course Rd ☎ 03 443 2299, ⓦ maudewines.com; map p.618. The lauded Wanaka winery now has a cellar door within walking distance from the centre. Sink into a sheepskin-draped seat on the all-weather terrace and enjoy the lake views as you taste your way through the Maude Range (four wines, $10) and/or Reserve Range (six wines $25) perhaps while snacking on a cheese or charcuterie board ($25–30). Mon & Thurs–Sun noon–5.30pm.

★ **Rhyme & Reason Brewery** 17 Gordon Rd ☎ 03 265 1101, ⓦ rhymeandreason.beer; map p.618. In Wanka's slowly gentrifying industrial estate, this brew bar is a great place to hang out on Saturday afternoons, when there's live music and local food trucks roll in. On other days, staff are happy to ring in your takeaway order while you work your way through a tasting flight ($15) concocted by Jessica Wolfgang, one of New Zealand's rising contingent of female brewers. Daily noon–11.30pm.

THE CARDRONA VALLEY

Cardrona Hotel Cardrona ☎ 03 443 8153, ⓦ cardronahotel.co.nz. Stop for a bite or a beer at this 1863 survivor which, after years of neglect, was spruced up and reopened in 1984, although the frontage is held in a state of arrested decay. In winter, skiers sink into the chesterfields around the fire, while in summer the beer garden bursts into life. There's a great range of drinks, modern pub meals such as venison and bacon burger with fries ($23) and "après" nachos ($16.50), plus B&B accommodation. Restaurant and bar daily 8am–10pm or later.

ENTERTAINMENT

Unless you catch a festival or a band passing through, entertainment extends to a night at the flicks.

Cinema Paradiso 72 Brownston St ☎ 03 443 1505, ⓦ paradiso.net.nz. The screens might have gone digital but you still sit in sagging old sofas, armchairs, airline seats or even a bisected Austin A30 at this quirky three-screener in a former Catholic church. The films range from Hollywood to art house, and there's always an interval during which everyone tucks into cookies, ice cream, coffee, booze and even pizza ($18–22) from the on-site café. Adults $15.

Ruby's 50 Cardrona Valley Rd, ☎ 03 443 6901, ⓦ rubyscinema.co.nz. A chic pair of small, digital cinemas (37-seat & a more luxe twelve-seater known as "the snug") entered through an intimate cocktail bar with Loren, Newman and Hepburn posters on the wall. Grab yourself a cocktail, wine or craft beer and a few nibbles and retire to the cinemas' huge leather recliners. Adults $18.50.

DIRECTORY

Internet Wanaka Internet, 3 Helwick St (generally daily 9am–6pm; ☎ 03 443 7429), has cheap rates.

Medical treatment Wanaka Medical Centre, 23 Cardrona Valley Rd (☎ 03 443 0710, ⓦ wanakamedicalcentre.co.nz). Clinic Mon–Fri 8am–6pm plus 24hr emergency care.

Pharmacy Wanaka Pharmacy, 41 Helwick St (daily 8am–8pm; ☎ 03 443 8000).

Post office 39 Ardmore St (Mon–Fri 9am–5pm).

Central Otago

Southeast of Queenstown and Wanaka, the **Central Otago goldfields** are strewn out along the winding Clutha River. This fascinating historic region is peppered with gold-town ruins from the 1860s, orchards and **vineyards** where you can taste some excellent wine. Many visitors also come to cycle the **Otago Central Rail Trail** (see page 634) which passes through the **Maniototo**, flat high country that feels like a windswept and ambient world apart, and provides the most interesting route to the east coast.

The reconstructed nineteenth-century settlement of **Cromwell**, 50km east of Queenstown, is a good jumping-off point for the former mining town of **Bendigo** and the wineries of **Bannockburn**, and has some great little wineries of its own. The twin towns of **Clyde** and **Alexandra** have fashioned themselves as bases for cycling the popular Otago Central Rail Trail, while **Lawrence** relishes its position as the gold rush's hometown. **St Bathans** and **Naseby** are worth sampling for their calm seclusion and subtle reminders of how greed transforms the land. Much of the area's pleasure is in even smaller places – the post office at **Ophir** or the old engineering works in the **Ida Valley** – and in the dozens of small cottages, many abandoned – a testimony to the harsh life in these parts.

Brief history

Predictably, Europeans first came in search of gold. They found it near **Naseby**, but returns swiftly declined and farming on the plains became more rewarding. This was especially true when **railway** developers looking for the easiest route from Dunedin to Alexandra chose a way up the Taieri Gorge and across the Maniototo. In 1898, the line arrived in **Ranfurly**, which soon took over from Naseby as the area's main administrative centre. With the closure of the rail line in 1990 an already moribund area withered further until the **Otago Central Rail Trail** caught on. In recent years, environmentalists have battled to save the landscape from **Project Hayes**, which would have been New Zealand's largest wind farm, a battle only won when the power company Meridian Energy backed down in 2012.

GETTING AROUND

CENTRAL OTAGO

By car and bike Driving or riding is the best way to see the region as public transport is limited.

By train The Taieri Gorge Railway (see page 580) runs daily from Dunedin to the Otago Rail Trail. On Fri and Sun it stops in Middlemarch, but on other days it turns around at Pukerangi and you'll have to cycle the 20km along the road to reach Middlemarch.

By bus SH8 follows the Clutha River pretty closely and is typically plied by four buses a day running between Dunedin and Queenstown. Most bus services between Wanaka and Queenstown stop in Cromwell. Trail Journeys (Oct–April daily; May–Sept on demand; ☎ 0800 030 381, ⓦ trailjourneys.co.nz) runs a service between Clyde and Middlemarch primarily for Rail Trail riders.

Cromwell

The service town of **CROMWELL**, 60km east of Queenstown, celebrates its gold-mining roots while hopping on the back of the region's food and wine renaissance; its new 4 Barrels Walking Wine Trail elevating it to a worthwhile overnight stop. Sadly, almost all of Cromwell's historic core is submerged below the shimmering surface of **Lake Dunstan**, formed behind the Clyde Dam, 20km downstream (see page 631). Cromwell may only be 120km from the coast, but this is as far from the sea as you can get in New Zealand, something that gives the area something of a continental climate that's perfect for growing stone fruit. A 13m-high, fibreglass **fruit sculpture** beside the highway highlights the long-time importance of nectarines, peaches, apples and pears, though these days cherries and grapes are probably more important.

4 Barrels Walking Wine Trail

Daily: Micha's Vineyard 10am–4pm, Aurum Wines, Scott Base and Wooing Tree Wines 10am–5pm, ⓦ facebook.com/4barrelscromwell
With the help of a beautifully illustrated free map available at the local i-SITE, you can now take your own half-day tour of central Cromwell's wineries via a self-paced 8km loop linking four wineries with great scenery along the way, including a lakeside

amble between **Micha's Vineyard** (if you're not much of a Riesling drinker, their "limelight" Riesling will change that) and **Aurum Wines** with its superb English-style garden. Tastings at Aurum are free, while the other three wineries charge a small fee redeemable on bottle purchases. You can tackle the loop in either direction, though if you get an early start towards Micha's, end your walk at **Wooing Tree Wines** for a relaxing lunch (and a sampling of their "Blondie" Blanc de Noir). Alternatively, **Scott Base** has a great little grazing menu, and Moa beer (created by Allen Scott's son, Josh) on tap.

Cromwell Historic Precinct

Lake Dunstan laps at the toes of **Cromwell Historic Precinct**, a short street of restored old shopfronts, most of which would now be submerged had they not been dismantled and rebuilt on the water's edge. On a fine day you can spend a happy hour browsing the art, craft and gourmet food shops before retiring for a libation to *Armando's*.

Goldfields Mining Centre

SH6, 7km west of Cromwell • Daily 9am–5pm; self-guided and guided tours $25 • ☎ 0800 111 038, ⓦ goldfieldsmining.co.nz

A footbridge across the Kawarau River accesses the **Goldfields Mining Centre**, a former mine site scattered along a river terrace. Among the old huts, flumes and rusty machinery, the most engaging part of the centre is the Chinese Village, ironically constructed as a film set in the early 1990s. You can take a **self-guided tour** in an hour or so, but it is far more informative to join the one-hour **guided tour** on which you get to handle some large gold nuggets, see a stamper battery cranked up using a water-powered Pelton wheel and try your hand at extracting a flake or two.

The site is also home to the *Wild Earth* restaurant and wine tasting.

Highlands Motorsport Park

Corner of SH6 and Sandflat Rd, 3km southeast of Cromwell • Daily: summer 8am–6pm; winter 9am–5.30pm • Go karts $45, Fastlaps $295, Ferrari $179 • ☎ 03 445 4052, ⓦ highlands.co.nz • National Motorsport Museum Daily 10am–5pm • $25

With no real motorsport tradition it was a bit of a surprise when, in 2013, the town opened a **motor racing circuit** with aspirations to host the New Zealand Grand Prix sometime in the future. But mostly the two tracks are a playground for those with a need for speed. There's everything from self-drive go karts to the chance to take a spin in a race-spec Ferrari 488 or even an Aston Martin Vulcan.

There's also a small **motorsport museum** with plenty of coverage of Kiwi legends Bruce McLaren (founder of F1 team McLaren) and 1967 F1 champion Denny Hulme. There are usually a couple of newer McLarens on display along with racers through the years in all sorts of shapes and forms.

ARRIVAL AND DEPARTURE   **CROMWELL**

By bus Cromwell acts as a hub for InterCity/Newmans, Ritches, Atomic, NakedBus and Catch-A-Bus, all stopping centrally on Lode Lane right by The Mall. You may well have to change buses here. Trail Journeys does a daily run to Dunedin via Middlemarch (Nov–March).

Destinations Alexandra (7 daily; 30min); Dunedin (9 daily; 3hr 30min); Lawrence (6 daily; 2hr); Middlemarch (1 daily; 2hr); Queenstown (10 daily; 1hr); Wanaka (6 daily; 45min).

INFORMATION AND ACTIVITIES

Information i-SITE, 2d The Mall (daily: 26 Dec–17 April 9am–7pm; 18 April–24 Dec 9am–5pm; ☎ 03 261 7999, ⓦ cromwell.org.nz). The region's main visitor centre provides the 4 *Barrels Walking Wine Trail* leaflet among loads of other brochures on the area, and contains a small museum packed with gold-mining memorabilia. Look out for the DOC's *Alexandria and Cromwell Tracks* brochure, also downloadable from the DOC website.

Roaring Wine Tours ☎ 03 398 7887, ⓦ roaringtours. co.nz. Led by a Court of Master Sommelier, these fantastic excursions take in up to six of Central Otago's best boutique wineries, some of which are not generally open to the public. Also offers a beer-tasting day trip with lunch ($215), with pick-ups for all tours available in Alexandra, Cromwell, Wanaka and Queenstown. Half-day $100; full day including lunch from $185.

11

ACCOMMODATION

★ **Burn Cottage Retreat** 168 Burn Cottage Rd, 3km north of town ☎ 03 445 3050, ⓦ burncottageretreat. co.nz. Three immaculate, high-standard self-contained cottages, peacefully set surrounded by vineyards and a stunning hosta garden. Cottages have sunny decks with barbecue and there's always a bowl of walnuts from the delightful owners' trees. Superb breakfast hampers cost $32, or $36 with fresh eggs. Cottages **$245**

Colonial Manor Motel 14 Barry Ave ☎ 03 445 0184, ⓦ colonialmanor.co.nz. You'll be well looked after at this clean and welcoming motel roughly midway between the town centre and the historic precinct. Good range of rooms including spa suites ($175). **$135**

Cromwell Backpackers 33 The Mall ☎ 03 445 1378. Set in a former medical centre, this super-clean small hostel is conveniently located for buses, restaurants and the 4 Barrels Walking Wine Trail. Towels, tea and coffee are included, and there's a New World supermarket two blocks west. Dorms **$34**, doubles **$87**

Cromwell Top 10 Holiday Park 1 Alpha St ☎ 0800 107 275, ⓦ cromwellholidaypark.co.nz. Large, quality campsite on the edge of town with a range of en-suite cabins ($115) and motel units ($150). Facilities include a hot tub, a TV room and a kids' playground with jumping pillow. Camping per site **$42**, cabins **$75**

Lowburn Freedom Camping SH6, 4km north of Cromwell. Large lakeside gravel parking area with toilets where freedom camping is allowed for up to three nights. **Free**

EATING AND DRINKING

Amigos 50 The Mall ☎ 03 445 8263, ⓦ amigosmexicangrill.co.nz. The tasty soft-shell tacos are a bargain at $5 each if ordered before 6pm ($7–8 each after 6pm), though there are plenty of other Mexican favourites to tuck into (mains $18–28). Daily 11am–10.30pm or later.

Armando's Italian Kitchen 71 Melmore Tce, Old Cromwell Town ☎ 03 445 0303, ⓦ armandoskitchen. com. Thin-crust pizza ($22–25), risottos and delicious gelato combine with Kiwi café staples in this casual joint overlooking the lake. Mon–Thurs & Sun 9am–4.30pm, Fri & Sat 9am–8pm.

Freeway Orchard 166 State Hwy 8b ☎ 03 445 1500, ⓦ freewayorchard.co.nz. Of the good handful of fruit stalls that encircle Cromwell, this is a top option for those who have a soft spot for preserves, as the popular Provisions of Otago shares the premises. Stock up on chutneys, salsas and fresh and dried fruit, the former blended to make wonderful fruit ice creams. Daily 8am–5pm or later.

Grain & Seed 71 Melmore Terrace, Old Cromwell Town ☎ 03 445 1077. Occupying a beautifully reconstructed 1870s seed and grain store, this cosy café is a top spot for coffee and cake, or a light breakfast (bacon butty $10) or sandwich (salmon "sammie"; $13). Daily 9am–4pm.

★ **Wild Earth Restaurant** Goldfields Mining Centre ☎ 03 445 4841. Stroll over the bridge across the Kawarau River to access this tasting room for top-quality Wild Earth wines, particularly Pinot Noir ($10 for five tastes). Wine-matched meals cooked in old French oak Pinot Noir barrels are served on the grass overlooking the river. Plump for five share plates cooked in a wine barrel barbecue called a stoaker ($85 for two) or opt for a single such as the stoaker-glazed pork ribs ($25.50). Cellar door daily 10am–5pm; restaurant until 6pm.

Bannockburn

There are remote clusters of cottage foundations and sluicings all over Central Otago, and dedicated ruin hounds can poke around the detritus in places such as the **Nevis Valley** and **Bendigo** (ask locally), but the most extensive workings are found at **BANNOCKBURN**, a scattered hamlet 9km southwest of Cromwell that's now more famous for its **wineries**; founded in the early 1990s, they have quickly established themselves as some of New Zealand's best. Almost a dozen are open for tasting; call in advance if you're visiting in winter.

Bannockburn Sluicings

Felton Rd • Open access • Free

Download the *Banockburn Sluicings Track* leaflet from the DOC website and make for the **Bannockburn Sluicings**, a tortured landscape that was once home to two thousand people, washing away the land to reveal the gold-rich seams below. Interpretive signs punctuate a ninety-minute **self-guided trail** that starts 1500m along Felton Road and weaves up to Stewart Town, home to dilapidated mud-brick huts and ageing pear and apricot trees.

ALL HAIL TO PINOT NOIR – THE CENTRAL OTAGO WINE STORY

It is only since the 1980s that **grapes** have been grown commercially in Central Otago, one of the world's most southerly wine-growing regions. The vineyards lie close to the 45th parallel, and a continental climate of hot dry summers, long cold winters and some of the largest daily temperature variations in New Zealand makes for tough growing conditions. This results in low yields, forcing wineries to go for quality boutique wines sold at prices which seem high (mostly $25–40) until you taste them.

The steep schist and gravel slopes on the southern banks of the Kawarau River were recognized as potential sites for vineyards as early as 1864, when French miner **Jean Désiré Feraud**, bored of his gold claim at Frenchman's Point near Alexandra, planted grapes from cuttings brought over from Australia. His wines won awards, but by the early 1880s he'd decamped to Dunedin. No more grapes were grown until 1975, when the owners of *Rippon Vineyard* planted some experimental vineyards near Wanaka (see page 619). It was another six years before the Kawarau Gorge was recognized as ideally suited to the cultivation of Pinot Gris, Riesling and particularly **Pinot Noir grapes**, with Alan Brady releasing the first commercial wines from *Gibbston Valley Winery* in 1987. Since then, free-draining river terraces with good sun and a bit of a slope to drain off the winter chill air have been exploited throughout the region. Local winemakers have garnered shelves full of trophies, especially for the elegant, fruit-driven Pinot Noirs which make up the bulk of production. Still, volumes are low with the whole Otago region only producing a tiny 2.4 percent of the country's output.

Dozens of cellar doors showcase the goods, all explained on the free and widely available *Central Otago Wine Map* (Ⓦ centralotagopinot.co.nz). You can drive to most of them, but you'll appreciate the experience a lot more if you join one of the wine tours that depart from Queenstown or Cromwell.

11

EATING AND DRINKING

BANNOCKBURN

Black Rabbit Kitchen & Bar 430a Bannockburn Rd ☎ 03 445 1553, Ⓦ facebook.com/black-rabbit-kitchen-bar. Set in a corrugated iron shed formerly known as *The Kitchen*, the *Rabbit* is a top spot for an Allpress coffee, or a hearty brunch or pub-style lunch. Stays open for dinner on the weekend. Mon–Thurs & Sun 8am–5pm, Fri & Sat 8am–late.

Carrick 247 Cairnmuir Rd ☎ 03 445 3480, Ⓦ carrick.co.nz. Fully organic winery overlooking Bannockburn Inlet that's good for tastings of its excellent wines ($5 for five) or lunch of Otago lamb cutlets with aubergine, pearl couscous, summer greens, lemon thyme and harissa ($38). Expect sophisticated Pinot Noir, and estate-grown Chardonnay, Riesling, Rose, Pinot Gris and even (unusually this far south) Sauvignon Blanc. Daily restaurant and cellar door 11am–5pm.

★ **Mt Difficulty Winery Restaurant** 73 Felton Rd ☎ 03 445 3445, Ⓦ mtdifficulty.nz. Local produce shines in dishes such as Manuka-smoked wild Fiordland venison strip loin with heirloom carrots, snow peas, balsamic roasted baby onions, almond puree and Pinot Noir, raspberry and balsamic vinegar glaze ($44) at this wonderful hillside restaurant, which also does a roaring trade in gourmet platters ($59.50 for two people). Naturally, all dishes can be wine-matched. If you only have time for a tasting, you can sample five for just $2 (bookings recommended). Daily restaurant noon–4pm, cellar door 10.30am–4.30pm, until 5.30pm Jan–Easter.

Felton Road Felton Rd ☎ 03 445 0885, Ⓦ feltonroad. com. There's no food at this cellar door overlooking the vines, just free tastings of five truly excellent wines. Tastings are by small-group tour on weekdays by appointment (usually two tours daily); the experience aimed at more dedicated wine drinkers (allow 2hr).

Clyde

SH8 cuts southeast from Cromwell through 20km of the bleak and windswept **Cromwell Gorge**, hugging the banks of Lake Dunstan to pretty and peaceful **CLYDE**. With several good places to stay and eat, this small former gold town makes a great base for forays around the region and on to the Otago Central Rail Trail.

Since the mid-1980s, Clyde has been dominated by the giant grey hydroelectric **Clyde Dam**, 1km north of town, which generates five percent of New Zealand's power and provides water for irrigation. Initially controversial, the dam is nevertheless considered something of an engineering marvel, with special "slip joints" providing the dam wall with flexibility in case of earthquakes.

Clyde Museum and the Herb Factory Museum

5 Blyth St and 10 Fache St • Both Sept–April Tues–Sun 2–4pm • Donation

Clyde's original 1864 stone courthouse is flanked by the **Clyde Museum**, worth a peek for its intriguing coverage of Clyde's botched Great Gold Robbery of 1870 when one George Rennie tried to make off with £13,000 in bullion and banknotes.

A couple of streets away, the **Herb Factory Museum** was established in the 1930s as New Zealand's first, and thrived by making use of the common thyme that still grows wild in abundance hereabouts.

ARRIVAL AND DEPARTURE   CLYDE

By bus Buses stop in Clyde on demand, pulling up on Sunderland St, which is where you'll find many of the town's accommodation, restaurants and amenities. Trail Journeys' Catch-a-Bus (☎0800 030 381, ⓦtrailjourneys.

co.nz) runs a daily return service from Dunedin to Cromwell via Middlemarch, Ranfurly, Alexandra, Clyde. Bags and bikes costs extra.

ACCOMMODATION

★ **Dunstan House** 29 Sunderland St ☎03 449 2295, ⓦdunstanhouse.co.nz. Comfy B&B in a former stagecoach stop with bags of character. Rooms are imaginatively decorated (half en suite at $190 and some with claw-foot bath), some opening out onto a wraparound veranda on the first floor. There's plenty of bike storage, a piano in the lounge, and a lovely buffet breakfast with home-made preserves and stewed fruits. $130

Hartley Arms 25 Sutherland St ☎03 449 270, ⓦhartleyarms.co.nz. Clyde's cheapest rooms with just one double, one twin, and one four-share room with queen and two bunks all sharing bathroom, laundry and cooking

facilities. Friendly and informative hosts. Closed July & Aug. Per person including continental breakfast $50

★ **Olivers** 34 Sunderland St ☎03 449 2600 & ☎0800 131 070, ⓦoliverscentralotago.co.nz. Don't pass up the opportunity to stay in this gorgeous eleven-room reworking of a former homestead right in the heart of town. Five of the rooms are in the former stables, which open out into a central courtyard, and all are completely different – schist wall, half-tester bed, claw-foot bath – while maintaining the same balance of modern comfort with period style. The five spacious premium rooms ($425) are especially gorgeous. Superb breakfast included. $235

EATING AND ENTERTAINMENT

The Bank Café 31 Sunderland St ☎03 449 2955. Streetside tables catch the morning sun at this central café, offering great coffee, eggs Benedict ($15.50), a good veggie burger ($14.50) and a friendly smile. Daily 9am–4pm.

Clyde Cinema 6a Naylor St ☎03 449 2379, ⓦclydecinema.co.nz. Sink into leather seats with a glass of wine for the latest mainstream and independent releases. Tickets $16.50.

★ **Olivers** 34 Sunderland St ☎03 449 2805, ⓦoliverscentralotago.co.nz. The former miners provisions store backing onto *Olivers* guesthouse has been beautifully transformed into a smart restaurant with interconnected casual bakery-cafe (*The Merchant of Clyde*) and brew-bar (*Victoria Store Brewery*). Bookings are highly recommended for dinner, which may see you feasting on the likes of pulled beef and mushroom ragu with papardelle, rocket, crispy

capers and pecorino ($26), with rhubarb crème brûlée for dessert ($16). Daily noon–2pm & 6pm–late.

Paulina's 6 Naylor St ☎03 449 3236, ⓦpaulinasrestaurant.co.nz. Grab a red leather booth and sample local produce with a South American twist at this central resto-bar, from quinoa salad with prawns, chorizo, corn, avocado, tomato and beans ($22) to wood-roasted half peri-peri chicken with corn, pineapple, feta and coriander salsa with hand-cut fries ($39). A short bar menu is served from 3–5pm. Daily noon–late.

Post Office Café & Bar 2 Blyth St ☎03 449 2488, ⓦpostofficecafeclyde.co.nz. This 1865 former post office has a fantastic beer garden, but it's also a good spot for a good-value feed, with dishes ranging from nachos ($12.50) to home-made pies with salad and fries ($18) to pan-fried Manuherikia salmon ($31). Daily 10am–10pm or later.

Alexandra

ALEXANDRA (affectionately known as Alex), 10km southeast of Clyde, sprang up during the 1862 gold rush, and flourished for four years before turning into a quiet, prosperous, service town for the fruit growers of Central Otago. Throughout the summer you'll find fruit stalls selling some delectable apricots, peaches and nectarines, and in December and January some of the world's finest cherries. While central Alex isn't particularly atmospheric, it has a clutch of excellent wineries on its doorstep including Kiwi actor Sam Neill's *Two Paddocks*, which unfortunately lacks a cellar door.

Central Stories
21 Centennial Ave · Daily 10am–4pm · Donation · ☎ 03 448 6230, �ⓦ centralstories.com

A huge water wheel marks the fascinating **Central Stories**, a social and natural history museum covering everything from geology to viticulture in the world's southernmost wine region. Learn about the heart-rending mystery of James Horn, whose father's deathbed letter will bring a lump to your throat, and the sorry tale of the rabbits, introduced into the area in 1909, which did what rabbits do – so well that they became a menace throughout the South Island. Despite criticism from animal welfare experts, the town holds an **Easter Bunny Hunt** every year in an effort to combat the problem.

ARRIVAL AND DEPARTURE   ALEXANDRA

By bus Atomic, InterCity and NakedBus all stop outside the i-SITE. Catch-A-Bus picks up wherever you want. Destinations Dunedin (6 daily; 3hr); Lawrence (6 daily; 1hr 15min); Queenstown (6 daily; 1hr 30min); Ranfurly (1 daily; 1hr).

INFORMATION AND ACTIVITIES

Information i-SITE, 21 Centennial Ave in Central Stories (daily: Nov–Easter 9am–6pm; Easter–Oct 9am–5pm; ☎ 03 448 9515, ⓦ centralotagonz.com).

Altitude Bikes 88 Centennial Ave ☎ 03 448 8917, ⓦ altitudebikes.co.nz. An abundance of treeless hills makes Alex a good base for mountain biking. Altitude Bikes rent mountain bikes from $40/day to get you out on the singletrack, and staff have the expertise for getting you on the Otago Central Rail Trail (see page 634). They also run guided single-track tours requiring intermediate skills or better: probably the best is the half-day Knobby Range ($149, including bike rental) across high-country tussock and down steep rocky trails with a ride to the start minimizing the amount of climbing. Mon–Fri 8.30am–5.30pm, Sat 9am–1pm.

ACCOMMODATION

Alexandra Lookout B&B 16 Lookout Drive ☎ 027 223 0767, ⓦ alexandra-lookout-bnb.co.nz. Friendly three-room B&B on the eastern bank of the Manuherikia River with mountain views and more character than most central hotels. Shared kitchen facilities. $220

Asure Avenue Motel 117 Centennial Ave ☎ 0800 758 899, ⓦ avenue-motel.co.nz Comfortable and central self-contained units with all the mod cons; some with spa bath. Studios $142, two-bedroom units $165

Marj's Place 5 Theyers St ☎ 03 448 7098, ⓦ marjsplace.co.nz. Marj is the mother hen at this welcoming hostel-cum-homestay in three houses on a quiet street. Homestay guests share a bathroom but get robes, a sauna and a spa bath plus access to a well-equipped kitchen with dishwasher. Most backpackers stay across the road, and there are good discounts for those looking to stay seven days or longer. Dorms $30, doubles $90

EATING AND DRINKING

Black Ridge 76 Conroys Rd ☎ 03 449 2059, ⓦ blackridge.co.nz. One of Central Otago's oldest wine producers, Black Ridge is dramatically set on a rocky ridge (hence the name) with lovely views across the vineyards. Tastings ($10) include an excellent rosé. Made with Pinot Noir grapes, rosés are a common feature of Central Otago wineries, and typically cost a lot less than the average bottle of Pinot Noir. Cellar door Mon–Fri 11am–5pm, Sat & Sun noon–5pm.

★ **Como Villa** 266 Earnscleugh Rd ☎ 03 449 2265, ⓦ comovilla.co.nz. Arguably Central Otago's most atmospheric boutique winery, *Como Villa* conducts tastings in the property's original 1865 stone house, now packed to the rafters with antiques, some found in a small underground cellar the current owners discovered in the 1980s, and painstakingly restored. Here you can taste five wines for $1 a pop, all aged for at least three years. Cellar door Nov–April daily 11am–5pm; May–Oct Sat & Sun 11am–5pm.

★ **Courthouse Café** 8 Centennial Ave ☎ 03 448 7818, ⓦ packingshedcompany.com. Licensed café in (and on the sunny lawns around) Alex's 1878 former courthouse, serving delicious home-baked food such as honey chicken salad with crispy noodles, macadamia

OTAGO CENTRAL RAIL TRAIL

One of the finest ways to explore the Maniototo is to **cycle** the Otago Central Rail Trail (OCRT), a largely flat 152km route from Clyde to Middlemarch that passes through all the main towns except for St Bathans and Naseby. It follows the hard-packed gravel trackbed of the former **Otago Central Branch railway line** and includes modified rail bridges and viaducts (several spanning over 100m), beautiful valleys and long agricultural plains.

Passenger trains ran through the Maniototo until 1990, a continuation of what is now the Taieri Gorge Railway (see page 580) but it wasn't until early 2000 that the trail opened, galvanizing a dying region. All sorts of accommodation has sprung up to cater to bikers' needs. Pubs and cafés located where the trail crosses roads aren't shy to advertise the opportunity to take a break.

The trail takes most people three to four days and combining the ride with the **Taieri Gorge Railway** makes a great way to travel between Clyde and Dunedin.

If you're just out to pick the **highlights**, aim for a couple of 10km stretches, both with tunnels, viaducts and interesting rock formations: Lauder–Auripo in the northern section, and Daisybank–Hyde in the east. A torch is handy for the tunnels.

The widely available *Otago Central Rail Trail* leaflet (free) outlines the route and elevation profile. The most comprehensive information on the web is at ⓦotagocentralrailtrail.co.nz, though a couple of commercial sites offer good practical information; try ⓦotagorailtrail.co.nz and ⓦrailtrail.co.nz.

BIKE RENTAL AND PACKAGES

Altitude Bikes ☎03 448 8917, ⓦaltitudebikes.co.nz. Alexandra-based operator offering a one-day, 47km OCRT highlights package with transport and bike rental ($89), a fully supported four-day package including B&B accommodation ($765) and all manner of freedom ride, bike rental and customized packages.

Bike It Now! 25 Holloway St, Clyde ☎0800 245 366, ⓦbikeitnow.co.nz. Offers top-quality bikes (from $40/half-day and $50/full-day) for use on guided and self-guided trips on all the local trails. Its three-day OCRT package with bike, transport and simple accommodation ($500) can be upgraded to more comfy digs ($645) and includes daily luggage transfers. The five-night variation costs from $760.

Cycle Surgery SH87 ☎0800 292 534, ⓦcyclesurgery.co.nz. Middlemarch-based company offering just about everything you might want to do from upright, step-through unisex bike rental ($40/day; tandems $70; panniers $5) and minibus shuttles to custom packages including Taieri Gorge Railway tickets, accommodation, bag transfers and meals. They cater for a wide range of budgets.

Not a Rail Trail ☎0800 429 253, ⓦnotarailtrail.co.nz. Guided trip specialist offering a four-day Clutha Gold/Roxburgh Gorge combo with a jetboat transfer between the centre of the gorge ($1475) including return transfers to Queenstown.

Trail Journeys ☎0800 030 381, ⓦtrailjourneys.co.nz. A big player on the OCRT scene, this Clyde-based operator uses Avanti bikes specially designed for the trail, and has a depot in Middlemarch. It offers bike rental and shuttle transport but specialize in itinerary planning, piecing together accommodation, bag transport and the like.

nuts and avocado ($23) plus a bunch of fresh salads, smoothies, cakes and coffee. Mon–Fri 6.30am–4.30pm, Sat 8.30am–4pm.

Tin Goose Café 22 Centennial Ave ☎03 448 5995, ⓦfacebook.com/thetingoosecafealexandra. Opposite the i-SITE, the *Goose* is handy for coffee and cake or a light lunch along the OCRT. Daily 6am–5pm.

Roxburgh

The quiet former gold town of **Roxburgh**, 40km south of Alexandra, sits hemmed in by vast orchards that yield bountiful crops of peaches, apricots, apples, raspberries and strawberries, all harvested by an annual influx of seasonal pickers. The season's surplus is sold from a phalanx of roadside stalls from early December through to May. Unless you're hungry, there's not a lot else to keep you here.

EATING

Faigan's Café and Store 1685 Teviot Rd, Millers Flat ☎ 021 206 4997, ⊚ facebook.com/faiganscafeandstore. Seventeen kilometres south of Roxburgh in the tiny riverside town of Millers Flat, friendly *Faigan's* is a great little Clutha Gold Trail pit stop. Drop in for a coffee or tuck into a *Faigan's* hamburger with raspberry and mint dressing ($19) or a venison and kumara pie with red wine jus ($20). There's a little provisions store in the back. Tues–Sun 8am–4pm.

Jimmy's Pies 143 Scotland St ☎ 03 446 9012, ⊚ jimmyspies.co.nz. Made here since 1960, the perfectly flaky pies are sold all over the South Island. Also sells an array of baked treats. Mon–Fri 7.30am–5pm.

Lawrence

From Roxburgh, SH8 runs 60km southeast to **LAWRENCE**, Otago's original 1861 gold town where, in May 1861, Australian Gabriel Read struck pay dirt. Twelve thousand gold-seekers scrambled to try their luck in the gold-rich Gabriel's Gully but the boom was over in barely a year. Its legacy is a sleepy farming town of barely 550 souls and a smattering of Victorian buildings, hastily constructed in a variety of styles. A few have now been converted into **galleries**, while another recently became a fancy chocolate shop (and worthy pit stop), the **Lawrence Mint**.

11

Gabriel's Gully Historic Reserve

3.5km north along Gabriel's Gully Rd • Open access • Free

Gabriel's Gully Road leads 3.5km north of Lawrence to **Gabriel's Gully Historic Reserve**, where an undulating 2.4km **walking loop** lined with information panels explaining the old workings should take you an hour or so to tramp. Amid the tailings, look out for the remnants of numerous water races, a raceman's hut site, a stamper battery, a mining tunnel and a powder magazine dotted around the gully.

ARRIVAL AND INFORMATION — LAWRENCE

By bus InterCity, Atomic and NakedBus all stop in the centre of town.

Destinations Alexandra (4 daily; 1hr 15min); Cromwell (6 daily; 2hr); Dunedin (6 daily; 1hr 20min).

Tourist information Lawrence Information Centre and Museum, 17 Ross Place (daily: May–Sept 9.30am–3.30pm, Oct–April 9.30am–4.30pm; ☎ 03 485 9222, ⊚ lawrence.co.nz). A combined information centre and museum that brings something of the heady early gold-rush days to life through imaginative displays (suggested donation $2). Also has free wi-fi.

Omakau and Ophir

Heading northeast from Alexandra, you climb steadily onto the high-country plain. After 26km, turn down Ophir Bridge Road which crosses a historic little **suspension bridge** across the Manuherikia River and continues 1km to **Ophir**, the region's original gold town. It still has its imposing and operational 1886 **Post & Telegraph Office** (Mon–Fri 9am–noon). **Omakau**, 2km to the north, has basic services.

ACCOMMODATION AND EATING — OMAKAU AND OPHIR

Chatto Creek Tavern 1544 SH85, 10km southwest of Omakau ☎ 03 447 3710, ⊚ chattocreektavern.co.nz. Classic Rail Trail stop with two comfortable restored rooms and a six-bed bunkroom in a 1886 schist pub. Lots of memorabilia and quality pub meals such as Stewart Island blue cod with chips and salad ($35) or crumbed chicken burger with Brie and apricot relish ($20). Rates include breakfast. Dorms $60, doubles $130

Pitches Store 45 Swindon St, Ophir ☎ 03 447 3240, ⊚ pitches-store.co.nz. This former general merchants' building now houses some of the classiest accommodation in the Maniototo, the rough-hewn schist walls contrasting nicely with the sophisticated modern decor. Out front, the café/restaurant offers an imaginative seasonal menu a few steps above most of what's available locally – think confit duck and prune rillettes with elderflower jelly and pickled baby vegetables ($18) followed by rabbit and Ophir thyme pie with black pudding, duck fat potatoes and Pinot Noir glaze ($35). Restaurant Nov–April daily 10am–9pm; May to early June & early Aug to Oct Mon & Thurs–Sun 10am–9pm. $295

GRAHAME SYDNEY

Many New Zealanders only know the Maniototo through the works of Dunedin-born Realist painter **Grahame Sydney** (W grahamesydney.com), who spends much of his time in the region. His broad, big-sky landscapes of goods sheds amid parched fields and letterboxes at lonely crossroads are universally accessible, and instantly recognizable to anyone visiting the region.

Prints and postcards of his work are found throughout the Maniototo and beyond, and originals hang in most of the country's major galleries. At first glance many of the works are unemotional renditions, but reflection reveals great poignancy. As he has said, "I'm the long stare, not the quick glimpse".

Oturehura

The main SH85 avoids the Ida Valley, but it is worth turning off at Omakau and detouring past a couple of the Maniototo's most interesting historical sights at Oturehura.

Hayes Engineering Works

Hayes Rd, Oturehua • Sept–May daily 10am–5pm • $12; guided tour $15; check website for "operating days" when guided tours are $20 • ☎ 03 444 5801, W hayesengineering.co.nz

All over the world, wire fences are still tensioned by parallel wire strainers designed by Ernest Hayes in 1902 at the **Hayes Engineering Works**, a site based around a frozen-in-time corrugated-iron workshop. Everything is as it was in 1952 when the company decamped to Christchurch – in the gloom, cutters and drill presses are linked by belts and pulleys to overhead shafts originally driven by wind, then hydro power and now the power-takeoff from an ancient tractor (still fired up on operating days).

Alongside the workshop stands the original 1890 mud-brick **cottage** (now a small museum and café) Ernest shared with his wife, Hannah. An integral part of the company, she set off on lengthy sales trips on her bicycle wearing an ankle-length skirt.

Next door is the somewhat idiosyncratic house they designed and built, decked out precisely as it was in the 1920s. They were engineers, not carpenters, so broken doors are fixed with metal bracing and one doorjamb was fitted with steel springs to prevent the door slamming shut.

Gilchrist's General Store

3353 Ida Valley Rd, Oturehua • Mon–Fri 7.30am–5pm, Sat 8am–4pm & Sun 10am–4pm • Free • ☎ 03 444 5808

Poke your head in to this quirky working museum, a still-operational 1929 grocery shop and post office lined with the original wooden shelving laden with ancient (and new) groceries. The place was once the hub of the valley, with twelve staff, but saw hard times and almost closed before being revived. Buy a pie, browse the books or just wander in for a chat.

ACCOMMODATION AND EATING   **OTUREHURA**

Oturehua Railway Hotel 3352 Ida Valley Rd ☎ 03 444 5856, W oturehuatavern.co.nz. Beside the OCRT, the historic inn serves pub grub (try the "big bike burger"; $22), Hummingbird coffee and craft brews in its sunny beer garden daily from 10.30am. Behind the main building, there's an en-suite unit with four single beds. $60 per person

St Bathans

Gallery ☎ 022 0776 6026, W stbathansgallery.co.nz

The picturesque former gold town of **ST BATHANS** is out on a limb 80km north of Alexandra and accessed 17km along St Bathans Loop Road from Becks. St Bathans boomed in 1863, but when the gold ran out in the 1930s everything went with it. These days it's virtually a ghost town, with a handful of residents and an attractive straggle of ancient buildings along the single road. The former post office exhibits photography, prints and engraving as **St Bathan's Gallery.**

Blue Lake

The few remaining dwellings overlook the striking **Blue Lake** where mineral-rich water has flooded a crater left by the merciless sluicing of Kildare Hill, once 120m high but now entirely washed away. A short track leads from the *Vulcan* to a vantage point over the azure waters, now used for swimming and boating.

ACCOMMODATION AND EATING	ST BATHANS
St Bathans Domain campsite Loop Rd, 1.3km northwest of St Bathans. Simple DOC site with water and toilets. <u>Free</u> **St Bathan's Jail and Constables Cottage** Loop Rd ☎ 0800 555 016, ⊕ stbathansnz.co.nz. Choose from a three-bedroom 1864 house with modern bathroom and kitchen and lovely gardens overlooking the Blue Lake, or a self-contained unit just behind with simple continental breakfast included.	Add $30 for each extra adult. Cottage <u>$220</u>, jail <u>$145</u> **Vulcan Hotel** Loop Rd ☎ 03 447 3629. Atmospheric 1882 hotel where local farmers and visitors prop up the wooden bar. Stop in for scones with jam and cream or book ahead for a home-style dinner in the dining room. You can also stay, though the nicest room (#1) is reputed to be haunted. Service can be hit and miss. Bar and restaurant daily 11am–9pm. <u>$120</u>

11

Naseby

The small settlement of **NASEBY**, 25km east of St Bathans and 9km off SH85, clings to the Maniototo some 600m above sea level. At its 4000-strong peak in 1865, Naseby was the largest gold-mining town hereabouts, but today numbers have dropped to around 100 huddled in a collection of small houses (many of them originally built of sun-dried mud brick by miners), with a shop, a garage, a couple of pubs, a café and a campsite.

Early Settlers Museum and Jubilee Museum

Dec–April Wed–Sun 1.30–3.30pm; donation

The story of the town and wider region is told through the tiny **Maniototo Early Settlers Museum**, corner of Earne and Leven streets, which is packed with black-and-white photos of past residents and also contains a small collection of items left by Chinese miners. Across the street, the **Jubilee Museum** houses the remains of an old watchmaker's shop together with displays on the local gold rush of the 1860s and 1870s.

INFORMATION AND ACTIVITIES	NASEBY
Information Naseby Information Centre, 16 Derwent St (Christmas to mid-Jan daily 10am–6pm; rest of year Mon & Fri Sun 11am–2pm, Sat 11am–4pm; ☎ 03 444 9961, ⊕ nasebyinfo.org.nz). Located in the former post office, this volunteer-run place has the *A Walk Through History* map of town and walking maps of the forest. **One Tree Hill Track** The visitor centre has maps showing three local walks, the best being this one (1600m; 1hr return), which starts on Brooms Street in town and snakes uphill along the eastern side of Hogburn Gully, past dramatic honey-coloured cliffs entirely carved by water.	**Mountain biking** If you've got your own wheels pick up a map from the information centre and head into the forest, threaded with lots of great single-track, mostly undulating without seriously steep climbs. **Naseby Curling International** 1057 Channel Rd ☎ 03 444 9878, ⊕ curling.co.nz. Naseby is New Zealand's home of curling. This occasionally takes place outside on cold winter days but most activity is at this indoor year-round venue. On the hill behind it lies the southern hemisphere's first luge track (daily: mid-June to late Aug; $35). Daily: Dec–April 9am–7.30pm; May–Nov 10am–5pm.

ACCOMMODATION AND EATING

Ancient Briton Hotel 16 Leven St ☎ 03 444 9992, ⊕ ancientbriton.co.nz. Classic Kiwi pub with a convivial bar, a sunny garden and excellent bar meals, including an award-winning roasted Provenance lamb shoulder with shallots, hummus, halloumi, roasted vegetables and a sweet sherry jus ($58 for two). The pub also doubles as the

Naseby Brewery producing porter, cider and fruit beers, and an annexe outside has pleasant rooms. $105

Black Forest Café 7 Derwent St ☎03 444 9820. Cosy café with good coffee and muffins, great cheese scones and light meals such as frittata ($10). Evening meals by arrangement. 9am–4pm; closed Tues.

Larchview Holiday Park 8 Swimming Dam Rd ☎03 444 9904, ⓦ larchviewholidaypark.co.nz. Pretty and tranquil forest campsite a 5min walk from town and across the road from the popular swimming dam complete with springboard. Also has two self-contained cottages ($100). Coin showers and no wi-fi. Camping $18, cabins $55

Naseby Lodge Corner Derwent and Oughter sts ☎0800 627 329, ⓦ nasebylodge.co.nz. A handful of modern

mud-brick and corrugated-iron one- and two-bedroom self-contained units cluster around the straw bale-built 2000ft restaurant which serves quality pub-style meals (from steak and veg to fish of the day) for around $30. Lodge and restaurant nightly Dec–April, by prior arrangement rest of year. $170

Old Doctors Residence 58 Derwent St ☎03 444 8358, ⓦ olddoctorsresidence.co.nz. Beautifully appointed B&B accommodation is in the mud-brick former dairy or a suite comprising the former doctor's surgery and the waiting room. There's a cosy guest lounge, a fantastic cooked breakfast, and a delightful included afternoon tea. $280

Dansey's Pass

The gravel Kyeburn Diggings Road runs east out of Naseby 16km to the *Dansey's Pass Coach Inn*. From here, the 50km north to Duntroon on SH83 is narrow, winding and unsuitable for medium and large campervans. But the route is barren and beautiful, one of the last untouched high-country passes with open hillsides covered in tussock. It is sometimes closed by snow between June and September: check in Naseby before setting out.

Old gold workings are visible from the roadside, where water-jets from sluices have distorted the schist and tussock landscape, leaving rock dramatically exposed.

ACCOMMODATION   **DANSEY'S PASS**

★ **Dansey's Pass Coach Inn** 781 Kyeburn Diggings, 16km east of Naseby ☎03 444 9048, ⓦ danseyspass. co.nz. Charming wayside inn with a bit of Wild West feel that's the only relic of the once 2000-strong gold-rush community. It was built from local schist stone in 1862 (the stonemason was reputedly paid a pint of beer for each stone laid). Stop in for a brew on leather sofas around the fire, grab lunch, or stay for dinner of lamb backstrap with Moroccan chutney ($30) in the conservatory restaurant. They close early if things are quiet, so call ahead before making a special journey. The nineteen rooms (en suites cost $20 extra) bare Victorian styled. Daily 8am–10pm or later. $140

Ranfurly

Centennial Milk Bar Tues–Sun: 10am–3pm • $2 donation

RANFURLY is the largest settlement on the Maniototo, though that's not saying much. It has enjoyed a resurgence, thanks to being roughly midway along the rail trail and a somewhat contrived attempt to brand itself as New Zealand's **Rural Art Deco** centre. In truth, the only vaguely noteworthy building is the sleek cream-and-green-painted 1948 Centennial Milk Bar on Charlemont Street East, which now operates as an Art Deco furnishings store. The town goes all out to make the best of what it has, particularly during the **Rural Art Deco Weekend** at the end of February.

INFORMATION AND ACTIVITIES   **RANFURLY**

i-SITE 3 Charlemont St East (daily: late Dec to mid-April 9am– 5.30pm; mid-April to late Dec 9am–5pm; ☎03 444 1005, ⓦ centralotagonz.com). Visitor centre housed in the former train station which has a free audiovisual show on the region (screened in a mini-train carriage) and pictorial displays tracing the history of the town and the Otago Central Railway.

Real Dog Adventures 5 Bypass Rd ☎03 444 9952, ⓦ realdog.co.nz. Take a sled dog ride (on land or snow) with a team of well-cared-for Alaskan malamutes ($110; allow 3hr), or simply take a tour of the kennels ($30; 45min).

ACCOMMODATION AND EATING

Hawkdun Lodge 1 Bute St ☎0508 444 975, ⊛hawkdunlodge.co.nz. This smart, modern, central hotel offers studio and one-bedroom suites (including an interconnected family unit; $290) alongside a kitchen, cosy TV lounge and an indoor spa bath that can be used at no extra charge. Continental breakfast included. Studios $112, units $170

Komako 634 Waipiata–Naseby Rd, 3km south of town ☎03 444 9324, ⊛komako.net.nz. Peony garden (blooming Oct–Dec) with three gorgeous B&B cabins right by the Rail Trail and surrounded by great views. Accommodation and dinner deals ($100/person), which could be a gourmet barbecue or a roast. Doubles per person $65

Maniototo Cafe 1 Pery St ☎03 444 9023, ⊛maniototocafe.co.nz. Tasty smoothies, salads, wraps and baked treats are on offer at this central café, which prepares packed lunches ($14) and gourmet BBQ dinner packs ($28) to order. Closes an hour or so early on weekdays during winter. Mon–Fri 7am–6pm, Sat & Sun 8am–5pm.

Maniototo Lodge 3 Ranfurly–Patearoa Rd, 1km south of Ranfurly ☎03 444 9780, ⊛maniototolodge.co.nz.

Charming and welcoming B&B in a solid-brick former presbytery with three shared-bath guest rooms equipped with bathrobes. There's a full cooked breakfast, and a two-course dinner ($45) or cook-your-own-BBQ platter ($30) on request, and as much local advice as you need. $190

Old Post Office Backpackers 11 Pery St ☎03 444 9588, ⊛oldpobackpackers.co.nz. Clean, comfortable and well-run hostel sleeping twenty in a variety of doubles, twins and five-bed dorms. Continental breakfast ($11) available. Dorms available late-Oct to April, doubles available only to pre-booked groups June–Sept. Dorms $33, doubles $75

Ranfurly Holiday Park Corner of Reade and Pery sts ☎0800 726 387, ⊛ranfurlyholidaypark.co.nz. Relaxed, spacious and central campsite with pitches, powered sites, and cabins and motel units sleeping up to eight ($120). Camping per site $32, cabins $60

Ranfurly Lion Hotel 10 Charlemont St East ☎03 444 9140, ⊛ranfurlyhotel.co.nz. A decent hotel restaurant in Art Deco surroundings serving burgers, roasts and the like. Daily 7.30am–10pm.

Middlemarch

⊛middlemarch.co.nz

At Kyeburn, 15km east of Ranfurly, SH85 (locally known as "The Pigroot") heads for the coast over to Palmerston while SH87 branches south, slowly winding through the eastern Maniototo between the Rock and Pillar Range and the Taieri River. Fifty barren yet scenic kilometres south, you'll reach the tiny community of **MIDDLEMARCH**, at the end of the Rail Trail and the Friday- and Sunday-only terminus of the **Taieri Gorge Railway** (see page 580). There's not much to it, but a number of local farms provide B&B accommodation, mostly for rail trailers.

ACCOMMODATION AND EATING   MIDDLEMARCH

Annandale 1 Snow St ☎03 464 3131, ⊛annandalebnb.co.nz. Lovely, central B&B in a characterful villa with comfortable rooms, modern bathrooms (one with a bath) all surrounded by a well-kept garden. Home-made preserves star in the continental breakfast. $150

Kissing Gate Café 2 Swansea St (SH87) ☎03 464 3224, ⊛facebook.com/kissingg8cafe. Grab a coffee or a light lunch at this pretty café in a cute old wooden cottage and its surrounding garden. Mon–Thurs 8.30am–4pm, Fri, Sat & Sun 8.30am–5pm.

The Lodge 24 Conway St ☎027 228 4789, ✉thelodge@middlemarch.co.nz. Modest but comfortable B&B accommodation in a central old villa with continental breakfast included. Add $30 for en suite. $100

Middlemarch Holiday Park 26 Mold St ☎03 464 3776, ⊛middlemarchholidaypark.co.nz. Bikers are always welcome at this modest site on the outskirts of Middlemarch which also has two-bedroom motel units ($95). Camping $20, cabins $65

11

Fiordland and Southland

DOUBTFUL SOUND

Fiordland and Southland

For all New Zealand's grandeur, no other region matches the concentration of stupendous landscapes found in Fiordland and Southland. Most of the southwest falls within the 12,500-square-kilometre Fiordland National Park, a raw, heroic landscape that embraces New Zealand's two deepest lakes, its highest rainfall, fifteen hairline fiords and some of the world's rarest birds. Fiordland itself is anchored by the small town of Te Anau on the beautiful shores of Lake Te Anau, launchpad for one of New Zealand's true showstoppers – Milford Sound, though the popular Milford Track and more isolated fiords such as Doubtful Sound are equally awe-inspiring.

The southeast might seem tame by comparison, but traversing the Southern Scenic Route affords vast, empty vistas of high pastures, rugged coastline and small towns and countryside little changed since the nineteenth century. New Zealand's southernmost city is **Invercargill**, a springboard for **Bluff**, the country's oldest European settlement, and **Stewart Island**, one of New Zealand's great backcountry destinations (a fantastic place to spot kiwi in the wild). Relatively few visit New Zealand's third island, but those that do are rewarded by its extraordinary bird life, particularly in **Mason Bay** and on **Ulva Island**. Invercargill also make a good base for a journey along the **Catlins Coast** towards Dunedin, incorporating the iconic **Purakaunui Falls**, wacky **Lost Gypsy Gallery** and the haunting **Cathedral Caves**.

12

Fiordland

Many visitors end their once-in-a-lifetime trip to New Zealand in **Fiordland**, the most remote and spectacular of the country's landscapes, most of it protected within Fiordland National Park. **Milford Sound**, in particular, has become one of the world's most popular "bucket list" destinations, and despite the growing number of visitors has remained a truly mesmerizing place. Many day-trippers who fly in from Queenstown see little else, but a greater sense of remoteness is gained by driving there along the achingly scenic **Milford Road** from the lakeside town of **Te Anau**. Better still, hike the **Milford Track**, widely promoted as the "finest walk in the world", though others in the region – particularly the **Hollyford Track** and the **Kepler Track** – are equally strong contenders.

A second lakeside town, **Manapouri**, is the springboard for trips to the West Arm hydroelectric power station, **Doubtful Sound** and the isolated fiords to the south.

One persistent feature of Fiordland is the **rain**. Milford Sound is particularly favoured, being deluged with up to 7m of rainfall a year – one of the highest in the world. Fortunately the area's settlements are in a rain shadow and receive less than half the precipitation of the coast. In any case, Milford Sound is particularly beautiful when it's raining, with ribbons of water plunging from hanging valleys into the fiords where colonies of red and black coral grow and dolphins, fur seals and Fiordland crested penguins cavort.

GETTING AROUND

By bus Almost all of Fiordland's buses ply the corridor from Queenstown through Te Anau to Milford Sound: most are tour buses, stopping at scenic spots and regaling passengers with a jocular commentary; others are scheduled services that disgorge trampers at the trailheads. Unless you are very pushed for time don't be persuaded to visit Milford from Queenstown, as it is an arduous journey that will lessen the Milford Sound experience – it's much better to stay overnight in Milford or visit from Te Anau.

KIWI

Highlights

❶ Kepler Track Hike one of New Zealand's "Great Walks", encompassing tussock-covered ridges, alpine vistas, tranquil lakes and untouched beech forest. See page 649

❷ Milford Sound Experience this world-famous fiord on a cruise or a kayak, dwarfed by soaring cliffs and plunging waterfalls See page 654

❸ The Milford Track Brave the rain (and the sandflies) to see why this enchanting four-day tramp really is "the finest walk in the world". See page 659

❹ Doubtful Sound Soak up the scenic grandeur and flourishing wildlife on a cruise through this isolated and pristine fiord. See page 663

❺ Dig This Invercargill Nothing lets off steam like smashing something to smithereens behind the wheel of a bulldozer; in Invercargill you really can do it. See page 671

❻ Stewart Island One giant nature reserve, relaxed Rakiura is rich in birdlife, the best place to see wild kiwi and a magical spot to kayak. See page 675

❼ The Catlins Coast The southern tip of New Zealand is a sparsely populated region of majestic waterfalls, giant Cathedral Caves, Curio Bay's fossilized forest and plenty of penguins, seals and Hector's dolphins. See page 682

HIGHLIGHTS ARE MARKED ON THE MAP ON PAGE 644

Te Anau

Ringed by snowcapped peaks, the gateway town to Fiordland, **TE ANAU** (pronounced Teh AHN-ow), stretches along the shores of its eponymous lake, one of New Zealand's grandest and deepest. To the west, the lake's watery fingers claw deep into bush-cloaked mountains so remote that their most celebrated inhabitant, the **takahe**, was thought extinct for half a century.

FIORDLAND AND SOUTHLAND

HIGHLIGHTS

1. Kepler Track
2. Milford Sound
3. The Milford Track
4. Doubtful Sound
5. Dig This Invercargill
6. Stewart Island
7. The Catlins Coast

0   50
kilometres

The main way-station on the route to Milford Sound, Te Anau is an ideal base and recuperation spot for the region's numerous tramps, including several of the most famous and worthwhile in the country. Top of most people's list is the **Milford Track**, which starts at the head of the lake, while the **Kepler Track** (see page 649) starts closer to town.

Fiordland Cinema

7 The Lane • Daily 9am–8pm; 4–10 screenings daily • *Ata Whenua: Shadowland* $10; mainstream movies $15 • ☎ 03 249 8844, ⓦ fiordlandcinema.co.nz

Don't leave town without visiting the **Fiordland Cinema**, which presents the 32-minute *Ata Whenua: Shadowland*. Filmed mostly from a helicopter, it shows Fiordland at its majestic best throughout the seasons with wonderful cinematography, an original soundtrack and no ponderous voiceover. Pick of the scenes are the snow-tipped mountain summits rising up out of a sea of clouds, and dropping from a forested gully out over a perpendicular waterfall. Screenings are interspersed with a selection of mainstream movies, the chairs are big and comfy, and you can take your espresso, beer or wine in with you (the *Black Dog Bar* is part of the complex, see page 648).

Te Anau Bird Sanctuary

SH95 • Open access sunrise to sunset; takahe feeding daily: Oct–March 9.30am; April–Sept 10.30am • Free • ☎ 03 249 7924, ⓦ doc.govt.nz/teanaubirdsanctuary

At the **Te Anau Bird Sanctuary** (Punanga Manu o Te Anau), on the shores of Lake Te Anau, you can amble through the park-like setting, and glimpse some of New Zealand's rarest birds, most of which are injured or captive-bred. Look out for kaka (indigenous parrots), kereru (New Zealand pigeons) and tui, as well as introduced mallard ducks and Canadian geese. The largest enclosure belongs to turkey-sized takahe, once thought extinct and painstakingly protected by the Department of Conservation (DOC); they can be hard to spot among the tussocks – your best chance of seeing them is at the daily feeding session.

Te Anau Glowworm Caves

Daily tours: Nov–March 10.15am, 2pm, 3.15pm, 5.45pm, 4.30pm, 7pm, 8.15pm & 9.30pm; April–Sept 2pm, 7pm; 2hr 15min • $83–88 • ☎ 03 249 6000, ⓦ realjourneys.co.nz (buy tickets online or at the Real Journeys Visitor Centre, 85 Lakefront Drive)

If you're not planning to visit the more impressive underground attractions at North Island's Waitomo (see page 203), make time for **Te Anau Glowworm Caves**. The town's full Māori name, Te Ana-au, means "cave with a current of swirling water" and it was a search for the town's namesake which led to their rediscovery in 1948. The tour feels a little processed but includes a pretty cruise to the western side of Lake Te Anau from the jetty adjacent to the visitor centre. After perusing the information panels at the Cavern House, guides then lead you underground in small groups, spending thirty minutes walking through the Aurora cave system, followed by a short underground boat ride through a glittering glowworm-festooned cavern and past a couple of churning waterfalls.

ARRIVAL AND DEPARTURE

TE ANAU

By bus InterCity runs Queenstown–Te Anau–Milford and Te Anau–Gore–Balclutha–Dunedin routes daily. In summer (late Oct to April) Tracknet (☎ 0800 483262, ⓦ tracknet.net) run buses daily between Queenstown, Te Anau, Milford Sound and Invercargill, plus Kepler Track and Manapouri shuttles, which must be must be pre-booked (in winter buses run between Queenstown, Te Anau and Invercargill Mon–Fri only). InterCity buses pick up and drop off at Kiwi Country, 2 Miro St (aka "Miro Street Bus Stop"), while Tracknet also departs Miro St, the DOC visitor centre on Lakefront Drive and several hotels, including the YHA. Topline Tours (☎ 03 249 8059, ⓦ toplinetours.co.nz) serves the Kepler Track trailheads ($5–10) and Manapouri ($20) on demand year-round.

Destinations The Divide, for the Routeburn Track (3–4 daily; 1hr 15min); Dunedin (1 daily; 4hr 40min); Invercargill (1 daily; 2hr 45min, with bus change in Mossburn); Kepler Track (3 daily; 10min); Manapouri (2 daily; 30min); Milford Sound (at least 6 daily; 3hr); Queenstown (at least 8 daily; 2hr 30min).

12

INFORMATION

Tourist information i-SITE, at 19 Town Centre between Lakefront Drive and Mokonui St (daily 8.30am–6pm; ☎03 249 8900, ⓦfiordland.org.nz); the Real Journeys Visitor Centre is at 85 Lakefront Drive (daily 8am–7pm; ☎03 249 6000, ⓦrealjourneys.co.nz); the Southern Discoveries Visitor Centre (for Milford Sound activities) is at 80 Lakefront Drive (☎03 441 1137, ⓦsoutherndiscoveries.co.nz).

DOC Fiordland National Park Visitor Centre, Lakefront Drive, 500m south of town centre ☎03 249 7924, ⓔfiordlandvc@doc.govt.nz. Stacks of track and hut information, some

useful tramping supplies and a Great Walks booking office (☎03 249 8514, ⓦdoc.govt.nz). Daily: Nov–April 8am–5pm; May–Oct 8.30am–4.30pm.

Outdoor gear rental Available from several places including Bev's Tramping Gear Hire, 16 Homer St (☎03 249 7389, ⓦbevs-hire.co.nz; Mon–Fri 9am–noon & 6–7pm). Individual items are charged by the day, but the per track rates are better value if you need gear for anything longer than an overnighter (sleeping bags $30/track); their Great Walks Package ($150 for 3–4 days), which has everything you

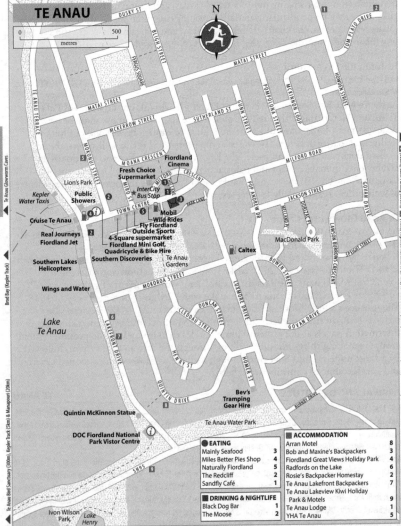

TE ANAU

● **EATING**
Mainly Seafood	3
Miles Better Pies Shop	4
Naturally Fiordland	5
The Redcliff	2
Sandfly Café	1

■ **DRINKING & NIGHTLIFE**
Black Dog Bar	1
The Moose	2

■ **ACCOMMODATION**
Arran Motel	8
Bob and Maxine's Backpackers	3
Fiordland Great Views Holiday Park	4
Radfords on the Lake	6
Rosie's Backpacker Homestay	2
Te Anau Lakefront Backpackers	7
Te Anau Lakeview Kiwi Holiday Park & Motels	9
Te Anau Lodge	1
YHA Te Anau	5

need, except boots and food, is another good option. Outside Sports, 38 Town Centre (☎03 249 8195, ⓦoutsidesports.

co.nz), has a full range of gear to sell or rent, including tents, backpacks and sleeping bags ($30 each for 4 days).

TOURS

Cruise Te Anau Lakefront Drive (at the end of Town Centre) ☎03 249 8005, ⓦcruiseteanau.co.nz. Scenic cruises aboard a restored kauri motor launch (daily 1pm; also 5pm Dec–March; 3hr; $105; daily 11am; 1hr; $49) plus overnight cruises including meals (2.30pm–9.30am; $1100 for two).

Fiordland Jet 84 Lakefront Drive ☎0800 253826, ⓦfjet.nz. Two-hour jetboat ride ($139) past three *Lord of the Rings* locations on the Waiau River (which served as the River Anduin in the movies) to Lake Manapouri. Several departures daily.

Fly Fiordland 4/52 Town Centre ☎0800 359346, ⓦflyfiordland.com. Scenic flights in small Cessna aircraft, from short (25–35min) zips over Milford ($335) or Doubtful

($245) sounds, to 1hr 15min flights over both ($375). Flights depart Manapouri Airport (pick-ups available).

Southern Lakes Helicopters 79 Lakefront Drive ☎03 249 7167, ⓦsouthernlakeshelicopters.co.nz. Helicopter flights from a waterside heli-pad start at $240 for 25min and range up to 3hr ($1995), including scenic flights over Milford, Doubtful and Dusky sounds.

Wings & Water 65 Lakefront Drive ☎03 249 7405, ⓦwingsandwater.co.nz. Floatplane flights are ideal for an aerial view of southern Fiordland. Milford Sound overflights (1hr; $530), Kepler Track overflights (20min; $225) and Doubtful Sound overflights (40min; $349) are among the top options.

GETTING AROUND

By bike Rentals are available from Te Anau Mini Golf, Quadricycle & Bike Hire at 7 Mokonui St (daily 10am–6pm; $30/half-day; $40/day; ☎03 249 7211, ⓦteanaubikehire.nz), Outside Sports (see page 647;

$30/half-day, $50/day) and Wild Rides, 68 Town Centre (Mon–Sat 10am–5pm; from $20/day; ☎03 280 0116, ⓦwildridesfiordland.co.nz), which also offers transport to trail heads.

12

ACCOMMODATION

Motels dominate the length of Lakefront Drive and Quintin Drive, a block back. Rates drop dramatically between June and August. Freedom camping is banned within 10km of Te Anau and there are "No Camping" signs in likely-looking parking spots well beyond that. There are, however, a couple of cheap DOC sites.

Arran Motel 64 Quintin Drive ☎03 249 8826, ⓦarranmotel.co.nz; map p.646. Attractive studios, one- and two-bedroom units, some with cooking facilities, and flatscreen TVs. Continental breakfast available ($11). $165

Bob and Maxine's Backpackers 20 Paton Place, off Oraka St ☎03 249 7429, ⓔbob.anderson@woosh. co.nz; map p.646. Barn-like purpose-built backpackers on the edge of town with simple but spacious and thoughtfully designed six-bunk dorms and one en-suite twin. The hospitable Bob and Maxine provide stacks of DVDs, free local calls, fresh fruit, free washing machines (dryer $3), bikes and dirt-cheap track drop-offs ($2). Dorms $38, twin $100

★ **Radfords on the Lake** 56 Lakefront Drive ☎03 249 9186, ⓦradfordsonthelake.co.nz; map p.646. Modern, scrupulously clean and well-managed motel with everything done to the highest standard. Some of the pretty rooms have great views, plus there's free espresso, oodles of TV channels, parkas to borrow and plenty of parking spots. Continental breakfast $19. $299

★ **Rosie's Backpacker Homestay** 23 Tom Plato Drive ☎03 249 8431, ⓦrosiesbackpackers.co.nz; map p.646. This small, relaxed backpackers sleeps just twelve in a family

home with lake and mountain views – and even after over twenty years of sharing their home with travellers, Rosie and her family are still warm, enthusiastic hosts (don't miss the home-made sourdough bread). Washing and drying available ($4 each). Book early as it fills up fast. Closed June & July. Dorms $36, doubles $84

Te Anau Lakefront Backpackers 48 Lakefront Drive ☎03 249 7713, ⓦteanaubackpackers.co.nz; map p.646. Ageing but friendly and well-organized 110-bed hostel spread across three buildings centred on a former motel. Dorms mostly come with their own bathroom and kitchen and some have great lake views. Pairs of doubles and twins generally share a kitchen and bathroom and there's a good barbecue area, which helps reduce pressure on the main kitchen. They're well set up for trampers, with $5/item gear storage, and you can camp ($20) on the back lawn. Dorms $34, doubles $88

Te Anau Lodge 52 Howden St ☎03 249 7477, ⓦteanaulodge.com; map p.646. Extremely comfortable accommodation in a substantially upgraded former Sisters of Mercy Convent. Rooms, many with superb mountain views, are styled in keeping with its 1936 origins and all are quite different; the deluxe rooms ($375) are particularly lovely. An excellent breakfast (included) is served in the wood-panelled former chapel, complete with organ keyboard; afternoon tea and cake are laid on in the commodious upstairs lounge. $250

YHA Te Anau 29 Mokonui St ☎03 249 7847, ⓔteanau@yha.co.nz; map p.646. Modern and comfortable two-storey hostel close to the town centre with large three- to eight-bed dorms, doubles (en suites $110), free gear storage, helpful staff, lounge with a separate TV room and an outdoors deck. There's a self-catering family cottage with double and twin rooms that can be booked separately or together. Free wi-fi up to 2GB/day. Dorms $\overline{37}$, doubles $\overline{100}$

CAMPING

Fiordland Great Views Holiday Park 129 Te Anau Milford Hwy (SH94), 2km east of town ☎03 249 7059, ✆stayfiordland.co.nz; map p.646. The cheapest of Te Anau's big holiday parks is set well back from the lake but facilities are pretty good, the kindly owner does cheap Kepler Track transfers, and organizes day-trips to Milford ($145) for guests that includes a good cruise, underwater observatory and lunch. Cabins (from $62) and self-catering units (from $120) available. Free wi-fi to 250MB/day. Camping per two-person site $\overline{40}$

Te Anau Lakeview Kiwi Holiday Park & Motels 77 Manapouri Rd, 1km south of Town Centre ☎03 249 7457, ✆teanauholidaypark.co.nz; map p.646. Vast, well-equipped complex with spacious tent and campervan areas, the *Steamers Beach* backpackers, lots of single rooms, modern facilities including a sauna, and a huge range of cabins and units including some gorgeous Marakura rooms ($289) with lake views. The free wi-fi is strongest in common areas. Camping $\overline{24}$, dorms $\overline{30}$

EATING

Mainly Seafood 106 Town Centre ☎027 516 5555; map p.646. The fish burgers ($12) from this friendly takeaway slip down a treat, but the venison burger ($11) is equally good and the mixed seafood Fisherman's Basket ($23.50) could be shared unless you've just finished a big hike. Daily 11.30am–8.30pm.

Miles Better Pies Shop 13 Town Centre ☎03 249 9044; map p.646. No-frills place with tasty pies in a range of fillings such as venison, steak and pepper, and Thai chicken (all $6.50), plus a few vegetarian and sweet varieties, to eat in or take away – grab the bacon and egg pie for an early start. Daily 6am–3pm.

Naturally Fiordland 62 Town Centre ☎03 249 7111; map p.646. While it's not the most authentic of Te Anau's four pizzerias, the pizzas here have good crispy bases with gently Kiwified toppings, and all come in 9" and 12" versions; try The Godfather (spinach, sun-dried tomatoes, olives, salami and feta; $18.80/$24.80) or a Little Sicily (a margherita with fresh tomatoes and herbs;

$13.80/$20.80). Pasta, coffee and cakes available too. Daily 11am–11.30pm.

★ **The Redcliff** 12 Mokonui St ☎03 249 7431, ✆theredcliff.co.nz; map p.646. This cosy timber cottage houses a semiformal restaurant that produces the best meals in Fiordland, a welcoming bar with seating in the garden out front and a nice little window nook. Dinner might be wild hare backstrap with glazed baby carrots ($38) or prime ribeye steak with truffle salt potato skins and mushroom mousse ($41). Daily: Oct–May 4–9.30pm, June–Sept 5–8.30pm; bar open daily 4pm–late

Sandfly Café 9 The Lane ☎03 249 9529; map p.646. The best of Te Anau's modest range of cafés is laidback and has heaps of sunny, roadside seating and indoor couches. They serve good coffee, a range of cooked breakfasts with the likes of steak sandwiches ($17), venison and Thai beef pies ($9) for lunch, along with piles of tempting cakes and pastries like berry brownies ($5). Daily 7am–4.30pm.

DRINKING AND NIGHTLIFE

Black Dog Bar 7 The Lane ☎03 249 8844, ✆blackdogbar.co.nz; map p.646. City-slicker cocktail bar in little old Te Anau – conveniently part of the Fiordland Cinema complex – with an intriguing line-up of New Zealand wines (including their very drinkable in-house Fiordland pinot noir and sauvignon blanc), whiskey, Fiordland lager and cocktails. "Kai iti" tapas plates ($15–19) available daily 4–9pm; happy hour daily 5.30–6.30pm. Wi-fi is free for 30min. Daily 9am–10.30pm or later (alcohol served from 10am).

The Moose 84 Lakefront Drive ☎03 249 7100, ✆themoosebarteanau.com; map p.646. Rambunctious locals' haunt (named in honour of the ten Canadian moose calves that were released at Dusky Sound in the 1900s), with low-cost drink deals, plus live music on summer Saturdays. Standard Kiwi pub grub in more-than-healthy portions, with burgers from $19.90 and dinner mains $24.90–39.90. Mon–Wed & Sun 11am–9pm, Thurs 9am–10.30pm, Fri 9am–11pm, Sat 9am–midnight.

DIRECTORY

Hospital The Fiordland Medical Centre at 25 Luxmore Drive (☎03 249 7007) is open Mon–Fri 8am–6pm, Sat 9am–noon. For urgent cases doctors are usually available 24hr (dial ☎111 for emergencies).

Internet Te Anau Library (Mon 1–6pm, Tues–Fri 9am–

5pm, Sat 10am–1pm) offers free wi-fi for 30min (per session).

Left luggage If your accommodation can't help, *Lakeview Kiwi Holiday Park* (see page 648) offer luggage storage at $10/locker for as long as you need.

Pharmacy Fiordland Community Pharmacy at 70 Town Centre (☎03 249 9268) is open Mon–Fri 8.30–6pm, Sat & Sun 9am–6pm.

Police station 196 Milford Rd (☎03 249 7600).

Post office 100 Town Centre (Mon–Fri 8.30am–6pm, Sat 9.30am–5pm).

Showers The Te Anau Terrace public toilet (daily 8.30am–1.30pm & 2.30–7pm) also has showers (daily 8.30am–1pm & 2.30–6.30pm; $5 for 8min), as well as shampoo and conditioner ($5) and towels ($6) to get you looking lovely post-tramp.

Vehicle storage Safer Parking, 48 Caswell Rd (☎03 249 7198, ⌨saferparking.co.nz), offer secure parking ($9/night) while you're on a tramp. Tracknet and Real Journeys can pick up here for transfers.

The Kepler Track

Offering mesmerizing alpine panoramas, lake vistas and tranquil beech forest, the **Kepler Track** (45–70km; 3–4 days) was created in 1988 and quickly designated as one of New Zealand's Great Walks. It was intended to take the load off the Milford and Routeburn tracks and has been so successful it has become equally popular. Tracing a wide loop through the Kepler Mountains on the western side of **Lake Te Anau**, the track has one full day of exposed subalpine ridge walking, and has the advantage of being accessible on foot from Te Anau. Typically walked **anticlockwise**, getting most of the climbing out of the way early, the track ranges from as little as 45km – if you use boats and buses – to 70km for the full Te Anau–Te Anau walk.

Well graded and maintained throughout, it is still lengthy and strenuous, particularly the long haul up to *Luxmore Hut*. The section between the *Luxmore* and *Iris Burn* huts is occasionally closed after snowfall. Top athletes complete the 60km **Kepler Challenge** (first Sat in Dec), a run around the track, in under five hours. The current record, set by Martin Dent in 2013, is 4:33:37.

12

Te Anau to Control Gates
5km; 45min–1hr; flat

Most hikers get the bus to the **Control Gates** (aka Kepler Track car park), but it is possible to walk, first heading south along Lakefront Drive, then right and following the lakeshore until the final right-turn to the control gates themselves, which regulate the water flow between lakes Te Anau and Manapouri. It's not a particularly interesting walk, but pretty enough.

Control Gates to Brod Bay
5.6km; 1hr–1hr 30min; flat

The track follows the lakeshore around Dock Bay and over Coal Creek, passing through predominantly beech and kamahi forests but with a fine stand of tree ferns. **Brod Bay** has good swimming off a sandy beach and makes a lovely place to camp.

Brod Bay to Luxmore Hut
8.2km; 3–4hr 30min; 880m ascent

Non-campers must press on from Brod Bay, following a signpost midway along the beach. The path climbs fairly steeply; after a couple of hours you sidle below limestone bluffs, from where it is almost another hour to the bushline and fine views over Te Anau and Manapouri lakes and the surrounding mountains. **Luxmore Hut** is almost one hour above the bushline. A 20min (return) side trip from the hut visits the short and fairly unexciting **Luxmore Cave**, its ceiling hung with skinny stalactites.

Luxmore Hut to Iris Burn Hut
14.6km; 5–6hr; 300m ascent, 900m descent

An exposed, high-level section where any hint of bad weather should be treated seriously. The track climbs to the highest point of the tramp, Luxmore Saddle (1400m), just below the summit of **Mount Luxmore** (from where you can hike up

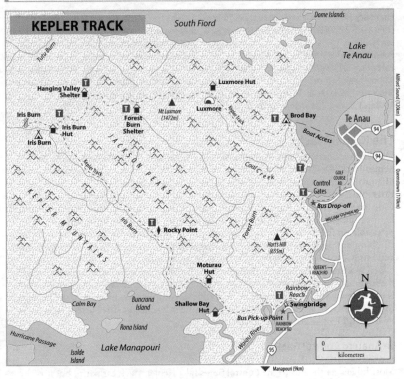

to the 1472m peak; 30min return), then descends to **Forest Burn Shelter** before following a ridge to **Hanging Valley Shelter** and turning sharply south to trace another open ridge towards **Iris Burn** – reached by zigzagging west into the forested Hanging Valley then following the stream to the hut and campsite in a large tussock clearing. It's worth doing the easy walk to the Iris Burn waterfall (40min return).

Iris Burn Hut to Moturau Hut
16.2km; 5–6hr; 300m descent

The track from the *Iris Burn Hut* passes over a low saddle before descending steadily past a large landslip and through beech forest and riverside clearings. About halfway you pass toilets at **Rocky Point**, then enter a short gorge before hugging the river for several magical kilometres. Just before Iris Burn spills into Lake Manapouri, the track swings east and skirts Shallow Bay to the pleasant lakeside **Moturau Hut**. If you're doing the track in three days, press on to the bus pick-up at Rainbow Reach, 6km further on.

Moturau Hut to Rainbow Reach
6km; 1hr 30min–2hr; flat

Most people finish their walk at **Rainbow Reach**, an easy walk through gentle beech forest from *Moturau Hut*. Keen trampers might want to continue on foot back to the Control Gates (additional 9.5km; 2–3hr; negligible ascent) on a track through mature lowland beech forest beside the Waiau River. There are opportunities for fishing and swimming, but the river flows swiftly, so pick your spot carefully.

ARRIVAL AND DEPARTURE

THE KEPLER TRACK

By bus The Kepler Track starts at the Control Gates, 5km southwest of Te Anau. Most people catch the Tracknet bus (late Oct to April only; $8; 10min; ☎ 0800 483262, ⊛ tracknet.net), which picks up at accommodation around town daily at 8.30am, 9.30am, 11.10am & 2.30pm, dropping off at the Control Gates. On the last day, most trampers stop 9.5km short of the Control Gates at the swingbridge over the Waiau's Rainbow Reach. Tracknet pick up at Rainbow Reach at 10am, 3pm, 4pm and 5pm (20min back to Te Anau); it costs $18 for a combined ticket to the Control Gates and return from Rainbow Reach.

By boat You can skip 5km of lakeside walking (and make a relaxed first day start) by boating across to Brod Bay from Te Anau wharf with Kepler Water Taxi (late Oct to April 8.30am, 9.30am & 4pm or by arrangement; returning 8.45am, 9.45am & 4.30pm; $25 one-way; ☎ 03 249 8364, ⊛ keplerwatertaxi.co.nz).

INFORMATION

Maps The trail information given in DOC's *Kepler Track* brochure (free) is adequate, but for more detailed information consult either the 1:55,000 *Kepler Track* map by NewTopo ($9.90) or the 1:40,000 *Kepler Track* map by Craig Potton Publishing ($25), both available from the National Park Visitor Centre.

Weather and track conditions The Te Anau National Park Visitor Centre has the latest weather forecast and track conditions. If you're hiking the Kepler Track in winter, see the winter-specific page at ⊛ doc.govt.nz/keplertrack.

Safety DOC do not track trampers' whereabouts. Let someone know your intentions through ⊛ adventuresmart.org.nz. Locator beacons are available for $30/3 days from Bev's Tramping Gear (see page 646) or the Mobil garage in Te Anau.

ACCOMMODATION

Booking Hut bookings are mandatory during Great Walk season (late Oct–April). You can walk in either direction, retrace your steps and stay up to two nights in a particular hut (three nights in the winter). Book as far ahead as possible – three months if you need a specific departure date or are part of a large group. It is easiest to book online (⊛ doc.govt.nz) from July 1 for the following season, though it is also possible to book by mail and in person at DOC visitor centres ($2). If the track is closed due to bad weather or track conditions, full refunds are given; however, new bookings can only be made if there is space. Changes can be made to existing bookings before you start ($10/booking).

Huts The three main huts – *Luxmore* (54 bunks), *Iris Burn* (50 bunks) and *Moturau* (40 bunks) – have a warden, gas stoves, cold water and flush toilets (but no showers): you'll need to carry your own pans and plates. Trampers are discouraged from using the simple and very small *Shallow Bay Hut*, just off the track beside Lake Manapouri. During the main season the Backcountry Hut Pass is not valid. Outside the main season, the huts lose their warden, gas stoves and running water, reverting to pit toilets until spring; during this period the Backcountry Hut Pass is valid. Great Walk season $65, off season $15

Camping Campers are forced to tackle the Kepler in one very short and two very long days using the campsites at Brod Bay and Iris Burn. Both have fifteen pitches, pit toilets and water. Great Walk season $20, off season $5

Milford Road

The 120km **Milford Road** (SH94), from Te Anau to Milford Sound, is one of the world's finest scenic highways. The two-hour drive can easily take a day if you grab every photo opportunity, and longer if you explore some of the excellent hiking trails outlined in the *Fiordland Day Walks* booklet, available free from the National Park Visitor Centre in Te Anau. Anywhere else the initial drive beside Lake Te Anau would be considered gorgeous, but it is nothing compared to the **Eglinton Valley**, where the road penetrates steeper into bush-clad mountains, winding through a subalpine wonderland to the seemingly impassable bare rock walls at the head of the Hollyford Valley. The rough-hewn Homer Tunnel cuts through to the sheer-walled Cleddau Valley before the road descends steeply to Milford Sound.

There's very little habitation along the way, and no mobile phone service, shops or **petrol** (fill up in Te Anau), but lots of great camping.

Eglinton Valley

Heading north from Te Anau, there's little reason to stop in the first 30km to the harbour at **Te Anau Downs**, where boats leave for the start of the **Milford Track** (see

12

MILFORD ROAD SAFETY

With all the fabulous scenery along the Milford Road it is easy for drivers to lose concentration. Bear in mind that there is heavy bus traffic Milford-bound from 10am to noon and Te Anau-bound between 3 and 5pm. Apart from the store in the Hollyford Valley, 8km off your route, there is nowhere to buy **food** until you reach Milford, so go prepared. There are single **petrol** and diesel pumps in Milford, but they often run out, so fill up in Te Anau before you leave.

   In winter (May–Oct or Nov) the subalpine section of the Milford Road is one of the world's most **avalanche-prone**. Since the last avalanche death on the road in 1983, a sophisticated monitoring system has been put in place and explosives are dropped from helicopters to loosen dangerous accumulations of snow while the road is closed. At this time, motorists are required to carry chains (available from service stations in Te Anau for $30/day). If there is a risk of snowfall you'll be stopped at the small kiosk five minutes' drive out of Te Anau to make sure that you have them and know how to fit them – and sent back to Te Anau if you don't. It's not uncommon for people to be stuck in Milford if the road does close. Always check weather forecasts with the DOC office in Te Anau before setting out; check the road status at ⓦ nzta. govt.nz/projects/sh94-milford-road.

page 659). The road then cuts east away from the lake, before veering north into the **Eglinton Valley** through occasional stands of beech, interspersed with open flats of red tussock grass. In November and December the flats are ablaze with pink, purple and white lupins – a pest, but a beautiful one.

12

Mirror Lakes

Particularly picturesque mountains hem the Eglinton Valley and, when the weather is calm, are reflected in the roadside **Mirror Lakes**, 56km north of Te Anau. Even without the reflective stillness it is a beautiful spot with boardwalks leading down to flax-fringed tarns, originally the bed of the Eglinton River.

Knob's Flat

Daily: May–Sept 8.30am–3pm; Oct–April 8am–5pm • Free

Most tour buses stop to use the last flush toilets before Milford at **Knob's Flat**, 6km beyond Mirror Lakes, where the amenity centre also contains display panels on the invasive species threatening the region (notably stoats and possums), plus the effects of avalanches that are a perennial danger June to November. The beech forests in this area are also home to New Zealand's only native land mammal, the **long-tailed bat**. **Camping** is permitted here.

The Divide

As you get nearer to the head of the Eglinton Valley the road steepens to **The Divide** (83km from Te Anau), which at 531m is the lowest east–west crossing of the Southern Alps. This is the start/finish of the **Greenstone** and **Caples** (see page 611) and **Routeburn** (see page 608) tracks, the last of which can be followed to **Key Summit** (5km return; 2–3hr; 400m ascent) for a shorter hike. The car park has a walkers' shelter with a notice board advertising the times of passing buses to Milford Sound (3 daily; 1hr 15min) and Te Anau (3–4 daily; 1hr), although it is better to prearrange a pick-up as there is no mobile reception up here.

   Pressing on a couple of kilometres towards Milford, you descend briefly into the top end of the Hollyford River, best seen from spectacular **Pops View** (also a likely place to see **kea**, the cheeky mountain parrot), just off the road (no buses are allowed here).

The Hollyford Valley

The Milford Road drops down from The Divide into the **Hollyford Valley**, which runs 80km from its headwaters in the Darran Mountains north to the Tasman

Sea at Martins Bay. Just beyond Pops View is the turning for the gravel **Lower Hollyford Road** that provides access to the **Hollyford Track** (see page 654). The fairly strenuous **Lake Marian Track** (2.4km return from the car park; 3hr) starts just 1km along Lower Hollyford Road, while the tiny settlement of **Gunn's Camp** (aka Hollyford Camp), lies 8km further on. This former 1938 public works camp now has simple accommodation, a museum devoted to the characters who have called the valley home, and a **shop** selling trampers' supplies along with postcards, books, maps and some rare bowenite pendants. The road runs another 8km beyond Gunn's Camp to the beginning of the Hollyford Track and the start of a short, steep walk to **Humboldt Falls** (30min return), a ribbon-thin cascade tumbling 200m. In the 1930s the road was slated to run all the way to Haast in Westland, a fact bemoaned by signs at Gunn's Camp – there are no plans to extend it any time soon.

Gunn's Camp Museum

Gunn's Camp (Hollyford Camp), Lower Hollyford Rd • Daily: Oct–March 8am–8pm; April–Sept 9am–7pm • $2, free to guests

Set half an hour aside for the tiny but fascinating **Gunn's Camp Museum** collection of pioneer artefacts (leather saddles, iron tools and fading photographs), intriguing paraphernalia relating to the one-time community at Martins Bay, stuff on the devastating floods that periodically afflict the region, the building of the Milford Road and the Homer Tunnel and the devastating fire here in 1990. A nice shot shows former owner, the late Murray Gunn, sitting in his kitchen back in 1989, and there's fascinating information on his pioneer father, **Davey Gunn**, who turned the camp into a base for tourism in 1951 (tragically, Davey drowned in the Hollyford River in 1955).

12

Homer Tunnel

After the Lower Hollyford Road turn-off, Milford Road continues west towards the Hollyford River's source, climbing all the while through ever more stunted beech trees to the huge glacial cirque of the Gertrude Valley. It is a magnificent spot, frequently strung with waterfalls and resounding to the sound of curious **kea**: do not feed them, as human food can kill them.

The road then cuts to the sea via the 1.2km-long **Homer Tunnel**, which punctures the headwall of the Gertrude Valley – it's named after explorer W.H. Homer who discovered the saddle pass to Milford Sound in 1889. Construction was started in 1935, but was badly planned from the start. Working at a one-in-ten downhill gradient, the builders soon hit water and were forced to pump it out continuously; a pilot tunnel allowing the water to drain westwards was finished in 1948. After a concerted push, the tunnel was completed in 1953, opening Milford Sound to road traffic for the first time. Each April, uninhibited locals compete in a race through the tunnel naked (apart from running shoes).

Despite recent improvements, the tunnel remains rough-hewn, narrow and dark. During peak periods in the summer **traffic lights** dictate one-way traffic (expect a wait of up to 15min; kea often patrol the line looking for snacks), but for the rest of the time you'll need to look out for oncoming vehicles.

The Chasm

The Homer Tunnel emerges at the top of a series of switchbacks down to the Cleddau River. Almost 10km on from the tunnel all buses stop at **The Chasm**, while their passengers stroll (15min return) to the near-vertical rapids where the Cleddau has scoured out a deep, narrow channel. Tantalizing glimpses through the foliage reveal sculpted rocks hollowed out by churning water or eroded into freestanding ribs that resemble flying buttresses. From here it is another 10km via the 1940 **Tutoko Suspension Bridge** to Milford Sound.

THE HOLLYFORD TRACK

Long, but mostly flat (accessible year-round), the **Hollyford Track** (56km; 3–4 days one-way; ⦿ doc.govt.nz/hollyfordtrack) runs from the end of the Lower Hollyford Rd (8km beyond Gunn's Camp) to **Martins Bay** following Fiordland's longest valley. It's a trail that offers dramatic mountain scenery as it snakes through the kahikatea, rimu and matai bush with an understorey of wineberry, fuchsia and fern. At Martins Bay, Long Reef has a resident **fur seal** colony, and from September to December you might spot rare Fiordland crested **penguins** (tawaki) nesting among the scrub and rocks. The track is a one-way tramp, requiring three to four days' backtracking (six decent huts are available on route, all with space for camping) – unless you're flash enough to fly out from the airstrip at Martins Bay or tough enough to continue around a long, difficult and remote loop known as the **Pyke–Big Bay Route** (9–10 days total; consult DOC's Pyke–Big Bay Route leaflet for details). Visit the excellent ⦿ **hollyfordtrack.com** for information on guided walks.

ACCOMMODATION

MILFORD ROAD

Campers will want to spend a night or two in one of the dozen simple DOC **campsites** along the Milford Road either on the grassy flats of the Eglinton Valley or the bush nearby. All have vault toilets and giardia-free stream water, and most have fireplaces; all are open year-round and are first come, first served (and take cash only May–Oct). All are outlined in DOC's free *Conservation Campsites* booklet: some of the best are listed below, in order of distance from Te Anau.

Cascade Creek Campsite SH94, 71km north of Te Anau. The closest DOC site to Milford Sound that's suitable for campers – still over 40km away. Tap water available and fly-fishing possible in the creek or Eglinton River. $13

Deer Flat Campsite SH94, 59km north of Te Anau. The pitches at this DOC campsite on the banks of the Eglinton River are scattered around, with a couple sheltered by patches of beech, the remainder on grassy flats nearby. Toilets and picnic tables available. $13

Gunn's Camp 8km along Lower Hollyford Rd ⦿ gunnscamp.org.nz. The only accommodation in these parts is this huddle of simple 1930s cabins that served as families' quarters for the long-suffering road-builders. An ongoing revamp includes a modern lounge and kitchen block, but the place retains its spirit – basic and with bags of character. Cabins generally have single beds or six-berth bunks ($30/bed); linen is available to rent ($5), but you'll

need a sleeping bag. There's generator power (7–9am & 6–10pm) and wood-fired showers, but no refrigeration, landline, mobile coverage or internet; very basic supplies are available from the small shop. Camping $20, double cabins $70

Henry Creek Campsite SH94, 23km north of Te Anau. The first of the Milford Road DOC sites is attractive with fifty (almost) lakeside gravel sites well spaced along the lakeshore and sheltered camping among the beech trees. Vault toilets and lake water only. $13

Knobs Flat SH94, 62km north of Te Anau ☎ 03 249 9122, ⦿ knobsflat.co.nz. Six very comfortable motel-style self-catering units in a remote location with great valley views from the verandas, but no TV, wi-fi or mobile phone reception. Guided nature walks through the Eglinton Valley are available ($20/hr; $75/half-day) and there's camping (no powered sites) with showers ($5) and a well-equipped camp kitchen ($5; use of showers, toilet and kitchen $20). A flax-girt bush bath makes a great spot for stargazing. Camping $20, doubles $130

Walker Creek Campsite SH94, 47km north of Te Anau. Small DOC site with valley views just 2km inside the national park on the banks of the Eglinton River. There's stream water, toilets and picnic tables plus plenty of room for campervans in secluded spots. $13

Milford Sound

The most northerly and celebrated of Fiordland's fifteen fiords is **Milford Sound** with its vertical sides towering 1200m above the sea and waterfalls plunging from hanging valleys. Some 16km long and mostly less than 1km wide, it is also one of the slenderest fiords – and yes, it is misnamed. Sounds are drowned river valleys whereas this is very much a glacially formed fiord. It is a wondrous place, though it is difficult to grasp its heroic scale unless your visit coincides with that of one of the great cruise liners – even these formidable vessels are totally dwarfed. When author Rudyard Kipling visited in 1891 he dubbed it the "Eighth Wonder of the World".

Perhaps counterintuitively, Milford is at its best in the rain, something that happens on over 180 days a year giving a massive 7m of **annual rainfall**. Within minutes of a torrential downpour every cliff-face sprouts a waterfall and the place looks even more magical as ethereal mist descends. Indeed, Milford warrants repeated visits: in bright sunshine (yes, it does happen), on a rainy day and even under a blanket of snow.

None of the other fiords quite matches Milford for its spectacular **beauty**, but what makes Milford special is its **accessibility**. The tiny airport hardly rests as planes buzz in and out, while busloads of visitors are disgorged from buses onto cruises – all day in the summer and around the middle of the day in spring and autumn.

The crowds can certainly detract from the grandeur, but don't let that put you off. Driving to Milford Sound and admiring it from the land just doesn't cut it; you need to get out on the water, either on a cruise or in a kayak.

Brief history

Māori know Milford Sound as **Piopiotahi** ("a single thrush"), and attribute its creation to the god Tu-te-Raki-whanoa, who was called away before he could carve a route into the interior, leaving high rock walls. These precipitous routes are now known as the Homer and Mackinnon passes, probably first used by Māori who came to collect *pounamu* from Anita Bay at the mouth of the fiord. The first European known to have sailed into Piopiotahi was sealer John Grono who, in 1823, named the fiord Milford Haven after his home port in south Wales. The main river flowing into the Welsh Milford is the Cleddau, so naturally the river at the head of the fiord is likewise named.

The earliest settler was Scottish adventurer **Donald Sutherland** (not to be confused with the Canadian actor) who arrived with his dog, John O'Groat, in 1877; he promptly planned a series of thatched huts beside the freshwater basin of what he called the "City of Milford", funding his explorations by guiding small numbers of visitors who had heard tell of the scenic wonder (Sutherland eventually died here in 1919).

All visitors arrived by boat or walked the Milford Track until 1953 when the road through the Homer Tunnel was finally completed, paving the way for the phalanxes of buses that today shuttle tourists onto cruises.

Milford Sound village

The settlement of **MILFORD SOUND** is tiny, comprising little more than a small airstrip, fishing harbour and a couple of lodges. The parking area lies around the **Discover Milford Sound Information Centre & Café** (daily: summer 8am–4pm, winter 9am–4pm; ☏03 249 7931). It's a ten- to fifteen-minute walk from here to the slick **Milford Sound Visitor Terminal**, the departure point for all the Milford cruises. You can buy tickets in the terminal but not much else – they have toilets and vending machines for drinks and snacks.

You're pretty much surrounded by water here, and should waste little time getting out on it, but if tales of his pioneering days have inspired you, pay homage at **Donald Sutherland's grave**, hidden among the staff accommodation behind the visitor centre. Alternatively take a five-minute **walk** up to a lookout behind *Mitre Peak Lodge*, or the **Piopiotahi Foreshore Walk**, which runs from the main car park along the fiord's sandy shore returning through beech woods to the settlement (30min loop; flat).

Mitre Peak

The view of Milford Sound is dominated by the iconic, triangular, glaciated pinnacle of **Mitre Peak** (1692m), named for its resemblance to a bishop's mitre. It actually doesn't look much like one, but pioneering Victorians were undoubtedly desperate to find an alternative to its Māori name, *Rahotu*, which some coyly translate as "member of upstanding masculinity" (though it really doesn't look much like one of those either).

MILFORD SOUND CRUISES AND KAYAKING

There's little point visiting Milford Sound and not spending time on the water, and fortunately there are numerous worthwhile ways to do just that.

DAY-CRUISES

The dramatic view from the shore of Milford Sound pales beside the spectacle from the water. The majority of cruises explore the full length of Milford Sound, all calling at waterfalls, a fur seal colony ("Seal Rock"), rare Fiordland crested penguins and overhanging rock faces; at **Stirling Falls**, boats nose up to the base of the falls, while suitably attired passengers are encouraged to edge out onto the bowsprit and collect a faceful of water (aka the "glacial facial").

The simplest option is one of the 1.5–3hr **day-cruises** (summer 20-plus daily; winter 10 daily; best booked a few days in advance in Jan, Feb & March) either on a large and comfortable catamaran or one of the more intimate small boats. The six cruise companies vary their **fares** during the day, with those leaving between 11am and 2pm around 20–30 percent more expensive than those at, say, 9am or 3pm. Otherwise, costs vary according to the size of boat, duration of trip and degree of interpretation, but all offer the same beautiful backdrop.

Cruise Milford ☎0800 645367, ⓦcruisemilfordnz. com. With the smallest boats on the sound (max. 40 passengers), this family-run cruise operator is a promising alternative should you wish to escape the tour groups that dominate elsewhere. 1hr 45min cruises cost $95.

Go Orange ☎0800 246672, ⓦgoorange.co.nz. Real Journeys' budget-friendly sister company offers good-value 2hr cruises ($45–80), with free snacks (from bacon sandwiches to fish and chips); they also offer a handful of kayaking/hiking trips from $118 for 4hr 30min (ⓦgoorangekayaks.co.nz).

Jucy Cruize ☎0800 500121, ⓦjucycruize.co.nz. Fun, budget-oriented cruises (90min–1hr 45min; $45–79) on a catamaran that takes up to 200 passengers, although it's rare for them to be that full. Sustenance is provided by an on-board branch of *Pita Pit*.

Mitre Peak Cruises ☎0800 744633, ⓦmitrepeak. com. With smallish boats (max. 75) and more personal service, there's undoubted appeal to these 2hr cruises ($70–82) and they're deservedly popular.

Real Journeys ☎0800 656501, ⓦrealjourneys.co.nz. The biggest cruise operator with a wide range of boats and professional service. Choose a basic scenic cruise (1hr 40min; $76–105) or a more leisurely nature cruise (2hr; $91–101); lunches (picnic $19; buffet $37) available, but Indian ($31) and Obento meals ($37) must be preordered.

Southern Discoveries ☎0800 264536, ⓦsoutherndiscoveries.co.nz. Mainstream options ranging from a basic cruise (1hr 45min; $46–99) to their Discover More cruise (3hr; $80–117) with lunch and a visit to the Milford Discovery Centre included.

OVERNIGHT CRUISES

Overnight cruises are all run by Real Journeys (☎0800 656501, ⓦrealjourneys.co.nz), which operates two motor cruisers each offering a slightly different experience. Both sail daily in summer from around 4.30pm–9.15am and take a leisurely cruise around Milford Sound, usually anchoring for a while at **Anita Bay** (Te-Wahi-Takiwai, "the place of Takiwai"), a former greenstone-gathering place at the fiord's mouth, but still sheltered from the wrath of the Tasman Sea. There's a chance to go kayaking, good meals and a night spent at anchor in sheltered Harrison Cove. Coach transfers or coach-flight combos are available from Queenstown and Te Anau.

Milford Wanderer The berths in this boat are mostly in cramped twin rooms that share bathrooms (though there are some quad-shares). All are equipped with duvets and towels, and a three-course set meal (drinks extra) also helps. Nov–March, twin-share $389, quad-share $339.

Milford Mariner Fairly luxurious 60-berth boat with reasonably comfortable twin or double en-suite cabins; dinner is a three-course buffet meal. Nov–March $489; Sept, Oct & April to mid-May $329.

KAYAKING

Rosco's Milford Sound Sea Kayaks 72 Town Centre, Te Anau ☎0800 476726, ⓦroscosmilfordkayaks.com. Range of Milford Sound-based kayaking trips with expert guides, including the wonderful Morning Glory (18km; 3hr 30min–4hr paddling; $219), with a dawn start, long paddle

then a water taxi back. The afternoon Twilight Wind & Waves (12km; 3hr 30min–4hr paddling; $179) follows a similar format (and will likely involve more wind and waves). Trips mostly run mid-Oct to mid-April, with the Sunriser (12km; 3hr–3hr 30min paddling; $155) available year-round.

Lady Bowen Falls and Stirling Falls

After heavy rain, Milford Sound can feel like a chasm of waterfalls but there are really only two major falls that keep going long after the rain stops – both best seen from the water. Right by Milford Sound village, the 161m **Lady Bowen Falls** (named after the wife of one of the country's early governors) is an impressive sight at any time, but truly thunders after heavy rain sending a vast spume of spray over any who approach.

Halfway along the fiord, the 155m **Stirling Falls** is almost as impressive and features on most cruise-boat itineraries and some kayak trips.

Milford Sound Underwater Observatory

Harrison Cove, optional stop on Southern Discoveries and Mitre Peak cruises only; 30–45min stop • $36 • ☎ 0800 264536, ⓦ southerndiscoveries.co.nz

About a third of the way along the fiord is the **Milford Sound Underwater Observatory**, a floating platform moored to a sheer rock wall in Harrison Cove (part of the Piopiotahi Marine Reserve). A spiral staircase takes you 10m down through the relatively lifeless freshwater surface layer to a circular gallery where windows look out into the briny heart of the fiord. Sharks and seals occasionally swim by, but most of the action happens immediately outside in window-box "gardens", specially grown from rare, locally gathered **coral** and plant species. Lights pick out colourful fish, tubeworms, sea fans, huge starfish, and rare red and black coral (the latter actually white when alive). Unless you're an experienced diver this is the only chance you'll get to see these corals, which elsewhere in the world grow only at depths greater than 40m.

Topside, there's diverting interpretation on the Milford Road, the construction of the Homer Tunnel, avalanche videos and the building of the centre in the mid-1990s.

12

ARRIVAL AND DEPARTURE

MILFORD SOUND

Milford Sound is on most visitors' itineraries, and during the season (Oct–April) there are plenty of operators to get you there from almost anywhere in the country. You can drive yourself along the Milford Road (see page 651), catch a bus the same way or fly direct from Queenstown (see page 594). Several companies combine forces offering coach/cruise/flight combos.

BY BUS

Numerous luxury tour buses make the 5–6hr journey from Queenstown to Milford Sound via Te Anau (complete with frequent photo stops and a relentless commentary), stopping briefly for a cruise before heading back to Queenstown – a hurried twelve- to thirteen-hour day usually starting 5–7am. A more palatable option is to base yourself in Te Anau and catch a bus from there – it's a leisurely eight hours to Milford and back, allowing you to concentrate on the most interesting section of the Milford Road and the cruise. The cheapest buses don't include cruises, leaving you to arrange your own upon arrival; InterCity runs Queenstown–Te Anau–Milford daily (from $66 one-way), while in summer (late Oct to April) Tracknet (see below), runs the same route daily. Destinations The Divide (3 daily; 45min); Queenstown (at least 5 daily; 5hr 50min); Te Anau (at least 5 daily; 2hr 15min–3hr).

BUS COMPANIES

BBQ Bus ☎ 03 442 1045, ⓦ bbqbus.co.nz. A great option from Queenstown, with stops for short bushwalks, a BBQ in the Hollyford Valley and a Milford cruise (or flight option; $619). Nov–April daily (13hr 30min round-trip from Queenstown; $180–220); May, Aug, Sept & Oct daily ($195–235; 12hr round-trip from Queenstown). Also available from Te Anau ($180; 8hr 15min).

Fiordland Tours ☎ 0800 247249, ⓦ fiordlandtours. co.nz. Te Anau-based owner-operator running small-bus tours to Milford Sound with accommodation pick-ups, good commentary, cruise and home baking ($169; lunch $20 extra).

Jucy ☎ 0800 500121, ⓦ jucycruize.co.nz. Budget trip from Queenstown for late-ish risers. Departs 8.25am, joins the 3.15pm Jucy Cruise and stops for a quick meal in Te Anau on the way back, returning 9pm ($125; $169 May–Sept).

Milford Sound Select ☎ 0800 477479, ⓦ milfordsoundselect.co.nz. Mid-sized glass-roofed coaches are a nice touch on these very competitively priced coach/cruise/coach tours from Queenstown (from $169 online; $189 regular).

Real Journeys ☎ 0800 656501, ⓦ realjourneys.co.nz. Upmarket coach/cruise/coach tours from Queenstown using wedge-shaped, glass-roofed coaches with slightly angled seats that give the best all-round views, and on-board wi-fi. There's good interpretation and a multilingual commentary. Operates all year ($199; 12–13hr) with pick-ups in Te Anau ($149; 7–8hr).

Tracknet ☎ 03 249 7777, ⓦ tracknet.net. Budget transport between Te Anau and Milford Sound, though you'll have to put up with detours to the trailheads. Oct–

April three times daily ($53 each way).

Trips & Tramps ☎ 0800 305807, ⓦ tripsandtramps. co.nz. Te Anau-based, interactive, nature-oriented trips start from a coach, cruise and walk option where you can either do a 2hr self-guided walk up Key Summit (see page 652) or join a nature guide on a few short walks (10hr; $169, picnic lunch included).

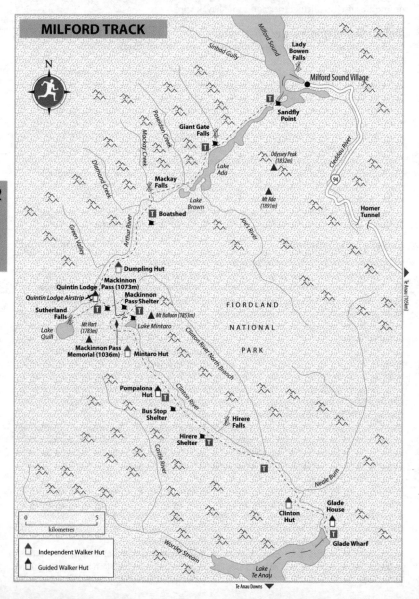

MILFORD TRACK

N

- 🏠 Independent Walker Hut
- 🏠 Guided Walker Hut

0   5
kilometres

Milford Sound

Sinbad Gully

Lady Bowen Falls

Milford Sound Village

Sandfly Point

Giant Gate Falls

Poseidon Creek

Mackay Creek

Lake Ada

Odyssey Peak (1832m)

Cleddau River

94

Diamond Creek

Mackay Falls

Lake Brown

Mt Ada (1891m)

Joes River

Homer Tunnel

Boatshed

Green Valley

Arthur River

Dumpling Hut

Te Anau (105km)

Quintin Lodge

Mackinnon Pass (1073m)

Mackinnon Pass Shelter

Quintin Lodge Airstrip

Sutherland Falls

Mt Hart (1783m)

Lake Quill

Lake Mintaro

Mt Balloon (1853m)

FIORDLAND

NATIONAL

PARK

Mackinnon Pass Memorial (1036m)

Mintaro Hut

Clinton River North Branch

Pompolona Hut

Clinton River

Bus Stop Shelter

Hirere Falls

Hirere Shelter

Castle River

Neale Burn

Glade House

Clinton Hut

Glade Wharf

Worsley Stream

Lake Te Anau

Te Anau Downs

12

BY PLANE

Visitors really pushed for time can do a simple overflight of Milford Sound from Te Anau (see page 644), Queenstown or Wanaka, but you really should land and take a cruise. Flights are, of course, weather dependent and operators won't fly you in to Milford unless they are fairly confident of getting you out again.

Milford Sound Scenic Flights 39 Lucas Place, Frankton, Queenstown 🕿 03 442 3065, 🖳 milfordflights.co.nz. Fly/

cruise combos from Queenstown, with 1hr scenic flights from $395, and fly/cruise/fly packages from $480.

Real Journeys 🕿 0800 656501, 🖳 realjourneys.co.nz. Major Fiordland operator flying from Queenstown and using their own cruise boats (fly-over $395; fly/cruise/fly from $490).

Wanaka Flightseeing 🕿 03 443 8787, 🖳 flightseeing. co.nz. Fly/cruise/fly trips from Wanaka give especially good views of Mt Aspiring and the Olivine Ice Plateau en route (4hr; $540; flyover from $455).

ACCOMMODATION AND EATING

The only place to eat at Milford Sound is the very basic café (daily 9am–4pm) inside the Discover Milford Sound Information Centre, though the lodging option below also offers meals.

Milford Sound Lodge 1.5km back from the wharf on SH94 🕿 03 249 8071, 🖳 milfordlodge.com. Book in advance to stay at this well-run lodge with sites for

campervans ($30 per person; no tent sites), spacious dorms and if you're splashing out, gorgeous riverside chalets (from $395) with large windows, underfloor heating and soft, super king-sized beds. The excellent in-house *Pio Pio Café* (daily 7.30am–8pm) and comfortable lounge are ample compensation for the cramped kitchen and pricey shop. Free wi-fi up 100MB/day for chalet guests only. Dorms $40,

The Milford Track

More than any other Great Walk, the 54km **Milford Track** is a Kiwi icon. Its exalted reputation is part accident and part history but there's no doubt that the Milford Track is wonderful and includes some of Fiordland's finest scenery. The track starts at the head of Lake Te Anau and follows the Clinton River into the heart of the mountains, climbing over the spectacular Mackinnon Pass before tracing the Arthur River to Milford Sound.

Some disparage the track as over-regimented, expensive and not especially varied, while others complain that the huts are badly spaced and lurk below the tree line among the sandflies. While these criticisms aren't unfounded – the tramp costs around $430 in hut and transport fees alone – the track is well managed and maintained, the huts clean and unobtrusive, and because everyone's going in the same direction you can charge ahead (or lag behind) and hike all day without seeing a soul. The Milford is also tougher than many people expect, packing the only hard climb and a dash for the boat at Milford Sound into the last two days.

Day 1: Glade Wharf to Clinton Hut
5km; 1–1hr 30min; 50m ascent

The first day is a doddle, starting at **Glade Wharf** and a 2km 4WD track that serves **Glade House** (accommodation for guided walkers only) at the top of Lake Te Anau. The path then crosses a swingbridge to the right bank of the gentle, meandering Clinton River. The track runs from here through dense beech forest, only occasionally giving glimpses of the mountains ahead beyond **Clinton Hut** (first night for independent walkers), where there are a handful of good swimming holes nearby.

Day 2: Clinton Hut to Mintaro Hut
16.5km; 5–7hr; 350m ascent

From Clinton Hut the track follows the right bank of the Clinton River to its source, **Lake Mintaro**, and the *Mintaro Hut*. Again, it's easy going and by the time you reach a short side track to **Hidden Lake**, Mackinnon Pass should be visible. The track steepens a little to Bus Stop Shelter, flattens out to **Pompolona Hut** (guided walkers only), and is a further hour to **Mintaro Hut** where, if it looks like it will be a good sunset, you should drop your pack and head up Mackinnon Pass.

Day 3: Mintaro Hut to Dumpling Hut

14km; 5–7hr; 550m ascent; 1030m descent

The walk to this point does little to prepare you for the third day. Though the surface of the broad path is firm and well-graded, less-experienced bushwalkers will find the haul up to **Mackinnon Pass** (1hr 30min–2hr) very strenuous. Long breath-catching pauses provide an opportunity to admire the wonderful alpine scenery, notably the headwall of the Clinton Valley, a sheer glacial cirque of grey granite. As the bush drops away behind you, the slope eases to the saddle at Mackinnon Pass (1154m), a great place to eat lunch, though you'll have the company of kea and the incessant buzzing of pleasure flights from Milford. A memorial to Quintin McKinnon and Ernest Mitchell (the first Europeans to discover the pass in 1888) marks the low point of the saddle, from where the path turns east and climbs to a day-shelter (with toilets and, in summer, a gas ring) just below the dramatic form of **Mount Balloon** (1847m).

From here it's all downhill, and steeply too, initially skirting the flank of Mount Balloon then following the path beside the picturesque Roaring Burn River down to the Arthur River. The confluence is marked by **Quintin Hut** (guided walkers only). Though it remains a private hut, toilets and shelter are provided for independent walkers – who mostly dump their packs for the walk to the base of the 580m **Sutherland Falls** (4km return; 1hr–1hr 30min; 50m ascent), the highest in New Zealand. **Dumpling Hut** is another hour's walk from *Quintin Hut*.

Day 4: Dumpling Hut to Sandfly Point

18km; 5–6hr; 125m descent

You're in for an early start and a steady walk to meet your launch (the last boat departs at 4pm). After rain this can be a magnificent walk, the valley walls streaming with waterfalls and the Arthur River in spate. The track follows the tumbling river for a couple of hours to the **Boatshed** (toilets), before crossing the Arthur River by swingbridge and cutting inland to the magnificent **Mackay Falls**. Though much smaller than the Sutherland Falls, they are equally impressive, particularly after rain. Don't miss Bell Rock, a water-hollowed boulder that you can crawl inside. The track subsequently follows Lake Ada, created by a centuries-old landslip, and named by Sutherland after his Scottish girlfriend. A small lunch shelter midway along its shore heralds Giant Gate Falls, which are best viewed from the swingbridge that crosses the river at the foot of the falls. From here it is roughly an hour and a half to the shelter at **Sandfly Point** along a good, broad track, the work of convicts put to work building it in the 1890s.

ARRIVAL AND DEPARTURE   MILFORD TRACK

By bus and boat Both ends of the Milford Track can only be approached by boat, and arrangements must be made at the same time as accommodation passes are issued. Independent walkers need to catch the Tracknet bus (late Oct to April 3 daily; 30min; $28) from Te Anau to the harbour at Te Anau Downs, 30km north of Te Anau, then the launch across Lake Te Anau to Glade Wharf (late Oct to April 10.30am, 1pm & 2pm; 1hr 30min; $88). There are early departures, but since the first day's walk is very easy, it is possible to make a late start using the 12.15pm bus and the 1pm launch. At the Milford end of the track, catch the launch from the aptly named Sandfly Point to Milford Sound (late Oct to April daily 2pm, 3pm & 4pm; 20min; $49.50). Tracknet buses back to Te Anau can be picked up at 9.25am, 2.30pm and 5pm (2hr 15min; $53).

INFORMATION AND TOURS

Seasons Hiking the track outside the main Oct–April season is not recommended since transport to the trailheads is very limited, some footbridges are removed and huts have no heating. Still, bookings are not required and the Backcountry Hut Pass is valid.

Leaflets and maps DOC's *Milford Track* brochure (free) is adequate, though for detailed information consult the 1:40,000 *Geographx Milford Track Map & Track Guide* ($24.99) or the 1:50,000 NZ Topo map *Homer Saddle* ($9), both available from the Fiordland National Park Visitor Centre. See also ⓦ doc.govt.nz/milfordtrack.

Weather and track conditions DOC in Te Anau have the latest weather forecast and track conditions.

Safety DOC do not keep track of trampers' whereabouts. Let someone know your intentions through ⓦ adventuresmart. org.nz. Due to the presence of avalanche zones along the track, anyone walking out of season should check conditions with DOC before setting out. Locator beacons are available for $30/3 days from Bev's Tramping Gear (see page 646) or the Mobil garage in Te Anau.

GUIDED WALKS

Milford Track Guided Walk ☎ 0800 659 255, ⓦ ultimatehikes.co.nz. For many years, the only way to tackle the Milford Track was on a guided walk. Some argue that this is still the best approach, with just your personal effects to carry and comfortable beds in clean, plain huts with hot showers, duvets, three-course dinners with wine and cooked breakfasts. Accommodation is in shared bunkrooms or double en-suites. Staff prepare the huts, cook the meals, make up the lunches and tidy up after you. The five-day, four-night package includes a pre-track briefing in Queenstown, trailhead transport, accommodation and food on the track, a night at the *Mitre Peak Lodge* and a Milford Sound cruise (Nov–April daily departures). The same company also runs guided walks on the Routeburn Track. A single-room supplement of $535 applies, with discounts available very early and late in the season (basically Nov and April). Bunk/person $2295, double/person $2695

ACCOMMODATION

Booking There's a rigid system of advance hut booking during the main hiking season (late Oct–April). You can only walk the track from south to north, spending the first night at *Clinton Hut*, the second at *Mintaro* and the third at *Dumpling*. No backtracking or second nights are allowed. It is easiest to book free online (ⓦ doc.govt.nz) from July 1 for the following season, though it is also possible through any DOC visitor centre. Pick up your accommodation passes from DOC in Te Anau up to two days in advance; you must get them before 9am if you're on the 10.30am boat or 11am if you're on the afternoon boat. Numbers are limited to forty per day, so you'll need to book well in advance; a couple of months if you are adaptable, six if you need a specific departure date or are part of a large group. If the track is closed due to bad weather or track conditions full refunds are made.

Huts and camping During the season, the three 40-bunk huts all have wardens and are equipped with flush toilets, running water (which must be treated), heaters and gas rings, but not pans and plates; the cost is $210 for the three nights. Outside the main season these huts lose their warden and gas rings, go back to pit toilets and cost $15 per night. There is no camping on the Milford Track.

12

Lake Manapouri

Even among New Zealand's bountiful supply of beautiful lakes, **Lake Manapouri** shines, its long, indented shoreline contorted into three distinct arms and clad with thick bush tangled with ferns. The lake sits at 178m and has a vast catchment area, guzzling all the water that flows down the Upper Waiau River from Lake Te Anau and unwittingly creating a massive hydroelectric generating capacity – something that almost led to its downfall. Completed in 1971, the **Manapouri Underground Power Station** remains one of the most ambitious projects ever carried out in New Zealand, some eighty percent of its output going to Tiwai Point aluminium smelter near Bluff, 160km to the southeast. The project was dogged by controversy from the start; the initial plan was to raise the level of the lake by up to 30m, and protests by the **Save Manapouri Campaign** (which were ultimately successful) became the foundation of the New Zealand environmental movement.

Manapouri

The small village of **MANAPOURI**, 20km south of Te Anau, wraps prettily around the shores of the lake at the head of the Waiau River, which the hydroelectric shenanigans have turned into a narrow arm of the lake now known as Pearl Harbour. Apart from being the gateway to **Doubtful Sound** (see page 663), Manapouri offers a few **hiking trails** that offer spell-binding views of the lake: accommodation and eating options are very limited, however.

Manapouri Underground Power Station

Oct–April daily at 12.30–1.30pm • Tours 3–4hr • $82 (picnic lunch from $19)

> **MANAPOURI HIKES**
>
> To access these walking trails you need to cross the Waiau River at Pearl Harbour.
>
> **Circle Track** (7km; 3–4hr loop; 330m ascent) Manapouri's most popular walk snakes west around the lakeshore before turning southeast to climb the ridge with stupendous views over the lake, then heads north back to the start.
>
> **Pearl Harbour to Hope Arm** (15km loop; 6–7hr; 200m ascent) Tranquil trail through the podocarp and beech forest west of Manapouri, with stellar lake views and an optional (and often muddy) side trip to Lake Rakatu (extra 2hr). Best done as an overnighter, sleeping at beachside Hope Arm Hut (12 bunks; $5) or Back Valley Hut (4 bunks; free). Both are first come, first served.
>
> **Pearl Harbour to Fraser's Beach** (30min one-way) Easy lakeshore track through beech forest, partly following the Old Coach Road Walk with fantails and silvereye flitting about the undergrowth; the views are magnificent on a clear evening.

Real Journeys (see page 656) are the only ones with access to the impressive, if controversial, **Manapouri Underground Power Station**. After a lake cruise, you can get a sense of the scale of the place from a scale model in the visitor centre, then a bus takes you down a narrow, 2km-long spiral tunnel to a viewing platform in the Machine Hall. All you see are the exposed sections of seven whirring turbines and panels assaulting you with statistics before you're whisked back to the bus. Note that the **power station will be closed until at least October 2018** for maintenance – check ⓦ realjourneys.co.nz for the latest.

12

ARRIVAL, INFORMATION AND TOURS
MANAPOURI

By bus Topline Tours (☎ 0508 249 8059, ⓦ toplinetours. co.nz) runs between Te Anau and Manapouri (year-round daily on demand; $20; 30min); Tracknet (see page 658) also make the trip twice daily (11.10am & 4.15pm; $18), dropping off at Real Journeys Visitor Centre, but you must pre-book.

Destinations Te Anau (1–2 daily; 20min).

Tourist information The Real Journeys Visitor Centre, 64 Waiau St (daily: Nov–Feb 7.30am–6pm; March–Oct 8.30am–5.30pm; ☎ 03 249 6000, ⓦ realjourneys.co.nz), is the best place for local information, and the start for Doubtful Sound trips (see page 663).

GETTING AROUND

By boat You can get around Manapouri on foot, but to access the best walking tracks you need to get across the Waiau River, which is less than 100m across.

Adventure Manapouri ☎ 021 925 577, ⓦ adventuremanapouri.co.nz. Runs a regular water taxi across the Waiau (Oct–April daily at 11am & 3pm; $20 return), a shuttle on demand (year-round $30 return), and rents rowing boats ($40/day; $60 overnight), which you can tie up and leave on the opposite bank while you hike.

ACCOMMODATION

Acheron Cottages 98 Hillside Rd (SH99) ☎ 03 249 6626, ⓦ manapouriaccommodation.co.nz. This justly popular lodge (reservations essential) has fine lake and mountain views from its two comfortable cottages, both with two bedrooms, fully equipped kitchens (complimentary milk, tea, coffee and hot chocolate), laundry, heating and a/c. $190

★ **Cathedral Peaks B&B** 44 Cathedral Drive (SH95) ☎ 03 249 6640, ⓦ cathedralpeaks.com. Three beautiful en-suite rooms, excellent cooked breakfasts and sensational views of the lake and Cathedral Peaks. $200

Freestone Backpackers 270 Hillside Rd (SH99), 3km east of Manapouri ☎ 03 249 6893, ⓦ freestone.co.nz. With its hillside setting, fabulous lake and mountain views, and accommodation in comfy wooden chalets (one en suite,

$98), this doesn't really feel like a hostel. Chalets have pot-bellied gas stoves, log fires, verandas and basic cooking facilities (no plug sockets, though); free wi-fi is available in the main house only, and there's a coin-operated laundry (the laundry room *does* have plug sockets). Closed June & July; cash only. Dorms $29, doubles $83

Possum Lodge 13 Murrell Ave ☎ 03 249 6623, ⓦ possumlodge.co.nz. An appealingly old-fashioned, peaceful and well-maintained campsite and hostel among beech trees where the Waiau River meets the lake. Some powered sites ($39) plus retro 1940s motel units ($110). Free wi-fi in public lounge. Camping per site $34, dorms $25

EATING

The Church 23 Waiau St ☎03 249 6001. Set on the lakefront in a converted church, this is currently the best place for a meal in Manapouri, with excellent burgers, pizza, seafood baskets, cheap beer, outside seating (if it's warm enough) and homely wood fire when it's cold (mains $18–27). Free wi-fi and free shuttle service to/from your accommodation. Mon–Wed & Sun 11am–10pm, Thurs–Sat 11am–1am.

Doubtful Sound

It was the building of the Manapouri hydro scheme in the 1960s that opened up the remote and blissfully untouched **Doubtful Sound** to visitors (Captain Cook spotted it in 1770 but didn't enter, as he was "doubtful" of his ability to sail out again in the face of winds buffeted by the steep-walled fiord). What was previously the preserve of the odd yacht and a few deerstalkers and trampers is now accessible to anyone prepared to take a boat across Lake Manapouri and a bus over the Wilmot Pass. Amid pristine beauty, wildlife is a major attraction, not least the resident pod of sixty-odd **bottlenose dolphins**, who frequently come to play around ships' bows and cavort near kayakers. **Fur seals** loll on the outer islands, **Fiordland crested penguins** arrive to breed in October and November, and the bush, which comes right down to the water's edge, is alive with kaka, kiwi and other rare bird species.

Like Milford, Doubtful Sound gets a huge amount of **rain**, but don't let that put you off – the place is at its best when the cliffs spring waterfalls everywhere you look after a downpour.

Though the rock architecture is a little less dramatic than Milford Sound, it easily makes up for this with its isolation. Travel between Manapouri to Doubtful Sound takes two hours, so to fully appreciate the beauty and isolation of the area it really pays to maximize your time there by staying overnight. Costs are unavoidably high and you need to be self-sufficient, but any inconvenience is easily outweighed by the glorious solitude – although it's becoming more popular for that very reason.

Dusky Sound

Captain Cook spent six weeks in isolated **Dusky Sound**, 40km south of Doubtful Sound, on his second voyage in 1773, while his crew recovered from an arduous crossing of the Southern Ocean. Time was mostly spent at Pickersgill Harbour where, at Astronomer's Point, it is still possible to see where Cook's astronomer had trees felled so he could get an accurate fix on the stars. Not far from here is the site where 1790s castaways built the first European-style house and boat in New Zealand. Marooned by the fiord's waters, nearby **Pigeon Island** shelters the ruins of a house built by **Richard Henry**, a pioneer of New Zealand's conservation movement, who battled here from 1894 to 1908 to save endangered native birds from introduced stoats and rats. Very few tour boats come down this way (the only way to visit), making it all the more rewarding if you make the effort (and have plenty of money).

ARRIVAL AND DEPARTURE   **DUSKY SOUND**

By tour Real Journeys (☎03 249 6000, ⓦrealjourneys. co.nz) operate several tours in the area, the shortest and cheapest of which is their Dusky Sound Discovery Expedition (book well in advance; 5 days; $2650–3000), which sees you cruising around Breaksea and Dusky sounds before hopping on a helicopter back to Manapouri.

The Southern Scenic Route

While in Fiordland, don't miss out on the beautiful fringe country, where the fertile sheep paddocks of Southland butt up against the remote wilderness of Fiordland National Park. The region's towns are linked by the underrated, pastoral

DOUBTFUL SOUND CRUISES AND KAYAK TRIPS

Spending the day (or preferably a couple of days) on Doubtful Sound is an unmissable experience, and the overall quality of the kayak and cruise operators makes it even more pleasurable.

Deep Cove Charters 03 249 6828, deepcovecharters.co.nz. For a small-boat overnight experience opt for the wonderful trips aboard the twelve-berth *Seafinn*, a modern cruiser with lots of space and a dedicated crew. As well as exploring the fiord and watching wildlife you can kayak and fish. All meals are included and accommodation is in slightly cramped doubles/twins with shared bathroom. Operates Nov–March. Bunk $600, twin-share $1330, double $1430.

Doubtful Sound Kayak Te Anau Lakeview Holiday Park, 77 Manapouri–Te Anau Hwy 03 249 7777, fiordlandadventure.co.nz. Operates a full-day guided trip ($299; 10hr; transport from Te Anau included), with 4–5hr paddling on Doubtful Sound into spectacular Hall Arm. Operates Sept to early May.

Go Orange Cruises 03 442 7340, gooorange.co.nz. A subsidiary of Real Journeys, these budget-oriented day-trips ($230–255) are the cheapest way to experience Doubtful Sound, with a 3hr cruise on the fiord, complete with breezy commentary and a variety of lunch options (from $25). The boat is smaller than some, taking a maximum of 45 passengers. Packages from Te Anau (same prices) and Queenstown ($269) available.

Go Orange Kayaks 03 442 7340, gooorangekayaks.co.nz. These energetic and awe-inspiring overnight kayaking trips ($411) give you maximum time on the water with 4–6hr days paddling quality fibreglass sea kayaks either side of a night spent at a simple bush camp beside the fiord, with three-($565) and five-day ($780) trips also available. No experience is needed but the minimum age is 16 and you'll need to bring your own food. Daily Nov to late April. They also do day-trips for $255.

Real Journeys Overnight Cruise 03 249 6000, realjourneys.co.nz. Spend the night anchored in Doubtful Sound aboard the *Fiordland Navigator*, a modern cruiser that's designed to look like an old-fashioned three-masted scow. You're away from Manapouri for a full 24hr, time enough to immerse yourself in this extraordinary landscape by kayaking or even swimming. Food and accommodation are excellent. Operates Sept to mid-May and there's a ten-percent YHA discount. Per adult prices: quad-share $419, double or twin-share $669, single $1171.

Real Journeys Wilderness Cruise 03 249 6000, realjourneys.co.nz. Doubtful Sound's original day-trip involves a boat trip across Lake Manapouri, a visit to the underground power station (if open) and a bus ride to Deep Cove. You then board a catamaran for the three-hour cruise out to the mouth of the fiord (where fur seals loll on the rocks) and back, making forays into the fiord's serene "arms" (where your wildlife-spotting chances are best) before the bus and boat trip back. Year-round; 1–2 daily; 8am cruise $250; 10.30am cruise $295; preordered lunch from $19.

charms of the **Southern Scenic Route** (southernscenicroute.co.nz), a series of small roads where sheep are the primary traffic hazard. From Te Anau it runs via Manapouri south, following the valley of the **Waiau River** to the cave-pocked limestone country around **Clifden**. From here a minor road cuts west to **Lake Hauroko**, access point for the Dusky Track, while the Southern Scenic Route continues south through the small service town of **Tuatapere** (the base for hiking the **Hump Ridge and South Coast tracks**), to estuary-side **Riverton** and on to **Invercargill**.

Clifden

CLIFDEN, 90km south of Te Anau, is barely a town at all but is of passing interest for the historic **Clifden Suspension Bridge**, at 111.5m the longest wooden bridge in the South Island, built over the **Waiau River** in 1899 and still open to foot traffic (it's signposted just off the main road, near the new bridge which replaced it in 1978). You can take **jet boat rides** from here (see 665).

Amateur spelunkers should allow time to tackle the **Clifden Caves** (open access; free), which are signposted around 1km north of the bridge off the Ohai-Clifden road (SH96). With no one to guide you there's a palpable sense of adventure when exploring this limestone labyrinth lined with flowstone and stalactite formations and dotted with glowworms. The passages are not too tight but you'll need to crouch, scramble and climb several short ladders, following a series of reflective strips; modest scrambling skills are handy and you'll almost certainly get wet feet traversing the cave pool at the end. Let someone know your intentions, and go with at least one other person – do not enter the caves during or after heavy rain as they are prone to **flash flooding**. Wear clothes you don't mind getting dirty and take at least **two torches** – you can expect to be underground for 1.5 to 2hr (you can return to the car park walking along Clifden Gorge Road).

JET BOAT RIDES

Southern Scenic Jet ☎ 03 225 5677 ⓦ wjet.co.nz. Jet boat rides (30–40min; $49; Nov–March daily 10am–4pm, departures on the hour) down the Waiau River from Clifden Suspension Bridge – expect lots of bird life, including the nesting sites of the world's most endangered seagull, the Buller's (or New Zealand) black beaked gull.

Lake Hauroko

Lake Hauroko, at the end of a 20km gravel road (Lilburn Valley Rd), 32km west of Clifden, is New Zealand's deepest lake (462m). Low bush-clad hills surrounding the lake create the "sounding winds" immortalized in its Māori name. The lake sits at the southern end of the epic **Dusky Track** (84km) – one of the longest (8–10 days) and most remote in New Zealand, and much tougher than any of the Great Walks. Experienced trampers considering tackling it should obtain information and condition reports from DOC offices in the region. At First Bay, the road-end, there's just a parking area and toilets, though you can **camp** some 7km back from the lake at DOC's *Thicket Burn* campsite (free), just a grassy field with toilets and tap water.

12

LAKE HAUROKO BOAT TRIPS

Lake Hauroko Tours 1260 Clifden–Orawia Rd, Clifden ☎ 03 225 5677, ⓦ wjet.co.nz. Operates a scheduled boat service to and from the Lake Hauroko end of the Dusky Track (1hr; $99 one-way) on Mon & Thurs (Nov–April), with shuttles from Clifden included. Also half-day cruises around the lake ($150). Advanced reservations essential.
Wairaurahiri Jet 1260 Clifden–Orawia Rd, Clifden ☎ 03 225 5677, ⓦ wjet.co.nz. Day-trips (from $249, including BBQ lunch) involve shooting across the lake, then

down the Wairaurahiri River to the coast by jet boat, (stops for guided nature walks included). Also offer Hump Track or South Coast Track tramper drop-off ($189).
Wairaurahiri Wilderness Jet 7 Main St, Otautau ☎ 03 225 8174, ⓦ river-jet.co.nz. Also operates jet boat rides across Lake Hauroko and down the Wairaurahiri River, which features some of the country's most thrilling Grade III whitewater rapids (5–6hr; from $230; BBQ lunch $30).

Tuatapere

Thinly spread on the banks of the Waiau River, 14km south of Clifden, **TUATAPERE** is the largest town in southwestern Southland (though that's not saying much; there are fewer than 600 inhabitants). It was once a major sawmilling hub, but a single sawmill and one stand of beech/podocarp forest is the only evidence that the town could once have justified its epithet of "The Hole in the Bush". As logging declined, the community banded together to create the excellent **Hump Ridge Track** (62km; 3-day loop), to encourage travellers to the area. The **South Coast Track** (61km one-way; 4 days) covers some of the same terrain, and both can be combined with jetboating along the Wairaurahiri River and Lake Hauroko.

Bushman's Museum

31 Orawia Rd • Nov–March 9am–5pm • Free (donation requested) • ☎ 03 226 6739

Next to the Hump Ridge Track information centre, the modest **Bushman's Museum** commemorates Tuatapere's lumber and milling heyday with old photos and timber milling equipment, providing a fairly rose-tinted version of pioneer history.

ARRIVAL AND DEPARTURE   TUATAPERE

By bus The Humpridge Shuttle (☏03 226 6739, ⓦhumpridgetrack.co.nz) is the region's only bus service (Nov–April only), operating between Tuatapere, Te Anau ($50 one-way; $75 return) and Invercargill ($60 one-way; $95 return) – connections to and from Queenstown ($95 one-way; $150 return) are booked through Humpridge

Shuttle, but operated by Tracknet. Advanced bookings essential.

Destinations Te Anau (1 daily 4.30pm; 1hr 15min); Invercargill (1 daily 12.30pm; 1hr 30min); Queenstown (1 daily 10.45am; 7hr); Rarakau Car Park, for the Hump Ridge Track (1 daily 8am; 30min).

INFORMATION

Hump Ridge Track booking office and information centre 31 Orawia Rd (daily mid-Nov to April 7.30am–6pm; ☏03 226 6739, ⓦhumpridgetrack. co.nz). Primarily set up for Hump Ridge Track hikers with

a small selection of tramping essentials and plenty of trail information. They can store valuables while you're in the wilds, and help with local accommodation and transport ($45 return to the trailhead at Rarakau car park).

ACCOMMODATION AND EATING

Tuatapere was once famous for its **sausages** (signs in the town still proclaim it "Sausage Capital"), but the last maker of traditional Tuatapere Sausages closed in 2015 (the recipe was concocted here in the 1980s). You might still be able to find some succulent local bangers at *Highway 99 Café/Bar* (daily 10am–8pm), 2 McFeely St, or in the surprisingly well-stocked Four Square supermarket, 73 Main Rd (which contains a simple canteen).

Last Light Lodge & Café 2 Clifden Hwy ☏03 226 6667, ⓦlastlightlodge.com. Once a forestry camp, this complex has been nicely converted into a holiday camp, with small, basic rooms (some triples from $101) and a few tent ($14 per person) and campervan ($16 per person) sites. The café is excellent, with plenty of seating outside, free wi-fi and a range of tasty dishes served all day – think tandoori curry ($28) or blue cod ($30). Café daily 8am–8pm (hours shortened May–Oct). $70

Tuatapere Motels & Shooters Backpackers 73 Main St ☏0800 009993, ⓦtuatapereaccommodation. co.nz. Slightly soulless but well-equipped combination of four spacious modern motel units, a backpackers with spa pool ($25/hr) and some tent sites ($18) and hook-ups ($19). Dorms 30, doubles $65

Yesteryears Café & Museum 3a Orawia Rd ☏03 226 6682. Owner Helen McKay whips up delightful home-made food in this former bakery decked out with a cornucopia of early twentieth-century kitchenware – a tribute to her and her husband's grandmothers, whose four jam pots hang on the wall (the "museum" is free). If you're in luck, she'll fire up the old coal range for pikelets with raspberry jam and cream, but otherwise there are pies, mince on toast ($6–10) and delectable date scones to keep you occupied – all to a soundtrack of golden oldies on the 1970s turntable. Oct–April daily 7am–5pm.

Te Waewae Bay

South of Tuatapere, SH99 follows the wind-ravaged cliffs behind the wide and moody **Te Waewae Bay**, where fierce southerlies have sculpted the much-photographed macrocarpa trees into extravagantly windswept forms. About 10km south of Tuatapere you get a spectacular view of the coast at **McCrackens Rest Lookout**. Just before Orepuki, the highway passes **Gemstone Beach**, a popular spot for beachcombing.

Orepuki and Monkey Island

The tiny one-street village of **OREPUKI**, 20km south of Tuatapere, is best known for its *Orepuki Beach Café*. About 3km beyond Orepuki, signs point to **Monkey Island** where there's a wide **beach**, magnificent sunsets and basic camping (free) with vault toilets. The tiny, namesake island just offshore (you can walk to it at low tide) has nothing to with monkeys sadly; the name is most likely a reference to the "monkey winch" once used to haul boats onto the beach, but you might see Hector dolphins frolicking in the lagoons nearby.

EATING	OREPUKI

★ **Orepuki Beach Café** Main Hwy ☎ 03 234 5211. Best known for exceptional chowder, but also cook their own beef, lamb and garden produce, delicious cakes and coffee. Daily 9am–5pm (usually opens later on Fri & Sat).

Cosy Nook

A further 4km south along SH99 from Monkey Island, signs point 5km west to **Cosy Nook**, a wonderfully picturesque cove hemmed in by granite boulders – you could easily imagine it along Scotland's west coast (the road ends up as a gravel, but passable, one-lane track). Indeed, one apocryphal story has a former resident, George Thomson, naming it after his Highland home village. The spot was once the site of one of the largest Māori settlements along this stretch of coast in the 1820s, with a *pa* (fort) on Matariki Island at the cove's mouth (which was returned to the Ngai Tahu people in 1997), though today all you'll see is a huddle of rustic holiday homes and old fishing shacks.

Colac Bay

Some 17km southeast of Orepuki, the highway regains the coast at the quiet community of **COLAC BAY**, a name eighteenth-century whalers derived from the local Māori chief, Korako. Apart from swimming and a nationally renowned **beach break** (known as "Trees", commemorated with a **giant surfer statue** outside the *Colac Bay Tavern*), the only reason to stop is to get some rest – self-contained **campervans** are allowed to park overnight on Colac Foreshore Road between the boat ramp and shelter shed (2 nights max; free).

Riverton

RIVERTON (Aparima), 12km east of Colac Bay, is one of the country's oldest settlements. Frequented by whalers as early as the 1790s, the town was formally established in 1836 by whaling captain John Howell – who is also credited with kick-starting New Zealand's now formidable sheep-farming industry. The small town is strung along a spit between the sea and the Jacob's River Estuary (actually the mouth of the Aparima and Pourakino rivers), where fishing boats still harbour. **St Mary's Anglican Church** (173 Palmerston St, opposite the museum) is one the prettiest in the region, completed in 1902 with a rare broached copper spire and beautiful rimu ceiling.

Te Hikoi: Southern Journey

172 Palmerston St • Daily: Oct–March 10am–5pm; April–Sept 10am–4pm • $8 • ☎ 03 234 8260, ⓦ tehikoi.co.nz

If you've any interest in the cultural history of the south coast, devote an hour to **Te Hikoi: Southern Journey**, a well-presented, modern museum, which kicks off with an absorbing fifteen-minute movie focusing on the unsettling times of early European contact. The subsequent tableau of a Māori muttonbirders' camp isn't entirely convincing but the tales of harvesting on the Titi Islands and the Māori seasonal food-gathering calendar show just how tough it was in these southern climes. Europeans didn't have it much easier, sealing, whaling and hacking out a living from the bush – though the charting of the virtual extinction of fur seals and the local right whale population by the 1830s might make you feel less sympathetic. Intermarriage between early European settlers and Māori women is highlighted, and there's also coverage of the 1880s Chinese gold-mining community at **Round Hill** (the remnants of which lie 5km back along SH99). The museum also doubles as the local **iSite information centre**.

ACCOMMODATION AND EATING	RIVERTON

Monkey's Backpackers 144 Palmerston St ☎ 020 4120 5732, ✉ monkeysbackpackers@gmail.com. Converted pub with dorms (no linen; bring a sleeping bag), singles and doubles, fully equipped shared kitchen, lounge/games room (with pool table and darts) and laundry. Tent sites from $15 per person. Dorms $20, doubles $50

★ **Postmaster Bakery** 166 Palmerston St ☎ 03 234 8153. The best coffee, sandwiches and cakes in town (as well as the locally celebrated cheese rolls), served in the grand old post office of 1911, with original polished wood floors and pressed tin ceilings. Free wi-fi. Cash only. Mon–Fri 7am–4pm, Sat & Sun 7.30am–4pm.

Invercargill

One of the southernmost cities in the world, **INVERCARGILL** is a surprisingly vibrant commercial centre and the gateway to **Stewart Island**, though the city of 60,000 boasts a growing tourism sector of its own. In addition to offering the chance to smash stuff up in your own bulldozer it's an especially popular destination for motorcycle fans – this is the home of *The World's Fastest Indian*.

Founded in the 1850s, Invercargill benefitted from the explosion in dairy exports in the early 1900s, while a second dairy boom in the 2000s has fuelled more recent growth. In 2000, community contributions allowed its main centre of learning, the **Southern Institute of Technology** (SIT), to offer free tuition for New Zealand and Australian residents (with lower than usual fees for international students), breathing new life into its arts scene and nightlife.

Town centre

While Invercargill's busy **town centre** sports mostly bland, functional buildings, the streets are studded with some real architectural gems, notably the pale yellow former **Town Hall** (now the **Civic Theatre**) of 1906 at 88 Tay St (on the main drag), the majestic **Victoria Railway Hotel** (1896) and several historic churches. The gorgeous Romanesque-Byzantine-style **First Presbyterian Church** (1915) at 151 Tay St features a striking 32m bell tower, while Catholic **St Mary's Basilica** at 65 Tyne St opened in 1905 and remains the city's most distinctive landmark, with a copper-clad dome and spectacular rose window.

12

Southland Museum and Art Gallery

108 Gala St, beside Queens Park • Mon–Fri 9am–5pm, Sat & Sun 10am–5pm • Free • ☎ 03 219 9069, ⓦ southlandmuseum.co.nz

Invercargill's chief attraction is the **Southland Museum and Art Gallery**, a giant white pyramid housing a well-laid-out collection over three levels. Upstairs, the fascinating "Beyond the Roaring Forties" exhibit focuses on New Zealand's **sub-Antarctic islands**, tiny windswept clusters such as the Auckland Islands and Campbell Island, lying hundreds of kilometres apart between New Zealand and Antarctica. Displays cover the shipwreck victims who have clung on to the islands, sometimes for years, sealers who subsisted while depressingly almost wiping out their quarry and meteorological teams who have weathered the storms with the albatross and penguins.

Southland's history is highlighted with a series of full-size Victorian household interiors and an exhibition on World War I, while downstairs, Māori artefacts include greenstone jewellery, rare canoes (discovered in 2011 and 2013) still being treated in water and intricately carved canoe prows from the 1600s. Burt Munro's exploits (see page 672) get glowing coverage alongside a replica bike made for *The World's Fastest Indian*.

Don't miss the **tuatara** – small, dinosaurian reptiles found nowhere else in the world – including Henry, who is thought to be well over a hundred years old. You can observe them in the glassed-in **tuatarium** at the back of the museum's ground floor.

Queens Park

Main entrance on Gala St • Animal Reserve daily 8.30am–4.30pm; Aviary daily 8am–sunset • Free

The vast **Queens Park** is Invercargill's prime green space and was set aside as a public reserve at the city's founding in 1857. Today there are lovely formal rose gardens, the Japanese Garden (built in 1997 by Japanese sister city Kumagaya), a farmyard-style Animal Reserve (featuring kunekune pigs, red deer and Enderby Island rabbits) and the walk-through Aviary (featuring native bird species, such as keas, kakas and parakeets), among other delights.

Invercargill Brewery

72 Leet St • Mon–Sat 10am–6pm; tours Mon–Fri 1pm • Tours $25 • ☎ 03 214 5070, ⓦ invercargillbrewery.co.nz

Connoisseurs of fine beer won't want to miss out on the **Invercargill Brewery**. There are walk-in brewery tours on weekdays, with samples of the standard range of beers included at the end (in the *Cellar Door*, which also opens on Saturdays). Brewer

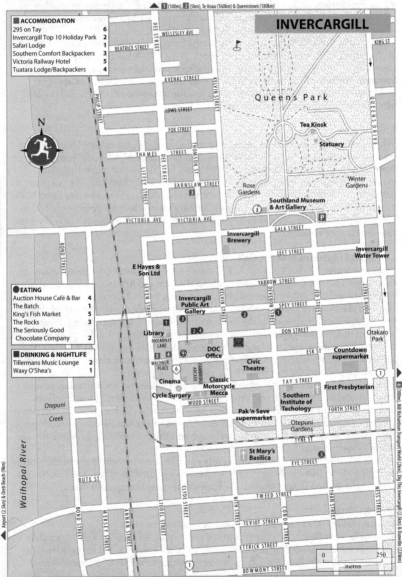

INVERCARGILL

ACCOMMODATION
295 on Tay	6
Invercargill Top 10 Holiday Park	2
Safari Lodge	1
Southern Comfort Backpackers	3
Victoria Railway Hotel	5
Tuatara Lodge/Backpackers	4

EATING
Auction House Café & Bar	4
The Batch	1
King's Fish Market	5
The Rocks	3
The Seriously Good Chocolate Company	2

DRINKING & NIGHTLIFE
Tillermans Music Lounge	2
Waxy O'Shea's	1

Steve Nally makes several varieties, including Stanley Green Pale Ale, named after the brewer's maternal grandfather and Wasp Honey Pilsner, flavoured with a touch of kamahi honey from the Catlins.

Invercargill Water Tower
107 Doon St, at Leet St • Closed to the public

The city's eastern skyline is dominated by the ornate 40m-high brick **Invercargill Water Tower**, a Romanesque, polychrome edifice that's surely far grander than it really needed to be. It was completed in 1889, but has been closed since 2012 due to earthquake concerns.

E. Hayes and Sons Ltd
168 Dee St • Mon–Fri 7.30am–5.30pm, Sat 9am–4pm, Sun 10am–4pm • Free • ☎ 03 218 2059, ⓦ ehayes.co.nz

Among the wrenches and hedge trimmers in Invercargill's premier hardware and homewares store, **E. Hayes and Sons Ltd**, is an eccentric collection of lovingly restored classic cars and historic motorbikes. Star attraction is the record-breaking bike ridden by **Burt Munro**, accompanied by some of his other bikes (Burt sold them to the Hayes family in 1977), replicas made for *The World's Fastest Indian*, British thumpers from the 1950s and 1960s, gleaming T-Birds and Corvettes and the shop's own 1956 Morris-Commercial delivery van.

Invercargill Public Art Gallery
5 Don St • Tues–Fri 10am–5pm, Sat noon–3.30pm • Free • ☎ 03 215 7432, ⓦ invercargillpublicartgallery.nz

Invercargill Public Art Gallery (formally Anderson Park Art Gallery) manages the city's surprisingly extensive public art collection, holding court in these temporary premises while its original Anderson Park home awaits some kind of renovation (the 1925 neo-Georgian mansion has been closed since 2014, however). The permanent collection of over 1000 pieces includes works by New Zealanders Charles Goldie, Rita Angus, Colin McCahon and Ralph Hotere, as well as contemporary artists such as Gregor Kregar.

12

Classic Motorcycle Mecca
25 Tay St • Daily 10am–5pm (last entry 4pm) • $20 ($40 with Bill Richard's Transport World) • ☎ 03 217 0199, ⓦ transportworld.co.nz/motorcycle-mecca

Aficionados will want to visit **Classic Motorcycle Mecca**, the latest of several moto-themed attractions to cash in on the Munro connection. Inside is the largest display of motorcycles in the country, some three hundred in all, ranging from rare antique 1902 Peugeot models to the latest touring bikes (previously housed in Nelson, the entire collection was sold to Transport World in 2016).

Bill Richardson Transport World
491 Tay St • Daily 10am–5pm (last entry 4pm) • $25 ($40 with Motorcycle Mecca) • ☎ 03 27 0199, ⓦ transportworld.co.nz

With literally hundreds of antique motor vehicles and petrol pumps on display, massive **Bill Richardson Transport World** is paradise for anyone with a passion for cars. Highlights include retro Volkswagen Kombis, Ford Model Ts, 1940s Diamond T trucks and rare 1930s Ford V8s (there's also an exhibit on the iconic *Pork Pie* movies filmed in Invercargill). Southland businessman Bill Richardson begin collecting in the 1960s, but passed away in 2005 – his family opened his collection to the public in 2015.

Dig This Invercargill
84 Otepuni Ave (1km from Transport World) • Daily 9am–6pm; digs daily 9am, 11am, 1pm & 3pm (plus 5pm Oct–April) • Rates range $20/50 for mini-digs (10–30min), to $169–385 for full digs (45min–1hr) • ☎ 03 217 0199, ⓦ transportworld.co.nz/dig-this

Invercargill's latest attraction is a dream for every grown-up little kid, with **Dig This Invercargill** offering a unique opportunity to operate bulldozers, excavators, mini excavators

BURT MUNRO – INVERCARGILL'S LOCAL HERO

Few New Zealanders, let alone anyone in the rest of the world, knew about **Burt Munro** (1899–1978) until Roger Donaldson's *The World's Fastest Indian* hit movie screens in 2005. All of a sudden everyone had heard of this eccentric **Invercargill mechanic** who, in 1967, aged 68, set the under-1000cc speed record of 295kph (184mph) on a 1920 Indian Scout bike at Bonneville Salt Flats in Utah (he actually hit speeds of 305kph/190mph during the attempt). He had spent years modifying the bike and testing it at Oreti Beach, just outside Invercargill. His stock has been rising around the town ever since the movie's release, with a display in the museum, a statue outside Queens Park, the original bike in E. Hayes and Sons Ltd shop, and the annual Burt Munro Challenge, four days of speedway and street racing, a hill climb and, of course, beach racing each November. Burt's record still stands.

and skid steers in a giant gravel pit. Experience is not necessary – it's a lot of fun, with "Dig & Destroy" an especially effective way of letting off steam. Bookings essential.

Demolition World

290 Bain St (5km south of the centre) • Mon–Fri 10am–5pm, Sat 9.30am–1pm • Free ("gold coin" donation requested) • ☎ 03 216 2441, ⓦ demoworld.co.nz

One of Invercargill's quirkier sights, **Demolition World** is a "village" constructed entirely from demolished buildings and recycled items, enhanced by a slightly spooky ensemble of mannequins and historic memorabilia, plus free-range chickens and the odd dog. Highlights include a "haunted" theatre, historic school, church and sweet store.

ARRIVAL AND DEPARTURE

INVERCARGILL

By plane Stewart Island Flights (see page 679) and Air New Zealand flights from Wellington and Christchurch land at Invercargill Airport (ⓦ invercargillairport.co.nz), 3.5km southwest of the city centre. For transport into town (10min) use Blue Star taxis (☎ 03 217 7777, ⓦ bluestartaxis.co.nz; $20); there is no public bus service, but long-distance companies will pick you up if you pre-arrange. Long-term airport parking costs $16 for the first day, $7 for the second, eventually dropping to a flat rate of $5/day from day five onwards.

Destinations Christchurch (5–7 daily; 1hr 15min); Stewart Island (3 daily; 20min); Wellington (1–2 daily; 1hr 55min).

By bus InterCity stops outside the i-SITE at 108 Gala St. Catch-A-Bus South (☎ 03 479 9960, ⓦ catchabussouth.co.nz) picks up from accommodation and Invercargill airport on their daily runs to Dunedin, Queenstown and Bluff. Stewart Island Experience buses also connect with each ferry departure in Bluff (see page 674).

Destinations Bluff (for Stewart Island; 5–6 daily; 30min); Dunedin (1–2 daily; 3hr 45min); Gore (3–4 daily; 1hr); Queenstown (2 daily; 3hr 45min).

GETTING AROUND

By bus The city's four bus routes (Mon–Sat only; ⓦ bussmart.co.nz), cost $3 (peak times) and just $1.60 to ride Mon–Fri 9am–2.55pm and Sat 10.30am–3.40pm. The main bus stop is dubbed Bus Smart Central (Dee St, just north of the central roundabout at Tay St).

By bike You'll get cycle trail maps and good-quality mountain bikes from Cycle Surgery, 21 Tay St (Mon–Fri 8.30am–5.30pm, Sat 10am–2pm; ☎ 03 218 8055, ⓦ cyclesurgeryinvercargill.co.nz), for $35/day.

INFORMATION

Tourist information i-SITE, 108 Gala St (Mon–Fri 8.30am–5pm, Sat & Sun 8.30am–4pm; ☎ 03 211 0895, ⓦ southlandnz.co.nz). Excellent visitor centre in the foyer of the Southland Museum, where you can pick up the *Invercargill Heritage Trail* leaflet, which details some

distinctive architecture around the city centre.

DOC Office Level 7, 33 Don St (Mon–Fri 8am–4.30pm; ☎ 03 211 2400). Information on walks and wildlife in the Catlins, Stewart Island and Fiordland.

ACCOMMODATION

Invercargill has a plethora of places to stay, with motels lining SH1 just outside the town centre. **Freedom camping** is not allowed in town or anywhere nearby –

the nearest DOC site is at Colac Bay (see page 668). All the listings below offer free wi-fi and free parking unless otherwise stated.

295 on Tay 295 Tay St ☎ 03 211 1295, ⊛ 295ontay.co.nz; map p.670. Very comfortable modern motel; the bland but pleasant rooms all have full kitchens, heated towel rails, electric blankets, minibars and hairdryers; downstairs units have spa baths too. Breakfast $12.50. $120

Invercargill Top 10 Holiday Park 77 McIvor Rd, 6km north of the city centre ☎ 03 215 9032, ⊛ invercargilltop10.co.nz; map p.670. Upscale parkland campsite with the typically high-standard Top 10 facilities, including a gas BBQ and pizza oven; cabins are $80, and comfy motel units $140. Wi-fi is $5/day. Camping per site $42

★ **Safari Lodge** 51 Herbert St ☎ 0800 885557, ⊛ safarilodge.co.nz; map p.670. Decorated with mementos of the owners' years in Mozambique, this luxurious four-room B&B is reminiscent of a Victorian explorer's mansion. The rooms are tastefully decorated and all have four-poster beds, while amenities include a billiards table and hot tub. Full breakfast and sundowners included. $230

Southern Comfort Backpackers 30 Thomson St ☎ 03 218 3838, ⊛ southerncomfortbackpackers.com; map p.670. Suburban BBH hostel in a neatly kept Victorian villa set among manicured lawns where a kids' playhouse has been put to use as a tiny double room ($60). There's a great modern kitchen and free luggage storage for those tramping on Stewart Island. Dorms $32, doubles $72

★ **Victoria Railway Hotel** 3 Leven St ☎ 03 218 1281, ⊛ hotelinvercargill.co.nz; map p.670. Grand central hotel built back in 1896 oozing historic character, now managed by friendly hosts Tom and Rose Shields – with only eleven rooms it feels more like a B&B. Rooms are compact but modern and comfy, with all the usual amenities, and the on-site bar and *Gerrard's Restaurant* are open to guests only, making a cosy spot to end to the evening. $120

Tuatara Lodge/Backpackers 30 Dee St ☎ 03 214 0954, ⊛ tuataralodge.co.nz; map p.670. High-ceilinged hostel in a converted bank building, right in the heart of town. While it's a little shabby around the edges, the rooms are decent (although some are windowless) and guests get a discount in the excellent café on the ground floor. Limited off-street parking. Dorms $28, doubles $75

EATING

Invercargill specializes in juicy Bluff oysters (freshest March–Aug) and blue cod, as well as Stewart Island salmon and muttonbird.

Auction House Café & Bar 20 Don St ☎ 03 214 1914, ⊛ theauctionhouse.co.nz; map p.670. Popular early breakfast café dishing up zingy coffee and a delicious Spanish sausage dish ($20) along with excellent cakes, scones and muffins; they also cook tasty lunches ($14.50–20.50), serve dinner from 5.30pm and have craft beer on tap. Mon 6.30am–4.30pm, Tues–Fri 6.30am–late, Sat 8am–late, Sun 9am–4pm.

★ **The Batch** 173 Spey St ☎ 03 214 6357; map p.670. Invercargill's best café is a light airy space with sofas and comfy chairs. They serve superb coffee and creative brunch dishes including dukkah (an Arabic spice) and feta poached eggs ($18), smoked cod cakes ($12.50) and sensational blue cod and mussel chowder ($17.50) along with their totally addictive "cinny scrolls" (cinnamon rolls; $5.50) and bacon and cheese scones ($4). Mon–Fri 7am–4.30pm, Sat & Sun 8am–4pm.

King's Fish Market 59 Ythan St ☎ 03 218 8450, ⊛ kingsfish.co.nz; map p.670. You can buy the fresh seafood on display to take away (priced by weight) or have it cooked to order while you wait (extra $1); they also do incredibly cheap, delicious blue cod and chips ($8.40–

14.50), fresh oysters (March–Aug) and mussels, whitebait fritters (in season; $8.50), dried muttonbird and Stewart Island salmon. There are a couple of small tables (inside and on the street) if you want to eat at the shop. Mon & Tues 9am–7pm, Wed–Fri 9am–8pm, Sat 10am–7.30pm, Sun 11am–7pm.

The Rocks Courtville Place, 101 Dee St ☎ 03 218 7597, ⊛ shop5rocks.com; map p.670. Longtime locals' favourite with bare brick walls and varied menu stretching from Sicilian seafood stew ($36.50) to ribeye steak finished with Kikorangi blue cheese sauce ($37.50). The more limited lunchtime menu has plenty of lower-priced options, with mains $18–23. Tues–Fri 10am–2pm & 5–9pm, Sat 11am–2pm & 5–9pm.

The Seriously Good Chocolate Company 147 Spey St ☎ 03 218 8060, ⊛ seriouslygoodchocolate.com; map p.670. This petite café is a perfectly good spot for a sausage roll or muffin and a coffee, but that would be missing the point. Sup on a super-rich hot chocolate while you choose from their fabulous selection of inventive creations all made on-site. Boxes of chocolates include a selection flavoured with Central Otago pinots, or with a Kiwiana theme (flavoured with jaffas, chocolate fish, hokey pokey and pineapple lumps). Mon–Fri 7am–4pm, Sat 9.30am–1pm.

DRINKING AND NIGHTLIFE

A number of the city's bars transform into dance venues as the evening wears on, though the town is usually quiet until Thursday night, and liveliest during university term time.

Tillermans Music Lounge 16 Don St ☎ 03 218 9240; map p.670. Behind this anonymous doorway on Don St lies a popular bar with pool tables; it's a focal point for

(often fairly offbeat) live music. Fri & Sat 11pm–3am.

Waxy O'Shea's 90 Dee St ☎ 03 214 0313, ⊛ waxys. co.nz; map p.670. Convivial and more convincing-than-average Irish bar with good – and occasionally live – music. They do a decent bangers and mash for $22.90 or steak and Guinness pie for $20.90. Daily 11am–10pm or later.

12

DIRECTORY

Internet Wi-fi is free at the museum/i-SITE and in the library; also free wi-fi hotspots along Esk St shopping mall.

Left luggage The i-SITE will hold bags during the day but not overnight (free).

Library 50 Dee St (Mon–Fri 9am–7pm, Sat & Sun 10am–4pm; ☎ 03 211 1444, ⓦ ilibrary.co.nz).

Medical treatment Southland Hospital, on Kew Rd (☎ 03 218 1949), has a 24hr accident and emergency department. For illness and minor accidents outside surgery hours,

contact the After Hours Doctors, 40 Clyde St (☎ 03 218 8821; Mon–Fri 6pm–6am, Sat & Sun 9am–4pm; appointment required; $105 per visit).

Pharmacy Inside the Countdown supermarket at 172 Tay St (pharmacy Mon–Fri 9am–8pm, Sat & Sun 9am–6pm); plus 24hr convenience store at Esk and Dee streets.

Police 117 Don St (☎ 03 211 0400).

Post office 51 Don St, near the junction with Kelvin St (Mon–Fri 9am–5pm, Sat 9am–1pm).

Bluff

The small but busy fishing town and port of **BLUFF**, 27km south of Invercargill, occupies a slender-waisted peninsula with its man-made harbour on one side and the wild Foveaux Strait on the other. Continuously settled since 1824, Bluff is the oldest European town in New Zealand and is starting to show its age. Parts look decidedly run down and, while most visitors are here to hop on the ferry to **Stewart Island**, the place has a great setting, a long history and some fine short walks. Unless you have your own vehicle, seeing the town will involve a good deal of walking, as it spreads along the shoreline for about 6km.

Bluff's famous oysters are celebrated at the annual **Bluff Oyster & Food Festival** (third weekend in May; ⓦ bluffoysterfest.co.nz), an event the local organizers claim is "unsophisticated and proud of it".

Bluff Maritime Museum

241 Foreshore Rd, 1km north of the ferry dock • Mon–Fri 10am–4.30pm, Sat & Sun in summer 1–5pm • $3

Bluff's small **Bluff Maritime Museum** contains historical displays focusing on whaling, the harbour development, oyster harvesting and shipwrecks. Pride of place is given to a triple-expansion steam engine and the 1909 oyster boat, *Monica II*, which sits outside the building.

Stirling Point

SH1, 2km south of the ferry dock

State Highway 1 ends at **Stirling Point**, not the South Island's most southerly point (that's Slope Point in the Catlins), but a fine spot with a multi-armed (and much photographed) **signpost** that balances Cape Reinga's at the other end of the country and the start of a couple of short **walks**.

Nearby, a massive **anchor chain sculpture** disappears into the sea, symbolically linking Stirling Point with Russell Beck's near-identical sculpture at Lee Bay on Stewart Island. In Māori lore, the South Island is demigod Maui's canoe, and Stewart Island is *Te Punga o Te Waka a Maui*, "The Anchor Stone of Maui's Canoe".

There are a couple of worthwhile **walks** from the car park at Stirling Point. The Foveaux Walkway (6.6km; 2hr one way; mostly flat) loops back towards town and has stupendous coastal views. The Topuni Track (2km one way; 45min; 265m ascent) is fairly steep and climbs to Bluff Hill Lookout for 360-degree views encompassing Stewart Island, 35km away. The lookout is also accessible by road from Bluff: follow Lee Street, opposite the ferry wharf, uphill for 3km.

ARRIVAL AND INFORMATION   BLUFF

By bus Catch-A-Bus South (see page 672) and Stewart Island Experience (☎ 0800 000511, ⓦ stewartislandexperience.co.nz) run regular bus services from Invercargill i-Site, *Tuatara Backpackers*, *Victoria*

Railway Hotel and the airport ($25 each way), to connect with the ferry (buses leave Invercargill 1hr before ferry departure). For details on sailings to Stewart Island, see page 679.

Tourist information Bluff's maritime museum acts as a de facto visitor centre. Check out w bluff.co.nz and pick up a *Bluff Heritage Trail* leaflet at Invercargill's i-SITE

ACCOMMODATION AND EATING

Bluff Lodge 120 Gore St ☎03 212 7106, w blufflodge. co.nz. Super-handy for the Stewart Island ferries, this peeling 1899 former post office now has five- and seven-bed dorms and three doubles, all sharing kitchen and bathroom facilities. The rooms are nothing fancy, but you can't complain at these prices. Linen is $5/person extra. Wi-fi is $3 for 30min or $5 till 10am following day; laundry $4; parking while on Stewart Island $4/night. Cash only. Dorms $20, doubles $45

Johnson's Oysters 8 Foreshore Rd ☎03 212 8665. Between March and August you can buy Bluff oysters around $23–27 for a dozen) direct at factory prices from several spots on Bluff's waterfront including this venerable establishment. March–Aug daily 9am–4pm.

Lands End Stirling Point 10 Ward Parade, Stirling Point ☎03 212 7575, w landsendhotel.co.nz. Overlooking Stirling Point's famous signpost, most of the stylish rooms here have brilliant views on clear days; happily there's heating for when the weather is less clement. All rooms are en suite with a continental breakfast in the café downstairs included. $265

Stewart Island

The Foveaux Strait separates the South Island from New Zealand's third main island, **STEWART ISLAND**, a genuinely special place of rare birds, bountiful seas and straight-talking people.

Most of Stewart Island is uninhabited and characterized by bush-fringed bays, sandy coves, windswept beaches and a rugged interior of rimu forest and granite outcrops. It is

12

STEWART ISLAND ADVENTURES

The dispersed nature of the sights on Stewart Island makes it well suited to guided trips and tours. Both **Ulva Island** and **Whalers Base** form part of various boat tours that take in Paterson Inlet and beyond. Energetic visitors can explore more thoroughly by sea-kayaking around the inlet's scattered bays and islands. The waters around Stewart Island are highly changeable; only extremely experienced kayakers should venture into these waters unaccompanied.

Phil's Sea Kayak 7 Leonard St, Halfmoon Bay (Oban) ☎03 219 1444, e philskayak@ observationrocklodge.co.nz. Excellent paddling trips around Paterson Inlet or along the coast north of Halfmoon Bay. Explore narrow inlets overhung by bush and see plenty of birdlife; exact itineraries are tailored to suit conditions and paddlers' experience, with prices from $90 for a 2hr sunset trip and $145 for a guided half-day tour, with hot drinks and buns included.

Ruggedy Range Wilderness Experience 14 Main Rd, Halfmoon Bay (Oban) ☎03 219 1066, w ruggedyrange.com. Furhana Ahmad leads fun and enthusiastic guided nature walks and hikes (from $130 for 3hr to $1050 for 3 days), sea kayaking (from $95 for 2hr to $230 for 1 day circumnavigation of Ulva), wild kiwi spotting (from $135) and scenic boat cruises (Ulva and Stewart islands; $120–140).

Stewart Island Experience The Red Shed, 12 Elgin Terrace, Oban ☎03 212 7660, w stewartislandexperience.co.nz. The main player on the island runs a number of trips and offers small discounts to those taking multiple trips. Its Wild Kiwi Encounter (4hr; $199) includes a cruise across Paterson Inlet to Little Glory Cove and The Neck, where a 45min guided walk by torchlight often reveals brown kiwis. The Village and Bays Tour (2–3 daily; 1hr 30min; $45) gets you onto a minibus and gives you the lie of the land around Oban, while the Ulva Island Explorer (Oct–April; 2hr 30min; $95) is a great introduction to the idyllic offshore island.

Ulva's Guided Walks (at Stewart Island Gift Shop, 20 Main Rd, Oban) ☎03 219 1216, w ulva.co.nz. Ulva Goodwillie was named after the island she now visits regularly on excellent 3–4hr guided walks ($130) which include plenty of botanizing and local Māori stories. Ulva also leads teams up with other companies to offer the Birding Bonanza, designed to pack in an evening kiwi-spotting expedition, a morning at Ulva island and an afternoon catamaran cruise (generally Mon eve–Tues afternoon; $480).

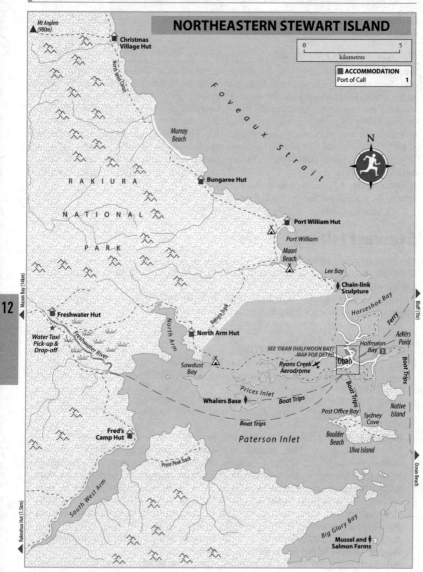

NORTHEASTERN STEWART ISLAND

Mt Anglem (980m)

Christmas Village Hut

North West Trail

Foveaux Strait

Murray Beach

R A K I U R A

Bungaree Hut

N A T I O N A L

Port William Hut

Port William

Maori Beach

Lee Bay

P A R K

Chain-link Sculpture

Horseshoe Bay

Ferry

Bluff (1hr)

Freshwater Hut

North Arm Hut

Rakiura Track

North Arm

SEE 'OBAN (HALFMOON BAY)' MAP FOR DETAIL

Halfmoon Bay

Ackers Point

Water Taxi Pick-up & Drop-off

Freshwater River

Sawdust Bay

Ryans Creek Aerodrome

Oban

Boat Trips

Maori Bay (14km)

12

Whalers Base

Prices Inlet

Boat Trips

Post Office Bay

Sydney Cove

Native Island

Fred's Camp Hut

Boat Trips

Paterson Inlet

Boulder Beach

Ulva Island

Pryse Peak Track

South West Arm

Big Glory Bay

Rakeahua Hut (1.5km)

Mussel and Salmon Farms

Ocean Beach

0   5
kilometres

ACCOMMODATION
Port of Call   **1**

known in Māori as Rakiura ("The Land of Glowing Skies"), although the jury is still out on whether this refers to the aurora australis – a.k.a. **southern lights** – occasionally seen in the night sky throughout the year, or the fabulous sunsets. The island was later named after William Stewart, the first officer on a sealing vessel that visited in 1809. Today almost all of Stewart Island's residents live from **conservation** work, **fishing** (crayfish, blue cod and paua), **fish farming** (salmon and mussels) and tourism. With the creation of **Rakiura National Park** in 2002 a full 85 percent of the island is now protected.

Almost the entire population of four hundred lives in the sole town, **Oban** (aka Halfmoon Bay), where boats dock, planes land and the parrot-shriek of kaka provides the soundtrack.

There's not much to do in town, but the slow island ways can quickly get into your blood and you may well want to stay longer than you had planned, especially if you're drawn to serious wilderness **tramping**, abundant **wildlife** in unspoilt surroundings and **sea-kayaking** around the flooded valley of **Paterson Inlet**.

Since 2013 a $5 **visitor levy** has been charged for Stewart Island. This is typically included in your flight or ferry ticket; the funds thus raised are used to maintain and improve visitor facilities.

Oban (Halfmoon Bay)

Scattered around Halfmoon Bay, **OBAN** comprises little more than a few dozen houses, a visitor centre, a tiny museum, a couple of stores and cafés, and a hotel with a bar. More houses straggle away up the surrounding hills, surrounded by bush alive with native birds. Without trying, you'll see tui and kereru and small flocks of squawking **kaka**, large rusty-brown native parrots that are almost never seen elsewhere in the country.

Rakiura Museum

9 Ayr St • Oct–April Mon–Sat 10am–1.30pm, Sun noon–2pm; May–Sept Mon–Fri 10am–noon, Sat 10am–1.30pm, Sun noon–2pm • $2 • ☎ 03 219 1221, ⓦ rakiuramuseum.co.nz

Devote some time to the **Rakiura Museum**, which focuses on local history including an 1816 globe still showing Stewart Island attached to the South Island, as Cook had depicted it. The small Māori collection contains a rare necklace made from several hundred dolphin teeth, while two giant sperm whale teeth add bite to a whaling display that includes delicate examples of scrimshaw.

Observation Rock

Excelsior Rd, 20min walk from central Oban

A short path through the bush leads to **Observation Rock**, a hilltop clearing with a wonderful panorama of Paterson Inlet and the island's highest peak, Mount Anglem (980m). As the sun sets you may be treated to a dozen or so kaka screeching and flying about.

Ulva Island

Paterson Inlet, 2km offshore • Daylight hours • Free

The birdlife in Oban is pretty special, but it pales next to that on the 2km-long, low **Ulva Island**, an open wildlife sanctuary that's been cleared of introduced predators through sustained local effort. On a series of easy walks to secluded beaches you'll see more native birdlife than almost anywhere else in New Zealand. The place is full of birdsong, its dense temperate rainforest alive with endangered saddleback, bellbirds, kaka, yellow- and red-crowned parakeets, tui, fantails, pigeons and robins, which approach visitors with fearless curiosity.

Everyone lands at **Post Office Bay**, whose former post office, built in 1872, is a remnant from the days when Ulva Island was the hub of the Paterson Inlet logging community. Armed with DOC's *Ulva Island: Te Wharawhara* brochure ($2; free online), you can find your own way along trails, though naturalist guidance on one of the tours means you'll spot a lot more. There's a pleasant picnic shelter beside the sand beach at **Sydney Cove**. For information on how to get to the island, see page 680.

Whalers Base

On the shores of Paterson Inlet, 7km west of Oban • If you're not visiting as part of a guided trip, catch a water taxi ($50 one-way); operators will fix a time to pick you up from Millers Beach

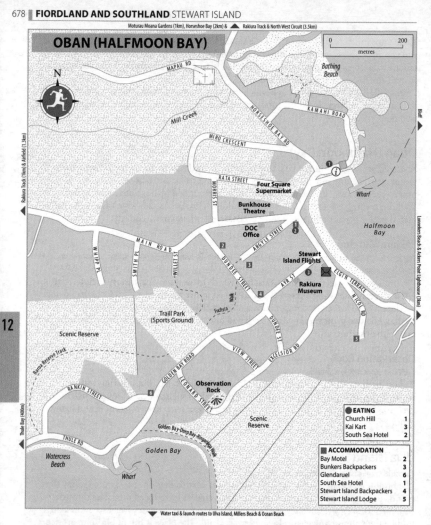

Moturau Moana Gardens (1km), Horseshoe Bay (2km) & ▲ Rakiura Track & North West Circuit (3.5km)

OBAN (HALFMOON BAY)

0   200
metres

Rakiura Track (1km) & Airfield (1.3km)

Bathing Beach

MAPAU RD

N

Mill Creek

HORSESHOE BAY RD

KAMAHI ROAD

Bluff ▶

Bluff ▶

MIRO CRESCENT

RATA STREET

Four Square Supermarket

Bunkhouse Theatre

MORRIS ST

MAIN ROAD

WHIPP PL

SMITH PL

WILLES ST

DOC Office

DUNDEE STREET

ARGYLE STREET

Stewart Island Flights

AVR ST

Rakiura Museum

ELGIN TERRACE

Halfmoon Bay

Lonnekers Beach & Ackers Point Lighthouse (3km)

Fuchsia Walk

Traill Park (Sports Ground)

Scenic Reserve

DUNDEE ST

VIEW STREET

EXCELSIOR RD

NICOL RD

Barnes Reserve Track

GOLDEN BAY ROAD

LEONARD STREET

Observation Rock

RANKIN STREET

Thule Bay (400m)

THULE RD

Watercress Beach

Golden Bay

Golden Bay-Deep Bay-Ringaringa Walk

Wharf

Scenic Reserve

▼ Water taxi & launch routes to Ulva Island, Millers Beach & Ocean Beach

12

● EATING	
Church Hill	1
Kai Kart	3
South Sea Hotel	2

■ ACCOMMODATION	
Bay Motel	2
Bunkers Backpackers	3
Glendaruel	6
South Sea Hotel	1
Stewart Island Backpackers	4
Stewart Island Lodge	5

Whalers Base is another wildlife-rich destination that can be included on boat and guided **kayaking trips**. A one-time overwintering spot for Norwegian whalers, it is accessed via **Millers Beach**, from where an easy twenty-minute coastal walk heads north from the beachside picnic shelter through native bush. Several eerie relics remain from 1924–32 when a fleet of Antarctic whaling ships was repaired here, and the beach is littered with objects left behind: old drums, cables, giant iron propellers, a boiler out in the water and, at the far end, a wrecked sailing ship deliberately sunk by the whaling company to create a wharf.

Mason Bay

Access from Oban by flight or by taking a water taxi to *Freshwater Hut* ($60 one way; 40min) then walking (15km; 3–4hr; flat but often flooded – check conditions before departure)

Stewart Island has become synonymous with **kiwi spotting** in the wild, something that is difficult to do on mainland New Zealand. There are kiwi spotting trips out of Oban, but the more adventurous option is to get yourself to **Mason Bay**, on the west coast, where you can stay overnight in the DOC hut and head out after dark in the hope of finding these elusive creatures. You'll almost certainly hear them, and have a fair chance of seeing them provided you don't go crashing about in the bush: just pick a spot and wait. Take a torch, but keep the beam pointed to the ground to avoid disturbing the birds.

Rakiura Track

39km loop; 2–3 days

Stewart Island's most popular overnight hike is the relatively gentle **Rakiura Track**, one of New Zealand's Great Walks. This makes a circuit from Oban, though you can shave 7km off the route by getting someone to drop you off and pick you up at the road-ends. DOC's *Rakiura Track* leaflet is adequate for route finding.

You can walk in either direction at any time of the year and there is no limit on the number of nights you can stay, but the majority of people walk anticlockwise. This gets the best coastal walking in early around Māori Bay and Port William, site of the first hut. The track then contours around a forested ridge to reach Paterson Inlet and the *North Arm Hut* before the final push back to Oban.

North West Circuit

125km; 9–11 days

It is a very big step up from the Rakiura Track to the **North West Circuit** around the island's northern arm: only the hardiest (masochistic) trampers should consider attempting it. The boggy terrain is energy sapping even in good weather and thigh-deep mud is not uncommon. Added to that, unless you organize a boat or charter flight to drop food at one of the coastal huts, you'll have to carry all your supplies.

The track itself alternates between open coast and forested hill country, offering a side trip (11km return; 6hr) to the 980m summit of Mount Anglem. DOC's *North West and Southern Circuit Tracks* leaflet gives a good overview, pinpointing the **ten huts**, which are mostly sited on the coast; there are no campsites. Make sure to stop in at the Oban DOC office if you're planning to hike the circuit, as the trail is frequently rerouted after storms.

ARRIVAL AND DEPARTURE — STEWART ISLAND

By plane Many people choose to fly to Stewart Island from Invercargill Airport, which avoids the nasty sea crossing but can still be a bumpy ride. Stewart Island Fights (☎ 03 218 9129, ⓦ stewartislandflights.co.nz) charges $125 one way or $215 return, with discounts available for BBH, YHA and student-card holders. Flights land 3km west of Oban; transfer between the airfield and the centre of town is included in the price of your ticket. The luggage allowance is 15kg/person; camping gas and fuels aren't allowed.

Destinations Invercargill (3 daily; 20min).

By ferry Foveaux Strait has a reputation for trying the stomachs of even the hardiest sailors, but if you're bringing a lot of luggage, want to carry camping stove fuel or just need to save money it is the way to go. Stewart Island Experience (☎ 0800 000511, ⓦ stewartislandexperience.co.nz) has fast catamarans (1hr; $79 one way, $139 return) running between Bluff and the wharf in central Oban at least once daily year-round, with up to five daily services in summer. A connecting bus picks up from Invercargill city and airport, costing $25 each way (there are connections to Queenstown and Te Anau Nov–April). There's secure parking at the Bluff terminal for around $10/24hr.

GETTING AROUND

Oban is a pleasant place to **walk** around, and unless you are staying in one of the more distant lodges you won't need any land transport. There are no roads outside the immediate vicinity of Oban, so straying further afield requires flying, taking a water taxi or walking.

By plane Stewart Island Flights (☎ 03 218 9129, ⓦ stewartislandflights.com) offer a "Coast to Coast" loop, flying from Oban to the beach at Mason Bay (weather and tide permitting), the quickest way to reach this remote spot. It costs $230 for the flight there and water taxi back, with a two-adult minimum: call them as they can often hook you up with others to make up numbers. Charter flights are available to Mason Bay, West Ruggedy Beach, Little Hellfire Beach and Doughboy Bay, all on the isolated west coast of Stewart Island.

By car and bike Stewart Island Experience (☎0800 000511, ⓦstewartislandexperience.co.nz) rents small cars ($85/4hr; $150/8hr), scooters ($77/4hr) and basic mountain bikes ($31/4hr; $41/8hr).

By boat Water taxis (typically speedboats with powerful outboard motors, carrying six to ten people) give great

flexibility. A handful of companies offer broadly similar services, including Kaian Water Taxi and Ranui Ulva Island Ferry (☎03 219 1013) operate a regular service to Ulva Island (Oct to early June daily departing Golden Bay Wharf at 9am, noon and 4pm; departing Ulva at noon, 4pm and 6pm; $20 return; cash only). All other companies run to Ulva Island on demand ($25 return; 10min) and to pretty much anywhere else you want to go (Mason Bay typically $60, Port William $50, Whaler's Base $50, all one-way); try Rakiura Water Taxi, 10 Main Rd (☎03 219 1487, ⓦrakiuracharters. co.nz) or Ruggedy Range (see page 675).

INFORMATION

DOC office/Rakiura National Park Visitor Centre Main Rd, Oban (Dec–March daily 8am–5pm; April, May, Oct & Nov Mon–Fri 8.30am–4.30pm, Sat & Sun 9am–4pm; June–Sept Mon–Fri 8.30am–4.30pm, Sat & Sun 10am–2pm; ☎03 219 0009, ⓦdoc.govt.nz). As well as all the usual DOC information there are excellent displays on the island's tracks, natural history, pioneering life on the island, pest control on Ulva Island.

Tourist information Oban Visitor Centre, The Red Shed, 12 Elgin Terrace (daily: Nov–April 7.30am–6.30pm; May–

Oct 8am–5pm; ☎03 219 0056). General island information with an emphasis on Stewart Island Experience trips and ferry crossings.

Weather and equipment Year-round, come prepared for all weather (often in the same day). This is particularly true for trampers who need to be ready for whatever the Stewart Island can throw at them: winds come straight across the southern ocean from Antarctica. Take several layers of clothing to cope with sun and rain, and don't forget sandfly repellent.

ACCOMMODATION

The island is never crowded (with only around 35,000 overnight visitors a year), but it's wise to book in advance if you visit between mid-December and mid-February. Likewise, huts can be busy Nov–March, so it's a good idea to bring a tent.

OBAN (HALFMOON BAY)

Bay Motel 9 Dundee St ☎03 219 1119, ⓦbaymotel. co.nz; map p.678. Top-class twelve-room motel where each fully self-contained unit has access to a deck with views over town and the bay. Quality furnishings, free transfers and great service. **$180**

Bunkers Backpackers 13 Argyle St ☎027 738 1796, ⓦbunkersbackpackers.co.nz; map p.678. The shoes-off policy gives a relaxed and welcoming feel to this hostel in a large double-fronted villa where everyone hangs out discussing plans in the lounge or around the barbecue. As well as comfy shared-bath doubles and twins there are four-and seven-bed dorms. Dorms **$35**, doubles **$82**

Glendaruel 38 Golden Bay Rd ☎03 219 1092, ⓦglendaruel.co.nz; map p.678. Comfortable and welcoming B&B a 10min walk from town, surrounded by native bush. The three rooms – one of which is a well-priced single ($135) – are all en-suite. Guests have their own lounge with telescope, and owner Raylene Waddell will do her best to ensure you have a great time on the island. **$275**

★ **Port of Call** Jensen Bay 2.5km east of town ☎03

219 1394, ⓦportofcall.co.nz; map p.678. Choose from a boutique B&B with a large bedroom in a large, sun-filled, contemporary house overlooking the bay, or a self-catering *bach* just across the road sleeping three with a full kitchen and use of a car. Transfers (from wharf or airfield) are included. *Bach* **$250**, B&B **$385**

South Sea Hotel 25 Elgin Terrace ☎03 219 1059, ⓦstewart-island.co.nz; map p.678. Century-old waterfront pub containing old-fashioned shared-bath rooms with TV; three rooms have sea views ($115) but these are also directly above the noisy bar. Light sleepers may prefer the four shared-bath doubles ($105) in a cottage and nine more modern en-suite units with their own kitchens ($170), both located behind the pub itself. Wi-fi in public areas ($2/hr). Shared-bath doubles **$115**

Stewart Island Backpackers 18 Ayr St ☎03 219 1114, ⓦstewartislandbackpackers.co.nz; map p.678. It's nothing swanky (and can be noisy), but the island's largest hostel offers large communal areas, ranks of comfortable-enough shared-bath doubles and twins and four-share dorms (no bunks) ranged around a central courtyard. Campers can pitch their own tents ($20; add $10 to rent a tent) in the sheltered back garden and use the hostel facilities. Laundry and dryer $5 each; free but patchy wi-fi. Dorms **$36**, doubles **$76**

Stewart Island Lodge 14 Nichol Rd ☎03 249 6000, ⓦstewartislandlodge.co.nz; map p.678. You're really

12

looked after at this very well-appointed lodge with six rooms all opening out onto a deck with superb views over Halfmoon Bay. The vistas are matched by those from the guest lounge where breakfast is served. Closed June & July. Shoulder season rates ($235) Aug, Sept, Oct, Nov, April & May. $295

DOC HUTS

Freshwater On the North West Circuit and handy on the way to Mason Bay this 16-bunk hut is accessible by water taxi from Oban. First come, first served; buy hut tickets from DOC in Oban. $5

Mason Bay Kiwi-spotters base themselves at this twenty-bunk hut tucked in behind the dunes, with heating and camping outside. First come, first served; buy hut tickets from DOC in Oban. Hut $5, camping free

North West Circuit There are ten huts along the North West Circuit including the two on the Rakiura Track (see page 679). The remaining eight huts (including *Freshwater*; see above) cost $5 a night (DOC backcountry hut pass valid) or you can buy a North West Circuit Pass ($35), which entitles you to ten hut nights in all huts except those on the Rakiura Track. Huts $5

Rakiura Track Hikers must book and pre-pay for the two huts (*Port William* and *North Arm*) and three campsites (*Māori Beach*, *Port William* and *North Arm*). Book online (there is a free computer for this in the Oban DOC office) or get DOC staff to do it for you ($2 booking fee). The huts are equipped with mattresses, wood stoves for heating only, running water and toilets; you'll need your own cooker. Huts Oct–April $24, May–Sept $22, camping $6

EATING AND DRINKING

Oban's Four Square Supermarket (daily 7.30am–7pm) at 20 Elgin Terrace offers a surprisingly good range of goods for those self-catering.

★ **Church Hill** 36 Kamahi Rd ☎03 219 1123, ⓦchurchhill.co.nz; map p.678. The island's most sophisticated dining is hidden away in a hilltop villa just above the ferry pier. The menu emphasizes local seafood, with starters including mussel patties with coriander and lemongrass ($19) and muttonbird and watercress dumplings ($22), and mains such as baked blue cod with brown butter and *kumara rösti* ($38), accompanied by an excellent wine list. Vegetarian options available; reservations recommended. Sept–Easter daily 5.30–10pm.

★ **Kai Kart** 7 Ayr St ☎021 268 7687; map p.678.

Billy Connolly once stopped by this fabulously quirky old pie cart, a glorified caravan decked out with leadlights and fresh flowers. You can order superb blue cod fish and chips ($15.50) or a fancy cod, venison, gurnard or mussel burger ($11–17.50) to eat inside or at the outdoor picnic tables, or get takeaway and tantalize the seagulls at the adjacent beach. Nov–Easter daily 11.30am–9pm.

South Sea Hotel 25 Elgin Terrace ☎03 219 1059; map p.678. The island's pub is very much its social centre. Muffins and coffee are served throughout the day, while lunch- and dinnertimes bring hearty portions of tasty pub food – and naturally their beer-battered cod and chips ($25) is particularly good. The lively bar has a Sunday pub quiz that shouldn't be missed. Breakfast 7–10.30am, lunch 11.30am–2pm, dinner 5.30–8pm.

DIRECTORY

Banks The island's only ATM, inside the 4-Square, doesn't accept international cards at present; fortunately most businesses take credit and debit cards, the water taxis being the only notable exception.

Cinema The Bunkhouse Theatre (10 Main Rd; ☎027 867 9381, ⓦbunkhousetheatre.co.nz) shows *A Local's Tail* (40min; $10) – a quirky look at the island's history and culture, "narrated" by a Staffordshire bull terrier – three times daily (11am, 2pm & 4pm) between Labour Day and Easter.

Left luggage Available at the DOC (small $10, rucksack size $20; no time limit), with access only during the office's open hours; Stewart Island Flights allows you to store extra luggage in Invercargill for free

Phone coverage Mobile coverage is good in Oban, fair around the bays to the northeast of Oban right to the island's northern tip, and sporadic everywhere else.

Post office 40 Elgin Terrace (Mon–Fri 7.30am–6pm, Sat & Sun 9.30am–5pm).

The Catlins Coast

The rugged coastal route linking Dunedin and Invercargill is one of the less-travelled highways on the South Island, traversing some of the country's wildest scenery along the **Catlins Coast**. Roaring southeasterlies and the remorseless sea have shaped the coastline into plunging cliffs, windswept headlands, white-sand beaches, rocky bays and gaping caves, many of which are accessible to visitors. The coastal highway is part of the **Southern Scenic Route** (ⓦsouthernscenicroute.co.nz), which also links Invercargill with Te Anau in Fiordland (see page 644).

THE CATLINS COAST

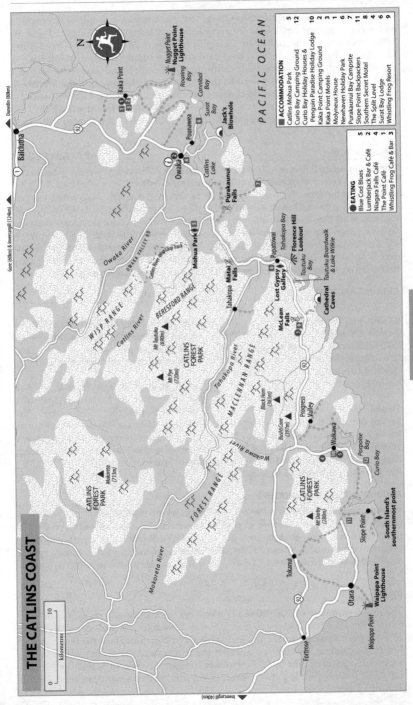

PACIFIC OCEAN

■ ACCOMMODATION

Catlins Mohua Park	5
Curio Bay Camping Ground	12
Curio Bay Holiday Houses &	10
Penguin Paradise Holiday Lodge	2
Kaka Point Camping Ground	1
Kaka Point Motels	6
Molyneux House	7
Newhaven Holiday Park	11
Purakaunui Bay Campsite	8
Slope Point Backpackers	4
Southern Secret Motel	6
The Split Level	9
Surat Bay Lodge	
Whistling Frog Resort	

● EATING

Blue Cod Blues	5
Lumberjack Bar & Café	2
Niagara Falls Café	4
The Point Café	1
Whistling Frog Café & Bar	3

12

The best way to enjoy the **Catlins Coast** is to invest at least a couple of days and take it easy – it's not possible to see everything in one day. From Waipapa Point in Southland (60km southeast of Invercargill), to Nugget Point in South Otago (just southeast of Balclutha), the wild landscape stretches unbroken, dense rainforest succumbing to open scrub as you cut through deep valleys and pass rocky bays and inlets. The coast is home to **penguins** (both blue and yellow-eyed), **dolphins**, many species of seabird and, at certain times of year, migrating **whales**. Elephant **seals**, fur seals, and increasingly, the rare New Zealand **sea lion** are found among the sand dunes, and **birds** – tui, resonant bellbirds and fantails – are abundant in the mossy depths of the forest.

INFORMATION
THE CATLINS COAST

Tourist information There is no i-SITE in the Catlins (though there is a decent information centre in Owaka), so make use of the outpost in the gateway town of Balclutha, 80km southwest of Dunedin; 4 Clyde St, in the War Memorial Hall (Nov–March Mon–Fri 8.30am–5pm, Sat & Sun 9.30am–3pm; April–Oct Mon–Fri 8.30am–5pm, Sat & Sun 10am–2pm; ☎ 03 418 0388, ⍵ cluthanz.com). It has all the usual information and booking facilities plus internet access. Visiting from the west, the

Invercargill i-SITE (see page 672) is your best bet. See also ⍵ catlins.org.nz.

Services There are no banks or ATMs in the Catlins; many places accept credit and debit cards but bring plenty of cash. There are very few petrol stations, and most pumps close around 5pm; fill up before you set off, then at Owaka (24hr card operated), Papatowai or Tokanui. There is another 24hr pump (credit card only) at Fortrose. Mobile phone coverage is poor away from the main settlements.

GETTING AROUND

BY CAR AND TOUR
The region is linked by the Southern Scenic Route (formerly SH92), which is sealed all the way, though virtually all the Catlins' attractions are reached on narrow gravel side roads. Without your own transport, visit on a guided tour – there is no public transport.

TOURS
Bottom Bus ☎ 03 477 9083, ⍵ bottombus.co.nz. Hop-on, hop-off service offered (three times a week in summer) as a supplementary trip by Kiwi Experience (though it attracts less of the booze-bus crowd). It loops from Queenstown to Dunedin via Invercargill and the

Catlins (main stop Curio Bay) over 3–7 days ($365). You can start anywhere, and there are Milford Sound and Stewart Island add-ons. Sector fares are also available with Dunedin–Catlins–Invercargill starting at $225.

Catlins Scenic & Wildlife Tours Mohua Park, 744 Catlins Valley Rd, Tawanui ☎ 03 415 8613, ⍵ catlinsmohuapark.co.nz. Entertaining and inspirational private tours (8hr day tours $350/person) led by committed conservationists sharing in-depth knowledge about the local ecology, history and geology. Advance bookings essential.

ACCOMMODATION AND EATING

Freedom camping Travellers in campervans have traditionally appreciated the abundance of peaceful wayside spots for sneaky overnight stays, but a combination of sheer numbers and misuse of these sites means freedom camping is now banned in the area and

instant fines have been imposed.
Self-catering Throughout the region you'll find very few worthwhile restaurants and cafés. It pays to bring your own supplies and self-cater where possible. You can get groceries in Owaka, and there is a small general store in Papatowai.

Fortrose

The tiny community of **FORTROSE** lies 45km east of Invercargill, at the mouth of the Mataura River. *Fortune Café* at 5 Moray Terrace (on the shorefront) has a 24-hour petrol pump (cards only) and there are public toilets near the boat ramp. Just to the south at low tide you can spot the remnants of the *Ino* in the shallows, a steamship wrecked here in 1886. From Fortrose, the Southern Scenic Route cuts inland to **Tokanui**, but it is more rewarding to stick to the minor coast road towards Waipapa Point.

Waipapa Point

Some 17km south of Fortrose (4km off the main road between Fortrose and Curio Bay, via passable gravel track), windswept **Waipapa Point** is the site of New Zealand's worst civilian shipwreck, in 1881, when 131 lives were lost on SS *Tararua*. The wooden, short 13.4m **Waipapa Point Lighthouse** (closed to the public) that now stands on the point was erected soon after in 1884 (it still operates, but has been automated since 1976), and you might spot sea lions and fur seals on the golden beach and around the rocky platform at its foot.

Slope Point

Open access, but road usually closed during Sept–Oct lambing season

Around 16km east of Waipapa Point, **Slope Point** is signposted off the main road (it's another 6km south on a dirt track), celebrated for being the southernmost tip of South Island. A walk through sheep paddocks (40min return) brings you to a wind-lashed promontory that's totally exposed to the Southern Ocean. A sign advises that it is still 4803km to the South Pole. Continuing east from Slope Point, the final 13km gravel section of the main road (aka Haldane-Curio Bay Rd) is being slowly sealed.

ACCOMMODATION   **SLOPE POINT**

Slope Point Backpackers 164 Slope Point Rd ☎03 246 8420, ⓦslopepoint.co.nz; map p.683. Friendly and great-value budget accommodation on a working sheep farm where kids (of all ages) are welcome to check out the animals. There's a selection of doubles, a self-contained unit ($90) and the three-bedroom *Getaway* (whole house $100). Laundry and drying $5 each. Free wi-fi, but only up to 20MB/day. $50

Curio Bay and Porpoise Bay

5km southwest of Waikawa (via Waikawa-Curio Bay Rd) • Open access • For surfing here, contact Catlins Surf (☎ 03 246 8552, ⓦ catlins-surf.co.nz), Curio Bay Campground Store, 601 Waikawa-Curio Bay Rd, which rents boards and wetsuits ($45/3hr 30min; surfboard only $25/3hr, $45/day), offers surfing lessons ($60/2hr) and gives you a chance to try stand-up paddleboarding ($75/2hr 30min)

Contrasting seascapes come together at a windswept headland that separates two of the most beautiful bays in a region packed with such things. To the northeast, the beautiful sandy crescent of **Porpoise Bay** forms a much calmer stretch of water where **Hector's dolphins** love to play (you can swim here safely, if you can stand the cold). To the south, the rocky wave-cut platform of **Curio Bay** is littered with the remains of a **petrified forest**, with fossilized Jurassic trees clearly visible at low tide. Over 170 million years ago, when most of New Zealand still lay beneath the sea, this would have been a broad, forested floodplain. Today, the seashore, composed of several layers of forest buried under blankets of volcanic mud and ash, is littered with fossilized tree stumps and fallen logs.

The road from Waikawa ends at a car park with a new **heritage centre** (with exhibits on the ecology of the area) and café. From here a path leads 400m to Curio Bay and the petrified forest; steps lead down to the rocks below. Return at sunrise or just before dusk when up to a dozen **yellow-eyed penguins** stagger ashore to their burrows in the bushes at the back the bay. Access to Porpoise Bay is through the adjacent *Curio Bay Holiday Park*, where you can park right above the beach.

ACCOMMODATION   **CURIO BAY AND PORPOISE BAY**

Curio Bay Camping Ground 601 Waikawa-Curio Bay Rd ☎03 246 8897, ✉curiobaycampingground@ gmail.com; map p.683. Wonderfully sited campsite where tent and powered sites come nestled between dense flax hedges to protect you from the sometimes ferocious winds. There are views across both Porpoise Bay and Curio Bay, and a tiny store sells supplies (daily 8am–8pm). Showers are $1/5min and for guests only. Powered sites cost $3 more per person. **$15**

Curio Bay Holiday Houses & Penguin Paradise Holiday Lodge 601 Waikawa-Curio Bay Rd ☏ 03 246 8552, ⊛ catlins-surf.co.nz; map p.683. The energetic owner of Catlins Surf operates a selection of four fully self-contained beachside holiday homes around Porpoise Bay (all with free wi-fi), as well as the backpacker-friendly *Penguin Paradise* in nearby Waikawa (612 Niagara Waikawa Rd; internet access at the museum next door). All of the holiday homes come with linen and towels provided. *Penguin Paradise* **$31**, holiday homes from **$120**

Waikawa

There's not much to the fishing village of **WAIKAWA**, 5km northeast of Curio Bay on Waikawa Harbour – just a few houses, and the pretty, wooden, former **St Marys Anglican Church** (daily: summer 10am–5pm, winter 10am–4pm; free), opened in 1932 and now maintained by the local museum (the church officially closed in 1994). The first sawmill was established in this area in 1858, with commercial fishing taking off in the 1920s – today none of the sawmills remain and farming and tourism are the most important money earners in the South Catlins.

Waikawa Museum

604 Niagara Waikawa Rd • Daily summer 10am–5pm; winter 10am–4pm • Donation • ☏ 03 246 8464

To learn something of the seafaring and logging life hereabouts, visit the small **Waikawa Museum**, which is overflowing with all sorts of historic curios, from a massive stash of intriguing black and white photos to artefacts salvaged from shipwrecks (including coins and bottles from the SS *Tararua*). The poignant section on World War I veterans has a small case containing a Bible with a bullet hole and the actual bullet that penetrated unfortunate local rifleman John Shortland in 1918. The museum building was originally the local school (which operated here 1912–72), and now doubles as the area's visitor centre.

EATING

Blue Cod Blues 610 Niagara Waikawa Rd; map p.683. Top-quality burgers ($7–10) and blue cod and chips ($8.50) from a nicely kitted-out wayside caravan managed by local character Kerri Stronach, with the odd table or two outside (next to the museum). Generally Oct–May Mon 11am–2pm, Fri–Sun 11am–2pm & 4.30–7pm; daily in high summer.

Niagara Falls Café 256 Niagara Waikawa Rd, 4km north of Waikawa ☏ 03 246 8577, ⊛ niagarafallscafe. co.nz; map p.683. Great licensed café in Niagara's refurbished 1895 schoolhouse surrounded by gardens and lawns. Everything is prepared on-site from natural ingredients and generally cooked as plainly as possible to bring out the flavours. Stop in for superb Atomic brand coffee and carrot cake, a whitebait main course ($27; available seasonally), blue cod with salad and house-baked bread ($28) or rack of lamb ($35). Wheat- and dairy-free options are available and select Kiwi wines all come by the glass. Late Oct to Easter daily 9am–11pm; Easter to late Oct Mon & Thurs–Sun 11am–4pm (closed June).

McLean Falls

Rewcastle Rd, 26km northeast of Waikawa, then 3km on a gravel track off the Southern Scenic Route • 30–40min return walk

North of Waikawa you re-join the Southern Scenic Route, with the picturesque 22m-high **McLean Falls** on the Tautuku River the most impressive and beautiful of the cascades hereabouts. From the car park a short trail runs through lush rainforest of podocarp, rimu and fuchsia, the climb steepening as you approach the multi-tiered waterfall beyond the lower churning section (known as The Chute). The best time to visit is late afternoon when sun strikes the forest around the main cascade. The falls were named after early settler Doug McLean, who once came here to bathe.

ACCOMMODATION

MCLEAN FALLS

Whistling Frog Resort 29 Rewcastle Rd, Southern Scenic Route (at the turning for McLean Falls) ☎03 415 8668, ⓦwhistlingfrogresort.com; map p.683. Excellent and professionally run complex (attached to *The Whistling Frog*), with sheltered campsites and powered sites, sharing communal barbecue areas, a cramped kitchen and a TV lounge. There are dorm beds available

($40pp), but the cute backpacker cabins ($85), with their own table and chairs on the tiny porch are a better deal if you're travelling in a pair; you'll need sleeping bags. There's a range of plusher accommodation from compact "Kiwiana" cabins ($110) to roomy one-bedroom chalets ($220). Camping per two-person site $39

EATING

Whistling Frog Café & Bar 27 Rewcastle Rd, Southern Scenic Route (at the turning for McLean Falls) ☎03 415 8338, ⓦwhistlingfrogcafe.com; map p.683. Some of the best dining in the Catlins at this cosy and welcoming café and bar. As well as the standard range of Kiwi breakfasts ($17), expect the likes of ribeye steak ($32), rack of lamb ($35) and delicious

vegetarian mushroom risotto ($28). There's wine by the glass and a good selection of beers, plus home-brew on tap (Whistling Frog Golden Lager and McLean Falls Ale). Oct–May daily 10am–6pm (dinner service begins 5–6pm by reservation only; closes when dinner service is complete).

Cathedral Caves

1069 Chaslands Hwy (Southern Scenic Route), 29km northeast of Waikawa, 2km off the main road • Late Oct–May accessible daily 2hr either side of low tide 7.30am–8.30pm • $5 • ⓦ cathedralcaves.co.nz

Just 3km on from the turning to McLean Falls, the ever-popular **Cathedral Caves** (owned by a Māori land trust), are the grandest of the fifteen or so caves that punctuate this part of the coast, their walls created by furious seas; the two sea-formed passages run for a total 200m, reaching up to 30m high. The 1km path – which winds from the car park down through mixed woodland to beautiful, **Waipati Beach** – is only open for two hours either side of low tide. The caves lie at the northeastern end of the beach; allow an hour for the walk down and back. Seasonal changes in the tides mean that the caves are closed each winter when the waves scour out much of the sand, generally reopening sometime in October: check the access situation on the website, or check the sign at turn-off on the main road.

Tautuku Estuary Boardwalk and Lake Wilkie

Southern Scenic Route (Chaslands Hwy), 5km southwest of Papatowai

Birders will appreciate a stroll along the **Tautuku Estuary Boardwalk** (2km return; 20–30min), a raised walkway nature trail over some estuarine marshes into fernbird territory. The gravel road turning to the boardwalk lies another 5km east on the Southern Scenic Route from the Cathedral Caves turn-off.

Another 1.5km east on the Southern Scenic Route, a small car park provides access to the **Lake Wilkie Walk** (30min return), through mature forest with interpretive signs explaining forest succession. The lake itself is a glacial remnant that has gradually shrunk as the forest has encroached.

Papatowai

Continuing northeast through the Catlins on the Southern Scenic Route you reach the small settlement of **PAPATOWAI**, 28km east of Waikawa (and 13km northeast of Cathedral Caves) on the Tahakopa River, with its general store, quirky gallery and a couple of good walks. Around 2.5km before you reach the village, stop briefly at the roadside **Florence Hill Lookout**, which presents a spectacular panoramic view of Tautuku Bay, a magnificent crescent of golden sand backed by extensive forest and the bulging Tautuku Peninsula. At the far end you can pick out the **Frances Pillars**, wave-lashed rock pinnacles made of conglomerate rock.

Lost Gypsy Gallery

Southern Scenic Route (Papatowai Hwy) • Late Oct to late April daily except Wed 10am–5pm • Free; "theatre" $5 • ⓦ thelostgypsy.com

Wild nature aside, the real highlight of the Catlins is the **Lost Gypsy Gallery**, a cheerful old bus beside the main road containing a wonderland of Blair Somerville's animatronics since 1999 – machines and toys ingeniously constructed from recycled materials and old electrical components. Almost everything in the bus is for sale (from teabag dunkers to dancing penguins) but Somerville showcases his best work in the **Winding Thoughts Theatre ... of Sorts**, in the garden just behind the bus. This highly amusing outdoor installation is a treasure-trove of wacky and often interactive home-made inventions that includes: a pedal-powered TV; a paua-shell waterwheel; a wonderful organ with each key activating sounds from an amazing array of objects; and just about anything imaginable in who-would-ever-think-of-that combinations. Somerville also runs a welcome **coffee** kiosk on-site.

ACCOMMODATION
PAPATOWAI

Southern Secret Motel 2510 Papatowai Hwy ☏ 03 415 8777, ⓦ southernsecretmotel.co.nz; map p.683. Though it looks like an ordinary home on the outside, this motel has four fabulous rooms done out in Pacific colours with mosquito-net-draped wrought-iron beds. The same people offer *Erehwon* and *Lancewood*, two eclectically decorated cottages. Motel doubles $110, self-contained cottage $135

Matai Falls

Southern Scenic Route, 8.5km north of Papatowai • 20–30min return walk

The easy walk to **Matai Falls** is as much a reason to visit as the fairly modest but pretty falls themselves. It winds through Table Hill Scenic Reserve among 10m-high native fuchsia trees, easily identified by their peeling pinkish bark and, in early summer, small red-and-blue trumpet flowers. A short extension of the path climbs above the first cascade to the **Horseshoe Falls**, a similar waterfall that extends much wider after heavy rains. You can extend your jaunt through the forest by taking the **Historic Rail Trail**, a one-hour return hike that begins halfway along the path to the falls.

Purakaunui Falls

Purakaunui Falls Rd, 11km northeast of Papatowai • 20min return walk

If there has been a good bit of rain recently (not unknown in these parts) don't miss the **Purakaunui Falls**, a gorgeous 20m-high, three-tiered waterfall in a scenic reserve of silver beech and podocarp. It is well signposted off the main Southern Scenic Route (9km on paved roads coming from Owaka; 9km on gravel roads coming from Papatowai), and accessed along a pleasant nature trail to a picnic area and viewing platform.

Owaka and around

The only settlement of any size within the Catlins is the farming town of **OWAKA**, 26km northeast of Papatowai on the Southern Scenic Route and little more than a crossroads where you'll find a few places to stay, a handful of restaurant/cafés and a petrol station.

Owaka Museum

10 Campbell St • Mon–Fri 9.30am–4.30pm, Sat & Sun 10am–4pm • $5 • ☏ 03 415 8323, ⓦ owakamuseum.org.nz

The well-curated **Owaka Museum** contains evocative exhibits on the area's significance to Māori and the coast's shipwrecks as well as sealer and whaler Captain Cattlin. The Owaka library is on-site and the staff can supply advertising and walks leaflets for the area.

Jack's Blowhole

A gravel road runs from central Owaka 8km across Catlins River to Jack's Bay, from where a farmland track (20–30min each way) leads up a valley and along the cliffs to **Jack's Blowhole**, an impressively wide 55m-deep hole in the ground, which connects with the sea through a 200m-long tunnel. Effectively the collapsed roof of a cave, the bottom of the blowhole is washed by surf at high tide when plumes of spray waft up.

INFORMATION	OWAKA AND AROUND

Tourist information Catlins Information Centre, inside the Owaka Museum, 10 Campbell St (Mon–Fri 9.30am–4.30pm, Sat & Sun 10am–4pm; ☎03 415 8371, ⓦcluthanz.com). Dispenses useful updates on eating and sleeping options, as well as DOC information.

ACCOMMODATION

Catlins Mohua Park 744 Catlins Valley Rd, 10km southwest then 7.5km inland ☎03 415 8613, ⓦcatlinsmohuapark.co.nz; map p.683. Four peaceful eco-cottages isolated on the edge of bush overlooking farmland; TV and phone-free zones, but there is free wi-fi at reception. The cottages are self-catering, so bring supplies, though meals are available on request. $225

Newhaven Holiday Park 324 Newhaven Rd, Surat Bay, 5km east of Owaka ☎03 415 8834, ⓦnewhavenholiday.com; map p.683. Delightful, small campsite bordering the estuary and just a 2min walk from the beach. Simple cabins and self-contained apartments ($130) come ranged around a central grassy area, and there's a vaguely 70s-styled retro caravan ($60) available too. Free but spotty wi-fi. Camping $35, cabins $70

Purakaunui Bay Campsite Purakaunui Bay Rd, 17km south of Owaka; map p.683. A DOC toilets-and-water site right on the coast with dramatic views of the cliffs, fire-pits and a ready supply of driftwood, plus good surfing. Cosgrove Island nature reserve is just offshore. First come, first served. Cash only. $8

The Split Level 9 Waikawa Rd ☎03 415 8868, ⓦthesplitlevel.co.nz; map p.683. There's little advantage to staying right in Owaka, but if you need to then try this warm and spacious 1970s house with a quad-share dorm, a twin and a double, all a decent distance from the well-appointed kitchen/lounge. There are also en-suite motel units (from $82) in a separate building. Dorms $33, doubles $74

Surat Bay Lodge 19 Surat Bay Rd, 5km east of Owaka ☎03 415 8696, ⓦsuratbay.co.nz; map p.683. Backpacker beds in a peaceful spot with good views, where the Catlins Estuary meets the beach. Tea, coffee, hot chocolate and local calls are free; there's free wi-fi too (up to 500MB). Dorms $32, doubles $84

EATING

Lumberjack Bar & Café 3 Saunders St ☎03 415 8747, ⓦlumberjackbarandcafe.co.nz; map p.683. This establishment is probably the best of Owaka's middling handful of places to eat and drink. The menu is pretty old-fashioned but it's a good spot for blue cod and chips ($31.80) or a decent ribeye steak with a choice of three sauces plus veg ($31) beside the big open fire. Daily 11am–2pm & 6–8.30pm, some winter closures.

Cannibal Bay

The long crescent of sand known as **Cannibal Bay** (named by an early explorer who thought human bones he found here were evidence of human feasting; in fact it was a Māori burial site) is an isolated but gorgeous spot at anytime, but the rocks on the north side are also a haunt for New Zealand sea lions. The bay lies at the end of a narrow, winding gravel road, some 11km southeast of Owaka. Keep at least 10m away from any sea lions you do see and back off quickly if they rear up and roar.

Kaka Point

The last key settlement inside the Catlins is **KAKA POINT**, 23km northeast of Owaka (and 22km south of Balclutha), a tiny holiday community with golden sands patrolled by lifeguards in summer, making it a good swimming and surfing spot.

ACCOMMODATION
KAKA POINT

Kaka Point Camping Ground 34 Tarata St ☎ 03 412 8801, ⓦ kakapointcamping.co.nz; map p.683. Grassy hilltop campsite with plenty of tree shelter. Facilities are basic, but it's got all the essentials, plus cheap cabins (doubles $60). Camping per two-person site $32

Kaka Point Motels 11 Rata St ☎ 03 412 8602, ⓦ catlins.co.nz; map p.683. Comfortable place with a range of spacious self-contained units, almost all with decking and wonderful ocean views. Economy units $115, studios $140

Molyneux House 2 Rimu St ☎ 03 412 8002, ⓦ molyneuxhouse.co.nz; map p.683. Very comfy B&B in a modern house offering just one deluxe suite with its own kitchen and great sea views from the deck. Continental breakfast ingredients provided. $215

EATING

The Point Café 58 Esplanade ☎ 03 412 8800; map p.683. This decent-enough café/pub is the only spot for a coffee ($4), seafood chowder ($15.50) or blue cod and chips ($30), but works best for a beer while watching the breakers (and dodging the sandflies) on the deck. Mon–Thurs & Sun 9am–8pm, Fri & Sat 9am–8.30pm.

Nugget Point

The Catlins go out with a bang at dramatic **Nugget Point**, a steep-sided, windswept promontory rising 133m above the sea 9km south of Kaka Point via a narrow road (sealed halfway). Just offshore lie **The Nuggets**, jagged stacks of wave-pounded rock whose layers have been tilted vertical over time. It is an impressive sight, visited on an easy, 900m track (30min return) which ends at a still-functioning 1870 **Nugget Point Lighthouse** (closed to the public), from where you can gaze down on lively groups of honking southern fur seals. Another short path leads from the car park to a clifftop viewpoint that overlooks a nesting colony of royal spoonbills.

At **Roaring Bay** (about 500m before the lighthouse car park), you can watch **yellow-eyed penguins** as they leave their nests at sunrise and descend the steep grassy cliffs to the sea or as they return just before dark (around 30min before sunset). Their progress is slow, so you need plenty of patience and insect repellent, and binoculars come in handy. A modern viewing hide is accessed along a 300m path from a dedicated car park.

Gore

The quiet Southland farming town of **GORE**, 70km west of Balclutha and 65km northeast of Invercargill, is a pleasant transit point at the intersection of routes from Dunedin to Te Anau and Invercargill. Dominated by the Hokonui Hills, Gore spans the Mataura River ("reddish swirling water"), and claims to be the **brown trout capital** of the world – celebrated by an enormous fish statue in the town centre. It also claims to be New Zealand's home of **country music** (not that anyone is fighting them for the honour), a scene that is most accessible during **Gold Guitar Week** (early June; ☎ 03 208 1978, ⓦ goldguitars.co.nz) when hundreds of would-be country stars and a few established performers roll into town for a weekend of low-key entertainment.

Hokonui Moonshine Museum

Hokonui Heritage Centre, 16 Hokonui Drive • Mon–Fri 8.30am–5pm, Sat 9.30am–3.30pm, Sun 1–3.30pm • $5

The entertaining **Hokonui Moonshine Museum** details decades of illicit whisky distillation deep in the local bush-covered hills. This "sly grogging" began as early as 1836 and reached a peak during a regional half-century of Prohibition that started in 1903. Alcohol freedom is still restricted in these parts, with all liquor sales and profits managed by a licensing trust. The visit ends with a dram of whisky loosely based on the old Hokonui recipe. In odd-numbered years, Gore hosts the biennial **Hokonui Moonshiners' Festival** (⊛moonshinefest.co.nz), with live music by local bands.

The Heritage Centre also contains the **Gore Historical Museum** (same hours; free), a high-quality collection of Victorian costume, vintage homewares and angling paraphernalia.

Eastern Southland Art Gallery

14 Hokonui Drive, at Norfolk St • Mon–Fri 10am–4.30pm, Sat & Sun 1–4pm • Free • ☎ 03 208 9907

Art lovers shouldn't miss the **Eastern Southland Art Gallery** with its nationally significant collection. The permanent exhibition centres on a fascinating collection of art bequeathed by expat Kiwi sexologist, Dr John Money, with Congolese ceremonial helmets and ranks of life-size Bambara ancestral figures displayed alongside richly coloured oils by Rita Angus and works by Dutch émigré Theo Schoon, who incorporated Māori iconography into his painting long before it was fashionable. Also on permanent display are career-spanning pieces gifted to the museum by one of New Zealand's most famous painters, the late Ralph Hotere.

Croydon Aviation Heritage Centre

1558 Waimea Hwy (SH94), 17km west of Gore • Museum Mon–Fri 9.30am–4.30pm, Sat & Sun 10am–4pm • $12; flights from $150/15min–$300/30min • ☎ 03 208 9755, ⊛ experiencemandeville.com

Fans of vintage aircraft shouldn't miss the **Croydon Aviation Heritage Centre** at the old Mandeville airfield, outside Gore, where you can watch the restoration of vintage planes (mostly 1920s and 1930s), take to the air in a Tiger Moth or a de Havilland biplane and have a leisurely wander around the museum containing a fleet of beautifully restored vintage aeroplanes. Refuel at the airfield café, *The Moth*.

ARRIVAL AND INFORMATION
GORE

By bus Gore lies on SH1 and the major bus route between Dunedin, Invercargill and Te Anau, with buses stopping outside the Heritage Centre on Hokonui Drive.

Destinations Christchurch (1 daily; 9hr); Dunedin (1–2 daily; 2hr 45min); Invercargill (2–3 daily; 50min); Te Anau (1 daily; 1hr 45min).

Tourist information 16 Hokonui Drive, inside the Hokonui Heritage Centre (Mon–Fri 8.30am–5pm, Sat 9.30am–4pm, Sun summer 10am–4pm, Sun winter 1–4pm; ☎ 03 203

9288, ⊛ gorenz.com or ⊛ goredc.govt.nz), with free maps and leaflets available outside.

Trout fishing During the fishing season (Oct–April) you can pit your wits against a brown trout on the Mataura River with tackle rented from B&B Sports, 65 Main St (☎ 03 208 0801, ⊛ bbsports.co.nz); they also sell national fishing licences ($20/day or $165/season, usually valid a full year from Oct to Sept).

ACCOMMODATION AND EATING

The Green Room 59 Irk St ☎ 03 208 1005. Casual wood-floored café next to Gore's St James Theatre that's good for soup, quiches, frittatas, early breakfasts or just a coffee and a slice of cake. Mon–Fri 6am–5pm, Sat 7.30am–1.30pm.

Howl at the Moon 2 Main St ☎ 03 208 3851. This cavernous but friendly joint serves coffee and snacks all day, with hot meals cooked to order at lunch and dinner, with the steak-and-lamb-rack orientated menu making occasional forays into more exotic territory, with Southern-style buttermilk chicken ($33) and pork and chive dumplings ($22). Light meals available for $20. Daily noon–2pm & 5.30–9pm.

Riverlea Motel 46 Hokonui Drive ☎ 03 208 3130, ⊛ riverleamotel.co.nz. Cosy and friendly motel in the heart of town, with fairly simple, clean and modern

rooms (from studios to two-bedroom units; $155), with Sky TV. **$135**

Wentworth Heights 86a Wentworth St, off SH1 3km northeast of town ☎ 03 208 6476, ⊛ wentworthheights. co.nz. Luxurious, semirural B&B with fabulous breakfasts, hot tub, and a warm welcome that few can match. Host Barry Perkins is also a fishing guide with great local knowledge. **$165**

The Thomas Green 30 Medway St ☎ 03 208 9295, ⊛ thethomasgreen.co.nz. City style comes to eastern Southland at this flash restaurant of mirrors, smart lighting and green and black chesterfields tucked behind the facade of a heritage building. The food is upscale pub style with the likes of mushroom and feta tart ($29) and seared venison served on beetroot puree ($37). Daily 10am–10pm or later.

12

MĀORI CARVING

Contexts

History

Many New Zealanders of European descent have long thought of their country as a model of humanitarian colonization. Māori often take a different view, however, informed by the repeated theft of land and erosion of rights that were supposedly guaranteed by a treaty. Schoolroom histories have generally been faithful to the European view, even to the point of influencing Māori mythology. In the last couple of decades, however, revisionist historians have largely discredited what many older New Zealanders know as fact. Much that is presented as tradition turns out to be the late nineteenth-century scholarship of historians who bent research to fit their theories and, in some cases, even destroyed evidence. What follows is inextricably interwoven with Māori legend and can be understood more fully with reference to the section on *Maoritanga* (see page 708).

Pre-European history

It's thought that the ancestors of modern **Māori** arrived from Polynesia in double-hulled canoes between 1150 and 1300 AD. Their journey was planned to the extent that they took with them the *kuri* (dog) and food plants such as taro (a starchy tuber), yam and *kumara* (sweet potato). The notion of a legendary "**Great Fleet**" of seven canoes arriving in 1350 AD seems most likely to be a Victorian adaptation of Māori oral history, which has been readopted into contemporary Māori legend.

The Polynesians found a land so much colder than their tropical home that many of their crops and plants wouldn't grow. Fortunately there was an abundance of marine life and large flightless birds, particularly in the North Island, where most settled. The people of this **Archaic Period** are often misleadingly known as "Moa Hunters" and while some undoubtedly lived off these birds, the moa wasn't present in all areas. By around 1350 settlements had been established all around the coast, but it was only later that there's evidence of horticulture, suggesting a later migration bringing plants for cultivation, or the beginning of successful year-round food storage, allowing a settled living pattern rather than the earlier hunters' short-lived campsites.

Either way, this marks the beginning of the **Classic Period** when *kainga* (villages) grew up close to the *kumara* grounds, often supported by *pa* (fortified villages) where the people could retreat when under attack. As tasks became more specialized and hunting and horticulture took up less time, the arts – particularly carving and weaving (see page 711) – flourished and warfare became endemic. The decline of easily caught birdlife and the relative ease of growing *kumara* in the warmer North Island marked the beginning of a northward population shift. When the Europeans arrived, 95 percent of

1250–1300 AD	c.1350	1642
Probable arrival of first Polynesians.	The traditional date of arrival of the "Great Fleet" from Hawaiki.	Dutchman Abel Tasman sails past the West Coast and anchors in Golden Bay.

POLYNESIAN MIGRATION

Modern scholarship suggests that humans from Southeast Asia first explored the South Pacific around five thousand years ago, gradually evolving a distinct culture as they filtered down through the Indonesian archipelago. A thousand years of progressive island-hopping got them as far as Tonga and Samoa, where a distinctly **Polynesian** society continued to evolve, honing seafaring skills to the point where lengthy sea journeys were possible. Around a thousand years ago, Polynesian culture reached its classical apotheosis in the **Society Islands** west of Tahiti, widely thought to be the hub for a series of migrations heading southwest across thousands of kilometres of open ocean, past the Cook Islands, eventually striking land in what is now known as New Zealand (Aotearoa).

the population was located in the North Island, mostly in the northern reaches, with most coastal settlements reaching down to Hawke's Bay and Wanganui.

European contact and the Māori response

Many **Europeans** were convinced of the existence of a *terra australis incognita*, an unknown southern land, and wanted to trade there. In 1642, Dutchman **Abel Tasman**, working for the Dutch East India Company, became the first European to catch sight of Aotearoa. He anchored in Golden Bay, where a small boat being rowed between Tasman's two ships was intercepted by a Māori war canoe and four sailors were killed. Without setting foot on land Tasman fled up the west coast of the North Island, going on to add Tonga and Fiji to European maps. Aotearoa was subsequently named Nieuw Zeeland after the Dutch maritime province.

Nieuw Zeeland was ignored for over a century until 1769, when **James Cook** (see page 695) paid the first of three extensive visits. Cook found Māori a **sophisticated people** with a highly formalized social structure and skills to turn stone and wood into fabulously carved canoes, weapons and meeting houses – yet they had no wheels, roads, metalwork, pottery or animal husbandry. After initial unfortunate encounters near Gisborne (see page 335) and Napier (see page 347), Cook managed to strike up friendly, constructive relations. The original settlers now found that their tribal allegiance wasn't enough to differentiate them from the Europeans and subsequently began calling themselves **Māori** (meaning "normal" or "not distinctive") while referring to the newcomers as **Pakeha** ("foreign").

The Coromandel Peninsula was one place where Cook deviated from instructions and unfurled the British flag, claiming formal possession without the consent of Māori, but was still able to return twice in 1773 and 1777. The French were also interested – on his 1769 voyage Cook had passed **Jean François Marie de Surville** in a storm without either knowing of the other's presence.

He may well have raised the flag in Coromandel, but it was on the highest point of Motuara Island in Queen Charlotte Sound that Cook first raised the Union Jack flag to claim NZ for England and the sound for his queen. Far exceeding his orders, the British made a point of excluding it from their list of colonies until well after 1820.

The establishment of the Botany Bay penal colony in neighbouring Australia aroused the first commercial interest in New Zealand and from the 1790s to the

1769	1830s	1835
Englishman James Cook circumnavigates both main islands.	Sealing and whaling stations dotted around the coast.	Independence of the United Tribes of NZ proclaimed.

JAMES COOK

Yorkshireman Lieutenant (later Captain) **James Cook** was a meticulous **navigator** who sailed the *Endeavour* into the Pacific to observe the transit of Venus across the sun. Following Admiralty instructions he then continued west, arriving at "the Eastern side of the Land discover'd by Tasman" where he observed the "Genius, Temper, Disposition and Number of the Natives" and encouraged his botanists, Banks and Solander, to collect numerous samples.

On three voyages between 1769 and 1777 Cook spent a total of ten months around the coast of Aotearoa, leaving his mark with numerous place names. Some of his **charts** were in use well into the twentieth century, and his only significant errors were showing Banks Peninsula as an island and Stewart Island joined to the mainland with a peninsula.

1830s New Zealand was part of the Australian frontier. By 1830 the coast was dotted with semi-permanent **sealing** communities which, within thirty years, clubbed the seals into near-extinction. The British navy rapidly felled giant kauri trees for its ships' masts, while others supplied Sydney shipbuilders. By the 1820s **whalers** had moved in, basing themselves at Kororareka (now Russell), where they could recruit Māori crew and provision their ships. This combination of rough whalers, escaped convicts from Australia and assorted miscreants and adventurers combined to turn Russell into a lawless place populated by what Darwin, on his visit in 1835, found to be "the very refuse of Society".

Before long, the Māori way of life had been entirely disrupted. **Intertribal fighting** soon broke out on a scale never seen before. Hongi Hika (see page 697) was the first off the mark, but the quest for new territory also fuelled the actions of Ngati Toa's **Te Rauparaha**, who soon controlled the southern half of the North Island.

The huge demand for **firearms** drove Māori to sell the best of their resources: one ton of *muka* (scraped flax fibre) for one musket was the going rate. This led to Māori relocating to unhealthy areas close to flax swamps, where flax production could be increased. Even highly valued tribal treasures – *pounamu* (greenstone) clubs and the preserved heads of chiefs taken in battle – were traded. European **diseases** swept through the Māori population, alcohol and tobacco became widespread, Māori women were prostituted to Pakeha sailors, and the tribal structure began to crumble.

Into this scene stepped the **missionaries** in 1814, the brutal New South Wales magistrate **Samuel Marsden** arriving in the Bay of Islands, a transformed man with a mission to bring Christianity and "civilization" to Māori, and to save the souls of the sealers and whalers. Subsequently Anglicans, Wesleyans and Catholics all set up missions throughout the North Island, ostensibly to protect Māori from the worst of the exploitation and campaigning in both London and Sydney for more policing of Pakeha actions. In exchange, they destroyed fine artworks considered too sexually explicit and demanded that Māori abandon cannibalism and slavery; in short, Māori were expected to trade in their *Maoritanga* and become "**Europeans**". By the late 1830s, self-confidence and the belief in Māori ways was in rapid decline: the *tohunga* (priest) was powerless over new European diseases which could often be cured by the missionaries, and some Māori had started to believe Pakeha that the Māori race was dying out.

1840	1840s	1852
Treaty of Waitangi. Capital moved from Kororareka to Auckland.	Cities of Auckland, Christchurch, Dunedin, Nelson, New Plymouth, Wanganui and Wellington established.	NZ becomes a self-governing colony divided into six provinces.

The push for colonization

Despite Cook's discovery claim in 1769, imperial cartographers had never marked New Zealand as a British possession and it was with some reluctance – informed by the perception of an overextended empire only marginally under control – that New South Wales law was nominally extended to New Zealand in 1817. The effect was minimal; the New South Wales governor had no official representation on this side of the Tasman and was powerless to act. Unimpressed, by 1831 a small group of northern Māori chiefs decided to petition the British monarch to become a "friend and the guardian of these islands", a letter that was later used to justify Britain's intervention.

Britain's response was to send the less-than-competent **James Busby** as British Resident in 1833, with a brief to encourage trade, stay on good terms with the missionaries and Māori, and apprehend escaped convicts for return to Sydney. Convinced that New Zealand was becoming a drain on the colony's economy, the New South Wales governor withheld guns and troops, and Busby was unable to enforce his will. Busby was also duped by Baron de Thierry, a Briton of French parents, who claimed he had bought most of the Hokianga district from Hongi Hika and styled himself the "sovereign chief of New Zealand", to "save" Māori from the degradation he foresaw under British dominion. In a panic, Busby misguidedly persuaded 35 northern chiefs to proclaim themselves as the "**United Tribes of New Zealand**" in 1835. As far as the Foreign Office was concerned, this allowed Britain to disclaim responsibility for the actions of its subjects.

By the late 1830s there were around two thousand Pakeha in New Zealand, the largest concentration around Kororareka in the Bay of Islands. Most were British, but French Catholics also consolidated their tentative toehold, and in 1839 British-born James Clendon was appointed American consul. Meanwhile, **land speculators** and colonists began taking an interest. The Australian emancipationist, William Charles Wentworth, had "bought" the South Island and Stewart Island for a few hundred pounds (the largest private land deal in history, subsequently quashed by government order) and British settlers were already setting sail. The British admiralty finally took notice when the Australian convict settlements, originally intended simply as an out-of-sight, out-of-mind solution to their bulging prisons, looked set to become a valuable possession.

A combination of these pressures and Busby's exaggeration of the Māori inability to manage their own affairs goaded the British government into action. The result was the 1840 **Treaty of Waitangi** (see pages 154 and 698), a document that purported to guarantee continued Māori control of their lands, rights and possessions in return for their loss of sovereignty, a concept open for misinterpretation. The annexed lands became a dependency of New South Wales until New Zealand was declared a separate colony a year later.

Settlement and the early pioneers

Even before the Treaty was signed, there were moves to found a settlement in Port Nicholson, the site of Wellington, on behalf of the New Zealand Company. This was the brainchild of **Edward Gibbon Wakefield**, who hoped to stem American-style egalitarianism and use New Zealand as the proving ground for his theory of "scientific

1858	1860–65	1860s
Settlers outnumber Māori.	New Zealand Wars between Pakeha and Māori.	Major gold rushes in the South Island.

HONGI HIKA

Hongi Hika from Ngapuhi *iwi* of the Bay of Islands was the first Māori chief to appreciate the value of firearms, and had already acquired several when missionary Thomas Kendall met him in 1814. At this time he was encouraging his people to grow crops that could be traded with Pakeha for guns.

In 1820 Hongi Hika ended up traveling to England with Thomas Kendall to work on *A grammar and vocabulary of the language of New Zealand*. While he was there he briefly became the toast of London society and was presented to King George IV as an "equal". Having little use for most of the gifts showered upon him, he traded them for 300 muskets. Eager to emulate the supreme power of the imperial king, Hongi Hika returned and set about subduing much of the North Island, using the often badly maintained and inexpertly aimed guns to rattle the enemy, who were then slaughtered with the traditional *mere*. Warriors abandoned the old fighting season – the lulls between hunting and tending the crops – and set off to settle old scores, resulting in a massive loss of life.

---

colonization". This aimed to preserve the English squire-and-yokel class structure but ended up encouraging absentee landlordism.

Between 1839 and 1843 the New Zealand Company dispatched nearly 19,000 settlers to "**planned settlements**" in Wellington, Wanganui, Nelson and New Plymouth. This was the core of Pakeha immigration, the only substantial non-Wakefield settlement being **Auckland**, a scruffy collection of waterside shacks which, to the horror of New Zealand Company officials, became the capital after the signing of the Treaty of Waitangi.

The company couldn't buy land direct from Māori, but the government bought up huge tracts and sold it on, often for ten or twenty times what they paid for it. In 1850 the New Zealand Company foundered, leaving settlements which, subject to the hard realities of colonial life, had failed to conform to Wakefield's lofty theories and were filled with mostly sturdy workers from labouring and lower-middle-class backgrounds.

In 1852 New Zealand achieved self-government and divided the country into six **provinces** – Auckland, New Plymouth, Wellington, Nelson, Canterbury and Otago – each run by their own Provincial Council. In addition to taking over land sales, it encouraged migrants with free passage, land grants and guaranteed employment on road construction schemes – a call heeded by those hoping for a better life away from the drudgery of working-class Britain. Māori still held the best land, growing potatoes and wheat for both local consumption and export to Australia, where the Victorian gold rush had created a huge demand. Pakeha were barely able to compete, and the slump in export prices in the mid-1850s saw many look to **pastoralism**. The Crown helped by halving the price of land, allowing poorer settlers to become landowners but simultaneously paving the way for the creation of huge pastoral runs and putting further pressure on Māori land.

Māori resistance and the New Zealand Wars

The first five years after the signing of the Treaty were a disaster, first under Governor Hobson then the ineffectual FitzRoy. Relations between Māori

1865	1867	1870s
Capital moved from Auckland to Wellington.	Māori men given the vote.	Wool established as the mainstay of the NZ economy.

THE TREATY OF WAITANGI

IN ENGLISH

The main points set out in the **English treaty** are as follows:
• The chiefs cede sovereignty of New Zealand to the Queen of England.
• The Queen guarantees the chiefs the "full exclusive and undisturbed possession of their Lands and Estates Forests Fisheries and other properties which they may collectively or individually possess".
• The Crown retains the right of pre-emption over Māori lands.
• The Queen extends the rights and privileges of British subjects to Māori.

IN MĀORI

However, the **Māori translation** presents numerous possibilities for misunderstanding, since Māori is a more idiomatic and metaphorical language, where words can take on several meanings. The main points of contention include the following:
• The preamble of the English version cites the main **objectives** of the treaty being to protect Māori interests, to provide for British settlement and to set up a government to maintain peace and order. On the other hand, the main thrust of the Māori version is that the all-important rank and status of the chiefs and tribes will be maintained.
• The concept of **sovereignty** in the Māori version is translated as *kawanatanga* (governorship), a word Māori linked to their experience of the toothless reign of **James Busby** (see page 696). It seems unlikely that the chiefs realized just what they were giving away.
• In the Māori text, the Crown guaranteed the *tangata whenua* (people of the land) the possession of their properties for as long as they wished to keep them. In English this was expressed in terms of **individual rights** over property. This is perhaps the most wilful mistranslation and, in practice, there were long periods when Māori were coerced into selling their **land**, and when they refused, lands were simply taken.
• **Pre-emption** was translated as *hokonga* – a term simply meaning "buying and selling", with no explanation of the Crown's exclusive right to buy Māori land, which was clearly spelled out in the English version. This has resulted in considerable friction over Māori being unable to sell any land that the government didn't want, even if they had a buyer.
• The implications of **British citizenship** may not have been well understood: it is not clear whether Māori realized they would be bound by British law.

and Pakeha began to deteriorate immediately, as the capital was moved from Kororareka to Auckland and duties were imposed in the Bay of Islands. The consequent loss of trade from passing ships precipitated the first tangible expression of dissent, a famous series of incidents involving the Ngapuhi leader **Hone Heke**, who repeatedly felled the most fundamental symbol of British authority, the big flagstaff at Russell. The situation improved to some degree with the appointment of **George Grey**, the most able of New Zealand's governors, who did more than anyone else to shape the country's early years. Soon Māori began to adapt their culture to accommodate Pakeha – selling crops, operating flour mills and running coastal shipping. Grey encouraged the process by establishing mission schools, erecting hospitals where Māori could get free treatment, and providing employment on public works. In short, he upheld the spirit of the Treaty, thereby

1876	**1882**	**1893**
Abolition of provincial governments. Power centralized in Wellington.	First refrigerated meat shipment to Europe. Lamb becomes increasingly important.	Full women's suffrage: a world first.

gaining enormous respect among Māori. Sadly, he failed to set up any mechanism to perpetuate his policies after he left for the governorship of Cape Town in 1853.

Under **New Zealand's constitution**, enacted in 1852, Māori were excluded from political decision-making and prevented from setting up their own form of government; although British subjects in name, they had few of the practical benefits and yet were increasingly expected to comply with British law. By now it was clear that Māori had been duped by the Treaty of Waitangi: one chief explained that they thought they were transferring the "shadow of the land" while "the substance of the land remains with us", and yet he now conceded "the substance of the land goes to the Europeans, the shadow only will be our portion". Growing **resistance** to land sales came at a time when settler communities were expanding and demanding to buy huge tracts of pastoral land. With improved communications Pakeha became more self-reliant and dismissive of Māori, who began to lose faith in the government and fell back on traditional methods of handling their affairs. Self-government had given landowners the vote, but since Māori didn't hold individual titles to their land they were denied suffrage, eventuating in the creation of special Māori seats in parliament. Māori and Pakeha aspirations seemed completely at odds and there was a growing **sense of betrayal**, which helped replace tribal animosities with a tenuous unity. In 1854, a month before New Zealand's first parliament, Māori held intertribal meetings to discuss a response to the degradation of their culture and the rapid loss of their land. The eventual upshot was the 1858 election of the ageing **Te Wherowhero**, head chief of the Waikatos, as the Māori "King", the leader of the **King Movement** (see page 201) behind which Māori could rally to hold back the flood of Pakeha settlement. Most were moderates making peaceful overtures that Pakeha chose to regard as rebellious.

Matters came to a head in 1860, when the government used troops to enforce a bogus confiscation of land at Waitara, near New Plymouth. The fighting at Taranaki soon consumed the whole of the North Island in the **New Zealand Wars**, once known by Pakeha as the Māori Wars and by Māori as *te riri Pakeha* (foreigners' anger). Māori were divided, with some settling old grievances by siding with the government against their traditional enemies. Through the early 1860s the number of Pakeha troops was tripled to around 3000, providing an effective force against less coordinated Māori forces. Though there were notable Māori successes, the final result was inevitable. Fighting had abated by the end of the 1860s but peace wasn't finally declared until 1881.

British soldiers had been lured into service with offers of land and free passage and, in a further affront to defeated Māori, many were settled in the solidly Māori Waikato. Much of the most fertile land was **confiscated**– in the Waikato, the Bay of Plenty and Taranaki – with little regard to the owners' allegiances during the conflict. By 1862 individuals could buy land directly from Māori, who were forced to limit the stated ownership first to ten individuals and later to just one owner. With their collective power smashed, voracious land agents lured Māori into debt then offered to buy their land to "save" them.

Between 1860 and 1881, the **non-Māori population** rose from 60,000 to 470,000, swamping and marginalizing Māori society. An Anglo-Saxon worldview came to

1910s	1914–18	1917
Rise of organized labour under the socialist Red Federation. Strikes at Blackball, Waihi and Auckland.	NZ takes part in World War I with terrible loss of life.	Temperance Movement closes pubs at 6pm. Only repealed in 1967.

dominate all aspects of New Zealand life, and by 1871 the Māori language was no longer used for teaching in schools.

Meanwhile, as the New Zealand Wars raged in the North Island, **gold fever** had struck the South, with discoveries near Queenstown in 1861 and later along the West Coast. For the best part of a decade, gold was New Zealand's major export, but its most noticeable effect was on population distribution: by 1858 the shrinking Māori population had been outstripped by rapidly swelling Pakeha numbers, most settling in the South Island where relations with Māori played a much smaller part.

Consolidation and social reform

The 1870s were dominated by the policies of Treasurer Julius Vogel, who started a **programme of public works** funded by borrowing on a massive scale. Within a decade, previously scattered towns in separately governed provinces were transformed into a single country unified by improved roads, an expanding rail system, 7000km of telegraph wires and numerous public institutions. Almost all the remaining farmable land was bought up or leased from Māori and acclimatization societies sprang up with the express aim of anglicizing the New Zealand countryside and improving **farming**. With no extensive market close enough to make perishable produce profitable, **wool** became the main export, stimulated by the development of the Corriedale sheep, a Romney-Lincoln cross with a long fleece. Wool continued as the mainstay until 1882, when the first **refrigerated meat shipment** left for Britain, signalling a turning point in the economy and the establishment of New Zealand as Britain's offshore larder, a role it maintained until the 1970s.

From 1879 until 1896 New Zealand slid into a "long depression", mostly overseen by the conservative "Continuous Ministry" – the last government composed of colonial gentry. During this time **trade unionism** began influencing the political scene and bolstered the Liberal Pact (a Liberal and Labour alliance). In 1890 the alliance wrested power and ushered in an era of unprecedented social change. Its first leader, **John Ballance**, firmly believed in state intervention and installed socialist **William Pember Reeves** as his Minister of Labour. Reeves was instrumental in pushing through sweeping reforms to working hours and factory conditions that were so progressive that no further changes were made to labour laws until 1936. When Ballance died in 1892 he was replaced by **Richard "King Dick" Seddon**, who introduced a graduated income tax and repealed property tax, hoping to break up some of the large estates. New Zealand was already being tagged the "social laboratory of the world", but more was to come.

In 1893, New Zealand was the first nation in the world to enact full **female suffrage**, (see below), followed five years later by the introduction of an **old age pension**. Fabian Beatrice Webb, in New Zealand that same year, declared that "it is delightful to see a country with no millionaires and hardly any slums".

By the early twentieth century, the Pakeha standard of living was one of the highest in the world. But things were not so rosy for Māori, whose numbers had plummeted from an estimated 200,000 at Cook's first visit to around 50,000 in 1896. However, as resistance to European diseases grew, numbers started rising, accompanied by a new confidence buoyed by the rise of Māori parliamentary leadership. **Apirana Ngata**, **Maui**

1920s	1935	1941
Initial prosperity evaporates as the Great Depression takes hold.	M.J. Savage's Labour government ushers in the world's first Welfare State.	Bombing of Pearl Harbor and World War II begins New Zealand's military realignment with the Pacific region.

ACCIDENTAL SUFFRAGE

In 1893, New Zealand became the first nation on earth to grant women the vote. Other territories (South Australia, Wyoming etc) had led the way with limited **women's suffrage**, but New Zealand threw the net wider. It is something New Zealanders are inordinately proud of even though it came about more by accident than any free-thinking principle.

When a radical electoral reform bill was up for consideration, Prime Minister Seddon let an amendment pass on the assumption that it would be rejected by the Legislative Council (an upper house which survived until 1950). Seddon then ordered a Liberal Party councillor to change his vote, his interference causing the ire of two other councillors who then voted for the bill, allowing it to pass by twenty votes to eighteen. It's also contended that female suffrage was approved in response to the powerful quasi-religious temperance movement, which hoped to "purify and improve the tone of our politics", effectively giving married couples double the vote of the unmarried man, who was often seen as a drunken layabout.

Regardless of the rationale, New Zealand set a precedent and other major Western nations eventually followed suit – Finland in 1906, all Australian states by 1908, Britain in 1918, and the US in 1920. It wasn't until 1919, however, that New Zealand women were given the right to stand for parliament, and they were not eligible to be appointed to the New Zealand Legislative Council until 1941.

Pomare and **Te Rangi Hiroa** (**Peter Buck**), who were committed to working within the administrative and legislative framework of government, became convinced that the survival of *Maoritanga* depended on shedding those aspects of the traditional lifestyle that impeded their acceptance of the modern world.

Seddon died in 1906 and the flame went out of the Liberal torch, though the party was to stay in power another six years. This era saw the rise of the **"Red Feds"**, international socialists of the Red Federation who began to organize Kiwi labour. They rejected the arbitration system that had kept wage rises below the level of inflation for a decade, and encouraged **strikes**. The longest was at Blackball on the West Coast, where prime movers in the formation of the Federation of Miners, and subsequently the Federation of Labour, led a three-month stoppage.

The 1912 election was won by William Massey's Reform Party, with the support of influential farmers (mostly sheep farming run holders). Allegiances were now substantially polarized and 1912 and 1913 saw bitter fighting at a series of strikes at the gold mines of Waihi, the docks at Timaru and the wharves of Auckland. As workers opposed to the arbitration system withdrew their labour, owners organized scab labour, while the hostile Farmers' Union recruited mounted "special constables" to help the government. Protected by naval and military forces, they decisively smashed the Red Feds. The Prime Minister even handed out medals to strike-breaking dairy farmers.

Coming of age

Though New Zealand had started off as the unwanted offspring of Mother England, it had soon transformed itself into a devoted daughter who could be relied upon in times of crisis. New Zealand had supported Britain in South Africa at the end of the nineteenth century and was now called upon to do the same in

1947	**1950**	**1951**
Full independence from Britain.	Parliament's upper house abolished.	NZ joins ANZUS military pact with the US and Australia.

World War I. Locally born Pakeha now outnumbered immigrants and, in 1907, New Zealand had traded its self-governing colony status for that of a Dominion. This gave the country control over its foreign policy, but did not stop New Zealanders flocking to the war effort. Altogether ten percent of the population was involved, 100,000 fighting in the trenches of Gallipoli, Passchendaele and elsewhere. Seventeen thousand were killed.

At home, the **Temperance Movement** was back in action, attempting to curb vices in the army brought on by drink. Plebiscites in 1911, 1914 and 1919 narrowly averted national prohibition but the "wowsers" succeeded to the point that from 1917 pubs would close at 6pm for the duration of the war, though it wasn't repealed until 1967. This "**Six o'clock swill**" – frenetic after-work consumption in which the ability to tank down as much beer as possible was raised to an art form – probably did more to hinder New Zealand's social development than anything else (and the emphasis on quantity over quality encouraged breweries to churn out dreadful watery brews).

The wartime boom economy continued until around 1920 as Britain's demand for food remained high. Pakeha **returned servicemen** were rehabilitated on newly acquired farmland; Māori returned servicemen got nothing.

New Zealand continued to grow, with ongoing improvements in infrastructure – hydroelectric dams and roads – and enormous improvements in farming techniques, such as the application of superphosphate fertilizers, sophisticated milking machines and tractors. Yet it was ill-prepared for the **Great Depression**. The already high national debt skyrocketed as export income dropped and the Reform government cut pensions, health care and public works' expenditure. The budget was balanced at the cost of producing huge numbers of unemployment. Prime Minister Forbes dictated "no pay without work" and sent thousands of men to primitive rural relief camps for unnecessary tasks such as planting trees and draining swamps. Although much-needed infrastructure was built during this time, the measures resulted in lines of ragged men awaiting their relief money, malnourished children in schools and former soldiers panhandling in the streets.

Throughout the 1920s the Labour Party had watered down some of its socialist policies in an attempt to woo the middle-ground voter. In 1935 it was swept to power and ushered in New Zealand's second era of massive social change, picking up where Seddon left off. Labour's leader **Michael Joseph Savage** felt that "Social Justice must be the guiding principle and economic organization must adapt itself to social needs", a sentiment translated by a contemporary commentator as aiming "to turn capitalism quite painlessly into a nicer sort of capitalism which will eventually become indistinguishable from socialism". Salaries reduced during the depression were restored; public works programmes were rekindled, with workers on full pay rather than "relief"; income was redistributed through graduated taxation; and in two rapid bursts of legislation Labour built the model **Welfare State**, the first in the world and the most comprehensive and integrated. State houses were built and let at low rental, pensions were increased, a national health service provided free medicines and health care, and family benefits supplemented the income of those with children.

Māori welfare was also on the agenda, with living standards raised to the Pakeha level, partly by increasing pensions and unemployment payments. Legal changes paved the way for Māori land to be farmed using Pakeha agricultural methods, while maintaining

1960s	1972–75	1975
Start of immigration from Pacific Islands. Major urbanization of Māori population.	NZ economy struggles to cope with huge oil price hikes and Britain's entry into the Common Market.	Waitangi Tribunal established to consider Māori land claims.

communal ownership. In return, the newly formed **Ratana Party**, who held all four of the Māori parliamentary seats, supported Labour, keeping them in office until 1949.

New Zealand's perception of its world position changed dramatically in 1941 when the Japanese bombed Hawaii's Pearl Harbor. The country was forced to recognize its position half a globe away from Britain and in the military sphere of America. As in World War I, large numbers of troops were called up, amounting to a third of the male labour force, but casualties were fewer and on the home front the economy continued to boom. By the 1940s New Zealand was one of the world's most prosperous countries, with an enviable quality of life and welfare safety-net.

More years of prosperity

The Reform Party and the remnants of the Liberals eventually combined to form the National Party which, in 1949, wrested power from Labour. With McCarthyite rhetoric, National branded the more militant unionists as Communists and succeeded in breaking much of the power of the unions during the violent 1951 **Waterfront Lock-out**. From the late 1940s until the mid-1980s, **National** became New Zealand's main party of government, interrupted only by two three-year stints with Labour in power. The country's underlying conservatism had now found its expression. Most were happy with the government's strong-arm tactics, which emasculated the militant unions.

Notions of the prosperous "Kiwi ideal" had huge appeal for Brits still suffering rationing after World War II, and between 1947 and 1975, 77,000 Brits became "**ten pound poms**", making use of the New Zealand government's assisted passage to fill Kiwi job vacancies.

By most measures New Zealand's wealth was evenly spread, with few truly rich and relatively few poor. The exception were Māori. Responding to the urban labour shortages and good wages after World War II, many now took part in a **Māori migration** to the cities, especially Auckland. Yet by the 1970s, unemployment, unrest and a disproportionate prison population were exposing weaknesses in the Pakeha belief that the country's race relations were the best in the world. Pakeha took great pride in Māori bravery, skill, generosity, sporting prowess and good humour, but were unable to set aside the discrimination which kept Māori out of professional jobs.

On the economic front, major changes took place under **Walter Nash**'s 1957–60 Labour government, when New Zealand embarked on a programme designed to relieve the country's dependence on exports. A steel rolling mill, oil refinery, gin distillery, aluminium smelter and glass factory were all set up. When **Keith Holyoake** helmed the next National government, in 1960, Britain was still by far New Zealand's biggest export market but was making overtures to the economically isolationist European Common Market. Britain was no longer the guardian she once was and in the **military** sphere New Zealand began to court Pacific allies, mainly through the ANZUS pact, which provided for mutual defence of Australia, New Zealand and the US.

Dithering in the face of adversity

In 1972 Britain finally joined the Common Market and New Zealand felt betrayed. Later the same year **oil prices** quadrupled in a few months and the

1970s–80s	1984	1985
Contentious sporting relations culminate in massive protests as a racially selected South African Springbok rugby team tours NZ.	The "Hikoi" land march brings Māori grievances into political focus.	French secret service agents bomb Greenpeace flagship the *Rainbow Warrior* in Auckland Harbour.

treasury found itself with mounting fuel bills and decreasing export receipts. The Labour government were defeated in 1975 by National's obstreperous and pugnacious **Robert "Piggy" Muldoon**, who denounced Labour's borrowing and then outdid them. In short order New Zealand had dreadful domestic and foreign debt, unemployment was the highest for decades, and the unthinkable was happening – the standard of living was falling. People began to leave in their thousands and the "brain drain" almost reached crisis point. Muldoon's solution was to "**Think Big**", a catch-all term for a number of capital-intensive petrochemical projects designed to utilize New Zealand's abundant natural gas to produce ammonia, urea fertilizer, methanol and synthetic petrol. It made little economic sense. Rather than use local technology and labour to convert vehicles to run on compressed natural gas (a system already up and running), Muldoon paid international corporations to design huge prefabricated processing plants which were then shipped to New Zealand for assembly, mostly around New Plymouth.

Factory outfalls often jeopardized traditional Māori shellfish beds, and a new **spirit of protest** saw *iwi* win significant concessions. Māori began to question the philosophy of Pakeha life and looked to the Treaty of Waitangi to correct their grievances. These were aired at occupations of traditional land at Bastion Point in Auckland and at Raglan, and through a petition delivered to parliament after a march across the North Island.

Māori also found expression in the formation of **gangs** – particularly Black Power and the Mongrel Mob – along the lines graphically depicted in Lee Tamahori's film *Once Were Warriors* (see page 726), which was originally written about South Auckland life in the 1970s. Fortified suburban homes still exist and such gangs continue to be influential among Māori youth.

Race relations were never Muldoon's strong suit and when large numbers of illegal **Polynesian immigrants** from South Pacific islands – particularly Tonga, Samoa and the Cook Islands – started arriving in Auckland he responded by instructing the police to conduct random "dawn raids" checking for "over-stayers", many of whom were deported.

Muldoon took a hands-off approach when it came to sporting contacts with apartheid South Africa and in 1976 let rugby administrators send an All Blacks team over to play racially selected South African teams. African nations responded by boycotting the Montréal Olympics, making New Zealand an international pariah. New Zealand signed the 1977 Gleneagles Agreement requiring it to "vigorously combat the evil of apartheid" and yet in 1981 the New Zealand Rugby Union courted a **Springbok Tour**, which sparked New Zealand's greatest civil disturbance since the labour riots of the 1920s.

Economic and electoral reform

Muldoon's big-spending economic policies proved unsuccessful, and in 1984 Labour was returned to power under **David Lange**. Just as National had eschewed traditional right-wing economics in favour of a "managed economy", Labour now addressed the dire economic problems by turning one of the world's most regulated economies into one governed by market forces. The long-standing belief that the state should provide for those least able to help themselves was cast aside as exchange controls were

1987	1990–96	1997
New Zealand becomes a Nuclear-Free Zone.	Continuation of free-market reforms and further dismantling of the welfare state.	National's Jenny Shipley becomes NZ's first female prime minister.

abolished, state benefits were cut, the maximum income-tax rate was halved and a Goods and Services Tax was introduced. Unemployment doubled to twelve percent, a quarter of manufacturing jobs were lost, and the moderately well-off benefited at the expense of the poor.

In other spheres Labour's views weren't so right-wing. One of Lange's first acts was to refuse US ships entry to New Zealand ports unless they declared that they were nuclear-free. The Americans refused, sticking to their 'neither conform nor deny' policy, and withdrew support for New Zealand's defence safety net, the **ANZUS** pact. Lange also gave **legal recognition to the Treaty of Waitangi**, for the first time since the middle of the nineteenth century. Now, Māori grievances dating back to 1840 could be addressed.

The rise in apparent income created consumer confidence and the economy boomed until the stock market crash of 1987, which hit New Zealand especially hard. In 1990 National's **Jim Bolger** took the helm, and throughout the deep recession National continued Labour's free-market reforms, cutting welfare programmes and weakening the unions by passing the **Employment Contracts Act**, under which individual workplaces came to their own agreements on wages and conditions. By the middle of the 1990s the economy had improved dramatically and what for a time had been considered a foolhardy experiment was seen by monetarists as a model for open economies the world over. Meanwhile, the gap between rich and poor continued to widen.

Political change

In 1996, New Zealand experienced its first MMP election (see page 706), which brought a new Māori spirit into parliament, with far more Māori MPs than ever before.

Bolger's poor handling of the first MMP coalition government saw him supplanted in a palace coup, with **Jenny Shipley** becoming New Zealand's first female prime minister. In the 1999 election, the **Green Party** came out of left field, long-sidelined but newly resurgent under MMP. They racked up six seats and helped form a government under Labour's **Helen Clark** – the country's first elected female prime minister. The 1999 election brought New Zealand's first Rastafarian MP, **Nandor Tanczos**, resplendent in waist-length dreads and a hemp suit, and **Georgina Beyer**, the world's first transgender MP.

The Labour-led coalition stopped the logging of West Coast beech forests and replaced the Employment Contracts Act with more worker-friendly legislation but failed to deliver on education and health care. Still, Labour was returned with an increased majority at the 2002 election.

Labour's popularity remained high until the 2003 **foreshore and seabed debate** in which Labour forced through legislation ostensibly guaranteeing beach-access to all, by declaring that the land in question was owned by the Crown. Māori perceived this as an affront to their sovereignty, and traditionally Labour-supporting Māori voters turned to the newly established **Māori Party**, co-led by former Labour MP **Tariana Turia**. At the 2005 election the Māori Party won four of the seven Māori seats but Labour was still able to cobble together a coalition without Māori Party support.

1999	2003	2003
Labour's Helen Clark becomes NZ's second female prime minister, and the first elected in her own right.	Privy Council in London replaced by a Supreme Court as NZ's highest legal body.	Continued immigration from East Asia brings the Asian population up to ten percent of the nation.

FIRST-PAST-THE-POST, MMP AND MĀORI SEATS

In the troubled economic times of 1993, when dissatisfaction with both major parties was running high, New Zealand voted to abandon its long-standing, Westminster-style, first-past-the-post voting system in favour of Mixed Member Proportional representation (MMP). This gave smaller parties an opportunity to have a greater influence, and New Zealand's Parliament has become all the more colourful for it.

Of the 120 MPs elected, around half represent their own area of the country ("electorate" or "seat") and half are elected from party lists. Voters get **two votes**. The first is for a person, who you hope will become your electorate MP. The second is for a party and is generally considered the more important as it determines the overall make-up of Parliament. A party's representation in Parliament is made up from the number of electorate seats they win plus a number of their list MPs determined by their percentage of the party vote.

To get any seats at all, small parties must exceed the threshold of five percent of the party vote, or win a constituency seat. If they win a seat, their representation is proportional to their party vote even if it's under five percent.

To further complicate matters, Māori voters can choose to vote either within the general system described above, or for one of the seven **Māori seats** which cover the country. All parties are entitled to field candidates in both general and Māori constituencies, though parties championing Māori concerns tend to win.

A **referendum** on New Zealand's electoral system was held at the same time as the 2011 general election, during which Kiwis resoundingly voted to retain the MMP system.

This, combined with the perception of the Labour government having outstayed its welcome after nearly a decade in power, saw a resurgent National Party, under former currency trader **John Key**, form a coalition government following the 2008 election.

Recent history

When much of the rest of the developed world struggled with the Global Financial Crisis from 2008, New Zealand fared reasonably well. Lefties will cite sound financial management under Labour but much of the credit goes to **booming international dairy prices**, particularly powdered milk, which almost doubled from 2007 to 2008 and remained high until 2014. Sheep farmers everywhere were converting to dairying and even arable regions like the Canterbury Plains now sprout cows on grassy circles created by kilometre-long irrigation booms. However, high nutrient loads leaching into depleted watercourses has led to a deep questioning in New Zealand about how much dairying is sustainable, but it may be the skyrocketing compliance costs for producers combined with the drop in milk prices which may turn farmers away from such practices.

In the early 1990s, 16 percent of Kiwi dairy exports went to the UK and 0.5 percent to China. Now those stats are reversed with the UK taking only 0.3 percent and China snaffling 25 percent. Much of that change has come about since 2008 when New Zealand became the first developed nation to sign a **free trade agreement** with China. In 2013, China became New Zealand's biggest trade partner (with $23 billion annually) just pipping Australia ($11 billion) with the USA ($6 billion), Japan ($4 billion) and Korea ($2 billion) as distant followers.

2008	2010–11	2011
New Zealand becomes first developed country to sign a free trade agreement with China.	Christchurch struck by severe earthquakes. The most devastating, in February 2011, kills 185 people.	New Zealand hosts – and wins – the Rugby World Cup. The country rejoices.

Firmly ensconced in Parliament until 2017, National sought to take control of Auckland by amalgamating a barely functional patchwork of seven councils under one unitary authority. To National's chagrin, this "Supercity" voted left-leaning **Len Brown** as its first mayor in 2010, followed by long term Labour MP Phil Goff in 2016. Auckland Council carries considerable heft and relations with the National Government were often fraught, especially over the council's approach to tackling the house prices that make Auckland one of the world's least affordable places to live. The two parties have also clashed over funding for the **City Rail Link**, Brown's dream of significantly improving Auckland's train system with a 3.4km-long $1 billion tunnel under the CBD. National's refusal to commit government funds threatened the 2021 completion date, but an agreement was worked out in 2017 that will see it eventually built.

Late 2010 wasn't a happy time. A 7.1 magnitude **earthquake** hitting Christchurch in September was followed by the loss of 29 men after an explosion at a botched coalmine development at **Pike River** on the West Coast in November. These were trumped in February 2011 when 185 people were killed by a massive aftershock in Christchurch (see page 506).

On the political front, Key's government repealed the Foreshore and Seabed Act in 2011 prompting Māori Party firebrand MP Hone Harawira to break away and form the **Mana Party**. Harawira took the Northland Māori seat of Te Tai Tokerau at the 2011 election and remained a thorn in the side of both the National government and the Māori Party. He lost his seat in 2014 after forming a disastrous alliance with the Internet party, founded by German Mega mogul, **Kim Dotcom**.

In opposition, a succession of Labour leaders have failed to dent John Key's popularity. Clark lieutenant **Phil Goff** fell after the 2011 election, **David Shearer** got rolled and, in 2014, Labour suffered its worst loss at the ballot box since 1922 under David Cunliffe. After polling under 25 percent and returning just 32 members in a 121-seat parliament, former union leader **Andrew Little** took over at Labour's helm.

Just eight weeks from the 2017 General Election, his leadership was contested and rising Labour star **Jacinda Ardern** took the helm of the party and "Jacinda mania" took the country by storm. The result of the elections were a hung parliament until a Labour-Greens-NZ First coalition formed with Ardern as Prime Minister. Closing the gap between rich and poor, along with housing and immigration issues now dominate New Zealand's modern political agenda.

2014	2016	2017
National re-elected for a third term under John Key, the first time any party has won an outright majority under MMP.	Kaikoura struck by a devastating 7.8 earthquake, cutting off the town along with highway and rail links for over a year.	Jacinda Ardern elected Prime Minister of the 6th Labour Government, replacing the three term reign of National.

Maoritanga

Contemporary Māori culture has seen a dramatic resurgence in recent decades, though it struggles in a broadly Anglo-European-dominated New Zealand. Around fifteen percent of the country's population identify as Māori, and many Pakeha also have Māori forebears. Indeed, Māori–Pakeha marriage since the early nineteenth century has created a complex interracial pool – a fact that led one academic to speculate "race relations will be worked out in the bedrooms of New Zealand". Ancestry remains the foundation of Maoridom but a sense of belonging is increasingly important and centres on *Maoritanga*. This embodies Māori lifestyle – embracing Māori social structure, ethics, customs, legends, art and language.

When the Pakeha first came to this Island, the first thing he taught the Māori was Christianity. They made parsons and priests of several members of the Māori race, and they taught these persons to look up and pray; and while they were looking up the Pakehas took away our land.
Mahuta, the son of the Māori King Tawhiao, addressing the New Zealand Legislative Council in 1903

Māori in the modern world

New Zealand's Māori make up a vital part of all walks of life – as lawyers, MPs, university lecturers, sporting, musical and media identities, even Governor-Generals. That said, average incomes are lower than those of Pakeha, almost half of all prison inmates are Māori and only around a quarter of Māori achieve post-school qualifications. These, along with dreadful health statistics, are among the imbalances that activists and politicians are working to redress.

Many Pakeha have long cited scenes of Māori and Pakeha elbow-to-elbow at the bar and Māori rugby players in the scrum alongside their Pakeha brothers as evidence of a harmonious existence. Yet this has ignored an undercurrent of Māori dissatisfaction over their treatment since the arrival of Europeans; the policy of **assimilation** relied on Māori conforming to the Pakeha way of doing things, making no concession to *Maoritanga*. Māori adapted quickly to European ways but were rewarded with the near-loss of their language and the loss of their **land**. It is impossible to overestimate the importance of this: Māori spirituality invests every tree, hill and bay with a kind of supernatural life of its own, drawn from past events and the actions of the ancestors. It is by no means fanciful to equate the loss of land with the diminution of Māori life force.

It's only really since the 1980s that the paternal Pakeha view has been challenged, with the country adopting **biculturalism**. As Māori rediscover their heritage and Pakeha comprehend what has been around for generations, knowledge of *Maoritanga* and some understanding of the language is considered desirable and advantageous. Recent governments have increasingly fostered a take-up in the learning of Māori language, resurgence in Māori arts and crafts and a growing pride in the culture by both Māori and Pakeha.

The sluggish pace of change led to an increase in Māori activism. The debate effectively led to the 2004 birth of the centrist Māori Party, and later the radical Mana Party. Activist Tame Iti and others obviously felt this was way too little and established a camp in the Urewera hills. During a strong-arm 2007 raid there was a "lock-down" of the local community at nearby Ruatoki and those arrested were charged as terrorists (later commuted to firearms offences). If anything, the then-Labour government's botched response heightened calls for greater self-determination.

Māori legend

Māori culture remains primarily oral with chants, storytelling and oratory central to ceremonial and daily life. Different tribal groups had different sets of stories, or at least variations on common themes, but European historians with pet theories often distorted the tales they heard and destroyed conflicting evidence, creating their own Māori folklore. Over time many of these stories have been taken back into Māori tradition, resulting in a patchwork of authentic and bowdlerized legends and helping create a common Māori identity.

Creation

From the primal nothingness of **Te Kore** sprang **Ranginui**, the sky father, and **Papatuanuku**, the earth mother. They had numerous offspring, including: **Haumia Tiketike**, the god of the fern root and food from the forest; **Rongo**, the god of the *kumara* and cultivation; **Tu Matauenga**, the god of war; **Tangaroa**, the god of the oceans and sea life; **Tawhirimatea**, the god of the winds; and **Tane Mahuta**, the god of the forests. Through long centuries of darkness the brothers argued over whether to separate their parents and create light. Tawhirimatea opposed the idea and fled to the skies where his anger is manifested in thunder and lightning, while Tane Mahuta succeeded in parting the two, allowing life to flourish. Ranginui's tears filled the oceans, and even now it is his grief that brings the dew, mist and rain.

Having created the creatures of the sea, the air and the land, the gods turned their attentions to humans and, realizing that they were all male, decided to create a female. They fashioned clay into a form resembling their mother, and **Tane Mahuta** breathed life into the nostrils of the Dawn Maiden, **Hinetitama**.

Maui the trickster and Kupe the navigator

Māori mythology is littered with demigods, none more celebrated than **Maui-Tikitiki-a-Taranga**, whose exploits are legend throughout Polynesia. With an armoury of spells, guile and boundless mischief, Maui gained a reputation as a trickster, using his abilities to turn situations to his advantage. Equipped with the powerful magic jawbone of his grandmother, he set about taming his world, believing himself invincible. He even took on the sun, which passed so swiftly through the heavens that people had no time to tend their fields. Maui, with the aid of his older brothers, plaited strong ropes and tied them across the sun's pit before dawn. The sun rose into the net and Maui beat the sun with his magic jawbone, imploring it not to go so fast. The sun weakened and agreed to Maui's request. Maui's legendary antics extend to the creation of Aotearoa (see page 710).

Māori trace their ancestry back to **Hawaiki**, the source of the Polynesian diaspora, for which the Society Islands and the Cook Islands are likely candidates. According to legend, the first visitor to Aotearoa was **Kupe**, the great Polynesian navigator. He was determined to kill a great octopus that kept stealing his bait; drawn ever further out to sea in pursuit, he finally reached landfall on the uninhabited shores of Aotearoa, the "land of the long white cloud". He named numerous features of the land before returning to Hawaiki with instructions for retracing his voyage.

Social structure and customs

Māori society is **tribal**, though mass migration from homelands to the cities has eroded tribal affiliations. In urban situations the finer points of *Maoritanga* have been rediscovered and the basic tenets remain strong, with formal protocol ruling ceremonies from funeral wakes to meetings.

The most fundamental grouping in Māori society is the extended family or **whanau** (literally "birthing"), spanning immediate relatives to cousins, uncles and nieces. A dozen or so *whanau* form localized subtribes or **hapu** (literally "gestation

MAUI FISHES UP THE NORTH ISLAND

Maui's greatest work was the creation of **Aotearoa**. Because of his reputation for mischief, Maui's brothers often left him behind when they went fishing, but one morning he stowed away, revealing himself far out to sea and promising to improve their catch. Maui egged them on until they were beyond the normal fishing grounds before dropping anchor. In no time at all Maui's brothers filled the canoe with fish, but Maui still had some fishing to do. They scorned his hook (secretly armed with a chip of his grandmother's jawbone) and wouldn't lend him any bait, so Maui struck his own nose and smeared the hook with his blood. Soon he hooked a fabulous fish that, as it broke the surface, stretched into the distance all around them. Chanting an incantation, Maui got the fish to lie quietly and it became the North Island, Te ika a Maui, the fish of Maui. As Maui went to make an offering to the gods, his brothers began to cut up the fish and eat it, hacking mountains and valleys into the surface. To fit in with the legend, the South Island is often called Te waka a Maui, the canoe of Maui, and Stewart Island the anchor, Te punga o te waka a Maui.

or pregnancy"), comprising extended families of common descent. *Hapu* were originally economically autonomous and today continue to conduct communal activities, typically through *marae* (see page 711). Neighbouring *hapu* are likely to belong to the same tribe or **iwi** (literally "bones"), a looser association of Māori spread over large geographical areas. The thirty-odd major *iwi* are tenuously linked by common ancestry, traced back to migration canoes, or *waka*. In troubled times, *iwi* from the same *waka* would band together for protection. Together these are the **tangata whenua**, "the people of the land", a term that may refer to Māori people as a whole, or just to one *hapu* if local concerns are being aired.

The literal meanings of *whanau*, *hapu* and *iwi* can be viewed as a metaphor for the Māori view of their relationship with their ancestors or **tupuna**, existing through their genetic inheritors, the past forming part of the present. Hence the respect accorded the **whakapapa**, an individual's genealogy tracing descent from the gods via one of the migratory *waka* and through the *tupuna*. The *whakapapa* is often recited on formal occasions such as **hui** (meetings).

Māori traditional life is informed by the parallel notions of **tapu** (taboo) and **noa** (mundane, not *tapu*). This belief system is designed to impose a code of conduct: transgressing *tapu* brings ostracism, ill fortune and sickness. Objects, places, actions and people can be *tapu*, demanding extra respect; the body parts of a chief, especially the head, menstruating women, sacred items, earrings, pendants, hair combs, burial sites, and the knowledge contained in the *whakapapa* are all *tapu*. The productivity of fishing grounds and forests was traditionally maintained by imposing *tapu* at critical times. The direct opposite of *tapu* is *noa*, a term applied to ordinary items that, by implication, are considered safe; a new building is *tapu* until a special ceremony renders it *noa*.

People, animals and artefacts, whether *tapu* or *noa*, possess **mauri** (life force), **wairua** (spirit) and **mana**, a term loosely translated as prestige but embodying wider concepts of power, influence, charisma and goodwill. Birthright brings with it a degree of *mana* that can then be augmented through brave deeds or lost through inaction. Wartime cannibalism was partly ritual and by eating an enemy's heart a warrior absorbed his *mauri*. Likewise personal effects gain *mana* from association with the *mana* of their owner, accruing more when passed to descendants. Any slight on the *mana* of an individual was felt by the *hapu*, who must then exact **utu** (a need to balance any action with an equal reaction), a compunction that often led to bloody feuds, sometimes escalating to war and further enhancing the *mana* of the victors. Pakeha found this a hard concept to grasp and deeds that they considered deceitful or treacherous could be considered correct in Māori terms.

The responsibility for determining *tapu* falls to the **tohunga** (priest or expert), the most exalted of many specialists in *Maoritanga*, conversant with tribal history, sacred lore and the *whakapapa*, and considered to be the earthly presence of the power of the gods.

Marae

The rituals of *hapu* life – *hui*, **tangi** (funeral wakes) and **powhiri** (formal welcomes) – are conducted on the **marae**, a combined community, cultural and social centre where the cultural values, protocols, customs and vitality of *Maoritanga* find their fullest expression. Strictly, a *marae* is a courtyard, but the term is often applied to a whole complex, comprising the **whare runanga** (meeting house, or *whare nui*), *whare manuhiri* (house for visitors), *whare kai* (eating house) and an old-fashioned **pataka** (raised storehouse). *Marae* belonging to one or more *hapu* are found all over the country, while pan-tribal urban *marae* exist to help Māori who have lost their roots.

Visitors, whether Māori or Pakeha, may not enter *marae* without invitation, so unless you're personally invited, you're most likely to visit on a commercially run **tour** (see page 713). Invited guests are expected to provide some form of **koha** (donation) towards the upkeep of the *marae*, usually included in tour fees. Remember, the *marae* is sacred and due reverence must be accorded the **kawa** (protocols).

Arts and crafts

The origins of **Māori art** lie in eastern Polynesia but half a millennium of isolated development has resulted in unique forms of expression. Eastern Polynesia has no suitable clay, so Māori forebears had no skills for pottery and focused on wood, stone and weaving, occasionally using naturalistic designs but more often the **stylized forms** that make Māori art unmistakeable.

As with other *taonga* (treasures), many examples were taken by Victorian and later collectors, but there is determined effort by *iwi* and Te Puni Kokiri (the Ministry of Māori Development) to restore *taonga* to New Zealand, including severed heads scattered through museums around the world.

Woodcarving

Māori handiworks' greatest expression is **woodcarving**. The essence of great Māori woodcarving is that as much care is given to the production of a humble water bailer as to the pinnacle of Māori creativity, *waka* (canoes) and *whare whakairo* (carved houses). Early examples of woodcarving feature the sparse, rectilinear styles of ancient eastern Polynesia, but by the fifteenth century these were replaced by the cursive style, employed by more traditional carvers today. In Northland, kauri wood was used, while elsewhere durable, easily worked totara was the material of choice. Carvers worked with shells and sharp stones in the earliest times, but the artist's scope increased with the invention of tools fashioned from **pounamu** (greenstone, a form of jade; see page 479). Some would say that the quality of the work declined after European arrival: not just through the demand for quickly executed "tourist art", but as a consequence of pressure to remove the phallic imagery found obscene by missionaries. As early as 1844, carving had been abandoned in areas with a strong missionary presence, and it continued to decline until the 1920s when Māori parliamentarian Apirana Ngata established Rotorua's pan-tribal **Māori Arts and Crafts Institute** – a foundation on which *Maoritanga* could be rebuilt.

The role of carver has always been highly respected, with seasoned and skilled exponents having the status of *tohunga* and travelling the country to carve and teach. The work is *tapu* and *noa* objects must be kept away – cooked food is not allowed nearby, and carvers have to brush away shavings rather than blow them – though women, previously banned, can now become carvers.

Māori carving exhibits a distinctive **style**. Relief forms are hewn from a single piece of wood with no concession to natural form, shapes or blemishes. Landscapes

WHARE

Originally the **chief's residence**, the *whare* gradually adopted the symbolism of the *waka* – some incorporated wood from *waka*. Each meeting house is a tangible manifestation of the *whakapapa*, usually representing a synthesis of the ancestors: the ridge-pole, the backbone; the rafters, the ribs; the interior, the belly; the gable, the head; and the barge-boards, the arms, often with finger-like decoration. Inside, all wooden surfaces are carved and the spaces filled with intricate woven-flax panels, *tukutuku*.

are symbolized (not actually depicted), perspective is not represented, and figures stand separately. Unadorned wood is rare, carvers creating a stylistic bed of swirling spirals, curving organic forms based on fern fronds or seashells and interlocking latticework. Superimposed on this are key elements, often inlaid with paua shell.

The most common is the ancestor figure, the **hei tiki**, a distorted human form, either male, female or of indeterminate gender. Almost as common is the mythical *manaia*, a beaked birdlike form with an almost human profile. Secondary motifs include the *pakake* (whale) and *moko* (lizard).

While the same level of craftsmanship was applied to all manner of tools, weapons and ornaments, it reached its most exalted expression in *waka taua* (**war canoes**), the focus of community pride and endeavour. Gunwales, bailers and paddles are fabulously decorated but the most detailed work is reserved for the prow and sternpost, usually a matrix of spirals interwoven with *manaia* figures. As guns and the European presence altered the balance of tribal warfare in the 1860s, the *waka taua* was superseded in importance by the *whare whakairo* (carved meeting house).

Greenstone carving

Māori carvers also work in **pounamu** (greenstone), supplied by pre-European trade routes originating in the West Coast and Fiordland; indeed, the South Island became known as Te Wai Pounamu, the Greenstone Water. The stone was fashioned into adzes, chisels and clubs for hand-to-hand combat, tools that took on a ritual significance and demanded decoration. *Pounamu*'s hardness dictates a more restrained carving style and *mere* and *patu* tend to be only partly worked, leaving large sweeping surfaces ending in a flourish of delicate swirls. Ornamental pieces range from simple drop pendants worn as earrings or neck decoration to *hei tiki*, worn as a breast pendant. Like other personal items, especially those worn close to the body, an heirloom *tiki* possesses the *mana* of the ancestors and absorbs the wearer's *mana*, becoming *tapu*.

Tattooing

A stylistic extension of the carver's craft is exhibited in *moko*, ornamental and ceremonial **tattooing** that almost died out with European contact. Women had *moko* on the lips and chin, high-ranking men had their faces completely covered, along with their buttocks and thighs; the greater the extent and intricacy of the *moko*, the greater the status. A symmetrical pattern of traditional elements, crescents, spirals, fern fronds and other organic forms, was gouged into the flesh with an *uhi* (chisel) and mallet, then soot rubbed into the wound. In the last couple of decades the tradition of full-face *moko* has been revived, as a symbol of *Maoritanga* and an art form in its own right; since 1999, *moko* artists have been eligible for government funding.

Weaving and clothing

While men carved, women concentrated on weaving and producing clothing. When Polynesians arrived in these cool, damp islands their paper mulberry plants didn't thrive and they were forced to look for alternatives. They found *harakeke* (New Zealand **flax**), the foundation of Māori fibre-work. The long, strong and pliable fibres, growing on lowland all over the country, were used for a myriad of reasons, from fishing lines to cordage for axe-heads and as floor matting. With the arrival of the Pakeha, Māori adopted European clothes, but they continued to wear cloaks on formal occasions and today these constitute the basis for contemporary designs.

Used in something close to their raw form for *raranga* (plaiting), flax fibres made *kete*, handle-less baskets for collecting shellfish and *kumara*, triangular canoe sails, sandals and *whariki*, patterned floor mats still used in meeting houses. For finer work, trimming, soaking and beating flax, a laborious process, produced stronger and more pliable fibre.

Most flax was neutral but Māori design requires some **colouring**: black is achieved by soaking in a dilute extract of hinau tree bark then rubbing with a black swamp sediment, *paru*; red-brown ranges of colours require boiling in dyes derived from the tanekaha tree bark and fixing by rolling in hot ashes; while the less-popular yellow tint is produced from the bark of the Coprosma species. Today synthetic dyes are used to create green.

Natural and coloured fibres are both used in *whatu kakahu* (**cloak-weaving**), the crowning achievement of Māori women's art, the finest cloaks ranking alongside prized *taonga*; the immense war canoe now in the Auckland Museum was once exchanged for a fine cloak. The technique is sometimes referred to as finger-weaving as no loom is used. The women work downwards from a base warp strung between two sticks. Complex weaving techniques produce a huge array of different textures, often decorated with *taniko* (coloured borders), cord tags tacked onto the cloth at intervals and, most impressively, **feathers**. Feather cloaks (*kahu hururu*) don't appear to have been common before European contact, though heroic tales often feature key players in iridescent garments. The appeal of the bright yellow feathers of the huia probably saw to its demise, and most other brightly coloured birds are now too rare to use for cloaks, so new feather cloaks are rarely made.

You'll come across some fine examples in museums, the base cloth often completely covered by a dense layer of kiwi feathers bordered by zigzag patterns of tui, native

EXPERIENCING MĀORI CULTURE

The most direct and popular introduction to Māori culture is a **concert and hangi** (feast), best experienced in Rotorua.

Both the concert and *hangi* once took place on a traditional *marae* though these days it is usually at some dedicated site or even inside a hotel. *Kawa* (*protocols*) governing behaviour dictate that *manuhiri* (visitors) must be challenged to determine friendly intent before being allowed onto the *marae*. As visitors, you elect a "chief" who represents you during this *wero*, where a fearsome warrior bears down on you with twirling *taiaha* (long club), flicking tongue and bulging eyes. Once a ritual gift has been accepted, the women make the *karanga* (welcoming call), breaking the *tapu*, followed by their *powhiri* (sung welcome). This acts as a prelude to ceremonial touching of noses, *hongi*, binding the *manuhiri* and the *tangata whenua* physically and spiritually.

And so begins the concert, performed in traditional costume. Highlights are the men's *haka* and the women's *poi* dance, in which tennis-ball-sized bulrush clumps are twirled rhythmically. The concert is followed by the *hangi*, a feast traditionally steamed in an earth oven or, in Rotorua, over a geothermal vent. Typically visits include learning at least a few words of the Māori language.

Beyond commercial concert and *hangi* ensembles, the following tours and lodgings offer opportunities to dig deeper into Māori culture. The website ⓦinz.maori.nz is also a handy resource to find Māori tourism operators around the country.

Footprints Waipoua Northland. See page 180.
Kapiti Island near Wellington. See page 387.
MāoriTours Kaikoura. See page 453.
TIME Unlimited tours Auckland. See page 78
Maraehako Bay Retreat East Cape. See page 331.
Tipuna Tours East Cape. See page 334.

pigeon and parakeet. More robust, *para* (rain capes) were made using the water-repellent leaves of the cabbage tree and a form of coarse canvas that could reportedly resist spear thrusts was used for *pukupuku* (war cloaks). Some *pukupuku* were turned into *kahu kuri* (dog-skin cloaks) with the addition of strips of dog skin, arranged vertically so that the natural fur colours produced distinctive patterns.

Weaving and plaiting are again popular; cloaks are an important element of formal occasions, whether on the *marae* for *hui* and *tangi*, or elsewhere for receiving academic or state honours. Old forms are reproduced directly or raided as inspiration for contemporary designs that interpret traditional elements in the light of modern fashion.

The haka, Māori dance and Māori music

The use of the *haka* (see box below) by what are often predominantly Pakeha sides might seem inappropriate but it is entrenched in Kiwi culture; there was a considerable backlash in 1996 when the All Blacks coach suggested the *haka* should be changed to mollify those Māori *iwi* who had been decimated by Te Rauparaha. The new, specially written *Kapa O Pango haka* was unveiled in 2005 but it hasn't completely replaced the Te Rauparaha version.

The drums of eastern Polynesia didn't make it to New Zealand, so both chants and the *haka* go unaccompanied. Along with the traditional bone flute, Pakeha added the guitar to accompany **waiata** (songs), relatively modern creations whose impact comes from tone, rhythm and lyrics. The impassioned delivery can seem at odds with music that's often based on Victorian hymns: perhaps the best known are *Pokarekare ana* and *Haere Ra*, both post-European-contact creations. Outside the tourist concert party, Māori music has developed enormously in recent years to the point where there are tribal and Māori-language music stations almost exclusively playing music written and performed by Māori, often with a hip-hop or R & B influence and a Pacific twist. The Māori TV channel continues this emphasis on home grown music. For more on music, see page 724.

THE HAKA

Before every international rugby match, New Zealand's All Blacks put the wind up the opposition by performing an intimidating thigh-slapping, eye-bulging, tongue-poking chant. Traditionally this has been the Te Rauparaha *haka*, just one of many such Māori posture dances, designed to display fitness, agility and ferocity. The Te Rauparaha *haka* was reputedly composed early in the nineteenth century by the warrior Te Rauparaha who was hiding from his enemies in the *kumara* pit of a friendly chief. Hearing noise above and then being blinded by light he thought his days were numbered, but as his eyes became accustomed to the sun he saw the hairy legs of his host and was so relieved he performed the *haka* on the spot.

Touring teams have performed the *haka* at least since the 1905 All Blacks tour of Britain, and since the 1987 World Cup for home matches as well. The performance is typically led by a player of Māori descent chanting:

Ringa pakia Slap the hands against the thighs
Uma tiraha Puff out the chest
Turi whatia Bend the knees
Hope whai ake Let the hip follow
Waewae takahia kia kino Stamp the feet as hard as you can
After a pause for effect the rest of the team join in with:
Ka Mate! Ka Mate! It is death! It is death!
Ka Ora! Ka Ora! It is life! It is life!
Tenei te ta ngata puhuru huru This is the hairy man
Nana nei i tiki mai Who caused the sun to shine
Whakawhiti te ra Keep abreast!
A upane ka upane! The rank! Hold fast!
A upane kaupane whiti te ra! Into the sun that shines!

Landscapes and wildlife

Despite its relatively small size, New Zealand is bursting with enormous diversity: subtropical forests, volcanic basins, boiling mud pools, geysers, rugged white-silica- and gold-sand-fringed coastlines and spectacular alpine regions. These landscapes support an extraordinary variety of animals and plant life, with almost ninety percent of the flora not found anywhere else in the world. Many habitats, plants and wildlife are easily accessible, protected within national parks and scenic reserves.

The Shaky Isles

The earliest rocks are thought to have originated in the continental forelands of Australia and Antarctica, part of Gondwanaland, a massive supercontinent to which New Zealand belonged. Oceanic islands were created by continental drift, the movement of the large plates that form the earth's crust, creating an island arc and oceanic trench about 100 million years ago.

Roughly 26 million years ago, New Zealand rose further from the sea and today's landscape evolved, through **volcanic** activity and continuous movement along fault lines, particularly the Alpine Fault of the South Island. On the boundary between the Australian and Pacific tectonic plates, New Zealand's North Island has the two plates crashing into one another, the Pacific plate pushed beneath the Australian to produce prolific volcanic activity. Conversely under the South Island the Pacific plate rides over the Australian, causing **mountain building** and creating the Southern Alps. This unique island combination generates about 15,000 **earthquakes** a year, although only 100 to 150 are big enough to be noticed, and has earned New Zealand the nickname "the Shaky Isles". In 2010 and 2011, severe quakes struck the Canterbury region around Christchurch, causing extensive damage and loss of life (see page 506). The volcanoes on the North Island periodically become impressively active: White Island (just off the coast of the Bay of Plenty) blows steam and is put on alert, while Mount Ruapehu is actively monitored after erupting in 2006 and 2007.

The end of isolation

New Zealand's flora and fauna evolved untouched until the first human reached Aotearoa, probably around 500 years ago. Before the arrival of Māori, the land was covered in thick **forest** composed of hundreds of tree species, and the only mammals were seals, whales and dolphins round the coast, and a couple of types of **bat**. Land mammals were non-existent, a unique situation, which allowed **birds** to take their place in the food chain; with no predators, many gradually lost the ability to fly. When Māori came, with their dogs and rats, then Pakeha, with all their introduced species, the birds could not compete. Those that survived (see page 720) now cling precariously to existence.

Māori impact pales in comparison with the devastation wreaked by **Europeans**. Cook's first exploratory visits left a legacy of wild pigs, sheep and potatoes, while in the early 1800s whalers and sealers bloodied the coastal waters, while logging campaigns cleared vast tracts of native bush for sheep and grazing cattle. Pioneers continued to tamper with the delicately balanced ecosystem in an attempt to create a "New England". **Acclimatization societies** sprung up in the late 1800s to introduce familiar animals and plants from settlers' European homelands – New Zealand would never have become the successful pastoral nation it is without the grasses, pollinating birds, bees and butterflies, sheep and cattle. But many releases were disastrous, either out-competing native plants and birds or killing them.

The lowlands

Archetypal paddocks full of **sheep**, often backed by shelter belts of macrocarpa trees, are within sight of the airports. Sheep number about 28 million, less than half the population of thirty years ago, with much of their grazing land turned over to other uses, particularly dairying. Elsewhere, land has been redeveloped for horticulture or **vineyards**, with vintners sometimes co-producing **olives**. Optimistic souls plant oak and hazel trees in the hope of creating a truffle industry.

Throughout both farmed and forested New Zealand you'll see native **cabbage trees** (*ti kouka*) with stout grey trunks (up to 10m high) topped by spear-shaped leaves and clusters of white flowers. Captain Cook and his men ate the leaf shoots, finding them vaguely cabbage-like.

Lowland forests

Much of the thick forest that greeted Māoriand early settlers was burned, logged, or cleared for farming, but pockets of **native bush** survive. The forests of Northland, the Coromandel Peninsula, the west coasts of both islands and on Stewart Island contain a wonderful variety of native trees. There are also hundreds of endemic native flowering plant species in lowland areas, whose blooms are almost all white or yellow. With no pollinating bees to attract there was little need for vibrant petals.

The **kauri** is the king of the forest, rising to 30m, two-thirds of it comprising straight, branchless trunk. It lives for over two thousand years and has long been revered by Māori canoe-builders, who enacted solemn ceremonies before cutting them down. European shipbuilders used them for masts and many more were turned into house weatherboards and floorboards. The tree was also the source of kauri gum, dug up and exported in the early twentieth century. In recent decades the kauri has been struck by **kauri dieback**, with whole forests succumbing to the fungus-like pathogen *Phytophthora taxon Agathis* (PTA). As scientists try to work out how to control it, authorities attempt to control its spread to unaffected pockets, particularly the Coromandel Peninsula. In early 2018, the entire Waitakere Ranges along Auckland's north western fringes was declared off limits to walkers.

Open spaces along forest edges and riverbanks are often alive with tui (see page 721) sucking nectar from golden clusters of **kowhai**, the national flower, which hang from trees whose wood was once fashioned into Māori canoe paddles and adze handles.

The North Island and the top third of the South are home to New Zealand's only native palm, the **nikau**. Its slender branchless stem bears shiny leaves, up to 30cm, long, pink spiky flowers and red berries, used by European settlers as pellets in the absence of ammunition.

Irregularly branched, growing to 20m, the **pohutukawa** is found as far south as Otago, in forests around the coast and at lake edges. Typically it bears festive, bright crimson blossoms around Christmas. Another red-blooming tree is the gnarled **rata**, found mostly in South Island forests but occasionally popping up around the North Island.

New Zealand is also known for its unusual family of pine species, or **podocarps**. One such is the majestic **rimu** (red pine), which grows to 60m, with small green flowers, red cones and tiny green or black fruit. It was heavily milled for its timber (the charcoal was mixed with oil and rubbed into Māori tattoo incisions) but is still widespread throughout mixed forests.

CONSERVATION AND WILDLIFE ORGANIZATIONS AND WEBSITES

Department of Conservation ⓦ doc.govt.nz. Government department charged with conserving New Zealand's natural and historic heritage.

Forest and Bird Protection Society ⓦ forestandbird.org.nz. New Zealand's leading independent conservation organization.

NZ Birds ⓦ nzbirds.com. Comprehensive site on everything feathery.

Kiwis for Kiwis ⓦ kiwisforkiwi.org. Independent charity campaigning to save the national bird from extinction.

THE SCOURGE OF THE BUSH: MAMMALIAN PESTS

Since human habitation began, 53 indigenous bird species have become extinct and New Zealand is now home to about eleven percent of the world's most endangered species. Settlement and the introduction of non-native plants and animals are responsible for devastating this country's unique ecosystem.

POSSUMS

Visitors to New Zealand soon become familiar with the nocturnal **possum** (officially brushtail opossum or *Trichosurus vulpecula*), if only as roadkill. Live specimens usually show up when you are tramping, their eyes reflecting your torchlight around huts at night. Although they look cute they are pests, causing enormous damage to flora and fauna, stunting trees by munching new shoots, eating native birds' eggs and killing chicks. Consequently, New Zealanders have an almost pathological hatred of this introduced Australian marsupial, and greenies who would never dream of wearing any other fur happily don possum garments.

Before the start of controlled European migration in 1840, enterprising individuals were liberating these cat-sized Australian natives in New Zealand, with the aim of establishing a fur industry. Releases stopped around 1930 but control measures were not introduced until 1951, when a bounty was paid on all possums with their skins intact. Until the late 1980s possums were killed for their fur, but successful anti-fur lobbying saw prices plummet. Hunting tailed off and possum numbers skyrocketed. There are now in excess of **forty million** possums, which currently eat their way through some 10,000 tonnes of vegetation every night, and are known carriers of bovine TB – endangering the dairy, beef and deer industries.

Possums are so widespread that hunting barely has any effect and the government is forced to spend around $80 million a year on possum control. The most cost-effective is aerial drops of **1080 poison**, a controversial substance banned in almost every other country in the world. Farmers claim it kills their stock while other opponents say it decimates the native birds it is designed to protect. Certainly native birds do die, but the decimation of the possum population allows such an increase in avian breeding success that bird numbers soon exceed their pre-poisoning levels. The issue remains contentious and will most likely be phased out as pressure mounts.

WILD PIGS, DEER, TAHR AND CHAMOIS

Captain James Cook is credited with releasing the first pigs into New Zealand for the wild variety, but the claim may go to French Explorer Jean-Francois-Mariede Surville, who gifted a sow and a boar to Māori in Doubtless Bay in 1769. These feral pigs (known as "Captain Cookers") are still rooting up the ground, although pig hunting keeps numbers down.

The forest understorey is hammered by the seven **deer** species introduced for sport from 1851 to the 1930s, and even today there are illegal releases of deer by hunters. Authorities are reluctant to advocate complete removal because of the political strength of the hunting lobby. In the first half of the twentieth century, the government also introduced the Himalayan **tahr**, a goat-like animal, and European **chamois**, both of which inhabit the high country of the South Island.

RABBITS AND MUSTELIDS

Rabbits were introduced to New Zealand from the 1840s, and though they don't pose a particular threat to native wildlife, the means used to try and stem the population certainly does. From the 1880s **ferrets**, weasels and stoats were introduced, but instead of targeting rabbits, these members of the mustelid family found the flightless birdlife (particularly their young and eggs in nests) easier prey.

DOGS, CATS, RATS AND MICE

Uncontrolled **dogs** can't resist playing with any flightless birds they might come across, and studies suggest they are responsible for 76 percent of adult brown kiwi deaths alone. There are an estimated 1.2 million **cats** in New Zealand, a quarter of them feral, and they kill numerous birds and lizards.

The *kiore* or Polynesian **rat** has been largely displaced by more aggressive Norway and ship rats, living everywhere from the treetops to the leaf litter, who ravage small bird and insect populations as well as devouring plant seeds and suppressing growth in the bush. **Mice** play a similarly devastating role.

Other podocarps include **matai** (black pine), **miro** (brown pine), **kahikatea** (white pine), and **totara**, which grow for up to a thousand years. The trunks were used by Māori to make war canoes while strips of the thick brown bark were woven into baskets.

Below the canopy of these trees you'll find an enormous variety of **tree ferns**, many hard to tell apart. The most famous, adopted as the national emblem, is the **ponga** (silver fern). Reaching about 10m in height, its long fronds are dull green on top and silvery white underneath.

The lowland forest is prime habitat for the bulk of New Zealand's endangered birds.

Rivers, lakes and wetlands

High mountains and plentiful rain mean that New Zealand is not short of rivers. Canterbury and the Waitaki sport distinctive **braided rivers**, their wide shingle beds and multiple channels providing a breeding ground for many birds, insects, fish and plants. Numerous lakes provide rich habitats; many of New Zealand's **wetlands**, on the other hand, have been drained for agriculture and property development, although some are preserved as national parks and scenic reserves. It's in low wetland areas that you're likely to come across the tallest of the native trees, the kahikatea (white pine), which reaches over 60m.

One bird you're bound to see in the vicinity of a lake is the **pukeko** (swamp hen), a bird still in the process of losing the power of flight. Also found in parts of Australia, the pukeko is mostly dark and mid-blue with large feet and an orange beak, and lets out a high-pitched screech if disturbed.

New Zealand is renowned for its freshwater fishing, with massive brown and rainbow **trout** and **salmon** swarming through the fast-flowing streams. All introduced species, these fish have adapted so well to their conditions that they grow much larger here than other places in the world; as a result, many native species have been driven out. Another delicacy found in New Zealand's waters is native **eels**, which, despite spending most of their lives in New Zealand rivers, migrate over 2000km to breed in the waters off Tonga.

Keeping anglers company along the riverbanks of the Mackenzie Country and Canterbury are the perilously rare **black stilts** (see page 720). The **common pied stilt**, a black-and-white bird, has been more successful in resisting introduced predators.

Another inhabitant of the Canterbury braided riverbank is the **wrybill**. This small white-and-grey bird uses its unique bent bill to turn over stones or pull out crustaceans from mud. The wrybill's close cousin, the **banded dotterel**, favours riverbanks, lakes, open land with sparse vegetation and coastal lagoons and beaches. A small, brown-and-white bird with a dark or black band around its neck, it breeds only in New Zealand, though it does migrate to Australia. Around fast-flowing streams you might see the increasingly rare **blue duck** (see page 720).

The highlands

With most of the lowland forests cleared for farming, you need to get into the hills to appreciate the picture that greeted Māoriand early European immigrants. The best bets are the Tongariro, Whanganui, Taranaki, Nelson Lakes, Arthur's Pass, Kahurangi and Aoraki/Mount Cook national parks – all cloaked in highland forests, particularly native beech trees, which, unlike northern hemisphere varieties, are evergreen. The 20m-high **mountain beech** (*tawhairauriki*) grows close to the top of the tree line and has sharp dark leaves and little red flowers. Also at high altitudes, often in mixed stands, are **silver beech** (*tawhai*), whose grey trunks grow up to 30m. Slightly lower altitudes are favoured by black and red beech. Often mixed in with them, the thin, straggly **manuka** (tea tree) grows in both alpine regions and on seashores.

New Zealand has five hundred species of flowering alpine plants that grow nowhere else in the world. Most famous is the large white-flowered yellow-centred **Mount Cook lily**, the world's largest buttercup. It flowers from November to January. On the high ground of the

THE KIWI

Flightless, dull brown in colour and distinctly odd looking, the kiwi is New Zealand's much-loved national symbol. Stout, muscular, shy and nocturnal, it is a member of the ratite family – which includes the ostrich, emu, rhea, cassowary and the long-extinct moa – and is one of the few birds in the world with a well-developed sense of **smell**. At night you might hear them snuffling around, using the nostrils at the end of their bill to detect earthworms, beetles, cicada larvae, spiders and koura (freshwater crayfish), berries and the occasional frog. Armed with sensitive bristles at the base of its bill and a highly developed sense of hearing, the kiwi can detect other birds and animals on its territory and will readily attack them with its claws. The females are bigger than the males and lay huge eggs, weighing a fifth of their body weight. After eighty days, the eggs hatch and the chicks live off the rich yolk; neither parent feeds them and they emerge from the nest totally independent. They sleep for up to twenty hours a day, which explains why they normally live to the age of 20 or 25.

Sadly there are probably fewer than 70,000 birds left and numbers in the wild are dropping. Kiwi are most easily seen in **kiwi houses** around the country in places such as Auckland Zoo, Otorohanga, Napier, Wellington and Hokitika. The best opportunities for seeing **kiwi in the wild** are:

Trounson Forest Northland. See page 183.
Tiritiri Matangi Auckland. See page 131.
Kapiti Island near Wellington. See page 387.
Okarito near Franz Josef. See page 484.
Mason Bay Stewart Island. See page 678.

KIWI SPECIES

Kiwi have traditionally been divided into three species – brown, little spotted and great spotted – but genetic research in recent decades subdivided new species off from the brown kiwi.

Great spotted kiwi Going by the Māori name *roa*, this is the largest kiwi species, with adult males averaging 2.4kg and females 3.3kg. They are the most rugged kiwi, and are happiest in subalpine regions with wet, mossy vegetation. Smaller birds range down into lowland and coastal beech forests. European explorers told stories of kiwi the size of turkeys with powerful spurs on their legs, whose call was the loudest. Their harsh home has also helped keep them relatively safe from mammalian pests. Living mostly in the northern half of the South Island, the population of around 15,000 is in slow decline.

Little spotted kiwi Also known as Kiwi Pukupuku, this is the smallest of the kiwi, with adults weighing 1100–1300g. The main population (around 1200 birds) is on Kapiti Island. Mellow and docile by nature, pairs often share daytime shelter, going their separate ways to feed, grunting to one another as they pass. They rarely probe for food, instead finding prey on the ground or in the forest litter. The best time to hear them is just after dark from high points around an island. Listen carefully for the male's shrill whistle and the female's gentle purr.

Brown kiwi These medium-sized kiwi are the most widespread, particularly in the central and northern North Island, where there are around 25,000 birds. They are famous for their bad temper and for being tough fighters of intruders on their territory. They live in a wide range of vegetation, including exotic forests and rough farmland.

Rowi (aka Okarito brown). Originally considered a subspecies of the brown kiwi, this is the rarest kiwi, with only around 375 surviving in the wild, all in the 11,000-hectare south Okarito Kiwi Sanctuary in South Westland. They're greyish in colour, often with patches of white feathers on their face. Males and females share incubation – unlike most kiwi, where the male does the lion's share.

Tokoeka The most numerous kiwi species with an estimated 30,000 birds. The rarest form is the small Haast tokoeka (around 400 left), which are most common around Haast's bushline and in subalpine grasslands, even digging their burrows in snow. The Northern Fiordland, Southern Fiordland and Stewart Island tokoeka are all larger and in steady decline. They are one of the most primitive and the most communal kiwi, sometimes seen poking about along the tideline within a few metres of one another.

South Island is the **vegetable sheep**, a white, hairy plant that grows cushion-like along the ground and, at a great distance, could just about be mistaken for a grazing animal.

NEW ZEALAND'S RARE AND ENDANGERED WILDLIFE

New Zealand has 69 birds and many more plants on the IUCN Red List of Globally Threatened Species (ⓦredlist.org). Among developed countries, only the United States has more. Of the birds, some 37 percent of New Zealand species (the world's highest percentage) are regarded as globally threatened, including most of the following.

BIRDS

Bellbird (*korimako*) Relatively common in forest and shrub, the shy, pale green bellbird is noted for its distinctive musical call.

Black stilt (*kaki*) This thin black bird with round eyes and long red legs is incredibly shy – if you do see one in the wild, keep well away. It is one of the world's rarest wading birds. Usually found in swamps and beside riverbeds, the best place to see them is in the specially created reserve near Twizel (see page 548).

Blue duck (*whio*) Uniquely among ducks, the *whio* (sometimes known as the torrent duck) spends most of its time in mountain streams, where it dives for food. One of four endemic species with no close relatives anywhere in the world, you can spot it by its blue-grey plumage, with chestnut on both breast and flanks. It also has an unusual bill with a black flexible membrane along each side, and yellow eyes (as seen on the $10 note). Its Māori name represents the male bird's call.

Fantail (*piwakawaka*) Relatively common forest dweller, seen constantly opening and closing the tail that gives it its name. It often flies alongside walkers on trails, not out of a desire for company but to feed on the insects disturbed.

Kaka Large parrot closely related to the kea, though it does not venture from its favoured lowland forest environments. You can recognize the bird by its colour: bronze with a crimson belly and underside of the tail and wings.

Kakapo The world's only flightless parrot, kakapo were once so widespread they were kept as pets. Now there are around 125 birds left, all on a couple of predator-free islands off the coast of Fiordland (off-limits to tourists).

Kakariki Bright green parakeets that come in yellow-crowned, red-crowned and orange-crowned varieties. Found at most wildlife sanctuaries and on offshore islands.

Kea The world's only alpine parrot.

Kereru (a.k.a. *kukupa*) With adults weighing in at around 650g, this is the world's second-largest pigeon. Its metallic green, purple and bronze colouring and pure white breast is often seen flashing through low-lying forests with its distinctive noisy wing-slaps. It is a very ancient New Zealand species, which seems to have no relatives elsewhere.

Kiwi See box, p.719.

Kokako Rare slate-grey bird with distinctive blue wattles (patches of skin) on each cheek. An abysmal flyer, it lives mainly in protected forests and mainland islands where trapping keeps predator numbers low. Closely related to the saddleback (see opposite) and featured on the $50 note.

Among alpine caves and rock crevices you might come across the black **alpine weta** (also known as the "Mount Cook flea"). Fewer species of bird inhabit the high country, but those that do are fascinating. In the Southern Alps you'll hear and see the raucous **kea** and perhaps the **New Zealand falcon** (for both see page 721). Subalpine areas host smaller birds like the yellow-and-green **rock wren** and the **rifleman**, a tiny green and blue bird with spiralling flight. Such areas are also the natural home of two of the country's rarest birds, the **takahe** and the **kakapo** (see page 720), neither seen outside tightly controlled areas.

The coast, islands and sea

New Zealand's indented coastline, battered by the Tasman Sea and the Pacific Ocean, is a meeting place for warm and cold currents, which makes for an environment suited to an enormous variety of fish. The warm currents, populated by hoki, kahawai, snapper, orange roughy and trevally, attract tropical fish like barracuda, marlin, sharks and tuna. The cold

Morepork (*ruru*) New Zealand's only native owl, this small brown bird is usually heard in the bush at night, and occasionally in town and city gardens. Both Māori and Pakeha names are supposed to represent its call.

New Zealand falcon (*karearea*) Seen occasionally in the north of the North Island but more often in the high country of the Southern Alps, Fiordland and the forests of Westland. New Zealand's only native raptor has a heavily flecked breast, chestnut thighs and a pointed head (as seen on the $20 note). Conservationists and winegrowers have reintroduced it to the Marlborough Plains where it may deter smaller, nuisance birds.

Robin There are three species of native robin, all glimpsed as they flit around the forest, often fearlessly pecking the dirt around your feet. They range from black with a cream or yellow breast to all black. Their prolonged and distinctive song lasts for up to thirty minutes, with only brief pauses for breath.

Saddleback (*tieke*) This rare but pretty thrush-sized bird is mostly black except for a tan-coloured saddle. Freely seen on Ulva Island, a wildlife reserve in Patterson Inlet, Stewart Island.

Stitchbird (*hihi*) Small with a slightly curved beak and distinctive yellow and white patches on its sides. There are thought to be a few left, some on Kapiti Island and Tiritiri Matangi, where you can see them using the feeding stations.

Takahe Rare turkey-sized bird once thought extinct.

Tui With its white throat and mostly green and purple velvet-like body, the tui is renowned for mimicking the calls of other birds and for its copious consumption of nectar and fruit. Its song has greater range than the bellbird and contains rather unmusical squeaks, croaks and strangled utterances.

Weka About the most common flightless native, the weka is a little like a kiwi but slimmer, far less shy, and generally dark brown with marked golden flecks, especially on its heavily streaked breast. Like the kiwi, the weka grubs around at dusk but can be seen regularly during the day: many are bold enough to approach trampers and take titbits from their hands. The bird's whistle is a loud and distinctive "kooo-li". There are four subspecies found in a variety of habitats throughout the country, including the Chatham Islands where they are still allowed to be eaten.

OTHER SPECIES

Tuatara This nocturnal lizard-like creature is a throwback to the age of dinosaurs and remains little changed over 260 million years. The tuatara lives on insects, small mammals and birds' eggs, a diet that sees them grow to 60cm in length and keeps them alive for well over a hundred years. Virtually all tuatara left live on offshore islands, so are best viewed in a zoo or kiwi house.

Weta A relatively common grasshopper-like insect that has lived in lowland forests for 190 million years. Several species live in the bush but they're hard to spot so you're most likely to see them in caves or zoos. The most impressive species is the giant weta (*wetapunga*), which ranks as the heaviest insect in the world, weighing up to 71g, and is said to have been the inspiration for Ridley Scott's *Alien*.

Antarctic currents bring blue and red cod, blue and red moki, and fish that can tolerate a considerable range of temperatures, such as the tarakihi, grouper and bass.

Marine mammals also grace these waters: the rare **humpback whale** is an occasional visitor to Kaikoura and Cook Strait, while **sperm whales** are common year-round in the deep sea trench near Kaikoura. **Orca** are seen regularly wherever there are dolphins, seals and other whales. Another frequent visitor is the **pilot whale**: up to two hundred pass by Farewell Spit each year; they're also seen in Cook Strait and the Bay of Plenty.

Common dolphins congregate all year round in the Bay of Plenty, Bay of Islands and around the Coromandel Peninsula. Of the three other species seen in New Zealand, **bottlenose dolphins** hang around Kaikoura and Whakatane most of the year, while **dusky dolphins**, the most playful, can be spotted near the shore of the Marlborough Sounds, Fiordland and Kaikoura from October to May. At any time of year you might get small schools of tiny **Hector's dolphins** accompanying your boat around Banks Peninsula, the Catlins and Invercargill.

Until recently there were few opportunities to see the Hooker's (or "New Zealand") **sea lion** except on remote Antarctic islands, but these rare animals, with their round noses and deep, wet eyes, now appear around the Catlins and Otago Peninsula. The larger New Zealand **fur seal** is in much greater abundance around the coast. You're most likely to come across them in the Sugar Loaf Marine Reserve off New Plymouth, around the Northland coast, in the Bay of Plenty, near Kaikoura, around the Otago Peninsula and in the Abel Tasman National Park. Both seals and sea lions can become aggressive during the breeding season (Dec–Feb), so remember to keep your distance (at least 30m). **Elephant seals** still breed in the Catlins; more extensive colonies exist on the offshore islands.

New Zealand has the world's greatest diversity of seabirds, with over 140 species drawn by the coast's fish-rich waters. Sadly, it also has the highest number of threatened breeding species, perhaps the most famous being the graceful royal albatross. A far more common sight is **little blue penguins**, which you'll see on any boat journey. The large **yellow-eyed penguin** is confined to parts of the east coast of the South Island, from Christchurch to the Catlins, while the **Fiordland crested penguin**, with its thick yellow eyebrows, is rarely seen outside Fiordland and Stewart Island. Other common seabirds include **gannets**, their yellow heads and white bodies unmistakeable as they dive into shoals of fish; and **cormorants** and **shags** (mostly grey or black), usually congregating on cliffs and rocky shores. On and around islands you're also likely to see the **sooty shearwater**, **titi** (also known as "muttonbirds"), while the **black oystercatchers** and the black-and-white **variable oystercatchers**, both with orange cigar beaks and stooping gait, can be spotted searching in pairs for food on the foreshore.

Green issues

New Zealand comes with an enviable reputation for being **clean and green**, but this is more by accident than design. With a population of 4.7 million and a relatively

---

SANCTUARIES, PARKS AND RESERVES

NORTH ISLAND

Bushy Park Wanganui. See page 310.
Goat Island Marine Reserve Northland. See page 139.
Kapiti Island near Wellington. See page 387.
Parry Kauri Park Northland. See page 137.
Poor Knights Islands Marine Reserve Northland. See page 149.
Pukaha Mount Bruce National Wildlife Centre Wairarapa. See page 395.
Rangitoto and Motutapu islands Auckland. See page 116.
Tiritiri Matangi Auckland. See page 131.
Waipoua and Trounson kauri forests Northland. See page 182.
Zealandia: The Karori Sanctuary Experience Wellington. See page 372

SOUTH ISLAND

Abel Tasman National Park See page 430.
Aoraki/Mount Cook National Park See page 551.
Fiordland National Park See page 642.
Kura Tawhiti Castle Hill Reserve. See page 536.
Mason Bay Stewart Island. See page 678.
Motuara Island Marlborough Sounds. See page 406.
Oamaru Blue Penguin Colony See page 569.
Orokonui Ecosanctuary near Dunedin. See page 585.
Ulva Island off Stewart Island. See page 677.

short recorded history, you might expect human impact to be limited, but in less than a thousand years (mostly the last 150) humans have converted three-quarters of the land to farming and commercial forestry. Just ten percent of native forest remains, while generous winds and flushing rainfall conveniently dispose of much of the country's **pollution**.

Land usage
European settlers and, later, returning World War I veterans spent years taming steep bush-covered hills only suitable for raising sheep. These **farms** were profitable when wool and lamb prices were high, but in recent years have become uneconomic; thus some areas are just left to revert to their natural state, through the **tenure review** process, opening them up to the public as parks and reserves. Far more often, marginal lands are planted with introduced **pines** and logged every 25 years, reducing them to unsightly hillsides of stumps. Meanwhile, the ever-growing need for housing, roads and associated infrastructure gobbles up productive farmland and threatens fragile wetland.

Pollution
In large parts of New Zealand you can inhale lungfuls of fresh air and gaze at crystal-clear lakes and rivers, but all is not idyllic. Due to poor public transport New Zealand's **car ownership** rates are some of the highest in the world. New Zealand also imports huge numbers of secondhand cars from Japan that would not be allowed off the boat in other countries, and there is no requirement for regular vehicle emission testing.

Mountain streams and alpine tarns look so clean and fresh you'll be tempted to drink straight from them. In most cases this is fine, but along well-trod routes the water might also harbour **giardia**, an intestinal parasite that can easily ruin your holiday. It is best to treat all drinking water, except in the most pristine headwaters. Freshwater rivers have recently become prey to the **didymo** algae (*Didymoshenia geminata*); boaties, anglers and kayakers should thoroughly clean all their gear before moving to another river to prevent it spreading. Additionally, modern intensive **farming** techniques, particularly the use of fertilizers, have polluted many lowland rivers, lakes and streams. On the bright side, **industrial pollution** is a relatively minor issue, but only because there is little manufacturing.

The search for power
With a population growing ever more power-hungry and a lack of major investment over the last thirty years, New Zealand's power supplies are inadequate, especially when hydro-generating lake levels get low in winter. Green **hydro** and **geothermal power** account for only two-thirds of electricity supply, compared to eighty percent in the late twentieth century, and even these clean generation methods are contentious: hydro reservoirs have destroyed natural habitats, especially riverbanks where threatened birds live. More geothermal stations are planned but over-extraction detrimentally affects geysers and boiling mud pools.

Building coal power stations (and converting to oil and gas stations) could make New Zealand electricity self-sufficient for over a hundred years, but at a considerable cost to the environment. Clean emission technologies are generally deemed the way forward. **Wind energy** meets resistance from those complaining of noise and visual pollution, and installed capacity is very low. For decades no one dared suggest New Zealand should invest in **nuclear power**, and even the power pinch and the need to follow Kyoto commitments has done little to make New Zealanders rethink the issue. Ongoing leakage of radiative water into the Pacific from the Fukushima nuclear disaster certainly helped re-galvanize attitudes.

The good news is that, despite government vacillation and the paramount interests of big business, an ever-increasing number of New Zealanders are working to preserve the country's unique environment.

Film and music

New Zealand has two film industries. The landscape provided the backdrop for internationally financed blockbusters, primarily Peter Jackson's *The Lord of the Rings* trilogy in the early 2000s and his three Hobbit films a decade later. Miniatures powerhouse Weta Workshop and postproduction unit, Park Road Post Production, have become familiar names and lent their skills to the likes of *The Chronicles of Narnia*, and the Avatar movies by James Cameron, who partly lives locally on his Wairarapa farm. Tax breaks and tweaked labour-rules have so far kept the work coming New Zealand's way.

Like most small countries, New Zealand lacks the resources and infrastructure to sustain a large-scale film industry but still manages to produce some fine movies. Between 1988 and 1994 alone, *The Navigator*, *An Angel at My Table*, *The Piano*, *Once Were Warriors* and *Heavenly Creatures* all rightly gained international recognition. Success has been patchy since but there's always hope for another "golden age of Kiwi cinema". Some touted 2014 as a new beginning with *The Dark Horse*, *What We Do in the Shadows*, *The Dead Lands*, *Housebound* and *The Pa Boys* all earning critical acclaim and seeing success at the box office. Since then, new films like Hunt for the Wilderpeople and Pecking Order have shown the versatility of local directors and broken all domestic box office records.

★ **An Angel at My Table** *Jane Campion, 1990.* Winner of the Special Jury prize at the Venice Film Festival. One of the most inspiring films New Zealand has produced, based on the brilliant autobiographies of Janet Frame (see page 728).

Bad Blood *Mike Newell, 1981.* A New Zealand/British collaboration set in New Zealand in World War II that relates the true story of Stan Graham, a Hokitika man who breaks the law by refusing to hand in his rifle. The ensuing events give rise to a discussion of the Kiwi spirit.

★ **Bad Taste** *Peter Jackson, 1988.* Winner of the Special Jury prize at the Paris Film Festival. Aliens visit earth to pick up flesh for an intergalactic fast-food chain and have a wild old time.

Black Sheep *Jonathan King, 2006.* Festival favourite telling the story of sheep-phobic Harry, who returns to the family farm where he discovers his brother has been playing with the sheep, genetically, and has inadvertently created man-eating weresheep.

★ **Boy** *Taika Waititi, 2010.* New Zealand's highest grossing movie is a coming-of-age drama set on the East Cape. Set in 1984, it finishes with the cast doing a brilliant Thriller-style *haka* to "Poi E", a huge hit that year.

★ **Came a Hot Friday** *Ian Mune, 1984.* The best comedy to come out of New Zealand, based on the novel by Ronald Hugh Morrieson (see page 729), concentrating on two incompetent confidence tricksters whose luck runs out in a sleepy country town.

Crush *Alison Maclean, 1992.* Offbeat, angst-ridden psychological drama set around Rotorua, where the boiling mud and gushing geysers underline the tensions and sexual chaos that arise when an American femme fatale enters the lives of a New Zealand family.

★ **The Dark Horse** *James Robertson, 2014.* Cliff Curtis is masterful as Genesis Potini in the true story of this Māori chess genius who struggles with bipolar disorder and a dysfunctional family. Deeply affecting and beautifully developed.

The Dead Lands *Toa Fraser, 2014.* Ultra-violence Māori-style. Set in pre-Pakeha Aotearoa, this bloody tale of honour and *utu* could be a standard coming-of-age movie if the director didn't seize every chance to showcase the traditional martial art of *mau rakau*.

Desperate Remedies *Peter Wells and Stewart Main, 1993.* This visually stimulating movie comments wryly on the melodramatic intrigues and desires of a group of Victorians on the edge of Britain's empire.

Eagle Versus Shark *Taika Waititi, 2007.* A low-key, well-realized love story starring Jemaine "Flight of the Conchords" Clement, with similar quirky humour.

Fifty Ways of Saying Fabulous *Stewart Main, 2005.* Clever adaptation of the book of the same name (see page 728) that grabs the spirit of the original and wrings out lots of laughs as well as poignancy.

★ **Forgotten Silver** *Peter Jackson, 2000.* Jackson, at his tongue-in-cheek best, constructs a fake documentary about a Kiwi movie pioneer, who invents film, sound, colour and the biblical epic, from flax, in the bush on the West Coast.

Goodbye Pork Pie *Geoff Murphy, 1980.* New Zealand's favourite comedy/road movie following the adventures of two young men in a yellow mini, the cops they infuriate, and the mixed bag of characters they encounter.

★ **Heavenly Creatures** *Peter Jackson, 1994.* Oscar-nominated account of the horrific Parker/Hulme matricide in the 1950s following the increasingly self-obsessed life of two adolescent girls. An evocative and explosive film that brings all Jackson's subversive humour to bear on the strait-laced real world and the girls' fantastic imaginary one. Kate Winslet's film debut.

The Hobbit *Peter Jackson, 2012–14*. Big budget, battle-heavy fantasy trilogy turning a four-hour epic of Bilbo's journey There and Back Again into eight hours of movie. Shot on location around the country, with miniatures and postproduction in Wellington.

Housebound *Gerard Johnstone, 2014*. Kiwis do horror. With characteristic pragmatism and dry humour this film undermines every scary movie convention and ends up celebrating diversity. Nothing is what it seems. Great fun.

Hunt for the Wilderpeople *Taika Waititi, 2016*. Comedy whose screenplay was based on the book *Wild Pork and Watercress* by Barry Crump. Sam Neill and Julian Dennison play "Uncle" Hector and Ricky Baker, a father figure and son who become the targets of a manhunt after fleeing into the New Zealand bush.

In My Father's Den *Brad McGann, 2004*. Depicts an emotional rough ride for an exhausted war journalist (Matthew Macfadyen) who returns home and becomes involved in an unexpected and engrossing journey of discovery that descends into murder mystery. From a novel by Maurice Gee (see page 728).

Insatiable Moon *Rosemary Riddell, 2010*. This low-budget Moondance winner was shot mainly round Ponsonby. It addresses issues of social evolution and progress, from the point of view of Arthur, street person and self-proclaimed Son of God. The community tries to close the care-in-the-community home in which Arthur lives and he becomes the catalyst of miraculous and magical events.

Kaikohe Demolition *Florian Habicht, 2004*. Even if demolition derbies are the furthest thing from your bucket list, check out this warm, low-budget doco of life in a small Northland town. A grower.

CONTEMPORARY KIWI MUSIC

Many people would have been hard pressed to name a single Kiwi contemporary band or artist until the meteoric rise of **Lorde**. Apparently from nowhere (well, Devonport actually) this wise-beyond-her-years 16-year-old arrived almost fully formed in mid-2013 with the release of "Royals", a #1 hit worldwide. With the release of her *Pure Heroine* album and the use of "Yellow Flicker Beat" as the lead song of movie *The Hunger Games: Mockingjay – Part 1*, Lorde's reputation grew. Bruce Springsteen even opened one of his 2014 Auckland concerts with a cover of "Royals".

Lorde may never be royal but the country doesn't lack rock royalty. Foremost among them is singer-songwriter **Dave Dobbyn** whose tunes provide the "soundtrack of the nation" both from his bands Th'Dudes and DD Smash and from his enduring solo career. Some consider the catchy Slice of Heaven (recorded with Herbs) an unofficial national anthem, while Loyal rings out whenever some national sporting team appear. Several of his songs appear on *The Great New Zealand Songbook* (Sony; 2009), a double CD – "Last Century" and "This Century" – that showcases a diverse cross section of Kiwi artists. Other high fliers on the all-time Kiwi playlist are **Tim Finn**, who founded seminal 1970s ban Split Enz, later joined by his brother **Neil Finn** who went on to helm Crowded House. Both have successful solo careers and are sometimes joined on stage by Neil's son, **Liam Finn**, one of New Zealand's most talented singer-songwriters and multi-instrumentalists.

There's always been plenty of indie rock with the jangly pop of **The Chills** threatening to break internationally in the mid-1980s. Subsequently bands like The Datsuns and the Mint Chicks have kept the flame burning.

The new millennium saw an explosion of Kiwi roots, reggae, dub and electronica with Pacifica influences, which continues to be fundamental to minorities as a mode of expression, with artists such as Katchafire, Trinity Roots, **Salmonella Dub**, the Black Seeds and **Fat Freddy's Drop** among the most successful. Salmonella Dub's **Tiki Taane** subsequently went solo, creating Always on My Mind, one of New Zealand's most successful songs ever. He also incorporates elements of Māori chants and instruments perhaps best heard on Tangaroa off his second album, *Past, Present, Future*.

Country and folk music have generally been quite fringe, though for the last thirty-odd years **The Topp Twins**, New Zealand's favourite yodelling lesbian sisters, have managed to cut through the prejudice with leftie politics and plenty of humour. The genre has gained wider acceptance with the rise of the Christchurch and Lyttelton scene which revolves around folkie songsmiths **The Eastern**, Delaney Davidson and Lindon Puffin.

Catching a gig is one of the best ways to tap into the country's music scene – ⓦ amplifier.co.nz lists upcoming shows, has downloads and sells CDs.

Lord of the Rings *Peter Jackson, 2001–03*. New Zealand hit the Hollywood big-time with Jackson's epic ten-hour Tolkien trilogy. The Kiwi scenery shone through the ground-breaking special effects and was as much a star as the actors.

★ **The Navigator** *Vincent Ward, 1988*. An atmospheric and stylistically inventive movie employing all Ward's favourite themes and characters, including the innocent visionary, in this case a boy who leads five men through time from a fourteenth-century Cumbrian village to New Zealand in the twentieth century in a quest to save their homes.

Once Were Warriors *Lee Tamahori, 1994*. A surging fly-on-the-wall-style comment on the economically challenged Māorisituation in modern south Auckland, bringing to mind the British kitchen-sink dramas of the 1950s and 1960s. More a study of class than a full-blown racial statement, it revels in human weakness and strength of spirit against a background of urban decay. Based on a novel by Alan Duff (see page 728).

Operation 8 *Errol Wright and Abi King-Jones, 2011*. Doco based on the real events of October 2007, when government agencies used the 2002 Terrorism Suppression Act as justification for arresting a number of Māoriactivists and its repercussions on wider society.

The Orator *Tusi Tamaese, 2011*. New Zealand-financed Samoan-language film, selected for the Sundance Film Festival and winner of the Venice Horizons Award, dealing with the unconventional life of a farmer and his efforts to protect his plantation and family.

Out of the Blue *Robert Sarkies, 2006*. Based on the true events of the Aramouna Massacre, in which thirteen people lost their lives to a local unemployed gun collector. A dark tale, concentrating on the heroism of the out-gunned seaside-town police and inhabitants.

The Pa Boys *Hinemoa Grace, 2014*. Almost the entire population of Tolaga Bay turns out for this tale of how a Māori reggae band's road trip turns, almost successfully, into a demonstration of how ancestral actions still affect the land and families today.

Patu *Merata Mita, 1983*. A powerful documentary recording the year of opposition to the 1981 Springbok rugby tour of New Zealand, which goes some way to showing the extraordinary passions ignited.

Pecking Order *Slavko Martinov, 2017*. This feel-good, feather-ruffling "flockumentary" follows a group of witty and distinctive poultry obsessives trying to take out the nationals as their 148-year old poultry club crumbles around them.

★ **The Piano** *Jane Campion, 1993*. With Holly Hunter, Harvey Keitel, Sam Neill and Anna Paquin. This moody winner of the Cannes Palme d'Or (and three Oscars) made Campion bankable in Hollywood. Its mixture of grand scenes and personal trauma knowingly synthesizes paperback romance, erotica and Victorian melodrama – and includes Keitel's stab at the worst Scottish accent of all time.

River Queen *Vincent Ward, 2005*. Production problems on the Whanganui River saw Ward depart before the project was finished, but what's left is a beautifully shot, over-simplified and uneven film worth a look just for the locations.

★ **Scarfies** *Robert Sarkies, 2000*. A darkly funny story about students taking over a deserted house in Dunedin only to discover a massive dope crop in the basement. Things get progressively more unpleasant when the dope grower returns.

Sione's Wedding *Chris Graham, 2006*. Lovely feel-good comedy about four immature Samoan-Kiwi thirty-somethings required to find girlfriends to attend their mate's wedding.

Sleeping Dogs *Roger Donaldson, 1977*. Perhaps the birth of the real New Zealand film industry, based on C.K. Stead's book *Smith's Dream*. Sam Neill plays a paranoid antihero hunted by repressive state forces. A slick thriller, which rushes to a violent conclusion.

Two Little Boys *Robert Sarkies, 2012*. A black comedy that becomes ever blacker as two former friends, a hot meat pie and ginger cat lead to the premature death of a Scandinavian footballer.

The Ugly *Scott Reynold, 1996*. Rave US reviews greeted this edgy comment on incarceration, reform and mistrust revolving around a serial killer who has been locked away and wants to convince the world he is cured.

Utu *Geoff Murphy, 1983*. This Kiwi classic portrays a Māoriwarrior in the late 1800s who sets out to revenge himself on the conquerors of New Zealand, in the form of a Pakeha farmer. A tense, well-acted representation of modern and historic issues.

Vigil *Vincent Ward, 1984*. Dark, rain-soaked story portraying a young girl's sexual awakening and her negative reaction to a stranger who is trying to seduce her mother.

Whakataratara Paneke *Don C. Selwyn, 2001*. The Māori*Merchant of Venice*, with English subtitles, an ambitious home-grown film that brings much local acting talent to the screen in an involved, if overly long, epic.

★ **Whale Rider** *Niki Caro, 2002*. Uplifting tale of 12-year-old Pai (Keisha Castle-Hughes) trying to win over her conservative Māori grandfather and claim the birthright denied her as a girl. Shot in the East Cape village of Whangara.

★ **What We Do in the Shadows** *Jermaine Clement and Taika Waititi, 2014*. Fly-on-the-wall comedy about house-sharing vampires in Wellington, the mundanity of their daily routine, and the fights they have with the local werewolf gang. Funny and sharp as their teeth.

★ **The World's Fastest Indian** *Roger Donaldson, 2005*. Feel-good movie that broke all box office records, about old codger Burt Munro, who in real life proved you don't have to be young to achieve your dreams – though being barmy helps. Anthony Hopkins in the lead role is marvellous and even does a passable Invercargill accent.

Books

Kiwis publish extensively, including a disproportionate number of glossy picture books, wildlife guides and things with "Middle Earth" in the title. Modern authors, inheritors of an increasingly confident tradition, regularly produce excellent novels, poems and factual material.

HISTORY, SOCIETY AND POLITICS

Carol Archie and Hineani Melbourne (eds) *Māori Sovereignty: The Māori Perspective*; and its companion volume *Māori Sovereignty: The Pakeha Perspective*. Every-one from grass-roots activists to statesmen gets a voice in these two volumes, one airing the widely divergent Māori visions of sovereignty, the other covering equally disparate Pakeha views. They assume a good understanding of Māori structures and recent New Zealand history but are highly instructive nonetheless.

Mark Beehre *Men Alone – Men Together*. Photographer and oral historian Mark Beehre documents the diverse lives of 45 gay men, recounting key events in their lives and those in New Zealand's social history before, during and after homosexual law reform.

James Belich *The New Zealand Wars*. Well-researched, in-depth study re-examining the Victorian and Māori interpretations of the colonial wars. A book for committed historians. *Paradise Reforged* is a history of New Zealanders from 1880 to 2000, concentrating on their relationship with the outside world.

Alistair Campbell *Māori Legends*. A brief, accessible retelling of selected stories with some evocative illustrations.

Garth Cartwright *Sweet As: Journeys in a New Zealand Summer*. Brickbats and bouquets are liberally handed out (often about different aspects of the same place) as the London-based music journalist visits his boyhood haunts and the wider Kiwi landscape. Art, music, politics and fish and chips are the main themes.

Ron Crosby *The Musket Wars*. Account of the massive nineteenth-century upsurge in inter-*iwi* conflict, exacerbated by the introduction of the musket, which led to the death of 23 percent of the Māori population, a proportion greater even than that suffered by Russia in World War II.

★ **Joan Druett** *Tupaia*. Fascinating tale of the Polynesian chief who joined James Cook's first visit to New Zealand and helped the great navigator communicate with Māori.

Adam Dudding *My Father's Island*. Award-winning memoir published in 2016, an insightful and deeply moving account of a son's changing perception of his father, starting off immersed in the morass of warts-and-all family politics through to his realization, and appreciation, that his editor father is amongst the forefront of the New Zealand literary scene.

Alan Duff *Out of the Mist and Steam*. A vivid memoir of the *Once Were Warriors* author's life that falls short of

autobiography, but gives the reader a good idea of the basis of inspiration for his novels.

A.K. Grant *Corridors of Paua*. A light-hearted look at the turbulent and fraught political history of the country from 1984 to the introduction of MMP in 1996.

Mark Inglis *Legs on Everest*. In 2006, 24 years after losing both lower legs to frostbite on Mt Cook, Inglis became the first double amputee to climb to the summit of Mt Everest. An inspirational read.

Hamish Keith *The Big Picture: A History of New Zealand Art from 1642*. A fascinating and rewarding tome for anybody interested in the progression from early Māori art through European influence to today's fusion of styles.

★ **Michael King** *The Penguin History of New Zealand*. Published in 2003, this is a highly readable general history of New Zealand, from Māori oral history to uneasy Māori–Pakeha relations and the Māori renaissance. *Death of the Rainbow Warrior* is a brilliant account of the farcical, and ultimately tragic, efforts of the French secret service to sabotage Greenpeace's campaign against French nuclear testing.

Gareth Morgan & Susan Guthrie *Are We There Yet?* Wealthy activist Morgan gives his view on the way forward as a nation, proposing compulsory Māori language learning in primary schools; an Upper House of Parliament with half the members elected by Māori; and changing the country's name to Aotearoa New Zealand. Some sound ideas which have rarked up the talkback stations.

★ **Claudia Orange** *The Story of the Treaty*. A concise illustrated exploration of the history and myths behind what many believe to be the most important document in New Zealand history, the Treaty of Waitangi.

Margaret Orbell *A Concise Encyclopaedia of Māori Myth and Legend*. A comprehensive rundown on many tales and their backgrounds that rewards perseverance, though a little dry.

Jock Phillips *A Man's Country? The Image of the Pakeha Male*. Classic treatise on mateship and the Kiwi bloke, an exploration of formative pioneering years, rugby, wartime camaraderie and the family-man ideal.

Anne Salmond *Amiria: The Life Story of Māori Women*. Reprinted classic describing the traditional values passed on to the author, set against a background of tribal history and contemporary race relations.

D.C. Starzecka (ed) *Māori Art and Culture*. A kind of Māori culture primer, with concise and interesting coverage of Māori history, culture, social structure, carving and weaving.

K. Taylor and P. Moloney (eds) *On the Left: Essays on Socialism in New Zealand*. Comprehensive collection of political essays spanning over a century that shows why New Zealand society has such a strong egalitarian spine.

Chris Trotter *No Left Turn*. Wonderful episodic history of New Zealand that convincingly argues that the country has been continuously shaped by "greed, bigotry and right-wing politics".

Dorothy Urlich Cloher *Hongi Hika*. Compelling biography dealing with the foremost Māori leader at the time of the first contact between Māori and the Europeans, and his subsequent participation in the Musket Wars.

FICTION

Graeme Aitken *Fifty Ways of Saying Fabulous*. Extremely funny book about burgeoning homosexuality in a young farm boy, who lives in a world where he is expected to clean up muck and play rugby.

Eric Beardsley *Blackball 08*. Entertaining and fairly accurate historical novel set in the West Coast coal-mining town of Blackball during New Zealand's longest labour dispute.

★ **Graham Billing** *Forbrush and the Penguins*. Described as the first serious novel to come out of Antarctica, this is a compelling description of one man's lonely vigil over a colony of penguins.

Samuel Butler *Erewhon*. Initially set in the Canterbury high country (where Butler ran a sheep station), but increasingly devoted to a satirical critique of mid-Victorian Britain.

Eleanor Catton *The Luminaries*. This complex whodunit set in gold-rush Hokitika in 1866 won the 2013 Man Booker Prize. At over 800 pages it is the longest winner and at 28 Catton was the youngest author. Part of its genius is the author's success at constraining the narrative within a straitjacket defined by chapter length, zodiac signs and lunar cycles.

Paul Cleave *The Cleaner*. Debut novel from Christchurch-based crime writer (and New Zealand's best-selling author) who turns his city into a grim and dysfunctional backdrop for complex tales taken from many perspectives. Continue with the sequel *Victim Joe* or his series centred on retired cop Carl Schroder.

Nigel Cox *Tarzan Presley*. Amusing reworking of the Tarzan myth where the hero grows up in New Zealand and then becomes the king of rock'n'roll – nothing if not ambitious.

★ **Ian Cross** *The God Boy*. Widely considered to be New Zealand's equivalent to *The Catcher in the Rye*, about a young boy trapped between two parents who hate each other and the violent consequences.

★ **Barry Crump** *A Good Keen Man; Hang on a Minute Mate; Bastards I Have Met; Forty Yarns and a Song; The Adventures of Sam Cash*. Just a few of the many New Zealand bushman books by the Kiwi equivalent of Banjo Paterson, who writes with humour, tenderness and style about the male-dominated world of hunting, shooting, fishing, drinking, and telling stories. Worth reading for a picture of a now-past New Zealand lifestyle.

Alan Duff *Once Were Warriors*. Shocking and violent social-realist book set in 1970s south Auckland and adapted in the 1990s for Lee Tamahori's film of the same name. Well intentioned and passionate.

Laurence Fearnley *The Hut Builder*. Mannered fiction concerning the life of a Kiwi poet, whose work never makes an appearance, and who happens to climb Mt Cook with Edmund Hillary.

★ **Janet Frame** *An Angel at My Table*. Though one of New Zealand's most accomplished novelists, Frame is perhaps best known for this three-volume autobiography, dramatized in Jane Campion's film, which with wit and a self-effacing honesty gives a poignant insight into both the author and her environment. Her superb novels and short stories use humour alongside highly disturbing combinations of events and characters to overthrow readers' preconceptions. For starters, try *Faces in the Water*, *Scented Gardens for the Blind*, *Towards Another Summer* and *Owls Do Cry*.

Maurice Gee *Crime Story; Going West; Prowlers; The Plumb Trilogy*. Novels from an underrated but highly talented writer. Despite the misleadingly light titles, Gee's focus is social realism, taking an unflinching, powerful look at motivation and unravelling relationships.

★ **Patricia Grace** *Potiki*. Poignant, poetic and exquisitely written tale of a Māori community redefining itself while its land is threatened by coastal development. *Baby No Eyes* is a magical weaving of real events with stories of family history told from four points of view. *Dogside Story*, shortlisted for the 2001 Booker Prize, is a wonderful story about the power of the land and the strength of *whanau* at the turn of the millennium. *Tu* is an astonishing novel about the Māori Battalion fighting in Italy in World War II, drawn from the experiences of the author's father and other relatives.

Peter Hawes *Leapfrog with Unicorns* and *Tasman's Lay*. Two from an unsung hero, cult figure and probably only member of the absurdist movement in New Zealand, who writes with great energy, wit and surprising discipline about almost anything that takes his fancy. Hawes has also written the not-to-be-missed *Inca Girls Aren't Easy*, a series of joyous, sad and slippery tales, under the name W.P. Hearst. A brilliant late addition to Hawes' eccentric canon, *Royce, Royce the People's Choice*, is a sort of *Old Man and the Sea* mixed with *Moby Dick*.

★ **Keri Hulme** *The Bone People*. The winner of the 1985 Booker Prize, and an extraordinary first novel, set along the wild beaches of the South Island's West Coast. Mysticism, myth and earthy reality are transformed into a haunting tale peopled with richly drawn characters.

★ **Witi Ihimaera** *Bulibasha – King of the Gypsies*. The best introduction to one of the country's finest Māori authors.

A rollicking good read, energetically exploring the life of a rebellious teenager in 1950s rural New Zealand – it's an intense look at adolescence, cultural choices, family ties and the abuse of power, culminating in a masterful twist. Look out also for *The Matriarch* and *The Uncle Story*, *Whale Rider* (adapted into a highly successful film) and *Star Dancer* by the same author.

Lloyd Jones *Mister Pip*. Intriguing 2007 Booker-shortlisted novel dealing with an unreported war on a remote South Pacific island where the schoolchildren's futures are entwined with a boy called Pip and a man named Dickens. Jones' 2009 collection of short stories, *The Man in the Shed*, showcases his sharp observations about contemporary NZ life.

Shonagh Koea *The Grandiflora Tree*. A savagely witty yet deeply moving study of the conventions of widowhood, with a peculiar love story thrown in. First novel from a journalist and short-story writer renowned for her astringent humour.

★ **Katherine Mansfield** *The Collected Stories of Katherine Mansfield*. All 73 short stories sit alongside fifteen unfinished fragments in this 780-page tome of concise, penetrating examinations of human behaviour in apparently trivial situations, often transmitting a painfully pessimistic view of the world – startlingly modern considering when they were written in the early twentieth century.

Craig Marriner *Stonedogs*. Frenetic, feral, culturally fraught tale of gang-controlled drug running between Rotarua, Auckland and Northland, portraying "a New Zealand the tourists and executives had better pray they never stumble upon".

★ **Ngaio Marsh** *Opening Night*; *Artists in Crime*; *Vintage Murder*. Just a selection from the doyenne of New Zealand crime fiction, who since 1934 has been airing her Anglophile sensibilities and killing off innumerable individuals in the name of entertainment, before solving the crimes with Inspector Allen. Perfect mindless reading matter for planes, trains and buses.

Owen Marshall *Drybread*. Sparingly written novel set between Christchurch and Central Otago that examines love and loss through its two protagonists: a mother returning to New Zealand to flee a court order from the US and an emotionally scarred local journalist pursuing her story.

★ **Ronald Hugh Morrieson** *Came a Hot Friday*. Superb account of the idiosyncrasies of country folk and the two smart spielers who enter their lives, in a visceral gothic comedy thriller focusing on crime and sex in a small town.

Also worth checking out are *The Scarecrow*, *Predicament* and *Pallet on the Floor*, all of which reveal Morrieson to have been the outstanding genius of this very New Zealand take on the genre.

Paula Morris *Rangitira*. Based on the true story of the author's forebear, Ngati Wai chief Paratene Te Manu, who in 1863 travelled to England. It begins with Paratene having his portrait painted by Gottfried Lindauer, which triggers memories of that fateful trip - from meeting with royalty in London, to the disintegration of the visit into poverty, mistrust, and humiliation.

Frank Sargeson *The Stories of Frank Sargeson*. Though not well known outside New Zealand, Sargeson is a giant of Kiwi literature. His writing, from the 1930s to the 1980s, is incisive and sharply observed, with dialogue true to the metre of New Zealand speech. This work brings together some of his finest short stories. *Once is Enough*, *More than Enough* and *Never Enough!* make up the complete autobiography of a man sometimes even more colourful than his characters; Michael King wrote a fine biography, *Frank Sargeson: A Life*.

★ **Maurice Shadbolt** *Strangers and Journeys*. On publication in 1972 this became a defining novel in New Zealand's literary ascendancy and its sense of nationhood. A tale of two families, with finely wrought characters, whose lives interweave through three generations – very New Zealand, very human and not overly epic. Later works, which consolidated Shadbolt's reputation, include *Monday's Warriors*, *Season of the Jew* and *The House of Strife*.

C.K. Stead *The Singing Whakapapa*. Highly regarded author of many books and critical essays who is little known outside New Zealand and Australia. This powerful novel focuses on an early missionary and a dissatisfied modern descendant searching for meaning in his own life. *All Visitors Ashore* is a masterpiece based around the harbourfront strike of 1951 and slyly alluding to Stead's literary contemporaries, while *Mansfield* is an evocative fictional musing about New Zealand's most famous short-story writer.

★ **Damien Wilkins** *The Miserables*. One of the best novels to come out of New Zealand, shorn of much of the colonial baggage of many writers and surprisingly mature for a first novel, it sharply evokes middle-class New Zealand life from the 1960s to the 1980s through finely wrought characters.

ANTHOLOGIES

Warwick Brown *100 New Zealand Artists*. Companion to the *Picador Book of Contemporary New Zealand Fiction*, but also allows room for sculptors, printmakers, photographers and graphic artists.

James Burns (ed) *Novels and Novelists 1861–1979, a Bibliography*. A sweeping and comprehensive introduction to the history of the New Zealand novel and the authors who made it a powerful art form.

Bill Manhire (ed) *100 New Zealand Poems*. Manageable selection that provides an excellent introduction to the poetry of the nation and the characters who penned the rhymes and verses.

★ **Owen Marshall** (selected by) *Essential New Zealand Short Stories*. A representative collection of fascinating tales by some of New Zealand's best-known and finest authors, including Frame, Ihimera, Mansfield, Shadbolt, Stead and Gee.

★ **Ian Wedde and Harvey McQueen** (eds) *The Penguin Book of New Zealand Verse*. A comprehensive collection of verse from the earliest European settlers to contemporary poets, and an excellent introduction to Kiwi poetry; highlights are works by James K. Baxter, Janet Frame, C.K. Stead, Sam Hunt, Keri Hulme, Hirini Melbourne and Apirana Taylor.

REFERENCE AND SPECIALIST GUIDES

John Kent *North Island Trout Fishing Guide* and *South Island Trout Fishing Guide*. Laden with information on access, seasons and fishing style, and illustrated with maps of the more important rivers.

FLORA, FAUNA AND THE ENVIRONMENT

★ **Andrew Crowe** *Which Native Tree?* Great little book, ideal for identifying New Zealand's common native trees – though not tree ferns – with diagrams of tree shape, photos of leaves and fruit and an idea of geographic extent.

John Dawson & Rob Lucas *New Zealand's Native Trees*. This magisterial tome is beautifully photographed and covers everything from distribution to detailed identification. *Their Field Guide to New Zealand's Native Trees* is more backpack-friendly.

Gerald Durrell *Two in the Bush*. Almost half of this slim volume is devoted to Durrell's 1962 visit while filming for a BBC wildlife documentary. Dated but a fascinating insight into both the times, the environment and the wildlife – mostly kaka, tuatara, takahe and penguins.

Julian Fitter *Guide to Wild New Zealand*. Fabulous collection of all the flora and fauna you are ever likely to encounter in an easy-to-manage package – the perfect field guide for experts and amateurs alike.

Susanne & John Hill *Richard Henry of Resolution Island*. Comprehensive and very readable account of a man widely regarded as New Zealand's first conservationist. The book also serves as a potted history of this underpopulated area of Fiordland, peopled by many of the key explorers.

Leonie Johnson & Tony Ward *Organic Explorer*. Small guide to the best in organic, eco- and vegetarian spots around the country with everything from wholefood shops and organic wineries to ecolodges.

Rod Morris & Hal Smith *Wild South: Saving New Zealand's Endangered Birds*. A fascinating companion volume to a 1980s TV series following a band of dedicated individuals trying to preserve a dozen of New Zealand's wonderfully exotic bird species, including the kiwi, kakapo, takahe and kea.

Neville Peat *Manapouri Saved*. Full and heartening coverage of one of New Zealand's earliest environmental battles when, in the 1960s, a petition signed by ten percent of the country succeeded in persuading the government to cancel its hydroelectric plans for Lake Manapouri.

Tim Rainger T*he Good New Zealand Beach Guide: North Island*. If golden strands, point breaks and surfcasting are your thing, don't miss this guide full of great photos, helpful maps and a few tall tales. No sign of a South Island companion volume yet.

Paul Schofield & Brent Stephenson *Birds of New Zealand: A Photographic Guide*. One for the campervan bookshelf, this is a complete guide to 365 species with over a thousand superb photos.

Kerry-Jayne Wilson *Flight of the Huia*. Focusing on Jurassic frogs and bizarre creatures such as the Alpine parrot, this book studies faunal change in New Zealand and current conservation issues.

TRAMPING, CYCLING AND ADVENTURE SPORTS

★ **Shaun Barnett** *Tramping in New Zealand*. Clear, concise and nicely photographed guide to forty of the best multi-day hikes in the country including most of the Great Walks. The maps show the terrain beautifully and there's a companion volume covering *100 Day Walks in New Zealand* with similar production values.

Graham Charles *New Zealand Whitewater: 180 Great Kayaking Runs*. A comprehensive and entertaining guide to New Zealand's kayaking rivers with maps and details on access, supplemented by quick reference panels with grades, timings, and handy tips.

Paul, Simon and Jonathan Kennett *Classic New Zealand Mountain Bike Rides*. All you need to know about off-road biking in New Zealand, with details of over three hundred rides. The brothers also publish *Classic New Zealand Road Rides*, *The New Zealand Cycle Trails* and others. Paul Kennett runs the ⓦ mountainbike.co.nz site.

Moir's Guide Away from the Great Walks, this is the most comprehensive guide to tramping in the South Island. It comes divided into two volumes: *North*, covering hikes between Lake Ohau and Lake Wakatipu; and *South*, which concentrates on walks around the southern lakes and fiords including the Kepler Track, plus the less popular Dusky and George Sound tracks.

Nigel Rushton *Pedallers' Paradise*. Separate light-weight *North Island* and *South Island* volumes covering recommended routes with distances, gradient profiles and places to grab a scone along the way.

Wavetrack New Zealand Surfing Guide *New Zealand Surfing Guide*. Pragmatic handbook to the prime surf spots around the New Zealand coast, with details on access, transport, the best wind and tide conditions and expected swells.

Language

English and *te reo Māori*, the Māori language, share joint status as New
Zealand's official languages (little known though is that sign language is the
country's third official language), but on a day-to-day basis all you'll need is
English, or its colourful Kiwi variant. All Māori speak English fluently, often
slipping in numerous Māori terms that in time become part of everyday
Kiwi parlance. Mainstream TV and radio coverage of any event that has
significance to Māori is likely to be littered with words totally alien to
foreigners, but well understood by Anglophone Kiwis. It is initially confusing,
but with the aid of our Glossary (see page 734) you'll soon find yourself
using Māori terms all the time.

A basic knowledge of Māori pronunciation will make you more comprehensible and
some understanding of the roots of place names can be helpful. You'll need to become
something of an expert to appreciate much of the wonderful oral history, and stories
told through *waiata* (songs), but learning a few key terms will enhance any Māori
cultural events you may attend.

To many Brits and North Americans, **Kiwi English** is barely distinguishable from
its trans-Tasman cousin, "Strine", sharing much of the same lexicon of slang terms,
but with a softer accent. Australians have no trouble distinguishing the two accents,
repeatedly highlighting the vowel shift which turns "bat" into "bet", makes "yes" sound
like "yis" and causes "fish" to come out as "fush". There is very little regional variation;
only residents of Otago and Southland – the southern quarter of the South Island
– distinguish themselves with a rolled "r", courtesy of their predominantly Scottish
forebears. Throughout the land, Kiwis add an upward inflection to statements, making
them sound like questions; most are not, and to highlight those that are, some add the
interrogative "eh?" to the end of the sentence, a trait most evident in the North Island,
especially among Māori.

Māori

For the 30,000–60,000 native speakers and additional 110,000 who speak it as a
second tongue, **Māori** is very much a living language. It is gaining strength all the time
as both Māori and Pākehā increasingly appreciate the cultural value of *te reo*, a language
central to *Māoritanga* and forming the basis of a huge body of magnificent songs,
chants and legends, lent a poetic quality by its hypnotic and lilting rhythms.

Māori is a member of the East Polynesian group of languages and shares both
grammar and vocabulary with those spoken throughout most of the South Pacific.
Similarities are so pronounced that Tupaia, a Tahitian crew member on Captain Cook's
first Pacific voyage in 1769, was able to communicate freely with the Aotearoa Māori
they encountered. The Treaty of Waitangi was written in both English and Māori, but
te reo soon began to lose ground to the point where, by the late nineteenth century,
its use was proscribed in schools. Māori parents keen for their offspring to do well in
the Pākehā world frequently promoted the use of English, and Māori declined further,
exacerbated by the mid-twentieth-century migration to the cities. The language reached
its nadir in the 1970s when perhaps only ten percent of Māori spoke their language
fluently. The tide began to turn towards the end of the decade with the inception of
kōhanga reo **pre-schools** (literally "language nests") where **Maoritanga** is taught and
activities are conducted in Māori. The national roll is around 9500 pupils. Originally

a Māori initiative, it now has some crossover and a few progressive Pākehā parents introduce their kids to biculturalism at an early age. Fortunate *kōhanga reo* graduates can progress to the small number of state-funded Māori-language primary schools known as *kura kaupapa*. For decades, Māori has been taught as an option in secondary schools, and there are now state-funded tertiary institutions operated by Māori, offering graduate programmes in Māori studies.

The success of these programmes has bred a young generation of Māori-speakers frequently far more fluent than their parents who, determined to recover their heritage, are attending Māori evening classes. Legal parity means that Māori is now finding its way into officialdom too, with government departments all adopting Māori names and many government and council documents being printed in both languages. Local Māori-language **radio stations** are now commonplace in the northern half of the North Island where the majority of Māori live (check out ⓦirirangi.net for locations and frequencies). But the real boost came in 2004 with the launching of **Māori Television**. Substantially government funded and less ratings-driven than its competitors, it has a dedicated audience and is well worth tuning into for a very different take on what's going on. Partly in English, partly in Māori and occasionally a synthesis of the two, there's a wonderful cross-fertilization of styles. You can expect everything from movies and sitcoms to discussion panels on Māori issues and lifestyle programmes such as *Pete and Pio's Kai Safari* and *Kai Time on the Road* (a cooking and Māori food show). There's even *Dora Matatoa*, the kids' show *Dora the Explorer*, and *SpongeBob Squarepants*, both of which have been dubbed into an engaging mix of Māori and Spanish.

In your day-to-day dealings you won't need **to speak Māori**, though both native speakers and Pākehā may well greet you with *kia ora* ("hi, hello"), or less commonly *haere mai* ("welcome"). On ceremonial occasions, such as *marae* visits, you'll hear the more formal greeting *tēnā koe* (said to one person) or *tena koutou katoa* (to a group).

Māori words used in place names are listed below, while those in common use are listed in the general Glossary (see page 734). If you are interested in learning a little more, the best handy reference is Patricia Turoa's *The Collins Māori Phrase Book*, which has helpful notes on pronunciation, handy phrases and a useful Māori–English and English–Māori vocabulary. Online resources include ⓦkorero.maori.nz and ⓦmaoridictionary.co.nz.

MĀORI PLACE NAMES

The following is a list of some of the most common words and elements you will see in **town and place names** throughout New Zealand.

Ao Cloud
Ara Road or path
Awa River or valley
Hau Wind
Ika Fish
Iti Small
Kai Food or eat
Kāinga Home, village
Kare Rippling
Kino Bad
Mā White, clear
Manga Stream
Manu Bird
Mata Headland
Maunga Mountain
Mihi Speeches or greetings

Moana Sea, lake
Motu Island or anything isolated
Muri End
Nui Big
O The place of
One Sand, beach
Pā Fortified settlement
Pae Ridge
Papa Flat, earth, floor
Pātere Chants
Puke Hill
Puna Spring
Raki North
Rangi Sky
Roa Long, high
Roto Lake
Rua Hole, cave, pit, two
Runga Top
Tahu Light

Tai Sea
Tāne Man
Tapu Sacred
Tara Peak
Te The

Tomo Cave
Wai Water
Waka Canoe
Whanga Bay, body of water
Whenua Land or country

Pronunciation

Pākehā – and consequently most visitors – may still have a distorted impression of Māori pronunciation, which is usually mutated into an anglicized form. Until the 1970s there was little attempt to get it right, but with the rise in Māori consciousness since the 1980s, coupled with a sense of political correctness, many Pākehā now make some attempt at Māori pronunciation. As a visitor you will probably get away with just about anything, but by sticking to a few simple rules and keeping your ears open, apparently unfathomable place names will soon trip off your tongue.

Māori was solely a spoken language before the arrival of British and French missionaries in the early nineteenth century, who transcribed it using only fifteen letters of the Roman alphabet. The eight **consonants**, **h**, **k**, **m**, **n**, **p**, **r**, **t** and **w**, and the digraph **ng** are pronounced much as they are in English. The five **vowels** come in long and short forms; the long form is sometimes signified in print by a macron – the flat bar above the letter that we've used in this section of the book – but usually it is simply a case of learning by experience which sound to use. When two vowels appear together they are both pronounced, though substantially run together. For example, "Māori" should be written with a macron on the "a" and be pronounced with the first two vowels separate, turning the commonly used but incorrect "Mow-ree" into something more like "Maao-ri".

Here are a few **pronunciation** pointers to help you get it right:

- Long compound words can be split into syllables which all end in a vowel. Waikaremoana comes out as Wai-kare-**moana**. Scanning our list of place-name elements should help a great deal.
- All syllables are stressed evenly, so it is not **Wai**-ka re-**moana** or Wai-kare-**moana** but a flat Wai-kare-**moana**.
- Māori words don't take an "s" to form a plural, so you'll find many plural nouns in this book – kiwi, tui, kauri, Māori – in what appears to be a singular form; about the only exception is Kiwis (as people), a Māori word wholly adopted into English.
- **Ng** is pronounced much as in "sing".
- **Wh** sounds either like an aspirated "f" as in "off", or like the "wh" in "why", depending on who is saying what and in which part of the country.

Glossary

ANZAC Australian and New Zealand Army Corps; every town in New Zealand has a memorial to ANZAC casualties from both world wars.

Aotearoa Māori for New Zealand, the land of the long white cloud.

Ariki Supreme chief of an *iwi*.

Aroha Love.

Bach (pronounced "batch") Holiday home, originally a bachelor pad at work camps and now something of a Kiwi institution that can be anything from shack to palatial waterside residence.

Back-blocks Remote areas.

Bludger Someone who doesn't pull their weight or pay their way, a sponger.

Bro Brother, term of endearment widely used by Māori.

BYO Bring Your Own (bottle to drink).

Captain Cooker Wild pig, probably descended from pigs released in the Marlborough Sounds on Cook's first voyage.

Chilly bin Insulated cool box for carrying picnic supplies.

Choice Fantastic.

Chook Chicken.

Chunder Vomit.

Coaster (Ex-) resident of the West Coast of the South Island.

Cocky Farmer, comes in "Cow" and "Sheep" variants.

Crib South Island name for a *bach*.

Crook Unwell.

Cuz or **Cuzzy** Short for cousin, see "bro".

Dag Wag or entertaining character.

Dairy Corner shop selling just about everything, open seven days and sometimes 24 hours.

Dob in Reporting one's friends and neighbours to the police; there is currently a dobber's charter encouraging drivers to report one another for dangerous driving.

DOC Department of Conservation. Operators of the national parks, conservation policy, track-administration and much more.

Docket Receipt.

Domain Grassy reserve, open to the public.

EFTPOS Card-based debit system found in shops, bars and restaurants.

Feijoa Fleshy, tomato-sized fruit with melon-like flesh and a tangy, perfumed flavour.

Footie Rugby, usually union rather than league, never soccer.

Freezing works Slaughterhouse.

Godzone New Zealand, short for "God's own country".

Good as (gold) First rate, excellent.

Greasies Takeaway food, especially fish and chips.

Greenstone A type of nephrite jade known in Māori as *pounamu*.

Haere mai Welcome.

Haka Māori dance performed in threatening fashion before All Blacks rugby games.

Handle Large glass of beer.

Hangi Māori feast cooked in an earth oven (see page 713).

Hapū Māori subtribal unit. Several make up an *iwi*.

Harakeke Flax.

Hard case See "dag".

Hikoi Walk (often as a protest).

Hogget The meat from a year-old sheep. Older and tastier (though less succulent) than lamb, but not as tough as mutton.

Hollywood A faked or exaggerated sporting injury used to gain advantage.

Hongi Māori greeting, performed by pressing noses together.

Hoon Lout, yob or delinquent.

Hori Offensive word for a Māori.

Hot dog A battered sausage on a stick, dipped in tomato ketchup. What the rest of the world knows as a hot dog is known here as an American hot dog.

Hui Māori gathering or conference.

Iwi Largest of Māori tribal groupings.

Jafa Just Another Fucking Aucklander. Semi-derogatory term now (over)used as a noun. "He's a bloody Jafa".

Jandals Ubiquitous Kiwi footwear, thongs or flip-flops.

Jug Litre of beer.

Ka kite See you later.

Ka pai It is good, well done.

Kai Māori word for food, used in general parlance.

Kaimoana Seafood.

Kāinga Village.

Karanga Call for visitors to come forward on a *marae*.

Kaumatuā Māori elders, old people.

Kawa-Marae Etiquette or protocol on a *marae*.

Kete Traditional basket made of plaited harakeke.

Kia ora Hello, thank you.

Kiore Polynesian rat.

kiwi The national bird and mascot of NZ, always set lower case.

Kiwi An alternative label for a New Zealander.

Kiwifruit In New Zealand they are always called kiwifruit, never "kiwis". Golden-fleshed kiwifruit are also available, and less acidic than their green counterparts.

Koha Donation, gift or present.

Kōhanga Reo Pre-school Māori language immersion (literally "language nest").

Kuia Female Māori elder.

Kūmara Sweet potato.

Kurī Polynesian dog, now extinct.

Lay-by Practice of putting a deposit on goods until they can be fully paid for.

Lucked in In luck. What "Lucked out" means elsewhere in the world.

Lucked out Out of luck. The meaning completely reversed on its way across the Pacific.

Mana Māori term indicating status, esteem, prestige or authority, and in wide use among all Kiwis.

Manaia Stylized bird or lizard forms used extensively in Māori carving.

Manuhiri Guest or visitor, particularly to a *marae*.

Maoritanga Māori culture and custom, the Māori way of doing things.

Marae Place for conducting ceremonies in front of a meeting house – literally "courtyard". Also a general term for a settlement centred on the meeting house.

Mauri Life force or life principle.

Mere War club, usually of greenstone.

Metalled Graded road surface of loose stones found all over rural New Zealand.

MMP Mixed Member Proportional representation – New Zealand's electoral system.

Moko Old form of tattooing on body and face that has seen a resurgence among Māori.

Munted Something broken or destroyed.

Muttonbird Gull-sized sooty shearwater that was a major component of the pre-European Māori diet and tastes like oily and slightly fishy mutton – hence the name.

Ngāti Tribal prefix meaning "the descendants (or people) of". Also Ngāi and Āti.

OE Overseas experience, usually a year spent abroad by Kiwis in their early twenties.

Pā Fortified village of yore, now usually an abandoned terraced hillside.

Paddock Field.

Pākehā A non-Māori, usually white and not usually expressed with derogatory intent. Literally "foreign" though it can also be translated as "flea" or "pest". It may also be a corruption of *pakepākehā*, which are mythical human-like beings with fair skins.

Pashing Kissing or snogging.

Patu Short fighting club.

Pāua The muscular foot of the abalone, often minced and served as a fritter, while the wonderful iridescent shell is used for jewellery and decoration.

Pavlova Meringue dessert with a fruit and cream topping.

Pike out To chicken out or give up.

Piss Beer.

Pissed Drunk.

Podocarp Family of pine, native to New Zealand including rimu, kahikatea, matai, miro, totara etc.

Pōhutukawa Gnarled native tree found around the coast of the upper North Island. Blooms bright red in mid-December and is sometimes known as New Zealand's Christmas Tree.

Poms Folk from Britain; not necessarily offensive.

Pounamu New Zealand greenstone, a unique type of jade.

Pōwhiri Traditional welcome onto a *marae*.

Prang Crash.

Pūhā Māori term for "sow thistle", a leafy plant -traditionally gathered by Māori and eaten like spinach.

Puku Māori for stomach, often used as a term of endearment for someone amply endowed.

Rangatira General term for a Māori chief.

Rapt Well-pleased.

Rattle your dags Hurry up.

Root Vulgar term for sex.

Rooted To be very tired or beyond repair, as in "she's rooted, mate" – your car is irreparable.

Rough as guts Uncouth, roughly made or operating badly, as in "she's running rough as guts, mate".

Sealed road Bitumen-surfaced road.

Section Block of land usually surrounding a house.

She'll be right Everything will work out fine.

Shout To buy a round of drinks or generally to treat folk.

Skull To knock back beer quickly.

Smoko Tea break.

Snarler, snag Sausage.

Squiz A look, as in "Give us a squiz".

Stoked Very pleased.

Sweet Cool.

Taiaha Long-handled club.

Tall poppy Someone who excels. "Cutting down tall poppies" is to bring overachievers back to earth – every Kiwi's perceived duty.

Tamarillo Slightly bitter, deep-red fruit, often known as a tree tomato.

Tāne Man.

Tangata whenua The people of the land, local or original inhabitants.

Tangi Mourning or funeral.

Taniwha Fearsome water spirit of Māori legend.

Taonga Treasures, prized possessions.

Tapu Forbidden or taboo. Frequently refers to sacred land.

Te reo Māori Māori language.

Tikanga Māori customs, ethics and etiquette – the Māori way of doing things.

Tiki Māori pendant depicting a distorted human figure.

Tiki tour Guided tour.

Togs Swimming costume.

Tohunga Māori priests, experts in *Maoritanga*.

True Left On the left facing downstream.

True Right On the right when facing downstream.

Tukutuku Knotted latticework panels decorating the inside of a meeting house.

Tupuna Ancestors; of great spiritual importance to Māori.

Ute Car-sized pick-up truck, short for "utility".

Varsity University.

Vegemite or **Marmite** Dark, savoury yeast-extract spreads. There's always debate between those who love Vegemite (Australian) and those who prefer Kiwi Marmite – sweeter and more appealing than its British equivalent – and of course those who loathe all of the above.

Wahine Woman.

Waiata Māori action songs.

Wairua Spirit.

Waka Māori canoe.

Waratah Stake, a term used to describe snow poles on tramps.

Wero Challenge before entering a *marae*.

Whakapapa Family tree or genealogical relationship.

Whānau Extended family group.

Whare Māori for a house.

Whare rūnanga Meeting house.

Whare whakairo Carved house.

Wop-wops Remote areas.

Small print and index

A ROUGH GUIDE TO ROUGH GUIDES

Published in 1982, the first Rough Guide – to Greece – was a student scheme that became a publishing phenomenon. Mark Ellingham, a recent graduate in English from Bristol University, had been travelling in Greece the previous summer and couldn't find the right guidebook. With a small group of friends he wrote his own guide, combining a contemporary, journalistic style with a thoroughly practical approach to travellers' needs.

The immediate success of the book spawned a series that rapidly covered dozens of destinations. And, in addition to impecunious backpackers, Rough Guides soon acquired a much broader readership that relished the guides' wit and inquisitiveness as much as their enthusiastic, critical approach and value-for-money ethos. These days, Rough Guides include recommendations from budget to luxury and cover more than 120 destinations around the globe, from Amsterdam to Zanzibar, all regularly updated by our team of roaming writers.

Browse all our latest guides, read inspirational features and book your trip at roughguides.com.

Rough Guide credits

Editors: Ann-Marie Shaw, Georgia Stephens, Aimee White
Cartography: Katie Bennett
Managing editor: Rachel Lawrence
Picture editor: Aude Vauconsant

Cover photo research: Aude Vauconsant
Senior DTP coordinator: Dan May
Head of DTP and Pre-Press: Rebeka Davies

Publishing information

Tenth edition 2019

Distribution
UK, Ireland and Europe
Apa Publications (UK) Ltd; sales@roughguides.com
United States and Canada
Ingram Publisher Services; ips@ingramcontent.com
Australia and New Zealand
Woodslane; info@woodslane.com.au
Southeast Asia
Apa Publications (SN) Pte; sales@roughguides.com
Worldwide
Apa Publications (UK) Ltd; sales@roughguides.com
Special Sales, Content Licensing and CoPublishing
Rough Guides can be purchased in bulk quantities
at discounted prices. We can create special editions,
personalised jackets and corporate imprints tailored to
your needs. sales@roughguides.com.

roughguides.com
Printed in China by CTPS

Help us update

We've gone to a lot of effort to ensure that the tenth
edition of **The Rough Guide to New Zealand** is accurate
and up-to-date. However, things change – places get
"discovered", opening hours are notoriously fickle,
restaurants and rooms raise prices or lower standards. If
you feel we've got it wrong or left something out, we'd like
to know, and if you can remember the address, the price,
the hours, the phone number, so much the better.

Please send your comments with the subject line
"**Rough Guide New Zealand Update**" to mail@
uk.roughguides.com. We'll credit all contributions and
send a copy of the next edition (or any other Rough Guide
if you prefer) for the very best emails.

Reader's update

Thanks to all the readers who have taken the time to write in with comments and suggestions (and apologies if we've
inadvertently omitted or misspelt anyone's name):

Sarah Binney, Bea Braun, Phil Cutcher, Jorrit R Dijkstra, Helen Hamberg-Black, Benny Hoffmann, Karen Johnston, Nora
Kestermann, David Marks, Pam McGrath, Pauline and John Trotter, Ruth Tuschling, Lucien Warner, Peter Wood

Photo credits

(Key: T-top; C-centre; B-bottom; L-left; R-right)

Alamy 5, 10, 13T, 16T, 16C, 18T, 18B, 19T, 19BL, 20T, 22B,
23T, 23B, 71, 89, 135, 186/187, 234/235, 273, 373, 483,
498/499, 535, 605, 640/641, 643, 667, 692
Danita Delimont.com/AWL Images 327
Doug Pearson/AWL Images 270/271
Getty Images 4, 8, 12, 15B, 19BR
Hemis/AWL Images 2
iStock 1, 9, 13B, 17T, 17B, 22TR, 22TL, 24, 68/69, 189, 237,

251, 305, 324/325, 341, 427, 459, 501, 563
Paul Whitfield/Rough Guides 16B, 21T, 21B, 26, 132/133,
171, 360/361, 396/397, 398/399, 560/561
Shutterstock 14, 15TR, 15C, 20B, 21C, 217, 363, 456/457
Tom Mackie/AWL Images 15TL

Cover: Fiordland National Park **Maurizio Rellini/
SIME/4Corners Images**

Acknowledgements

Gerard Hindmarsh would like to thank Tourism West Coast, Destination Marlborough and Nelson Tasman Tourism.
Stephen Keeling would like to thank the folks at Fiordland National Park Visitor Centre, Destination Fiordland, Gunn's Camp and Arthurs Pass Visitor Centre; Ashley Andrew and the generous team at Jucy car rentals; my fellow writers; and all the friendly New Zealanders that made researching this guide such a pleasure. Thanks also to Ann-Marie Shaw, Georgia Stephens, Andy Turner and Rachel Mills for all their hard work and editing back in the UK; and lastly to Tiffany Wu, the world's greatest travel companion.
Shafik Meghji Thanks to all the travellers and locals who helped out along the way. A special thanks to: Georgia Stephens, Andy Turner and Aimee White at RG HQ; Tessa Andersson at Accor Hotels; Emma Crequer at YHA New Zealand; everyone at Solscape in Raglan and ArtHouse in Tauranga; Jason Bleibtreu at River Birches; Danielle Goodall at White Island Rendezvous; Jean, Nizar and Nina Meghji; and Sioned Jones.
Rachel Mills would like to thank Andy Turner, Helen Abramson, Georgia Stephens and Aimee White at Rough Guides HQ, plus Emma Crequer at YHA. A huge thank you to my beautiful Toi Toi family who make me want to pack my bags and move to New Zealand.
Ian Osborn Thanks to my darling travel companion for all those beautiful meals cooked from the back of our camper and the conversations we shared as we crawled along the SH2 … my sincere appreciation is extended to all hosts and informers on our travels, notably Dean, Zarli, Chris Lee and Ella Blake all from Wellington; Lisa from Martinborough; Matt Moore of Gisborne; Monty Manuel for his insight into Mt Hikurangi; Bill Martin from Te Araroa; and the lovely folks at Wairoa iSite. A special mention goes to the three local lads who helped dig my camper out of the sandy car park at the wild Whakamahia Beach in Wairoa.
Sarah Reid Thanks firstly to the Rough Guides team, particularly to Andy for the opportunity to work on this book, and to Annie for your stellar editing. Thanks also to the legends at the Queenstown, Wanaka, Central Otago and Dunedin tourism boards for your great tips and hospitality, and to the other wonderful tourism providers who made me feel so at home in Otago. Lastly, thanks to my wonderful friend Laura for joining me on one of my favourite road trips to date, and to my huzzo Tim for keeping the home fires burning.

ABOUT THE AUTHOR

Gerard Hindmarsh is a Nelson-based freelance travel journalist, broadcaster and author.
Stephen Keeling has been travelling to New Zealand since 1999. Before writing his first travel guide, he worked as a financial journalist and editor in Asia for seven years, a job that included covering the Kiwi dollar loan and bond market (which really exists). He has written numerous titles for Rough Guides, including books on Puerto Rico, Taiwan, Colombia and The Philippines. Stephen lives in New York City.
Shafik Meghji is an award-winning travel writer, journalist and broadcaster based in south London, who has worked on more than thirty Rough Guides to destinations in Australia, Asia, Europe, Latin America and North Africa. He writes regularly for print and digital publications around the world, including BBC Travel, Adventure.com and Time Out, and talks about travel on podcasts, the radio and TV. He is a member of the British Guild of Travel Writers, a fellow of the Royal Geographical Society and a trustee of the Latin America Bureau. shafikmeghji.com. Twitter: @ShafikMeghji. Instagram: @shafikmeghji.
Rachel Mills is a freelance writer and editor based by the sea in Kent. She is a co-author for Rough Guides to India, Vietnam, Ireland and England, as well as New Zealand, a country that she first fell in love with more than ten years ago. You can follow her on Instagram @rachmillstravel.
Ian Osborn Since his mid-twenties, Ian has lived around the South Pacific as a photographer, travel writer, Rough Guide author and most recently as owner of the online travel portal Beautiful Pacific. Today he splits his time between friends and family in his homeland England, with his children in Brisbane and living in Fiji with his Rotuman wife, Sia.
Sarah Reid still can't believe it took her more than thirty years to make her first trip to New Zealand, despite growing up just across the Tasman Strait. Based in Byron Bay (when she's not travelling), she writes for a wide stable of travel publishers across the globe, edits a sustainable travel-focused blog, ecotravelist.com, and now visits NZ more regularly. You can also follow her on Instagram @ecotravelist.

Index

Map symbols

The symbols below are used on maps throughout the book

Chapter boundary	Parking	Arboretum	Radio mast
Motorway	Transport stop	Entrance/gate	Wind turbine
Major road	Helipad	Ski area	Bird Sanctuary
Minor road	Point of interest	Swimming pool	Campground
Pedestrian road	Tourist office	Surf/beach	Lodge
4 Wheel drive	Post office	Kayaking	Shelter
Steps	Internet access	Spring	Boat
Railway	Hospital	Bridge	Ferry terminal
Tram	Garden	Cave	Church (town maps)
Cable car	Golf course	Ruins	Stadium
Ferry route	Vineyard	Waterfall	Building
Footpath	Castle	Mountain peak	Park/forest
Airport (international)	Church (regional maps)	Mountain range	Beach
Airport (domestic)	Statue	Gorge	Cemetery
Fuel station	Museum	Viewpoint	Glacier
Toilets	Observatory	Lighthouse	Marsh

Listings key

- Accommodation
- Eating
- Drinking/nightlife
- Shopping